YALE UNIVERSITY PRESS
PELICAN HISTORY OF ART

FOUNDING EDITOR: NIKOLAUS PEVSNER

CHRISTOPHER GREEN

ART IN FRANCE
1900–1940

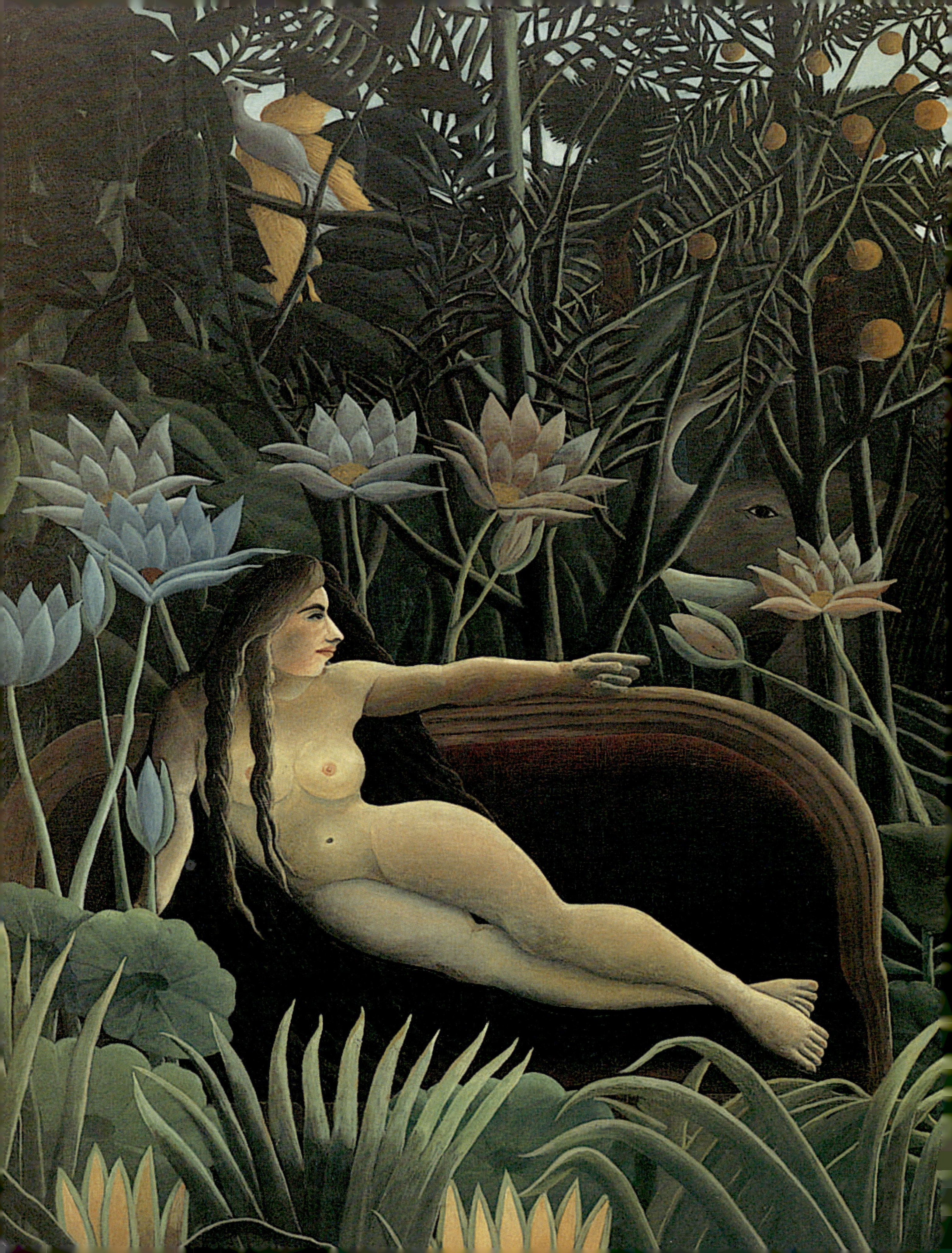

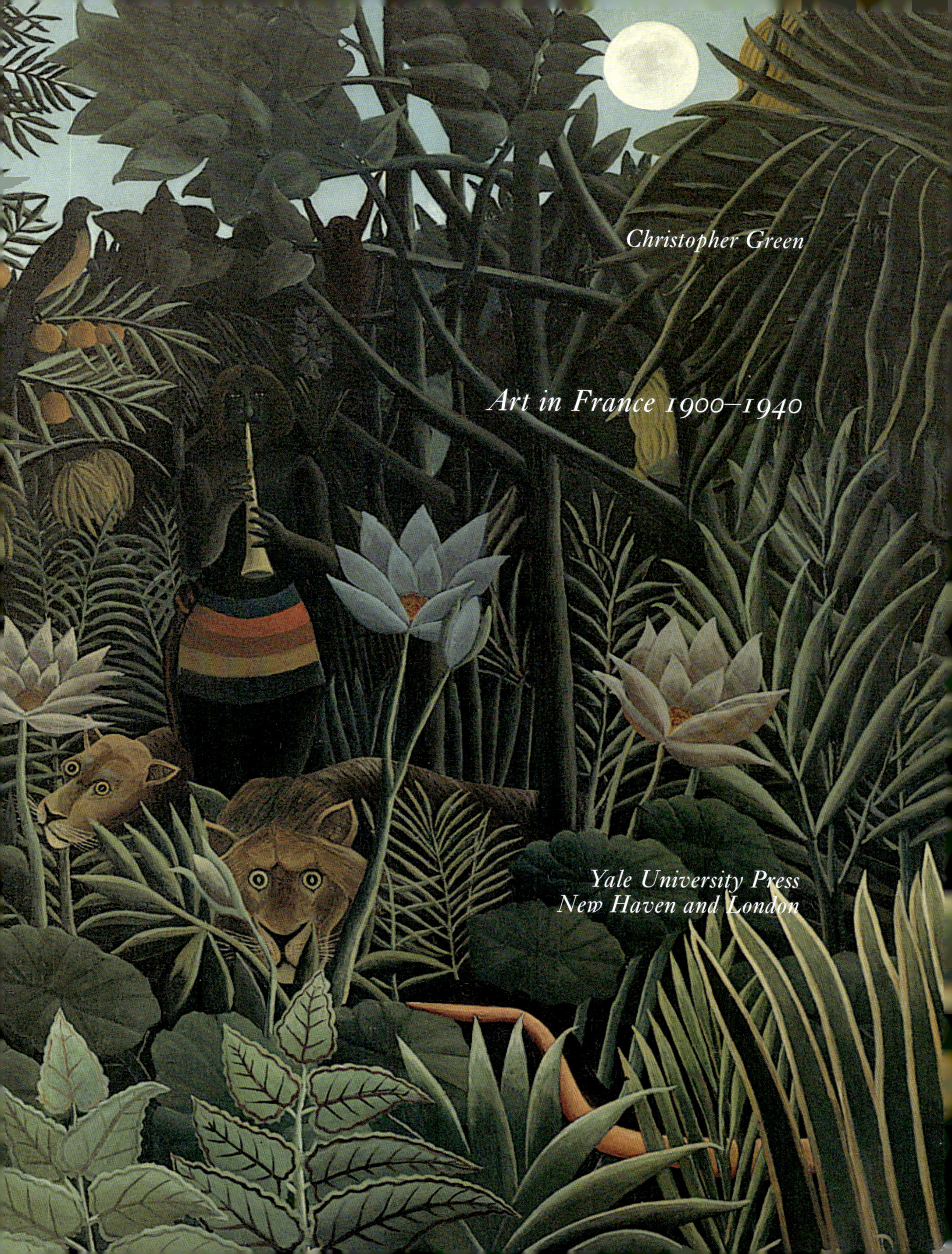

Christopher Green

Art in France 1900–1940

Yale University Press
New Haven and London

To the research students who have worked with me
at the Courtauld Institute

Set in Ehrhardt by Best-set Typesetter Ltd., Hong Kong
Printed and bound by CS Graphics, Singapore

Designed by Beatrix McIntyre

Library of Congress Cataloging-in-Publication Data

Green, Christopher, 1943 June 11
Art in France: 1900–1940 / Christopher Green.
p. cm. – (Yale University Press Pelican history of art)
Includes bibliographical references and index.
ISBN 0–300–08401–3 (cloth: alk. paper)
1. Art, French. 2. Art, Modern – 20th century – France.
I. Title. II. Series.
N6848.G73 2000
709′.44′09041 – dc21

99-089522

Title page illustration: Henri Rousseau, *The Dream*, 1910. Oil on canvas, 204 × 298 cm. The Museum of Modern Art, New York. Gift of Nelson A. Rockefeller

Contents

Acknowledgements

Art in France, 1900–1940 has a personal history for me which goes back three decades and more to my earliest engagement with French art in the twentieth century. Across those decades I have accumulated more debts than can possibly be recalled here; but my gratitude to all who have helped me over many years remains warm and undiminished. The book itself was drafted in the twelve months between October 1997 and September 1998. I could not have written it without that period of concentrated looking, reading, thinking and writing. My first and most fundamental debt is to the Leverhulme Trust, which made this possible with the award of a Senior Research Fellowship.

Confidence, bordering on foolhardiness, is needed to set out on a project like this. I am not self-sufficient enough to have that kind of confidence without the backing of others who I respect. The unstinting support and warm encouragement I have had from Dawn Ades, Eric Fernie, John Golding, John Milner and Michael Podro has been essential. So too has been that of many colleagues in the Courtauld Institute, those who teach with me in the 'Modern Section' most consistently of all. At certain points in the development and writing of the book, crucial contributions have been made by my friends Christian Derouet, Hélène Lassalle and Alan G.Wilkinson. I especially want to record here my gratitude for Hélène Lassalle's speedy response to my request to help find a photographer to record a mural in the Sorbonne. The photographer she found, Jacques Faujour, deserves my special thanks too for the dispatch and quality of his work in difficult circumstances. Another friend who supplied a much-needed photograph, and to whom I am extremely grateful, was Liliane Caffin Madaule.

I do not believe that lone scholarship, the usual research mode in the Humanities, can produce a book of this kind. Certainly, I could not have written many sections, or developed key arguments, without my own research as a 'lone scholar', but, besides my enormous debt to the many others who have produced significant research in the field, I owe a major debt to the students who have worked with me. Where I have drawn directly from their work, I have made specific acknowledgements in the body of the book to those students as well as to other specialists, but here I would like to underline my debt to the research students of the Courtauld Institute by naming names. All of the following have been my teachers in the field: Fiona Bradley, Fay Brauer, Sophie Bowness, David Cottington, Penelope Curtis, Simon Dell, Patrick Elliott, John Finlay, Matthew Gale, Romy Golan, Memory Holloway, Valerie Holman, William Jeffett, Julia Kelly, Elizabeth Legge, David Lomas, Sanda Miller, Jennifer Mundy, Gavin Parkinson, Alexandra Parigoris, Cathy Pütz, Penelope Rook, Julian Stallabrass, Michael Stone-Richards, John Welchman, Sarah Wilson and Jonathan Wood. The book is dedicated to the students who have worked with me: not only those I have named, but those others, working on art outside France, who have helped me keep alert to new possibilities.

Three of those named above were also among the friends and colleagues who helped me manage the passage from draft to final text by reading the book in its early drafts. A writer's hope is that their text will be so absorbing that, for anyone reading it, time will simply disappear. This is, of course, an illusion: the hours and days given by those who read my drafts were, I know well enough, very real; and I know too the pressures that can make freeing even the briefest periods so difficult. Mark Antliff and Patricia Leighten read drafts of the later parts of the book, and made key suggestions, which have led to changes of considerable importance; Sanda Miller read the earlier parts in a very raw state, and, as only a friend could, rammed home the importance of accessible prose; Fay Brauer and John Milner read the book in its entirety and gave me the sharpest point-by-point critiques which were of enormous value; my colleagues at the Courtauld, Margaret Garlake and Sarah Wilson, also read the book in its entirety, and both, from their very different perspectives, made me aware of gaps to be filled, errors to be avoided and judgements in need of reconsideration.

Yale University Press has provided the guidance, tactful editing and unruffled professionalism which is now so much what I expect from them that I am in danger of taking it for granted. It was John Nicoll who suggested that I write the book for the Pelican series, when I first brought him the idea of a book on art in France between 1900 and 1940. The knowledge that he was behind the project throughout was immensely important to me. Sally Salvesen, the editor of the Pelican series, has kept an expert eye on the project from its early synoptic stages to the end; her confidence in it has also kept me going. Sally Nicholls has collected together the photographs for the book and cleared the reproduction rights with great patience and resourcefulness. And Beatrix McIntyre has edited the text and designed the book with judicious skill, retaining her humour and good nature throughout, whatever the pressures.

Over many years, Charlotte, Abigail and Toby have made even the most challenging things (this book included) seem possible. Theirs has been the biggest contribution of all. I sometimes wonder how they have had the forbearance, quite apart from the generosity of spirit, to give me so much.

Preface

The beginning and end of this history are marked by events. It begins with the arrival in Paris of art from across the world for the massive Exposition Universelle of 1900. It ends in 1940 with the flight from Paris of many who, over the intervening four decades, made the city a centre of innovation in the visual arts of enormous international importance. It begins too with the election of the centre-Left Waldeck-Rousseau government, an event which consolidated the idea of France as a liberal democracy dedicated to reason and progress, and ends with German invasion and the brutal defeat of all those ideals.

I have not, however, written this history as the unfolding of a single narrative culminating in the international triumph of French art and the end of the Third Republic. To have done so would have sustained the idea of a progressive evolution in which works of art are simply stages, and, with this, the idea that the history of art in the twentieth century is a history of movements, one following and superseding another. Artists did indeed identify with or resist movements in France, and on certain levels their work spoke from positions related to movements as collective realities. I have myself written about French art in terms of the debates that developed around movements, in particular Cubism; and, indeed, artists in their Cubist or Dadaist or Surrealist personae make frequent appearances throughout this book. But to write a history on this scale as a history of movements would, I believe, be far too restrictive. So diagrammatic a picture would inevitably mask the fact that artists speak through their work from within their own narratives and their own contexts. It would also pen their work into a cultural area fenced off from other histories, an area in which art changes and acquires meaning on its own terms alone, and in which the social and the political are 'background'. My aim has been to write a history that allows artists and works of art, looked at individually, to be set not against but in a much wider landscape, one actively shaped by politics and social change interacting with the eruption and movement of ideas.

This book may not tell a story with an easily delineated plot, but I have structured it so as to facilitate ease of access. At the same time, I have structured it so as to enable its use by readers with different levels of knowledge, from the least to the most developed. Part One has been written as an introduction for anyone who is a newcomer to the field, and also as a foundation on which the rest of the book is built. The remaining five parts take five slices right through the period, looking at its art from five distinct vantage points. There is a logic to the sequence of these five parts, even if there is no single narrative: they are designed to be read in succession by anyone who wants to read the book as a whole. But they are also designed to be approached separately by those whose interest is in one or more of the areas they cover. Each one stands on its own as a way into a particular topic: a concise historical study in its own right.

Overall, the book is constructed in two halves. The first three parts prepare the way for the last three. Thus, following Part One's introduction, Parts Two and Three survey the whole field of art across the period and chart change within it, Part Two looking at art-world lives and careers, Part Three looking at new theories and practices. By contrast, Parts Four, Five and Six, are interpretative, and look more selectively at the art of the period according to themes. Some awareness of the material covered in the first half of the book has been assumed in the writing of this second half, whether it has been acquired from other reading or not.

As a guide to the book, I shall set out briefly the contents of the six parts. Each consists of a short introduction and two chapters.

Part One deals with history. Chapter 1 looks at the Paris Exhibitions of 1900, 1925 and 1937 as a way of introducing the social, economic and political history of France in the period. Each in its own spectacular way used art and architecture to create a glamorised representation of France at that moment, and so they bring together history in the widest sense with the history of art, sometimes misleadingly, sometimes revealingly, always eloquently. The chapter ends with a discussion of how art in France from the previous forty or fifty years was shown at the 1937 Exhibition, bringing out the ways in which France was held up as the source and origin of a new and triumphant international 'independent art'. Chapter 2 introduces the history of art as such in the period by looking at the history of modern movements according to which it has most often been written. Thumbnail histories of the major movements – Fauvism, Cubism, Dada, Surrealism and non-objective art – are given, but in such a way as to make apparent the inadequacy of an overall view that depends on these movements as its defining categories. Part One ends by scrutinising the term 'avant-garde' and by asking how avant-gardism in France is to be understood in relation to social and political change: how it relates to orthodoxies of every kind, not only artistic.

Part Two deals with the lives of artists and of others involved in the visual arts in the period, and brings out the constraints that shaped them. Chapter 3 explores the role of the State as client and patron of artists, considers what was 'official' and what was 'independent' art, how so-called 'academic' and anti-academic artists approached the marketing of their work, and how the distinctions between the categories most especially of painting and sculpture, but also of 'fine' and 'commercial' art were challenged. Finally, it brings out the importance of art critics and especially of art dealers and collectors as the engine of the success of modernism both in France and abroad. Chapter 4 looks into the ways in which 'independent' success and failure were evaluated, and then the conditions that allowed them. It highlights the problems faced by foreign artists and women artists in France, before analysing the careers of a selection of major modern figures, most prominently Picasso, Matisse and Duchamp. Portraits and self-portraits of artists (photographs as well as paintings) are given special prominence here because of the insights they offer. The analysis is geared to bring out the tensions that existed between the need to succeed in the market and the need to practice art freely, on its own terms alone. Part Two ends with Duchamp's refusal of the very idea of a career in art while developing one anyway, and making sure it would be remembered.

Part Three deals with artistic innovation and the theories and practices of modernism. Initially, modern practices are placed in relation to those of such 'academics' as Henri Gervex and Léon Bonnat. The focus is exclusively on artist's statements, artist's ways of working and what they actually produced: the works themselves. Necessarily, the section has a strong narrative form, following, as it does, successive developments. The thread that holds it together is the increasing importance given to the relationship between the work and the spectator. Chapter 5 moves from Matisse's 'decorative' aesthetic to the 'conceptual' art of the Cubists, concentrating on the question of aesthetic 'autonomy' – the self-sufficiency of the work of art – and culminating with the idea of the tableau objet (picture-object) and the possibility of abstraction. Chapter 6 moves from an analysis of Cubism as a system of signs which allows identities to change, into the metamorphic practices of the Dada and Surrealist artists. It culminates with the incorporation of words into works of art and the arrival of the 'Surrealist object'. Part Three ends with the point that the approach to interpretation in the second half of the book will favour the spectator, as modernist art did, and look more at how works could invite responses than at what artists intended them to say.

Part Four takes as its theme modernity. Chapter 7 deals with the representation of modernity as 'progress' in science and technology. It takes in newly disseminated ideas of chemical transformation, space and time, and new developments in transport and communication – the motor car and wireless – and explores how they are represented by artists ranging from the quasi-Impressionist 'academic' Albert Besnard to Cubists such as Gleizes and Léger. It looks too at old and new techniques of representation, in particular painting in relation to photography. Finally, it considers the representation of science in the hugely popular Palais de la Découverte at the 1937 Exposition Internationale. Chapter 8 deals with the role of modern spaces and people in art, approaching them in the context of social and political change in France. It opens with the growth of consumerism, and its impact through department store display and advertising on art, moves on to the 'modern' woman as a theme in the work of artists as various as Marie Laurencin, Le Corbusier and Suzanne Valadon, before confronting class and class conflict as the subject matter of politically engaged artists especially in the 1930s. Part Four ends with the modernists of the Left opposed by the claim of Socialist Realists like Boris Taslitsky and André Fougeron to be the only effective artist-propagandists of Revolution.

Part Five takes as its theme tradition and nationalism. It starts by introducing the opposition in France between a dominant territorial idea of the nation, which is liberal and expansive, open to the assimilation of immigrants, and an authoritarian, organic idea of the nation, growing in influence during the period, which stresses racial 'purity' and exclusion. The central topic throughout is ownership of the 'French Tradition', a notion which itself is shown to be unstable. The central question is: can modernists in France redefine that tradition convincingly enough to belong? And, if so, are they to be aligned with an exclusive or an inclusive idea of the French nation? Chapter 9 deals with Matisse, Denis, Maillol, the Cubists (foreign and French) and Derain, culminating in the push to align Cubism with a 'Latin' idea of the 'French Tradition' during the 1914–18 war. Chapter 10 takes the inter-war period, and deals with the fortunes of the idea of a Latin French Tradition alongside that of a France of 'petit pays' sustaining regional diversity in culture. These are explored in the context of high immigration and the growth across the political spectrum of xenophobic, often anti-semitic reaction. The 'classical' work of such major modernists as Picasso, Braque and Léger is included, alongside that of other figures then considered highly significant in the period, among them Dunoyer de Segonzac and Marcel Gromaire.

Part Six looks at the resistance of artists to 'modernity' and 'tradition', both of them taken as fundamental to the ideal of civilization. It is the most substantial of the thematic sections of the book, and deals with material that can still provoke, material that is often rebarbatively counter-cultural. Chapter 11 singles out the theme of 'primitivism' in the pre-1914 period. It focuses especially on Picasso, Brancusi and Henri Rousseau. It explores the way modern art was 'primitivized' in relation to the non-European and to the peasant cultures of Europe, and also the way 'naïvety' became an ideal for artists in a society dedicated to education as its primary civilising and democratising mission. Chapter 12 focuses especially on the work of the Dadaists, the Surrealists and their dissident counterparts. It takes in the writing of such figures as André Breton, Georges Bataille and Michel Leiris, as well as the work once again of Picasso, and of such figures as Duchamp, Masson, Miró, Giacometti and Dalí. A central concern is the way artists and writers did not simply oppose the progressive and the rational by appropriating the regressive, irrational aspects of psychoanalysis, but worked to de-civilize culture altogether. Topics opened up here include the non-European as savage 'other', the artist as magician, infantilism, Bataille's notions of 'bassesse' and the 'informe', and the death drive in opposition to Eros: violence and ultimately war against love. The book ends with a section written around Picasso's Guernica of 1937 as an allegory of the death drive victorious, and as political propaganda. It takes up the question of art and political opposition across the whole period 1900-40, from the anarchist activism of the 1900s to the anti-Fascism of the build up to war in the 1930s.

One final point needs to be made about the book as a whole. My approach throughout gives priority to history. While the themes I have chosen and the issues I have explored are certainly determined by my vantage-point from the turn of the millennium, and are driven therefore by contemporary agendas and an awareness of contemporary theoretical positions, the historical situation of a work is always a factor in the critical judgements I have made, whatever its impact or lack of impact now. In France between 1900 and 1940, there were artists treated today as major who were habitually dismissed as minor – Duchamp most remarkably

– and there were artists treated today as minor who were celebrated as major – de Segonzac, for instance. Historians cannot help but colonise the past to exploit it for the present, but my book has been written with a strong sense of the distance between now and then. Art historians can only deal with works of art as they confront them in their present; Duchamp is given far more space here than de Segonzac, even if both his and de Segonzac's work are looked at in their historical contexts. My book is written to open the way for a richer responsiveness to the kind of work I look at. But I have not approached the art of what is now the first half of the last century as if it is only worth serious attention when it helps develop our critical agendas: as if it was made for us today.

Christopher Green, 5 June 2000

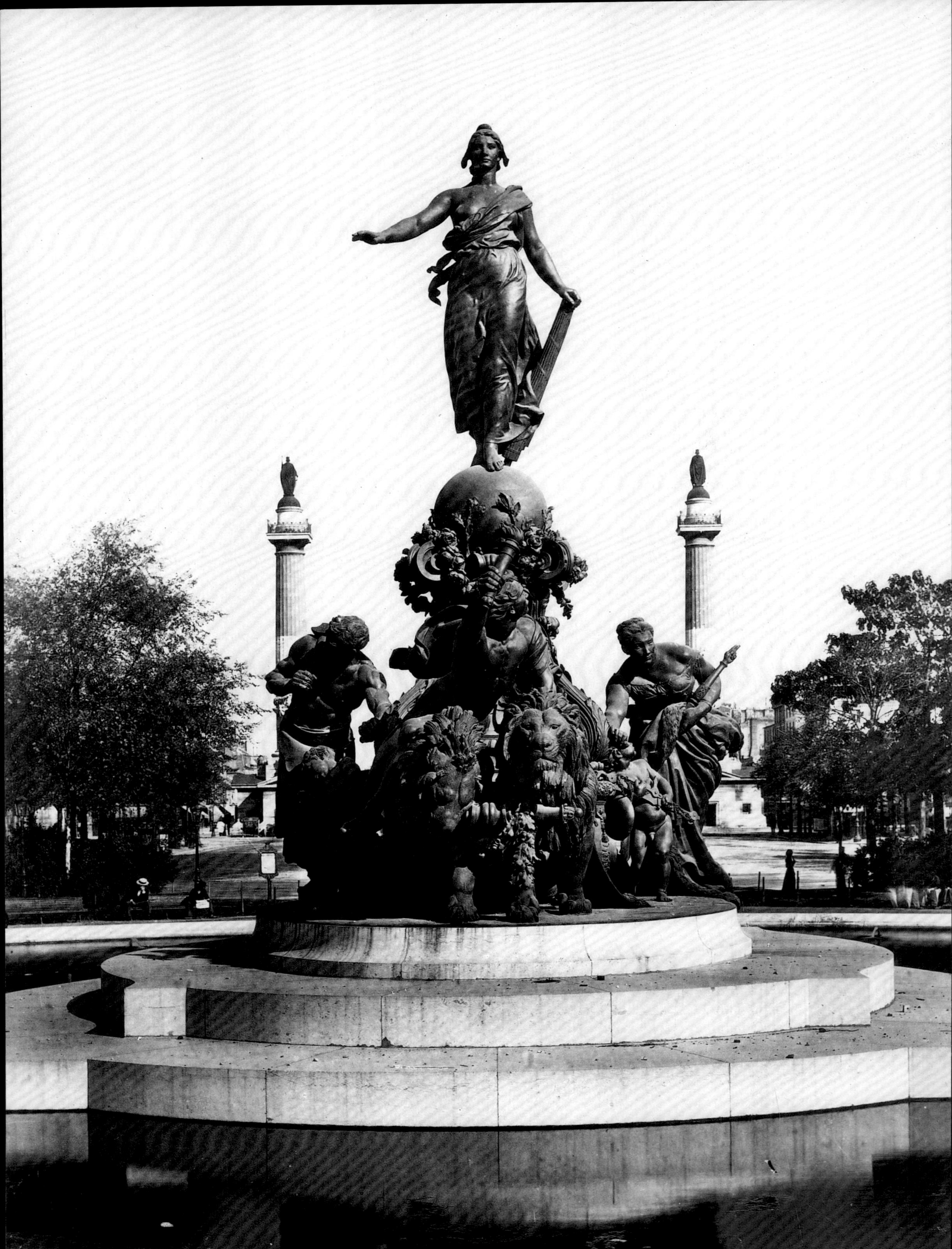

PART ONE

Art Made History

INTRODUCTION

'Nation' is encountered now either at speed as a traffic roundabout on the eastern fringes of Paris or in the routines of city travel as a major junction on the Métro. The huge monument in bronze around which the traffic sweeps, Jules Dalou's *Triumph of the Republic* [1], celebrates the end of France's monarchs and Emperors unnoticed by most. On 19 November 1899, its inauguration made it the focus of a great popular event; around it gathered dense crowds of workers and ordinary Parisians who had walked in orderly but noisy procession decked out with red flags along the faubourg Saint-Antoine to add their massed presence to its confident endorsement of the Third Republic.[1] It had taken Dalou (1838–1902) twenty years to realise the monument for its triumphant inauguration on the eve of the twentieth century.

Today its allegorical rhetoric has few listeners above the din of the traffic; in 1899, even the least educated of its mass audience would have found the allegories eloquent. The female figure of the Republic advances, one breast bare in accepted 'radical' style, the Phrygian red bonnet of the Revolution on her head. She stands poised upon a globe, her right hand raised in a gesture at once of protection and of command. Her platform is in rumbling movement; it is a chariot pulled by the People in the implacable form of pair of lions, its wheels helped round by the muscular male figure of Work, sledgehammer over shoulder, and the equally powerful female figure of Justice, appropriately draped. The chariot is accompanied by children, given the accoutrements of Education, Equity and Wealth; the heroic figure of Liberty points the way with his flaming torch, mounted insouciantly upon the lions, while Peace, carrying the attributes of abundance, distributes (no doubt fairly) her largesse of flowers and fruit in the chariot's wake.

Early the following summer, the fifth of France's Universal Exhibitions opened, the Exhibition of 1900, inaugurating three of the grandest expressions of Third Republic pride to survive to 2000: the Grand and the Petit Palais, and the Pont Alexandre III which joins them to the Right Bank. Georges Récipon's nude god in bronze launching a quartet of leaping horses into the sky above the cours la Reine entrance of the Grand Palais [2] is titled *Harmony Triumphing over Discord*; it offers Baroque elan rather than sturdy poise as an expression of faith in the new century's inevitable Republican triumph over the discord of the nineteenth century. The 1900 Exhibition was presented by France's minister of Commerce and Industry, Jules Roche (future father-in-law of the Cubist painter Albert Gleizes), as a 'record from which will be given the material and moral conditions of contemporary life.'[2] The mission of the exhibition, like all the Universal Exhibitions since 1855, was to give spectacular form to France as a modern industrial nation; for Roche, the 'moral conditions' of that modernity were the values of the new Republic: liberty, reason and democracy. The Exhibition of 1900 was the successor to the Exhibition of 1889, which had set up the Eiffel Tower as the symbol of material progress in confrontation against the traditionalist Roman Catholic envangelism of Sacré Coeur, rising on the hill of Montmartre across Paris. 1900 too gave modernity a central role, as spectacle in the galerie des machines, which survived from 1889, and beneath the Baroque cladding of the two Palais in the space-spanning steel frames that made them possible. The thresholds of the Pont Alexandre III – a still more advanced reinforced concrete structure – are guarded by monumental sculptures by Gustave Michel, which allegorize in female form the France of the Renaissance, of Louis XIV, of the Middle Ages and of modern times; the corseted figure of modernity holds in her left hand a statue, easily interpreted as the twentieth century at its birth.[3]

Paris had to wait nearly four decades for its next Universal Exhibition, the 'Exposition internationale des arts et des techniques dans la vie moderne' of 1937. In between there had been an extravagant 'Exposition internationale des arts décoratifs et industriels modernes' and an exotic 'Exposition Coloniale', in 1925 and 1931 respectively, but only this had the sweep and ambition of a Universal Exhibition. Its dedication to 'modern life' rivalled 1900, and yet even thirty-seven years later it offered in its monuments and its officially commissioned art most conspicuously a combination of stylishness (often backward-looking) and allegory. Both in 1900 and in 1937, a major modern theme was electricity, given its most spectacular expression as light – electric light had been a key factor in exhibition-making since its introduction into art galleries from 1879. In 1937, there were dramatic night-time multi-media shows and even electric cars to ferry visitors between pavilions, and, indeed, one of those pavilions was dedicated to 'electricity and light' [5]. The Pavillon de l'électricité et de la lumière was designed by the programmatically modernist architects Georges Pingusson and Robert Mallet-Stevens, its curved blank façade serving as screen for image projections and as back-cloth for the drama of a live spark that leapt a seven-metre gap in front of it. On the curving interior wall of its foyer, the painter Raoul Dufy (b.1877) covered an immense surface (60-by-10 metres) to produce the celebrated mural, *The Muse of Electricity* (*Fée électricité*) [3], where a roll-call of the Great Men behind the discovery and exploitation of electricity, accompanied by allegorical figures, were floated onto the canvas in drifts of weightless colour instantly recognisable as 'modern'.

1. Facing page. Jules Dalou, *Triumph of the Republic*, 1899. Place de la Nation, Paris

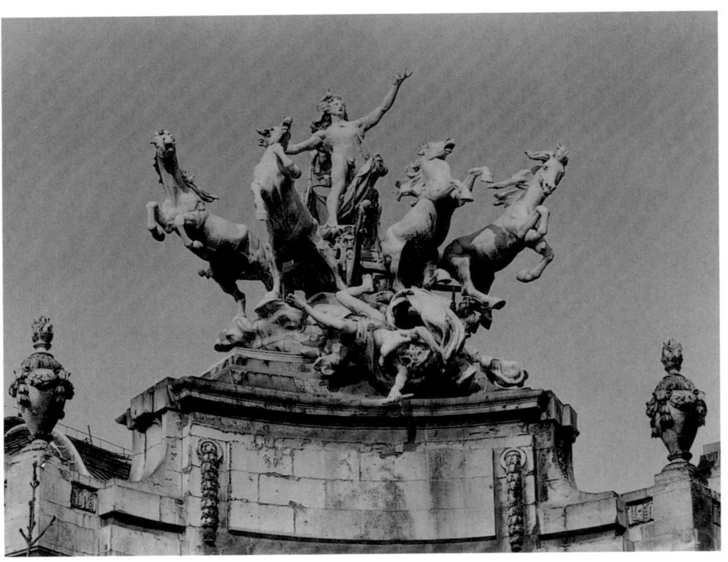

2. Georges Récipon, *Harmony Triumphing over Discord*, 1900. Grand Palais, Paris

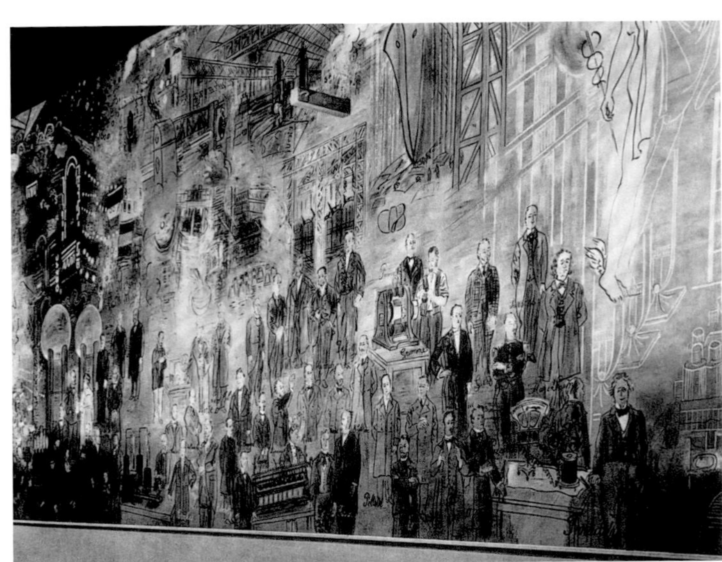

3. Raoul Dufy, *The Muse of Electricity* (*Fée électricité*), 1937. Musée d'art moderne de la Ville de Paris

4. View of the Exposition internationale des arts et des techniques dans la vie moderne, Paris, 1937, showing on the left the German Pavilion by Albert Speer, and on the right the Soviet Pavilion by Boris Iofan, with sculpture by Vera Mukhina

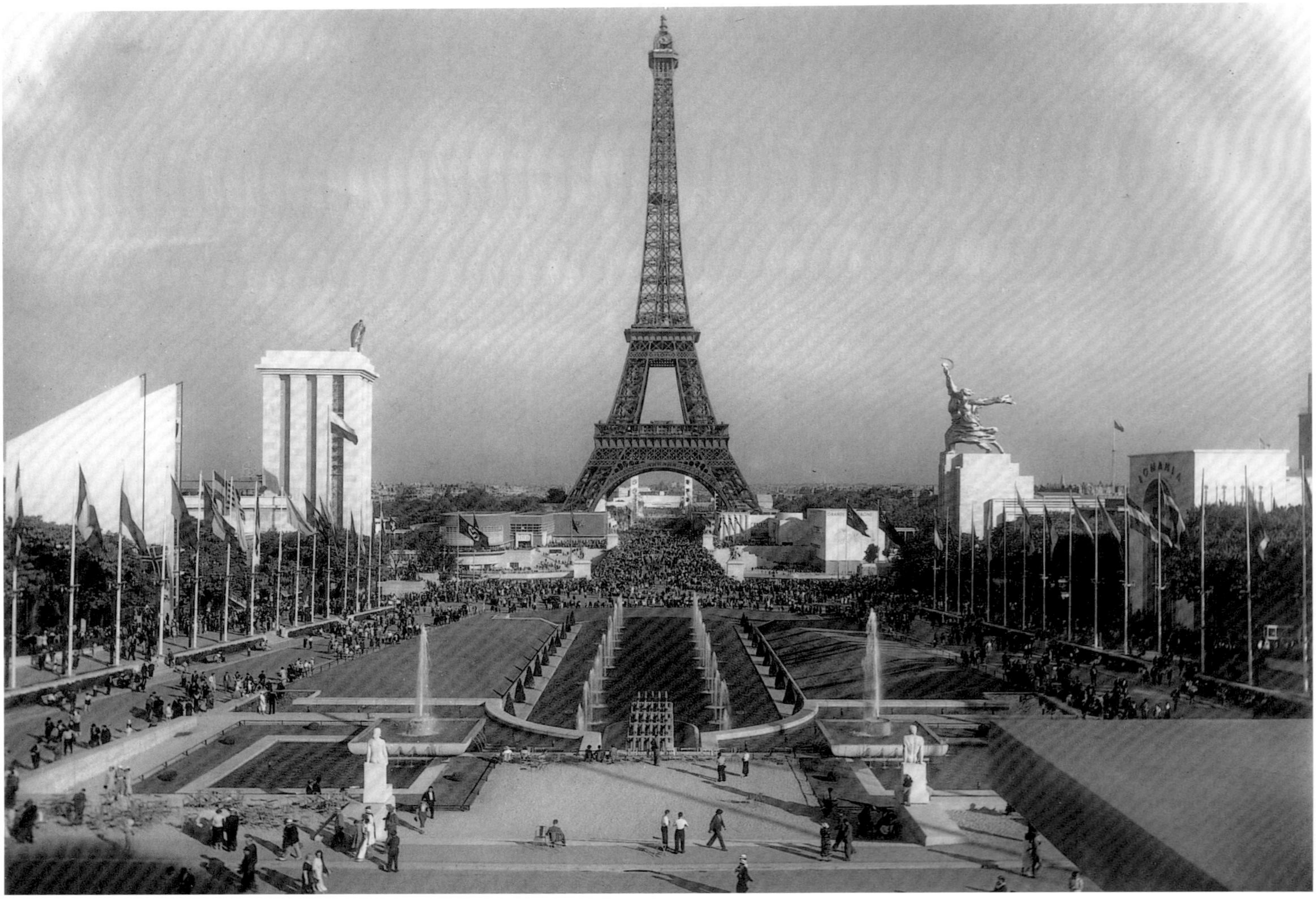

If hope and the triumph of republican 'harmony' over the conflicts of the nineteenth century had been a dominant theme of the 1900 Exhibition, the hope for peace presided over the Exhibition of 1937. The rebuilt Palais du Trocadéro – the Palais de Chaillot – embraced the main site of the exhibition [13], and, behind it, in the Place du Trocadéro, the 'International Peace Campaign' (Rassemblement Universel pour la paix) erected a tower wrapped around with olive branch decorations, the column of Peace; at its foot was a low semi-circular pavilion whose four rooms took its many visitors from the horrors of the 1914–18 war and of the then current Spanish Civil War to the hope embodied in the League of Nations, representative, it was declared, of nearly 1.5 billion of the 1.8 billion people of the world. 'What government,' asked a wall text, 'would dare unleash war if it had to confront all of humanity, standing firm in its pacific and powerful sovereignty?'[4]

The answer lay below the wide terraces of the Palais de Chaillot, over which the Peace Column presided, in the theatrical confrontation of the Soviet and German pavilions, the enormous figures of Vera Mukhina's *Worker and 'Kolkhozian' Woman* hurling themselves across space against Alfred Speer's impassive tower with its crowning feature, the eagle of the Third Reich [4]. The Exhibition of 1937 acted as a huge stage for the anxieties of a world on the edge of conflict, a stage whose decor was dominated by allegories of peace, progress and reason, the increasingly desperate expressions of republican virtue and collective hope. Deep beneath the Palais de Chaillot and the Peace Column, a new National Theatre was built as one of the permanent legacies of the exhibition. Above one of the two grand staircases that gave access from the Place du Trocadéro the one-time Prix-de-Rome winner (1907) and ocean-liner muralist, Louis Billotey, has left a stylish allegorical fresco painted in cement, *Tragedy* [6]; its central presiding figure, Fate, balances on the palms of her hands Man and Woman, an echo (doubtless unconscious) of the statuette figure of the nascent twentieth century held by modern France on the Pont Alexandre III, and an anticipation (doubtless unconscious) of imminent disaster: the end of the Third Republic that would follow the surrender of France in 1940.

It is between the poles of confidence and conflict monumentalised in the Exhibitions of 1900 and 1937 that any history of art in France between 1900 and 1940 is necessarily situated. The distance travelled between these poles by the Third Republic requires a closer scrutiny before the question of 'art' as one of its features is addressed; the Exhibitions of 1900 and 1937, coming together with the Decorative Arts Exhibition of 1925, give triangulation points for such a survey.

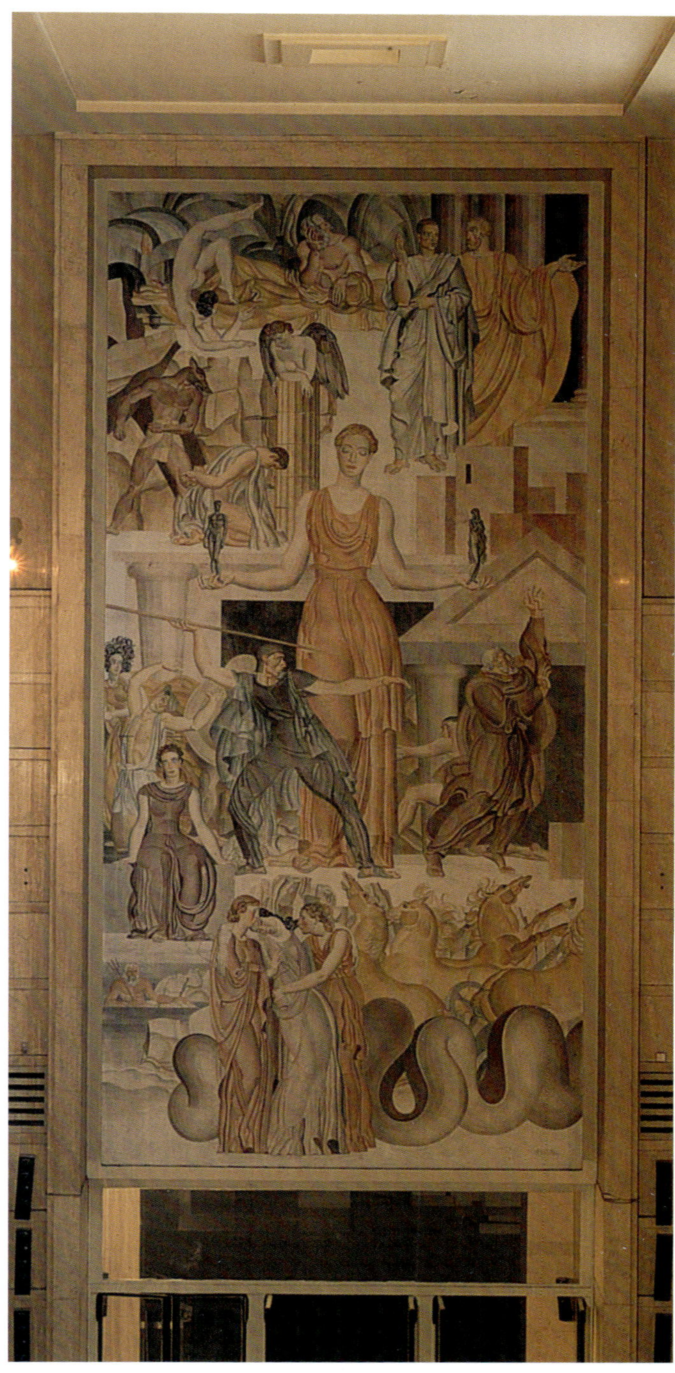

6. Right. Louis Billotey, *Tragedy*, 1937. Fresco in cement. Théâtre du Palais de Chaillot, Paris

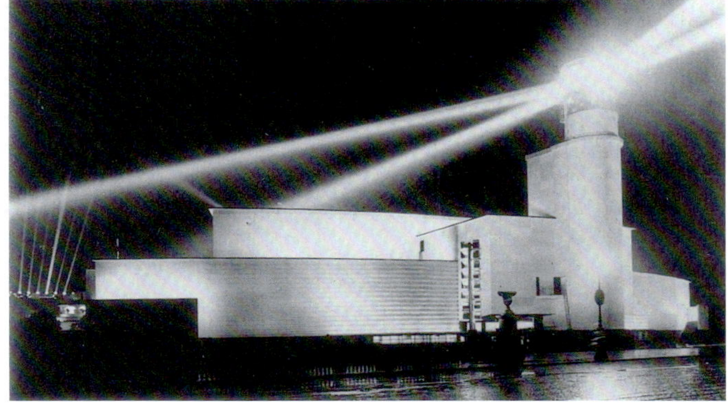

5. Georges Pingusson and Robert Mallet-Stevens, Pavilion of Electricity and Light (Pavillon de l'électricité et de la lumière), Exposition internationale des arts et des techniques dans la vie moderne, Paris, 1937

CHAPTER 1

Monuments to the Third Republic: the Great Exhibitions of 1900, 1925 and 1937

BEFORE AND AFTER 1900

The sense of well-being was pervasive at the Great Exhibition of 1900: the Third Republic presented a confident face. There were two major contributing factors behind this. One was the beginning of the end of the Dreyfus Affair with President Loubet's signing of Dreyfus's pardon on 19 September 1899; the other was the election in June 1899 of Waldeck-Rousseau's 'radical' administration, followed in May 1900 by widespread republican successes in the local elections. The Affair had been triggered by false accusations of espionage against an army officer. It had exposed the slippery relativity of symbols, for the scandalous imprisonment and exile of Captain Alfred Dreyfus, son of a Jewish manufacturer from Mulhouse, had turned him into a symbol on the Right of the danger to France of republican laxity, and, on the Left, of the need for republican institutions and a free press to defend Truth and the liberty of the individual. The Affair had also exposed the potential for violent confrontation still to be extracted from the social and political differences keeping apart Roman Catholic, Bonapartist and monarchist believers in traditional hierarchies and libertarian believers in the new secular institutions and democratic rights of the Republic; but in 1900 those conflicts seemed resolved on the side of the Third Republic.

The exhibition staged its republican vision of France in Paris as the ancient yet modern metropolitan centre of an infinitely diverse country and of an expanding colonial empire, the capital of a nation now to be counted in the 'concert of nations'.

The ancient and the modern coexisted in the juxtaposition, for instance, of the elaborate reconstruction of 'Vieux Paris' especially conceived for the exhibition by Albert Robida, complete with 'authentic' hostelries, and the Paris Métro, with its Art Nouveau station entrances by Hector Guimard, whose first line was opened by President Loubet on 19 July (during the exhibition).

The interdependence of metropolis and provinces was perhaps most splendidly demonstrated by an event too vast even for the steel-vaulted expanses of the new Salle des fêtes in the Grand Palais. It was the banquet held on 22 September 1900 (the anniversary of the Republic) for the mayors of France. More than twenty thousand attended, seated at 606 tables under canvas in the Jardins des Tuileries, each guest supplied with two bottles of wine; they sung of themselves, gathered under the red, white and blue of the French Republic, like a great 'bouquet of flowers'. The Exhibition of 1900 was a Parisian amusement park, planned from Paris by a civil-servant-run Conseil général just as national government remained centralised under the prefects and sub-prefects of the Napoleonic system, but from 1884 the mayors of the local Communes were elected, and the building or enlargement of town-halls all over France signalled their new democratic role in the Republic. Between 1900 and 1914, Paris remained a special case, the one major modern city in a still predominantly rural country: a city of nearly three million, hardly challenged by the only other two cities of more than half-a-million, Lyon and Marseille. And between 1900 and 1914, the Radicals who came together in 1901–3 to form the first modern political party in France, consolidated their dominance as the party of government not because they had the support of Paris, the city of government, but because of their dispersed, uncoordinated network of supporting groups across the provinces: power was enjoyed in Paris, but it was won in the country.[1]

Just as 'authentic' old Paris was displayed in idealised reconstructions, so too was the 'authentic' exoticism of France's new colonies: the expanding colonial power of the Third Republic was made the source of novel diversions, not a demonstration, as its early advocate Jules Ferry had said it was in the 1880s, of France's civilising role outside Europe. Paul Morand was to publish a memoir of the 1900 Exhibition in 1931, the year of the 'Exposition Coloniale' in the Bois de Vincennes. 'I pass my days,' he wrote, 'in this arab, negro, polynesian town, which stretches from the Eiffel Tower to Passy, gentle Parisian hillside which all of a sudden carries on its back Africa, Asia, the immense universe of which I dream.'[2] Despite the unabashed pleasure taken by such as Morand in the colonies as settings for dream projection, in 1900 colonial expansion was one of the routes to real European power and, for individual French citizens, to real wealth. 1900 was the year when three French expeditionary columns, which had set out from the Sahara, the Congo and the Sudan, came together in Chad after destroying the empire of Rabah; the prospect was offered of a French Republic whose 'civilising' law might one day stretch from the Mediterranean to the Congo. It would not be rival colonial ambitions that took Europe into war in 1914, but it was as a colonial as well as a European power that France pursued her triple entente policy with Britain, Russia and Italy against Germany from 1905. In 1900, the Pont Alexandre III, symbol not only of the Republic's commitment to modern engineering but also of her developing entente with Tsarist Russia, declared a bombastic new confidence in France's European future.

The right-wing press mounted a campaign against the 1900 Exhibition, as a metropolitan threat to the moral values of the French in all their regional diversity. In fact, it attracted thousands of visitors from all over France, who encountered that bombastic new confidence everywhere: a can-do mentality summed up, as Pascal Ory has pointed out, by the Nitrate of Soda pavilion, which took the form of a temple topped by a figure of the Republic in her Phrygian bonnet housing a pillar made of blocks mounted one on top of another to symbolise the unstoppable rise in production from 1830 to 1899.[3]

On 1 June 1911, René Guilleré, lawyer and president of the Société des artistes décorateurs, published a proposal for an 'Exposition internationale des arts décoratifs' to open in 1915; this was one of the first moves in preparations for the Decorative Arts Exhibition that would open more than half a decade after the 1914–18 war in 1925, and it focused on that aspect of the 1900 Exhibition which Guilleré and the Society considered most important, the alliance between modern industry and modern design (as 'decorative art'), especially as represented in Samuel Bing's Pavillon de l'Art Nouveau and in Guimard's brand new métro stations. If, however, war had not been declared in August 1914 and another Universal Exhibition had followed the Exhibition of 1900 in 1915, it is likely that its idealised portrait of the Third Republic would have lacked something of the unqualified optimism of 1900.

Certainly, growth in industrial production was a feature of the period 1900–14, indeed far stronger growth than in the last decades of the nineteenth century. The Eiffel Tower was iron, the frames of the Grand and Petit Palais were steel. The 1890s saw the French metallurgical industry shift from iron to steel and to the new plants of Lorraine; between 1900 and 1914 steel production more than tripled, after nearly doubling to 1.5 million tonnes in the 1890s. Most spectacular, however, was the growth of the new industries: chemical, electrical and car-manufacturing. Between 1900 and 1913, electrical production expanded from 340 million kilowatts to 1,800 million, and by 1914, France was Europe's largest car-manufacturer, led by Renault and Citroën. Between 1896 and 1913, growth in the French national product averaged 1.6%, a long way behind the USA and Germany, but close to Britain. Incomes for the dividend-gaining middle classes rose more than satisfactorily. It remains easy to dub the period to 1914, the Belle Epoque.[4]

The dynamic advance of the Third Republic as an industrial economy was, however, only partial. In 1914, most workers remained in the old industries, especially textiles, which were slow to use credit for expansion and to respond to technological innovation; and most remained employed in small family firms with less than fifty employees, the vast majority artisanal enterprises with less than four. As representatives of the traditionally strong luxury goods industries of France, the artists and craftspeople working in the 'decorative arts' were more typical than the new specialist workers employed by André Citroën. René Guilleré's 'modern' dream of the ideal place of decorative artists working for manufacturers as individual aesthetic inventors was not attuned to the capitalist dynamism of the new industries. French business remained predominantly old-fashioned: the easy-going companion of the still dominant, and still more stagnant rural sector, which was exclusively the preserve of small peasant farming but for limited areas of capitalist farming in the Paris basin and the North and in the wine growing areas of the South West.

At the same time, while the dominant group in national politics, the new Radical Party, had lost its reforming zeal and became the party of middle-class pragmatism by 1914, the potential for revolutionary conflict within the republic had been heightened by the formation on the Left of a Marxist Socialist Party in 1904 (the SFIO – French Section of the Workers' International) and, on the Right, by the emergence of a violently anti-republican and anti-Semitic organisation dedicated to the return of the monarchy. This was Action française, still tiny, but through its daily newspaper (founded in 1908) and its eloquent editor, Charles Maurras, disruptive on a national scale.

Had there been a Universal Exhibition in 1914, even without the explosion of the Balkan Crisis that August, it would have been an event infused with external as well as internal tensions, for the years 1911 to 1914 saw a major crisis in Franco-German relations over rival colonial ambitions in Morocco (resolved humiliatingly in Germany's favour) and a consequent intensification of French nationalism which provoked concerted Socialist anger on the streets. By 1914 radical republicans shared some of the nationalist passions and prejudices of Action française; in this at least the centre Left had moved strongly to the Right. Traditionalist nationalism had been given a republican dimension. Inspired by the intransigence of the independent Socialist, Jean Jaurès, the Socialist Party (SFIO) fought the three-year military service legislation of 1913 that accompanied this shift with demonstrations, and the danger of war with the fantasy threat of an international General Strike.

In 1900 the Universal Exhibition could represent the hopes and values of secular republicanism as a new consensus built on the defeat of the nationalist Right, the potential of industry and the emerging strength of France as a European and colonial power. On 4 August 1914, in the Chamber of Deputies, Raymond Poincaré, the president of the Republic, pleaded for a 'Union Sacré' to supercede the political differences of peacetime as France mobilised for war; the consensus had been an illusion, Poincaré's plea was imperative. The Union would always be fragile; it had collapsed by 1917.

BEFORE AND AFTER 1925

Painting and sculpture were given a central role in the Exhibition of 1900. They filled the Petit and the Grand Palais in grand displays of France's cultural leadership. The Petit Palais contained a huge Retrospective Exhibition of French Art, which took the story up to 1800, and the Grand Palais contained an even larger Centennial Exhibition of French Art, 1800–1900 (the Centennale), which actually finished in 1890 and was placed in knowingly competitive juxtaposition with an exhibition of a decade of 'fine art' from 1889 to 1900 (the Décennale). The Centennale, which showed over 3000 exhibits, including 672 paintings and 420 sculptures, filled over three-quarters of the west wing of the Grand Palais; the Décennale filled over three-quarters of the vast main body of the palace, shunting the small foreign showings into confined marginal areas. A feature of the Centennale was its curator Roger Marx's decision to show decorative arts – furniture – with 'fine art'. His rationale for this is summed up by Emile Molinier (curator of the Louvre) in his preface to a luxury collection of half-tone reproductions of works from the exhibition: 'We have wished for the most intimate possible mixture of painting, sculpture and interior decoration . . . It will show once again how false is the concept of two arts, the great and the industrial: the unity

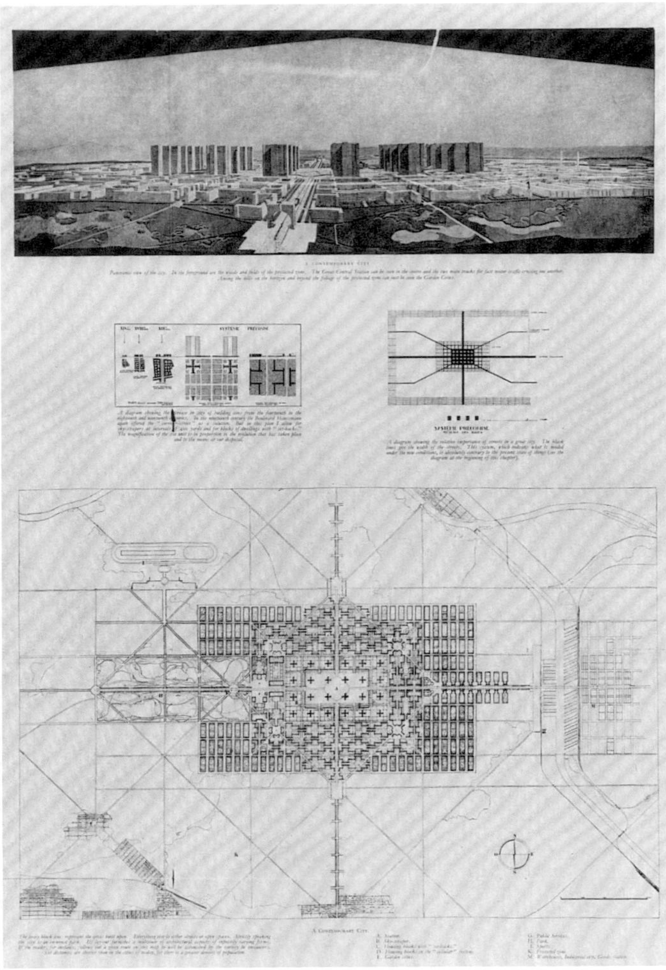

7. Le Corbusier, *Contemporary City for Three-Million*, 1922. Panoramic View and Plan, as published in Le Corbusier's *Urbanisme* (Paris, 1925)

of art is a principle, it should be a veritable dogma . . .'[5]

Roger Marx, a senior civil servant from the Fine Arts administration, followed here the lead of a major late nineteenth century advocate of the decorative arts, Antonin Proust, president of the Union centrale des arts décoratifs (1881–9); the decorative arts were given the key role in unifying the arts to create a new 'social art'.[6] By 1912, Roger Marx had published a manifesto on the theme: *L'Art social*, and had seen the ideal of a 'social art' become the cornerstone of cultural policy on the reforming parliamentary Left, most influentially in a book published the year before by the republican-socialist deputy for Blois, Joseph Paul-Boncour, *Art et démocratie*. Roger Marx's vision was of 'art for all, in everything and everywhere', the product of a new cooperative relationship between artist, manufacturer and consumer, which would socialise art by making it useful.[7] Paul-Boncour saw the spread of popular education with the secularisation of society under the Radical administrations of 1900–5 as grounding such a development in the collaboration of the educated middle classes and the working class, something he believed a real possibility.[8] This was the utopian framework within which the proposals for an international exhibition of decorative arts were placed by René Guilleré in 1911. Significantly, Roger Marx had himself proposed such an exhibition a couple of years before to mark the end of the conflict between art and technology. Guilleré imagined mass-produced yet beautifully designed drain-covers and automobile radiator-caps.[9]

There was another far from utopian framework for Guilleré's proposal in 1911: France's competitive position as a producer of modern design against such major rivals as Britain and Germany, and the newly emergent Italy. By 1924 and the final preparations for the International Exhibition of 1925, the ideal of 'social art' had been almost entirely displaced by overriding commercial priorities, as commissions and committees of the ministries of Public Instruction and of Industry and Commerce took over control. There were sections in the 1925 Exhibition for 'street art' and 'garden art', but its reputation was made by luxury designing, not by beautiful drain-covers: its mission was manifestly to boost France's luxury goods production.

It was its failure as a modern social project that provoked the concentrated fire of the modernists, led by the architect Le Corbusier and the critics Marie Dormoy, Gabriel Mourey and above all Waldemar George. Along with the Soviet Pavilion by Melnikov, George singled out Auguste Perret's theatre (a temporary demonstration in timber of the possibilities of reinforced concrete), Mallet-Stevens's contributions, including his Pavillon de Tourisme, and Le Corbusier's Pavillon de l'Esprit Nouveau [8] as the only 'modern' buildings in the exhibition.[10] Le Corbusier's tiny pavilion, erected late and against official disapproval, stood for the standardisation of design right down to furnishings, and was conceived as just one residential unit in a vision of an ideal *Contemporary City for Three-Million* [7].[11] For George, as for Le Corbusier, an incoherent medley of individualist luxury designs had taken over a project which should have offered planned solutions to the problems of modern society as a whole. He accused 'French and foreign decorators' of working 'only for the privileged class,' and, referring to one of the stars of the show, added: 'To have called an ensemble, as Ruhlmann has: 'the Town House of a Rich Collector' testifies either to a cynical spirit or to a

8. Le Corbusier, L'Esprit Nouveau Pavilion (Pavillon de l'Esprit Nouveau), 1925 (interior). Exposition Internationale des arts décoratifs et industriels modernes

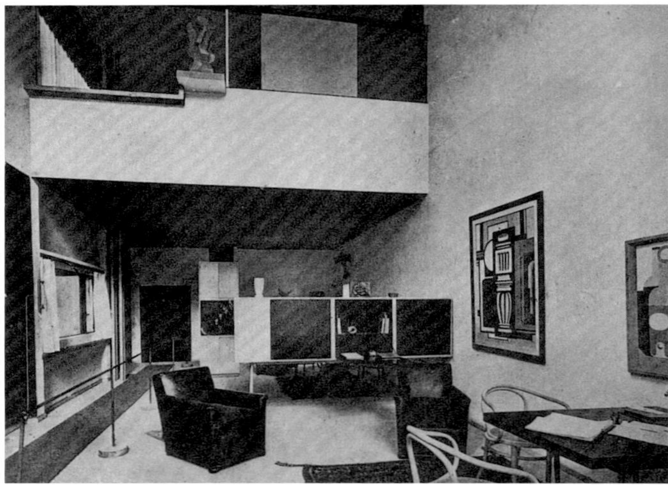

remarkable lack of awareness' [10].[12]

The single housing-unit which featured as Le Corbusier's Pavillon de l'Esprit Nouveau was designed for an imaginary middle class of managers and technocrats servicing business and government. Ruhlmann's sumptuous private palace was designed for an existing haute bourgeoisie and more broadly to appeal to the aspirations of the lesser middle classes, who could imagine themselves being 'rich collectors' too. It offered wealth and up-to-date good taste as a spectacle; an ersartz glimpse of post-war spending power as glamorised by the highly productive French film industry and the mass-circulation illustrated press. Le Corbusier and Waldemar George claimed to confront the realities of social problems and the real aspirations of modern society; in fact, Ruhlmann and his collaborators, the architect Pierre Patout, the sculptor Joseph Bernard, the metal-worker Edgar Brandt, and designers of precious objects like Jean Puiforcat or Pierre Legrain addressed actual classes of people with actual, current desires. It was these people who sampled fashion on-board Paul Poiret's pleasure barges moored on the Seine, and who were attracted by the stylish showmanship of the department store pavilions: the Bon Marché, the Galeries Lafayette, the Grands Magasins du Printemps [9]. The 1925 Exhibition stood for an obviously actual conjunction – the conjunction which Antonin Proust, Roger Marx and Joseph Paul-Boncour had rejected: culture and the middle classes.

In 1925 as in 1900, the middle classes were the dominant force in French society; it was they, especially the lesser middle classes known in the 1870s and the 1880s as the 'new strata', who brought back to power the Radicals in the 1924 Left coalition, the 'cartel des gauches', after a half-decade of right-wing dominance in the Chamber from 1919, and brought back with them the rationalist libertarian values of 1900–14. Indeed, the 1925 Exhibition is one testimony to a mid-twenties desire to remake in the image of a new modernity the Belle Epoque, imagined as a time of realised ambitions and sated appetites.

Berstein calculates the relative class populations in

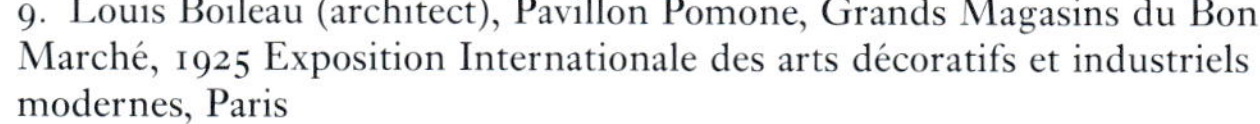

9. Louis Boileau (architect), Pavillon Pomone, Grands Magasins du Bon Marché, 1925 Exposition Internationale des arts décoratifs et industriels modernes, Paris

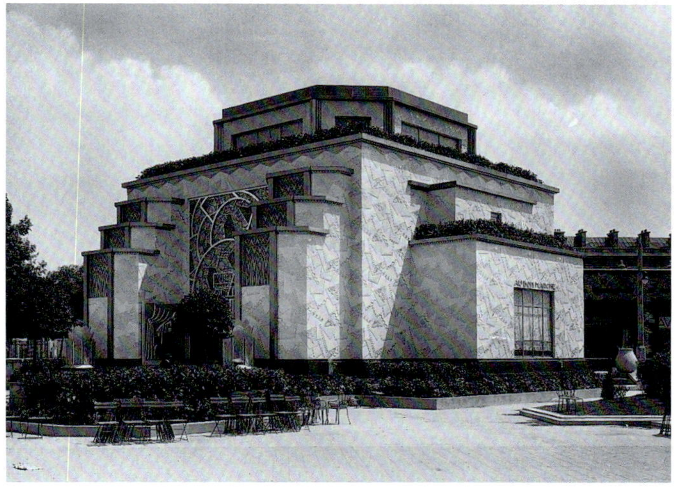

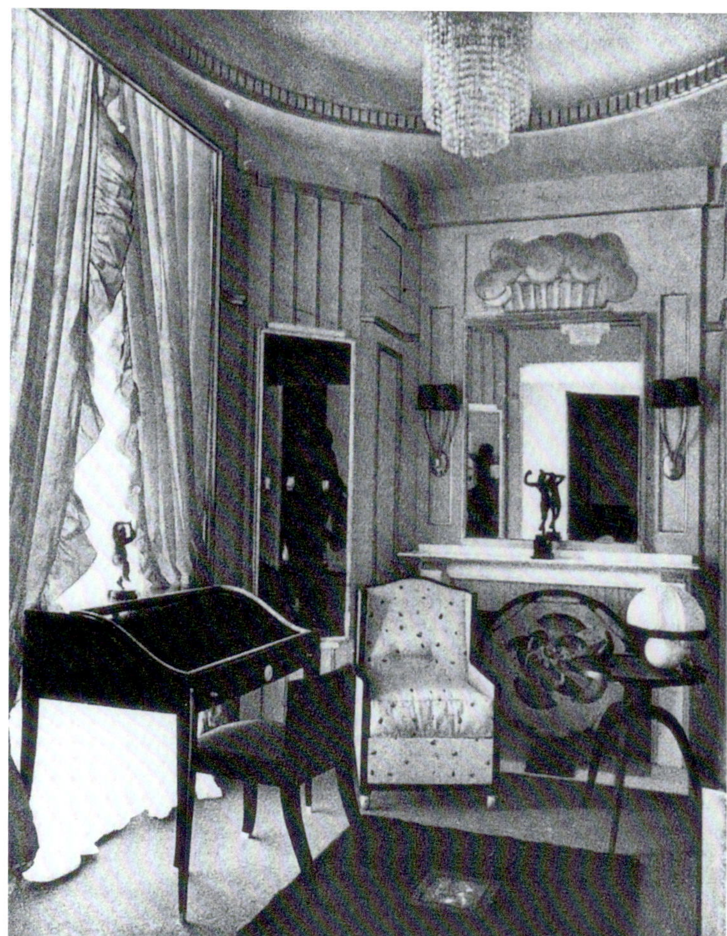

10. Ruhlmann Group. Pierre Patout (architect). *Town Mansion of a Rich Collector*, 1925. Boudoir. Exposition internationale des arts décoratifs et industriels modernes, Paris

France around 1930 as fourteen million peasants, thirteen million workers and fourteen million 'bourgeois'. Of the fourteen million bourgeois he calls twelve million middle class and adds to them some eight or nine million small and medium landowners living in the country on the proceeds of leased farms, a total of at least twenty million in a population of forty-two million.[13] What distinguished the middle classes most obviously from the condition of the workers and the peasants was the relative security of economic independence; what distinguished the bourgeois within the middle classes was a lycée education (until 1928, fee-paying). The middle classes were emphatically plural: they ranged from small provincal bankers, manufacturers and traders, through the liberal professions, the senior civil service and those living off investments, to a petty bourgeoisie of junior civil servants, white-collar workers, shopkeepers, small builders and craftsmen, many of whom qualified economically, but lacked the education of the bourgeois. Certainly, the nationalist and clerical Right recruited from these classes, but secular, individualist republicanism dominated, and within the lesser middle classes there was widespread hostility to hierarchical privilege and capitalist big business. As Mayeur and Reberioux have remarked of the pre-1914 middle classes, what finally brought them together was the fact that they did not work with their hands, and what most frequently characterised their behaviour was social aspiration: the belief in the openness of the system to their ascent.[14] With their one all-purpose maid, and, if they could afford it, their Citroën 5CV, the lesser middle classes ran scaled-down versions of the comfortable households of the bourgeois rich. It was its lavish appeal to this kind of social emulation that made of the 1925 Exhibition a popular as well as an élite success.

Its appeal to dominant middle-class values was consolidated by the prominent role it gave women. Thus, in Louis Dejean's gilded figure *Welcome* greeting visitors into the exhibition at the Porte de la Concorde [11] the female body was offered as a transcendent surrogate into whose blankness to project an agreeable persona and in which to discover a desired physical and spiritual state: a generous responsiveness. At the same time, the prominence given to fashion not only by Poiret's pleasure barges but also by the fashion section in the Grand Palais, the Pavillon de l'élégance and by Sonia Delaunay's *Simultaneous Boutique* underlined the importance of women more as consumers than as the designers of decorative luxury [44]. Right across the middle classes the gender roles of the nineteenth century had been maintained, even after the much-praised effort women had made to fill men's jobs in industry and agriculture during the 1914–18 war; active working women like the artist Sonia Delaunay and the couturier Jeanne Lanvin, coordinator of the fashion section and the Pavillon de l'élégance, were rare exceptions. In 1924, secondary school curricula became identical for boys and girls, but there were still manifold obstacles to women's careers: they were excluded from the magistrature, boycotted by the liberal professions generally and kept out of the adminstrative civil service by the rule that only those who had done military service were eligible. Their place remained the home, whether stylishly bourgeois or penny-pinching. The catastrophic losses of the war had led to a renewed idealisation of motherhood, and to draconian anti-contraception and anti-abortion laws. In 1922, the Senate had thrown out legislation to give women the vote; women would be denied the vote until 1944.

In its stylish consumerism the 1925 Exhibition approached the confidence of 1900, and many of the themes of 1900 were there again: Paris as metropolitan centre for a France of the regions was symbolised by an ideal 'Village français' built on the Esplanade des Invalides; France as the centre of a colonial empire – significantly enlarged after the Treaty of Versailles – by the ubiquity of exotic woods and skins from Africa and the Far East in the luxury furnishings on display. Seven years after the victorious conclusion of the Great War, however, there were signs of an uncertain future even for the middle classes. The Belle Epoque was, after all, beyond revival. In April 1925, Etienne Clémentel stepped down as finance minister as his deflationary, high-debt policies led to a weakening of the franc to a level far below that of 1914, and the flight of capital abroad. The year before, it had become clear that France would not be able to force Germany to keep up the reparation payments agreed at Versailles. At the same time, the Radical regime was confronted now by a splitting in two of the Marxist Left, and the birth at the Socialists' Congrès de Tours (1920) of the Parti Communiste français (PCF), an altogether new kind of danger to the middle classes.

11. Louis Dejean, *Welcome*, 1925. In front of the Porte de la Concorde, Exposition Internationale des arts décoratifs et industriels modernes, Paris

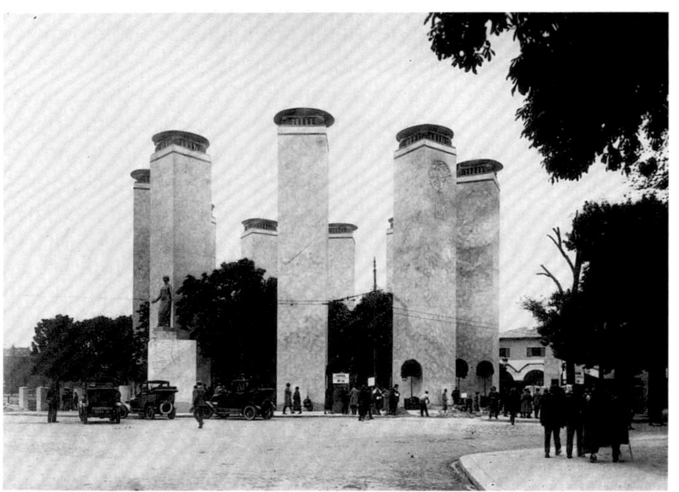

BEFORE AND AFTER 1937

Shifted to the sidelines in 1925, painting and sculpture were everywhere in the 'Exposition internationale des arts et des techniques dans la vie moderne' twelve years later. The raw figures for 1937 are scarcely credible. The State alone commissioned 464 painters, 577 sculptors and 336 'artisans décorateurs'.[15] The painters were chosen from well over 2000 candidates; all candidates in all categories had to be French nationals. The last of the Universal Exhibitions, this was by far the largest, involving huge new construction projects – the Palais de Chaillot and the new modern museums, the Palais National des Arts (now the Palais de Tokyo) – the latter, of course, an extravagant demonstration of the status accorded to painters and sculptors. Those commissioned were chosen and monitored by a two-tier committee system, whose guiding principle in commissioning for the new public palaces, the most important sites of all, was the harmonious integration of architecture, the decorative and the fine arts.

There was, indeed, a comfortable unanimity in the relationship between the nude neo-classicism of the palaces of 1937 and the sculptural and mural styles that discreetly clothed them [6, 14], but it was achieved against powerful opposition from the committees, especially from the new Director of the Fine Arts administration, Georges Huisman, who had become the passionate advocate of a 'modernist concept of art, politics and the State.'[16] What is more, painting and sculpture as such, apparently unchallenged at the heart of the exhibition, were themselves under threat everywhere as the dominant media of visual art, and the threat now was not of absorption into the 'decorative arts', but of imminent marginalisation before the surging rise of the new media: film, photography and advertising. National and theme pavilions used photography and film as information technology; for the first time a Universal Exhibition had a pavilion of advertising; and one of the popular successes of 1937 was the Pavillon 'Photo-Ciné-Phono', with its piped Mozart and Louis Armstrong and its 1,200 seater cinema. There might have been thousands of active painters and sculptors in France, but some had begun to use photography and even film, and 'talkies' were showing in 4,000 cinemas across the country.

Conflict and the pervasive sense of a culture and a society under threat were features of the 1937 Exhibition even where certainty and harmony seemed most apparent, and the divisions exposed were as much internal to French society as they were external: the Soviet-Nazi confrontation [4] made a melodrama of conflicts that threatened not only war but the deepest values of the Third Republic.

Any examination of the organisation of the exhibition exposes fundamental divisions and abrupt discontinuities, which bear the direct impress of destabilising political change. Serious planning had been initiated in 1932, the year after the French economy began to feel the effects of the world Depression; at that stage the possibility was at least entertained of responding to the criticisms of 1925 by using this opportunity to build a modern urban development with a suburban site – Le Corbusier submitted a project for an 'Exposition Internationale de l'Habitation', which was quickly eliminated.

From 1932 to 1934, there was a bewildering series of moderate governments, each pursuing ineffectual deflationary policies, as the majority Radicals tried to form administrations without involving the Socialists (SFIO). In the twelve months between January 1933 and January 1934, there were four different administrations, the first led by the old 'art-and-democracy' idealist, Paul-Boncour. At the end of 1933, the Stavisky scandal broke, the machinations of a devious financier – a Russian Jew – being used by *Action française* and the right-wing press to 'expose' the malign influence of 'wogs' ('métèques') and the corrupt cronyism of democratic politicians. It was the trigger for violent street demonstrations against the regime on 6 February 1934, demonstrations that involved not only the fast-growing right-wing Leagues with their disciplined thuggery, but also the French Communist Party. Fourteen died. The government under Daladier fell, to be succeeded by yet another, led by Gaston Doumergue. Through all this, an ambitious overall plan for the exhibition – close to the final plan – was developed with the committed support of the Radical Minister of Public Instruction, Anatole de Monzie (who had attended the opening of Le Corbusier's Pavillon de l'Esprit Nouveau in 1925), but the fall of the Daladier government put paid to de Monzie and resulted in the immediate cancellation of the entire project. It was revived in May 1934 when the Ville de Paris agreed to share the costs with the State, and in July a new 'commissaire général' was appointed, Edmond Labbé.

At the end of 1933, the title of the project was: 'Exposition internationale des arts décoratifs et industriels et de la vie ouvrière et paysanne, et de la coopération intellectuelle'. With Labbé, it would be given its simpler final title, but the confusion of conflicting objectives remained: the exhibition would continue to oppose art and industry, worker and peasant, nationalism and internationalism, all within a force-field of violent political difference, without any prospect of resolving the tensions.

The riots of 6 February 1934, so close, it could seem, to a coup d'état, opened the door to fascism wider. Fascism would never take root in France as a genuinely mass movement, but by 1937 fascist thinking was producing disruptive echoes in the writing of intellectuals more brutally eloquent even than Charles Maurras, figures like Robert Brasillach and Drieu de la Rochelle: the revolutionary Right had moved on from monarchism. As Drieu put it in 1934: 'A monarchist is never a true fascist . . . which is to say that a monarchist is never a true modern: he just does not have the brutality, the barbarous simplicity of a modern.'[17] And in 1936, Jacques Doriot founded the first large-scale fascist party in France, the Parti Populaire Français (PPF), which Drieu joined. It was for a mass coalition of the working and the middle classes that Doriot campaigned.

6 February 1934, at the same time opened the way to an anti-fascist alliance of the broad Left, the Front Populaire, which was made possible by the Soviet realisation of the danger to the Revolution of Hitler's Germany. This led from the summer of 1934 to Commintern encouragement of the French Communist Party to develop a common front with the Socialists and even the Radicals against fascism. In the elections of April 1936, the resulting electoral pact brought the Front Populaire into power, and the Exhibition of 1937 opened in the last month of its first administration under the Socialist leader Léon Blum. The Communists would not join a cabinet composed of Socialists and Radicals, but they were a key component in a government coalition. And it was a government that met an outburst of strikes on gaining power by forcing agreement from the employers to fifteen percent pay-rises, acceptance of compulsory collective bargaining, and the recognition of trade-union rights; a government that legislated a forty-hour week and statutory paid holidays for workers. The majority right-of-centre press had the fuel to feed the fears of the property-owning, small-business-running middle classes, who were confronted at the exhibition by delayed openings, the result of strikes, and by crowds of workers, brought from all over the country on excursion fares and let in on cheap ticket deals offered to workers' organisations.

Edmond Labbé, Commissaire Général of the exhibition, was close to the conservative centrist Gaston Doumergue. His experience lay in technical and craft training, especially in the regions, and his vision was of industry coexisting with the crafts and of a regionally diverse France where the proletarianised worker would never supplant the artisan and where neither would pose a threat to the respectable middle classes.[18] He was well supported by his deputy, Paul Léon, a deeply conservative Fine Arts civil servant, who was largely responsible for the choice of Prix-de-Rome winning architects rather than modernists to design the new public palaces. Léon Blum was a Parisian bourgeois who had rejected the bourgeoisie and, as a Marxist, considered the lesser middle classes irrelevant beside the immanent force of the proletariat, which indeed had become politically significant in France by 1930. He shared the orthodox socialist faith in technology as a progressive good which would free men for leisure, and so for education, outdoor recreation and the arts. In the early years of the century, he had also made a reputation as a critic and poet, publishing alongside Gide and Valéry, before launching his career as a politician. Inevitably, he took a direct and energetic interest in the 1937

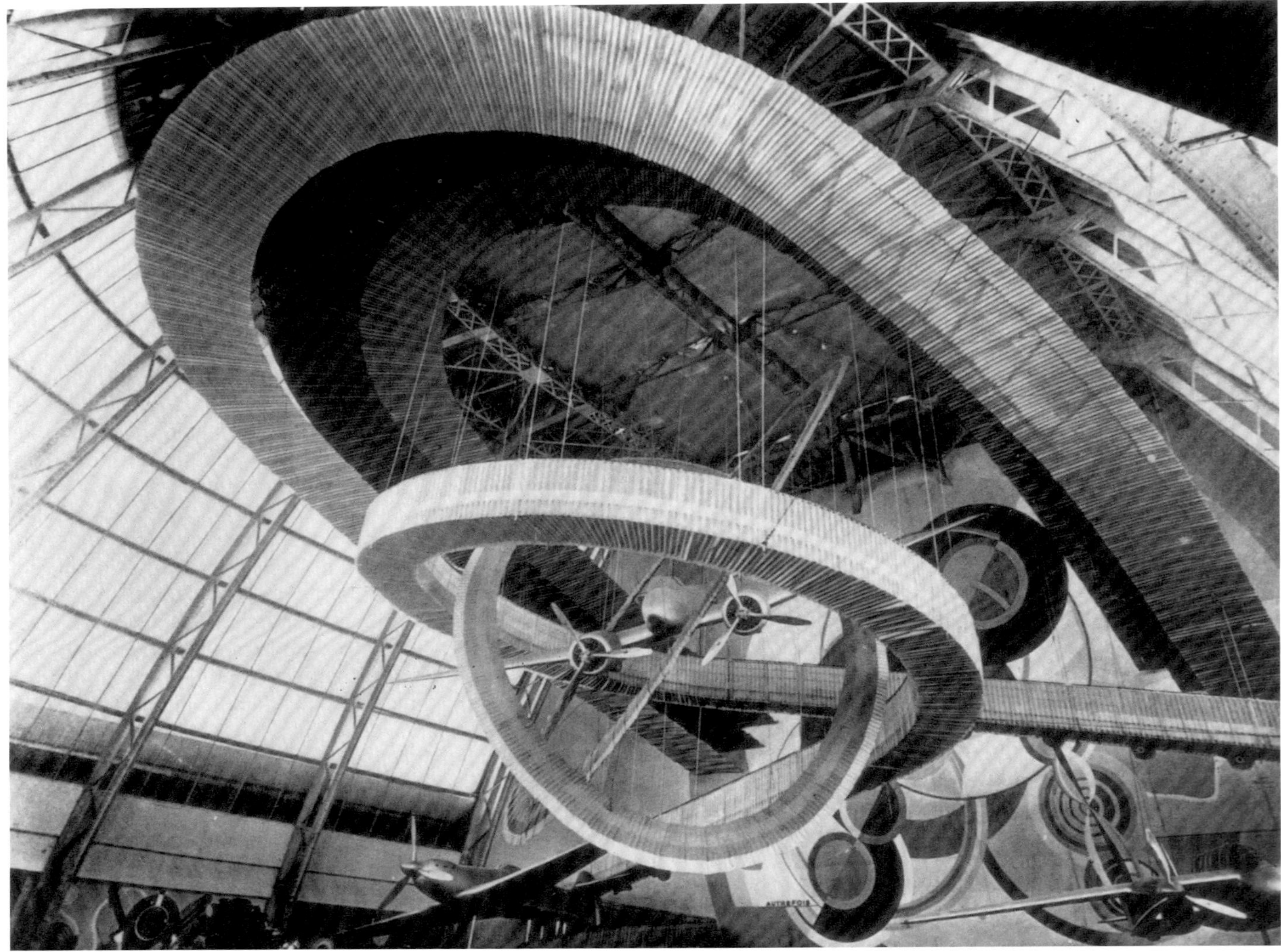

12. F. Aublet and R. Delaunay, 'Art and Light' (Art et Lumière), Hall, Aeronautical Pavilion (Pavillon aéronautique). Exposition Internationale des arts et des techniques dans la vie moderne, Paris, 1937

Exhibition throughout the year between the formation of his cabinet and its opening, as did his young Minister of Public Instruction, the Radical Jean Zay. Inevitably too, the result was initiatives that challenged Labbé's and Léon's traditionalist republican vision, and so heightened the tensions contained in the exhibition.

Besides the great 'Roman' palaces with their endless Versaillesque flights of stairs and monumental park statuary [13], Labbé's exhibition gave special prominence to a 'Centre Rural', conceived as a modern model for rural development, and to a 'Centre régional', for which local architects designed pavilions representing the regions of France usually in modernised versions of regional vernaculars [272].[19] Blum, by contrast, saw to it that the west wing of the Grand Palais, which had housed the Centennale in 1900, was turned into a science museum, under the direction of the Nobel Prize-winning physicist (and active Socialist) Jean Perrin: the Palais de la Découverte. He saw to it that Le Corbusier was given a site, as it happened right beside the 'Centre rural', on which to build a Pavillon des Temps Nouveaux, a high-tech tent dubbed in Soviet agitprop language, a 'Travelling Museum of Popular Education' which was dedicated to combined urban and rural development. And he saw to it that one of the major spaces in the already resolutely modern Pavillon aéronautique was painted by a team under the leadership of the abstract painter Robert Delaunay [12].[20]

Blum's interventions, and those more broadly of the Front Populaire, in widening access to the exhibition repeatedly drew attention to the divisions now so deep and dangerous in French society: not only between classes, but also between progress and tradition, city and country, the older generations and the young. On a world stage, France was exposed as a riven country, its commitment to liberal republicanism threatened by authoritarian solutions to the apparent corruption of democracy, on the Left as well as the Right: a country factionalised by conflicting responses to youth and innovation and by conflicting attitudes to the urban and the rural, the industrial and the traditional. Against the formidable cohesion of the totalitarian pavilions – the Italian, as well as the German and Soviet – this was easily read as weakness. The cluster of exotic entertainments and craft sales-points built on the Ile-des-Cygnes in the Seine, as postscript to the huge 1931 Exposition Coloniale, established France as a colonial power once again, but there was more than enough material for diagnosing the decline of French society in 1937.

From the election of the Front Populaire, the 1937 Exhibition had been part of its 'great projects' policy for the creation of jobs (for artists as well as construction workers, as we have seen). The Depression had hit late in France and with a relatively soft impact. Indeed, the dynamic new industries of the 1900s actually continued to expand. Electical power production rose from sixteen to twenty-one billion kilowatts between 1930 and 1938, and hydroelectric development continued – the starring role of electricity in the exhibition was deserved. The petroleum, chemical and the newer aluminium industry all did well – a sleek aluminium skin sheathed the heavy Baroque of the main entrance of the Palais de la Découverte; and car-production from the huge Citroën and Renault plants built in the twenties was rising in 1937. Where the Depression hit was in the older, more conservative industries, which employed most workers, above all the textile industry; the production of cloth halved in the decade to 1938. The Depression revealed the continuing dominance of the small family firm in French industry, resistant to credit and investment, uninterested in export, insistent on tariff protection; ironically, it was their archaic practices that softened the effect of the withdrawal of American credit and markets, so devastating elsewhere.[21] French industry, overall, was stagnant; French business archaic. In the 1930s, the average age of machines used in French factory production was twenty years, against seven in Germany, four in Japan.

Though the census of 1931 for the first time put the urban population (51.2%) higher than the rural (48.8%), France remained much more a rural country than any other comparably developed economy. Urban meant towns of more than two thousand; it included hundreds of little provincial towns with less than 5000 inhabitants, still dominated by agriculture. Labbé's rural and regional centres spoke to a France – middle-class as well as peasant – which was still real and strong; but where many felt menaced by the urban and the modern. The Front Populaire initiative of a Musée des arts et traditions populaire, in its early stages in 1937, was a recognition both of the place of rural France in the French imagination, and of the imminence of its loss.[22]

And France was an ageing country, for the 1930s was the decade when the demographic effects of 1914–18 worked their way through in the form of a significantly diminished generation of newly active adults. German and British war losses did not approach those of the French in proportional terms: 10.5% of the active male population in France were killed. 1.1 million were left disfigured or maimed. The presiding presence of the *Peace Column* in 1937 was backed by the visceral pacifism of millions of war-veterans, and for good reason. The result two decades after the massacre was a drastic reduction in the number of fertile young people, which had begun around 1931. In 1900, there had been 400,000 of each sex aged between eleven or twelve and seventeen or eighteen; in 1931, this had almost halved for both, the drop being more marked for males.[23] France was dominated by the age-group between the early thirties and the fifties, with a preponderance of older women. In 1937 there was something desperate as well as false about the celebration of youth encouraged by the Front Populaire.

For the Exhibition of 1925 a 9 metre-high bronze cast of *France* by Emile-Antoine Bourdelle (b.1861), then perhaps the most celebrated living French sculptor, was erected in front of the main entrance to the Grand Palais [14]. After his death, Bourdelle's figure of a female warrior *France* scanning the horizon reappeared in a painted plaster version on the terrace of the new Palais de Tokyo in 1937; in those twelve years its strident victor's message had become less than compelling. It must have seemed to some an oddly militant companion to the *Peace Column* at the top of the Avenue Président Wilson in the Place du Trocadéro, and both of them were equally out of tune with Picasso's response to the bombing of the Basque town Guernica, his allegory of war as murderer in the Spanish Pavilion [333]. The defensive pacifism of French foreign policy helped in the evasion of European war for two more years. When it came in September 1939, France proved to have neither the watchfulness nor the military capability to resist the invasion that followed in the spring of 1940.

The social and political effects of dominant middle-class attitudes – rationalist, individualist, conservative – and a slow decline towards stagnation, nostalgia and division are central themes in any history of the Third Republic between the Exhibitions of 1900 and 1937. How extraordinary, then, that openness to innovation and sustained dynamic activity should be dominant themes in most historical analyses of art in France during those years, especially since art was so largely the preserve of the middle classes. Fundamentally, the cultural is not separable from the social and the political even in such a case, but it is simple enough to see how the first historians of art in France in the early twentieth century could have told their stories as if art had its own special history of triumph, utterly separate from a history that otherwise ended in defeat.

13. Arial view of the 1937 Exposition Universelle including the Soviet and German pavilions with above, Jacques Carlu, Louis-Hippolyte Boileau and Léon Azéma, *The Palais de Chaillot*, 1937

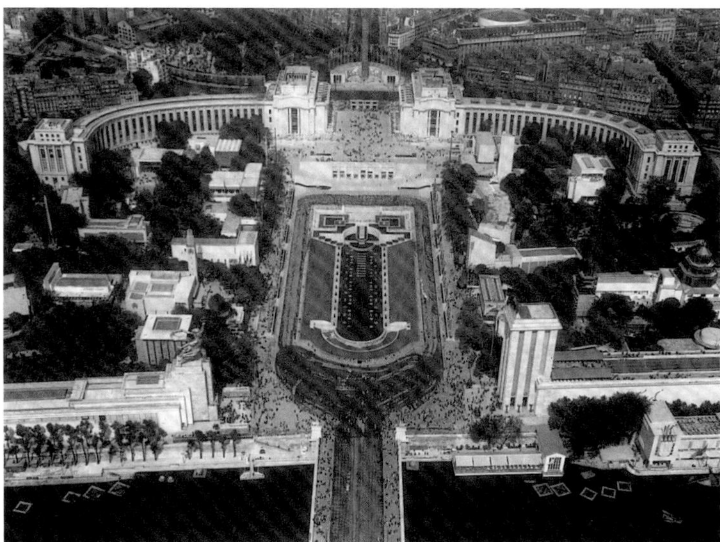

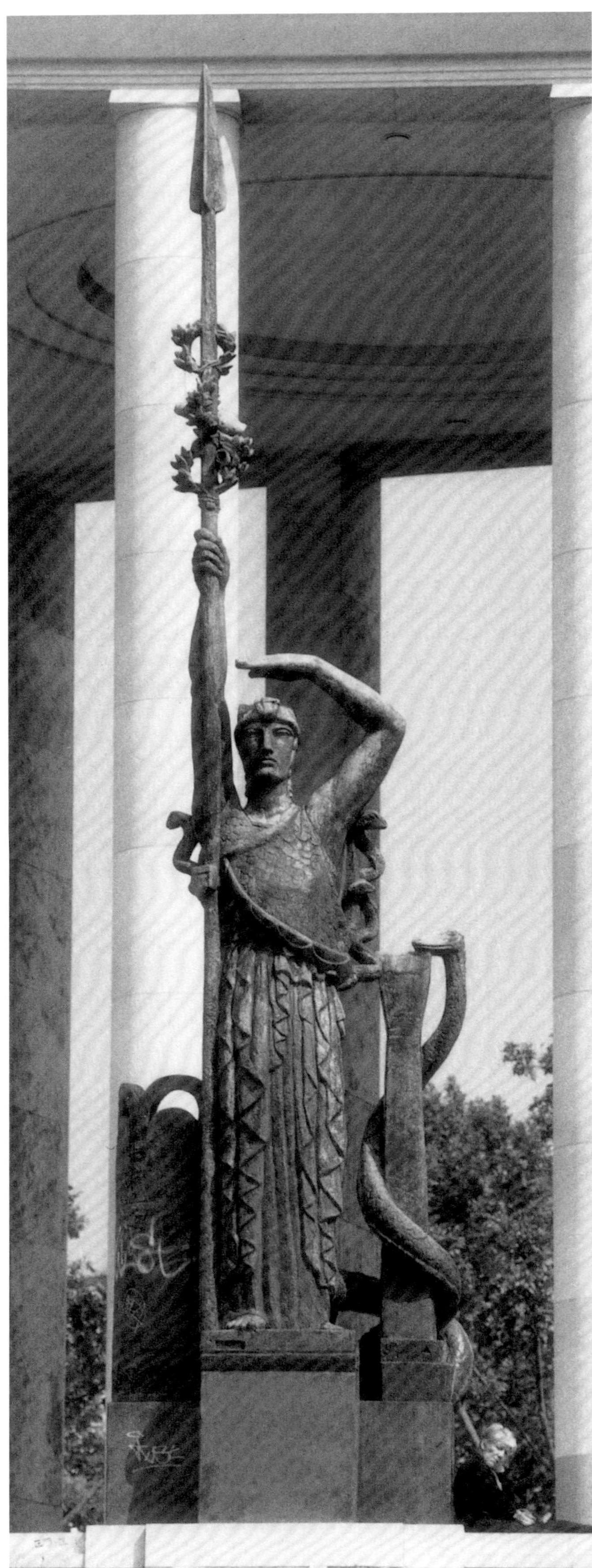

14. Antoine Bourdelle, *France*, 1925. Bronze, h. 9.00 m. As erected on the terrace of the Palais de Tokyo, Paris

ART IN FRANCE, 1900–40: FRENCH AND TRANSATLANTIC PERSPECTIVES

The history of art in France was given a major role in 1937, as it had been with the Centennale and the Décennale of 1900. Another of Léon Blum's interventions was to ensure that the brand new museums of modern art for the State and the Ville de Paris in the Palais de Tokyo would open with what he called an 'encyclopaedia' of French 'master-pieces'. The vast exhibition, 'Chefs d'oeuvre d'art français', included works of craft and decorative art and the products of the untutored (including the Douanier Rousseau), and so challenged hierarchies even as it reinforced the French canon of high art that stretched from the Master of Flémalle to Cézanne. Surveys of the art of 1900–37 were shown in exhibitions put on by the Ville de Paris in the Petit Palais and with State support in the Jeu de Paume. These two exhibitions stand for two quite distinct ways of representing art in France in 1937.

The Petit Palais exhibition was put together by its curator Raymond Escholier to celebrate the Ville de Paris's support of what was described as 'independent art' through the period. By independent art what was meant was the work shown in the annual salons of the Société des artistes indépendants, which had been founded as an open, unselected alternative to the jury-selected Salon de la Société des artistes français in 1884; the exhibition was called 'Les Maîtres de l'art indépendant, 1895–1937'. Independent art, Escholier declared in his preface to the catalogue, 'was emphatically not all contemporary French art. It was one of its aspects, that which, for thirty years, has made an impact abroad . . .'[24] It was what he thought of as significant modern art; it was art that defied the huge decorative paintings by Alfred Roll, Albert Besnard and others who had ignored the Indépendants, which filled to bursting the ceilings above in the Petit Palais with early twentieth-century echoes of the rococo. Escholier laid out the show as a series of solo exhibitions, whose relative size acted as a measure of the importance of each artist. Visitors making the circuit of the palace could encounter an overpowering accumulation of exhibitions bringing together more than twenty-five works each, interspersed with smaller groupings of work by a mass of artists. Among those who reached the twenty-five work threshold were, in the sequence in which they would have been seen: Vlaminck (thirty-eight), Derain (thirty), Matisse (sixty-one), Rouault (forty-two), Maillol (sixty), Denis (thirty-nine), Bonnard (thirty-three), Vuillard (thirty-one), Dufy (thirty-four), Utrillo (thirty-six), Braque (twenty-nine), Lhote (thirty-four), Léger (twenty-seven), Maria Blanchard (twenty-eight), Picasso (thirty-two), Zadkine (forty-seven), Laurens (thirty-three) and Lipchitz (thirty-two). There would have been a loose yet distinct sense of progression and of groupings as one moved between generations and styles, but overwhelmingly individual artistic identities would have been what left their mark.

One of the priorities of Louis Hautecoeur, curator of the

collection of recent French art at the Musée du Luxembourg, was to bring together French and foreign modern art in the modern art museum planned to replace the Luxembourg in the Palais de Tokyo. Before 1937, foreign modern art owned by the State had been housed in the Jeu de Paume. It was André Dezarrois, curator of this 'foreign' collection, who initiated the Jeu de Paume's rival to the Petit Palais Indépendants show; he did so helped by the Surrealist poet-collector Paul Eluard, and Christian Zervos, editor of the influential modernist periodical *Cahiers d'art*. Georges Huisman chaired an organising committee that brought together with these three a potent and select group, including the young curator and Communist fellow traveller, Jean Cassou, who would be the first post-war director of the Musée National d'art moderne, and a roll-call of major moderns: Braque, Léger, Marcoussis, Matisse and Picasso. The exhibition's title was 'Origines et développement de l'art internationale indépendant', quite as telling a title as 'Les Maîtres de l'art indépendant'. The stress here was not on a French institution, but on independent art as an international phenomenon; it was not on individual 'masters', but on historical 'development'.

The year before, Alfred H. Barr had brought together a show at the Museum of Modern Art in New York, which was to act as a blueprint for Anglo-American histories of modernism into the 1970s: *Cubism and Abstract Art*. Barr had produced a history of interconnecting linear developments describing the ascent of movements out of 'Synthetism' and 'Neo-Impressionism' in the 1890s, through Cubism and ultimately into 'Abstract Art'; the frontispiece of his catalogue was that history reduced to a diagram. The Jeu de Paume's 'Origines et développement' was a French version; it replaced a history of master artists with a history of master movements. The catalogue and the installation told a story, each room a chapter: a story comparable with and yet crucially different from the one Barr plotted from across the Atlantic. The French story gave a more integral role to Surrealism (no doubt because of Eluard's involvement) and it treated abstract art, called here 'non-figurative', more as something found right across the period after 1910 than as a climax. But most important of all it underlined the role of French art as source and origin.[25] The unsigned preface declares the 'foreign schools' to be the centre of gravity of the exhibition, but justifies the inclusion of art by French artists as to explain 'the sources to which these [foreign] artists' had gone.

The sequence of movements started with the French of the late nineteenth century, including a Bibémus quarry painting by Cézanne, the Douanier Rousseau's *Snake Charmer* and a neo-impressionist Henri-Edmond Cross from Matisse's collection. Next was the 'Fauve' room, entirely filled with French painting. Then came the major 'Cubist' room, this time including 'foreign' artists with the French, but only foreigners who had worked in France: Picasso, Gris, Marcoussis, Lipchitz. Braque showed his *Portuguese* of 1911 [105] alongside a comparable Picasso, and Matisse knowingly showed his *Moroccans* and *Piano Lesson* of 1915–16 as 'cubist' pictures. There followed a room dominated by Surrealist or Surrealist-related painting, where again almost all the 'foreigners' had spent important periods in France: Chagall, de Chirico, Ernst, Miró, Dalí.

The last two rooms, which ranged across movements and periods, included Klee and Baumeister, artists who had never been based in France, but many more who were French or again Paris-based. The overall message of the exhibition was clear: the history of art between the 1890s and 1937 as a story of 'origins' and 'development' was to be understood in terms of movements driven by artists, French and 'foreign', *in France*.

In the late 1930s Alfred H. Barr might have agreed, but his book and exhibition of 1936 was the first move in the globalisation of the story of modernism: in the making of a kind of historical writing that would represent the succession of movements as supranational, and the making ultimately of the global modernism and post-modernism of the late twentieth century. The end of the 1930s was perhaps the last moment when even the French could exhibit the 'international' development of modern art as the dynamic history of modern movements in France.

The idea of movements as the makers of significant change in art was, by 1937, long established in France. Surprisingly, 'Origines et développement de l'art internationale indépendant' was the first and the only attempt in France before 1940 from a position free of engagement in an -ism, to represent the history of art after 1900 so rigorously and comprehensively as a history of movements. Adherents to or defenders of movements, often pictured cultural history as chains of -isms culminating in theirs, but the less *parti pris* critical syntheses that followed the first of real importance, André Salmon's 1912 *La Jeune Peinture française*, while acknowledging movements, placed the emphasis much more on groups and individuals, as Escholier did in the Petit Palais.

Salmon opened his 1912 accolade to the energy of the painters of the 1900s by writing of the end of 'schools' and the emergence of 'families of artists'.[26] He wrote of the 'fauves' and the 'cubists' as such 'families', both led by dominant personalities (Matisse and Picasso), and otherwise he promoted a disparate succession of individuals under the heading 'Living Art'; he was always to be suspicious of movements. In 1922, the emerging critic Waldemar George collaborated with the older and better-known art-journalist, Louis Vauxcelles, to write the twentieth-century section of an *Histoire générale de l'art français de la Révolution à nos jours*. Vauxcelles, as we shall see, was the journalist personally responsible for launching the terms 'Fauvism' and 'Cubism', yet this is a history that oscillates uncomfortably between movements, groups and individuals, with just that loose sense of progression found in *Maîtres de l'art indépendant*. Its only overall strategy is the search for lines of continuity by which, as its general editor André Fontanas maintained, to group together precursors and successors in an on-going history of broad tendencies.[27]

This had been the strategy of Roger Marx in selecting the Centennale of 1900 to tell a story, and it is found again in the treatment of art in France in major general histories of 1928 and 1935, the first by Henri Focillon, then the most distinguished establishment art historian in France, holder of the Chair at the Sorbonne, the second edited by René Huyghe, Deputy Curator of the Louvre.[28] Huyghe announces that his editorial policy is to break up the 'history of contemporary art' into sections each dealing with a 'group of artists' and each consisting of an introduction by himself followed by heteroclite clusters of monographic studies.[29] The very structure of the book placed groups and individuals in tension, the groups defined sometimes by movements, sometimes not. Thus, he introduces Cubism as the modern French expression of the 'Cartesian' spirit and then promptly allows any coherent notion of it as a movement to be pulled apart by strongly contrasting treatments of individuals, ranging from himself on the 'Spanish' Picasso and the 'French' Braque, to Cassou on the 'lyrical cubism' of Braque, Marcoussis and Juan Gris, and Raymond Cogniat on the 'methodical cubism' of Léger. The idea of the group here was no longer socially defined, and in a 1939 treatment of 'the contemporaries' in French painting, Huyghe preferred to divide the artists of the century into generations.[30] He identified six generations by their birth dates: 1855–65, the generation 'still under the sign of Impressionism'; 1865–70, the generation in whom 'the last echoes of Impressionism are united with a modernising art'; 1870–80, that of the Fauves and of those who had moved towards 'a more willed, classical construction' (including many who painted murals for the Palais de Chaillot); 1880–90, that of Cubism and its competitors; 1890–1900, that of the Surrealists; and finally, those born after 1900, who are seen to be moving 'towards a neo-humanism'. The -isms remained, but so hugely enlarged that they now could embrace whole generations: those generations conceived as the loosest possible groupings of individuals.

Throughout the period, awareness of generations is a feature of art-writing – André Salmon's phrase 'young painting', given poignancy by the unspoken loss of so many young between 1914 and 1918, became increasingly orthodox between the wars. I shall, therefore, routinely give the birth-dates of artists in this book; their generation always mattered. The question of movements, groups and individuals is altogether less simple. Individuals often defined their positions for and against movements, and often came together in groups, but as often those who did attach themselves to movements or groups were quick to assert their independence. What is more, the history of modernism as a history of movements inevitably produces a picture of art 'developing' by its own dynamics free of society; it enhances the false sense of disjunction between the cultural and the social. There *were* movements, just as there was a Socialist and a Communist Party in France, but the way artists behaved on the ground was much more in tune with the France of self-interested individuals and small groups of the like-minded – free-thought societies, café discussion circles, Masonic lodges and so on – the France that somehow held together to form that loose coalition of the middle classes, the Radical Party: except this 'Radical' France was dispersed across the provinces, and the 'Radical' artists virtually all inhabited Paris. They were metropolitan, like the Universal Exhibitions.

An awareness of the history of movements is a necessary complement to the study of individual artists, but more important is the realisation that movements, groups and individuals were almost always in tension, theories and practices working against as well as with each other. To this extent, the ramshackle histories of 'contemporary art' published by George and Vauxcelles, Focillon and Huyghe come closer to representing art in France as it was experienced by its practitioners in the period than Barr's diagram of movements ever could. It is, nonetheless, necessary to open the way to a more complex understanding by sketching out as clearly as possible the history of modern movements in France along the broad lines of Barr's and the Jeu de Paume's versions at the end of the 1930s: to introduce Fauvism, Cubism, Dada and Surrealism as -isms. I shall do so, however, in such a way as to bring out the tensions between them and those individuals who were identified with them; and the often conflicting images of them composed by their historians.

CHAPTER 2

Modern Movements in France, 1900–40

MAKING FAUVISM

There was an obvious rightness in 1937, when Raymond Escholier decided to place at the start of his exhibition 'Maîtres de l'art indépendant' so strong a concentration of paintings by the artists referred to as the 'fauves'. All of them had been important early exhibitors in the Salons des Indépendants in the opening decade of the century, and they first came together to show as a recognisable group there early in 1905. One of their number, Henri Matisse (b.1869), chaired the hanging committee of the Indépendants that year, and brought onto it Charles Camoin, Henri Manguin, Albert Marquet and Jean Puy, all but the last old friends from his student days in the 1890s in the Ecole National des Beaux-Arts studio of Gustave Moreau. They saw to it that they showed together that year, along with others they felt close to, including another of their Beaux-Arts peers, Georges Rouault (b.1871) (then the new curator of the equally new Gustave Moreau Museum), a Montmartre-based Dutchman, Kees van Dongen (b.1877), two painters from suburban Chatou, André Derain (b.1880) and Maurice Vlaminck (b.1876), and a pair of provincials from Le Havre, Raoul Dufy (b.1877) and Emile-Othon Friesz (b.1879). The group-showing stood out enough among the 4,269 exhibits in the Salon for the periodical *La Nouvelle Revue* to remark on the clustering of ex-students of Gustave Moreau, and for Louis Vauxcelles (already a significant newspaper critic) to pick out Matisse as the leader of this 'school' in the republican daily *Gil Blas*.[1]

A major reason for Matisse's elevation to chair of the Indépendants' hanging-committee was his close relationship with Paul Signac (b.1863), anarchist, Neo-Impressionist and vice-president of the Société, with whom he had spent the summer of 1904 at St Tropez, and his major contribution was a large canvas worked up in the autumn from oil sketches made there; he used a line from Baudelaire for the title: *Luxe, calme et volupté* (*Luxuriant, voluptuous and calm*) [86]. This picture associated him with the Neo-Impressionists, considered dominant in the Salon that year. For critics to begin to attach the idea of a new and special -ism to him and his friends, strong stylistic distinctiveness was required. Matisse spent the summer of 1905 with Derain in the little Mediterranean fishing port of Collioure, close to the Spanish border; on his and Signac's advice, Camoin, Manguin and Marquet went to St Tropez; Vlaminck painted as usual in Chatou. The following November they all showed again, this time in a single room ('Salle VII') in the Salon d'automne, a selective counterpart of the Indépendants.[2] The Collioure landscapes of Matisse and Derain above all established the distinctiveness of the painting of this group, and Vlaminck's Chatou pictures equalled their uncompromising vigour [15, 16, 88, 89].

Notoriety brought these artists an intensity and range of press attention they had not known. The mass-circulation picture magazine *L'Illustration* gave them full-page coverage [17], the Impressionists' historian, Camille Mauclair, descended to name-calling, and, in a press that was by no means mostly dismissive, Vauxcelles obliged by supplying the epithet that would eventually become the root-word of the group's -ism: 'fauve'. Noting the presence of two quattrocento-style figurative sculptures with these new paintings in Salle VII, Vauxcelles famously wrote: 'the artlessness of these busts comes as a surprise in the midst of the orgy of pure colours; Donatello at home among the wild beasts ("fauves").'[3] Matisse would quickly be accused by the painter-critic Maurice Denis (b.1870) of veering towards the abstract because of the excessive exercise of intellectual control, but the aggression and apparent *lack* of control in the facture of their paintings helped the term 'fauve' stick; 'pure colour' would always be identified as a key feature of Fauve painting.[4]

It is perhaps surprising that 'Fauvism' as a label took until 1907 to be taken into common journalistic use; by that date, most are agreed, the movement was already breaking up. In between, the artists had exhibited individually and in various permutations in the Indépendants of 1906 and 1907, the Salon d'automne of 1906, and in the galleries of the dealers Berthe Weill and Ambroise Vollard, who had been the supporters of most of them since before 1905.

From among the -isms, Fauvism would always be the term most easily used and yet most often qualified. The reason is, on the one hand, that it entailed no theory to complicate matters, and on the other, the difficulty of disentangling the idea of any coherent movement from the momentary convergence of short-lived groups. Only one serious, extended theoretical statement is associated with it: Matisse's 'Notes of a Painter', which codified his personal position, not that of any group, and was published in 1908, after Fauvism ceased to have historical valency.[5] Otherwise, Fauvism has been identified with the practices of at least some of the artists who exhibited together at the Indépendants and the Salon d'automne of 1905, most centrally of all Matisse, Derain and Vlaminck.[6] It is as easy to dwell on the differences as the similarities between these practices: the pictures Vlaminck painted in Chatou in 1905 obviously invite different conclusions from those Matisse and Derain painted at Collioure – they use thick paint densely, never sparely, seldom lightened by the exposure of the white-primed canvas. And the alliance in Salle VII at the Salon d'automne of 1905 brought together what had been clearly distinct developments in groups of artists whose differences are as telling as the fact that they briefly came together between 1904 and 1907. Even Matisse, orchestrator of the group as exhibitors, told Fauvism's first important monographer, Georges Duthuit, that he had 'no idea what "fauvism" means.'[7] Vauxcelles, inventor of the term 'Fauve', wrote of 'fauves' freely enough when he came to deal with

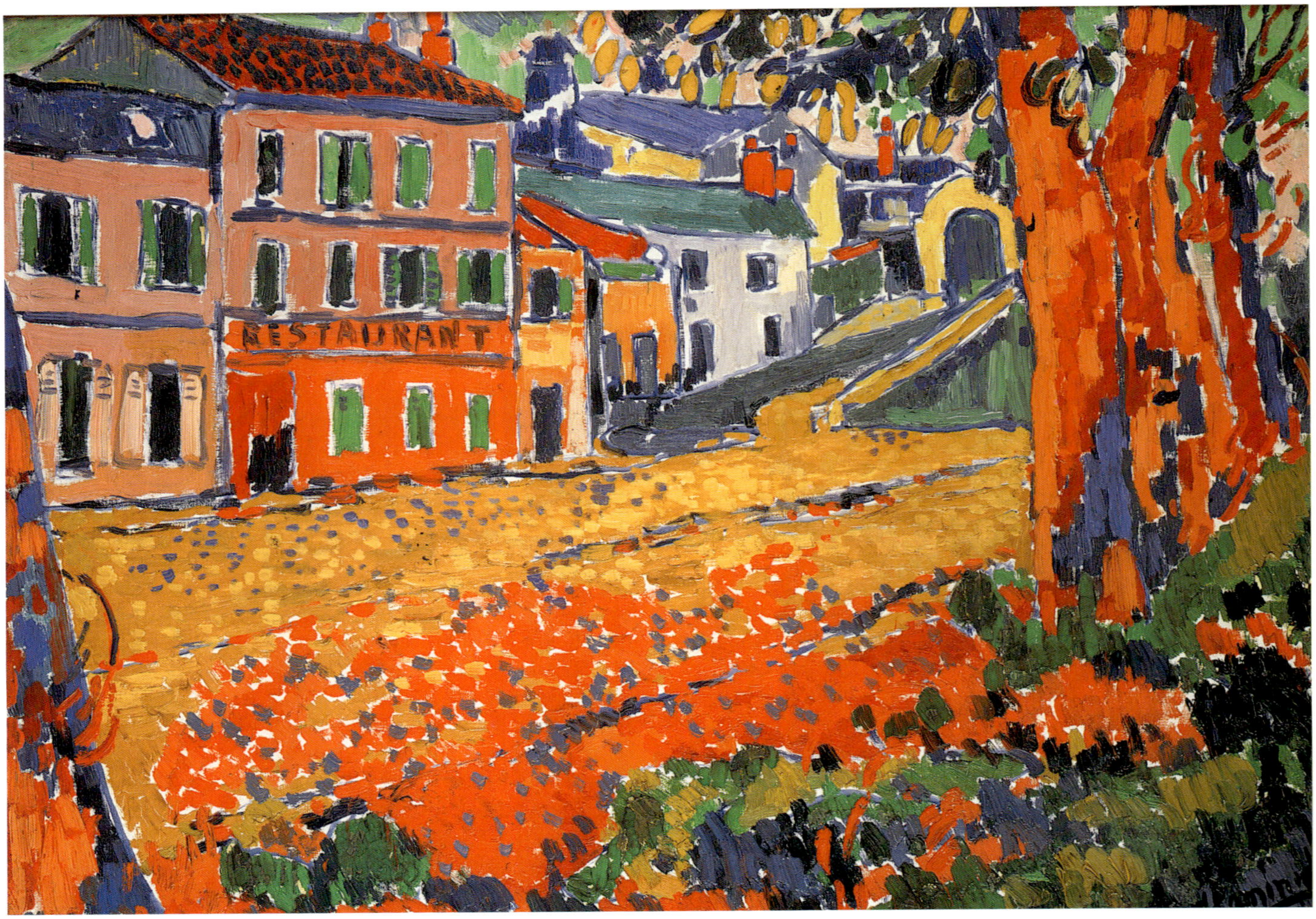

15. Maurice Vlaminck, *The 'Restaurant de la Machine' at Bougival*, 1906. Oil on canvas, 60 × 81.5 cm. Musée d'Orsay, Paris

16. Henri Matisse, *View of Collioure*, 1905. Oil on canvas, 59.5 × 73 cm. The State Hermitage Museum, St Petersburg

17. Page from *L'Illustration*, 4 November 1905

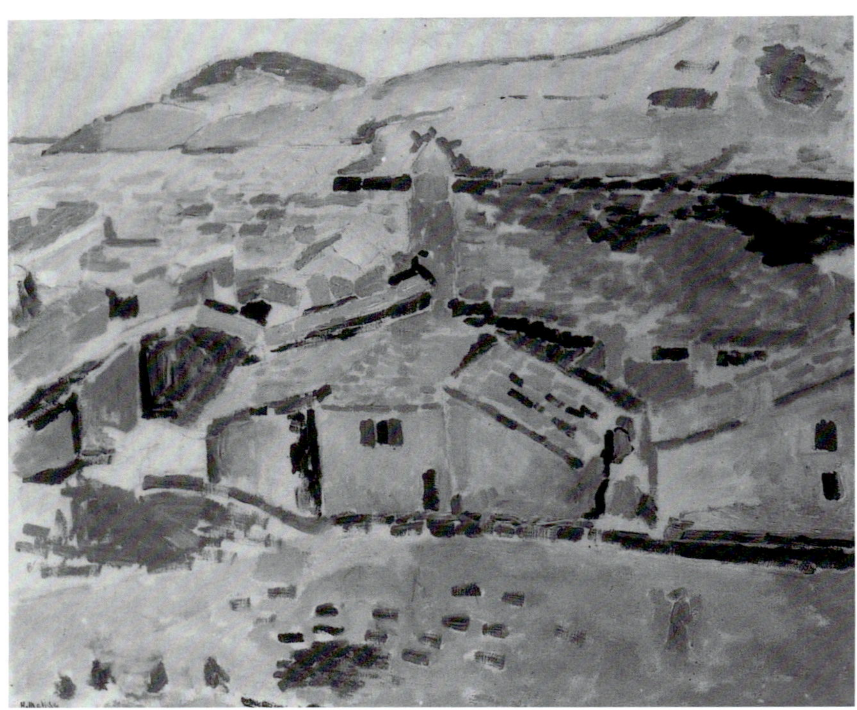

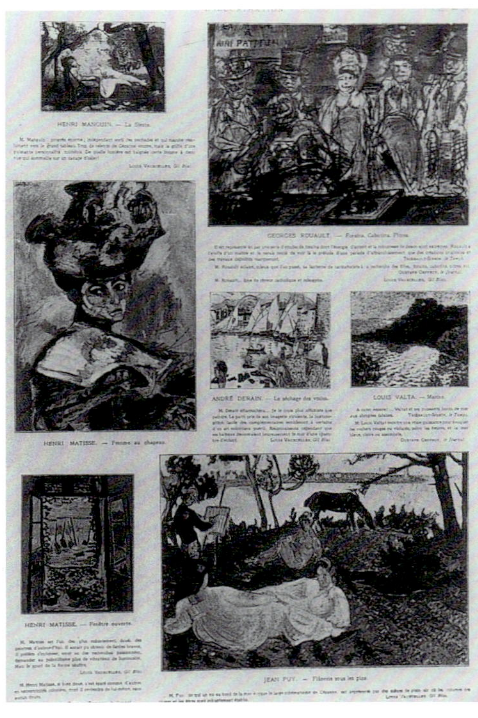

HENRI MANGUIN. — La Sieste.

GEORGES ROUAULT. — Forains, Cabotins, Filles.

HENRI MATISSE. — Femme au chapeau.

ANDRÉ DERAIN. — Le séchage des voiles.

LOUIS VALTA. — Marine.

HENRI MATISSE. — Fenêtre ouverte.

JEAN PUY. — Flânerie sous les pins.

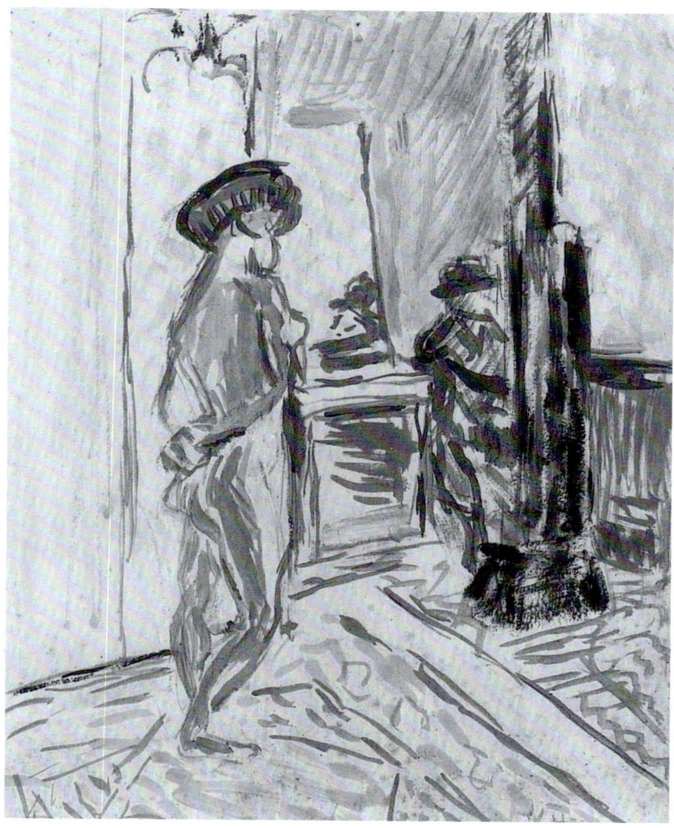

18. Henri Matisse, *Marquet Painting in Manguin's Studio*, 1904–5. Oil on canvas, 91.1 × 72.1 cm. Musée National d'Art Moderne, Paris

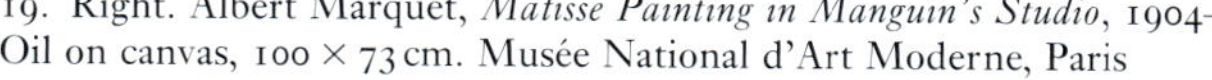

19. Right. Albert Marquet, *Matisse Painting in Manguin's Studio*, 1904–5. Oil on canvas, 100 × 73 cm. Musée National d'Art Moderne, Paris

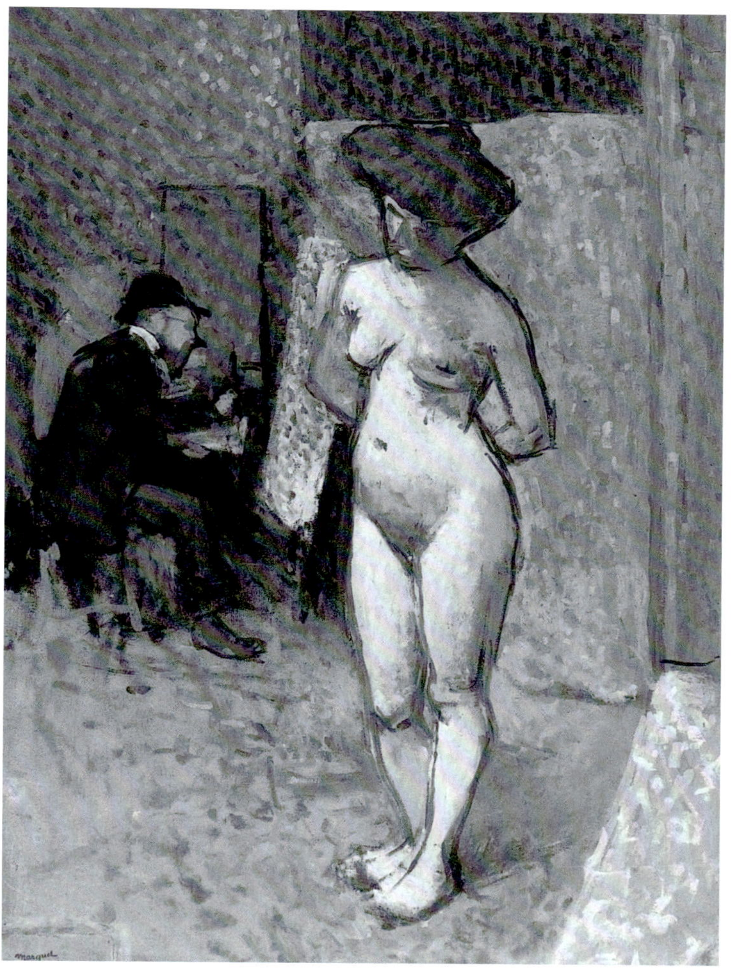

them in the *Histoire générale de l'art français de la Révolution à nos jours* in 1922, but he wrote of them emphatically as painters developing and interacting individually; he saw no need to *define* what he still called Fauvism.[8]

Told in this way, as the story of individuals and groups converging, any account of the Fauves has three strands: the strand that extends from Gustave Moreau's studio in the Ecole National des Beaux-Arts; the strand that extends from Derain and Vlaminck's meeting at Chatou; and the strand that extends from Le Havre to Paris, with the development of Dufy, Friesz and a younger painter who did not show with the Fauves until the Indépendants of 1906, Georges Braque (b.1882). Van Dongen is not identified with any of these strands, though it was Matisse who advised Vollard to show him in November 1904.

The key relationship in the first strand is that between Matisse and Marquet. They are seen to have produced 'proto-Fauve' nudes while working with others, mostly originally from Gustave Moreau's studio, in the independent school, the Académie Carrière, as early as 1899 – proto-Fauve because of the brilliance of their colour and the casual informality of their handling. A second crucial proto-Fauve moment is identified at the turn of 1904–5, the period of the execution of Matisse's *Luxe, calme et volupté*, when he, Marquet and Manguin worked on models hired to pose in Manguin's studio, freeing the colour relationships of their still Neo-Impressionist *taches* from the rigours of Signac's method by working at speed from observation [18, 19].

The Derain–Vlaminck relationship of the second strand started in June 1900 with a celebrated serendipitous meeting on the Chatou–Paris line when a commuter train was derailed, the day after which they painted together for the first of countless times. Derain already knew Matisse well from the Académie Carrière, and introduced Vlaminck to him at a major Van Gogh exhibition in the galerie Bernheim-Jeune in 1901, but between 1901 and 1904 Derain's work was interrupted by military service, and the Derain–Vlaminck strand did not effectively tie up with Matisse and the others from the Beaux-Arts and the Académie Carrière until late 1904. In 1905 the two Chatou friends painted each other at the moment that they became part of the triumvirate which would be at the heart of the Fauve episode [20, 21]. Vlaminck made pugnaciously smudged vermillion and pink stand metaphorically for Derain's intense engagement with his art; Derain came closer to a quickly sketched record of his companion, allowing the angle of the bowler and the set of the head to assert

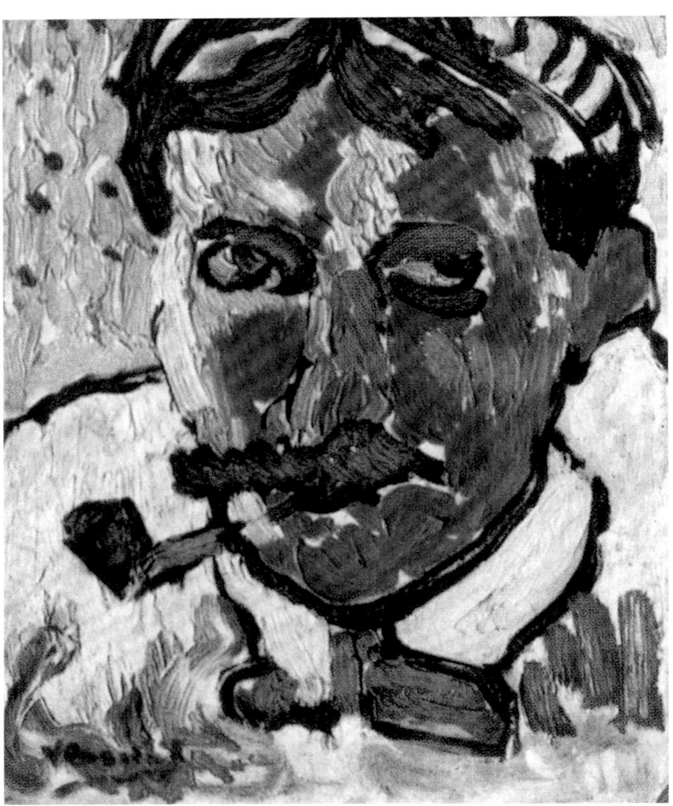

20. Maurice Vlaminck, *Portrait of André Derain*, 1905. Oil on canvas, 27.3 × 22.2 cm. Private Collection

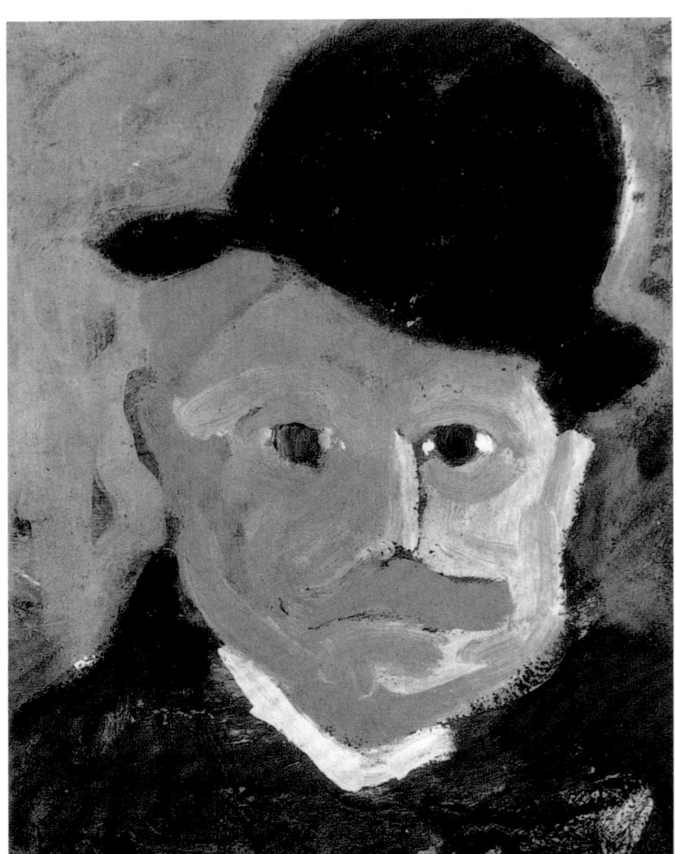

21. André Derain, *Portrait of Maurice Vlaminck*, 1905. Oil on canvas, 41.3 × 33 cm. Private Collection

Vlaminck's sturdy truculence. The frequency of mutual portaiture among the Fauves is itself a measure of the importance of personal relationships to what they produced: the interpersonal character of Fauvism. As Derain and Matisse, in their new painter's relationship at Collioure, developed the style they would unveil together at the Salon d'automne of 1905, they too painted each other. Derain's studious Matisse has the even gaze of the intellectual Maurice Denis would divine in his painting, and the image is built up in paint with studious deliberation [22]. What came of the alliance between Derain and Matisse was very different from what came of that between Derain and Vlaminck. It is a relationship at its closest, in fact, not in such companiable portraiture, but in the remarkable reciprocity of their Collioure landscapes [16, 88].

The third strand, that of the three painters from Le Havre, was a development only initiated from 1905; Braque's important contribution to it would not be made, in fact, until late 1906 and 1907 [23]. Moreover, the Havrais Fauves not only arrived on the scene late, but remained somewhat apart. Dufy and Friesz were old and close friends who had trained together in Le Havre and then as municipal scholarship winners, in Léon Bonnat's studio at the Beaux-Arts. Braque, who came to Paris to study for a diploma in painting and decoration, in 1900 (the date of Dufy and Friesz's arrival), started to work seriously alongside Friesz in 1906. All of them responded to Matisse and his friends at the Indépendants and the Salon d'automne of 1905 and 1906, and all of them are conventionally included under the Fauve label; indeed, in John Elderfield's major history of Fauvism as a movement, Braque is called the 'most important Fauve practitioner of [the] late manner'.[9]

From early on, attempts to *define* Fauvism have focused on the case of Matisse. Salmon in 1912 (who eccentrically includes Picasso among the Fauves) gives Matisse most space and calls him its 'inventor'. The unsigned introduction to 'Origines et développement de l'art internationale indépendant' in 1937 discusses Fauvism exclusively in terms of his work. And the most ambitious later attempt, John Elderfield's, though allowing the distinct contribution of Vlaminck and the often anticipatory role of Derain, defines what he calls 'true Fauvism' mostly through analyses of Matisse's painting.[10] Besides Braque's late Fauve style, Elderfield identifies two 'true' Fauve styles: what he calls the 'mixed technique' style of Derain and Matisse at Collioure, with its plurality of different coloured marks and patches, and the 'second Fauvist style', characterised by flat colour areas, which he calls the 'classic flat-color Fauvism of 1906–7'.[11] For him, what makes both styles 'true' follows from Matisse's determination to 'affirm the planarity of the surface as a taut, stretched membrane, very different from the softer, more pliant surface of Impressionist painting'.[12] Subject matter has not been an issue in attempted definitions of Fauvism; it has been accepted that the Fauves' range of landscape, figure, occasionally still-life and 'Golden Age' subjects was not new.[13]

There are obvious disjunctions between such 'definitions'

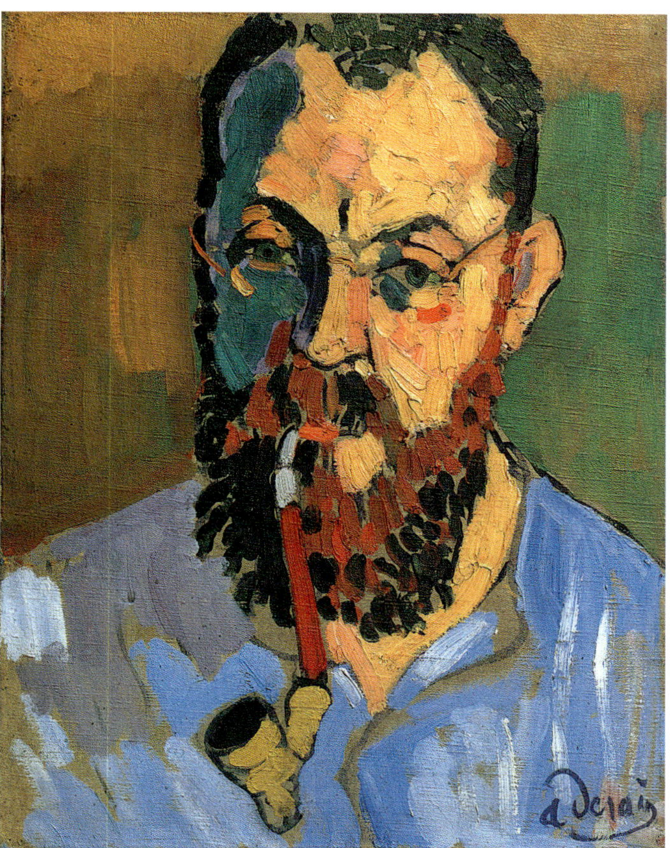

22. André Derain, *Portrait of Henri Matisse*, 1905. Oil on canvas, 46 × 34.9 cm. The Tate Gallery, London

and the perceptions of Fauve painting developed in response to it by contemporaries. Matisse himself was aware of the arbitrariness and flatness of his colour, but never claimed for it any definitive role within Fauvism as a movement. Elderfield is at pains to analyse out of the movement one of those whose work was reproduced on the famous page of *L'Illustration* in 1905, Louis Valtat [17], rightly pointing not only to the stylistic differences in his work, but to the fact that he came from an older and separate artistic grouping.[14]

Yet, should a hindsight notion of 'true Fauvism' based on the work of Derain and above all Matisse take precedence over contemporary perceptions based on the actual conditions of artistic groupings and public exhibition? Besides Valtat, what are we to make of another obviously distinct painter included on the *L'Illustration* page, Georges Rouault? Most monographs on Fauvism set him aside too. And, if we are to talk of a 'true Fauve' style (or styles), why should those who approach such a style from outside the small groups and the brief period called Fauve be excluded? After 1907, other artists, mostly younger, associated with other groupings produced paintings that could be analysed as 'truly Fauve' (or almost) and sometimes were called 'Fauve' at the time, for instance Francis Picabia, Jean Metzinger, Robert and Sonia Delaunay, all of whom tend to be placed under other -ism headings, as we shall see.

Patently, attempts to define Fauvism and to deal with it both as a convergence of groups and as a movement raise more questions than they answer.

MAKING CUBISM

Since Alfred Barr's *Cubism and Abstract Art* of 1936, the -ism suffix has denoted significance with scope: -isms, it has been accepted, changed things on the scale of global histories. In Paris before 1914 it was a suffix used by critics to convey suspicion tinged with scorn, or quite simply scorn.[15] The parodic invention of -isms was a journalistic sport by 1912. The poet-critic, Guillaume Apollinaire, author of one of the first books on Cubism, *Méditations esthétiques. Les Peintres cubistes*, figures in what may or may not be an actual interview published by the popular magazine *Fantasio* that year, where he holds forth on a cavalcade of -isms culminating in the 'transcendent school of excentroconcentroconcepticorationaloorphism.'[16] Artists knowingly used group exhibiting tactics and the collective banner of the -ism as publicity strategies at a time when the psychology of advertising was fast developing. They could be both attracted and repulsed by the practice, one reason for the later stand-offishness of Matisse towards Fauvism, and the reluctance of those quickly recognised as the first Cubists, the latecomer Fauve Braque and Pablo Picasso (b.1881), to be called Cubists. Not only did the -ism undermine individual artistic identity, it could also suggest an insatiable appetite for fame at the expense of serious commitment.

Fauvism only slowly and inconclusively became an -ism, Cubism achieved that status quickly and comprehensively; and it achieved it even before there were group showings of Cubists. It was Braque whose work was first talked of in the press in terms of 'cubes'. In the summer of 1908, he worked at L'Estaque, surrounding himself with landscape motifs associated with Cézanne, a retrospective of whose painting had been held at the Salon d'automne of 1907. Flat colour had given way gradually in Braque's painting to angular, flat facets, modelled with warm and cool tones like enlargements of Cézanne's mosaics of planes, which in the L'Estaque landscapes, Braque made rock right across the picture surface in

23. Georges Braque, *The Small Bay, La Ciotat*, 1907. Oil on canvas, 44 × 55 cm. Musée National d'Art Moderne, Paris

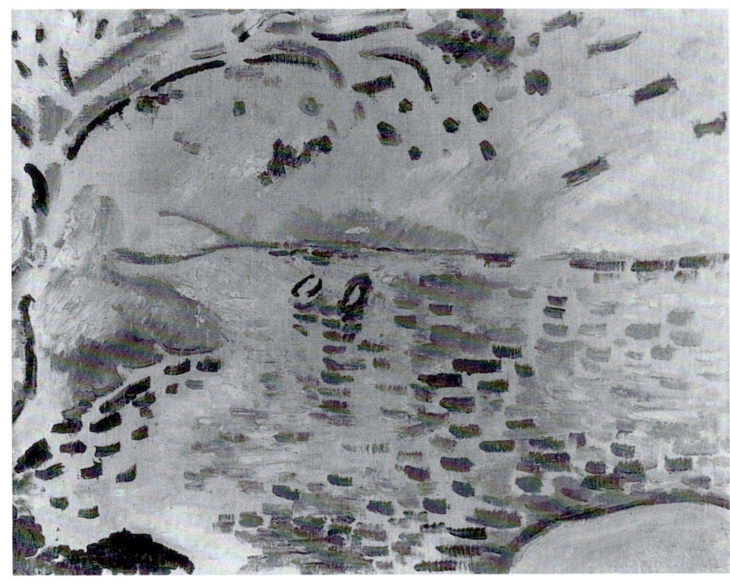

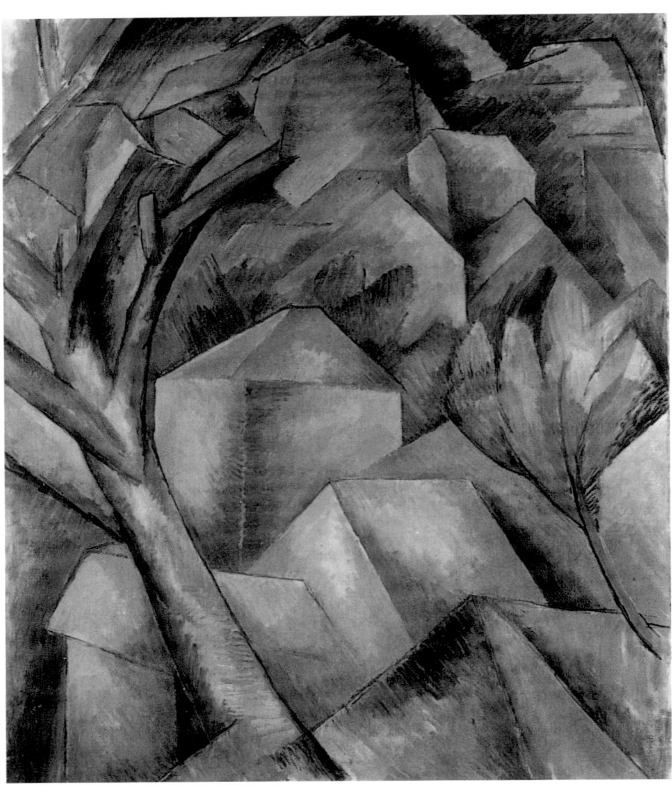

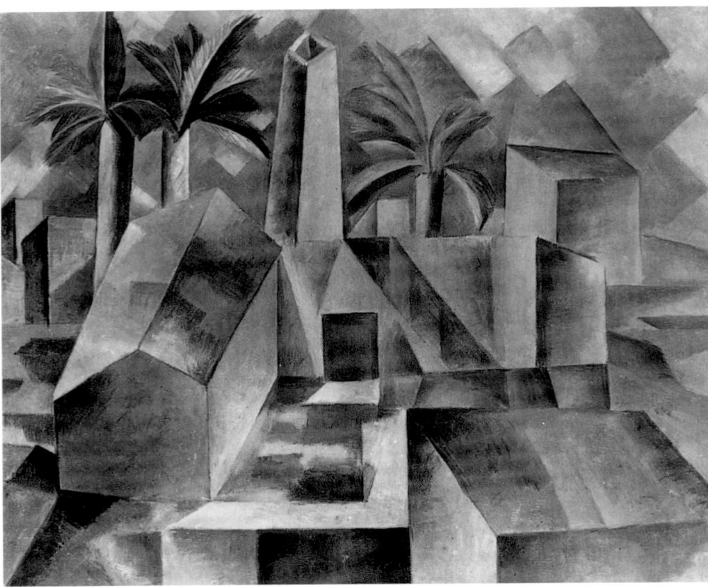

24. Georges Braque, *Houses at L'Estaque*, 1908. Oil on canvas, 73 × 60 cm. Kunstmuseum Bern (Hermann and Margrit Rupf Foundation)

25. Pablo Picasso, *Factory at Horta de Ebro*, 1909. Oil on canvas, 53 × 60 cm. The State Hermitage Museum, St Petersburg

emulation of trees and hummocky ground and houses on a hillside [24]; the effect of a substructure of geometric solids led Vauxcelles to apply the epithet cubes, when some of these pictures were shown by Daniel-Henry Kahnweiler in November 1908.[17] By April 1909, the critic Charles Morice could remark in the literary review *Mercure de France* that Braque was 'a victim – setting Cubism aside – of an admiration for Cézanne that is too exclusive or ill-considered'.[18] By June 1910, the epithet 'cubic' had been applied to paintings by Braque's friend Picasso, including a landscape which was in part a response to his L'Estaque landscapes [25].[19]

By the end of 1910, there were not just two but three painters to whom the term Cubism could be applied, even though still no group showing of Cubism had occurred. André Salmon, writing as critic for the newspaper *Paris-Journal*, picked out a *Nude* by Jean Metzinger (b.1883) as alone 'defending Cubism', at the Salon d'automne.[20] And shortly afterwards it was Metzinger who began the process of supplying theories for Cubism, writing on Picasso and Braque in the German periodical *Pan* before the end of the year. He 'does not deny the object,' Metzinger wrote of Picasso, 'he illuminates it with his intelligence and feeling'.[21] The 'intelligent' representation of things was to be a claim increasingly made for Cubism; something kept deliberately distinct from the direct representation of sensations then identified with Impressionism.

Unlike Fauvism, Cubism would, from 1910 on, always be a movement complicated by a heavy overlay of theory, but theories of Cubism produced from the inside did not fully emerge until 1912–13. They were elaborated with brilliance but inconsistency in Apollinaire's *Les Peintres cubistes* (1913), and in a little book by Metzinger written in collaboration with a 'Cubist' colleague, the painter Albert Gleizes (b.1881), *Du Cubisme* (1912). Also influential were the writings of the critic, Maurice Raynal, another from the circle of Apollinaire, Picasso and Braque. Salmon's *La Jeune Peinture française* supplied an 'anecdotal history of Cubism' at the same time, confirming the now agreed status of Picasso (rather than Braque) as Cubism's 'inventor'. It was precisely at this moment, between early 1911 and late 1912, that Cubism became the name of a movement given a public face by group showings in the Indépendants and the Salon d'automne. The term, thus, became identified with a set of theories and a group simultaneously: its status as a movement was doubly consolidated.

Just as Matisse had engineered the group showing of the Fauves at the Indépendants of 1905, so an alliance involving Gleizes and Metzinger engineered a group showing in the now celebrated 'Salle 41' of the 1911 Indépendants. It brought together work by Henri Le Fauconnier (b.1881), Robert Delaunay (b.1885) and Fernand Léger (b.1881) as well as Gleizes and Metzinger. These artists had been meeting in Le Fauconnier's studio and the Montparnasse café the Closerie des Lilas for months. The major painting in progress in Le Fauconnier's studio had been an allegory of abundance with a superstructure of post-Cézanne facets [26]; it joined Léger's massive metallic *Nudes in a Forest* and Delaunay's twisting and fractured *Eiffel Tower* as one of the stars of a public demonstration of Cubism [27, 28]. The press did its job in March 1911 – Cubism acquired high name-recognition – but it was really with the group showings more easily engineered at the Autumn Salons of 1911 and especially 1912 that Cubism became a big enough phenomenon to attract mass-circulation celebration, invective

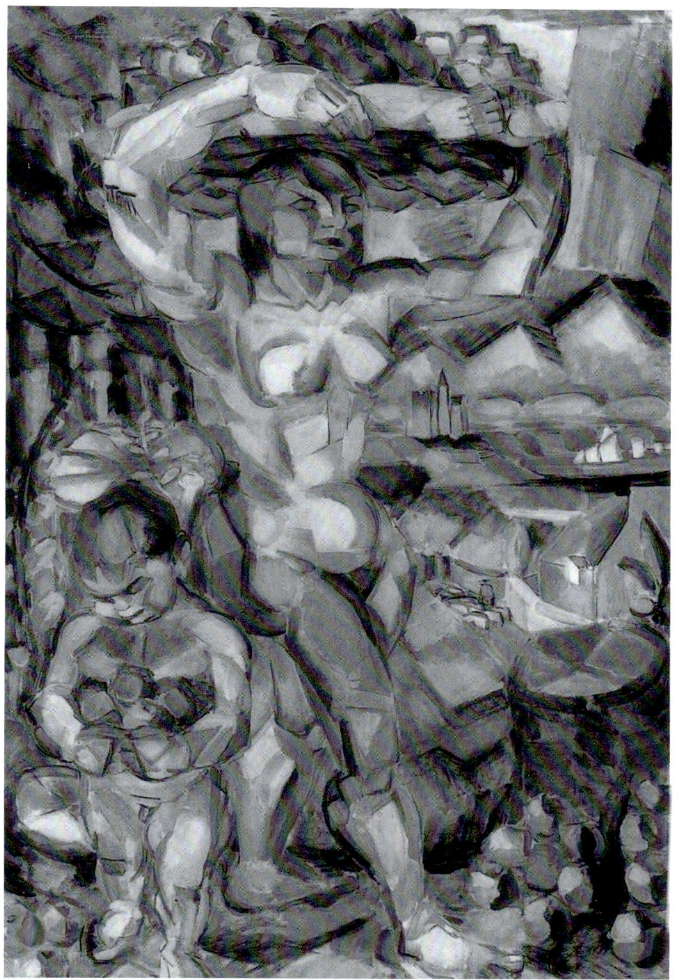

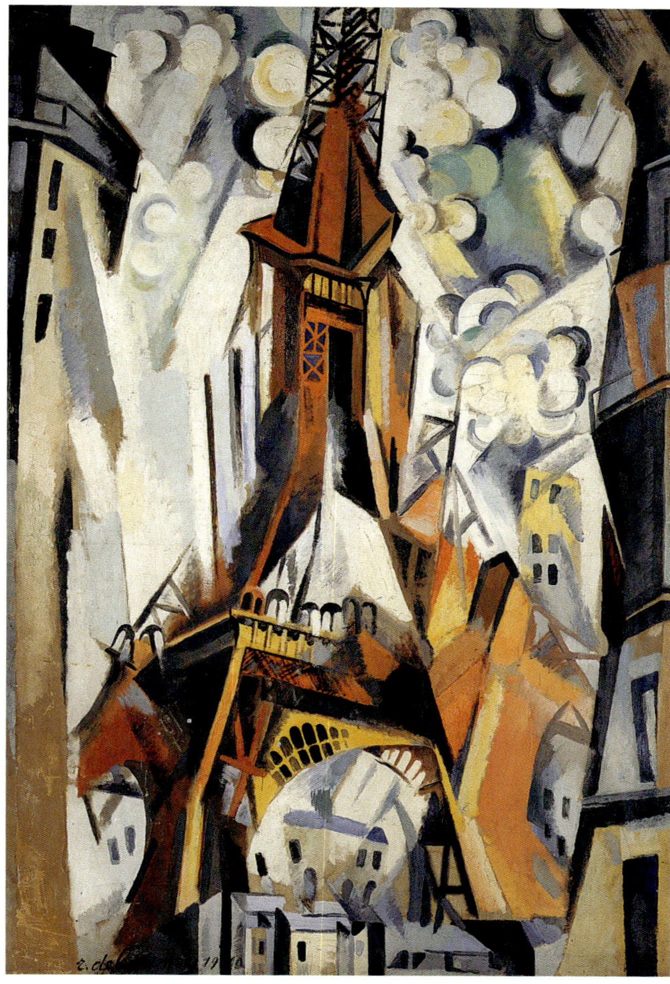

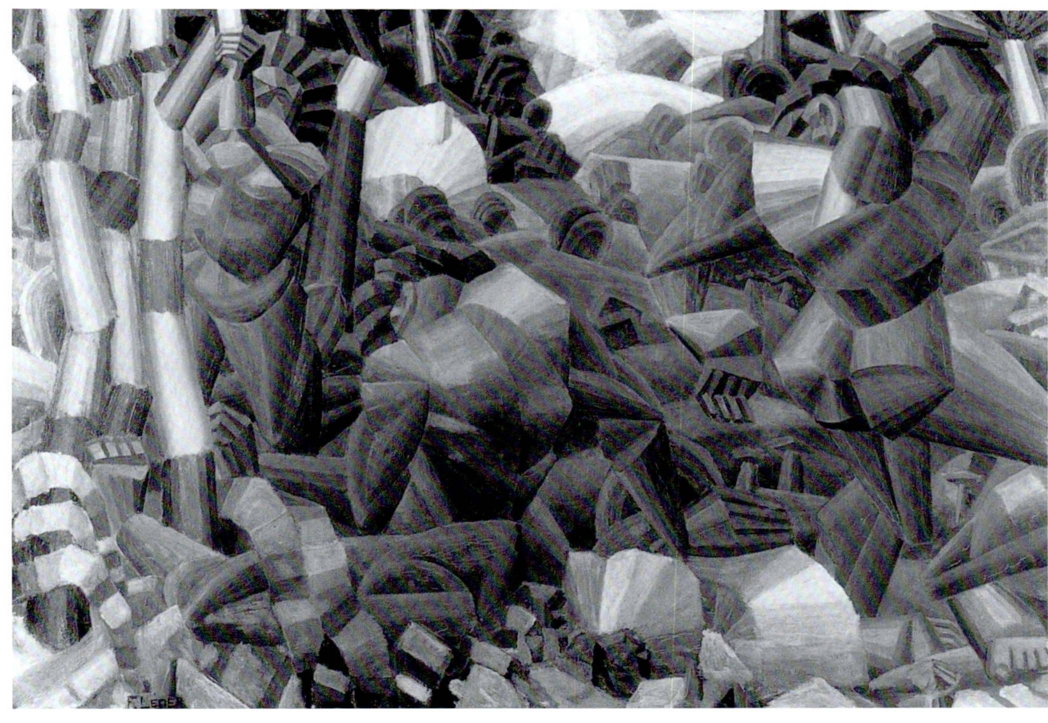

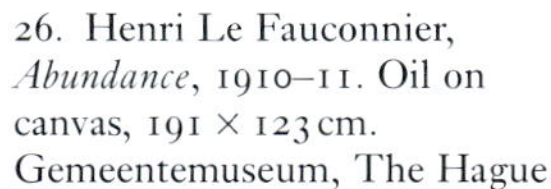

26. Henri Le Fauconnier, *Abundance*, 1910–11. Oil on canvas, 191 × 123 cm. Gemeentemuseum, The Hague

27. Robert Delaunay, *The Eiffel Tower*, 1910–11. Oil on canvas, 200 × 97 cm. Emanuel Hoffman-Stiftung, permanent loan to the Kunstmuseum, Basel

28. Fernand Léger, *Nudes in a Forest*, 1910–11. Oil on canvas, 120 × 170 cm. Rijksmuseum Kröller-Müller Museum, Otterlo

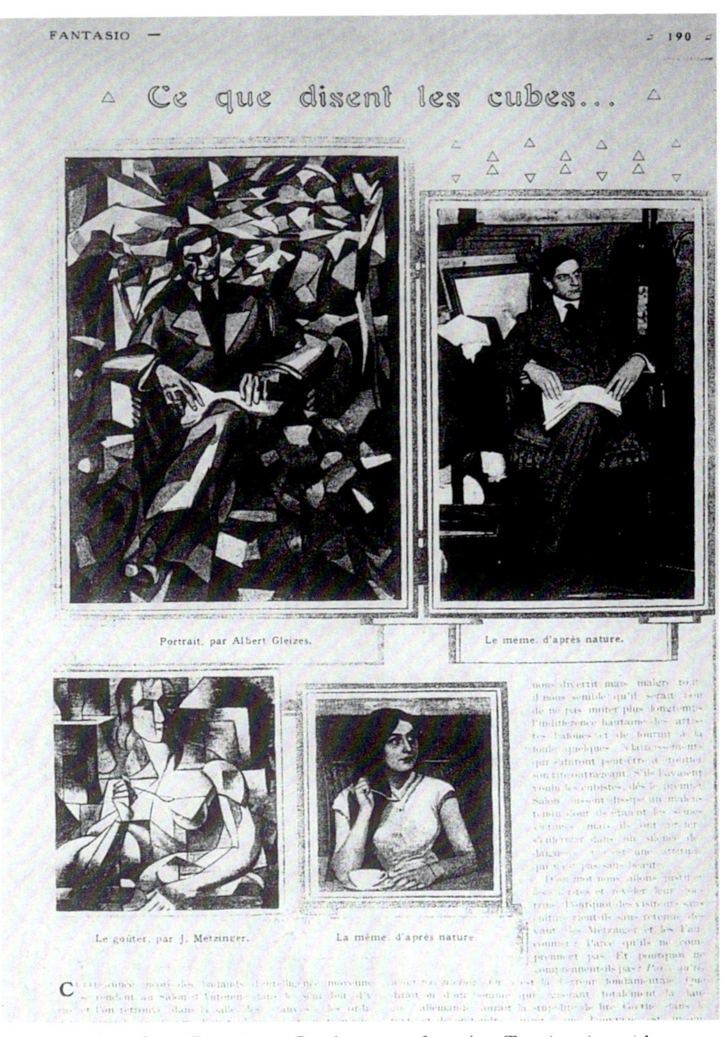

FANTASIO — 190

Ce que disent les cubes...

Portrait, par Albert Gleizes.

Le même, d'après nature.

Le goûter, par J. Metzinger.

La même, d'après nature.

29. Page from *Fantasio*, 15 October 1911, featuring *Tea-time (1911)* by Jean Metzinger (below), and *Portrait of Jacques Nayral (1911)* by Albert Gleizes (above)

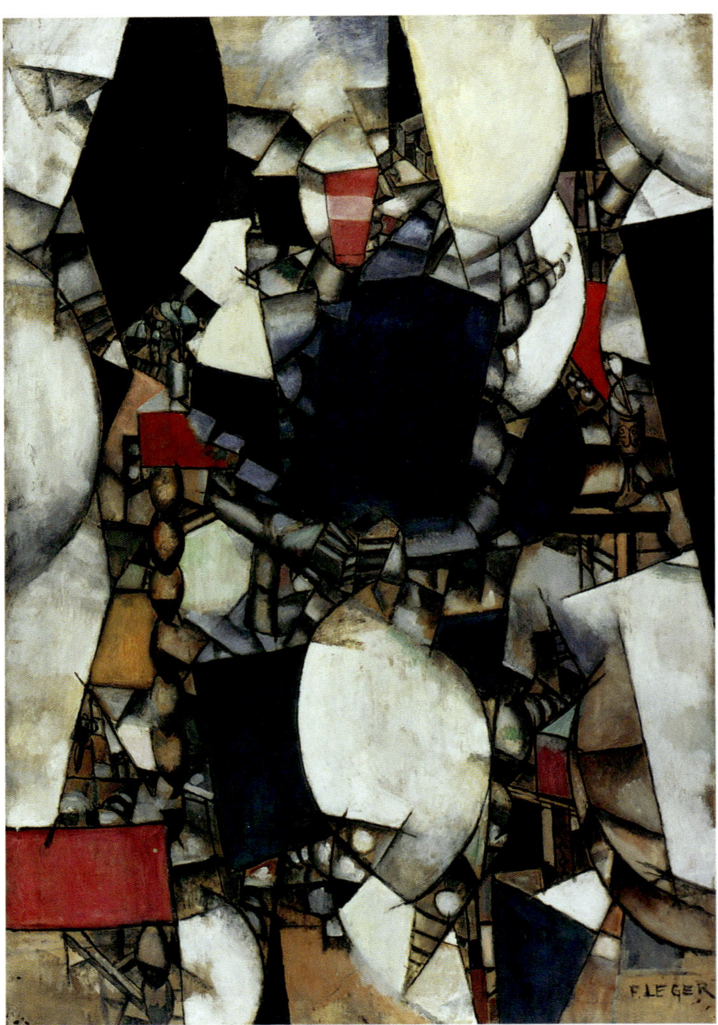

30. Fernand Léger, *Woman in Blue*, 1912. Oil on canvas, 193 × 130 cm. Kunstmuseum, Basel

and satire. There were images to go with the onslaught of words. In November 1911, *Fantasio* illustrated a trio of Cubist portraits by Léger, Gleizes and Metzinger juxtaposed with photographs of models posed as if they were the sitters [29]; it was accompanied by a heavily ironic commentary.[22] The following year, Léger's next major contribution to the Salon d'automne, his *Woman in Blue* appeared on the front page of two mass-circulation newspapers, *Le Matin* and *L'Eclair* [30].[23]

With the Salon d'automne of 1912, in fact, Cubism became a political issue. It provoked sharp exchanges in the budget debate in the Chamber of Deputies as a result of an open letter sent to the press by a prominent Socialist member of the Conseil municipal de la Ville de Paris, Monsieur Lampué, who, according to *Paris-Journal*, himself had exhibited at the Indépendants. The complaint was that the Salon d'automne was giving 'the most trivial vulgarities one can imagine' a platform in a State building, the Grand Palais. Marcel Sembat, also a prominent Socialist, collector of independent art and husband of a Salon d'automne exhibitor, spoke eloquently for the defence.[24]

What was missing, of course, from the Cubist showings at the Indépendants and the Salon d'automne of 1911–12 was any work by Picasso and Braque, even though the press repeatedly referred to them as initiators. 'What is a Cubist?' asked the tabloid-style *Petit Parisien* in April 1911. 'It is a painter from the Braque–Picasso school.'[25] After 1908, these two had sold increasingly to Daniel-Henry Kahnweiler, already Derain's and Vlaminck's dealer, who discouraged them from contributing to the Salons, preferring to avoid the rough-and-tumble of -ism controversies.[26] In 1913, Léger would join Picasso and Braque as a Kahnweiler Cubist and so would a newcomer among the Salon Cubists, the young Spanish friend of Picasso, Juan Gris (b.1887), who had made his debut as a Cubist with a *Homage to Pablo Picasso* at the Indépendants of 1912 [31]. It is the split between the exclusivity of Kahnweiler's Cubists, especially Picasso and Braque before 1913, and the public Cubism of Le Fauconnier, Metzinger, Gleizes and the others who made names for themselves in the Salon scandals of 1911–12, that exposes the contradictions inherent in Cubism as an historical phenomenon and opens to question the attempts that have been made from the 1960s to define it and to pinpoint its key significance for twentieth-century art.

The writing of the history of Cubism's formation has developed two distinct plot lines, one primary, the other secondary: the story of a 'true' or 'essential' Cubism – directly comparable to Elderfield's 'true Fauvism', with Picasso and Braque playing the role of Matisse – has taken over as the primary plot. This was already the case in the 1920s in Kahnweiler's own little book, *Der Weg zum Kubismus* (The Rise of Cubism) published in Munich in 1920, and the first serious historical treatment of the movement, Guillaume Janneau's *L'Art cubiste. Théories et réalisations* of 1929. Janneau was able to write of Picasso and Braque achieving 'rigorously Cubist' practices by 1911–12, on the way to 'the pure doctrine of Cubism', repeatedly underlining their primacy.[27] With Barr's decision to give Cubism the fundamental role as the generator of all those modernist movements that he saw culminating in abstraction in 1936, the primacy of the Picasso–Braque story and the status of their Cubism as 'true Cubism' was assured, so was the eventual reduction of the Salon Cubists to the condition of historical etceteras. Ironically, as Cubism the movement emerged from France with a global role in histories of international modern art, Cubism as it had first existed in public form – the work of the groups that made it an -ism at the Indépendants and Salons d'automnes in 1911–12 – was at best marginalised and at worst rendered irrelevant to any 'essential' account of Cubism. The individuals who did least for the collective emergence of the movement *became* the movement in its essence, as some, like Salmon and Apollinaire at the time, claimed they always were: the movers of the movement behind the scenes.

What then of 'true Cubism' and its definitions? If one follows in sequence the successive versions of the Picasso–Braque primary storyline and the attempted definitions of Cubism that usually accompany them, one does not, I believe, build a master story of the ascent towards an 'essential' understanding of what Cubism 'truly' was, one becomes aware of the openness of Picasso and Braque's work between 1907 and 1914 to later, changing critical agendas. And with each successive version, the starting date of significant Cubist art has tended to change.

Salmon begins his 'anecdotal history' of 1912 with a rambling, contradictory account of Picasso's *Demoiselles d'Avignon* painted in 1907 [282]; and in 1920 Kahnweiler too identifies it as the 'beginnings of Cubism.' The intense engagement of this picture with sexuality contrasts forcibly with the austere calm of Braque's and Picasso's Cubist painting of 1909–12, but Kahnweiler manages to write about it as if Picasso's central concern was the most basic of *pictorial* problems: that of representing three-dimensions on a two-dimensional surface. Salmon dwells on its capacity to shock, but what he stresses is not the expressive in Picasso's nudes, it is *how* they are represented. For him, they are the result far more of *con*ception than of *per*ception; he calls them 'white numbers on a black-board'. Salmon was the first to link the painting to non-European culture, but, though he wrote of Picasso 'seeking anwers . . . among the enchantments of Oceania and Africa', he played down 'the occult' and instead insisted that Picasso's 'demoiselles' approached above all 'a total representation of man and things'.[28]

Flatness and the conceptual were to become the two poles of discussions of Cubism as defined through the work of Picasso and Braque. At first, it was the conceptual pole that took precedence; this was the focus of an influential article by Raynal published in *Gil Blas* in 1912, 'Conception et vision'. For him, as for Salmon, the key principle of Cubist painting was the primacy of the mind over the eye; the key manifestations of that primacy were geometry and, most telling of all, the shifting of viewpoints.[29] Later historians have found it easy to see both in the *Demoiselles d'Avignon*; the latter most dramatically in the swivelling of the head of the croucher on the right into three-quarter and full-face view, which threatens dislocation from her back-view back.[30] When Braque met Picasso in 1907 through Apollinaire, it was above all the conceptual freedom offered by the shifting of viewpoints in the *Demoiselles* that left its mark. His response was a large, awkward nude, its swivelling head above a fusion of three-quarter view and full-face buttocks [32].

Janneau's 'pure doctrine of Cubism' was ultimately a reiteration of Raynal's conceptual theory, but he anticipated later versions of the Picasso–Braque story by suggesting for Braque 'a certain anteriority'. It was he who was the first to single out the Braque of the L'Estaque landscapes, as the beginning of Cubism proper [24].[31] Picasso remained unchallenged as the inventor of Cubism in Barr's version of the story, but with John Golding's 'history and analysis', first published in 1959 and the starting point of later twentieth-century versions, Braque's primary role in Janneau's

31. Juan Gris, *Homage to Pablo Picasso*, 1912. Oil on canvas, 93 × 74.1 cm. The Art Institute of Chicago (Gift of Leigh B. Block)

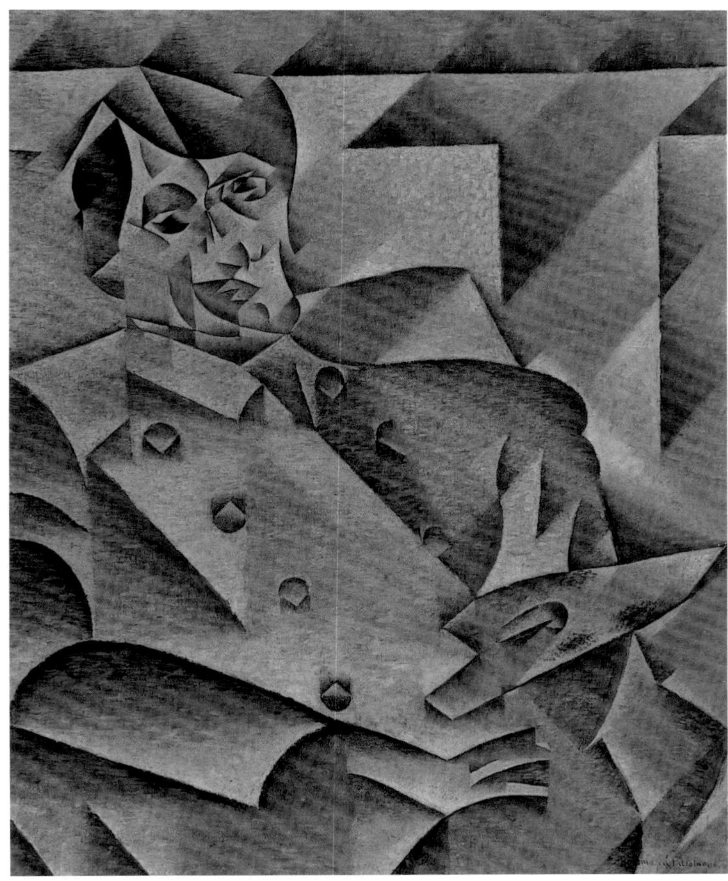

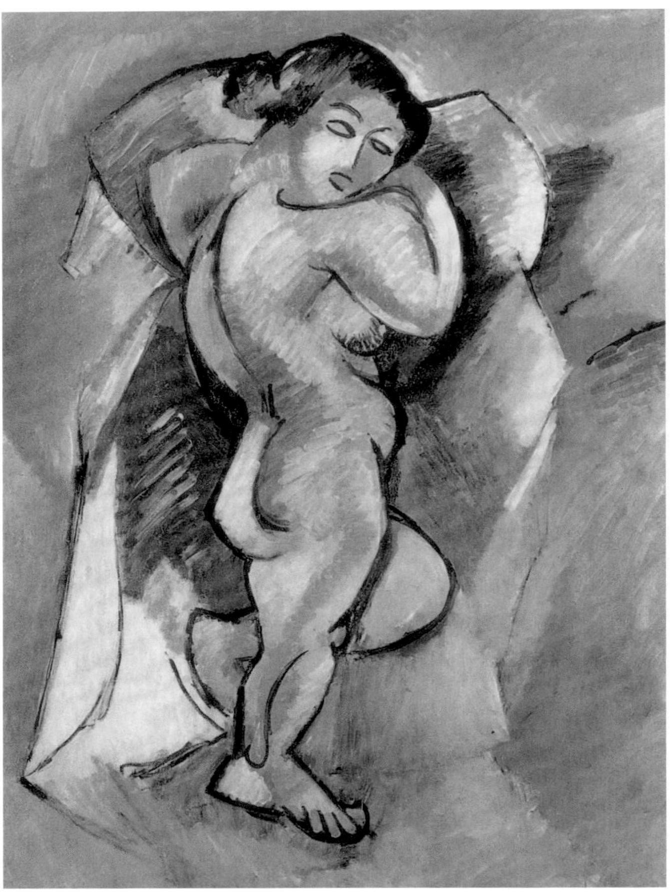

32. Georges Braque, *Large Nude*, 1908. Oil on canvas, 142 × 102 cm. Private Collection

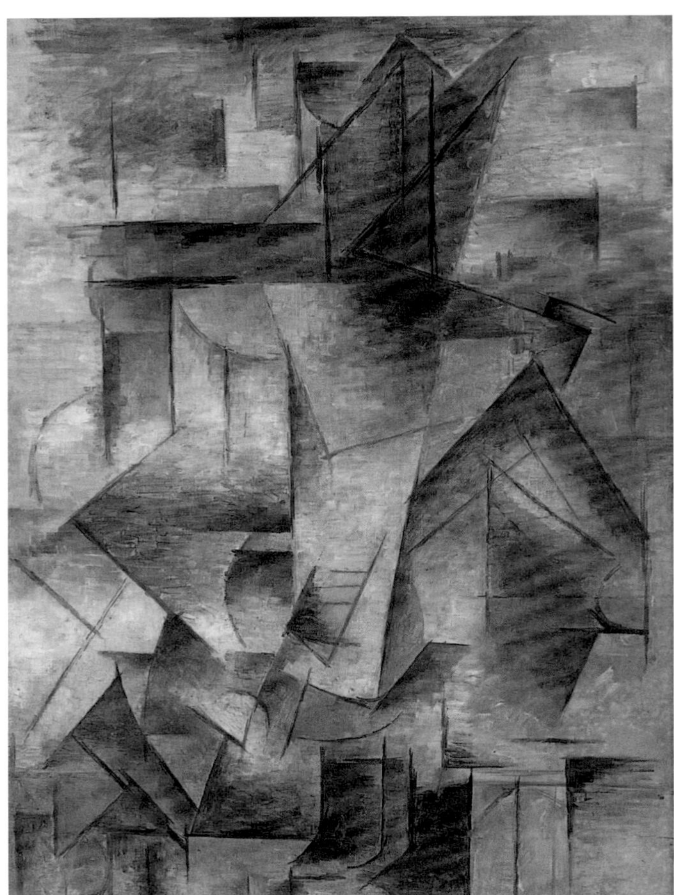

33. Pablo Picasso, *Guitarist*, 1910. Oil on canvas, 100 × 73 cm. Musée National d'Art Moderne, Paris

study was restored, to be underlined most influentially of all by the work of William Rubin between the 1970s and 1989, the date of the apotheosis of Braque and Picasso's Cubism in Rubin's huge exhibition, *Pioneering Cubism*, at the Museum of Modern Art, New York. With this shift of status and roles from Picasso to Braque went a major change in the definition of Cubism. What was essential to Rubin's definition was neither the geometry nor the shifting viewpoints that are to be seen in Braque's L'Estaque pictures, it was their capacity to suggest depth while keeping a strong sense of the actual flatness of the picture surface. Applying the priorities of the dominant American critical agenda of the 1960s – Clement Greenberg's formalism – Rubin found in Braque's flattened facets a key early stage in a history of modern painting's return to the basic material essentials of painting: form rendered by means of coloured pigments or other substances applied flat on to the flat picture-plane. Now, the emphasis was on *per*ception, not *con*ception: the experience of seeing in depth as the eye tracks tilted facets across a two-dimensional surface. And a crucial factor in this was a device dubbed *passage*: the sliding of one painted surface into another through Cézannian broken contours.

Such an idea of what is essential to Cubism has not necessarily led the tellers of the story to date its 'essential' beginnings to 1908, rather than 1907 and the *Demoiselles d'Avignon*. For Kahnweiler, of course, what was proto-Cubist in the *Demoiselles* was Picasso's visible struggle, ultimately a failure, to solve the problem of rendering three-dimensions in two, yet for him *the* breakthrough occurred not with Braque's L'Estaque landscapes nor with Picasso's response to them [24, 25], but two years later in the summer of 1910, with a series of paintings made by Picasso at the little port of Cadaquès in Catalonia, where the technique of *passage* allowed the facets of figures and objects so freely to overflow contours that they virtually disappeared [33].

At the end of the twentieth century, the application of another critical agenda led not to a new date for Cubism's beginning, but to the fixing of a still later date for the most important of Cubism's discoveries. The key work in this modification of 'essential Cubism's' history is Picasso's metal construction, *Guitar* [129], probably first made as a cardboard model in the autumn of 1912, a few months after Picasso's first collage *Still-life with Chair-caning*, and at the same time as Braque's invention of *papier-collé* (the sticking to the canvas of materials such as cloth, and of cut-out pieces of paper, including newspaper) [128, 104]. The work of two writers, Rosalind Krauss and Yve-Alain Bois has been crucial. Their critical agenda is structuralist and post-structuralist, and stresses the way the use of simple interchangeable signs denoting features and objects detaches sign from referent while still allowing things to be represented; something that only begins to occur with real clarity at this point, especially in Picasso's constructions and *papiers-collés*.[32] Alfred Barr's major contribution to the codification of the study of Cubism was the distinction between a kind of Cubist painting based on breaking things down through a part-by-part analysis, involving the shifting of viewpoints, and a kind based on the building up of images from schematic conceptual signs for features: 'Analytic' and 'Synthetic' Cubism. I shall show how far this was an over-simplification in Part Three. Barr established 1912 as the date marking the break between the two, and linked it to the development of collage and *papier-collé*. Krauss's and Bois's version of the story gives a special initiatory significance to that break, and especially to the invention out of collage of construction, but at the same time it restores primacy to Picasso, and shifts the terms of discussion from forms and processes to language.

I shall return to the questions raised by these attempts to define an essential Cubism in Part Three, but what has to be stressed here is their exclusive focus on the work of Picasso and Braque as definitive, and their striking differences. Most important, however, in any *historical* analysis of Cubism is the disjunction between Picasso's and Braque's Cubism and that of the Salon Cubists – it becomes necessary to talk not of an 'essential Cubism' but of many Cubisms.

The gap between the Salon Cubists and Picasso and Braque (with Gris added as the third of a triumvirate) is the gap between groups more separate from each other than the Fauves around Matisse had been from the Havrais Fauves. In 1914, Gris made a papier-collé, *The Bottle of Anis del Mono* [34], which offers the bottle label as a heraldic device for his alliance with Picasso and Braque under Kahnweiler's protection. It features three medals won for the excellence of the drink: one refers to Madrid, one to Paris, one to Badalona (an industrial suburb of Barcelona). Gris came from Madrid, Braque was now a Parisian, and Picasso had come to Paris from Barcelona. Nothing could better underline the inward-turning privacy of the art of these three at this moment: the message is a private one between friends, and, as the label says, the resulting work is to be consumed by those few in the know as a 'Distallacion especial'. Until Picasso's move away in 1912, they had lived in or adjacent to Montmartre and all three mixed in a circle of post-Symbolist poets which revolved around Apollinaire and an even longer-standing friend of Picasso's, Max Jacob. Their Cubism found strong echoes in the elusive Symbolist poetry of Stéphane Mallarmé, which all of them knew; their watchword was 'purity', symbolised in Apollinaire's writing by the flame. 'Fire,' he had written in 1908, 'is the symbol of painting . . . Fire has the purity that suffers the existence of nothing foreign to itself and cruelly transforms into itself whatever it touches.'[33] The colours on the palette in Gris's *Homage to Picasso* flair in the form of flames.

The public Cubists, including the fourth of Kahnweiler's Cubists, Léger, lived on the Left Bank, in the Latin Quarter and Montparnasse, and in the Western outskirts of Paris at Courbevoie and Puteaux. They interacted within a very different milieu also featuring writers, which elevated the dynamism of lived experience above the 'purity' of art. Gleizes in particular had been involved with the writers

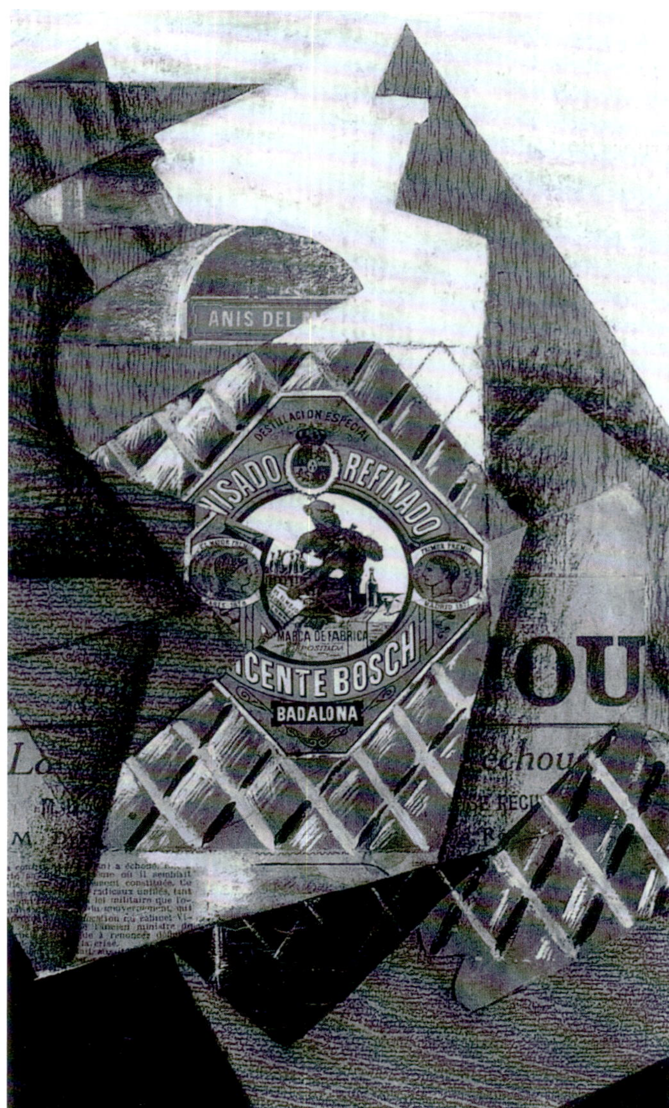

34. Juan Gris, *Bottle of Anis del Mono*, 1914. Papier collé, oil and charcoal on canvas, 41.8 × 24 cm. Judith Rothschild Collection, New York

Jules Romain, René Arcos and Alexandre Mercereau in a failed experiment in communal living on the Tolstoyan model, the Abbaye de Créteil. These were writers who admired the verve of Emile Verhaeren and Walt Whitman above the hermeticism of Mallarmé, and they and the artists were drawn to the thinking of the most influential living French philosopher of the period, Henri Bergson, whose conviction that knowledge at its most profound lies in the immediately experiential they shared. Where Picasso and Braque used figures, still lives and landscapes as starting points, often to be almost obliterated in the pursuit of a Mallarméan idea, works like Léger's *Nudes in a Forest* and Le Fauconnier's *Abundance* [28, 26] featured subjects that counted in their own right and which said so baldly. Though Metzinger clearly knew Picasso's and Braque's work at least by 1910, Daniel Robbins has convincingly argued, indeed, that Le Fauconnier, Gleizes and Léger may even have built the planar structures of their paintings without any secondary dependence on that work.[34] What is encountered in the Cubism of the Salons is not 'the Braque–Picasso school' at all, but a different range of Cubist styles with a different set of priorities, produced within different milieux.

Finally, there is the question of when Cubism ended. Most writers on Cubism since Barr have made an ending to their accounts of the movement around 1921 or sometimes earlier, and yet most commentators on the Decorative Arts Exhibition of 1925, writing in 1925, picked out Cubism as one of its dominant themes. The pavilions of Robert Mallet-Stephens and the sculpture of Jan and Joël Martel were, for instance, seen as new applications of a Cubist aesthetic given a decorative dimension. Certainly Cubism was domesticated by later practitioners like the Martels as slick visual enhancements of 'modern' environments – one of the Martels' successes in 1925 was a group of reinforced-concrete Cubist trees planted in a garden of ruthlessly clipped hedges by Mallet-Stevens [35]. Despite this, however, a look at what the artists were exhibiting and the critical debates in the specialist and the non-specialist press after the 1914–18 war demonstrates clearly that Cubism remained for most the cutting-edge of vanguard art until at least 1924, to be celebrated or attacked as such.[35] Further, what are fundamentally Cubist priorities continued to direct the still inventive use of Cubist pictorial and sculptural techniques in at least some of the work of a wide range of artists, including Picasso, Braque and Gris, and several others identified as Cubists before the war, for instance Léger and Gleizes. A few new Cubists emerged in the war too, most importantly the sculptors Jacques Lipchitz and Henri Laurens. What is more, between 1917 and the early 1920s, Raynal had been joined by the poet Pierre Reverdy, another Montmartre friend of Picasso, Braque and Gris, in developing a more all-embracing theory of Cubism based on the Apollinairian principle of 'purity', which took over from the conceptual and the Bergsonian experiential theories as the dominant theory of Cubism in what was considered its most advanced form.[36] Indeed, the painter-critic André Lhote called this later Cubism '*a priori*' or 'pure' Cubism; by which he meant, not an 'essential Cubism' predicated on the work of Picasso and Braque alone,

35. Jan and Joël Martel, *Trees*, 1925. Reinforced concrete (garden designed by Robert Mallet-Stevens) Exposition Internationale des arts décoratifs et industriels, Paris

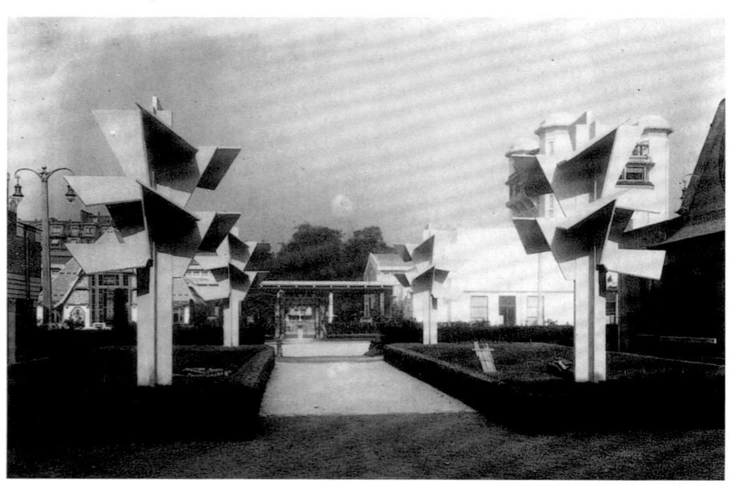

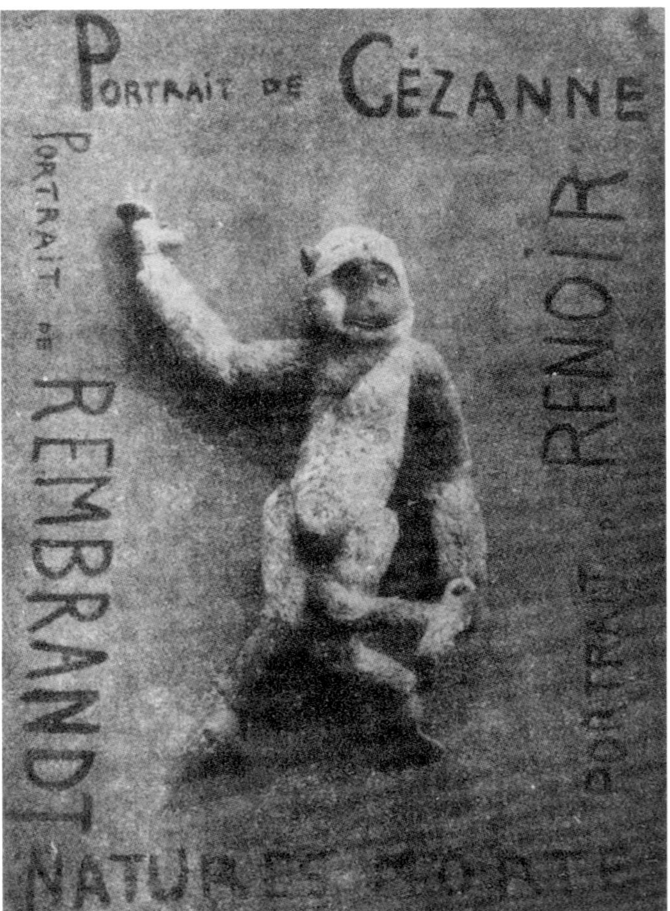

but a distillation of the varied, often motif-based Cubisms of all the Cubists of the pre-1914 period.[37]

That later twentieth-century accounts and definitions of Cubism, with their sometimes exclusive focus on the work of Picasso and Braque between 1907 and 1914, should have ignored this period of intense activity and debate from 1918 to 1925 is the final demonstration of the gap between Cubism as an essence to be *defined* and thus adapted to changing critical agendas, and Cubism as an *historical* phenomenon. The one is too restrictive to be able to take in the diversity and extension of the other. Again, the contradictions raise more questions than they answer.

MAKING DADA

On 13 April 1919, the poet André Breton wrote to a new friend Louis Aragon expressing a frank distaste for their literary vocation: 'For me, poetry, art, ceases to be an end, becomes instead a means (of publicity). Publicity ceases to be a means so as to become an end, Death of art (for art's sake). Subversion.'[38] He, Aragon and a third young poet, Philippe Soupault, had published a few months earlier the first number of a periodical, which, for all their scepticism, they called *Littérature*. Breton's commitment to art as a means of subversive publicity showed an acute awareness of the potential of group action and the -ism for penetrating mentalities, not merely forcing change in the *forms* of art. It

36. Left. Francis Picabia, *Dada Picture*, 1920. Media, support, size and whereabouts unknown. Presumed destroyed

37. Max Ernst, *The Master's Bedroom*, 1920. Collage, gouache and pencil on paper, 16.3 × 22 cm. Private Collection

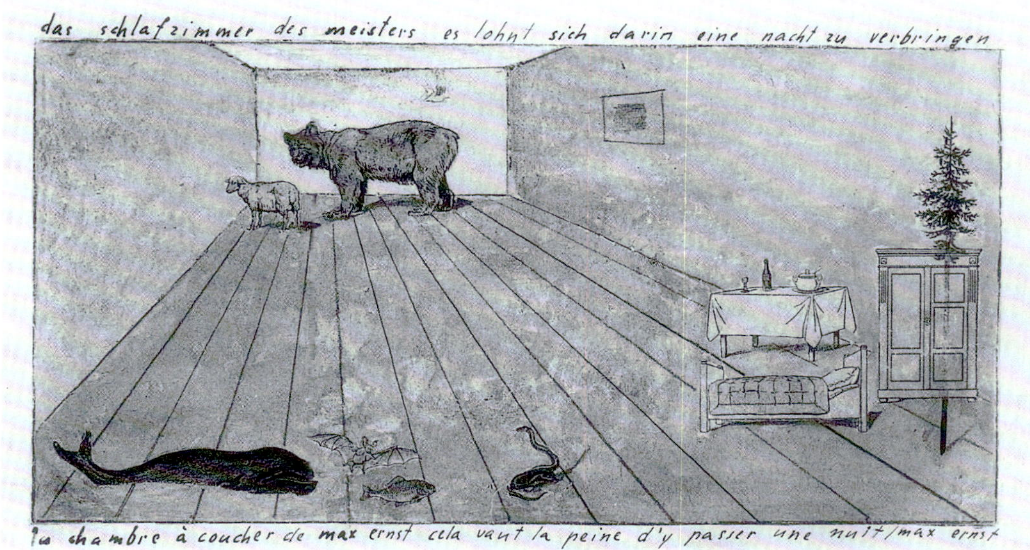

was encouraged by knowledge of the activities of Francis Picabia, a latter-day Fauve who had become a Salon Cubist, publisher (from 1915) of an insolent periodical *391*, an artist-writer whose evasion of active war-service from 1915 to 1918 had taken him to Barcelona, New York and Switzerland. But it was sparked more immediately by another scurrilous periodical, *Dada*, the product (from 1917) of a small group of writers and artists in neutral Zurich, and especially by the nihilistic aggression of one of their number, Tristan Tzara, a Romanian.

Breton and Tzara were in touch, and in September 1919, Tzara wrote to Breton describing how *Dada* had been the creation of a few friends who found they had 'nothing in common with futurism and cubism.' It was, he insisted, an illusion to call it a 'Movement'; he refused any responsibility for the 'school launched by journalists and commonly called Dadaism'.[39] In fact, Zurich Dada owed a great deal to the model provided by Italian Futurism of a movement as a vehicle for cultural subversion. It did without a strong leader – there was no Dada equivalent of Futurism's patron and undisputed chief, F.T. Marinetti; but it took over Futurism's tactic of provocation through public performance (Marinetti's roaring recitals of 'free-word' poetry, or Luigi Russolo's noise concerts), and Futurism's use of the manifesto to grab attention. In Paris, Dada was to exist in the coming together and the concerted subversive activity of the *Littérature* group around Breton, added to by Tzara, and Picabia, the latter supported by a motley crew of associates, including his old Paris friends Marcel Duchamp (another one-time Salon Cubist) and Georges Ribemont-Dessaignes. Picabia in particular was continually to hold up Cubism to ridicule for being in its post-1918 form so 'serious', so principled in its 'purity' and for selling out to the commercial campaigning of the dealer who had taken over from Kahnweiler in the war, Léonce Rosenberg: for being, in a word, a movement. His *Dada Manifesto* of March 1920 made Cubism its target: 'They have . . . cubed violins, cubed guitars, cubed illustrated papers, cubed shit and the profiles of young girls, now they must cube money!!! DADA wants nothing, nothing, nothing, it acts to make the public say: "we understand nothing, nothing, nothing".'[40]

This refusal of the idea of the movement by what was perceived as a movement, certainly between early 1920 and spring 1922 (as long a period as that of Fauvism), has led historians of Dada to refuse definitions and to identify Dada in terms of group activity by those who, usually in passing, adopted the Dada label – brief passages of concerted action produced by individual encounters. Michel Sanouillet's major history of Paris Dada plots its course through a furious flurry of manifestos, exhibitions, periodical publications, performances and 'soirées', where poems, statements or objects and images acquire meaning, but never more than circumstantially; it resists any idea of an 'essential Dada' style or practice.[41]

The key opening move was the arrival of Tzara in Paris to stay in the apartment of Picabia's new mistress, Germaine Everling, on 17 January 1920. The key meeting place was the Café Certa, a little Basque bar in a covered gallery of shops close to the Avenue de l'Opéra, a long way from the Cubists' haunts in Montparnasse. The key moments of concerted publicity-seeking action in 1920–1 were the performance-events, and the exhibitions.

The events began with the matinée held on 23 January 1920 in a small room in the Palais des fêtes (function rooms) on the rue Saint-Martin. The opening half featured Breton reading a text on Léger, Gris, the Italian painter de Chirico and Lipchitz, work of all of whom was on show. It was followed in the second half by a performance apparently dismissing all visual art as pointless: Picabia's exhibition of a blackboard on which he had made a few chalk marks for Breton to rub out. Visual art was now something which could perform to an audience, as Picabia's *Dada Picture* did when he showed it on stage at the Dada soirée of 27 March 1920 in the Théâtre de l'œuvre [36]. Here monkeys are made of three giants of the canon: Cézanne, Renoir and Rembrandt.

The key exhibitions were Picabia's at the galerie Au Sans

Pareil in 1920 and at the Barcelona Dalmau galleries in November 1922 (strictly speaking actually post-Dada), the solo show of the Cologne-based Dada, Max Ernst (b.1891), in May 1921, and the Salon Dada of June 1920 held in the Studio des Champs-Elysées, a chic theatrical venue on the Avenue Montaigne. Picabia also made calculatedly provocative showings in the Indépendants and the Autumn Salons between 1919 and 1922, including his absurdly titled *L'Oeil cacodylate* at the Salon d'automne of 1921, which consisted of nothing more than signatures and inscriptions supplied by his not necessarily Dada friends. The Ernst show consisted of thoroughly un-Cubist collages usually incorporating popular encyclopaedia engravings juxtaposed with nonsense captions [37]. And the Salon Dada of June 1920 was put together as an anti-art rejoinder to a Cubist show earlier in the year, an attempted revival of the pre-war Cubist exhibition that accompanied the 1912 Salon d'automne, the Salon de la section d'or. The Dada response included paintings by non-painters: Tzara showed three works entitled *Mon*, *Cher* and *Ami*.

1920 saw completed the very brief life-cycles of two or three new Dada periodicals, including *Proverbe*, edited by one of the Breton circle, Paul Eluard, and *Z*, edited by Paul Dermée, a young Belgian writer, who showed himself too interested in poetry and art to be accepted as a Dada beyond 1920. Picabia's *391* and *Littérature* continued, however, to be the key Paris Dada periodicals, with Picabia happy to contribute to the latter so long as he was not intent on disrupting Breton's initiatives.

If there was a Dada mentality, in Paris Tzara kept to it with most constancy; if there was a Dada behaviour, the mischief-maker Picabia was its avatar. The force that subverted Dada from within was given its concentrated strength by Breton; it was generated by that will to find coherence and purpose which was the target of both Tzara's and Picabia's most disruptive activities, inside as well as outside Dada. Breton's heretical determination to make a movement of Dada after all, produced Surrealism.

MAKING SURREALISM

In the lecture he delivered to accompany Picabia's Barcelona exhibition of November 1922, André Breton looked back over the history of movements since the beginning of the century and announced: 'I consider that Cubism, Futurism and Dada are not, when all is said and done, three distinct movements . . . To consider in succession Cubism, Futurism and Dada is to follow the ascent of an idea which has now reached a certain height and which awaits only a new impulse to continue to draw the curve which has been assigned it.'[42] He had, it seems, set aside Tristan Tzara's warnings of 1919 against the idea of Dada-ism and indeed Tzara's clear distinction between the Dadas and Cubism and Futurism too. Breton now thought in terms of a gathering forward thrust in which *one* movement did not merely follow others, but took their force into itself: consumed all that went before.

Telling the story of the end of Dada and the beginning of Surrealism has appeared reassuringly easy, because the one entails the other, and they join in a sequence of episodes driven along by a single leading character, Breton, episodes in which attempts are made to draw coherent conclusions and above all a direction from Dada practices. Indeed Breton was constructive enough to initiate discussions early in 1922 involving not only Dadas but artists positively sympathetic to Cubism, which were aimed at holding a conference to address the question of the 'new spirit'; it was to be called the Congrès de Paris. Predictably, Tzara sabotaged the project. Picabia supported it, but Sanouillet has suggested that he did so only to promote confusion; Breton's support of Picabia's Barcelona exhibition at the end of the year was, in fact, his last attempt to make something positive of the Dada practices for which Picabia still stood.[43]

The sequence of episodes marking the end of Dada and the beginning of Surrealism gave way to a phase lasting through 1923 when Breton was unsure where his initiatives were leading; it is often referred to as the 'époque floue'. Then came the publication of two texts that unequivocally signalled an end and declared a beginning: the first, early in 1924, was an anthology of Breton's Dada and post-Dada essays, presented as the route to a new starting-point: *Les Pas perdus* (Lost Steps); the second, in October 1924, was his *Manifesto of Surrealism*.

Through Breton's 'lost steps' two concerns emerge which would initially become, for him, the core features of Surrealism: first, the conviction that language has nothing to do with the true and the false, with meaning as a 'reality' to be directly communicated; second, the conviction that desire rather than reason gives meaning to language, and that the main route to an art infused with desire is 'psychic automatism'. The first of these concerns – language – was addressed in a piece published in *Littérature* at the end of 1922, 'Les Mots sans rides' (Words without Wrinkles). Here Breton traced links between the word-games of ex-Dadas like Duchamp (b.1887) and Robert Desnos and the poetry of Apollinaire and Mallarmé. The second concern – psychic automatism – was addressed initially in an essay dedicated to experiments the group was making with hypnosis-induced trances also at the end of 1922, 'L'Entrée des Médiums' (The Entrance of the Mediums). In that piece Breton used the term 'surrealism' specifically to mean 'a certain psychic automatism which corresponds well enough to the condition of dreaming'.[44] The terrain was prepared thus for the isolation of psychic automatism as the defining principle of the Surrealist movement, and this duly occurred in the *First Manifesto*. As if in a dictionary, Breton wrote: 'Surrealism. *n.masc.* pure psychic automatism, by which an attempt is made to express, either verbally, in writing or in any other manner, the true functioning of thought, in the absence of all control by the reason, excluding any aesthetic or moral preoccupation.'[45] This definition was grounded in psychiatry, above all in Freudian psychoanalysis (Breton had received the beginnings of a psychiatric training in the war). Surrealist practice was to use 'free association' automatist techniques to discover images in the Freudian Unconscious.

From the start, then, Surrealism had a definition and a problematic, the problematic of language. It also had a leader, a group identity and a programme. Support for the programme came from Aragon's *Une Vague de rêves* (A Wave ofDreams), published like the *Manifesto* in October 1924. For Aragon too, automatism was central, and language, no longer a means of communication to be trusted, was a material, a stuff of the imagination with unpredictable powers. Surrealism, indeed, was the first -ism developed in France in which the fact of the group and the idea of the movement coalesced from the outset to make a straightforwardly comprehensible unity. In this whole, however, were pulled together, as was intermittently the case in Dada, not merely different individual activists but wholly different kinds of activity, including what were still referred to as 'poetry' and 'painting', despite the continuing Dada-like distaste for the 'aesthetic'. Surrealism would always be, for Breton, an idea requiring definition, but its engagement with the Freudian Unconscious, and its commitment to language as the speaking of desire, constituted a direct challenge to the very processes of categorisation fundamental to the making of definitions. Between 1925 and the mid-1930s, Breton would be attracted to the tough materialism of the French Communist Party on the level of political theory and practice, but by committing Surrealism to the imagination he would always open his project at best to the Party's suspicion and at worst to its absolute anathemas. The Surrealist project concerned the individual as an independent questing personality, and yet the quest, Breton would increasingly believe, was only possible under a group discipline as ruthless as that of the Communist Party. He learned from the Party how to treat others much as the Party treated him.

38. Page from *La Révolution surréaliste*, no. 1 (Paris, 1 December 1924)

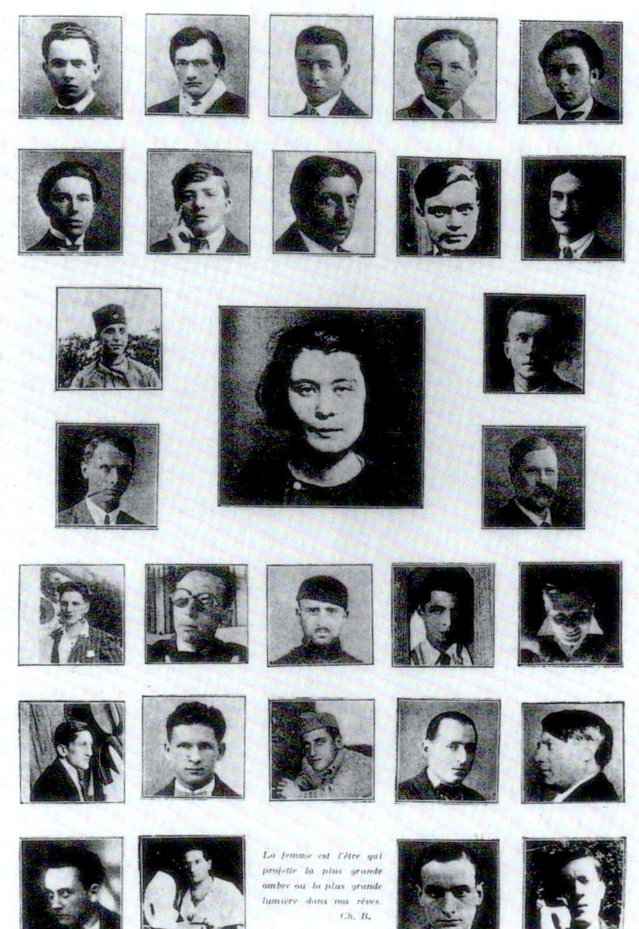

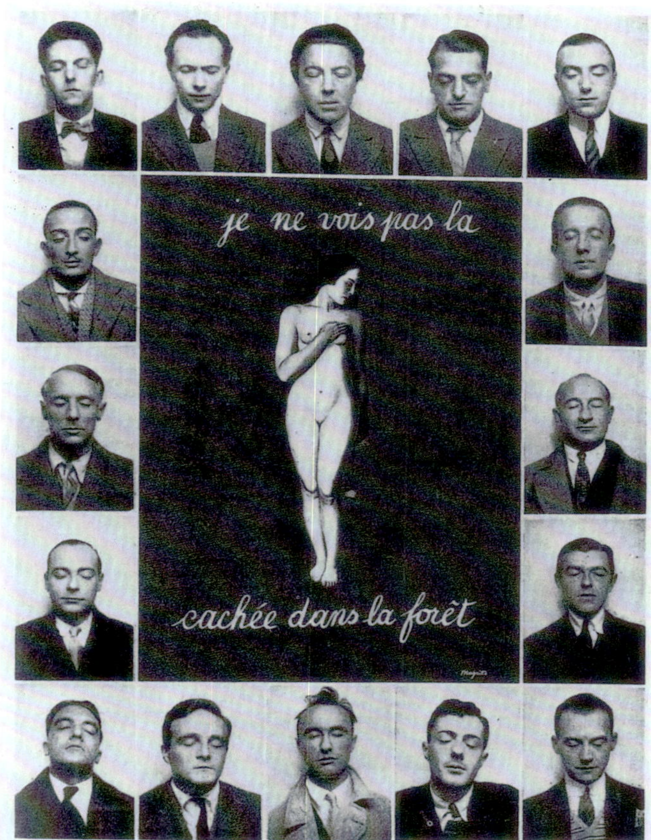

39. Page from *La Révolution surréaliste*, no. 12 (Paris, 15 December 1929)

David Sylvester has called Surrealism a religion, 'with a view of the world, a code of behaviour,' and 'a joy in the membership of a community of the like-minded' which required total commitment.[46] Jacqueline Chénieux-Gendron has written of it as 'a way of living and thinking, a madness of living and thinking which, refusing the world as it is – since the 'real' is often only a habit – proposes both to 'transform the world' (Marx) and to 'change life' (Rimbaud).'[47] The comprehensiveness of the demands it made on those who engaged with it went with a powerful sense of revolutionary mission; it was fundamentally this aggressive commitment to changing social as well as mental and linguistic structures that drew it to the ideal of Communist revolution. The titles of its two periodicals bill Surrealism as an instrument of revolution: *La Révolution surréaliste* (1924–9) and *Le Surréalisme au service de la révolution* (SASDLR – 1930–3). To the force of 'love' (desire) was to be added the violence of hate. When Breton produced a *Second Manifesto of Surrealism* in 1929, he started by driving the point home: 'One can understand why Surrealism was not afraid to make for itself a tenet of total revolt, complete insubordination, of sabotage . . . , and why it still expects nothing save violence. The simplest Surrealist act consists of dashing down into the street, pistol in hand, and firing blindly, as fast as you can pull

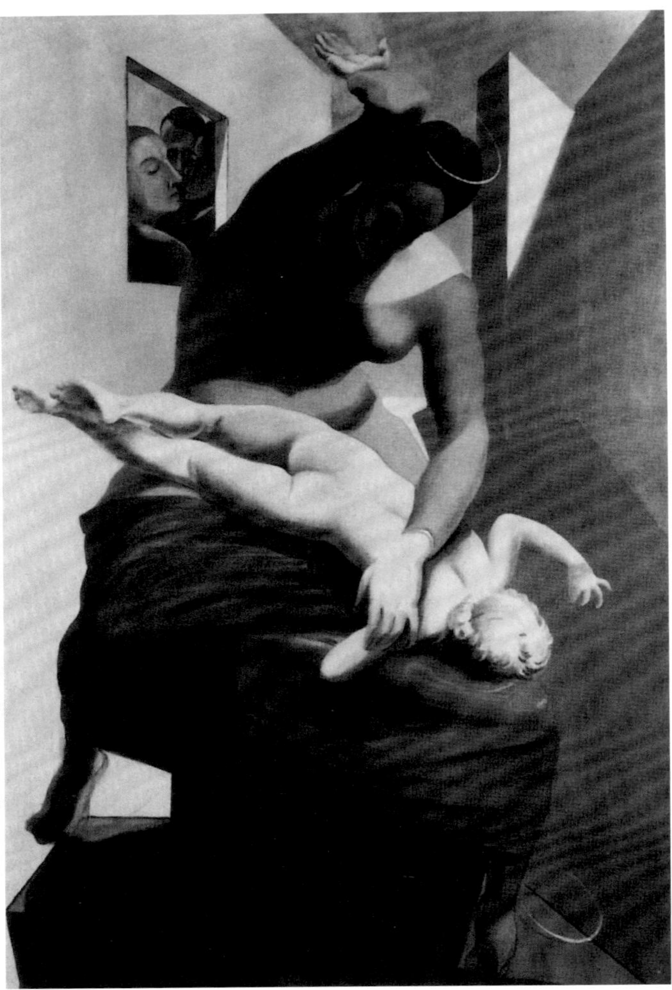

40. Max Ernst, *The Infant Jesus Chastised by the Virgin Mary before Witnesses (M.E., A.B. and P.E.)*, 1926. Oil on canvas, 196 × 130 cm. Museum Ludwig, Cologne

the trigger into the crowd.'[48]

There was a biographical dimension to the intensity of this commitment to the revolutionary transformation of bourgeois France. In 1917–18, Breton and Aragon had worked in the medical services responsible for the hundreds of thousands of casualties whose sanity had been threatened or destroyed on the Front. Accepted social and political values had condoned that madness. At the start, the anger that sharpened the edge of Dada and Surrealist insolence was a compensatory echo of the massacre of 1914–18. The youth of the first Surrealists was flaunted as a rare privilege. Breton opened his *Pas perdus* by announcing his age, twenty-six; Aragon, also twenty-six, made a point of telling his readers so too in *Une Vague de rêves*.

As a revolutionary sect, Surrealism formed its own micro-society set against the values and habits of a sane and sensible macro-society. For Breton, Surrealist texts, objects and visual images were made in and for that micro-society – that group – whose shared refusal of accepted beliefs and values opened up a Surrealist way of life, as a constant provocation and exhortation to the vast majority left outside, with their dominant nationalism and their faith in common sense. The Surrealists might have engaged in mass politics, and, in the visual arts, might have showed an unflagging talent for attracting attention, but their texts and periodicals were not forms of 'publicity' in any outgoing popular sense. *La Révolution surréaliste* sold no more than a thousand copies of its last number; *Le Surréalisme au service de la révolution* (*SASDLR*) sold just 350 copies of its first two numbers.[49] The first and last numbers of *La Révolution surréaliste* featured photographs commemorating the Surrealists as a group of the elect. In the first they are arranged around the fierce features of the anarchist murderess Germaine Berton; in the second (the group's personnel significantly changed) they are arranged around René Magritte's painting *I do not See the . . . Hidden in the Forest* (*Je ne vois pas la . . . cachée dans la forêt*) [38, 39], their eyes shut against the banal 'reality' of the everyday. It was a group that would always be dominated by males, submitting to dreams and desires which converged on women.

The moment when Breton made his most uncompromising demand for rigorous adhesion to group values was 1929, the moment of the *Second Manifesto* and the replacement of *La Révolution surréaliste* by *SASDLR*. 'Rigour' and 'purity' are two words that recur in the *Second Manifesto*; it ends with a plea to the few who will change their lives for Surrealism: 'Is everything to be risked, yes or no, merely for the joy of glimpsing in the distance – at the very bottom of the crucible in which we propose to fling our wretched comforts, what remains of our good reputation and our doubts pell mell with the pretty gewgaws of sensibility, and the radical notion of impotence and the stupidity of our so-called duties – *the light which will no longer be the one that fails*?'[50] The priestly hauteur and exaltation of the tone is characteristic (so is the syntax stretched almost to breaking-point).

The *Second Manifesto* was preceded by a purge of the 'impure', who Breton believed had joined without the total commitment necessary. It was a purge consciously modelled on the techniques of public exposure and criticism practiced by the Communist Party. Breton had joined the PCF with four others from the group early in 1927, and had immediately made his first expulsions for lack of revolutionary zeal; Soupault was one of them. In February 1929, he sent a letter to a wide range of intellectuals, both Surrealists and others, asking two questions. The first was: 'Do you believe that, all things considered . . . , your activity should or should not be definitively limited to an individual form?'[51] The second concerned the definition of shared individual positions or of a group programme. Those who sent answers considered unacceptable were to be excluded from a meeting which was to follow on 11 March at 9:30 p.m. in the Bar du Château, on the rue du Château. In fact, several of the excluded came, witnessing accusations directed especially at the editors of a periodical only loosely associated with the Surrealists, *Le Grand Jeu*. There were walk-outs and the *Second Manifesto*, appearing in the last number of *La Révolution surréaliste*, then printed the names of the expelled produced by the exercise, complete with charges, mostly of literary and artistic careerism and/or failure to conform to revolutionary dialectics.

One of those expelled was the painter André Masson (b.1896); he, Joan Miró (b.1893) and Max Ernst had been among the first artists to be closely associated with *La*

Révolution Surréaliste. Miró too showed scant enthusiasm for submission to a group identity in 1929, but was kept on; Ernst at this point was one of the 'purest'. Threatened three years before (alongside Miró) with expulsion for working with Serge Diaghilev's Russian ballet for the bourgeoisie, Ernst had published a sacriligeous manifesto painting in *La Révolution* as a mark of his loyalty: the infant Jesus chastised by the Virgin Mary before witnesses – himself, Breton and Paul Eluard [40].

Breton gave special prominence among the expelled to a group centred on the little magazine *Documents* (1929–30), the first number of which had appeared as if a riposte to the Bar du Château meeting. This included the writers Georges Limbour and Michel Leiris; but the most special treatment of all was reserved for Georges Bataille. Briefly, *Documents* and Bataille represented what, for Breton, was a group of dissidents, standing against the Surrealist dialectical ideal as expressed in the *Second Manifesto*. Here Breton had committed Surrealism to the search for a 'certain point in the mind at which life and death, the real and imaginary, the past and future, the communicable and the incommunicable, the heights and the depths cease to be perceived contradictorily.'[52] Bataille wanted a direct engagement with material reality, not some sort of takeover of the 'real' by the imagination (desire) at the expense of reality's baseness. His answer to Breton's letter had been: 'Too many fucking idealists!' Breton, by the same token, dismissed him as an old-fashioned materialist obsessed with the horrific and the disgusting: 'Monsieur Bataille loves flies.'[53] In 1929 Bataille was Breton's 'other' by which to define what was inside and outside the group: what Surrealism was and was not. In the mid-1930s Louis Aragon's defection to the French Communist Party at the moment when Breton separated from it would place him in that role as champion of 'Socialist Realism' and Bataille's successor.

Artists may not have been the key figures in the development of Surrealism as a group and a movement with definitions and theories, but they were crucial to Surrealism as a developing practice able to grab the attention of those outside it. Breton devoted to visual art no more than a footnote in the *Manifesto* of 1924, but from *La Révolution surréaliste* no. 1, it was a feature, although the periodical showed a remarkable openness to photography as well as painting and drawing, and to the untrained and the popular as well as artists. No. 1 opened with a photograph of a mysterious wrapped object (a sewing-machine) by Duchamp's American Dada friend Man Ray (b.1890), his *Enigma of Isidore Ducasse* [41], and included a naïve drawing by the non-artist, Max Morise, a photograph of carnival floats and a Buster Keaton film-still, as well as reproductions of drawings by Masson, Ernst and de Chirico (b.1888) and of a late Cubist construction by Picasso. In no. 4 (15 July 1925) Breton included the first of a series of articles on 'Le Surréalisme et la peinture', which he would publish as a book in 1928, appropriating Picasso (with his tacit acquiescence) for the movement by means of a eulogy to Cubism as a kind of proto-Surrealism. Cubism was represented as an imaginative release from the material world, a movement, however, which had remained too much concerned with materiality. Picasso would never explicitly identify with the group.

Non-artists and untrained artists as well as professionals selling to collectors always had a place in the Surrealist magazines, as did popular culture, photography and film. The last number of *La Révolution* (15 December 1929) included the screenplay of *Un Chien andalou*, the film Salvador Dalí (b.1904) made that year with Luis Buñuel (both are included in the Surrealist group photograph [39]). The opening number of *SASDLR* (July 1930) illustrated stills from their full-length follow-up *L'Age d'or*. Surrealist visual culture was most lavishly illustrated in the periodical *Minotaure* which followed *SASDLR* between 1933 and 1939. It may not have been taken over by the group until 1939, but Breton was a major influence on its contents from the beginning. For the first time it gave luxury illustration to a wide range of Surrealist visual phenomena besides painting and sculpture, including, for instance, a piece of soap or a loaf of bread captioned 'Involuntary Sculptures' [159] and Hans Bellmer's savagely dismembered dolls [332]. Non-European visual culture was also a feature of the Surrealist periodicals.

Yet, the role of the traditional media, painting, sculpture and drawing in Surrealism cannot be underestimated; nor can the significance of 'professional' artists. 1925 saw an exhibition of 'Surrealist Painting' in a private gallery, the galerie Pierre; it gathered together Picasso, de Chirico, Man Ray, Masson, Miró, Ernst and the Alsatian Hans (Jean) Arp (b.1886), a refugee to Surrealism from Zurich Dada. Between 1926 and 1927, Breton, who with Éluard bought art that he admired, ran a galerie Surréaliste which showed such new arrivals as Dalí and Yves Tanguy (b.1900), besides Ernst and Arp. What is more, the work of artists could and did have an influence on the development of the Surrealist agenda. Masson's, Miró's and Ernst's adaptation of automatist writing techniques to drawing and painting between 1924 and the late 1920s reinforced the belief in automatism [135, 306, 313]. Dalí's reaction against the passivity of such early automatist practices, where loss of control ideally went with loss of conscious intervention, was the active transformation

41. Man Ray, *The Enigma of Isidore Ducasse*, 1924. Photograph, as published in *La Révolution Surréaliste*, no. 1 (Paris, 1 December 1924)

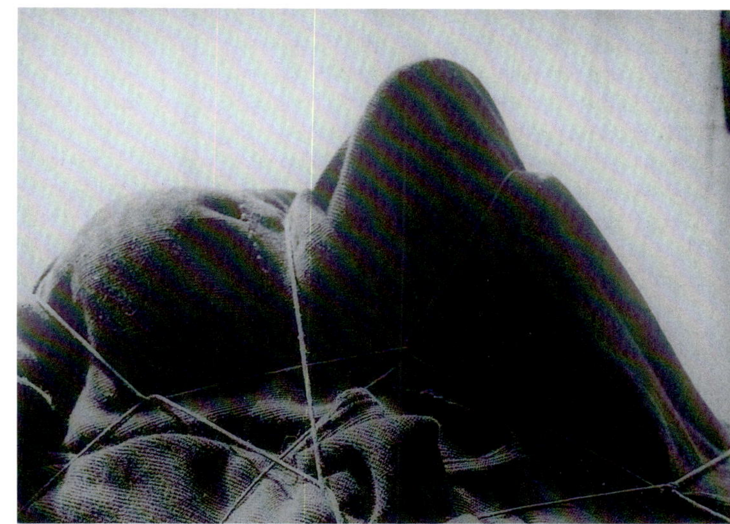

of reality by the imposition of a paranoid's vision; after Breton's *Second Manifesto*, it opened the way to a new phase in the Surrealist quest for the reconciliation of the dream and the 'real'. That phase received a further impulse from Dalí's response to the request in 1931 for proposals for new group action, his suggestion that the group should focus attention on the 'Surrealist object'. When it did so a crucial initial stimulus was supplied by not only Dalí but Miró and the young Swiss sculptor Alberto Giacometti (b.1901).

Indeed, it could be said that visual artists gave presence to the public face of Surrealism more pervasively than even Breton did during the 1930s. From the outside, he could appear the theoretical back-up to a movement dominated by artists. This was especially so as Surrealism became international. Artists and writers without French in the U.S. or Britain could respond to the illustrations in *Minotaure* but not to Breton's verbose subtleties. And the vehicle of Surrealism's internationalisation was the art exhibition, most importantly the two major exhibitions of international Surrealism outside France, in London (1936) and Mexico City (1940). Such an exhibition in Paris, held at the galerie des Beaux-Arts in 1938, was able to assemble seventy Surrealist artists from fourteen countries. By the late 1930s, among the countries with active Surrealist groups besides Britain and Mexico, were Belgium, Czechoslovakia and even Japan. When the core of the French group around Breton went into exile in 1940 to escape occupied France, they found a situation in New York in which Surrealist art had very effectively prepared the way for their arrival.

Ultimately, the unity and coherence even of the Surrealist movement was as much an illusion as the 'essential' unities critics and historians have found in Fauvism and Cubism; and the relations of the painters to it are as good a way as any of revealing this. Breton's expulsions themselves, of course, expose the tension between individual stances and practices taken to be Surrealist and the group solidarity he believed essential to Surrealism. Was Masson's painting any less Surrealist between 1929 and his mid-1930s reconciliation with the group? Miró, accepted by many as the 'chef de l'école' in the mid-1920s, asserted his preference for individual action in 1929 and repeatedly distanced himself, but was not expelled. And he and Picasso were prominent in *Documents*, while continuing in a state of Surrealist grace. Along with Masson, they were all the friends of the 'dissident' Leiris. Dalí meanwhile, whom Bataille was keen to claim for *Documents* as an exemplary 'base materialist' (painter of excrement and ants rather than flies), was welcomed by the ever-competitive Breton in 1929–30, despite his obvious dissident appeal. Even Bataille himself was to move briefly back into the group's activities in 1935.

Most recent historical and critical analyses of Surrealism and the major Surrealist painters and sculptors have assumed a Surrealist orientation – an engagement with psychoanalytic themes and with the problem of language – that embraces Dada and the dissidents as well as those who were loyal members of the Surrealist group. The simple conjunction of movement and group has been increasingly ignored, as writers from Dawn Ades to Rosalind Krauss and Hal Foster have placed Bataille and *Documents* at the heart of a broad intellectual current that refuses Breton's exclusions.[54]

MODERN MOVEMENTS AND 'ABSTRACT ART', 1912–40

French commentators who attempted surveys of art in France between 1900 and the 1930s from within the period tended to marginalise or even exclude Dada and Surrealism altogether. Vauxcelles and George in their survey of 1922 fail to give Dada a mention; Focillon in his of 1928 says nothing about Surrealism. The first to make serious mention of Surrealism in such a survey was the pre-1914 defender of the Cubists Maurice Raynal in his *Anthologie de la peinture en France de 1906 à nos jours* of 1927, which was more a critical summing up of the situation in the mid-twenties than a history. Raynal wrote of Surrealism as a movement engaged in 'politics, sociology, philosophy, medicine, dance, music, commercial transactions, and also literature', which had influenced a disparate crew of artists. He writes of the 'extra-pictorial' and 'Freudism', and sums up: it is 'a fashionable movement more German than French, more literary than plastic, above all because of a pathological influence which does not correspond to the art trends at home'.[55] It was easier to push Dada and Surrealism out into a nebulous zone both foreign (worse, German) and outside art than to confront the challenge they presented for the traditional media of painting and sculpture and ultimately for the very category, art.

The French State employed not a single major Surrealist painter or sculptor on the public projects of the 1937 Exhibition, despite the fact that André Masson was French, had studied in the fresco-painting studio of Paul Baudouïn at the Ecole National des Beaux-Arts and in 1937 was running a hugely popular 'professional studio in decoration' ('Atelier "professionnel" de décoration') for the PCF institution, the Maison de la culture. In this context, the Jeu de Paume's inclusion of Surrealist painting in the culminating rooms of its show 'Origines et développement de l'art internationale indépendant' alongside the latest abstract painting was especially remarkable. The conventional French view was in one way closer to Alfred Barr's: Surrealist painting was best given separate treatment as something within its own essentially literary tradition (Barr put on an exhibition of 'Fantastic Art, Dada, Surrealism' as counterpart to *Cubism and Abstract Art*). The newest art was abstract – the painting of, say, Robert Delaunay and his team in the railway and aviation pavilions [12] – and in France abstraction, it was solemnly repeated, had already been overtaken by the Neo-Humanist return to the figure, to be seen all over the terraces and walls of the Palais de Chaillot (not, of course, Barr's view) [6, 13].

In fact, however strong the various abstract sequels to Cubism had become internationally in the 1930s, in France abstract art – or as it was termed in 'Origines et développement', non-figurative art – had not gathered the concerted group support at any time since 1912 that could give it a significant place in any history of movements. In the Jeu de Paume exhibition, Robert Delaunay was there in the two final rooms as one of the original non-figurative painters, alongside Kandinsky (b.1866) and Mondrian (b.1872); he and the much younger Jean Hélion (b.1904) were the only French painters shown who could have been called non-figurative in terms comparable with the Russian and the Dutchman. Otherwise, there were a few foreign non-figurative artists associated with pan-European movements: César Domela, Antoine Pevsner and Naum Gabo, as well as the obstinately non-ism individuals, František Kupka and Alberto Magnelli. In the catalogue, Mondrian is 'chef' of 'Neo-Plasticism', and Gabo and Pevsner representatives of 'Constructivism', but 'non-figurative art' is used as a larger, more all-embracing label. It is, in contra-distinction to Surrealism, a grand synthesis in which is reconciled the discoveries of Cézanne (Cubism) and Matisse (Fauvism); its beginnings lie not in the work of Kandinsky, but in the Paris-based work of Picabia (during his Salon Cubist phase), the Cubist sculptor Alexander Archipenko (b.1887) and Delaunay. Jean Hélion, who showed a work of 1935 certainly comparable to *Standing Figure* of that year [125], is treated as an individual innovator who has restored complexity in an art reduced to geometrical over-simplification by the 'Neo-Plasticists'.

As *Standing Figure* shows clearly enough, Hélion's acquisition of complexity after 'Neo-Plastic' beginnings amounted to a re-figuration of the non-figurative; between 1939 and 1944, this would lead him to a direct, forceful, if quirky figuration [126]. His ambivalent relationship with the non-figurative can stand for a less than committed French engagement with the idea of an end to figuration. Picabia, Archipenko and even Delaunay were similarly ambivalent. Two of them, Picabia and Delaunay, were singled out by Apollinaire in his *Les Peintres cubistes* of early 1913 as 'orphic cubists', in the company of two other Salon Cubists, Duchamp and Léger (then not yet a Kahnweiler painter); Kupka (b.1871) may also have been named as one of them in a lecture the poet gave at the Salon d'automne of 1912. Apollinaire defined 'orphic cubism' as: 'The art of painting new ensembles with elements not borrowed from visual reality, but entirely created by the artist and endowed by him with a powerful reality.'[56] Kupka was, in fact, the only one of these artists for whom this can be convincingly argued. Delaunay and Léger produced work which was certainly endowed with 'a powerful reality', but which was derived from visual experience and was believed to produce an *equivalent of that experience*. Both found nothing contradictory in oscillating between figuration and what Apollinaire called 'pure painting'. Duchamp and Picabia were always explicitly concerned with representation at some level, however inaccessible. Orphism would never be established in France as a movement properly distinct from Cubism.

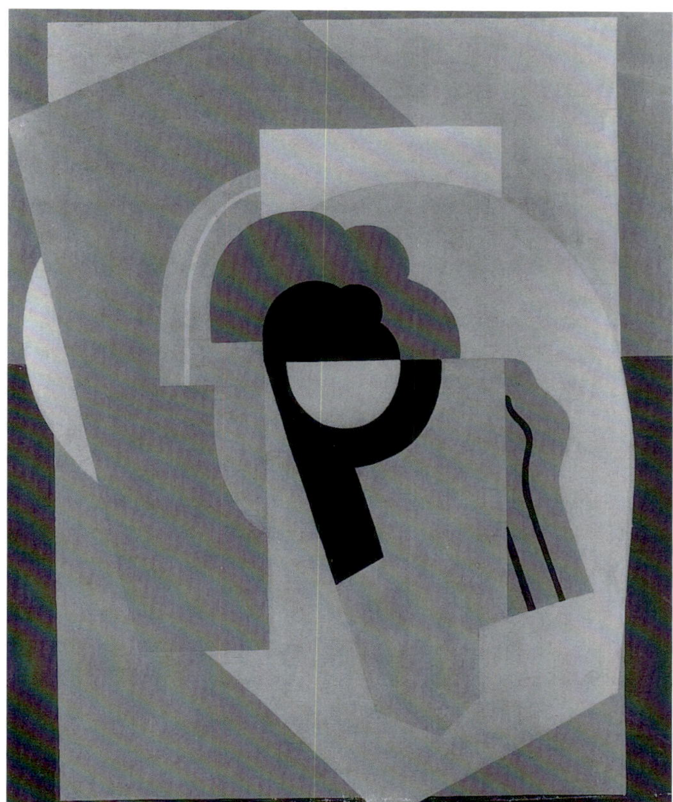

43. Albert Gleizes, Composition, Picture, 1921. Tempera on panel, 91 × 71.5 cm. Tate Gallery, London

42. Auguste Herbin, Polychrome Relief, 1920. Painted wood. 84.5 × 66 cm. Musée d'Art Moderne de la Ville de Paris, Donation Henry-Thomas.

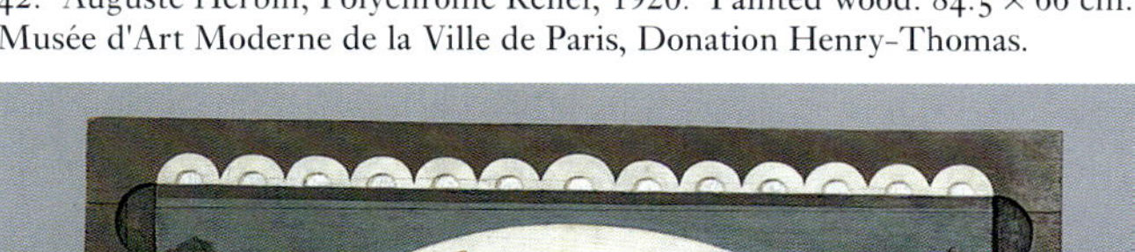

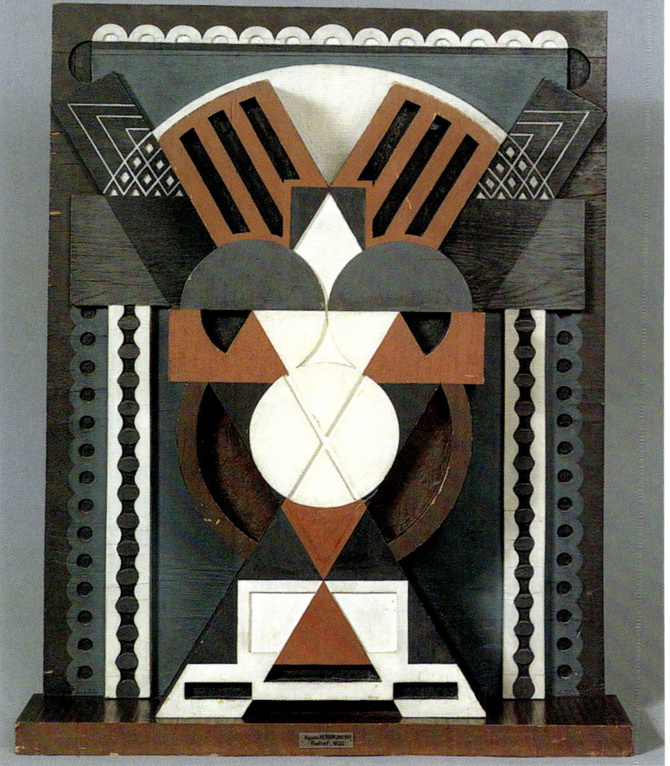

Between 1920 and 1925, Kupka acquired two energetic followers in Félix Del Marle (b.1889) and Pierre-Antoine Gallien. In 1924–5, Del Marle, as art editor of *Vouloir*, a little magazine published in Lille (his home town), briefly gave Kupka a platform for his ideas; but his loyalty was short-lived and Kupka soon found himself isolated as *Vouloir* moved on to other enthusiasms, and as Del Marle and Gallien's alliance broke down amid bitter recriminations.[57] Two further non-figurative developments are worth recording too. First, there is the case of Auguste Herbin (b.1882), who followed up an early career as an experimental cubist equally responsive to Picasso and Braque and to Salon Cubism, with near abstract ornamental canvases and painted wooden reliefs in 1919–20 as one of Léonce Rosenberg's L'Effort Moderne painters [42]. Herbin's experiment was, however, isolated and short-lived – he set it aside in the early 1920s – and the rationale for his symmetrical abstractions was explicitly decorative. He envisaged a new art integrated into a new monumental architecture: an architecture which was structurally innovative but which preserved a place for ornamental embellishment, like that of Le Corbusier's one-time mentor, Auguste Perret. The second case is that of the Salon Cubist Albert Gleizes, who, between 1920 and 1925, took Cubist synthesis towards a level of 'purity' beyond Orphism, intent on leading a return to what he believed were the fundamental compositional principles of French wall painting in the thirteenth century [43]. Like Kupka, in the early 1920s, Gleizes too found followers, most importantly the Irish women artists, Mainie Jellett and Evie Hone; and the dealer-publisher Povolozky gave him a platform for both his work and his theoretical writing. The mid-1920s, however, saw him turn his back on the metropolitan avant-garde and set up an artists' community, Moly Sabata, in the Rhone valley south of Lyon at Serrières. Here a trickle of new followers joined him, among them the Australian painter and ceramicist Anne Dangard, but his retreat from Paris inevitably marginalised his effort.

Despite the undoubted commitment of Kupka and the leadership of Gleizes, there would be no French group of non-figurative artists long enough lived and with a clearly enough defined purpose to compare either with the Cubists or the Surrealists. Indeed, when a Polish associate of Gleizes, Y.V. Poznanski, organised a wide-ranging exhibition at the rue de la Ville l'Evêque in 1925, with the portentous title 'L'Art d'aujourd'hui' (Art of Today), its attempt to establish 'abstract art' as the 'art of today' in France manifestly failed. A strong contingent of artists from across Europe showed, but the French representation was incomplete – Kupka refused to exhibit – and did not amount to a coherent statement. Furthermore, the decision to show leading Cubists and Orphists (Picasso, Gris and Léger included) as mere precursors was unconvincing. Gleizes apart, none of the Cubists selected had, of course, committed themselves to 'pure painting'.

Most importantly, non-figuration as a self-sufficient art without a decorative function came to France from abroad. It came with Mondrian's Neo-Plasticism when he returned to Paris in 1919 (he had developed his own Dutch Cubism there between 1912 and 1914), but for half a decade excited minimal interest and led to no grouping. It came again in 1923 with the organisation by Theo van Doesburg (b.1883) of a De Stijl exhibition at Léonce Rosenberg's Cubist galerie de l'Effort Moderne, and then a little later with his decision to run the international De Stijl magazine and movement from Paris. De Stijl provided a major contingent in the 1925 exhibition 'Art d'aujourd'hui', and the year after, it was towards van Doesburg and De Stijl that Del Marle's *Vouloir* moved after its engagement with Kupka. In 1927, Del Marle published a French translation of a major piece by Mondrian, 'Home – Street – City', which took the Dutchman's Neo-Plastic painting as a model for the urban environment as a whole. Del Marle went as far as reconstructing his own studio in Lille as a 'home' within such an environment. More than Mondrian, it was, however, van Doesburg's indomitable energy that provided the initial impetus behind two significant attempts to form Paris-based non-figurative groups capable of providing a platform for the defence of non-figuration: 'Art Concret', which came briefly into being in 1930, and 'Abstraction-Création', in whose formation he was involved just before his sudden death in 1931, but which survived until 1935.

'Art Concret' was van Doesburg's own initiative. It was a tightly organised group with rigorous non-figurative principles; Hélion was one of the six members. 'Abstraction-Création' was altogether more representative of the anything-goes co-existence of figuration and non-figuration among post-Cubist artists in Paris. It brought together 'Art Concret' painters (Hélion included) with many who approached figuration, as Hélion would soon, continuing the lax pluralism of another short-lived alliance, which van Doesburg had not seen fit to join, 'Cercle et carré'. This latter generated an exhibition and three numbers of its own periodical in 1930; it was the initiative of a Belgian, Michel Seuphor (b.1901) who was, like van Doesburg, a veteran of the 'international Constructivism' so pervasive across the rest of western Europe from the early 1920s.

I shall not offer any simple answer to the question of why no major non-figurative movement was initiated or took root in France. One observation is worth making, however. The idealism of Wassily Kandinsky's Blaue Reiter, of Mondrian and van Doesburg's De Stijl, and of the international Constructivism of such as Seuphor, theorised visual art as a means for the expression or embodiment of a transcendent Idea. As we shall see in Chapter 5, avant-gardism in France in the form it took with Fauve and Cubist art rejected the late nineteenth-century Symbolist concept of the painting, sculpture or text as the revelation of some essence – idea – veiled behind the surface of phenomena. In visual art its fundamental starting point was the concrete presence of the art-object, the 'tableau-objet', *as such*, and its key problem was that of *re*presentation – how to make an art experience not merely relate to but take into itself, embody the intensity of life experiences. With such priorities, non-figurative art, vacuum-packed in its theories, could seem an intangible irrelevance.

AVANT-GARDES, DOMINANT VALUES AND HISTORIES

A history of modern movements, global or French, has the advantage of clarity and thrust. Barr's and the Jeu de Paume's exhibitions in 1936–7 must have made exhilarating viewing. What they delivered, however, was a picture of a highly reductive kind shaped by a critical agenda in favour of what was becoming international modernism, and at the same time their international priorities extracted the art and artists they selected from their specific, nationally bounded worlds. Before turning to the question of art *in France* as distinct from art in the western world, it helps to set out some of the exclusions made by the history of movements; it has been a history as ruthlessly dogmatic as André Breton was at the centre of the Surrealists in 1929.

Even if one's sole interest is modernism, twentieth-century art in France before the 1940s was much more than the art contained in modern movements (however defined). There was highly productive life in Fauves, Cubists, Dadas and Surrealists before and after their lives in these movements. Quite obviously Matisse's painting after 1908 is not the less important for being outside the category 'Fauve'; neither is Picasso's 'classical' figure painting in relation to the category 'Cubist'. There were artists of real significance in modernism who hardly touched movements, and were not taken up by them; Kupka was one, so were Chagall, Soutine and Modigliani, as was a woman artist like Suzanne Valadon. There were artists who never took a leading role in the movements they touched, but who produced major work. The most startling example is Marcel Duchamp, who was briefly a major Cubist because of the impact of his *Nude Descending a Staircase, No. 2* when it was shown in the New York Armory Show in 1913 [78], and who was repeatedly acknowledged as a major figure by Breton, but was considered by most contemporary observers of art in France an irrelevance.[58] Again there is a significant woman artist who remains on the margins of any history of movements, Sonia Delaunay. Sonia would never have argued with her husband Robert's leadership role in Apollinaire's Orphism and in French non-figurative art generally; she painted – she was in his team in the railway and aviation pavilions in 1937 – but after 1912 she achieved the most impact, especially in the 1920s, in that nebulous area between the decorative and the fine arts, designing Orphic fashion to light up the rising and the risen bourgeoisie. Her *Simultaneous Boutique* on the Pont Alexandre III was one of the great fashion successes of the 1925 Decorative Arts Exhibition [44].

And if one looks beyond modernism, if, for instance, one makes, as we did at the beginning, a tour of the international Exhibitions of 1900, 1925 and 1937 and considers (however sketchily) the art shown in them, a simple point becomes clear: twentieth-century art in France before 1940 was much more than modernism. It is at this point that the question of the specificity of art, even modern-movement art *in France* begins to emerge. The writing of history with a modern-movement agenda has one even more obvious effect than leaving out or distorting the achievements of certain modernists: it gives the impression that with every new move forward (moves are always forward) all previous practices become obsolete. The fact is that in the 1920s Claude Monet (1840–1926) was painting the *Nymphéas*, his set of mural-scale canvases wrapped around the basement space of the Orangerie in the Tuileries gardens, arguably one of the most important single works completed in the decade following 1918 [73]. The fact is also that right into the 1920s decorative paintings were being executed in major public spaces by such officially endorsed figures as Albert Besnard (1849–1934), working with Baroque compositional and allegorical modes and a late-Impressionist colour range (Besnard was one of those who had figured prominently in the decoration of the Petit Palais before 1914 [165]). Modernism as 'independent art' first of all defined itself in a *French* context, however much its strength came of its success as a product for export; it developed in relation to an extraordinarily diverse 'other', which continued to be widely accepted as French art even as late as 1937 in the grand new public palaces [6, 13].

The greatest limitation imposed by a history of movements, however, lies in its historical refinement. It might seem that I have introduced two absolutely separate histories in the opening part of this book. The history of art in France told as a history of movements is so internally self-sufficient that it constructs a strikingly coherent picture of a dynamic cultural history distinct in all its features and its patterns, as I have suggested, from the history of the Third Republic between the comforts of 1900 and the defeat of 1940. My conviction is that all art in France in the period – including the art usually wrapped up in modern movements – is most richly approached as an integral part of a political and social as well as a cultural history. This is not simply a matter of the 'official' or commercial support systems within which art was produced, or of art's national and international markets. It is more profoundly a matter of the relation of artists' lives, practices and products to the values dominant in that society, a society, as we have seen, dominated by the classes they mostly belonged to and worked for: the republican middle classes. In different ways, at different stages in this book the question will be addressed: how does this statement, this work, this way of living relate to the liberal and democratic, secular and materialist, enlightened and rational, progressive yet traditional values so solidly at the heart of Third Republic society at least into the early 1930s? It is a question whose terms change fundamentally as

44. Sonia Delaunay, *Simultaneous Boutique*, 1925. Pont Alexandre III, Exposition Internationale des arts décoratifs et industriels modernes, Paris

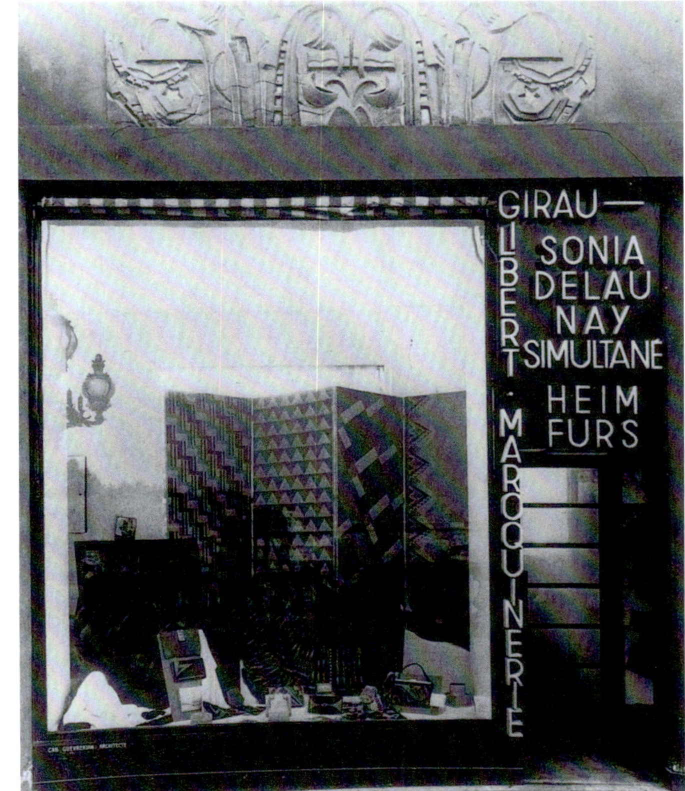

that society's givens are challenged by both Left and Right especially from 1934, and as modernism – setting Breton's 'revolutionaries' aside – is given a certain official stamp under the Front Populaire. Art in France across the period could both represent and threaten the dominant values of those who elected the mostly Radical-dominated majorities in the Chamber of Deputies, political leaders epitomised perhaps by Edouard Herriot between the wars, who in typical Radical style dressed up a deep resistance to change with progressive rhetoric. Those values went with a continuing belief in the status and efficacy of 'art'; a belief still held with pride by those who built and decorated the Palais de Chaillot and the Palais de Tokyo in 1937.

Modernism as a concept associated with the possibility of social and political change is often discussed under the heading 'avant-garde'. Especially influential has been the view set out in the late 1960s by Peter Bürger, which attempts to isolate an authentic (essential?) avant-gardism defined by its capacity for effective political and social critique. Bürger argues that such an avant-garde did not properly emerge until the Dadas of the late teens and early twenties; he writes of modernism before 1914 – that of the Fauves and the Cubists – as 'Aesthetic'.[59] There can be no doubt that the Dadas and the Surrealists in Paris acted as such a critical force, though not with the direct and sustained political engagement found especially in Berlin Dada and the subsequent work of George Grosz and John Heartfield. Such a project, aimed specifically at subverting accepted values, is clearly enough stated, as we have seen, by Breton writing to Aragon in 1919, and was more or less a factor in all the practices associated with Dada and Surrealism. I would argue, further, that its sheer scope and intellectual ambition was something that was a more likely development in France than in any other liberal democracy of the early twentieth century, for in France the 'intellectual' – the thinker, the writer, the artist – was scorned or celebrated not merely for their individual contributions to French culture but as a force, indeed *a class* with the potential to trigger change.

Mayeur and Reberioux point out that the noun 'intellectual' seems first to have been used in the French language in the period of the Dreyfus Affair, around 1900. During the Affair, all but a very few vanguard writers were supporters of Dreyfus – Dreyfusards – committed to the stance first articulated in Emile Zola's 'J'accuse'; Mallarmé and Apollinaire were, and so were such painters as Signac, Pissarro, Bonnard and Vuillard.[60] By 1900, against the huge majority of the press, intellectuals, identified strongly with the Left, were changing opinion and influencing values. The confidence that came with that moment – the confidence in writing and any other 'artistic' activity as a dissident force for change – was still there in the magisterial tone adopted by a Breton and an Aragon as they lived their dissidence and proclaimed their anathemas in the 1930s. The work of artists as part of a larger cultural project of critique was given an importance it has rarely been given outside France, until the rise of French 'Theory' in America and England from the 1970s.

Yet, the model of the avant-garde project as critique does apply to the art and practices of modernists before 1914; the moves they made were not just 'aesthetic', though they were certainly that. Both Matisse and the Cubists were attacked for being 'intellectuals' when they should have been artists. Cubism, as a practice concerned with the very question of representation as well as the 'conceptual' in art, was at one level an epistemological enterprise aimed at the heart of Third Republic common sense, one reason for the passionate anger of those who tried to exclude it from the Grand Palais in 1912. Fauve painting, as a statement of belief in the total liberty of the artist echoed, in the case of Vlaminck explicitly, the then current anarchist critique of an industrial society moving towards large-scale organisation for the profit of the great capitalists.

Dominant values in the Third Republic could be challenged from the Right as well as the Left – by Maurras or Drieu de la Rochelle as well as Aragon or Breton. The challenge from modernism came almost exclusively with a Left bias or inflection, though it often came with no political label attached, which does not mean that modernists necessarily mounted any challenge at all. Often their work could actually be read as an endorsement of dominant values or remained profoundly ambivalent, open to contradictory responses. Whatever threat they offered was always to be responded to in a society much of whose visual culture until the thirties unambiguously and with blithe rather than fierce confidence celebrated the Third Republic's values and submitted to its institutions. My intention is to open the way to an encounter with that visual culture of the acceptable, even if the centre of gravity in this book will be modernism. Twentieth-century artists were not all modernists or dissidents in France before 1940; and indeed the culture of the *un*acceptable was to be accepted astonishingly quickly after 1945.

PART TWO

Lives in Art

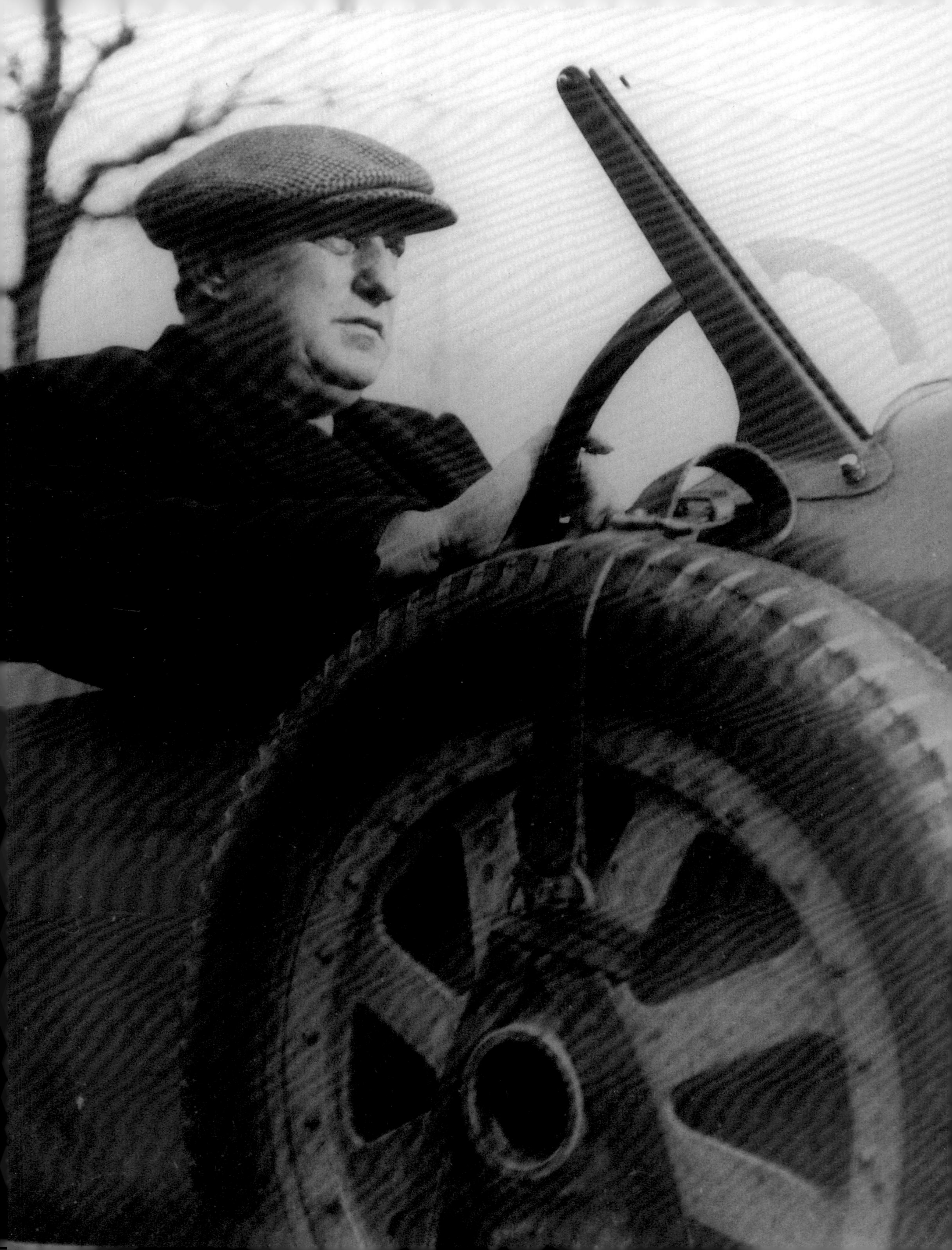

PART TWO

Lives in Art

INTRODUCTION

On 1 June 1904, Henri Matisse's first solo show opened at Ambroise Vollard's gallery on the rue Laffitte. In the catalogue, the leading art-world figure Roger Marx wrote that the painter had renounced fashionable success for 'the challenges of struggle and the bitter honour of satisfying himself'.[1] This claim to total independence from material constraints or ambitions was and is continually made for modernist artists in the late nineteenth and early twentieth centuries. Here, tellingly, it is made by a figure who had used his influence to persuade the dealer Vollard to give Matisse his show, a figure who also happened to be a high official in the Beaux-Arts administration of the Third Republic: 'Inspecteur principal des musées départementaux'. Even a leading modernist like Matisse could only pursue his self-imposed challenges with the support and encouragement of figures like Roger Marx. Even he worked under certain enabling conditions. And even he worked in a world that included, besides the private Salons and galleries, State institutions (the Beaux-Arts administration being one).

Part Two of this book is concerned with the conditions under which artists and those around them lived and worked. Chapter 3 deals with the world in which all artists made their careers. Chapter 4 will deal with the careers made by some artists – successful modernists.

CHAPTER 3

Framing Lives

DEMOCRACY, DIVERSITY AND DIRECTION: OFFICIALS AND INSTITUTIONS

'We have to have either dogma, that is the Institute, or complete liberty.'[1] In 1880, Emile Zola reduced the problems faced by those organising the large-scale display of art in France to a stark choice between the élite academic control exercised by the Institut, a survival of the *ancien régime*, and anarchy. This was Zola's response to the government-funded Salon of that year, whose hugely expanded and at the same time democratised jury (entirely elected by artists) accepted the vast total of 7,000 works. As Patricia Mainardi has shown, Zola's alternatives sum up a real opposition between those who wanted to restrict selection according to imposed aesthetic ideals, and those who wanted to open selection to as many as possible, an opposition which went with two notions of what the Salon exhibition should do: show highly select works 'to be seen', or show works in profusion 'to be sold'. And these two notions went with the idea of two kinds of institution with two sets of principles: one closed, hierarchical and dedicated to an élite ideal of art, the other open, liberal and commercial – as Ingres had put it, the Salon as 'bazaar'.[2]

In 1881, the Salon was privatised; it became the 'Société des artistes français', funded and run by its members. It was a typical Third Republic creation, aiming to provide a market place for art whose very quantity and diversity would be a measure of democratic 'liberty'. The choice, however, between direction and democracy, selection and diversity, remained unresolved, to some extent within the Artistes français itself, and very clearly in the rivalry between the competing artists' societies (all of them private) that proliferated around it. The same can be said too of the State as art buyer and patron, as we shall see.

The rhetoric and style of the Artistes français was democratic enough, but in 1911 two budget reports on the State and art, one by M.J. Simyan, the other by Paul-Boncour, sought to expose the workings of hierarchical Academic power in a highly effective network of cronies. This network tied the Society to the committee of the Beaux-Arts administration, which distributed commissions and bought for the State, and to the Conseil Supérieur of the Ecole Nationale des Beaux-Arts (ENBA) along with its teaching Ateliers. The constitution of the Artistes français was actually further opened up in 1901 under its president the academician Jean-Paul Laurens (1838–1921). It had a huge governing committee of ninety members, and equally wide representation on the juries for its four sections, which were all elected: the painting jury numbered seventy, the sculpture jury, a hundred; the jury for graphic art, sixteen. The limits on numbers of works shown were hugely generous: 1,500 pictures and 500 drawings in the painting section, for instance.[3]

What Paul-Boncour and Simyan brought out was the way cronyism, backed by artists in positions of power, undermined this apparent openness. The problems centred around the prestige to be gained from medal-winning and the exposure to be gained from being displayed well. The number of jury votes determined whether you were skied or hung on the centre-line (a key factor in winning an award);

Facing page. Detail of Man Ray, *Andre Dérain in his 'Delage' Car*, 1925 [66]

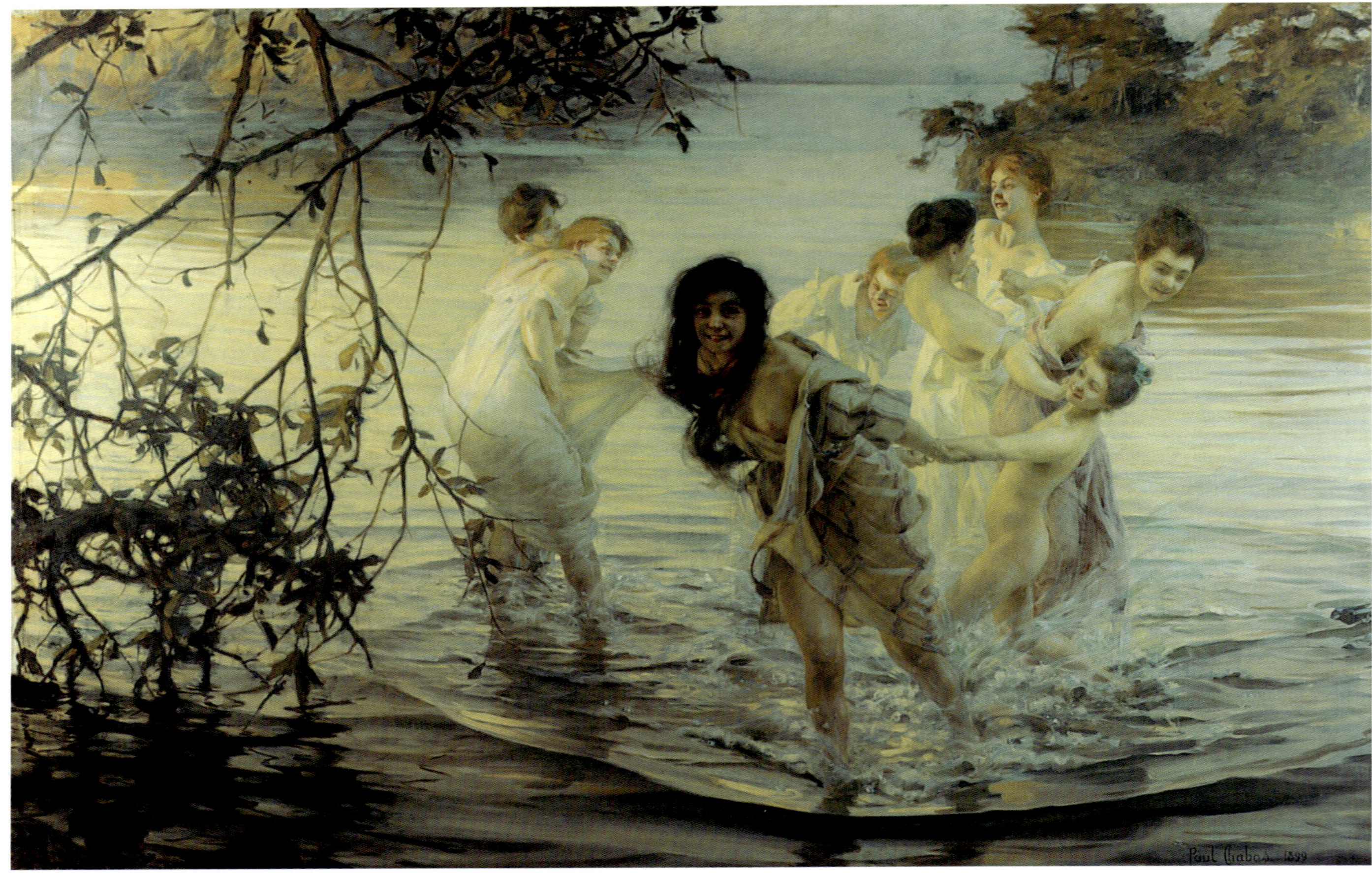

45. Paul Chabas, *Joyous Frolics*, 1899. Oil on canvas, 202 × 315 cm. Musée des Beaux-Arts, Nantes

and voting at every level sustained the prominence of academicians, especially those who ran Ateliers in ENBA, all of them men, most over sixty. Election to the Académie des Beaux-Arts itself – a section of the Institut – was by academicians and was for life. When the sculptor Denys Peuch (b.1854) was elected in 1905, he was the youngest member, at fifty-one; tenure averaged twenty-five years. As late as 1913, the academicians Bonnat, Cormon, Laurens, Humbert, Merson, Ferrier, Morot and Flameng were elected for three-year terms on the painting jury, and Mercié, Couteau, Verlet, Marquestre and Peuch for the sculpture jury. Paul-Boncour and Simyan almost certainly exaggerated in 1911, but there is no doubt that cronyism did operate within and between the Society and ENBA; students and ex-students gained by voting with and for their influential academician teachers, and academicians from supporting each other.

By 1900, the double aspect of the 'Artistes français' – democratic bazaar and symbol of established authority – had led to two counter organisations, both private societies of artists: the Indépendants founded in 1884 and the Société Nationale founded in 1890. The Indépendants countered its authority by having neither juries nor medals; anyone could show, though, as we saw in Chapter 2, great advantages were gained by being elected on to its hanging committees, as Matisse and his friends were in 1905, and Le Fauconnier and his friends were in 1911. The Nationale countered not the authority but what was perceived as the indiscriminate commercial diversity of the Artistes français, and did so by the more stringent use of jury selection, and by establishing a narrower electoral base of already successful artists. It represented a breakaway group of highly successful artists, several of them academicians or future academicians, who openly wished to consolidate their position as guarantors of aesthetic excellence and leaders of taste. Its founder members were exempt from jury selection. Among them were such stars as Meissonier, Puvis-de-Chavannes, Carrière, Besnard, Dagnan-Bouveret, Gervex and Roll, as well as Rodin and Dalou. There were no medals, but to be elected as a 'sociétaire' by the existing 'sociétaires' carried with it the more than adequate recompense of influence on what was shown and how. It confronted the heady jumble of the Artistes français with luxury installations which gave exhibits space.

The Salons of both the Artistes français and the Nationale were held in the State's Grand Palais. The Indépendants did not achieve real State backing until well after 1918; its president would only be given a designated seat on the otherwise widely representative Conseil Supérieur des Beaux-Arts in 1938, and its Salon was held annually in spaces provided rent-free by the Ville de Paris, not the State.

As very much the extra-Academic 'other' of the Artistes français and from 1890 the Nationale too, the Indépendants produced its own secession, the Salon d'automne, whose first Salon in 1903 was also supported by the Ville de Paris rather than the State. But the Salon d'automne quickly achieved a certain degree of State support, and indeed entered the Grand Palais the following year. It did so partly because it was, like the Nationale, a society for those who wanted a selective showcase, not just the rag-bag diversity of the open market. In this instance, however, it was a showcase for the new kinds of 'independent art' that the Indépendants had spawned. It had small, highly select juries, elected annually, eighty percent of whom were 'artistes fondateurs' or 'membres sociétaires'; and it underlined its welcome for 'tendencies' by organising choice monographic exhibitions of the artists judged most influential on current developments (Renoir, Redon and Lautrec in 1903; Puvis-de-Chavannes, 1904; Manet, 1905; Gauguin, 1906; Cézanne, 1907; Corot, 1909). Another reason for its early recognition by the State was the involvement from the beginning of Beaux-Arts civil servants and politicians: Roger Marx, organiser of the Centennale in 1900, author of *Art social* and Inspecteur principal des musées des départements, was a 'membre sociétaire' and among the honorary members were the curator of the Musée du Luxembourg (the museum of contemporary French art), Léonce Bénédite, and influential politicians, including M.J. Simyan. One can see how easy it was for the controversy caused by the Cubists in the Salon d'automne to penetrate the Chamber of Deputies.

The four great societies of artists, the Artistes français and the Nationale, the Indépendants and the Salon d'automne, dominated a world of Salons which included smaller Salonnets and societies like the 'Femmes peintres'.[4] From the early 1920s the private gallery system would begin to oust the Salons as the most important supplier of spaces for buying, selling and showing works of art. Nonetheless, right through to 1940, the Salons had a role, one which was double: answering the private demands of dealers and collectors, but also the public demands of the State.

Across the whole 1900–40 period, the State, in the form of its Beaux-Arts administration acting as buyer and patron, played out its own conflict between the impulse to openness, diversity and democracy, and the impulse to control, selection and direction: another mirror of the unresolved tensions within the Third Republic. Democracy and diversity dominated the rhetoric of its representatives until 1936–7, at which point the impulse towards direction (always there) finally pushed aside all pretence at openness when the State decisively endorsed modernism, as I shall show. The switch was confirmed after 1945 by the cultural policies of the Fourth and the Fifth Republics.

The opposition between selection and diversity was there plainly enough in the competitive confrontation of the Centennale and the Décennale in the Grand Palais at the 1900 Universal Exhibition. Against Roger Marx's careful selection of art from 1800 to 1889 for the Centennale, with its arrangement of 'masterpieces' in sequences to bring out continuity between 'tendencies', the Décennale offered neither any overall theme, nor even any emergent 'tendencies', but rather a mass of individuals pursuing different subjects in dozens of different manners. The jury selecting French artists for the Décennale was a compromise between the autocratically imposed and the democratically elected: half were elected by the Artistes français and the Nationale, a quarter appointed by government and a quarter by the Académie. There were sub-Impressionists like Albert Besnard (b.1849) in the show, but the Impressionists themselves were excluded (because they did not submit, it has been suggested), and so were the modern-movement leaders of the 1880s and 1890s, figures like Gauguin and Seurat, Bonnard and Vuillard. Otherwise, the Jury accepted everything from female allegories of naturalness, like Paul Chabas' *Joyous Frolics* [45] and 'realist' portraits of great men, like Léon Bonnat's *Portrait of Renan*, to brutal dreams of exotic savagery, like the sculptor Emmanuel Frémiet's *Orang-outang Attacking a Savage* which is closely related to *Gorilla Dragging a Warrior by the Hair,* [46].

In 1937, broadly the same confrontation between the selected and the diverse was repeated in the opposition between the Jeu de Paume's international contemporary art show, with its clear view of who and what counted in the ongoing 'development' of movements, and the major State commissions for the Palais de Chaillot. Almost all those commissioned to decorate the Palace were chosen from the highest of three categories of artists listed by a committee on which both the director of the 'Beaux-Arts', Georges Huisman, and the curator of the Musée du Luxembourg, Louis Hautecoeur, sat, with artist-representatives, including academicians and two painters shown among the Petit Palais' *Maîtres de l'art indépendant*, Emile Othon-Friesz and Dunoyer de Segonzac. There was, therefore, selection, but it went right across generations and 'tendencies'. Braque,

46. Emmanel Frémiet, *Gorilla Dragging a Warrior by the Hair*. Terracotta, h. 24 cm. Musée d'Orsay, Paris

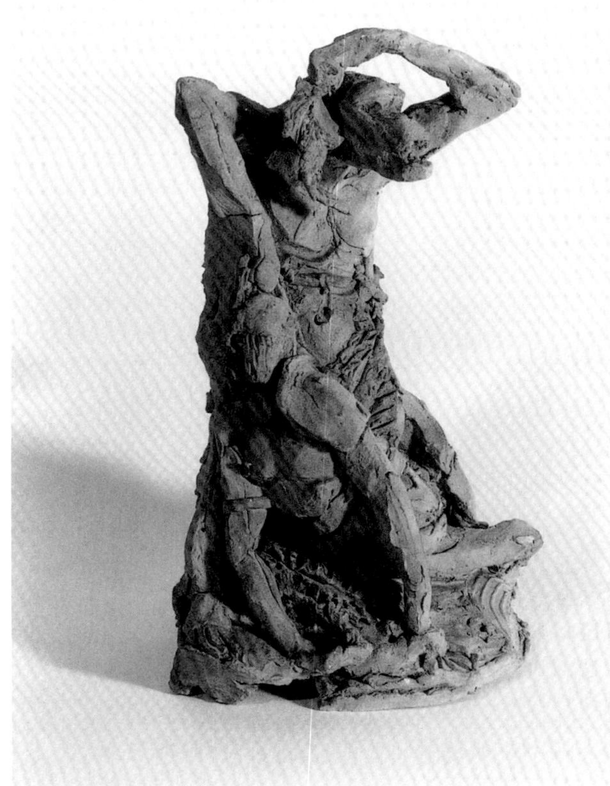

the renowned Cubist, was chosen to paint one of the frescos on cement for the stairs down to the National Theatre, as the pair to Louis Billotey's stylish neo-classicism [6]; he declined the invitation.

The modernist Huisman was the last director of 'Beaux-Arts' in the Third Republic; and his Front Populaire zeal coupled with his commitment to the moderns set him apart. Otherwise, between 1900 and his 1934 appointment, the directors and the politician under-secretaries of state (sous-secrétaires d'état) who supplanted them between 1905 and 1919, had cultivated a dispassionate eclecticism founded upon the democratic ideal of full representation – from the academicians to the 'masters of independent art': diversity. This had been the attitude behind the commissioning and purchasing policy of both the dominant figures in the early twentieth-century 'Beaux-Arts' administration: the first under-secretary-cum-director, Henri Dujardin-Beaumetz (1905–11), a battle painter turned moderate-Radical deputy, and Paul Léon, an exemplary bureaucrat who ran Dujardin-Beaumetz's office before restoring the position and power of the director in 1919 and using that power to the full until 1932. When in December 1912 Léon Bérard, under-secretary successor to Dujardin-Beaumetz, spoke up for tolerance of the Salon d'automne and its Cubists in the Chamber of Deputies, his was the standard argument of democratic liberalism: 'Yes, the State must remain neutral, which is to say that in the face of all these groups, it cannot apply to the advantage of any one against the others the coercive authority of an official aesthetic.'[5]

In fact, such vapid permissiveness veiled the actual operation of preferences. Léger's *Woman in Blue* [30] was the most reproduced of the Cubist pictures in the Salon d'automne of 1912; the State would not buy its first Léger until 1936. Indeed, as the work of Marie-Claude Genet-Delacroix has brought out, the very interaction of directors, under-secretaries and committees within the Beaux-Arts administration itself testifies to the tension between this constantly advocated drive towards impartial diversity and a more covert will for directed decision-making: between the forms of liberal democracy and the behaviour of individuals and groups used to directing affairs.[6] The most telling demonstration of this is, Genet-Delacroix shows, the history of the largest and longest lived of the Beaux-Arts committees, the Conseil Supérieur des Beaux-Arts (CSBA), apparently the highest, certainly the most diverse and democratic of its committees, actually relatively powerless by the 1900s.

In 1905, the CSBA had eighty members; in 1909, ninety-one; in 1923, ninety-three. Throughout, it balanced permanent and annual appointees, and politicians, officials and artists, though there was a progressive shift towards civil servants.[7] As Genet-Delacroix maintains, it came to stand for the transfer of power from traditional, personally directed authority (monarchical) to collective, representative bodies acting anonymously (the republic). But nothing could conceal the fact that the CSBA was an unwieldy vehicle for decision-making, and it continued to vote on little more than the annual Prix du Salon and travelling bursaries for young artists, meeting only once a year, while meaningful decisions on State purchases and decorative or monumental commissions were made by smaller consultative committees and sub-committees skilfully manipulated by the under-secretary or director of the Beaux-Arts administration. Individually, these management figures were subordinate to the Minister of Public Instruction (to whose ministry the Beaux-Arts was attached), but ministers changed so regularly that *de facto* directorial power was rarely challenged. In Dujardin-Beaumetz's office and as director himself, Paul Léon served under fifty-eight ministers! The two ministers in the earlier twentieth century who made a difference were the Radical supporter of modernism, Anatole de Monzie between 1932 and 1934, and the dynamic young Front Populaire minister, Jean Zay. Both reformed the Beaux-Arts committee structures to make them more professionally executive and more aligned with modernist priorities – more dirigiste.

From the time of Dujardin-Beaumetz and his predecessor Henri Roujon, purchases were run by an independent Works of Art Committee (Comité des travaux d'art), under which sub-committees proliferated, dominated by administrators until there were seven by 1939. Successive directors and under-secretaries tended to operate through the smaller sub-committees. Most purchases went to the provinces, but those judged the most important were reserved for the Luxembourg, where diversity was encouraged by restricting the number of works hung by any one artist (partly because of lack of space); a rule broken by the Impressionists brought in with the Caillebotte Bequest in the 1890s. For public patronage an independent 'Consultative Commission' was set up, reporting to the Office of Works of Art and the Beaux-Arts director; yet further committees were set up for the Exhibition of 1937.

The democratic principle operated to the extent that there was a considerable overlap between these real, functioning vehicles of policy and the membership of the CSBA, but their proliferation went with the recurrent realisation that smallness makes for decisive action. It is revealing that when, under de Monzie, a new committee was set up to buy for national collections, it was called the 'little commission' (petite commission), with its thirteen members, in contradistinction to the thirty-nine member descendent of the Comité des travaux d'art, the 'big commission' (grande commission). In 1939, Huisman reformed the 'grande commission' itself; it ended up with just seventeen members – another small body, this one dealing with all the most important purchases.[8] Professional curators and administrators totally dominated these miniaturised, more and more goal-oriented bodies.

It was the old-style civil servants who ensured the refusal of 'tendencies' in the Palais de Chaillot in 1937 – Louis Hautecoeur and Paul Léon in his role as deputy to the Exhibition's general secretary (secrétaire-générale). On the organising committee of the Jeu de Paume's international contemporary art show with its clear modernist criteria, was Jean Cassou, novelist and poet as well as administrator and curator. He effectively represented the new breed of curator, committed to modernism and ready to operate with real professionalism against the old amateur – yet democratic – spirit of diversity.

In his annual report for 1938, Huisman, who had chaired

the committee for the Jeu de Paume exhibition, argued strongly for the takeover of the professional curators from artist representatives; for him, artists always excluded too much. He envisaged a more direct relationship between administrators and artists, discerning curators negotiating one-to-one with major modern masters, securing the kind of works for the new Musée National d'art moderne in the Palais de Tokyo that the art market had put out of the State's reach.[9] Since the mid-1920s, there had been demands from the supporters of the independents for curators who could approach artists as their 'friends', in other words no longer from a position of all-inclusive detachment.[10] In the end, the Front Populaire's demand that the State actively take the initiative for the benefit of France's institutions rather than for that of the infinitely diverse art community put an end to all pretence of impartiality. The highly selective story of the modern movements with their modern masters became the official story of art in France in the twentieth century, and the result was a highly selective purchase and exhibition policy, finally put into practice with total commitment by Jean Cassou when he took over as director of the Musée National d'art moderne in 1945. Between that date and the museum's post-war opening in 1947, Cassou acquired by gift or purchase, often at reduced prices, the core of a major collection of modernist masterpieces; most were obtained directly from the artists, who found this new kind of approach based on cultivated curatorial expertise irresistible.[11] The institutionalisation of liberal democracy was replaced by personal authority given a new kind of professional inflection, a brand of authority whose rhetoric was progressive, not traditional: the rhetoric of modernism.[12]

DIFFERENT ARTISTS, DIFFERENT MARKETS

Between 1920 and 1922, Fernand Léger (b.1881) used the 'independent' Salons – the Salon d'automne as well as the Indépendants – to show a succession of enormous canvases; they included, *The City* [176] in the Indépendants of 1920, the first after the war, and the *Grand Déjeuner* and *Mother and Child* [247, 249], in the Autumn Salons of 1921 and 1922. Pictures on such a scale were specifically excluded from the contract he had signed in 1918 with Léonce Rosenberg, D-H. Kahnweiler's wartime replacement as the leading Cubist dealer. They were painted to make an impact: to consolidate Léger's reputation as one of the leading moderns. It is easy to think of such major works as throw-backs to the great Salon history paintings of the nineteenth century, which similarly were painted more to be seen than to be sold. In fact, they were painted both as 'masterpieces' *and* as tactical moves in an integrated commercial strategy. They prepared the market for smaller canvases 'to be sold'; and were never so far above the market that they could not themselves be sold. Scale was not only a measure of aesthetic ambition, it demanded a response; from the right response (celebration or notoriety) came prestige. Writing to Léger in October 1926, Rosenberg advised him always to think of his 'prestige': 'Money,' he added, 'is only the consequence of well-established prestige, towards which business flows by itself'.[13] As early, indeed, as 1900, it had become virtually impossible to separate aesthetic idealism, whether traditionalist or modernist, from the commercial workings of the art world.

In all four major Salons, including the 'aristocratic' Nationale and the modernist Salon d'automne with its selectively marshalled 'tendencies', showing 'to be seen' and 'to be sold' had come together. What differed was the degree of emphasis on either market openness or the optimum conditions for display: the Artistes français and the Indépendants went for the former, the Nationale and the Salon d'automne went for the latter. But, as Mainardi has shown, in both cases their spaces were geared to commerce: the seductions of the department store, with its designed installations and flattery of the customer's good taste providing an alternative model to the chaotic cornucopia of the bazaar.[14]

Obviously, there were growing private markets for art in the Salons and the dealers' galleries; it is less often realised that public bodies constituted a major market too, most important of all the State. In the Third Republic, the State acted as both collector and patron; in both cases, it distributed not only prestige but income. The prolific generosity of the Beaux-Arts at the 1937 Exhibition was, of course, a way of combating the Depression by giving artists employment. The State openly gave priority to the material support of painters, sculptors and decorative artists as well as acting as the patron of monumental art.[15] In the earlier years of the Third Republic, the roles of customer and patron had been altogether more clearly separated in policy terms. When the State privatised the Salon in 1881, as the Artistes français, it switched its support entirely to purchasing. Until the mid-1930s, its role in the Salons would always be to administer financial stimulants in relatively small doses to promote the vigour of otherwise unsubsidised markets. It was this aspect of policy that went especially with the rhetoric of diversity and individualism. Speaking in the Chamber of Deputies in 1881, the republican Edouard Lockroy had already identified, by contrast, the State's main aims as patron rather than collector: 'art,' he declared, must be seen as 'an especially powerful means of national education and industrial prosperity'.[16] The decorative-arts policies that led to the Exhibition of 1925, at first galvanised by Antonin Proust and Roger Marx, were geared to promoting 'industrial prosperity'; between the early 1880s and 1914, a massive programme of mural painting and monumental sculpture for new or refurbished public buildings became the instrument of a policy of national education by art. This latter, which transformed public buildings not only in Paris but in thousands of communes across France, was driven by republican idealism certainly, but the high-profile prestige it often guaranteed artists coupled with the sheer scale of its munificence inevitably gave it a major market role.

The Beaux-Arts budget was always a tiny proportion of the national budget, and a small proportion of the Education (Instruction Publique) budget too.[17] Yet, State purchases, even when modest, gave real encouragement, and when compared with prices for easel-paintings and privately bought sculpture, State commissions could bring something approaching financial ease, not just security. In the early 1920s, Léger was asking 25,000 francs for his great Salon pictures, as against the rather more normal 1,300 francs asked at Rosenberg's 1919 Léger exhibition for *The Propellors* [178], a typical medium-sized dealers' picture.[18]

25,000 francs was exactly the sum paid to the academician and Ecole professor Cormon for his State commissioned commemorative painting of the reception of the 'mayors of France' at the Elysée Palace in 1900; it was also the sum agreed for Jean-Paul Laurens' decorative paintings for the great staircase of the Capitol at Toulouse in 1902 [47].[19] In the 1900s, a good petty-bourgeois annual income was 3,000 to 4,000 francs. After 400% wartime inflation, each of these commissions would have been worth 100,000 francs by the early 1920s. Brauer records that on 22 January 1912, Léon Bérard, Under-Secretary of State at the Beaux-Arts, wrote to his colleague in government Raymond Poincaré suggesting caution when considering Gaston La Touche, a founder-member of the Nationale, since he had already received 62,000 francs from State commissions since 1905![20] When Paul Léon saw to the commissioning of a large-scale version of Bourdelle's *France* [14] for the Decorative Arts Exhibition of 1925, the sculptor was not only paid a substantial fee, but given a studio in the State's dépot des marbres on the rue de l'Université, which he was allowed to keep until his death. As well as names, substantial livings, replete with privilege, were to be gained from the State.

And the opportunities for the prestige of large-scale exposure, especially from the commissions that went with the grand decorative and 'educational' schemes for public buildings, were phenomenal; much more so, in fact, before 1914 than in the 1930s. Cash and prestige were good companions in what was experienced as a virtuous circle of support by most artists caught up in it; consciences were, of course, cleared by the sense of service to the new Republic. The enormous scale of the State enterprise, and the range and often spectacular verve of the mural painting produced in response by dozens of painters between the early 1880s and 1914 has been revealed by Pierre Vaisse.[21] Its starting point was the mid-1870s project for the redecoration of the Panthéon, which was followed in the decades up to 1914 by programmes for the Nouvelle Sorbonne, for railway stations, theatres, provincial museums and prefectures, and for the newly empowered town halls of the regions, some of them vast projects (Toulouse, Lyon, Tour, for instance), which were financed and run as partnerships usually dominated from the centre by the State. The one municipality capable of initiating a programme ambitious enough to compete with the Beaux-Arts was the Ville de Paris. Between the early 1880s and 1914, it provided the boost of considerable funds and a tidal wave of republican enthusiasm, completing huge schemes of decoration in the rebuilt Hôtel de Ville, the town halls of the arrondissements and inner suburban boroughs of Paris, and – the culmination – from 1903 in the Petit Palais.[22]

47. Jean-Paul Laurens, *The First Official Meeting of the 'Jeux Floraux'*, 1912. The Great Staircase of the Capitole at Toulouse

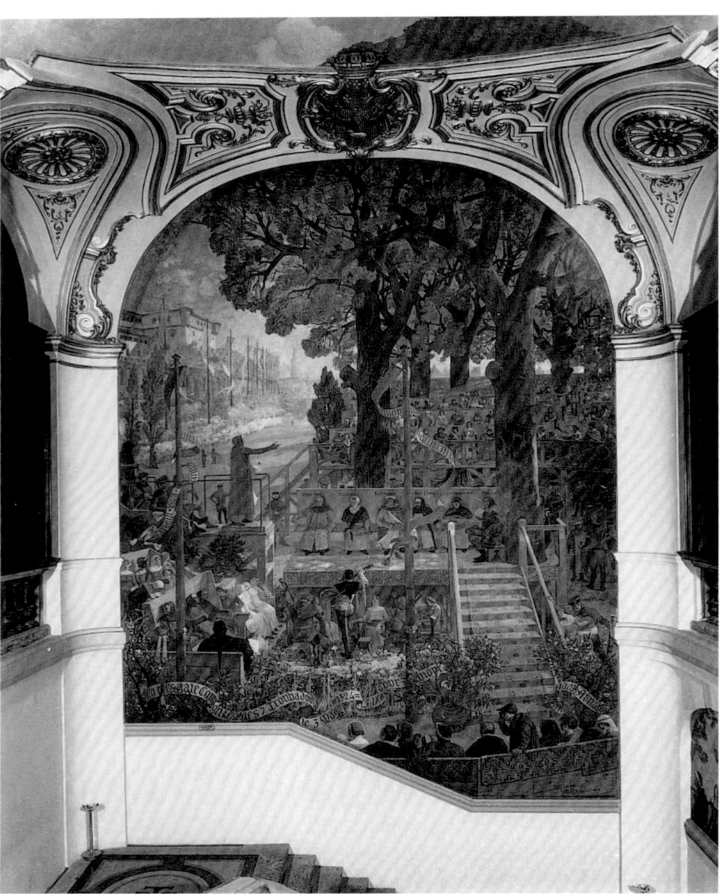

The prodigious scale of the achievement has not been answered by a comparable breadth and depth of response. Sometimes, no doubt, this is because of the relative inaccessibility of the spaces painted – Besnard's murals for the Ecole de Pharmacie in the Sorbonne, for instance. And sometimes in the more public spaces – theatres or town hall Salles de mariage, for instance – because of the abstruseness of the allegorical conceits elaborated, often bringing together contemporary fact and transcendent symbolism in unlikely juxtapositions. Yet, acres of painting, accessible in both senses, were produced by artists whose technical control across such daunting surfaces and whose self-confidence can be breathtaking: Jean-Paul Laurens in the Capitol at Toulouse, say, or Henri Gervex (b.1852) in the Paris Hôtel de Ville [47, 83].

The sheer self-confidence and command of the sculptors working for public spaces can be astonishing too, even if their staging of eulogies has found a diminishing audience. The Nouvelle Sorbonne and the Hôtel de Ville provided opportunities on a large scale for sculptors as well as painters, and there were statues to be made for the façade of the Palais de Justice between 1911 and 1914, but for them the market for large-scale monumental statuary was not dominated by the State and the Ville de Paris to the extent that it was for painters looking for walls to cover.[23] Many of the monuments erected in public squares, parks and cemeteries across France were initiated by private societies or committees which raised funds by subscription, sometimes backed by press campaigns, and oversaw the work from the first maquettes through to the final piece. The débâcle of the Balzac monument, which ended in 1902 with the academician Alexandre Falguière's sedentary mortal replacing Rodin's striding superman, was entirely the responsibility of the private Société des gens de lettres. Dalou's extraordinary motorised triumphal arch memorialising the engineer Emile Levassor [184] and Maillol's feminised homage to Cézanne

[149] and many more such monuments came about because of groups of enthusiasts, not just in Paris. Maillol conceived and developed his Cézanne monument between 1910 and 1914 for Aix-en-Provence, funded by the proceeds of sales donated privately by prominent artists, including Monet, Renoir and Matisse.

There were occasions when the State acted alone, but almost always private committees had to act with the cooperation of the State or municipality, in agreeing a site. Sometimes, committees and public bodies acted together; or public bodies came to the rescue when great projects were threatened. Laurent Marquestre's monument to the Radical premier of 1900, Waldeck-Rousseau, and Gustave Michel's monument to the Republican leader of the 1880s, Jules Ferry, were heavily subsidised by the State. In 1906 and 1910 respectively they were inaugurated as major assertions of Republican power in one of the most sought-after public sites in the capital, the State's Jardin des Tuileries [148]. In 1925, the city of Aix-en-Provence finally refused Maillol's Cézanne monument on the grounds that the artist himself was not monumentalised; by 1927, the State had provided a site in the Tuileries for it, a conclusive demonstration of Cézanne's unquestioned stature by that date and an inestimable contribution to Maillol's prestige.

It has been calculated that in the period 1870–1914, between 153 and 160 statues were erected in public sites in France; the word 'statuemania' has been coined for it. The period 1915–25 saw only five such statues, an episode almost of 'statuephobia'. Painters too faced a big fall in areas of wall and ceiling to be covered. But for sculptors there was more than adequate compensation in the huge demand for war memorials, which provided work for belated Cubists like the Martel brothers as well as out-and-out traditionalists like the extreme right-wing Camelot du roi, Maximé Réal de Sarte, specialist in patriotic statues of Jeanne d'Arc. The Musée de l'armée records 37,708 war memorials erected in the more than 40,000 communes. 30,000 were erected between 1920 and 1925.[24] The great majority of memorials cost less than 10,000 francs, and were selected from catalogues distributed by individual sculptors willing to produce in quantity at reasonable prices, like one H. Jacomet from the Vaucluse who offered either a Victory or a common soldier (poilu) for 3,500 francs.[25] But major monuments were erected in the primary cities for huge sums. Poisson's *Monument aux morts* at Le Havre cost a million.

Between the late 1920s and the Exhibition of 1937, the sculptors, like the painters, were increasingly short of work for public spaces. The nine years from 1925 to 1934 saw a dramatic drop in the number of sculptor-decorators employed: from 3,050 to 1,650.[26] These are figures that apply, of course, to artisan-sculptors, but they show how demand for all kinds of public sculpture dropped, before the immense artificial fillip provided for painting and sculpture alike by the Front Populaire's great projects. 1937 was a last spectacular but brief wave of support for public art, most of it financed by the State, before the sudden end of the Third Republic in 1940.

Through most of the twentieth century, it was conventional to make a sharp distinction between 'independents' and artists who received 'official' support, a distinction which concerns not only their art but their lives. The 'statuaire' sculptors of public monuments in France and the painters involved in the grandest of the State's and the Ville de Paris' decorative programmes were set up as an undifferentiated defining 'other' against figures like Matisse, Braque and Léger, and especially the foreign moderns, figures like Picasso and Brancusi, who were often disqualified from competing for State commissions. The implication was that 'official' careers were so beholden to the 'official' establishment and so weighed down by honours and rewards that such artists could only supply tired formulas where the moderns, released from mere material ambition, could dare. Different degrees of 'freedom' in art were calibrated with different degrees of 'independence'. Before 1918, there were indeed distinctive kinds of career for painters and sculptors in France, and being a 'sociétaire' of the Artistes français or the Nationale rather than of the 'independent' Salons, coupled with significant involvement in public art, marked defining differences. But, as we shall see, the independents were no less immersed in the liberal commercial reality of the Third Republic and, as their response to the modernist patronage of the Front Populaire shows plainly enough, in the end they were no less open to official endorsement.

We are dealing here with different lives in art with different market opportunities and different ways of achieving that crucial attribute, prestige. Léger did not only sell through dealers, his career culminated in 1936–7 with official commissions and the entry of his work into the State's museums. In the same way, the great beneficiaries of State commissions in the 1900s, like Léon Bonnat of the Artistes français, used the open market of the annual Salon to find private sitters and collectors, while a sculptor who always had commissions for monuments like Denys Puech [163] never ceased to produce portrait busts for bourgeois apartments. As Vaisse has argued, in class terms, their private customers were little different from the mostly middle-class clientele of the moderns, and the sheer stylistic diversity of their work makes it impossible to talk of an official art in any collective sense.[27] Moreover, as I have already suggested, the State and the Ville de Paris themselves constituted markets. There were major differences in lifestyles and artistic practices, but lives in art were not lived anywhere in France out of the reach of markets, whether in the name of avant-garde movements or of Public Instruction. In the markets available for artists, public as well as private, what differed were the strategies for building prestige and success.

The modernist history of heroic masters and modern movements sketched in Chapter 2 reveals the tensions between contradictory strategies followed by ambitious independents: the use of what Mainardi has called individualist market differentiation and the collective tactic of the group Salon or gallery showing. The most successful moderns managed to establish themselves as utterly distinct individual artists *and* as important contributors to a group identity: they were what their names stood for and yet shared in the provocative exposure provided by a major -ism, sometimes while denying any such involvement. From before 1910, Picasso was the inventor of Cubism, and from 1925 he was an honorary Surrealist, but more than either a Cubist or a Surrealist he was always celebrated and reviled as 'Picasso'. The poet-critic André Salmon had anecdotalised Picasso's role at the beginning of Cubism from 1911, yet in 1919 he could write of him as 'all alone between the sky and the earth'.[28] His success reconciled the two counter-identities – individual and collective – more completely than any other artist's. Between 1917 and the early 1920s, Léonce Rosenberg's galerie de l'Effort Moderne deliberately presented its Cubist artists as a disciplined collective; but when the dealer brought in Maurice Raynal to write monographs and articles on his Cubists, Raynal made a point of isolating them as originals. 'Each man,' he wrote of Juan Gris in 1920, 'creates his private beauty . . .'.[29] For avant-garde independents such as these, prestige came with serious attention in the press and sales to big-spending collectors, foreign as well as French; -isms could make the breach, names sustained the breakthrough. It was difficult to make a name without an -ism, though exceptional differentiation associated with an interesting biography did the trick for a Modigliani, an Utrillo or a Suzanne Valadon.

Before the mid-1920s, both 'independent' individuality and group identity went, broadly, with that exaggerated sense of difference from artists considered 'official' already mentioned; the distinction was not one arrived at later, it was made in the period. The Impressionists steadily gained official success from the acceptance of the Caillebotte bequest in the 1890s onwards, reaching a first climax in 1914 with the opening of the Camondo bequest in the Louvre. But Monet showed the typical resistance of independents to official acceptance when he expressed serious reservations about being included alongside the officially successful in Roger Marx's Centennale of 1900.[30] The same kind of hesitation no doubt helps explain Braque's decision not to accept the commission to paint one of the frescos for the Palais de Chaillot in 1936. Both, of course, produced major work for the State in the end: Monet, his *Nymphéas* cycle for the Orangerie [73], Braque a ceiling in the Louvre itself after 1945.

The strategies for building prestige developed by the most successful of the artists of the Nationale and the

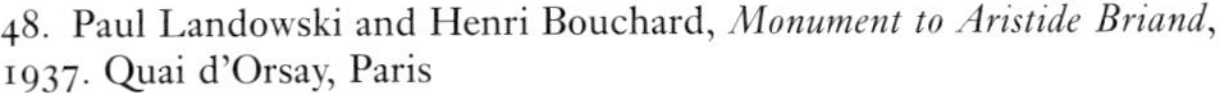

48. Paul Landowski and Henri Bouchard, *Monument to Aristide Briand*, 1937. Quai d'Orsay, Paris

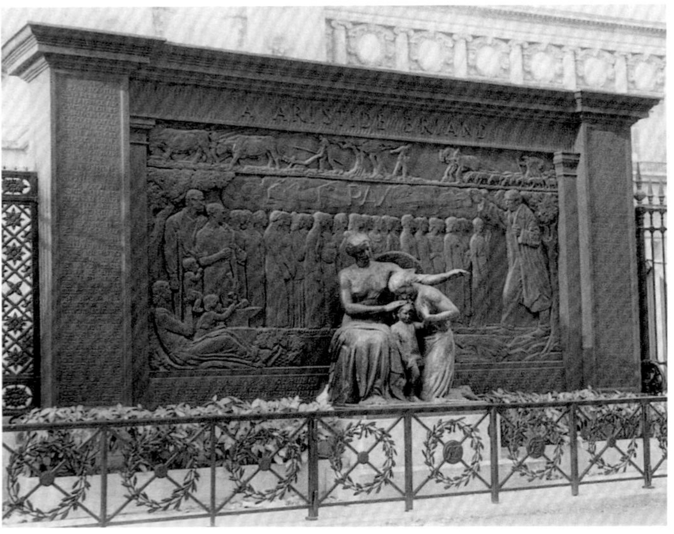

Artistes français (whether calculated or not) were indeed utterly different: official recognition and distinction was the nub. In 1910, Louis Vauxcelles, a critic uncompromisingly committed to the independents, offered the following verbal caricature of the ideal officially sanctioned artistic career; he is guying the careerist sentiments of a member of the Artistes français hanging committee: 'We want to enjoy the fruits of life, to receive State commissions, the smiles of M. Beaumetz, the cravat of Commander [of the Légion d'honneur], to own town-houses on the avenue de Villiers, to draw the portraits of fashionable ladies, to sit in the Institut between M. Dagnan-Bouveret and M. Flameng.'[31] The two academicians named were highly successful society portraitists, who had achieved both official recognition and financial rewards in plenty. But Vauxcelles' list of the markers of success was actually lacking, he could have added at least two further items: positions of influence in the great State institutions – above all, the Ecole and the Académie française at the Villa Medici in Rome – and positions of influence on official bodies.

The prestige supplied by official endorsement impacted directly on the success of such artists in their markets, both with public bodies and in such luxury private establishments as the galerie Georges Petit or Bernheim-Jeune. Vaisse gives the telling example of Léon Bonnat in 1892 reimbursing the Cardinal de Lavegerie [98] for his portrait, so that the State could buy it for the Luxembourg; and Curtis records a letter of 1929 to the academician-sculptor Henri Bouchard concerning the projected *Monument to Marshal Foch*, suggesting he obtain references not only from artists and critics, but from members of the Beaux-Arts ministry.[32] Bouchard (b.1875) did not get the job, but not for lack of contacts; starting in 1907, he received fourteen State commissions in a long career, developed in tandem with his friend from the Villa Medici, Paul Landowski. Both were laureates of the 'Premier grand prix de Rome' (Landowski, 1900; Bouchard 1901) and both sat on the commissioning committee for the 1937 Exhibition. Landowski became director of ENBA in 1939, where Bouchard was a 'chef d'atelier', and they worked together on the massive monument to the one-time Socialist Aristide Briand, erected on the Quai d'Orsay in 1937 [48]. Theirs were careers patterned on that of earlier 'Premier grand prix de Rome' laureates like Denys Puech, who won in 1884 and also went on to play a role on Beaux-Arts committees and in State institutions: he was director of the Villa Medici between 1921 and 1933. But it was certainly two painters, Léon Bonnat and Albert Besnard who balanced dazzling private success and weighty public prestige most impressively. They achieved a level of market success along with positions of influence within the organs of the State unrivalled by any of their contemporaries.

Bonnat was born in 1833; he was six years younger than Cézanne and a year older than Degas. Besnard was born in 1849, he was a little younger than Monet and Renoir. Both remained highly influential until their deaths: Bonnat's in 1922, Besnard's in 1934 – Besnard was given a State funeral in the Louvre. Bonnat valued stylishness, a clear line and a sharp eye; his portraits were sought after [98], and he was deeply respectful of Ingres; he lent several Ingres drawings from his own collection to the Centennale in 1900.

Camille Mauclair, the early historian of Impressionism, was Besnard's first biographer. Mauclair made a point of separating him both from the Impressionists and from 'official painting', but he was certainly one of the first to make the loose handling and coloured shadows associated with Impressionism officially acceptable. Like Bonnat, he was selected by Roger Marx for the Centennale, but his breakthrough picture from the 1886 Artistes français, the *Portrait of Mme. Roger Jourdain*, was discussed in Marx's catalogue text in the wake not of Ingres but of Manet. Both adapted easily to large-scale mural painting, and capitalised with superlative skill on a succession of major commissions, especially Besnard [165, 166].

Bonnat remained loyal to the Artistes français, while Besnard was one of the founders of the secessionist Nationale in 1890, but they shared a common devotion as members of the artistic great and good to the major Beaux-Arts institutions of the State. Besnard was director of the Villa Medici in Rome between 1913 and 1921; Bonnat was director of ENBA from 1909 to 1922, and then was succeeded by Besnard. Both gave their time on the committees of the Beaux-Arts, but no-one could exceed the zeal of Léon Bonnat: his ubiquity was a phenomenon, commented upon by Paul-Boncour in his budget report of 1911. Genet-Delacroix has charted his membership of the CSBA in four different capacities for forty-two years, between 1880 and 1922, during which period he also served on the Conseil des Musées Nationaux (president in 1892), the Conseil de la Réunion des Musées Nationaux (president in 1899) – the latter an important committee deciding on bequests – the Consultative Commission on State purchases, and the Commission des Beaux-Arts of the Ville de Paris. Bonnat was an ever-present influence on the distribution of prestige until his death in 1922; and, of course, his own prestige was unchallenged as a result, at least from the official vantage point of Dujardin-Beaumetz or Paul Léon. Naturally, Bonnat and Besnard both became academicians (in 1881 and 1912, respectively), and both received the State's confirmation of reputations well earned, ascent through the grades of the Légion d'honneur.

Vauxcelles' scorn for the kind of success grasped with such tenacity by Bonnat and Besnard went with a ruthless desire to extinguish all official art. Bonnat countered by using his position tirelessly to defend the State institutions against the entryism of the emergent moderns. From the vantage point of the independents, Bonnat and his kind stood for a weakened 'official art' which would be defeated: from Bonnat's vantage point, the independents stood for a threat whose increasing strength had to be resisted. From both directions, the division beween official and independent artists seemed real and complete, but, despite the apparent sway of a figure like Bonnat, already before 1914 commentators from the independent side could see where their strength lay. The French State as a market may hardly have acknowledged the existence of post-Nabis modern painting, but other markets, not necessarily in France, were buying. This was Salmon's boast in *La Jeune Peinture française* of 1912, and when, in 1913, Apollinaire accused Bonnat of being the single individual most to be blamed for the paucity of work from 'the modern French school' in the Luxembourg, he went on to claim that the best collections of modern French art were actually in Berlin.[33]

As we shall see when we look at the activities of dealers and collectors, it would be the strength of independent art in the growing international as well as French art market during the 1920s that prepared the way for the State's volte-face in the 1930s. It would be the private market that changed the orientation of the State as a market for art in France, making Huisman's and Cassou's dedication to modernism possible, so that the 'independent' and the 'official' finally became one and the same. The signs were already there by the mid-1920s.

If Bonnat was an uncompromising opponent of everything independent, even the surviving Impressionists, by 1923, the year after Bonnat's death, Besnard was willing to negotiate an accommodation with the moderns of the Salon d'automne; he could not ignore their emerging prestige. He was one of the leaders of the Nationale who initiated a joint Salon with the Salon d'automne that summer, the Salon des Tuileries. His own full-size cartoon for the State-commissioned tapestry, *The Return to Strasbourg of the French Universities*, was shown alongside work by not only one-time Fauves like Friesz, but the Cubists Metzinger, Marcoussis and Gleizes.

To coincide with the Decorative Arts Exhibition of 1925, an officially endorsed exhibition on the model of the Centennale opened at the Pavillon Marsan; it was called 'Cinquante ans de peinture française' (Fifty Years of French Art), and among its selectors was Louis Vauxcelles. The supporters of independent art represented it as a triumph. It was organised in two parts. The first was pre-1914, amassing sixty modernist works against a rump of just sixteen from the sociétaires of the Artistes français and the Nationale. There were four Cézannes against one Bonnat and not a single Besnard. In the second part which took the period after 1914, only one work was allowed for each artist; it included Vuillard, Bonnard, Matisse, Derain, Vlaminck, Dufy, Friesz, Picasso and Braque. According to André Salmon, it was pressure from the private lenders of the Monets, Cézannes and other modern works that pushed out the Bonnats and Besnards.[34]

By the mid-1920s, the shift in the orientation of the Beaux-Arts administration was clearly underway. In April 1926, the Luxembourg re-opened after re-hanging under its new curator, Charles Masson. Bonnat and Besnard were still there with Jean-Paul Laurens and Henri Gervex, but so now were Bonnard, Matisse, Vlaminck, Marquet and Friesz; and the Impressionists of the Caillebotte bequest formed the new centrepiece of the museum. It would no longer be so easy to separate the independent from the official; the independents had begun to win the attention of the State as buyer and patron. And both Louis Vauxcelles and Henri Matisse had begun their own 'independent' ascents through the grades of the Légion d'honneur.[35]

FIXING AND UNFIXING CATEGORIES: PAINTERS, SCULPTORS AND OTHERS

For Bonnat and Vauxcelles, the division between the 'official' and the 'independent' was a frontier never to be crossed. Besnard's willingness to shake hands with those on the other side in 1923 betrays the existence of a no-man's land of equivocation. There were increasing numbers of artists in the 1920s who worked in a vaguely defined area that was both officially endorsed *and* recognised by hard-liners like Vauxcelles to be authentically independent. Indeed, there had been artists working thus since the first decade of the century. Bonnard, Vuillard, Denis, Roussel, Vallotton – the Nabis generation born in the later 1860s – were unquestioned qualifiers for the Petit Palais retrospective of the Indépendants in 1937, but they had been welcomed into the Salons of the Nationale by the 1900s. What is more, Henri Marcel, the director of the Beaux-Arts before Dujardin-Beaumetz took over in 1905, bought from Vuillard, Denis and Vallotton. In 1913, the State paid 7,000 francs for Denis' *Annunciation*, a special purchase earmarked for the Luxembourg.[36] When for a few months Anatole de Monzie first became Minister in 1925, he went as far as appointing Matisse and Friesz to the Consultative Commission; not only now was their work thought worthy of the Luxembourg, but they were actually involved in the decision-making for State purchases.[37]

And yet, it was not so much painters who worked in that no-man's land between the official and the independent; much more equivocal was the status of the leading independent sculptors. André Salmon followed up his *La Jeune Peinture française* of 1912 with *La Jeune Sculpture française*, mostly written before 1914, but not published until 1919. Salmon's post-war Preface dismisses the idea of 'Left' and 'Right' in art altogether; he accepts that those on the 'Left' risk the disappointment of failing to enter the museums or to win the Légion d'honneur (not strictly true, as we have seen), but insists that they are not blind followers of 'that barbarous cult of novelty'.[38] Such a righteous distaste for innovation was something far more easily argued for the most celebrated independent sculptors than for the painters.

A decade later A.-H. Martinie published a more wide-ranging and more historically structured survey of twentieth-century French sculpture than Salmon's. Its major categories were 'Academicism and Eclecticism' as against 'The Independents', and the leading independents named are all sculptors of the same generation as the Nabis or just a few years younger: Bourdelle (b.1861), Maillol (b.1861), Despiau (b.1874), and Joseph Bernard (b.1866).[39] Bourdelle was consistently to be set somewhat apart – the hero of his own reaction against the overwhelming presence of Rodin (who lived until 1917). The other three, led by Maillol, but inspired before 1910 by a sculptor who died young, Lucien Schnegg, are seen to represent a more concerted reaction, one that favours idealised stylisation against gesticulating expression, and that revives pre-Hellenic archaism in the pursuit of universals. Vauxcelles had grouped Schnegg, Despiau and Maillol together against those who were 'Rodinising' as early as 1911.[40]

49. Constantin Brancusi, *A Corner of the Studio*, photograph illustrated in *Cahiers d'art*, no. 8–9 (Paris, 1929)

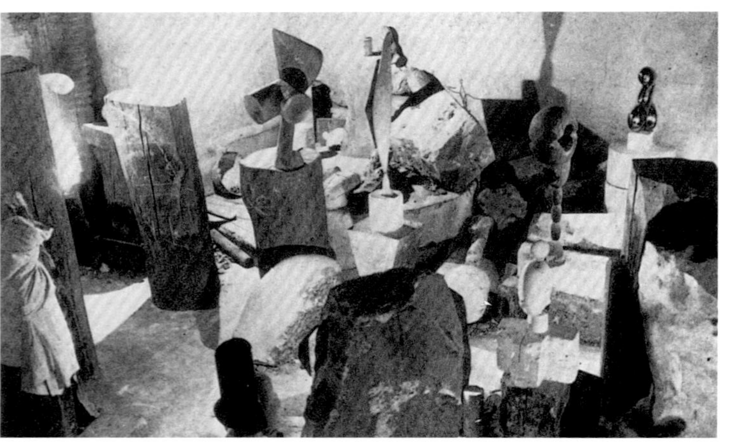

This was the hefty yet elevating figure-style that was to ornament the walls and terraces of the Palais de Chaillot and the Palais de Tokyo in 1937; from 1919, it was quickly made official – while remaining 'independent'. Indeed, independent sculpture had clearly begun to achieve official recognition before 1914. Despiau's bust of *Paulette* [100], his pert characterisation of a girl from his native region, the Landes, had been bought for 2,000 francs from the Nationale in 1910.[41] The following year he became a chevalier of the Légion d'honneur, as Bourdelle had in 1909; Maillol would follow them in 1920. Much was made of the fact that none of these sculptors were Prix de Rome winners like the 'academics' Puech, Landowski or Bouchard. They would never win comparable numbers of State commissions, but they showed in the Nationale until 1923, when they joined Besnard, Aman-Jean and the other Nationale 'sociétaires' in the Salon des Tuileries, where Maillol and Despiau continued to show into the 1930s. Their 'independent' status was never unequivocal in the sense that Matisse's or Léger's was.

Patrick Elliott has argued persuasively that the relative conservatism of independent sculpture in France stemmed from the very different conditions of sculptural as distinct from pictorial production. He quotes Louis Hautecoeur of the Luxembourg in 1929 on the sculptor's resistance to 'the contagion of theories' as the counterpart to the physical character of sculpture; this was a common view at the time.[42] The official or independent status of a Maillol or a Despiau might have been ill-defined, but sculpture as such was widely thought to be a category absolutely distinct from painting: an art and a practice with its own training, its own exhibition spaces and its own literature. Salmon, Vauxcelles, Huyghe and all who surveyed art in France before 1939 were careful to deal with sculpture on its own.

To go right through the training and early practical experience of a sculptor was to take on an identity which could come as close to the artisan as to the artist. Artisanal and peasant origins were routinely stressed: Maillol and Bourdelle from remote beginnings in the South (French Catalonia and the Tarn), Bernard and Despiau, the sons of artisans (Bernard son of a mason and Despiau, son of a master plasterer). Salmon's book gives us a Bourdelle teaching at the Académie de la Chaumière (an independent art school) with a mission to guide the young back to the integrated craft practices of the artisan and away from the industrialised division of labour (he is careful to play down the need for assistants and division of labour in the production of any large-scale monument). Of Maillol, he writes that he has the 'beautiful instinct of the artisan' and compares his monuments to 'the vases of a potter.'[43] Despiau and Bourdelle both progressed before 1910 from early craft training through the Ecole studios and then work experience as assistants (praticiens) for Rodin. This gave them a training not only in the arts of drawing and sculpture but in sculptural techniques. These varied from the production of clay maquettes, to the scaling up of plasters, to working with specialist 'metteurs au point' and carvers, or with the bronze foundries to produce finished large-scale works suitably polished or patinated.[44] The status of monumental sculptor (statuaire) was hard-earned; much harder earned, it could seem, than the status of painter – a fact underlined by the costs and practical difficulties of showing sculpture. In the Salons, sculptors mostly showed plaster models in the hope of commissions or clients capable of paying for full-scale execution in stone or bronze. By the same token, dealer exhibitions of sculpture were rare.

And yet, in France between 1900 and 1940 both the craft specificity of sculpture as a practice and the clarity of the distinction between sculpture and painting were fundamentally challenged. By the 1930s, the very status of sculpture as a definitively self-sufficient category was in danger. Those responsible for this were the very few avant-garde sculptors associated with Cubism and Surrealism; and painters. Maillol was an early warning of what could happen. He was untrained, and had begun as a painter close to Denis and the Nabis: he was a new sort of hybrid, a painter-sculptor. But where Maillol set aside his role as a painter, those who represented the real threat did not. Besides Martinie's survey of sculpture, 1928 saw the publication of another by Adolphe Basler, who made a point of discussing the 'always topical' 'controversy over painter-sculptors and sculptor-painters.' He looked back as far as Daumier and Degas, and named Matisse, Derain, Picasso and Modigliani, before accusing the Cubists of pretentious games of artifice at the expense of ancient sculptural principles.[45] In 1916–17 even one of the Cubists, the Lithuanian Jacques Lipchitz, who had preferred the more liberal Académie Julian to the Ecole, felt compelled to reject polychromy (reintroduced in sculpture by Picasso and Alexander Archipenko) for very similar reasons. The threat from painters to the integrity of sculpture was widely and deeply felt.

Maillol was French, as were painter-sculptors like Degas. Renoir, Derain and Matisse. Many of the sculptural avant-garde altogether, were not. Modigliani (Italian), Archipenko (Russian) and above all Picasso (Spanish) stood out. They had neither the ingrained prejudices nor hard-earned skills of sculptors trained in the French ENBA system who had worked as 'praticiens' for the great monumental 'statuaires'; they came from outside. Moreover, the supra-artisanal idea of the artist for which so many modernist painters stood – the idea of the intellectual, the metaphysician or the magician – had its effect on the image of certain sculptors whose training and whose work was emphatically sculptural and who never lost their artisanal identity, most important among them, the Romanian Constantin Brancusi (b.1876) and the Swiss Alberto Giacometti (b.1901). Just how subtly yet drastically the intrusion of painters and painters' images into the practices of sculptors could undermine the categorical distinction between them is there to be seen in the increasing quantities of photographs of sculptors' and painter-sculptors' studios published in modernist periodicals between the wars.

In 1929, *Cahiers d'art* published photographs of 'corners' of Brancusi's studio with a text by the expelled Surrealist Roger Vitrac [49]. The images and the words hold in balance the idea of Brancusi as craftsman, working material with his hands, and the idea of him as 'sorcerer' who endows what he touches with 'occult meaning'. His hands 'work like the waters of the tides rolling antique marbles' across the sea-floor – a natural force; but his power is metamorphic, alchemical, no less than any painter admired in the Surrealist milieu.[46]

In 1933, the brand new periodical *Minotaure*, published first a photo-essay by Brassaï featuring Picasso's studios with a text by André Breton, and then a few months later, a cluster of photographs of corners in sculptor's studios with a text by Maurice Raynal.[47] As published, Brassaï's photographs gave more prominence to Picasso's sculpture studio at the Château de Boisgeloup than to his Paris painting studios on the rue la Boétie; and sculpture was present in most of the photographs he took in Paris. Startlingly, he transformed the Boisgeloup sculpture studio into a place of magic illumination by beaming the headlights of Picasso's Hispano-Suiza onto the plasters massed there [50]; it becomes a place of dematerialisation, where the artisan and

50. Brassaï, *Picasso's sculpture studio, Château de Boisgeloup*, 1932. Photograph illustrated in *Minotaure*, no. 1 (Paris, 1933)

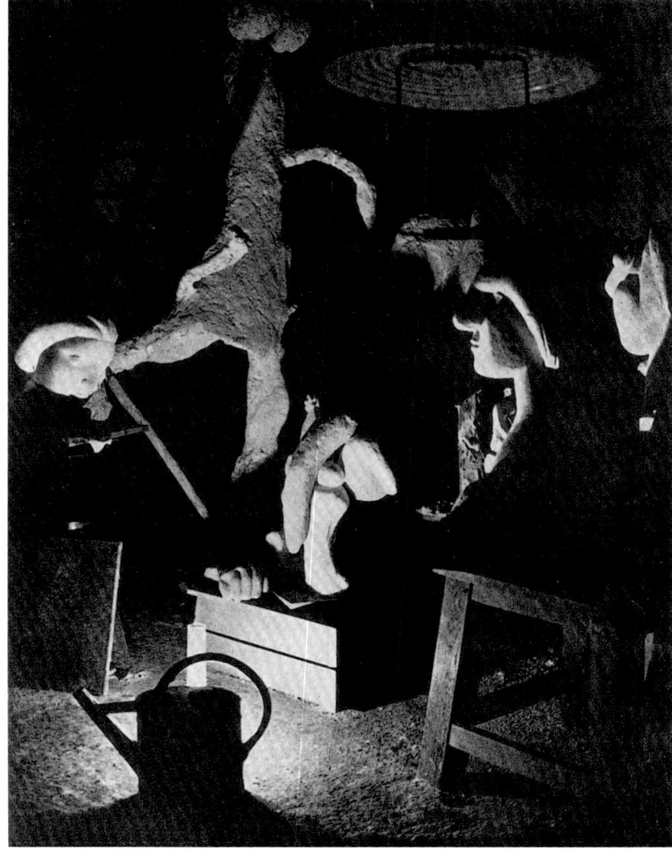

his tools can hardly be imagined. The studios of both Brancusi and Lipchitz appeared with Raynal's text – Brancusi's photographed by himself as before, Lipchitz's spot-lit as Picasso's had been – so did the studios of Maillol and Despiau [51, 52]. The full-page photograph of Maillol's studio is a carefully composed grouping of finished pieces; but on the stand in the foreground tools have been left, and one of the smaller photographs opposite in his double-spread shows him delicately scraping at the already smooth marble flank of his *Ile de France*, finished that year, an idea he had been perfecting since 1907. Despiau also displays finished work – dominated by the seried ranks of his now-fashionable busts. Rather than tools, however, he displays himself in person to represent his artisanal identity; he is proudly seated with his production, an experienced workman, his sleeves rolled up.

Maillol and Despiau stand for the old craft of sculpture; they work in spaces that could not be further removed from the magical spaces occupied by Brancusi, Lipchitz and Picasso. Brancusi's studio stands for an idea of the artist no less prevalent among painters, as I show in Chapter 12. Brassaï's record of Picasso's studios leaves an image of a modern artistic practice that simply ignores the distinction between sculptors and painters; Picasso moves from one identity to the other as easily as his Hispano-Suiza limousine takes him from Paris to Boisgeloup.

Professionalised skills, clear distinctions between occupations and trades, these were the bedrock of both provincial and metropolitan or big-city attitudes to work in the Third Republic. They would remain basic as mass-production methods crossed the Atlantic to create the new category of 'specialised worker' in France's dynamic new industries, especially during and after the 1914–18 war (when unskilled workers were given highly differentiated repetitive tasks). They were replicated not only in the separation of the artisanal sculptor from the painter, but in the clear distinctions made between fine arts (Beaux-Arts) and the many other activities tangential to them: the decorative arts (promoted, of course, quite separately as 'art social', as shown in Chapter 1), the arts of caricature and poster-designing, of photography and film-making.

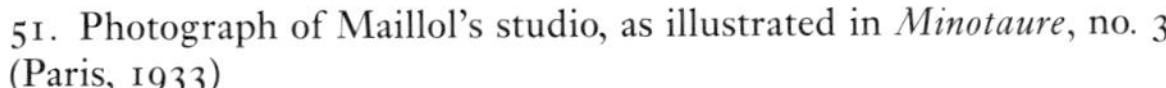
51. Photograph of Maillol's studio, as illustrated in *Minotaure*, no. 3 (Paris, 1933)

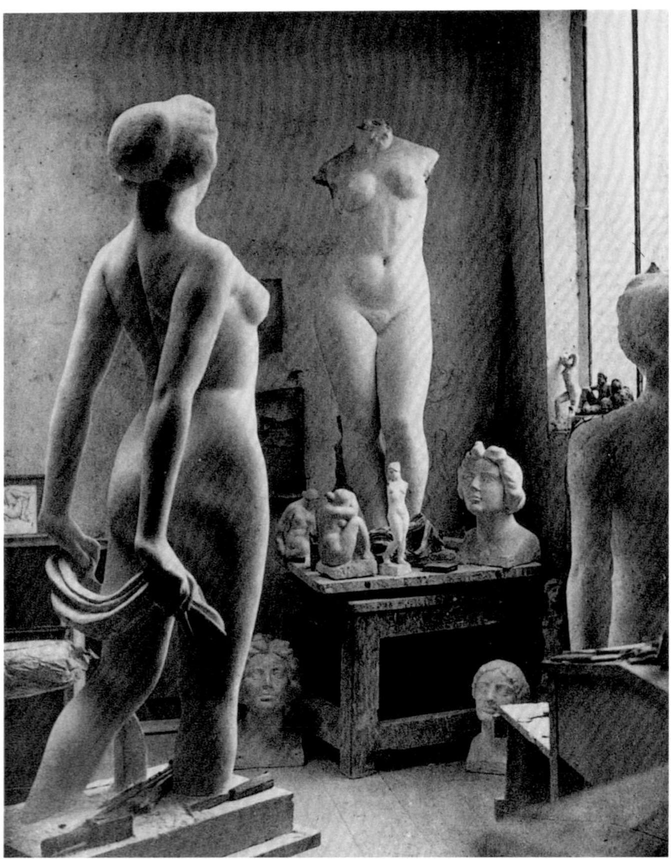

Before 1914, caricature in the popular illustrated press – periodicals like *Le Rire*, *Le Charivari* and *Assiette au beurre* – gave hundreds of artists work. Some of them moved between drawing for the magazines and painting, for instance, Kupka, Marcoussis, Villon and Gris, but a clear division was made between the two activities. There were highly respected caricature specialists, like Adolphe Willette and Jean Forain; one of Denys Puech's Paris monuments was to the nineteenth-century caricaturist Gavarni (1904). But the young and ambitious tended to become painters at the expense of caricature when they achieved the necessary support from the market. In his monograph on Gris, the dealer Kahnweiler, who made the move possible for him, represents caricature as an inferior necessity jettisoned with relief.

By 1912–13, when Gris gave up caricature for painting (slowly, not all at once), the career of caricaturist was actually less and less an alternative; photography was replacing lithography in the mass-circulation illustrated press. After his 1920 arrival in Paris, the American Man Ray would use portrait and fashion photography to support his Dada-Surrealist activities; and others, including Léger and René Magritte, designed advertising images as an occasional sideline in the 1920s and 1930s, following the late nineteenth-century example of Toulouse-Lautrec. In 1926 the middle-of-the-road independent periodical *L'Art vivant* published a regular feature on posters, the last of which recorded Léger's opinions on poster-design as 'art'.[48] By the end of the 1920s, Man Ray and others associated with Cubism and Surrealism had begun to challenge the boundaries between the practices of 'artists' and photographers or film-makers. By then, it was increasingly difficult to say what artists could or could not be.

Modernism in France did not merely unfix the categories of 'official' and 'independent' after 1914; it unfixed the categories of painter and sculptor along with many others.

POETS AND PROFESSIONALS: WRITING ON ART

Whether official or independent, whether painters or sculptors, whether respectful of orthodox categories and hierarchies or not, artists in search of a reputation needed the press; and, just as the artists' societies and the Beaux-Arts administration were mirrors of the unresolved tensions within the Third Republic, so was the art press between 1900 and the Second World War. Its immense expansion during the period parallels and complements that of the private dealer system; both were the products of a liberal market economy. The last sections of this chapter are devoted to the writers, dealers and collectors who, increasingly more than State patronage, consolidated, even created reputations for artists, above all for modernists.

The law of 29 July 1881 provided an extremely liberal legislative framework for the press. All government restrictions were removed, though the right of reply was retained. Between the 1880s and the 1900s, there was a remarkable expansion in the number, the circulation and the diversity of newspapers, journals and periodicals, and with the Dreyfus Affair at the turn of the century, the press became an acknowledged political force, capable of changing opinion. Mostly, newspapers had strong political colouring, and politicians were directly involved in the founding of several important dailies. When Picasso, Braque and Gris produced their first *papiers-collés* in 1912–14, they tended to cut up mass-circulation newspapers, in particular *Le Matin* and *Le Journal*, both of which were on the centre Right, supportive of nationalism and three-year military service, but the critics most sympathetic to them – Apollinaire, Salmon, Raynal – wrote most of all for papers on the Anarchist and Socialist Left, *L'Intransigeant*, *Paris-Journal* and *Gil Blas*.

Perhaps predictably, the critics who eulogised the great establishment artists like Bonnat, Besnard and Jean-Paul Laurens and the institutions dominated by the Ecole and academicians, above all the Artistes français, wrote for the newspapers of the Right. These varied from Royalist like *Le Gaulois* and *L'Eclair* to just stridently conservative like *L'Echo de Paris* and the mass-circulation *Le Petit-Journal*.[49] The revolutionary Royalism of *Action française* found art-critical expression in the traditionalism of Louis Dimier. And yet, the temptation to pair radical art and radical criticism with the radical Left because of press affiliation, is seriously undermined by the case of Salmon, who was happy to move from *Gil Blas* to the Royalist newspaper *Le Soleil*, in the days of hysterical nationalism just before the August 1914 declaration of war. Writers on the cultural 'Left' (as Cocteau was to call it during the war) could be politically ambivalent – or even conservative – while activists on the political Left could be firmly on the cultural 'Right'. Lampué, the politician who opened the attack on the Cubists in the Salon d'automne of 1912 by publishing his letter to the under-secretary for the Beaux-Arts in *Le Matin*, was a Socialist. Much later, in the mid-to-late 1930s, the Communist Left, led by Aragon, would use the organs of the French Communist Party (PCF), *L'Humanité* and especially the periodical *Commune*, to stand against the modernists and for an overtly traditional 'realism'.

With the expansion of the press came the professionalisation of art criticism. By the early 1900s, Arsène Alexandre and Thiébault-Sisson were supplying regular columns respectively to *Le Figaro* and *Le Temps*. From 1903, these two began to sign their pieces, and Louis Vauxcelles started his regular signed column 'La Vie artistique' in *Gil Blas*; he would keep it going to 1914, on the way, of course, naming the 'fauves' and the 'cubists', but writing on art right across the spectrum. Gaston Sauvebois, his editor, took him seriously enough to give his coverage of all four major Salons the front page in 1910. Salmon was taken on by

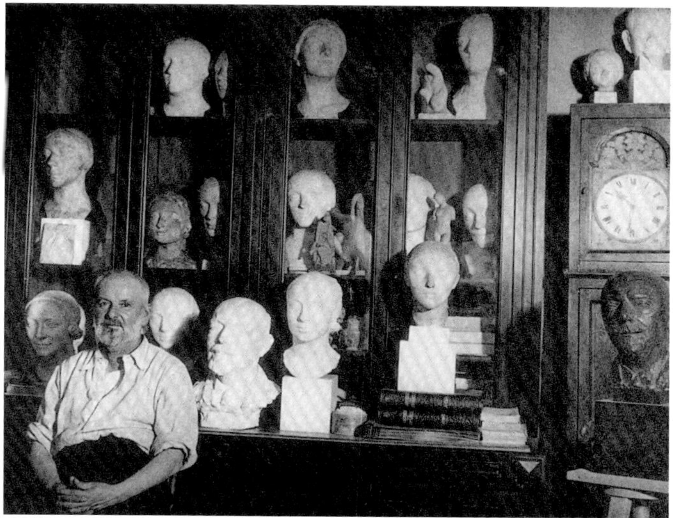

52. Photograph of Despiau in his studio, as illustrated in *Minotaure*, no. 3 (Paris, 1933)

L'Intransigeant after providing witty coverage of the Indépendants of 1909. When he moved to *Paris-Journal* as 'La Palette' early in 1910, Apollinaire replaced him, and when he moved from *Paris-Journal* to join Vauxcelles writing for *Gil Blas* in April 1912, Raynal replaced him there. By 1912, he and Vauxcelles were at the centre of a network of writers, supportive of independent art and close to independent artists, who could produce opinionated copy at speed, in quantity. They were consummate professionals, given their head by seasoned editors like Léon Bailby of *L'Intransigeant*. Salmon got to the point of producing three columns a week for *Paris-Journal*.

In 1920, Salmon published a follow-up to his *La Jeune Peinture* and *La Jeune Sculpture française*, an equally hurried survey of the scene this time from a clearly post-war vantage-point. The title he gave it stressed survival after the massacre: *L'Art vivant*, living art. He launched the book with the bold declaration: 'We have killed the old criticism.' 'It is,' he claimed, 'the criticism of the poets that has delivered the public from the most enduring prejudices.'[50] He and Apollinaire had both made their names as poets and had published first in the literary reviews, continuing as literary modernists right through to 1914 and beyond. They brought real verbal wizardry to the routines of newspaper journalism, but there can be no doubt that they helped create a new professional art-writing in France which delivered opinions more often than it offered challenging ideas or revealing word-pictures.

After 1918 (and the death of Apollinaire), bread-and-butter criticism moved to new weeklies alongside the dailies: Salmon wrote for the weeklies *L'Europe nouvelle* and *La Revue de France*; Vauxcelles for a weekly that gave him an unusual amount of space, *Le Carnet de la semaine* (all of them had comparatively large circulations); Raynal wrote for *L'Intransigeant* from 1921 to 1928. After 1914, Raynal had no pretensions to be a poet, but there is a clear distinction between his newspaper columns and the searching, laboriously thought-through pieces he wrote for avant-garde outlets like *L'Esprit nouveau* or Léonce Rosenberg's *L'Effort moderne* monographs. He could write with the kind of intensity and commitment found in the most ambitious art-writing of the poets Reverdy and Apollinaire, and, like Apollinaire, he could made a clear distinction between professional journalism and the critically engaged. In *L'Art vivant*, as in his little books on 'young' art of 1912 and 1919, Salmon could produce moments of real critical excitement – as in his passages on Picasso's *Demoiselles d'Avignon* and his metal *Guitar* – but his daily and weekly columns rarely offered more than the judgemental professionalism he affected to despise.

The crucial distinction in writing on art was not so much that between poet-critics and professional critics, as that between those engaged in critical combat from within groups or movements and those operating as disengaged observers, open to everything. Here too, we encounter the pull between the democratic belief in diversity and the compulsive need to direct developments. By the end of the 1920s, this had developed into a stand-off between professional journalism, whether written by poets or not, and the committed writing of those artists, poets and polemicists who contributed to the engaged modernist periodicals: the one encouraging diversity, the other pointing the way.

Diversity promoted by professional criticism was to be encountered not just in the large-circulation dailies and weeklies, but in the new illustrated art magazines of the 1920s. They used half-tone photographic reproduction and large formats to attract a wide audience of exhibition-goers and collectors to independent art in the most all-inclusive sense. The leaders here were *L'Amour de l'art*, founded in 1920, which started out under Vauxcelles' editorship, and *L'Art vivant*, which grew out of the middle-brow *Nouvelles littéraires*, and was described as 'the domaine' of Jacques Guenne and an early exponent of the artists' interview, Florent Fels.[51] Both these periodicals stood for a determinedly non-avant-garde position, against what they represented as the intellectual abstraction of 'pure' Cubism and the literary impurities of Surrealism, but also against what was represented as the repression of the academics. Their diversity was not that of Dujardin-Beaumetz and Paul Léon, it did not embrace Bonnat and Puech; it embraced instead the now widening range of independent styles shorn of the academics, from Bonnard and Denis to Picasso. The leading moderns were taken seriously, but as individuals contributing to a cornucopia of styles, not as -ism ideologues. One of the post-war professionals produced in this context was Waldemar George, who followed Vauxcelles as editor of *L'Amour de l'art* in 1924. Like Raynal on *L'Intransigeant*, George was actually a committed champion of the Cubists, before advancing (as he saw it) to the so-called 'Neo-Humanism' of *Formes*, the periodical he ran between 1930 and 1933. George on *L'Amour de l'art* and Raynal on *L'Intransigeant*, were in their different ways careful to mute their partisan convictions and to promote breadth of coverage. It is telling that they were both replaced because they were considered not plural enough (George in 1927, Raynal in 1928).

Nothing could be further from these disparate collections of reproductions and opinions than the concentrated sense of purpose found in the avant-garde periodicals of the inter-war period, especially those that revolved around or were published from within the post-Cubist and post-Dada modern movements. These included the painter Ozenfant and the architect Le Corbusier's so-called Purist *L'Esprit nouveau* (1920–5), Van Doesburg's *De Stijl* and *Art concret*, Seuphor's *Cercle et carré*, and especially *La Révolution surréaliste*, *Documents* and *Le Surréalisme au service de la révolution*. Texts and illustrations here worked together actually to *make* the movements they represented by means of the ongoing succession of their numbers. The writing in these periodicals explicitly operates to exclude as well as include; there is no professional's willingness either to appeal to the prejudices of the reader or to compromise so as not to lose the reader. A major reason for Breton's exclusion of Roger Vitrac and Robert Desnos from the Surrealist group in 1929 was their decision to earn money from journalism. Desnos's professional writing for newspapers like *Paris-Soir* had, asserted Breton in the *Second Manifesto*, devoured Desnos the poet.[52]

Among the art magazines looking for a wider readership in the 1920s was *Cahiers d'art*, founded and edited throughout a long life that ran from 1926 far beyond 1945 by Christian Zervos, a Paris-based Greek. Zervos, it could be said, professionalised engaged modernist writing and publishing in France. He was the art press equivalent of the new pro-modernist curators of the mid-to-late 1930s epitomised by Jean Cassou (who wrote on occasion for *Cahiers d'art*). Zervos managed to combine cultural radicalism with professionalism as editor and critic to a degree not anticipated by the divided early 1920s practices of Raynal and Waldemar George, and so did his early associate on *Cahiers d'art*, Tériade. Working with the publisher Albert Skira, Tériade was even able to professionalise the publishing of Breton and his group; it was he who collaborated with Breton to place Surrealism in the lavishly illustrated setting of *Minotaure* from 1933.

Especially after 1918, the art press was rarely free of the art market in France, and this applies not just to critics like Vauxcelles and George, who regularly worked with dealers, but to the art press at its most combative. The lives of the modernists, whether artists or polemicists, were tightly interwoven with the lives and interests of dealers and collectors. After the young dealer Paul Guillaume started his own periodical, *Les Arts à Paris* in 1916, dealers' periodicals increasingly involved independent critics, and these could be highly combative. Certainly the most controlled convergence of an aesthetic and a commercial campaign in this form was Léonce Rosenberg's *Bulletin de l'effort moderne* (1924–8), which combined sequences of black-and-white plates to advertise Rosenberg's stock with the principled publication of major theoretical texts by leading critics, above all Raynal, and by the leading gallery artists, Gleizes, Mondrian and Léger included.

There is nothing surprising in so interactive a relationship between key modernist theorists and a key modernist dealer, for the dynamism of the dealers was the engine of modernism. It was the art market that provided the thrust behind the eventual ascendancy of the moderns over the painters and sculptors of the Artistes français and the Nationale. In the long term, the private market proved an altogether more powerful stimulus than the market provided by the State, with its museum collections, its grand commissions and its final accolade, the Légion d'honneur.

WINNING FOR MODERNISM: THE DEALERS AND COLLECTORS

The fortnightly *L'Art vivant* was a convivial combination of the opinionated and the newsy. The perfect vehicle for this was the 'Enquête' (Enquiry), a genre much used in newspaper and magazine journalism in the 1920s: the publication of the replies of leading opinion-formers to a set of leading questions on a topical issue. In 1925 *L'Art vivant* ran an Enquête on whether there should be a new Musée français d'art moderne decisively oriented towards independent art and what form it should take. By the time Georges Charensol summed up the results in October sixty-three replies had been published since July from artists, critics, dealers, collectors and curators. Many – for instance, the artists Gleizes and Kisling – dismissed the idea of museums altogether as utterly inimical to independent art; but thirty-six wanted such a museum and around a dozen of these wanted a museum completely free of the State. The dealer Paul Guillaume contemptuously dismissed the State's curators as 'those parasites of politics who we call euphemistically civil servants', but he was vague about who should take over from them, averring only that they should be sufficiently 'intelligent, informed, disinterested, passionate and impartial'.[53] For the collectors Dr Tzanck and the Belgian René Gaffé it was clear who these paragons were: the collectors. In 1923, Tzanck had formed a 'Société des Amateurs et Collectionneurs' whose central project was just such a privately run museum. Its collection was to be formed from gifts and loans; Guillaume too wanted private generosity altogether to replace State patronage.

Such a museum was founded in New York in 1929, the Museum of Modern Art, which would become Alfred H. Barr's headquarters of international modernism in the 1930s. The only attempt at such a thing in France would be the Musée d'art vivant founded in 1937, the initiative of an alliance of dealers, critics, curators and collectors led by the dealer Jeanne Bucher. It consisted of a loan collection exhibited at the Communist Maison de la culture on the rue d'Anjou; there was work by artists as important as Matisse, Picasso, Braque, Bonnard, Arp, Laurens and Lipchitz. It survived for just six months. Tzanck's and Bucher's initiatives and *L'Art vivant*'s Enquête are markers of one major development: the exponential growth of the art market and the clear linkage of that growth to the national and international hegemony of modernism. Barr's modern movements developed with and partly because of the international art market, a system which can seem diametrically opposed to the institutions of the State. The broad truth of this sometimes invites a simple-minded alignment of modernism with free-market capitalism against the collectivist Left. The importance of starting by avoiding such simple political equations is underlined by the conjunction between the dealer Jeanne Bucher and the Maison de la culture; she herself was sympathetic to the Left, and several leading figures in her private enterprise museum were Communist or Socialist Party sympathisers and members, including Cassou and the distinguished scientist collector, Henri Laugier, a regular client of hers.[54]

The emerging importance of the dealers is demonstrated by the fact that in France during the early 1920s, gallery exhibitions took over from the Salons of the artists' societies as the spaces in which to show in order to make an impact. In 1926 Vauxcelles could write of leading artists refusing to send to the Indépendants, commenting that its 'star' was 'fading'.[55] These abstentions were triggered by changes in its organisation, but artists would not have left what had been *the* exhibition space for the new, if there had not been more effective alternatives. The ultimate international success of 'modern art' would be consolidated by the Museum of Modern Art in New York, but it was a success kick-started by the energy of dealers who managed its export across Europe and the Atlantic with a risk-taking élan found only in the most dynamic of new French industries after 1900.

The beginnings of this development were little and local, though by the late nineteenth century there were major Parisian galleries exporting recent French art for high prices, notably Durand-Ruel which had already given Impressionism its international profile by the mid-1890s. In the early years of the century, the successful artists of the Nationale and the Artistes français showed in the plush retail spaces of such galleries: besides Durand-Ruel, the galerie Georges Petit, for instance, and, especially influential, the galerie Bernheim-Jeune, run by Gaston and Josse Bernheim with the critic Félix Fénéon as manager. In the first decade of the century, Bernheim-Jeune followed up the emergence of the Nabis in the 1890s and the Fauves in 1905–7 by taking on a select few of their leading figures: first of all Bonnard and Vuillard, then, in 1909, Matisse. But it was not with such major enterprises that Salmon's 'young' painters, including Matisse, first found exhibition spaces outside the Indépendants and the Salon d'automne; it was with small, fledgling enterprises, one or two of which would become big enough to challenge even the Bernheims between the wars.

In 1905 the galerie Weill put on a group show including many of the Fauves alongside their famous display at the Salon d'automne. At that date Berthe Weill's was one of only two galleries (properly speaking) which showed 'young' contemporary art in Paris. The other was Ambroise Vollard's, which had already given Picasso and Matisse their first solo shows (1901 and 1904); Vollard had built an Impressionist stock in the 1890s and an unrivalled stock of Cézanne and Gauguin. Besides them, there were one or two outlets that were closer to bric-a-brac shops than galleries, like Père Soulier's and Clovis Sagot's in Montmartre, and that was all.

Collectors looking for new independent painting kept in touch with the Souliers and the Sagots, sometimes introducing themselves into the milieux of the artists, or hunting through the thousands of works on show at the Indépendants and the Salon d'automne, buying directly from the studios much more than from dealers. The Americans in Paris Gertrude and Leo Stein made their first purchases of Picasso and Matisse directly from them in 1905 and 1906 respectively; it was through the two collectors that the artists first met in 1906. Gertrude and Leo, and their brother Michael with his wife Sarah, would buy both directly and at the galleries from then on. Perhaps the most systematic such collector, André Level, also bought both directly in the studios and from the galleries; he bought from Bernheim-Jeune as well as Vollard and Weill. Level's buying was systematic because it was a business venture. He presided over a group of thirteen partners, four of them his relations, who from 1904 collectively invested 2,500 francs a year for ten years, with an eye on an auction-house profit; they called themselves the 'Peau de l'ours' (Skin of the Bear). By 1907, he had bought Matisse, Marquet, Manguin and Puy from among the Fauves, as well as Picasso. At the Hôtel Drouot Peau de l'ours Sale on 2 March 1914, there were ten Matisses and twelve Picassos. The profit realised was spectacular enough to be news; it was the first comprehensive public demonstration of the market potential of modernism. The 145 paintings sold for 116,545 francs on an outlay of just 27,500 francs, giving a gain, after expenses had been deducted, of 75,845 francs. Picasso's *Family of Saltimbanques* (1904) sold for 12,650 francs having cost 1,000 francs [53]. To their eternal credit, the Peau de l'ours partnership agreed to cede 20% of their profit to the artists, a decade before legislation in France established a 'droit de suite' for artists.[56] The entire operation, with its combination of passion and calculation, profit and generous patronage, sums up the contradictions that would be inherent in the interaction between commerce and independent artists from the pre-1914 period on. Indeed, Level as an individual sums up those contradictions: he thought of himself as a collector, but became a dealer too in the 1920s, as the main backer of the galerie Percier.

Vollard and Berthe Weill provided models for new gallery ventures before 1914, and by that date the potential of the market for independent art was obvious enough to have produced a scattering of new small galleries ready to invest in 'young painting'. The most daring and, in its business methods, the most innovative had been opened in 1907 by a young well-capitalised German from Mannheim, Daniel-Henry (Daniel-Heinrich) Kahnweiler. He was already buying from Matisse, Vlaminck, Derain, Van Dongen and Braque that year, and put on the Braque exhibition that introduced the term 'cubist' into the critical vocabulary in November 1908. Unlike Berthe Weill, however, he was not to use selling on commission from temporary exhibitions as his basic strategy; his model was Vollard, and from 1909 he concentrated on building an unequalled stock of what he considered the most important new painting, selling just enough to keep his operation viable. By that date he was buying in quantity from Picasso, who was selling also to Vollard, Sagot and another young German, Wilhelm Uhde. In 1910, he bought sixty Picassos. He did not advertise, he did not even put his stock in the window of his little gallery on the rue Vignon; he did not need to, the press created the necessary interest, especially Apollinaire and Salmon in *L'Intransigeant* and *Paris-Journal*. Indeed, he was one of the first to discourage his artists from showing in the Salons, as mentioned in Chapter 2. From the outset, he thought in terms of the exclusive, not diversity. He sold to a small circle of clients, including Gertrude and Leo Stein, Roger Dutilleul and an old friend, Hermann Rupf from Bern. Between 1910 and 1914, he lent work by his artists prodigiously outside France, starting in Munich and Cologne, but by 1912–13 he was sending pictures across the Channel to London, across the Atlantic to New York and across the Steppes to Moscow. His aim was the creation of an international market as big as the one already built for Impressionism; he contributed significantly to the groundwork that made possible the international success of modernism between the wars.

But what was especially new about Kahnweiler was the fact that he was critically and aesthetically engaged with his artists to an unprecedented degree; he was an intellectual as well as a businessman, one of those who turned the avant-garde project towards critique (in his case, aesthetic not social or political critique). Like them, he profited from and yet resisted the -ism labels; Picasso and Braque were the Cubists least involved in Cubism as a public movement, and, when he took them on, Gris and Léger loosened their attachment to it. On the surface, he lived a perfectly correct bourgeois life in his apartment on the rue George-Sand, and he sited his gallery in the rue Vignon close to the great galleries of the Right Bank, but he was intensely involved with his artists, thinking through with them the implications of what they were doing. Picasso photographed him in his studio in 1911, just as he did other friends of his, including Salmon [54]; they were all the same generation. The contracts he signed with Picasso, Braque, Derain, Gris and Léger in 1912–13, not only gave him the exclusive right to all their production, it gave them each a monthly salary, binding them into a close, almost family circle of aesthetic risk-takers.[57]

Exiled from France during the 1914–18 war, because of his German nationality, Kahnweiler lost his entire stock to the French government, which auctioned it with that of Wilhelm Uhde, another independent dealer, between 1921 and 1923. On his return to Paris in 1920, he continued as a major dealer, with a French business partner André Simon to protect him against the risk of future sequestrations. He rebuilt his stock and his relations with many of his pre-1914 artists, and he took on new artists, most notably Henri Laurens, the Cubist sculptor who emerged during the war, and his one Surrealist, Masson, but it was not he who was most significantly behind the conclusive international success of modernism.

The major figures after 1918 were Paul Guillaume and the brothers Léonce and Paul Rosenberg. They were young too: like Kahnweiler, from the generation of the Cubists. The Rosenbergs were the sons of a successful dealer, Alexandre; they had separated and divided their inheritance in 1910. Their strategies were distinct, and so were their fortunes. Léonce, starting with Picasso in 1915, took over Kahnweiler's Cubists, and by 1919 was contracted with or buying from most of the artists in France associated with Cubism. His galerie de l'Effort Moderne was conceived as a centre from which to mastermind the aesthetic takeover of European modernism by a disciplined Cubism in tune with 'tradition'. Paul was in secret partnership with the immensely wealthy Impressionist and Old Master dealer Georges Wildenstein, and combined building a substantial stock of nineteenth-century art with contracting the moderns who he believed had the most commercial potential. He started by taking over Picasso from Léonce

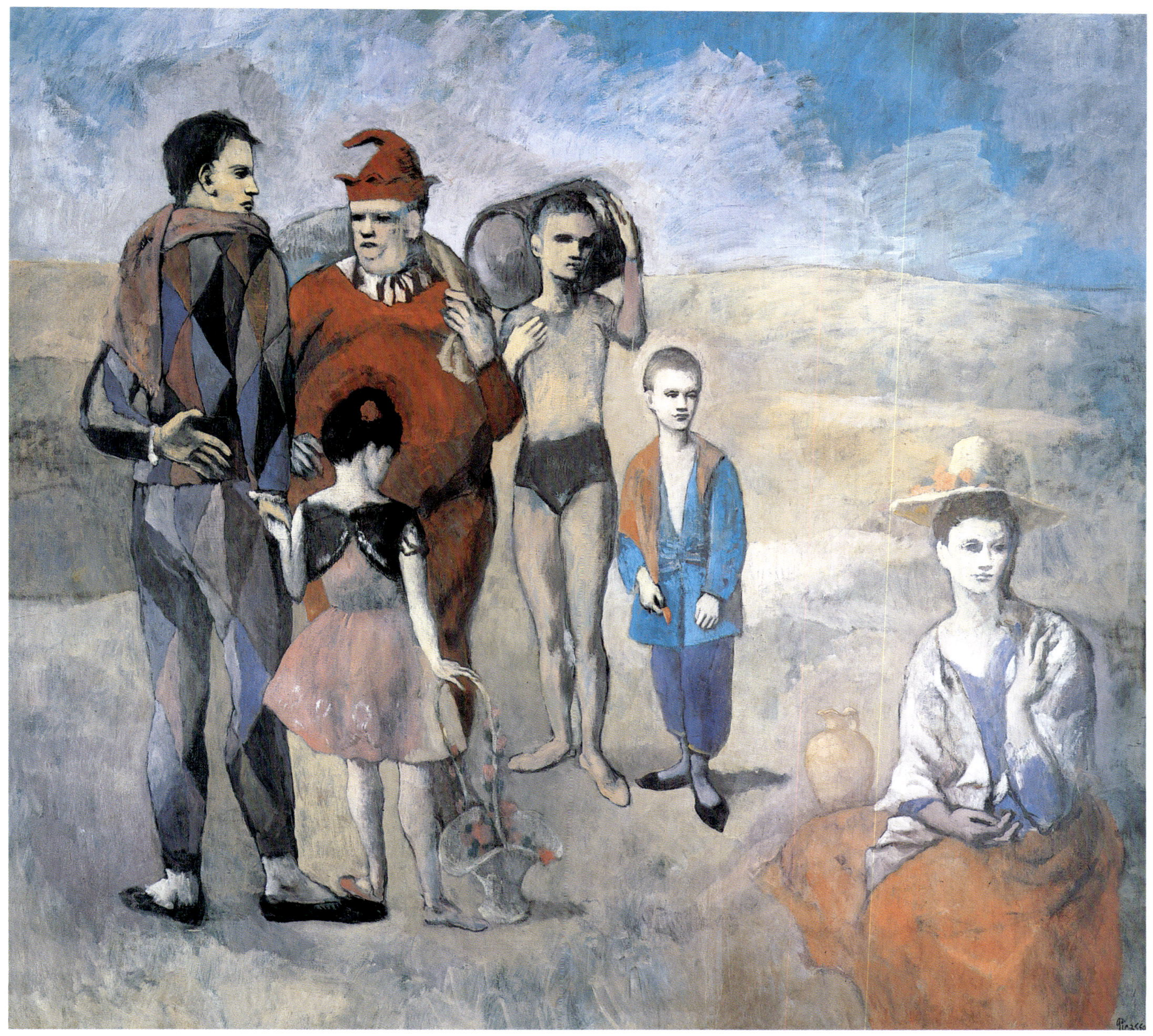

53. Pablo Picasso, *Family of Saltimbanques*, 1905. Oil on canvas, 212.8 × 229.6 cm. National Gallery of Art, Washington D.C. Chester Dale Collection

early in 1919, and during the 1920s gave contracts to Marie Laurencin, Braque and Léger (who switched from Léonce in 1928). Léonce wrote dogged aesthetics besides publishing his *Bulletin de l'effort moderne* and attempted to impose intellectual discipline as well as tight contracts on his artists. Paul kept aloof from theory and offered real money to his chosen few; he joined the line of the well-connected fashionable dealers like Gaston and Josse Bernheim. Paul would weather the Depression in the early 1930s, Léonce would not.[58]

The case of Guillaume is distinct. His career amounted to the ideal middle-class ascent; the son of petty-bourgeois first-generation Parisians, he transformed himself into a grand-bourgeois socialite, his mansion-museum at 20, Avenue de Méssine, a public display of big-spending consumerism at its most stylish and exclusive. On the way, he operated at every conceivable level as a dealer, so that his career offers a sort of typology of dealing in Paris in the early twentieth century. He started as one of the very first to deal in African art, buying and selling without a gallery, initially as an employee in a luxury car salesroom. Encouraged by Apollinaire's support and his widening acquaintance among the artists of Montmartre, he opened a little gallery at 6, rue Miromesnil in 1914, buying artists like Modigliani and de Chirico alongside tribal art. Unlike others who started in a small way before and after 1914 (Charles Vildrac in 1912 or Pierre Loeb and Jeanne Bucher in 1924 and 1925 for instance) he saw the importance of a smart address from the beginning. During the war, he added Derain to his artists, an important gain, dealing from an apartment in the sought-

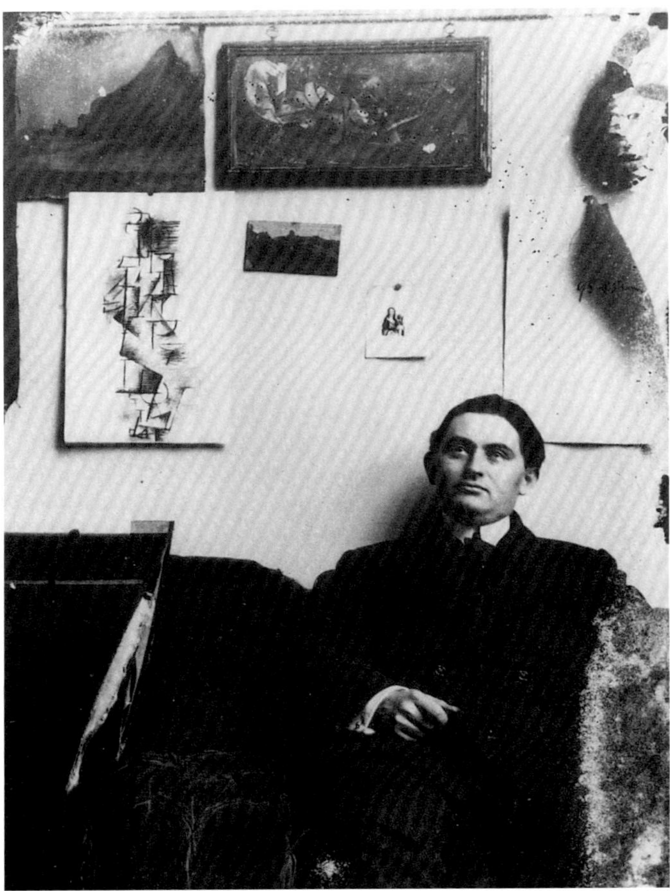

54. Pablo Picasso, *D-H. Kahnweiler in Picasso's studio*, 1911. Photograph

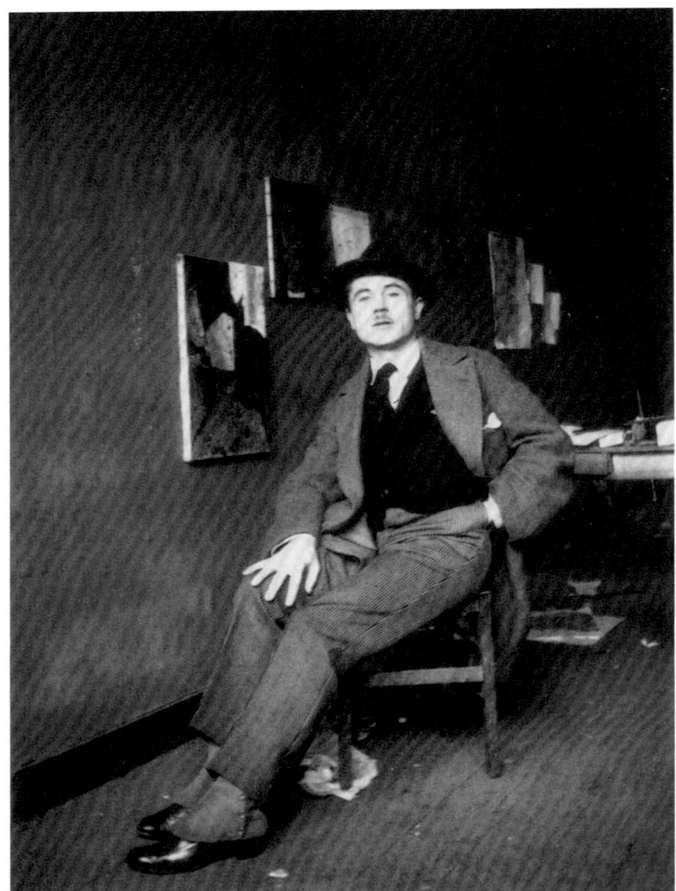

55. Amedeo Modigliani, *Paul Guillaume in Modigliani's studio*, 1915. Photograph

after Avenue de Villiers, before opening a better-appointed gallery at 128 rue Faubourg Saint Honoré in 1917 and finally in 1921 moving to luxuriously appointed premises on the rue La Boétie, by then the centre of the fashionable Right Bank art trade. Paul Rosenberg's gallery was on the same street, and Léonce's close by in a town house on the rue de Baume. Most small galleries selling the moderns in the 1920s were on the Left Bank, around the rue de Seine or in Montparnasse; Guillaume was both a small and a big dealer on the Right Bank. He would add Soutine and Lipchitz to his artists in the 1920s, and all three of them would profit hugely from the intensive buying and commissioning campaigns of the American educationalist-collector Dr Albert Barnes from 1923.[59]

In 1915, Guillaume and Modigliani took photographs of each other in the studio the dealer had rented for his protegé on the rue Ravignan in Montmartre. Modigliani's photograph of Guillaume [55], and the photograph Picasso took of Kahnweiler in his studio four years earlier [54], can sum up the contradictions inherent in the relationships between engaged modernist dealers and their artists. Guillaume, friend of Apollinaire and Max Jacob, habitué around 1910 of the same Montmartre cafés, is welcome in such a stark bohemian space as this; but, in his sharply cut suit and spats, his jaunty pose cannot conceal his awkwardness. Kahnweiler too was welcome in Picasso's messy studio on the Boulevard de Clichy, and strikes a more relaxed reflective attitude, but his sombre stockbroker's suit and stiff collar jar against the casual confusion around him. Their engagement with the work of their artists was real, and in Kahnweiler's case deep, but it was their commercial acumen that brought them and their artists success. They moved between artists who they thought of as working in a space outside society, above commerce, and operations driven by the most concrete appreciation of the artwork's potential as a commodity.

The very early 1920s brought a brief downturn while the flooding of the market by the Uhde and Kahnweiler Sales depressed prices for Cubist art between 1921 and 1923, but by the mid-1920s the market was booming. The French economy as a whole may not have regained the zest of the 1910–14 period, but, even allowing for inflation, in 1926 prices across the whole range of independent art, including the Cubists, were moving far ahead of their levels at the Peau de l'ours Sale. A key demonstration was the Paris sale on 28 October that year of a major part of the huge collection formed by an American lawyer John Quinn, who had died in 1925. He had used a French agent H.P. Roché to help him buy especially remarkable groups of Picassos and Brancusis in the early 1920s. Paul Guillaume set a record for Picasso, paying 79,000 francs for a neo-classical Picasso at the Palais Galliéra section of the sale; Matisse's *Blue Nude* [283] sold for 101,000 francs; and the Douanier Rousseau's *Sleeping Gypsy* for a staggering 520,000 francs. The prices were discussed in the art press with astonished relish. Three years later, in 1928, the Vicomte de Noailles would pay Kahnweiler 175,000 francs for a Picasso. Huge profits were made by collectors as well as dealers.

It was on the back of the 1920s art-market boom that Guillaume and the Rosenbergs developed their international strategies. In 1923, Paul Rosenberg and his partner Wildenstein launched an ambitious solo Picasso show in New York and Chicago, which was planned as the spearhead of a sustained campaign in the States. Léonce watched carefully, planning his own travelling show of Léger. Paul set his prices too high, however, and the Picassos did not sell, so his brother set aside the Léger project and both of them concentrated through the mid- and late twenties on selling to American collectors in Paris. New York shows were organised by dealers and agents like Michael Brenner, Joseph Brummer and Marcel Duchamp, but Guillaume and Kahnweiler also chose to concentrate more on selling to Americans in Paris than across the Atlantic. And the Americans came to buy: Quinn, Barnes, Chester Dale (by the end of the 1920s) and many others. Collectors and dealers from across Europe converged on Paris too, as they had before 1914, but in Europe the big Paris dealers worked differently, Kahnweiler opening up the market in the Weimar Republic by putting on shows with his German-based partner Flechtheim, for instance, Léonce Rosenberg putting on exhibitions and sales in Rome or Geneva or Amsterdam.

Though the effects of the Depression on France were belated and muted, the international character of the market in modernism ensured that it would be hit. Smaller dealers disappeared – Jeanne Bucher was out of action between 1932 and 1935; and even the big and successful lowered their profiles – having bought thirty-nine Picassos between April 1929 and April 1930, Paul Rosenberg bought just one Picasso a year for the next three years.[60] But the platform for French modernism's international success had been laid firmly enough; Alfred Barr made his crucial trips to Europe prior to the great Museum of Modern Art exhibitions of 1936 in the depressed early thirties, and in those years artists like Ernst, Magritte and Léger followed Picasso with their first New York solo shows.

The great American collectors of modernism in the twenties built survey collections with agendas. Dr Barnes and A.E. Gallatin actually turned them into instructive displays, Barnes at his foundation in Merrion outside Philadelphia built in the mid-1920s, Gallatin with his Museum of Living Art in New York University. They anticipated and then echoed Alfred H. Barr's ruthless drive to cut through the plurality of developments in Europe, especially France, to produce a diagrammatic history of movements. In France there were one or two collectors who were engaged enough with particular movements to build collections with clear agendas. The Swiss banker Raoul La Roche built such a collection of Cubist and Purist work before 1925, advised by the Purists Ozenfant and Le Corbusier themselves. But the public images of the major collectors most committed to modernism had more to do with the living of desirable lifestyles than with any instructive aesthetic ideal; La Roche's display of dedication to an aesthetic even to the point of austerity was rare [188].

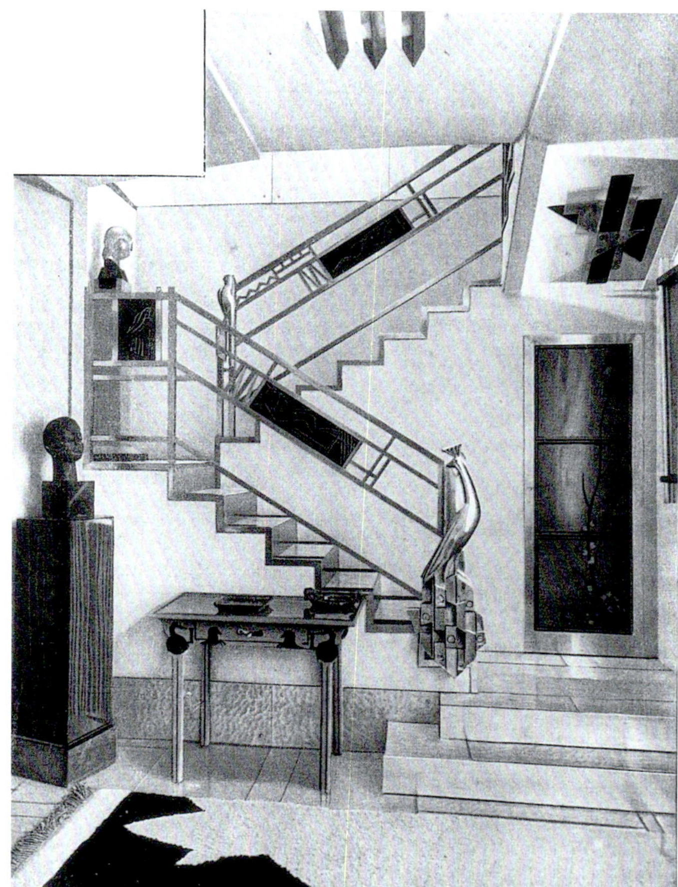

56. Josef Czaky, Staircase, Jacques Doucet's Studio House, rue Saint-James, Neuilly, 1928

In October 1929, the couturier Jacques Doucet, one of the style-makers of the late nineteenth and early twentieth century, died; he was in his late seventies. In 1930, the mass-circulation *L'Illustration* ran a photographic feature on the studio house in the rue Saint-James, Neuilly, into which he had moved in 1928. The fashion magazine *Fémina* had done the same for his far more palatial apartment at 46, Avenue du Bois in 1925. What readers saw here was the perfectly designed environment of the model consumer: an individualist with the means to construct a total image of himself by applying aesthetic judgement through exacting patronage and purchase. At Neuilly, Léonce Rosenberg's sculptor Josef Csaky designed a staircase under Doucet's close supervision above which Picasso's *Demoiselles d'Avignon* hung framed by the Deco-Cubist bookbinder and designer Pierre Legrain [56]. Doucet's studio was entered through a great iron and glass double-door designed by Lalique, one of the stars of the 1925 Exhibition, and the Cubist sculptor Lipchitz had designed a shallow-cut relief for the pink-marble chimney piece. Besides Picassos, paintings by Matisse, Ernst, Miró and Picabia hung in this small gem of a building, designed as a frame for art, ancient and exotic as well as brave and modern.[61]

In 1928, the established decorative arts periodical *Art et décoration* published a photographic feature on the Vicomte and Vicomtesse de Noailles' Villa at Hyères, where the indoor swimming pool, designed largely by the Vicomte himself, had just been completed. The building was the work of the most prominent modern-movement architect at the 1925 Exhibition, Robert Mallet-Stevens [57]. The de Noailles were outrageously modern, but without the austerity of a Raoul La Roche; they stood for youth as well as wealth. In 1929, articles were to appear in *Vogue* on the vigorous fitness routines in which Charles and Marie-Laure led their guests at Hyères. What is more, they combined a taste for the extremes of Cubism, Surrealism and architectural modernism with the maintainance of the Vicomtesse's inherited Parisian mansion, an 'hôtel' of unrivalled opulence filled not only with their Picassos, Légers and, from 1929, their Dalís, but with an inherited Old Master collection too. Dalí was to recall his pleasure at seeing his painting *The Dismal Sport* between a Cranach and a Watteau in the hôtel on the Place des Etats-Unis. Though aristocrats, the de Noailles offered another model for the aspirant middle classes, again one where designing the spaces for collections could become a kind of self-portraiture, revealing the daring of individuals willing to make choices: the expression of identity by the consumption of art.[62]

The art historian Malcolm Gee has surveyed both the dealers and the collectors in France before the Depression. Among the collectors, he has drawn distinctions between confident aristocratic and upper-middle-class figures, like the de Noailles or Doucet, La Roche or Level, and lesser figures – professionals like the dentist Dr Tzanck and the medical practicioner Dr Girardin – who tended to buy less narrowly and more conservatively. Collecting was a pursuit whose diversity demonstrates in itself the plurality of the middle and upper middle classes in France, as well as the continuing attractions of the aristocracy as a focus for aspiration. Yet, equally revealing is the ease with which categories could become unfixed in the practices of dealing and collecting, just as they could in the practices of avant-garde artists. Collectors and dealers could be patrons as well as buyers of modern art. Doucet financed Pierre Reverdy's little magazine *Nord-Sud*, and funded the making of the prototype for Duchamp's *Rotative Demisphere* in 1924–5. Wildenstein financed Georges Bataille's *Documents* in 1929–30, paid Masson an allowance in the mid-1930s, and lent Breton his galerie des Beaux-Arts for the International Surrealist Exhibition in 1938. The most daring collectors of modernism could also be daring patrons of film: Doucet began to form a collection of films and film-scenarios in 1927; the de Noailles staged screenings of Man Ray's as well as Buñuel's and Dalí's films under the Sicilian Baroque ceiling of the ballroom in their Paris mansion, and paid a cool million to

57. Robert Mallet-Stevens, *The De Noailles Villa*, Hyères, 1923–8. Exterior of the swimming pool and gymasium

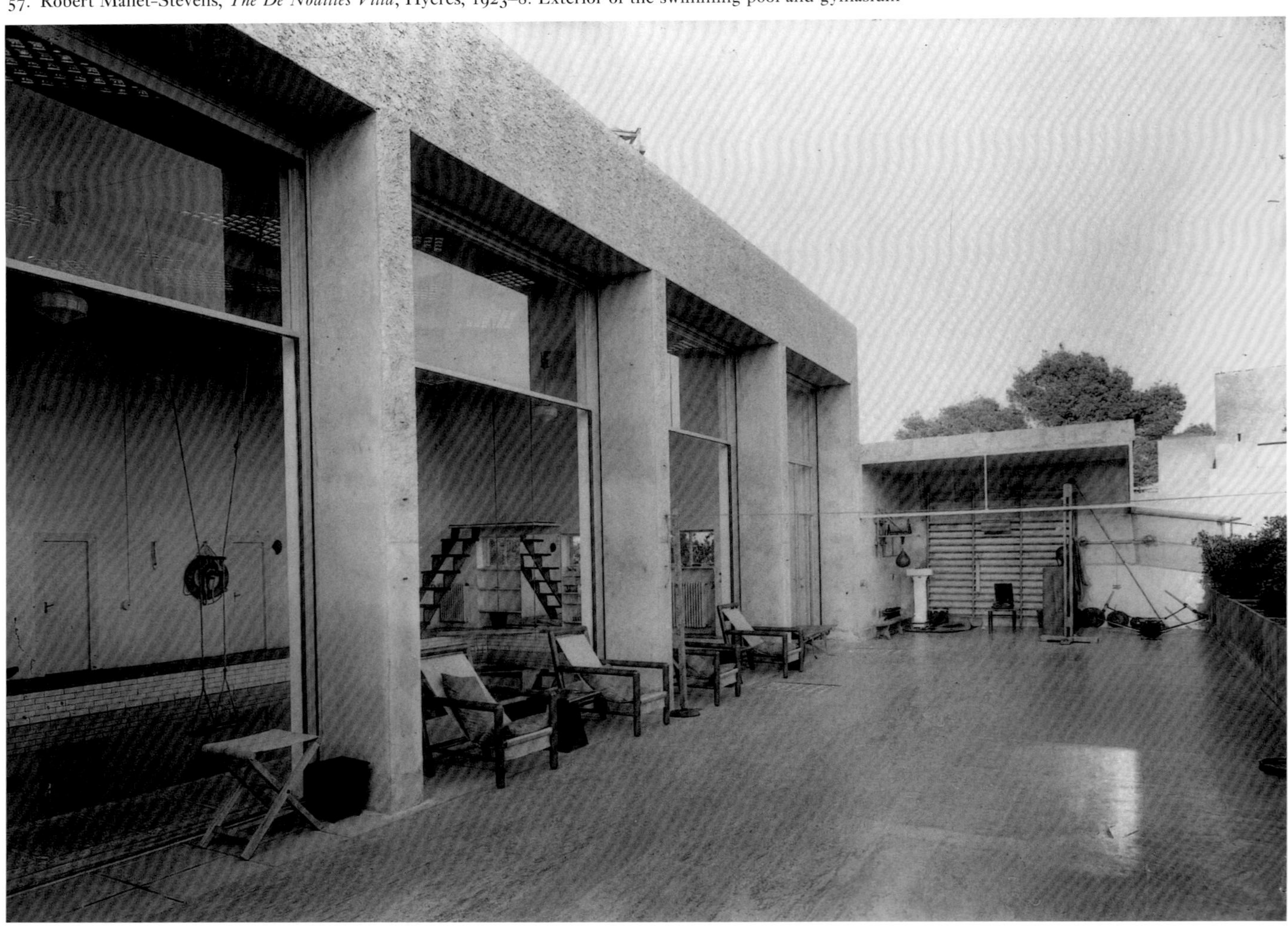

finance the Spaniards' full-length *L'Age d'or* in 1929. Modernism could certainly provoke a willingness to cross boundaries among its supporters.

At the same time, just as collectors could become dealers and dealers collectors, artists and writers could become collectors and even dealers. Nothing could more clearly bring out both the degree to which the making of art and the art market became enmeshed together during the period, nor the contradictions inherent in this process and in the lives of independent artists under the Third Republic. There were artists known for their collecting; Guillaume admired not only Lipchitz the sculptor but Lipchitz the discerning collector, who bought Delacroix and Watteau as well as African and Cubist art. Marcel Duchamp, as we shall see in Chapter 4, speculated on the art market and intermittently operated as a dealer from 1926; Charles Vildrac continued to publish his poetry when he set up a gallery on the rue de Seine in 1912; and even Paul Guillaume found time to paint as a part-time Cubist. But the most telling case of all is that of André Breton, who consistently used *La Révolution surréaliste* as a platform from which to attack speculation in the art market, while himself buying from the studios, in the galleries and at auction, and for brief periods coming close to being an out-and-out dealer. Between late 1920 and 1926, his and Aragon's advice directed Doucet's buying – he was behind the purchase of the *Demoiselles d'Avignon* (1923–4). And in 1926–8 and in 1938–9, he opened his own small Left Bank galleries, the galerie Surréaliste and the galerie Gradiva, which combined hard-headed (not necessarily successful) commerce with a Surrealist agenda. This way, Breton could promote the distribution through society of what Aragon described in 1926 as the drug of Surrealism, and help finance a Surrealist way of life for himself and artists like Tanguy.[63]

Breton's continually changing collection, installed in the two studio-apartments he successively occupied in Pigalle, at 42, rue Fontaine [58], created a transgressive counterpart to the desirable spaces of consumption designed by Doucet and the de Noailles. It became a changing image of the free operation of desire as Bretonian Surrealism conceived it, collapsing conventional categories even in its earliest stages in the 1920s to bring together modern paintings and sculptures not only with tribal and popular images but also with the most disparate objects salvaged from everyday life. It provided an alternative space for an alternative life lived against the middle-class grain, and yet this was a life funded at crucial moments by profit in a buoyant art market. Independent art almost never escaped the market in France between 1900 and 1940; and neither did independent artists.

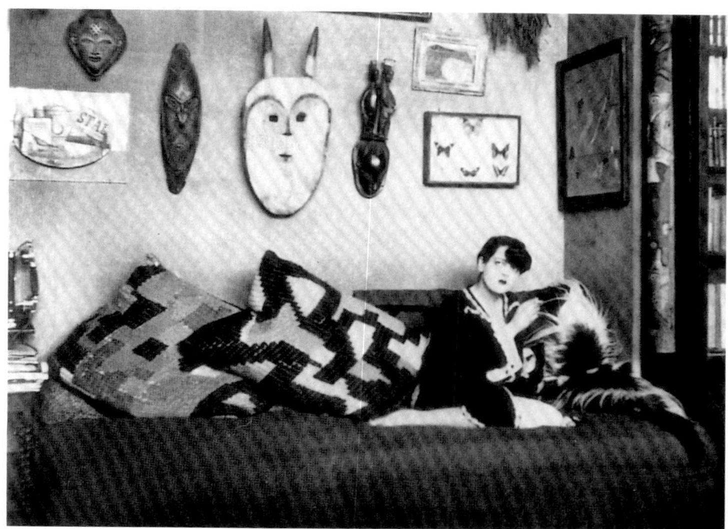

58. Simone Breton in André Breton's apartment at 42, rue Fontaine, Paris, *c.* 1927

CHAPTER 4

Celebrated Lives

THE CONDITIONS OF SUCCESS

In 1927, *L'Art vivant* followed up its Enquête on the desirability of a museum of modern art, with another which asked whether 'money, commerce, speculation' had a good or bad influence on art, and whether 'spiritual creators' (artists) were to be placed on the same plane as 'manual labourers'. Many, especially the dealers who replied, could see no problem, since art with 'quality' was by definition independent of monetary motivations, and was obviously superior to 'work'. The consensus view was that the thriving market which had reached its peak by the late 1920s had delivered freedom of creative action to those artists independent ('true') enough to grow with it.[1]

The twentieth-century roots of this ideal of total artistic freedom lay in the anarchism of the 1890s and 1900s, expressed in, for instance, the views of Jean Grave, editor of the anarchist periodical, *Les Temps nouveaux*. For Grave in *La Société future* (1895), the artist producing 'free art' is the model of the free individual, whose work is not a 'punishment', as it is under Christianity and capitalism, but a need, because it follows his 'tastes', 'without constraint'.[2] By the 1920s, it was not necessary to be an anarchist to believe in the artist as the paradigm of the free individual liberated from the profit motive. For the supporters of independent art, this was certainly the dominant view. And yet, one or two commentators were sceptical. The determinedly catch-all *L'Art vivant* had published articles by the Socialist critic Léon Werth in 1925 which analysed the material situation of artists with devastating candour. He had no doubt that in so buoyant a market, economic conditions could change 'the character of the artist', and he recalls wryly an artist-friend's concierge remarking: 'It's a good job . . . now . . . isn't it . . . painting?'[3] In Werth's opinion artworks had become fashionable commodities in France, and art galleries 'as beautiful as the premises of car-dealers'.[4] In a limited but real sense Léon Werth was right, by 1925 many successful independent artists had become producers of very expensive luxury goods, just like Meissonier, Bonnat and Besnard before them; they benefited accordingly.

The respondents to the *L'Art vivant* Enquête of 1927 were perhaps even more discomfited by the question of class than that of money. Many attempted to place artists in a sphere removed not just from monetary motivation but from class divisions too. Even Marcel Gromaire, a painter whose realist subject matter proclaimed a Left-leaning engagement with class, insisted that 'the artist is outside casts. He is at the service of all and of no-one'.[5] But again there is evidence that a few in the period were aware of the question of class as an issue for artists as well as everyone else. James Herbert cites Vlaminck, when he had become a country-house and car-owner in the mid-1920s, walking in the Normandy countryside and coming across a team of reapers; he is carrying his canvas and paintbox. 'Good-day, Monsieur,' Vlaminck recalls them saying: 'respectful . . . of the 'Monsieur' I am. I felt shame not to be working.'[6] Vlaminck (a self-proclaimed anarchist in the 1900s) knew that his paintbox gave him middle-class status. From the early 1920s, Fernand Léger loudly proclaimed the hope that artists and workers would come together. His 1923 lecture, 'The Machine Aesthetic', published the following year in the *Bulletin de l'effort moderne*, explicitly sought a working alliance between the skilled artisanal worker, the maker of precision parts or the mechanic, and the artist. His *Mechanic* of 1920 [179] ennobles its subject. What Léger's desire for contact with the working class ultimately reveals, however, is not the appropriation of a working-class identity for himself, but rather a wish for the kind of collaboration between the middle classes (including artists) and the working classes that Joseph Paul-Boncour had set up as an ideal in an influential book *Art et démocratie*, published in 1911. This theory would underpin the entire electoral strategy of the Popular Front in 1936. Even Léger insisted on the superiority of the artist: for him, one who does not merely fabricate, but who 'invents'.[7]

As we shall see, successful independent artists, including Léger, achieved a level of material security that was the dream of all the aspirant middle classes, whether it was the artists' personal dream or not. And one of the privileges given by that security was the preservation of a space in which to live as if released from the usual restraints of middle-class convention. The illusion of total freedom was often maintained, but it had to be paid for. There were many indicators of an artist's success, but there is no doubt that from the 1914 triumph of the 'Peau de l'ours' sale, one of those indicators was prices at auction, and another was whether or not an artist had a contract with a gallery, and then whether that gallery was a well-connected operation on the Right Bank or a small concern on the Left Bank. The new art periodicals with wide readerships, *L'Amour de l'art* (from 1920) as well as *L'Art vivant* (from 1925), made a practice of reporting the best prices attained in the salerooms during the 1920s and early 1930s. And indeed, when *L'Art vivant* added to its 1925 Museum of Modern Art Enquête a request for respondents to list their top ten artists, there was a very high correlation between the artists who got the most votes, and those whose prices were highest. In order of popularity, the final top ten were: 1. Matisse, 2. Maillol, 3. Derain, 4. De Segonzac, 5. Picasso, 6. Utrillo, 7. Rouault, 8. Bonnard, 9. Braque, 10. Vlaminck.[8]

Three points are worth making about this list; they all contribute to a grasp of the nature of recognition for artists in the period. First, the list throws into relief the distance between the canon as established by an informed French consensus in this snapshot instance from the mid-1920s and the canon at the turn of the millennium. Duchamp, Brancusi and Mondrian, for instance – now accepted as undisputed major figures – are missing, and present are figures now marginalised: De Segonzac, Utrillo, and the Derain and Vlaminck of the 1920s. The conditions for recognition have changed as the critical agendas after 1945 have changed and the shape of historical accounts with them. Second, there is only one foreigner, Picasso, and he is placed well below the position in which his prices and his international profile would have placed him. The Enquête concerned the possibility of a *French* museum of modern art, and the vast majority of respondents were French. Other foreigners, including Brancusi, did appear in individual lists, but they were rare. Picasso emerged as a special case. Achieving recognition for a foreigner in France was not the same as it was for a Frenchman, and this is corroborated by the limited exposure given to foreign artists in French surveys of art in France written in the period. Third, and finally, there are no women on the list. One or two, most frequently Marie Laurencin, appear on individual lists, but not enough to qualify in the final top ten. Achieving recognition was certainly not the same for male and female artists in France, whether French or foreign.

So, before we look at some of those who became then or who have become since 'modern masters' (a term whose gender implications are as appropriate as they are telling), I shall look at the experience of foreigners and women in pursuit of recognition. Both had boundaries to cross.

CROSSING BOUNDARIES: FOREIGN ARTISTS IN FRANCE, 1900–40

Klüver and Martin have asserted that in the period 1900 to 1930, between 30 and 40% of the artists in Montparnasse were not French.[9] The private artists' societies were increasingly open to foreign exhibitors after the 1880s. In the reforms of the Artistes français led by Jean-Paul Laurens in 1901, the most conservative of the Salons ended restrictions on foreigners, though its juries remained exclusively French. From its formation in 1890, the Salons of the Société Nationale had been open in this way. The Indépendants imposed no restrictions on nationalities, and through the 1900s showed rising proportions of foreign artists, as did the Salon d'automne, which organised a series of foreign exhibitions to promote internationalism: Scandinavian and Russian in 1906, Belgian in 1907, Finnish 1908, Italian 1909, and the German decorative arts, 1910 Sections of the press expressed concern about an 'invasion', especially in the period of rising nationalism between 1911 and 1914. And one of the most common charges against Cubism in the Salon d'automne controversy of 1912 was that it was foreign, and worse, given the disaster of the Franco-Prussian War (1870–1), German-backed.

From within the independent art world, however, the influx of foreign artists into Montmartre and especially Montparnasse was seen as a marker of the rise of French modernism. When the officially backed survey of 'Fifty Years of French Art' at the Pavillon Marsan in 1925 included Picasso (always the exception) among 'the French masters', André Salmon saw it as a symbolic recognition of the artistic meeting of nations in Paris: 'Paris! Paris, the new Rome.'[10] From 1918, the Luxembourg might have been kept for the French, and foreign artists shown separately in the Jeu de Paume, but the French State both bought and honoured foreign artists. In 1912, the Swiss Ferdinand Hodler, a regular exhibitor at the Salon d'automne, received the rosette of a chevalier of the Légion d'honneur. There was a long history of openness to foreigners behind the internationalism of the Jeu de Paume's 1937 exhibition, 'Origines et développement de la peinture internationale contemporaine'.

Foreign artists, however, remained foreign, magnets for prejudice like any other immigrant; and the openness of French society to immigration in general and to artistic immigration in particular bred reaction. Foreign artists were often made to feel their difference, even inadvertently by the most welcoming. Between 1908 and 1911, Matisse ran an Academy largely for Americans, Germans and Scandinavians; he was an exemplary internationalist, and would be an active member of the committee for the Jeu de Paume's 1937 show. Yet, when he visited the Russian sculptor Ossip Zadkine's studio around 1913, Zadkine remembers feeling that 'what he [Matisse] saw seemed to him foreign, I mean: foreign, not French' – a comment as much on Zadkine's own continuing sense of otherness (even in the 1960s, when the recollection was published) as on anything Matisse might have said.[11] Zadkine and the polyglot company in Matisse's Academy were part of a wider phenomenon in France than the convergence of foreign artists on Paris. In 1914, there were 1.6 million immigrants in France, nearly 3% of the population, the highest figure in Europe. These were mostly workers (both urban and rural), the greatest numbers Italian and Belgian, with smaller numbers of Spaniards, Germans, Swiss and from 1906, Poles.[12] After 1918, the need for male workers to replace the millions massacred on the Front led to a massive rise, driven by government policy. By 1931, the figure was nearly 3 million, approaching 7% . In 1921, foreign residents in Paris were 5.3% of the population; by 1931, the figure was 9.2%.[13] Concentrations were much higher, of course, in certain neighbourhoods, among them Montparnasse. The vast majority of artists who came to Paris were almost exclusively cultural not economic immigrants, a fact underlined by the point that the greatest artistic immigration was between 1905 and 1914, not during the years of rapid immigration growth after 1918, and that the dominant national groups were different: the Americans and the Russians came in the greatest numbers, Italians, Spaniards and Poles less so.

Artist immigrants were certainly different socially and in their motivation from worker immigrants: they mostly came from comfortable middle-class backgrounds, encouraged by training in cosmopolitan urban centres: New York or Barcelona, Munich or Cracow, Vienna or St Petersburg. Genuinely poor artist-immigrants with no support from back home, like Chaim Soutine, were rare. But whatever their origins, these cultural immigrants were also, like foreign workers, the victims of the terrifying waves of xenophobia that came, first following the Moroccan crisis in 1912, and then, with more sustained and more violent menace, in paranoid response to the 1920s government-sponsored expansion of immigration. Their work in this context, above all in the context of anti-Semitism, is a major topic in

Chapter 10 and is explored at length there. Here it is worth simply recording that the continuous virulence of xenophobic, often anti-Semitic reaction, in French society between the Dreyfus Affair and Marshal Pétain's 'New Order', went against dominant values in the France of the Third Republic, and even more clearly against those in the milieux of independent art.

At the same time, Zadkine's sense of otherness when confronted by the Frenchness of Matisse just before the 1914–18 war should be placed in the context of his response to the declaration of war on 3 August 1914, and that of many other foreign artists and writers. On 29 July 1914, the Swiss Blaise Cendrars and the Italian Ricciotto Canudo, had published a ringing declaration of loyalty to France in many newspapers. 'Foreigners, friends of France, who . . . have learned to love and cherish her like a second fatherland, feel the imperative need to offer themselves to her'.[14] Zadkine was among those who joined up (in January 1916), so did Apollinaire, with his Polish parentage (in 1914), and many other artists, including the Polish Jews Kisling and Marcoussis, and the Czech Kupka. The correspondence of those who did not join up – among them the Spaniards Gris and Picasso – often reveals that they too identified closely with their French friends on the Front. In Kisling's case, his war service qualified him for naturalisation. Many others not thus qualified made the same decision to become French especially after the naturalisation process was eased in 1927. The anti-foreign, anti-Semitic reaction gathered strength in a decade when the number of naturalisations increased tenfold.

As State policies and those of the artists' societies make clear, the France of the Third Republic offered a genuinely open prospect to such cultural immigrants, however violent the xenophobic reaction might have been. When not long after the Armistice of 1918 Zadkine married, he married a French woman from Algeria, the painter Valentine Prax; her father was French Catalan, her mother Sicilian, one of the witnesses was the Japanese painter Foujita. They were guests of Zadkine's French friend Henry Ramey in the provincial South-West near Montauban. In France such multi-national events could happen, though in the independent art world the presence of an ethnic non-European – a Japanese – was rare (despite Foujita's stylish ubiquity). France's attraction to foreign artists was immensely strong.

59. The low building is 13 rue Ravignon, Paris, known as the 'Bâteau-lavoir'

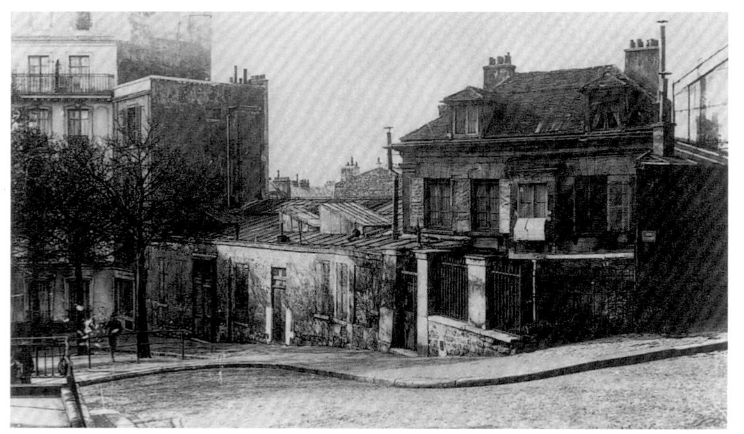

The nationalism (often ethnic) which grew especially from 1911, affecting even the liberal Left, developed in opposition to a continuing outward-looking belief in the civilising mission of the French Republic, which is already there in Ernest Renan's famous 'Qu'est-ce qu'une nation?' of 1882. As Renan saw it, the foundation of nationhood was the community of memory: 'To have suffered, worked, hoped together; . . . that is what one really understands despite differences of race and language'.[15] Kisling and other foreigners who fought in 1914–18 were given the right of citizenship because they had become part of Renan's community of memory. In the last years of the nineteenth and the first of the twentieth century, in a Europe dominated by hierarchical monarchies and Empires, France offered republican 'liberties' (of the press, of assembly, etc.), and positively welcomed political refugees, militant Russians and Russian Jews especially (25,000 to 45,000 in the 1900s, mostly in Paris).[16]

The artists who came between 1900 and 1914 were almost never political refugees, but the rhetoric of liberty appealed, and so did the 'free' students' way of life available in Paris as nowhere else. Places as 'free students' (actually fee-paying) in the ateliers of the Ecole Nationale des Beaux-Arts (ENBA) were available for both sculptors and painters, for instance the sculptors Zadkine and Lipchitz, who both worked in the studio of Antonin Injalbert in 1910. There were courses at the relatively new Ecole des Arts Décoratifs, and others run by the Ville de Paris. And then besides there was an enormous range of 'free academies' (again fee-paying), some, like the Académie Colarossi offering no more than models and space to work in, some offering courses with artists of reputation. There was, for instance, Bourdelle's renowned sculpture course at the Académie de la Grande-Chaumière (from 1906), the teaching of the one-time Nabis, Bonnard, Denis, Sérusier and Vuillard at the Académie Ranson (in Montmartre until 1911, in Montparnasse thereafter), and the school run by the academician Ferdinand Humbert. Braque and Marie Laurencin were among Humbert's students, and many French artists who bypassed ENBA studied in the 'free academies' – another much used by the French was the Académie Julian, which had four branches across Paris – but what Laurencin's recollections of the Académie Humbert stress is the enormous range of nationalities she found around her there in 1903–4.[17] Matisse followed a well-worn path when he started his academy in 1908; so would Léger and Ozenfant in the courses they ran from the early 1920s at the Académie Moderne in Montparnasse, and Friesz and Lhote in their Montparnasse Académies founded after 1918. The academies started by the independents from the Académie Ranson forward, were magnets for ambitious young artists in foreign cities, made aware of the roll-call of Parisian -isms and 'modern masters' by the dealer-driven export of French art.

In the 1920s and 1930s, the most important of the foreign artists to arrive in Paris and spend significant periods there were already artists with the beginnings of reputations at home. This is true, for instance, of Man Ray, Max Ernst, Joan Miró, René Magritte and Salvador Dalí, among the Surrealists, and of Theo van Doesburg or Torres-García among those drawn to non-figuration. They went not to study, but to take part; as Miró put it when he was planning his first visit in the summer of 1919, he wanted to go there 'as a *fighter* and not a *spectator*'.[18] A major exception was Alberto Giacometti, son of a leading Swiss Impressionist, who started off in Paris between 1922 and 1925 studying with Bourdelle at the Grande Chaumière, continuing more sporadically until 1927. Others who developed reputations back home, came to learn from particular 'masters' or movements: the Japanese American sculptor Isamu Noguchi, who was in Paris in 1927–8, was one of very few taken on as a student-assistant by Brancusi. The American Stuart Davis, who was there in 1928–9, came to learn from the one-time Cubists like Léger, though he worked with none of them. Noguchi was one of the first to come with a Guggenheim fellowship; by the late 1920s the patronage of visits to Paris was becoming institutionalised.

In the earlier period, before 1914, foreign artists who made reputations in Paris went more often as beginners to study, like Zadkine and Lipchitz, or the Russian Jewess Sonia Terk (Delaunay) and the American Patrick Henry Bruce. But there were several too who already saw Paris as the modernist capital where names were to be made. František Kupka, from a peasant background in Czechoslovakia, settled definitively in 1906 having studied (with private patronage) and exhibited successfully in Vienna. Jules Pascin, from a wealthy Bulgarian Jewish family, arrived in 1905 having already made a reputation with drawings in the German illustrated magazine *Simplicissimus*. Picasso, son of a Professor in the Barcelona School of Fine Arts, arrived, first of all in 1900, having made the beginnings of a modernist reputation in Barcelona, much as Miró and Dalí would, the first in 1920, the second in 1929.

Both before and after 1914, the places where foreign artists met each other (and French artists too) were the ENBA ateliers and the academies, the often run-down studio complexes where they settled, and the cafés. In the 1900s, there were still little communities of artists in Montmartre, the best remembered of which was centred on a ramshackle studio building on the Place Ravignan known as the 'Bâteau-lavoir' (the laundry barge) [59]. Here Picasso and Gris were neighbours between 1906 and 1911, and the poets Apollinaire and Jacob were frequent visitors . Spaniards in particular were drawn to the still provincially scaled streets of Montmartre, with its ready-made seedy bohemia. By 1911 when the Académie Ranson moved there from Montmartre, Montparnasse's status as the major centre for communities of artists, especially foreigners, was firmly estabished. The shifting populations of incomers were housed in studio complexes like the Cité Falguière close to Montparnasse station and especially La Ruche (the bee-hive). This was a complex on the western fringes of the neighbourhood which was opened by the Minister of Public Instruction in 1902 as an officially approved (but not funded) artists' community, complete with its own tiny theatre. Zadkine, Modigliani, Soutine and Chagall all had one of the wedge-shaped studios in the domed central building of La Ruche at one time or another between 1910 and 1914 (as did Léger).

Before 1914, the café meeting-places that provided the right welcome and ambiance for these alternative communities were often dominated by foreigners. They included the Lapin agile in Montmartre, and, in Montparnasse, the Dôme [60] (opened in 1898) and the Rotonde (from its purchase in

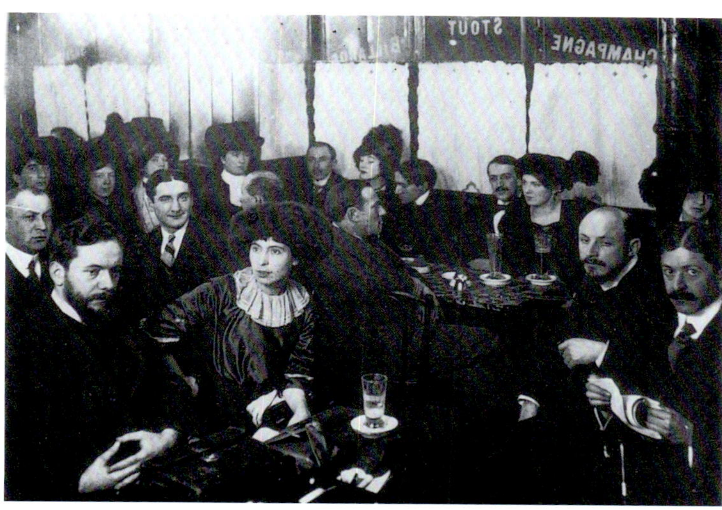

60. German-speaking artists and friends photographed at the Dôme in Montparnasse *c.* 1910. Among them are the German artists Hans Purrmann, one of the instigators of Matisse's academy, (third from right), Rudolf Levy (centre, in profile, facing right), and the Bulgarian Jules Pascin (centre, in profile, facing left)

1910 by Victor Libian, who offered artists exchange deals and credit as well as bonhommie). The Dôme was on the carrefour Vavin, where the Boulevard du Montparnasse crosses the Boulevard Raspail; the Rotonde was nearby. Another café, the Closerie des Lilas, not far along the Boulevard du Montparnasse, was a centre more for French groupings, especially around Paul Fort, poet-editor and founder of the literary periodical *Vers et prose* in 1905. In the 1914–18 war the Rotonde took over from the Dôme as the place to be, but in the 1920s, under new management, both continued to attract artists and in 1924–5 they were both enlarged. A little later they were joined along the Boulevard du Montparnasse by a vast dancehall brasserie, La Coupole, whose spectacular opening in 1927, with decor by artists including Léger, Friesz and the Russian Marie Wassilief marked the apogee of Montparnasse as a multi-national art centre.

The stories of artists like Joan Miró, who arrived in 1920, and Man Ray, who arrived in 1922, show that after 1918 assimilation could be almost immediate. Man Ray, as Duchamp's friend, came straight into Breton's Dada group. Miró, with introductions to Picasso and Maurice Raynal and contacts through his Barcelona dealer Dalmau, was quickly showing at the galerie La Licorne, and in the studio complex at 47 rue Blomet where he moved in 1921 for the winter, was taken into the circle of French artists and writers around André Masson. Language and national groupings tended to keep together longer and more effectively before 1914. In a few highly significant instances such groupings formed active and energetic clusters of artists, writers, dealers and collectors which gave each other mutual support and at the same time supplied French modernism not only with new recruits but also with new clients who had pan-European or transatlantic connections. Two instances are especially important: the German speakers who met in the front room of the Dôme and the Americans who revolved around Gertrude and Leo Stein's home on the rue de Fleurus (also in Montparnasse); they were groupings that overlapped, because the Americans frequented the Dôme too.

Kenneth Silver places a circle of Jews from Eastern Europe centred on Pascin at the core of the German-speaking group [60], but includes also non-Jewish Germans: Wilhelm Lehmbruck, Hans Purrmann, Oskar and Greta Moll. More important perhaps than any of the artists involved were those beginning to collect and deal, some of whom would emerge as key figures: Wilhelm Uhde, Alfred Flechtheim, Adolphe Basler, and Paul Cassirer (with Flechtheim to become an influential gallery owner in Germany, buying significantly from France).[19] The Stein circle included Gertrude and Leo's brother Michael and his wife Sarah. Gertrude wrote as a tough-minded modernist in her own right, a fascinating and attractive figure for artists as different as Picasso, Matisse and Robert Delaunay. Both the sibling pair and the married couple were intensely engaged in buying the most adventurous art, and had the means to do so. The better-connected Americans who came to be modernists in Paris quickly found their way to the Steins: Patrick Henry Bruce and Arthur B. Frost in 1906, both of whom would become close to the Delaunays, and in 1908 Stanton Macdonald Wright, Frost's future partner in what they would call 'Synchromism' in 1913. Others who came into and out of that circle were the photographer Edward Steichen, who provided a crucial bridge between Paris and the dealer-photographer Alfred Steiglitz in New York, and Walter Pach, the organising force behind the enormously influential Armory Show in New York early in 1913. Steichen made Matisse's first New York drawings show happen at Steiglitz's Little Galleries in 1908, and Pach engineered his first paintings show at the Montross Gallery in 1915. It was also from the Stein circle, this time in concert with the Dômiers, that the initiative for Matisse's academy came. Sarah Stein, Patrick Henry Bruce and Hans Purrmann were all involved.

The overlapping communities of foreign artists, writers, dealers and collectors in Paris from 1900 were a major factor in the internationalisation of French modernism. In the end, the American connection, immeasurably strengthened between the wars as we have seen, would provide a lifeline for French as well as foreign artists under the occupation in the winter of 1940–1, when invitations from the Museum of Modern Art in New York brought across the Atlantic Léger and Masson as well as Ernst and Chagall. In France, foreign artists were certainly subject to different pressures than the French, especially of a hostile xenophobic kind, and they were fitted only slowly and at first awkwardly into the French picture of independent art in France. But what is striking is the degree to which they and their communities found the space in which to thrive in Paris and to cross-fertilise with French artists. Foreigners were among the most conspicuously successful independents in Paris by 1925, whatever *L'Art vivant*'s top ten seems to indicate. At that moment no informed commentator would have questioned the prominence in the market and the art press of Lipchitz

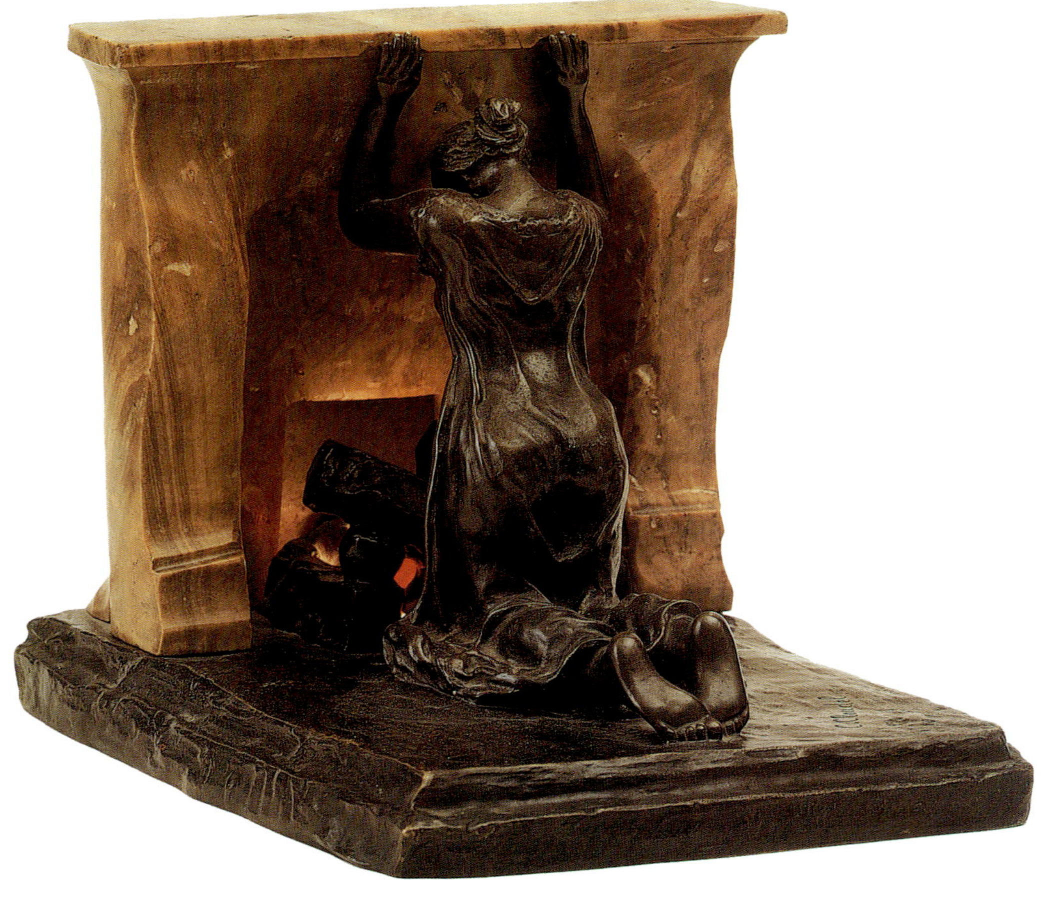

61. Camille Claudel, *Profound Thought*, 1905. Bronze and onyx, h. 24 × l. 22 × d. 27.5 cm. Lucie Audouy Collection

or Chagall, Soutine or Foujita. For a foreign artist, even for Max Ernst, an illegal immigrant in 1922 from France's unforgiven invader Germany, the borders around the French art world were easily crossed.

CROSSING BOUNDARIES: WOMEN ARTISTS IN FRANCE, 1900–40

Superficially it could seem that it was at least easier for women to cross the borders around the French art world than for them to cross those around most other careers in France, even in the 1900s. If it was not until the 1920s that women began significantly to penetrate the training institutions of the professions, by 1900 they were already entering the Ecole Nationale des Beaux-Arts in numbers. From 1889, Madame Berteaux, the formidable president of the 'Union des femmes peintres et sculpteurs', had launched a campaign, first for special women's classes in ENBA, and then when the first forty-six women had entered such a class in 1896, for access to the ateliers. In 1903 access was conceded, and women could compete for the Prix de Rome.[20] In 1911, the Grand Prix de Rome for sculpture went to a woman; the year before the first woman pleaded in a French assize court.[21] It would not, however, be from ENBA that the women artists who became recognised in the independent art world would emerge, but from private tuition and especially the 'free academies'. At first, in the late nineteenth-century schools like the Académie Julian provided separate studios for women at double the cost, but by 1910 mixed classes were available in most, and the list of French and foreign women who worked in them is long. To mention just a few, there were, besides Marie Laurencin at the Académie Humbert alongside Braque, Sonia Delaunay at the 'Palette' in 1905, Marie Wassilief, a Russian like Sonia, alongside Sarah Stein and Patrick Henry Bruce with Matisse in 1908, and Alice Halicka, who later married Marcoussis, in the Académie Ranson in 1912. Marie Wassilief set up her own academy in her studio on the Avenue du Maine in 1909, where Maria Blanchard, later a l'Effort Moderne Cubist, studied that year. By 1910, the popular writer Octave Uzanne could write of 'a perfect army of woman painters' invading 'the studios and the Salons'.[22]

For a figure like Uzanne, this 'army' represented a threat, but the artists' societies and the dealers seem not to have attempted any form of systematic exclusion. By the 1900s women were showing in all the major Salons, from the Artistes français to the Salon d'automne, and indeed the image chosen for the cover of the catalogue of the 1908 Salon d'automne was a woman artist at her easel. The woman dealer Berthe Weill showed a succession of woman artists, starting in 1902 with Jacqueline Marval (who would make a considerable reputation) and including Halicka and Laurencin. And after 1918, even male dealers specialising in high-profile modernism gave contracts to women: Paul Rosenberg to Laurencin, D-H. Kahnweiler to a 1920s newcomer Suzanne Roger. Neither is there evidence of the systematic exclusion of women by critics sympathetic to modernism or the authors of surveys of independent art. Apollinaire dedicated an article to 'Les femmes peintres' in *Le Petit Bleu* in April 1912, and also that year, André Salmon's *La Jeune Peinture française* included a chapter dedicated to 'L'Art féminin du XX siècle'; both handed out praise to selected women independents. In 1922, Louis Vauxcelles also devoted a chapter of his section on twentieth-century painting in the widely read *Histoire générale de l'art français* to women painters, and he too acknowledged the existence of some who had made an impact.

One name recurs in all three of these texts, that of Apollinaire's mistress of the period 1908–13, Marie Laurencin (b.1883). By 1925, when she was named in the top tens of some of the respondents to *L'Art vivant*'s Museum of Modern Art Enquête, Laurencin certainly fulfilled all the criteria of success; and so did one other woman painter, Puvis de Chavanne's, Renoir's and Lautrec's model from the 1880s, Suzanne Valadon (b.1867). Valadon was included in a package deal with her son Maurice Utrillo on contract to Bernheim-Jeune, and in her own right commanded good prices and respectful reviews in the art press. In 1932, Josse Bernheim and his partners in the prestigious galerie Georges Petit gave not only Picasso but Valadon a solo retrospective; hers was opened by Edouard Herriot, President of the Republic. According to René Gimpel, Rosenberg paid Marie Laurencin a princessly 50,000 francs a year, probably from her hugely successful exhibition of 1921 onwards.[23] By the mid-1920s, she had become a sought-after portraitist in the emancipated high-society world of such socialite collectors as the Baronne Gourgaud [203] and had designed for Diaghilev's Ballets Russes.[24]

Salmon's and Apollinaire's decision to isolate women's art as a special topic in 1912, and that of Vauxcelles ten years later, demonstrates clearly enough that the question of women in modernism was seriously addressed in the period. And the relative prominence of Laurencin and Valadon can make it seem that as art education, exhibiting spaces and the press opened up to the arrival of women, success in the independent art world came too. But such success was exceptional, and no woman achieved the kind of impact achieved by Picasso and Matisse, or even figures like Ernst or Miró; no woman got into a position where she could alter the course of a modern movement. And when women made reputations, those reputations tended to be circumscribed by the term 'feminine', given weakening rather than positive connotations, as we shall see. Understandably, the two studies that have looked at women modernists in the period, Gill Perry's and Whitney Chadwick's, have dwelt far more on the reasons for their relative marginalisation then and since than on their impact.[25]

In 1922, Louis Vauxcelles ended his section on modern sculpture for the *Histoire générale de l'art français* with a eulogy to 'a great artist the survival of whose merit is assured': Camille Claudel (b.1864). He was aware of the tragedy of her confinement since 1913 in an asylum, and made his contribution to the survival, against the grain, of her fame as a sculptor. The case of Claudel and especially the example of a work that was exhibited in optimum conditions in 1900 at the moment of her greatest fame, can introduce well the problem of the marginalisation of woman artists across the whole period between 1900 and 1940. In the Décennale at the Universal Exhibition of 1900, Claudel showed three pieces; they included an early version of *Profound Thought*, an idea reprised in bronze and onyx in 1905 [61]. During the exhibition, her teacher and one-time lover Rodin had mounted his own exhibition in a pavilion especially constructed on the Place de l'Alma, where he showed his *Gates of Hell* for the first time. Claudel's *Profound Thought* gives us a female figure on her knees, thin drapes clinging to her soft flesh, braced against a chimney piece, her dreams living in the flames in the hearth: an allegory of desire projected inwards embodied in a figure which is both vulnerable and erotic. The year she made the bronze and onyx version of the idea, Rodin's *Thinker*, enlarged from the figure which presides over the *Gates*, was erected on the steps of the Panthéon [62]. Claudel's piece is the obverse of *The Thinker*'s forceful, masculine, outgoing inwardness. It represents female creativity as dream, a passive yearning, not an active muscular effort to understand, and it contains female creativity within the frame of the hearth. Vauxcelles insisted on the independence of her sculpture from Rodin's, but she remains, like all women artists who achieved recognition in the period, a woman given her crucial opportunities by male intervention: Rodin's personal involvement and his influence, even after their relationship broke down in the 1890s. And her image of female creativity breaking through yet contained by the domestic hearth finds repeated echoes in the history of women artists in the period. For women artists, success had to be achieved against powerful domestic constraints and in milieux where men alone could initiate and where women were appreciated exclusively on male terms.

62. Auguste Rodin, *The Thinker*, as installed in 1905 on the steps of the Panthéon, Paris

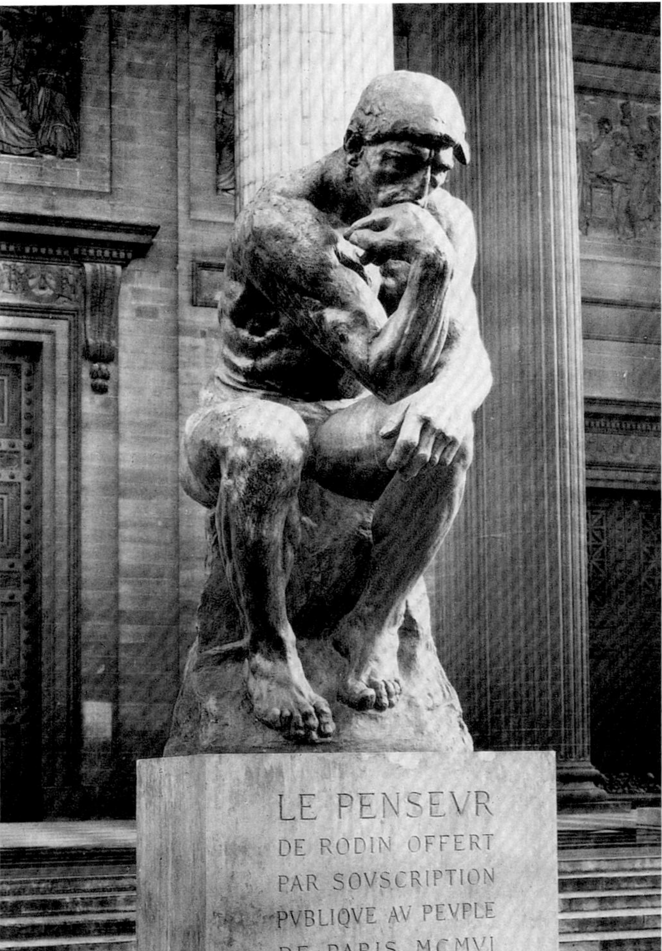

In his 1929 *Second Manifesto of Surrealism*, André Breton made extravagant claims for the importance of women to Surrealism with the declaration: 'The problem of woman is all that is marvellous and troubling in the world.'[26] In the first number of *La Révolution surréaliste* Germaine Bertin, the anarchist murderess of the extreme right-winger Marius Plateau, leader of the paramilitary Camelots du roi, is featured as a symbol of revolution surrounded by Man Ray's photographs of the Surrealist group [38]. Women were from then on accorded a certain revolutionary and creative status in Surrealism, but, as Chadwick underlines, no significant woman Surrealist emerged before 1929, and when women Surrealists did their passport into the group was male interest.

Meret Oppenheim (b.1913), from a German and Swiss background, became a maker of Surrealist objects from 1933 [158] after meeting Giacometti at the Dôme and then being invited to show with Giacometti and Arp at the Salon des surindépendants in 1933. Remedios Varo (b.1913) came into the group in 1937–9 having married the Surrealist poet Benjamin Péret. Leonora Carrington was brought back by Ernst from the opening of his solo show at the Mayor Gallery in London in 1937. All of them had the advantage of well-off backgrounds and Varo and Carrington had begun serious studies in Madrid and London respectively, but all needed men to invite them to be active Surrealists; and in most cases those men were their lovers. The same was so of virtually all the woman artists involved in or peripheral to the Fauves and the Cubists. Gill Perry's discovery, Emilie Charmy, whose work in the early 1900s anticipates certain aspects of Fauve painting, only entered the milieu around Matisse when she became involved with Charles Camoin in 1906. It was Braque and Apollinaire who brought Laurencin into the circle around Picasso in 1908. Sonia Delaunay's engagement with Apollinaire's new category of 1912, 'orphic Cubism', was part and parcel of her partnership with Robert. And it was Diego Rivera and Juan Gris who encouraged Léonce Rosenberg to take an interest in Maria Blanchard in 1917. Women were brought into the significant groups and movements by men. The presence of a border controlled by men and the difficulty of making an active contribution when invited across it is exposed clearly enough by Breton's apparently magnanimous recognition of the 'problem of woman' in 1929. For him the 'problem' was actually not women's at all, but men's: it was the problem of male love. Woman could be a symbol of creative freedom, but her role was most importantly to become the *object* of love – a screen for the projection of desire.

Social conventions and intellectual orthodoxies on the Left as well as the Right converged to restrict and weaken any idea of the active woman, either within society or in revolt against it. As Maurice Agulhon has pointed out, in the period 1900–14 women are very rarely reported taking part in strikes or street demonstrations; male labour activists, like middle-class family men, thought their place was at home.[27] In the major Union organisation, the CGT, anti-feminism was explicit: working women were seen as a threat to working men. Female membership was just 9.8% in 1911.[28] The anarchist periodical *Assiette au beurre*, a stalwart of the Left, published two special numbers lampooning feminism in April 1910 and September 1911, with drawings by Juan Gris, who was already beginning to experiment as a Picassian Cubist. Gris might later have encouraged Maria Blanchard with great generosity, but he was more than willing to attack feminism, and in doing so he voiced a widespread dislike even in such modernist circles of the woman activist, one that was perfectly consistent with a 'revolutionary' stance in art just as it was in politics.

Such a reluctance to identify women with revolution went with a view of the 'feminine' that was perhaps the most effective brake of all on radical female achievement in art. Vauxcelles' treatment of women artists in his *Histoire générale de l'art français* of 1922 began with a discourse on the domestic entrapment of women. He deplored especially the academic orthodoxies displayed annually in the Salons of the Union des femmes peintres et sculpteurs, and he sketched a depressing picture of the prospects for any young girl with an eye on a career as an artist. His stereotype is middle class and 'docile'. She starts by being taken every day by her maid to the Académie Julian, and obediently following instruction. On holiday, she brushes watercolours at the seaside or in the mountains, her work conforming to 'bourgeois' and 'professorial' convention, and when she takes her own studio all she can manage is to go on obediently doing what she has so painstakingly learned. In an extraordinary passage anticipating the essentialist feminism of the 1970s, he appeals to women to dare to set aside male academic instruction and to 'be' women: he envisages a possible *women*'s modernism. 'Inequality will disappear the day when woman wishes to express in art what she has to say and not what man has already said.'[29]

The bourgeois domestic ideal for women and the constraints it imposed upon them, was certainly a major factor in their containment. Perry has shown the extent to which Emilie Charmy's comfortable Saint-Etienne family kept an eye on her in Paris, where at first she lived with her brother as chaperon, and Perry has also brought out the difficulties imposed on the Russian artist Marevna by single parenthood.[30] But a more internalised and more profound constraint was imposed by dominant notions of 'femininity', often articulated by men but also often sustained by women artists themselves. And, as much as any other critic, Vauxcelles was responsible for a view of the 'feminine' in art that dwelt on docility, the anti-intellectual, the intuitive and the attractively available, as his extended analysis of Marie Laurencin in the *Histoire générale* makes amply plain. Since Apollinaire's pre-1914 writing on her – especially in his 1912 piece 'Les Femmes peintres' – Laurencin had become the epitome of the modern woman artist whose art was quintessentially 'feminine'.

Valadon was in many ways her polar opposite, a female exception to every rule. She was the illegitimate child of a poor domestic servant; she had none of the education of a bourgeois woman before the sculptor Bartholomé, one of the artists for whom she modelled, showed her drawings to Degas and he began to give her private tuition. A 'masculine' vigour, even brutality, was found in her work [205, 207]. Laurencin was also born illegitimate, but her mother was discretely supported in a petty-bourgeois lifestyle by her politician father, and so she was lycée educated and brought up to middle-class aspirational values. She continued to live with her mother through the years of her Cubist beginnings (despite Apollinaire's attentions). 'Grace' was the quality Apollinaire found above all in her work in 1912; for him, a specifically 'feminine' quality. It was a quality cultivated in her close collaborative relationship from before 1914 with the interior-designer André Groult and his wife Nicole, sister of the couturier Paul Poiret. For Vauxcelles in 1922, she had invented in her painting an ideal female type, 'a Marie Laurencin', a child-woman, slender and delicate, always discovered in 'feminine' pursuits, combing her hair, playing the mandolin, caressing a horse 'that resembles a unicorn', dreaming. All her sitters, indeed, became 'Marie Laurencins', including the Baronne Gourgaud [203].[31] When in 1923 Man Ray photographed her, he softened the focus in such a way as to enhance her Marie Laurencin-ness [63], and when in 1928, Marcel Jouhandeau published a little monograph on her, he used a self-consciously childlike prose to tell stories about this 'eternal little girl'.[32] The pervasiveness of such a view of the 'feminine' across the modernist groups is perhaps summed up by the fact that the Surrealists – so far outside the ambiance of Marie Laurencin – idealised above all the child-woman (the 'femme-enfant'). The cover of *La Révolution surréaliste* no. 9–10 (1 October 1927) offers an

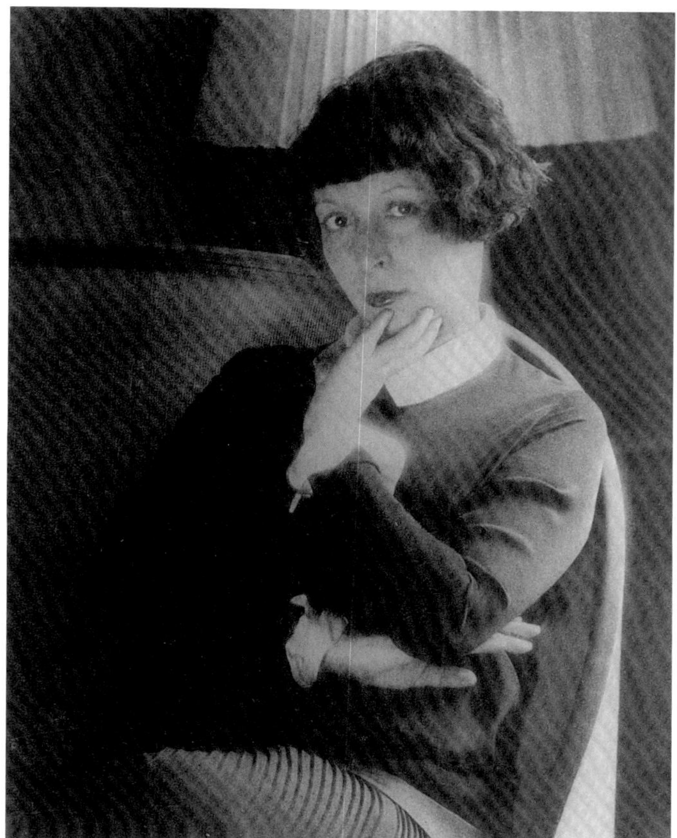
63. Man Ray, *Portrait of Marie Laurencin*, 1923. Photograph

adult woman in schoolgirl outfit sitting at a school desk as the image of inspiration.

Woman artists before 1940 broke their way into art education and careers as artists, but they were still unable to construct their own 'feminine' mentalities, languages and behaviours, even within the alternative social spaces provided by the independent art world of the studios and the cafés. Only rarely too could they break free from the normative domestic frameworks erected around them by middle-class expectations, and often those that did had already crossed borders to arrive. Many of the women artists whose lifestyles were most challenging, including the women Surrealists, were foreign. For women, being foreign could be an advantage; a Meret Oppenheim or a Leonora Carrington had the advantage of having escaped the comfortable conventions of home-based 'femininity'.

BEING A MODERN MASTER: MATISSE AND PICASSO, BRANCUSI, MONDRIAN, GIACOMETTI AND OTHERS

In 1932, the year after the Depression began to hit the art trade in France, Picasso's dealer Paul Rosenberg cooperated with two of his leading rivals, Josse Bernheim and Etienne Bignou, to make possible a full-scale Picasso retrospective at that venerable symbol of artistic celebrity, the galerie Georges Petit. It opened in June, the anniversary of a Matisse retrospective in the same huge exhibition halls, but the 236 works listed in the catalogue exceeded the number of Matisses shown by nearly 100 and it gave a far more comprehensive coverage across all the periods of Picasso's career. Picasso himself lent work, as did many of those who had been involved in his rise, including Vollard, Kahnweiler and André Level. So did several newer supporters from Europe and the States, most generously Chester Dale, a backer of Bignou's and Bernheim's enterprise, who had bought the star of the 1914 'Peau de l'ours' sale, *The Family of Saltimbanques* [53] in February 1931.[33] The opening was reported in Europe and across the Atlantic as an evening for diamonds and tails, 'champagne [and] microscopic sandwiches'.[34] Picasso hung the show himself, with a collagist's contempt for stylistic homogeneity and linear chronology, and the independent art press collectively gasped. Most flattering of all, Christian Zervos's glossy modernist *Cahiers d'art* produced a fully illustrated special number and Zervos published the first volume of a projected catalogue which was intended to give illustrated coverage of all of Picasso's work, every drawing and sketchbook page included. By its provisional completion there would be thirty-three volumes.[35] 1932 marked the beginning of Picasso's career at the age of fifty-one not simply as a celebrity modern master but as an historical figure, one who with Zervos would actually collaborate in the construction of his own historical image.

1932 was the date also of the Hungarian Brassaï's first

64. Brassaï, *Picasso's studio at 23, rue Boétie, Paris*, 1932. Photograph published in *Minotaure*, no. 1 (Paris, 1933)

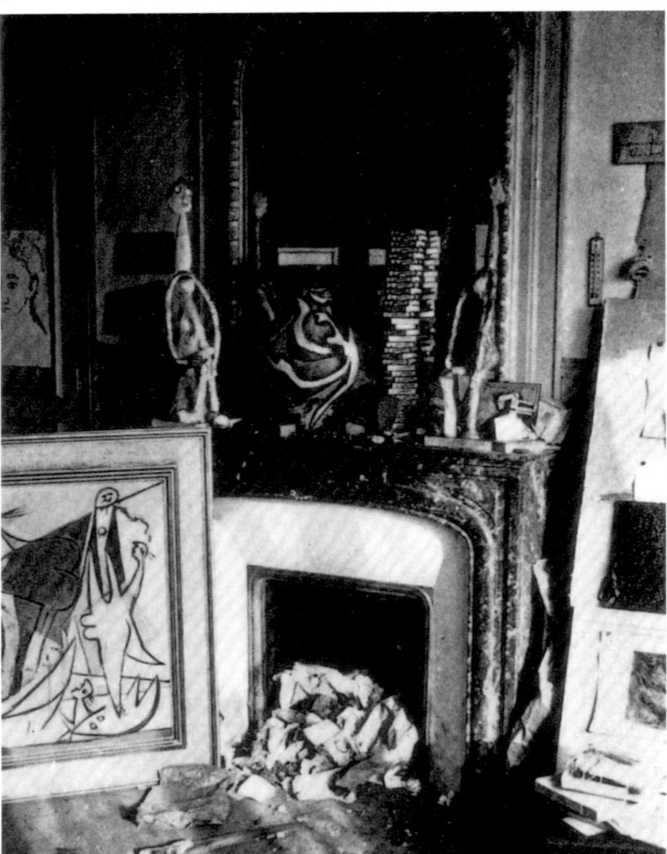

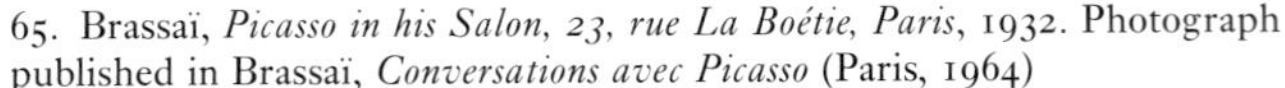

65. Brassaï, *Picasso in his Salon, 23, rue La Boétie, Paris*, 1932. Photograph published in Brassaï, *Conversations avec Picasso* (Paris, 1964)

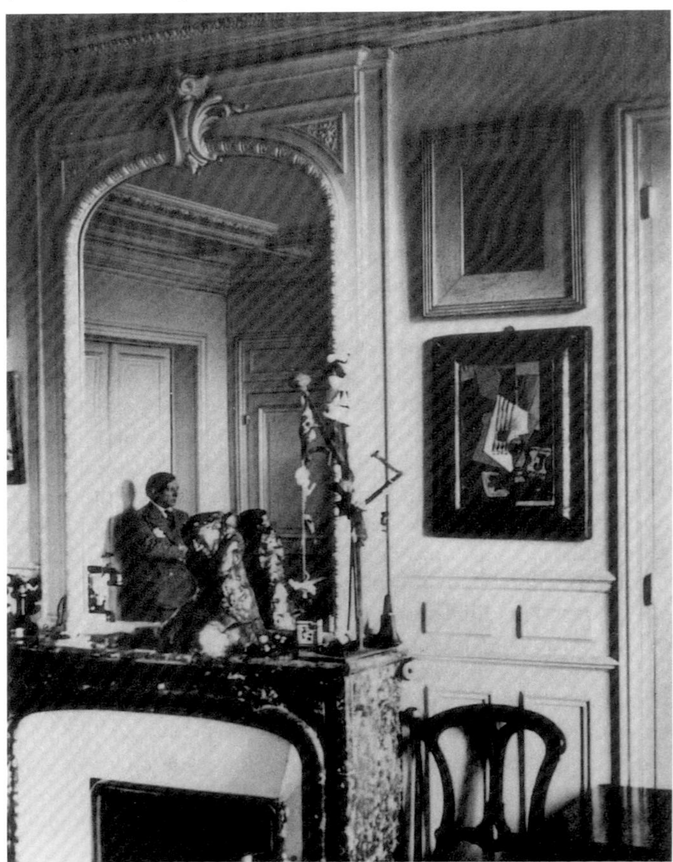

photographic session with Picasso, some of the results of which were published in the Surrealist backed periodical *Minotaure* a year later [64]. One of the photographs taken then that was not published at the time [65] offers a glimpse of Picasso in suit and tie, arms folded, caught in the mirror of the stylish salon of the apartment found for him in 1918 by Paul Rosenberg above his gallery on the rue La Boétie. Only the strange construction on the marble mantelpiece suggests that the obviously successful figure held within this bourgeois frame is an artist. For Brassaï even the presence of Picasso's work on the walls did not modify the effect of sumptuous conformity; it could, after all, have been the salon of one of the rich collectors *of* Picassos. By 1932, the artist had acquired all the signs of spectacular material success to go with his prestige as a modern master: 'a Hispano-Suiza driven by a liveried chauffeur, suits from the leading tailors, pedigree dogs, a double "grand bourgeois" apartment, a little château in Normandy – he had just bought Boisgeloup – a bank-vault and a mistress . . . there was nothing missing'.[36]

Picasso and Matisse (the latter in his early sixties in 1932), remained celebrated and productive as established modern masters throughout that decade of crises. But the decade when artistic and material success married as a result of modernism's international 'triumph' was the 1920s. It was between 1905 and 1914 that Matisse and Picasso made their reputations as modern masters, a fact confirmed just before war was declared in 1914 and just before the Armistice of 1918, first by their unrivalled prices at the 'Peau de l'ours' and then by the respect given to a joint Picasso-Matisse exhibition at Paul Guillaume's new gallery on the rue du Faubourg Saint-Honoré.

In the 1920s the buoyancy of the art market made it seem briefly that being a modern master was a privilege open to many lesser independents. In the mid- and later 1920s, the popular press made much of the glamour lent to the alternative, 'free' lifestyles of artists by sudden injections of wealth. Foujita was an especial favourite because of the way he exoticised French individualism. There were photographic features on his life in the brand new studio-house into which he moved with his French partner Youki (Lucie Badoul) in 1926 (the year after he had become a chevalier de la Légion d'honneur alongside Matisse) and then on the two of them holidaying the following year at the fashionable resort of Deauville. The mid-1920s saw many successful independents moving, like Foujita and Youki, into smart new studio-houses in the hinterland of Montparnasse around the Parc Montsouris and the Avenue Denfert-Rochereau. Auguste Perret, one of Le Corbusier's teachers, designed studio-houses there for both the modernist portrait-sculptor, Chana Orloff, and Georges Braque in the Villa Seurat, a little street not far from Foujita and Youki. Further west, in the comfortable sixteenth arrondissement, Robert Mallet-Stevens built for both himself and the sculptor brothers Jan and Joël Martel. His name was considered to carry enough weight for the development to be called the rue Mallet-Stevens; it attracted much press attention when it was opened in 1927. Further still to the west, in the developing suburbs of Boulogne-sur-Seine, close to the Parc des Princes, Le Corbusier himself built a double studio-house

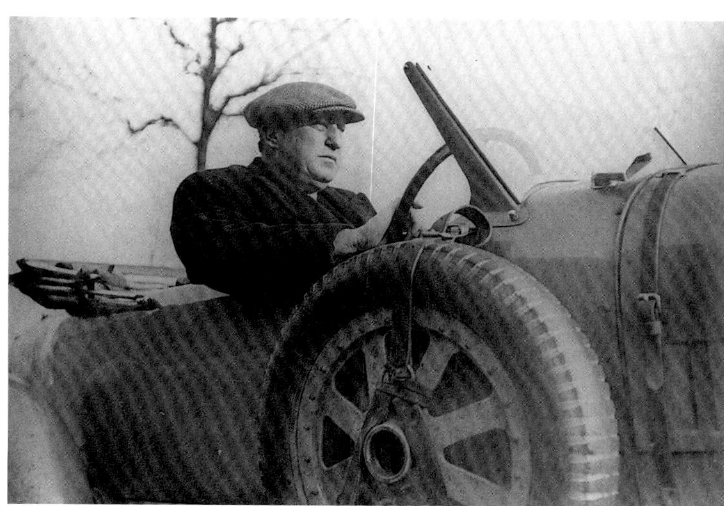

66. Man Ray, *André Derain in his 'Delage' Car*, 1925. Photograph

for Lipchitz and another Russian immigrant sculptor, Oscar Meitschaninoff. It was completed in 1925; in the case of Lipchitz, a direct consequence of Dr Albert Barnes's prodigiously extravagant visit to Paris in 1923.

As with material success in any other middle-class sphere, further key signs of status for artists were houses in the country and cars. Suzanne Valadon, her alcoholic but high-earning artist-son, Maurice Utrillo, and her partner, André Utter, bought the small medieval château de Saint-Bernard at Meyzieux (near Villefranche-sur-Saone) in 1923, long before Picasso bought Boisgeloup. Vlaminck, who like Utrillo and Valadon had a contract with Matisse's dealer Bernheim-Jeune, converted an old farm in the Norman countryside near Dreux in 1924–5, adopting the air of 'a gentleman farmer with his tweed jacket, flat hat and eternal red neckerchief'.[37] A little before, in 1922, Léger bought a more modest villa in the still green but fast developing Fontenay-aux-roses just south of Paris, to which he invited friends like the Kahnweilers and the Raynals to relaxing outdoor Sundays. Fontenay-aux-roses was at the end of a tramline, easily accessible from his Montparnasse studio on the rue Notre-Dame-des-Champs. And Valadon's highly unusual family group (Utter was nineteen years her junior) often made the trip to Meyzieux from Montmartre by taxi, but many, including Vlaminck, were conspicuous consumers of expensive cars. Vlaminck was photographed for *L'Art vivant* both with a motorbike and in his Chenard in 1925. Derain, in the 1920s an even more widely recognised modern master than his one-time Fauve friend from Chatou, drove to his motifs in Provence in a Buggatti, and insisted on being photographed by Man Ray at the wheel of another of his expensive open-top cars, an eight-cylinder 'custom-made job' as the photographer described it [66]. He recalled Derain saying that it 'was more beautiful than any work of art'.[38] Man Ray himself marked his success as a fashion and society photographer by buying a Voisin.[39]

It is an indicator of the role artists could play by the 1920s as models for a special kind of stylish but still essentially middle-class individualism, that Man Ray used his portrait photographs of artists as a kind of publicity to attract

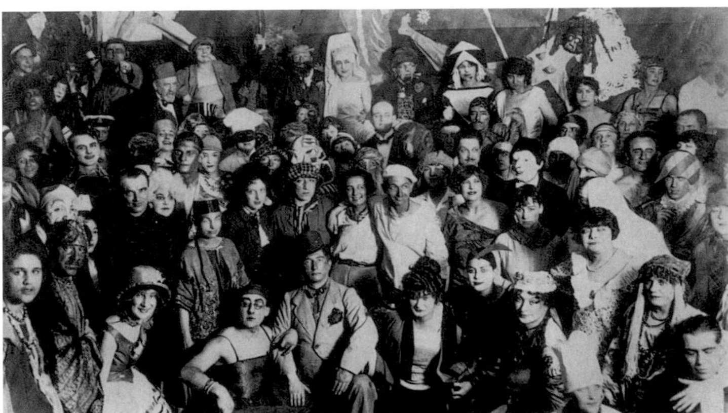

67. *Maison Watteau Ball*, 23 March 1924.

high-spending sitters into his studio from the business and society worlds. Starting in 1922, he photographed a whole gallery of modern masters, including Picasso and Matisse as well as Derain and the modern mistress, Laurencin [63], often not taking a fee so as to encourage sitters.[40] He was, in fact, an ever-available intermediary between apparently incompatible worlds, as much because of his social mobility as because of his function as a professional photographer. He moved easily between the milieux of the Surrealists and high society, as indeed did many others in the Surrealist group when invited by the de Beaumonts or in the late 1920s by the de Noailles.

As Melissa McQuillan has observed, the themed balls put on by the de Beaumonts and the de Noailles in the 1920s, were themselves social hybrids. They pulled together the elegance of the aristocratic seventeenth and eighteenth-century masked ball and the extrovert eccentricities of the artists' balls [67] that had developed especially in Montparnasse in the wake of the Beaux-Arts students' 'Bal des Quat'z'Arts' of the 1890s.[41] By 1922, many of those who dressed up with bohemian abandon for the 'Fête du Nuit' at the Bal Bullier dance hall in Montparnasse, also made spectacular entrances at de Beaumont's 'Bal des jeux'. The 'Fête de nuit', like the balls organised by the Union des artistes russes, was a charity as well as an artists' ball, and tickets were available for the former at all the Right Bank dealers who sold to the de Beaumonts and their friends. Such events in the 1920s (and there were many) made an extrovert masquerade of the confluence of a now professionalised bohemia and the worlds of its aristocratic and bourgeois clientele. Even collage, the most formidable of challenges to the aesthetics of elegance, was appropriated in the interests of high-society chic when the de Noailles held their 'Bal des matières' in 1925, where guests appeared in everything from celophane to paper doilies.

The sheer glamour of independent art and artists in the 1920s made a spectacle of what was a problematic conflict for the most engaged of the modernists, one that was grasped in terms of incompatible times as well as worlds. It is picked up by Léon Werth in his sceptical articles of 1925 for *L'Art vivant* on the commodification of art, where he contrasts what for him is the current market-driven reality, and what he sees as an ideal pre-1914 freedom, when 'painters painted for themselves alone, for a few friends, a few enthusiasts and a few dealers . . .'[42] In 1933, the year after Picasso's Georges Petit retrospective, his partner of the period 1904–12, Fernande Olivier, published a memoir – another sign of his emergence as an historical figure – *Picasso et ses amis*. It is a sort of lament for a bohemia lost in the pre-war past. 'How does [he] feel now,' she asks, 'about those days when nothing in the world would have induced him to wear a proper shirt, a stiff collar or a hat?'[43] She gives an overwhelming sense of a lost innocence with the coming of wealth. At the same time, intermittently through her memoir Fernande Olivier brings out a contrast between her bohemian image of Picasso before 1910 and her memory of Matisse. She recalls the two of them at Gertrude and Leo Stein's rue de Fleurus soirées, Picasso 'shy' and out of place, Matisse 'the type of the great master . . .'. She writes of a Matisse who 'argued, affirmed, set out to convince . . . very much in control of himself'.[44]

Fernande Olivier recalls Matisse as 'nearly forty-five', when he was actually in his late thirties in 1907–8, a telling mistake, because he had always appeared reassuringly solid and mature (enough for Derain to ask him to persuade his parents that painting was a serious career, when he finished his military service in 1904). Gertrude Stein later stressed the rivalry between Picasso and Matisse, which she remembered beginning at the rue de Fleurus in 1908 with Picasso's jealousy of Matisse's closeness to her. Since then, they have become not only the two most celebrated modern masters in France of the 1900–40 period, but the paradigms of two distinct kinds of modern master, the models for many. Picasso as the bohemian foreigner, who would never be fully

68. Pablo Picasso, *Self-Portrait ('Yo Picasso')*, 1901. Oil on canvas, 73.7 × 59 cm. Private Collection

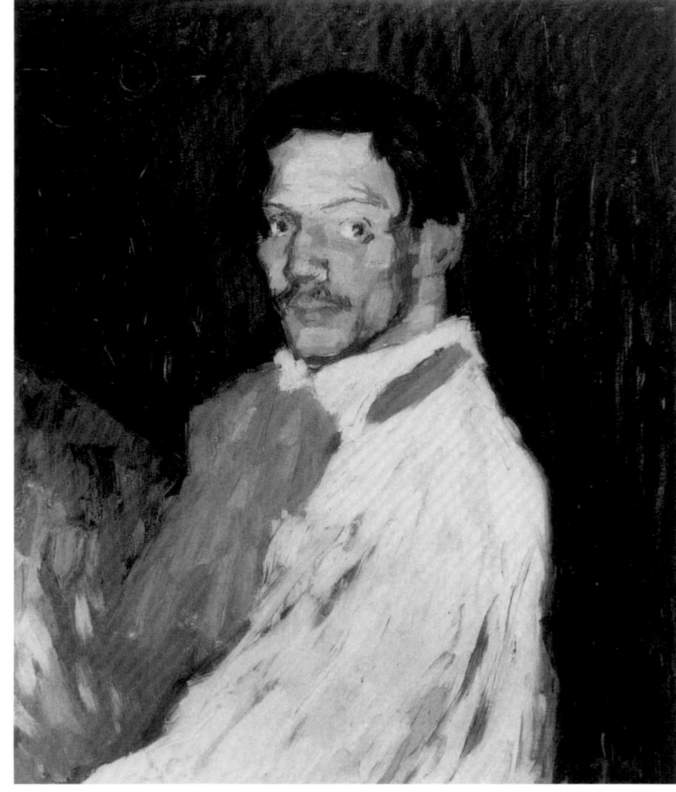

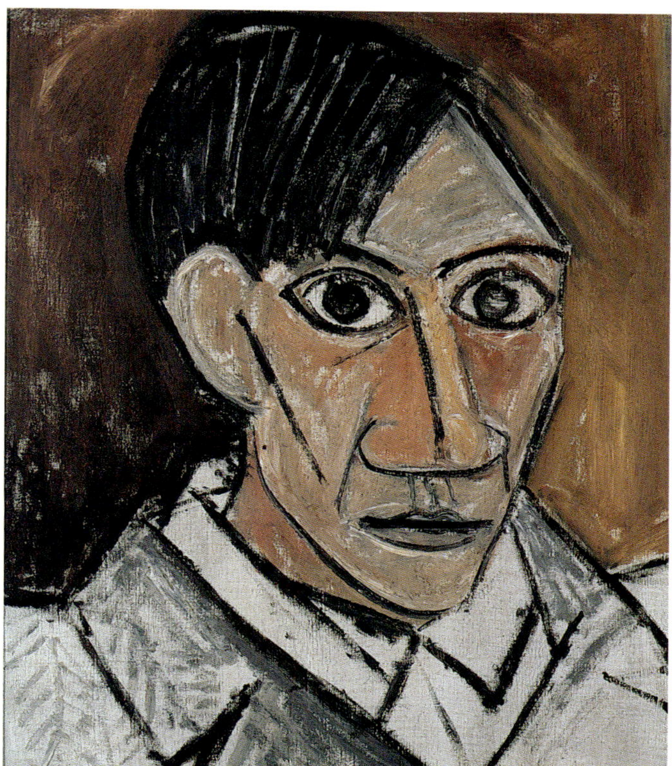

69. Pablo Picasso, *Self-Portrait*, 1907. Oil on canvas, 50 × 46 cm. National Gallery, Prague

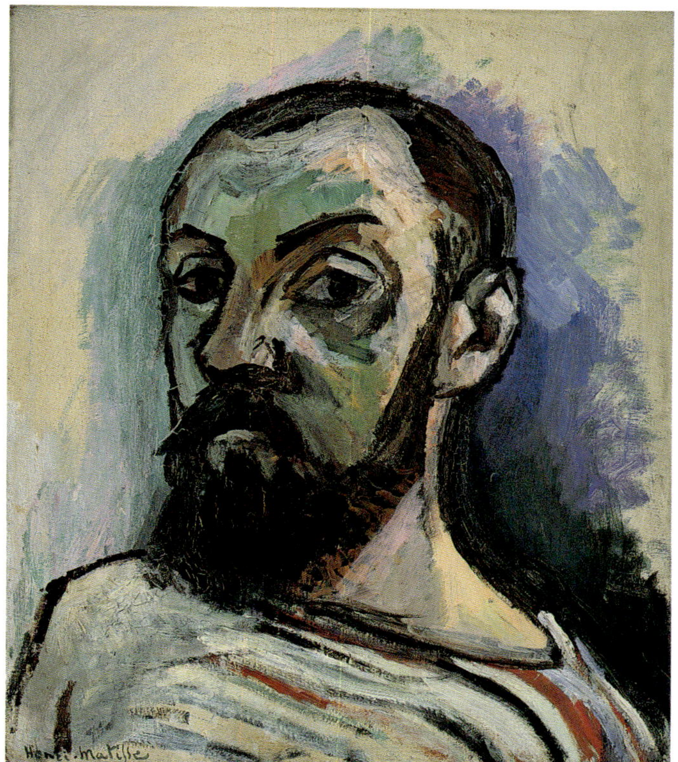

70. Henri Matisse, *Self-Portrait*, 1906. Oil on canvas, 55 × 46 cm. Statens Museum fur Kunst, Copenhagen (J. Rump Collection)

absorbed into the bourgeois world, despite that apartment on the rue La Boétie; Matisse, the Frenchman, who was always a bourgeois. As we shall see, this is an exaggerated polarity that conceals complexities in both cases, but theirs remain the two most revealing stories of modern-master celebrity. They each bring out, in their very different ways, the conflict experienced by most ambitious modernists between total commitment as artists and the pursuit of market success. Especially revealing are surviving portraits of them (painted and photographic), above all their self-portraits.

Picasso arrived in Paris, probably just before his nineteenth birthday in October 1900, already reputed enough to be represented in the Spanish showing at the Universal Exhibition. Through a Catalan contact, Pere Mañach, he was introduced to Berthe Weill, and on that very first stay Weill sold three pastels and gave him a contract of 150 francs a month (it did not last). When, after working in Barcelona and Madrid, he came back to Paris in May 1901, he already had a show organised with Vollard; the work sold, according to Richardson, because he consciously designed it for the post-Lautrec French market.[45] That year in Paris, he painted himself in bravura style as an artist confident of his talent, adding the Nietzschian inscription: 'Yo Picasso' (I Picasso) [68].[46] His exposure to early material success was, however, brief, and during his so-called Blue Period (1901–4) in Barcelona and Paris, when poverty was his central theme, he was indeed poor. On his third Paris stay, late in 1902, he shared a hotel room with the poet Max Jacob, sleeping in the bed in relays. It was in April 1904 that Picasso moved into the impoverished bohemia of the 'Bâteau-lavoir' and Montmartre [59], and it was there that he met Fernande, a neighbour; from now on he was based in Paris. By spring 1907, when he painted himself [69] in the primitivised style of the *Demoiselles d'Avignon* (on which he was at work), his canvases were being bought again, by Gertrude and Leo Stein among others; the previous autumn he had completed a portrait of Gertrude for which she had sat many times. The 1907 *Self-Portrait* is not, however, an image of confidence; it bristles with anxious intensity. Fernande's bohemian Picasso was above all to be characterised by total commitment to his work, and by anxiety. That artistic self-image was not to alter as he achieved recognition and material success, constantly bringing out the disjunction between the ideal of total creative engagement and the lavish social life its products made possible into and beyond the 1920s.

It was two years before Picasso's 1907 *Self-portrait* that Derain painted Matisse at Collioure reflectively sucking on his pipe [22]; he gives us the image of the artist as thinker, but an image no less of concentrated commitment. The following autumn, in 1906, Matisse painted himself with an incisive directness that anticipates the Picasso [70]. He is represented without any of the attributes of the bourgeois. In his collarless vest, Matisse is stripped off for work; not an anxious artist, but a brooding, searching one. And yet his bourgeois credentials as an artist actively constructing a career were already clear enough. Hilary Spurling has shown how, in 1902–3, a devastating financial and human crisis precipitated by the ruin of his parents-in-law – innocents caught up in a typical Third Republic banking scandal – had forced on Matisse a hard-headed commitment to earning for his family through his painting, however tough his attitude to its expressive and aesthetic demands remained.[47] By late 1906, his skilful manipulation of the fast-expanding market for his Fauve painting was bearing fruit. The group-show strategy at the 1905 Autumn Salon had brought Leo and Gertrude Stein to the studio, after they had paid the 500 franc asking price for his *Woman with a Hat*; they had been followed by Michael and Sarah, who had brought their Baltimore friend, Etta Cone. Matisse had always been a professional, even before his parents-in-law's ruin in 1902–3. He had accepted State commissions to copy Old Masters into the 1900s, and from 1903, as his focus on his earning power sharpened, his enterprise and resourcefulness in building his market would have been a lesson to any aspiring small businessman. In 1903, he attempted unsuccessfully to put together a consortium of collectors to pay him a monthly salary. In 1904–5, he used his influence with Signac to pack the committee of the Indépendants and cleverly worked the elections and committees of the Salon d'automne to resist the opposition of its president, Frantz Jourdain. Even before the autumn Salon of 1906 opened, Signac's dealer Druet had bought all the pictures he sent. In 1907–8, he personally managed his expanding affairs with Bernheim-Jeune and foreign collectors, including the major German patron Karl-Ernst Osthaus from Hagen and the hugely wealthy Russian collector Sergei Shchukin. When in March 1909, Shchukin commissioned from him the decorative panels *Dance* and *Music* [82] for the staircase of his Moscow Palace, he paid him 27,000 francs for the two, a price to match those the great official decorators like Besnard and J.P. Laurens were receiving from the French State. And at the end of 1909, he negotiated conspicuously good terms when finally he signed a contract with Bernheim-Jeune, retaining the right to manage his 'decorative' commissions independently.

And yet there is no doubt that this shrewd operator, whose experience of crisis as a family man so strengthened his awareness of the bottom line, continued throughout to see himself as the totally engaged artist of the 1906 *Self-portrait*. Matisse too, like Picasso, offers conflicting images of the worldly and the unwordly, the careerist and the independent creator incapable of compromise. Both in their work absolutely refused easy solutions; neither was tempted by the coming of success to demand less of themselves. Their self-images as artists would not allow them to, and indeed a dealer like Kahnweiler and collectors like Gertrude Stein and Shchukin demanded no less than total engagement from them, going further to demand it from themselves too. There is a revealing letter from Shchukin to Matisse, written in November 1910 to mark his decision to accept the *Dance* and the *Music* panels, where he portrays himself, the collector, as a risk-taker on the model of Matisse the artist. He accuses himself of having lacked courage when he first saw what Matisse had done (at the Salon d'automne): 'One must not desert the field of battle without attempting the struggle . . . They will shout, they will laugh, but as I am convinced of the rightness of your path, perhaps time will be my ally and in the end I will be victorious.'[48] When the panels were hung in Moscow in December, he wrote that he hoped 'to like them one day'.[49] Years later, in her 1938 Picasso monograph, Gertrude Stein was to claim ugliness as one of the necessary qualities of innovative art, especially Picasso's. She put it thus: 'In the effort to create the intensity and the struggle to create this intensity, the result always produces a certain ugliness . . .'. By purchasing Picasso's 'ugliness', she too partook of his uncompromising self-image as an artistic explorer.[50]

Fernande Olivier recalls the stubborn determination with which Picasso refused to be distracted from his central concerns as an artist. She remembers his refusal of an offer of 700 or 800 francs (a considerable sum) to produce drawings for one of the caricature magazines as 'heroic in the circumstances'.[51] But she also recalls how patiently he played a waiting game with the dealers, never going to them, and certainly by 1909, he was handling the growing demand for his work with some skill. That year, the dealers Sagot, Uhde, Vollard and Kahnweiler were all competing for him. In 1909 he did well enough to move out of the 'Bâteau-lavoir' down the hill from Montmartre, to a comfortable apartment with studio on the Boulevard de Clichy, where he and Fernande took on a maid. When, at the end of 1912, he moved into a Montparnasse apartment on the Boulevard Raspail and signed his contract with Kahnweiler, he was able to negotiate terms at least comparable with Matisse's at Bernheim-Jeune. His personal accounts show that in 1913 Kahnweiler paid him 51,400 francs in all, an income approaching that of many academicians.[52] Ultimately, if Matisse was a canny businessman yet totally committed to his art, Picasso was a totally committed artist yet a canny businessman.

And, though both chose difficult confrontations with the superficially 'ugly' as they pushed into their personal unknowns behind the studio doors, their work *was* materially changed by their business dealings; at least on the level of such generalities as scale, format and rhythm of production. Matisse's succession of decorative commissions from Osthaus and especially from Shchukin meant that between 1908 and 1911, his energies went into working with generous expanses of colour across surfaces often several metres wide: the *Dance* and *Music* panels are almost four metres across. Before Kahnweiler decided in 1909 to invest in as much of Picasso's production as he could get out of him, Picasso had worked in long sequences of studies and smaller oils towards large canvases, though not as large as Matisse's decorations: *The Family of Saltimbanques*, the *Demoiselles d'Avignon* and finally *Three Women* [53, 282, 288]. As Matisse had with *Luxe, calme et volupté* and *The Joy of Life* in 1904 and 1906, he hoped that respect and prestige would accrue to large statements of this kind, though he did not use the independent Salons to stage them, his admirers came to him. Kahnweiler's commitment from 1909 was open-ended: he wanted engaged experimental art, on the edge. Accordingly, from 1909 Picasso began to work in sequences of smaller, less resolved paintings, moving in the end, at the moment of his contract with the dealer, into the ad hoc, conspicuously provisional domain of collage and construction. Shchukin and Kahnweiler opened up new possibilities for continued uncompromising exploration in both Matisse's and Picasso's cases, but the nature of the agreements they reached with the artists still determined certain of the parameters within which they worked.

Again, the 1914–18 war brought changes in the market of

the two artists which seem to have affected how they worked. Matisse lost his big decorative commissions, and in 1915–16, before he signed a new contract with Bernheim-Jeune in 1917, sold to the Cubists' dealer Léonce Rosenberg. He continued to paint on a huge scale when he could, taking ideas initiated before the war – for instance, *Bathers by a Stream* [84] – to tough new conclusions of extraordinary ambition. But there is every reason to believe that the tangential relationship of these and his smaller canvases of the period to the Cubism of Picasso and Gris relates as much to the climate of expectation created by Rosenberg's Cubist convictions as to Matisse's then fruitful relationship with Gris. Léonce Rosenberg also bought Picasso's work, of course, before the Spaniard moved decisively to Paul in 1918–19, and Picasso's decision mostly to set collage and construction aside during the war could well relate in part to both the Rosenbergs' preference for conventional oil painting. In the early 1920s, Picasso went back to his pre-1909 rhythm, producing smaller canvases interspersed with large-scale statements, as he found clients for the large-scale like John Quinn in New York alongside his dealer clients

71. Pablo Picasso, *Self-Portrait in front of 'Construction with Guitar Player'*, 1913. Photograph, original print, 16.6 × 10 cm. Musée Picasso, Paris

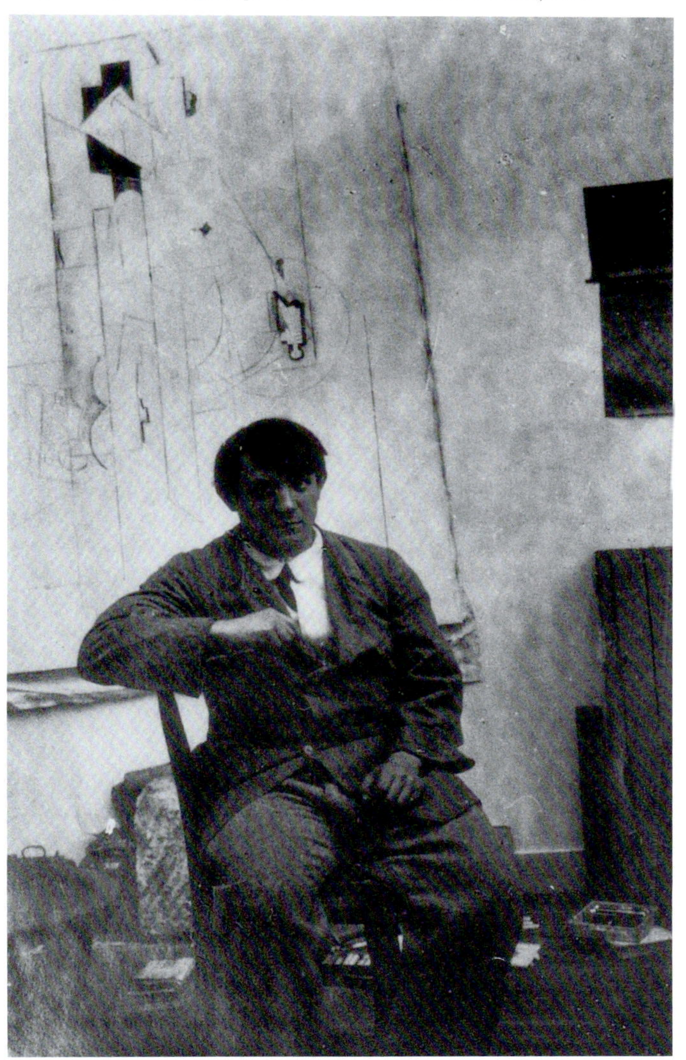

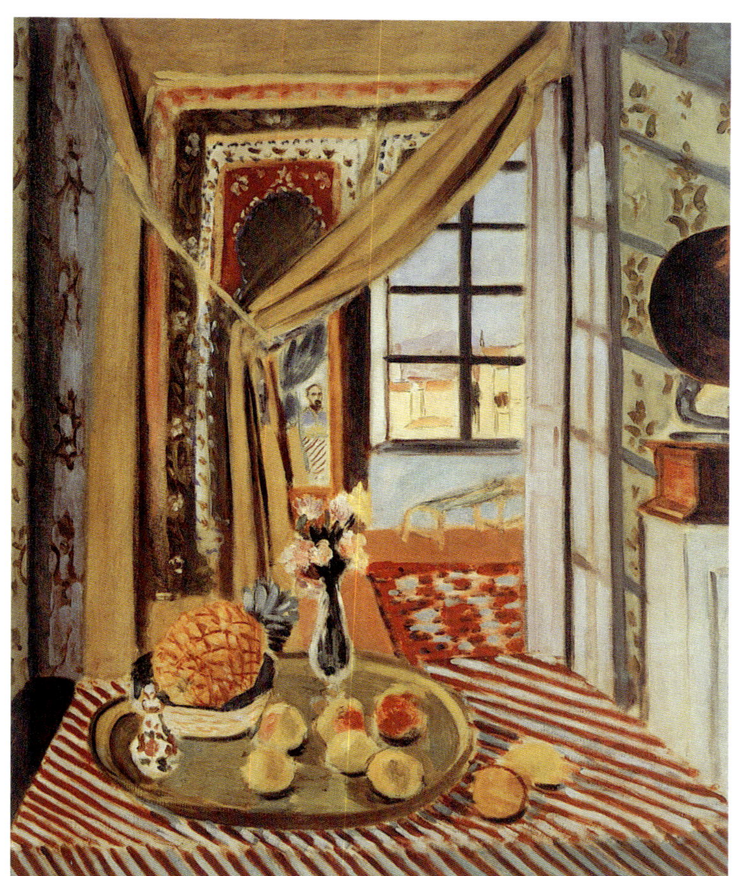

72. Henri Matisse, *Interior with Phonograph*, 1924. Oil on canvas, 100.5 × 81 cm. Private Collection

Paul Rosenberg and Kahnweiler in Paris. Sequences of portrait and still-life-scale canvases are punctuated by major works: in 1921, the two versions of *Three Musicians* and also *Women at the Fountain* (offered to Quinn), in 1925 *Three Dancers*, in 1927–8, *The Studio* and *Painter and Model* (the latter bought by Kahnweiler) [318, 328]. From 1917, Matisse, encouraged by the generous terms for smaller sub-40-size pictures granted in his new Bernheim-Jeune contract, returned to the modest scale of his pre-Shchukin work, as he settled into a pattern of summers in his substantial home at Issy on the western outskirts of Paris, and winters on the Côte d'azur in Nice.[53]

Following Matisse's and Picasso's very different experiences as emerging and then established modern masters repeatedly brings out, thus, the competing demands of their art and their pursuit of market success: the contradictions so easily missed if one looks only at their work. Both stood for total engagement as artists and yet at the same time for a worldly and highly effective engagement with the realities of the market place. But in the final analysis, Picasso's self-image remains more that of the anxious artist enclosed in a studio world, and Matisse's more that of a successful artist inhabiting the upper end of comfortable middle-class society. Two self-portraits make the contrast plain, one a photograph taken by Picasso of himself in front of a large unfinished canvas in 1913 [71], the other a sumptuous orientalised interior, with a tiny self-portrait caught in a mirror, painted a decade later by Matisse in his apartment at Place Charles-Félix in Nice [72]. Picasso sits stiff and intense in rumpled work clothes, his hastily knotted tie between curling collars. He is in a desolate studio space, his materials and brushes scattered like debris on the bare floorboards. Behind him is work manifestly in progress; work he is worrying over, a canvas which for a moment became an element in an extraordinary studio construction, also recorded by Picasso the photographer [161]. That photographed construction, Anne Baldassari has argued, could be itself a displaced self-portrait. Picasso can become his own Cubist invention, a guitar-player whose world is exclusively the studio, a space where objects – wine-bottles, clay pipes, newspapers – have existences ultimately as the components of still-lifes, and where the artist is dedicated only to art.[54] Matisse's *Interior with Phonograph* of 1924 absorbs him as working painter into his own riotously patterned, highly individual version of a bourgeois home. He is caught as Brassaï caught Picasso in the mirror of his rue la Boétie salon in 1932 [65], enveloped in the stylish space of his social life, but this is the space in which he regularly sets up his easel to paint everything from still-lifes to odalisques. His self-image as an artist can happily survive in these rooms where ordinary appetites are aroused and duly satisfied.

Matisse's Nice paintings of the 1920s often bring the studio into the domestic spaces of his social life. Picasso's move to 23 rue la Boétie after his 1918 marriage to the Ballets Russes dancer Olga Koklova deepened the split that had existed since 1909 between his studio and his social worlds. Brassaï's photographs and recollections of 1932 document that split: the spotless bourgeois apartment downstairs, the filthy studio apartment upstairs, where fag ends desecrate the waxed polish of the costly parquet [64, 65]. The two studio pictures of 1927–8, especially *Painter and Model* of 1928 [328], give a mythic presence to the studio as a special space in which the artist operates apart from and above society, in the case of *Painter and Model* as a savage magician – an image of the artist I explore further in Chapter 12. Picasso's semi-detached but always significant relations with Breton and the Surrealists from 1924 and with Michel Leiris in the circle of the periodical *Documents* in 1929–30, allowed him to take on for a second time a leading avant-garde role, but now firmly in the context of a socially as well as culturally critical project. In the mid-1920s, Picasso became the first modern master in the twentieth century to use fame as the platform for a subversive, critical practice, aimed against the

73. Claude Monet photographed *c.* 1924 in the large studio at Giverny in front of one of the *Water-lilies decorations*, 1916–23, later installed in the Musée de l'Orangerie, Paris

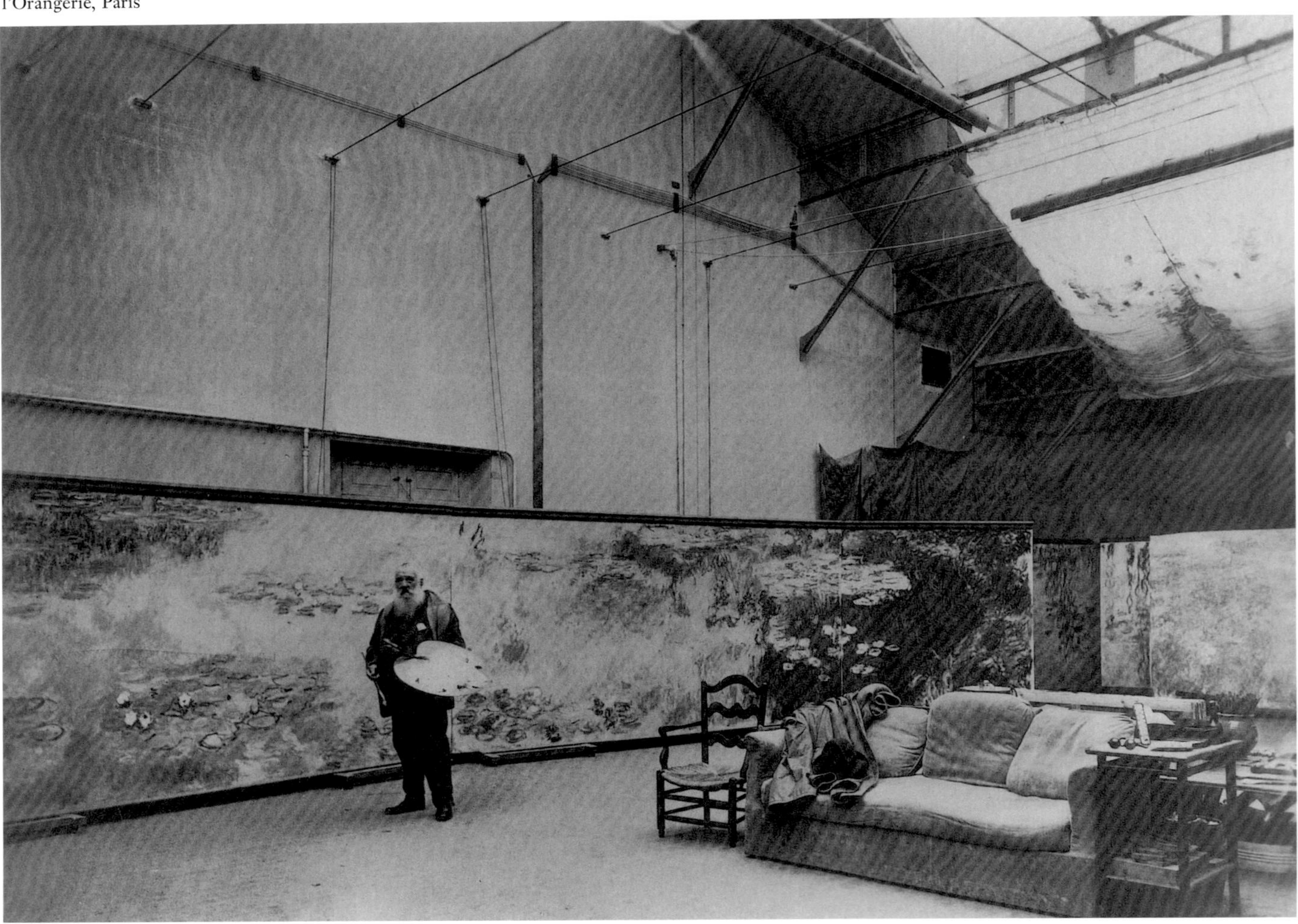

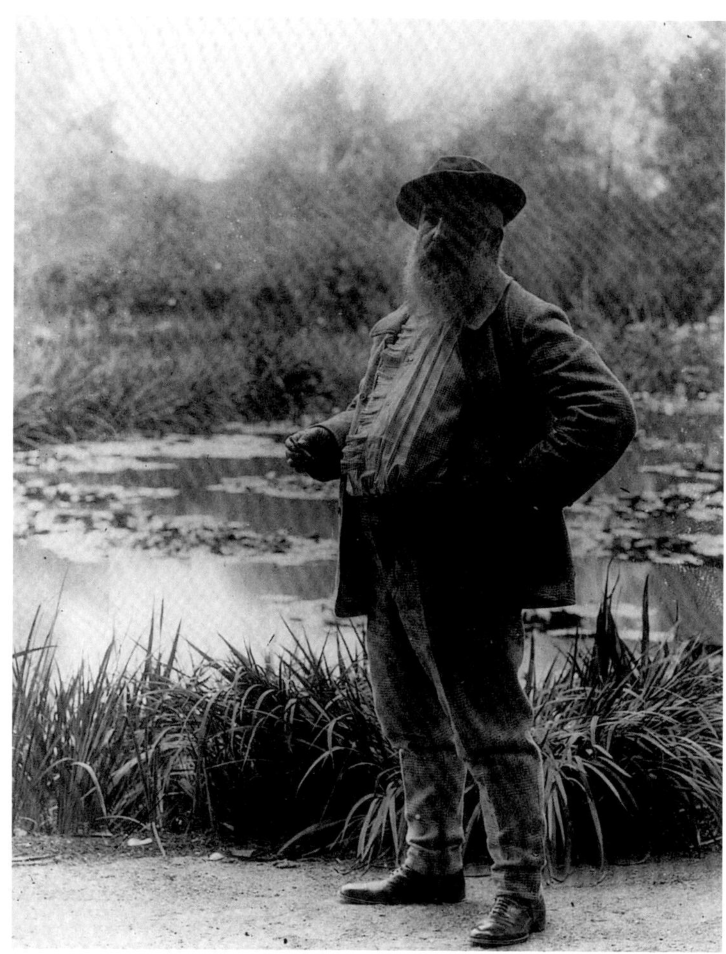

74. Claude Monet in his garden, by the waterlily pond with the Japanese bridge in the background, 1905. Photograph

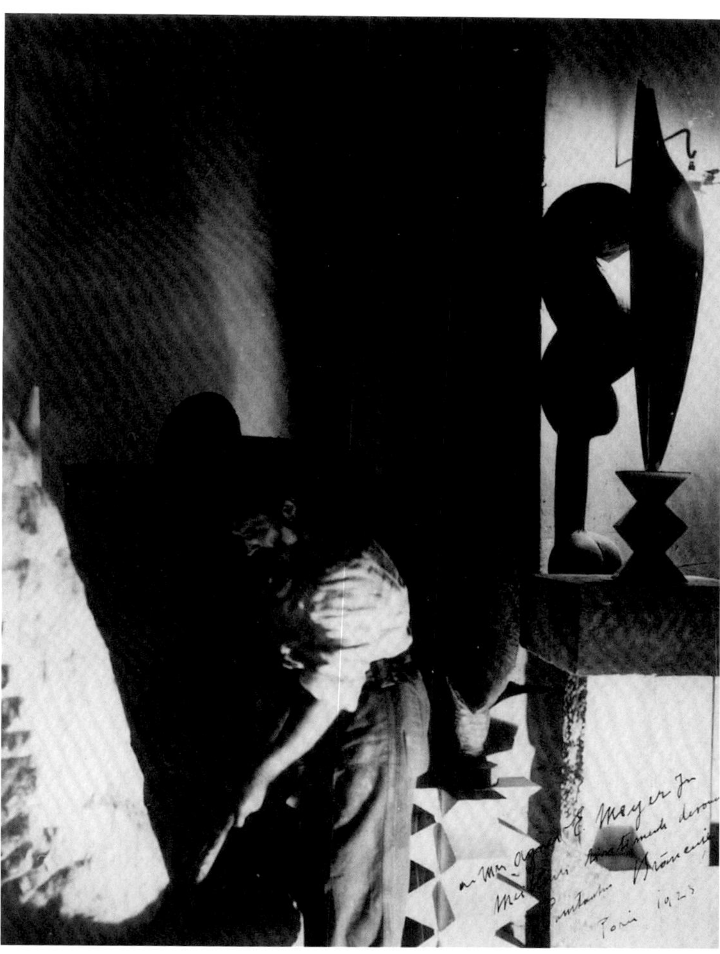

75. Constantin Brancusi, *Self-Portrait in studio*, *c*.1923. Photograph. Original print, 34.2 × 27.5 cm. Philadelphia Museum of Art, Gift of Elizabeth Lorentz

society that celebrated him; careers like those of Andy Warhol or Josef Beuys have followed the pattern he set. So long as he continued in his conventional marriage to Olga and his socialite's rue la Boétie life, the split between his artistic and these other identities became even more a necessity. The split would only begin to heal when he moved into 7 rue des Grands-Augustins on the Left Bank in 1937, two years after his divorce from Olga.

Matisse's successful fusion of life with his artistic practice, and its image, the transformed domestic space, had its best-known early twentieth-century forerunner in Monet's home at Giverny. Not, however, in the spacious custom-built studio in which he painted the large water-lily series [73], but outside in his garden, which by the 1920s had become a place of pilgrimage. The public image of Monet was of the grand old man wrapped up in an Impressionist world of reflecting water studded with water-lilies, hemmed in by a profusion of flowers always in bloom [74]. Just as in 1926 *Cahiers d'art* published Matisse photographed with a model in his Nice apartment, so in 1925 *L'Art vivant* published Monet photographed in his garden. In both these cases, a middle-class environment is aestheticised, turned into a space of fulfulled desires, entirely shaped according to the vision of the artist who owns it. By contrast, the avant-garde artist's dissenting self-image led especially from the early 1920s to the making of studio spaces that fused domestic life and work, creating spaces that were, like Picasso's rue la Boétie studio, utterly *alien* to middle-class environments. They housed artists whose careers to a greater or lesser extent refused the material signs of success, whose careers were often developed in contradistinction to Monet's and Matisse's. I shall look briefly at three such spaces, the studios of Brancusi, Mondrian and Giacometti, and the careers of the artists who shaped them.

Brancusi himself photographically documented his work in his studio, and, like Picasso, set up his own photographic self-portraits in that changing environment. Corners of the studio with arrangements of sculptures were occasionally published in the art press [49]; his self-portraits, including a strikingly lit photograph taken around 1922 [75], tended to remain private. Here, like Monet in his garden, Brancusi the sculptor-craftsman is totally enveloped by the world he has literally carved out in the space around him, a space transformed by his sculptures and sculpted bases rather than by water and flowers. Already known in his native Romania when he had arrived in Paris in 1904, he had built a market first among the small Romanian community there and then as one of the circle of the Steins at the rue de Fleurus. As I

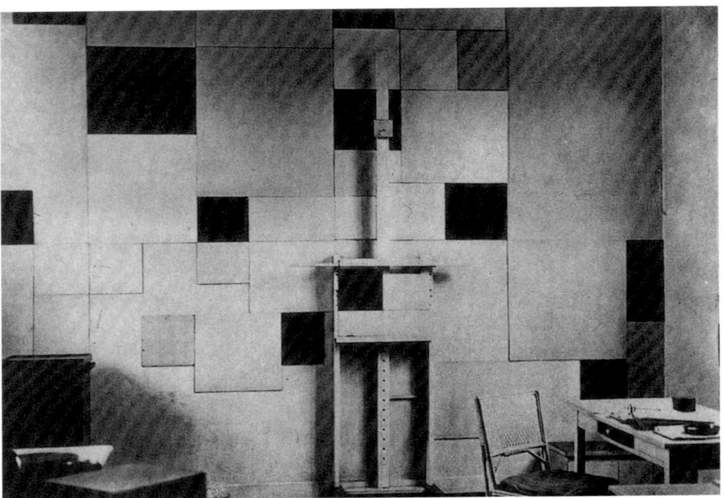

76. Michel Seuphor, *Mondrian's Studio at 26 rue du Départ*, c.1930. Photograph published in *Cercle et carré*, no. 3 (Paris, 1930)

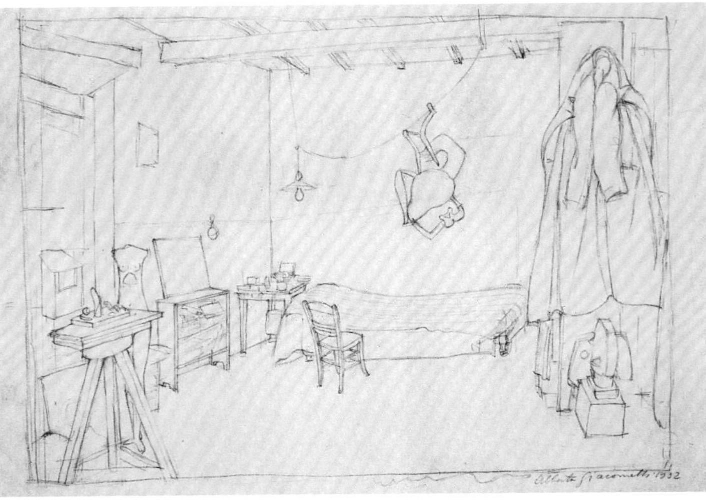

77. Alberto Giacometti, *The Studio*, 1932. Pencil on paper, 31 × 32.1 cm. Offentliche Kunstsammlung, Basel, Kupferstichkabinett

show in Chapter 11, he played on his genuine peasant origins as he developed primitivised idioms and direct carving practices between 1907 and 1914; in the 1920s he then experienced his own transaltantic rise to prominence helped by his friend Marcel Duchamp and by the indefatigable acquisitiveness of John Quinn. Indeed, so strong was his American market that he was able almost entirely to ignore the Parisian Salons (after 1920) and the Parisian dealers. But he did not leave his shed-like studio in the Impasse Ronsin, a backwater in the heart of Montparnasse, proof against its big-city surroundings. He changed studios in the Impasse Ronsin at the end of the 1920s, but would never move out of it. There, set apart from the metropolis but often visited by close friends like Duchamp and Léger, he perfected his own never static but 'pure' Brancusian environment. Noguchi remembered it as a world of unrelieved whiteness when he knew it in 1927–8, from the white of the circular plaster table around which guests ate Brancusi's renowned Romanian suppers to the white of his dog, the whole framed by whitewashed walls.[55]

In the mid-1920s, Mondrian's studio became as well-known as Brancusi's. Occasionally, photographs of it appeared in the art press, though more in the Netherlands and Germany than in France. One that was published in France shows it around 1930; it appeared that year in Michel Seuphor's short-lived periodical founded to promote non-figuration in France, *Cercle et carré* [76].[56] Mondrian had come first to Paris as a well-established Dutch modernist in spring 1912, and had quickly immersed himself in Picasso's and Braque's Cubism while continuing to show and to sell in the Netherlands. He too would not budge from the same studio complex whatever the temptations of success, though, when he emerged as a leading avant-garde figure in the mid-1920s, he did not experience anything like the market support enjoyed by Brancusi. His studio home was at 26, rue du Départ, in the unrelentingly urban neighbourhood of Montparnasse station, from very shortly after his arrival in 1912 until he finally left in 1938; only the war kept him away between 1914 and 1919. From 1919, he lived and worked in a cramped five-sided space, his bed only partially partitioned off from the main area, and gradually from the early 1920s he transformed it into a 'Neo-Plastic' space: the prototype of what he wrote of in his 1926 essay 'Home – Street – City' as a visionary project for entire cities 'spiritually' transformed.[57] That year, 1926, with the help of his Belgian artist-friend Vantongerloo, another early member of Theo van Doesburg's De Stijl group in Amsterdam, Mondrian took his transformation of the studio walls up to the ceiling; but he would never stop changing the juxtapositions of the moveable colour rectangles that were his compositional building-blocks. It is this space, like Brancusi's always open to alteration, that was recorded in *Cercle et carré* in 1930: the home in the studio as a work of art. The placing of the chair implicitly invites the artist into the space; Mondrian is, even in his absence, the controlling presence, the maker of this particular world, a very special individual who has chosen to resist material ambition.

In the spring of 1927, about the time he finally ceased attending Bourdelle's classes at the Académie de la Chaumière, Alberto Giacometti moved with his brother Diego into an ill-served studio at 46, rue Hippolyte-Mandrin. It was just north of the rue d'Alesia, not far from the expensive new studio homes of Foujita, Braque and Orloff on the fringes of Montparnasse. There was a shared toilet in the corridor, and no electricity or running water. He would sometimes sleep in a nearby hotel and often spent the summer in Maloja, a little village in the Italian/Swiss Alps he had known since his childhood, but mostly he was to live and work in the rue Hippolyte-Mandrin until his death in 1966. By 1929, he was showing at the galerie Jeanne Bucher, and that year the de Noailles bought a piece of his there. Between 1930 and 1933, he became an important new addition to the Surrealist group, and in terms of patrons and sales he was quickly successful. In 1930, there was a commission for the de Noailles' villa at Hyères; in 1932, there was a first solo show at the galerie Pierre Colle. In 1934, there was a first New York show at the Julien Levy Gallery and in 1936, his *Palace at 4 a.m.* [325], given its first exposure in *Minotaure*, was bought by the Museum of Modern Art. But he chose to go on living as well as working in the dark cave-like space of his studio, his own graffiti scratched into the cracked plaster on the walls, the filth from his work sessions with metal, wood, clay and plaster around him, and by 1933 that space was already a central aspect of his self-image. The studio appears suggestively photographed in the same number of *Minotaure* as the *Palace at 4.a.m.* (itself a kind of dream studio space) – one of those recorded to illustrate Maurice Raynal's essay on sculptors' studios [51, 52], but so different from them all, except perhaps Brancusi's.[58] The year before, he had recorded it in two meticulously all-inclusive pencil drawings sent to an Italian admirer, among the first of his visitors to go away haunted by the image of the studio. One of the drawings [77] delineates with undifferentiated scupulousness his overcoat, hung like the sculpture (now lost) suspended from the ceiling, a flimsy chair, an improvised dressing-table, his bed and such pieces as *Model for a Square* (on the modelling stand to the left) and *Walking Woman* (behind it). The artworks have become just everyday objects; the everyday objects, art. Everything and nothing here is art. In all its dimensions, conceptual and palpable, this is Giacometti's world, observing Giacometti's categories.

Breton scorned commerce and yet himself operated as a dealer to keep a place in society for the artists he admired. As unabashedly as Picasso, he brought together avant-garde intransigence with a willingness to manage his affairs effectively.[59] He despised the careerist compromises that drew a writer like Robert Desnos to journalism. But all those artists who operated at the centre of Surrealism's attack on the dominant values of French society, even an artist like Giacometti who so conspicuously refused the trappings of material success, accepted, like Breton, that in order for an artist's work to be seen there had to be exhibitions and so there had to be dealers and collectors to back them. There had to be careers. A career in that sense was successfully avoided by only one artist whose life and work has been remembered and celebrated: Marcel Duchamp.

The case of Duchamp finally brings home the disjunction between earlier and later canons. Since the publication of the first monograph on him, Robert Lebel's in 1959, he has become a modern master to equal or even exceed Matisse and Picasso in stature. In the 1960s and 1970s, he emerged as *the* model for a critical avant-garde practice capable of keeping all who respond to it off-balance. Before 1940, though not so much in America, his contribution was hardly visible; indeed, in France he was rarely mentioned outside the Surrealist circle, and then only as an artist who had squandered his gifts.[60]

However marginal he appeared then in France, Duchamp's is a case that demands special attention. It is unique, but still it decisively reveals the contradictions and complexities inherent in the ever dependent relationship between avant-garde artists and the well-off middle-class circles that supported them, however subversive their work. It is a case also that points the way towards the globalisation of modernism more emphatically than even those of Matisse and Picasso, because Duchamp invented the role of artist-without-a-career on a transatlantic stage.

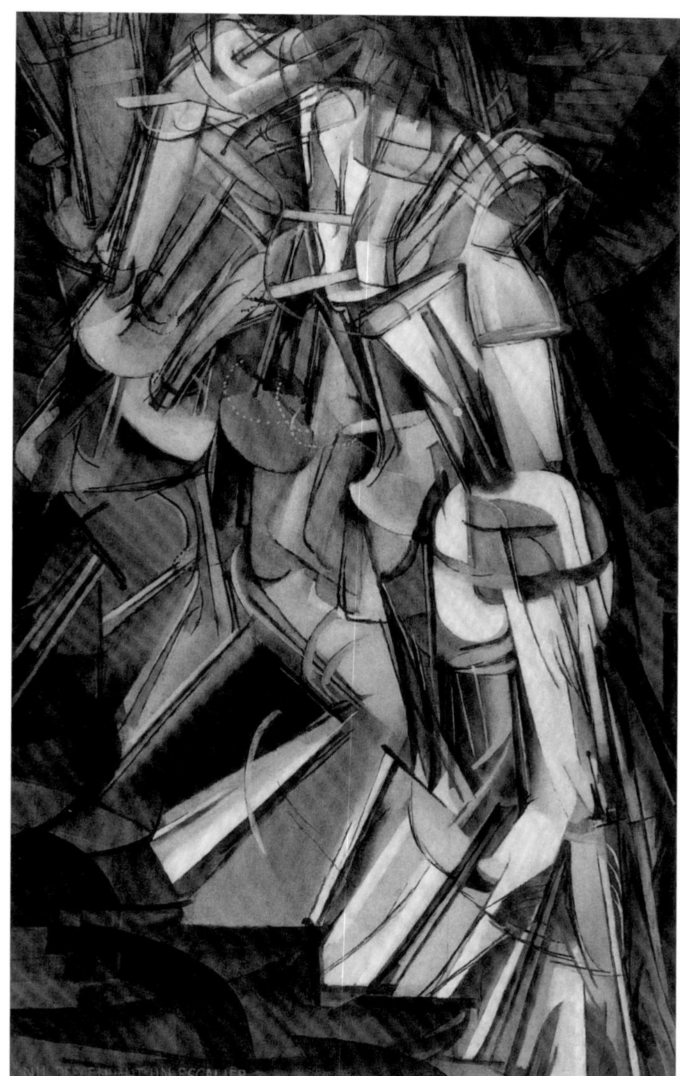

78. Marcel Duchamp, *Nude Descending a Staircase, No. 2*, 1912. Oil on canvas, 146 × 89 cm. Philadelphia Museum of Art, The Louise and Walter Arensberg Collection

BEING MARCEL DUCHAMP: A SINGULAR DOUBLE-LIFE

Like many independents, Duchamp bypassed ENBA (he failed the entrance exams in 1905), and instead developed a dual career as caricaturist and serious aspirant painter. His brother Gaston, signing himself 'Jacques Villon' in the illustrated magazines, had done so from the mid-1890s. Duchamp's moment as an emergent modernist came when, with his artist brothers, the sculptor Raymond Duchamp-Villon and the painter Jacques Villon, he took part in the Cubist group-showing at the Salon d'automne of 1911. Early in 1912, there was a brief impediment to his rise to prominence when Gleizes and Metzinger objected to the inclusion of his *Nude Descending a Staircase No. 2* [78] in the Cubist showing at the Indépendants of 1912. Duchamp always maintained that the sticking-point was his elaborate descriptive title which was actually written on to the far-from-descriptive painting; he also maintained later that it was the

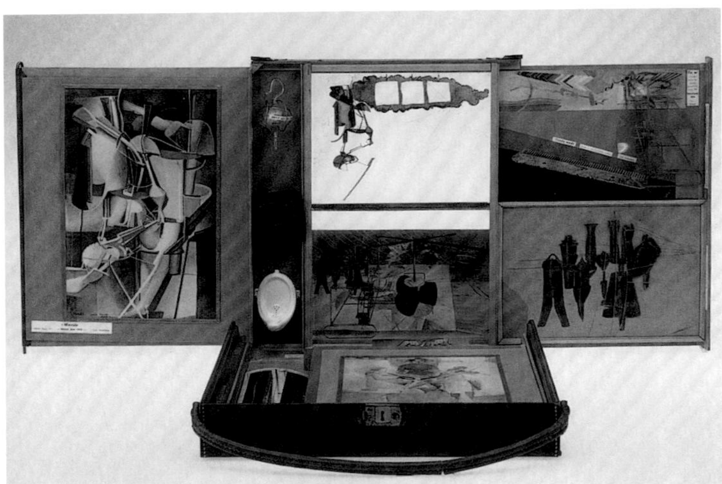

79. Marcel Duchamp, *Boîte-en-valise (Box in a Suitcase)*, 1941, Deluxe Edition, View III. Miniature replicas and colour reproductions of works by Duchamp contained in a cloth-covered cardboard box enclosed in a leather valise. Philadelphia Museum of Art, Louise and Walter Arensberg Collection

title that made the work the centre of the press hullabaloo that met the Armory Show in New York in March 1913.[61]

Duchamp only heard about his fame in the United States as the painter of *Nude Descending* when Picabia, a close friend, arrived back months later from a transatlantic trip accompanying the show. But even before he had agreed to send work to the Armory Show, he had convinced himself that the collective demands of the Cubist group and the obligation to follow up avant-garde notoriety with market success encroached too oppressively on his independence. Already in November 1912, he had enrolled on a State-run course in librarianship and, using the influence of Picabia's uncle, Maurice Davanne, director of the Bibliothèque Sainte-Geneviève in the Sorbonne, took on a job there early in 1913 at five francs a day. Like his artist-brothers, he had a modest allowance of 150 francs a month from his father in Rouen too. The hours were easy, three-and-a-half a day, and freed from pressure he was able to develop in total privacy the idea for an altogether new kind of artwork to be executed on glass, the *Large Glass*, or to give it its full title, *The Bride Stripped Bare by her Bachelors, Even* [150, 302].

From that point on, without any fanfare, Duchamp quietly developed a double-life strategy, designed to give him freedom from both modern movement groupings and the market. He gave himself the chance to pursue his own projects on his own terms by earning a living in undemanding routine jobs. A rheumatic heart-murmur saved him from the front, and in 1915 he crossed the Atlantic to the city of his scandalous Armory Show triumph, New York. There he continued to work on the *Glass*, mostly in a one-room bachelor studio in the Lincoln Arcade Building on Broadway between 65th and 66th Streets, earning two dollars an hour by giving French lessons. At one point he worked as a librarian in J.P. Morgan's private library and at another as personal secretary to a French army captain on a military mission to the city.[62] He also began to acquire wealthy friends. His notoriety and his Armory Show contacts, notably Walter Pach, gave him an immediate introduction on arrival to the collectors Walter and Louise Arensberg, and through them his circle of faithful supporters widened. It was through the Arensbergs, too, that he met Man Ray, whose double Parisian life as artist and society photographer would, of course, be modelled on Duchamp's example. It would also involve, however, unlike Duchamp's strategy, a means of earning which has since become treated as an art, complicating matters. By 1919 and 1921, when he returned for several months at a time to France, Duchamp numbered among his rich transatlantic friends John Quinn and Katherine S. Dreier alongside the Arensbergs. In 1920, he helped Dreier found the Société Anonyme, a pioneer organisation for collecting and showing modern art in New York. It anticipated both the Barnes Foundation and the New York Museum of Modern Art, as well as Gallatin's Museum of Living Art. Back in France, where he was again based between 1923 and 1941, his double-life continued, with Jacques Doucet added to his supportive entourage in 1923. He left the *Large Glass* 'definitively unfinished' in the Arensbergs' New York apartment. Where Matisse, Picasso, and most other modern masters (including Brancusi) cultivated wealthy collectors of their work, Duchamp collected the collectors themselves, not to buy his work, but to support his singular activities; he seldom produced anything for them to buy.

At the same time, he maintained his own earnings and indeed in the 1920s tried his hand as a businessman to improve them: first, in a failed bookshop attached to a dyers in New York (1922), and then (1924–5) in a project to develop a system to beat the Casino at Monte Carlo, for which he issued bonds (among his investors where figures as various as Doucet and Marie Laurencin). Indeed, he saw nothing problematic in speculating both on his own and in partnership with his French friend from New York Henri-Pierre Roché (Quinn's European agent) in the art market he so despised. In 1926, he used his friendship with Picabia to buy a 'collection' of Picabia's work, which he then sold for an immediate 10% profit at the Hôtel Drouot. Then, Quinn having died in 1924, he and Roché negotiated the purchase of some thirty Brancusis from the American's unrivalled collection of the Romanian's work. This formed the core of a major Brancusi show put on by Joseph Brummer in New York in 1926, and the sale one by one of the Brancusis Duchamp still owned after that exhibition financed his life and his projects through the 1930s.

Duchamp the artist was not productive; he had made sure that he was under no pressure to produce, and anyway he repeatedly claimed that work bored him. In New York between 1915 and the early 1920s, he engaged in the avant-garde activities of the Arensberg circle and besides working on the *Large Glass* took into the public arena an idea which was to have great consequences, the 'readymade'. In France, he served as a much appreciated stimulant on the fringes of the Dada and Surrealist groups. But especially after he moved into a bare two-room apartment at 11 rue de Larrey in 1927, he focused his creative energies almost entirely on chess, at least until the mid-1930s. He was selected for the French international chess team, and in 1932 published a serious study of end-games. And yet, however subterranean Duchamp's activities as an artist became, he remained throughout the 1930s a presence within the most radical section of the French avant-garde, around André Breton.

Indeed, he began, with considerable care, to plan for his future as an historical figure.[63] Even Duchamp's non-career ended up a career.

In 1934, with the help of a Brancusi sale and the collateral from another Brancusi sculpture, he financed the private publication of ninety-four pages of the notes, sketches and photographs he had accumulated mostly in 1912–13 in the development of the *Large Glass*. They were printed in a limited edition of 300, with a deluxe edition of ten, and distributed in boxes clad in green suede. He intended *The Green Box* as an accompaniment, indeed an essential component of the *Glass*, and went to enormous lengths to give the notes 'authenticity' by reproducing as exactly as possible the original inks, pencil leads and papers – down to the smallest tear. An almost immediate result of this enterprise was the publication of the first essay dedicated to the *Large Glass*, Breton's 'Phare de la mariée' (Lighthouse of the Bride), which appeared in *Minotaure* in December 1934; it has been the starting point for historical analyses of the work ever since. Very soon afterwards, in 1935, Duchamp started on another retrospective project, the meticulous miniaturised reproduction using the stencil pochoir technique of his entire oeuvre, including already lost or destroyed readymades. The project would not be completed until 1941, when he produced the first *Boîte-en-valise* (*Box in a Suitcase*) [79]. The enclosure in a suitcase of the record of his 'œuvre complète' from over thirty years of slow-motion, virtually secret activity says a great deal. In New York and Paris, he had avoided the accumulation of possessions. He and his 'art' were always ready to move. The *Green Box* and the *Boîte-en-valise*, however, mark what was certainly for Duchamp more than a flicker of interest in his 'œuvre's' survival prospects. It can be no accident that these two projects summing up his achievement followed so closely upon Matisse's and Picasso's huge retrospectives of 1931 and 1932, and the first volume of Zervos's 'œuvres complètes' catalogue of Picasso. Duchamp was another modern master who used the record of his 'work' to begin constructing an historical identity for himself in the 1930s.[64]

The random disorder of the notes in the *Green Box* and the ironic comment on the modern museum contained in the *Boîte-en-valise* reveal a peculiarly Duchampian attitude to the documentation of an 'œuvre'. He was the obverse of the great paradigmatic moderns, Matisse and Picasso, in almost every way. His ideas and projects after 1912 were never dependent in any way on the market; he learned to exploit collectors and to speculate in the market himself. Before 1940, he was never free of the need to earn; but he never allowed his own 'art' to earn a living for him. Perhaps most striking of all, not only did he reduce art to the condition of a problem without solutions, he also refused to play the role of artist in any of its accepted forms. There are no images of Duchamp the artist or of his 'studio' (photographed or painted) in the art press between the wars. He might have kept his own name, unlike his artist-brothers Raymond (Duchamp-Villan) and Gaston (Jacques Villon), but when his image did appear it was invariably under assumed identities: photographed by Man Ray in the early 1920s, for instance, in cross-dressed disguise as Rose or Rrose Sélavy, a female alter-ego of his own invention [303]. Duchamp *as* Duchamp appeared most memorably for a 1920s French art audience in René Clair's film *Entre'acte* (1924). Man Ray was there too; they were playing chess [80].

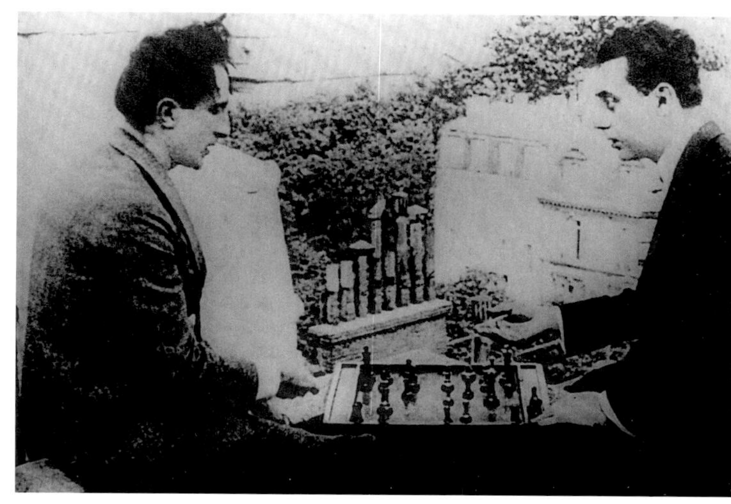

80. René Clair, Still from the film *Entr'acte* (Duchamp and Man Ray playing chess) 1924

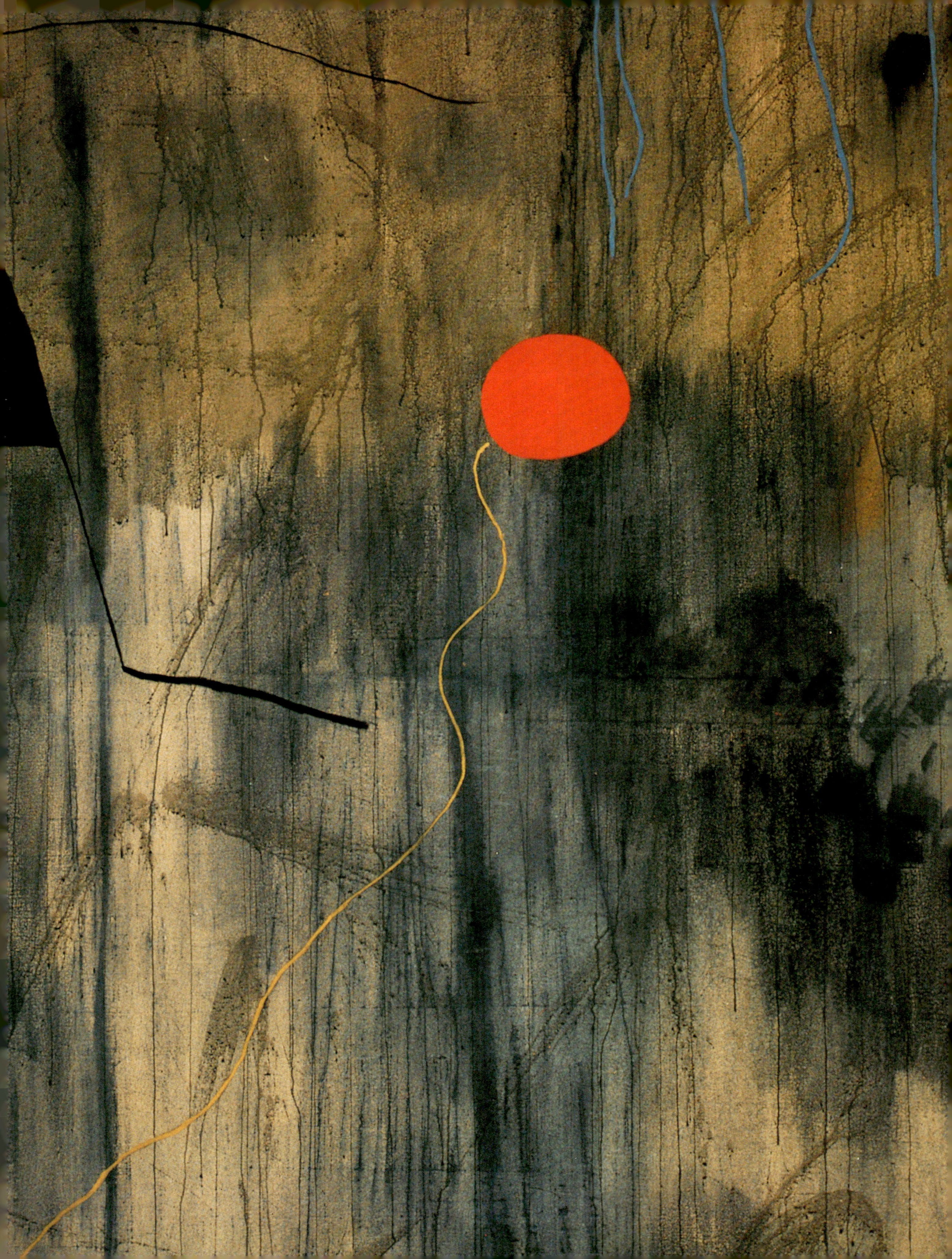

PART THREE

Making Art

PART THREE

Making Art

INTRODUCTION

Parts One and Two of this book look at histories and lives. Part Three is focused on works of art. Above all, Part Three is concerned with the 'how' of works of art, not the 'what'. Many modernist works of art were predicated upon 'formalist' ideals: the conviction that the 'what' and the 'how' are one and the same, that meaning at its most profound resides in the formal properties of the work, in *how* it is put together. Such a conviction, of course, fixes works of art in an autonomous aesthetic sphere, separate from society, as much of the theory associated with modernism in France outside the Dada-Surrealist milieu does. In fact, modernist as much as non-modernist works of art were caught up in the major social, political and cultural conflicts of the period; and the ways in which this affected what they said is a major concern of the second half of this book.

Part Three also deals with what was new in the modernist art of the period. The material that will be discussed here is, therefore, primarily works by key modernists, alongside statements and theoretical writings both by them and their champions in the press. Such a concentration on the new in the work of leading modernists carries the obvious danger of perpetuating the kind of storyline that picks out individual modernist heroes rather than movements: a storyline in which irresistible innovative revolutionaries pit their courage against comfortable academics who are protected by institutional support and who are working with exhausted conventions. Part Two has, I hope, constructed a different picture, one in which independent and academic artists competed for dominance in a single-market system which included both private individuals and public institutions. It should also be clear that before 1914, the art supported by State institutions and the more conventional bourgeois collectors was not exhausted: it was confident, highly accomplished and bewilderingly diverse. The 'others' against which modernists defined themselves were many. They included the recent modernism of older generations who were still very much alive (Monet and Signac for Matisse, say, Matisse for Picasso, Picasso for Miró). They also included the current work of the conventionally successful (the fashionable portrait painters and those who contributed to the great decorative schemes in the Hôtel de Ville and the Petit Palais, figures like Bonnat, Gervex or Besnard).

CHAPTER 5

Representing Nature; Seeing Art

EXPRESSION AND DECORATION: FROM 'ART NOUVEAU' BING TO MATISSE

At the Salon d'automne of 1910 two sets of mural paintings destined for great town-houses were shown by leading independents. One was by Maurice Denis (b.1870), a painter-theorist who stressed his membership of 'the generation of 1890' (b.1865–70), the generation inspired, as he understood it, by Van Gogh, Gauguin and Cézanne. It consisted of four small and four large panels, which were trapezoidal in shape in order to fit the octagonal dome of the studio in Charles Stern's newly built 'hôtel' on the Boulevard Lannes in Paris. Together they were entitled *Florentine Evening*, drawing attention to their early Italian Renaissance echoes. In a Mediterranean setting of cypresses, olive trees and rose bowers they evoked subjects from Bocaccio's *Decameron*: their titles were *The Poem*, *Bathers*, *The Song* [81] and *Dances*. The other set of mural paintings was the pair of huge canvases painted by Matisse (b.1869) for the staircase in the Trubetskoy Palace, Sergei Shchukin's Moscow home. Despite the total lack of Italian Renaissance resonance in Matisse's huge canvases, their subjects, *Dance* and *Music* were very much in tune with Denis' [82]. And when Matisse had started work on them in 1909, a third canvas whose subject also echoes Denis' had been begun as part of the set, *Bathers by a Stream*. Found to have no place in the scheme, it would be completed as an easel painting in its own right several years later in 1916 [84].[1] The arts and in particular dance and music have a long history in European decorative painting, a history whose Baroque and Rococo high points were recalled twenty years earlier in two of the ceiling panels for the lavishly appointed ballroom of the Hôtel de Ville, which were executed around the time of the emergence of 'the generation of 1890'.[2] Their subjects were *Dance* and *Music across the Ages*. Henri Gervex's *Music across the Ages* meets the decorative challenge with particular panache [83].

Gervex exploits the motion and space-making techniques of post-Baroque ceiling painting to create effects only possible after the 1870s. His muses and musicians tumble out of a turbulent sky from above a modern singer on stage:

Facing page. Detail of Joan Miró, *Birth of the World*, 1925 [316]

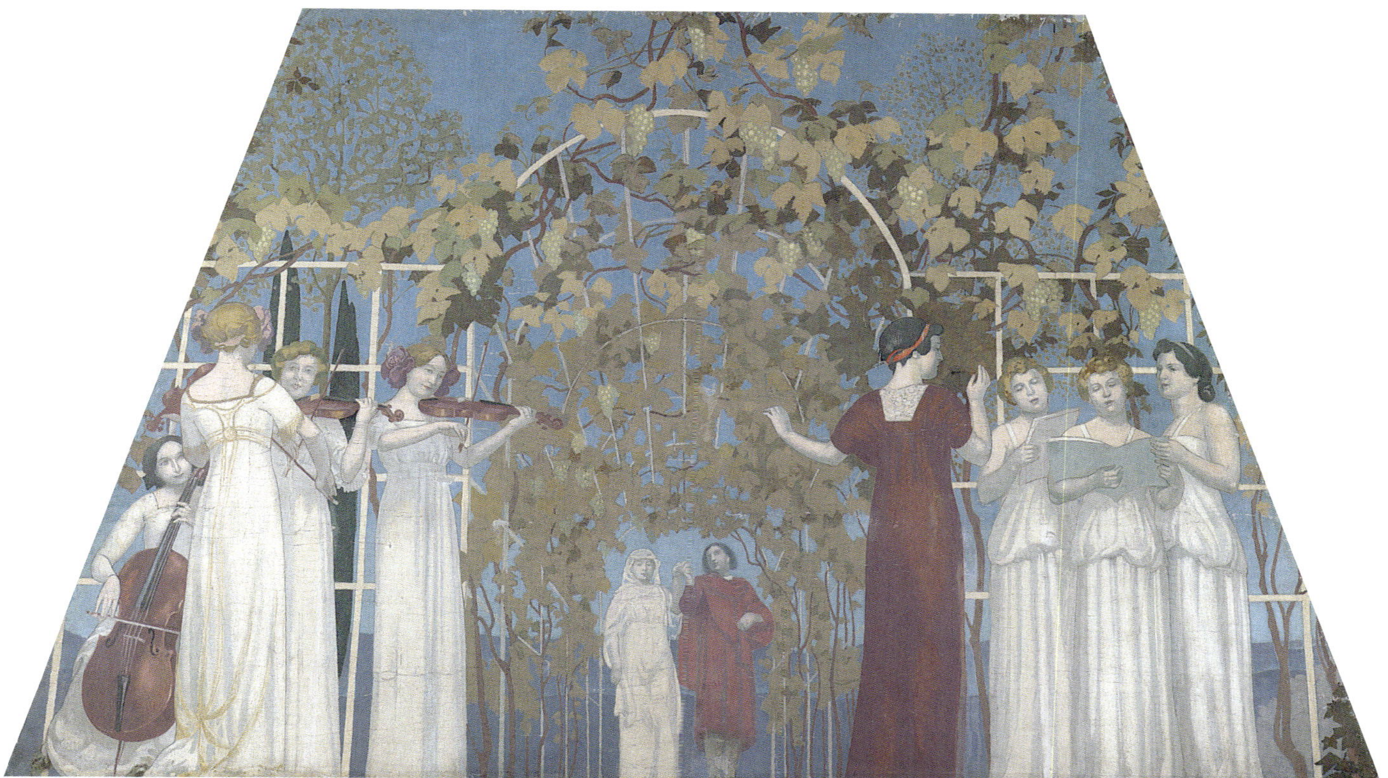

81. Maurice Denis, *The Song*, 1910. Fresco-technique on trapezoidal canvas, 213 × 364 and 212 cm. Musée du Petit Palais, Paris

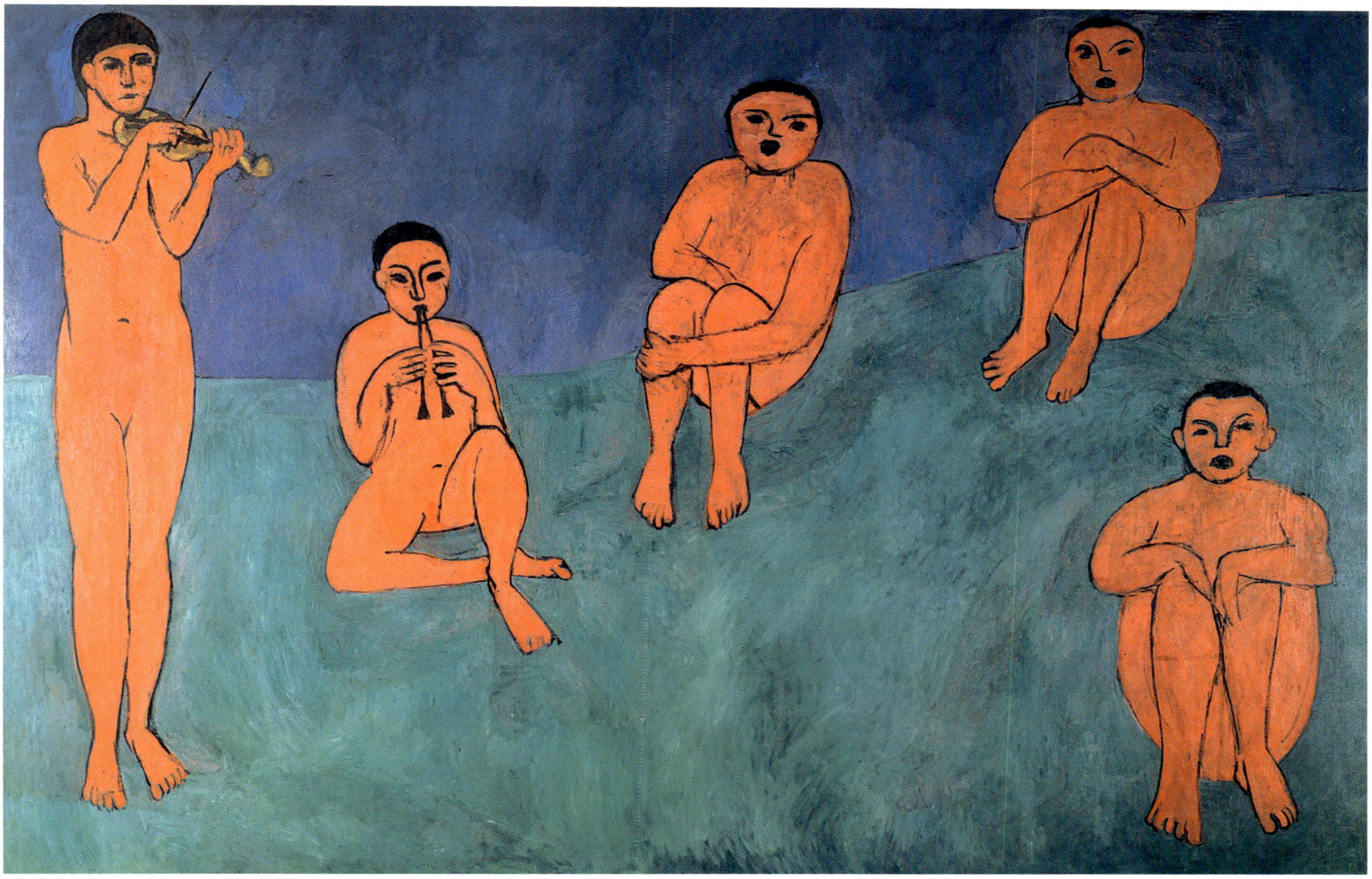

82. Henri Matisse, *Music*, 1910. Oil on canvas, 260 × 389 cm. The State Hermitage Museum, St Petersburg

Tiepolo and Degas in near collision, watched by Parisian mondains in a *quadra tura* box at the theatre. The 'allegorical' and the 'real' cohabit in an elaborate perspectival and atmospheric illusion of deep space, just as they do in Alfred Roll's or Albert Besnard's ceiling paintings of the 1900s for the Petit Palais [165]. Against this, the surface-hugging blue and green of Denis' skies and foliage in his 1910 panels, and the lucid arrangement of the figures in relation to the picture-plane can seem comparatively flat. But, though Denis, in emulation of Puvis de Chavanne's reticent Neo-Classicism, avoids spectacular illusions of plunging recession, he achieves an effect of space opening out around the dome by using ornamental garden features to arrange an orderly retreat from the picture plane into perspectival depth. The low viewpoint adopted in all the panels introduces the idea of vistas we can only imagine: a space for the mind as well as the eye.

Vistas are not even alluded to in Matisse's *Music* and there is neither perspective nor the suggestion of atmosphere: there are none of the devices either of post-Baroque or post Neo-Classical mural painting. Five schematically outlined male nudes coloured brick-red are placed against broad areas of blue and green. The scuffed and scumbled surfaces of the blue and green make them at once tactile and vibrant, but suggest neither relief modelling nor recession; the clash of red against blue and red's complementary, green, is a clash of flat-colour quantities. If *Music* (and the same is so of *Dance*) can seem to open up a space, it is the effect of colour and paint marks alone – an effect that makes the figures appear to hang in front of the depths sensed in the tactile blue and green.

83. Henri Gervex, *Music across the Ages*, 1888–9. Oil on canvas fixed to the ceiling. Salle des fêtes, Hôtel de Ville, Paris

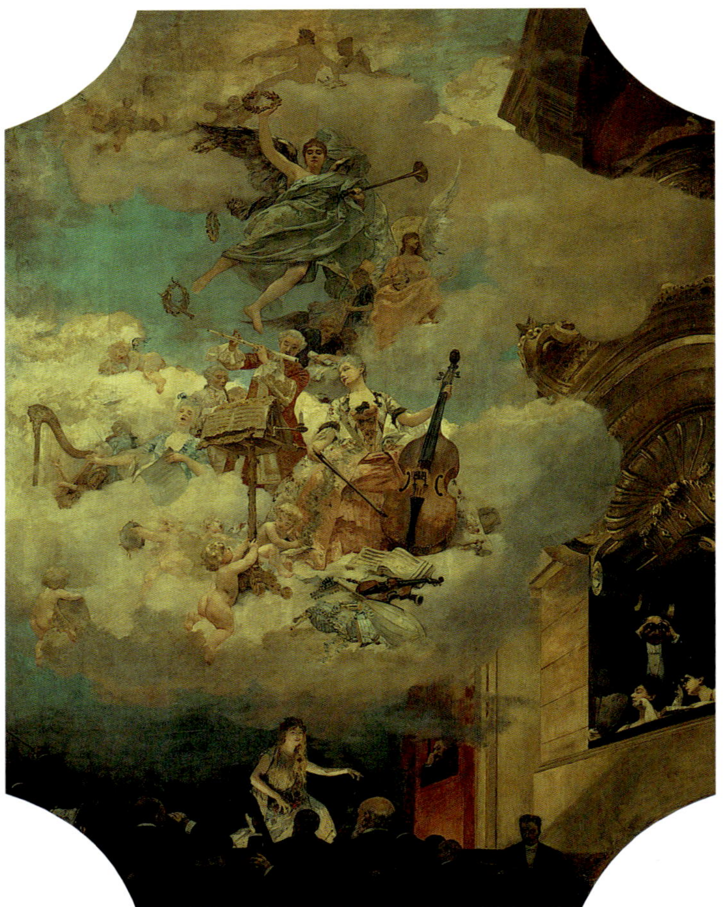

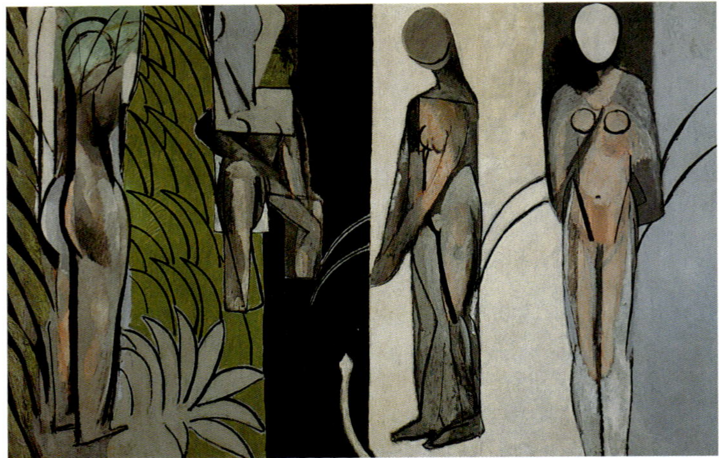

84. Henri Matisse, *Bathers by a Stream*, 1909–16. Oil on canvas, 261.8 × 391.4 cm. The Art Institute of Chicago. Charles H. and Mary F. S. Worcester Collection

Both Maurice Denis and Matisse thought of modernist painting as essentially 'decorative', and periodically through their careers underlined the point by painting for large-scale decorative schemes. 'Notes of a Painter' of 1908 was Matisse's major theoretical statement before the 1930s, and indeed, was the single attempt to put into words a credo for any who might follow him and the Fauves. Composition is the core artistic practice as Matisse conceives it in that text. 'Composition,' he writes, 'is the art of arranging in a decorative manner the diverse elements at the painter's command to express his feelings'.[3] Decoration and expression come together at the heart of the new painting, as they had for Denis and the Nabis in the 1890s. They were, however, not necessarily easily reconciled one with the other, and indeed a stress on self-expression can be thought to contradict a stress on decoration.

In 1895, Denis and another of the Nabis, Paul Ranson, had been involved as decorative painters with the impresario of the decorative arts Samuel Bing in the designing and installation of his Parisian retail gallery, the galerie de l'Art Nouveau. Ranson painted murals of pastoral scenes for the show dining room designed by the Belgian architect-decorator Henry Van der Velde [85]; Denis painted murals and designed the furniture for the show bedroom. Its prospectus stated the function of Bing's enterprise to be as 'a gathering place for all works marked by a clearly personal sentiment',[4] but at the same time Bing could write to Denis insisting that there should be 'a perfect consistency of style' in each room.[5] There is evidence, thus, at the beginning of the Art Nouveau enterprise of conflict between the aspiration to personal expression and the need for architectural wholeness. In 1910, Denis was content to paint as an individual subordinating his work to the space supplied to him by Charles Stern; he conceived the movement and depth of his panels on the terms dictated by its architectur-

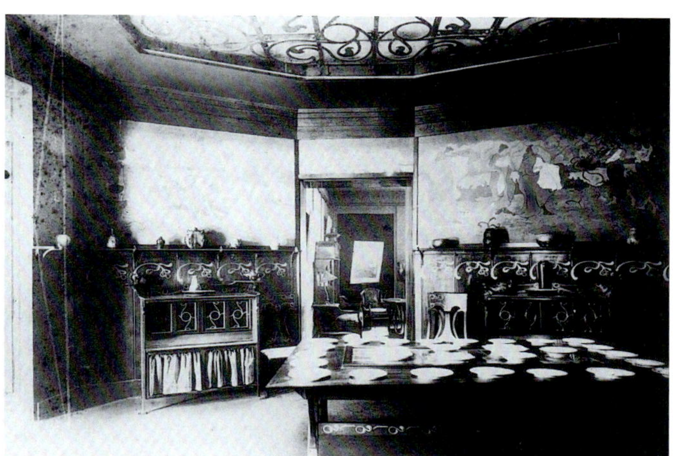

85. Henri Van der Velde, with murals by Paul Ranson, *Dining-room, Galerie de l'Art Nouveau*, Paris, 1895

al frame.[6] Matisse ignored all but the basic measurements of the architectural frame. His *Dance* and *Music* panels were painted to take over any interior: personal expression had become the controlling imperative.

However respectful they could be to the architectural demands of interiors, it was 'the generation of 1890', following that of the mid-1880s, who first appropriated the decorative aesthetic associated with Samuel Bing for the theorisation of a self-sufficient and individually expressive pictorial art. This decorative aesthetic had been developed on the basis of Japonisme (Bing's first enthusiasm) and English decorative art theory, which stressed the inappropriateness of illusionist space and naturalist form for art designed to enhance architecture, as well as the expressive potential of line and colour (the writings, for instance, of Walter Crane and Arthur Heygate Macmurdo in the 1880s and 1890s). Decorative painting was presented as self-sufficient and two-dimensional, an assertion of the flatness of the wall in the planar ensembles of architecture; its ornamental function freed it from the imitation of appearance. Where Henri Gervex pierced the wall and opened up an illusionist space for modernised allegorical reverie, Denis and his Nabis friends working for Bing's 'Art Nouveau' covered the walls with flat screens of line and colour, styling their figures in response to Van der Velde's ornamental vocabulary as well as to their memories of Gauguin's Synthetism. Even in 1910 with the Stern murals, Denis balanced his orderly construction of perspectival recession against a treatment of figures as idealised formal ciphers and colour areas as flat pattern.

From the 1880s, the decorative aesthetic among modernists was not confined to mural painting, and by 1900 it had become a feature of the thinking not only of those who consciously followed Gauguin and Van Gogh, but of those who considered themselves the scientific heirs of the Impressionists. In 1898, Paul Signac (b.1863), Georges Seurat's ally from the 1880s, published a series of articles in *La Revue Blanche*, which he then put together as a book, *D'Eugène Delacroix au néo-impressionnisme*. Here he identified the representation of light as the central task of modern painting, and claimed that 'Neo-Impressionism' – the art of himself and such friends as Henri-Edmond Cross and the Belgian Theo van Rysselberghe – was the logical conclusion to the intuitions of Delacroix and the Impressionists as painters of light. Yet, this theory too, with its focus on the idea of painting as representation, insisted on art's decorative self-sufficiency. 'Even paintings of small dimensions by the neo-impressionists,' Signac wrote, 'can be presented as decorative.' They 'restore light to the walls of our modern apartments, enclose pure colours in rhythmic lines, and share the charm of oriental carpets, mosaics and tapestries – are they not also decorations?'[7]

In 1908 with the 'Notes of a Painter' and in 1910 with *Dance* and *Music*, Matisse was plainly the heir to both Signac and 'the generation of 1890', but his appropriation of a decorative aesthetic for painting was far more insistent on the expressive independence of the artist from architectural imperatives. Everything about these 'decorative' canvases asserted Matisse's commitment to a self-driven, self-sufficient exploration of painting as painting. *Music*, like *Dance*, refuses any superficial echo of architectural styles; the working of the surface conveys the long-drawn-out process of making at the expense of any display of craft, skill or consistency; it is the result of unplanned acts of marking and erasure, and says so. The artist de-skills as a craftsman in order to re-skill as a self-expressive painter. *Bathers by a Stream*, completed as an independent easel painting, says so still more assertively: no figure is 'finished' with any consistency, the standing nude on the left offers passages of modelling and passages of schematic line-drawing over grey. One leg is firmly contoured, the other is merely hinted at with a single broken line, everywhere there are visible *pentimenti*.[8] In the 'Notes', long passages are devoted to the process of 'composing'; they concentrate entirely on the artist's individual phase-by-phase relationship with each painting, sculpture or drawing, a relationship developed over time, and one that in painting always takes account of the rectangle of the canvas as a whole. Even in painting with a decorative function, for Matisse, it is only the self-sufficient space

86. Henri Matisse, *Luxe, calme et volupté*, 1904–5. Oil on canvas, 98.5 × 118 cm. Musée d'Orsay, Paris

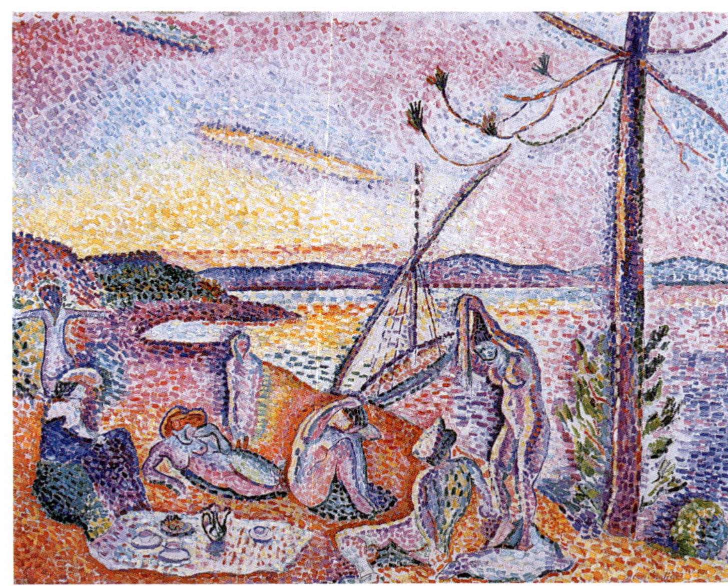

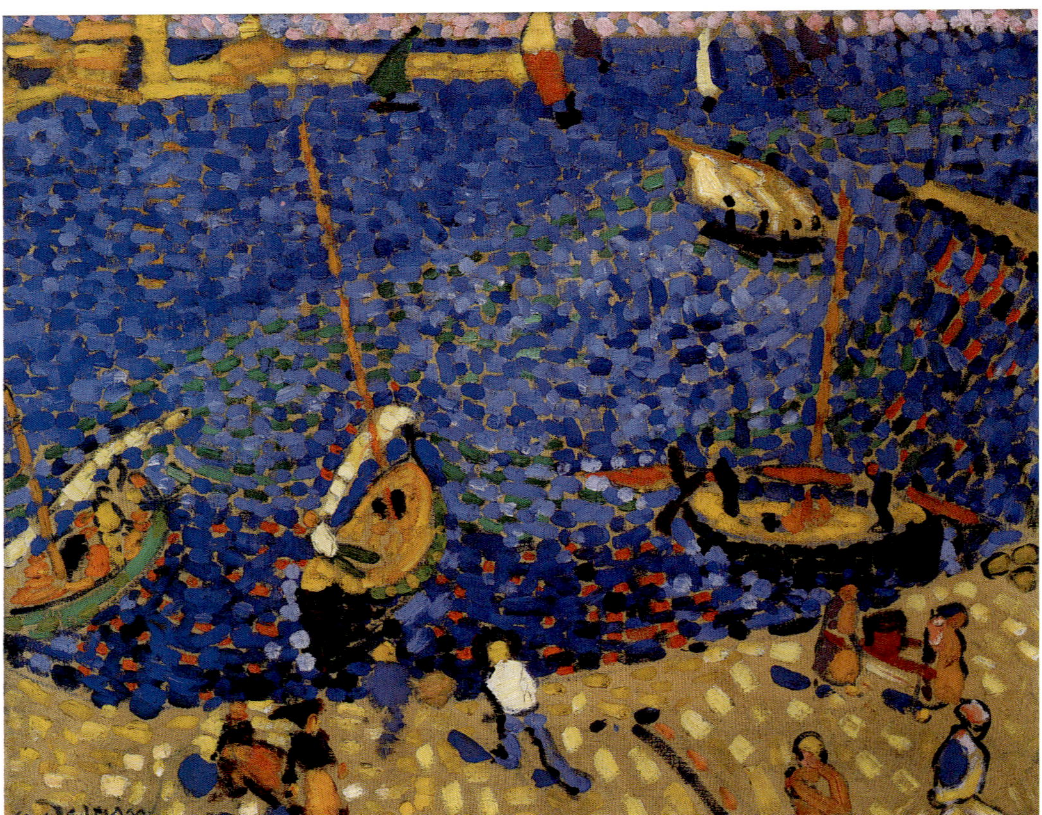

87. André Derain, *Boats at Collioure*, 1905. Oil on canvas, 60 × 73 cm. Kunstsammlung Nordrhein Westfalen, Düsseldorf

within the frame that matters; and within that what matters most, according to the 'Notes', is 'expression'.

And yet, what Matisse says he expresses is emotion felt, not before painting, but before nature. Matisse's expressive theory of decorative painting, like the theory of painting developed by Maurice Denis in the 1890s and 1900s, declares the self-sufficiency of the work of art while yet declaring its continued dependence on the artist's experience of nature. In this they share Signac's Neo-Impressionist belief that painting simplifies (abstracts) *in order* to represent. Matisse's first Fauve style emerged from brief but intense experimentation with Neo-Impressionist technique; so did André Derain's. Derain (b.1880) did not publish theory, and Matisse made a point of stressing the difficulty of finding words for painting, especially for an artist. But in the 'Notes' he did find words for what he thought he and those who painted like him were doing, and both the concepts and the vocabulary he developed in his theory have their sources above all in Neo-Impressionist and post-Nabis theory, especially as set down by Signac and Denis. If we are to grasp how his notion of the decorative related to his notion of the expressive, it is by examining in tandem how he worked in relation to nature (the model or motif), and how he conceived the relationship between seeing the composition develop as he drew, painted or sculpted, and seeing nature. Denis and Signac provide a verbal context for this; Signac and his close friend Henri-Edmond Cross (b.1862) a pictorial one too, since Matisse directly responded to their painting.

Matisse made his learning experience with Signac and Cross very public by showing at the Indépendants of 1905 the ambitious composition that resulted from a summer spent with them at Saint-Tropez in 1904: *Luxe, calme et volupté* [86]. It takes up both the arcadian subject matter of Cross in the early 1900s [228] and Signac's and Cross's divisionist technique; Signac bought it, the ultimate compliment. Derain did not make such a public display of respect, but among the earlier pictures he painted when he joined Matisse at Collioure in the summer of 1905, some obviously adapt divisionist technique: for instance, *Boats at Collioure* [87].

Matisse had first read Signac's *D'Eugène Delacroix au néo-impressionnisme* in the *Revue Blanche* serialisation of 1898; his earliest attempts to adapt the theory are in paintings of 1899.[9] By Neo-Impressionist theory, he understood a post-Impressionist belief that shadows as well as lights are coloured (violet, blue or blue-green), that coloured light modifies local colour, and that only unmixed, 'pure' colours should be used by the painter. He understood too that the painter should work for a balance of 'cool and warm hues, pale and intense tones', constantly aware of the effect of colours on one another by contrast and analogy (especially the three complementary contrasts involving primary colours – red and green, blue and orange, yellow and violet).[10] He understood, further, that the ambition to produce in the viewer's eye an optical mixture of the coloured components of light had been replaced by an ambition to create coloured harmonies by the distribution of contrasts across the picture surface, and that this shift from scientific naturalism to chromatic composition entailed the rejection of the *pointilliste* dot.[11] The dot had been replaced by the 'touch' ('tache'), a coloured mark which was too large to be absorbed into the pallid veil produced by the 'optical mix-

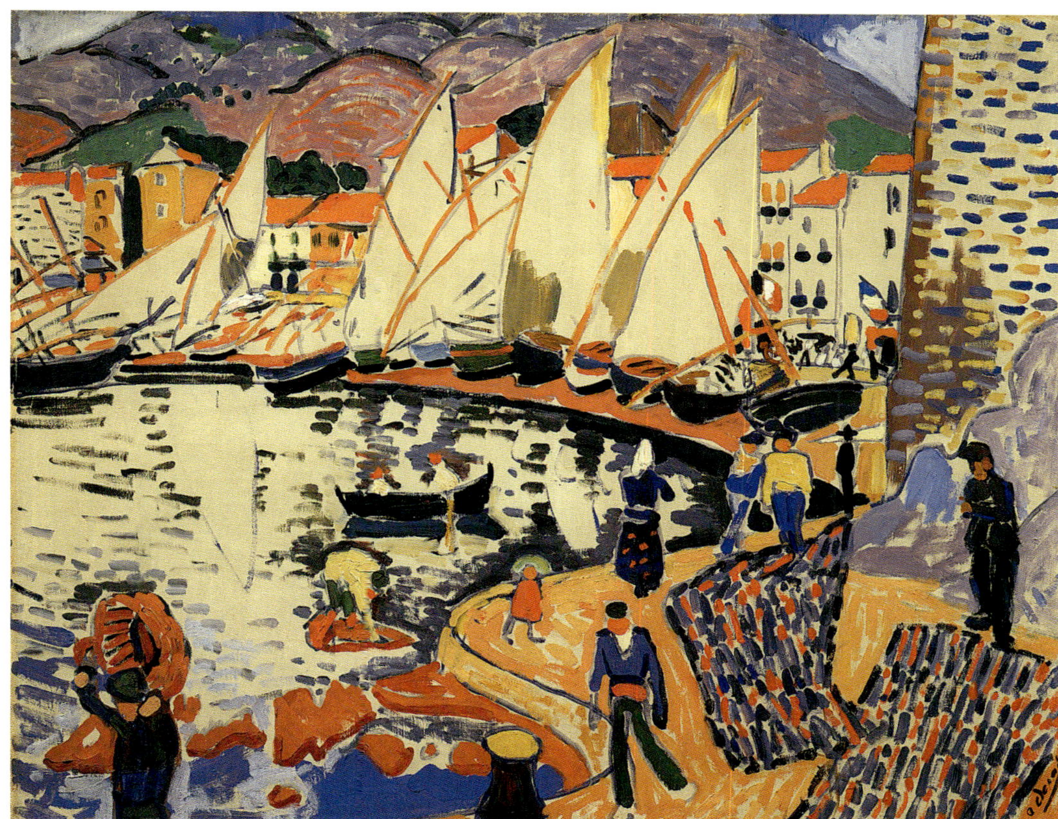

88. André Derain, *Drying Sails*, 1905. 82 × 101 cm. Pushkin Museum of Fine Art, Moscow

ing' of tiny coloured dots; and the 'touch' was to be treated as a pure pictorial element, varied according to the size of the canvas and the demands of the composition. Indeed, colour materialised in the 'touch' was to be treated like the pure tones of a musical scale. Finally, Matisse understood that, for Signac and Cross, these individually discernible coloured marks, each one a material element, combined to create the radiant effect of dematerialisation in light. It was by recreating light in nature with coloured pigment that Neo-Impressionist painting remained representational, and as such it always began with the artist's response to nature.

All the aspects of such a comprehensive understanding of Neo-Impressionist theory are displayed in *Luxe, calme et volupté*, even the dependence on nature; it may conjure an imaginary scene, but its first step was a landscape of the bay of Saint-Tropez painted from nature [226]. But the touches are broader and more varied than in Signac and Cross; they are more easily seen as discrete coloured marks because the white ground is allowed often to show between them; and the contrasts are more abrupt. In *Boats at Collioure* [87], Derain paints on a dark-brown ground, so the colour touches do not stand out so stridently, but their size is not diminished to take account of the small format, and the closely analogous blues of the sea dominate to such an extent that wide, solid planes of colour are suggested, broken by sudden reds in direct confrontation with the blues. Together at Collioure in 1905, Matisse and Derain developed a variety of coloured marks, an acute awareness of the interaction of colours and the prepared ground of the canvas (usually white), and a readiness to use primaries in broad surface areas that exceeded at every point Neo-Impressionist theo-

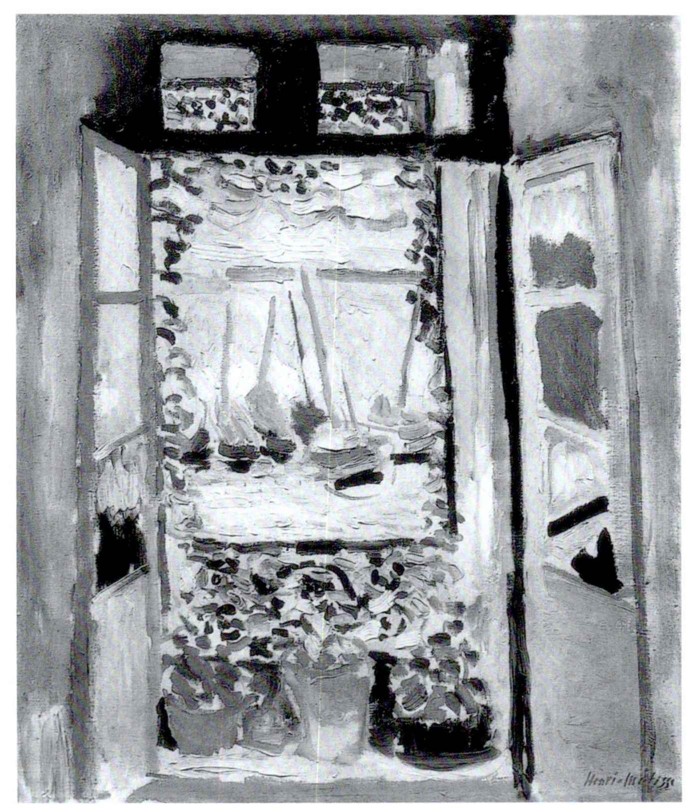

89. Henri Matisse, *Open Window, Collioure* 1905. Oil on canvas, 55.2 × 46 cm. Mrs. John Hay Whitney Collection

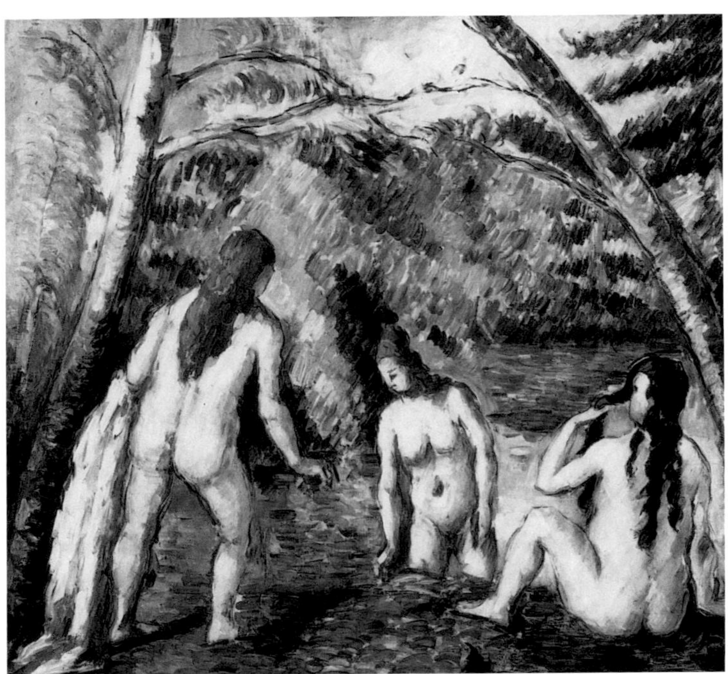

90. Paul Cézanne, *The Three Bathers*, *c*.1884–5. Oil on canvas, 50 × 50 cm. Musée du Petit Palais, Paris

ry. This is as true of Derain's *Drying Sails* [88], as of Matisse's *View of Collioure* [16] or his *Open Window, Collioure* [89]. Thus, the broad areas of white, primed canvas in Derain's *Sails Drying*, the massed yellows of the quay, the sinuous pink streak of the beach and the solid blues of the mountains together set off collisions of primaries, often saturated and not lightened by the admixture of white.

Matisse's and Derain's Collioure subjects could be taken in at a glance, but so strong was the emphasis on the pictorial contrasts of mark, texture and colour that Maurice Denis could write about these paintings at the 'Fauve' Salon d'automne of 1905 as if they were virtually abstract. This is beyond 'literary' or 'decorative artificiality', he exclaimed, 'it is something still more abstract, it is painting outside of every contingency, painting in itself, the pure act of painting'.[12] Matisse's sequel to that summer at Collioure, his *Le Bonheur de vivre* (*The Joy of Life*) [227], moved Signac to uncomprehending exasperation when he saw it before it was shown at the 1906 Indépendants. Though this too was developed from landscapes painted in the dazzling sun of the South, mere accuracy in the capture of the harmony of light in nature was clearly no longer Matisse's ambition.[13]

For Denis responding to the Collioure paintings in 1905, their 'abstraction' – the arbitrariness of their colour, pink for a beach, red for a hillside – went with the intellectual control

91. Henri Matisse, *Back II*, 1913. Bronze, 188 × 116 × 14 cm. The Museum of Modern Art, New York. Mrs Simon Guggenheim Fund

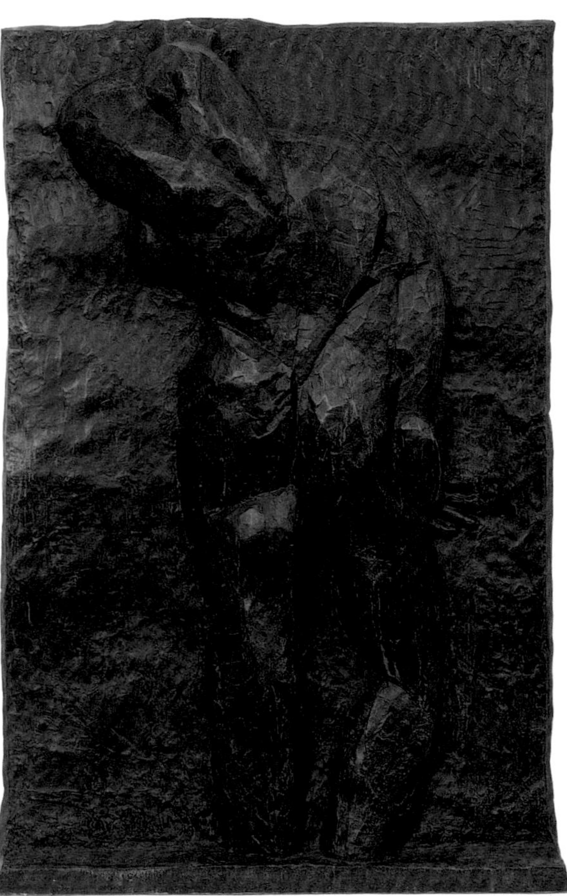

92. Henri Matisse, *Back III*, 1916. Bronze, 190 × 114 × 16 cm. The Museum of Modern Art, New York. Mrs Simon Guggenheim Fund

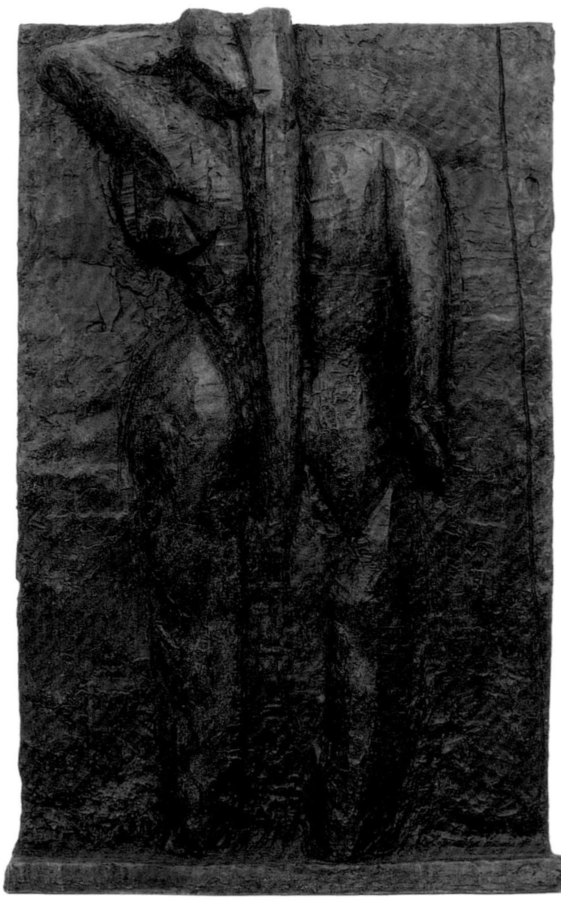

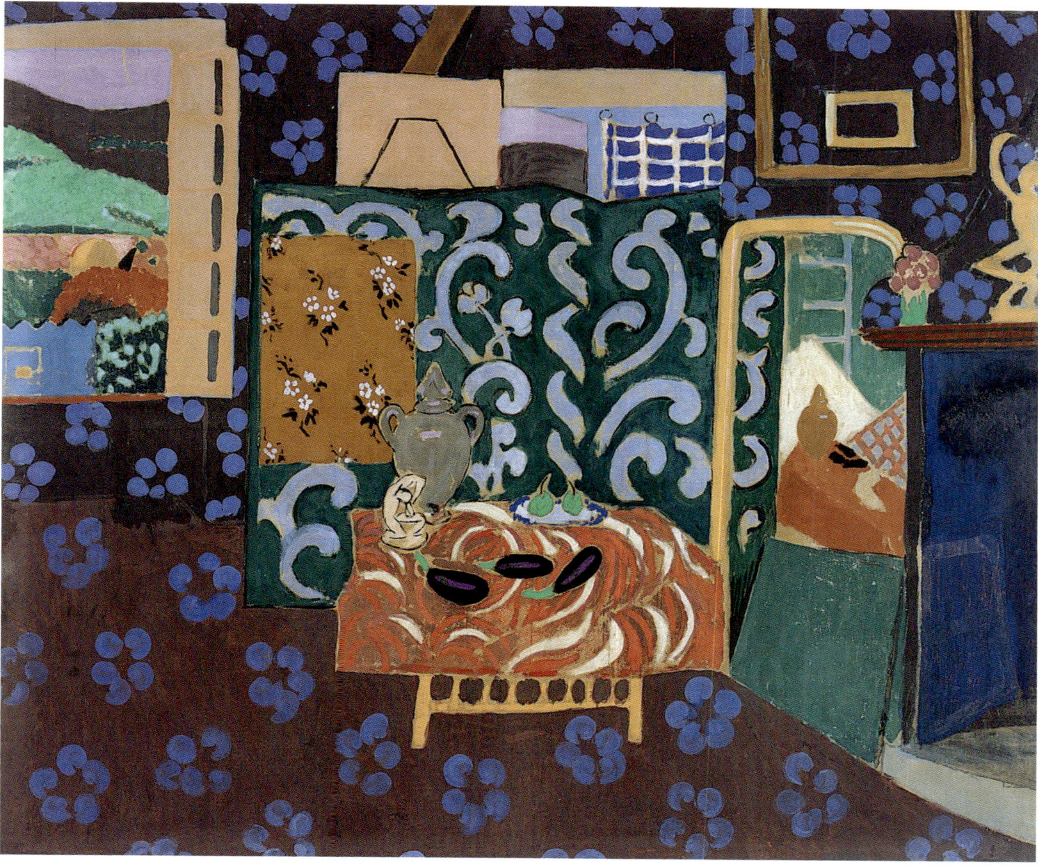

93. Henri Matisse, *Interior with Aubergines*, 1911. Mixed medium on canvas, 212 × 246 cm. Musée de Grenoble

of colour theory at the expense of intuition in front of nature.[14] According to Matisse's American supporter, Sarah Stein (soon to be his pupil), the painter challenged Denis in front of *Le Bonheur* to 'tell him whether the feat of calculating all those relations would not be a far more extraordinary thing than composing them intuitively', and Denis was forced to agree.[15] The 'Notes' were published in part to elaborate Matisse's answer to such criticisms; very soon afterwards, Denis declared that he was persuaded. Indeed, he actually presented the 'Notes' as clinching evidence that 'the young' 'are less theoretically minded and they believe more in the power of instinct'.[16] Matisse's and Denis' reconciliation, initially in front of *Le Bonheur*, underscores the close alignment of their theories, however different their work.

This was especially so where the relationship of nature to art was concerned, and here, for both, the model was not so much Signac or Gauguin, but rather Cézanne. Matisse had owned Cézanne's small yet massively substantial *The Three Bathers* [90] since 1899, and in his figure painting alongside his sculpture he had repeatedly applied a developing understanding of that picture through the 1900s; the reworking of *Bathers by the Stream* would represent an ongoing reassessment of those lessons, so would the modelling of the second and third of Matisse's *Back* series in 1913 and 1916 contemporary with the later phases of the *Bathers'* development [91, 92]. In 1907, the year after Cézanne's death and the year of the major Cézanne retrospective at the Salon d'automne, Denis published the single most influential article on him to appear in France before 1914.[17] Three years earlier, a painter of Gauguin's generation, Emile Bernard, had followed visits to the old man's studio at Aix with another much-read article which included a selection of his sayings; they would repeatedly be cited by those who saw Cézanne as the main source of new art.[18]

For Matisse as for Denis, Cézanne's art brought together the enduring – what Matisse called the 'absolute' – with the instantaneous and ephemeral – the direct experience of nature. According to the sayings quoted by Bernard, he experienced nature in terms immediately translatable into his limited vocabulary of mosaic-like colour planes. This was what he called his 'sensation'; it was his, not everyone's. What mattered was the 'organisation' of *his* sensation both before nature and in the making of the painting. For Matisse, in his own work as much as Cézanne's, only thus could transitory experience be made enduring in a picture or sculpture. And Cézanne (as quoted by Bernard) insisted that for this to be possible, optical response and abstract intelligence had to work together: 'There are two things in a painter: the eye and the brain . . . The painter must work towards their mutual development, with the eye through its vision of nature, with the brain through the logic of organised sensations, which provide the means of expression.'[19] Expression for Matisse was the expression of *his* sensation in front of nature: nature felt intensely and with immediacy but in terms translatable into *his* pictorial vocabulary. For him, expression and his pictorial means – his coloured marks and areas – were inseparable, as was his experience of nature and of art, however unlike nature his work could seem. 'I am unable,' he wrote in the 'Notes', 'to distinguish between the feeling I have about life and my way of translating it'.[20]

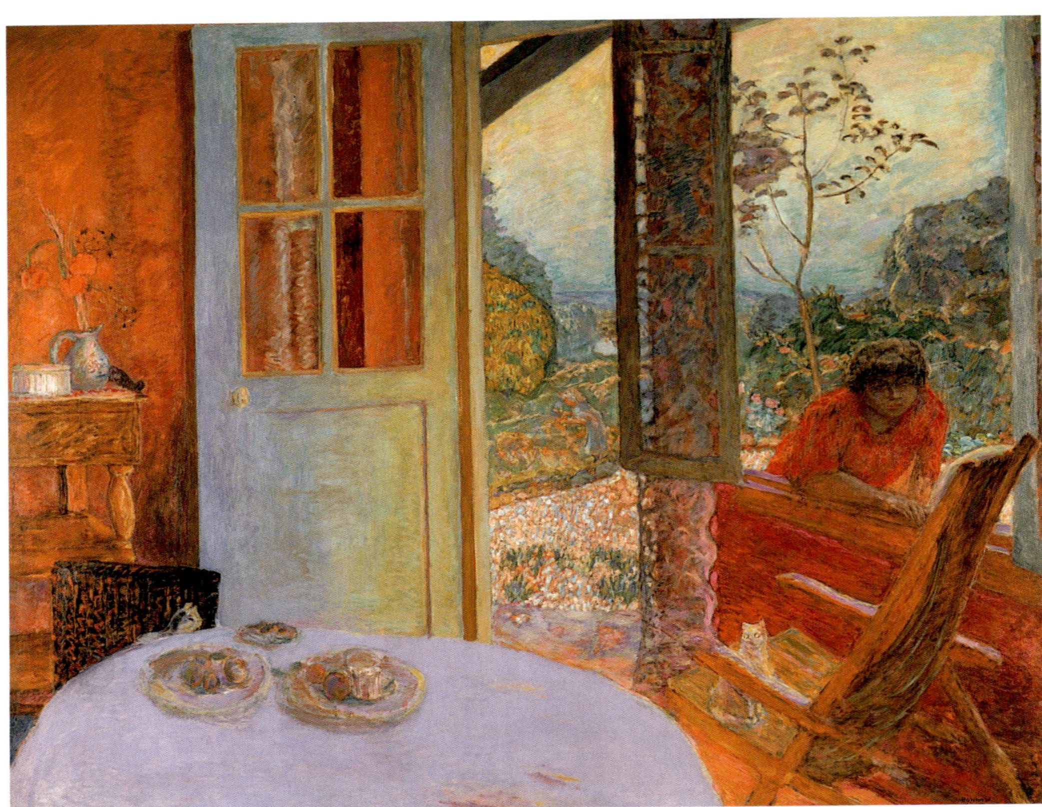

94. Pierre Bonnard, *The Dining Room in the Country*, 1913. Oil on canvas, 164.5 × 205.7 cm. The Minneapolis Institute of Arts

Sarah Stein's record in 1908 of Matisse's teaching gives an insight into what this actually led to in his practice. 'When painting,' he instructed his students, 'first look long and well at your model or subject . . . In painting a landscape you choose it for certain beauties – spots of colour, suggestions of composition. Close your eyes and visualise the picture; then go to work, always keeping these characteristics the important features of the picture.'[21] At Collioure the process of translation was usually quick and nature was always directly confronted. By 1908 and especially from 1909, with the painting of the large decorative compositions (*Music* included), the process was often more drawn out, and the starting point could be in memory and imagination, as well as nature directly confronted. But the principle remained the same, an initial feeling experienced in the visualisation of something as a pictorial or sculptural composition, which returned and developed with each phase of work. For Matisse, even in front of the motif or model nature was to be seen as art. The long process of working such compositions as *Music* and the *Bathers* might seem to have been a matter of altering relationships internally, within the painting, but Matisse saw the outcome as something which produced an intensity of feeling *equivalent* to his 'sensation' before nature. As he put it towards the end of the 'Notes': the painter 'must have the humility of mind to believe that he has painted only what he has seen. I like Chardin's way of putting it: "I apply colour until there is a resemblance".'[22] The painting or sculpture did not describe what was seen in nature, it presented the spectator with an equivalent.

Such a view of decoration and expression, and of art in relation to nature, was shared in its broad outlines by Matisse and Denis. It was also essentially the view of the painters around Matisse in general, though Elderfield is right to suggest that only Derain and Vlaminck achieved a degree of arbitrariness in their use of colour and mark comparable with Matisse's, and then only before 1908.[23] It was also essentially the view of the others of 'the generation of 1890' who continued to develop as artists beyond 1900.

Denis was a powerful thinker and a lucid theorist, but a timid painter. Of his allies from the 1890s, none approached him in prowess as a writer, but one produced a body of work whose brilliance so far exceeds Denis' as to challenge even Matisse's. This was Pierre Bonnard (b.1867), who alone of the ex-Nabis responded with real daring to Matisse's painting. Bonnard's *The Dining Room in the Country* [94], shown in the Salon d'automne of 1913, was a new beginning for him as a composer and colourist on a grand decorative scale. It came as a sequel to the series of decorative interiors painted by Matisse in 1911, the year following *Dance* and *Music*, among them *Interior with Aubergines* [93]. Bonnard would be habitually treated as a belated Impressionist in the art press, especially in the 1920s, and there can be no doubt that his complex minglings of cool and warm hues and his vibrantly brushed surfaces invite such a characterisation, as does the effect he preserves of direct contact with things seen in nature. But already in *The Dining Room in the Country* his use of interleaved violets, blue-greens, pinks and hot reds is clearly not descriptive; he too pursues equivalence in the pictorialised terms of his own 'sensation', and makes first and foremost a painting.

There are important conclusions that follow from the decorative theory and practice developed around Matisse and the 'generation of 1890'. First, nature is seen only *in* the work of art. In the case of painting, the picture surface is not a transparent plane through which a structured illusion of nature is seen, it is a material surface on which coloured marks and drawn lines are disposed and it is in the action of these on the spectator that any effect of light and space in nature is to be experienced. It follows from this that the painter's priority is not so much to capture what he or she sees in nature, but rather to provoke the spectator's eye to move and explore in response to the coloured marks and lines on the canvas. The emphasis has shifted from the relationship between the painter and nature, to that between the work of art and the viewer.

John Elderfield has shown the degree to which Bonnard's manipulation of different chromatic intensities after 1913 controls optical response, especially as the eye moves between awareness of things in peripheral vision (usually involving areas of coloured shadow) and sharp focusing.[24] Many have shown how in works like Matisse's *Open Window, Collioure* [89] the inflection of brushed lines and variously drawn and smudged 'touches' combine to direct the eye across the surface, optically creating a pictorial space. The way such works are painted and sometimes their subject matter can act as analogues or metaphors of the experience of seeing that they provoke. Matisse's open window and Bonnard's open windows and mirrors [223] are invitations to active looking; the Golden Age in the classical form of *Le Bonheur de vivre* and the domesticated form of *The Dining Room in the Country* offer analogues of the paradise for the eyes presented by the paintings as paintings. Yet, in these cases, the paradise for the eyes has to be worked for. An *active* spectatorship is required, one comparable with the active and self-critical spectatorship of the artist in front of the work in the phases of its making, and it is this that the exposure of the traces of that process on the surface of the painting declares. The viewer is asked to emulate the always open-ended, exploratory process of making in the process of looking: to look creatively. Finally, this is a kind of art that is emphatically individualist, both for the artist and the spectator: one intensely personal 'sensation' leads to another.

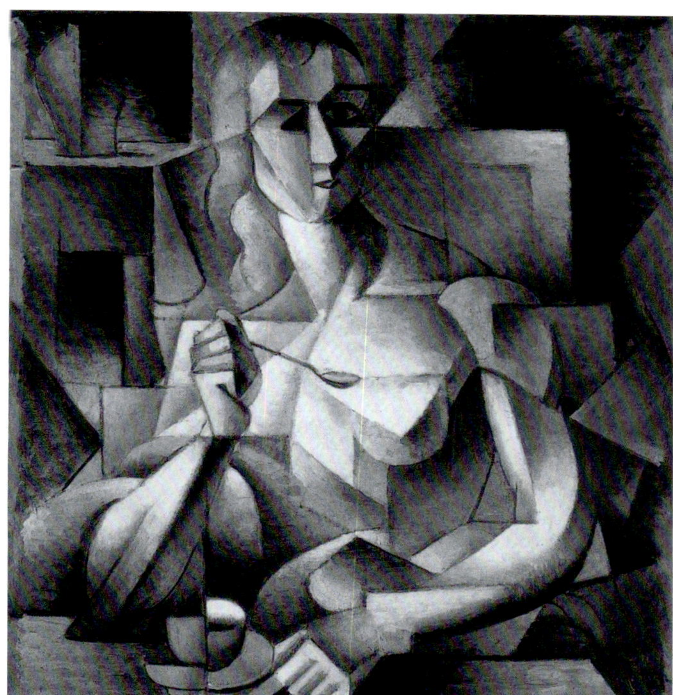

95. Jean Metzinger, *Tea-time*, 1911. Oil on wood, 75.6 × 69.5 cm. Philadelphia Museum of Art, Louise and Walter Arensberg Collection

96. Henri Matisse, *Portrait of Mme. Matisse*, 1913. Oil on canvas, 145 × 97 cm. The State Hermitage Museum, St Petersburg

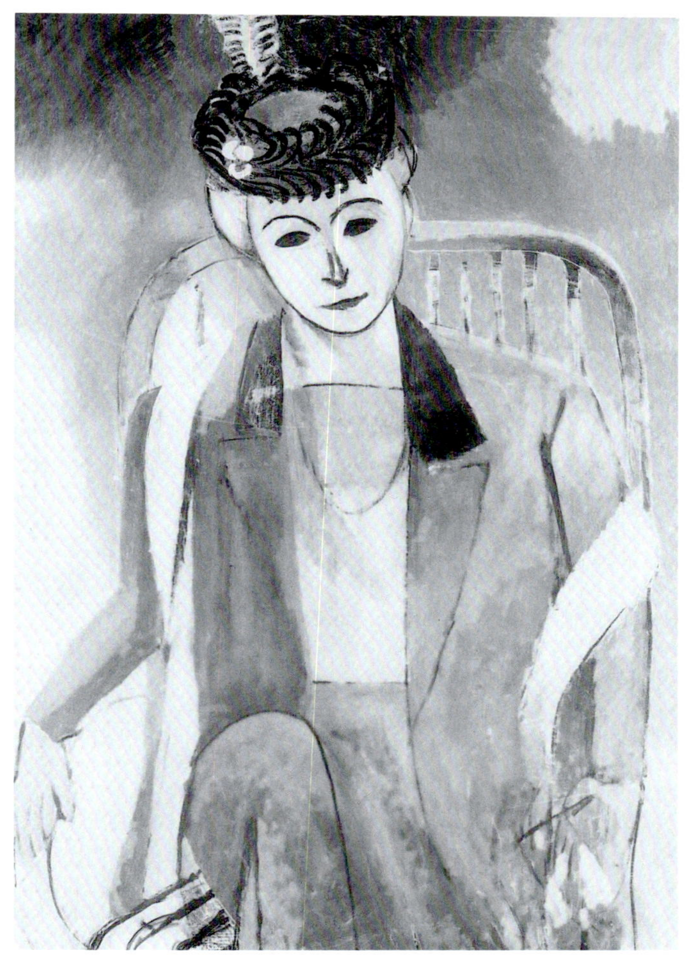

LIKENESS AND DEFORMATION, ANALYSIS AND SYNTHESIS: FROM MATISSE INTO CUBISM

It could be said that what the decorative and expressive new painting of Matisse and Bonnard produced was pictures that were at once unlike and like nature. Responses to early modernism in France dwell on the factor of unlikeness: a word often used was 'deformation'. When in 1907, Matisse exhibited his *Blue Nude* [283] at the Indépendants, the critic Louis Vauxcelles itemised the things about it he could not 'understand'. They included the 'flat and weighty' right arm of the 'mannish nymph', and above all the fact that 'the buttocks of the deformed body determine an arabesque of foliage that motivates the curve of the woman'.[25] Even a supporter of the Cubists and especially of Picasso, André Salmon, could identify the grotesqueness of the distortions in Picasso's *Demoiselles d'Avignon* [282], completed in 1907, as the main cause of the horror it aroused among those who saw it in the artist's studio. The nudes' faces, according to

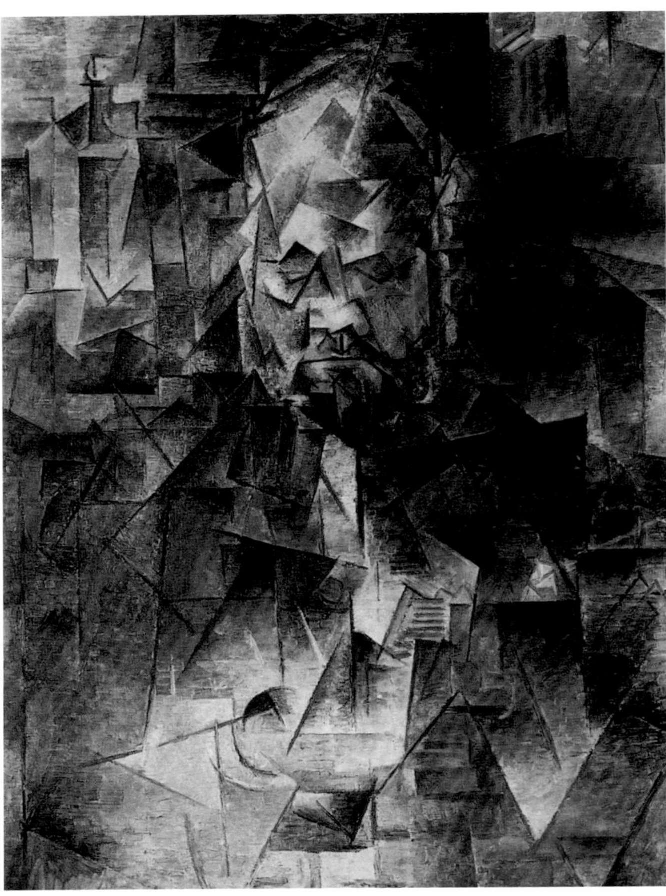

97. Pablo Picasso, *Portrait of Ambroise Vollard*, 1909–10. Oil on canvas, 92 × 65 cm. Pushkin Museum of Fine Art, Moscow

Salmon in 1912, are 'masks almost entirely freed from humanity'; their 'inhumanity' inspires 'a sort of terror'.[26]

Portraiture was, of course, *the* genre where likeness mattered, and the crux of likeness in portraiture is the face. The inhumanity of the 'demoiselles', for Salmon, is concentrated in their masked faces. Significantly, portraiture figured at key points in the most experimental work of leading modernists before 1914. One can point to Vlaminck's, Derain's and Matisse's interactive portraits of 1905–6, or Matisse's *Portrait of Mme. Matisse* of 1913 [96]; to Picasso's portraits of 1906–7, including his *Self-portrait* of 1907 [69], or his portrait series of 1909–10 [97, 106]; and to Juan Gris's portrait of Picasso himself, Gris's *Homage* of 1912 [31], or to a work like Jean Metzinger's portrait-format *Tea-time* [95].

In Picasso's *Portrait of Ambroise Vollard* of 1909–10 [97] a near-caricature likeness of Vollard, centred on his face, emerges heavily yet luminously out of the otherwise illegible faceted structure. A likeness dominates, but it is threatened by Picasso's new formal vocabulary. In Gris's *Homage* [31], a work predicated upon an acute understanding of pictures like the Vollard portrait, the one relatively small region of the painting where the ordered grid of planes fuses with the displacement of features to defy the recognition of a likeness, is the face. The title written on the painting, the blue tunic and the easily identified lock of hair over the forehead are all that could tell even those who knew Picasso's appearance that he was the sitter. Gris's more controlled version of Picasso's vocabulary has almost obliterated likeness. Nothing so comprehensively threatening to likeness occurs in Matisse's *Portrait of Mme. Matisse*, among the first of his distinctly personal responses to the Picasso of the Vollard portrait [97] and the Gris of *Homage*, but the masking of the face rids it of the quirks of character. Like all Matisse's portraits, it began closer to a naturalist likeness, which was gradually effaced in pursuit of new pictorial relationships; Mme. Matisse sat over 100 times. She is said to have cried when she saw the mask that had replaced a likeness which had been at first a delight to her.[27] When the picture was shown at the Automne of 1913, Salmon commented: '[Matisse's] woman in blue wears a wooden mask smeared with chalk . . .'[28]

As portraits, all of these pictures define themselves against the model of the 'official' portrait provided by the suave contemporaneity of a Gervex [201] or the consummate traditionalism of a Bonnat (b.1833). Bonnat's spectacular *Portrait of Cardinal Lavigerie*, for example, was shown at the Salon des Artistes français of 1888 alongside his official portrait of the republican politician Jules Ferry, and by the 1900s was a star in the Luxembourg museum [98]. Here, the generous width and height of the space in which Bonnat seats his sitter is constructed with brilliant economy: the sharp forward edge of the table, the piled books and the shadowed folds of the screen behind completing the effect. This stage for the figure is crucial to the impression of grandeur and nobility. But despite such a setting and the distracting luxury of red and gold, the head presides. As one critic put it in 1888: 'This material brilliance does not distract one from what counts above all, from that living head, which takes control because of its moral beauty.'[29]

Matisse's rationale for putting aside the technical pyrotechnics of such portraiture was, of course, simple. The flat, decorative demands of the painting, based on the expressive drive of the artist, required a decisive rejection of all that conspired to produce so compelling an illusion of a 'living head'. Painting took over from the sitter, just as sculpture (emphatically not flat) did for Constantin Brancusi (b.1876) in his series of busts of his Hungarian acquaintance *Mlle. Pogany* begun the year before the *Portrait of Mme. Matisse* in 1912, when they are compared with, for instance, Charles Despiau's *Paulette* of 1910 [99, 100].

Bonnat did far more than copy nature, but for Matisse the distinction between his own work and that of an artist like Bonnat was simply the difference between copying and the decorative expression of sensation. 'I cannot copy nature in a servile way,' he writes in the 'Notes'; 'I am forced to interpret nature and submit it to the spirit of the picture'.[30] When Yvonne Landsberg sat for him in 1914, a mutual friend recalled that Matisse re-painted the entire picture at each sitting, a single change leading to revisions across the whole picture surface.[31] The case of Brancusi in relation to Despiau is less straightforward. Despiau (b.1874), was concerned not merely with likeness but with interpreting form in idealised sculptural terms too. He was, after all, thought of as an independent, not an academic. Here, according to Matisse's decorative aesthetic, distinctions would have been made only between degrees of interpretation: degrees of simplification or deformation.

Such an approach to deformation and likeness operated

entirely on the level of perception – what was *seen*: to the eye, the work was at once unlike and like the model. In theory and sometimes in practice, the level at which likeness was grasped by the Cubists was far more conceptual than perceptual. This applies both to the so-called 'true Cubism' of Picasso, Braque and Gris, and to the varied Cubist practices of Léger, Gleizes, Metzinger, the Duchamp brothers and Le Fauconnier or of the sculptors Lipchitz, Laurens and Archipenko.

Cubist theory before 1914 was dominated by a view of Cubist practice that privileged conception over perception.[32] Just before the opening of the Salon d'automne of 1911, Gleizes (b.1881) published a major article on Metzinger (b.1883), who must just then have been completing *Tea-time* [95]. Representation, argued Gleizes (as Matisse had), was fundamental, but what Metzinger aspired to was 'to inscribe the total image'. This total image combined the evidence of perception with 'a new truth, born from what his intelligence permits him to know'. Such 'intelligent' knowledge was the accumulation of an all-round study of things, and so it was conveyed by the combination of multiple viewpoints in a single image. This accumulation of fragmented aspects would be given 'equilibrium' by a geometric, a 'cubic' structure.[33] Metzinger's *Tea-time* [95], a work that attracted much attention at the Salon d'automne of 1911, is like a pictorial demonstration of Gleizes's text. Multiple perspectives and a firm overall geometric structure (almost a grid) take control of a near pornographic subject:

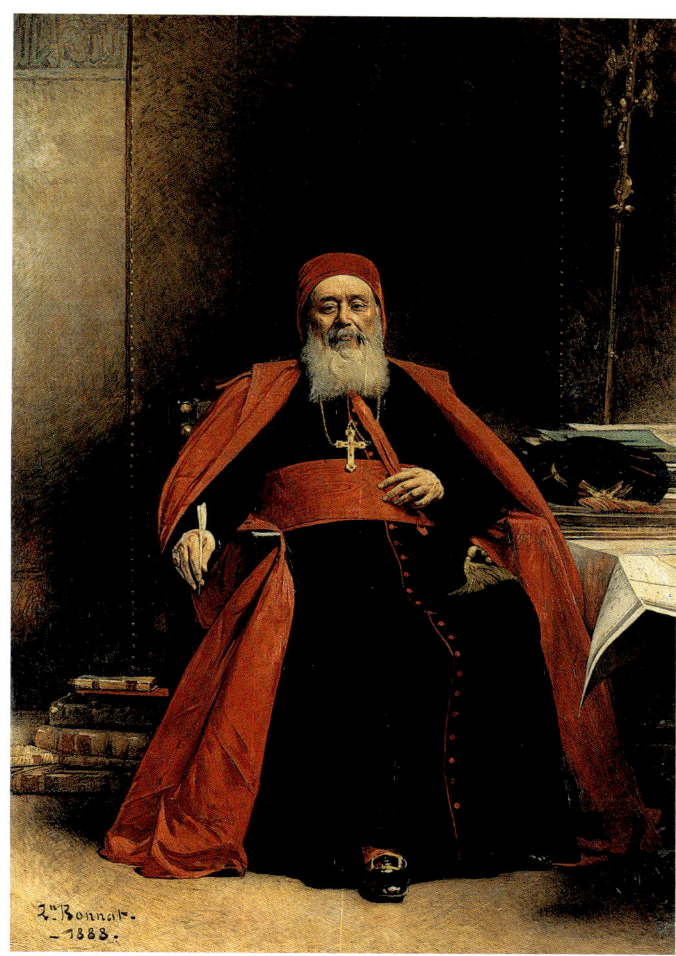

98. Right. Léon Bonnat, *Portrait of Cardinal Lavigerie*, 1888. Oil on canvas, 239 × 164 cm. Musée du Château de Versailles

99. Constantin Brancusi, *Mlle. Pogany*, 1913. Bronze on a limestone base, 43.8 × 27 × 30 cm. The Museum of Modern Art, New York. Acquired through the Lillie P. Bliss Bequest

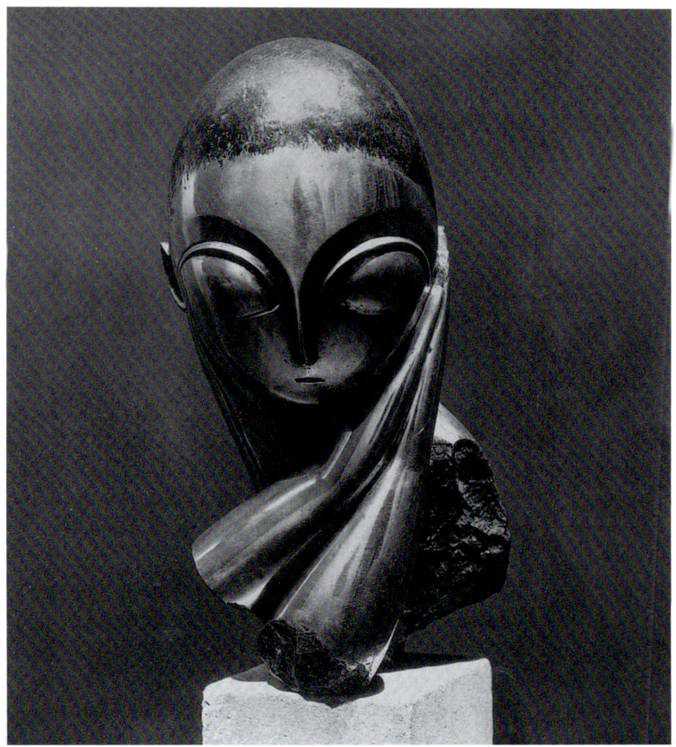

100. Below. Charles Despiau, *Paulette*, 1910. Marble, 41 × 30 × 20 cm. Musée National d'Art Moderne, Paris

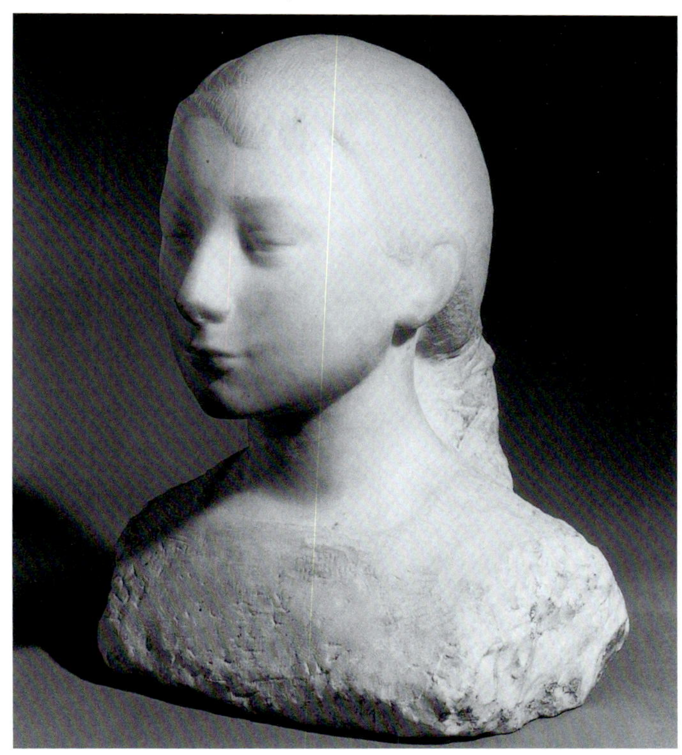

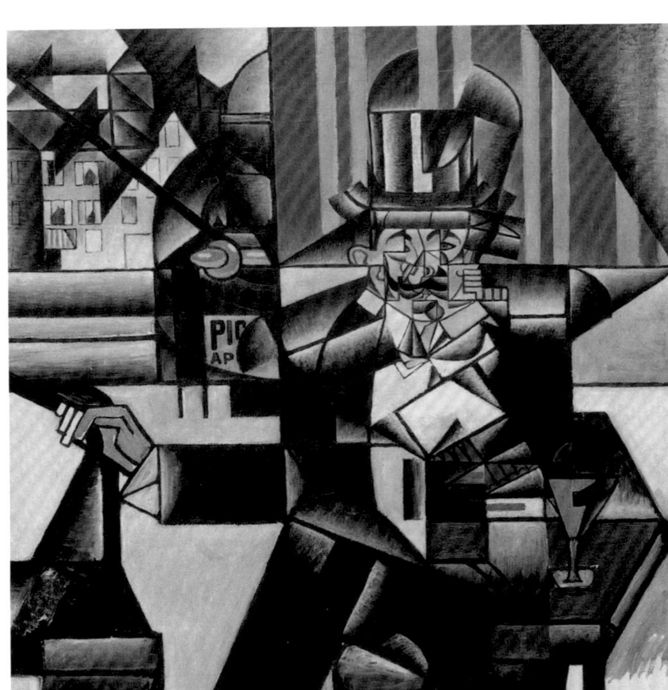

101. Juan Gris, *Man in a Café*, 1912. Oil on canvas, 128.2 × 88 cm. Philadelphia Museum of Art, The Louise and Walter Arensberg Collection

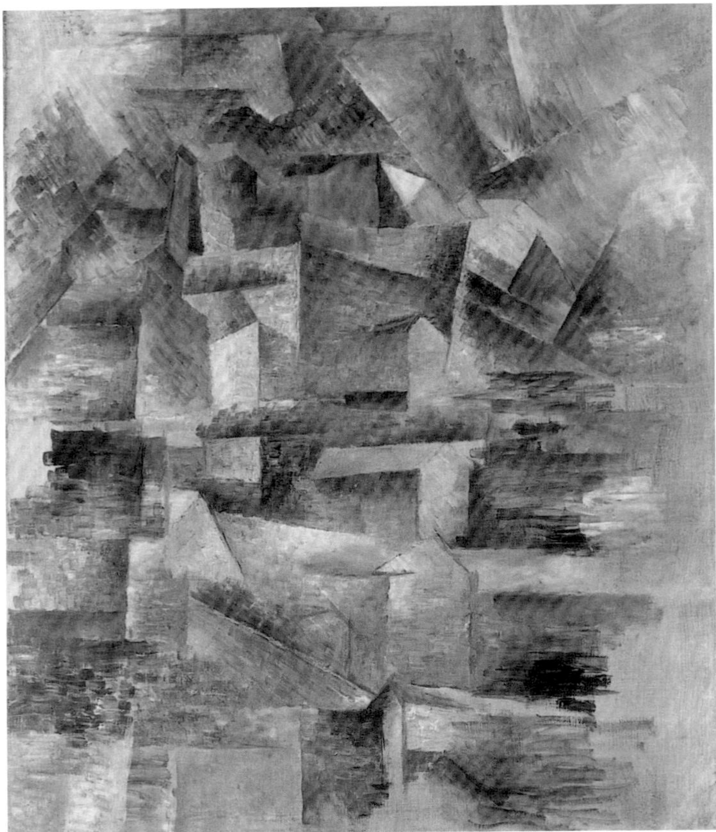

102. Georges Braque, *Rio Tinto Factories at L'Estaque*, 1910. Oil on canvas, 65 × 54 cm. Musée National d'Art Moderne, Paris

'intelligence' subdues the senses.

More influentially than Gleizes, it was Maurice Raynal, friend both of many Salon Cubists and of those around Picasso, who codified the conceptual view of Cubism. He did so in his article of summer 1912, 'Conception and Vision'. Raynal too identified multiple or mobile perspective as the means to a conceptual rather than a perceptual representation of things. 'We never, in fact, see an object in all its dimensions at once,' he wrote. 'Therefore what has to be done is to fill in the gap in our seeing. Conception gives us the means.'[34]

The Cézanne publicised by Emile Bernard in 1904, wanted the brain always to work *with* the eye of the artist. Early Cubist theory put the mind in control. The eye was considered no more than an analytical tool, which made possible a conceptual synthesis. The pursuit of a synthesis in art that would remove painting and sculpture from too fixed an anchorage in the material world had been a feature of Gauguin's 'Synthetism'. And the idea of a 'synthesis' growing out of 'analysis' was central to Denis' understanding of the lesson of Cézanne. For both him and Matisse, however, analysis (seeing) was inseparable from synthesis (painting), hence Matisse's confession that he was unable to distinguish between his 'feeling' in front of nature and his 'way of translating it'. By contrast, already in Gleizes's 1911 article on Metzinger, a clear separation between analysis and synthesis is declared by the promotion of a two-stage process of artistic creation. First, the multiplication of the 'visual field' by an aspect-by-aspect analysis of things from different viewpoints, then the putting of it together again by geometry to create equilibrium. In 1912, Raynal was to repeat this model of Cubist practise, and that year, following Metzinger's as well as Picasso and Braque's lead, Juan Gris (b.1887) exhibited a series of works which can seem to be demonstrations of this two-stage process in action.[35] It included his *Homage to Pablo Picasso* [31] and also works like *Man in a Café* [101], a painting shown at a Salon independently organised by and for the Cubists at the end of 1912, the Salon de la Section d'Or.

However illegible Picasso's face in *Homage*, each of its features is clearly based on study, either first-hand or from a photograph, the results of which have then been displaced and realigned to fit the overall two-dimensional grid controlling the composition. The analytic and synthetic elements are, however, most lucidly united and most sharply differentiated in a work like *Man in a Café*, where specially adapted grids are applied to the head and to the glass and cigar-box on the table, and where within each of the units of these grids a different aspect of a different feature is contained. Just how carefully Gris fused together the observed features and his grids is there to be seen in pencil and charcoal studies.[36] On both levels, as the fragmentary outcome of analysis, and as the cohesive geometric outcome of synthesis

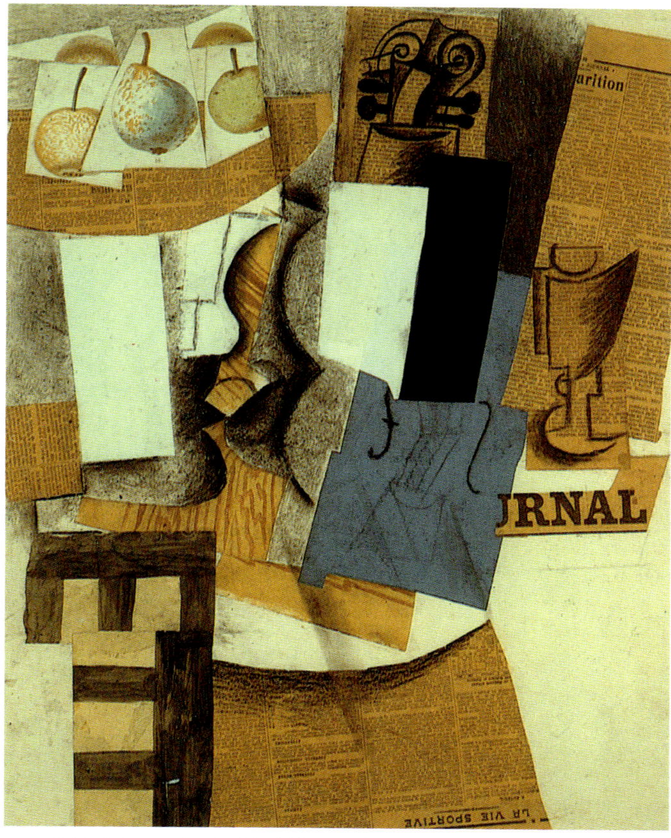

103. Pablo Picasso, *Fruit-dish, Violin and Wineglass*, 1912–13. Pasted paper, watercolour, chalk, oil and charcoal on cardboard, 65 × 50.5 cm. The Philadelphia Museum of Art, A.E. Gallatin Collection

these are, in Raynal's terms, the purest and most lucid of conceptual paintings.[37]

The terms 'analysis' and 'synthesis' were to become basic to the understanding of Cubist art from Alfred H. Barr's *Cubism and Abstract Art* in 1936 until at least the 1970s.[38] The two-stage theory of the process of making art, beginning with analysis and ending with synthesis, was adapted to define two stages in the history of Cubism altogether: 'Analytic Cubism' before 1912, 'Synthetic Cubism' after 1912. For Barr, despite Gleizes's or Raynal's claims, Cubist painting before the end of 1912 remained based essentially on perception: on a process by which things seen were broken down into their component parts – a process of empirical analysis. According to his scenario, only with the introduction of simpler, more schematic ways of representing things as a result of Braque's and Picasso's development of Cubist papier-collé and construction [103, 104] did synthesis properly speaking take over. By this Barr meant the building up of compositions using entirely conceptual components – abstract forms and invented signs.

Barr's scenario applies almost exclusively to the work of Picasso, Braque and Gris, but even when applied in that restricted area it is so reductive as to be seriously misleading in the period before 1914. In fact, both before and after 1912, the way these artists worked cannot be called either exclusively analytical or exclusively synthetic: it was both more complex and more unpredictable than that. Moreover, it is important to realise that, Picasso (b.1881) and Braque

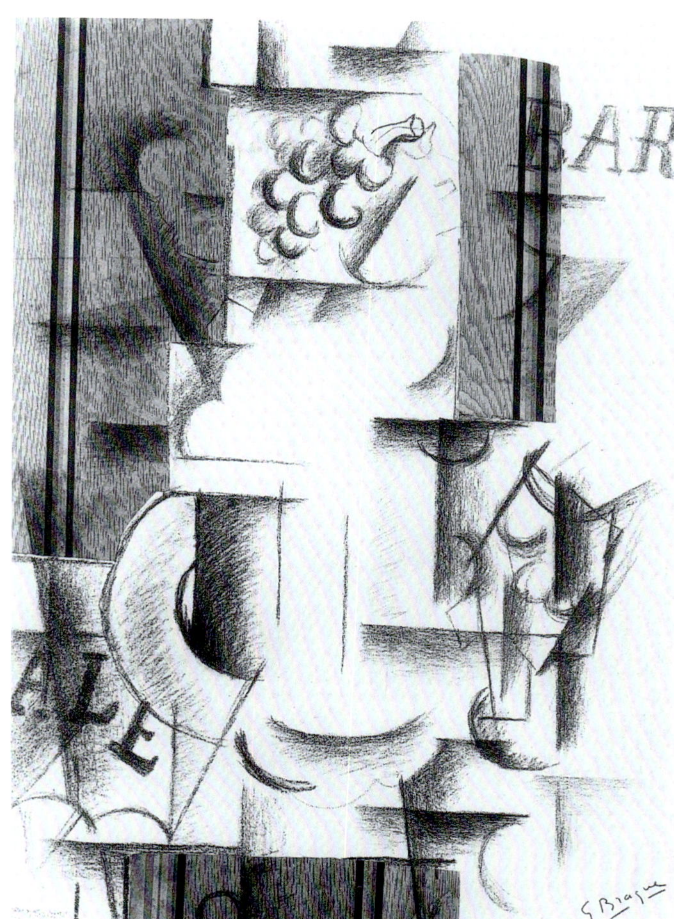

104. Georges Braque, *Fruit-dish and Glass*, 1912. Charcoal, wallpaper, on paper, 62 × 44.5 cm. Private Collection

(b.1882) resisted theory, unlike Gleizes and Metzinger. Their emphasis was always on the open-ended making of art. Gris was attracted by theory, especially after 1914, as we shall see, but even he worked less programmatically than is often realised. The inadequacy of Barr's scenario featuring Analytic and Synthetic Cubism is clearest if one looks first at Picasso's and Braque's work in the so-called Analytic period, especially between 1910 and early 1912.

Matisse almost always painted portraits from the life. By 1909, Braque was painting landscapes as much from memory as from the motif. But in 1910, Picasso did ask his portrait subjects, including Vollard and Kahnweiler, to sit for him [97, 106]; and Braque's *Rio Tinto Factories at L'Estaque* of September 1910 [102] was one of two landscapes based on work in front of the motif. Neither Picasso's Kahnweiler portrait, however, nor Braque's landscape could be called simply analytic on the terms of Barr's historical scenario.

An examination of the portrait in relation to other figure compositions of 1910, suggests that Picasso neither worked away from more naturalistic images, nor reconstructed Kahnweiler's head on the basis of anything like a straightforward feature-by-feature analysis. Rather, he seems to have worked from a very simple schema for the head, consisting of a couple of overlapping rectangles with secondary curves; this was elaborated and given its shimmering skin of

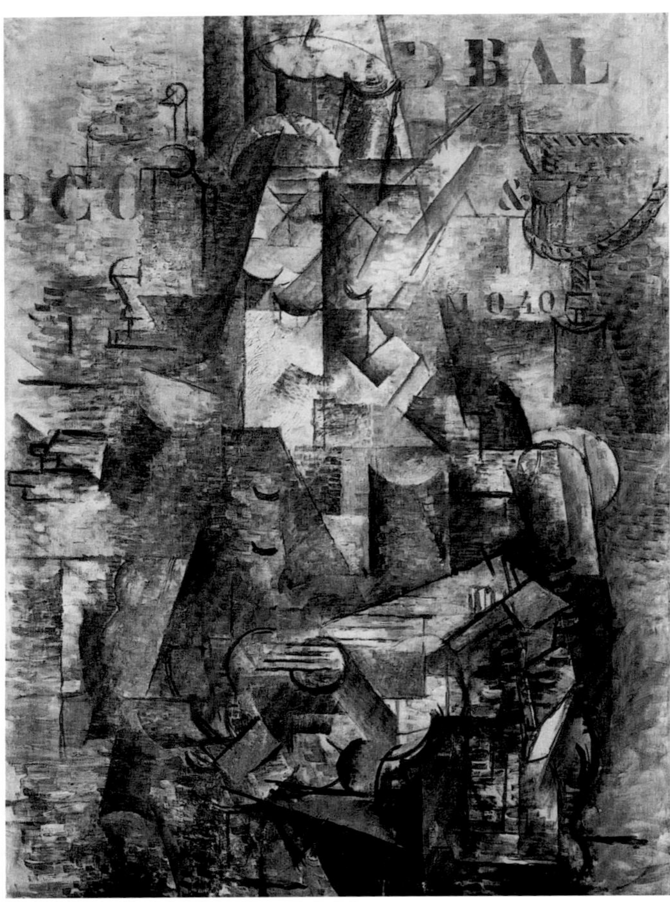

105. Georges Braque, *The Portuguese*, 1911. Oil on canvas, 117 × 81 cm. Oeffentliche Kunstsammlung Basel, Kunstmuseum. Gift of Raoul La Roche

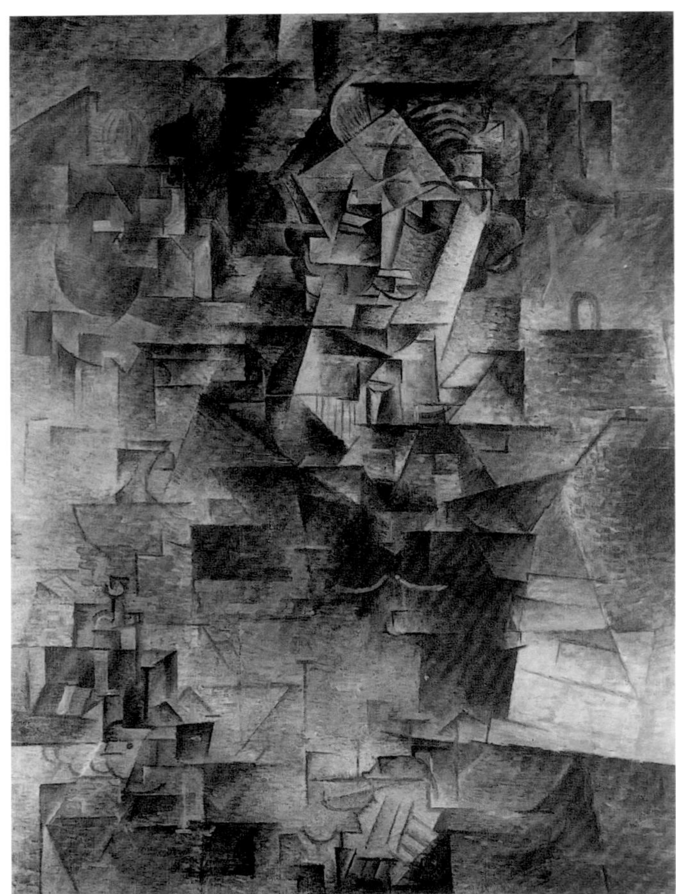

106. Pablo Picasso, *Portrait of Daniel-Henry Kahnweiler*, 1910. Oil on canvas, 100.6 × 72.8 cm. The Art Institute of Chicago. Gift of Mrs Gilbert W. Chapman in Memory of Charles B. Goodspeed

facets as its surroundings were elaborated. The features – eyes, brows, nose, etc. – depicted from different viewpoints were then added.[39] In other words, when he analysed he did so on the basis of a simple synthesized schema: analysis and synthesis working together in a process so open-ended and complex that, in practice, they can no more be disentangled than in the case of Matisse.

Braque introduced synthesis in his Rio Tinto landscapes by arbitrarily structuring the space of his motif rather than inventing simple signs as a starting point. He constructed a shallow relief-like architecture of tilting planes in warm and cool tones obviously evocative of Cézanne's by then celebrated L'Estaque paintings. That particular colour range and the use of 'touches' applied in orderly clusters plainly invoke not only Cézanne but Signac and Neo-Impressionism too: kinds of painting firmly based on the first-hand experience of nature. But any empirical analysis of the scene has been ordered on the canvas by horizontals which cross the picture surface from the thinly worked flanks, suggesting a partial grid. These horizontals are completely arbitrary: they impose a synthetic structure on the piled-up flattened fragments of the factory buildings. Analysis and synthesis are once again continually interactive; in practice, there is no simple development from one to the other.

Even the apparently exemplary case of Juan Gris's Analytical Cubism in 1911–12 is not as clear-cut as it seems. Thus, for instance, one surviving drawing for the head of *Man in a Café* is covered with rubbings out revealing that the grid was not a rigid given which determined how the features were to be analysed, but was itself changing as the analysis developed. Even here, analysis and synthesis actually worked together in close interaction.[40]

It is hard to see anything analytical in the work Braque and Picasso produced when they were together at Céret in the South West in the summer of 1911, nor in their work of the following autumn and winter. Braque's *The Portuguese* [105] had a subject – an immigrant sitting in a Céret café in front of dance posters – but he has been utterly taken over by the scaffold that articulates the space around him.[41] Picasso's *Man with a Clarinet* [107], probably painted in the months following his return to Paris from Céret, grew out of suites of pen drawings made in the South [108, 109]. The most schematic of these drawings [108] show clearly how figure and geometric framework were conceived together, not separately. The more developed drawings show how the process of elaboration threatened legibility, so that in the painting the set of the arms and the positioning to the right of the sheet music on its stand can only be discerned with reference to the drawings (the one illustrated here [109] does not include the music-stand). In the painting, the head and shoulders were originally intermeshed with a more complex planar scaffold on either side; by partially painting this out Picasso exposes the synthetic character of his sign-making more clearly than in most of his contemporary work. Such instances show that Picasso's and Braque's painting of 1911–12 was actually *more* synthetic than analytic: they arrived at fragmentary suggestions of resemblance, but worked almost exclusively with invented signs. The results were so complex and obscure that Kahnweiler later dubbed them 'hermetic'.[42]

When Picasso and Braque moved into so-called Synthetic Cubism late in 1912, they often included obvious analytical fragments among their simpler signs for things, so that even then the relationship between analysis and synthesis could be interactive. Thus, in Picasso's *Fruit-dish, Violin and Wineglass* [103] of 1913 and Braque's *Glass, Bottle and Newspaper* of 1914 [110], multi-perspectival glasses, unmistakably based on part-by-part analyses, are drawn over cut-out paper planes beside signs for other things. In Braque's case these signs are exclusively synthetic. In Picasso's they range from the detailed depiction of the violin tuning keys to the most schematic of ciphers (the cut-out signs for the fruit-dish and the body of the violin). Indeed, such post-papier-collé composing repeatedly confronts the most schematic of signs with not merely fragments of analysis, which act as traces of things seen, but with *actual* fragments from everyday life. The incorporation of printed illustrations of fruit in Picasso's fruit-bowl and of actual newspaper cuttings in both these works is, in the pictorial circumstances, provocatively matter-of-fact. In the Picasso, however, the newspaper is cut to form the sign not for a newspaper but for the bowl of the fruit-dish: a fragment of 'reality' (newspaper) is appropriated for the invention of another synthesised sign standing for something else (not a newspaper).

Alfred H. Barr's scenario, with its simple progression from Analytic to Synthetic Cubism, was not altogether his own invention. It was, in fact, the sequel to developments that occurred actually in Cubist theory and practice between 1914 and the early 1920s, though without the encouragement of Picasso and Braque. A leading role in these developments was played by Juan Gris, and it involved several of the Salon Cubists. After 1918 Gris repeatedly differentiated his more recent painting, pictures like *The Man from the Touraine* of 1918 [240] and *Guitar and Fruit-dish* [112] of 1919, from his pre-1914 work, and used the distinction between painting based on the analytical dissection of things and painting dedicated to synthetic purity to do so. For him, Synthetic Cubism did indeed displace Analytic Cubism, at least in his own work. In 1917, a development had begun in his practice that reached a crucial stage in the summer of 1918, which he spent at Beaulieu-lès-Loches in the Touraine, in close contact with Metzinger, Lipchitz and the newcomer Cubist Maria Blanchard. The key to it was pictorial rhymes. So simple had his signs denoting things become by then that very similar schemas could denote quite different things, creating rhymes. In *Man from the Touraine*, the eyes rhyme with the buttons of the peasant figure, his hand

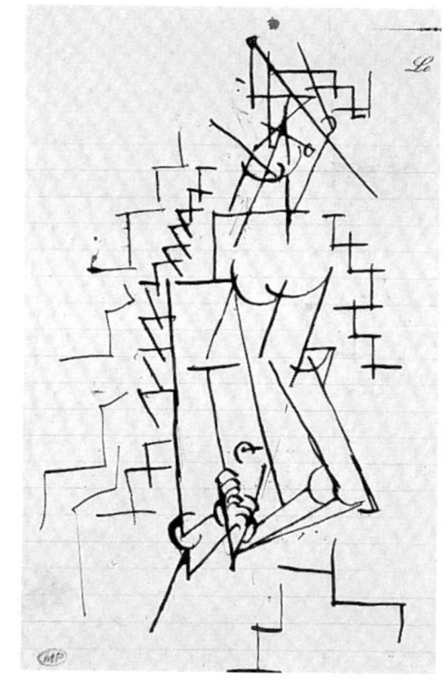

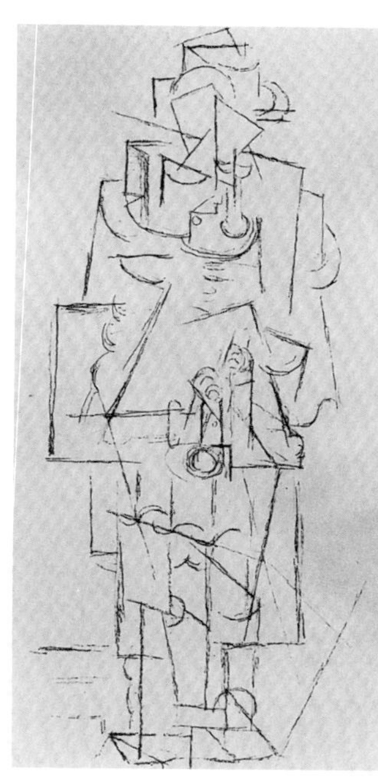

108. Pablo Picasso, *Bust of a Woman from Céret*, 1911. Pen on headed paper 26.8 × 21.4 cm. Musée Picasso, Paris

109. Pablo Picasso, *Man with a Clarinet*, 1911. Ink on paper, 29 × 23 cm. Whereabouts unknown

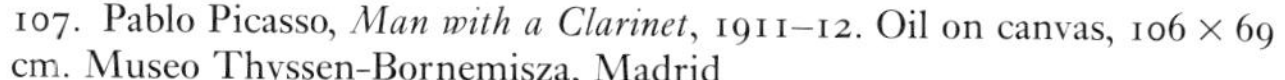

107. Pablo Picasso, *Man with a Clarinet*, 1911–12. Oil on canvas, 106 × 69 cm. Museo Thyssen-Bornemisza, Madrid

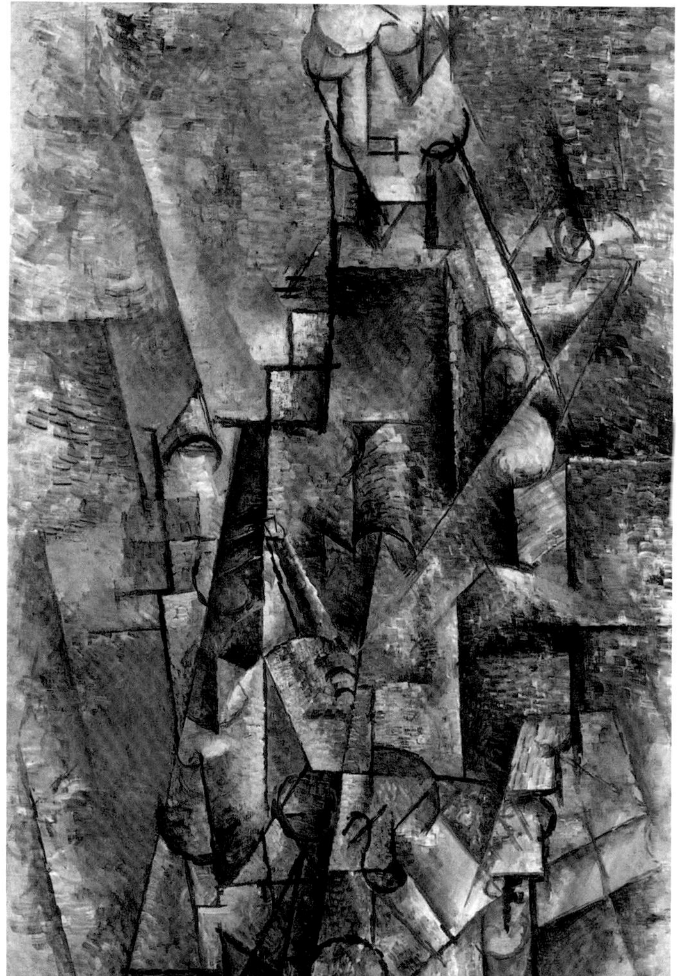

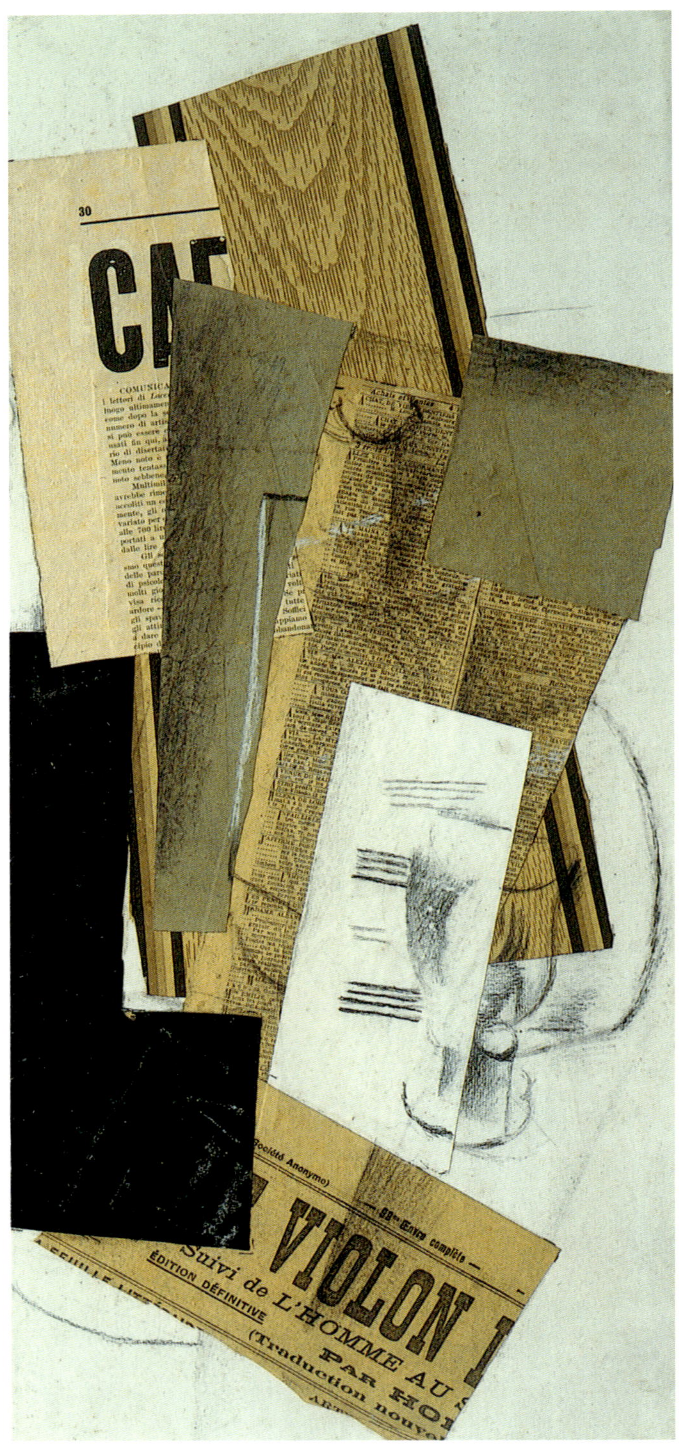

110. Georges Braque, *Glass, Bottle and Newspaper*, 1914. Pasted paper on paper, 62.5 × 28.5 cm. Private Collection

with his sleeve, the structure of his brow, cheek and nose taken together with the neck and square-rimmed top of the bottle. What this meant was that Gris could start with the simplest arrangements of coloured shapes and find in them a whole range of possible signs for things: he could start in the abstract (the purely conceptual) before arriving at representation. In a statement of 1921, Gris called his procedure the 'deductive method' (moving from the abstract to the

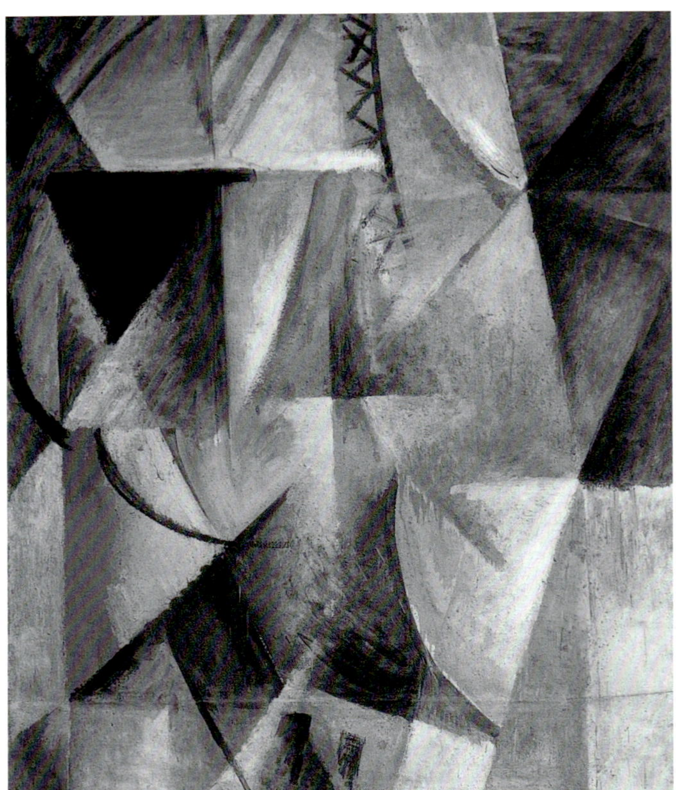

111. Robert Delaunay, *Simultaneous Window*, 1912. Oil on canvas, 112.5 × 91.5 cm. Musée National d'Art Moderne, Paris

concrete) and wrote of making a bottle *from* a cylinder, not a cylinder from a bottle. For him, the 'deductive method' was the guarantee of the purity of his synthesis: the things in his paintings would always be based on abstractions, as cerebral as algebraic formulae.[43]

This was a theory which, from 1917, encouraged the claim to be repeatedly made that a new degree of conceptual purity – a higher synthesis – had been reached in the Cubism of Gris and others associated with the Cubists' new Paris dealer, Léonce Rosenberg. The poet Paul Dermée, who was close to all of them, claimed as much for both Metzinger and Lipchitz in 1919 and 1920 [242, 238].[44] Dermée's mentor Pierre Reverdy, a poet-critic especially close to Gris, had claimed as much for Cubism altogether in 1917.[45] In this context, post-1918 Cubism around Gris and Léonce Rosenberg's galerie de L'Effort Moderne, became firmly identified with a refined form of Platonic idealism, according to which Cubist art constructed the Ideas of things, not things as they exist in day-to-day experience. André Lhote, a painter-critic who was much respected for his essays in *La Nouvelle Revue française*, could write of a new kind of Cubism which he called 'a priorism': a Cubism that aspired to reaching an essence believed to be in things before and beyond empirical experience, that is to Immanuel Kant's synthetic *a priori*.[46] In this highly distilled version of Cubist theory, synthesis in Cubism came back to its point of origin in the idealism of Matisse and Denis. As we have seen, they too believed that the 'absolute' was to be found by giving things an enduring form in art.

And yet, the fact is that neither Gris nor his Cubist allies after 1917, actually followed this idealised process consistently. They might sometimes have started by drawing geometrical schemas, but it is clear that often their subject-matter was fixed from the start, at least in general terms, and even where there was no actual model or motif involved at any stage, their work always responded to experiences of things in the world. The solid stability of Gris's *Man from the Touraine* is literally, not merely metaphorically, architectural. Even the colour range, from slate grey and tile brown to pale limestone buffs evokes the building materials of the Loire valley. And in this case, the subject was probably an actual peasant neighbour at Beaulieu. There remained an element of analysis in even the purest synthetic work of the purest of the Cubists.

'PURE PAINTING' AND THE TABLEAU-OBJET: CUBISTS, ORPHISTS AND MATISSE

Generally speaking, the simpler Picasso's, Braque's and Gris's signs became, the more legible they became too. Moreover, this simplification went with the apparently matter-of-fact introduction of fragments extracted from the debris of daily life in collage and papier-collé. And yet this development did not simplify but complicated further their approach to representation, something underlined by the seemingly matter-of-fact titles added to their works by Kahnweiler. Clearly, in the case both of Picasso's papier-collé containing 'fruit-bowl, violin and wineglass' [103] and Braque's containing 'glass, bottle and newspaper' [110], knowing the objects to which they refer tells the viewer very little about what she or he sees. This conflict between subject matter advertised by titles and the character of the work is also there too in pre-collage and papier-collé paintings like *The Portuguese* and *Man with a Clarinet* [105, 107], where an element of mystery enters in as well. The viewer is told the subject, but must work even to imagine the presence of a Portuguese and a musician.

Looking back at his 'hermetic' works, Picasso chose to dwell on their relation to things as they are experienced in life: their density, weight, presence. Suggestion is the key, he said, to that relationship. 'It's not a reality you can take in your hand. It's more like a perfume – in front of you, behind you, to the sides. The scent is everywhere, but you don't quite know where it comes from.'[47] Such an approach to the relationship between painting and object, which refuses the literal altogether in favour of sustained equivocation, has often rightly been aligned with the late poetry of the Symbolist poet Stéphane Mallarmé, written at the end of the nineteenth century. It echoes Mallarmé's reluctance to name the objects that inspired his disparate clusters of epithets and images. Picasso's French was apparently not good enough for him to have got much from Mallarmé's complex manipulation of the French language, but Braque was, of course, French, and they were surrounded by writers deeply appreciative of Mallarmé (Apollinaire included) who would almost certainly have known the poet's key statement of 1891 concerning words and names: 'To name an object is to destroy three-quarters of the pleasure we take in the poem, which is derived from the enjoyment of guessing by degrees; of suggesting it.'[48] For Guillaume Apollinaire, the Mallarméan eva-

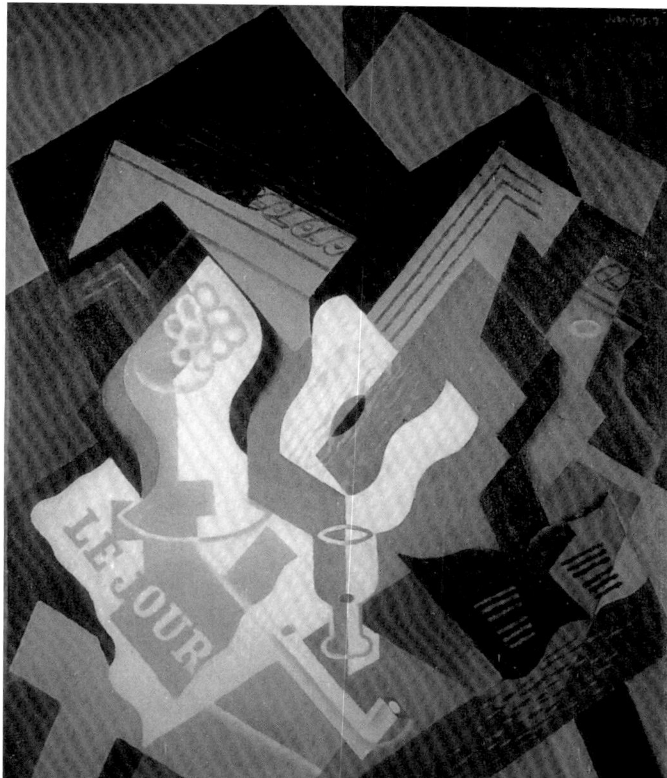

112. Juan Gris, *Guitar and Fruit-dish*, 1919. Oil on canvas, 92 × 73.5 cm. Henie-Onstad Kunstsenter, Høvikodden

sion of the named object (of nominalism) had led by 1912 to a new faith in the painting or the poem *as such*, at the expense of subject matter altogether. From 1908, Apollinaire had drawn attention to the 'purity' of the early Cubist painting of Picasso and Braque, but in 1912 he found it at its most extreme in what he called 'Orphic Cubism'.[49] Above all, he found it in the work of Robert Delaunay (b.1885).

Early in 1912, Apollinaire published an article advocating what he called 'pure painting'. He declared that: 'If painters still observe nature, they no longer imitate it', and that 'the young painters of the avant-garde schools' are engaged in painting which is 'not yet as abstract as it would like to be'.[50] As if in response to this, which amounted to an invitation, Delaunay painted a series of canvases in the spring and summer of 1912 in which he overlaid the traces of a postcard view of the Eiffel Tower with screens of prismatic colours which were arranged within Braque-like grids, his *Simultaneous Window* series [111]. True to Mallarméan suggestion, he left a hint of an 'object', but one almost completely veiled by 'pure painting' (usually, the silhouette of the Eiffel Tower sinks into the picture surface coloured a retiring green, the complementary of the rust red of its actual colouring). Early the following year, the *Windows* featured in a solo show of Delaunay's work at Der Sturm gallery in Berlin, and the painter published a short text; it was titled simply 'Light'. Here he returned to Signac's claim that light was the ultimate subject matter of painting: light recreated on the canvas by simultaneous colour contrast. His 'pure painting' amounted to the painting of the pure chromatic components of light (as understood by Signac and others),

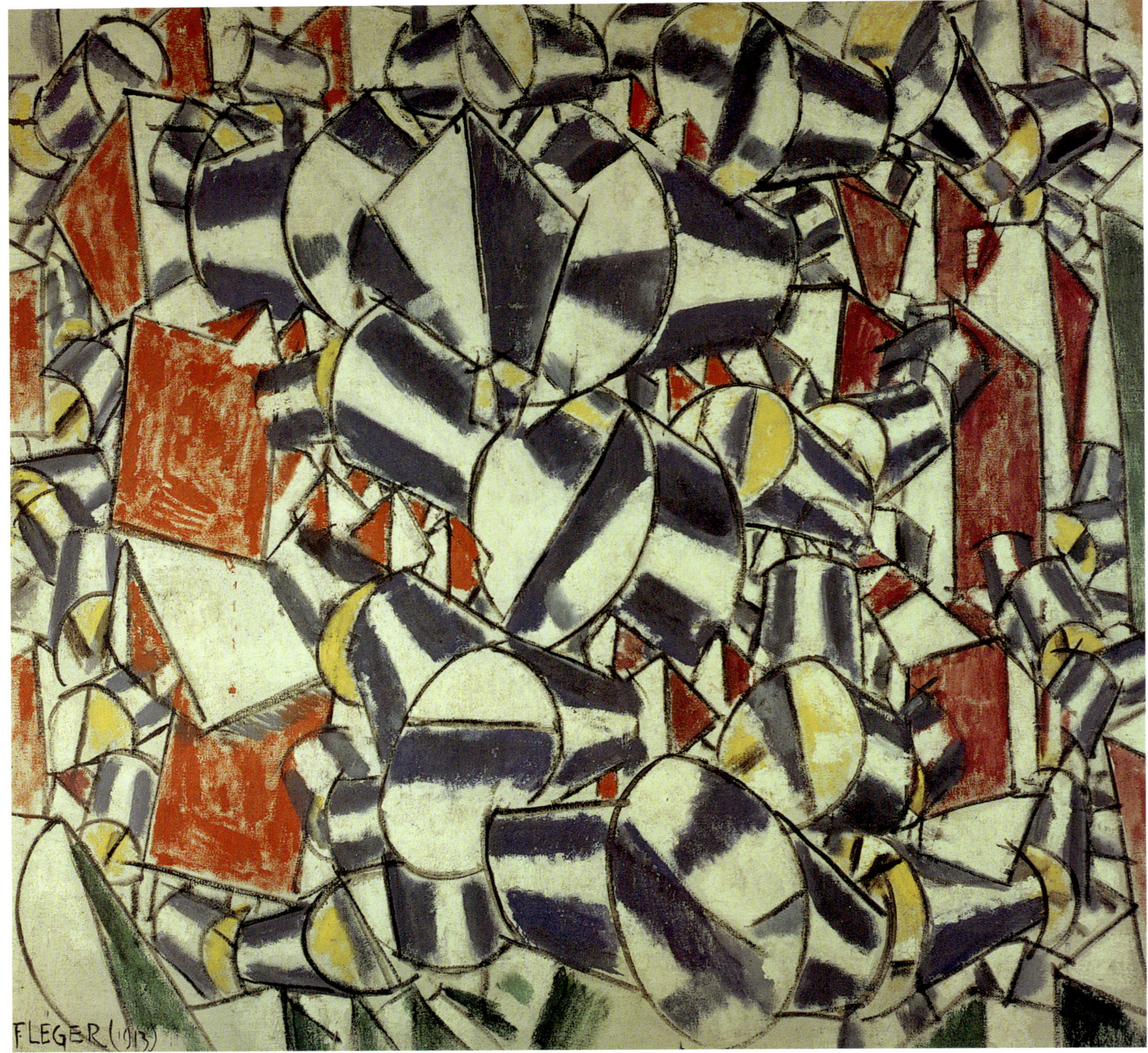

113. Fernand Léger, *Contrasts of Form*, 1913. Oil on canvas, 169.5 × 175.5 cm. Galerie Rosengart, Lucerne

not the objects revealed by the action of light in the world. It was to this especially that Apollinaire alluded when he attempted a definition of Orphic Cubism in his early 1913 anthology, *Les Peintres cubistes*. 'It is the art,' Apollinaire wrote, 'of painting new ensembles with elements borrowed not from visual reality, but entirely created by the artist and endowed by him with a powerful reality'.[51] Both Signac and Matisse had stressed the artificiality of colour in painting, however much it was to be used to represent nature; Delaunay focused on pictorial colour structures at the expense, it seemed, of nature. He accepted that subject matter could be *added to* his colour structures, especially images evoking modernity [172], but not that his colour structures should be *based on* subject matter.[52]

Delaunay's 'pure painting' of 1912–13 eliminated the naturalist residue from Neo-Impressionism and transformed the Divisionist touch into the Cubist facet, bringing brilliant colour into the hitherto shadowy spaces of Cubism. It also applied a very sophisticated understanding of colour theory, using not only Signac and his primary source M.-E.Chevreul's *De la loi du contraste simultané des couleurs*, but Ogden H. Rood's *Modern Chromatics* (first published in America) as well. Signac's *D'Eugène Delacroix au néo-impressionisme* had appeared in a new edition in August 1911. Like both Chevreul and Rood, he maintained that the key to the perception of light is the movement stimulated by the simultaneous contrasts of spectral colours, a movement based on the interaction of different wavelengths (quantities). For

Delaunay, this movement was an effect particularly to be experienced in the meeting of juxtaposed colours, or as he understood it the 'intervals' between them. His colour structures were designed to incite the eye to motion, and at the same time to achieve a proportionate balance analogous to the 'harmony' he believed, like Signac, was inherent in all experiences of light. He used various of Rood's suggested techniques in pursuit of this harmony: the direct juxtaposition of closely related colours (orange-red, yellow, orange-yellow, say), and the direct juxtaposition as well of colours which are relatively distant from each other in the Newtonian colour-circle (blue and yellow, say). Like Rood too (and Matisse), he allowed himself tonal modulation within hues (using darker or lighter pigments), believing that this did not diminish the effect of simultaneous contrast.[53] Despite the undeniable purity of his chromatic means and the uncompromising tone of his rhetoric, Delaunay's painting remained, however, at once analytic and synthetic, just like Picasso's and Braque's Cubist work of 1910–12. Even his *Circular Form* series of 1913, in which he can seem to have entirely got rid of subject matter, was actually based on first-hand studies of sun and moonlight in Louveciennes.[54]

Almost a year later than Delaunay, Fernand Léger (b.1881) was another to respond to Apollinaire's invitation to be a 'pure painter'. In 1913 he painted a series which he titled simply *Contrasts of Forms* [113], and which were apparently just as 'pure' as Delaunay's *Circular Forms*. They too were produced alongside works with subjects, though his subjects were less explicitly modern than Delaunay's: landscape, still-life, figures [174], sometimes posed to look like portraits. In his case, indeed, he used his 'contrasting forms' as the components of a simple, easily read repertoire of signs for things; he did not merely *add* signs to his pictorial structures, as Delaunay did. But, in a lecture published in 1913 conspicuous for its bold clarity, Léger outlined a theory of painting which was resolutely 'pure'. He wrote of a 'pictorial realism' (to be distinguished from all simple realisms) whose aim was 'the simultaneous ordering of the three great plastic quantities: lines, forms and colours', and he concluded uncompromisingly: 'Pictorial contrasts used in their purest sense (complementaries) of colours and line, of form, are from now on the armature of modern painting.'[55] His recourse to the idea of simultaneous contrast was, like Delaunay's, Neo-Impressionist in origin, but he went further in excising the residue of naturalism by advocating, not prismatic colour as the representation of light, but line, form and colour as concrete pictorial elements. The painting was, for him, a *material* reality, not a dematerialised analogue of light in nature; that was the message of the phrase 'pictorial realism'. It found an echo in Apollinaire's talk of the painter endowing pictorial elements with 'a powerful reality'.

In the *Contrasts of Forms* and the figurative works related to them [113, 174], Léger uses white highlights and volume-giving contours to create the effect of solid form (a kind of illusion), but everything about his quick, rough technique acts to assert the material flatness of the work as an object covered with pigment and medium. The canvases are as coarse as sacking and covered with a thick glue-based priming (usually grey). Léger draws with black and scrubs on the patches of colour and white in such a way that lines and colour patches are kept separate. The viewer, thus, can be simultaneously aware of volumetric forms and of flat line and colour. Ultimately, he sustained the belief in painting as the creation of a reality equivalent in its intensity to his first-hand experience of things: the belief in painting as *both* 'pure' *and* representational shared by so many modernists, from Signac and Denis to Matisse and Delaunay. His 1913 lecture carried the telling title, 'The Origins of Painting and its Representational Value'; and a second lecture, published in 1914, expanded on the capacity of painting to 'represent' modern experience. Moreover, even the *Contrasts of Forms* have their beginnings in painting with subject matter. Léger arrived at the 'purity' of these compositions by transforming landscapes, giving landscape forms a solidity more easily associated with still-life and figure painting.[56] As a 'pure painter', he too analysed as well as synthesised.

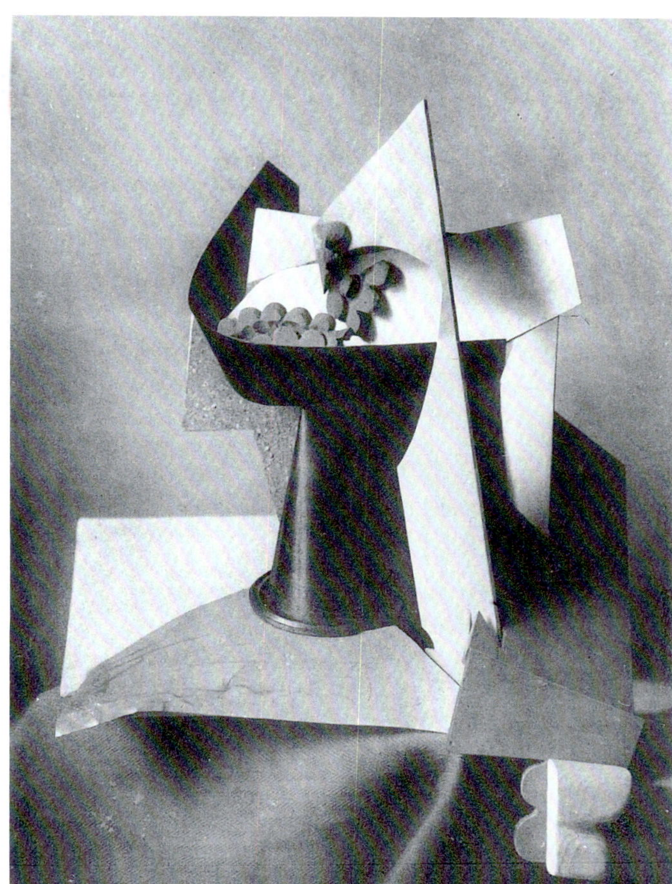

114. Henri Laurens, *Fruit-dish with Grapes*, 1918. Wood and painted steel, 68 × 62 × 47 cm. Claude and Mme. Claude Laurens Collection

Yet, the sheer brutality of his stress on the material fact of the work of art, underlines a point which applies right across the whole range of Matissean and Cubist art in the early decades of the century: the fundamental importance of approaching the painting *as an object*, the notion of the 'tableau-objet' (picture-object). With this, as we saw in the case of the artists around Matisse, went the new emphasis placed on the relationship between the work and its viewer. The material matter-of-factness of Braque's and Picasso's use, first of rough-textured surfaces, then of collaged material and cut-out paper shapes, was another way of making the point that the painting was an object. Indeed, the drive to materialise the work took Picasso into construction – the making of three-dimensional objects – first working with cardboard, then with cut and bent metal or with wood, (often roughly sawn) and actual debris (from pieces of turned wood to condensed milk cans) [front cover, 129]. And constructing in three-dimensions could mean constructing in *actual* space.

Post-collage and papier-collé Cubist space, however, was never literal, even when actual space was involved. The picture-object was always a 'picture' as well as an object. It could be a very material thing, and yet still suggest apparently infinite spaces. And this was so as much in the Picassian sculpture-object, the Cubist construction, as in the flat collage or papier-collé. It was so not only in the case of Picasso's sculpture-objects, but of Alexander Archipenko's from 1912 too, and of those made by Henri Laurens (b.1885) between 1915 and 1918 [114]. In the flat, the way such a pictorial space was created in collage and papier-collé is perhaps most cogently demonstrated by Braque's papier-collés of 1912–14, for example his *Glass, Bottle and Newspaper* of 1914 [110]. The newspaper cuttings and the sample of false-wood-graining wallpaper are flat and palpably material, but they are stuck over and under one another in combination with pieces of black and green coloured paper in such a way that they can suggest a space *in front* of the canvas. It is an imagined, dematerialised space which the viewer creates for her or himself from the actual overlappings of material fragments. Drawn lines and shading on top of these surfaces suggest further relationships in space, this time by the illusionist manipulation of shape and shading. In the end, the viewer's options for the imaginative creation of spaces in the work are increased almost *ad infinitum*. As with Matisse, active spectatorship is demanded if this very material thing is to be imaginatively dematerialised.

The incorporation of actual space in the three-dimensional sculpture-object complicated things still further, because Picasso, Archipenko and Laurens all used pictorial devices in their constructions to suggest spatial relationships that *contradicted* the actual. Laurens, like Braque on the flat, offers a particularly cogent demonstration of how papier-collé devices were translated into three-dimensions. Except for a small piece of turned wood standing in for the table leg, his *Fruit-dish with Grapes* of 1918 [114] is constructed from cut pieces of metal, whose sharp corners jut jaggedly out, uncomfortably tactile. One or two are given textured surfaces, but those with transparently brushed surfaces of white and grey themselves evoke spaces. Around the fruit-dish core they all perform the function of the overlapping space planes of papier-collé, opening the way to the creation of comparably dematerialised spatial relationships. And, again as in flat papier-collé, the sign for a solid thing can be a space, here an actual space: the sign for the bowl of the fruit-dish is thrust forward as a shaped void cut out of one of the metal space planes.

This kind of play between the materiality of sculpture and the Cubist art of dematerialisation was not simply confined to construction. From 1916, Lipchitz (b.1891) too used a simple planar vocabulary as a sculptor, but did so almost exclusively in the traditional materials of stone and bronze. In Lipchitz's case, in fact, the actual material weightiness of these elements increased the force with which their material actuality was denied: as can be seen, for instance, in the sturdy bronze of 1918 *Seated Man with a Guitar* [238], where voids often stand in for volumes and vice versa.

It is significant that when Matisse responded positively to the Cubist work of those around Picasso (between 1913 and 1917), he paid attention above all to Cubist space and the Cubist accent on the picture-object. He did not become a 'conceptual' painter in the sense that Picasso and Braque were; but he now worked to produce not merely paintings, but tactile paintings-as-objects, and he adapted obviously Cubist devices for the purpose.

This is already clear in the grand still-life painted in autumn 1914, *Artist and Goldfish* [115], which includes to the right the crossed legs of the artist and a square palette with his thumb poking through the hole.[57] The black vertical strip in front of which the table top and fishbowl are suspended can be seen either as a plane laid over the atmospheric blue depth outside the window or as a still-deeper depth dug like a channel cutting the painting in two, top to bottom. If the black is seen as in front of the blue, the cylinder of the pale bowl with its bright vermillion fish is pushed forward into an imagined space in front of the picture plane; if not they hover indeterminately somewhere close behind the surface. The structure of interlocking planes overlaps the scrolls of the balcony railing, especially on the right. Since the rough, discontinuous drawing of those scrolls is experienced as drawn *onto* the blue, these planes, especially the white of the square palette, are pushed out at the viewer too. Cubist spatial complexities are marshalled within an overall architecture of strips (in the case of the black axial strip joining edge to edge), which relates to Gris's work of 1913 and 1914 (the two were together at Collioure in the summer of 1914). There is no collage or papier-collé here, but the thick, coarsely worked surfaces and above all the way Matisse has scraped and scored them, often with the sharp end of his brush, gives them a material presence as tactile as any Picasso or Braque collage. Architectures of vertical strips, suggestions of space in front as well as within those flat structures, the shuttling of forms backwards and forwards in relation to the viewer, and unevenly worked surfaces involving scraping down and repainting, all these are features of Matisse's most experimental paintings of 1916, *Bathers by a Stream* among them [84]. He found his own ways of adapting his decorative, expressive priorities to the demands of the Cubist picture-object.

What the accommodation reached between Matisse and post-papier-collé Cubism underlines finally is the broad compatibility of the Matissian stance and that of the Cubists around Picasso and Braque. In the end, both were most fundamentally concerned with finding ways of moving beyond not only late nineteenth-century naturalism (in its Impressionist guise especially) but also late nineteenth-century Symbolism. Both wanted a kind of art that neither

115. Henri Matisse, *Artist and Goldfish*, 1914. Oil on canvas, 146.5 × 112.4 cm. The Museum of Modern Art, New York. Gift and Bequest of Florene M. Schoenborn and Samuel A. Marx

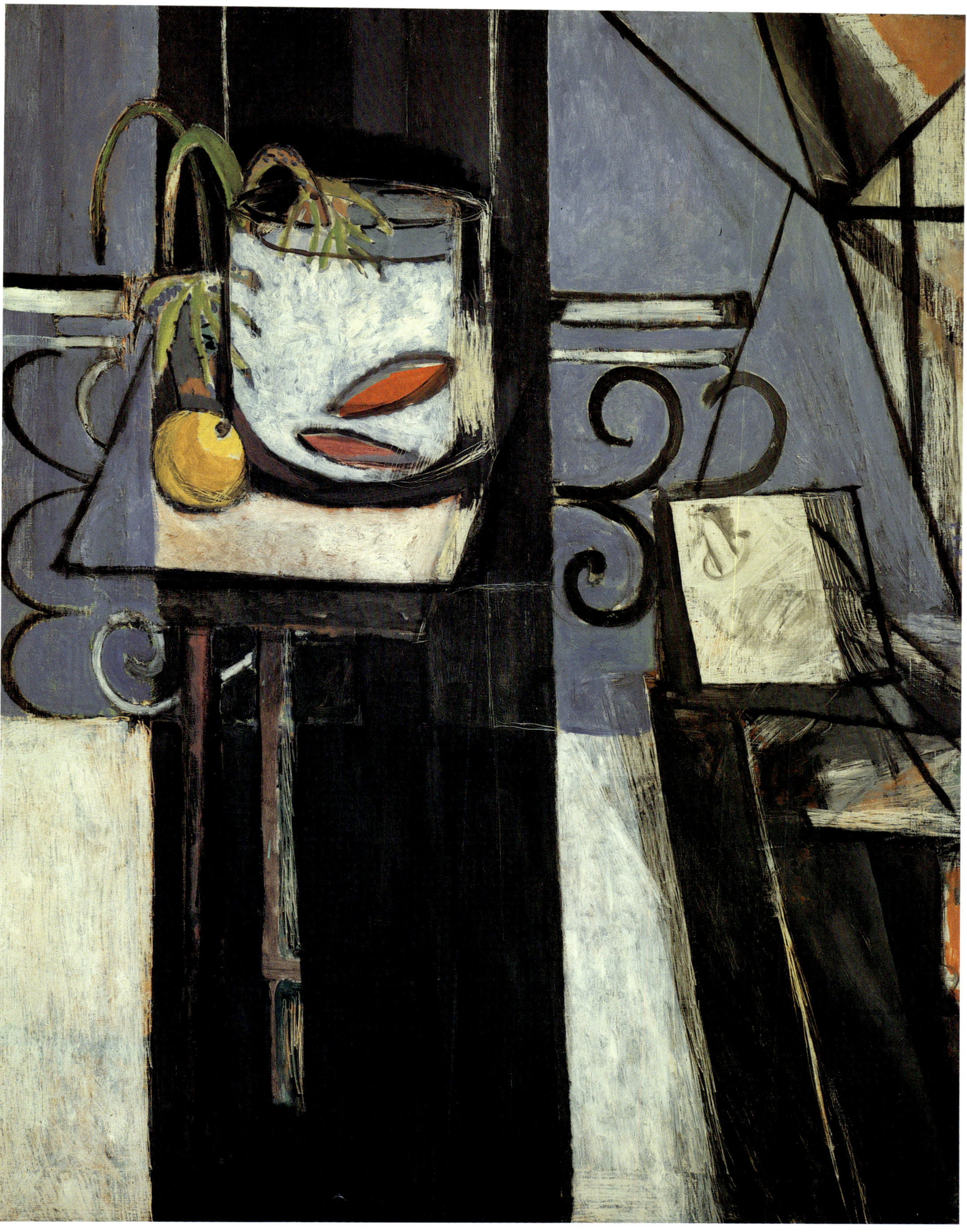

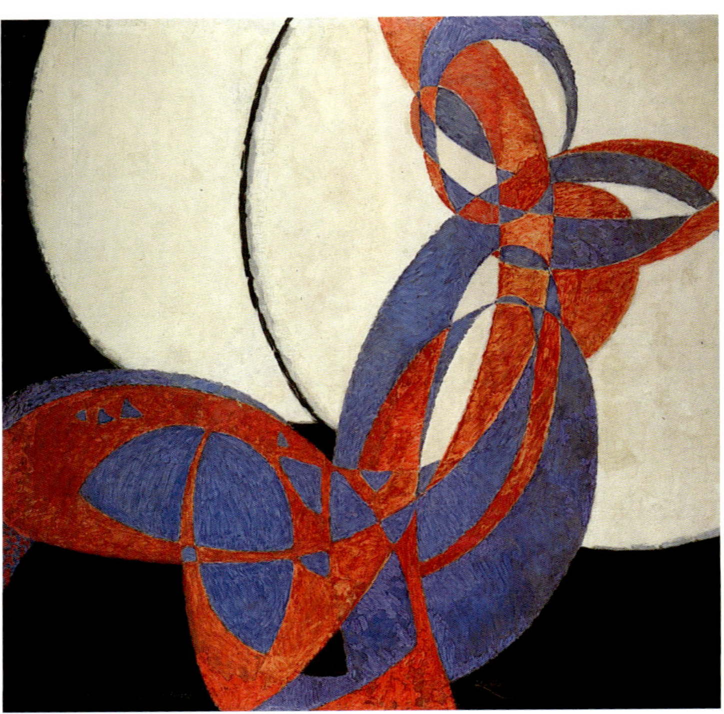

116. František Kupka, *Amorpha, Fugue in Two Colours*, 1912. Oil on canvas, 211 × 220 cm. National Gallery, Prague

described the look of nature nor symbolised an idea, but which found a material equivalent for nature at its most intensively experienced and ways of embodying *in* the art-object ideas of essence. And for both, if art was concerned with absolutes, those absolutes – essences – were revealed through individual experience in front of nature and in the making of the work of art.

When, in 1924, Gris gave Cubist theory perhaps its most unadulterated idealist shape in his lecture 'On the Possibilities of Painting', this point was elaborated at length. In the end, even Gris, the most Platonic of the Cubists, placed the stress on individual experience at its most concrete. Like Matisse and indeed Signac, Gris argued in 1924 that the fundamental principles of colour and form were constant, but he too resisted the temptation to go on from there to argue that art could actually arrive at the Platonic Idea in its *final* perfection. He argued instead that the artist could only reveal 'the world of ideas' in terms of his or her very specific experience of the visual, an experience that was unmeasurable, always open to change: an experience given its material embodiment in works of art, each one a thing distinct from the last, offered to the eyes of the viewer.[58]

THE IDEA IN THE WORK: KUPKA AND MONDRIAN

Robert Delaunay and Fernand Léger came close to the level of 'purity' envisaged for painting by Apollinaire in 1912, but not across the whole range of their painting. That year, however, saw one artist in Paris begin to produce nothing but 'pure painting', František Kupka (b.1871). In 1912, Kupka showed a large canvas at the Salon d'automne whose title invoked the analogy between painting and music, *Amorpha, Fugue in Two Colours* [116]. It was one of two exhibits which responded to this analogy by proposing an art of uncompromising non-figuration. Kupka may also have shown comparable painting that autumn at the Cubists' Salon de la Section d'Or; if so, Apollinaire's definition of Orphic Cubism as painting with elements 'entirely created by the artist' may very well have first been formulated in a lecture delivered in front of his work.[59]

Throughout the inter-war period, Kupka retained personal and professional links with his native Czechoslovakia (newly formed after 1918 as an independent state by the Treaty of Versailles). His training in Prague and Vienna, and his engagement with metaphysical ideas, notably the writings of Goethe and of the German Theosophist Rudolf Steiner, set him apart in Paris. However, he was Jacques Villon's and Raymond Duchamp-Villon's neighbour at Puteaux, and closely in touch with all three Duchamp brothers. A small number of French artists would produce work as uncompromisingly pure as Kupka's, including Félix Del Marle, Jean Gorin and Jean Hélion in the inter-war years, as outlined in Chapter 2. But, those who led the way in France to such an extreme were foreigners. Besides Kupka, the key figures were the Dutch artists Piet Mondrian (b.1872) and Theo van Doesburg (b.1883). All of them shared a deep involvement in metaphysics, the metaphysics associated above all with the Theosophical movement, founded as a fusion of Eastern and Western religious traditions by the mystic Helena Petrovna Blavatsky in the

117. František Kupka, *Child with a Ball*, 1908–9. Pastel on paper, 62.2 × 47.5 cm. The Museum of Modern Art, New York. Gift of Mr and Mrs František Kupka

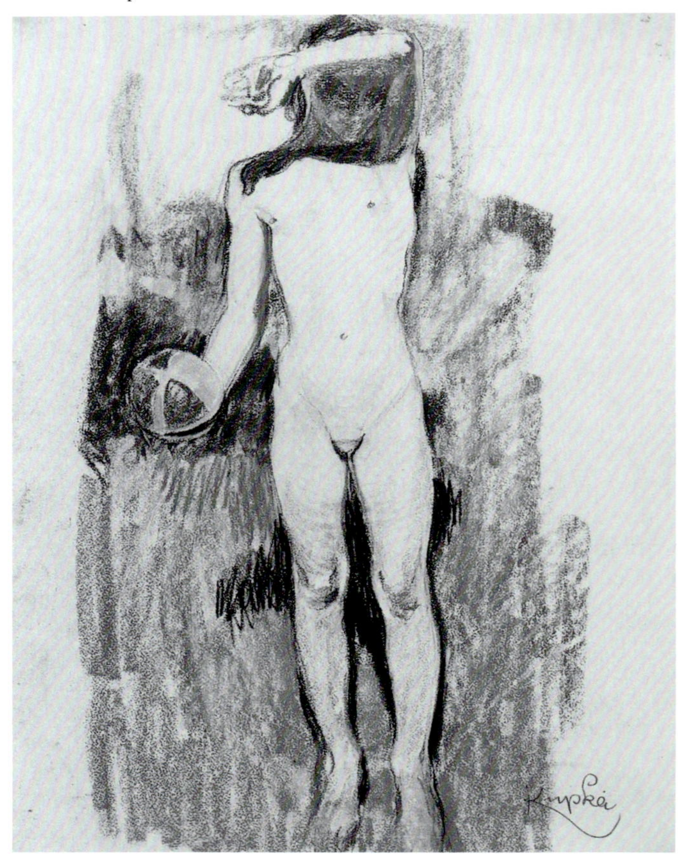

late nineteenth century. This alone made them at best eccentrics in relation to most sections of French middle-class society, including those who were involved in the art world. A look at the two rather different cases of Kupka and Mondrian can bring out most of the points at which non-figurative art could diverge from and converge with the theory and practice of French modernism generally in the period from the 1900s.

Kupka may have had a metaphysical agenda, but he developed his 'pure painting' on the basis of a long-drawn-out study of the perception of light in nature alongside the components of pictorial composition, a study of light as colour and the action of paint-marks rooted in Signac's *D'Eugène Delacroix au néo-impressionnisme* and, from among its sources, Chevreul's *De la loi du constraste simultané des couleurs*. He too moved between analysis and synthesis, given confidence by Neo-Impressionist theory, and, in his notes (published and unpublished) of 1910–13, he too repeatedly insists on the role of 'perceived "reality"' (his phrase) in the development of pictorial ideas.[60] Both *Amorpha, Fugue in Two Colours* and his equally uncompromising *Vertical Planes III*, which was shown at the Indépendants of 1913, emerged from earlier series and suites of studies that were often translations into pictorial terms of subjects observed in nature. *Amorpha, Fugue* began in studies of Kupka's daughter naked in his Puteaux garden with a coloured ball [117]. *Vertical Planes* began in a series of paintings where Kupka moved from Neo-Impressionist dabs to long vertical strips, as in, for instance, *Study for the Language of Verticals* [118], probably of 1911. The stimuli behind the series included reflections on water, piano keys, coloured light filtered through medieval stained glass and an area of reflected light on the wall in an earlier self-portrait.[61]

Such varied starting points in 'perceived "reality"', did not, however, weaken Kupka's commitment to the non-figurative. In *Language of Verticals*, he erases all traces of things studied in nature. The picture was later exhibited with the subtitle 'Red Background'. Its title as inscribed on the canvas, coupled with this additional subtitle, underline the fact that it was presented as a purely pictorial experiment, closer in spirit to Léger's *Contrasts of Forms* than Delaunay's *Simultaneous Windows*. In his writings of 1910–13, Kupka pointed out that red is a colour which has the effect of always appearing to advance in relation to other colours; this gives a clue to the nature of the experiment attempted in *Language of Verticals*.[62] Solid 'advancing' reds (with pink) form the 'background' for suspended planes of white, pale greenish and yellowish greys, and overlapping bands of green and black. The result is a successful experiment in pictorial flattening through colour: in making 'background' and 'foreground' fuse.

At the same time, Kupka did not depend on things seen alone as the starting points for his pictorial ideas. He noted, indeed, that what he called 'subjective images', by which he meant his own entirely cerebral inventions, could be a 'point of departure'.[63] The pictures he showed at the Salon d'automne of 1913, with their neo-scientific titles *Positionings of Mobile Graphic Elements I* and *II*, seem to have been pictorial ideas at least initially generated by 'subjective images' (to use Kupka's own phrasing) alone. And, though he was prob-

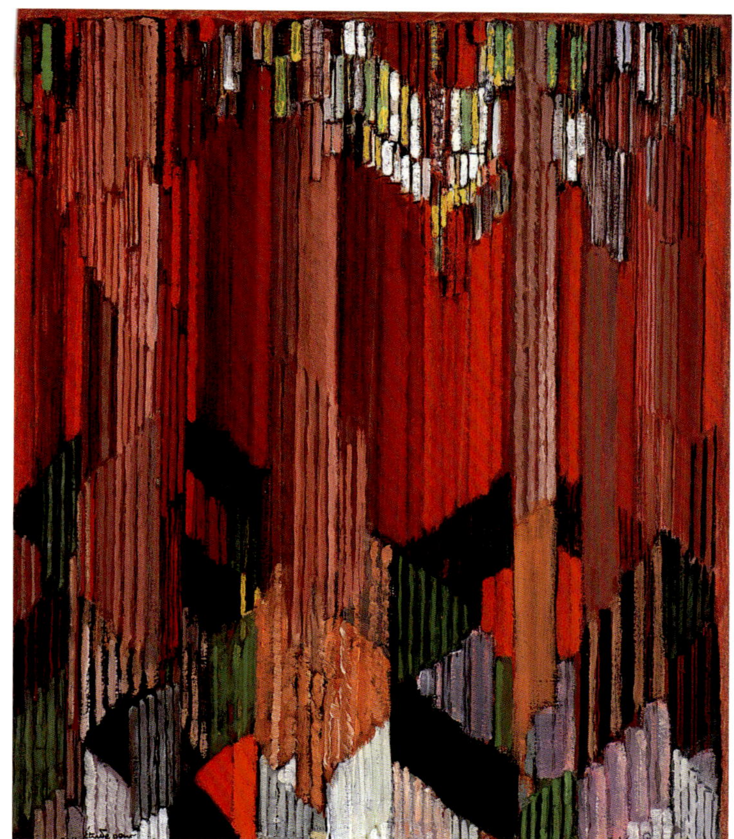

118. František Kupka, *Study for the language of Verticals*, 1911. Oil on canvas, 78 × 63 cm. Museo Thyssen-Bornemisza, Madrid

ably unaware of Wassily Kandinsky's major theoretical tract *On the Spiritual in Art* before the summer of 1913, his approach to the conception and development of pictorial ideas closely paralleled that of the Munich-based leader of the Blaue Reiter from at least 1911. He wrote of the artist externalising an 'inner impulse' (analogous with Kandinsky's 'inner necessity'), of giving that impulse 'graphic' shape and then fixing it in pictorial space. Whether a pictorial idea's origins lay in things seen or in the mind, it was, for Kupka, the externalisation of something 'inner', something within himself, and it was developed through a series of studies very much as Kandinsky worked towards his 'Compositions'. Major paintings were not the result of a process of open-ended exploration as they were for Picasso and Braque or for Matisse, they were the result of a process which gradually gave visible form to the 'inner impulse'.[64] And for Kupka, what Matisse called the absolute was to be discovered *in* such 'inner impulses', not in the artist's 'sensation' of nature, however 'pure'. Looking at things and learning to manipulate the components of pictorial composition could not in themselves be enough. Indeed, he wrote that every mark or colour touch, even if simply 'technical', inevitably carried a trace of 'the psychic element' (his phrase), even the chaos of colours on an artist's palette.

Something of the expressive force that he believed existed in a picture like *Language of Verticals*, which might seem a simple technical experiment, is conveyed by the following two observations extracted from his writings of 1910–13. 'There is in the vertical,' he writes, 'all the majesty of the sta-

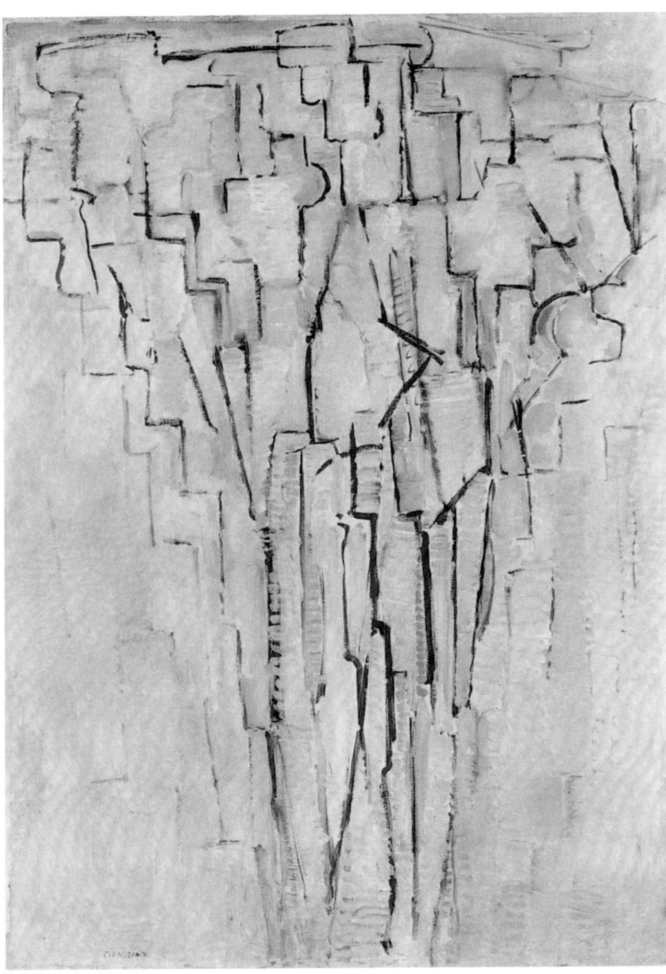

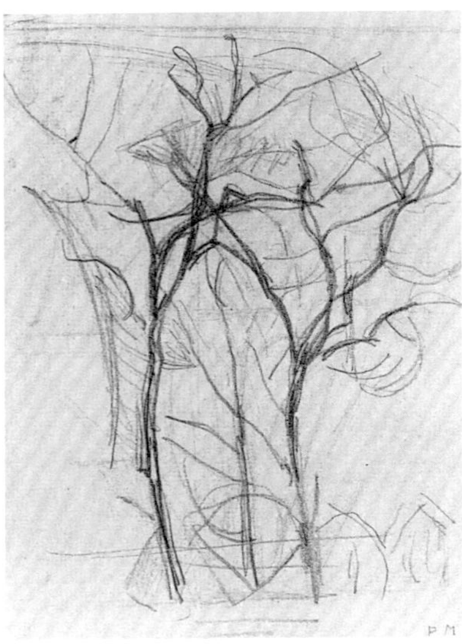

119. Piet Mondrian, *The Tree A*, 1913. Oil on canvas, 100.5 × 67.5 cm. Tate Gallery, London

120. Piet Mondrian, *Trees*, 1912. Pencil on paper, 17.3 × 12.4 cm. Private Collection

121. Facing page. Piet Mondrian, *Composition with Trees 1*, 1912. Oil on canvas, 81 × 62 cm. Gemeentemuseum, The Hague

122 Facing page. Piet Mondrian, *Composition with Yellow, Blue, Black, Red and Grey*, 1921. Oil on canvas, 88.5 × 72 cm. Stephen Mazoh and Co., Inc.

tic. It contains at once top and bottom, reuniting them, but dividing space *horizontally*. Repeated as a series of parallels [as in *Language of Verticals*], the vertical expands horizontally in tense and dumb anticipation.' A few pages earlier he had written: 'Silence is static, vertical tetrahedron.'[65]

In the end, Kupka's metaphysical agenda placed him closer to the Symbolists of the late nineteenth century than to the most radical modernists in France of the 1900s and 1910s. He did not think of the universal (Matisse's 'absolute') as directly embodied in the material fabric of the work of art; it was, for him, an inner meaning *behind* it, as it was behind nature. He wrote of 'the language of the inner voice', and claimed for the true artist 'the faculty of penetration': access to 'that which is most intimate in the human soul'.[66]

Even from a radical modernist standpoint, Kupka's work appeared extreme in France before 1914, as it would still between the wars. And yet, the practice that lay behind such results would have seemed conservative. He developed his ideas, after all, following a method in line with the teaching of composition in academies across Europe (including the Ecole National des Beaux-Arts), as he acknowledged. Each major painting was the outcome of a series of studies which applied the full range of his technical knowledge to the development of an idea. Among modernists in France, Léger was to work in a comparable way from 1917, producing studies on paper and smaller versions of each idea on canvas, before painting what he called the 'definitive state'; although in 1913–14 he had worked, like Picasso and Braque, in an open-ended experimental way with roughly painted suites of canvases, as we have seen. Generally, however, modernists in France at their most experimental refused the certainties of Kupka's quasi-academic method, the method that lay behind the great decorative mural projects of the 1900s. They preferred to keep the idea under fundamental critical review right up to the point at which it was left. Indeed, in the case of Picasso and Braque, the idea was something arrived at only at the end: something previously unknown. For Kupka, the pictorial idea was something known from the start, however vaguely, which was finally and definitively fixed. His very working method was the analogue of his metaphysical belief in the supremacy of Idea over matter. In the case of Mondrian, a closely related belief in the superior 'reality' of the Idea found pictorial embodiment in a practise as open as Picasso's and Braque's, though from 1916 his paintings became more and more finished. Mondrian's actual work, therefore, whatever his metaphysical agenda, has a capacity to invite an exploratory, empathetic spectatorship, and has a material presence, the equal of the most admired experimental work of Matisse and the Cubists.

He arrived from Amsterdam for his first Paris stay in the spring of 1912, so he was there for the Cubist Salon de la Section d'Or and the scandal of the 1912 Salon d'automne (with Kupka's *Amorpha* pictures on show). He remained until the summer of 1914, when the outbreak of war kept him in the Netherlands. Mondrian came to Paris a respected Dutch innovator with his metaphysical agenda almost

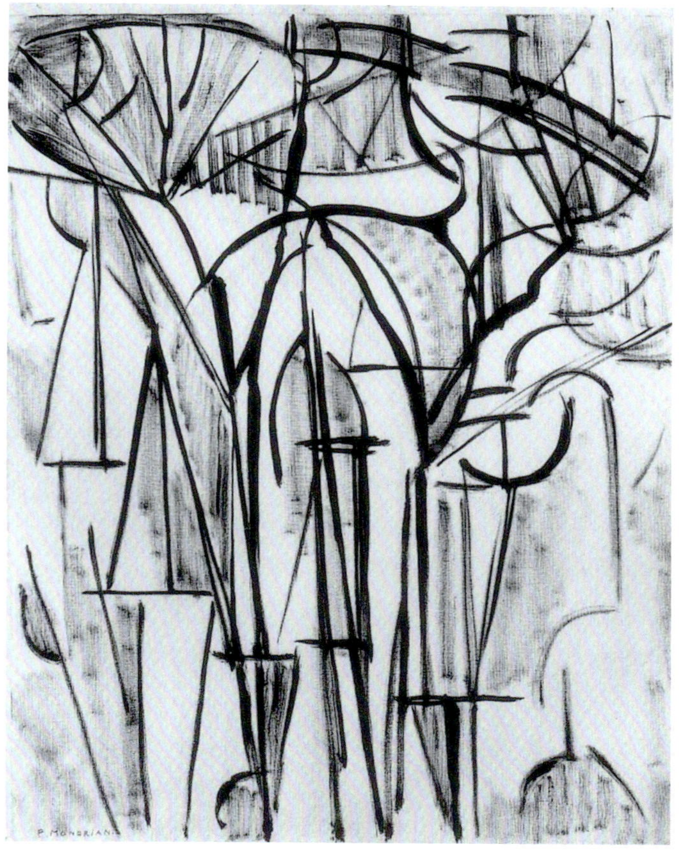

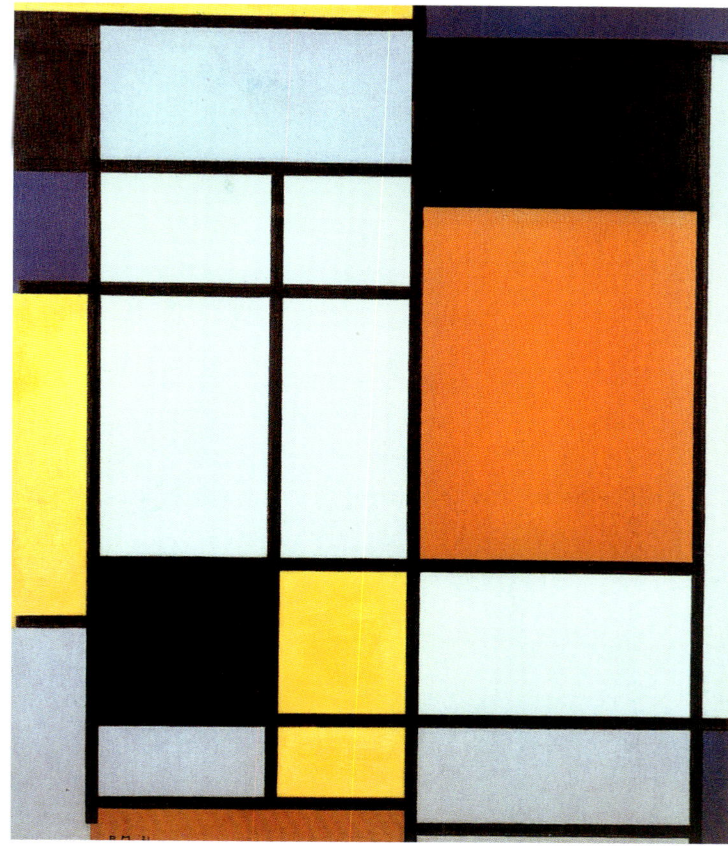

fully formed. He had seen recent Picassos and Braques in Amsterdam, and, though he met Le Fauconnier and Léger soon after arriving, he focused almost exclusively on the work of Picasso which he saw at Kahnweiler's gallery. In those two and a half years he developed a practise as challenging in its openness to risk as the pictures by Picasso that Kahnweiler called 'hermetic' (and as demanding for the viewer). It produced paintings [119] which replaced the definitive images of much of his Dutch work with images that were both more veiled and more provisional: open invitations to creative viewing closely comparable at first to the Picasso of *Man with a Clarinet* [107].

Mondrian's commitment to abstraction at the expense of the representation of nature is clear already in his first Paris period from his correspondence and from two sketchbooks in which he jotted down thoughts as they came to him.[67] So are the metaphysical foundations of his stance; he had attended Rudolf Steiner's lectures in the Netherlands in 1908 and had become a member of the Theosophical Society in 1909. Set down on paper, his approach can seem as single-minded in its drive towards the conclusive fixing of the Idea as Kupka's. In January 1914, he wrote to the Dutch critic-collector, H.P. Bremmer, of the inspiration given him by nature, and then added: 'but I want to approach truth as closely as possible and therefore abstract everything until I reach the essential of things (although always still an external essential!)'.[68] A key subject in his earliest Paris work of 1912–13 was the tree – apple trees and Dutch elms stripped of leaves. It was a motif easily reduced to two-dimensional linear traceries on the picture surface, and the linear structure of a work like *The Tree* [119] is evidently developed from sketches of trees similar to those that survive, torn from a sketchbook, probably made before Mondrian's departure from the Netherlands [120].[69] Certainly such a picture can seem to be the outcome, therefore, of an elaborate but fundamentally straightforward process of abstraction directed towards the fixing of a single ideal image. And yet the way it leaves unconcealed the overpaintings and erasings of its making says otherwise, as in all Mondrian's canvases of this phase. The viewer is invited into the process of the image's materialisation; he or she is not simply presented with a complete idea, as with Kupka's *Amorpha* or *Vertical Plane* paintings.

Indeed, Mondrian's practice in 1912–14 took further than Picasso and Braque did themselves, a suggestive confusion endemic in all of their work of 1911–14. His work did not merely blur the distinction between the finished and the unfinished but between drawing and painting. Thus, alongside *The Tree* or just before it, he made a painting which is closer to the surviving sketchbook drawings, *Composition with Trees I* [121], working exclusively in black and white to produce what is plainly a painting-as-drawing. This is a painting with all the marks of immediacy and of the provisional that are associated with drawing when it is approached as the medium of inspiration and exploration. In a real sense, *all* his paintings of 1912–14 are paintings-as-drawings, even when they introduced stronger colour – pinks and blues – just before the coming of war.

It seems that at this time Mondrian himself thought of abstraction as a process which not only led to the gradual

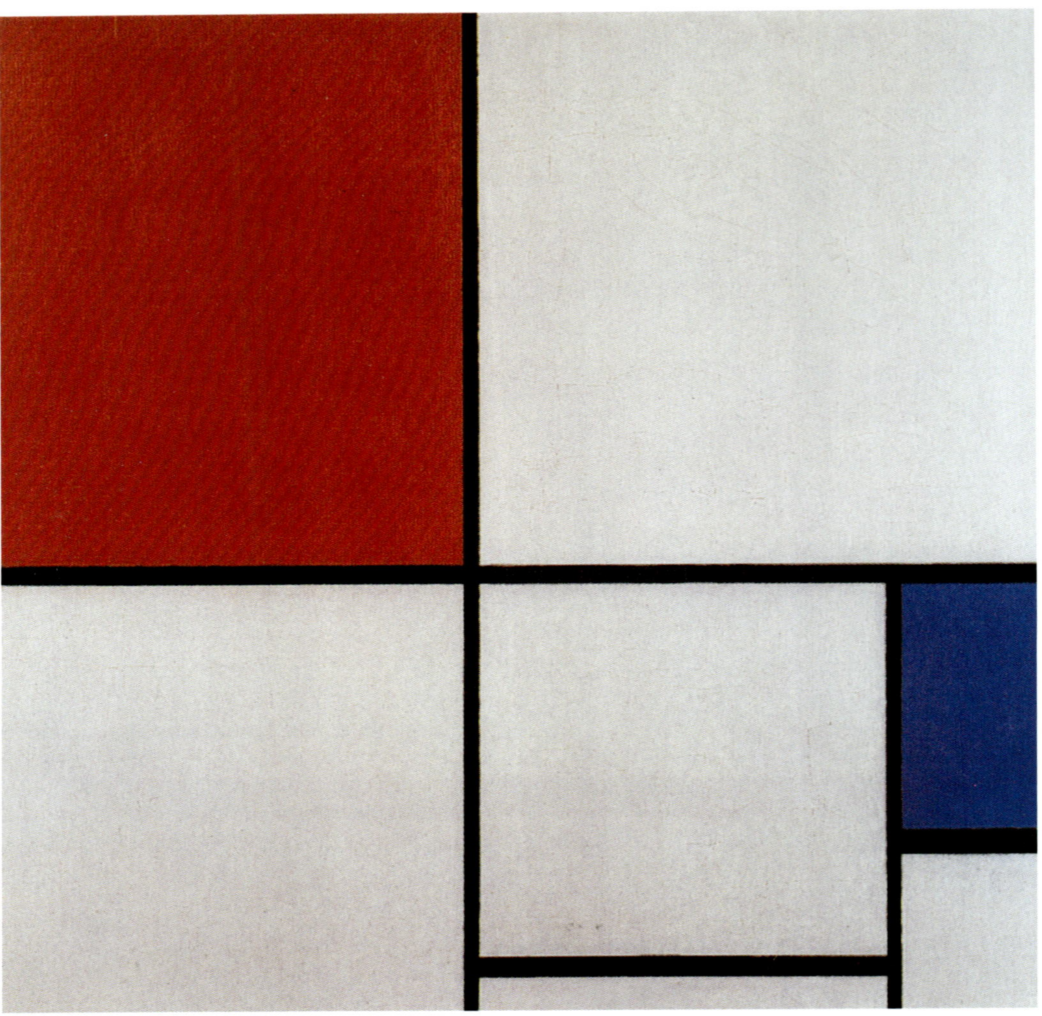

123. Piet Mondrian, *Composition A*, 1932. Oil on canvas, 55 × 55 cm. Kunstmuseum, Winterthur, Bequest of Clara and Emil Friedrich-Jezler

elimination of the motif but to dematerialisation. In one of his sketchbooks he wrote: 'The elimination of matter also eliminates the imitation of matter. We arrive at the representation of other things such as laws which hold matter together.'[70] Once again, there is no mistaking the metaphysical thrust of such sentiments. In a work like *The Tree*, the visible pentimenti exposing the way the linear structure around the flanks has been progressively over-painted, act as a metaphor of the materialisation of the image through dematerialisation. The irony is that it is a metaphor experienced only by taking in the materially tactile qualities of the painting, only by affirming the painting's material presence. It was this inescapable fact that Mondrian recognised when he told Bremmer that 'the essential' he arrived at was 'always still an external essential!' His absolute, like Matisse's, was embodied, he believed, in the painting-as-object; each one distinct from any other and arrived at in the experience of its making.

When Mondrian returned to Paris in the summer of 1919, he had confirmed his status as a leading Dutch avant-gardist by taking an active role with Van Doesburg in the formation and early development of the De Stijl group. With Van Doesburg, and the De Stijl painter Vilmos Huszar, he had developed both his thinking and his painting so far that he had already published in the periodical *De Stijl* the main tenets of his mature theory (dubbed 'Neo-Plasticism'), and was on the threshold of his mature non-figurative work as a painter. He had entirely rid his work of recognisable subject matter in 1916; and between then and 1919 had progressively expunged from his painting figure/ground relationships and the suggestions of depth that went with them, using linear grids as all-over flattening devices. Little more than a year after his return to Paris, he produced his first fully fledged Neo-Plastic paintings, among them *Composition with Yellow, Blue, Black, Red and Grey* of 1921 [122].

One can talk of such a work as fully fledged Neo-Plasticism, because it is a complete realisation of the theory set out first in *De Stijl* between its foundation in 1917 and 1920, and then in Mondrian's little pamphlet published in 1920 by Léonce Rosenberg's galerie de L'Effort Moderne, *Le Néo-Plasticisme*. Yve-Alain Bois has shown how that theory was a re-casting of Mondrian's earlier metaphysics in response to a wartime reading of Hegel through the intermediary of his Dutch follower, G.J.P.J. Bolland, and has brought out the key importance of this new stimulus.[71] By 1914, Mondrian already believed that by reducing the elements of painting (colour and line) to the simplest relationships (between contrasting colours and lines in opposi-

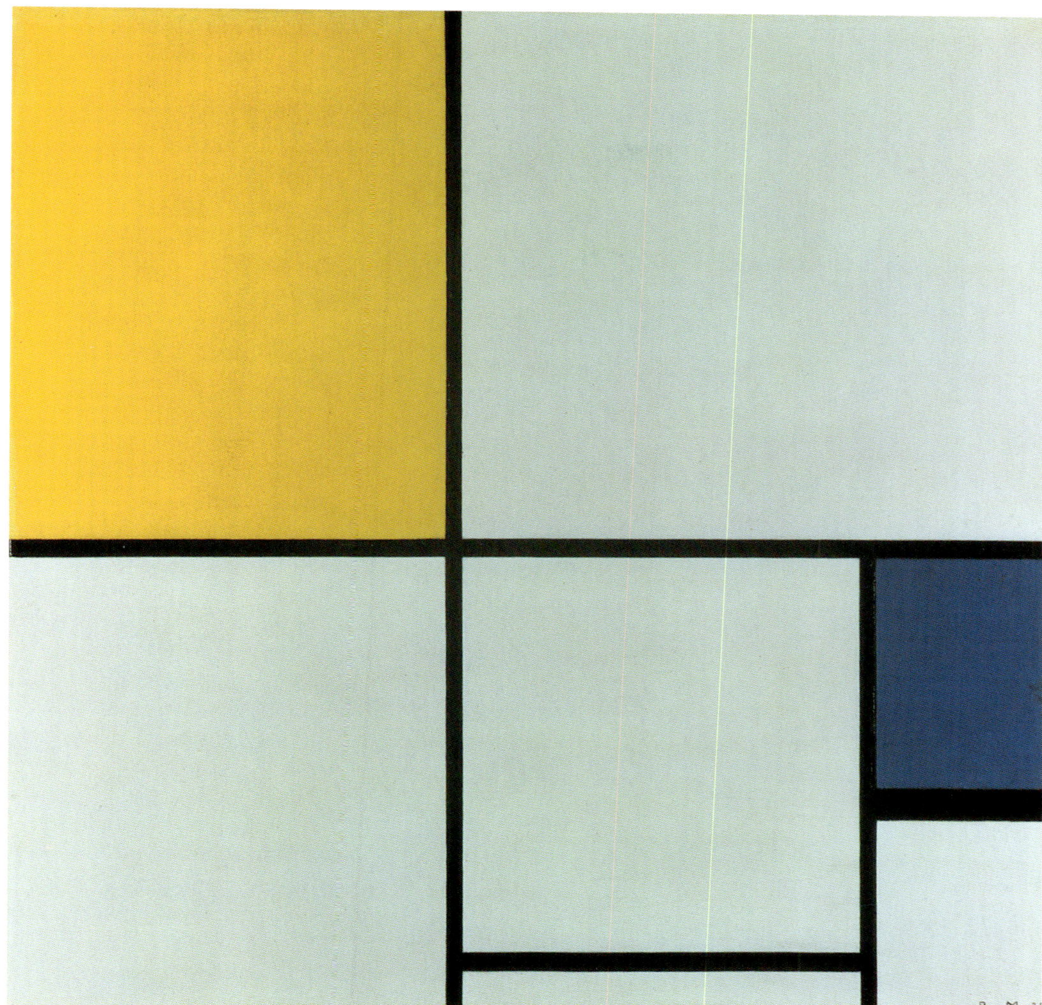

124. Piet Mondrian, *Composition with Yellow and Blue*, 1932. Oil on canvas, 55.5 × 55.5 cm. Fondation Beyeler, Riehen/Basel

tion), the order of relations basic to all existence could be represented: between male and female, the individual and the universal, mind and matter. What Hegellian dialectics taught him was that the resolution of oppositions on every level – philosophical and aesthetic – had to be an ongoing, dynamic process of equilibration, in which the opposing elements existed only as the function of their *relationships*, not as *individual* forms. The open-ended Cubist practice he had adapted from Picasso was given confirmation by a theory whose engagement with universals was profoundly compatible with his earlier thinking. He was driven to reduce the elements of painting to the simplest possible opposites: the three primary colours, the black line in the vertical and horizontal positions and non-colour; and to treat the activity of painting as a continual process of resolution, where the relationships between colour and non-colour, vertical and horizontal are all there is to experience.

The new dynamic way in which he now approached picture-making is summed up by the fact that now he thought of the action of opposites in the work as simultaneous negation and affirmation.[72] In a piece like *Composition with Yellow, Blue, Black, Red and Grey*, Mondrian worked for an equilibrium in which every oppositional relationship between vertical and horizontal, colour and colour, colour and non-colour held their mutual powers of negation and affirmation in balance. In such a painting, no colour rectangle or straight line can be experienced as a separate element, since it is affirmed, or, as Bois puts it, produced by its opposite. Nothing exists outside relationships. By comparison with the work of Mondrian's first year back in Paris, such a painting's fully fledged Neo-Plasticism lies in the sheer clarity of its oppositions (the dense black of the lines and the saturation of the primaries especially), and in the fact that an irregular asymmetry has replaced the regular grids that had guided the linear structures of the earlier non-figurative compositions. Mondrian now started out from an inherently unbalanced asymmetrical set of relations within which balance could only be reached by the placing and relative saturation of his colour rectangles against the areas of non-colour. The kind of pictorial equilibrium he achieved in such circumstances would always involve tensions: resolved but not denied.

Before 1914, the practise of painting-as-drawing had built the openness of Mondrian's method into the image. In his Neo-Plastic work, each piece was resolved as immaculately as possible, concealing the dynamics of its dialectical development. The openness inherent in his new pictorial dialectics was there to be seen only in the sometimes startling difference between one similar painting and another.

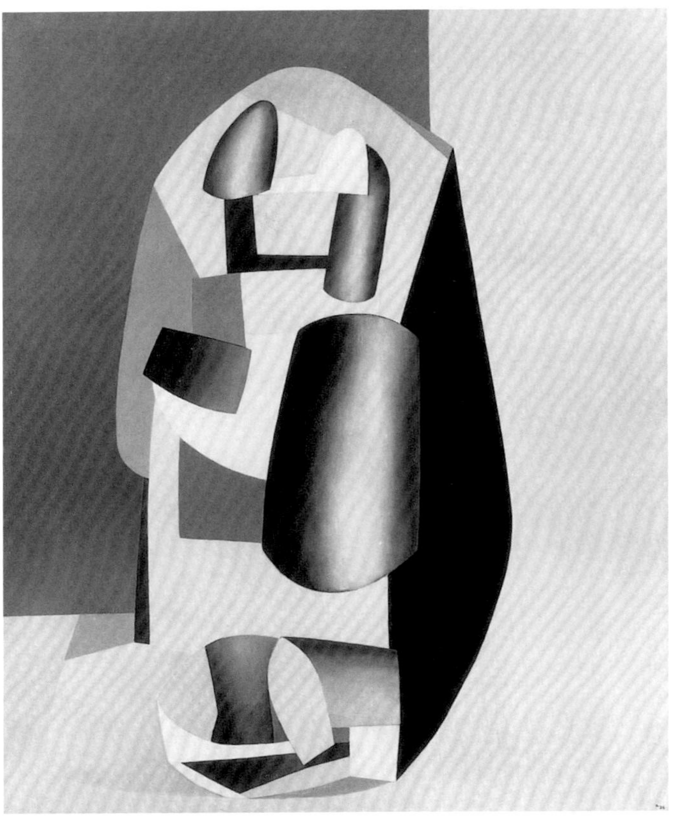

125. Jean Hélion, *Standing Figure*, 1936. Oil on canvas, 146 × 114 cm. The Metropolitan Museum of Art, New York. Gift of the Joseph Cantor Foundation, 1982

A particular series of Neo-Plastic paintings shows Mondrian drawing attention to difference by repetition – similarity – more decisively than any other. It was painted between 1929 and 1932, and consists of eight square canvases of comparable size whose format is divided by verticals and horizontals in an almost identical way; *Composition A* and *Composition with Yellow and Blue* [123, 124] are two of the four Mondrian painted in 1932. One of the 1932 variants introduced a double line for the main horizontal, otherwise the single crossing, the placing of the single extended vertical and horizontal and of the enclosed white plane, usually a square, is repeated but for minimal differences in each work. Those differences in these two cases involve the exact size of the small coloured rectangle to the right, and the exact thickness of the lines. So precise had Mondrian become in his guaging of relationships on the picture surface that by the late 1920s he was arriving at the linear division of the canvas in charcoal and pencil directly on the primed surface; incredibly, minute shifts in positioning occurred at this early stage even in these 'identical' linear structures.[73] However closed it appeared, his practise remained open as he worked with eye and hand, refusing calculation. Decisions about the placing of colour were made soon after the division of the surface was fixed, and it is here that the main scope for variation exists between variants. In this case different primaries, red and yellow, fill the same upper left rectangle and the proportion of the blue rectangle lower right is subtly altered, as is the intensity of the blue.

This series seems to have been painted partly as a belated response to Mondrian's serious difference of opinion with his old ally Van Doesburg in the mid-1920s, when Van Doesburg's decision to use the anti-gravitational 45° diagonal led to Mondrian's withdrawal from De Stijl. Van Doesburg (and a growing critical concensus) charged Mondrian's Neo-Plasticism above all with being incapable of change. For Mondrian, to restrict so rigidly the room for change was actually to sharpen awareness of it to an infinitely acute point. As he put it in 1930: 'Neo-Plastic tries to express *the invariable and the variable at the same time and in equivalence*.'[74]

Photographs of paintings of this size in the rue du Départ studio show how Mondrian framed them. He tacked on to the flanks of the stretcher strips of white-painted wood recessed slightly from the picture surface and fixed each work on a white painted board which echoed its format and was slightly larger (many of these frames still survive, as in these cases). The effect was to combat any suggestion that the painting is a surface in which the viewer is to imagine depth, and to push that surface out at the viewer as a flat material area covered in pigment and medium. At the same time, the lines direct the eye outwards unchecked, the surrounding white allows the white inside the painting to expand outside, and simultaneously lights up the colour planes where they abut it. Mondrian's framing is calculated both to underpin the presence of the work as a flat picture-object and to enhance its effect as a radiant trap for the eye that pulls the gaze in and then pushes it outwards across the expanse of wall around it.

One unexpected material property of these works is that the lines are densely black yet relatively thinly painted and the brilliant-white surfaces are built up thickly all across the picture plane, so that the verticals and horizontals become shallow channels recessed into the paint. Where there could be depth, there is the most tactile surface. Space is flat expanse; light is not in the painting, it is emitted by it. This is the picture-object stripped of its last illusions: those of Matisse's pictorial spaces created from colour, and of Cubist advancing and retreating planes.

As a Neo-Plastic painter, Mondrian could still think in terms of symbols. In 1930, he wrote of light as a symbol of the future, placing his work at the point of a new dawn which looked towards 'full daylight', and certainly the brilliant white and saturated primaries of his painting in the early 1930s are attuned to the ancient theme of light as revelation.[75] But he was aware that such symbolic meanings were a secondary accretion, added to the work, which at its most essential was, for him, the material embodiment of the universal, an individual material manifestation of Spirit. In an echo of Léger's phrase 'pictorial realism', Mondrian referred to his painting as 'abstract-real', never abstract. Its dematerialised Idea – its dialectical equilibrium – was rendered material for each viewer. Far more than Kupka's and no less than Matisse's, Picasso's or Léger's, this was painting that placed the relationship between work and viewer first.

ART AND 'EVOLUTION'

Mondrian's vision in 1930 of Neo-Plastic art as a 'new dawn' opening a way towards 'full daylight' was of a piece with his vision of art in history as a whole. The most persistent les-

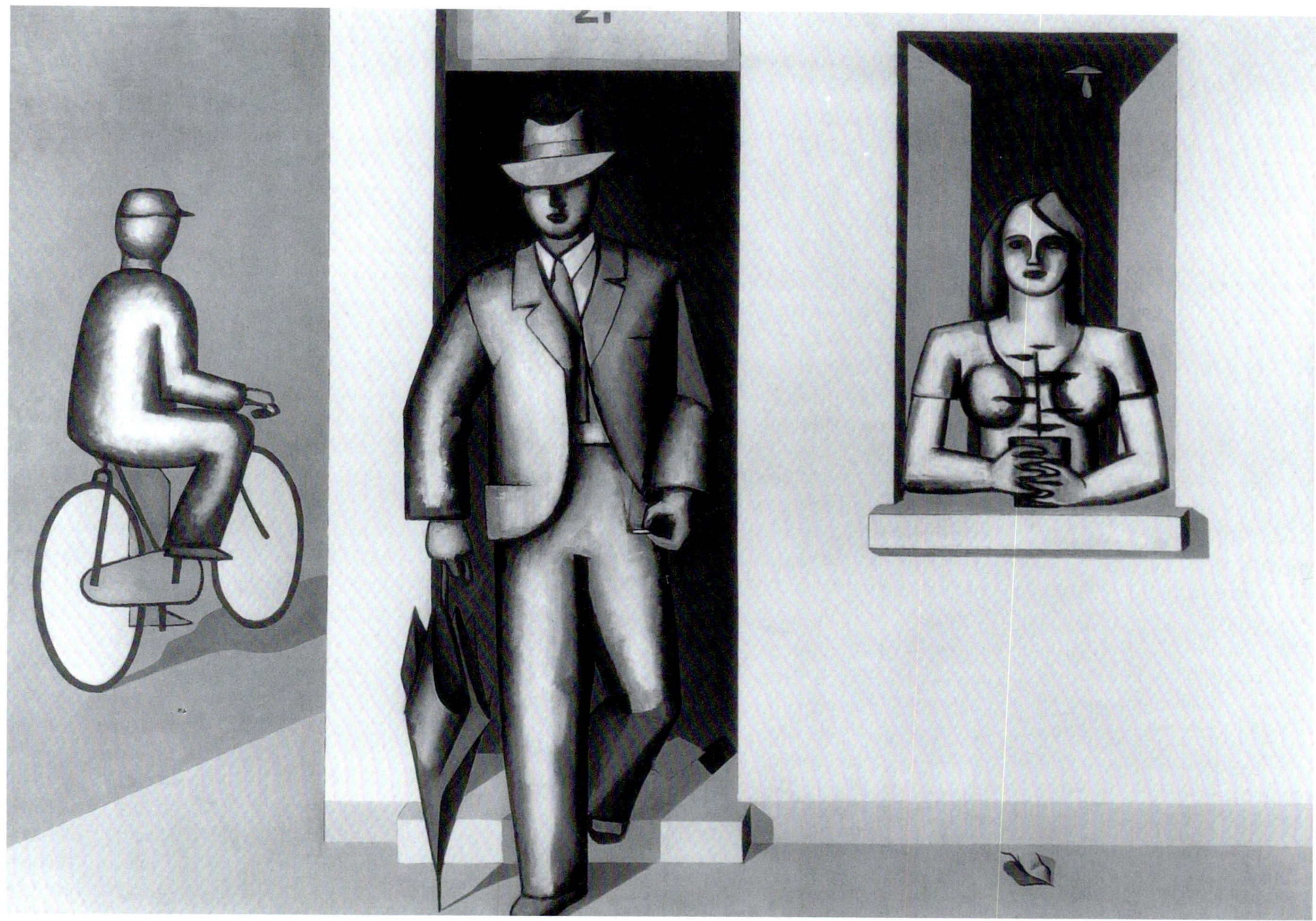

126. Jean Hélion, *For the Cyclist*, 1939. 134 × 184 cm. Musée National d'Art Moderne, Paris

son that he learned from Theosophy was the conviction that there was a history of the spirit to be divined in the history of art, and that it was to be understood as revealing Man's evolution towards the perfection of the Idea. Hegellian dialectics applied to painting were easily adapted to this belief: each painting became a stage on the way. Within this framework, Mondrian placed Cubism as a stage on the way to Neo-Plasticism. He called Cubism 'Morphoplastic', distinguishing it from the 'Neo-Plastic' because of its continued need to refer to subject matter. Such a vision of art in history, of course, can in one sense seem to be a schematic anticipation of Alfred H. Barr's famous diagram of the progression of movements towards 'abstract art'.

The structure of this chapter, moving inexorably from expression and decoration, through Cubism to Apollinaire's 'pure painting' and Neo-Plasticism, could be taken to serve as a support for such an evolutionary view. I end, therefore, with a reminder that in many individual cases among the modernists working in France in the period, the sequel to the development of a relatively or even comprehensively 'pure' style was often its rejection. There is no irreversible historical logic to be divined in the 'evolution' of most artists, taking them away from the representation of nature towards non-figuration. Matisse followed his experimental work of 1913–17 with what is usually treated as a return to painting nature directly (with the Impressionists consciously recalled) [262]. Picasso followed his post-papier-collé work with the development of classicising styles alongside his still-developing *a priori* Cubism, especially from 1917 [251]. When Léger returned from the front in 1917, he made much of 'returning to the subject', as he put it, though he had never entirely left it behind [175]. And Jean Hélion, perhaps the most original of the French non-figurative painters to learn from Mondrian and Van Doesburg, completed an 'evolution' between the early 1930s and 1940, which started in strict non-figuration and ended in a return to figuration [125, 126].

What is clear, however, is that such modernist 'returns' did not mean the rejection of the basic convictions about art and representation established in the first two decades of the century. Even modernist art which allowed attention to focus on subject matter once again, was conceived and made primarily to offer an experience of art, to incite from the viewer creative spectatorship.

CHAPTER 6

The Languages and Objects of Art

METAMORPHOSIS AND THE SEMIOTICS OF CUBISM

Neither Picasso's early use of collage (the incorporation into painting of fragments from daily life) nor Braque's early use of papier-collé (the sticking on of cut-out pieces of paper) could be called lucid. Both Picasso's first collage, *Still-life with Chair-caning* of spring 1912, and Braque's first papier-collé, *Fruit-dish and Glass* [128, 104] of autumn that year, retain the equivocal suggestiveness of their 'hermetic' work from the previous two years. The signs for objects levitate from or sink back into shadowy depths; and stuck-on materials are not what they seem to be. The chair-caning in Picasso's collage is actually shiny oilcloth printed with a trompe-l'oeil chair-caning design, and Braque's cut-out pieces of *faux bois* only sometimes refer to wood panelling. Lucidity, at once in the use of materials and signs, was something Picasso achieved when he made his earliest papiers-collés and constructions alongside one another at the end of 1912, works like *Man with a Hat* and the metal *Guitar* [127, 129].[1]

Paradoxically, with Picasso's more easily legibile use of signs and more explicit use of materials went a new kind of suggestiveness in the spatial dimension. Thus, in the case of *The Guitar*, the actual cylinder projecting from the flat planes is instantly read as the sign of a negative void, the instrument's sound-hole. Those reversals of actual spatial relations set in play in the Cubist sculpture of Laurens and Lipchitz after 1915 have their starting point here: Picasso's metal *Guitar* was the first Cubist construction. Construction brought out the contradictions exposed by the notion of the picture-object far more directly than papier-collé, and indeed it can be argued that it was the sheer immediacy with which *The Guitar* did so that made possible the lucidity found in both his early papiers-collés and his early Cubist sculpture.[2]

Picasso's constructions were not taken by Kahnweiler for his gallery, or shown before 1914, but they were illustrated in the periodical *Soirées de Paris* with photographs supplied by the dealer; and indeed photographs of them were even put on display as exhibits in a show across the Channel in London.[3] Those who knew Picasso's work were aware of the importance of the constructions as an entirely new kind of artwork with far-reaching implications for sculpture. Either just before or just after the 1914–18 war, Salmon was provoked by them to frame his book, *La Jeune Sculpture française*, with remarkable passages on the object and art. He ends with 'that immense metal guitar', and with Picasso's studio, which contained, he says, 'not one work of art in the old sense, [and] was furnished with the newest of objects'. '"What is it?"' Picasso is recorded rhetorically asking Salmon. '"Is it to be placed on a pedestal, that thing there? Is it to be hung on the wall? What is it, painting or sculpture?" Dressed in the blue overalls of the Parisian artisan, Picasso replied in his beautiful Andalusian voice: "It's nothing, it's el guitare (sic)!"'[4]

The problem of the sculpture-object could not be more plainly put. Picasso's *Guitar* is directly relevant to the two-dimensional art of papier-collé, because it destroyed the distinction between painting and sculpture. The way is opened to a new kind of artist who does not merely draw while painting, but sculpts as a painter and paints as a sculptor, producing neither paintings nor sculptures, but two- or three-dimensional *objects*. Matisse was a painter-sculptor working with the conventional techniques of oil-painting and clay modelling for bronze casting. His *Back II* of 1913 [91] is painterly in the way its Cézannian facetting encourages a surface scanning of the relief; his *Bathers by a Stream* [84] is sculptural in its relation to *Back III* [92]. But neither are object-works in the same sense as Picasso's constructions, because their allusion to the other medium does not involve its *actual* incorporation. As a painter-sculptor Matisse played one medium *against* the other to sharpen his sensitivity to the pictorial and the sculptural, not to collapse one *into* the other. With the constructions, Picasso consolidated the object-ness of *both* painting and sculpture; by doing so, he was able to move between them with a new inventive abandon.[5]

And yet, the spaces suggested by Picasso's papiers-collés and constructions which are in conflict with their actual material properties are not the result of seeing these pieces as physical objects. Their space, rather, is created by a fundamentally imaginative, conceptual process of viewing. Just as now Picasso, the artist, could metamorphose from painter into sculptor with ease, so the viewer can alter the material facts in front of her or him by imaginative viewing. In both *The Guitar* and a two-dimensional work like *Man with a Hat*, the key to this could not be less material: it depends on the explicitness of the signs Picasso has invented *for* things. The materiality of the construction and the papier-collé is *seen* by the viewer; the 'idea' of immaterial spatial relationships made available by both works is something *read*. Such spatial relationships can only be grasped when the signs for things are read. Thus, most strikingly, it is only when the cylinder in *The Guitar* is read as a sign for the sound-hole that it can dissolve into the idea of a void punched through a surface.

Semiological analyses of Cubist work have brought out how the functioning of the sign in them (from autumn 1912 onwards) lays bare the semiotic workings of language in the very largest sense, and indeed the fundamental condition of all human communication (including visual art) *as* 'language', as sign-systems in action.[6] It has been argued that the ultimate importance of *The Guitar* lies not so much in the way it collapsed painting into sculpture, as in the way that it revealed two general principles fundamental to lan-

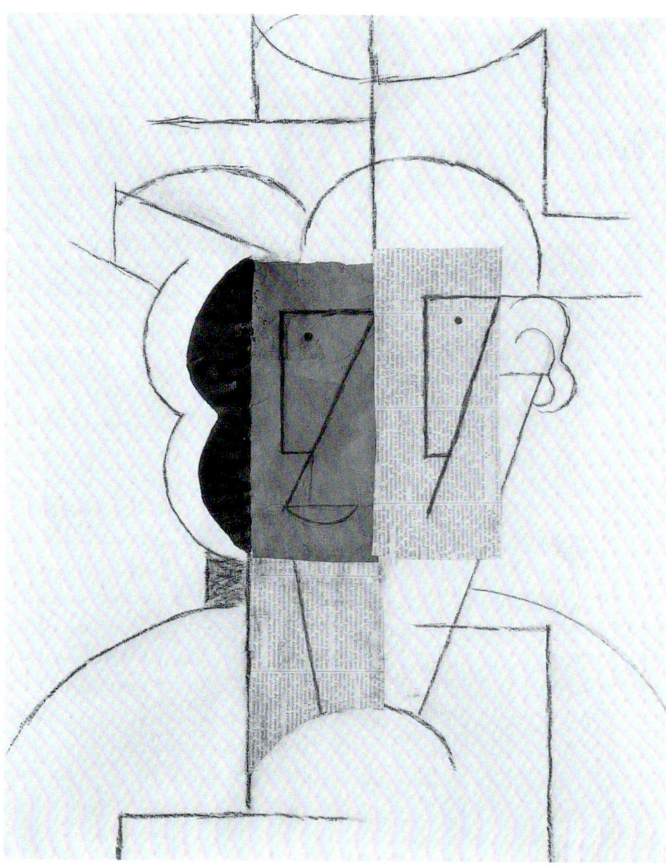

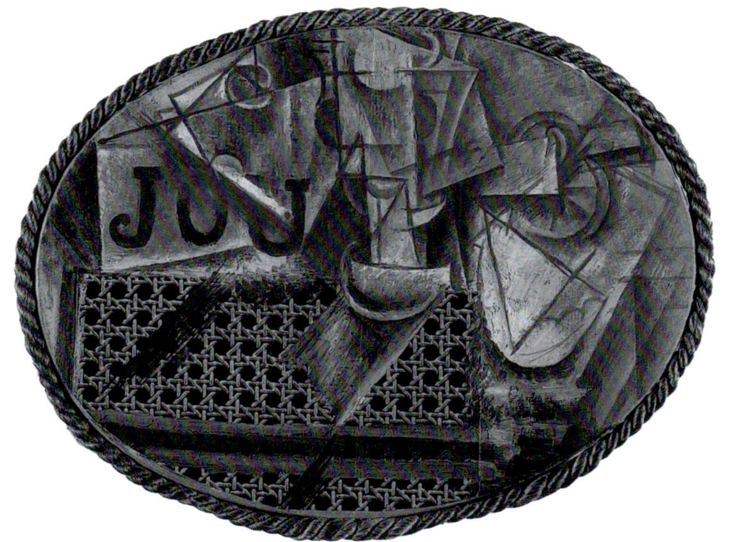

127. Pablo Picasso, *Man with a Hat*, 1912. Pasted paper, charcoal and ink on paper, 62.2 × 47.3 cm. The Museum of Modern Art, New York. Purchase

128. Pablo Picasso, *Still-life with Chair-caning*, 1912. Collage of oilcloth and pasted paper on canvas, 27 × 35 cm. Musée Picasso, Paris

129. Right. Pablo Picasso, *Guitar*, 1912–13. Construction of sheet metal, and wire, 77.5 × 35 × 19.3 cm. The Museum of Modern Art, New York. Gift of the artist

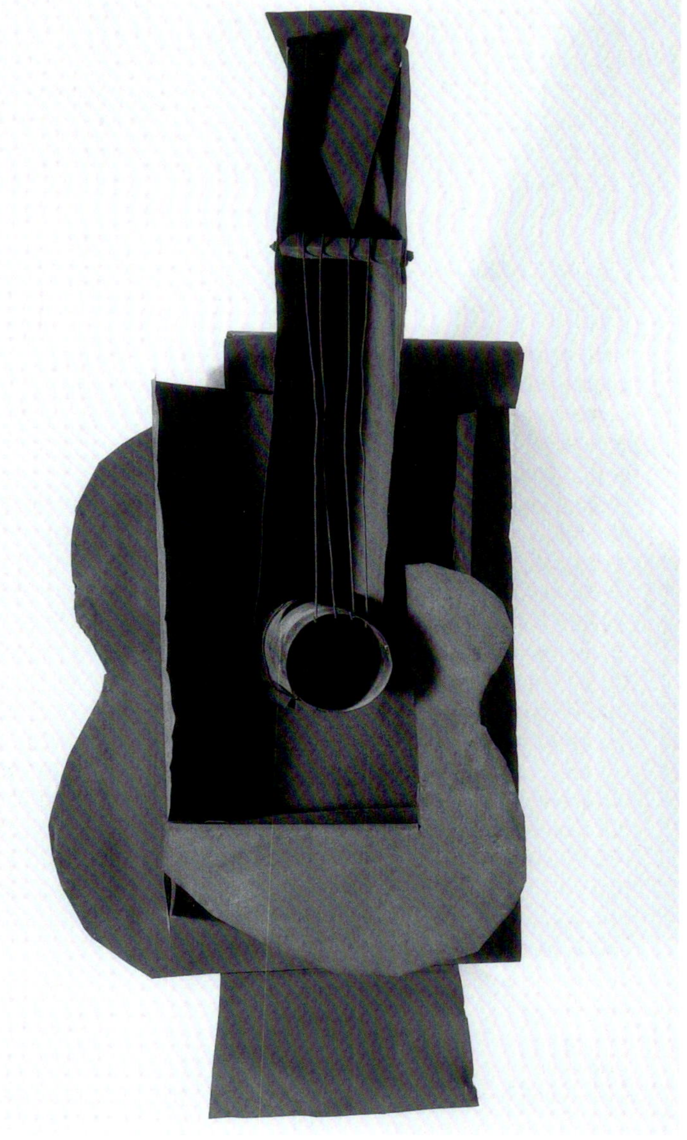

guage, and by doing so allowed their wilful exploitation.[7] These principles were fundamental to the structural approach to language which was first codified at this time in Geneva by Ferdinand Saussure. Their importance for understanding how Picasso began to use signs in 1912 is in no way diminished by the fact that he and his friends almost certainly knew nothing of Saussure.

First, Picasso's signs were not specific to the things they denoted – a cylinder could just as well denote a bottle as a guitar sound-hole. There is no *necessary* relation between the sign and what it denotes (its referent). The arbitrariness of the sign is revealed. Further, it becomes clear that any specific meaning (referent) attached to a sign depends not on its particular form but on its context. It is the positioning of the cylinder in relation to curved edges which are legible as the flanks of a guitar that allows it to be read as a sound-hole, and of dots in relation to lines legible as 'nose' and 'ear' that allows them to be read as eyes. Signs are given meaning in context, within systems of relationships, and the key to this, apart from their positioning, is the clear differentiation of one from another, dot from straight line from curved line. The value of the line or dot as sign is given by its incorporation into a *conceptual* system of signs. These thoroughly

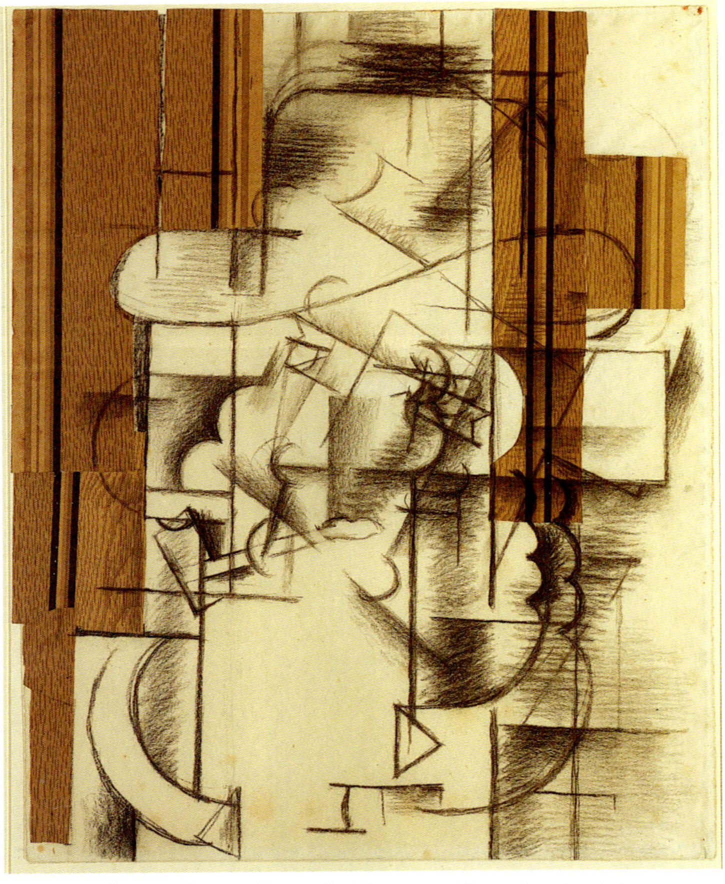

130. Georges Braque, *Man with a Pipe*, 1912. Charcoal and pasted paper on paper, 61.9 × 49 cm. Oeffentliche Kunstsammlung Basel, Kupferstichkabinett

material works are given 'meaning' *only* when they are dematerialised conceptually.[8] The emptiness of a void (that empty recess around the cylinder 'sound-hole') can be filled by the intelligent imagination finding a positive sign within a system of relationships (a sign for the guitar's body).

So far my assessment of how Cubist pieces work for viewers or 'readers' has only treated the property of flatness in two-dimensional compositions incidentally. Kahnweiler, William Rubin and other commentators have not been wrong, however, to give the problem of the representation of three-dimensions in two-dimensions key importance in Picasso's and Braque's Cubist painting. In 1909–12, Picasso and Braque's use of faceting was obviously extrapolated from Cézanne's loose, planar mosaics of the 1890s and 1900s. And, in the same way, it has the effect of translating everything, including all suggestions of space and volume, into terms which replicate the rectangle of the picture format, asserting therefore its existence as a flat plane. The desire to continue working with this kind of tension, reminiscent of Cézanne, between the suggestion of volume and space and the assertion of the flatness of the canvas was what led to the extraordinarily elaborate obscurity of the so-called 'hermetic cubist' works; in Picasso's case, the veiling of their often basically simple signs [106, 107]. For Picasso, to have presented such signs in painting with the easily read lucidity of many of the drawings of 1911–12 would have risked producing illusionist representations of what looked like sculptural constructions. The partial painting out of the flanks of *Man with a Clarinet* [107] hints at what could have happened if the figurative sign here had been fully isolated and clearly defined in its space. The 'figure' would have been seen as a solidly constructed thing in an illusion of space behind the picture plane.

One major effect of the development of collage and especially papier-collé was that the material flatness of the picture surface could be asserted without deploying those elaborate grey and brown scaffolds of planes. It could be done simply by gluing on pieces of material and paper, leaving the drawing of signs to work with the utmost simplicity alongside and over them. There was no risk of the work becoming a window into depth. Following this, it would become enough to use painted planes of comparable breadth and opacity, doing without actual pieces of material or paper. A material development, therefore, was crucial to the simplification of both Braque's and Picasso's use of signs, and with that came the realisation of their conceptual potential. The semiotic lesson learned thus would never be forgotten by either of them. If the relationship between signs and their referents was arbitrary and changeable, infinite possibilities were opened up for the imagination. New signs could be invented to denote many things, and then could be made to mean still other things. It was above all the realisation of the potential released by the uncoupling of signs from any fixed relation to referents that made Picasso's and Braque's discoveries of 1912–14 so seminal in France.

Between 1912 and 1914, both were well aware of the newly open character of their signs, and used it. Braque's *Fruit-dish* [103] was quickly followed by a closely related papier-collé, *Man with a Pipe* [130], itself closely comparable with Picasso's *Man with a Hat* [127]. It is as if Braque has taken the imaginary spaces opened up by the white expanses between the cut-out pieces of paper as a screen for projection. The positioning of the pieces of paper is almost repeated from *Fruit-dish*, and the broad outlines of the fruit dish remain, but a stiff collar replaces its round base and the rim of a hat replaces the rim of the dish above, while into the emptiness in between, the features of a face with pipe have been very partially suggested in charcoal. In this case, Braque has used his imagination to produce a 'man with a pipe' for the viewer, and has supplied enough legible information to make the reading almost obligatory. In the later, more complex papier-collé, *Glass, Bottle and Newspaper* [110], the information he supplies is far less definitive. The drawing allows the viewer to read a bottle and a glass on a table, but the piece of newspaper below bears the word 'violon' in heavy type and the general arrangement of planes invites the viewer to discover a violin behind the bottle and glass on the table. Not only the space suggested by overlapping planes and drawing, but also the very *things* represented are now in the power of the viewer: it is he or she who decides what is to be found here, as much as Braque. This kind of manipulation of the openness of sign-systems, allowed the artist to change the things he represented as he worked, and sometimes, as in this case, it invited the spectator to change them too. Picasso's *Man with a Hat* is not quite wholly within a sign-system which gives exclusively figurative meanings to dots and lines; there are hints of other possible readings involving musical instruments: the double curve on the left is patently an echo of the guitar flanks in the metal *Guitar*. Increasingly, Picasso would leave his signs on the edge, between possible readings.

I showed in Chapter 5 that the work of those around Matisse, and certain important aspects of Cubist practice, including that of Mondrian, used drawing-as-painting and the lack of finish to accentuate the creative spectatorship demanded of the viewer and so to emphasise the priority given to the relationship between the viewer and the art work.[9] The kind of empathetic spectatorship invited is retrospective in this instance: the process of making is re-lived imaginatively. The often rough workmanship of Picasso's constructions and of Braque's and Picasso's papiers-collés continued to invite such an empathetic experience, but something else was added.[10] The viewer was asked to complete the work her or himself by reading its signs. And, of course, in this open situation no final completion was promised: the viewer was asked to go on imagining what might be there, to become, much more fully and actually, the artist. This was the most enticing metamorphosis on offer.

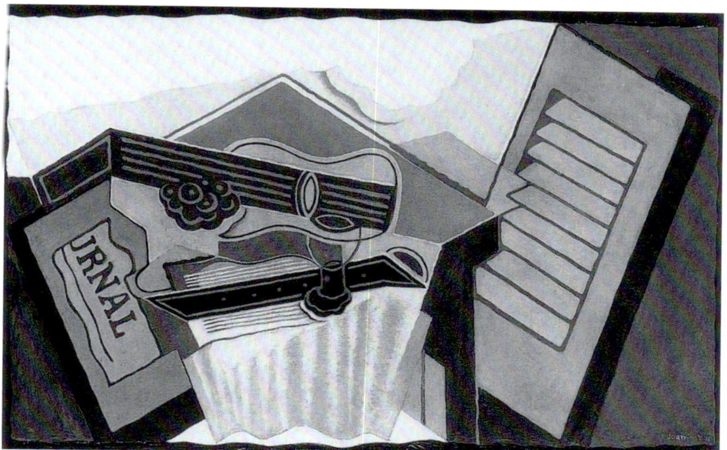

131. Juan Gris, *The Cloud*, 1921. Oil on canvas, 65 × 100 cm. Hamburger Kunsthalle

METAPHOR AND METAMORPHOSIS: SURREALISTS AND CUBISTS

Juan Gris's manipulation of pictorial rhymes after 1917, the key to his purified version of 'synthesis' in Cubist painting, was obviously one of the benefits that accrued in his case from the realisation that signs are arbitrary, and so can change their referents: the things they denote. Others like Blanchard and Lipchitz profited in this way too.

In 1923, probably after discussions with Gris, Maurice Raynal wrote a piece which identified the visual rhyme in the painter's work with metaphor. Visual rhyming operated to bring things together and by doing so to produce, in the mind, something new. Raynal relates this to a particular kind of verbal metaphor called by the Greeks 'catacresis'. In catacresis, as he explains, words with established meanings (referents) are combined to designate a new thing, for instance 'leaf of paper' or 'mill-sail'. 'The inventive spirit,' he writes, 'takes from two different things the resources to construct a third'.[11] In Gris's *Guitar and Fruit-dish* of 1919 [112], a structural rhyme makes the guitar echo the fruit-dish with its bunch of grapes; in this way the viewer is allowed to read a guitar/fruit-dish and a fruit-dish/guitar, two new things. In *The Cloud* of 1921 [131], Gris gives the viewer a grapes/cloud and a cloud/grapes, quite apart from a guitar-sound-hole/mouth-of-a-glass/mouth-of-a clarinet. Verbally, the result is often clumsy; as a visual image it is always elegant and concise.

As Raynal insists, metaphor, whether verbal or visual, is completely conceptual, an imaginative operation, producing a thing that exists only in the mind of the reader or viewer. Yet, as used by Gris it can invite the eye to work with the imagination to create new ideas of things which are highly suggestive of sensations: sensations involving all the senses, touch, taste and hearing as well as sight. Thus one thing can partake of the sensory associations generated by another: in *The Cloud*, there are fluffy grapes and squashy clouds. Gris works particularly often with mouth rhymes, here linking the mouth of the clarinet and of the glass with the sound-hole of the guitar, as if all could make sound, and the sound made could be drunk. Such late Cubist painting exposes the fact that even on the level of the conceptual, placed in its purest register, the invention and manipulation of signs preserves a place for the sensory, sometimes the sensuous experience of things. The hardness or softness of Gris's line, the particular qualities of each surface, the warmth or coolness of colours, work *with* the signs and the rhymes and the metaphors. The way the viewer is invited to experience paintings like *Guitar and Fruit-dish* and *The Cloud* fuses reading and seeing, as in fact the Cubism of Picasso and Braque always does too.

Raynal on metaphor in Gris applies in a new way a notion first formulated in 1918 to define the modern poetic 'image' by their mutual friend, the poet Pierre Reverdy. By that date there was a growing conviction in the overlapping milieux of writers and artists which included both Reverdy's periodical *Nord-Sud* and André Breton's proto-Dada *Littérature* that the histories of poetry and visual art were converging in the wake of the pre-1914 Cubist work of Picasso, Braque, Gris and others. Indeed, another of the circle of Reverdy and *Nord-Sud*, Paul Dermée, could write in 1919 of a single 'aesthetic', 'discovered long ago by Mallarmé and Rimbaud' which had 'spread with marvellous effect into Cubist painting and the literature of the new spirit'.[12] According to this view, the Mallarméan aversion to the simple naming of things had led not merely to the replacement of description by suggestion, but to the separation of words in poetry from their normal referential usage in everyday life. Mallarmé and Rimbaud, in the verbal medium, had anticipated the separation of sign from referent in Cubist visual art.

Reverdy's notion of the poetic image provided, in effect, a new underpinning for the separation of poetic language from the merely functional, its purification. He focused not on the single word but on the way words in combination could create unlikely yet what he called 'right' conjunctions of ideas. 'The image,' he wrote, 'is a pure creation of the spirit. It cannot be born of a comparison but [only] of the coming together of two more or less remote realities. The more the conjunctions of two . . . realities are distant and

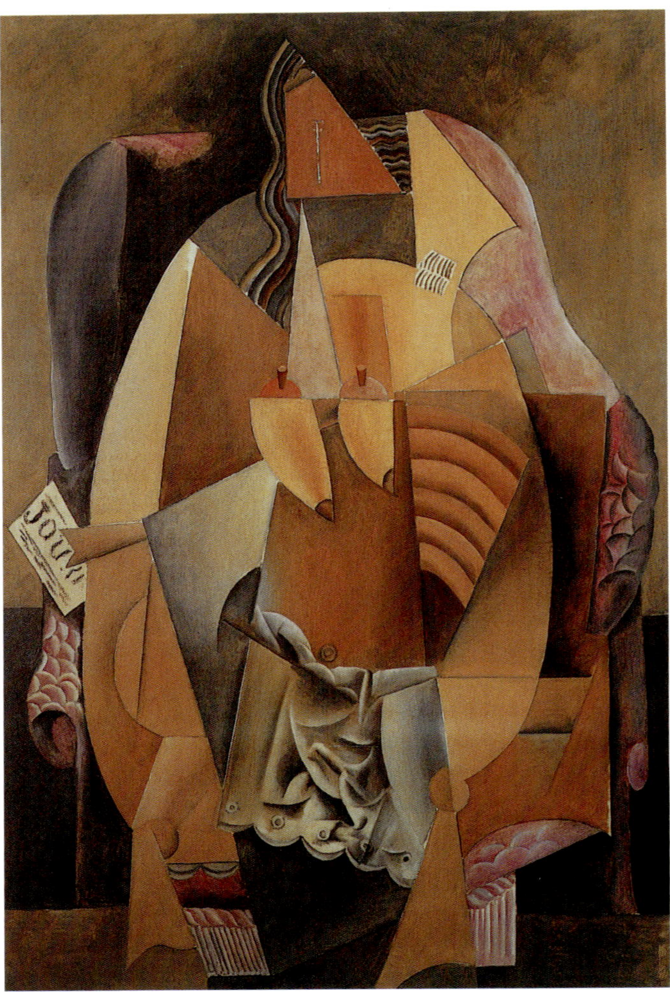

132. Pablo Picasso, *Woman in an Armchair*, 1913. Oil on canvas, 148 × 99 cm. Private Collection

right, the more the image will be strong – the more it will have emotional power and poetic reality.'[13] He had in mind such images from his own current poetry as 'The sun punctures its eye-ball', where the words 'sun' and 'eye-ball' take on new valencies within the fabric of the poem because of their surprising yet 'right' conjunction.[14] Gris's cloud/grapes or guitar/fruit-dish are poetic images of the same order.

When in 1924, the year following Raynal's piece on metaphor in Gris, André Breton wrote the first *Manifesto of Surrealism*, the notion of the poetic image was given an important place in his account of what Surrealist 'psychic automatism' produced. Breton had corresponded with Reverdy as a result of his 1918 definition of the image, and even then had pinpointed crucial disagreements between them. In 1924, while acknowledging his debt to Reverdy, he pinpointed them again. There were two key points of difference. First, Breton resisted the idea that new, unexpected conjunctions – images – should be *willed* by the poet. Reverdy, like Gris, manipulated his material (words), conscious of an end, the well-crafted poetic composition. He actively invented images. Breton believed that the strongest images were not willed but *found*; the Surrealist theory of 'psychic automatism' advocated, as shown in Chapter 2, the *passive* reception of images in dreams or automatic writing. Second, Breton resisted the idea that conjunctions should be 'distant and right'. For him, there could be no inherent rightness in an image, what mattered was the image's 'power of disorientation', as Marguerite Bonnet has phrased it.[15] 'For me,' Breton writes, 'the strongest [image] is that which constitutes to the highest degree arbitrariness . . .'.[16]

Reverdy believed that an image was both strong and 'right', when it brought out an unexpected and yet essential oneness unifying two 'distant realities'. Raynal wrote of Gris's metaphors responding to a 'constructive necessity' and so containing 'a true judgement'. Bringing together a guitar and a cloud revealed essential qualities held in common.[17] Such an idealist concern with essences was compatible with the Platonism so often associated with Gris's work in the 1920s. It was, however, utterly at odds with Breton's vision of an unruly poetic force liberated from the Freudian Unconscious in the form of images. Ideally, Reverdy, Raynal and Gris saw the separation of sign from referent and its manipulation to create images as pure synthesis. Breton saw the opening up of the sign and the discovery of images as a route to unending and always disorienting metamorphosis.

Breton's Surrealist images were not merely fusions of 'distant realities', but instants of contact experienced like 'the spark' (a word he used) leaping between electrical contacts. It was in the sudden '*light of the image*' that its force was felt, a light that revealed 'limitless expanses where one's desires are exposed . . .'. The Surrealist image 'upset' the equilibrium of 'the spirit' so valued by a Reverdy or a Gris.[18] For Breton (with some justice), the Cubist who more than any other had anticipated the imaginative freedom and the destabilising force of Surrealism was Picasso. The scope offered the imaginative by the shadowy obscurity of the hermetic cubist pictures gave one of those works, for him, the status of a prophecy, holding up the promise of an art which could release the imagination from all restraint. In the first of a series of articles in *La Révolution surréaliste* on 'Surrealism and Painting', Breton wrote in 1925 of *Man with a Clarinet* [107] as 'the tangible proof of that which we continue to assert, to know, that each one of us is in a position to accompany an always beautiful Alice into Wonderland.'[19] But it was Picasso working with the metamorphic potential of his signs in the clearly delineated terms of his papiers-collés and constructions who most compellingly anticipated the image-making of the first Surrealist painters, a fact never more apparent than when sex became a factor (as it never did at all explicitly in the cases of Braque or Gris). As if to underline the point, Breton gave special prominence in 'Surrealism and Painting' to a painting of 1913 which more confrontationally than in any other case used the explicitness of Cubist signs to make a sexually explicit image, *Woman in an Armchair* [132]. Calling it 'the woman in a chemise', Breton credits this picture with putting the idea in his mind of seeing 'the toys of our whole life spread before us like those of our childhood'.[20]

Superficially, *Woman in an Armchair* has the sombre look of the hermetic paintings; it is entirely in oils, without either collage or papier-collé. But the bulbous presence that lends a fleshy glow to the dark interior is as easily read as any of the more schematic papier-collé figures. The suggestiveness of the image does not lie in the veiling of recognisable features.[21] Head perched on tapering neck, a double-take of breasts (perky and pendulous), flipper-hands and feet, even the belly-button and a showing of underarm hair, all can be itemised, and so can the cushioned leather of the chair's arms. What unsettles, besides the apparent monstrousness of the torso so shamelessly exposed, is the fact that every one of these straightforwardly itemised features could either be or is on the point of becoming something else, usually something absurdly inappropriate to a painted nude, something that repulses more often than it attracts. The belly-button is a button, like the buttons along the scalloped edge of the chemise (it can be undone); the breasts are sharpened teeth or blades and also containers with stoppers that can be pulled out; the fin-hands and feet turn the entire woman into a bloated flatfish and the interior into an undersea world. Her disparateness is that of a doll stitched together from bits and pieces. Breton's image of toys was well-judged: toys can become anything in the games of the imagination. Picasso has used the openness of his signs to metamorphosis as a new instrument of suggestion, and raised the stakes by his selection not merely of a nude figure-subject, but of a woman so obviously undressed for male eyes.

133. André Masson, *The Statue*, 1925. Oil on canvas, 55 × 35 cm. Museo Thyssen-Bornemisza, Madrid

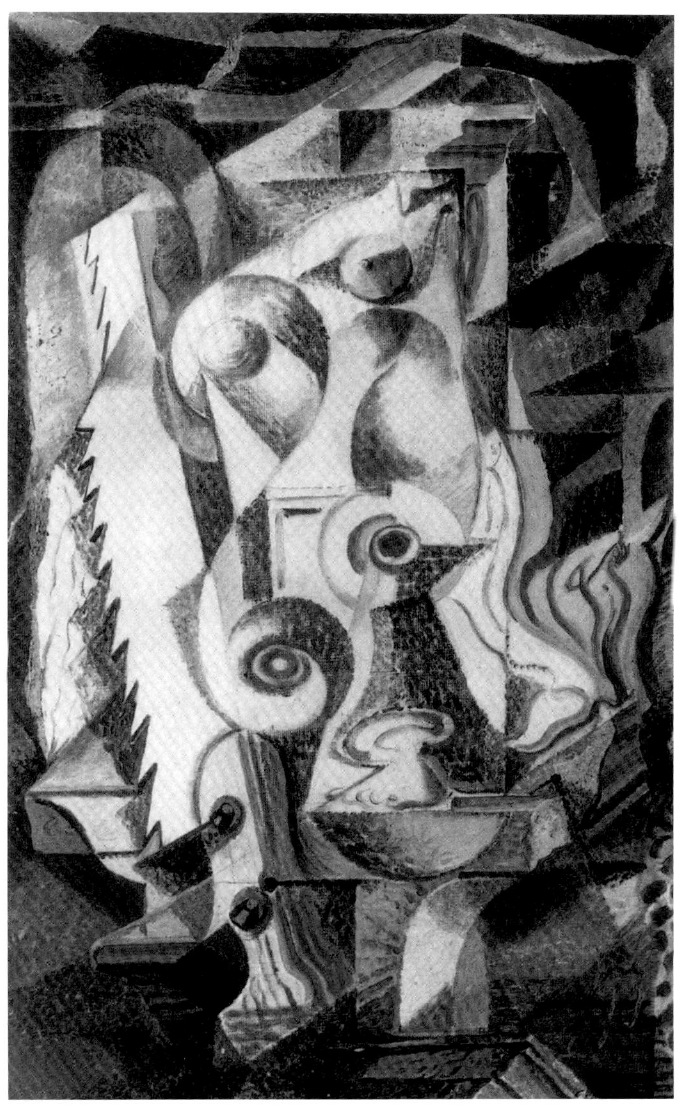

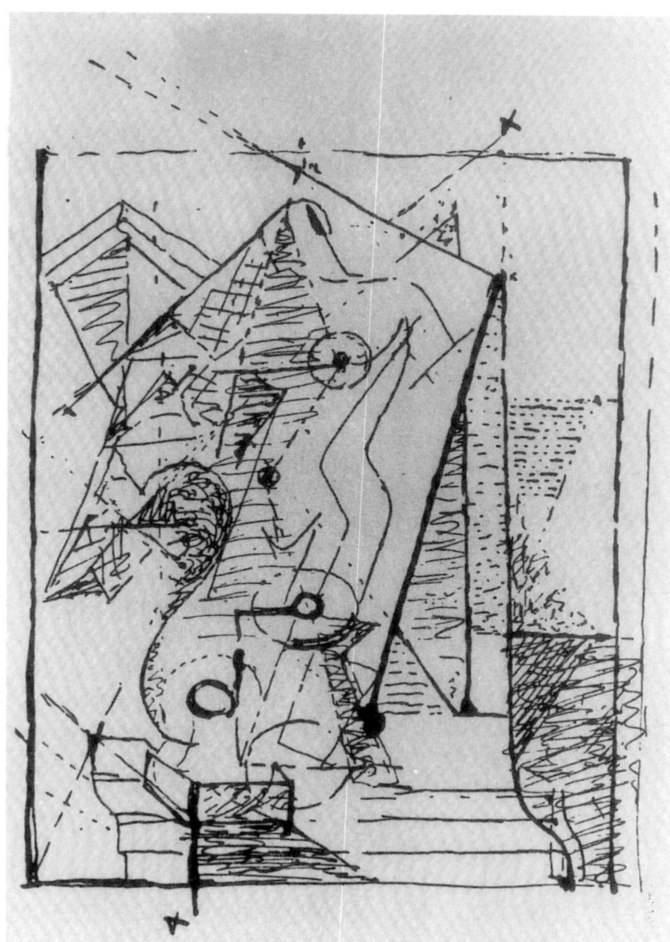

134. André Masson, *Drawing*, 1924. Dimensions and whereabouts unknown. Illustrated in *La Révolution surréaliste*, no. 1 (Paris 1 December 1924) p. 27

The Cubist work of Braque and Gris, and usually Picasso too, tended to keep to the conventional genres – figure-subjects, landscape, still-life. From the start, early Surrealist painting in the mid-1920s either subverted those genres in the spirit of Picasso's *Woman in an Armchair*, or ranged outside them. Two of the artists recognised by Breton in 1925–6 as the Surrealist successors to Picasso used the potential of the Cubist metamorphic sign for the generation of Surrealist images especially productively: André Masson (b.1896) and Joan Miró (b.1893). Both took it in new directions with more highly charged, often erotic subjects.

In Masson's case, surprisingly, the springboard for a Surrealist use of the open Cubist sign was not the work of Picasso, but that of Gris in the early 1920s, at his most uncompromisingly pure. Masson did not meet Breton until February 1924, when he had already begun to make what would later be called 'automatic drawings'. These were encouraged by studying Nietzsche, the pre-Socratic philosopher Heraclitus and the German Romantic poets,

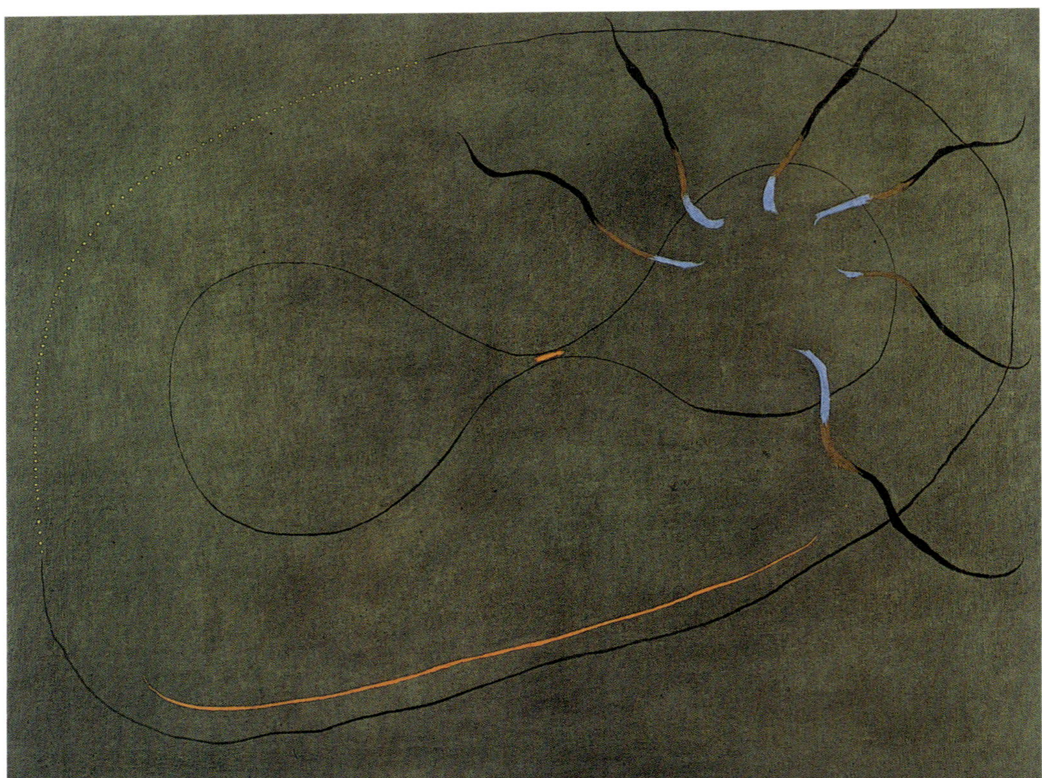

135. Joan Miró, *The Kiss*, 1924. Oil on canvas, 73 × 92 cm. Jose Mugrabi Collection

and by seeing the work of Paul Klee in reproduction. He was Miró's neighbour at 45 rue Blomet, during the Catalan's winters in Paris between 1923 and 1925, and they worked together in a milieu which included writers soon to be involved in Surrealism: Michel Leiris and Robert Desnos. But he was also, with Leiris, part of the circle around Kahnweiler's new post-war galerie Simon, with which he had signed a contract in 1922, and at Kahnweiler's Sunday lunches he met Gris. They became close enough to holiday together, with Leiris, in the summer of 1924. Stylistically, the paintings of 1925 by Masson that were shown that year in the exhibition of Surrealist Painting at the galerie Pierre and those illustrated in *La Révolution surréaliste*, have the appearance of stiff postscripts to Picasso's and Braque's hermetic Cubism of 1911–12, with a new and unsettling range of subjects, obviously identifiable as Bretonian Surrealist images. It is at the deeper level of the automatist generation of those images, not the superficial level of their compositional containment within a scaffold of hermetic Cubist facets, that his debt to Gris is apparent.

One of those first Surrealist works by Masson of 1925 is *The Statue* [133], which is especially revealing of how images could be generated for them because of its connection with a drawing published upside down in the first number of *La Révolution surréaliste* in December 1924 [134]. The drawing could almost be used as an illustration of how Gris's so-called 'deductive method' is supposed to have worked. Anticipating *The Statue*, a female torso rises from a water jug in the drawing alongside the volutes of an unravelled scroll. Torso, jug and scroll can all be seen to have emerged directly out of a ruled and measured geometrical framework punctuated by circles and elipses, a framework very close to the kind that kept Gris's compositions in order. The most disturbing conjunction in the painting – the insertion of the saw alongside the nude torso – came later, but Masson is observed exploiting the capacity of simple shapes to become signs just as Gris had, and then proliferating rhyming relationships across the surface to bind the signs together, sustaining their force as metaphor. Jug spout, paper-scroll, breasts, saw-handle screws, all are fused together by rhymes, having been generated out of nothing but line and shape. In the earliest of his 'automatic drawings', Masson worked directly in pen on paper, without pencil under-drawing, generating and proliferating images broadly in this way. However in these drawings a looser, more calligraphic line is the norm, a line more easily read as spontaneous.

The drawing associated with *The Statue* appeared in the opening number of the Surrealist periodical as one of the illustrations for the first Surrealist text on automatism and painting, Max Morise's 'Enchanted Eyes' (published six months before Breton's first piece on 'Surrealism and Painting'). Here Morise consolidated Masson's position as 'automatist' draftsman by claiming that pictorial automatism generated images more directly by way of the drawn or painted mark than by the depiction of dreams.[22] He also gave support in anticipation to a major part of Joan Miró's earliest Surrealist work. Despite his relations with Masson and writers like Leiris, Miró did not meet Breton until early 1925; but shortly afterwards a solo show at the galerie Pierre and inclusion in the 1925 exhibition of 'Surrealist Painting' established him at the centre of Breton's project. The poet's support for him as a Surrealist would be qualified in the second manifesto of 1929, but even here Breton allowed that he was 'the most Surrealist among us', precisely because of his acknowledged talent for regression, his ability to turn everything into toys.

Miró spent the summer of 1924 (the summer before Breton's first *Manifesto* and Morise's 'Enchanted Eyes') at his parents' farm in Montroig, deep in the Catalan countryside. One of the most elaborate products of that summer was *The Hunter (Catalan Landscape)* [322], a canvas begun the summer before. It can be read now as a catalogue of metaphors discovered in rhymes, often absurd metaphors but unsettling enough to be called Surrealist images. The spare drawing recalls the simple schemata of Picasso's early papiers-collés; the triangular head of the hunter with its circle-and-dot eye and its pipe is certainly a deliberate reference. Family connections had ensured an introduction to the by now celebrated Picasso when Miró arrived in Paris for the first time in 1920, and by 1924 they were as closely in contact as Masson and Gris. Picasso rather than Gris is the significant relationship here. In the picture, one thing is almost always the echo of another, sometimes as if exchanges and metamorphoses are occurring before our eyes. The fish on the sand in the foreground borrows the hunter's ear and moustache, which becomes a rabbit's ear and whiskers. Its tongue, stuck out to trap a fly, is red and curled like its gut, which will be fed the fly. An eye on the horizon emits rays in

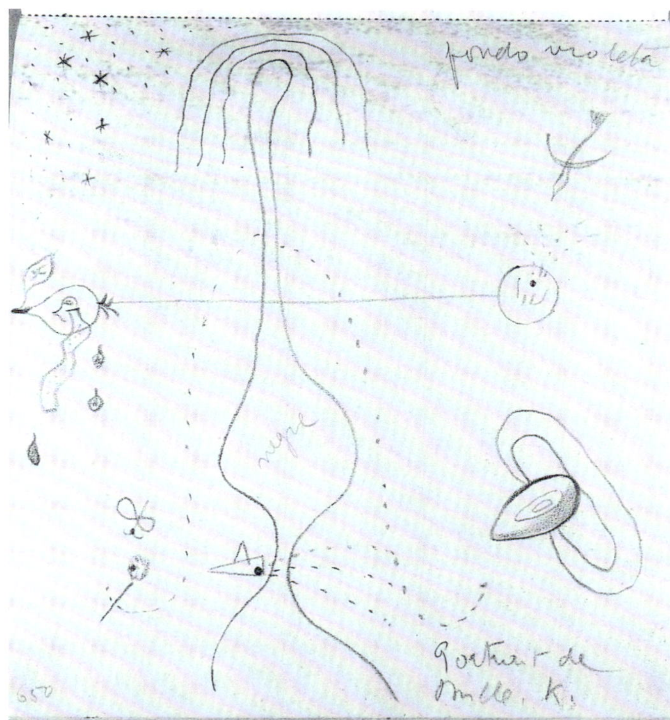

137. Joan Miró, *Portrait of Mlle. K*, 1924. Pencil on paper, 19.1 × 16.5 cm. Fundació Joan Miró, Barcelona

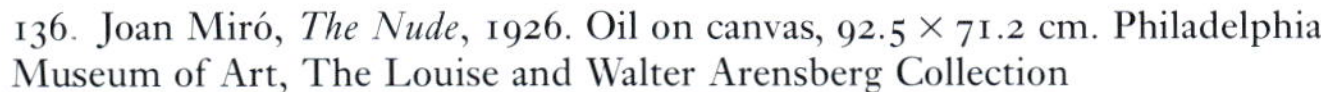

136. Joan Miró, *The Nude*, 1926. Oil on canvas, 92.5 × 71.2 cm. Philadelphia Museum of Art, The Louise and Walter Arensberg Collection

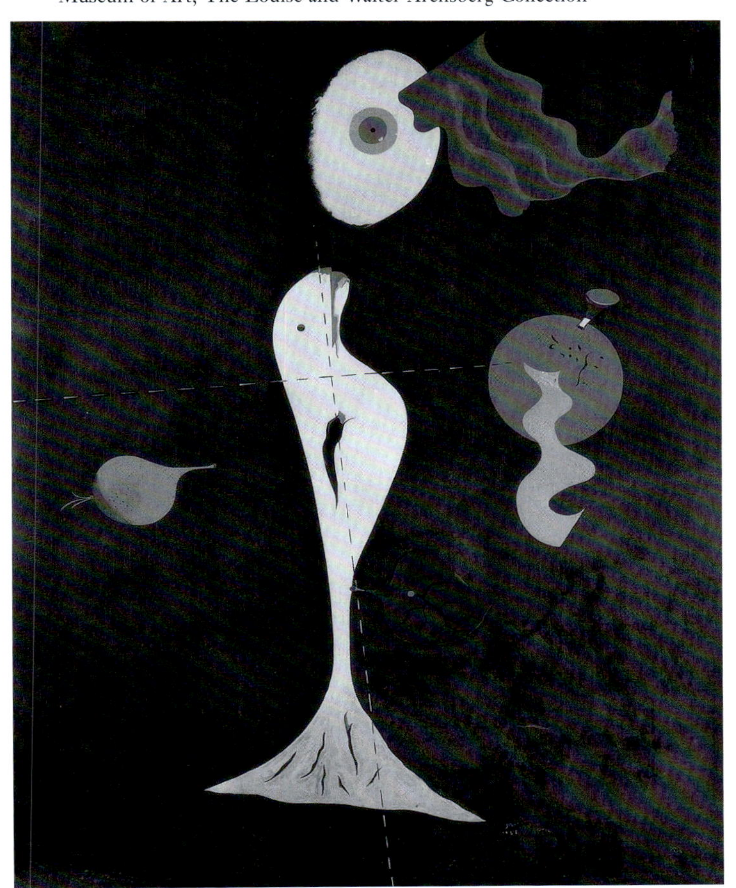

ruled lines; the hunter's grain-like penis, floating beneath his open legs, emits seed (or urine) in curved trails. The sun in the sky echoes the grain form of the male sex, but its rays turn into legs and it becomes a spider in the sky (one of Miró's signs for female genitalia).

Miró's automatist practices from the summer of 1924 were more often simple and vague in their pictorial results than complex and clear like *The Hunter*. Already that summer he was capable of a work as elementary in its forms and as open to plural readings as *The Kiss* [135], a picture whose title is calculated to sexualise response and whose theme of contact was, of course, echoed by Breton's metaphor of the spark for the image. The picture could serve as an emblem for all Surrealist image-making: the emotional force released by the contact of two sexually charged 'distant realities'. Miró, indeed, both in his complex and his simple work of the mid-1920s fuses the discovery of poetic metaphors in the imagination with the generation of visual imagery in a way that, from a Bretonian perspective, is exemplary. A particularly good demonstration of this is a work dated 1926 whose beginnings lie in the summer of 1924, *The Nude* [136], and this is so, because we know more than usual about how Miró approached the discovery of its imagery.

The evidence is in a letter he wrote to Leiris that August, where he describes arriving at the starting point of *The Nude*, which was a sketchbook drawing with the inscribed title *Portrait of Mlle.K* [137]. Miró writes:

> Figuration, of one of my latest x's [pictures] . . . Portrait of a charming lady friend from Paris – I begin with the idea of touching her body *very chastely*, beginning with her side

> and going up to her head . . . A vertical line for the breasts; one is a pear that opens and scatters its little seeds (those wonderful little hearts of fruit). On the other side, an apple pecked at by a bird. Sparks fly out of the wound caused by this pecking. Below, going across the sex (I insist on my very chaste and respectful intentions) a comet with its luminous tail; blond hair; one hand holds a flower with a butterfly circling around it; the other hand is trying to take hold of an egg that is turning, a luminous circle around it – in the upper corner of the canvas are stars.[23]

The canvas, not actually to be painted for another two years, pares down the imagery, but much is still there. The onrush of metaphors has come to a halt in simple rhyming signs painted with definitive precision. The egg has become the head, the torso has become a fish (an echo of Picasso's flatfish-woman in a chemise) from which a fig-leaf sex is extruded; but the apple and pear breasts are still hung on either side, though now Miró peels the apple instead of the pear.

In both Masson's and Miró's case their pictorial automatism was indirect. They started by finding images in drawing and then translated the results into painting; the look of spontaneity, even in Miró's most apparently casual paintings, was misleading (intentionally). Pencil under-drawing is part of the process in Masson's *Statue*, and not only *The Kiss* but the most celebrated of Miró's automatist paintings of the early Surrealist period, *The Birth of the World* [316] is transposed from a sketch, which was in turn developed from another.[24]

138. Max Ernst, *Invention*, 1922. Illustration for Paul Eluard and Max Ernst, *Répétitions* (Paris, 1922)

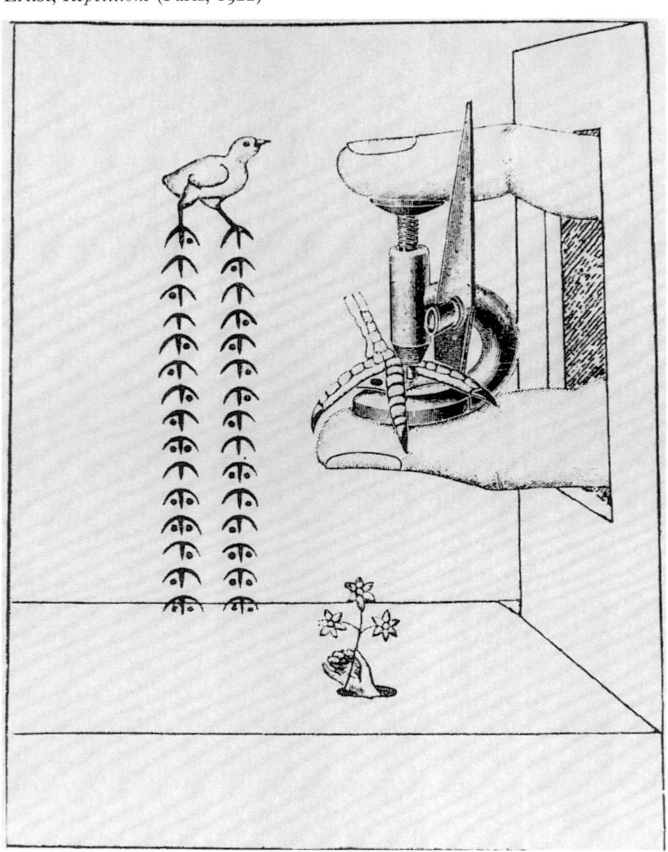

Drawing was not the route to the discovery of images initially taken by Max Ernst (b.1891), the third young artist to be recognised as a leading Surrealist by Breton in 1924–5. Neither did Ernst's obviously proto-Surrealist work of 1920–4 lend support to Max Morise's advocacy of mark-making as the most legitimate form of pictorial automatism. Ernst's route also had its starting point in pre-1914 collage and papier-collé, but rather than taking the metamorphic openness of Cubist signs as his springboard, he took the juxtapositional nature of collage and papier-collé composition instead. In one sense, the collage technique of, for instance, the small works on paper he showed at the galerie Au Sans Pareil in May 1921 [37] was as indirect and dependent on covering his traces as Masson's and Miró's practice of translating from drawing. Picasso and Braque left exposed the physical abutment of one cut-out piece of material or paper against another, and so the material basis of all their juxtapositions. Ernst, conversely, applied drawing, gouache or watercolour carefully to conceal all the joins between the cut-out images from which he fabricated his collages, and he often used subsequent photographic reproduction to conceal their identity as collages altogether.

At first, Ernst's contact with Breton's circle was mostly at one remove. He could not attend the opening of his exhibition in 1921 because the German authorities had confiscated his passport; and did not come to Paris until summer 1922 (without one). But the impact of the collages sent for the Au Sans Pareil show from Cologne was immediate. It was their unsettling juxtapositions that brought from Breton his first allusion to the 'spark' struck by the meeting of 'distant realities' in poetic images.[25] Breton holidayed briefly with Ernst that year in the Austrian Alps, after a trip to Vienna to visit Freud (a disappointment). His Dada colleague Paul Eluard came on the trip with him, and later spent a week with Ernst in Cologne. One result of Eluard's stay was their collaboration in publishing a collage book, *Répétitions*, which appeared in 1922. It led to a sequel, *Les Malheurs des immortels*, also published that year in Paris. Eluard's poems for *Répétitions* were themselves collages, juxtaposing ready-made fragments mostly from earlier poems. And the collages by Ernst that 'illustrated' them, for instance, *Invention* [138], were not made in response to the poems, but were also ready-made: Eluard pre-selected them on his Cologne visit in 1921.[26] The collage juxtaposed by Eluard with the poem 'Invention' is of particular importance, because it was the germ of a painting in 1922, *Oedipus Rex* [139], one of a series of oils executed in a plausible realist style by Ernst between 1921 and 1924. These paintings take collage juxtapositions as their starting points, and so are usually referred to as collage paintings. *Oedipus Rex* was quickly bought by Eluard.

The material for Ernst's collages sometimes included material as such (bits of wallpaper or textile), but those most closely related to the collage paintings use images rather than material: etched, engraved and photographed images (something only incidentally found in pre-1914 Cubist collage and papier-collé). These reproduced images were cut out from such sources as retail catalogues, back numbers

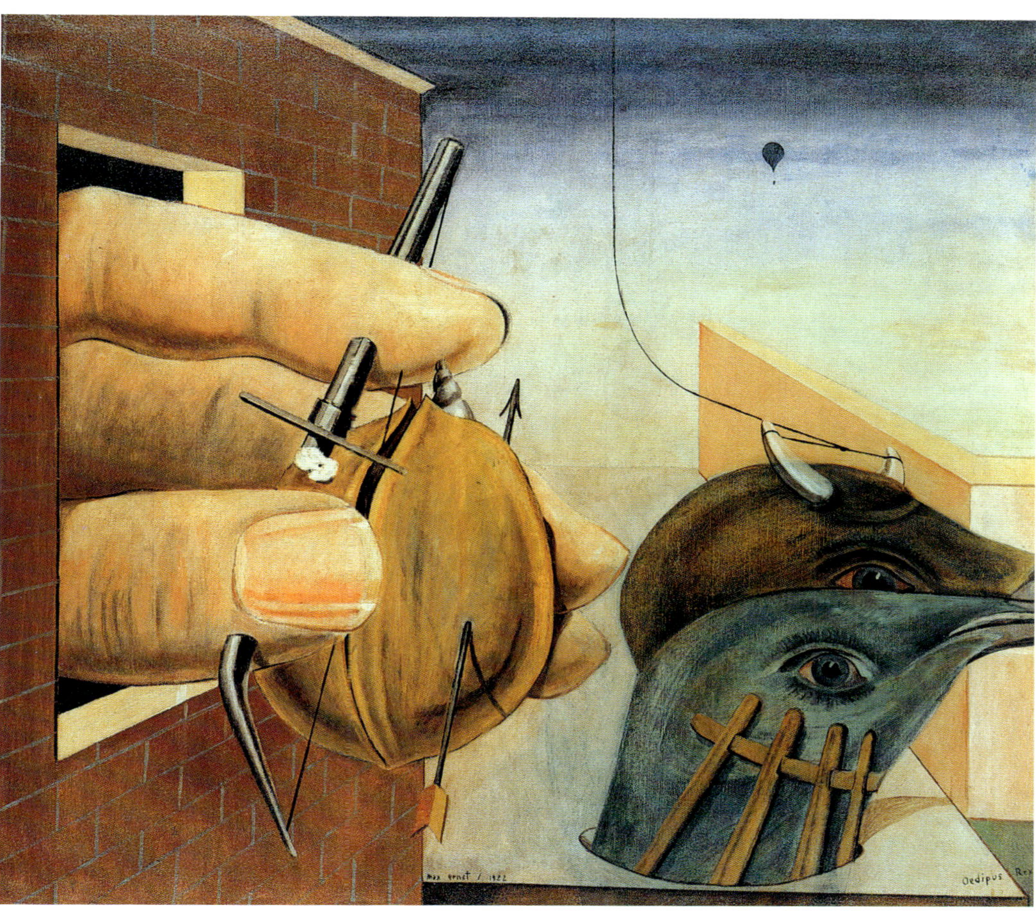

139. Max Ernst, *Oedipus Rex*, 1922. Oil on canvas, 93 × 102 cm. Private Collection

of the popular science periodical *La Nature* and from a German teaching-aids catalogue, the *Bibliotheca Paedagogica*. The source of the fingers holding the walnut in *Oedipus Rex* was an engraving in *La Nature* illustrating an elementary experiment in physics to demonstrate elasticity. The source of the mechanism held uncomfortably between two fingers in *Invention* is an engraving of a device for piercing bird's feet (a bird's foot remains attached as if severed).[27] Ernst placed his unexpected juxtapositions of images in either agoraphobic or claustrophobic worlds under translucent skies; they were presented as if the material of dreams. He did not record dreams in his collages and collage paintings (the practice Max Morise found so unconvincing), he presented his collage finds as if imagining possible dreams, as if foretelling his own and his viewers' dreams. It was this conjunction of the collage process and the idea of the painted dream that privileged the ready-made image over not merely collaged material as such, but the invented sign. As Louis Aragon put it in 1923, Ernst was a 'painter of illusions', the very reverse of everything that stood behind the phrase, the *tableau-object*.[28] Images in conjunction always took precedence over the physical fact of the work.

In the later 1920s and the 1930s, Ernst would return to collage practices in the context of Bretonian Surrealism, but he was enough of a group loyalist to respond positively to the emphasis given to the automatism of the mark during the first year of *La Révolution surréaliste*, as Miró and Masson developed their versions of it. There was, however, in his mark-making practice a tendency towards the use of ready-made starting points and mechanical processes of reproduction which was his own, and which, not very far below the surface, betrayed links with collage. Ernst's search for a more direct technique led to his increasing use of the pencil and charcoal-rubbing technique he dubbed 'frottage' from 1925, which spawned a painterly variant, involving scraping, dubbed 'grattage'.[29] In both techniques, images were discovered by rubbing over pieces of material and such objects as fishbones, buttons and threads. By 1927, grattage had been combined with the chance markings obtained by dropping paint-covered string onto the picture surface to generate some of Ernst's most powerful images, for instance, *The Horde* [306]. Images were isolated by overpainting, after the processes of scraping and dropping string. The lasso line in a work like *The Horde* can give the impression of something close to frenzy, but the deliberate exclusion of will (even in its most spontaneous register) from the initial mark-making process is clear even here, and a look at one of the first frottages in relation to the object over which the rubbing was made conveys the degree to which the process could be mechanised in 1925.

Earthquake [140] was one of the opening frottages in a collection that Ernst put together in 1925 under the title *Natural History*: it evokes disaster on a cosmic scale. It comes as a surprise, confronted with so Romantic an image, to find it underpinned by strict regularity: the apparently measured intervals between the concentric circles. In fact,

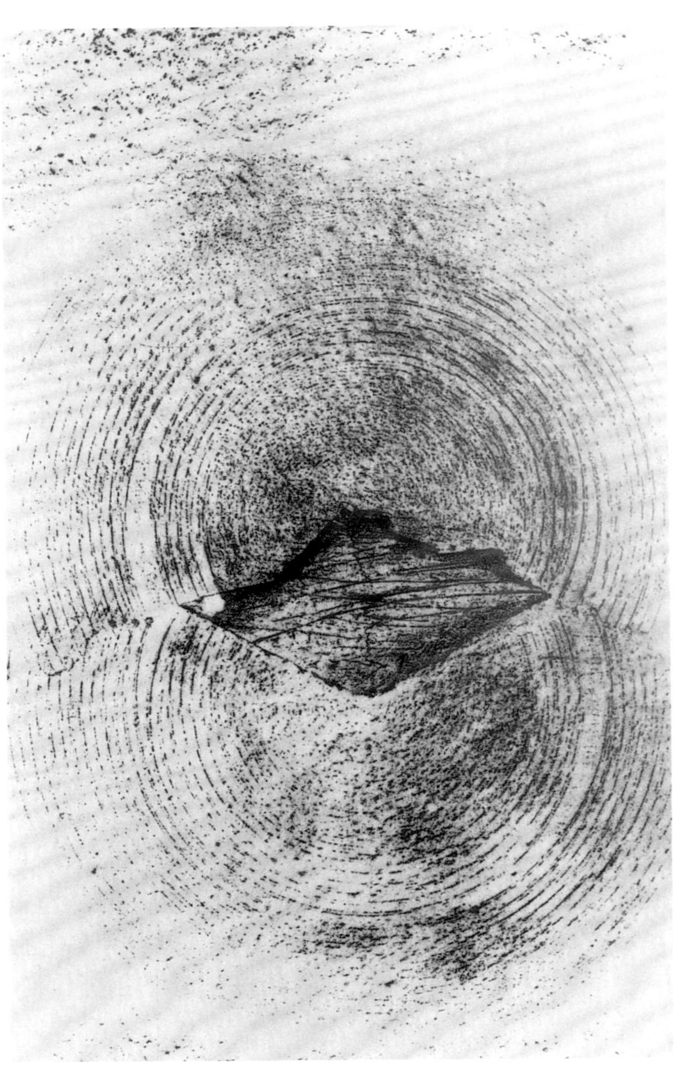

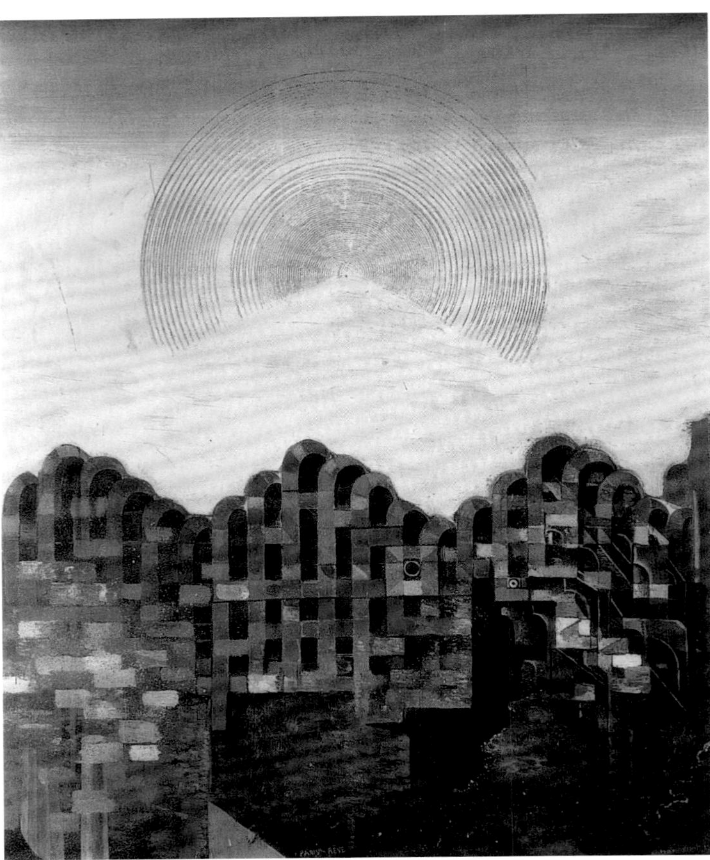

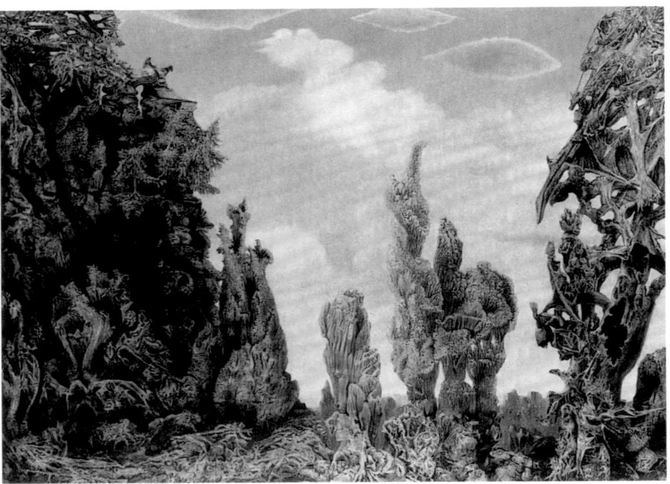

140. Max Ernst, *Earthquake*, 1925. Frottage from Max Ernst, *Histoire Naturelle*, 1925

141. Max Ernst, *Paris-Dream*, 1924–5. Oil on canvas, 71.1 × 61 cm. Yale University Art Gallery, Gift of Société Anonyme

142. Max Ernst, *The Fascinating Cypress*, 1940. Oil on canvas, 73.7 × 100.3 cm. Private Collection

these intervals have not been obtained by a geometric instrument (a pair of dividers or a compass) they have been obtained by rubbing over lines incised into the surface of an earlier painting, which were themselves obtained by pivoting a comb (with two teeth missing) in wet paint.[30] It is not certain exactly which of a small group of paintings using this combed motif was rubbed over, but it could have been *Paris-Dream* [141], a work made by Ernst just before the first frottages at the turn of 1924–5. To use a comb in so routine a way to inscribe an image was in itself to work with something given (the tooth pattern) as in collage; to generate another image by rubbing over it was to make the process still more automatic (with all the mechanical implications of the term).

Ernst would repeatedly be attracted by quasi-mechanical techniques which concealed their collage character, often, as in the grattages, under thick paint-surfaces. In the mid-1930s, Oscar Dominguez, a later recruit to Breton's cause, invented the technique of 'decalcomania'. First developed with gouache, it entailed covering a sheet with the medium applied in varying degrees of dilution, then pressing another sheet down on it and lifting it, perhaps several times, before the gouache dried. The result was, as Breton pointed out, a surface like Leonardo da Vinci's famous wall, a screen of suggestive patches and blurs into which images can be projected.[31] Ernst was quick to adapt the technique to oils, using glass as the surface to press down, producing in this random and yet mechanical way the starting point for a series of paintings that magically combine the randomly covered sur-

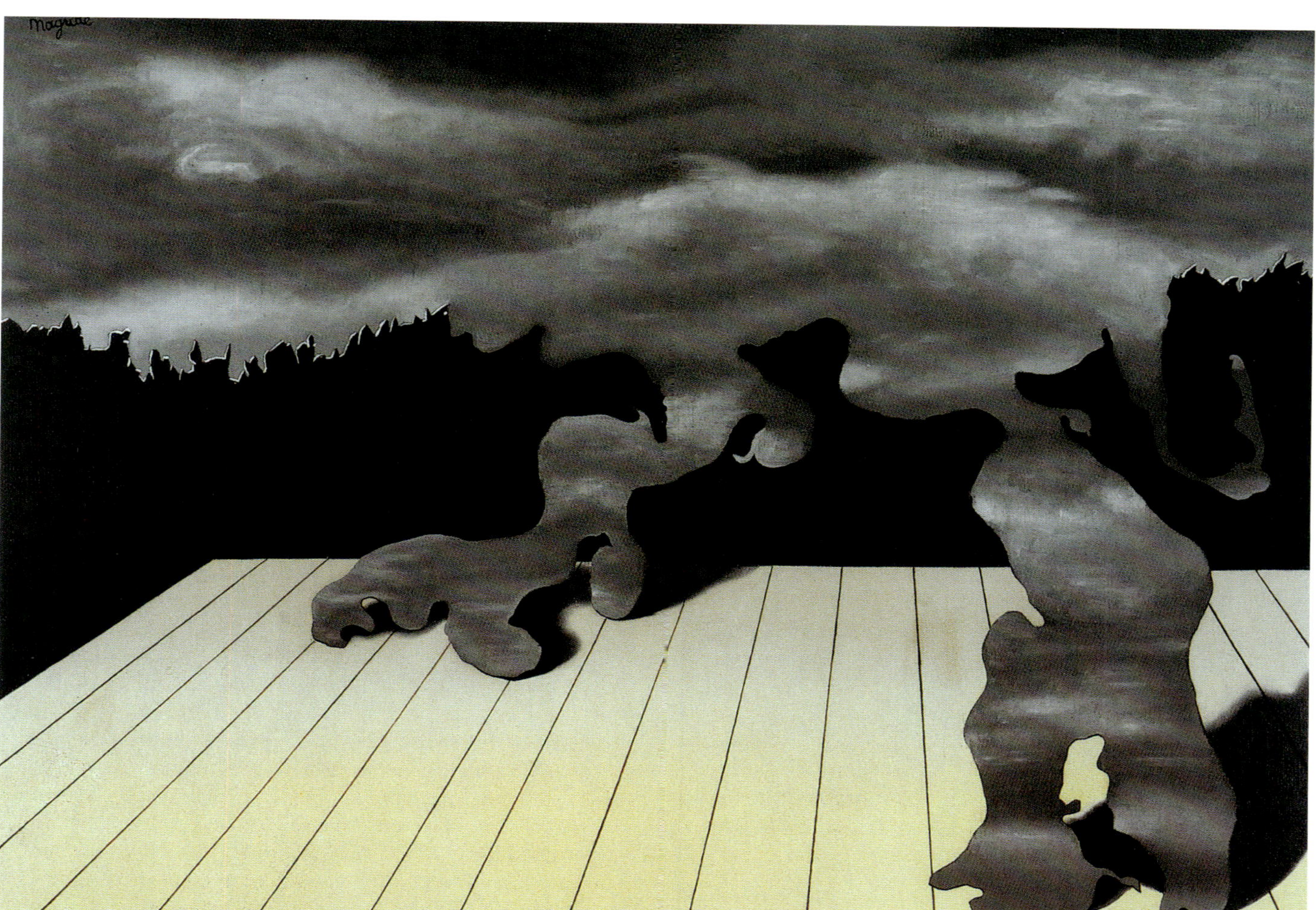

143. René Magritte, *The Muscles of the Sky (Les Muscles célestes)*, 1927. Oil on canvas, 54 × 73 cm. Mmes. Brigitte Friedlender-Salik and Véronique Dwek-Salik, Brussels

faces of mark-making automatism with the 'realism' of the collage paintings. Decalcomanic works like *The Fascinating Cypress* [142], which was painted in 1940 just before Ernst fled France, give that realism a new pitch of stage-lit intensity; mark-making processes did not necessarily prevent Ernst from being Aragon's 'painter of illusions'.

Between 1927 and 1930, two younger artists were taken up by Breton, who might have qualified as painters of illusions following the model of Ernst, but who took the imaginary (rarely the actual) collaging of images in new and different directions: René Magritte (b.1898) and Salvador Dalí (b.1904). Both used plausible realist techniques to depict worlds transformed in unsettling ways, but both used such techniques to go well beyond the painting of possible dreams.

Magritte was the first arrival, moving to the eastern suburbs of Paris in September 1927, and staying until the tense aftermath of the second Surrealist *Manifesto* in 1930. He came with a reputation already formed as one of the members of the earliest European satellite of Bretonian Surrealism, the Brussels group. Probably the first canvas he painted in Paris was *The Muscles of the Sky* (*Les Muscles célestes*) [143], which he initially titled 'The legs of the sky' in a letter that autumn to a friend.[32] Not much later, he painted *Discovery* [144].

The first is an entirely imaginary invention; in the second areas of wood-graining are imprinted on the flesh of a ready-made image of a nude, copied from a postcard pin-up.[33] Both are easily read as commentaries on the collage and papier-collé innovations of Picasso and Braque: the first, on their spatial, the second on their material implications for painting. In 1936, Magritte would write of Cubism as the consequence of Cézanne's problematisation of 'pictorial representation', and he would define the problem revealed as the gap between things in painting and their visual appearance in the world (the semiotic condition of all art). For him, the outcome of this was the problematisation of appearance itself.[34] What he painted from 1925, looking more directly at Braque's and Picasso's example than Ernst, was not the settings for possible dreams, but pictorial conundrums designed to jolt the viewer into active critical reflection.

In *The Muscles of the Sky* he paints a plunging moonlit stage with a backdrop of trees silhouetted against the sky, and then denies all that his carefully drawn perspective tells us by 'cutting out' pieces of stage and silhouetted trees so that the sky can flow forward to form ghost-like figures on stage. Ghost-like they may be, but Magritte attaches cast shadows to make these figures more palpably at once 'really' in front and 'really' behind their background. In *Discovery*

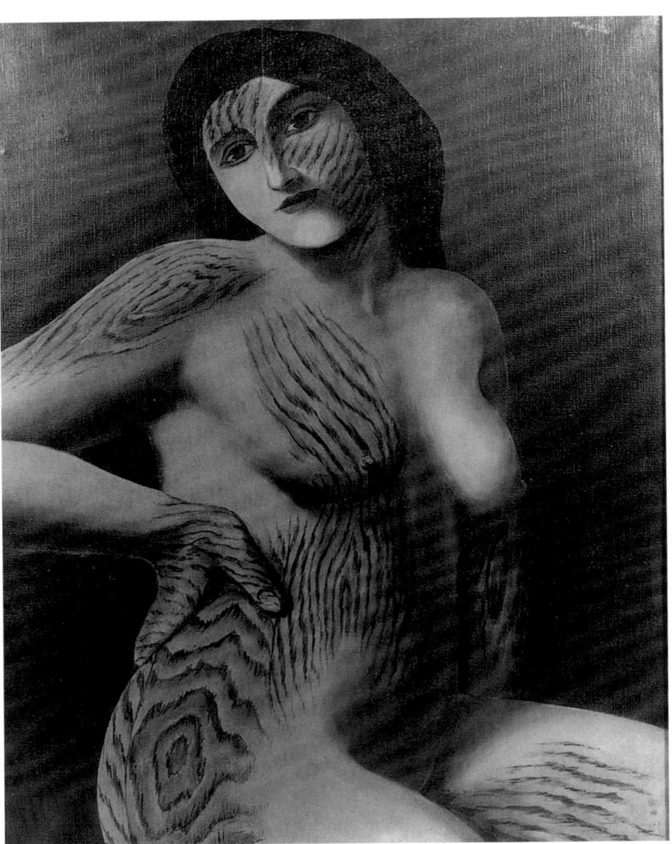

144. René Magritte, *Discovery*, 1927. Oil on canvas, 65 × 50 cm. Musées royaux des Beaux-Arts de Belgique, Brussels

he paints metamorphosis as a function not of open signs but of interchangeable material surfaces, skin and wood, obviously alluding to the first *faux bois* wallpaper papier-collés [103]. The picture went with others where areas of wood-graining appear against the sky. The effect is of appearances themselves rendered metamorphic through the process of representation. Braque's first papier-collé questions the way we see and read works of art; Magritte disrupts the way we see 'reality' itself through pictorial representation.

'The miserable conceptual mental expedient hidden by the word "reality" is nowadays the object of systematic denunciation, the revolutionary consequences of which are indisputable.' This was Breton's and Eluard's opening to the brief insert that they added to Dalí's text *La Femme visible*, when he published it early in 1930.[35] The transformation of the real by the force of the imagination was always at the heart of the Surrealist enterprise, verbal and visual, and Dalí's dramatic entrance into the Surrealist milieu at the moment of the second *Manifesto* in 1929, was instantly seen in this light. He came to Paris, to shoot the film *Un Chien andalou* with Luis Buñuel, and spent the summer in Cadaqués in Catalonia for the shooting of some of the scenes in their sequel, the full-length *L'Age d'or*. Both films disrupted the narrative expectations of cinema, exploiting its unquestioned veracity to heighten the impact of manifestly impossible events. The complement to his involvement with the 'realist' art of film was his decision in 1929 to fuse the collage practice he had developed earlier in Catalonia with the meticulous depiction of deep landscape spaces under brilliant Mediterranean skies. It could well be that one stimulus behind this was exposure to Ernst's collage-paintings (including *Oedipus Rex*), which were easily available to him in Paul Eluard's apartment.[36] Among his first paintings of this kind was *Illumined Pleasures* of 1929 [145], a work almost instantly bought by Breton. *La Femme visible* and another text by Dalí, 'The Putrified Donkey', published in *Le Surréalisme au service de la révolution* (*SASDLR*), marked his emergence in 1930 as a writer too. His writings expounded new theory in an arresting poetic language packed with hybrid words and neologisms to such effect that, far more than any other leading Surrealist artist, he was established as a writer on art as well as a painter. In that dual role, he remained a force within Breton's group until the mid-1930s, when his 'irresponsible' politics (as Breton put it) led to his gradual separation from the group. *The Metamorphosis of Narcissus* [324] was painted in 1937, after he had become unacceptable to Breton. Yet, fundamentally, in terms of theory and practice, *Illumined Pleasures* and *The Metamorphosis of Narcissus* remain of a piece, underlining the integrity of Dalí's position in the 1930s.

A distinction can be made, however, between Dalí's painting of the period around 1929–30, and an increasing proportion of his production – including *The Metamorphosis of Narcissus* – from the early 1930s through the rest of the decade. Canvases like *Illumined Pleasures* and *The Invisible Man* [327] are accumulations of images, in broad terms comparable in their relationship to collage with Ernst's collage-paintings. *The Metamorphosis of Narcissus* is not an accumulation of images, it is painted as if it is the result of a single act of the imagination which has produced a single transformed scene: its brand of metamorphosis manifestly has little to do with collage. *Illumined Pleasures* includes a small area of actual collage (a fragment of a black-and-white illustration of a church façade), which is carefully integrated into the painting as if not collage at all. And yet the pictures within the picture make a theme of collage as a juxtapositional process. It is as if Dalí has cut out images from a catalogue illustrating the hallucinatory images produced by his own delirium. Many recur in other paintings of the period: the roaring lion of Freudian passion, the woman's profile with glazed smile, here turned into a jug with handle, the eggs, the grasshopper, the guilty hands. The difference from Ernst's practice is clear. Dalí does not juxtapose ready-made images from popular sources, striking sparks from their unexpected encounters, he depicts images which he claimed appeared to him whole, often – as with the grasshoppers – images from his childhood which filled him with inexplicable dread. His compositional process is in emulation of their irresistible appearance one after another, a piling up of images: in the case of *Illumined Pleasures* a picture-show of images, in that of *The Invisible Man* the seeming result of serial extrusions, where one image emerges out of another.

What joins such accumulations of images to such a concentrated visionary work as *The Metamorphosis of Narcissus* is the idea of paranoia. 'The Putrified Donkey' begins with an extraordinary sequence of claims for paranoia as 'a force and power' equivalent to, but the opposite of, 'hallucination'. Dalí's distinction is crucial: hallucinations appear to a passive recipient, paranoia is an 'active' mental instrument of transformation by which the individual can 'systematise confusion and contribute to the total discrediting of . . . reality'. Paranoid images – his images – are as 'real' as hallucinations, but the individual – he – actively imposes them on things, driven by the compulsion to *see* them in the world, a compulsion infused with horror and desire. Picasso and Braque in 1912–14 had realised the metamorphic potential of the schematic sign. Magritte, with cool intellectual clarity, had realised the metamorphic potential of appearances when subjected to the procedures of pictorial representation. Dalí, with irresistible conviction, advocated the metamorphic potential of vision itself. And in 'The Putrified Donkey' in 1930, he placed at the heart of 'the mechanism of paranoia' the 'double image': 'that is to say, the representation of an object, which, without the slightest anatomical or figurative modification, can be at the same time the representation of something completely different.' And that double image, he contended, could proliferate to become an 'image of multiple meanings'.[37] Picasso's metamorphic signs, Gris's rhymes-as-metaphors, Reverdy's and Breton's encounters between 'distant realities' are, for Dalí, there to be seen in the way things actually appear.

Probably early in 1931, he met Jacques Lacan, who was working on a doctoral thesis applying Freudian psychoanalytic method to the problem of paranoia, and who was struck by the closeness of his ideas to Dalí's in 'The Putrified Donkey'. When the thesis was completed the following year, Dalí found his insights endorsed and fleshed out with all the apparatus of academic research.[38] Lacan's main conclusion was that paranoid delusion is not the result of rational deduction based on false judgements (and therefore at a remove from sensuory perception), but is experienced directly: it *is* the paranoid's reality. Perception itself is restructured; in Dalí's vocabulary, confusion is systematised.

The double image was given a central role in *The Invisible Man* [327], on which Dalí worked over a long period, between 1929 and 1931, and details of it, focusing on the double image, were reproduced in *SASDLR* with 'The Putrified Donkey'. But here and mostly in the paintings executed around 1930 the double image was just one kind of image among many others without the potential to multiply. The result was that, however startling the detail in which Dalí depicted his 'simulacra', the impression could remain, not of the systematic restructuring of reality, but of the mere recording of images from dreams and hallucinations, of ersatz dreamscapes in the line of Ernst's, with heightened realism. When Dalí gave the double image unchallenged precedence, he gave particular force as well to the idea of a world systematically transformed in all its aspects and in an instant of recognition. *The Metamorphosis of Narcissus* can be read as a double narrative – one that doubles that of Dalí with that of the figure from ancient myth, Narcissus, who drowned himself because of his love of his own reflection in the water. It is presented not, however, as a sequence of events but as a single scene dominated by a double, indeed a multiple image, whose echoes ripple outwards from the centre. Narcissus sunk down in contemplation of himself is doubled by a hand; his head is a pebble that becomes an egg held by the hand; it sprouts the Narcissus flower which, the

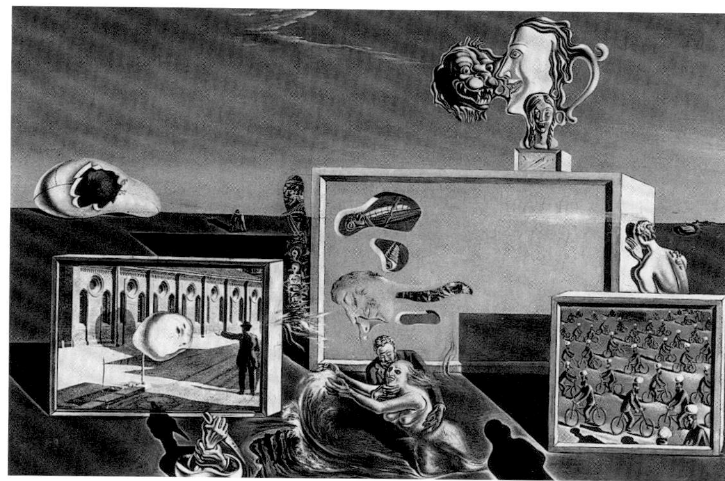

145. Salvador Dalí, *Illumined Pleasures*, 1929. Oil and collage on composition board, 23.8 × 34.7 cm. The Museum of Modern Art, New York. The Sidney and Harriet Janis Collection

myth recounts, grew in his place. Ovid's myth of metamorphosis doubles the metamorphic action of paranoia, and the theme of reflection doubles that of representation.

It was as his capacity to realise such concentrated images developed that Dalí arrived at the stronger version of the theory first expounded in 'The Putrified Donkey', for which he minted the term 'paranoiac critical method', where the active imposition of the paranoid vision on reality itself becomes something under the control of the artist: a 'critical method'.[39] Dalí's eulogy to academic technique of 1935 was written under the banner of the paranoiac critical method. His paintings had become: 'Instantaneous and hand-done colour photography . . .'[40] The metamorphic potential of the visual arts was revealed by Braque and Picasso as one outcome of their *rejection* of everything to do with the 'academic' naturalism of a Léon Bonnat [99]. Among the most influential outcomes of that revelation was Dalí's *recuperation* of academic realism in the service of metamorphic paranoia.

In 1929, Michel Leiris wrote a 'definition' of metaphor for the dissenting Surrealist periodical *Documents*. It amounted to a definition of the real *as* metaphor. Leiris rejected both objective reality and the idealist's 'thing in itself' (the Platonic Idea). He replaced them with the notion that all knowledge is based on the mental construction of analogies: the seeing of one thing in another – 'a play of transpositions, symbols, which one can call metaphoric'. Clear distinctions are lost in metaphoric fusions: 'As the sky is a subtle terrain, the terrain is a heavy sky.' There are no definitions, he concludes, so that even his own 'definition' of metaphor is 'metaphoric'.[41] The passage from collage, papier-collé and Cubist construction through automatism to the metamorphoses of Dalinian paranoia was opened up by a growing faith in the reality of metaphor and the metaphoric nature of reality. Such a position led in the extreme case of Dalí to the denial of the picture-object as a tangible material thing and the return of pictorial realism in a spectacular new form. But, when the whole range of practices developed by leading Surrealists is looked at, it is a position that is seen actually to have reinforced the crucial change in the relationship

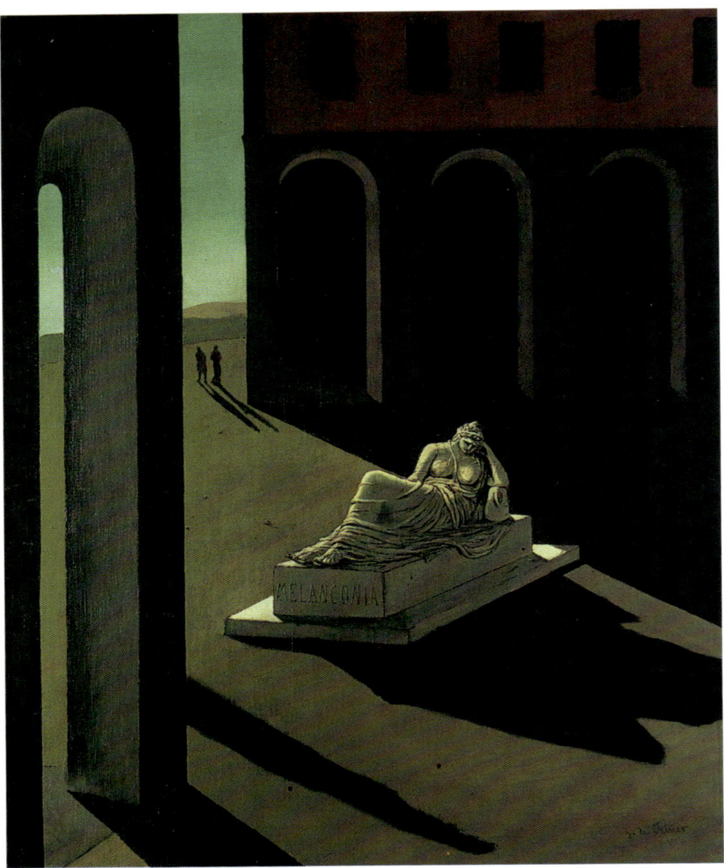

146. Giorgio de Chirico, *Melanchonia*, 1912. Oil on canvas, 78.5 × 63.5 cm. Estorick Collection of Modern Italian Art, London

between the artwork and the viewer that came with the arrival of the picture-object early in the twentieth century.

From the start, Bretonian Surrealist theory minimised the significance of the artist. Poetic images were *found*, not made; they were not the artists' but everyone's. Artworks too were metaphors and so, at least in theory, open in relation to any viewer's transforming powers. Obviously, mark-making automatism at its most abstruse in the work of Miró and the *frottages* and *grattages* of Ernst encouraged an active transformative engagement from the viewer. More than in, say, Picasso's *Man with a Hat*, it is the viewer who completes the work. In the same way, Magritte's images demand to be addressed by active problem-solving minds (which are promised continual frustration). In the case of Ernst's collages and collage paintings, it has been shown that they were the result of a knowing manipulation of precisely the kind of images analysed by Freud in major works like *The Interpretation of Dreams* and even in the less widely read case studies. *Oedipus Rex* is particularly good evidence of this, as I show in Chapter 12; in Freudian terms, it is indeed a possible dream. Such manipulations were made with an awareness that Freud did not give fixed significations to symbols, and thought of them rather as changing their signification according to individual circumstance and the way they are combined.[42] So even here, where fixed symbolic meanings might be inferred, in fact the onus was placed on the viewer to respond as an individual with his or her own psychic history.

It is Dalí who was most seriously tempted to place things in fixed symbolic relationships, where the viewer is left with almost no alternative but to follow where he leads. *The Metamorphosis of Narcissus* is certainly a case in point, and there can be no doubt that most readings will end by focusing attention on Dalí at the expense of the viewer. Applying the Freudian model, much of the work produced by those who were at one time or another leading Surrealists placed *both* viewer *and* artist in the dual role of analyst and analysand, requiring an active investment from the viewer as the analogue of the artist. Dalí increasingly was the exception; he took for himself alone the role of maker *and* interpreter of images, offering himself – in the guise of 'a madman' who is 'not mad' – as a case for analysis.[43] It was far more in this than in his devotion to the academic standards of Léon Bonnat that he betrayed the fundamentals of modernist practice as they were established in France before 1940.

ALLEGORY AND MYTH: FROM DE CHIRICO TO 'GUERNICA'

The dreamscapes of Ernst, the mindscapes of Magritte, and Dalí's haunted settings for paranoia have one shared precedent: the so-called 'metaphysical' paintings of Giorgio de Chirico (b.1888). All three were proud to confess their debt. Magritte called him his 'master'. De Chirico was in Paris between 1911 and 1915, and in the key years 1913–14 was one of the circle around Apollinaire. By the time he returned to Italy, much of his work from his first Paris period had been bought up by Paul Guillaume, and so it was easily accessible to Breton and his friends. Eluard and he were early collectors of de Chirico after the war, but, though Ernst, Magritte and Dalí would come to know his painting at first hand, their first and most often recalled encounters with his images were in reproduction. In Ernst's case this was the grey half-tones seen in an Italian monograph as early as 1919, in Magritte's case a black-and-white photograph seen as early as 1923.[44]

Dalí devotes a passage to de Chirico in the preface he wrote for his own exhibition at the galerie Pierre Colle in 1933. Predictably, he picks out de Chirico's conservation of 'all the essential academic conventions', but he adds that the Italian has 'sensationally revolutionise[d] the anecdote.'[45] The Dalí of the Narcissus picture and the de Chirico of 1911–15 were linked not just by a shared deadpan 'realism' (found also in Ernst and Magritte), but by the stories they told and their reasons for telling them pictorially. Both used the figures of classical myth to make myths of their own histories, a practice that was spreading, especially in Surrealist circles, by the early 1930s. But where Dalí made his mythologisation of himself so visible in the figure of Narcissus, a key reason for the impact that de Chirico's exploitation of myth made in France between the wars was the fact that the heroic role he gave himself in his own mythology seems to have been invisible.

De Chirico used classical mythology to build a highly personalised iconography, where the key themes are fate, art and the artist. *Melanchonia* of 1912 [146] is one of a series of pictures centred on the statue of a brooding Ariadne. She is both living and dead on her pedestal in the dreamscape, a

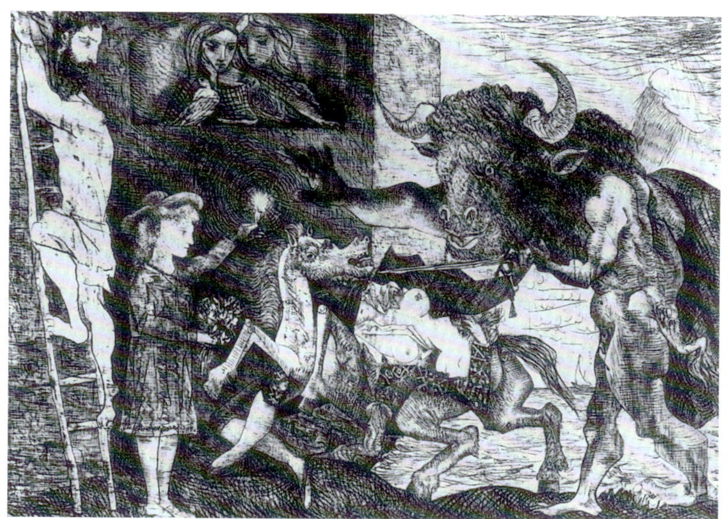

147. Pablo Picasso, *The Minotauromachy*, 1935. Etching and scraper, 49.8 × 69.3. Musée Picasso, Paris

simple stimulus to reverie, but this moment in Ariadne's story signifies within an iconography of artistic creation. Lost in thought, she is as Theseus left her on the island of Naxos, deserted, and awaiting an unknown fate. As a figure, she is caught between the divine powers of Apollo and Dionysus, since Theseus has departed for games dedicated to the god Apollo and she will be discovered on Naxos by the young Dionysus who will take her for his bride. Friedrich Nietzsche was de Chirico's major philosophical source; Apollo (associated with sculpture and harmony) and Dionysus (associated with creation as frenzy) were the two poles of the aesthetic established by the German philosopher in his first book, *The Birth of Tragedy*.[46]

Such networks of allusion – in other instances often revolving around de Chirico and his brother – are there to be read in most of de Chirico's adaptations of classical myth. But, though his writings of the 1920s make no secret of the mythic dimension he gave his life alongside his art, what he called 'enigma' was the quality most repeatedly praised in his painting.[47] By 1926, Breton had rejected him for what he saw as a betrayal of his early work motivated by greed, but, back in Paris between 1924 and 1929, he had influential champions, among them Jean Cocteau and Waldemar George, who claimed for the Italian a status the equal even of Picasso. For them, as much as for Breton responding to the pre-1919 de Chirico, what gave his painting its unsettling force was its *resistance* to interpretation. As Cocteau saw it, the 'miracle' of de Chirico's painting was that it made the ordinary attain such a degree of enchantment as to suggest, but never declare, a metaphysical beyond. His work was taken to offer a lexicon of signs to which the key was missing.[48]

Treated thus, de Chirico's painting was opened away from him and outwards to its viewers, including Breton, who always acknowledged the importance of the early work. It demanded the same level of participant spectatorship and individual responsiveness as the collagist Ernst or even the automatist Miró. And just such an openness characterises some of the most important appropriations of ancient myths by artists in and around the Surrealist group during the 1930s, the most important case of all being Picasso.[49] Classical myth was a factor in Picasso's work long before Breton's attempt to claim him for Surrealism in the mid-1920s. But there are obvious Surrealist aspects to the use he made of mythological figures and settings in the suite of etchings, the 'Vollard Suite', that formed the 1930s prelude to his great allegorical mural of 1937, *Guernica* [333]. What is more, he met Dalí soon after the young painter's arrival in Paris in 1929, and the way he revived his own superlative academic skills in the Vollard Suite etchings echoes Dalí's technical exhibitionism. Most impressively this is so of an etching produced independently of them, which exceeds them in ambition, *The Minotauromachy* [147]. Picasso too uses a totally convincing realism to create a mythic world where metamorphosis is always possible and everything is metaphor. Nothing could more comprehensively demonstrate the gap between ambitious modernism by the 1930s and the art both of earlier generations and of the French academic tradition than the refusal of fixed meanings displayed in such a mythological image.

In 1900, allegory was the dominant mode in monumental sculpture and large-scale mural painting. It remained a living form in the Paris Exhibition of 1937, at least outside the Spanish Pavilion where *Guernica* was shown, in such murals as Raoul Dufy's *The Muse of Electricity* and Louis Billotey's *Tragedy* [3, 6]. Around 1900, allegories like Dalou's *Triumph of the Republic* or Laurent Marquestre's *Monument to Waldeck-Rousseau* [1, 148] used a repertoire of mythological

148. Laurent Marquestre, *Monument to Waldeck-Rousseau*. Inaugurated in the Jardin des Tuileries, Paris, 1906

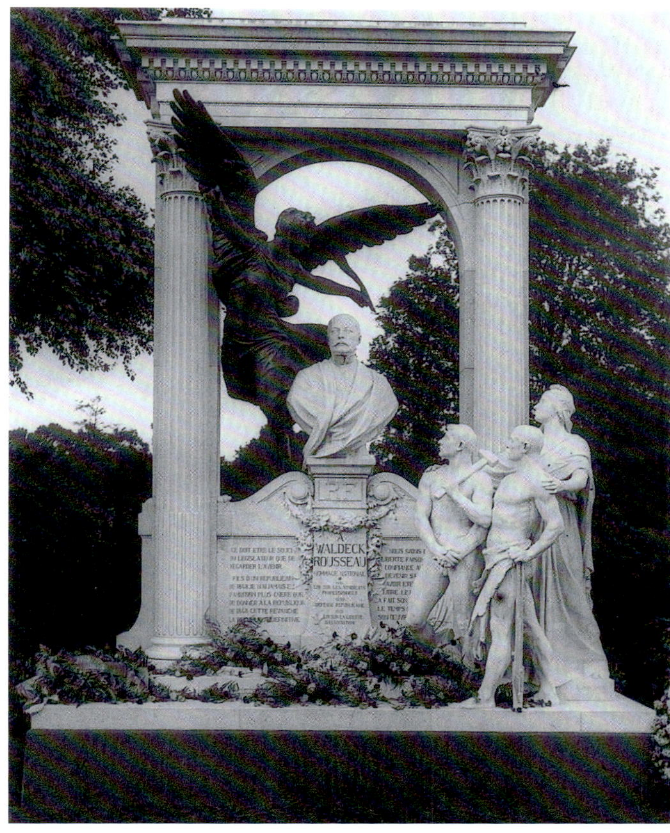

figures which, as discussed at the beginning of Part One, constructed instantly legible symbolic scenarios. In the latter, a distinctly contemporary politician, with distinctly contemporary workers, is visited by Fame (the bronze figure of which no longer survives); in the former, apart from another contemporary worker, Liberty, Justice and Peace are easily recognised. As a city of monuments, Paris could be read like a book. In the decorative schemes of the Hôtel de Ville and the town halls of the arrondissements, figures from classical myth were routinely used to allegorise the city and the values of the Republic. Robert Delaunay's *City of Paris* [162], with its centrepiece of the Three Graces as an allegory of Paris, works with and against this orthodox public art, and is deliberately comparable in its mural scale: it too profits from the instant legibility of symbols in current allegorical usage. Allegory so used, especially in its appropriation of figures from ancient myth, depends on that easy legibility.

Maillol was celebrated as a 'classical' independent, because he was prepared to generalise his mythological figures to such an extent that they no longer remained allegorical in so full a sense. This was something that made his *Monument to Cézanne* [149] appear pointless (empty) to the councillors from Aix-en-Provence who refused it. His were figures left iconographically vague enough to become screens for the projection of appropriate meanings, depending on their context. But de Chirico's apparently purposeless and sometimes complex recycling of the figures and the stories of ancient myth opened up that repertoire of personages and symbols to so unrestricted a field of possible meanings that the word 'appropriate' no longer applies. And Picasso went futher still, with images that often appear actually easier to read as allegory. In *The Minotauromachy*, Picasso gives us characters who might be read as Theseus, the Minotaure and Ariadne, in a setting which might be read as outside the Labyrinth. But there are interlopers, the dead female matador and the eviscerated horse, and all of them are caught in an event related only in the loosest possible way to the point in the story evoked, which is on Crete, before Theseus took Ariadne to Naxos. Ariadne (if it is she) has a light (like Liberty or Truth), not a thread to guide her through the Labyrinth; the Minotaure is out of his den; Theseus (if it is he) does not confront him, but climbs a ladder to escape. Just as Ernst had offered complex new combinations of Freudian dream images to be read and responded to from any outside vantage point, so Picasso offers figures from mythology without any key to fix their meanings. He passes the responsibility of making meaning to the viewer.

In *Guernica*, Picasso replaced the mythological monster of the Vollard Suite and *The Minotauromachy* with a bull and recalibrated the screaming horse, subtracted the dead female matador and added the broken statue of a fallen warrior and female victims (conventional figures in allegories of war). The anti-modernist Left attacked the work precisely for its refusal of clear meanings, as I show in Chapter 12. A decade later, Picasso could not have made his own position in relation to such questions plainer. Asked by Alfred H. Barr via Kahnweiler whether the horse represented defeated Spanish nationalism and the bull the victorious people, he replied: 'There are some animals. That is all, so far as I'm concerned. It's up to the public to see what it wants to see.'[50]

The modernist appropriation of the figures of allegory and of classical myth underlines once again and in yet another way, the shift that I have tried to elucidate. It is the one theme common to the extraordinarily diverse manifestations of modernism at its most innovative in France from Matisse and Derain at Collioure in 1905 to Picasso in the Spanish Pavilion at the Exhibition of 1937: the empowering of the viewer, sometimes at the expense of the artist. Nothing could be further from the blatancy of the iconographical programmes of a Laurent Marquestre or a Louis Billotey.

149. Aristide Maillol, *Monument to Cézanne*, 1907–25. Bronze. In the Jardin des Tuileries, Paris

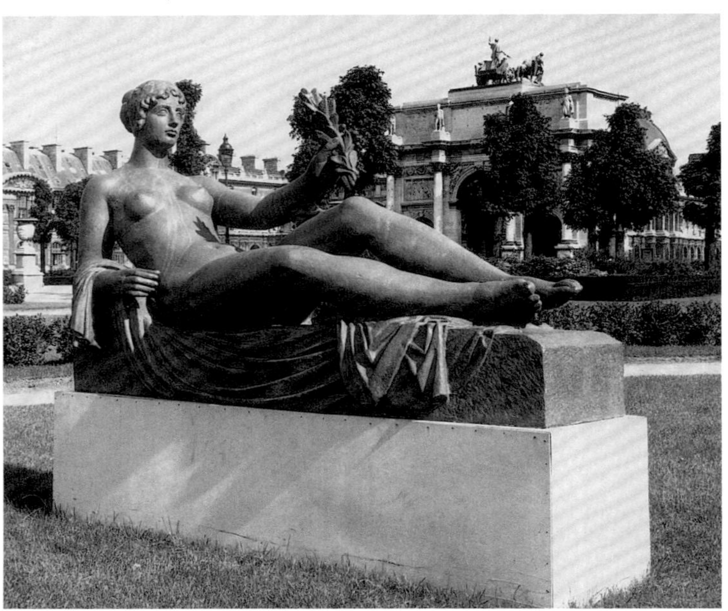

WORDS AND THINGS: FROM DUCHAMP'S 'LARGE GLASS' TO THE 'SURREALIST OBJECT'

Commenting in 1913 on Picasso's introduction of 'real objects' – 'a piece of newspaper, a piece of oilcloth printed with chair-caning' – Apollinaire made the following observation. The object in such works 'constitutes the internal frame of the painting, marking the limits of its depth just as the frame marks its exterior limits.'[51] Three days after this observation appeared in the periodical *Montjoie!*, Apollinaire's book *Les Peintres cubistes* was published. In the section he devoted to Francis Picabia (b.1879) he tackled Picabia's habit of writing his titles on his paintings. They must, he said, 'play the role of an internal frame, as do authentic objects and precisely copied inscriptions in the pictures of Picasso'.[52] At that moment in March 1913, the poet-critic pinpointed two factors newly introduced into painting which were to have devastating effects: the object and the word.

The challenge to established orthodoxies thrown down by some modernists went beyond alternative kinds of image and image-making. The most basic assumptions about representation and meaning were put in question, and so was the very status of the artwork as Art. They did not, of course, 'kill' Art. Much painting and sculpting continued untouched, as we have seen. But a region of doubt was opened up which could not be closed off once it was glimpsed. The tools with which they proposed to take apart, illusion by illusion, the immense authority of art in Western Europe after the sixteenth and seventeenth centuries, were the object and the word. Apollinaire was well aware of the threat posed to that 'tradition' thus, hence his recourse to the analogy of the frame. The object finally blocked up perspective's window; words opened a new space of thought and imagination.

In March 1930, nearly two decades after Apollinaire's welcome for the object and the word in painting, the galerie Goemans held an exhibition of collage. In it several of Picasso's and Braque's early papiers-collés reappeared in a new avant-garde context, in the company of recent collages by emergent artists like Dalí and Miró, as well as products from a mid-1920s return to collage by Picasso himself [317]. The show received the enthusiastic support of the Surrealists, and Louis Aragon wrote a text for the catalogue, 'In Defiance of Painting' (La Peinture au défi), which was perhaps the single most influential statement on collage made from within the Surrealist circle. Here Aragon acknowledged Picasso's and Braque's first step towards the rehabilitation of the object, but gave a special importance to Picabia and Marcel Duchamp (b.1887) for seeing the 'logical consequences' of collage. These two, claimed Aragon, had replaced technique with choice: the choice of the readymade. Personal technique had been replaced by the 'personality of choice'. And, he remarked, these were painters who used the objects they chose 'like words.'[53] Choice is an entirely mental procedure. With the final objectification of painting and sculpture, Aragon realised, the mind could at last take over from the senses as the maker of meaning. Apollinaire also paired Picabia with Duchamp (their friendship had begun late in 1911), but saw Picabia as the initiator. In fact, in the period 1912–14, Duchamp took the 'logical consequences' of collage for the object and the word furthest, and he did so, both on the simple level of 'choosing' ready-made things and on a far more complex level, where word and object become so closely enmeshed that there is no longer any question of objects merely being 'like' words: they exist *through* words.

The complex counterpart to Duchamp's readymades was the *Large Glass*, *The Bride Stripped Bare by her Bachelors, Even* [302], which was mostly conceived, though not made, before Duchamp's departure for New York in 1915. When the *Glass* appeared in *Le Surréalisme au service de la révolution* in 1933, Breton would describe it as an 'object painted on transparent glass'. Notes by Duchamp dated 1915 were published here as accompaniment. They ensured that it could *only* be experienced through words (with algebraic comparisons added for good measure).[54]

When Picasso told André Salmon that his construction *The Guitar* [129] was no more than 'el guitare (sic)', both of them knew that one thing it was *not* was a guitar. The word for the thing represented could not be enough. When D-H. Kahnweiler titled Braque's papier-collé [110] *Glass, Bottle and Newspaper*, the word 'violin' remained there in the work to introduce doubt among those other seemingly

150. Marcel Duchamp, *The Bride Stripped Bare by Her Bachelors, Even*, 1912–23. As illustrated with a key in *Minotaure*, no. 6 (Paris, winter 1935) p. 48

unequivocal words. Words in Picasso's and Braque's collages and papier-collés typically worked against their own and their titles' simple naming function (nominalism); they helped prise open signs everywhere. There are no words in Duchamp's 'object painted on transparent glass', his *Bride Stripped Bare*, but the way it works with and against the verbal accompaniment of the 'Notes' excerpted by Breton in 1933 and then published by Duchamp in 1934 in *The Green Box*, takes further in an astonishingly elaborate way the relationship between the image and the titles that he had written on to his paintings from late 1911 [78].

The *Glass* itself was still in New York, when Duchamp published *The Green Box*. It remained as he had left it in 1923, 'definitively unfinished' after the meticulous labour he had put in there from 1915 making his notes and drawings and fragments of 1912–15 into an object; its glass had been shattered in transit from its first exhibition in Brooklyn in 1926. In France, it would be known in the 1930s only by reproduction (like the reproduced notes in the *Box*), pristine, unbroken, and exclusively in the Surrealist context of *SASDLR* and *Minotaure*. When, in 1935, Breton followed up the appearance of *The Green Box* ('a capital event') with his *Minotaure* article 'Lighthouse of the Bride', he illustrated it with a numbered key [150] and set out all of its parts as a close reading of the notes identified them.

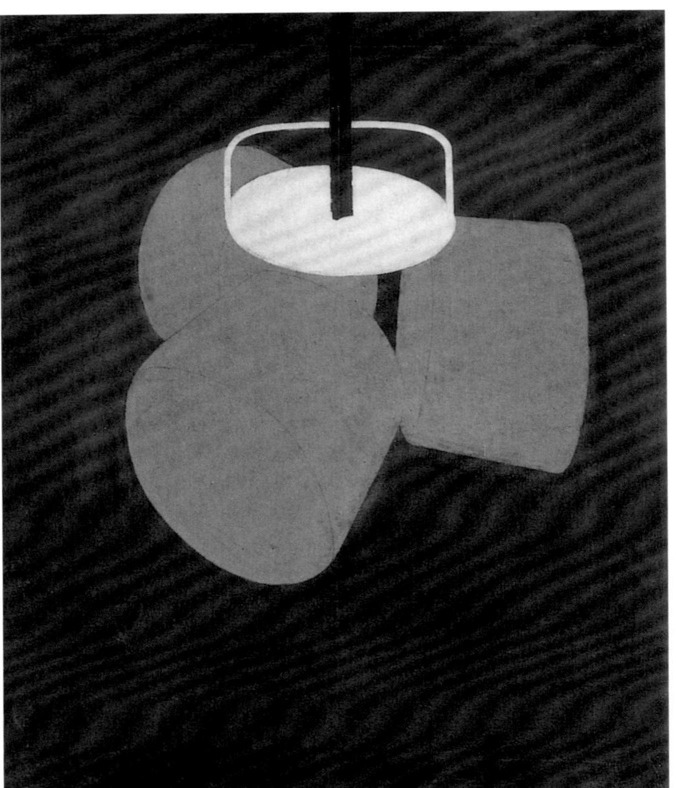

151. Marcel Duchamp, *Chocolate Grinder No. 2*, 1912. Oil and pencil on canvas, 73 × 60 cm. Kunstsammlung Nordrhein-Westfalen, Dusseldorf

1. *Bride* (or *hanged woman*) reduced to what could be taken for her skeleton in the canvas of 1912 which carries this title [301]. 2. *The Inscription at the top* (obtained with the 3 *air pistons* a, a′, a″ surrounded by a sort of *milky way*). 3. *Nine malic moulds* (or the *Eros machine*, or the *bachelor machine* or the *cemetery of uniforms and liveries* (gendarme, armourer, keeper of the peace, priest, café employee, department store supplier, flunkey, undertaker, station-master). 4. *Glider* (or *chariot*, or *sledge*) supported by runners p and p' sliding in a track. 5. *Water-mill*. 6. *Scissors*. 7. *Sieves* (or *line of discharge*). 8. *Chocolate Grinder* (b. *bayonet*, c. *tie*, r. *rollers*, l. Louis XV *base*). 9. Region of the *splashes*. 10. *Oculist Witnesses*. 11. Region of the *gravity controller* (or *gravity carer*, not represented). 12. *Shots*. 13. *Bride's dress*.

This catalogue of imponderables was rendered still more unfathomable by Breton's subsequent account of the working of this mechanism dedicated to 'the phenomenon of love: the passage of woman from the state of virginity to that of non-virginity . . .' The three *air pistons* send *orders* to the bachelor machine below, in which the *nine malic moulds* (malic rhymed with phallic) receive the *illuminating gas*, which travels along the capillaries in solidified form, becoming *explosive liquid*, while the *Glider* recites its litanies ('Slow life. Vicious circle. Onanism', etc.). As it moves, the *Glider* opens the *Scissors* producing the *splashes*, in which form the *illuminating gas* is projected back upwards, through the circles of the *Oculist Witnesses*, reaching the canon which fires it as *shots*, but only crossing the divide of the dress if the *gravity controller* (not represented) is in balance, according to the 'Wilson-Lincoln system'. The union desired as a result of the blossoming of the bride and her stripping is never achieved, and the *chocolate grinder*, set somewhat apart, continues 'to grind his chocolate himself'.[55] In the guise of a nominalist listing of the parts followed by instructions as to the mechanism's functioning, Breton uses the notes as he understands they should be used to mystify with each successive clarification. But on one point he is unequivocal: this 'object painted on transparent glass' projects its mysteries into mental space, and does so through the medium of words.

Duchamp fabricated the *Large Glass* in a manner as dissimilar as possible to the way painters executed paintings on canvas in 1912–14. He used his own version of mechanical drawing to project the parts of the bachelor machine below; he drew with lead wire, fixing it to the glass with varnish; he sealed his colours under the glass with lead foil; and in the case of the *sieves* he used a three or four month accumulation of dust for colour ('a delay in glass'). It was far more like a complex manufactured object than the 'creation' of a painter, and its transparency allowed the things around it – floorboards, skirting boards, wall panels – to be incorporated. It constructed a space of projection by mechanical drawing in an actual space of appearance. It is both as an object

152. Marcel Duchamp, *Bottle-Dryer 'Antique certifié'*, 1961 version of lost original. Galvanized iron, 50 × 33 cm. Philadelphia Museum of Art, Gift of Jacqueline, Paul and Pierre Matisse, in memory of their mother Alexina Duchamp

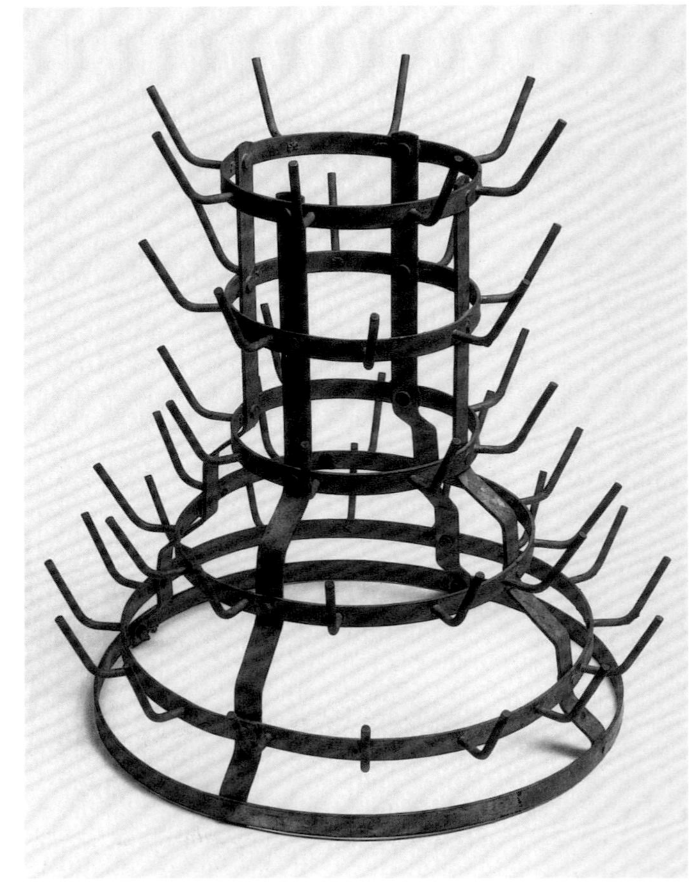

and as an object transformed by words that it is the counterpart to the readymades.

Behind the *Chocolate Grinder* in the *Glass* lie two exact pictorial depictions executed in 1913 and 1914; they are titled simply *Chocolate Grinder No. 1* and *No. 2* [151]. Duchamp had known the grinder which was their motif for years; it was in the window of a sweet shop in his home town of Rouen. In a sense therefore, these depictions were records of an unobtainable 'readymade'. The first readymades properly speaking had no titles at all. *Bottle-dryer* was a bottle-dryer: a tiered metal construction incorporating pegs on which wine bottles were put to dry [152]. Duchamp bought it in 1914 from a department store beside the Hôtel de Ville, and only gave it a title – '*Certified Antique*' – when he bought a replacement for the lost 'original' ten years later.

As an 'antique', it was, like all his readymades, something merely to possess, not to use. That title brings out the essentials of the operation involved with the selection of each readymade: the object was deprived of its usefulness, and detached therefore from its normal context, where meaning followed from function. It was an operation that exactly replicated the detachment of the sign from its normal naming, referring or describing function. When Duchamp titled his readymades, he underlined the visual and verbal dislocations involved: the new name allowed fresh accretions of meaning (never stable or fixed) to replace the 'name' of the thing. Most notoriously, there was his upended porcelain urinal shown in New York in 1917 as the work of 'R. Mutt', which, as Breton phrased it in 'Lighthouse of the Bride', 'went under the title *Fountain*' [300], a phrasing that gives the title the character, not of a name, but of a disguise.[56] The readymades made blatant what was only implicit in Cubist collage and construction: the fact that not only words and images, but objects too could be open signs. And what their titles did was to forge the first link in any number of possible semiotic chains to be forged by the viewer, where not merely signifieds (meanings) can endlessly change, but signifiers too (the generators of meaning, now objects as well as representations of objects). Once the urinal becomes a fountain and the bottle-dryer an antique, their identities have been unfixed for ever.

During the war, alongside Duchamp in New York, Picabia pioneered the use of dislocating titles with ready-made images mechanically reproduced – technical diagrams, photographs, etc. – in his periodical *391*. These readymade images found their way to Paris before Duchamp's first trip back to the city in 1919. Aragon was right to put Picabia and Duchamp together as the first to demonstrate the 'logical consequences' of collage for the object. Picabia's impact from within early 1920s Dada circles was far more immediate than Duchamp's. The colossal force of Duchamp's impact went far deeper, but was only felt gradually, especially after 1930 – a 'delay' in history. Before that date, however, neither Picabia nor Duchamp, exposed the polysemic potential of words and objects in juxtaposition more effectively than René Magritte, who between 1927 and 1929 added his own cogent addenda to their readymade agenda; he did so, not with objects, but with paintings.

The twelfth and final number of *La Révolution surréaliste* (15 December 1929), in which Breton's second *Manifesto*

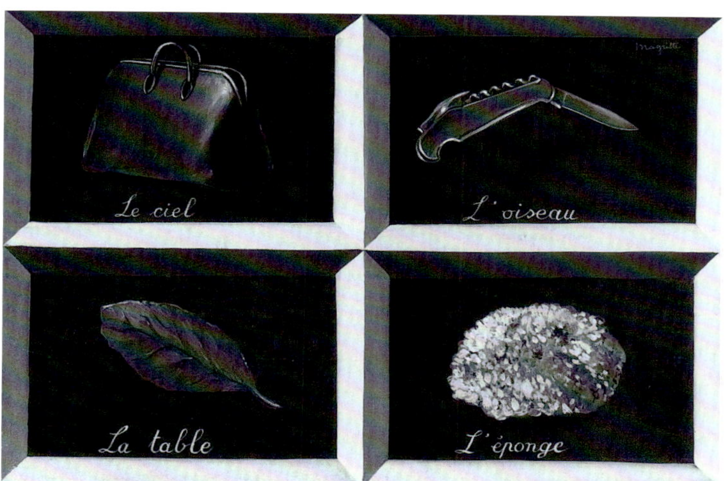

153. René Magritte, *The Key to Dreams*, 1927. Oil on canvas, 38 × 55 cm. Staatsgalerie moderner Kunst, Munich, Theo-Wormland-Sammlung

appeared, included a short piece by Magritte, 'Words and Images'. It began: 'An object is not so attached to its name that one could not find another that fits better,' after which there followed a deliberately banal drawing of a leaf captioned 'Canon'. In this piece Magritte reflected summarily on a sequence of paintings which he had begun late in 1927 with *The Key to Dreams* [153] and had brought to the clearest possible conclusion early in 1929 with *The Treason of Images* [307]. Both use a highly informative painting technique and blank backgrounds as in department store catalogues, combined with copy-book 'hand-written' captions to widen the gap between words and images. A sponge is a 'sponge', a leaf is a 'table', and, in *The Treason of Images*, the words 'This is not a pipe' caption the profile image of a bakelite pipe. The point, commented Magritte's Belgian writer-friend Paul Nougé in 1936 *vis-à-vis The Key to Dreams*, is that 'the word never reproduces the object, it is external to it and more or less indifferent.'[57]

That word 'indifferent' might seem to connect with a principle central to Duchamp's notion of the readymade. He aspired to total neutrality in relation to the objects he chose: 'The choice of a readymade is always based on visual indifference . . .'[58] But what marks out Magritte's word/object fusions is the fact that the deadpan indifference of their handling as painting and writing produces something that asks for a response. The naming of images can be 'the key to dreams'. In 1929, he offered a definition of poetry in *La Révolution surréaliste*: 'Poetry is a pipe'.[59] The pipe in *The Treason of Images* was 'not a pipe' because it was so much else: a symbol of modernity from Le Corbusier's and Ozenfant's Purist periodical *L'Esprit nouveau*, and, as a recent reading has brought out, a fusion of male (stem) and female (bowl), with untold possible consequences. It was preceded by a painting of 1928, *Pipes in love with the Moon*, which offered three pipes in a provocatively aroused condition.[60] Nougé's analysis of *The Key to Dreams* mentioned above, allowed that the picture 'leads one towards serious meditations', but also suggested that it was 'a poetic machine'.[61] Obviously, to bring together objects and words with other referents could be a way of producing 'poetic images' in the Reverdian and the Bretonian sense: meetings of 'distant realities'. It was certainly not as matters of 'indifference' that Breton first envisaged a possible future for the object in Surrealism, it was as a product of and a trigger for dreams, much more a 'poetic machine' than the source of 'serious meditations'. The 'Surrealist object', when it emerged with that nomenclature in 1931, would almost exclusively be approached on the terms of poetry (understood in the Surrealist sense) and the dream.

From before 1920, Breton was willing to use collage techniques to make poems, plundering such sources of readymade names and phrases as the telephone book and newspapers.[62] But it is with an object 'found' in a dream that he first anticipated the 'Surrealist object'. In a text of 1924, he recalled dreaming of finding a book in an open-air market near Saint-Malo whose spine 'consisted of a wooden gnome with a white beard, cut in the Assyrian style, which reached down to his feet'. It had pages of 'thick black wool'. 'I would like,' he commented, 'to put various objects of this kind into circulation, and it seems to me that their fate would be eminently problematic and disturbing'.[63] Periodically until 1931, exhibitions of objects were suggested in the Surrealist milieu, or the circulation of dream objects like Breton's 'rather curious book'. In *Le Paysan de Paris* (1926) Aragon took the lowliest objects for sale in the shopping arcade, the 'Passage de l'Opéra', as starting points for an unchecked imaginative delirium.[64] And in *Nadja* (1928) Breton singled out for special mention objects that seduced him in the flea market at Saint–Ouen on the northern fringes of Paris. But it was not until December 1931 and the appearance of *SASDLR* no. 3 that the 'Surrealist object' emerged as a significant feature of Surrealist practice. It did so as the preserve both of writers and artists, substantiating Aragon's point that the readymade substituted 'choice' for 'technique' (skill) and so allowed anyone into the act. *SASDLR* illustrated objects assembled by artists (Giacometti, Miró, Dalí and Valentine Hugo), but also objects assembled by two non-artists, Dalí's Gala and Breton himself.

There were two types of object illustrated in *SASDLR*, one is represented by Dalí's piece, later dubbed *Scatalogical Object* [154], the other is represented by Giacometti's *Suspended Ball* [155]. They were either assemblages of found objects or imagined objects specially constructed (by craftsmen working to designs). If the recycling of finds had a prelude in Breton's and Aragon's writing, the realisation of new, imagined objects had a prelude in painting, above all in the work of Yves Tanguy (b.1900), which Breton had shown at the galerie Surréaliste in May 1927. The pictures he showed there, for instance *Mama, Papa is Wounded!* [156], were the result of mark-making automatism, but used a suggestive 'realism' loosely analogous to that of Ernst's collage paintings to realise the animate/inanimate things that undi-

154. Salvador Dalí, *Scatalogical Object*, 1931. Mixed media, 48 × 24 × 14 cm. Whereabouts unknown.

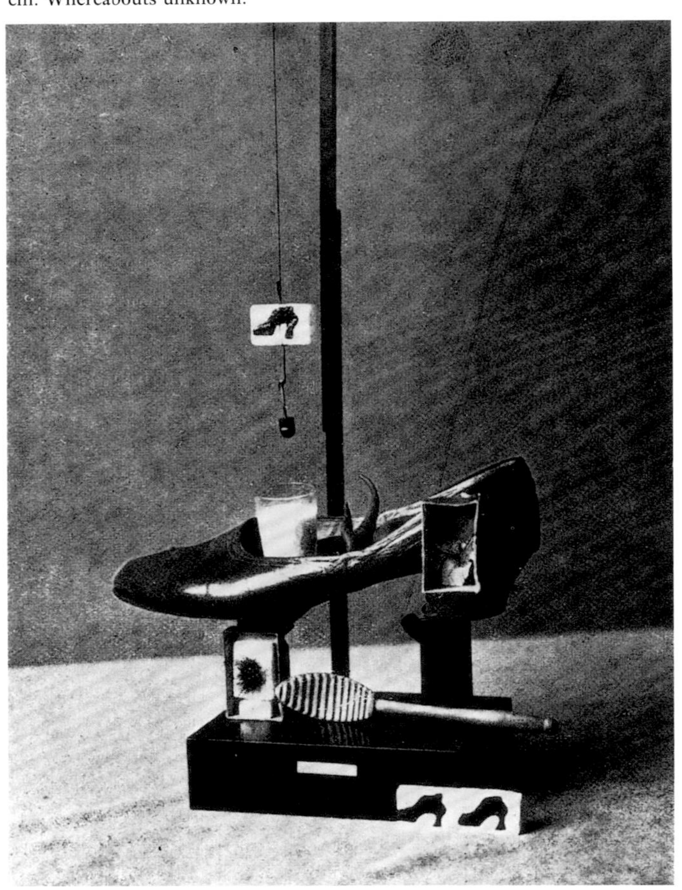

155. Alberto Giacometti, *Suspended Ball*, 1930. Plaster, metal and string. h. 61 cm. Alberto Giacometti Foundation, Kunsthaus Zurich

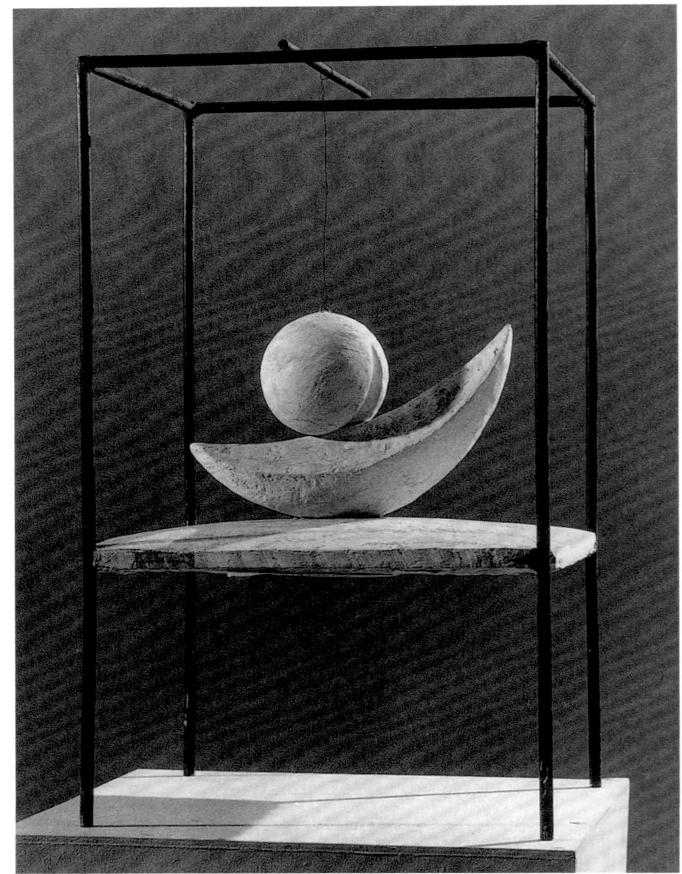

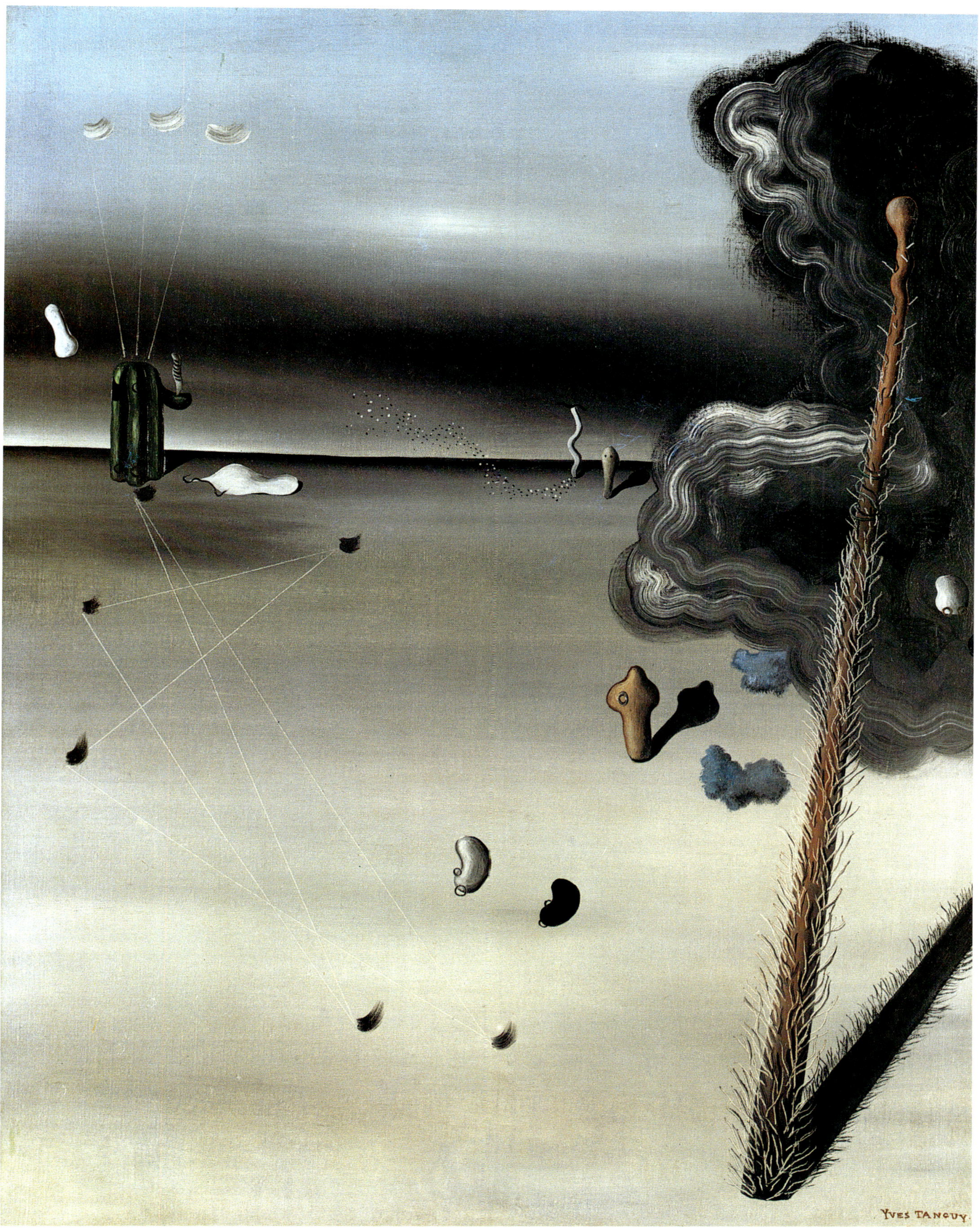

156. Yves Tanguy, *Mama, Papa is Wounded!*, 1927. Oil on canvas, 92.1 × 73 cm. The Museum of Modern Art, New York. Purchase

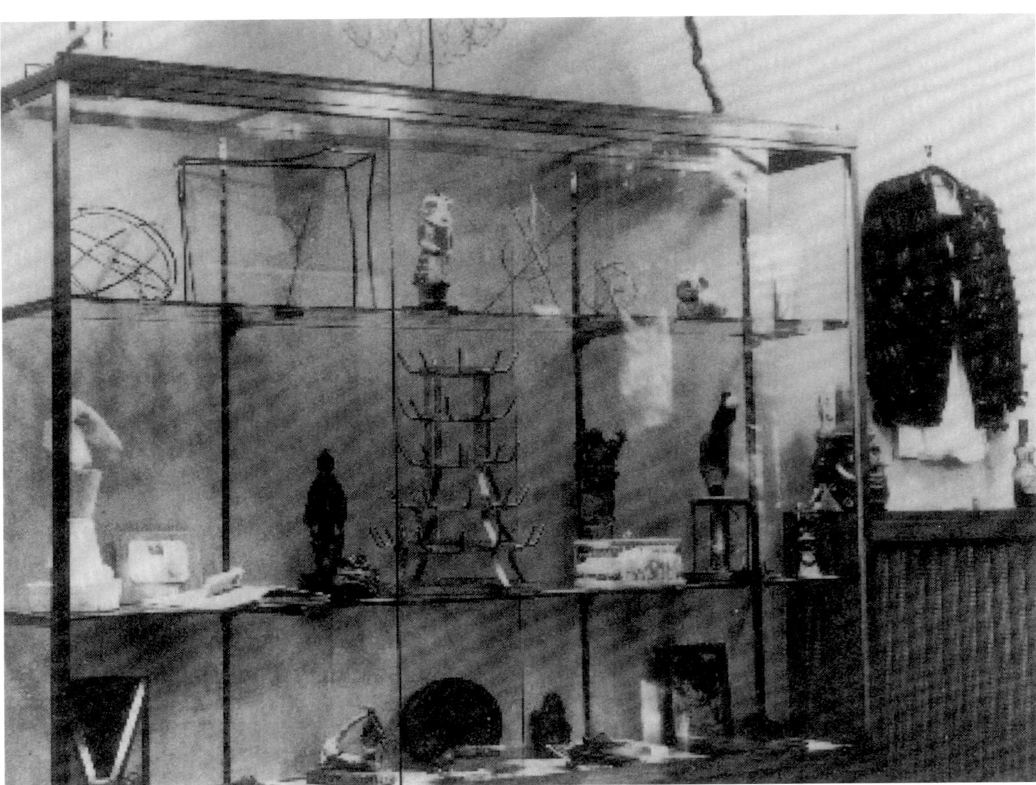

157. Man Ray, Photograph of the *Surrealist Exhibition of Objects*, 1936. Galerie Charles Ratton, Paris

158. Meret Oppenheim, *Luncheon in Fur (Le Déjeuner en fourrure)*, 1936. Fur-covered cup, saucer and spoon; cup 10.9 cm diameter; saucer 23.7 cm diameter; spoon 20.2 cm long; overall height 7.3 cm. The Museum of Modern Art, New York. Purchase

rected drawing threw up. The invitation to dream was completed by the addition of titles lifted randomly by Tanguy and Breton shortly before the exhibition from a huge study of paranormal phenomena published in 1922, Charles Richet's *Traité de métapsychique*. In *SASDLR* no. 3, Tanguy supplied a short text with drawings which was dedicated to objects imagined for exploration by hand as well as eye; they were left as unrealised projects, like Breton's dream book with black wool pages.[65] Through the 1930s, he would continue to paint an imagined world of objects, unlike yet suggestively like objects in the known world, progressively increasing their 'realism' as the words for his titles continued to send out invitations to dream.

Giacometti's *Suspended Ball* derived its capacity for inducing discomfiture from the relationship of the ball to the wooden, sliced-melon form it encounters. As photographed in *SASDLR* no. 3, the groove cut into the ball just where the two forms can touch is invisible, and it seems that the ball rests on or is sliced into by the sharp edge of the other form, as if it is hurt by the contact, an imagined sensation increased by the realisation that the suspended ball can move, rubbing against the cutting blade. When seen from views where the groove in the ball is not obscured, a lack of fit between cut and blade becomes obvious; the ball will never swing right through, and so will always encounter pain as whoever swings it encounters frustration. None of the objects illustrated in *SASDLR* no. 3 were given titles to invite the imaginative participation of the viewer, but all except Miró's incorporated movement, requiring active or imagined participation to make them function, and all used that movement as itself the trigger for erotically directed imaginative engagement. Dalí published a text introducing the idea of 'symbolically functioning objects' to go with his *Scatalogical Object*, where 'functioning' involving movement and transformation were the key features.[66] This assemblage of objects functions when a lump of sugar, on which is stuck the image of a high-heeled shoe, is lowered by string into a glass of milk inside an actual high-heeled shoe, and so melts, inviting repetition of the action with new lumps of sugar *ad infinitum*. The fetishistic shoe, like Magritte's pipe, can be both 'symbolic' of the male (whose object of desire it is) and the female (when it becomes the receptacle for that desire, dissolving it and inducing the endless repetition of the act). There are obvious allusions to semen (male) and lactation (female).

By 1934, the object was at the very centre of the Surrealist enterprise, so that Breton could write: 'It is essentially the *object* on which the increasingly lucid eyes of Surrealism have remained open in recent years.'[67] It had dominated the two final numbers of *SASDLR* in 1933 (nos. 5 and 6), and almost literally submerged the paintings included in an exhibition of Surrealism at the galerie Pierre Colle that year. 1936 would see its Surrealist high point, the 'Surrealist Exhibition of Objects' held at the galerie Charles Ratton [157]. Photographs show among the more than 200 objects exhibited, readymades by Duchamp, including the *Bottle-Dryer*, Alaskan, New Guinea, and Oceanic masks, Cubist constructions by Picasso, found vegetable and mineral specimens. Also included were objects discovered by Max Ernst at the Institut Henri Poincaré illustrating mathematical propositions, Dalí's *Aphrodisiac Jacket* (where glasses of peppermint liqueur were attached to a jacket on a hanger) and Giacometti's *Suspended Ball*. Everything was juxtaposed apparently at random. Among the stars of the

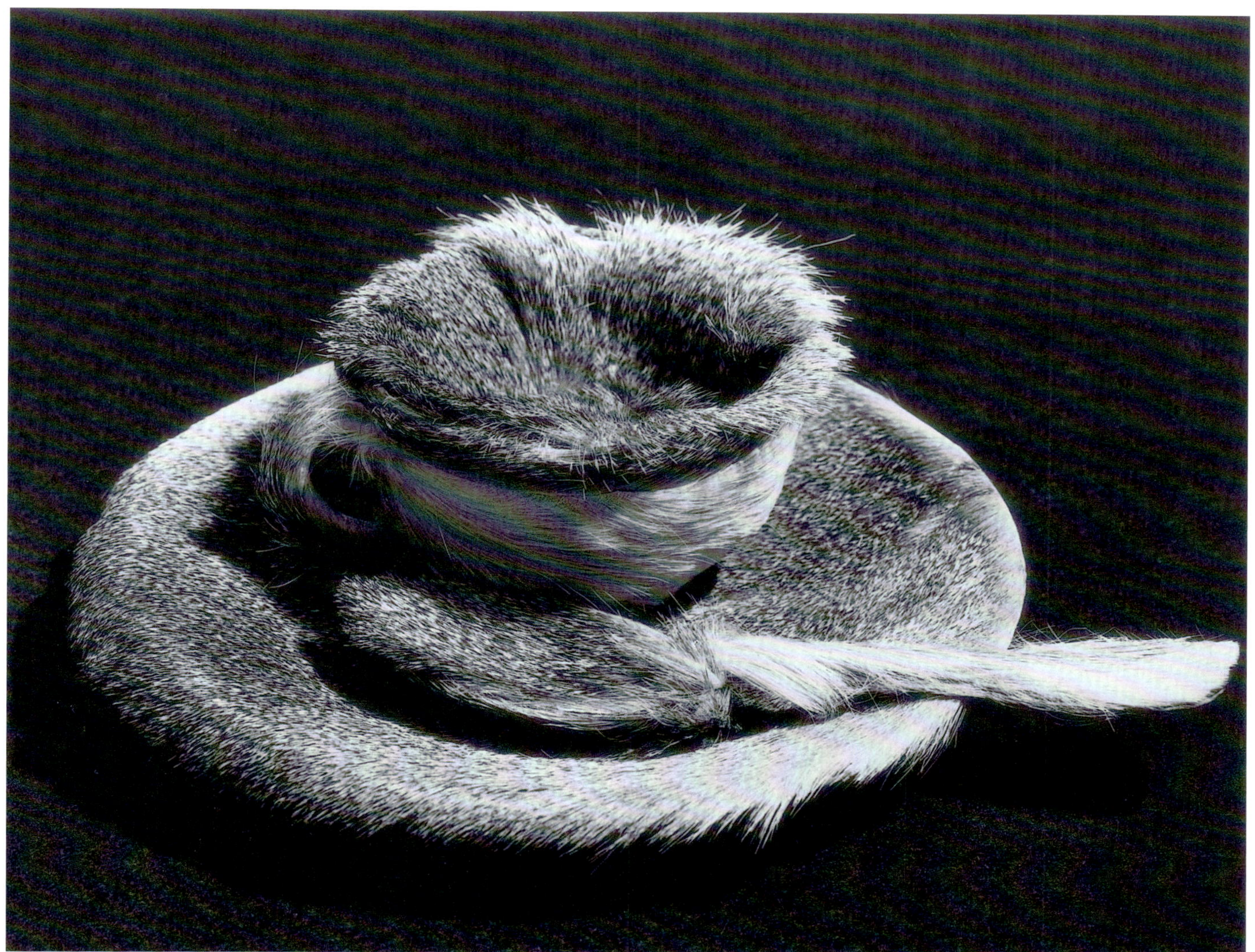

show was Meyer Oppenheim's *Luncheon in Fur* (*Le Déjeuner en fourrure*) [158], which can sum up the successive dislocations at the level of object and word that by 1936 had opened the way to object finds and manufactures on this prolific scale. It is a cup, spoon and saucer covered in fur. The fur stands between seeing and using. One sees to imagine, not as a preliminary to use. The fur eroticises; easily engendering the cup (as female) and spoon (as male), allowing imaginary acts involving stroking. Breton was responsible for the title, which combines allusions to Edouard Manet's scene of erotic encounter, *Le Déjeuner sur l'herbe* (*Luncheon on the Grass*), and to Sacher-Masoch's fictional celebration of eroticised pain *Vénus en fourrure* (*Venus in Furs*). No doubt the connotations of consumption (drinking) relate to Dalí's obsession with the edible and the imbibable (including liquids to be drunk). Once more the viewer is drawn into an imagined active participation, though one above all stimulated by touch, a sense rarely excited by Dalí in so sensual a way.

Aragon's notion 'the personality of choice', as I have indicated, places the conceptual above the material: it is the mental process of choosing that matters. More importantly still, it was the object released into the imagination (often by words) that gave the 'Surrealist object' and its predecessors 'reality'. As Nougé put it in 1930, from a Surrealist perspective, the object 'owes its existence to the action of our mind which invents it'.[68] Right from 1913 and the earliest dissemination of Picasso's sculpture-objects, the actual material presence of a work-as-object was not essential to its capacity to survive: I have mentioned already the photographs of Picasso's constructions shown actually as exhibits in London that year. Photographs were enough to make such things operational as 'poetic machines', a fact that became increasingly evident.

After its brief non-appearance in the New York Independents exhibition of 1917, Duchamp's *Fountain* functioned solely because of the photograph by Alfred Stieglitz published in the New York periodical, *The Blind Man* [300], until its first re-make in 1950.[69] Man Ray's first readymade, *The Gift*, an iron chosen in 1921 on whose ironing surface carpet tacks were glued in a row (an 'assisted readymade' therefore), was stolen from his solo exhibition of that year, and only existed thereafter in his photograph of it. It was first remade in 1949 but that was also lost and survives only as a photograph. Man Ray was to provide the image that appears on the opening page of the opening number of *La Révolution surréaliste* in December 1924. It is a photo-

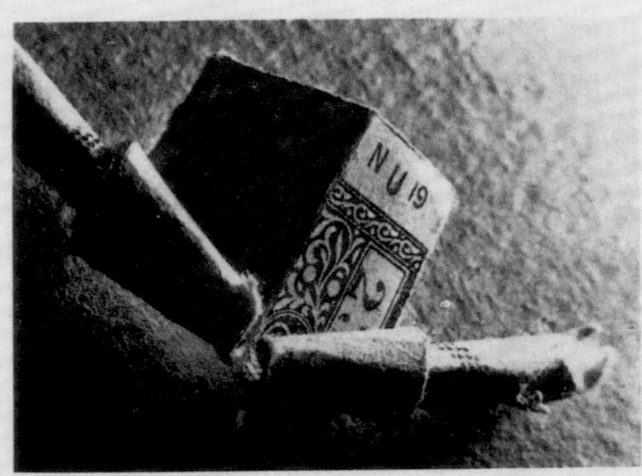

BILLET D'AUTOBUS ROULÉ " SYMÉTRIQUEMENT ", FORME TRÈS RARE D'AUTOMATISME MORPHOLOGIQUE AVEC GERMES ÉVIDENTS DE STÉRÉOTYPIE.

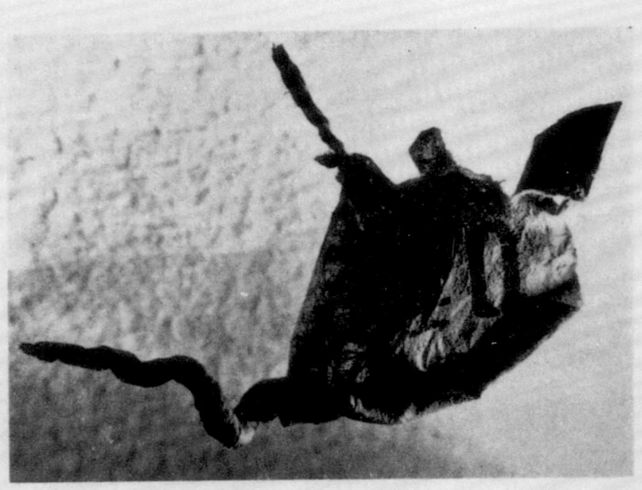

NUMÉRO D'AUTOBUS ROULÉ, TROUVÉ DANS LA POCHE DE VESTON D'UN BUREAUCRATE MOYEN (CRÉDIT LYONNAIS) ; CARACTÉRISTIQUES LES PLUS FRÉQUENTES DE " MODERN'STYLE ".

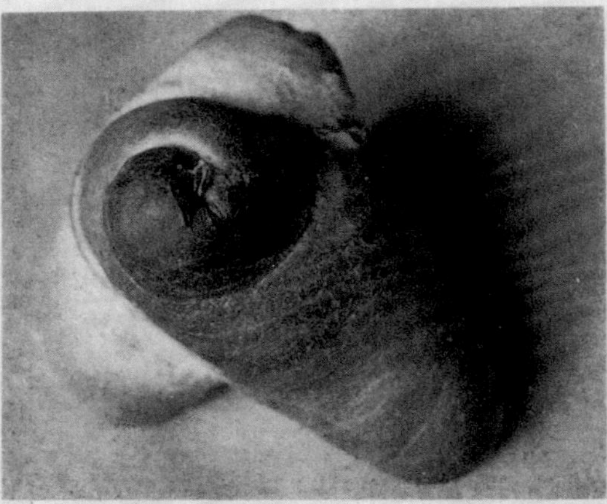

LE PAIN ORNEMENTAL ET MODERN'STYLE ÉCHAPPE A LA STÉRÉOTYPIE MOLLE

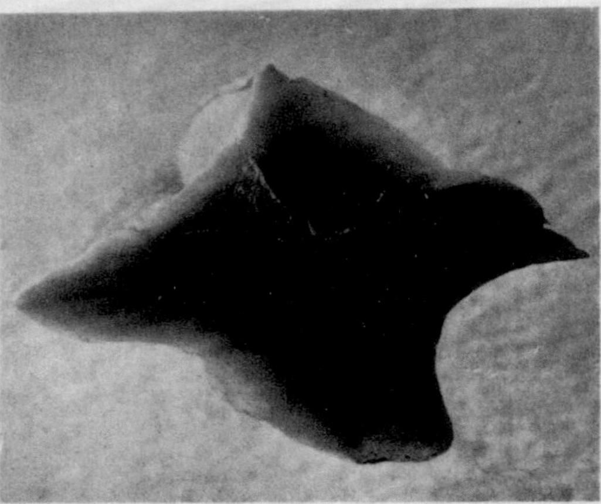

MORCEAU DE SAVON PRÉSENTANT DES FORMES AUTOMATIQUES MODERN'STYLE TROUVÉ DANS UN LAVABO.

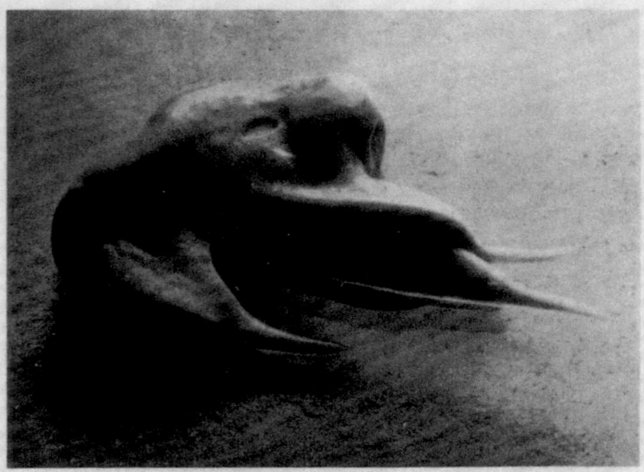

LE HASARD MORPHOLOGIQUE DU DENTRIFICE RÉPANDU N'ÉCHAPPE PAS A LA STÉRÉOTYPIE FINE ET ORNEMENTALE.

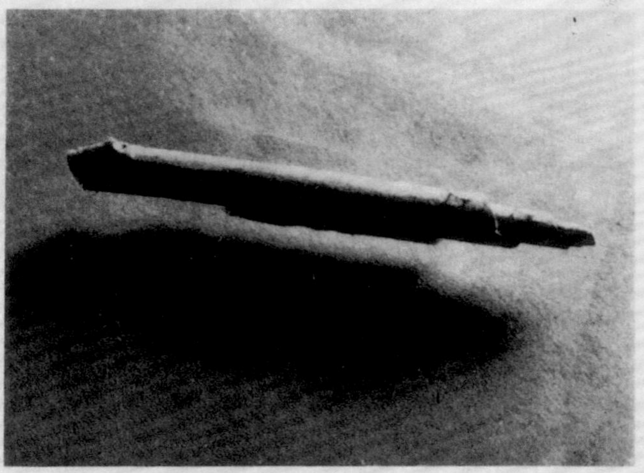

ENROULEMENT ÉLÉMENTAIRE OBTENU CHEZ UN " DÉBILE MENTAL ".

SCULPTURES INVOLONTAIRES

graph of another lost readymade, captioned here *The Enigma of Isidore Ducasse* [41]: the photograph of a sewing machine rendered darkly suggestive by concealment under a blanket bound by cords. This was photography used to reveal by concealment, the unbounded world of metaphor opened up when, in the Surrealist *Manifesto* of 1924, Breton had invoked an image 'found' by the poet Lautréamont: the meeting of an umbrella and a sewing machine on a dissecting table. Isidore Ducasse was the 'real' name that the pseudonym Lautréamont concealed.

Photography, indeed, in the hands of Man Ray and others in the Surrealist circle – notably Jacques-André Boiffard, Brassaï, Raoul Ubac and Dora Maar – was unrivalled in the exposure of the non-material, the imaginative reality of things, whether the camera was turned on objects chosen or fabricated by artists and writers or not. The very 'realism' of photography made it an especially surreal medium.[70] The objective status claimed for objects is doubled in the photograph, while the photograph's capacity to lift its object out of context and to estrange it by choice of angle, cropping, and lighting can give photography a special role in exposing the condition of the real as sign.

Nowhere was this act of dislocation more disorienting in its invitation to invent the object than in a page of photographs by the Hungarian photographer Brassaï, published above the general caption, 'Involuntary Sculptures', in *Minotaure* no. 3 (December 1933) [159]. Here it is angle and lighting that makes ordinary things strange, and they are made still stranger by the seemingly nominalist accuracy of their individual captions, added apparently by Dalí to complement his article 'On the Terrifying and Edible Beauty of Modern Style Architecture', whose opening page is opposite. Thus, one of them 'is' an 'ornamental and modern-style loaf of bread' and another 'is' a 'piece of soap presenting automatic modern-style forms found in a basin'. Photographic images of objects derail simple (if perversely phrased) nominalist titles. The object and the word are back together again, opening up a space in between for the imagination to fill. Here the realism of photography makes that space seem unreal; mostly, photography in the service of Surrealism made the unreal seem real. The Surrealist Exhibition of Objects of 1936 included photographs. One was Dora Maar's *Portrait of Ubu* [160], a print that transforms the foetus of a creature of uncertain identity into an object and, through its title, brings it back to life as a mindless monster, the heir to Alfred Jarry's stage monster with a pig's snout, 'Père Ubu'. Photography was the medium that came closest to realising the conviction expressed by Breton in 1930: 'The imagination is that which is on the way to becoming real.'[71]

Besides an object of his own, André Breton's contribution to the number of *SASDLR* that launched the 'Surrealist object' in 1931 was 'Phantom Object'. In this article, with Dalí's symbolically functioning objects in mind, he warned against choosing objects which were too 'systematically determined' and therefore functioned too efficiently as symbols. 'Latent meaning,' he counselled, should not coincide too completely with 'manifest content'.[72] When he responded to the objects in the galerie Charles Ratton in 1936, he observed that the kind of object selected, 'however finished it may be, goes back to an uninterrupted series of latencies which are not particular to it and which call for its transformation.'[73] He applied psychoanalytical language to the process of dislocation and transformation that we have followed in this account of the Cubist and 'Surrealist object' (whether photographic images or not). There is one further level of dislocation and transformation for us to encounter; it emerges if the question is asked, latent meanings for whom? Attempting to answer inevitably returns us to the viewer. The work-as-object, the readymade, the 'Surrealist object', invite the interpretative attention of subjects, viewers, who re-invent them each time they are seen. Viewers in their looking supercede the act of choosing, or imagining, or manufacture that came first. Each viewer becomes the new subject in the object, just as unstable in her or his transformations as the object itself.

159. Brassaï, *Involuntary Sculptures*, 1933. Photographs as illustrated in *Minotaure*, no. 3 (Paris, December 1933)

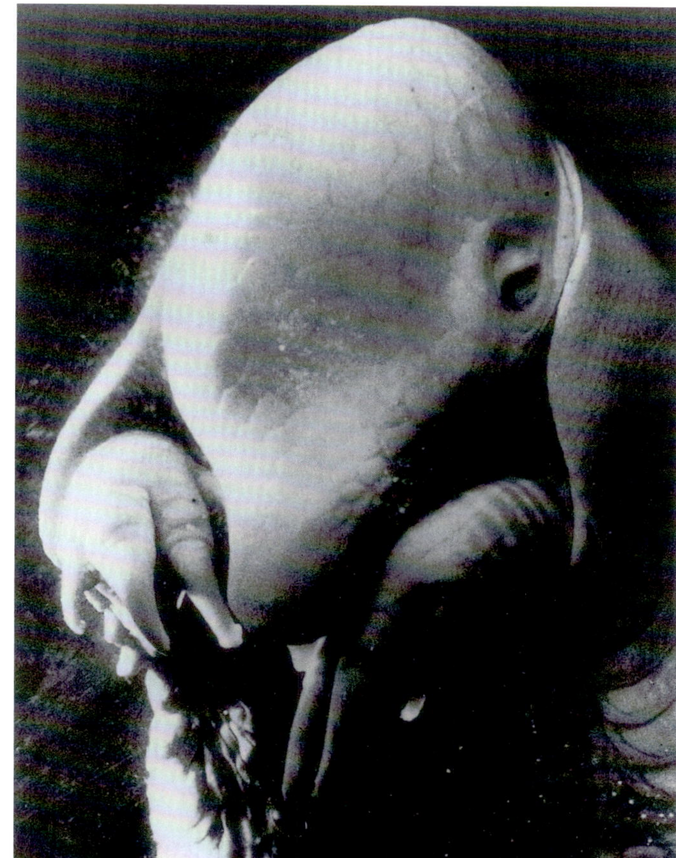

160. Dora Maar, *Portrait of Ubu*, 1936. Photograph

Two works can sum up the degree to which the normal relations between object and subject were disrupted. The first is a photograph Picasso took in 1913 of a construction which was almost immediately dismantled [161] and is only known from his photographs (he too was a photographer). It consists of a newly begun Cubist figure-painting, with newspaper arms attached so that they can fold outwards; the figure is 'playing' a real guitar which has been suspend-

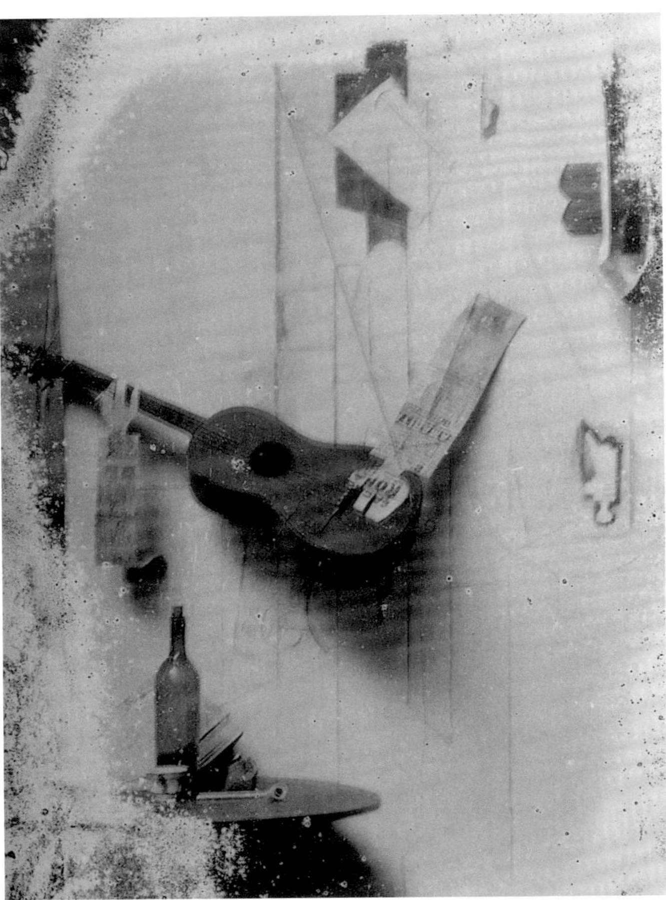

161. Pablo Picasso, *Photographic composition with 'Construction with Guitar Player'*, 1913. Photograph, original print, 11.8 × 8.7 cm. Musée Picasso, Paris

ed in front of the canvas; a real pedestal table stands in front, on which are arranged a wine-bottle, clay pipe and newspaper. As we saw in Chapter 4, this has been read by one commentator as a self-portrait: Picasso, on this reading, is the subject projected into the object, playing his guitar.[74] And yet, if this was how he imagined it, this is not how the photograph asks its viewers necessarily to imagine it. In the end, he, Picasso, is only a tentative suggestion in a provisionally phtographed construction, a subject easily displaced. The second work to consider is *The Large Glass*. One unavoidable effect of its glass support is reflection. When Duchamp was patiently realising its components, the image it reflected was his. Now, the image it reflects – the subject in the object – is each new viewer.

ART AND 'REVOLUTION'

'This world is splitting apart,' wrote Louis Aragon in 1930 . . . 'Follow the smoke that is rising, the whiplash of spectres in the world of the bourgeoisie. A flash of lightning is smouldering beneath their bowler hats. Truly there is witchcraft in the air.'[75] By the close of 1932, Aragon's commitment to the French Communist Party had separated him from Breton's Surrealist group; he had chosen political revolution. But the word 'revolution', with all its political connotations, remained a commonplace of discourse on the new in visual and verbal culture, as it had been since the beginning of the century. The Fauves at the Salon d'automne of 1905 and the Cubists at the Autumn Salons of 1911 and 1912 had both been dubbed 'revolutionaries'. Before 1914, radical modernism in France was 'revolutionary art'. In 1924 and 1930, the Surrealists made a point of incorporating the word 'revolution' in the titles of their periodicals.

Within the confined if diverse world of art, I have shown in Part Three how the modernists did indeed challenge orthodoxies and sometimes went further to challenge fundamental assumptions. Even if the institutions of culture were slow to respond to artists working in and around Surrealism, the changes wrought in French visual culture were comprehensive enough by the last years of the Third Republic to be called revolutionary: they had changed the basic criteria of critical judgement. But, as Parts One and Two show, this 'revolution' did not achieve real dominance until the mid-1930s, though the noise of it was heard from the beginning. And again, art in France through the period, whether 'revolutionary' or not, was produced in a society whose dominant liberal and conservative values were not seriously undermined, until invasion cleared the way for the new fascisized Right's revenge on the Third Republic: a 'revolution' ruthlessly directed against the one to which Aragon was committed.

It is, however, worth bringing out one consequence of the shift from artist to viewer that the modernist revolution in visual culture effected. To explore the social and political inflections of art in this period, especially modernist art, is not primarily to explore it in relation to the artists who produced it. They cannot be forgotten, but nor can those who were the first viewers of their art. The possible meanings that art could have for those viewers has to be a central concern. In a real sense, the shift from artist to viewer, is a function of a major shift that occurred between the products of capitalist industry and its consumers. As I show in Chapter 8, Aragon's 'personality of choice' is the analogue of the advertisers' realisation in the period that to choose any commodity – from a fashion item or a car to a work of art – was to make a personal statement, to confirm an individual identity by forming and activating desires.[76] When one looks at art in relation to the themes that are the concern of the second half of this book – modernity and tradition, civilisation and the 'primitive', republican and anti-republican politics – the question is both what artists could say and how far their work confirmed or challenged the values of their viewers.

PART FOUR

Representing Modernity

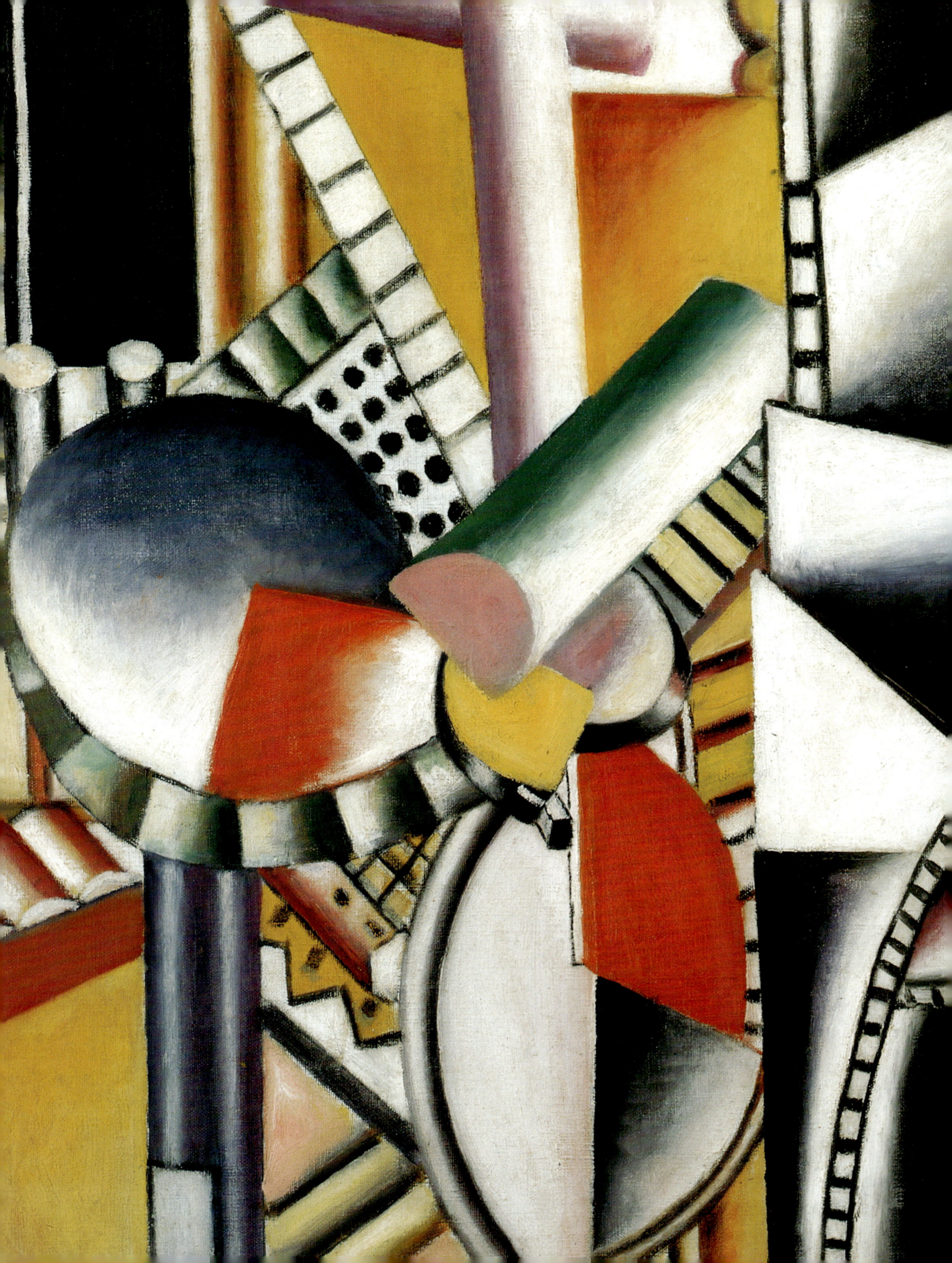

PART FOUR

Representing Modernity

INTRODUCTION

And I shall construct a hangar for my aeroplane with the fossilised bones of mammoths.

Blaise Cendrars, 1913[1]

The modern spirit prevails; this novelty for our epoch will re-establish the link with the epoch of the Greeks.

Amédée Ozenfant and Charles-Edouard Jeanneret (Le Corbusier), 1918[2]

Writing just before the 1914–18 war, Blaise Cendrars – adventurer, poet and ally of Guillaume Apollinaire – brought together prehistory and the infancy of aviation in a line from a long poem inspired by memories of the Trans-Siberian railway. The year before, in 1912, Robert Delaunay (b.1885), painter-friend of both Cendrars and Apollinaire, showed a huge canvas, *The City of Paris* at the Indépendants [162]. Delaunay used his 'simultaneous contrasts of colours' to bring together the Eiffel Tower, the roofs and the quays of Paris and the Three Graces of antiquity, which he had adapted from a reproduction of a Pompeian fresco. As the 1914–18 war neared its end, the painter Ozenfant and the painter-architect Le Corbusier (b.1887) published a pamphlet to announce a new beginning, *Après le cubisme* (After Cubism). Here they united what they called the 'modern spirit' and antiquity. Nearly a decade later, Man Ray (b.1890) photographed the Avenue de l'Observatoire in Paris with its embellishment by the academician Denys Puech (b.1854), the *Monument to François Garnier* of 1898 [163]. Above a cylindrical pedestal Garnier, a famous explorer, is surrounded by personifications of the rivers of Asia. But Man Ray's camera angle does not allow the bust of the hero to rise clear into the sky: the gimcrack rococo of the Ball Bullier dance hall and the hectoring dazzle of posters the size of buildings turn this survivor of the monumental tradition into just another item of urban clutter.

These instances make a single point: none of the themes addressed in Parts Four, Five and Six – modernity, tradition and resistance against modernity and the ideal of civilisation – can be entirely isolated from the others. To speak of or to represent things considered utterly modern did not mean that the pre-modern, the anti-modern or the traditional were necessarily set aside or even marginalised. Aviation and fossils, the Eiffel Tower and the Three Graces, modern thinking and the 'epoch of the Greeks' could all come together within the mentalities that produced 'modern' images between 1900 and 1940. And, whether separate or combined they could all be politically inflected, both by the artists that represented them and their spectators.

It remains, however, possible to address modernity as a theme across the four decades of the period, for a rhetoric of modernity was developed in words and images, a rhetoric which can at times make it seem that the modern is all that counts. Chapter 7 will address modernity as an experience, and the problems of its representation. Chapter 8 will address the questions raised by what was experienced and represented: the places and the people of modernity.

CHAPTER 7

The Experience of Modernity and the 'New Spirit'

REPRESENTING MODERN IDEAS: ABSTRACTION, SCIENCE AND BERGSONISM

In 1923, Dr René Allendy founded a 'Society for the philosophical and scientific examination of new ideas'. It brought together artists, writers and scientists of various kinds; Ozenfant, Juan Gris and Fernand Léger all delivered lectures at the Sorbonne under its auspices in 1923 and 1924. Allendy, a medical practitioner and philosopher of science, kept in touch with many in the 1920s art world. He gave support to the widely shared conviction that the syntheses offered by Cubist and post-Cubist art were part of a large-scale progressive phenomenon, embracing the new in every field, what Ozenfant and Le Corbusier, as quoted in the Introduction to Part Four, referred to as the 'new spirit'. In 1920, Ozenfant and Le Corbusier had asserted that 'after Cubism' came 'Purism', a movement that would pull together all the aspects of the modern to create a post-war synthesis. They called the periodical with which they promoted the idea between 1920 and 1925 *L'Esprit nouveau* (The New Spirit). Writing for a readership of modernist writers and artists in 1923, Allendy argued that the early twentieth century had seen a re-orientation of thinking towards the unity of synthesis. He found it in social and international institutions (Unionism and the League of Nations), and in psychology and physics. Thus, in physics, for example, he stressed the replacement of the old opposed notions of matter and energy by a single notion of matter as

Facing page. Detail of Fernand Léger, *The Propellors*, 1918 [178]

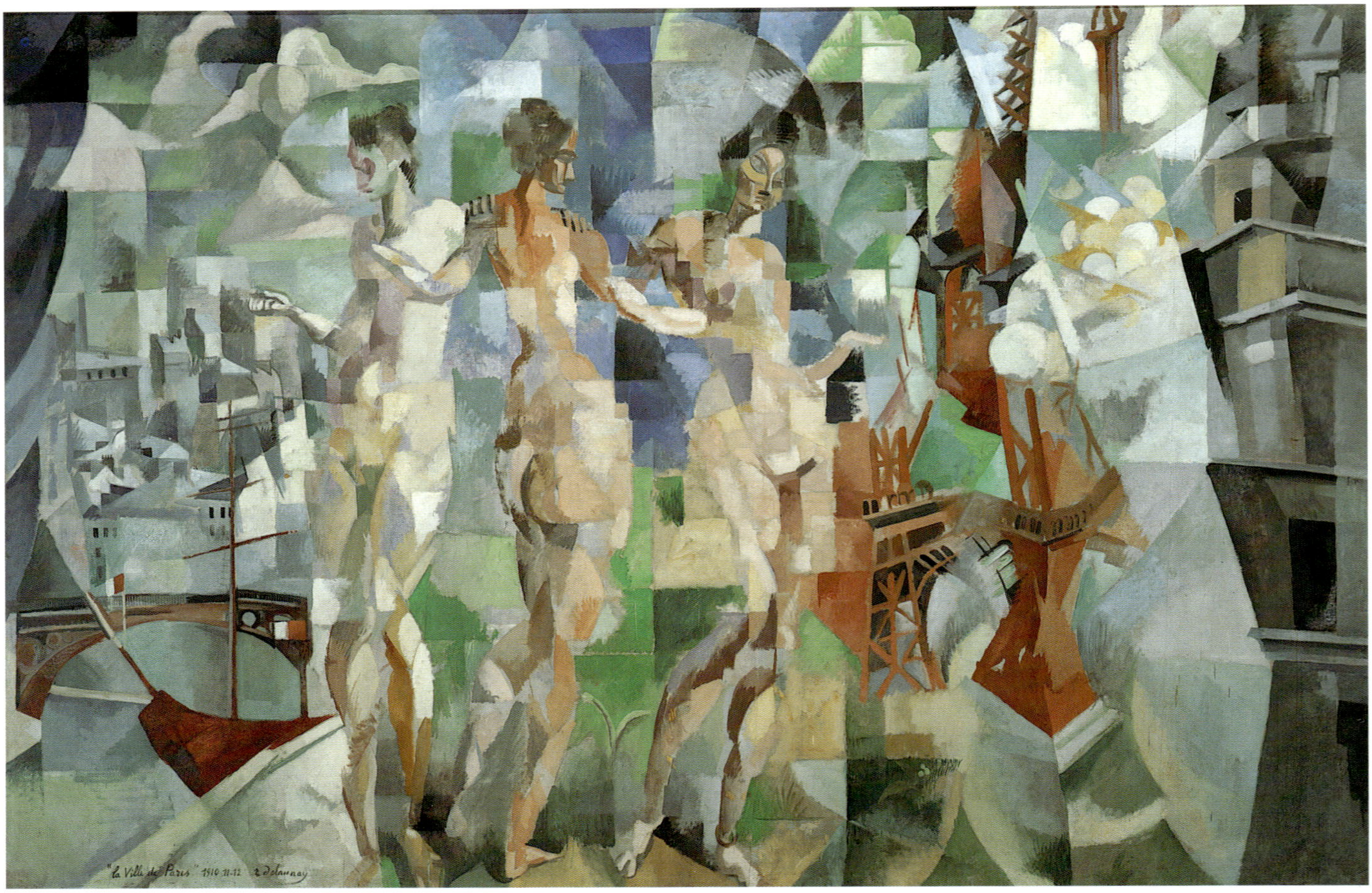

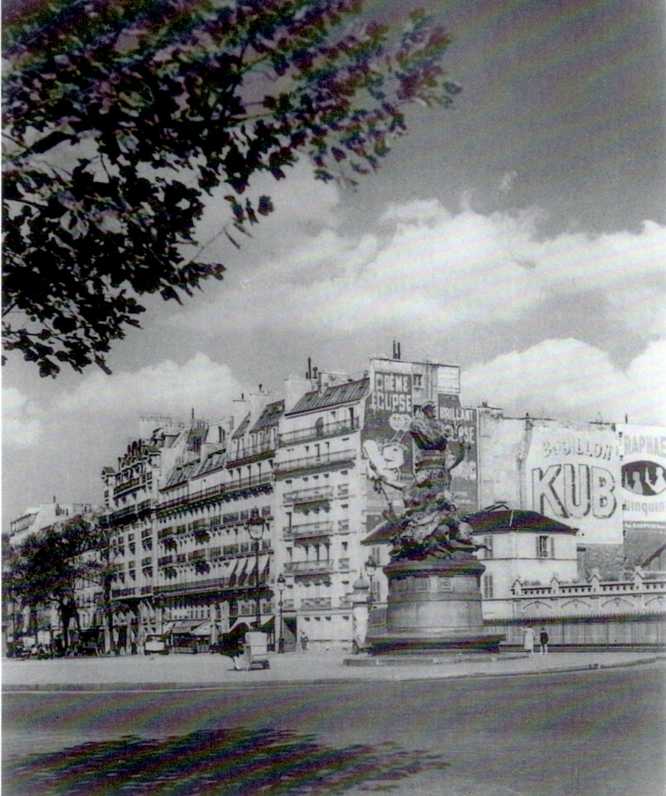

162. Robert Delaunay, *The City of Paris*, 1912. Oil on canvas, 411 × 265 cm. Musée National d'Art Moderne, Paris

163. Man Ray, *Avenue de l'Observatoire*, c.1926. Photograph

'nothing but an aspect of universal energy', and pointed to Einstein's rejection of the old separation of space and time.[1]

It was also in the early 1920s that the progressive modernist ideas of Piet Mondrian (b.1872), Theo van Doesburg (b.1883) and De Stijl began their slow, never more than shallow penetration of the Parisian post-1918 avant-garde. The first steps were made in 1920, shortly after Mondrian's return to Paris, with the publication of two short books by the Cubists' dealer, Léonce Rosenberg: Van Doesburg's *Classique – Baroque – Moderne* and Mondrian's *Le Néo-Plasticisme*. Both argued an evolutionary case for the non-figurative as modernity in art. Throughout *Le Néo-Plasticisme* Mondrian opposes the 'new spirit' to the 'old mentality', identifying the new with an engagement with the relations between forms (the 'plastic') and the old with an engagement in forms as such (the 'morphoplastic'). Art rooted in the observation of nature is old, because it depends on natural forms; art concerned with relationships replaces natural forms with resolved abstract tensions and thus reveals 'the birth of the new'. Music, for Mondrian, was an especially powerful 'obstacle to the new spirit', because of its

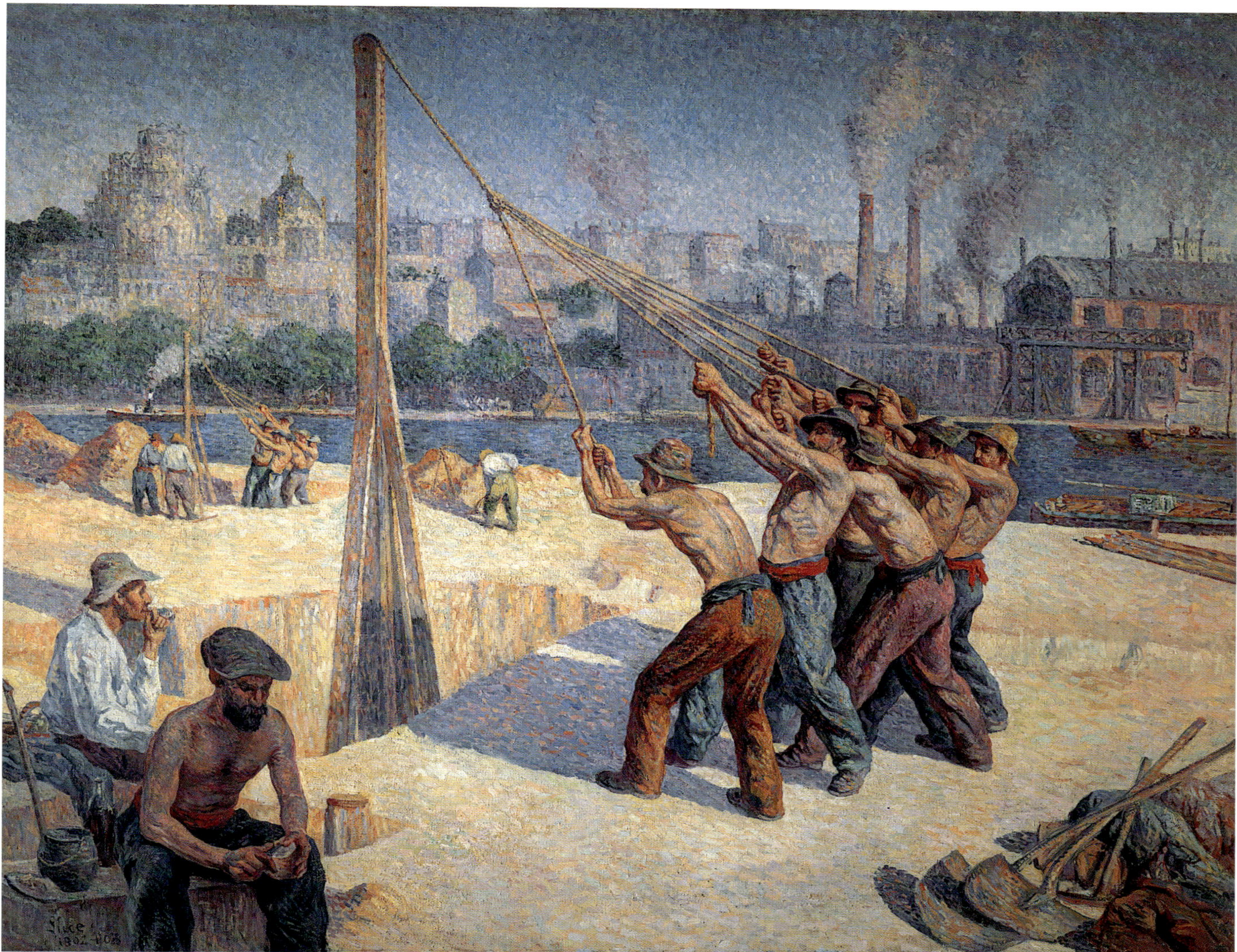

164. Maximilien Luce, *The Stone Workers, Quai de la Seine at Billancourt*. 1902–3. Oil on canvas, 153 × 195 cm. Musée d'Orsay, Paris

appeal to 'natural' emotion, but he saw hope in jazz, which he first encountered in Holland around 1916, and about which he would continue to enthuse through the 1930s. 'In the midst of traditional music . . . ,' he writes, 'there appears, perhaps somewhat brutally, the *jazz band*, which dares abrupt demolitions of melody and dry, unfamiliar, strange noises that oppose rounded sound . . .'.[2] By 1930, he was writing that the Neo-Plastic art of relationships created 'free rhythm' as opposed to 'natural rhythm', some idea of which was to be grasped 'by listening to "American jazz" '.[3]

For both the Purists and Mondrian the 'new spirit', however abstract its conception, raised no representational problem for the artist. Painters, sculptors or architects either worked within the 'new spirit' or not: their work presented rather than *re*presented it. What this entailed in Mondrian's case was the notion of parallel evolutions in modern thinking and art, both moving away from natural forms towards abstract relationships in the quest for the 'universal'. What this entailed in the Purists' case allowed a more explicit relationship between art and not only modern thinking but modern things (which will be explored later in this chapter), but not a relationship that required the representation of the modern or modern ideas as such. Before 1914, many modernists were, however, concerned with representing the modern as such; they all came up against, therefore, the problem of how not simply to *be* modern, but to paint the modern. And at its most fundamental the problem was how to find modern means for the representation of modern ways of thinking.

This was a problem, as we shall see, that concerned artists associated with Cubism. Not surprisingly, it concerned a wide range of non-Cubist artists too. Signac's Neo-Impressionism was, of course, a 'scientific' and therefore a modern means of representing what were sometimes explicitly modern subjects, in the case of Maximilien Luce (b.1858) often urban and industrial [164]. But non-independents with 'official' endorsement tackled the problem too, and the Cubists' attempts to develop modern means for representing modern things and ways of thinking are tellingly illuminated by considering such a case: that of Albert Besnard (b.1849) as painter in the service of science.

When, in 1914, the defender and early historian of the

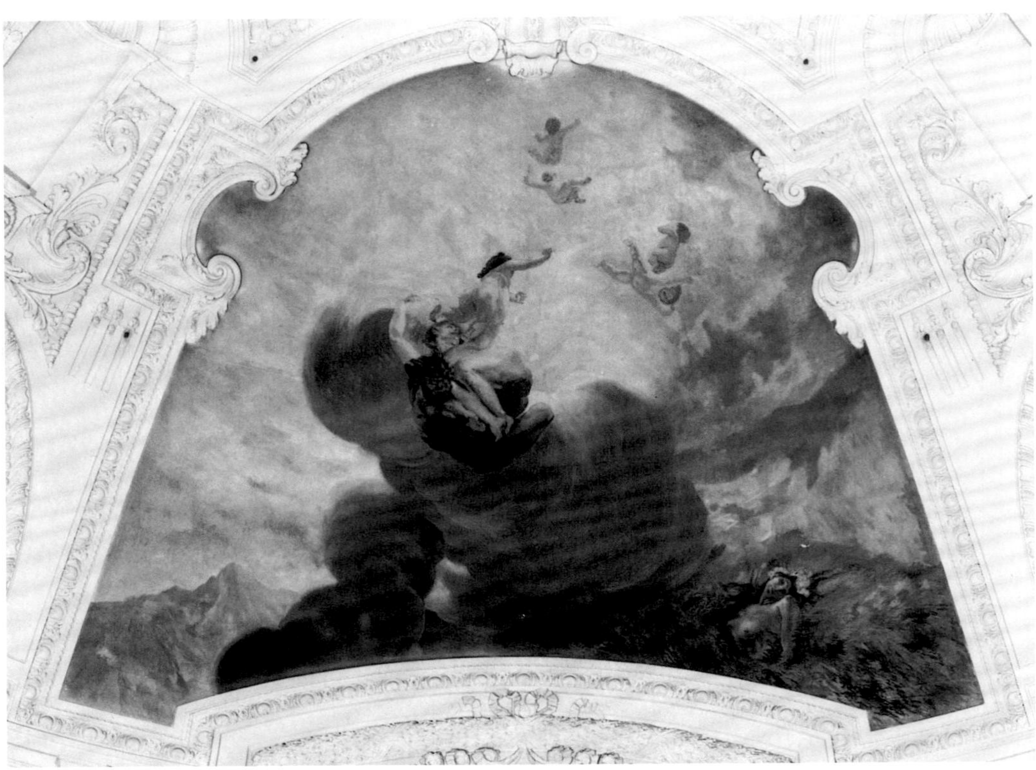

165. Albert Besnard, *Matter*, 1904–7. Oil on canvas fixed to the wall, 60 m². Panel for the dome of the Petit Palais, Paris

166. Opposite. Albert Besnard, *The Rebirth of Life in Death*, 1896. Chemistry School Lecture-Theatre, now the Amphithéâtre de Gestion-Oury, Sorbonne

Impressionists Camille Mauclair published a monograph on Besnard, he devoted a chapter to 'Scientific Symbolism in M. Besnard's decorations'. It was a topic which had already been taken up by Mauclair's friend Paul Adam at the turn of 1911–12. Both celebrated modernity in evolutionary terms, but in evolutionary terms very different from Mondrian's with his 'abstract' notion of the 'new spirit'. Where Mondrian would give primacy to philosophy, following Hegel, Mauclair singled out science alongside art. Science, for him, as for many progressives, was the new religion, whose 'palaces', the Universities, were 'the temples of a new belief'. This new belief, embracing the conclusions of all the sciences ranging from physics to organic chemistry and biology, he summed up with the terms 'transformism' and 'creative evolution'. 'If,' he asked, 'the idea of redemption has found thousands of images for its representation, why should not the idea of transformism, of creative evolution, find as many?'[4] Like Adam, he picked out such images in the murals Besnard had painted for two of the Sorbonne's science faculties, for the ceiling of the Salon des sciences in the Hôtel de Ville and in one of the panels he had painted for the dome of the Petit Palais, *Matter* [165, 166]. The panels for the Petit Palais were commissioned in 1904; *Matter* was shown at the Salon de la Nationale in 1907, with another panel, *Thought*.

Mauclair reads *Matter* as an allegory of liberation from the material. A nude, half-buried in a fruitful earth, watches her own struggle against a satyr, 'symbol of the soul . . . of Matter', who tries to drag her downwards. She sees herself free of the satyr, gesturing upwards after the weightless, soaring forms of infants. Traditional allegorical figures are used to convey a new progressive idealism.[5] For Mauclair, as for Adam, however, Besnard's most effective representation of the belief in 'transformism' as a truth substantiated by the sciences is his mural, *The Rebirth of Life in Death* (*Vie renaissant de la mort*), painted for the Sorbonne's chemistry lecture theatre in 1896 [166]. The central image here is a woman at the moment of death. She lies, head downwards, sprawled on her back, the blue-green of her flesh signalling the immanence of decay. The sun above burns a scorching gold. It is, comments Mauclair, a sun which will 'create from this dead flesh, atomic fermentation'. A child sucks at her breast and the milk overflows into the grass, where the serpent of Genesis lurks, 'symbol of hidden, omnipresent life'. On the right, the child becomes, we need Mauclair to tell us, Adam, who lifts Eve up to pick fruit from a tree in an Eden through which flows a river. Nature here is softly abundant under a warm light. On the left, the river burns among infernal volcanoes in a glow of unearthly pinks beneath a sky weighed down by heavy greys and greens. 'Water and Fire unite, a mass of human forms, corpses . . . calcified matter . . . on the point of new metamorphoses'. Mauclair sums up: 'The essential ideas of science are here represented by exact, timeless images. The allusion to Genesis . . . is directly tied to the scientific principle hidden beneath this legend. There is no need for any allegorical accessory, any supernatural figure.'[6]

This odd conjunction of science and images of biblical, organic and geological genesis (one thinks of Cendrars' aircraft hangar constructed from mammoth bones) can be examined by attending to those key terms: 'transformism' and 'creative evolution'. Paul Adam offers another juxtaposition, aligning Besnard's painting with the ideas of the most influential philosopher in France between the 1890s and the 1920s, Henri Bergson. It is this that Mauclair builds on, clearly with Besnard's support. The year of the exhibition of

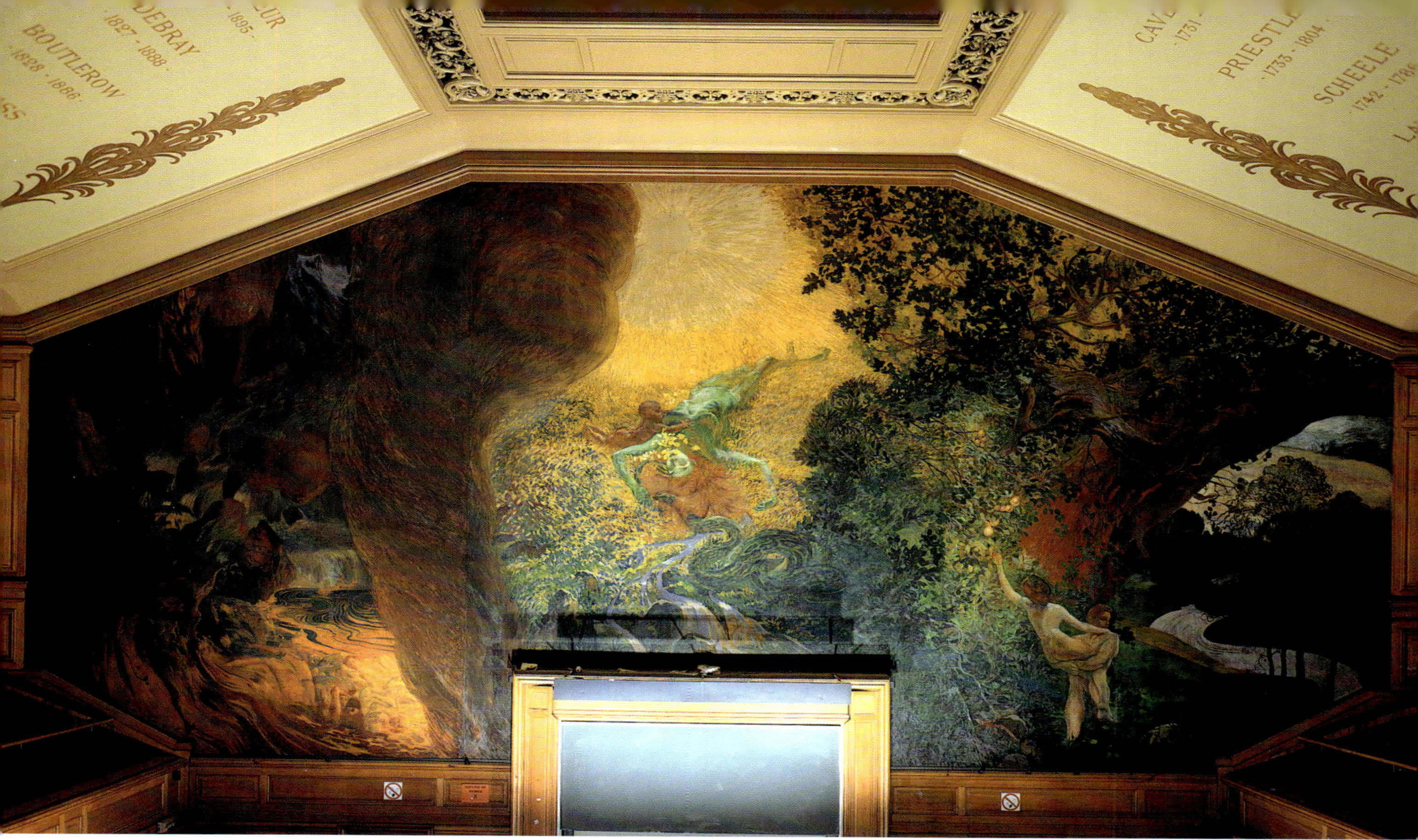

Matter, 1907, was also the year when Bergson's major book, *L'Evolution créatrice* (Creative Evolution), was published; the painting's theme draws on the earlier book, *Matière et mémoire* (Matter and Memory) of 1896. In the 1900s, Bergson gave philosophical weight to the late nineteenth-century Symbolist reaction against the positivism of Auguste Comte, and especially against the belief that reality can only be grasped by logical reasoning based on observation and measurement. To the idea of reality understood in terms of what is seen and is therefore quantifiable, Bergson opposed the idea of an inner essence grasped only in the complexity and flux of individual experience. That essence he called 'la durée' ('duration'), for where observation could reduce spatial relations to measured quantities, experience at its most intense and profound was, he argued, temporal, engaging memory and anticipation so that past, present and future flow together. Duration was experienced in the material world, but, in its perpetual motion, was freed from the material, as Besnard's nude in the Petit Palais cupola is freed from the satyr, her image represented three times as if moving in a psychological time dimension. Adam ends his analysis by quoting at length both from Bergson and from a major article of 1910 which had adapted Bergson's theory of creative evolution to the unquantifiable time and space of Symbolist poetry, the literary critic Tancrède de Visan's 'M. Bergson's Philosophy and Contemporary Lyricism'.[7] It is clear that if Bergson used science, most obviously the biological theory of evolution, to underpin his anti-positivist argument, Besnard used allegories of Bergsonian 'creative evolution' to represent what for him was the thrust of modern scientific thought: beyond positivism.

The Salon Cubists were deeply involved with Bergson's ideas.[8] Mark Antliff has shown how pervasive Bergson's influence on them was and has brought out the significance of de Visan's contribution.[9] Gleizes' and Metzinger's writing, including their *Du Cubisme* of 1912, is infused with Bergsonism. So is the writing of poets associated with the Abbaye de Créteil around 1907 and the Cubists' meetings at Puteaux in 1911–12, for instance, Alexandre Mercereau, Henri-Martin Barzun and Jules Romains. Others have shown the relevance of Bergson's emphasis on time and movement to the ideas of the Italian Futurists, especially as they were expressed in 1912–13 in Umberto Boccioni's French texts on painting and sculpture.[10] Delaunay's adaptation of the quasi-scientific colour theory of Chevreul and Rood to the faceted surfaces of 'hermetic Cubism' was, he asserted in 1913, directed to revealing through optical movement 'the vital movement of the *world*', a deeply Bergsonian aim.[11]

Such adaptations of Bergson's theory of creative evolution were, in the consistent anti-positivism they shared with de Visan, Besnard, Mauclair and Adam, at once for and against modernity as it was understood in the period. This kind of Bergsonism led to a stress on two factors in almost all representations of modernity by modernists before 1914. First, they focused on modernity as an *experience*, an experience which was the more modern the more it was dynamic and temporal. Second, the means of representation themselves signified modernity if they could seem to penetrate beyond factual observation (the measurable) and draw attention to time. Moreover, it needs to be stressed that the Bergsonian critique did not necessarily imply a rejection of the material progress that positivist science had made possible. Bergson recognised the role of observation and reason in the sphere of the practical (from medicine to engineering); his argument was geared to bringing out the inadequacy of observation and reason in the pursuit of deeper understanding.

Besnard, as we have seen, allegorised science in terms of Bergsonian creative evolution both in *Matter* and in *The Rebirth of Life in Death*. Adam's invocation of Bergson, however, is instigated not by the painter's allegories but by his portraits. For him, Bes nard's use of colour and brushwork makes everything, even in his portraits, seem 'in flux, in the process of appearing'.[12] The same had been claimed by Mauclair for Monet's later Impressionism, and given similarly metaphysical implications. The modern (Bergsonian) representation of experience in its temporal dimension was as much a question of the 'how' as the 'what', and this was more obviously so of Salon Cubist painting. The year Besnard's *Matter* was installed in the dome of the Petit Palais, 1911, Le Fauconnier's *Abundance* [26] was one of the stars in the inaugural Salon showing of Cubism in 'Salle 41' at the Indépendants. Le Fauconnier, like Besnard, allegorises creative evolution, echoing a prose poem published by Mercereau earlier in the year, *Paroles devant la vie*. He places a mother and her child in a setting of symbols of the evolutionary role of humanity, as cultivators and labourers on land and water.[13] But it was more in the appropriation of Cézannian faceting to the rhythmic articulation of the picture surface than in the modernisation of the traditional allegory of abundance that the work laid claim to modernity of vision. Mother, child, fruit and setting are caught up in unbroken sequences of angular planes, pulling them together to produce a pictorial analogy for the durational continuity of experience.

At the Salon d'automne of 1911, such a meaning could be attributed to Cubist faceting without the help of allegory, for instance in Gleizes's *Portrait of Jacques Nayral* or even Metzinger's less obviously mobile surfaces in *Tea-time* [29, 95]. And Gleizes (b.1881) and Metzinger (b.1883) explicitly connected Cubist techniques to the representation of Bergsonian duration in their *Du Cubisme* a year later, writing of 'the expression of notions of depth, density, and duration, considered inexpressible', by means of 'a complex rhythm' and 'a veritable fusion of objects'.[14] For them multiple perspective (clearly a factor in *Tea-time*) was a durational technique. They write of moving 'around an object to seize several successive aspects' and then, in 'a single image' reconstituting the object 'in duration'.[15] Furthermore, Linda Henderson has shown how the anti-positivist appeal to the complexity of durational experience in *Du Cubisme* is made using concepts drawn not only from Bergson but from the new non-Euclidean geometry that was attracting attention in France during the 1900s. This originated above all through the widely read books of a remarkable scientific populariser, Henri Poincaré.[16] The names of nineteenth-century mathematicians – Lobachevsky, Boljai and Riemann – were circulated by Poincaré and reappear together or separately in texts by Apollinaire or Mercereau or Gleizes and Metzinger between 1911 and 1914. They offered alternative geometries to Euclid's, where in curved spaces his fifth postulate – that only one parallel to a given line can be drawn through a given point – did not hold. This was Poincaré's evidence for his argument in *La Science et l'hypothèse* (1902) that the postulates of Euclidean geometry were merely conventions, not *a priori* truths, and that a fundamental distinction was to be drawn between the intellectually constructed spaces of geometry and the physically and psychologically known spaces of experience. Geometric space, said Poincaré, was continuous, infinite and three-dimensional. 'Perceptual' space was made up of three component spaces – visual, tactile and motor: it was heterogeneous and not necessarily three-dimensional at all.

Such thinking could seem to give new scientific credibility to the Bergsonian accent on the complexities of experience as distinct from the abstract simplifications of reasoning. It is not surprising, therefore, to find it regurgitated in *Du Cubisme*. 'To establish pictorial space,' Gleizes and Metzinger write, 'we must have recourse to tactile and motor sensations, indeed to all our faculties'.[17] By being concerned with perceptual rather than geometric space, painting is, in Bergsonian terms, concerned with movement through time as well as space: duration. Given the stress on the direct experience of the work of art right across modernist practice from 1900, such conjunctions of the new mathematics and Bergsonian thinking could appeal to those who were not Cubists too. By the time Matisse wrote his 'Notes on Painting' in 1908, he was well aware of Bergson.[18] In 1916, as he developed his own quasi-Cubist pictorial spaces, he wrote to Derain that he was reading *La Science et l'hypothèse*, singling out one of Poincaré's most obviously Bergsonian hypotheses: that 'movement exists only in the destruction and construction of matter'.[19]

In the context of Cubism, there was one further concept that seemed to bring together new mathematical thinking with Bergsonian anti-positivism in a way relevant to pictorial representation, the fourth dimension. In 1912, Apollinaire, Gleizes and Metzinger all suggested the presence of a fourth dimension in Cubist painting. Again it was especially Poincaré who was responsible for its dissemination in France. By 1911–12, however, it had given rise to what was virtually a popular science-fiction genre: the imagining of non-three-dimensional worlds, or of people who can experience four-dimensions or only two.[20] In 1912 Gaston de Pawlowski, editor of the newspaper *Comoedia*, published a Wellsian fantasy, *Voyage au pays de la quatrième dimension* (Journey to the Land of the Fourth Dimension). He serialised it on the front page of *Comoedia* that year, and the third episode actually appeared alongside a reproduction of a Metzinger. Typically, Pawlowski appropriated the idea of a spatial dimension to be projected beyond the third (as the third is from the second) in order to reveal the limitations of a positivist dependence on material observation: to imagine the possibility of seeing beyond appearances. He conceived the fourth dimension in Platonic terms as 'a manner of envisaging things in their eternal and immutable aspect'.[21] It was an entirely abstract intellectual dimension, freed from space and time: a Bergsonian dimension where 'one finds oneself blended with the entire universe, with so-called future events, as with so-called past events'.[22] The question raised by such ethereal notions was, of course, simple: if the fourth dimension was beyond the range of normal optical vision, how could it be represented? On offer were complex diagrams developed from the work of an Englishman, Charles Howard Hinton, which used superimposed cubes and axonometric projection, each cube denoting a stage in the passage of a four-dimensional figure through three-dimensions. In France, E. Jouffret had published books in 1903 and 1906 which used non-Euclidean geometry and complex versions of perspective ('perspective cavalière') to go beyond Hinton in what was called hyperspace philosophy.[23]

The fourth dimension lends a certain intellectual exoticism to the fragmentary theory of Cubism emergent in 1911–12: the connection is announced, but never explained. It is therefore unhelpful to attempt to analyse any work related to Cubism as an explicit representation of the fourth dimension. Linda Henderson has pulled together the evidence for knowledge both of non-Euclidean geometry and of hyperspace philosophy in the milieux of Picasso and the Salon Cubists, demonstrating the key role of an insurance actuary Maurice Princet, who frequented the cafés and studios of Montmartre, in introducing them to Poincaré's ideas. It has also been established that Gris, Metzinger, Diego Rivera and Gino Severini actively searched for ways of painting four-dimensionally in 1916–17 (though what this entailed remains obscure), and striking similarities have been noted between the faceted structures of Braque's and Picasso's Cubist work around 1910 and Jouffret's 'perspective cavalière' (though without any necessary causal connection).[24] But whether or not the four-dimensional can actually be demonstrated in Cubist painting, the significance of a notion that was so widely circulated in France at the moment of Cubism's emergence into the public eye and that was immediately linked to it should not be underestimated. For many of those who found modernity in Cubist art, that modernity was tied up in a quasi-scientific, quasi-philosophical view of the world which, as we have seen, went beyond observation and logic, so that in fact a major attraction of the notion of a fourth dimension was its very resistance to representation. One artist who was unequivocally a dabbler in hyperspace philosophy in 1912–15 was Marcel Duchamp (b.1887); Duchamp exploits Poincaré's hypotheses and cites Jouffret in the notes of the *Green Box*. His series of 1912 paintings on the theme of *The Bride* [301] seem to have involved the idea of the fourth dimension (he may have intended to show her passage as a four-dimensional figure through our three-dimensions), and the impossibility of its pictorial representation was certainly one factor in Duchamp's decision finally to reject 'retinal' for a conceptual art.

All-over faceting plus multiple perspectives, which brought time into the space of the image and suggested the possibility of a fourth dimension beyond perception, gave modernity of vision to Cubist painting; things were represented in terms that themselves signified modernity. Moreover, despite Picasso's resistance to philosophical analyses of his work, many of the more sympathetic viewers of his and Braque's Cubism would have thought of them as modern in this sense. But such means of representation were developed in the ancient medium of oil painting and could be modern without representing either modern subjects or specifically modern experiences, as was certainly the case in Metzinger's *Tea-time* or in Picasso's and Braque's figure paintings and still-lifes. In the next section my topic will be the representation of specifically modern subjects and experiences, and my starting point will be the durability of oil painting as the favoured 'artistic' medium for their representation.

REPRESENTING MODERN EXPERIENCE: PHOTOGRAPHY AND PAINTING, FUTURISTS AND SIMULTANISTS

Cubist faceting imposed interpenetrative movement upon often static subjects; multiple perspective did the same by suggesting the movement of the artist around a subject. In 1910, the *Technical Manifesto of Futurist Painting*, published both in French and Italian, announced the Futurists' intention to paint the 'dynamic sensation itself' in a world in which 'everything moves, is in flux.'[25] Like the French Bergsonists, they believed dynamism to be a property of all experience, but one of their strategies in its representation was to be the painting of things in motion, and here they remarked that the phenomenon of the after-image could imprint the image of a moving horse upon the cheek of a woman and multiply the number of its legs. By 1912, among the Futurists who showed at the galerie Bernheim-Jeune's exhibition of Futurist painting, Giacomo Balla was especially involved in the representation of physical motion by the multiplication of still images, and in 1911–12 one of the Salon Cubists, Marcel Duchamp, took it up too. Among his first attempts was *Sad Young Man on a Train* [167] painted in December 1911; the most resolved was *Nude Descending a Staircase, No.2* of early 1912 [78]. When, in 1912, Gleizes and Metzinger excluded *Nude Descending* from the Cubist showing at the Indépendants, one reason was almost certainly the echoes it carried of Futurist dynamism; the Bernheim-Jeune exhibition had opened only a month before, in February 1912, as a direct challenge to Cubist avant-garde leadership.

Balla and Duchamp shared a common source, chronophotography. This was one of several advances in the application of photography to science at the end of the nineteenth century. Its inventor was a leading French physiologist, Etienne-Jules Marey, who combined a camera with the revolving magazine of a repeating pistol to produce his photographic-gun in 1882. This Marey adapted to develop a fixed-plate chronophotographic camera, which used a revolving slotted-disc shutter placed first between the photographic plate and the lens and then in front of the lens, so that ten distinct images of a subject in movement shot in one second could appear on a single plate, i.e. in a single continuous image of motion [168]. During the 1880s he refined the apparatus to produce one-hundred images per second. The dematerialisation of Duchamp's figures in motion, the way their dissolution into multiple images renders them transparent, gives them an obvious chronophotographic aspect – more so than Balla's work, because of the monochrome palette – though they recall Marey's earlier chronophotographs, before he had resolved the problem of overlappings between images and the confusion they caused. A further factor in Gleizes and Metzinger's unease when confronted with *Nude Descending* would have been this connection (which they cannot have missed), for it lent Duchamp's

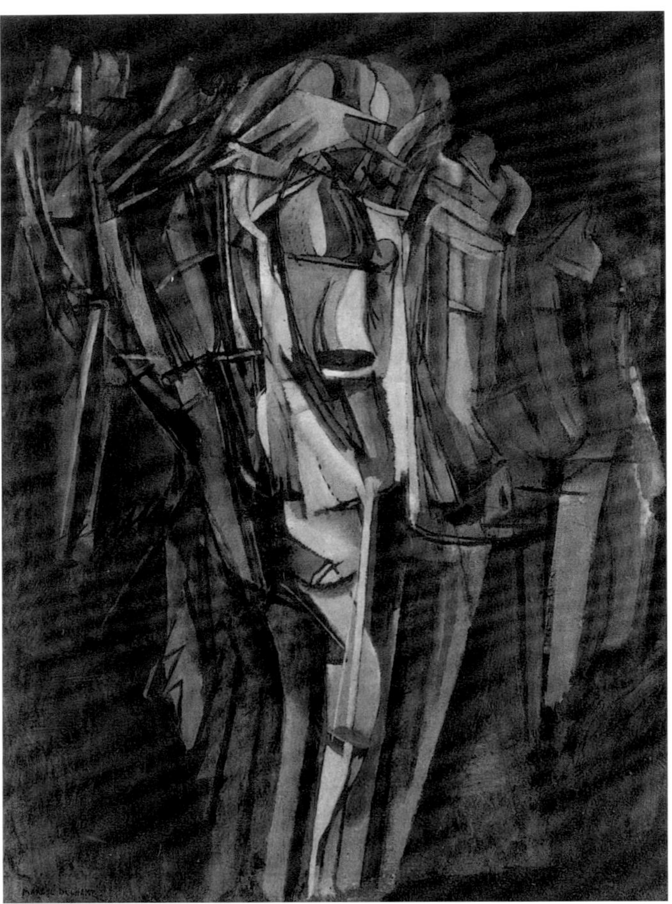

167. Marcel Duchamp, *Sad Young Man on a Train*, 1911–1912. Oil on cardboard, 100 × 73 cm. The Solomon R. Guggenheim Foundation, New York, Peggy Guggenheim Collection, Venice, 1976

painting the look not of science in the service of Bergsonian 'transformism', but of science at its most bluntly positivist. Marey had developed chronophotography as a precision tool for the recording of motion. With the results of dissection, it supplied the empirical evidence required for his investigation of the relationship between physiological structure and different kinds of bodily movement. Chronophotography, like other photographic techniques that extended vision beyond the normal capacities of the eye (microphotography or astronomical photography), produced documents of record, designed to allow analysis based on measurement. Later Duchamp would stress the diagrammatic character of *Nude Descending*. Marey's own development of chronophotographic technique entailed dressing his moving subjects in dark clothing and marking their joints with shiny buttons connected with metal bands in order to produce a clear white-on-black image, a photographic record given diagrammatic clarity [168]; the aim of chronophotography was to ease the translation of movements into diagrams.[26]

And yet, Duchamp's appropriation of photography actually brings out the distance between scientific photography in the period 1900–14 and ambitious modern painting, including that of Gleizes and Metzinger, for his representation of movement can never be reduced simply to a diagrammatic record and no more. It is significant that Duchamp used chronophotography in its earlier, less-easily legible form. In *Sad Young Man on a Train* he creates a highly suggestive image of a figure carried along by the movement of the train, and does so by using the overlappings that Marey had found too confusing. Not only is the figure dematerialised, but in its dematerialisation a mood is suggested with the title as trigger, the emotional state of sadness. The work becomes not an objective record but a subjective evocation, and its subject is actually Duchamp himself: he is the young man, represented in memory ruminatively smoking a pipe, on the train between Rouen and Paris. *Nude Descending* is closely related to a drawing intended as an illustration of a poem, 'Encore à cet astre' ('Once more to that star') by the second-generation Symbolist Jules Laforgue, and the 'pervasive melancholy' of Laforgue has been found by commentators in the painting, giving it a 'mood' dimension too.[27] Duchamp uses chronophotography in its most suggestive, transparent form to rob bodies of the bodily, and so to open them in representation to kinds of response that are highly subjective. Given his wry humour, the irony of adapting a means of objective documentation to such unquantifiable subjective ends must have added to the attraction of the technique. This was certainly not art submitting to photography's new status as 'the true retina of science' (postitivist science, that is).[28] Indeed before 1914, modernist art altogether, whether Cubist or not, defined itself against the condition of photography as 'objective' surrogate of the retina, and it did not

168. Etienne-Jules Marey, *Jump from a Height with Knees Straight*, from the series of chronolithographs entitled 'Analysis of the Jump', 1884

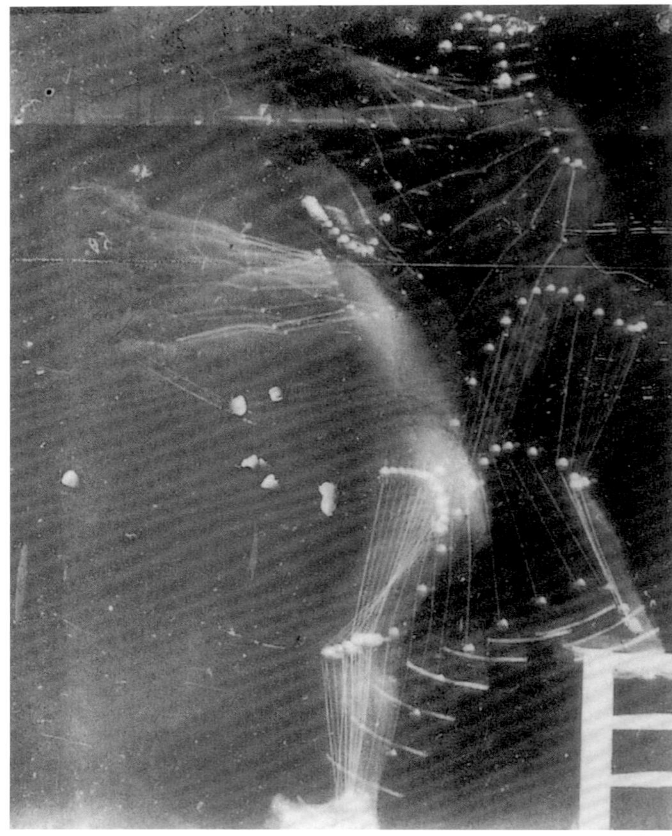

do so only in relation to scientific photography.

Between the 1880s and 1914, photography began to develop its reputation as the true retina of serious observers of modern society. The aura of authenticity that went with its supposed objectivity gave it a special role in providing a modern record of progress, and it was used as such alongside displays of graphs and other diagrams to demonstrate advances in education and hygiene in the progressive Third Republic at the Universal Exhibitions of 1889 and 1900. That role as the instrument of record spread to include everything from the accumulation of evidence in support of social reform (the magnesium flash allowed photography of lives in the darkest spaces) to the collection of snaps of family holidays and events by those in the middle classes who could afford the new portable box cameras with pliable celluloid films made available around 1900. And the scope of its dissemination expanded to include the thousands of purchasers of postcards from 1901, and the mass readerships of newspapers and illustrated magazines with the introduction into the French press of half-tone mechanical reproduction from 1902. Painters were quick to exploit photography as an instrument of record, including many modernists. Bonnard used photography as well as sketching en route to paintings from the early 1890s. Picasso photographed himself, his friends, motifs and work in the studio, beginning around 1908 [54, 71].[29] Indeed, the best remembered photographic recorder of Paris in the first three decades of the century, Eugène Atget (1857–1927), set up as a photographer in 1898

169. Eugène Atget, *Au Tambour*, 1908. Photograph. Caisse nationale des Monuments historiques et des Sites, Paris

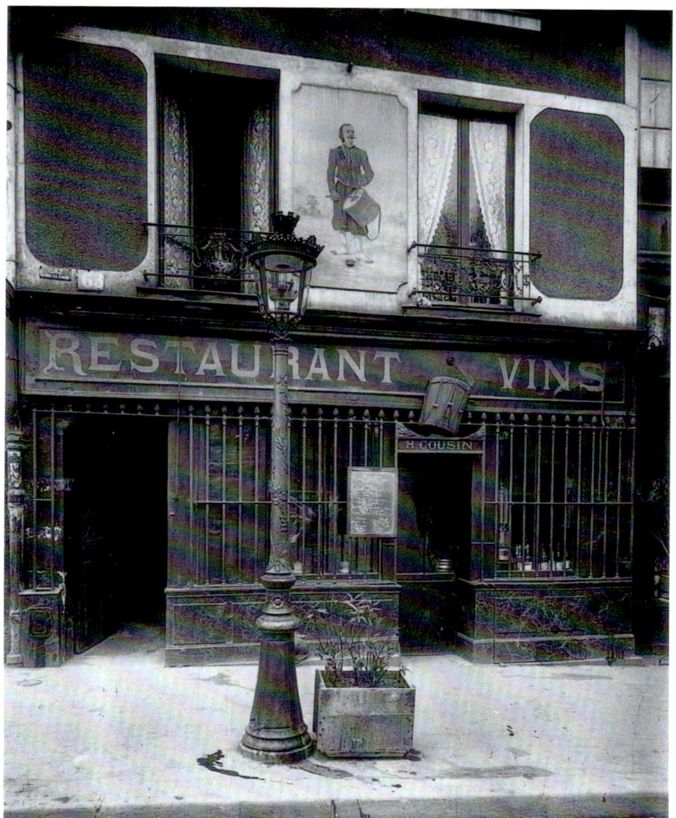

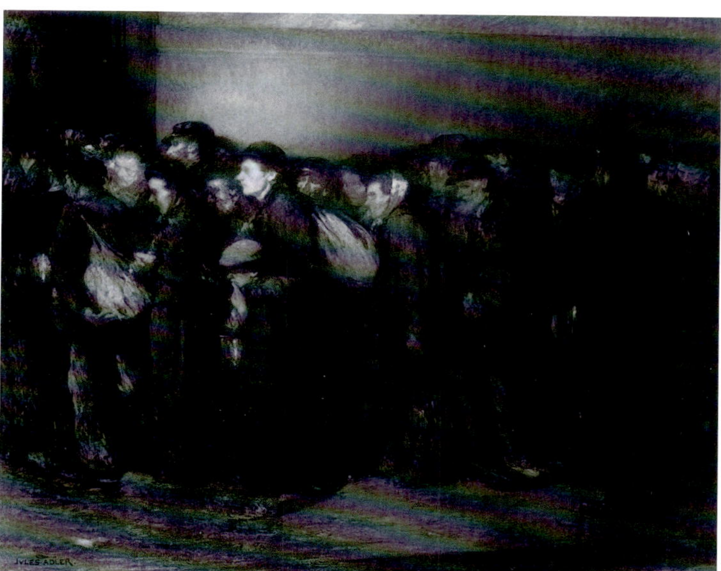

170. Jules Adler, *Soup Kitchen for the Poor*, 1906. Oil on canvas, 220 × 352 cm. Musée du Petit Palais, Paris

to answer the demand among painters for documentation to help with settings [169].

Yet, if professional photography was dedicated to documentation, ambitious amateur photography, the so-called pictorialism of the Photo Club de Paris rather than the snaps of family albums, was dedicated to art, and as such to the denial of photography's documentary role. The point of sophisticated processes like Robert Demachy and Constant Puyo's gum bichromate process and of the effects of blurring created by Puyo's 'artists' lenses' was to allow subjective intervention: to go beyond objectivity.[30] These pictorialist photographers worked broadly in a painterly, late nineteenth-century Impressionistic and naturalistic manner and were of no interest to the modernists, who preferred to use documentation, especially their own, and postcards, when they worked from photographic sources. But when the modernists dismissed photography in favour of painting, they did so using arguments close to those for pictorialist photography against the document. Painting allowed the complexity and intensity of the subjective *experience* of modernity to be represented in ways, as we have seen, that could involve both the conceptual and the temporal, and with an immediacy and force, it was firmly believed, outside the range of photography. Matisse's theory of expressive deformation in the 1908 'Notes of a Painter' diminished photography as well as Impressionist painting. Léger's theory of pictorial 'realism' in his first Académie Wassilief lecture of 1913 did the same, with a calculated side-swipe at photography, which was taken further in his second lecture of 1914.[31]

Between 1900 and 1914, there was a continuing market for painters recording modern subjects in styles derived from nineteenth-century Realism and Impressionism. For example painters like Jules Adler (b.1865) annually documenting the lives of the poor at the Artistes français [170] or like Henri Gervex (b.1852) at the Société Nationale celebrating the lives of the stylishly comfortable. But such painters were obviously under threat from the instantaneity,

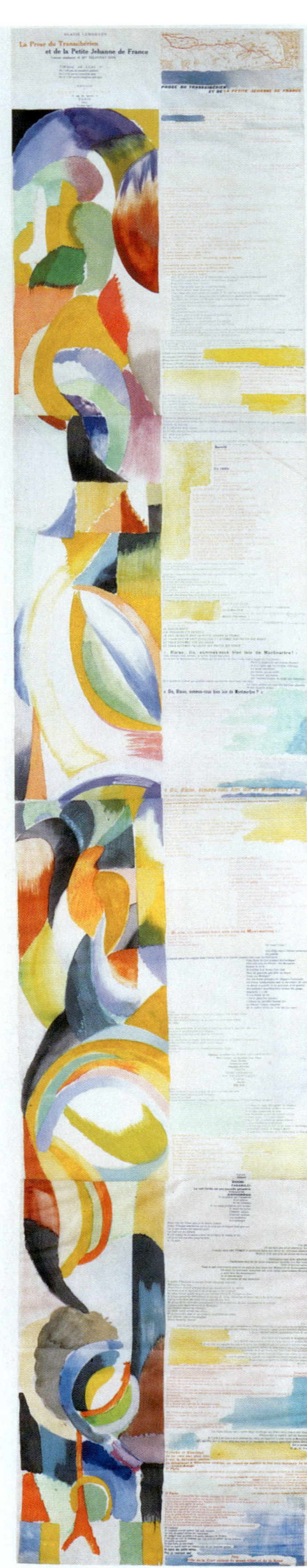

171. Sonia Delaunay and Blaise Cendrars, *Prose du Transsibérien et de la petite Jehanne de France*, 1913. Text with pochoir colour accompaniment, single folded sheet, h. 200 cm. Tate Gallery, London

cheapness and apparent authenticity of the photograph (though 'realist' painting would prove far more durable than the graphic illustrators of the popular press). The modernist decision to move outside the scope of photography evaded the challenge and opened up other possibilities for the painting of modern subjects, especially for artists working in Cubist- and Futurist-related manners. Such artists before 1914 found the stimulus for new ways of representing the force of their experience of modern subjects not in photography but in certain of those modern subjects themselves: the new means of transport, from the railways to aviation, and the new means of communication, from telegraph to wireless. The stimulus provided came of the fact that these modern developments brought with them new experiences of space and time which in turn suggested new means for their representation; and it was a stimulus mediated by writers, among them Cendrars and Apollinaire.

Man's 'brain is an endless road where thoughts, images, sensations whirr and run . . . at 100 kilometres-an-hour . . . Life everywhere rushes headlong . . .'. Octave Mirbeau's elegy to a car journey, *La 628-E8*, was published in 1908 with illustrations by Bonnard. It belonged to a literary genre which endowed the experience of speed with the capacity to change humanity by altering the very nature of perception, opening up access to the dematerialised experience of duration with a new immediacy. The year 1908 saw also the publication in France of a collection of poems by the man who would be the leader of the Futurists, F.T. Marinetti, which included his ode to the automobile 'A mon Pégase' (To my Pegasus); Marinetti was then based in Paris, and among his mentors was Camille Mauclair's friend, Paul Adam.[32] The experience here of driving faster and faster, finally without brakes, becomes one of flight, of losing contact with 'the filthy world' and soaring into 'the great bed' of the stars. For Marinetti, the theme would coalesce with a Nietzschean vision of the deification of Man; in his *Mafarka le futuriste – roman africain* (published in French in 1910), Mafarka flies off with an escort of condors to dethrone the sun. If speed dematerialised perception, telegraph, wireless and the telephone (already in use in Paris by 1900) destroyed distance, bringing everything instantly close. 'It rains in London, it snows in Pomerania, . . . in Paraguay there's nothing but roses, while Melbourne roasts'. As early as 1904, Paul Claudel could claim in *Connaissance du temps* (Knowledge of Time) that each morning the press, in instant touch with everywhere, drew for its readers 'the physiognomy of the earth', bringing 'the present in its totality . . . before our eyes'.

When Robert Delaunay painted his *Eiffel Tower* series in 1910–11 [27], he painted the tower not simply as a feat of modern engineering, but as the wireless mast of Paris, and it was as such that Cendrars wrote of it in 1913 in one of the first of his nineteen 'elastic poems':

Antique God
Modern beast
Solar spectacle
Subject of my poem
Tower
World tower [tour du monde]
Tower in movement[33]

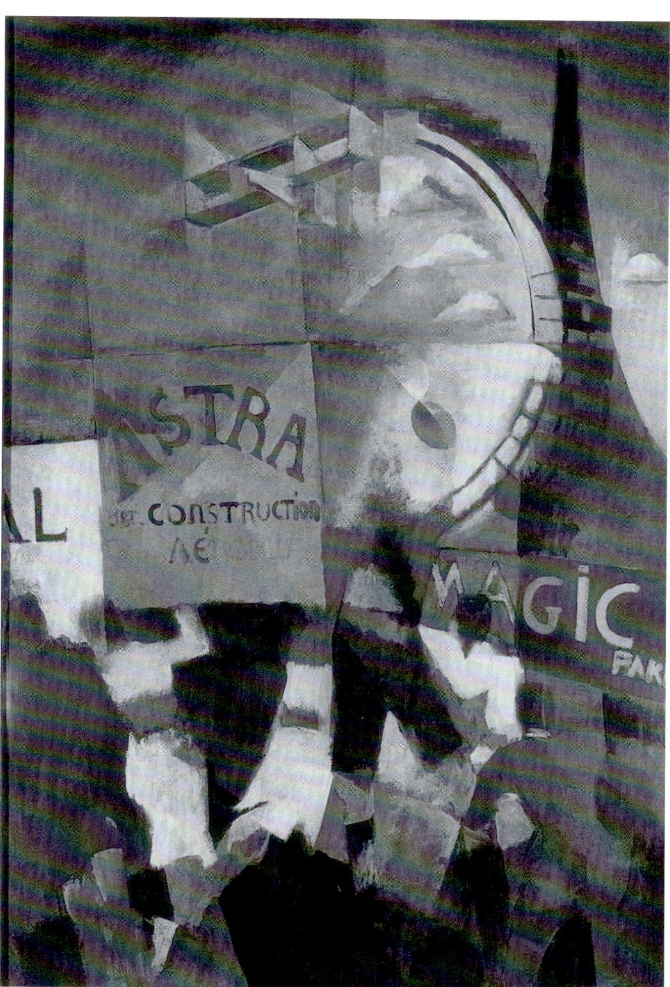

172. Robert Delaunay, *The Cardiff Team (3rd Representation)*, 1912–13. Oil on canvas, 195.5 × 132 cm. Van Abbemuseum, Eindhoven

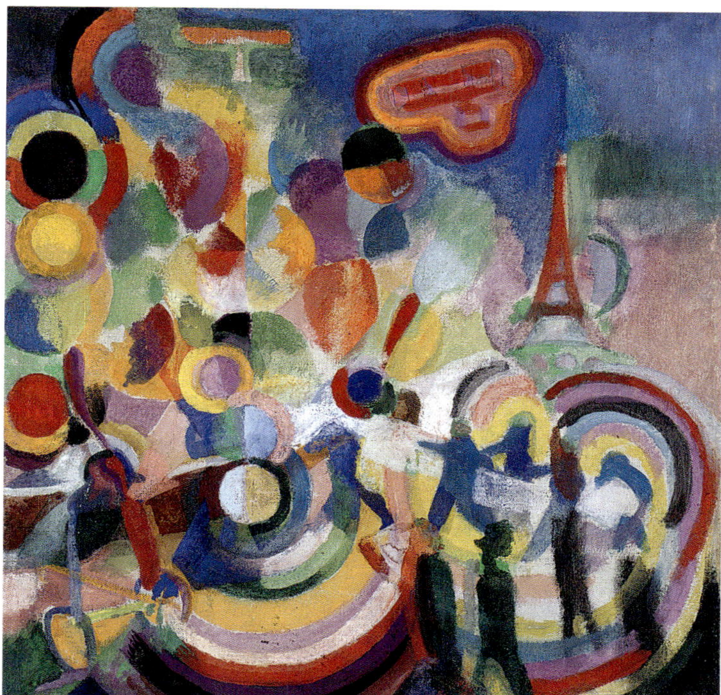

173. Robert Delaunay, *Homage to Blériot*, 1914. Oil on canvas, 460 × 460 cm. Musée de Grenoble

Cendrars' 1913 *Prose du Transsibérien* also ends with the image of the Tower, and uses throughout a vocabulary dominated by nouns and verbs, telegraphic in its concreteness and concision, to produce a poetic equivalent of the Bergsonian interpenetration of past and present, the distant and the immediate, in psychological time and space. The speed of the train and the instantaneity of modern communication repeatedly signifies the role of technological progress in accelerating and thus deepening that experience. The year 1913 saw *Prose du Transsibérien*'s publication as 'the first simultaneous book', a limited edition in which the text was given an accompaniment of simultaneously contrasting colours by Sonia Delaunay using the pochoir stencil technique. It was designed so that it could be opened out to display text and colours in their entirety [171]. The term 'simultaneous' here referred as much to the simultaneity of images from different times and places in the poem as to the simultaneity of colour contrasts or that of word and image; and Sonia Delaunay uses the image of the Tower to close her colour composition just as Cendrars does to close his poem. That year, 1913, her painting along with Robert's became 'simultaneous' in an analogously total way: colour movement continued to convey the 'movement of the world', as in Robert's *Windows* [111], but modern images sometimes brought together from different places and times were added, often accompanied by words. Such a possibility had, of course, already been anticipated by Robert's ambitious contribution to the Indépendants of 1912, his *City of Paris*, where the Graces come all the way in space and time from Pompeii, summoned up with the aid of mechanical reproduction, to settle into an anthology of city views, including the Tower [162].

As a means of representing modernity using modern images, simultaneity in painting came to Paris, in fact, just before Robert Delaunay's *City of Paris*, with the Bernheim-Jeune gallery's exhibition of Futurist painting. Boccioni's catalogue preface declared the Italians' intention to paint the 'simultaneity of the ambiance', using dislocation to synthesise both 'what is remembered and what is seen.'[34] The Paris-based Futurist, Gino Severini (b.1883) (an old acquaintance of Delaunay's), had already painted an exemplary synthesis of the remembered and seen in his *Memories of a Journey* of 1911, jumbling together images from a train journey between Venice and Paris in anticipation of Cendrars' railway poem. Delaunay's *City of Paris* arranges its images more coherently; it uses modern and ancient images simultaneously to pitch modernity, as we saw in Chapter 6, against the traditional allegories of Paris painted for official decorative schemes by artists like Besnard.[35] It took Cendrars' verbal accumulations of modern images to free his simultanist painting from the aura of traditional allegory, not only in the 1913 *Prose du Transsibérien* but also in the earlier *Pâques à New York* (Easter in New York), whose themes included steamer travel and transatlantic immigration.[36] At the beginning of 1913, Delaunay showed his *Cardiff Team (3rd Representation)* in the Indépendants, one of two large-scale treatments of the same theme [172], jux-

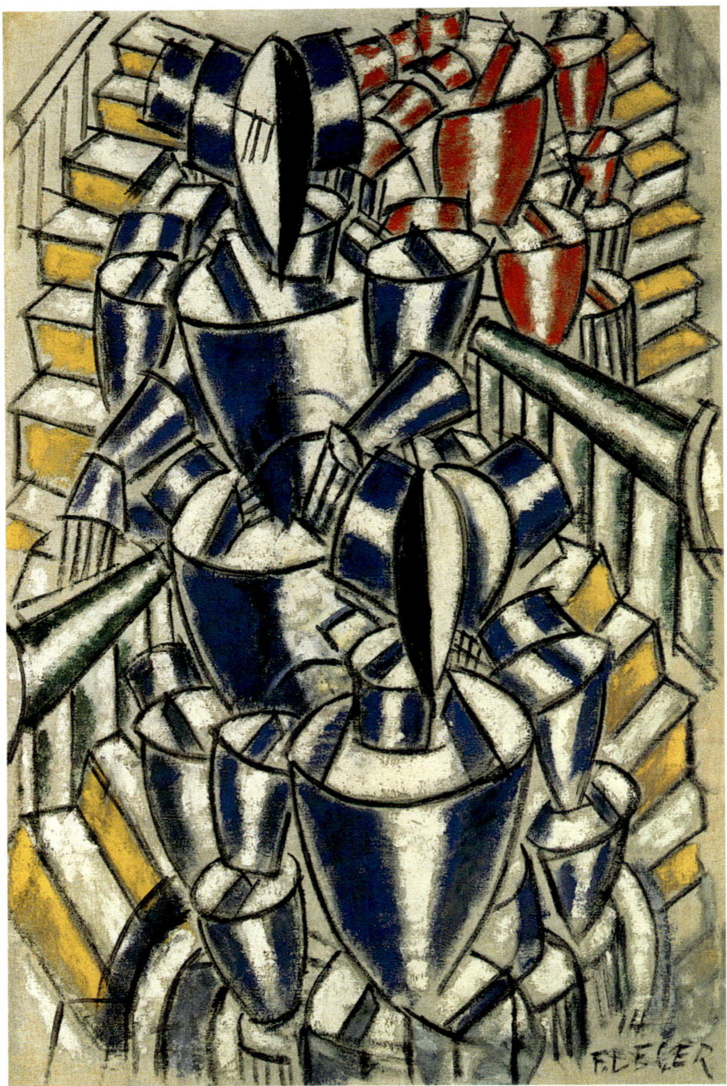

174. Fernand Léger, *The Staircase*, 1914. Oil on canvas, 144.5 × 93.5 cm. Moderna Museet, Stockholm

taposing rugby players taken from a press photograph with advertising hoardings, the Tower and the box-kite form of an early aeroplane to declare unequivocally the modernity of the experience of colour and movement that he offered.[37] From then until 1914, modern images would repeatedly intrude on his 'pure painting' in staccato, Cendrars-like juxtapositions, reaching a grand culmination in his *Homage to Blériot* [173] painted for the Indépendants of 1914 and dedicated to the flyer first to cross the English Channel (in 1910). By 1914, a few months before the declaration of war, aeroplanes could sometimes be seen flying from the field at Issy-les-Moulineaux to circle the Eiffel Tower, but Delaunay's images of mechanics, planes and the Tower jostle among the target-disc arc lamps allowing no more than a residual sense of spatial and temporal unity, as the setting sun is dethroned by electricity.

The years 1913–14 were the climax of the 'dynamic' representation of modernity in simultaneous accumulations of modern images both in painting and poetry. The Paris-based Futurists Severini and Félix del Marle (b.1889) produced simultanist representations of the Métro and the city, and 'simultaneity' became a feature of several short-lived literary movements: Henri Guilbeaux' 'Dynamism', Nicolas Beaudouin's 'Paroxism' and the one-time Abbaye-de-Créteil-writer Henri-Martin Barzun's 'Dramatism'. Apollinaire responded to the impetus supplied by Cendrars by giving modern imagery a conspicuous role in his poetry from 'Zone' late in 1912, as he continued to be closely involved with the Delaunays, and invented his own simultanist fusion of word and image, the 'calligram'.

Indeed, through Apollinaire the idea of simultaneity as the essence of the experience of modernity penetrated even the work of Picasso, Braque and Gris, however independent it might seem from the programmatic representation of the modern as such. Certain of Apollinaire's poems of 1912–13, notably 'Les Fenêtres' (The Windows) and 'Rue Christine', inject overheard snatches of conversation, producing a linguistic simultaneity too, so that contrasting colloquialisms are juxtaposed. There is an obvious relationship between Cubist collage or papier-collé and Apollinaire's calligrams. There is also a relationship between his conversation poems and the appropriation of manufactured wallpapers or combinations of text and image in the popular press (advertising and news) for Cubist collage. In a collage like Picasso's *At the Bon Marché* [190] the disparate and fast-changing colloquialisms of popular imagery are juxtaposed. Here and in the conversation poems, modernity is in language itself, verbal and visual: in the transient variety of mechanically reproduced images and of speech. The mobility of language in its popular forms was one of the current topics of French linguistic research in the work of scholars like Arsène Darmestater, Michel Bréal and the sociologist A. Meillet. All are cited in Alexandre Mercereau's *La Littérature et les idées nouvelles* of 1912, as he attempts to oppose the massive weight of the idea that the French language is a static monolith rooted in Latin by revealing 'the life of words' in their daily use.[38] Before 1914, it was certainly possible to read a collage like *At the Bon Marché* along the lines of Mercereau's interpretation of the simultaneity of popular language: to read it as yet another modern display of 'creative evolution' in action.

REPRESENTING WAR AND PEACE: LÉGER AND THE PURIST 'NEW SPIRIT', 1913–28

The cultural politics that went with Bergsonism were not unitary. A belief in Bergsonian creative evolution could go with extreme forms of individualism, given the stress on subjective experience. And it could also go with the almost mystical collectivism implicit in what Jules Romains called 'Unanimism', his belief in the unifying power of group emotion, enhanced by the new mass phenomena – sporting events, strikes, city life in Paris. It could go with the social-democratic pacificism of Albert Gleizes on the threshold of war, and with the anti-democratic promotion of violence by the anarcho-Syndicalist Georges Sorel, whose *Réflexions sur la violence* (1908) was one justification for Marinetti's brutal opening to the first *Manifesto of Futurism* in 1909: 'War, sole hygiene of the world.' In the 1920s, the Sorelian aesthetics of violence would accompany Marinetti in Italy into fascism, while one of Sorel's French admirers, Georges Valois, would found France's first fascist party, 'Le Faisceau'. Yet, between the wars Bergson (d.1941) would be the culminating point of the philosophy course taught in the lycées, his essentially progressive vision of evolution and his accent on individual experience considered highly compatible with the values of French liberal democracy.[39] In this context, the cultural politics of modernists drawn to modernity as a Bergsonian dynamic experience must often have appeared ambivalent, open to conflicting readings.

In his Académie Wassilief lectures of 1913 and 1914, Fernand Léger (b.1881) was ambivalent neither about his modernism nor his focus as a painter on the dynamism of modern experience, and yet the ideological inflection of his pre-First World War work is not clear-cut. He opened the 1914 lecture with an assertion that 'pictorial realisation is the result of modern ways of thinking', and proceeded to show how this modern mentality was determined by the dynamism of experiences produced by modern commerce and technology. He eulogised railway travel (like the Delaunays, he was close to Cendrars) and the visual violence of advertising hoardings in the countryside, scorning the campaigns of the early environmentalists.[40] His adaptation of the theory of simultaneous contrast was geared to finding a pictorial equivalent for the visual dissonance of working machinery and the new environments of city and suburb; the cylindrical volumes and metallic highlights of his *Contrasts of Forms* [113] cement the connection with mechanisms, the strident colour with urban and suburban spaces.

The Futurists acknowledged him as the most Futurist of the French, and indeed his 1914 lecture comes close to plagiarising Boccioni.[41] There is much certainly to compare between Léger's and Boccioni's uncritical passion for urban and industrial modernity. Italy, like France, was still in the early stages of urbanisation, and Léger (brought up in Argentan, a little Norman town embedded in its rural hinterland), like Boccioni, was a provincial dazzled by technology and big-city life in a predominantly rural country. In the decade and a half before 1914, as I show in Part One, there was enormous growth in French industrial production, particularly in the new industries. Between 1895 and 1914, the number of cars in France rose from 300 to 107,000 and aircraft production was quick to start growing too.[42] There is good evidence that Léger was an enthusiastic visitor to the Salon de l'aviation in 1912, when it was held alongside the Salon d'automne in the Grand Palais, where he would have seen the aero-engines displayed, stripped and polished like works of art on pedestals.[43] He gave the look of engines to the figures he painted in 1913–14 with the most positive motives [174]. We have already seen how optimistic believers, like him, in progress as creative evolution, thought only technology capable of improving human faculties.

Léger's wartime correspondence, after his mobilisation in summer 1914, reveals a reluctant soldier deeply antagonistic to the bellicose patriotism of propagandists like Maurice Barrès and drawn to the anti-bourgeois Left. And yet his pictorial celebration of the machine and of dissonance in its pre-war Futurist context (contrast equalling conflict) was obviously open to nationalist and militarist readings.[44] The growth in industrial production did not only go with transport and news, consumerism and leisure, between 1911 and 1914 it went with the growth of armaments. In the build-up to the war after the Moroccan crisis of 1911, armament production was behind the huge expansion in the metallurgical industries; by 1913–14, the French State was spending over a third of its budget on arms.[45] In the tense atmosphere that accompanied the passing of a three-year conscription law in 1913, where the polarisation of Left and Right became that of pacifism against militarism, Léger's aero-engine figures carried connotations that for some would have contradicted what seems to have been his personal distaste for aggressive patriotism. It is perhaps not surprising that of the painters associated with Cubism, Léger was the one who most memorably took on front-line experience as a subject; and what he produced seems similarly to have invited conflicting responses.

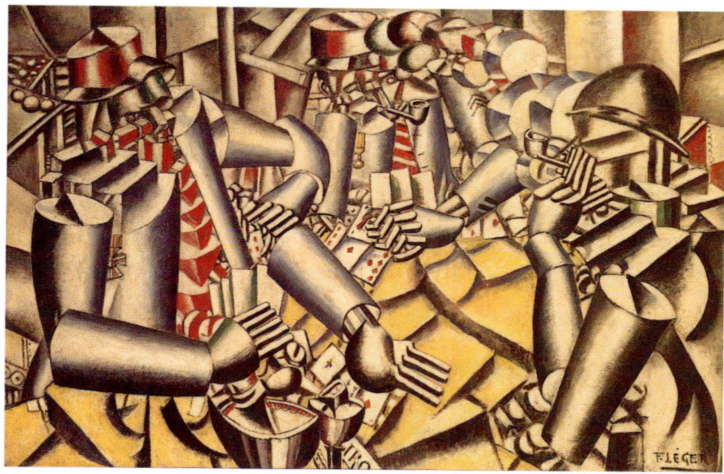

175. Fernand Léger, *The Card-Game*, 1917. Oil on canvas, 129 × 193 cm. Kröller-Müller Museum, Otterlo

Like most French independent painters on the front in 1914–18, Léger found even modernist techniques inadequate in the face of mechanised warfare. There are a few sketches of artillery pieces and a series of Verdun destroyed by shelling, but he focused above all on the common soldiers he served with. He was a sapper and a stretcher-bearer in the Argonne in 1915, and a stretcher-bearer on the Aisne front and at Verdun in 1916, before (in slightly dubious circumstances) being invalided out in 1917.[46] His subjects echo those of the photographs from the front that filled the mass-circulation illustrated magazines *L'Illustration* and *Le Monde illustré*. He used a simplified graphic version of his pre-war figure style and so spelt out plainly enough the symbiosis between men and machines on the front, but he gave new emphasis to their individual humanity (as the magazines did) in drawings he probably intended to show but never did. And when, after the Armistice, he exhibited with Léonce Rosenberg in February 1919, the acknowledged centrepiece of the exhibition was *The Card-game*, a large canvas painted in military hospital, which is based on some of these drawings [175]. It is a work in which men-as-engines, decorations pinned to their armour tunics, are made human by the stolid patience that their card-game conveys. In eight months, the battle of Verdun, whose

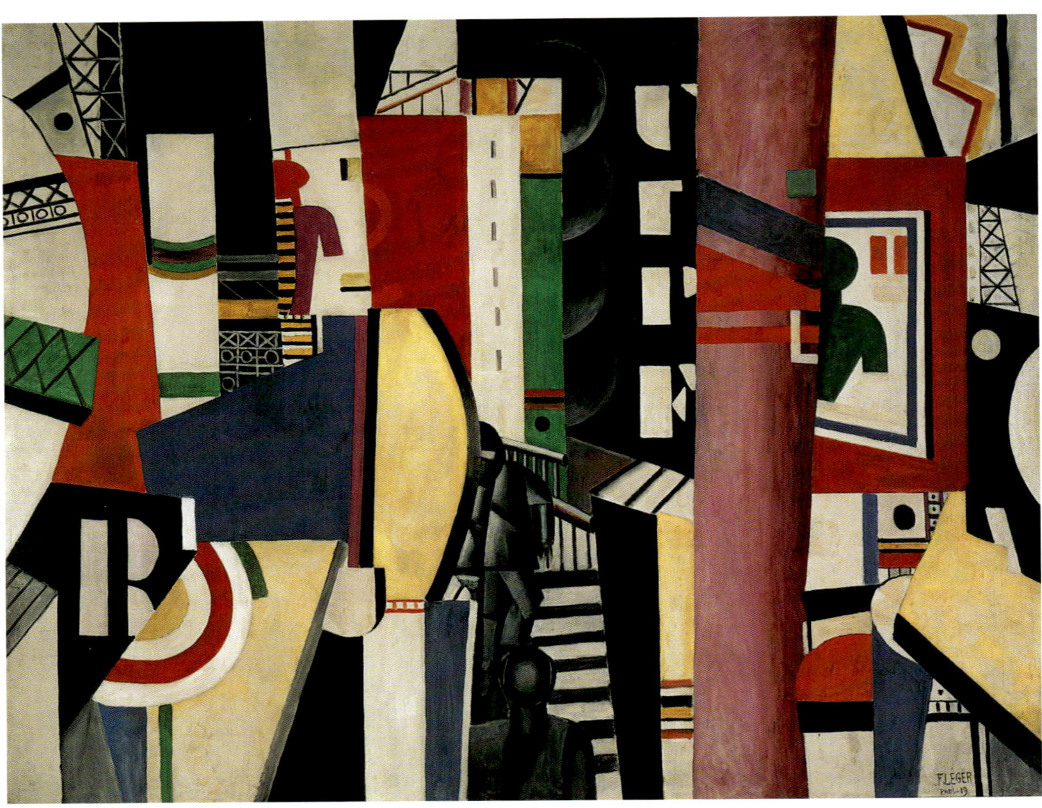

176. Fernand Léger, *The City*, 1919. Oil on canvas, 227 × 294 cm. Philadelphia Museum of Art, Philadelphia. A.E. Gallatin Collection

177. Fernand Léger and Dudley Murphy, Stills from *Ballet mécanique*, 1924. As illustrated in *L'Esprit Nouveau*, 1924

178. Facing page. Fernand Léger, *The Propellors*, 1918. Oil on canvas, 80.9 × 65.4 cm. The Museum of Modern Art, New York. Katherine S. Dreier Bequest

179. Facing page. Fernand Léger, *The Mechanic*, 1920. Oil on canvas, 116 × 88.8 cm. National Gallery of Canada, Ottawa. Purchased 1966

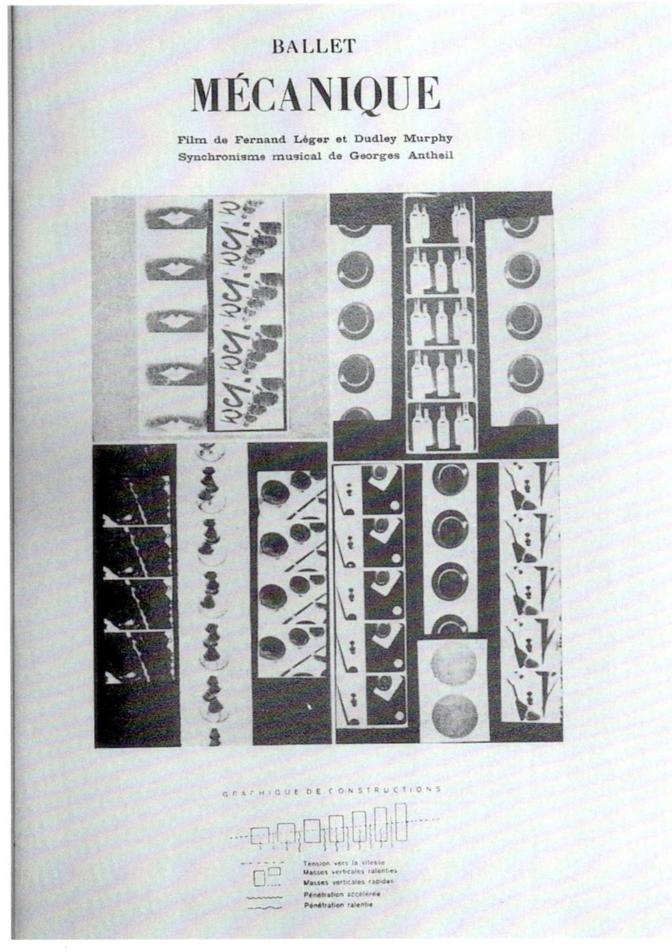

dénouement Léger witnessed, killed more than 300,000 Frenchmen. His correspondence shows how aware he was of the calculated control behind such casualty figures, especially in the minutely planned use of artillery bombardments; a letter of 1915 actually aligns that cold control with the 'abstraction' of Cubism.[47] And yet, in 1919 he was to publish a text in which the beauty of the French 75 calibre gun is extolled, and that murderous beauty can seem to be extolled too in *The Card-game*; these are not merely men-as-engines, they are also men-as-guns.[48] Moreover, the picture was shown with works like *The Propellors* whose eulogising of the machine is unequivocal [178].

The 1914–18 war demonstrated as no previous war had, the destructive power of mechanisation. It did not diminish Léger's awed faith in technology, but even he realised quickly that the aggressive dynamism of the pre-war celebration of modernity, with its equation between the machine and violence, had become unacceptable. In 1919–20, he was the only leading modernist still to use simultanist techniques of spatial and temporal fragmentation to celebrate modernity, having ignored them before 1914. But he did not use them simply to dramatise commercial and technological progress, he used them to celebrate Paris as the capital city of peace. One of his letters in 1915 claims that the horror of living on the front has so intensified his awareness of the value of the simplest things that he has developed a new appetite for everything about Paris. 'How I shall eat Paris up if I have the happiness of returning there.'[49] It is this image-by-image consumption of Paris as a centre of peacetime life that Delaunay's simultanist techniques allowed Léger to paint in *The City* [176], his major contribution to the 1920 Indépendants (the first after the war). He sets out signboard

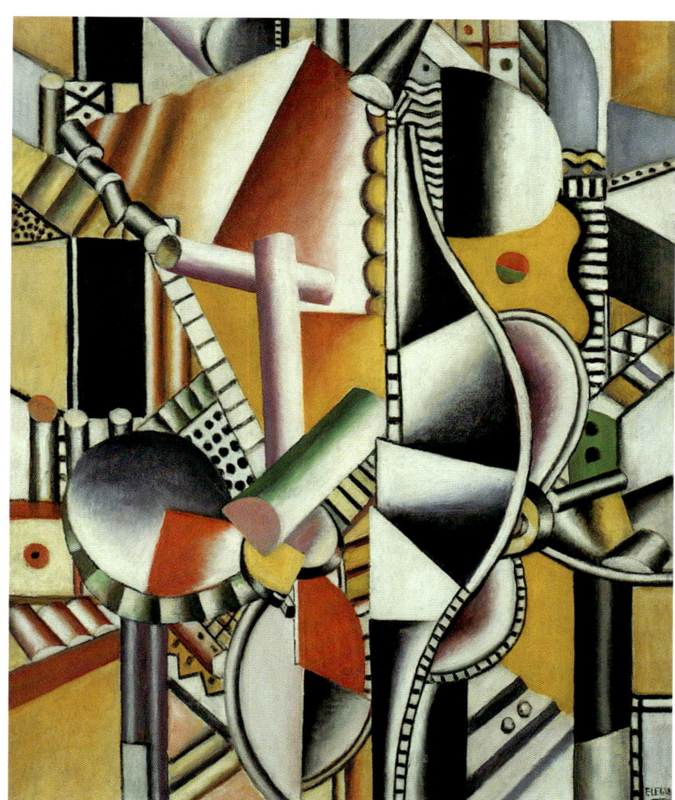

That year he painted *The Mechanic* [179], giving a hieratic wholeness and stability to the image of a modern working man in peacetime. The following year, he showed in the Salon d'automne a large composition featuring nudes, where the mechanisation of the human figure is allied to the formal properties of classical figure-painting in the line of Poussin and David [247]. During the 1920s, Léger's figurative retreat from the dynamics of modernity as an experience of spatial and temporal fragmentation widened. It embraced his painting of urban and suburban landscape, machine elements and manufactured objects too; indeed, his painting of modernity altogether.

Between 1920 and 1924, Léger became a theatre designer and experimental film-maker as well as painter, and in these mobile media he remained concerned with dynamism as a manifestation of modern energy. The film he made with the American Dudley Murphy in 1924, *Ballet mécanique*, used cinematic techniques of fast-cutting to produce intense effects of fragmentation and movement. Mirrors were employed to complicate appearances, as in the photography of a pictorialist like Alvin Langdon Coburn, and masking to fragment them. But machines and manufactured objects were also often presented whole [179], and it was whole that they appeared in paintings like *The Siphon* of 1924 and *Composition with Hand and Hats* of 1927, the latter a work painted in direct response to the displays of objects in the film [180, 191].

letters, piled-up windows, a column of smoke, a pair of machine-men descending a staircase, catwalks, derricks and mannequins, as if making a catalogue of urban images, each one savoured individually and displayed thus against a dazzling architecture of flat colour planes. Pictorial intensity goes with the itemisation of modern phenomena – the optical excitements of peacetime modernity, which are ranged against abstraction-as-death.

Between 1918 and 1920, Léger was alone among major modernists painting pictures for peacetime using the pictorial analogues of modern experience developed before 1914. The sheer negative force of the experience of war, even as it was felt at one remove behind the lines, shifted attention from the capacity of post-Cubist techniques to convey the dynamic intensity of the modern as an experience, to their capacity to construct. Except for Léger, by 1918 all of the Cubists associated with Léonce Rosenberg's galerie de l'Effort Moderne had opted for pictorial construction against dynamism and simultaneity, the sculptors Lipchitz and Laurens along with the painters [238]. As I show in Part Five, this went with a stress on connotations of tradition rather than modernity, but Paul Dermée, a poet close to most of the L'Effort Moderne Cubists, made a point in 1917 of drawing an analogy between the emerging preference for structure and mechanised production. 'The work of art,' he wrote, 'must be conceived as the working man conceives the manufacture of a pipe or hat, the position of every part should be determined strictly according to function and importance.'[50] The focus has switched from the speeded-up experiences generated by technology to the logical procedures of production and the construction of the object produced. In 1920, Léger made the switch too.

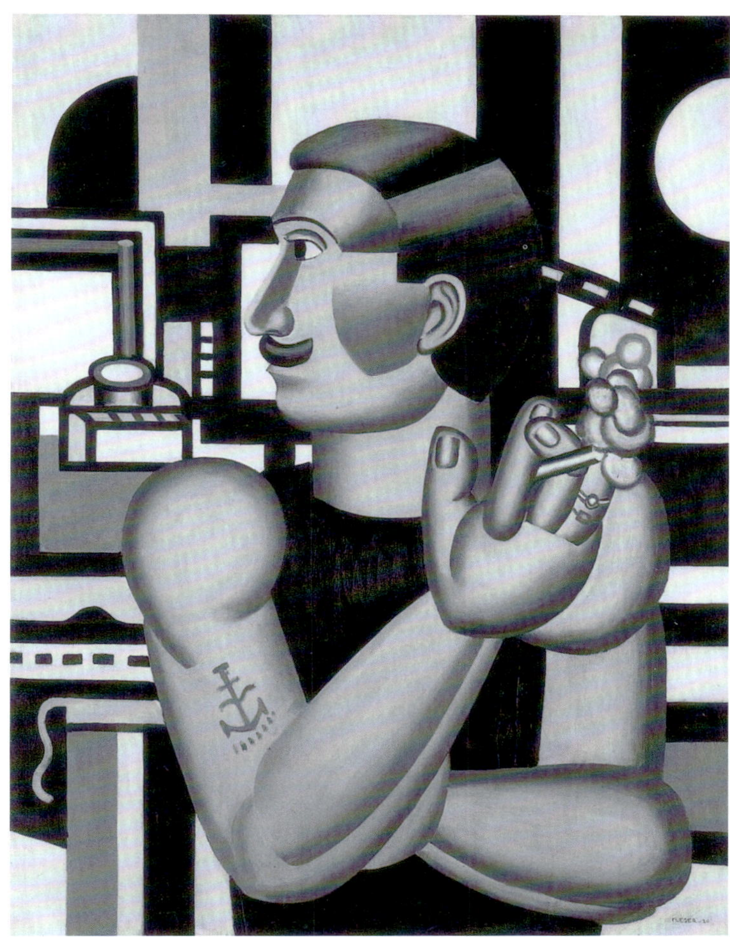

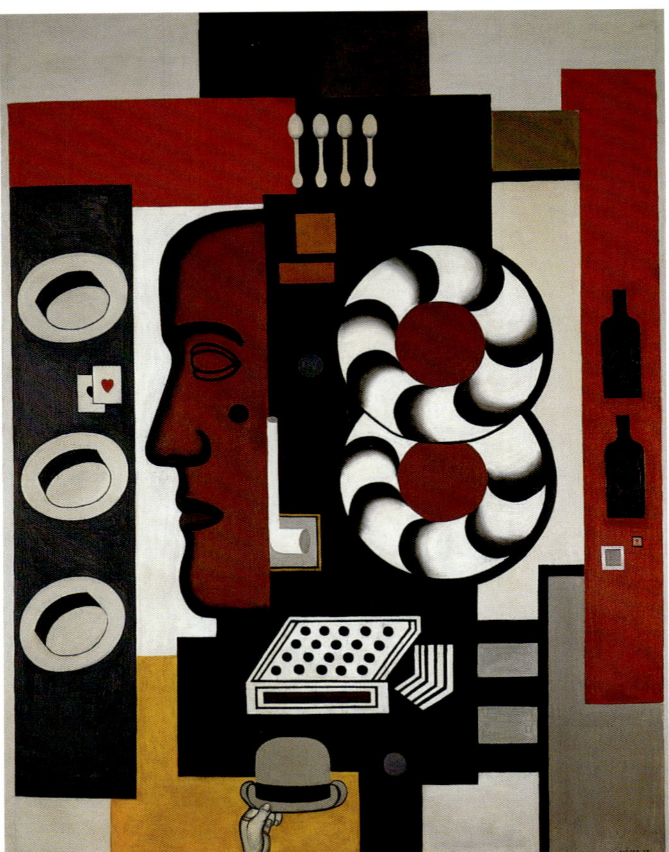

180. Fernand Léger, *Composition with Hand and Hats*, 1927. Oil on canvas, 248 × 185 cm. Musée National d'Art Moderne, Paris

Moreover, in such still-life arrangements of modern products, everything was done to contain them in stable planar structures, to resist effects of motion, as if Léger wished to set painting up against modern theatre and the new medium, film, as a medium defined by its immobility. In *The Siphon*, the arc of water squirted into the glass is as motionless and as informative as a diagram.

This 'call to order' in Léger's painting of modernity might have followed alongside the call to order in L'Effort Moderne Cubism generally, but its focus on the modern in its allusions to mechanisation and its selection of mass-produced objects as still-life subjects aligned it more tellingly with another immediately post-war development. This was Ozenfant and Le Corbusier's 'new spirit': the Purism they promoted as the next stage 'after Cubism'. Between 1920 and 1925, Ozenfant and Le Corbusier (who retained his real name Jeanneret as a painter until 1923) painted neither figures nor exclusively modern manufactured objects, but they explicitly linked their structured compositions of clearly represented still-life objects to a campaign for a modern Humanism committed to the constructive, to order in mechanised production [181, 277]. Léger's statements on art, like his painting, reveal as much his independence from the Purists as areas of agreement between them, but along with the Cubists Lipchitz, Laurens and Gris he did not hesitate to contribute to Le Corbusier's Pavillon de l'Esprit nouveau in 1925 [8], and he regularly featured in their periodical, *L'Esprit nouveau*. It was in *L'Esprit nouveau* that he first published on *Ballet mécanique* (the stills in 179 appear as they were reproduced there in 1924).[51] What seems an uncomplicated shift from a Bergsonian stress on the dynamism of experience to a revived positivist accent on 'objective' display within structured settings is, in fact, best illuminated by probing the Purist theory of the 'new spirit' in the context of modernity as it was celebrated in *L'Esprit nouveau*.

'There is a new spirit: it is a spirit of construction and synthesis guided by a clear concept.' This was how Ozenfant and Le Corbusier announced the 'new spirit' of Purism in 1918.[52] Half a decade later, they wrote of this new spirit as a condition provoked by the city: '. . . the streets, the houses, almost uniformly squared up by windows, the neat strips of the pavements, the lines of trees with their almost identical circular fences, the regular punctuation of street-lighting . . . confine us still and always in geometry.'[53] 1924 also saw Léger return to the theme of his 1920 *City* [176]. In *Animated Landscape* [182], one of three related pictures, he extracts the machine-men on a staircase from their fragmentary urban spectacle, dresses them in up-to-date business suits and displays them whole, dominated not by the simultaneity of city images but by a confining urban geometry.

The lucid constructive spirit claimed as the dominant post-war spirit by the Purists was unequivocally positivist. In every domain, including the development of cities, it was, they asserted, characterised by a logical problem-solving mentality, which measured and analysed on the basis of methodical observation. Number – quantification – was fundamental to modern knowledge, number for measurement and calculation. In 1924, Le Corbusier was developing the case for rational urban planning which would be presented in his book *Urbanisme* the following year, and one of the articles published en route in *L'Esprit nouveau* was 'Statistics'. 'Statistics,' he wrote, 'is the Pegasus of urbanism. Horribly dull, thorough and without passion . . . , it is the springboard of lyricism . . .'.[54] For the Purists, science at its least fancifully systematic was the means by which the laws basic to existence were accessible, and those laws were most clearly expressed in numbers. Art, including the art of city planning, was inspired only if it was grounded in those laws. Nothing could be further from the imprecision, the unquantifiable flux of Bergsonian duration, or from Marinetti's motorised Pegasus of 1908 flying free of the material world. In the very first issues of *L'Esprit nouveau*, Le Corbusier replaced Bergson's modern hero, the artist, with the engineer. Engineers, he informs his readers with relish in 1924, 'are calm . . . , modest . . . , positive'. They 'represent the forces of nature by "a" and "β" . . .'.[55] They design for a world fit for Léger's mechanic.

The material progress achieved by humanity, according to Ozenfant and Le Corbusier, was not to be understood as creative evolution but rather as a process of mechanical as against natural evolution, whereby everything designed and manufactured for human use becomes more and more efficient according to a general 'Law of Economy', the less efficient being ruthlessly eliminated as a result of 'Mechanical Selection'. Precision and economy are to be actively pursued in every sector of human production, including painting.

The Purists' still-lifes are carefully planned, composed on

the basis of the Golden Section ratio and modular systems, and executed exactly, leaving as little indication of personality through brushwork as possible [181, 277]. The restricted range of objects presented in them were chosen as 'type-objects', thought of as formally perfected by the process of 'Mechanical Selection': mechanical extensions of the naturally evolved perfection of the human body.[56] The Purists adapted Cubist multiple perspective to the elucidation of such objects (ignoring the possibility of durational representation). In 1918, they wrote of the 'privileged aspect', that which was most informative, taking as their paradigmatic instance the profile view of a jet of water, in anticipation of Léger's *Siphon*. Léger never applied proportional systems, did not restrict himself to Purist type-objects, and was not at all rigorous about using 'privileged aspects'. But he too minimised individual brushwork and planned his compositions, between 1920 and the end of the decade accentuating the look of precision-painting, especially in his aptly dubbed 'definitive states'.

If Bergsonist champions of the experience of modernity often left their images ideologically ambivalent, the post-war champions of the 'new spirit' did not. With positivist certainties went political clarity, as Mary McLeod has shown.[57] Ozenfant and Le Corbusier's obsessive stress on logic and precision as the key to solving contemporary problems, and their appreciation of assembly-line efficiency as an unalloyed benefit, represented an endorsement of those most committed to technological progress in French politics and industry, those who followed the American creed of 'Scientific Management' developed in the 1880s by the engineer F.W. Taylor. The Purists expressly acknowledged 'Taylorism' from 1918. 'Instinct, groping, and empiricism,' they wrote of it then, 'are replaced by scientific principles of analysis, organisation and classification'.[58]

Taylorism had clear ideological connotations in post-war France. Its time-and-motion principles and assembly-line methods had been given enormous encouragement by

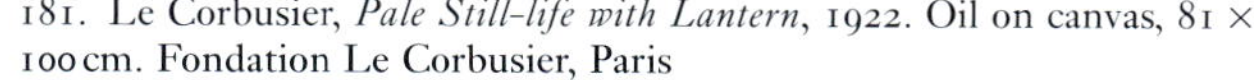

181. Le Corbusier, *Pale Still-life with Lantern*, 1922. Oil on canvas, 81 × 100 cm. Fondation Le Corbusier, Paris

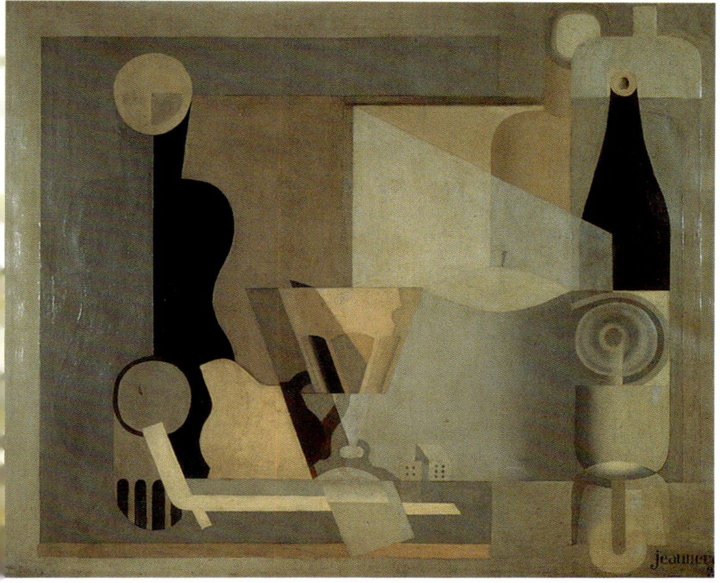

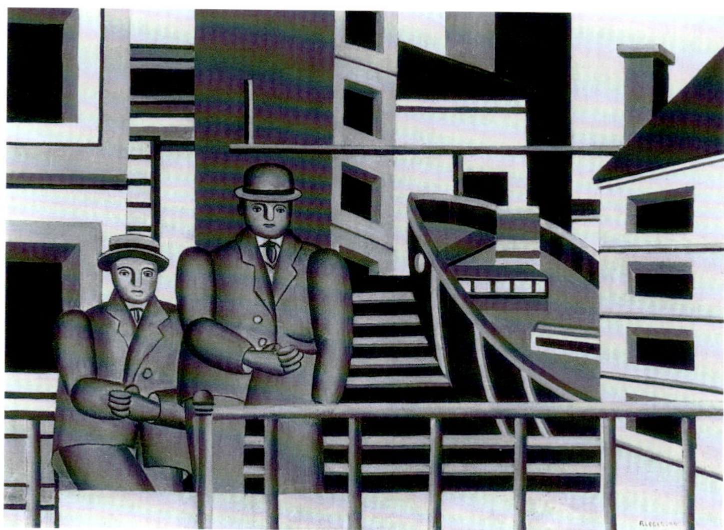

182. Fernand Léger, *Animated Landscape*, 1924. Oil on canvas, 50 × 60 cm. Philadelphia Museum of Art, Philadelphia. Given by Bernard Davis

the demands of wartime production and post-war reconstruction, winning over innovative industrialists including Louis Renault, André Citroën and the aircraft and car manufacturer Gabriel Voisin, as well as the most technologically progressive Radical politicians, above all Louis Loucheur, minister of reconstruction in 1919, and Edouard Herriot, the dominant Radical figure of the 1920s and early 1930s.[59] In tune with the moderate reforming direction of Radical politics, it offered the prospect of scientific solutions to social problems paid for by increased productivity rather than by attacks on property rights or by the redistribution of income.

During the Purist period not only did Le Corbusier present big business as 'a healthy and moral organism', and seek sponsorship from industrialists (notably Voisin), but he also cultivated good relations with progressive Radical politicians (notably Loucheur who was also an industrialist), while, after the 1924 general elections, *L'Esprit nouveau* supported the success of the 'cartel des gauches' under Herriot, commending 'a peaceful revolution'.[60] In *Urbanisme* (1925), Le Corbusier would present his plans as an investment opportunity for risk-taking capitalists and an alternative to Communist revolution. The efficiency of the 'new spirit' was to solve the kind of social problems that left 25% of Parisians still living on average two to a room in 1926, without threatening the liberal economic system. Léger's correspondence with his dealer Léonce Rosenberg reveals that in 1924 he shared Le Corbusier's admiration for the dynamism of big business.[61] His business-suited figures in the city paintings of 1924 [182] could as well be modern businessmen as engineers: they were new modern heroes to place alongside the mechanic. Such faith in 'American' methods, whether combined with moderate politics or not, was a minority phenomenon in 1920s France: Loucheur's Taylorism did not get far even when he was in government in 1928, the anti-American conservatism of the small bourgeois businessmen who were still the dominant force in French manufacturing saw to that. But neither did the realities of the situation diminish the optimism of the Purists (or it seems of Léger): their conviction in the growing potential of the 'new spirit' as a force for good held firm into the mid-1920s.

Positivist and rationalist Ozenfant and Le Corbusier's 'New Spirit' certainly was, yet at a deep level it remained involved with the *experience* of modernity above all, and so did Léger's painting, along with the work of his students and admirers. Indeed, in 1924, Ozenfant must have surprised some by insisting on the consistency of his views with Bergsonian philosophy. *L'Esprit nouveau* no. 22 carried an essay by him with the telling title 'Certainty'. Here he argued that the only certainty was the experience of the 'vital instant'. 'The past is made up of abolished certainties which dissolve according to their distance from the instant . . . where we experience ourselves living'. Past and future are no more than 'probability, possibility, ineffability'. The facts of science are ultimately hypotheses too, and Ozenfant repeats Bergson's view that science attains certainty in the practical sphere alone; it cannot, in the words of the positivist philosopher Ernest Renan, 'resolve the enigma of things'. The measurable laws of nature are universal, Ozenfant contends, but only within the limits of human perception: they are human constructions imposed on the world. 'Science holds as an axiom that our senses and the instruments which extend them give us a vantage point on reality; in fact, it merely projects man upon a screen which is nothing but himself . . .'.[62] It was thus that Purism proposed a Humanist positivism, one that recognised the centrality of human experience; and ultimately Ozenfant and Le Corbusier understood the 'new spirit' as a problem-solving, precisionist mentality created by the *experience* of modernity: the experience of mechanisms and their products, of cities and the new means of communication as manifestations not of simultaneous flux but of order.

183. Jacques Lipchitz, with two plasters of *Prometheus Strangling the Vulture*, 1936–7. Larger plaster, h. 914 cm. Destroyed. The Estate of Jacques Lipchitz, courtesy, Marlborough Gallery, New York

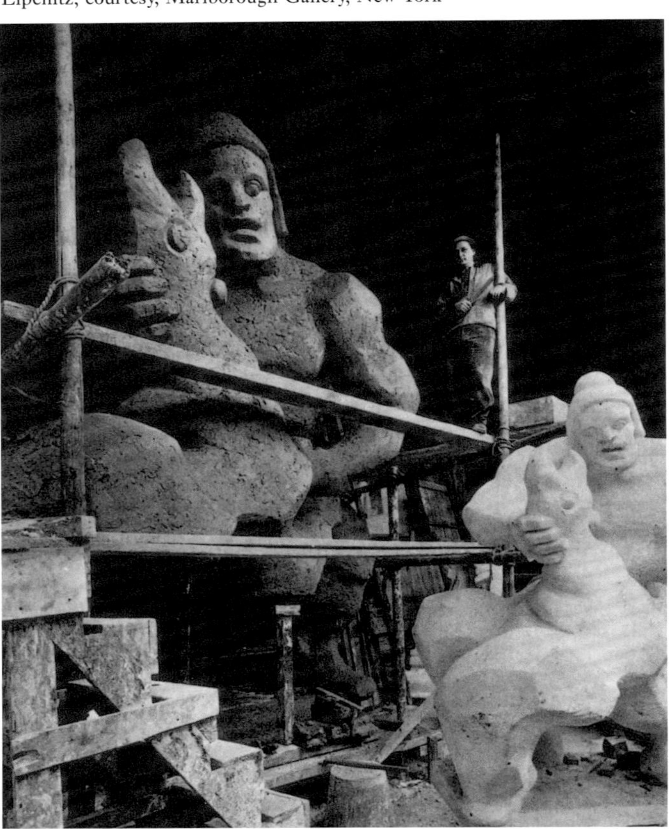

Purist theory can so stress the positivist and the rational that the statement it makes about modernity as an experience is obscured; this was never the case with Léger. His work might be more structured and lucid in the 1920s than it was in 1913–14, but its use of contrasts to give pictorial intensity through dissonance continues unabated. Moreover, all his published statements, including his most influential piece, his lecture 'The Machine Aesthetic' delivered in 1923, embedded talk of geometry and order in descriptions of encounters with modernity, from the cars and planes on display at the automobile and aviation Salons, to the most banal of manufactured objects arranged in shop windows.[63] His was as selective a view as the Purists' of a France where advances might have been sustained, but where society as a whole was only slowly modernising. It was mediated by an idealist concern with order which had a strong ideological thrust. And yet to the extent that it was stimulated by intensely lived experiences, it could seem simply to be their product: a matter of fact. Léger began his lecture on 'The Machine Aesthetic' with what is presented as a statement of fact: 'More and more modern man is living in a geometrically controlled order.'[64] Modernity for early twentieth-century modernists was always an idea, but *their* experience of it could make their modernity seem to be the only reality.

THE PALAIS DE LA DÉCOUVERTE: REPRESENTING SCIENCE AND TECHNOLOGY AT THE EXHIBITION OF 1937

In 1928, Le Corbusier was briefly engaged in an attempt to win over the political and the industrial élites in France from within the Third Republic's democratic system. Alongside figures like the First World War military strategist Marshall Foch and the one-time minister of commerce, Etienne Clementel, he joined a short-lived organisation, the 'Redressement français', formed by the future president of the Compagnie française de petroles, Ernest Mercier (an exemplary technocratic businessman); it made little impact.[65] In 1927, Le Corbusier had also shown interest in Georges Valois' French fascist movement, whose periodical, *Nouveau siècle*, held up his city projects as a vision of the ideal fascist city. And between 1930 and the mid-1930s he was among those who countered the instability of Third Republic politics by promoting authoritarian alternatives to liberal democracy, as I show in Chapter 8.[66] His engagement, however, in technocratic capitalist initiatives and authoritarian attacks on the Third Republic did not prevent him from becoming one of the modernist beneficiaries of the Front Populaire's electoral success at the 1937 Paris Exhibition, where he received a late commission to build a Pavillon des temps nouveaux as a result of the direct intervention of the Socialist prime minister, Léon Blum. The name Le Corbusier was so closely associated with the concept of modernity by the mid-1930s, that modernising democratic socialism was as open to sponsoring what it stood for as the modernising factions of the anti-democratic Right.

The title of the 1937 Exhibition, the International Exhibition of Arts and Techniques in Modern Life, underlined its commitment to modernity, and Blum's many interventions in its organisation were often aimed at strengthening the connection between modernist art and modernity. Technological and scientific progress tended thus to lose any associations it might have had with the Right. It was made a central theme of the politics of the Left, and many modernist as well as anti-modernist artists, including Fernand Léger, became active on the Left, a development encouraged above all by the formation in 1934 of the Popular Front as an alliance against fascism drawing together the French Communist Party, the Socialists and the Radicals.

It was in this context that the Palais de la Découverte, installed in the specially modernised nave and galleries of the west wing of the Grand Palais, became one of the great successes of the exhibition. It attracted over two and a quarter million visitors, including 600 groups organised by educational bodies and the Trades Unions, a success impressive enough to persuade Jean Zay, the young Radical minister of public instruction, to extend its life after the closure of the exhibition and then to establish it as a State institution in 1938.[67] Ultimately, the Palais de la Découverte was the responsibility of an inspired and inspirational scientist, Jean Perrin, who had won the Nobel Prize for physics in 1926 (and had contributed to *L'Esprit nouveau*). Perrin's project was interactive: he wanted to provoke visitors to find out about science for themselves, hence the title, 'Palace of Discovery'. Art played an integral part in this, as a medium by which to give impact to the effects of scientific advance, and as a means by which to convey science's fundamental importance to human life and knowledge. One of Perrin's priorities was to demonstrate a parallel between artistic creation and scientific invention. Largely on his initiative, twenty painters and six sculptors were commissioned for the project: Lipchitz, Laurens and Léger made contributions alongside less advanced modernists like André Lhote and Marcel Gromaire. Paired exhibitions were held in the Palais, one setting out the stages of scientific and technological progress, the other, 'Science and Art', juxtaposing reproductions of works of art with scientific instruments and a selection of modernist paintings that ranged from Monet to Picasso and the Cubists (including Delaunay and Léger). The architecture of Le Corbusier featured. Art and science were represented as equally progressive and as linked in their advances, the complementary aspects of the development of human knowledge. Progress was not merely material, but, as Perrin put it, 'will assure the progressive enfranchisement of men and, thanks to the leisure gained, the possibility to make available to all the joys of Art and Thought.'[68] Art and Science, like the Purists' 'new spirit' of the 1920s, came together, the twin benefits of progress.

Perrin was a member of the Socialist Party, and held political office in Zay's ministry as a member of the Popular Front government. The politicisation of the union between art and science in the context of the Popular Front was unequivocal. It was given dramatic public exposure by a controversy caused by one of Perrin's commissions, Jacques Lipchitz's sculpture *Prometheus strangling the Vulture* [183], the plaster for which was placed outside the Palais. Prometheus – who stole fire from the gods – was represented in traditional allegorical terms as knowledge murdering ignorance, but he was given a revolutionary's Phrygian bonnet and the vulture was easily read as the eagle of the Third Reich. Science was thus appropriated for the revolutionary Republic against fascism; the early twentieth-century socialist Jean Jaurès had, after all, claimed that science was 'naturally republican'.[69] It was as symbol of the fusion of modernism and socialism under the umbrella of science that the *Prometheus* by Lipchitz (b.1891) became the focus of a campaign led by the newspaper *Le Matin* from the conservative Right. The decision in 1938 to establish the Palais as a permanent State institution triggered near-hysterical demands that 'this sample of art as the Popular Front conceives it' should be removed.[70] It was destroyed as part of the planned demolition of the exhibition's temporary structures, an act interpreted on the Left as victory for the Right.

Within this very specifically late 1930s context of political confrontation, the Palais de la Découverte represented modernity in many of the ways explored by modernists from the 1900s onwards. There was no place here for the dramatised naturalism of early attempts to come to terms with the excitement of the new, no modernised equivalents of Jules Dalou's *Monument to Emile Levassor*, where he depicts in stone the engineer driving his motor car hectically out

184. Jules Dalou, *Monument to Émile Levassor*, completed 1907. Marble. Porte Maillot, Paris

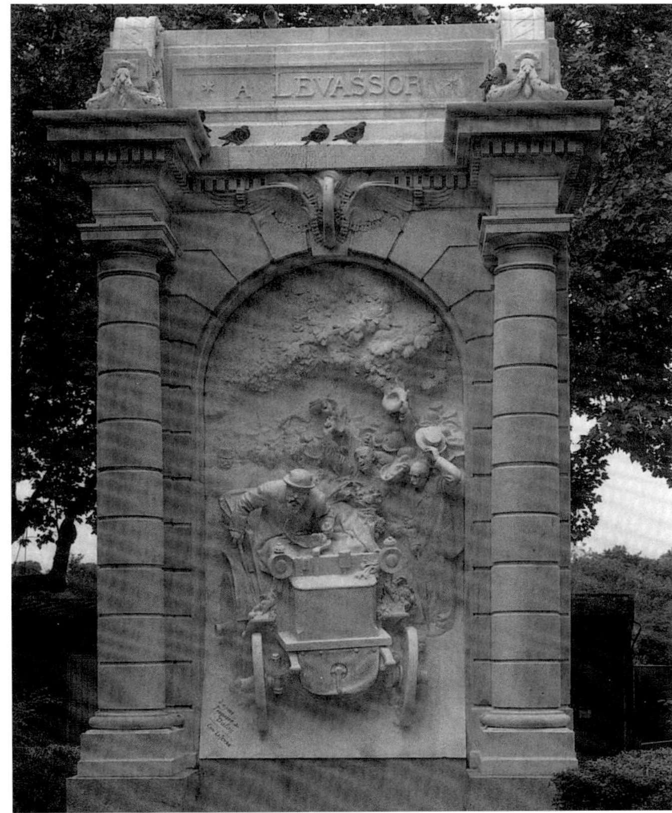

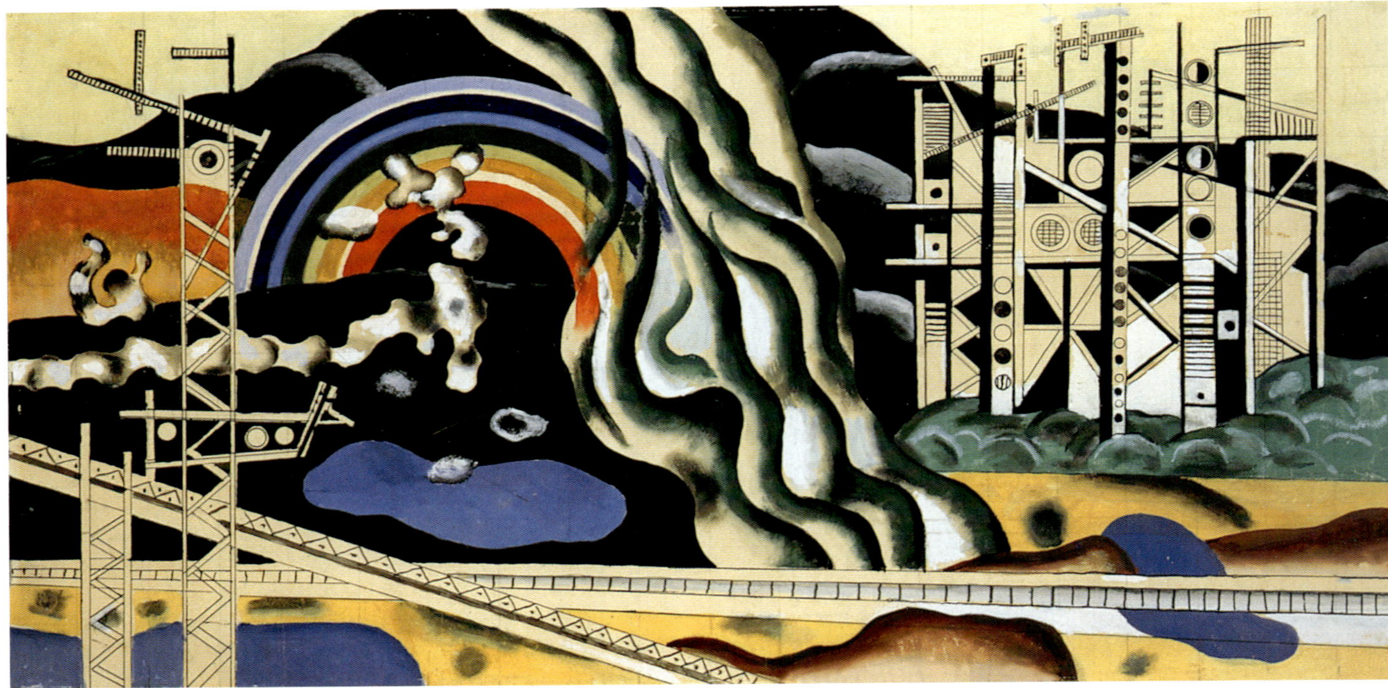

185. Fernand Léger, *The Transmission of Energy*, 1937. Study. Musée Fernand Léger, Biot

towards the viewer [184]. There were, however, sub-Cubist depictions of conventional late nineteenth-century subjects, like Lhote's *Coke Furnaces*, and, as in the case of Lipchitz's *Prometheus*, updated allegories too. And there were treatments of themes which retained strong early twentieth-century connotations of 'Transformism' and 'creative evolution': Laurens' reliefs dedicated to earth, water, night and day. The constructive precision of the Purist 'new spirit' was there in the exhibiting of scientific instruments and machines as such, and most monumentally, in the vast cylinders of the electrostatic generator displayed in blue light in the main rotunda of the Palais, but just as tellingly in the smaller rotunda dedicated to 'Pi', where surfaces were covered with the then calculated 707 decimals of Pi in celebration of numbers.[71] Then, hung in the main nave of the Pavilion, there was Léger's huge painting *The Transmission of Energy*, which employed pictorial dissonance and the fragmented spaces of Bergsonian simultaneity together in celebration of the great new hydroelectric schemes of the inter-war years [185]. It was executed by Léger's students to his exacting plans, another display of precision painting approached more as a process of manufacture than as an expressive activity.

France's collective pride in the progress made by the Third Republic's scientists and advanced industries was deserved. Perrin was one of a generation of remarkable French scientists, and established, besides the Palais de la Découverte, the Centre National de la Recherche Scientifique (CNRS) to build scientific research into the institutional fabric of the State. As I show in Chapter 1, France's new industries, including hydroelectricity, maintained their impetus in the depressed 1930s. But in one area of production significant growth came too late: production for war. Science and technology in the Front Populaire's Palais de la Découverte were expressly at the service of peace. Car production in France may have risen from 200,000 to 227,000 between 1936 and 1938, but, as Weber acerbically notes, in 1938 budget allocations for military transport stood at 30 million francs while those for horse-fodder for the army stood at a staggering 128 million.[72] The scientific and technological progress celebrated by artists in France, from Albert Besnard to Fernand Léger, could not prevent the German victory of 1940.

CHAPTER 8

Modern Spaces; Modern Objects; Modern People

DOMESTIC MODERNITY: FROM THE MAISON CUBISTE TO THE PAVILLON DE L'ESPRIT NOUVEAU; FROM COLLAGE TO LÉGER'S MANUFACTURED OBJECTS

The modernity represented by the Delaunays and Léger before the 1914–18 war and by the Purists alongside Léger after the Armistice, was, for them reality: it was the essential experience of the modern. However selective and idealised their modernity, it was believed to be there for anyone to respond to: a contemporary experience, on the one hand of dynamism and simultaneity, on the other of precision and order. The modern for such modernists in the early twentieth century had, however, another dimension which was transparently ideal. It could also be thought of as a condition to be imagined and desired: something that did not yet exist, except in the minds of certain far-seeing individuals or in a few isolated yet paradigmatic cases, mostly no more than exhibition installations or paper projects. Modernity was an idea that oscillated between the experienced and the imagined.

Ideal modern worlds were most effectively displayed to modernism's publics in exhibitions, and were made most concrete when shown in the form of the domestic interior, because imagined rooms for imagined lives could be constructed as 'life size' exhibition installations easily enough. Such installations, offering an image of possible modern spaces on a domestic scale, were a staple of the department stores and the Universal Exhibitions of the late nineteenth century (continuing into the twentieth) and of the decorative arts section which was given a special prominence in the Salon d'automne from its foundation in 1903. At Samuel Bing's galerie de l'Art Nouveau [85] and at his pavilion in the 1900 Universal Exhibition, images were presented of a possible modernity. And, as in the great department stores, the Grands magasins du Louvre or the Bon Marché, these images were designed to create desires in potential consumers that might lead to purchases and the actual realisation of that modernity in the domestic spaces of middle-class homes. It was in this context that a modern home in which Cubist art had a place was imagined for the Salon d'automne of 1912; the installation was instantly dubbed the 'Maison Cubiste' (Cubist House). And it was in this context too that Le Corbusier (b.1887) imagined a Purist home to display at the 'decorative arts' Exhibition of 1925, the Pavillon de l'Esprit nouveau [8, 186–9]. As I shall show later in this chapter, Le Corbusier's Pavilion was conceived and displayed as just one housing unit in a plan to rebuild the centre of Paris and in a 'Contemporary City for Three Million' [7, 8, 186], but these vast and still entirely cerebral visions were only to be grasped in terms that could relate to actual lives in the life-sized spaces of the Pavilion.

Led by the spectacular success of the Bon Marché from 1869, the department stores had initiated the formation of a mass-consumer society in France, which by 1914 was becoming a reality not just in Paris but for those across the provinces who visited the city by rail or who made their purchases by mail-order from the store catalogues.[1] Besides the low prices produced by economies of scale and organisational efficiency, the key to this transformation was the department stores' focus on display: image. As Michael Miller has shown, what was sold was the image of a modern, bourgeois way of life; one that was always changing with fashion and that never existed in its entirety, but one whose luxury, comforts and pleasures were to be desired and could, at least partially, be bought in the form of goods, including from the 1880s whole domestic interiors.[2] The 'Maison Cubiste' was put together in 1912 by a young artist-decorator André Mare, who with others like Gustave Jaulmes and André Groult was one of a new grouping of designers, the so-called 'coloristes'.[3] These designers worked in a way especially well adapted to the new marketing imperatives. They did not develop all-embracing styles to which every detail of furnishing and decor, including works of art, had to be subordinated, like Bing's Art Nouveau designers. Instead, they composed ensembles which brought together individually assertive, often contrasting elements; it was a strategy which offered images of possible wholes – ensembles – but allowed the objects and embellishments that made them up to be sold separately, including the paintings.

In *Du Cubisme*, written as the 'Maison Cubiste' was being assembled, Gleizes and Metzinger made a point of stressing the autonomy of works of art, the importance of not subordinating them to decorative schemes. Mare's ensembles were accepted as frames for Cubist works because they allowed paintings and sculptures their independence, creating a play of contrast, hence the involvement not only of Gleizes and Metzinger themselves, but of Marie Laurencin, the Duchamp brothers from Puteaux (Raymond Duchamp-Villon designed the façade) and Mare's old friends Léger and Roger de la Fresnaye.[4] What was displayed was an image of a home in which Cubist art could be experienced as part of modern bourgeois life: an image that could, it was blithely presumed, create a demand not only for the services of Mare and his collaborators on the design side, but for Cubist art too. Mare called the sitting room in which paintings by Gleizes, Metzinger, Laurencin and Léger hung, the 'salon bourgeois' [187], a title Léger described as 'perfect' in a letter written to him at the planning stage. 'Your idea,' Léger enthused, 'is absolutely *splendid* for us, really *splendid*. People will see Cubism in its domestic setting, which is very important.'[5] To view it, the visitors to the Autumn Salon passed through the full-scale plaster model of the ground-floor of the façade designed by Duchamp-Villon [189], a façade judged, despite its Cubist detailing, to appeal to the taste for

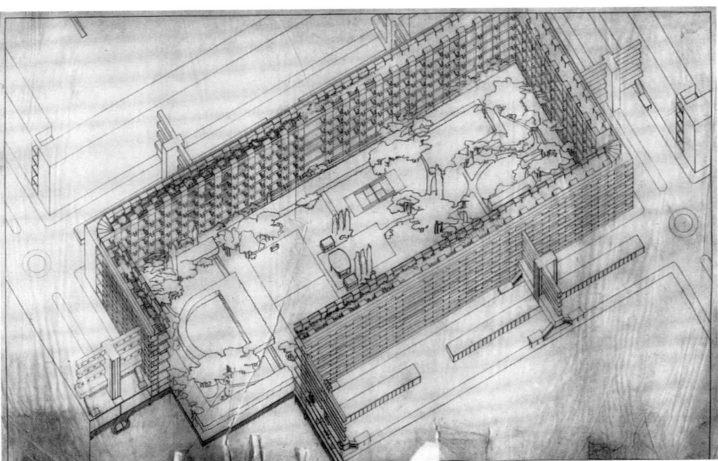

186. Le Corbusier, *Block of Dwellings on the 'Cellular' System*, 1922. Drawing as illustrated in *Urbanisme* (Paris, 1925)

late eighteenth-century domestic architecture as a model of bourgeois comfort and style.

The marketing methods of the department store spectacularly corroborated Karl Marx's observation in *Capital* that when objects become commodities their value is detached from their physical nature as the products of labour: they are 'fetishised' (to use his term), becoming more image than object. One effect of the formation of mass markets by the department store was the arrival, in the first three decades of the century, of modern advertising: selling by image-making. Art historians have drawn attention to the manifold connections between the history of modernism and the history of advertising in that period.[6] Simon Dell's recent analysis successfully parallels the shift in modernist art towards an emphasis on the relationship between image and viewer with a change in advertising theory and practice between 1900 and 1930 from an emphasis on demonstrating the usefulness of the product by giving information to the exploitation of 'psychological' suggestion as a means of arousing desire.[7] In advertising (as in modernist art) this shift was underway in France before 1914, led by O.J. Gérin and C. Espinadel, whose *La Publicité suggestive* of 1911 set the pace. By the early 1920s, advertising as an art of suggestion was the current orthodoxy, given weight by the work of the economist Charles Gide, whose argument that desire had replaced utility in the creation of value led him to write in 1921 of a 'socialism of consumers', where individual desires combine to create a collective force.[8] Modern marketing in the post-war decade has been shown to have actually underwritten the dominant individualism of French middle-class society on every level, a point hammered home by Francis Elvinger's *La Marque* (The Brand name) of 1922. For Elvinger, advertising creates desire in each consumer as an individual response focused on an individual product, a brand name. It is 'the individuality of the product' that is bought, and where need (and therefore use) is to be thought of as general, desire always has a particular object: 'I need to eat; to satisfy this need, I desire *pâtes Bertrand* (Bertrand's pastes).'[9] And what was desired and bought by consumers, according to the advertisers, was above all the social status suggested by the image. Advertising images went beyond need to create desire by holding up the promise of a way of life and a status which could be obtained just by purchasing selected products. The personal choice of individual things could create identity on both a private and a public (social) level.

And yet, if it is easy enough to see the overlap between the 'Maison Cubiste' and the marketing of images developed by advertising and the department stores, it is not so easy to see any overlap between the display of modernity presented in the Purist Pavillon de l'Esprit nouveau and the highly skilled manipulation of consumer desire in the 1920s. After all, as Chapter 7 showed, Purist theory constantly reiterated a commitment to functional efficiency, in other words, to use-value determined by need, and nothing could be more unlike the sumptuous exhibitionism of the department store pavilions at the 1925 decorative arts Exhibition [10] than the Pavillon de l'Esprit nouveau [8]. Le Corbusier's prelude to the Exhibition was a series of articles published in *L'Esprit nouveau* which mounted a concentrated attack on the very idea of 'decorative art'.[10] A particular target was the collaboration encouraged between 'decorative artists' and manufacturers, whose aim was the aestheticisation of industrial production, Roger Marx's 'Social Art' (introduced in Chapter 1). Le Corbusier furnished and fitted out the Esprit nouveau pavilion with what he insisted on calling 'equipment'.[11] He revelled in the idea of using standardised ready-made furniture and fittings – Thonet bentwood chairs, L'Innovation cupboards. He praised especially the storage units which he adapted as space dividers (between kitchen and living areas, for instance), and which he proudly announced could be bought from the Bazaar de l'Hôtel de Ville (one of the older department stores). It is now clear that some of this equipment was actually custom-made, the tubular metal dining table manufactured by the hospital suppliers L. Schmittheisler, for instance, but the anti-decorative, functionalist rhetoric of the pavilion is not dimin-

187. André Mare, The 'Salon bourgeois', The Cubist House (Maison Cubiste), Salon d'automne, Paris, 1912. To left, Jean Metzinger's *Woman with a Fan* (1912); reflected in mirror, Fernand Léger's *Level Crossing*, 1912

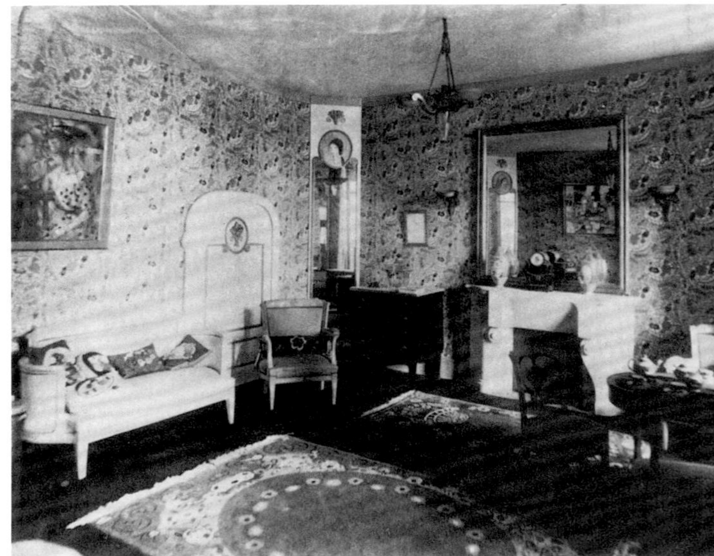

ished by this. The fitting out of his pavilion was not to be compared with the composition of ensembles by ex-coloristes like Mare or Groult (both of whom designed for the 1925 Exhibition), but rather with the equipping of factories, sports halls or garages.[12]

What is more, the urbanist project of which the pavilion represented a part [186], seemed explicitly to place it outside the terms of middle-class consumerism. This was not an image of a possible bourgeois way of life to be realised by aspiring and discerning individuals in modern French society as then constituted. It was an image of a way of life which could be indiscriminately available for millions at low cost in a Taylorist modern society that did not yet exist.[13] It was merely an element in a projected solution to the problem of low-cost housing, a solution that went further than functional design to envisage the bringing together of the working and middle classes in an ideal corporate unity, as we shall see later.

Desire, personal choice and the fetishism of the commodity were allowed into the apparently air-tight functionalism of the Purist pavilion by the presence of art, both in the works of art by Léger, Gris, Laurens, Lipchitz and by Ozenfant and Le Corbusier themselves, as well as in the 'architecture' of the building. Indeed, ultimately even the equipment assembled in the pavilion could become desirable, fetishised, not only because repressed sexual desires could be projected into the most uncompromisingly useful objects, but because they had been chosen personally by Le Corbusier and so could come to represent him.[14] His was a brand name to rival any in modern design: a distinctly attractive compound of modern professionalism and creativity.

The role of art in Purist theory was, in fact, defined in contradistinction to that of equipment. Works of art were by definition without utility. Ozenfant called them 'machines for producing emotion'; Le Corbusier insisted that they were produced by and aroused 'passion'.[15] Architecture was

188. Le Corbusier, Hall of the *Villa La Roche*, 1924. Square du docteur Blanche. Entrance hall, with displayed below Georges Braque's *Musician*, 1917–18,

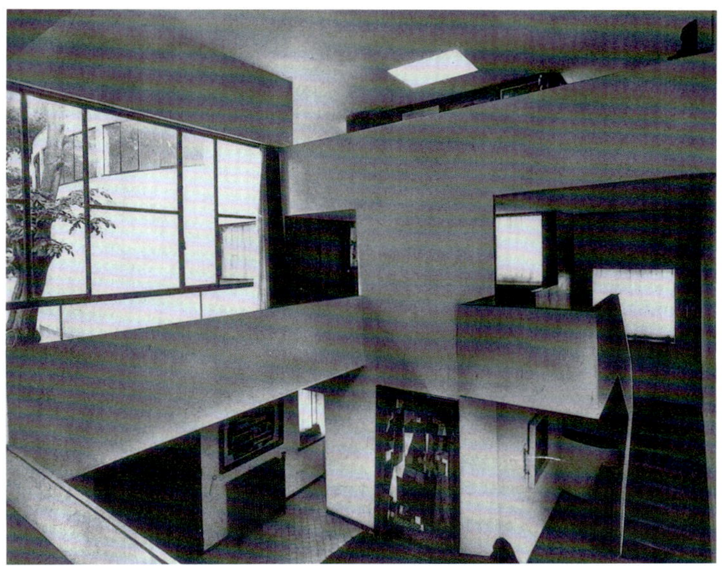

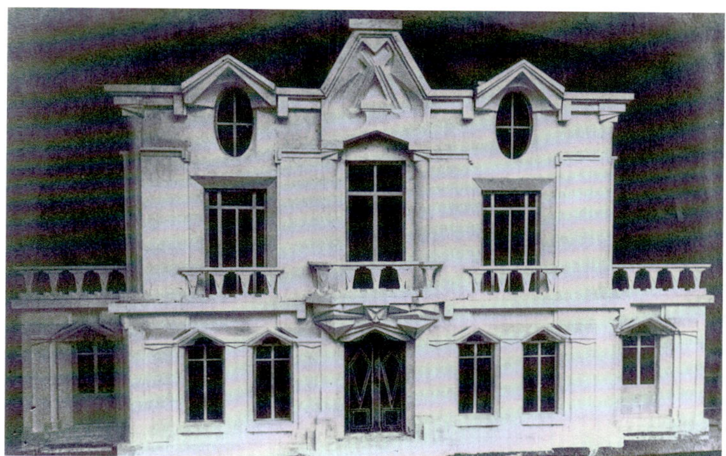

189. Raymond Duchamp-Villon, Facade of the *Maison Cubiste* (The Cubist House), Salon d'Automne, 1912. Plaster model. Destroyed

at once functional and beautiful, the product of rational problem-solving *and* of irrational 'plastic' creation. Le Corbusier's book of 1923, *Vers une architecture*, based on articles in *L'Esprit nouveau*, gave equal emphasis to both. Purism held in balance, thus, a concern for use-value and a concern for the value of the useless: art. The latter amounted to an invitation specifically to the middle class as well as more generally to the irrational and emotive. It made the pavilion and its contents desirable, as did the unequivocal bourgeois status of those who were commissioning dwellings from Le Corbusier by 1925. Some of the 'equipment' used in the pavilion was borrowed from the recently completed house designed by him for the banker Raoul La Roche. Here, as in the pavilion, colour was used in a dulled-down version of Theo van Doesburg's De Stijl polychromatic architecture to underscore the status of the building as art, and the spacious interiors were designed as much as a setting for La Roche's splendid collection of Cubist and Purist painting as the domestic interiors of a home [188]. La Roche himself certainly thought of it as above all a work of art, and by the end of the 1920s was opening the house and collection twice a week to visitors. Despite Le Corbusier's rhetoric of self-denial, even the Pavillon de L'Esprit Nouveau had a role in the consumer culture so extravagantly endorsed by the Exhibition of 1925.

There are many indicators that when the Cubists decided to incorporate the paper detritus of the mass media into their work, including press advertising, they grasped its appeal to the irrational: the dimension of suggestion. Apollinaire's 1913 eulogy to Picasso as collagist dwells on the material factuality of the 'real objects' he used, but adds provocatively 'surprise laughs wildly in the purity of light'.[16] It was a little before this statement that Robert Delaunay (b.1885) incorporated posters into his *Cardiff Team* [172], scattering his images of modernity around placards bearing the words 'Astra, construction' and 'Magic, Paris': leaving their suggestions open, as psychological attractions. The collages of Picasso, Braque and Gris, juxtapose styles of attraction as well as images and words: sometimes styles of lettering, sometimes brand-name labels against newsprint ads, often commercial graphic images alongside their own Cubist

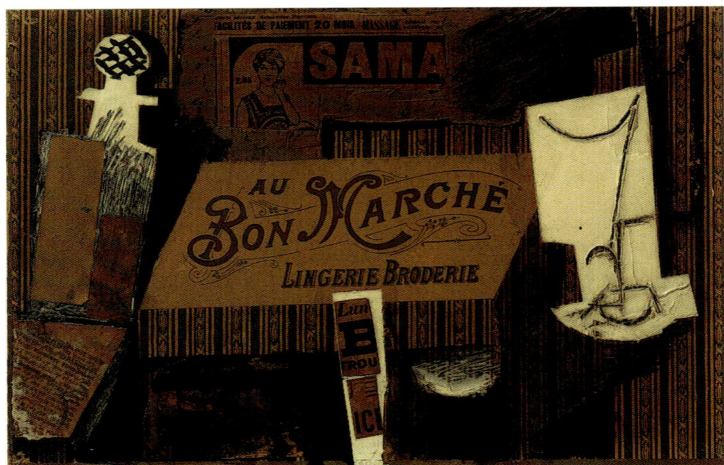

190. Pablo Picasso, *At the Bon Marché*, 1913. Oil and pasted paper on cardboard, 23.8 × 35.9 cm. Museum Ludwig, Köln

styles. By the isolation or fragmentation of words, brand names can be detached from the products they announce – as in Delaunay's 'Astra' (the name of a manufacturer of airships) – entirely losing their capacity to inform and becoming, like the partial signs around them, suggestions and nothing more.[17] Braque (b.1882) repeatedly used suggestions of music: Bach, Valse, Violin [110]. Picasso (b.1881) often left names hanging: Figaro, Suze, Vieux Marc . . .

In one case, Picasso's tiny 1913 collage, *At the Bon Marché* [190], department-store consumerism comes into explicit conjunction with desire, when the suggestions offered are wittily sexualised (a joke at the expense of a store, the Bon Marché, which made a policy of prudishness). Here Picasso places a fragment of a press advertisement for a 'white sale' (a linen sale) at the Samaritain store above an elegantly lettered card publicising the linen and embroidery (lingerie broderie) department of the Bon Marché store. These two elements can be read together with the cut-out words below, 'trou ici' ('hole here'): above, there is the head and shoulders of a woman coquettishly posed, then comes underclothing ('lingerie'), under which is her sex ('hole here'), and every part of her is a 'bargain' ('Bon Marché').[18]

Léger's *City* of 1919 [176], in the simultanist mode of Delaunay's *Cardiff Team*, incorporates lettering. It evokes posters as well as street signs. Later he was to agree with Cendrars' suggestion that the picture was partly a response to the visual excitement of the huge posters in the Place Clichy, the largest in Paris, the site, as he put it, of 'the birth of publicity'.[19] He was himself to design posters in the early and mid-1920s, and was an acknowledged influence on the poster designing of the then most-renowned poster designer in France, Cassandre. But, in the context of consumerism, his work in that decade exploits more the fetishisation of the object as such than the 'psychological suggestion' put in play by advertising. Certainly his practice of presenting objects in matter-of-fact isolation in *Ballet mécanique* and in works related to it like *Composition with Hand and Hats* [177, 180] parallels the marketing practice of the department store catalogues and much product advertising in the press. Biscuits were advertised in illustrated magazines like *Le Monde illustré* very much as they appear in the 1927 picture. In the case of the 1924 painting *The Siphon* there was a specific advertising source, a Campari advertisement in the newspaper *Le Matin* [192, 193].[20] And yet, in this, the clearest case known of direct influence, what the connection demonstrates is the way Léger (b.1881) erases every trace of the advertisement as an image: he comprehensively detaches the banal representations of hand, glass and siphon from their brand-name context. No trace of the word 'Campari' on the glass remains to situate it in a suggested way of life where desires are satisfied by purchasing the right drink into which to squirt soda. It is the simple functioning relationship between siphon and glass, activated by the hand, that becomes the subject.

This is, however, an exception; Léger's objects are rarely represented functioning thus. One critic ridiculed him in 1923 as the painter of 'pseudo-machines "which do not work" '.[21] And in an interview in the same year, he resolutely lifted the 'manufactured object', which he identified as the basis of his work, out of the sphere of use-value, where it functioned efficiently, and into the sphere of art, the beautiful. Le Corbusier's polarised distinction between equipment and art is echoed, except that for Léger the 'beauty' of functional objects – their desirability – could override their usefulness. 'I try,' he said, 'to create with mechanical elements a *beautiful object*'. And then: 'The manufactured object is there, absolute, polychromatic, clean and precise, beautiful in itself; and it is the most extreme competition that the artist has ever experienced.'[22] The irrational sphere of 'beauty' into which the object is thus brought in his paint-

191. Fernand Léger, *Mona Lisa with Keys*, 1930. Oil on canvas, 91 × 72 cm. Musée Fernand Léger, Biot

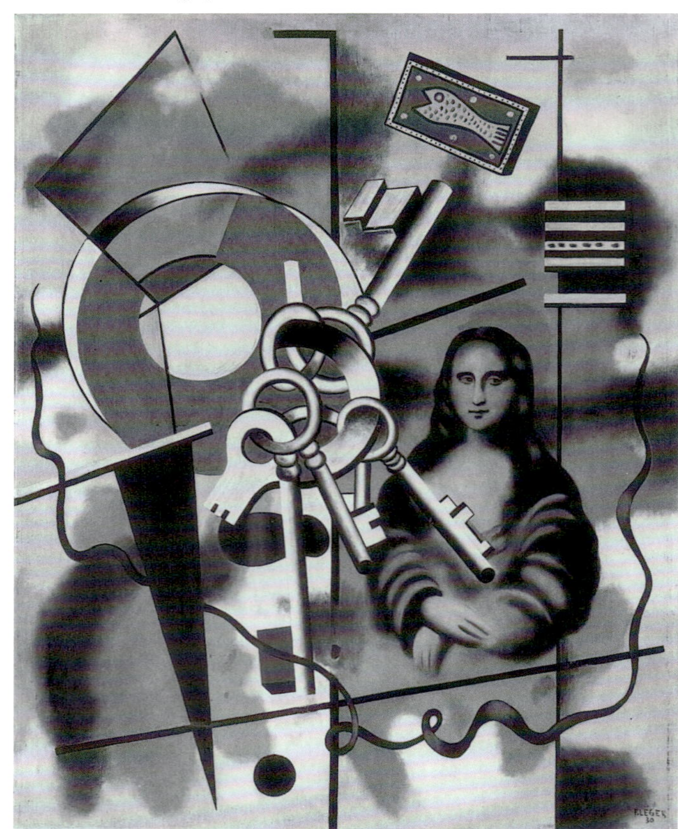

192. Far right. Fernand Léger, *The Siphon*, 1924. Oil on canvas, 65.1 × 46.3 cm. Albright-Knox Art Gallery, Buffalo, New York. Gift of Mr and Mrs Gordon Bunshaft, 1977

193. Advertisement for Campari, from *Le Matin*, 12 September 1924, p. 3

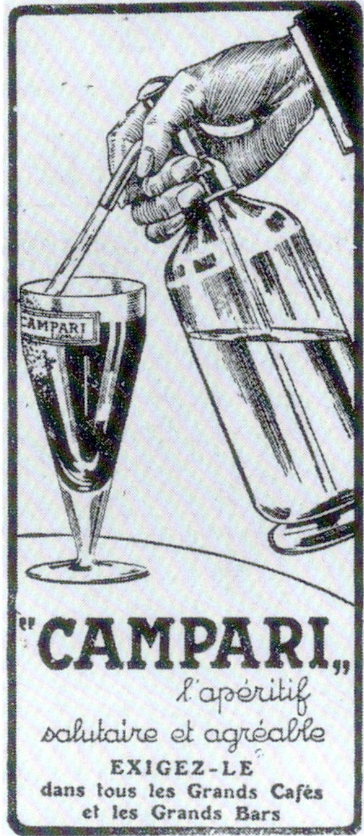

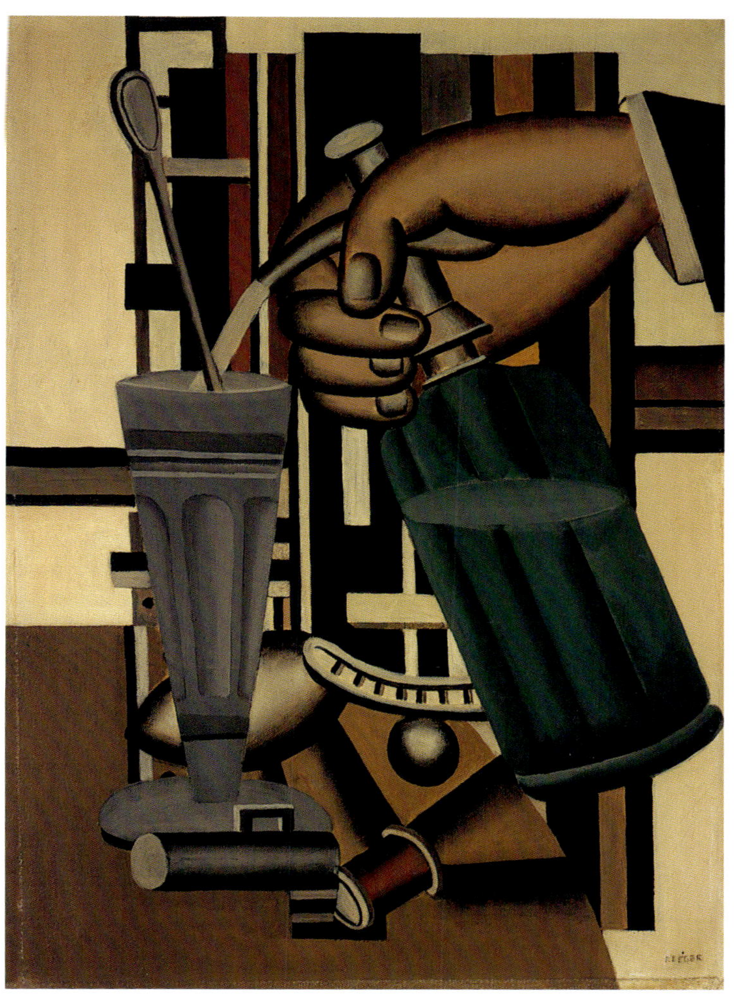

ing is, of course, a sphere in which it becomes above all desirable, but desirable on the exclusive terms of art (as Léger understood it), a sphere in which, he would later insist, sexual attraction had no place.

At the end of the 1930s, Léger produced a series of paintings that released manufactured objects to float in only vaguely articulated spaces; among these was *Mona Lisa with Keys* [191]. Here an apparently random collection of objects, removed entirely from the sphere of use-value and at the same time from any overt reference to brand-named desire, become suggestive enough seriously to threaten Léger's desexualised ideal of beauty. The image of the Mona Lisa, transformed into a manufactured object by mechanical reproduction, acts as a cipher of the suggestiveness of art (*art*, not advertising). Suggestion invites projection: the possibility of projecting sexual meanings into the keys and the ring is obvious.

Léger's paintings of objects in space have often been compared to the irrational juxtapositions of Surrealist painting, especially that of Magritte, whose own deadpan exploitation of manufactured objects such as pipes can seem to be a Surrealist commentary on Léger's work and on the Purist mechanically selected object [307]. It is a relationship that brings out the modernity of the Surrealists' notion of the object more than Léger's, or the Purists', for with the emergence of the 'Surrealist object' between 1931 and 1936, the fetishisation of the object in mass-consumer society received its most telling modernist response. Given the Surrealists' deep antipathy to bourgeois and utopian notions of modernity, nothing could be more ironic. When in 1930 Louis Aragon characterised collage as a practice that exposed the 'personality of choice' rather than the 'personality of technique', he clearly aligned it with the art of suggestion in advertising: the art of arousing desire.[23] The object in Surrealism, from Magritte's pipe in *The Treason of Images* [307] to Meret Oppenheim's *Luncheon in Fur* [158], represents the total and, for the Surrealists, the final submergence of usefulness by desire.

MODERNITY AND GENDER: WORKING WOMEN AND INDEPENDENT WOMEN; WIVES AND MOTHERS

The department stores generated such extremes of desire among 'respectable people' that by the 1900s serious psychological studies were being devoted to the emergence of kleptomania on an unprecedented scale.[24] The condition was considered to be restricted almost exclusively to women, since women, as Zola had observed in his notes for his department store novel *Au bonheur des dames* (1883), were considered the quintessential new consumers.[25] The modern woman as bourgeois consumer (not thief), dressing fashionably, appearing in desirable venues appropriately turned out, or making the home, would be a constant performer in advertising images, especially from the 1920s, when the act of consumption (especially taking pleasures) became the typical theme of advertisements.

In 1934 Le Corbusier and his wife Yvonne moved into the

penthouse apartment he had designed for them near the Parc des Princes. That year he published a photographic record of their new home in the second volume of his architectural 'Oeuvres complètes'. A shot of the studio shows the artist-architect, the modern man, at a table working, surrounded by paintings which are the product of his creative energy. A shot of the kitchen ('one of the essential rooms in the home') shows Yvonne decoratively turned out, the modern woman, a housewife, and behind her a set of gleaming pans, newly purchased [194, 195]. In modernity as Le Corbusier conceived it, both during the Purist period and afterwards, the producers were almost exclusively male. Men were the constructors of the 'new spirit' in the 1920s and those who would initiate what he called the second machine age in the 1930s. His modern heroes, the engineer, the entrepreneur, the industrialist, the political leader, the architect, the artist, all represent aspects of a male productive principle. In Léger's painting too, the heroic is exclusively male and, in peacetime, productive: represented most obviously, by the moustachioed *Mechanic* and the business-suited men in the 1924 city paintings [179, 182]. His praise in the statements with which he developed his machine aesthetic in the mid-1920s is reserved for the producers of the manufactured object alone: the mechanics and especially the artisans, always male. Both the dynamism and the precision of Léger's modernity are represented as masculine qualities, even in the case of his mechanised female figures. In a text published in 1924, he describes 'the manufactured and "mechanical" object . . . slowly subjugating the breasts and curves of woman.'[26] Such an image of the masculine as creative and productive, defined *against* the image of the feminine as passive and consumerist was a cliché in modernist and non-modernist art throughout the period.

The decades between 1900 and 1940, however, did see the slow, repeatedly obstructed emergence in France of an active, creative modern woman, in fact as well as image.

194. Le Corbusier's studio at *24, rue Nungesser-et-Coli*, Paris, 1931–4. Photograph published in *Le Corbusier et Pierre Jeanneret. Oeuvre complète de 1929–1934*, p. 149

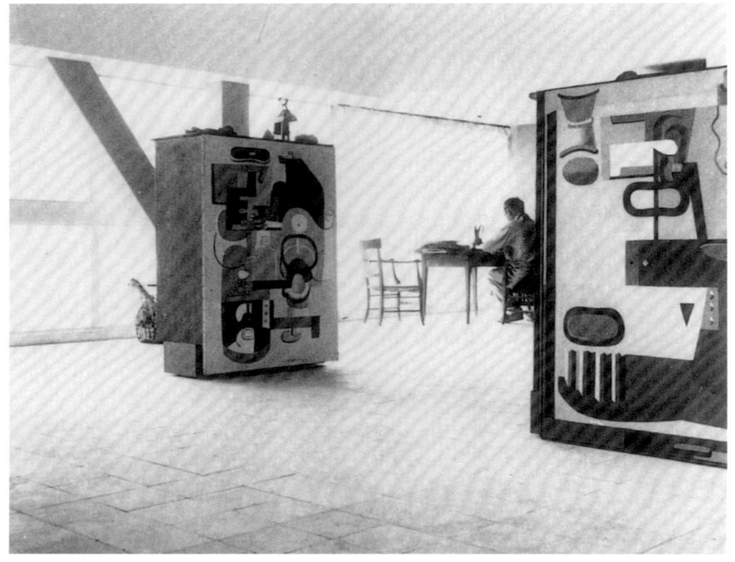

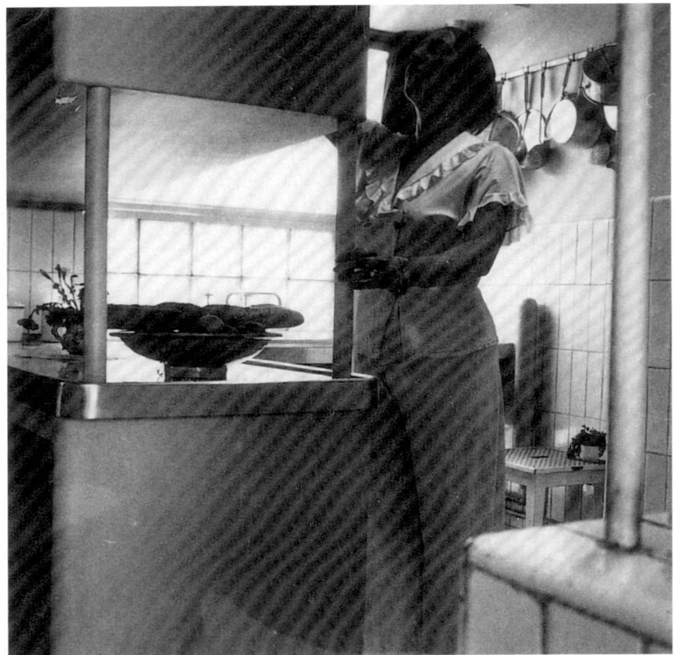

The surprise is not that this occurred, but that active images of women, representing modern aspiration and actuality, are so rare in independent art, especially where it is most engaged with the idea of modernity, and that this includes art produced by women (for instance, Sonia Delaunay and Maria Blanchard).

As women entered the Ecole National des Beaux-Arts (from 1896) and began to compete for the Prix de Rome (from 1903), education for women was gradually opening a way for them to enter professional careers other than school teaching. In 1914, half the 2,000 girls who attended lycées were still destined for teaching, but there were also women doctors, lawyers, architects and journalists, as well as artists.[27] At the same time, on the other hand, the Unions, led by the CGT, resisted the rise of the working woman, and shared the middle-class ideal of woman as wife and mother at the hearth. By 1914, women actually accounted for 36.6% of the active working population outside agriculture, but they neither had the vote nor could stand for election, and when they worked it was mostly in lower-paid jobs, as typists, postal employees and sales girls.[28] Such occupations did lead to a new kind of independence for some. Department store 'demoiselles' could earn good petty bourgeois salaries of more than 3,000 francs a year, and often had left provincial homes to come to Paris. In fiction and the press they were treated as a significant new phenomenon, whose tendency to moral laxity was a threat, but they were a minority in the department-store workforces. They seem typically to have been on the lookout for marriage, and any sign of moral irregularity led to instant dismissal.[29]

The massive depletion of the male workforce brought about by the Great War at every level of industry and agriculture seemed by 1917–18 to have accelerated the feminization of work and the prospects of real emancipation for women. Writers like Léon Abensour and Marie de la Hire eulogised the response of women to President René

195. Left. Le Corbusier, Apartment at 24, rue Nungesser-et-Coli, Paris, 1931–4. Kitchen with Yvonne Le Corbusier. Photograph published in *Le Corbusier et Pierre Jeanneret. Oeuvre complète de 1929–1934*, p. 150

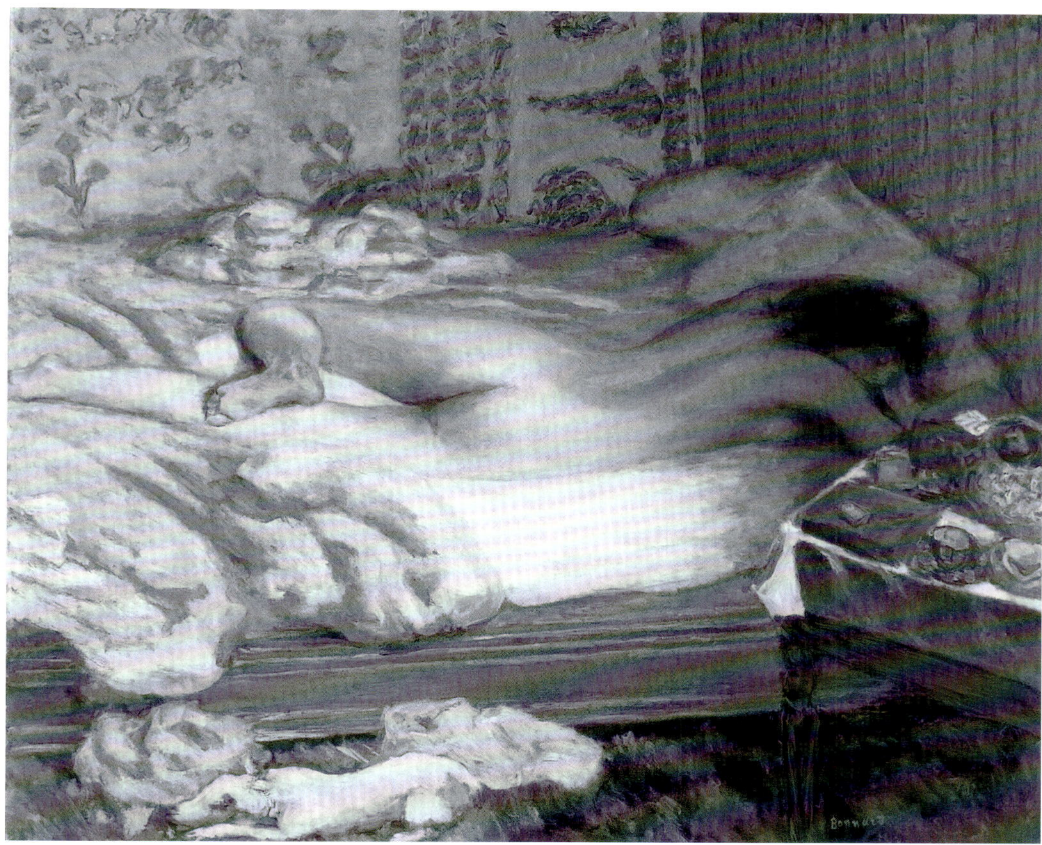

196. Pierre Bonnard, *Siesta – The Artist's Studio*, 1900. Oil on canvas, 109 × 132 cm. National Gallery of Victoria, Melbourne, Australia. Felton bequest, 1949

Viviani's resounding 1914 appeal for them to replace 'in the field of work those who are on the field of battle'.[30] The militant feminists of Marguerite Durand's *La Fronde* ceased their campaigning for the vote and civil rights, and dedicated their energies to the wartime 'Union Sacrée'; but the sheer numbers of new women workers in the factories, and the takeover by women of such civil roles as mayor and local councillor across the nation made it seem that a threshold was about to be crossed. Even three years after the Armistice in 1921, Abensour could write of women being ready 'to gather the fruit of their long struggles'.[31] With the dynamic image of working women recorded in a film officially made by the army 'cinematographic section' went other images popularised through the press, postcards and fiction, including that of a still more sexually liberated modern woman. If the figures for divorce dropped sharply during the war, those for illegitimate birth in France rose from 8.4% in 1913–14 to 14.2% in 1917; prostitutes were the favoured female visitors to the front.[32] 1920 saw the publication of Colette's novel *Chéri*, a portrait of liberated sexuality in a world surviving from the late nineteenth century, that of courtesans made independent by wealth, the *grandes cocottes*. It was avidly consumed by women as much as men. In 1922, the year following Abensour's confident prediction of women's final emancipation, Victor Margueritte's *La Garçonne* appeared, a portrait of a new kind of woman, determined to experience sexual pleasure (lesbian as well as heterosexual) with the abandon of the most promiscuous young men: a female 'boy', challenging gender stereotypes, capable of living outside bourgeois marriage and the family (she runs an art gallery on the rue la Boétie).

The 1920s produced a new range of popular images of modern female independence, from the cigarette smoking *midinettes* with their cropped haircuts to the stars of high society, like Marie-Laure, the Vicomtesse de Noailles, but the optimism of supporters of militant feminism like Léon Abensour was quickly disappointed. Significantly, the final image of the film made by the army's 'cinematographic section' about women in the war, was a woman waiting at the hearth for the return of her soldier husband. Both government and organised labour responded to the demographic implications of the huge war losses by renewing with fresh vigour the demand that women should stay at home and bear children. In 1921, legislation stipulated fines and imprisonment of up to six months for distributing birth-control propaganda or contraceptives, criminalising what one character in *La Garçonne* describes as the Malthusian prerequisite for the liberated lifestyle explored there.[33] Indeed, so great was the shock caused by Margueritte's novel that it was banned from Paris book shops and he was stripped of the Légion d'honneur.[34] And yet, in this obdurately resistant context there was a continued strengthening of the position of active working women, however gradual, a process that was consolidated under the Popular Front between 1936 and 1938. By the end of the 1930s, a third of those gaining the baccalauréat were girls. In 1935, 10% of the lawyers at the Paris bar were women.[35] In *La Garçonne*, Léon Blum's *Du Mariage* is held up as a prime text for sexual liberationists opposing the institution of marriage. Blum's Popular Front administration was the first in France to give government posts to women.

As I have indicated, the images of modern women that predominated in independent and modernist art throughout the period 1900–40 set aside the idea of women as active, creative producers. They tended, rather, to sustain the conventional resistance to women's emancipation in work and in democratic politics by merely modernising established 'feminine' stereotypes, stereotypes which characterise the feminine as essentially passive and receptive. I shall look at modern women in such images under four headings: the sexually liberated woman, the emancipated society woman, the wife and mother, and the banalised everyday companion.

Many of the women who became involved in the bohemias of Montmartre and Montparnasse at the beginning of the century were women who had left home in the provinces to find independence in Paris, in the new style of department store 'demoiselles' and their like. They were often independent enough to live with lovers rather than marry, and indeed the account left by Marevna (Maria Vorobëv, b.1892), woman painter and wartime lover of Diego Rivera, candidly exposes the importance of female sexual availability in this world: sex as a currency of exchange.[36] Most were not painters, like Marevna, though there were others, for instance Jacqueline Marval (b.1866), partner of the successful painter Jules Flandrin.[37] Picasso's partner Fernande Olivier was an independent woman of this kind (though she did not come from the provinces). Marthe Boursin, who became Marthe Bonnard, and Charlotte Herpin, who became Josette Gris, were such women too; they both changed their names to consolidate their independence, the one from a poor background in the region of Bourges, the other from a petty bourgeois background in the Touraine.[38]

197. Kees Van Dongen, *The Spanish Shawl*, 1913. Oil on canvas, 195.5 × 130.5 cm. Musée Nationale d'Art Moderne, Paris

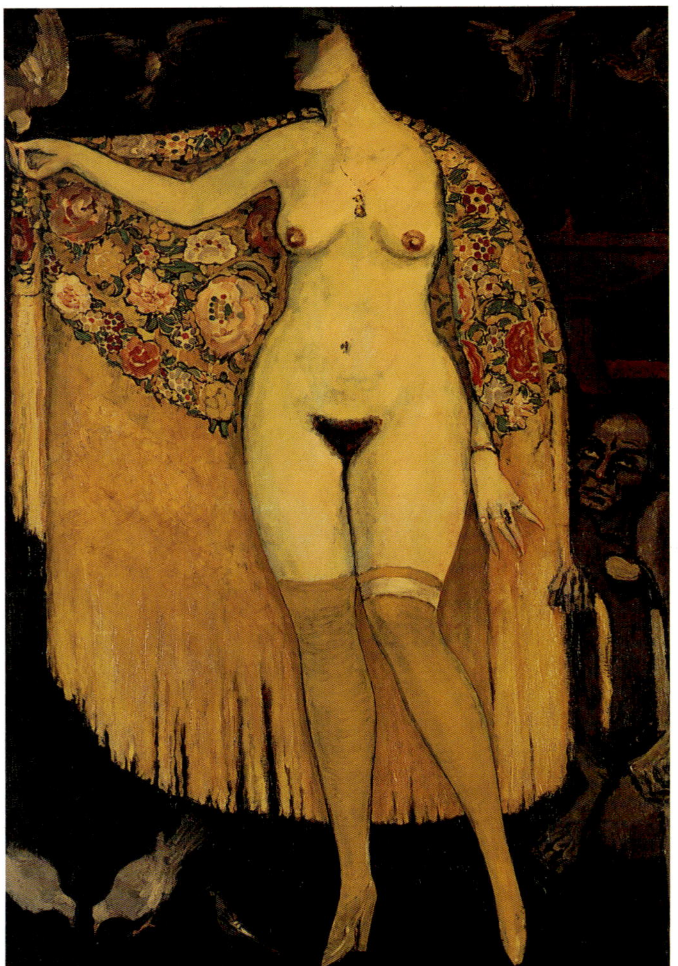

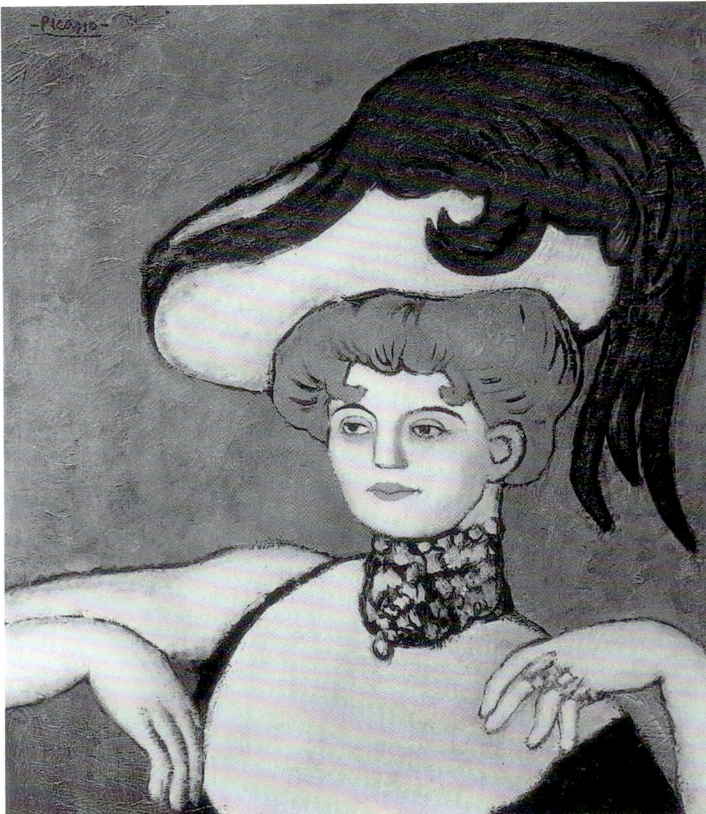

198. Pablo Picasso, *Woman with a Necklace*, 1901. Oil on canvas, 65.3 × 54.5 cm. Private Collection

In the late 1890s and the early 1900s, working with his box camera as an aid, Bonnard (b.1867) repeatedly painted Marthe as a modern sexually liberated (and for the male, sexually liberating) woman. An image such as the magnificently lassitudinous *Siesta* of 1900 [196] draws no line between the aftermath of freely exchanged love and of sex as a commodity for sale. Marthe could just as well be a prostitute here as what she actually was, the mistress with whom Bonnard enjoyed 'free love' (Bonnard was a committed anarchist, who became a friend of Léon Blum). The prostitute had, of course, become an established icon of modernity in the late nineteenth century, especially through the work of Toulouse-Lautrec. She continued as such into the twentieth century, her sexual availability often ambiguously merged with that of the new, independent woman-as-lover, and always subject to, shaped by masculine desire. Picasso included paintings of prostitutes and their privileged equivalent courtesans, in his exhibition of 1901 at Vollard's gallery. His *Woman with a Necklace* [198] shows that the promise (for men) of liberated sexuality did not have to be naked: a certain lavish fashionable look was enough. Richardson has suggested that this is

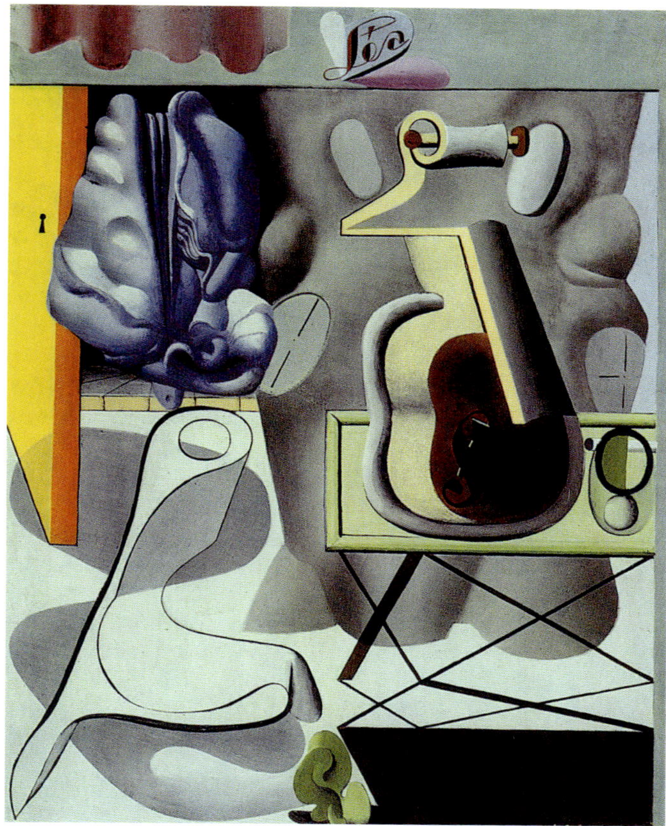

199. Le Corbusier, *Léa*, 1931. Oil on canvas, 146 × 114 cm. Private Collection

the famous actress-courtesan, 'La Belle Otéro', one of the *grandes cocottes* brought to mind by Colette's pearl-necklaced Léa in *Chéri* twenty years later.[39] Such women were as much the modern subjects of socially acceptable anti-modernists like Henri Gervex as they were of radical modernists. Bourgeois society could absorb their modern sexuality in images; but available women offered naked to the male gaze could still cause scandal in 1914. Derain and Vlaminck both painted Fauve versions of a typical Lautrec subject, a dancer at the Rat Mort. It was, however, the more marginal Fauve, Kees Van Dongen (b.1877), who was especially drawn to such subjects, and at the Salon d'automne of 1913 Van Dongen succeeded in causing a major scandal with his *Spanish Shawl* [197]. This image of exhibitionist exposure and of desire personified in the shape of a deformed cripple gazing at the display offered caused enough shock for the police to remove the work, the inevitable press controversy following on.

The painting of such subjects continued through the 1920s, by then, however, never with comparably scandalous results. Foujita earned his dazzling success in the early 1920s with the help of stylish yet sharp up-datings of Manet's *Olympia*, and among those who continued to paint available modern nudes were Jules Pascin, Moïse Kisling and even that most respectable of middle-of-the-road independents, Dunoyer de Segonzac. Surprisingly perhaps, Le Corbusier painted a late addendum to the early twentieth-century theme of the modern woman and liberated sexuality. His painting *Léa* of 1932 [199] carries an obvious allusion to Colette's Léa in *Chéri*, fictional vehicle of female sexual independence. Related works on paper show a naked woman emerging from the holiday cabin door; she is replaced by the oyster (referring to Léa's jealously guarded pearls) as the analogue of the female genitalia (the female pearl).

Sexual independence in the form of modern women made available to the modern masculine gaze quickly lost its capacity to surprise. What remains surprising, however, is the fact, comprehensively demonstrated by Gill Perry, that such subjects were taken up by several prominent women painters, including Emilie Charmy (b.1872), a close friend of Colette in the 1920s, and Jacqueline Marval.[40] Charmy's *Sleeping Nude* of the mid-1920s [200] is an image of a woman's pleasure in her own body (she may be masturbating), but also of liberated abandon. Perry's conclusion, that women painters often could only represent female sexuality as it was shaped by the male gaze, is irrefutable.

The emancipated society woman was not represented as first and foremost to be defined in terms of any supposed sexual independence. She was represented rather as the ultimate female consumer, defined by her 'feminine' sense of style and her discerning membership of the clientele of the great fashion houses – before 1914 Worth, Doucet or Poiret, after 1918, Poiret (until his bankruptcy in 1925) joined by new figures like Lanvin and Coco Chanel. 'Artistes français' and 'Société Nationale' painters like Gervex, Besnard and François Flameng painted society women thus, for instance in Gervex's portrait of his wife showing off her costume for a reception at the Austrian Embassy in 1908 [201]. The earnings of such artists were enough to pay the huge costs of the major couturiers (between ten and a hundred thousand francs could be spent a year on being fashionable).[41] Leading modernists painted society women much less often, but in the early post-war years Van Dongen and Marie Laurencin (1883) emerged as sought-after society portraitists, as did Man Ray in photography. There was no overlap between the images of top consumers that they produced, for instance

200. Emilie Charmy, *Sleeping Nude*, *c*.1925. Oil on canvas, 65 × 80 cm. Private Collection

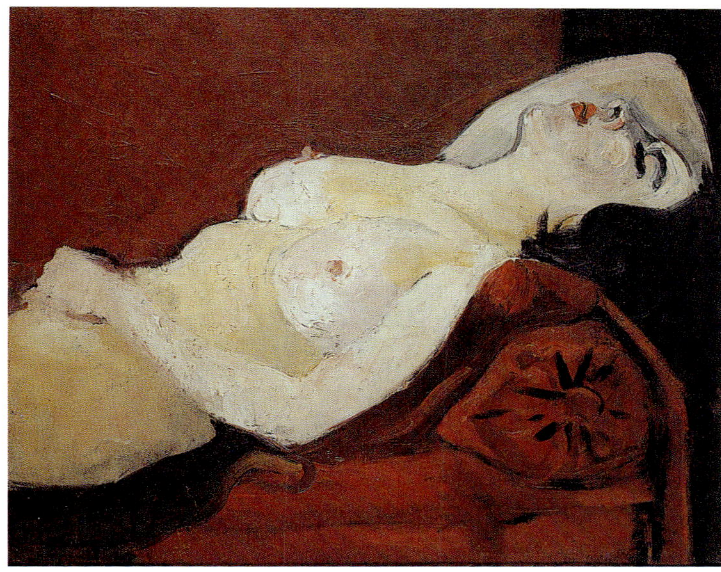

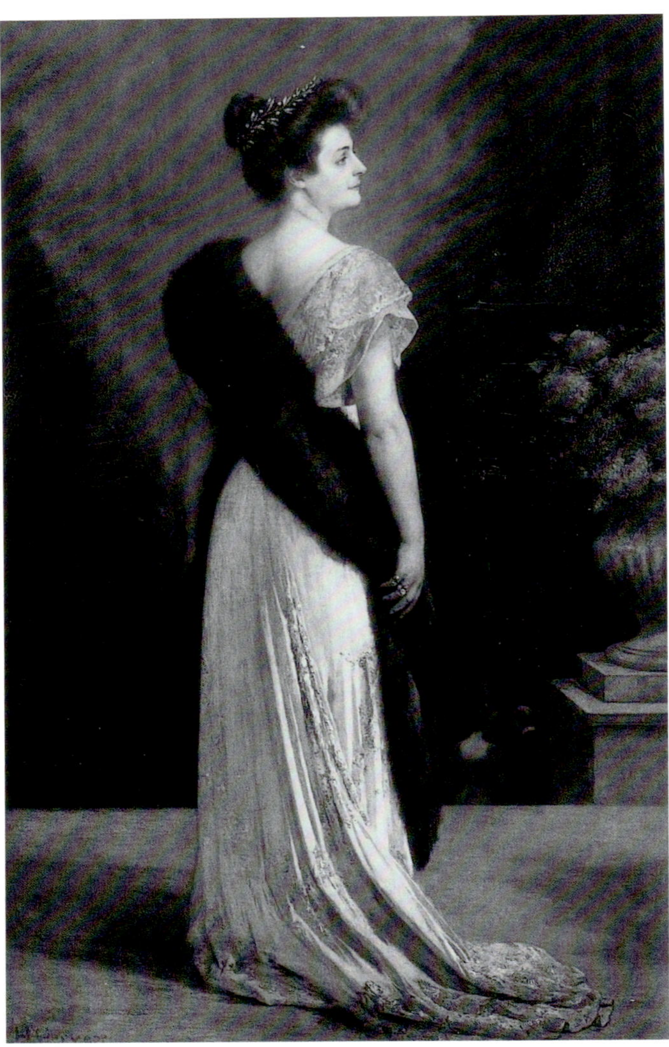

201. Henri Gervex, *Portrait of Mme. Gervex*, 1908. Oil on canvas, 221 × 136 cm. Musée des Beaux-Arts, Nancy

Laurencin's *Portrait of the Baronne Gourgaud* of 1923 [203], and those painted by modernists of sexually liberated women, the overlap was rather with the fashion model photographed for the developing fashion press. One leading woman modernist, of course, made her own contribution to fashion, Sonia Delaunay, with her Atelier Simultané (set up in 1924), and her collaboration with the furrier Heim at the 1925 Exhibition [44]. Offering images of sexual availability for male consumption was not to be confused either with creating modern images for big-spending society women or with painting them as top consumers.

Such exceptional modern women are presented as such: they are out of the ordinary, and the very sumptuousness of colour in Van Dongen and the very refinement of line and hue in Laurencin say so. By contrast, ordinariness (in costume and setting) is the pervasive characteristic of the maternities and family scenes that became common during the Great War and in the period of the pro-natalist campaigns that followed. Modern women here were more to be imagined buying what they needed from the ready-to-wear departments of the Bon Marché or the Samaritaine than setting trends. Madame Matisse had run her own milliner's shop in Paris early in the century, and posed with considerable fashion sense for Matisse's *Woman in a Hat* of 1905 and her portrait of 1913 [96]. By 1913, she probably could have afforded to buy from the couturiers, but Matisse (b.1869) never paints her in family situations as anything other than a middling, middle-class woman. That is certainly what she is when he paints her in the summer of 1919 taking tea in the garden at Issy-les-Moulineaux with Marguerite, Matisse's daughter, and the dog [202]. Picasso's maternities of the early 1920s identify the theme of motherhood with notions not of modernity, but of timelessness and tradition. In the same years, on the other hand, Maria Blanchard (b.1881), herself hunchbacked, childless and unmarried, produced a

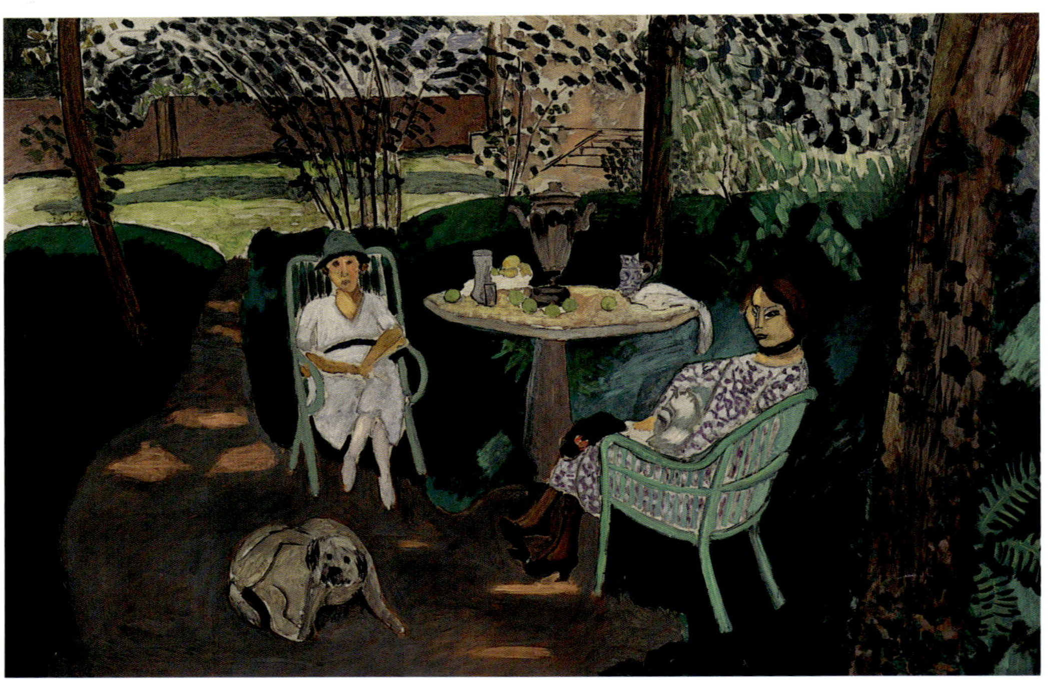

202. Henri Matisse, *Tea in the Garden*, 1919. Oil on canvas, 140.8 × 211.3 cm. Los Angeles County Museum of Art, Bequest of David L. Loew in memory of his father, Marcus Loew

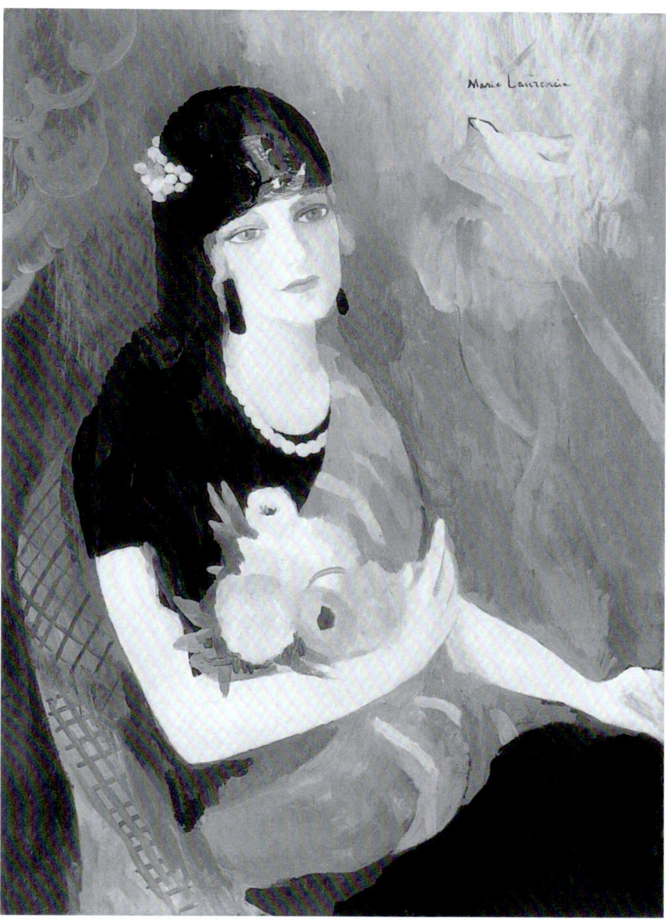

203. Marie Laurencin, *Portrait of the Baronne Gourgaud with a Black Mantilla*, 1923. Oil on canvas, 51 × 36cm. Musée National d'Art Moderne, Paris

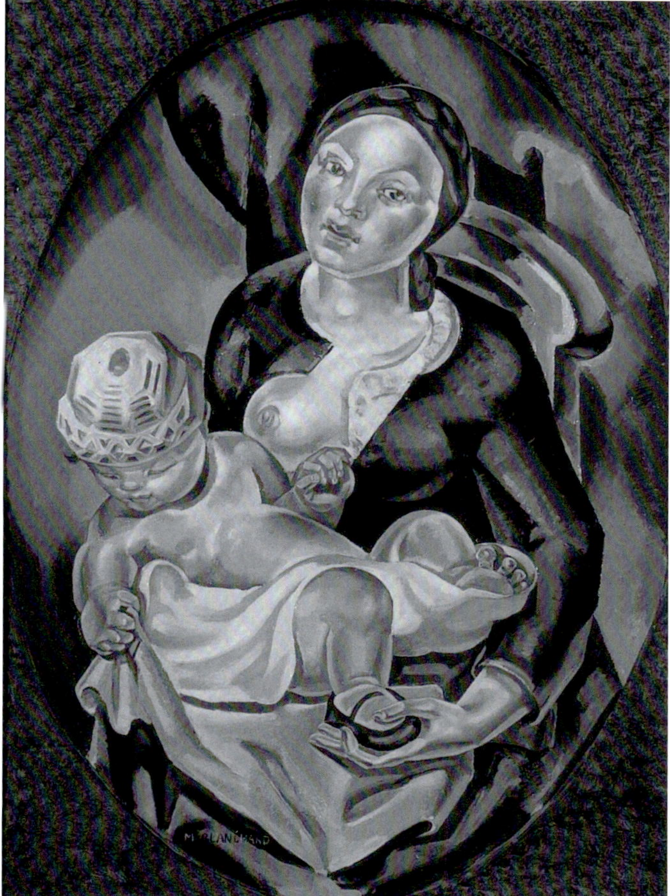

204. Maria Blanchard, *Maternity*, 1921–2. Oil on canvas, 101 × 75cm. Musée National d'Art Moderne, Paris

succession of images of the modern ordinariness of motherhood which capture a desired condition of female fulfilment with special intensity. There is fatigue in the face of the mother in her oval *Maternity* of 1921–2 [204], but pride too in the way she offers her child to the viewer, the infant's rattle and bonnet just the sort of mass-produced items she might have bought from the Bon Marché.[42]

It was, however, Léger who, early in the 1920s, produced the most ambitious modernist representation of family life as a desired manifestation of modernity in its newest and yet most ordinary aspects. He did so in the huge painting he showed at the Salon d'automne of 1922, *Mother and Child* [249], which was probably based on a visit to his suburban weekend home at Fontenay-aux-roses by the critic Maurice Raynal, his wife Germaine and their young son. The scene is a lower-middle-class version of Matisse's *Tea in the Garden*, except the child is not adult like Marguerite. Léger's mother-figure sits on a deckchair, literally surrounded by bargain-price purchases, all of them shining and new – furniture, vases, table- and kitchen-ware; she is as confident and as contented a consumer as Yvonne Le Corbusier would be in her new kitchen in 1934 [195]. Here the very precisionist perfectionism with which she and her child are painted acts as a metaphor for her demanding standards as a consumer. It is in this that she shares in the 'new spirit', that she is a *modern* mother.

Ordinariness may be given monumentality in Léger's *Mother and Child*, but even here the representation of modern woman in her domestic setting is not far from banality. Much of the most challenging painting of modern women in the first decades of the century crossed the line from ordinariness into banality, by focusing on the day-to-day existences of women released equally from the demands of the desiring male gaze, from the pressures of fashion and from the duties of motherhood and home-making. Into the 1920s perhaps the strongest images of femininity thus banalised were painted by a woman artist, Suzanne Valadon (b.1865). From the mid-1920s, it is possible to see Bonnard's bathroom paintings of Marthe, begun in 1925, as the most compulsively developed sequence of such images. One can, it is true, find a veiled eroticism in certain of these works, but especially where he paints Marthe from above [206], leaving no hint of the voyeur's key-hole view, the erotic becomes overwhelmingly ordinary however extraordinary the work's pictorial qualities. Bonnard too can take the signifier of liberated female sexuality, unashamed nakedness, and render it banal.

Valadon's *Neither White nor Black* of 1909 [205] comes after dozens of harsh examinations of domestic nudity on paper, which start from the bathing themes of her mentor,

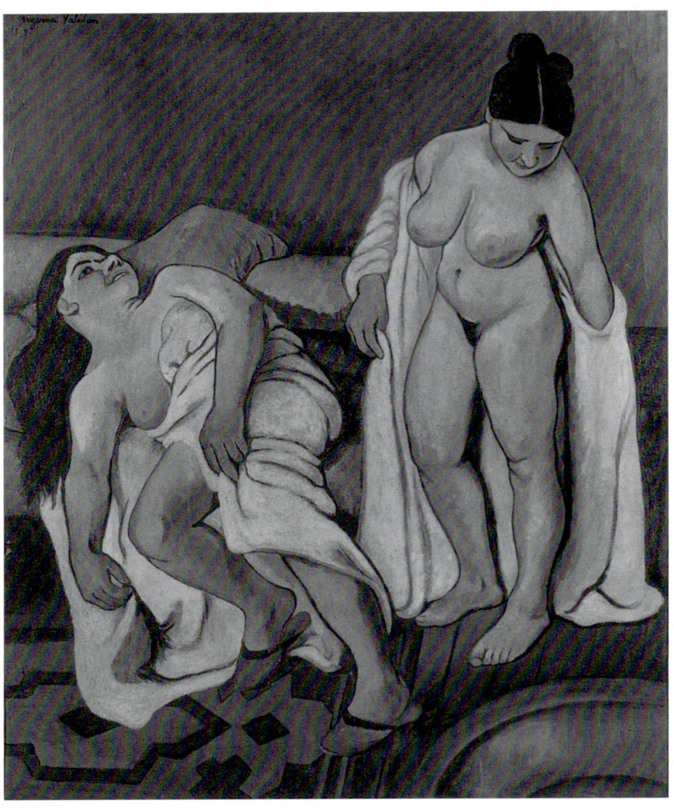

Degas. The matter-of-fact informativeness of her hard line, delivering every bulge of these unlovely bodies to the viewer has been called cruel, but the slow ease with which these two women dry and dress conveys a comfortable acceptance of what and who they are: a total lack of interest in how desirable they might be to any male voyeur. Bonnard's laborious yet always chromatically felicitous evocations of Marthe oiling, soaping or drying herself in the bathroom at Le Cannet, or simply stretched out in the iron bath [206], suggest that she is still as unblemished as in 1900, though she had by now been his wife for many years, and she was actually in middle-age. But especially where she lies immobile, her body has ceased to be the object of his or any imagined male viewer's desire; it has become simply an accepted companion in the routines of daily existence, and as such, something to be painted as no more than a reflecting membrane in an envelope of air, water and steam. Valadon did paint sexually available nudes in the 1920s, but in 1923 she painted her own sexually independent postscript to Manet's *Olympia*, *The Blue Room* [207]. Manet's naked courtesan is replaced by a casually dressed smoker. There could be no more direct and uncompromising refusal of the stereotyping impress of masculine desire in its early twentieth-century French forms.

205. Suzanne Valadon, *Neither White nor Black (Two Figures after the Bath)*, 1909. Oil on card, 101 × 82 cm. Musée National d'Art Moderne, Paris

206. Pierre Bonnard, *Nude in the Bath*, 1936. Oil on canvas, 93 × 147 cm. Musée d'Art Moderne de la Ville de Paris

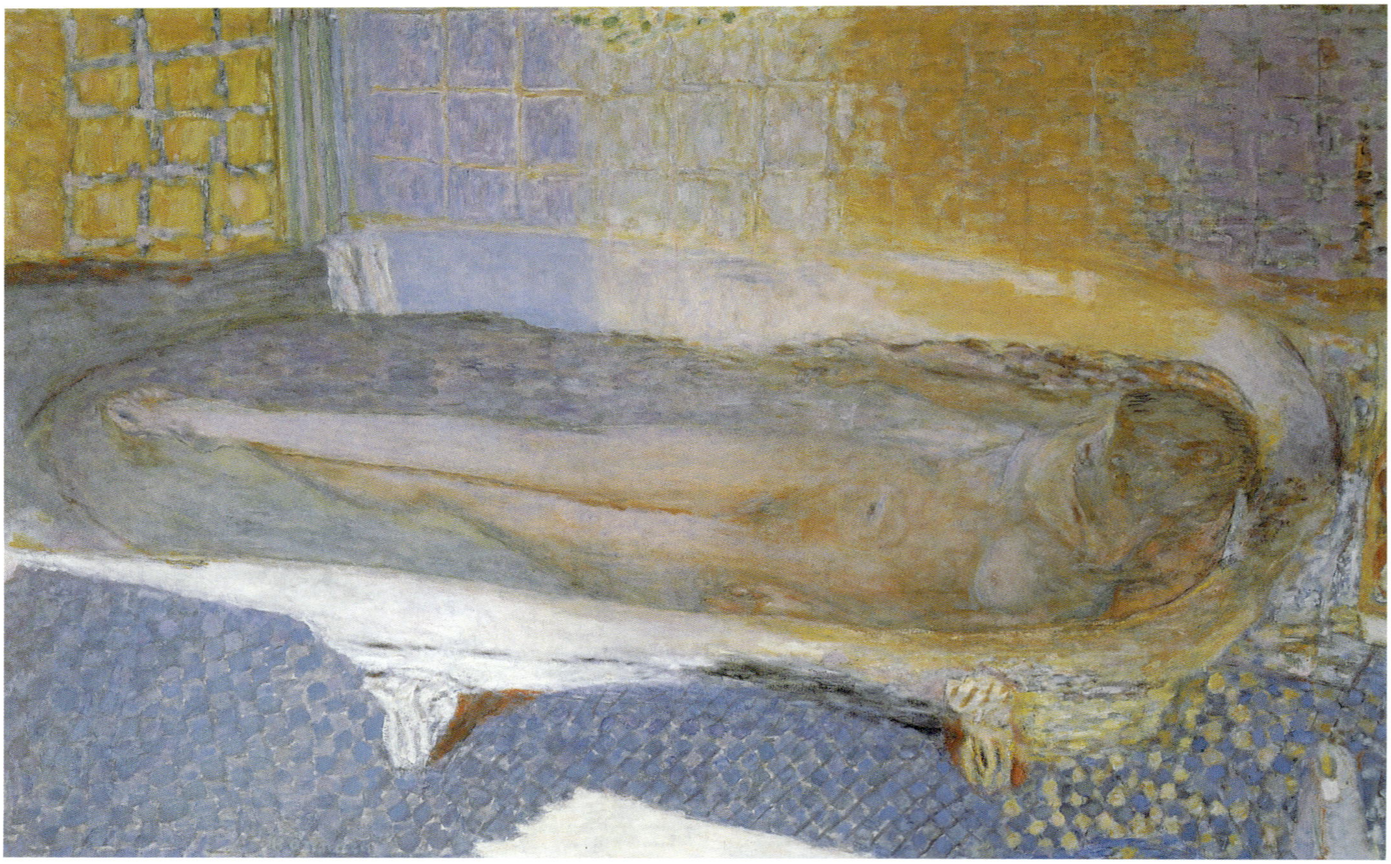

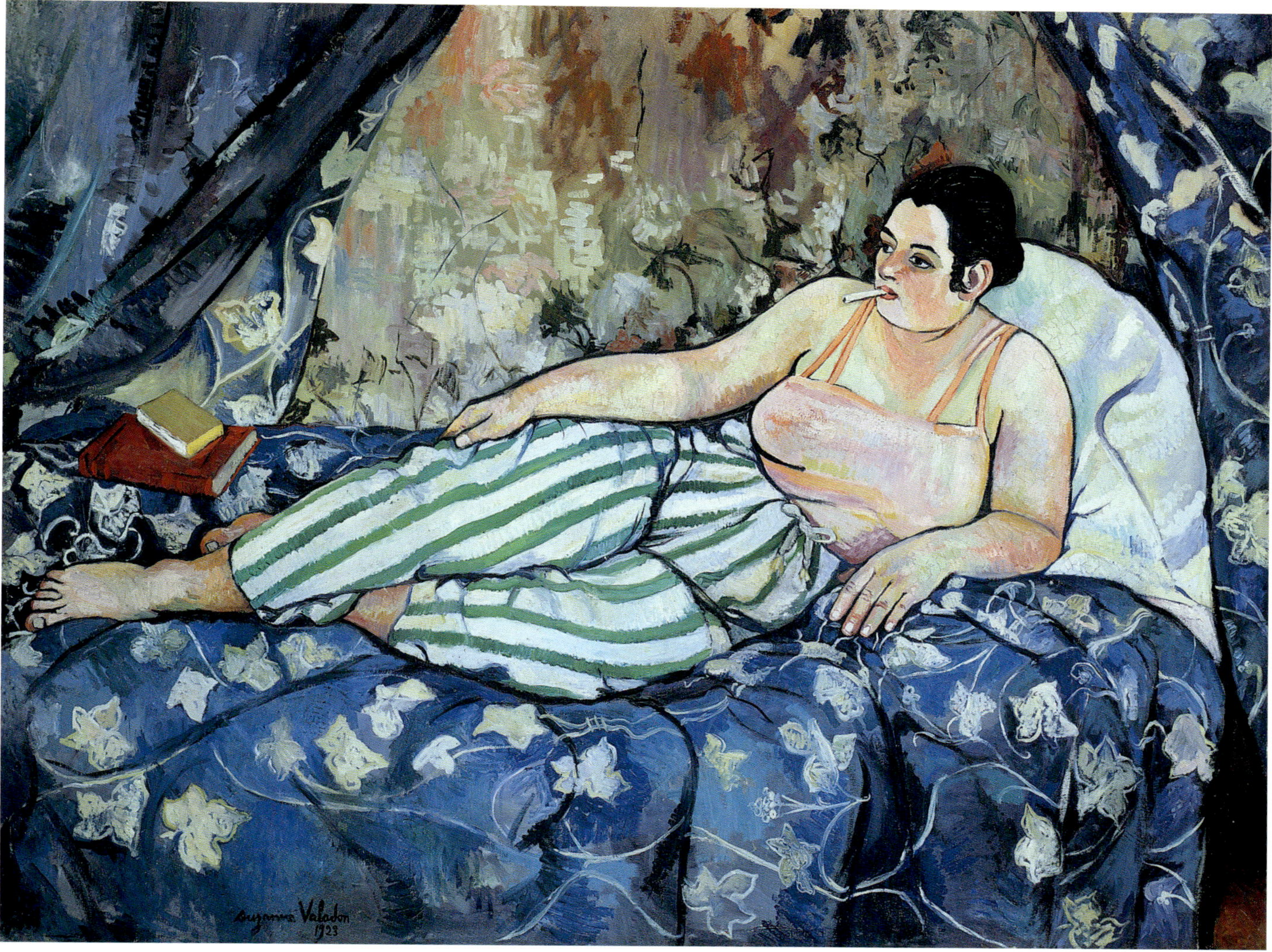

207. Suzanne Valadon, *The Blue Room*, 1923. Oil on canvas, 190 × 116 cm. Musée National d'Art Moderne, Paris

REPRESENTING MODERN SOCIETY: CLASS, POLITICAL ENGAGEMENT AND THE 'REALISM' DEBATE IN THE 1930S; WORLDS OF WORK AND LEISURE

Gender, inevitably, is a question inseparable from that of class; and both class and gender are themes ultimately addressed in the representation not merely of individuals but of people in society. With the polarisation of politics in the 1930s, artists and architects who were concerned with modern people in modern society increasingly brought an explicit political agenda to the modernity they observed or dreamed. Like the modernists who aimed to represent modernity as an experience, they too were caught between the real and the ideal, the experienced and the imagined. The degree to which an engagement with the notion of modernity could partner idealised notions of the class structure of modern society is already clear in Le Corbusier's Taylorist vision of a 'City of Tomorrow' in the 1920s.

Taylorism aimed to replace 'natural' hierarchies with a meritocratic class system centred on the division between managers and workers. Led by the great entrepreneurial capitalists, 'Scientific management' was to eradicate class struggle by ensuring good wages and conditions for all workers and allowing free passage into the managerial class on merit. 'The right man for the right job is coldly selected,' Le Corbusier declares confidently in 1923, '. . . and the man who is made of the right stuff to be a manager will not remain a workman; the higher places are open to all'.[43] The *Contemporary City for Three Million* [7], which he exhibited at the Salon d'automne in 1922 and then in the Pavillon de L'Esprit Nouveau in 1925, was planned to provide for a population meritocratically divided thus. Le Corbusier's book *Urbanisme* specifies precisely who, in class terms, is to live where. The pavilion was conceived as a 'cellular' unit in blocks of 660 units to be built for managers and administrators, in easy reach by Métro of the cruciform office blocks in the city centre [186]. The mass of the working class (approaching 2.5 million of the 3 million population) were to live in 'garden cities' outside the city proper, whether they worked in the industrial zone or the centre. 'Great men and our leaders' were to be provided with 'luxury' housing, like the management class's 'cells' close to the centre. These top men included artists, architects and engineers alongside business and political bosses.[44] Art, for Le Corbusier, was above all for this elite. 'Art,' he had written in 1921, 'is only necessary sustenance for the élites whose job it is to commune with themselves so as to lead. Art is in essence lofty.'[45] The business and professional classes so admired by the Purists and Léger in the 1920s did exist, but for Le Corbusier they were primarily to be thought of as the models for an ideal managerial class in an ideal future modernity.

In a catalogue text of 1938, Le Corbusier once again asked who the public for art was. He continued to stress the élite nature of aesthetic experience, but now he set aside the question of class. Anyone could develop the necessary 'qualities', including the 'ardent men of the collective society' commissioning 'public art'.[46] In 1935, he had published a second urbanist book, *La Ville radieuse* (The Radiant City), which set out the vision of a city for a classless society, where housing was allotted according to need in undifferentiated slabs of cellular units [208]. 'If the city were to become human,' Le Corbusier now declared, 'it would be a city without classes'.[47] *La Ville radieuse* was largely composed of articles published in two periodicals: between 1930 and 1932, *Plans*, after 1932, *Préludes*. Both were the organs of a marginal but extremely active political offshoot of the early twentieth-century French labour movement, Regional Syndicalism. In 1932, Le Corbusier became a member of the movement's Central Committee. His move towards Regional Syndicalism had come in 1929–30, after his flirtation with Georges Valois' short-lived French fascist party, le Faisceau, and with Mercier's Redressement français. It was the result of his total disillusionment both with capitalism and with parliamentary democracy, and his embrace of uncompromising authoritarian solutions as the only means of ensuring the efficient management of resources for the social good. In *La Ville radieuse*, he repeatedly vilified 'the civilisation of money', a society driven by profit, as the cause of every social ill and every economic catastrophe, most immediately the Crash, whose effects began to reach France in 1931.

208. Le Corbusier, Residential Block, VR Type, 1930–4. Photograph of model published in *La Ville radieuse*, 1935

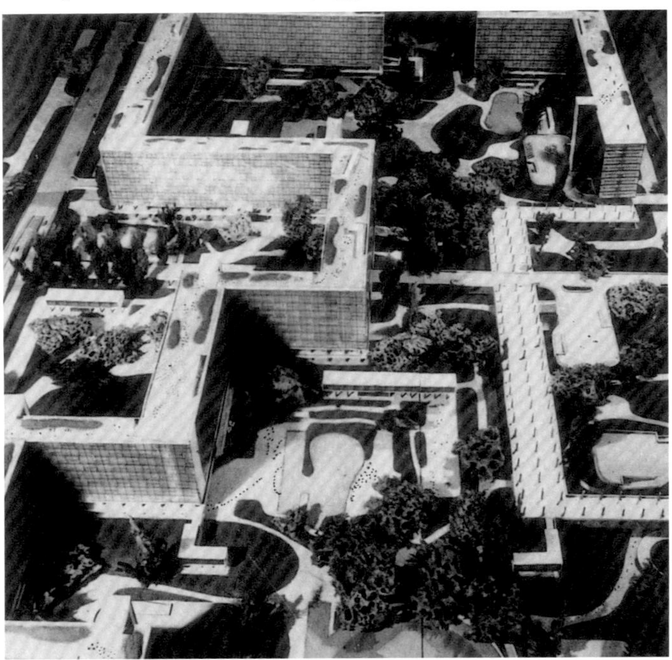

As a Regional Syndicalist, Le Corbusier advocated an hierarchical system of government, where each productive unit elected its management, managements elected regional representatives according to trades, and these in turn elected representatives at a higher governmental level. It was a system which allowed everyone the notional possibility of power, but broke the link between the lowest levels of representation and government. The activists with whom he worked, Philippe Lamour, Hubert Lagardelle and the physical culture advocate, Dr Paul Winter, had all been involved in Valois's 'Faisceau', and were attracted by the notion of strong, unelected leadership at the top of this pyramid; Lagardelle retained ties with the anti-capitalist Left of Mussolini's Italian Fascist Party. Le Corbusier dedicated *La Ville radieuse* to 'Authority', and made an absolute distinction between production (industry), which was to be hierarchically organised from the top down, and leisure, including 'civic' activities and sport, which was to be participatory and open to all. Following Valois and Lagardelle, he presented this future society as neither Capitalist nor Communist; a society without big bosses and without a proletariat.[48]

With the emergence between 1934 and 1938 of the Popular Front, Regional Syndicalism, already excluded from the larger labour movement, was rendered still more marginal. In 1935, *Prélude* ceased publication, and that year Le Corbusier presented his Radiant City project to the Paris branch of the Communist led Maison de la culture shortly after its installation at 12, rue Navarin. He would never become a Communist, and briefly, with the formation of Marshall Pétain's authoritarian 'New Order' government in Vichy after the German invasion, would be tempted again to collaborate with the fascist Right in pursuit of his 'radiant' Utopia, but he was one of many artists and intellectuals brought into the cultural politics of the Left by the inclusive strategy of the Popular Front. Marxist theory, as followed both by Maurice Thorez, leader of the French Communist Party (PCF), and by Léon Blum, leader of the French Socialist Party (SFIO), also envisaged a classless Utopia. It presented that vision, however, as the prize to be won only by the victory of the proletariat; and it conceived Capitalist modernity in terms of a highly reductive division between the proletariat and the ruling bourgeoisie. The parties of the emerging fascist Right in the mid-1930s recognised the significance and potential anti-democratic force of the lower middle classes, Marx's petty bourgeoisie. They sought to use nationalist and racial prejudice to weld an alliance between them and the proletariat. The Marxist Left, Blum included, were prepared to forge an anti-fascist alliance with the lower middle classes, but in the end dismissed them as politically insignificant, a class subject to monopolistic Capitalist power and so merely a proletariat in the making. Alongside Le Corbusier, those drawn into the cultural debates on the Left in the period of the Popular Front, focused therefore on the proletariat, on the place of the peasant, agricultural labourer and especially the industrial worker in society and on what they could gain from art.[49]

Approaching both these debates and the work produced by the artists involved in them depends on first appreciating the sheer breadth of the alliance created by the Popular Front strategy. The strategy was launched after the street riots of February 1934 by the Communist Party (on the initiative of the Soviet Commintern), but both in the political and the cultural sphere it tied in democrats and anti-democrats, liberals and Marxists, of the most contradictory kinds. Le Corbusier was not the only figure to have been attracted by authoritarian politics on the Right to be willing to work with the Popular Front; another was the critic Waldemar George, whose Neo-Humanism I discuss in Part Five. Blum was himself a literary figure, with a reputation established alongside such luminaries as André Gide before 1914, and he always stressed the cultural dimension in the Socialist world for which he worked. The key figure behind the Popular Front's cultural alliance on the Left was, however, Paul Vaillant-Couturier, a leading member of the Central Committee of the PCF from the Party's formation in 1921, editor-in-chief of its newspaper *L'Humanité*, and secretary-general of the 'Association des écrivains et artistes révolutionnaires' (AEAR), out of which the Maisons de la culture movement emerged in the 1930s. In October 1934, he extended the hand of welcome offered to all anti-fascists by Thorez specifically to writers and artists, assuring them that they were welcome even if all they offered was 'vague sympathy for the USSR and an emotional horror of war'. 'We ask of no one,' he added, 'a certificate of Marxist faith'.[50] The one-time Surrealist Louis Aragon, Party activist and editor of *Commune*, the periodical of the AEAR, became the Secretary-General of the Maisons de la culture movement, and figures close to the Party like Jean Cassou were deeply involved, but so were non-Party-members like André Gide, André Malraux and the SFIO Party member Jean Perrin. Among the artists drawn into the debates and exhibitions organised on the Left, especially by the Maisons de la culture, there were passionate activists like Jean Lurçat, Boris Taslitzky, Edouard Pignon and André Fougeron, but also many non-Communist Popular Front supporters, including André Lhote and Fernand Léger (who would not join the PCF until after the Liberation of 1944).

The key issues discussed in the cultural debates on the Left of the 1930s converged on the primary question, should art be for the proletariat, and the secondary question that followed from it, how could art relate to the proletariat? The distance between possible stances is summed up by that between a statement signed by a group of future Popular Front artists and writers, including the painters Edouard Goerg and Marcel Gromaire, in October 1934, and an essay published by Aragon in 1935. In the first, published by the periodical *L'Esprit*, the signatories declare: 'Art is not made for the proletariat, or for the revolution, neither is one obliged to make art for the bourgeoisie. Art is made for Man.'[51] Aragon is equally adamant. He argues for the re-education of the artist as activist, and asserts his conviction that: 'Intellectuals are the brothers in equality of the labouring peasants and the workers.'[52] Aragon's essay was published in an anthology which made a major contribution to the debates on the Left, *Pour un réalisme socialiste* (For a Socialist Realism). It was the prelude to a series of discussions organised in May 1936 by the Maisons de la Culture, which focused on the means and ends of modern painting; the major contributions to them were edited by Aragon and published that year as *La Querelle du réalisme* (The Realism Quarrel). These discussions consolidated the position of the 'realism' question at the centre of all attempts to address the relationship between art and the proletariat, indeed between art and any possible mass public.

Working from a Soviet-inspired agenda, in *Pour un réalisme socialiste*, Aragon had presented the argument against modernism (including Surrealism) and for artists to become 'realists in the spirit of socialism' and so 'excellent engineers of souls'. Such a position did not imply the mere imitation of appearances, or the mindless painting of obvious socialist subjects. Aragon included in his 1935 anthology a statement by Léon Moussinac, PCF film critic of *L'Humanité*, where he dismissed not only abstract art, but propaganda art: the painting of a workers' leader or the masses around a red flag was not to be considered enough. Subject matter was to be chosen to function ideologically, Moussinac said, to strike against petty bourgeois values.[53] Moreover, in *La Querelle* as published, Aragon himself spoke against a Popular Front 'naturalism'. 'Human expression,' he wrote, 'will not . . . be dictated to by the forces of nature, it will be the result of human forces', in other words, shaped by the socialist view of 'reality'.[54] Bringing to mind the example of Jacques-Louis David, he spoke of a 'revolutionary romanticism'; inspiring historical subjects could be 'socialist realist', however 'romantic'.

Such a rejection of 'naturalism' meant that there was at least some common ground between Aragon and those who made the case for modernism. Among his opponents in the 'Quarrel' were Léger and Le Corbusier. Léger had been especially close to the architect in the 1930s, and had published in *Plans*, but he had never been pulled into the fascisizing currents of authoritarian politics. His argument against socialist realism amounted to a recasting of the arguments for a new 'pictorial realism' that he had first presented in 1913. Now, in 1936, emphasis was especially given to the role of education in building a mass public for an art whose 'reality' was its own concrete presence, not any subject matter to which it might refer. He deplored what he saw as a patronising refusal to accept the capacity of the working class to see the modernity in modernist art. It was as if, he said, these 'brand new men' were decreed 'incapable of rising to the new realism which is their epoch, in which they live, where they work, which they manufacture with their own hands'.[55] Aragon's reply poured scorn on the fetishisation of manufactured objects that he saw as the foundation of Léger's 'new realism'. For him, it merely sustained the values of a consumerist society; it made no ideological intervention. 'Slave, you paint your chains.'[56]

Non-Communist modernists, like Léger, were as effective as Popular Front activists in visual culture as Communist realists. Interviewed in 1938, Léger picked out two authentically new forms of art for the new epoch, 'Mural art and the great popular spectacles.'[57] His own achievement as a Popular Front artist was indeed above all as muralist and stage or 'popular spectacle' designer. From 1923, he had been an advocate of the mural, working first with the sculptor Josef Csaky on an installation at the Indépendants and then with the architect Robert Mallet-Stevens to supply a mural for an installation at the decorative arts exhibition of 1925.[58] In the 1920s, he stressed the possible link between mural painting and street-scale advertising, arguing for sober, restful compositions as an antidote to the dynamism of urban experience, and for total abstraction as the key to architectural adaptation.[59] The result was a series of easel paintings intended for architectural environments which echoed Mondrian's orthogonal asymmetries in a muted Corbusian colour range. Such activity in the mid-1920s had been isolated and its ambitions mostly limited to the domestic sphere, though he spoke of polychromatic cities to the Soviet poet Mayakovsky. From 1934, his advocacy of the mural became part of a strong muralist movement in the mainstream of the Popular Front cultural alliance; he shared in a collective enterprise with large ambitions for art in public spaces and the promise that they could be achieved. At the Paris Exhibition of 1937, to some extent and for a limited time, they were.

Léger was a member of an extremely active 'Association de l'art mural' from not long after its foundation in 1934 by a man who was a painter, a sculptor and a glass maker whose working name was Saint-Maur. According to Ory, it held at least five Salons between the first in 1935 and a manifesto-exhibition in 1938. Among those on its first 'Comité d'honneur' were Gromaire, Lhote, Bonnard, Derain, Dufy, Kandinsky (now resident in Paris) and Ozenfant; a list that conveys its stylistic and ideological pluralism.[60] It tended to the Left, and was touched by the realism debate, the reverberations being felt, as in the USA, of the Mexican muralists (Rivera, Siqueros and Orozco); but it found room both for the 'new realism' of Léger and for the post-Orphist 'pure painting' of Robert Delaunay. Their modernist murals at the Exhibition of 1937 [12, 185] were part of a concerted attempt to develop a mural art in France capable of transforming the decor of modernity not merely in domestic but in large public spaces.[61]

Even events kept within the elite confines of the cultural world could mimic the popular in the mid-1930s. There were attendances of around 2,000 for the debates of the *Querelle du réalisme*, needless to say almost all of them artists and writers.[62] When asked in 1937 what popular theatre was, Léger answered that all theatre became 'popular' when the audience went above 3,000, because then, inevitably, 'the people' were present, which created 'a certain spirit'.[63] In the early 1920s, he had designed for the fashionable bourgeois audiences of Rolf de Maré's Ballets Suisses working very much in the same public sphere as Picasso or Gris had with Serge Diaghilev's Ballets Russes, now in 1937 his priority is theatre for 'the people'. Again, he declares himself part of a movement thus, for the production of such 'popular spectacles' became the ambition of many on the Left in the period of the Popular Front.

A major attempt at such a spectacle was the production of Romain Rolland's French Revolution drama, *Le Quatorze Juillet* (first performed in 1902) at the Alhambra Theatre in Paris in the summer of 1936. It acted not only to revive the memory of 1789, but also as a celebration of the electoral victory of the Popular Front of spring 1936; its hero was 'the

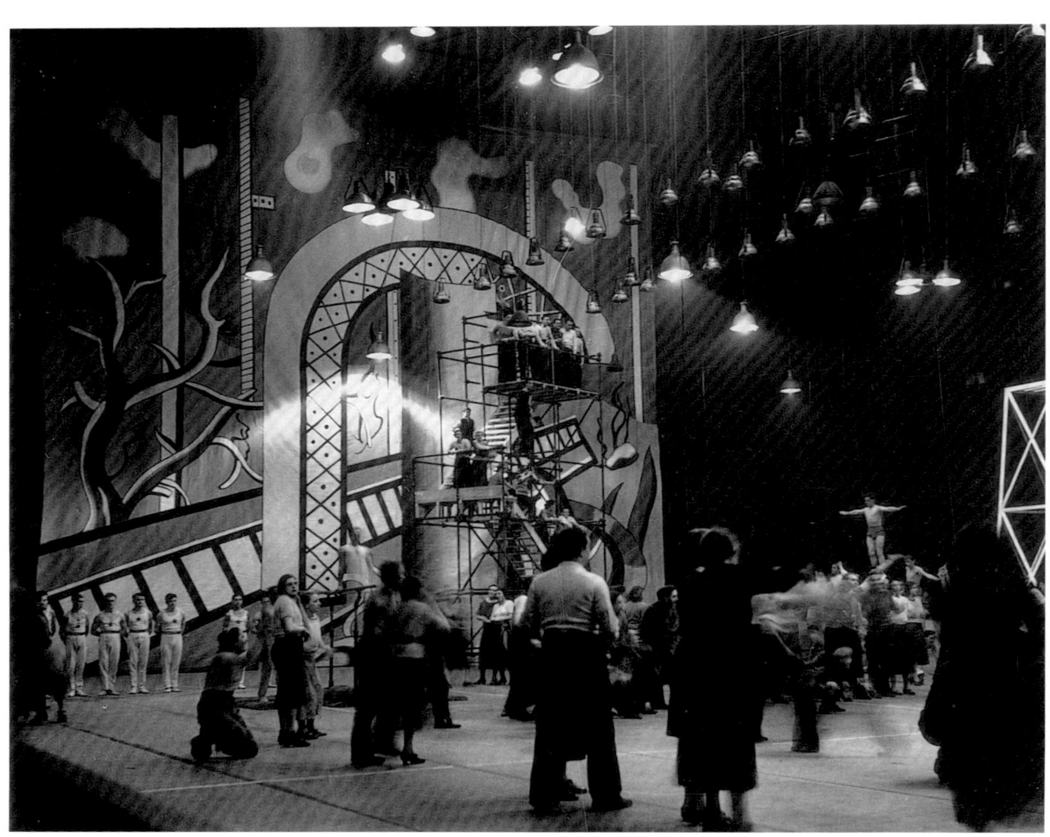

209. Fernand Léger, *et al.* Performance of Jean-Richard Bloch's *Birth of a City*, 18 October 1937

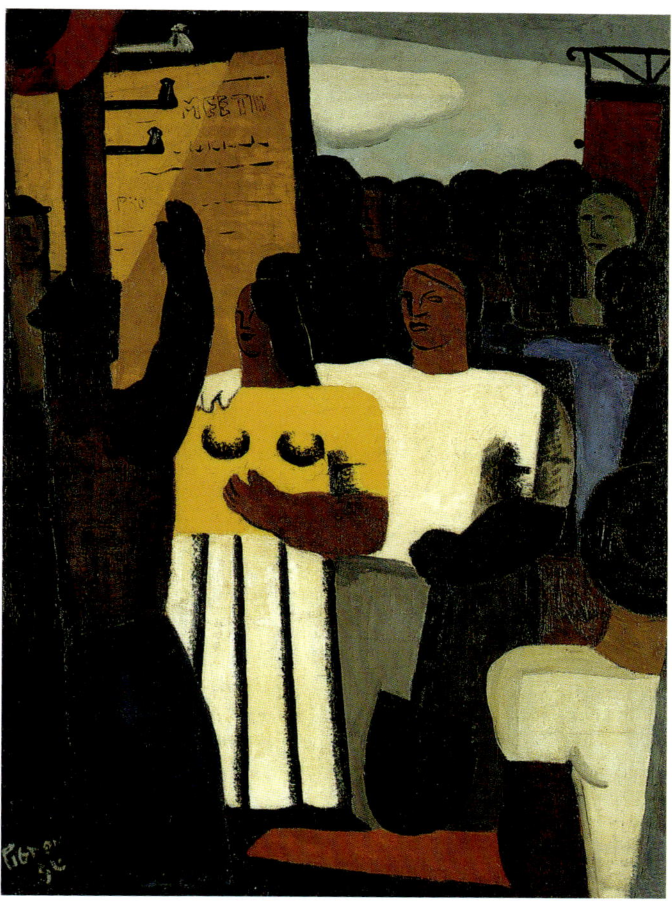

210. Edouard Pignon, *The Meeting*, 1936. Oil on canvas, 130 × 95 cm. Musée National d'Art Moderne, Paris

people', and 150 actors represented 'the people' on stage. It also involved artists. During rehearsals, the artists' association of the Maisons de la culture put on an exhibition at the theatre, offering a typically unprogrammatic mix which brought activists like Taslitzky and Pignon together with Gromaire, Lhote and even Matisse. A gouache by Picasso served as the maquette for the safety curtain.

Léger himself had just one opportunity to work on a theatrical production whose scale could really justify calling it a 'popular spectacle' following his definition. This was *Naissance d'un cité* (Birth of a City), a production which marshalled hundreds of performers to tell the story of a community born anew ('cité' is a word that refers as much to a community as to a 'city') [209]. As Jean-Richard Bloch, the Marxist writer of the scenario put it, on this scale the individual actor became 'an insect', so the action consisted 'of mass movements, very powerful, very simple, very clear'.[64] The spectacle was performed on 18 October 1937, during the Paris Exhibition; it took place in an authentically popular venue, the Vélodrome d'hiver, a cycle-racing stadium [209]. Music was produced by Darius Milhaud and Arthur Honnegger, and sets by Léger. Bloch's storyline was Utopian in the grandest manner: a colony founded on a desert island, led by an engineer, enriched by oil, threatened by imperial interests, finally saved by a League of Nations decision to pool world resources and so usher in an era of

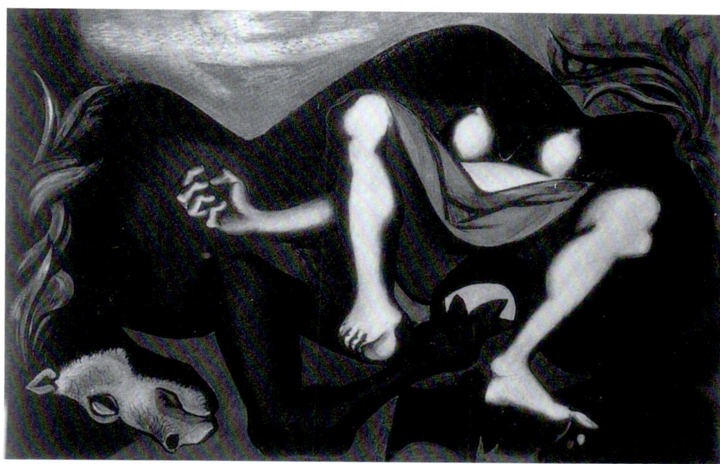

211. André Fougeron, *Spain the Martyr*, 1937. Oil on canvas, 154 × 110 cm. Estate of the artist

endless peace. And yet everything was done to give it the immediacy of the here and now: horns and sirens, the noise of vehicles, news flashes, and a search-lit finale with a cycle race, wrestling and athletic events; the chorus was a radio announcer, broadcast by two amplified speakers. Initially, film was to be projected onto a huge screen, but in the end an equally huge drop curtain was used designed by Léger, from behind which scene changes were wheeled in on trolleys.[65] Léger's statements on theatre in the 1920s had stressed the transformation of the actor into an object; here he collaborated in the transformation of crowds into actors: the protagonists in a dramatised vision of the building of a classless future. In Jean-Richard Bloch's words to the 1934 Congress of Writers in Moscow: 'The great Socialist aim is to be a society without classes.'[66]

Léger called *Naissance d'un cité* 'a vast fresco, at once realist and lyrical'; he made a point of underlining its claims to 'realist' status.[67] By comparison, his own 'new realist' easel painting along with the many other kinds of 'realist' prints and easel paintings produced under the Popular Front banner can seem feeble, however banal the populism of Bloch's spectacle. And yet, activists produced and showed such work in considerable quantities, and they did so with the encouragement of a succession of historical exhibitions devoted to possible models for new realisms. Rembrandt prints were shown at the Bibliothèque Nationale, Corot at the Orangerie, and twenty-five Courbets in the Paris Maison de la culture, all in 1936.[68] Courbet's manifesto of Realism, *The Artist's Studio*, had been hung in the Louvre in 1934. Style was distinctly variable in Popular Front realism – it is better to speak of realism*s* – but subject matter was primarily the generator of meaning, even for those who did not align themselves with Aragon's 'Pour un réalisme socialiste'. In 1936, 'Les Indélicats' (loosely translateable perhaps as 'the Brutes'), a group of activist artists formed in 1932, showed albums of linocuts at the galerie Billiet-Vorms, a gallery run by a nephew of the Communist critic Joseph Billiet with a commitment to realist work. In 1934, the gallery had called a group show 'Le Retour au sujet' (The Return to the Subject). Each of the Indélicats' albums took subjects from a list of specified themes: 'Unemployment',

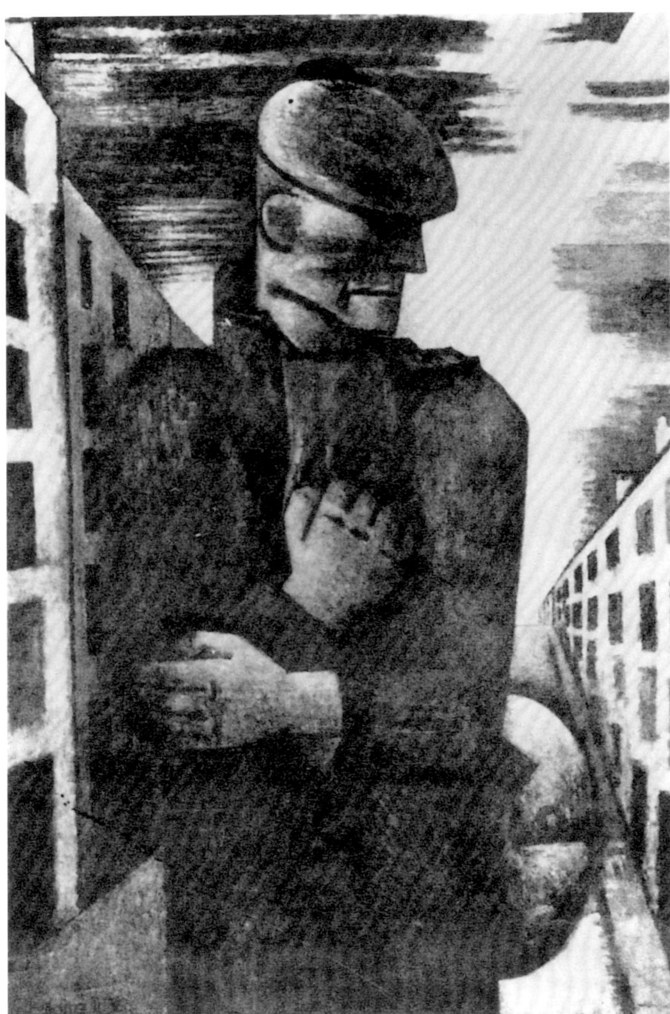

212. Marcel Gromaire, *The Unemployed Man*, 1936. Oil on canvas, 104 × 78 cm. Private Collection

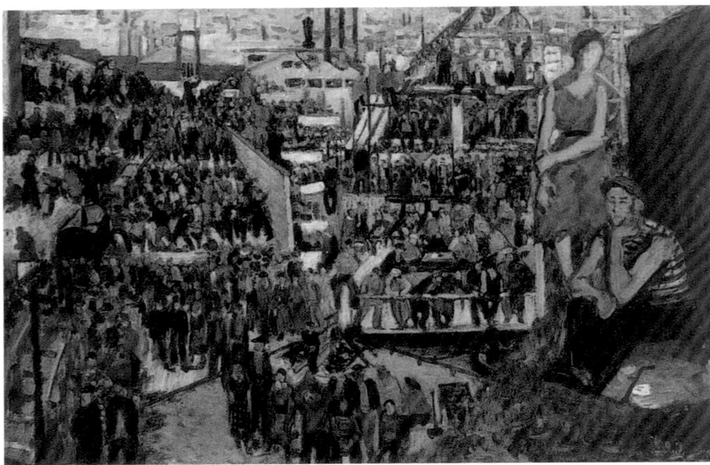

213. Boris Taslitzky, *The Strikes of May 1936*. Oil on canvas, 40 × 60 cm. The artist's collection

'War', 'the 14th July', 'Colonisation', 'Taboos', 'the Crisis', 'the Elites', 'the Sporting', 'Long live Life'[69]. Certain of these themes have a strong 1930s flavour, 'Taboos' and 'the Crisis', for instance. But most overlap, like the subject matter of most realist work of the Popular Front period, with the themes addressed by politically committed social realist painters at the turn of the century, painters of social types and spaces as stylistically opposed to one another as the Neo-Impressionist Maximilien Luce [164] and the 'realist' Jules Adler [170]. Obviously, such themes were often treated very differently in the period of the Popular Front, and could be read with different ideological inflections, but just as obviously there are significant continuities. I shall look at just a few instances from the later period.

Edouard Pignon and André Fougeron both showed with 'Les Indélicats' in 1936. Pignon (b.1905) in particular could not be aligned with socialist realism, but both painted strong realist subjects, for instance Pignon's *The Meeting* of 1936 [210], which adapts a late Cubist style to the job of plain speaking (in visual terms) with a workers' meeting as subject matter. Beneath that symbol of immediate communication, a telegraph pole, a half-naked labour leader addresses a manuel worker with sturdy female companion in front of a massed proletarian audience. The compositional structure is flat and planar; the figures are heroic in their solidarity, the pictorial descendants of Léger's *Mechanic*. In its flatness, the result invokes Picasso as well as Léger, but in its easy legibility is closer to the altogether more straightforward modernism of André Lhote (b.1885); Lhote had applied a simplified Cubist style to popular subjects from before 1914, he continued to do so in his murals for the Palais de la Découverte in 1937. Both Pignon and Fougeron were artists from working-class backgrounds, Pignon from the mines in the North, Fougeron from the poor Paris neighbourhood of Belleville; both were PCF members. Fougeron (b.1913), a self-taught painter, had been unemployed for a year when he showed with 'Les Indélicats'.[70] His *Spain the Martyr* of 1937 [211] crosses Picassian distortion (especially of feet and hands) with a brutal Caravaggist chiaroscuro to dramatise a subject whose ideological function could not be more transparent. It is one of many 'revolutionary romantic' responses in France to the Spanish Civil War, responses made in the context of Blum's refusal to commit French arms or forces against General Franco. Its instant legibility as an image of defencelessness in the face of armed and murderous aggression contrasts with the openness of Picasso's imagery in *Guernica* [333]; it came afterwards. Such images smothered the rhetoric of peace that was so loud a feature of the 1937 Exhibition, and that Jean-Richard Bloch allowed to take over the finale of *Naissance d'un cité*.

Boris Taslitzky (b.1911) was a young PCF member, actively involved in the Maisons de la culture movement, who spoke on Aragon's side in the *Querelle du réalisme* debates. At an exhibition organised by the galerie Billiet-Vorms to accompany the debates in 1936, he showed a major painting completed that year of the Popular Front-organised *Procession to the Père Lachaise Cemetery* of 1935.[71] He was especially drawn to mass demonstrations as a subject. In 1937, Vaillant-Couturier had claimed that mass industrial action the year before had produced its own 'folklore', an art of songs, chants, posters and placards.[72] Taslitzky as a participant in marches and demonstrations between 1934 and 1937 had certainly contributed to this folklore himself. His

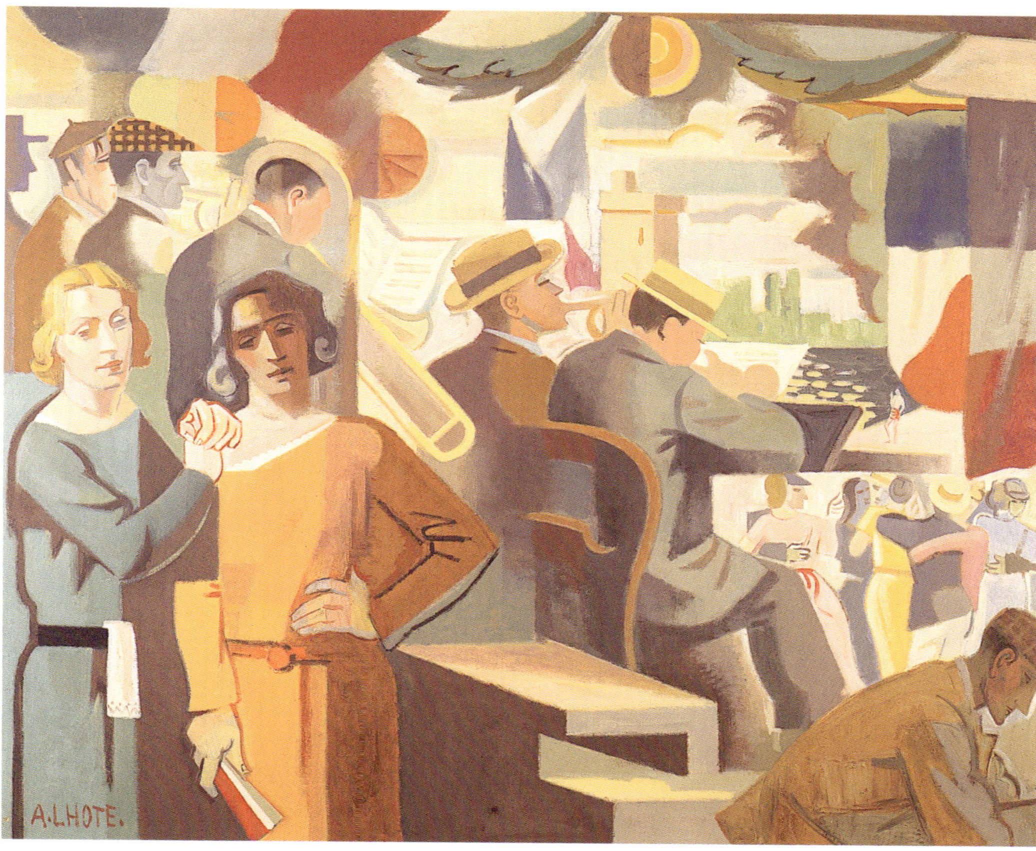

214. André Lhote, *The 14th July at Avignon*, 1923. Oil on canvas, 145 × 175 cm. Musée des Beaux-Arts, Pau

Strikes of May 1936 [213] composes massed groups of workers into carefully balanced areas, producing an image of purposeful organisation presided over by a youthful proletarian couple, whose relaxed poses anticipate a more leisured future, a future free from conflict. It underlines the hope that comes with discipline, monumentalising the strikes that followed the election of Blum's Popular Front majority: strikes and occupations which had led to a government-brokered deal with the employers' organisations, agreeing trades-union recognition and substantial wage-rises, the 'accords Matignon'.

Marcel Gromaire (b.1892) had been a Left-leaning painter of social spaces and social types through the 1920s, though, as we have seen, he was happy in 1934 to sign a declaration rejecting propaganda art. Stylistically, his work used far lower levels of post-Cubist simplification than Lhote's or Pignon's, to give pictorial solidity and structure to popular subjects that were consistently legible. He was not an activist of Pignon, Fougeron or Taslitzky's ilk, but he spoke in the *Querelle* debates, stressing his sense of affinity with the 'popular realism' of the Douanier Rousseau and the naifs. The degree to which painting whose subjects continued an early twentieth-century realist tradition could be appropriated by Popular Front imperatives is demonstrated by the fact that his painting of 1930, *The Unemployed Man* [212], was retitled *The Striker* by the organisers of a 1938 exhibition at the Paris Maison de la culture. A representation of deprivation and powerlessness, which connects with realist representations of poverty decades earlier, becomes a Popular Front image of unbreakable resistance. The figure's

215. Marcel Gromaire, *The Canoe*, 1930. Oil on canvas, 81 × 65 cm. Musée d'art moderne de la Ville de Paris

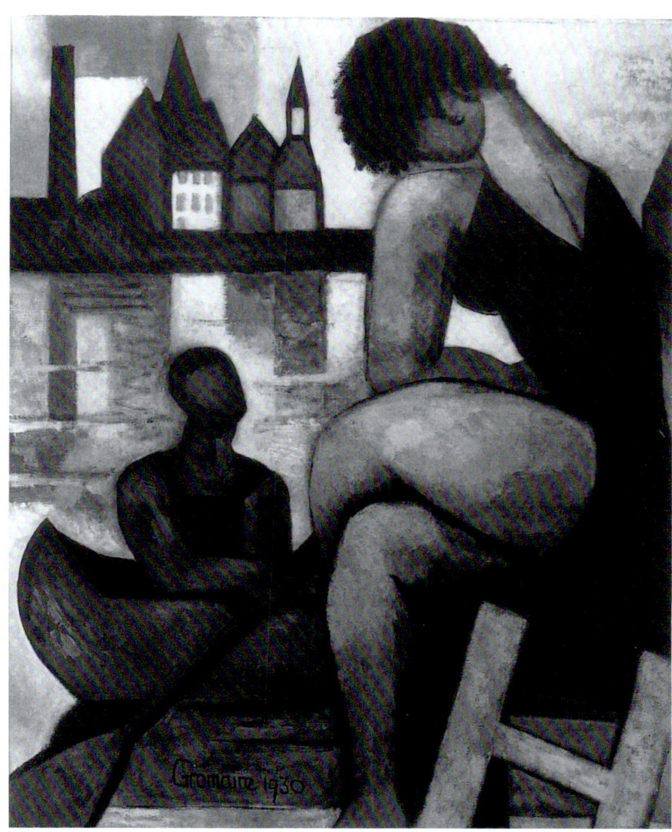

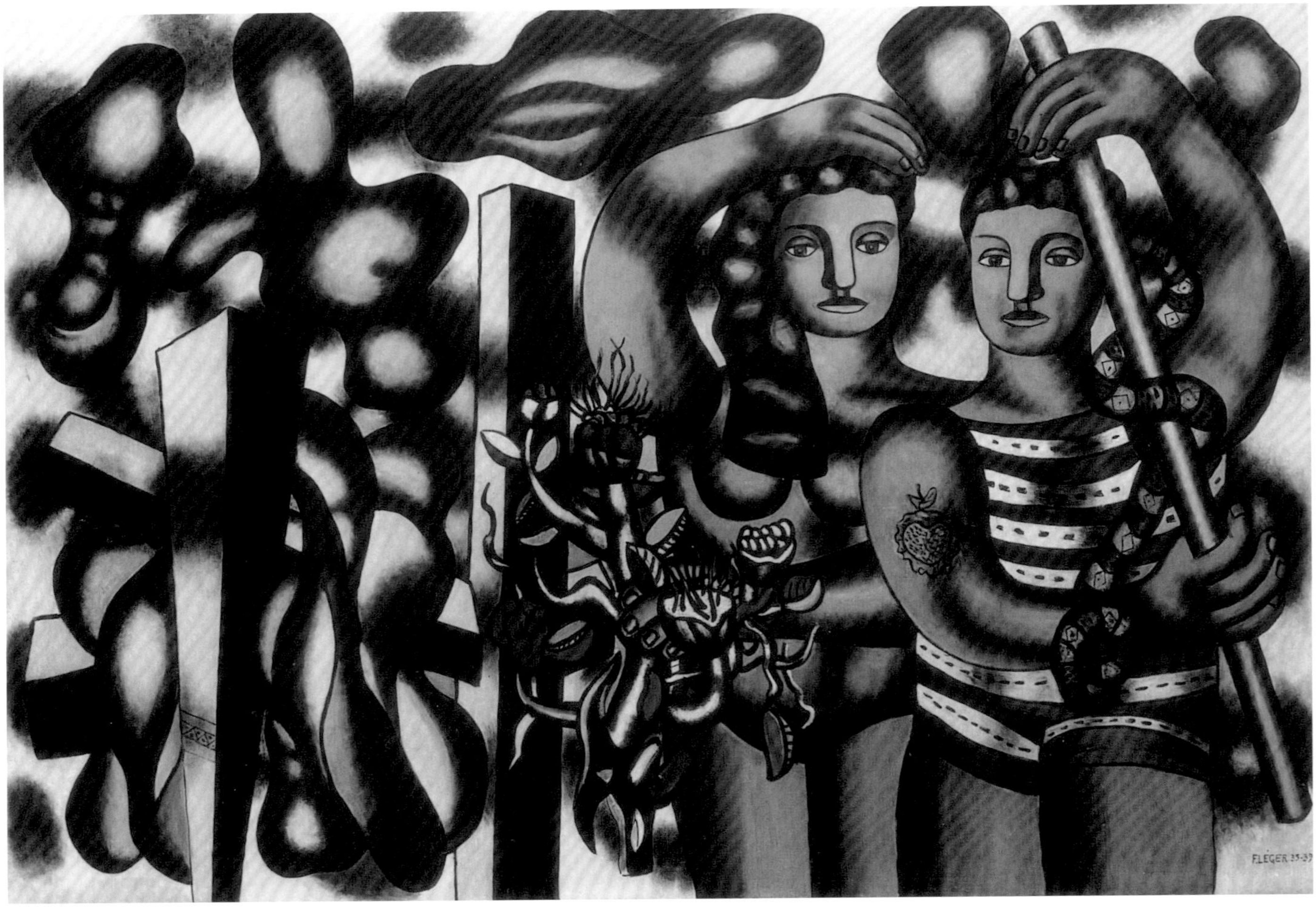

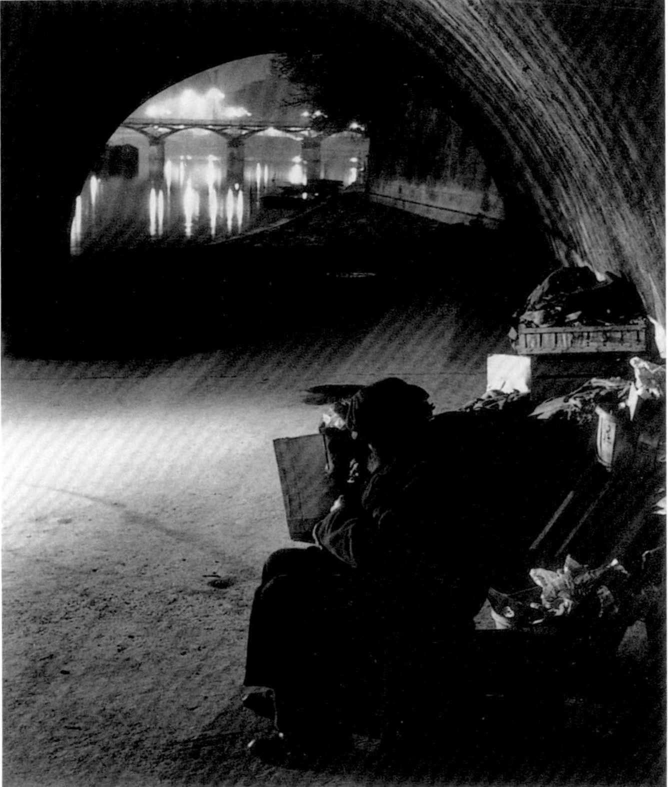

clenched fists invited the switch; the clenched fist had wide currency in the mid-1930s as a gesture of militant proletarian solidarity.

One of Gromaire's themes through the 1920s was leisure, as it was one of Lhote's and indeed one of Léger's, for instance in his *Mother and Child* of 1922 [249]. Leisure does not feature as such in the list of themes for the 'Indélicats'' linocuts exhibition of 1936, but it overlaps, of course, with sport which does, and sport had been a theme in the modernist painting of modernity since Delaunay's *Cardiff Team* in 1913 [172] and indeed earlier.[73] A whole range of modern leisure pursuits of the 1930s featured in *Naissance d'un cité*, above all sport. For Bloch, they were crucial to the representation of 'the principle desires and habits of the modern masses.'[74] The politics of leisure was at the very heart of Popular Front idealism and policy making. For Blum, the corollary of social justice was a harmonious balance between work and leisure, and within leisure, culture, sport and regular holidays were to come together to complete each individual's fulfilment. Such an aspiration is there, of course, behind Le Corbusier's division between

216. Top. Fernand Léger, *Adam and Eve*, 1935–9. Oil on canvas, 228 × 334 cm. Kunstsammlung Nordrhein-Westfalen, Düsseldorf

217. Brassaï, *Tramps under the Pont-Neuf*, 1930–2. Print, 39.4 × 29.7 cm. Musée d'art moderne de la Ville de Paris

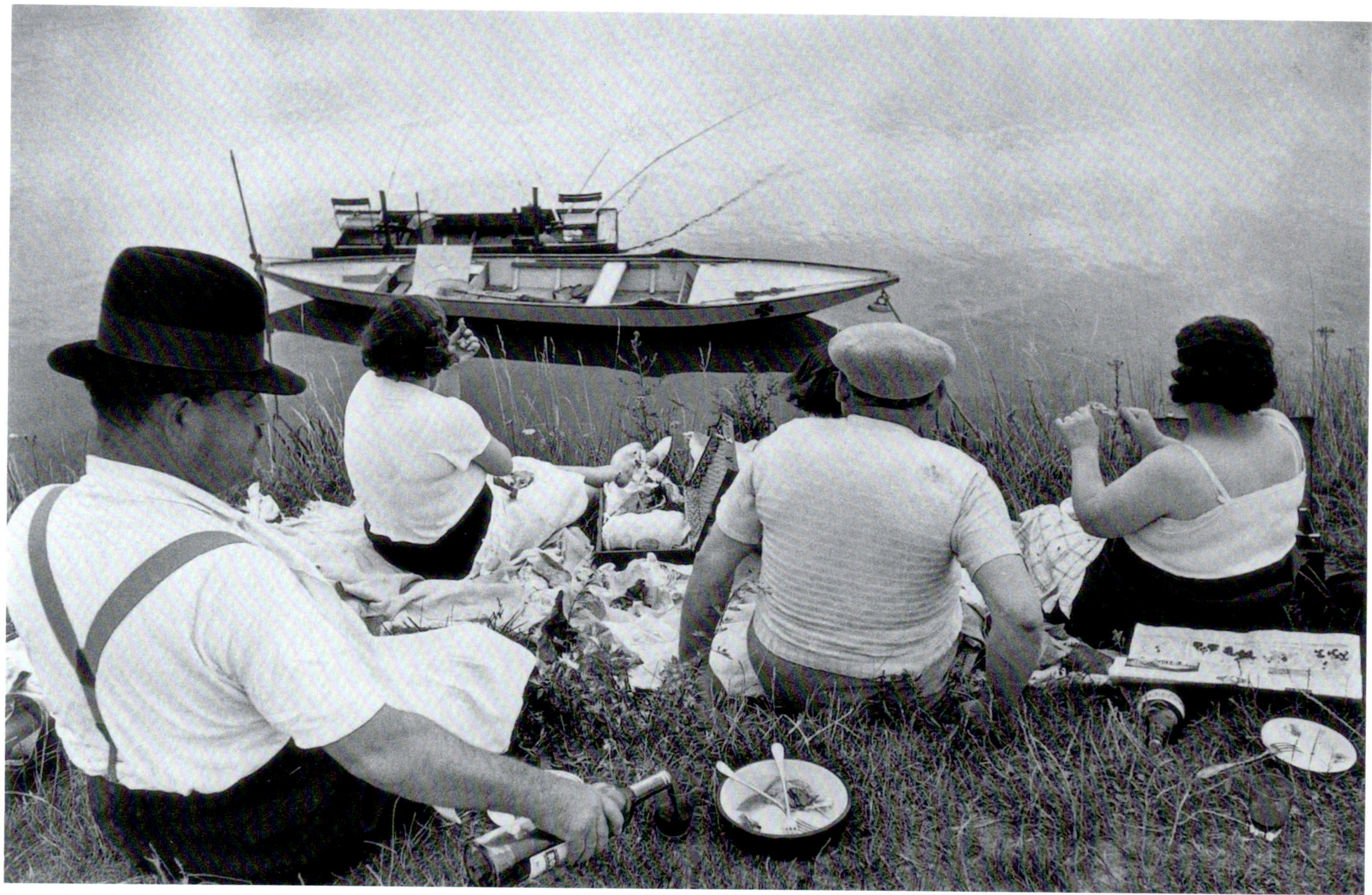

218. Henri Cartier-Bresson, *The First Paid Holidays, 1936*, 1936. Magnum Photos, Paris

organised work and participatory leisure in his 'radiant city'; sports fields were to be at the foot of every housing slab, and running tracks and solaria on their flat roofs [208]. The right to leisure and the importance of sport were points at which socialist and fascist aspirations met. In 1935, the PCF reissued the text which was the foundation of the socialist politics of leisure, Paul Lafargue's *Le Droit à la paresse* (The Right to Idleness) of 1891; and in 1936 a world congress on the uses of leisure was held under Nazi patronage in Hamburg.[75] When the Popular Front legislated for paid holidays in 1936, and when Blum's administration placed culture, sport and leisure together in an enlarged Ministry of Education, they were competing on the side of socialist civilisation against the populist success of European fascism. Moreover, the legislation came at the end of a determined inter-war campaign in France: the Chamber had voted twice for paid holidays (1928 and 1932), on both occasions being rebuffed by the Senate.

Lhote's *The 14th July at Avignon* of 1923 [214] and Gromaire's *The Canoe* [215] of 1930, belong to a strong vein of undemanding leisure painting produced in the 1920s and 1930s, which acquires a sharp ideological edge in the period of the Popular Front. Lhote's image of noisy holiday pleasure crosses the theme of popular leisure with that of Republicanism: Bastille Day in peacetime (boaters were the one type of head-wear considered classless). Gromaire's image of relaxation on the water gives the sporting woman a central role (women were often dominant in leisure painting), and opens up the theme of the weekend. This is a scene not of holiday beaches at Deauville or Dinard, but of urban relaxation outside working hours; this is a sub-industrial riverside. Léger's *Mother and Child* is, of course, also an image inspired by the weekend (his weekends at Fontenay-aux-roses).

'It's advisable all the same to slow down on the road to Deauville. Take a bit of a look to right and left.'[76] As early as 1929, Léger was publishing in the press on the importance of taking holidays seriously, and of the car and the road as the route to a new dimension of leisure. Between the wars cars remained a luxury beyond the working classes, though mass-production widened their middle-class market. Le Corbusier, however, like Léger, believed Henry Ford's promise that lowering costs would bring cars even to the working class; his 'second machine age' of the 'radiant city', a Utopia liberated from the great capitalists, promised as much too. Where his 1920s 'City for Three Million' had opposed a closed geometrical plan of the modern city against the formlessness of the countryside [7], his Ville radieuse opened the city up to its green surroundings. The plan was bilateral, strung out along a dominant axis to allow optimum orientation in relation to the sun, its zones are separated by areas of green, and much was made of the roads that linked it up with a country-wide network. 'In the face of the new phenomenon of the road,' Le Corbusier wrote, '[which] opens up from today a brilliant civilisation to replace the railway, urbanisation spreads out into the towns and the countryside, across the whole land'.[77] The countryside, as setting for leisure, had become part of a vision of modernity; and indeed he even envisaged an industrialised 'radiant farm' to complete a modernised 'radiant' vision of a whole world. Leisure brought nature into the notion of the modern even for the most extreme of 'scientific' urbanists. *Léa* [199] was the product of one of many holidays spent living 'in nature' (on one occasion with Léger) at Cap Ferret on the Bassin d'Arcachon, south of Bordeaux, holidays made possible by Le Corbusier's touring Voisin. It is a modernist image of the holiday as release from work and repression; its imagery of liberated sexuality functions within an imagery of modern leisure.

Modernism, then, continued to produce art dedicated to the representation of modernity alongside the non- and anti-modernist realisms of the 1930s, and to do so in ways easily read in terms of socialist ideology. Indeed, Le Corbusier's megalomaniac vision of a 'radiant' world is certainly the most forceful demonstration of the distance between the dominant values of middle-class, conservative and Radical-voting France, and the new values of the Left factions in the Popular Front. For the French middle classes, the future to be refused was not merely one in which class disappeared with the victory of the proletariat, but one in which consumerist individualism disappeared with the imposition of central planning and social 'engineering'. It is worth remembering that it was the resistance of small businessmen as much as that of big business that staved off the revolution for which Blum and the Left fought between 1934 and 1940.

What is more, modernists like Le Corbusier and Léger, dedicated to an ideal of modernity, painted subjects that often underlined the convergence of their vision with the ideology of the Left. Léger's *Adam and Eve* of 1934 [216], the primal modern couple, is easily read as a couple related to the young workers who preside over Taslitzky's *Strikes of May 1936*. Such modernism was plainly compatible with the values of 'socialist realists'. The argument between them was more about means than ends. It was, after all, under the Popular Front, as I show in Part Two, that modernism gained real recognition at an official level, in the Beaux-Arts administration and among the museum curators. Modernism was accepted as very much a valid contribution to the Front's programme by such new establishment figures of the activist Left as Jean Cassou. Yet, what such a confrontation between modernism and socialist realism brings out in the final analysis is the point that modernism escaped one major, indeed probably *the* major challenge that faced every realist painter of French society: the challenge from photography and film. From around 1930, it was a challenge that acquired renewed force.

Léger had held up his 'new realism' as the modern painter's answer to the problem of photography in 1913–14; technical advances gave vastly increased weight to his arguments now. The extraordinarily rapid emergence of talking films from 1929 and the equally rapid emergence of modern photo-journalism with the commercial distribution of the new Leica camera from the mid-1920s, rendered the kind of commentary on modernity offered by painting less and less compelling. Brassaï's photographs of destitution [217] or of the underside of city life, and Henri Cartier-Bresson's photographs of urban poverty and of the first paid holidays for workers [218] achieved a degree of penetration and of immediacy beyond any painterly realism. Photo-journalist magazines, led by the brilliantly edited *Vu*, made such images instantly available, potentially to the largest of mass publics. The 'realism quarrel' was one held exclusively among painters; the real quarrel, however, for painters committed to realism in 1936 was with the new media. The picturing at the galerie Billiet-Vorms that year of all those categories identified as modern and as worthy of socialist attention by the 'Indélicats' – 'Unemployment' or 'the Taboo' or 'the Sporting' and leisure – was more and more clearly now the business of photographers and film-makers.

Aragon's key statement on the visual arts in his *Pour un réalisme socialiste* of 1935 was an essay on the photomontages of John Heartfield; Heartfield is held up as a revolutionary whose work has superceded painting even more effectively than collage. 'Photomontage,' Aragon writes, 'like theatre, is an art designed for the masses'.[78] When Léger supervised displays of photographs and photomontages for Le Corbusier's Pavillon des temps nouveaux at the 1937 Exhibition he would have seen no threat to his work as a painter in these new media. Aragon too did not lose his faith in painting. But in a socialist realist context the threat would have been clear enough. In 1937, as part of the Left's campaign for French engagement on the side of the Republicans in Spain, a show was put on by the Paris Maison de la culture with the title 'Espagne 1930–1937, No pasaran'; Aragon wrote the preface. It consisted of works on paper by six artists, including such activist realists as Jannot, Goerg and Masereel; and photographs.[79]

PART FIVE

History, Tradition and the French Nation

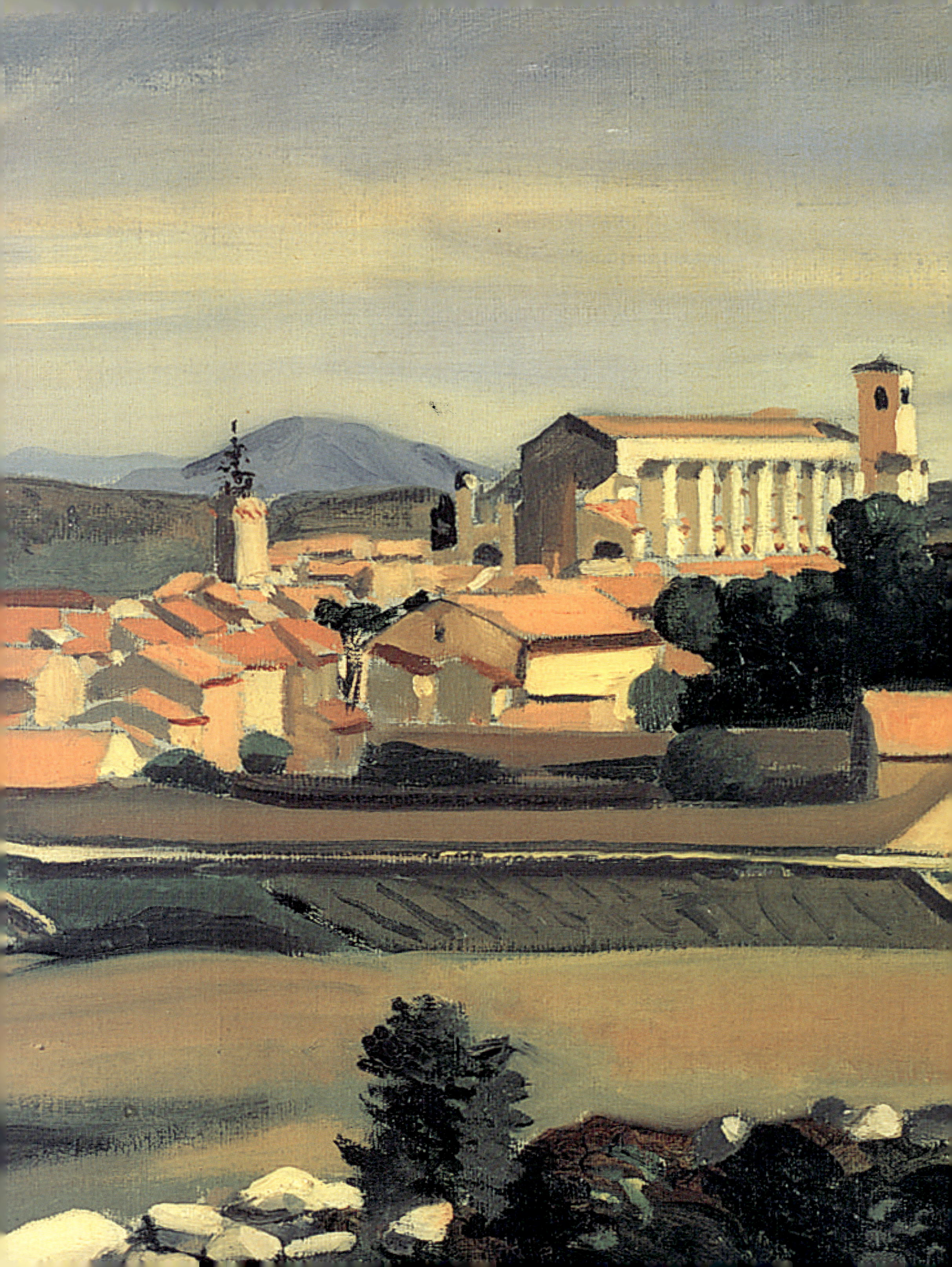

PART FIVE

History, Tradition and the French Nation

INTRODUCTION

Looking back from 1928, the academic art historian Henri Focillon remarked on the importance of the decision made at the foundation of the Salon d'automne in 1903 to combine the showing of 'young French painting' with regular retrospectives of masters from the recent and not so recent past. 'It imposed,' he said, 'a notion of tradition, sometimes a little slack and artificial, but supported by the most eloquent examples'.[1] From 1905, the Salon d'automne took on two such shows a year, starting with what was presented as a pairing of opposites, the 'revolutionary' Manet and the 'classic' Ingres; it was a pairing designed to reveal their complementarity. The catalogue of the 1905 Autumn Salon was prefaced by Elie Faure, then emerging as a champion of a populist art history responsive to modernism. 'Like Puvis [de Chavannes] last year,' he announced, 'Ingres and Manet are going to affirm for us quietly that the revolutionary of today is the classic of tomorrow'.[2]

From the beginning of the century, modernism in France was as regularly linked to notions of tradition as it was to notions and experiences of modernity, and this was often done by artists using the simplest of stylistic and iconographic references. The work of modernists no less than that of artists whose work was endorsed by 'official' success can often be straightforwardly linked to the past. The directness of such referencing of the past is clear in two cases, one 'independent' and modernist, the other official: Robert Delaunay (b.1885), whose *Windows* of 1912 [111] represented for the modernist critic Guillaume Apollinaire 'pure painting' in its paradigmatic form, and the sculptor Henri Bouchard (b.1875), winner of the 'Premier grand prix de Rome' in 1901, beneficiary of many major commissions for monuments from 1907.

Among Robert Delaunay's preludes to 'pure painting' were three series of paintings with Gothic subjects: the interior of the church of Saint-Séverin in Paris, the spire of Notre-Dame-de-Paris, and the hilltop cathedral of Laon in Picardy [219]. The latter was painted early in 1912, just before the 'pure' *Windows* series with their emphatically modern Eiffel Tower references; both the other Gothic subjects were returned to after 1912 in new variants or with the repainting of old ones. Alongside his repertoire of modern images, Delaunay continued with this repertoire of Medieval images. Between 1933 and 1935, Henri Bouchard produced the huge, relief sculpture in stone for the tympanum of the newly built church of Saint-Pierre de Chaillot in Paris [220]. It is plainly a twentieth-century version of the twelfth-century tympanum of the abbey church at Conques in the southern Auvergne, at once modern and Romanesque in its wall-hugging compilation of many parts. Two years later, Bouchard produced one of the largest figure sculptures fully in the round for the International Exhibition of 1937, the *Apollo* cast in bronze at enormous expense for the terrace of the Palais de Chaillot, not far from Saint-Pierre [221]. It is plainly a twentieth-century version of an archaic Greek *kouros*. Bouchard's respectful adaptations, overpowering in their confidence, are very different from Delaunay's supple transformations of Gothic motifs, but both artists salute past models to situate their modern art in a notion of tradition.

Just what this notion of tradition is, however, cannot be at all straightforwardly outlined in either case. In the 1930s, Bouchard was ready to identify with both the Romanesque and the Greek. Just before the 1914–18 war, Delaunay was ready to identify not only with the Gothic but with Roman antiquity, as demonstrated by his recourse to a Pompeian fresco of the Three Graces for the centrepiece of his *City of Paris* [162]. We are dealing here with not one but two or more notion*s* of tradition, and they are notions that can bring together diverse styles from different times and different places (inside and outside France). Between 1900 and 1940, artists in France did not merely identify with a tradition, they continually recreated 'tradition', spawning new

219. Robert Delaunay, *The Towers of Laon*, 1912. Oil on canvas, 163 × 130 cm. Musée National d'Art Moderne

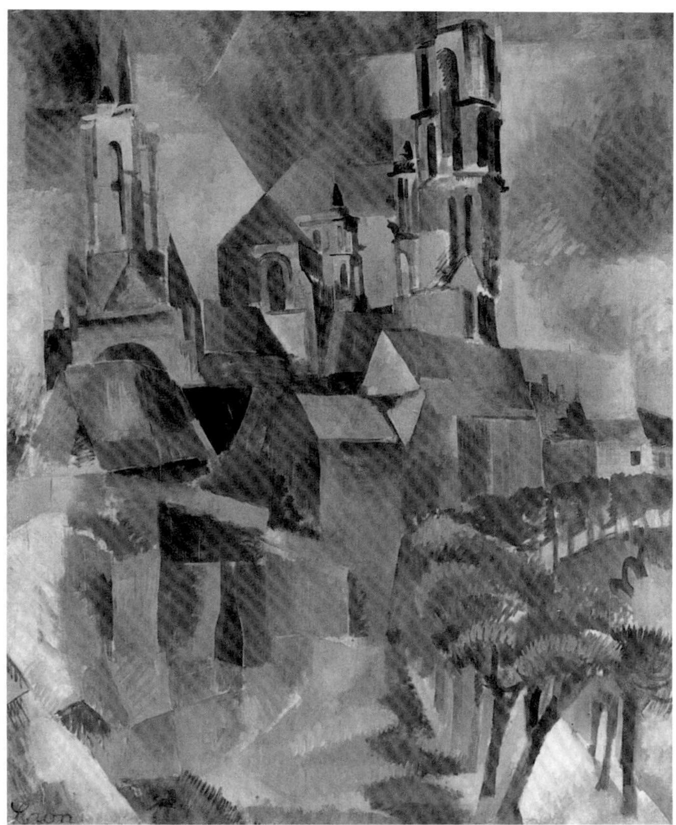

Facing page. Detail of André Derain, *View of Saint Maximin*, 1930 [236]

notions of it alongside the critics and art historians. And tradition was at every point employed as a notion that underpinned developing beliefs within French society concerning national identity. Tradition, it will become clear, was often treated as universal, and therefore above politics. In fact, profoundly attached as it was to the burning question of national identity, the notion of tradition would always arouse political passions.

Diversity in unity was fundamental to notions of both tradition and national identity in France throughout the period. What this entailed in the dominant understanding of French nationhood within France needs to be outlined at the outset, as well as its broadest overlaps with dominant historical representations of the French Tradition. So much was at stake: what France was and who the French were, nothing less.

In 1912, Elie Faure published the second volume of his *Histoire de l'art*. It dealt with medieval art, and centred on an account of France's central role in its genesis, by then an accepted given in French art-historical writing due to the work above all of Emile Mâle, Focillon's predecessor in the chair of art history at the Sorbonne. Faure's eulogy to the Gothic becomes a eulogy to France. The Gothic exists in contrasting French schools, each with its own character and yet this transformation of 'the whole land of France into a forest of stone' produces what Faure calls 'the spiritual unity of will and faith' peculiar to 'the French mind'. It is a mind, he writes, 'that must remain close to . . . [France's] soil, to her rivers, to the winds that cross her skies'.[3] It was Henri Focillon who wrote the preface to the catalogue of the huge exhibition 'Chefs-d'oeuvre de l'art français' initiated by Léon Blum at the International Exhibition of 1937. He called the 'Masterpieces' exhibition a 'portrait of France', and provided a flattering portrait of diversity in unity across time. 'Each epoch of French art has its particular physiognomy', he wrote.[4]

Focillon's allusion to France as the subject of a 'portrait' places his text in a venerable lineage, which goes back to the historian Jules Michelet's early nineteenth-century picture of France as an heroic 'personality' who has transcended the racial diversity of 'her' component peoples. Michelet was the acknowledged foundation of the two pictures of France presented to Third Republic society which were most profoundly opinion-forming. These were Ernest Lavisse's primary school textbook introducing French history known as the 'Petit Lavisse', and the geographer Paul Vidal de la Blanche's *Tableau de la géographie de la France*, which served as the first of the twenty-seven volumes making up Lavisse's *Histoire de France*. The 'Petit Lavisse' virtually monopolised history teaching at primary level, which was itself dominated by history as a subject; it first appeared in 1885, and then in progressively more nationalist republican versions in 1895 and 1912. It was still being revised between the wars, after countless reprintings. Vidal's *Tableau* was published in 1903 and was aimed at the more select market of lycée and university students, but it too went through many editions.[5]

Lavisse writes the history of France as a story of unification, initiated by the monarchs, consolidated by the Revolution and finally by the Third Republic. 'The kings unified France; the people defended it.'[6] Vidal set out to answer the question: 'How did a fragment of the earth's surface which is neither a peninsular nor an island and which from the standpoint of physical geography is not, strictly speaking, a unit, come to achieve the political status of a country and ultimately become a nation?'[7] His 'picture' is constructed as a series of interlocked contrasts, moving from one clearly distinct locality to another; rivers, in particular the Loire and the Seine, are identified as the routes to unification, allowing the crucial cementing of ties between North and South, between the Ile-de-France and the rest of France in all its diversity. As we shall see, the

220. Henri Bouchard, Tympanum of the church of Saint-Pierre de Chaillot, Paris. 15m. × 28m. 1933–5

221. Henri Bouchard, *Apollo*, 1937. Bronze. h. 7m. Terrace of the Palais de Chaillot, Paris

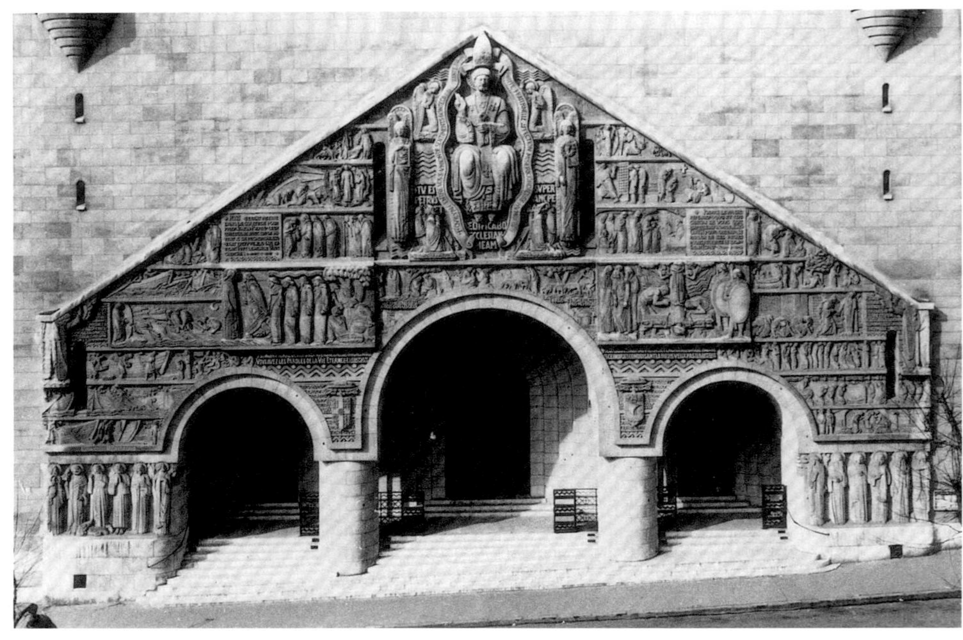

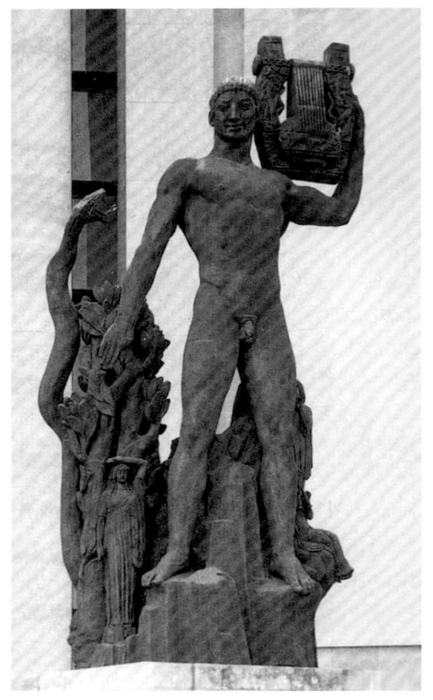

question of tradition would continually centre on the question of the 'Gothic' North and the 'Latin' South.

It is telling that Lavisse should have asked Vidal to provide a geography as the introduction to his definitive *Histoire de France*, for the dominant notion of nationality throughout the period was far more profoundly centred on the ideal of a territorial community bound together by the will of the people than on the ideal of a community of descent, bound together by ethnicity. The Universal Exhibition of 1889, widely seen as a triumphalist endorsement of the future of the Third Republic, coincided with legislation that confirmed an open, expansive approach to citizenship, one which originated in the Revolution. Fundamentally, that legislation remained unchanged to 1940, though requirements for naturalisation were liberalised in 1927 and then restricted more tightly than before with the fall of the Popular Front. Descent – 'jus sanguinis' – was acknowledged in 1889 as a condition of French citizenship, but only in the most limited sense. All second-generation immigrants, domiciled in France, had French citizenship automatically conferred upon them by right of residence – 'jus soli' – whatever their parents' race or country of origin. Behind this legislation lay, as Rogers Brubaker has shown, a political rather than ethnocultural concept of the State, and two key enabling factors. First, a deep belief in the superiority of French civilization as a beacon of liberty, and second, following from this, a deep faith in France's capacity to assimilate immigrants (with education – including the 'Petit Lavisse' – one of the chief instruments of assimilation).[8] The case was put thus in the Senate debate of 1889: 'France is not only a race, but especially a fatherland (patrie) . . . she possesses that eminently colonial capacity of absorbing in herself the peoples to whom she transports civilisation'.[9] The term 'race' is used here as Michelet used it: the French 'race' is a fusion of races, it is multi-racial and ethnically open to modification. Senator Isaac, who made the statement, was a Jew. What mattered was 'patrie': the shared history of peoples in a territory unified by their political will.

In France, just as the nation was thought of as essentially a territorial community, tradition was rarely a matter simply of lineages connected through time; it was usually a matter of place too, of connections across territories centred on the geographical space between the Atlantic and the Mediterranean. At the same time, just as the nation was thought of as outward-looking, always capable of absorbing the 'foreign', tradition was conventionally considered a product not only of internal developments but of new stimuli assimilated from outside. For Focillon in 1937, any survey of French 'masterpieces' was bound to hold in balance the contributions of the 'indigenous' peoples of France and the impact of 'invasions'.

I have sketched here the dominant orthodox view of nationhood and citizenship in France between 1900 and 1940. There was an energetic and active counter-view, according to which France was thought of as much more fundamentally an organic, not merely a political whole, a community of descent, ethnoculturally defined, for all the ethnic diversity of its peoples. This counter-view was driven above all by activists who used culture as their mode of political intervention, and so it permeated the discourse of tradition, in its independent as well as its official forms.[10] Moreover, it became increasingly strong and strident, especially as the Depression began to affect France from 1931, able with growing success to exploit the latent xenophobia and anti-Semitism at every level of French society, until it took control with the 'New Order' of Marshall Pétain. It should, however, be remembered that even in the 1930s, this was a counter-view, its stridency always met by a dominant liberal orthodoxy, not only from the Left but from the Radical Party in the centre. Nowhere was resistance to it more uncompromising than in Montparnasse and the rue la Boétie, the centres of the art world.

CHAPTER 9

Modernism and the Re-invention of Tradition, 1900–18

'ONE MUST BECOME CLASSICAL AGAIN BY WAY OF NATURE': FROM DENIS AND MAILLOL TO MATISSE

In 1906, Camille Mauclair, one of Impressionism's first historians, published a garulous polemic with the title *Trois crises de l'art actuel* (Three Crises in Art Now). The second and most grave of the crises he identified was the danger that 'the conquests of impressionism' would be ignored, and this was so important to Mauclair because Impressionism, he claimed, represented a renewal of a quintessentially French 'tradition'. This tradition linked Renoir and Manet to the masters of the eighteenth century, Fragonard and Boucher. In its Impressionist manifestation it combined the spontaneous with the logical, a direct responsiveness to light in nature with a 'scientific technique', and, as such, could be called 'classical'. Revealing a nascent ethnocultural nationalism, which would develop into anti-Semitic xenophobia between the wars, Mauclair wrote: 'In reality, [Impressionism] was not only a return to the national spirit, to the genius of our race, but once again to classicism, that is to say, to the cult of the primordial elements of art.'[11] On the 'classical' basis of this new technique, he held up the promise of a modern art which would go beyond the 'naturalism' of 'the first Impressionists'. He wrote of a 'second Impressionism', concerned above all with the painting of 'inner meaning', and among the artists he picked out as its leaders was Maurice Denis (b.1870). In Denis he found a painter responding directly to light in nature using Impressionist chromatic technique, and yet painting religious and mythological subjects while openly invoking the art of the past, from the Florentine to the Gothic, out of a deep 'respect for pictorial classicism'.[2]

Mauclair rightly made much of Denis's debt to Italy. The self-conscious classicism of his decorative murals for Charles Stern [81] came in significant part from a passion for the Tuscan Quattrocento and for later Renaissance Roman painting fed by visits to Italy which had begun in 1895. But the critic conspicuously ignored another stimulus which Denis had long insisted upon, Paul Cézanne; for him the springboard of a modern classicism. Indeed, Mauclair made a point of ridiculing the idea that 'the grossness of M. Cézanne's visions and means' should be aligned with 'the taste, the severe aesthetic, the linear science of Ingres,' the 'true god' of classicism.[3] Mauclair's notion of a modernist French tradition whose new foundation would be Impressionist technique was steadily marginalised by modernist criticism from 1906 on; Denis's belief that a renewal of the French tradition depended on the example of Cézanne quickly became a modernist article of faith.

Superficially there is nothing obviously Cézanne-like about Denis's painting in the 1900s; one reason for Mauclair's approval. The references to a lineage that would include Poussin, Ingres and Puvis de Chavannes as well as Italian Renaissance art are much clearer than any echo of Cézanne in works like his arcadian *The Shepherds* of 1909 [222]. The clue to Cézanne's presence as the 'classical' example behind such a picture lies in their reconciliation of the 'real' and the 'ideal'. Denis's flute-playing shepherd and half-draped muses relax on a clifftop above the bay at Perros-Guirec in Brittany, where the year before the painter had bought a villa. Their Mediterranean Arcadia is transported to France's North-West coast. A classical world is seen in the world Denis painted at first hand: in nature. In both cases, classicism is aligned with structured composition, by which intense colour relationships discovered in response to nature are organised.

'One must become classical again by way of nature, that is, by way of sensation.' This statement by Cézanne from a letter to the artist-critic Emile Bernard sums up what was to become a widely shared understanding of his 'classicism'. It went with his advice that the 'eye' and 'brain' should work in tandem, the eye by its 'vision of nature', the 'brain by the logic of organised sensations'. Both statements were included among Cézanne's 'Opinions' published in 1904 along with an essay by Bernard, where he argues that Cézanne achieved the 'classical by way of nature' precisely because he began with his spontaneous experience of nature and only then sought to 'organise' his 'sensations'.[4] Broadly, such an idea of classicism as the complementary resolution of the spontaneous and the organised, of nature experienced directly and 'logic', was echoed by Mauclair, even if he dismissed Cézanne; it was to remain fundamental to most ideas of classicism and especially of the French tradition formulated in the period up to 1940, whether or not with Cézanne named as founding father. Denis, much more than Bernard, was the one who ensured that Cézanne, understood basically in this way, became the paradigm for so many artists in search of a modernist classicism.

Denis did so above all in a long essay published as a response to the Cézanne retrospective at the Salon d'automne of 1907. Here penetrating passages on the always tense, rarely resolved relationship between seeing and pictorial construction in Cézanne's way of working, coexist with

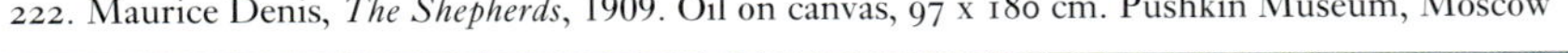
222. Maurice Denis, *The Shepherds*, 1909. Oil on canvas, 97 x 180 cm. Pushkin Museum, Moscow

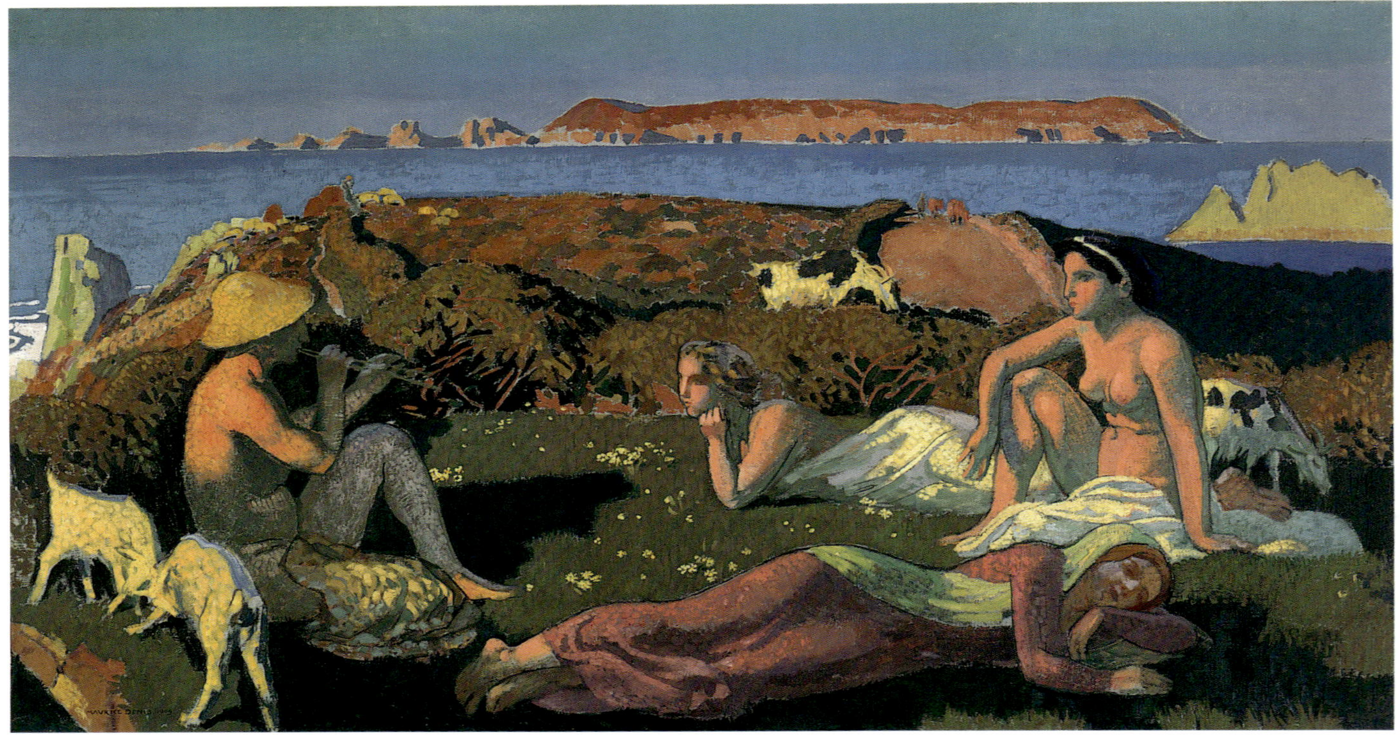

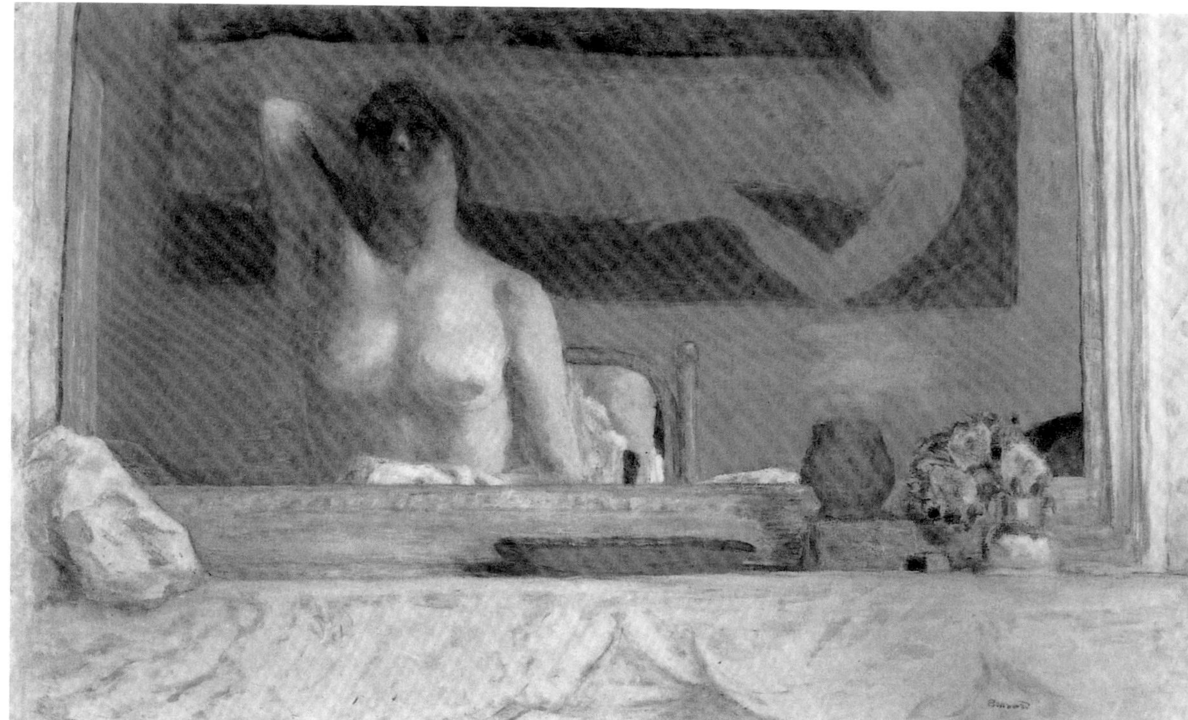

223. Pierre Bonnard, *The Mantlepiece*, 1916. Oil on canvas, 80.7 × 126.7 cm. Margoline Collection

224. Aristide Maillol, *The Mediterranean*, 1900–1905. Limestone, height 114 cm. Sammlung Oskar Reinhart 'Am Römerholz', Winterthur

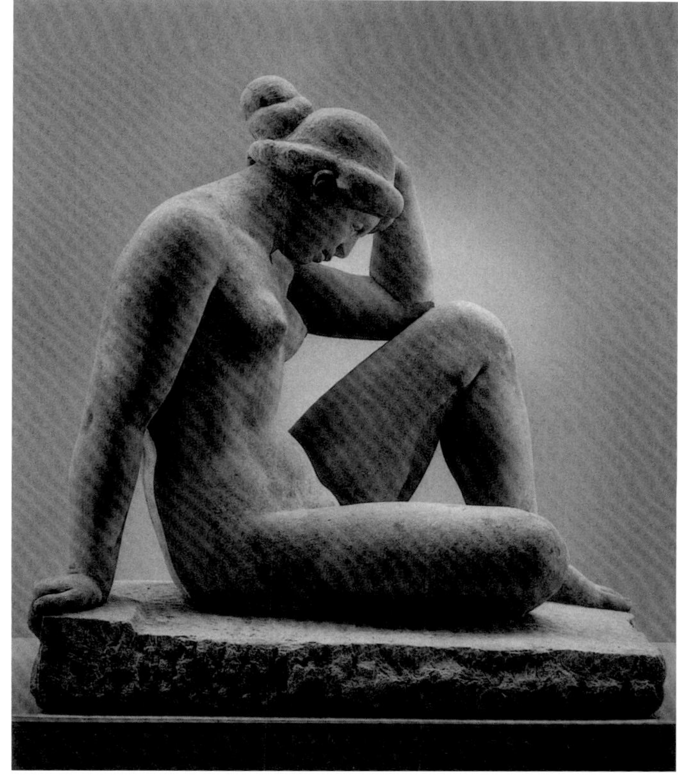

the resounding claim that he is the 'Poussin of impressionism', an artist who has created 'classicism' out of 'impressionism'. As Denis presents him, Cézanne's classicism is innate; he actually *sees* with a classical feeling for 'style'. In his case, spontaneity is not given measure at one remove, it is itself measured. He does not imitate past masters, he finds their 'discipline' in himself: 'He is so naturally a painter and so spontaneously classical'.[5] Such a view of Cézanne, which can accept the unfinished in his painting, which holds in balance a positive appreciation of the open-endedness of his working practice and of its discipline, and which does all this under the defining term 'classicism', carried obvious attractions for experimental modernists who wished to identify with some notion of tradition, most prominently Matisse. It did not, however, free Denis of his own compulsive need for the tidily resolved and the finished. From the Nabi generation – what Denis called the generation of 1890 – Bonnard was the painter most memorably to attempt to be 'spontaneously classical', to create a 'classicism' out of 'impressionism'. He sometimes left clues as to the lineage with which he identified even in his paintings of the everyday, especially after 1914. In *The Mantlepiece* of 1916 [223] the pose of the nude in the mirror has been shown to derive from that of *The Dying Niobid*, a fifth-century Greek marble; the painting on the wall behind is by Denis.[6]

Denis's influential view of what a modern French 'classicism' could be, was not confined to painting alone. Indeed, before the essay on Cézanne it was given an earlier clear exposition in an article on a sculptor, a sculptor who was to become almost as important a paradigm of such a classicism as Cézanne: Aristide Maillol, another of the generation of 1890. That article appeared in November 1905 as an accompaniment to the showing at the Salon d'automne of a lifesize plaster by Maillol (b.1861) titled simply *Woman*. The same year, a carved limestone version was begun too [224]. In the early 1920s, this sculpture would be re-titled *The Mediterranean*; by then it was recognised as the key work in the formation of Maillol's mature style and that title gave reverberating emphasis to its connection with a 'Latin' notion of the classical tradition. Maillol had been refining the idea of this sculpture, on paper and in clay, since 1900. The full-scale version in clay from which the plaster and limestone pieces were produced was made possible by a commission from the German collector-patron Count Harry Kessler; Maurice Denis had made the contact for Maillol. Between 1904 and 1914 Denis and Maillol were particularly close, working in a milieu that included many involved in a classical revival with modernist credentials oriented towards the 'Latin' Mediterranean. André Gide, with whom Denis had been in Rome in 1898, was one of them, and the literary periodical with which he was involved, the *Nouvelle Revue française*, provided an effective networking centre within this milieu from its first number in February 1909. Another important connection, again a close friend of Denis's, was Adrien Mithouard, editor of *L'Occident*, in which Denis's article on Maillol appeared, as well as many of his other key writings.[7] Maillol's major works, *Pomona* [225], *Flora*, *Spring* and *Summer* were conceived in 1909 as a foursome to complement Denis's major cycle of decorative paintings, the *History of Psyche*, installed in the Russian collector Ivan Morosov's Moscow palace in 1912. The muse, seated bolt-upright in Denis's *The Shepherds* (also bought by Morosov) pays a reciprocal homage to Maillol's *Mediterranean*.

225. Aristide Maillol, *Pomona*, 1908–10. Bronze. h. 164 cm. Museum am Ostwall, Dortmund

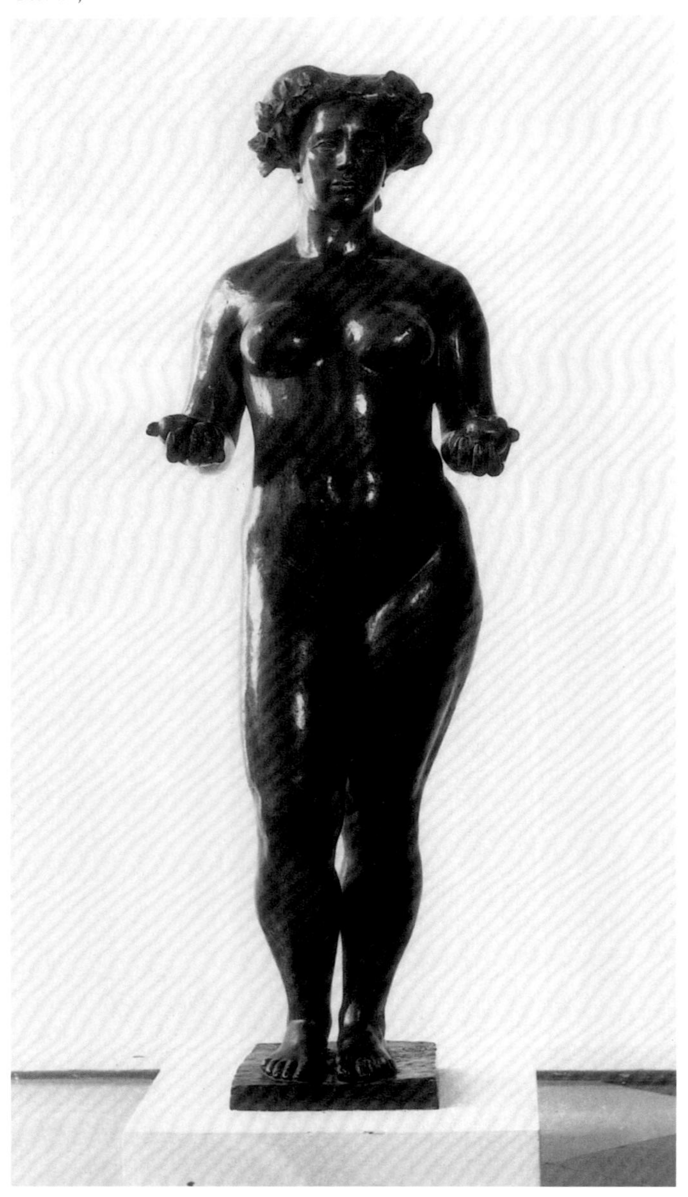

Denis's essay on Maillol of 1905, anticipating the 'spontaneous' classicism found two years later in Cézanne, started by claiming that for him classicism was not something acquired, it was a 'gift': a gift characterised by 'naïve sensuality', 'simplicity' and 'nobility'. Denis went on to link the sculptor's 'classical art' to the Greeks and to insist that 'the [Greek] sculptor of the school of Phidias', never suppressed the model, but fused 'the mathematics with which he ordered every detail' in a supreme corporeal harmony, making 'the idea (pensée)' real. Maillol is presented, like Cézanne, as 'this great classic', responding directly to nature, with the 'sensibility of a child'. The earth and the heavens, the real and the abstract merge in the warm bath of Denis's prose: Maillol's sculpted females are 'fleshly architectures which would be cold without the tremble on the skin, the hesitancy and tenderness of gesture'.[8] His surfaces, always lovingly cared for, become, like Cézanne's nervous brushstroke and fragile contours, the sign of responsiveness to life: nature as the source of classic harmony.

According to his biographer Judith Cladel, when in 1900 Maillol brought back to Paris his first clay model of *The Mediterranean*, it was Henri Matisse (b.1869) who helped him prepare the mould for casting the first plaster. The two were close, and Matisse also paid serious attention to Denis's opinions. In a 1913 interview published in New York, Matisse echoes Denis in calling Cézanne 'classic', and later, looking back in another interview of 1925, he too singles out the unfinished, the open-ended hesitancy of Cézanne's painting as fundamental to his 'lesson'.[9] In his mind, the direct and always open experience both of seeing nature and of painting was indissolubly linked to classicism, and the model was Cézanne. Even as a Fauve, he hoped to become a 'classic' in what for him was the most traditional sense. He went on, in that interview of 1925, to recall his teaching at his Academy in 1908. 'I especially took pains to inculcate in them a sense of tradition,' he said. 'Needless to say, many of my students were disappointed to see that a master with a reputation for being revolutionary could have repeated the words of Courbet to them: "I have simply wished to assert the reasoned and independent feeling of my own individuality within a total knowledge of tradition".'[10]

It was perhaps no accident that the landscapes Matisse and Derain (b.1880) painted in Collioure on the Catalan coast, close to Maillol's hometown of Banyuls, were shown in a room at the Salon d'automne of 1905 featuring a bust and a torso in a Quattrocento Italian manner by one Albert

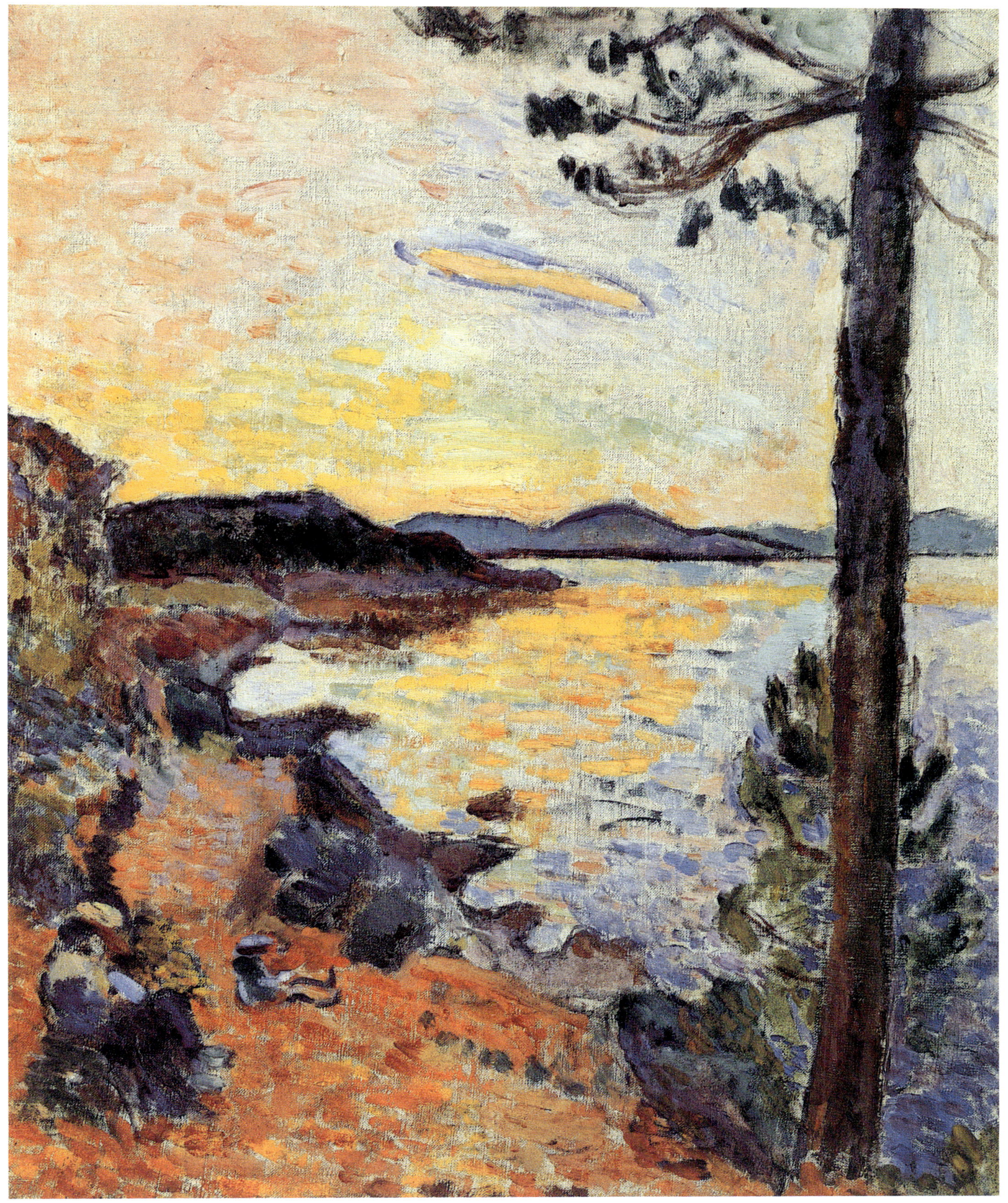

226. Henri Matisse, *By the Sea (Gulf of Saint-Tropez)*, 1904. Oil on canvas, 64.1 × 50.5 cm. Kunstsammlung Nordrhein-Westfalen, Düsseldorf

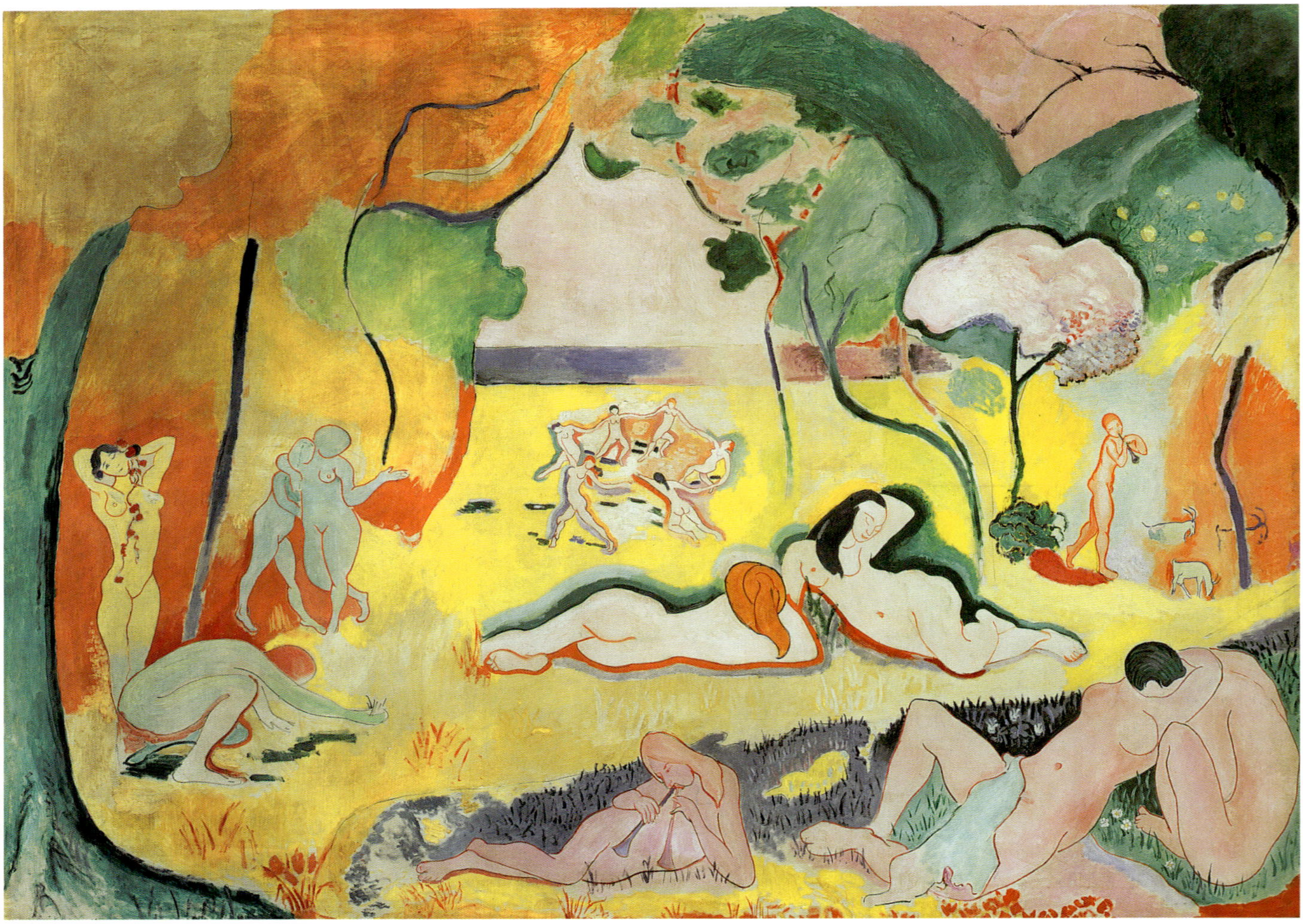

227. Henri Matisse, *Le Bonheur de vivre* (*The Joy of Life*), 1906. Oil on canvas, 174 × 238.1 cm. The Barnes Foundation, Merion, Pennsylvania

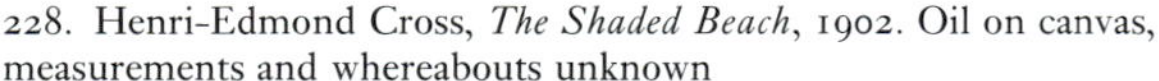

228. Henri-Edmond Cross, *The Shaded Beach*, 1902. Oil on canvas, measurements and whereabouts unknown

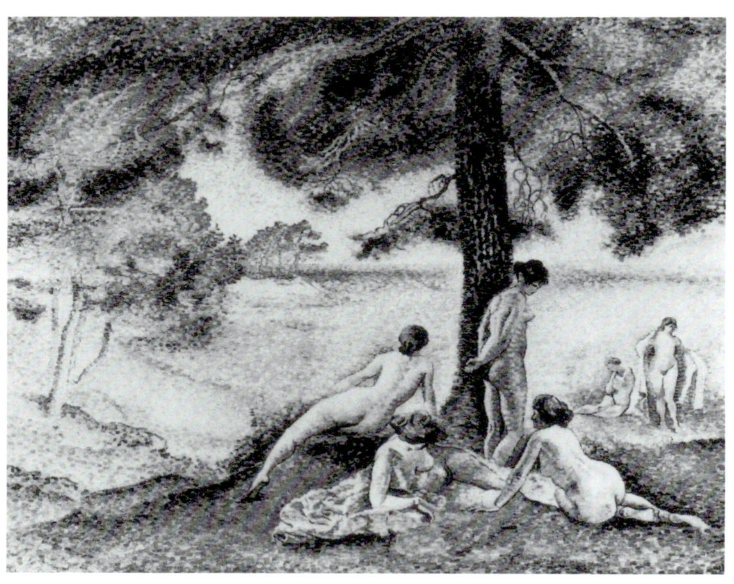

Marque. Vauxcelles might have written deflatingly of Donatello 'among wild beasts (fauves)', but Matisse and the others who hung the room may very well have found something positive in the juxtaposition, for it placed their work in contact with a notion of tradition indelibly associated with the Mediterranean. Derain and Matisse's landscapes have been shown sometimes to echo the seventeenth-century compositions of the Roman Campagna by Claude and Poussin, themselves routinely echoed in the picture postcards which now met the growing demand of the middle-class tourist market in the South.[11] Herbert picks out a small picture painted the summer before by Matisse, during his stay at Saint-Tropez with Signac and Henri-Edmond Cross, *By the Sea (Gulf of Saint-Tropez)* [226]. Certainly such echoes are visible in the placing of its repoussoir pine tree to the right and in the comfortable enclosure of the hills which gently holds the figures of Matisse and his family enfolded.[12] Even, however, in such Collioure landscapes of 1905 as Matisse's *View of Collioure* or Derain's *Drying Sails* [16, 88], where the echoes are more muffled, the brilliant colour gives heat and light to landscapes far more readily associated with the Arcadian idyll than Denis's cliffs at Perros-Guirec in the North. The notion of a Latin tradition identified here is as

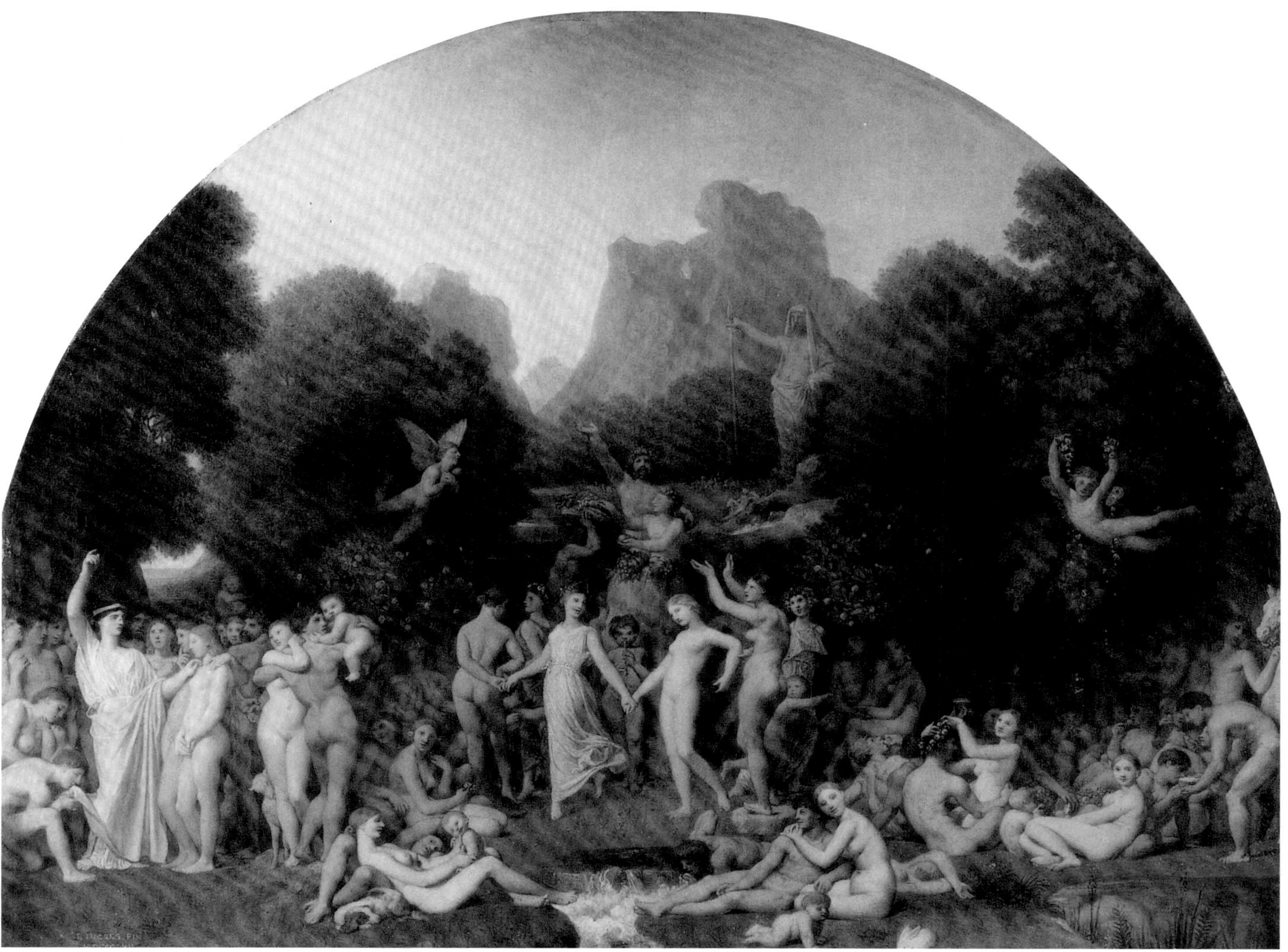

229. Jean-Dominique Ingres, *The Golden Age*, 1862. Oil on paper mounted on wood panel, 46.3 × 61.9 cm. Fogg Art Museum, Harvard University Art Museums, Bequest of Grenville L. Winthrop

much a question of place as it is of cultural lineage. Derain and Matisse, the first from the Ile-de-France, the second from Picardy in the North, had taken the train from Paris to the South, a small demonstration of what Vidal de la Blanche, in his *Tableau de la géographie de la France*, called the southernisation of Paris made possible by the river-valley routes that opened the city to the Mediterranean. Vlaminck's Chatou landscapes were there alongside their Collioure landscapes as reminders of Paris and the Ile-de-France. Fauve landscape painting would always, taken all together, present its own 'picture (tableau) of the geography of France'.[13]

The eloquence of place and cultural lineage had already been brought together in *Luxe, calme et volupé* [86], the large, figure composition that Matisse painted for the Autumn Salon of 1904 based on his Saint-Tropez oil sketch *By the Sea*. The Mediterranean coast had set the scene for a figure composition explicitly placed in the classical figurative tradition as defined by Poussin, Ingres and Puvis de Chavannes. This was a painting explicitly placed too in the context of Neo-Impressionist 'modern' continuations of that tradition, most obviously Henri-Edmond Cross's Arcadian idylls, where female nudes (usually unaware of male voyeurs) also inhabit the pine-wooded coast near Saint-Tropez [228].

It was not until the Indépendants of 1906, however, that the new, far less modulated 'fauve' style developed by Matisse and Derain at Collioure was taken beyond the implicit Latinity of place and explicitly linked to that figurative classical tradition. Matisse alone made the claim of belonging to that lineage; he did so with his sole exhibit at the Salon d'automne, his *Bonheur de vivre* (*Joy of Life*) [227]. The work wears its sources on its sleeve, the better to transform them. Most obviously, Matisse evokes Ingres's *Golden Age* of 1862 [229], while there are strong echoes too of Ingres's *Grande Odalisque*, which in 1906 was hung alongside Manet's *Olympia* in the Louvre, an event of incalculable significance to the modernists' claims to be the real 'classics'. The traditional is rendered revolutionary by Matisse's saturated colour and unfixed spatial relations, just as the bringing of Ingres into proximity with Manet at their paired Salon d'automne retrospectives in 1905 had rendered Ingres suddenly 'revolutionary'.[14]

Matisse's bid for inclusion in a notion of tradition with so strong a Latin flavour certainly placed him alongside such ardent supporters of Latinity as Denis and Maillol. It also could seem to place him alongside a newly emergent nationalist movement on the far Right of politics, Action française,

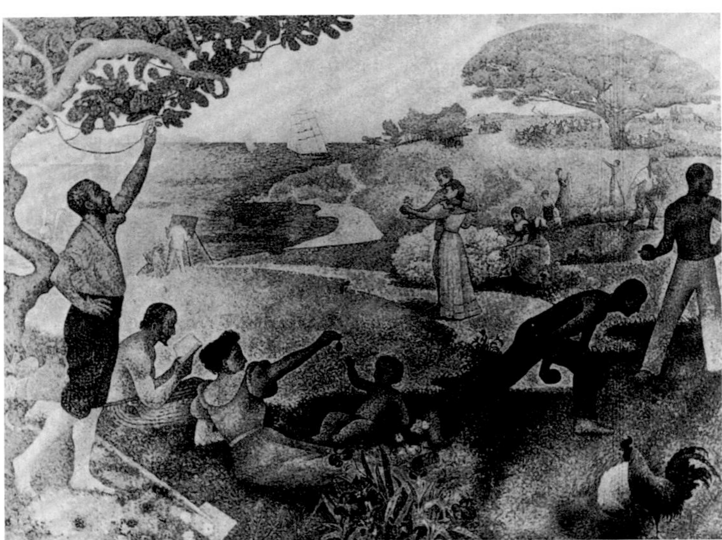

230. Paul Signac, *In Time of Harmony*, 1895. Town Hall, Montreuil-sous-Bois

for the notion of the French tradition as quintessentially Latin was among its core patriotic myths.

Action française had its origins in the most virulent anti-Dreyfusard activity of the late 1890s. It began with a small-circulation review edited by a dangerously talented polemicist, Charles Maurras. Maurras committed the movement to 'total royalism' and to what he called 'integral nationalism'. He refused the idea that a liberal Republic could maintain the unity of France, and advocated instead control, hierarchy and monarchy. He also refused the expansive idea of the French nation as a political unity held together by the democratic will of its peoples, and advocated instead the ideal of an ethnocultural community of descent, violently hostile to 'foreigners' and racial minorities, above all Jews. By 1905, there was a Ligue d'Action française; and in 1908 the little periodical became a daily newspaper backed especially by the family of the hugely successful popular novelist Alphonse Daudet: Léon Daudet, his son, became one of Maurras' most aggressive literary allies. Before 1914, the circulation of *l'Action française* remained small, but its attacks on republican politicians, Germans and Jews became the trigger for street violence in the Latin Quarter, led by the movement's own semi-militarised thugs, the Camelots du roi. At the same time, as a writer and cultural thinker Maurras was respected, especially by those who professed a commitment to classicism, as was the art critic of *L'Action française*, Louis Dimier, a noted historian and polemicist for classicism. Maurras's cultural ideas, though not Action française's taste for invective and street violence, attracted sympathy from a few in the 'independent' art world, including Maurice Denis and Aristide Maillol. Cladel states that for a while Maillol intended to retitle his famous Salon d'uutomne sculpture of 1905, *La Pensée latine*, 'a phrase,' she adds, 'which must be taken in the sense understood by Charles Maurras'; this was almost certainly in the 1900s, long before it was given the still Maurrasian title, *The Mediterranean*.[15]

Matisse had nothing whatever to do with Action française, either the movement, its leaders or its publications, but there is no doubt that his espousal of Latinity could have seemed for some to make a cultural statement that was inescapably political, a statement which in one way or another connected with the rhetoric of the new Right. The question is: how far would his Latinity have been responded to necessarily as a partisan statement from the Right?

There can be no denying the all-embracing commitment to Latinity for which Maurras and Action française stood, nor the depth of Maurras's identification with his own Provençal origins. 'The essential,' Maurras wrote in 1903, 'is that there exists a Latin civilisation, a Latin spirit, the vehicle and complement of hellenism, interpreter of reason and of athenian beauty, durable monument of roman strength'.[16] The core of that spirit and that civilisation was France, and he could not imagine France without Provence or Provence without France. Rightly, Herbert has pointed to the effectiveness with which Action française identified itself with the idea that Latin culture *was* French culture, the sheer relentlessness with which it claimed exclusive possession of the idea in the 1900s. And certainly others constructed their notions of the French tradition in explicit opposition to the movement's attempt to monopolise Latinity. Thus, Mauclair's notion of the French tradition as a lineage connecting the Impressionists with Fragonard and Boucher in the eighteenth-century was expressly formed to support the secular, progressive Republic. It was also expressly directed against Action française's promotion of a Latin France.

The Roman connection would always be backward for Mauclair, even when he himself became an authoritarian anti-Semite later. As he put it in 1905, his own brand of 'classicism', like his nationalism, was 'anti-roman'.[17]

Yet even Maurras, with all his rhetorical skills, did not achieve monopolistic control of the Latin notion of the classical tradition in the 1900s. It had already been appropriated by late nineteenth-century Symbolists, particularly at the point where Symbolism, anarchism and the pro-Dreyfus campaign converged. If Matisse's *Luxe, calme et volupté* invoked the poetry of Baudelaire, his *Bonheur de vivre*, despite its title, invoked that of Stéphane Mallarmé, specifically Mallarmé's evocation of Arcadia as an erotic dream, *L'après-midi d'un faune*.

> These nymphs, I want to perpetuate.
> So clear.
> Their light carnation, that drifts on the air
> Drowsing with tufted slumbers
> Did I love a dream?

Aptly, Jack Flam has juxtaposed *Bonheur de vivre* with the opening lines of the poem. He has also brought out the way the picture's special combination of intensity and suggestiveness, of chromatic directness and spatial elusiveness creates a painterly analogue for Mallarmé's reverie.[18] Denis's and Cross's idylls share this Mallarméan echo, and they were not alone in finding inspiration there. Of the generation of 1890, Ker-Xavier Roussel and Bonnard were also producing dreamlike Mallarméan idylls in the mid-1900s. Such atmospheres and images might seem now to

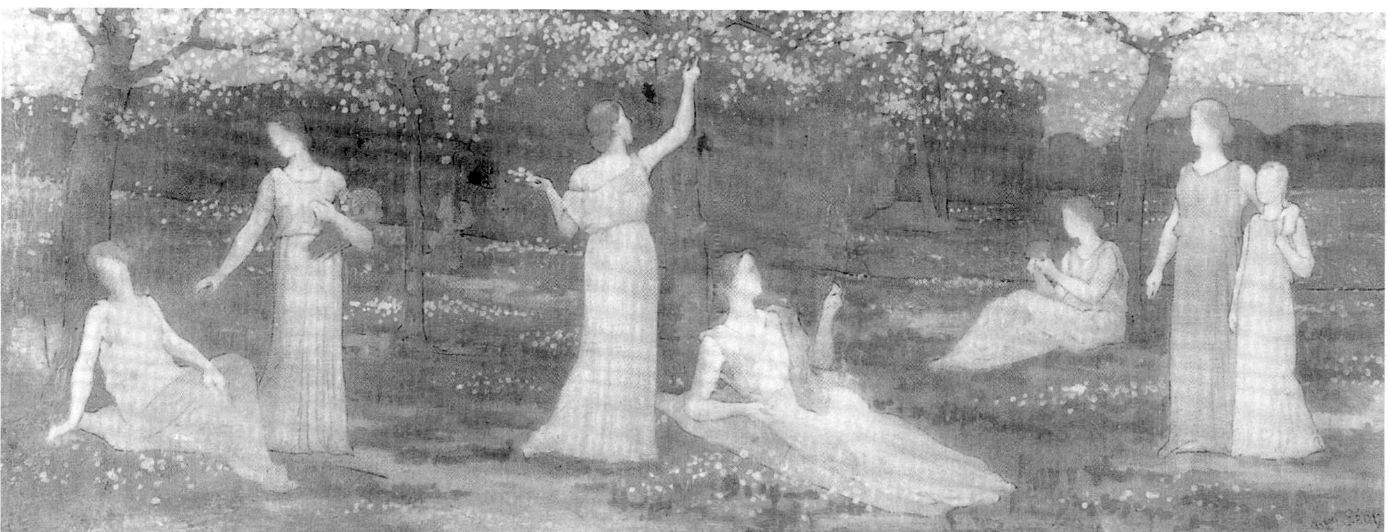

231. Alexandre Séon, *The Virgins*, study for the mural for the Salle des mariages in the Town Hall of Monteuil-sous-Bois, 1892. Oil on canvas, 24 × 64 cm. Musée du Petit-Palais, Paris

signify at best an escape into hedonistic irrelevance, but around 1900 they could be seen as the other side of a political activism that also produced Maximilien Luce's anarcho-syndicalist homages to labour [164]. As modern Arcadias they invited association with Paul Signac's anarchist dream of an ideal future, *In Time of Harmony* (1894), though they deprived that dream of its key components, modern dress and the imagery of work and leisure [230]. Mallarmé was an active defender of Dreyfus against the anti-Dreyfusard Right; Bonnard, who continued to paint Latin paradises into the war years, remained the anarchist he had been in the 1890s.

What is more, the lineage of Poussin and Ingres, and the adaptation of classical myth or mythological personnages to the building not of a monarchist but of a republican myth were features of the huge State-driven decorative programme that transformed the public buildings of the Republic from the 1880s. Signac's *In Time of Harmony* was such a public commission; it was painted for the town hall of Montreuil-sous-Bois. Puvis de Chavannes, as a modern intermediary with a Latin classical past, was often the model for artists commissioned to decorate the town halls of Paris's arrondissements and outer suburban boroughs; for instance in Alexandre Séon's murals, also painted for the town hall of suburban Montreuil [231]. By 1900, the official republican credentials of 'pictorial classicism' in its most recognisably Latin forms were so firmly established that even the eloquence of Maurras and Louis Dimier could not take it over altogether for the anti-republican Right.

And one simple point is clear, the experimental modernism of Matisse and Derain, however strongly it invoked Latinity, was as unacceptable to Maurras and Dimier at *l'Action française* as it was to Camille Mauclair; they could see the future only in terms of a return to a lost past, not in terms of the possession of a developing present. When in 1925 Matisse quoted Courbet (a cult figure of the Left), it was to underline how the desire for 'total knowledge of tradition' could go with an uncompromising individualism of a kind that was utterly unacceptable on the authoritarian Right. Certainly, to invoke Latinity was to allow identification with the 'natural', hierarchical ideal of France pedalled by Action française. But equally Matisse's *Bonheur de vivre* could have been taken to appropriate the myth of Latinity for modernist libertarianism, imbuing it with a forward-looking, risk-taking confidence in tune with its moment, 1906, when the 'radical Republic' led by liberal bourgeois ideals could still generate hope in middle-class France, even if that optimism was already sorely tried by the events that led to the collapse of the Bloc des gauches that very year.[19] The myth of a Latin France was a cultural weapon. Possession of it was contested by the democratic centre as well as the anti-democratic Right. It would remain up for ideological grabs for the next four decades.

Again, the rebarbativeness of Matisse's attitude to tradition is clear: he proudly attached himself to a notion of tradition that brought Ingres and Cézanne together, but only on his own uncompromising terms. The masters of the past were to be challenged as well as emulated. In 1907, he is quoted thus by Apollinaire: 'I have never avoided the influence of others . . . I believe that the personality of the artist develops and asserts itself through the struggles it has to go through when it is pitted against other personalities'.[20] Such an attitude, respectful yet self-assertive, capable often of aggression towards its models, incapable of straightforward fidelity to the past as a source of authority, was typical of the modernist relationship with notions of tradition at its most productive. It was not an attitude that the fundamentally conservative Denis would have found appealing, but it was one that all Matisse's Fauve allies would have shared, at least to some degree. It was certainly the attitude the Cubists brought to bear on the masters of the past and the notions of tradition that attracted them: Picasso and Braque as well as the artists who showed in the Salle 41 at the Indépendants of 1911 and at the controversial Salon d'automne of 1912.

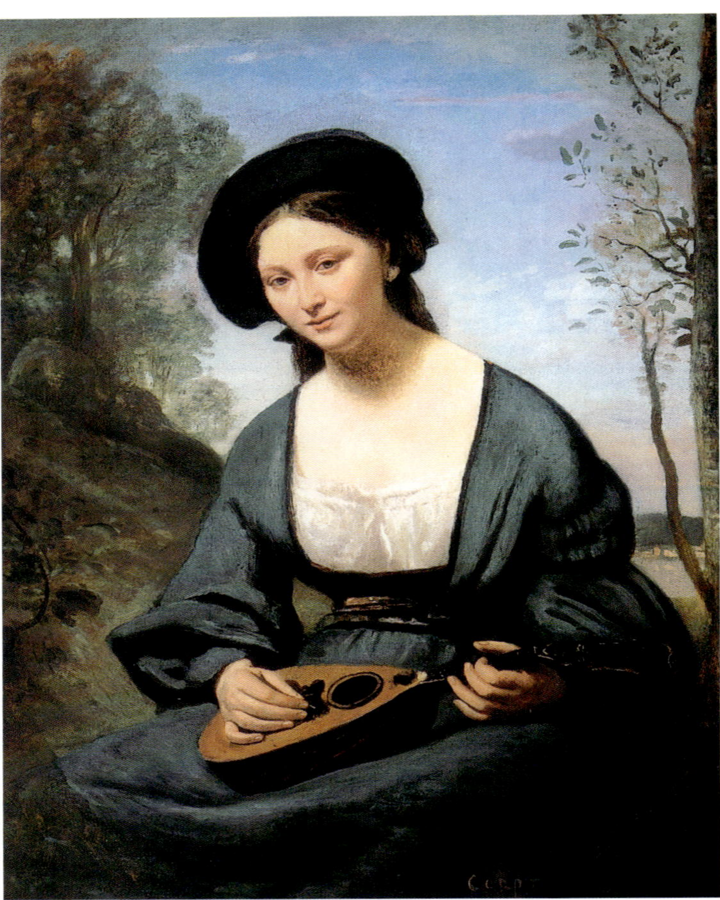

232. Camille Corot, *Woman with a Toque*, *c.*1850–5. Oil on canvas, 113 × 87.5 cm. Private Collection

THE CHALLENGE OF TRADITION: THE PRESENCE OF THE PAST IN THE WORK OF THE CUBISTS AND OF DERAIN, 1907–14

The past is not ignored altogether in pre-1914 art writing which addresses Braque's and Picasso's Cubism, but the cultural references, sometimes taking in the non-European, tend not to infer attachment to any recognisable notion of tradition, certainly not a French classical tradition. Between 1907 and 1912, however, Braque and Picasso repeatedly used subjects and stylistic features that alluded to the past in ways that could evoke such notions.

In Picasso's case the degree of aggression towards some of the masters referred to is such that ties with all notions of tradition can seem to be irrevocably broken; a sympathetic commentator like André Salmon certainly thought they were. Picasso's *Demoiselles d'Avignon* [282] can be related to Titian's treatment of the story of Diana and Actaeon – posturing nudes in a curtained space surprised by a male intruder – but only in a spirit of impudent cultural vandalism. When Salmon wrote of the smile of the *Mona Lisa* in the context of the *Demoiselles*, he only did so to enhance the shock of the picture's denial of the European past.[21] Even here, however, the references to an El Greco then in Paris and to the crouching nude in the little Cézanne *Bathers* owned by Matisse [90] makes a positive statement that could link the work to a then developing modernist notion of tradition which brought the Spaniard and the Provençal Frenchman together, a notion that reached outside France and indeed Europe.[22]

Most plainly positive and most explicit in its invocation of tradition was a small group of canvases painted by both Picasso and Braque at the moment of their closest collaboration, in 1910. This was another result of the Salon d'automne's policy of mounting salutary retrospectives. Here the stimulus was the exhibition of Corot's figure paintings at the Salon d'automne of 1909 (another nineteenth-century French 'master' with Italian, especially Roman credentials). One of the works on view was Corot's *Woman with a Toque* [232]. Within six months, Braque and Picasso had each produced two paintings in direct response to the challenge of such Italianate figures with their delicate silvery tonalities.

Braque's *Woman with a Mandolin* in Munich [233], like one of Picasso's responses, uses an oval format to reach beyond Corot to French decorative painting of the eighteenth century. Marie Laurencin too would use the oval format, for instance in work she contributed for the ornamental corner furnishings of the Salon Bourgeois in the 1912 Maison Cubiste [187]. But where she deliberately accented the decorative possibilities of Cubism and her sense of connection with the eighteenth century, Braque can seem deliberately to have called up such associations in order to give emphasis to his *anti*-decorative, *twentieth*-century sense of pictorial purpose. His ornamental female subject is broken apart, as contours fracture and planes slip into one another, while the austerity of monochromy is preferred to the pleasures of colour. From the vantage point of the 1920s with hindsight, however, precisely this kind of 'hermetic Cubist' painting, in the work of Picasso as well as Braque, would be called 'classic', and commentators like the Purists, Ozenfant and Le Corbusier, would dwell on the stability of its planar structures as a sign of continuity with tradition understood in the broadest supra-national sense.[23] Besides the openly Corot-like subject of Braque's *Woman with a Mandolin* and its Corotian silvery lights, the dabbed touches of paint placed like building blocks, and the angular faceting insidiously introduce associations with Neo-Impressionism and Cézanne. Connections with the past were, thus, invited on every level, by treatment as well as subject matter, making it possible to link even this kind of pictorial iconoclasm with notions of tradition. In this case, these were notions centred on France, combining the eighteenth century of Boucher, so admired by Mauclair, with the nineteenth century of Corot and Cézanne, and the early twentieth century of Signac and Cross. As we shall see, Picasso's invocations of tradition after 1914 would always preserve an ironic, subversive, sometimes vandalistic aspect.[24] By the 1920s, Braque, on the other hand, would be recognised by his most loyal supporters, without even a hint of irony, as one of the leading modernist representatives of the French tradition along with Matisse.

From 1911, the Cubism of the Salons repeatedly used subject matter to declare a relationship with the past. At the Indépendants of 1911, Léger's *Nudes in a Forest* [28] was clearly connected to a hypothetical chain of nudes in landscape settings which linked Cézanne's *Bathers* to the seventeenth century; while Le Fauconnier's *Abundance* [26] was placed squarely in a classical allegorical lineage. At the Salon d'automne of 1911, Metzinger's *Tea-time* [95] offered a conventional portrait subject, with echoes of Corot (the girl's hint of a smile led to provocative talk of the Mona Lisa of Cubism). And, at the 1912 Salon d'automne, even Léger's *Woman in Blue* [30], a work given special exposure as an iconoclastic provocation, took the most conventional of subjects, one that especially recalled Cézanne's late portraits of his wife and his *Woman with a Coffee-pot* then in the Pellerin collection. Cubism was constantly 'pitted against other personalities', past masters, in the spirit of Matisse's 1907 remark to Apollinaire quoted above; and constantly, by the same token, called up notions of tradition, with the empowering presence of Cézanne (always alluded to stylistically) the implied point of exchange between past and present.

Such references were easily adapted to existing notions of the French tradition, which for the viewing public (of which the majority was hostile at the Salons) must have amplified the destructive force of each Cubist showing. It was, in fact, as a direct threat to both national tradition and national identity that Cubism was most violently attacked in 1911 and especially 1912, not only in the right-wing press but from the Radical centre and even some sectors of the independent socialist Left too. It was regarded as a foreign invasion aided and abetted by a cultural fifth column of French artists. The question of Cubism was caught up, thus, in the sudden intensification of militant nationalism that characterised the years between 1911 and 1914 in France, a change of climate relentlessly encouraged by Action française's promotion of xenophobic paranoia.

The Salon d'automne of 1911 coincided with the culmination of the Morocco crisis, when, with a German gunboat lying off Agadir, the French government under the radical Caillaux was forced to cede to Germany part of France's new colony in the Congo in return for continued rights of economic exploitation in Morocco. Between that date and the election of Raymond Poincaré's administration in January 1913, the democratic Right and the conservative centre came together with Action française and the anti-democratic Right in a nationalist campaign that led to the Poincaré government's extension of conscription from two to three years, against the furious pacifist opposition of the socialist Left around Jean Jaurès. Alongside Maurras, republican nationalism had thrown up at the end of the 1890s a propagandist with perhaps even greater literary gifts, Maurice Barrès, a champion of the Latin image of France, equally contemptuous of the Chamber of Deputies, who did not identify patriotism with monarchy. Barrès's championship of a less restrictively neo-classical idea of classicism than Maurras's opened conservative nationalism to a wider cultural constituency. His novels and polemics mounted an argument for a natural French classicism: an innate French balance between realism and order, the product of the continuity of tradition in the immensely varied yet single land of France. It was an argument very much in tune with those who found just such a balance in the 'classicism' of Cézanne and Maillol.[25] Between 1911 and 1914, nationalism, as its appeal grew, became widely associated with a Latin image of French culture, Maurrasian or Barrèsian, defined against the irrational barbarism of a caricature

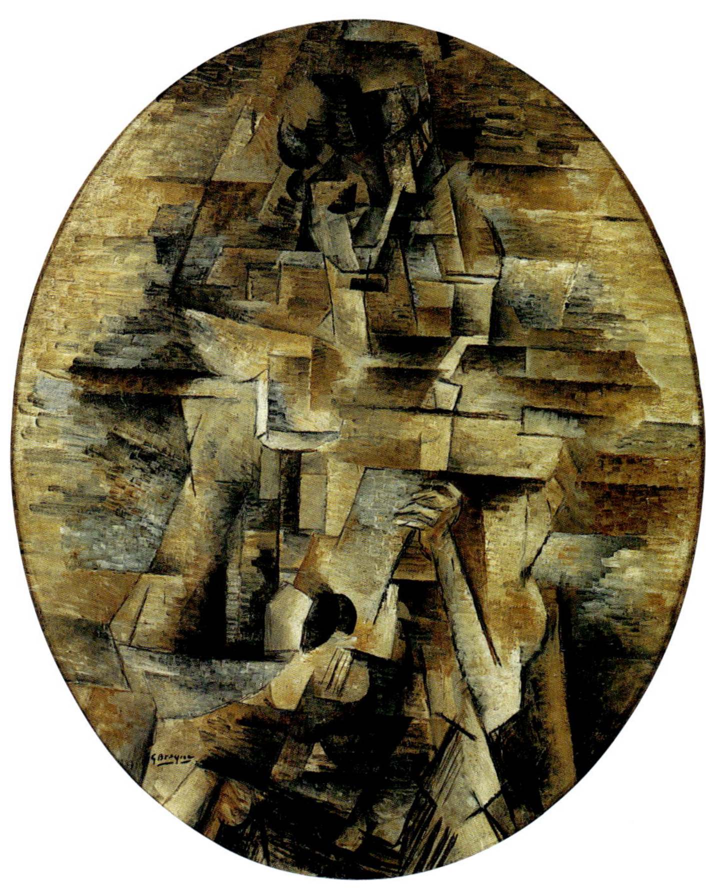

233. Georges Braque, *Woman with a Mandolin*, 1910. Oil on canvas, oval, 91.5 × 72.5 cm. Bayerisches Staatsgemäldesammlungen, Munich

notion of German culture. This was so across a political spectrum now inclusive of increasing numbers of ardent republicans, who in all other ways were hostile to Barrèsian conservatism. Mauclair did not suddenly embrace Latinity, but it was as a republican patriot who believed in a natural French classicism, one who would in fact be drawn to Barrès's vision, that he attacked the Cubists.

In this period too a new word entered the world of cultural dispute, 'métèque', the acrid flavour of which is perhaps best approximated by 'wog'. It was a hold-all term for foreigner with strong racist undertones, which spread into common usage from *L'Action française*. When, in the autumn of 1911 Apollinaire was briefly held as a suspect in connection with the theft of the *Mona Lisa* from the Louvre, Léon Daudet, writing in *L'Action française*, drew attention to his real name, Wilhelm de Kostrowitzky, before finding him guilty as a Polish Jew (he was not in fact Jewish) and a 'métèque'.[26] Briefly, both as poet and champion of the Cubists in the press, he was a favourite 'métèque' target of the Right in papers like *L'Œuvre* and periodicals like *Les Guêpes*. It is no coincidence that the attacks on Cubism in the autumn of 1911, obsessively preoccupied as they were with the idea of invasion, should have been accompanied by a virulent campaign led by Daudet in *L'Action française* against 'Jewish-German espionage'.[27] Louis Vauxcelles, a critic of the liberal republican centre, kept his distance from

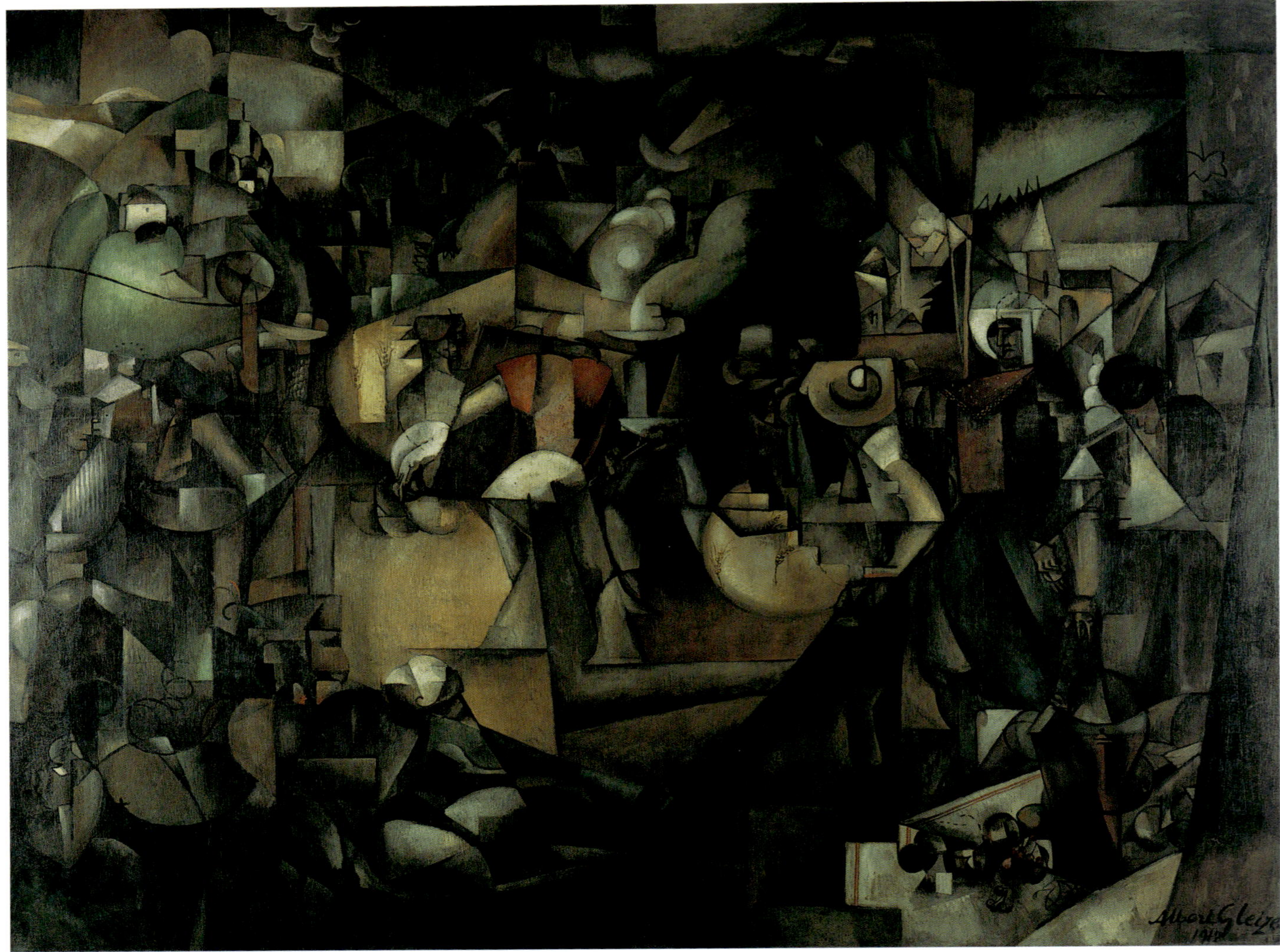

234. Albert Gleizes, *Harvest Threshing*, 1912. Oil on canvas, 269 × 353 cm. Private Collection

this kind of extremism, but even he, in *Gil Blas*, a newspaper of the democratic Left, argued that the abstraction of Cubism, its apparent denial of nature as starting point, set it apart from the engagement with nature that he saw as crucial to French painting, from Poussin to Ingres and Cézanne (he was another who embraced an idea of the French tradition as realist and ordered without in any sense being a Barrèsian conservative). This was an argument which not only identified Cubism as foreign to a particular notion of the French tradition, but, in the context of that xenophobic moment, implied a commitment to national defence of a clearly nationalist kind.

Hemmed in thus by attackers who insisted on the foreign character of Cubism, there was one artist in particular among the Salon Cubists who staked a claim for Cubism as a quintessentially French art. This was Albert Gleizes, and he did so by bringing to bear a notion of the French tradition which directly challenged Action française along with those republican nationalists who had committed themselves to the equation between France and Latinity. His alternative was clearly identified with the anarcho-syndicalist Left, and yet, like Maurras's, it was based on strong racist foundations. It attached Cubism to the idea of a 'Celtic tradition', and of a fundamentally Celtic rather than Roman France.

Gleizes and Metzinger, as Bergsonians, focused on the mobility of modern experience as one means of realising the dynamism of 'duration' ('la durée').[28] This commitment to modernity as an increasingly intense experience of movement in time did not, of course, separate the modern from the past, since the modern could only be thought of as within duration. The artist was, for them, an individual intuitively breaking down temporal barriers, bringing the past into the present. Already in September 1911, a year before he and Metzinger published *Du Cubisme* together, Gleizes was writing of art as a constant process of 'renaissance', and of Cubism as caught up in a moving stream out of the past into the future. It was in this spirit that, at the beginning of 1913 he asserted, as if all in his milieu would agree: 'We consider . . . that the works of the most independent artists today have their origins in our national tradition'.[29] He made this assertion in a two-part article published by the periodical *Montjoie!*; this piece was given the portentious title 'Cubism and Tradition'. In 1911, Gleizes had identified Cubism with a 'French Tradition', whose qualities of 'grandeur, clarity, equilibrium and intelligence' stemmed from the 'Greco-Roman traditions' of the West.[30] In 1913, he identified Cubism with Gothic art, which for him was fundamentally Celtic, and rejected David and Ingres as imitators of an Italian art 'impregnated with Greek antiquity'. In between he had embraced wholeheartedly the Celtic nationalism of Robert Pelletier's Ligue Celtique, as had many others in the Puteaux milieu.[31]

Cubism, thus, became explicitly nationalist (at least according to Gleizes) in contradistinction to the Latin nationalism associated at its most extreme with Action française and the revolutionary Right. In social historical terms, this was a brand of nationalism connected with the early nineteenth-century historian Augustin Thierry's claim that the French common people were Gallic (Celtic) and had been ruled over by a Frankish aristocracy descended from German invaders. In political terms, it went with a vision of society organised communally by means of corporate bodies (unions) based on trades which would return to the corporate Guild system of the Middle Ages, a system imagined to have been essentially Gallic.[32] Far from being naturally hierarchical (Maurras's vision of the French), the Gauls – for these nationalists, the most French of the French – were imagined to have been natural republicans. In cultural terms, the French tradition was thought of as reaching its first summit with the Gothic cathedral, the paradigm of a Celtic art whose discipline was intuitively realised and which, in a fully Bergsonian sense, transcended reason.[33] In this mythology, the history of French art becomes a story of resistance against invaders, with the Romans and the Italians demonised as threats to a native 'race, full of sap' (to use Gleizes's words). Maurice Denis's sacrosanct Italian Renaissance becomes 'the most dangerous pressure' ever exerted upon French art. And if, for Gleizes, Cézanne has a role as a link in the chain of tradition, it is above all as a link with a Gothic, not with a Latin classical past.[34]

Through 1912 and 1913, Gleizes's choice of subjects was calculatedly nationalist. His huge canvas, *Harvest Threshing* [234] was the centrepiece of the Cubists's Salon de la Section d'Or of Autumn 1912. It takes a theme fundamental to Vidal de la Blanche's vision (as discussed in the Introduction to Part Four) of the 'physiognomies' of France: the shaping of its 'pays' (localities) by human habitation and exploitation, in response to the innate demands of climate and physical geography (the landscapes painted by French artists throughout the period are almost invariably settled, rarely untouched). The land these peasants harvest has provided not just the grain they thresh but the stone of their dwellings; and each of the three villages guarding the fields that are harvested is dominated by its Medieval church. That year, Gleizes painted Chartres cathedral too, and in 1913 his most ambitious picture, *The City and the River*, an oil sketch for which is all that survives [235], is a composition which makes a Gothic church tower its dominant feature but which includes also fragments of modern engineering. A Gothic past and a changing present are brought together around the Bergsonian image of the river. In both instances, Cubist innovations are used to create surface rhythms and to merge one thing with another as expressions of the mobility of the relationship between past and present,

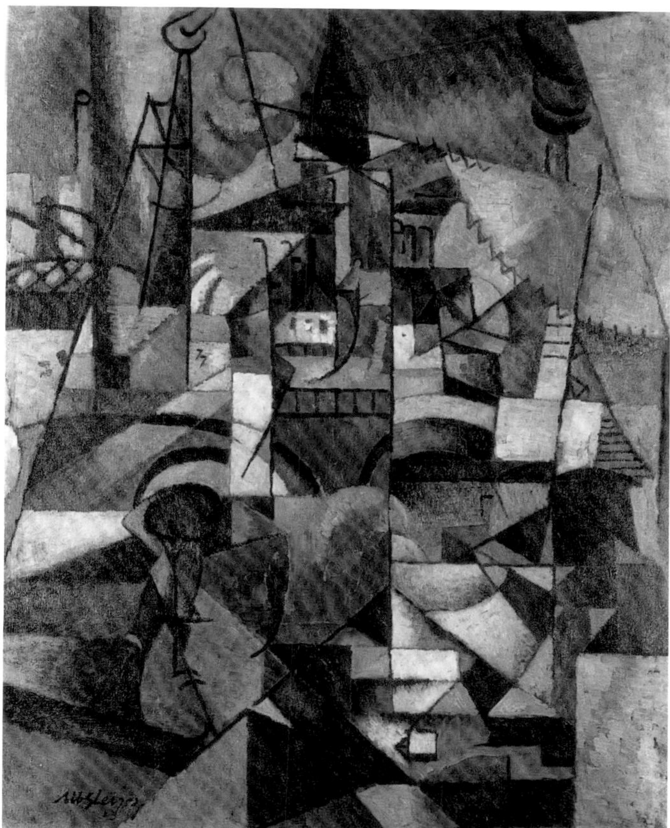

235. Albert Gleizes, *The City and the River*, 1913. Oil on canvas, 79.2 × 63.2 cm. Ursula and R. Stanley Johnson Family Collection, Chicago

but that relationship is tied into a notion of tradition which is exclusively 'Celtic' and French.

In such a context, Robert Delaunay's twin engagement with Medieval and modern images – the towers of Laon alongside the Eiffel Tower – could obviously take on strong connotations within the politics of culture [27, 219]. And yet, in his case there was nothing exclusive about his devotion to the Gothic, as his Roman Graces make clear in *The City of Paris* [162]. Celtic nationalism did not take sole possession of the Gothic subject, just as Action française's 'integral nationalism' did not take sole possession of the notion of a Greco-Roman French tradition. Indeed, for many determined to find the past in modern art, the Latin and the Gothic were actually complementary: they went together. They were different but linked manifestations of that balance between 'realism' and reason, spontaneity and discipline which was believed to have been given its new paradigmatic form in the painting of Cézanne. And their complementarity was a demonstration of the success with which France had unified North and South.

Thus neither Denis nor Maillol were, ultimately, exclusive partisans of Latin classicism. The third section of Denis's 1905 article on the sculptor dealt with the question 'Greek classic or Gothic classic?', finding in his work both. And in 1910, Maillol would send Denis a postcard of the columnar figure-sculptures of Chartres' south Porch with the note: 'In it are reconciled two successive traditions, fifth-century Greek and thirteenth-century Christian, two arts which have realised two ideals of humanity, by the fullness

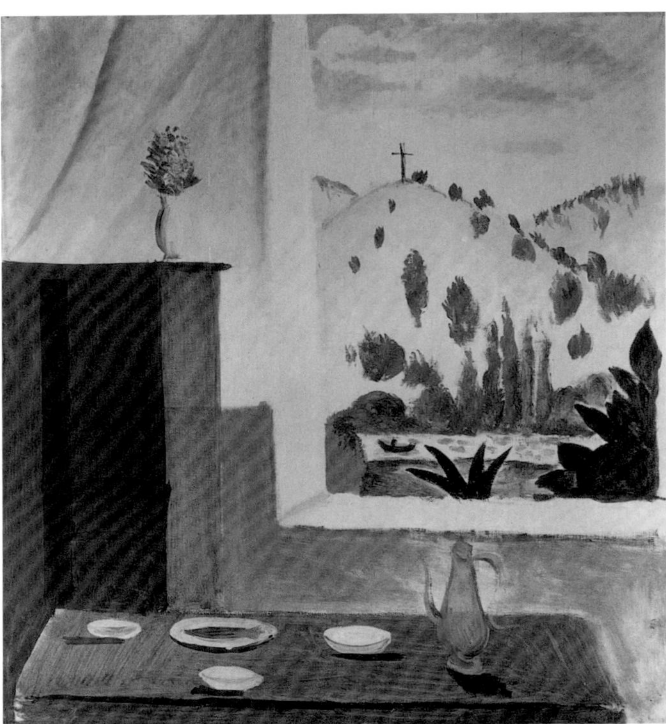

236. André Derain, *The Calvary*, 1912. Oil on canvas, 65.5 × 57.5 cm. Oeffentliche Kunstsammlung Basel, Kunstmuseum

of form.'[35] At the same time, the painter from the milieu of Picasso and Braque who most openly aligned his work with a notion of tradition in the years just before the 1914–18 war, André Derain, combined evocations of the Gothic with just as powerful evocations of Tuscany and the South. Since Derain developed his very personal form of post-Fauve traditionalism in the context of Cubism, and since his painting (alongside Maillol's sculpture) would come to represent for many the most impressive modern expression of the dominant post-war notion of tradition, his case seems the right one for concluding here.

When the by then deeply conservative critic Waldemar George surveyed Derain's career in 1935, he took him as the French painter who had given the new art a 'sense of history', and he set him apart as such from 'a Picasso, a Braque, a Matisse, those painters of the unadulterated present'. Many would have disagreed with him about Picasso, Braque and Matisse, but most would have agreed about Derain. Again in that monographic survey, George drew attention to Derain's 'medieval epoch' as 'perhaps his golden age', pointing to the period between 1911 and 1914, when he painted such canvases as *The Calvary* and *Saturday* [236, 237]. He called this work 'French medievalism', but wrote of windows opening 'onto the landscapes of the Tuscan primitives'; the Gothic fused with the Italian South.[36]

Derain had moved out of his high-colour Fauve style from 1907 in the company not of Matisse so much as the Montmartre circle around Picasso and Braque and the writers Salmon, Apollinaire and Max Jacob. His Paris base was in Montmartre from 1908 to 1910, and he was with Picasso at Cadaquès in the summer of 1910. His own profound exploration of Cézanne between 1908 and 1913 did not persuade him to open up contours and allow planes to slip into one another, as in the case of Picasso and Braque; he preserved the contour as a clear line of demarcation and the subject as something plainly stated, working for dense fullness of form combined with lucidity. With this he developed, especially between 1911 and 1914, an extraordinary richness of historical reference, a scholarly subtlety and care in the invocation of past styles utterly unlike the challenging approach developed by Picasso and Braque in, for instance, their Corotesque figures of 1910.

His 'medievalism' has been shown to have embodied not only a deepening identification with notions of the French tradition that unified North and South, but a solemn yet passionate involvement in long-established Roman Catholic iconographies.[37] Painted in 1912 at Vers in the southern 'département' of the Lot, *The Calvary* offers objects on an upward-tilted table treated with a Northern French and a Cubist acceptance of multiple viewpoints in front of a hill surmounted by a cross which is painted with a Quattrocento Tuscan dryness reminiscent of Piero della Francesca or Alesso Baldovinetti. The placing of the outdoor cross turns the table into an altar and endows the objects with sacred meaning: they become the vessels of the Eucharist in the Catholic mass, and thus symbolic of the transformation of the bread and wine into the flesh and blood of Christ. In 1910, Derain's friend, the Catholic poet Paul Claudel, had written of this transformation – 'Transubstantiation' – as a Christian expression of European Platonism, bringing out the affinity between Christian and Greek thought. *Saturday*, a picture finished in 1913 but possibly worked on from as early as 1908, takes as its subject 'le Samedi saint', in Holy Week, and gives a domestic scene an appropiate air of ritual gravity, over which the priestlike central seated figure presides. George associates it again with Tuscan Quattrocento painting – Botticelli and Filippo Lippi – but Jane Lee is right to stress the stylistic echoes of one of the most celebrated discoveries of the major exhibition of the 'French Primitives', held at the Louvre in 1904, the *Pietà* of the fifteenth-century Avignon School from Villeneuve-lès-Avignon.[38]

Derain probably saw that exhibition in 1904. If he did, he may or may not have realised that it had been organised with a very clear nationalist agenda in mind, one which could not have been called specifically Celtic but which was directed against the Latin nationalist agenda nonetheless. Its curator, Henri Bouchot, made no secret of his belief that the post-fifteenth-century Italian Renaissance influence on French art was the cause of decline, nor that art in France between the eleventh and the fifteenth centuries was in a profound sense especially representative of the French. It was this exhibition that for the first time collected together works of that period from North and South to create the category of the 'French Primitives'. It took as its starting point the eleventh century because this was the moment when, announced the catalogue preface, 'the national genius, till then formed of diverse elements . . . began to be aware of itself'. And blame for the failure to recognise hitherto the presence of that genius in the art of this early period was placed squarely on the French habit of welcoming the foreign. 'It would be said that, fated to be dispersed, because of our geographical situation and our ethnic composition, open because of our territory and our com-

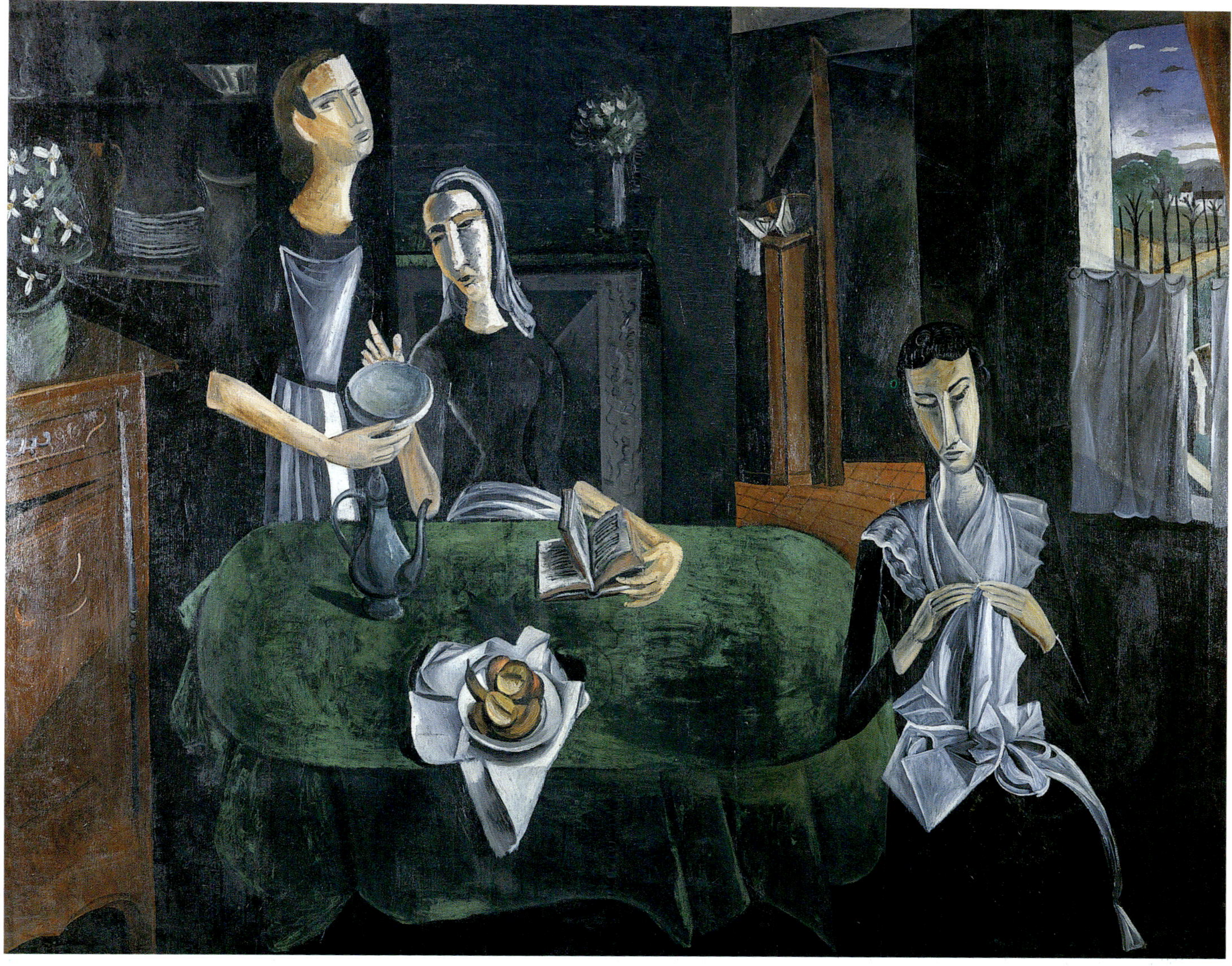

237. André Derain, *Saturday*, 1913. Oil on canvas, 181 × 228 cm. Pushkin Museum, Moscow

plex souls ceaselessly to receive, welcome, [and] attract contacts from outside, we will always be ready also to forget, in this generous need for assimilation . . . , the fundamental and enduring qualities of our own genius!'[39]

Derain, in 1911–14, was as ready to look at Piero della Francesca's painting as at the Villeneuve-lès-Avignon *Pietà*; he certainly did not share such doubts about looking outwards. Nor did he set his face against the Latin notion of the French tradition; he painted landscapes as evocative of the early Rome-based Corot as of Cézanne during these years. His case once again demonstrates that by referring to particular styles from the past, painters did not necessarily place their work in a fixed, clearly delimited cultural or ideological framework, like the one outlined by the catalogue of the 'French Primitives' exhibition, and neither did they necessarily attach their work to a particular notion of tradition. There were artists who did – Denis and Gleizes are cases in point – but this tended to be the exception, not the rule. The war brought a change; by the 1920s, the exception had become the rule, as we shall see.

BEING MODERN AND TRADITIONAL IN WARTIME: HOME-FRONT CUBISM, 1914–18

During 1916, the sculptor Jacques Lipchitz (b.1891), a Lithuanian non-combatant working as one of the youngest recruits to Cubism in Paris, made a significant change of practice. He ceased making polychrome constructions indebted to Picasso's constructions of 1912–15, and dedicated himself to sculpture in stone and bronze. In December that year he wrote to his dealer Léonce Rosenberg confessing how he had been tempted by polychromy (an 'unhealthy tendency'), and declaring a new conviction: 'Sculpture must be made as architecture is made. It's like that, indeed, that the ancients made it as well as the Egyptians and the Assyrians and also the French of the cathedral of Chartres.'[40] The work he produced in 1917–19, for instance *Seated Man with a Guitar* of 1918 [238], was 'architectural' in a way totally alien to, say, Maillol's *Pomona*, and the past he invoked here was less culturally confined than either Gleizes's Celtic or Denis's Latin traditions, but he too identified with Chartres and the cathedrals of France.

Also late in 1916, Juan Gris (b.1887), another of Rosenberg's foreign Cubists on the home front, painted an adaptation from a black-and-white photograph of a Corot mandolin player, and alongside it a full-length Cubist portrait of his partner Josette in restrained Corotesque pose, crystallised within a geometric armature abstracted from Corot's figure compositions, and overlaid with cool silvery tonalities also suggestive of him [239]. In 1917, he would paint an adaptation from one of Cézanne's portraits of his wife, and in the summer and autumn of 1918, working in the Touraine, one of Vidal de la Blanche's core regions of the French nation, he would paint a series of figure pieces with local peasant subjects whose solid simplicity followed partly from his admira-

238. Jacques Lipchitz, *Seated Man with a Guitar*, 1918. H. 76.2 cm. Estate of Jacque Lipchitz, courtesy, Marlborough Gallery, New York

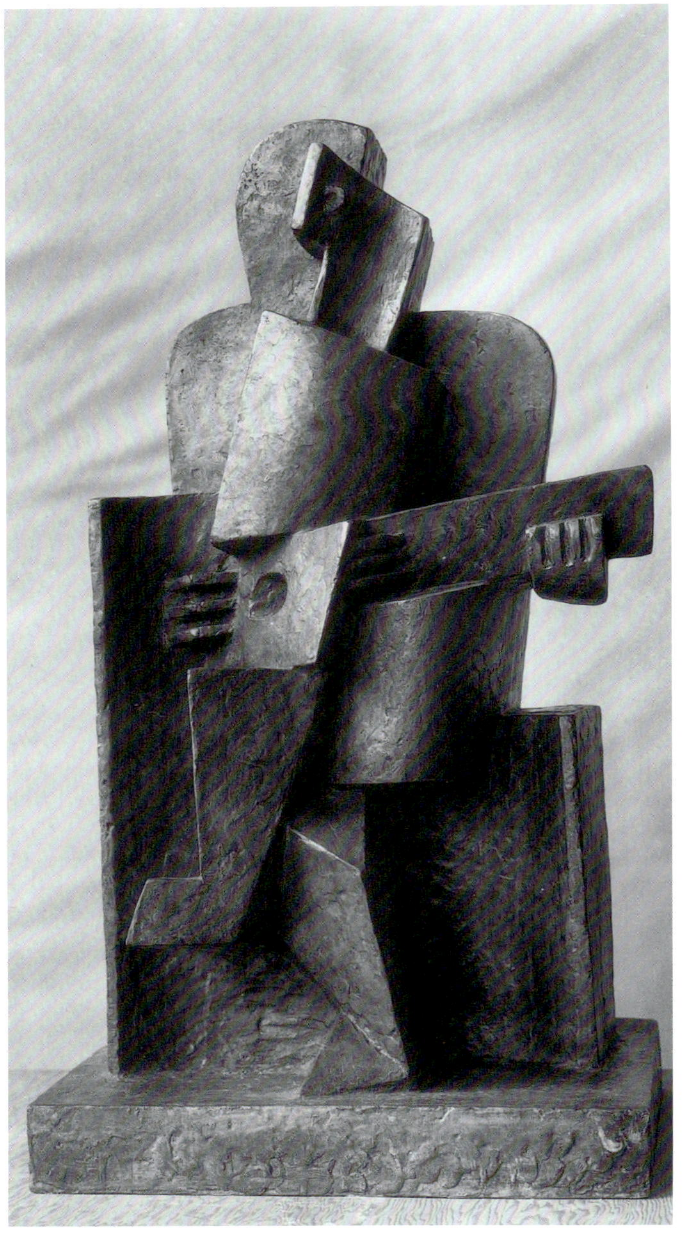

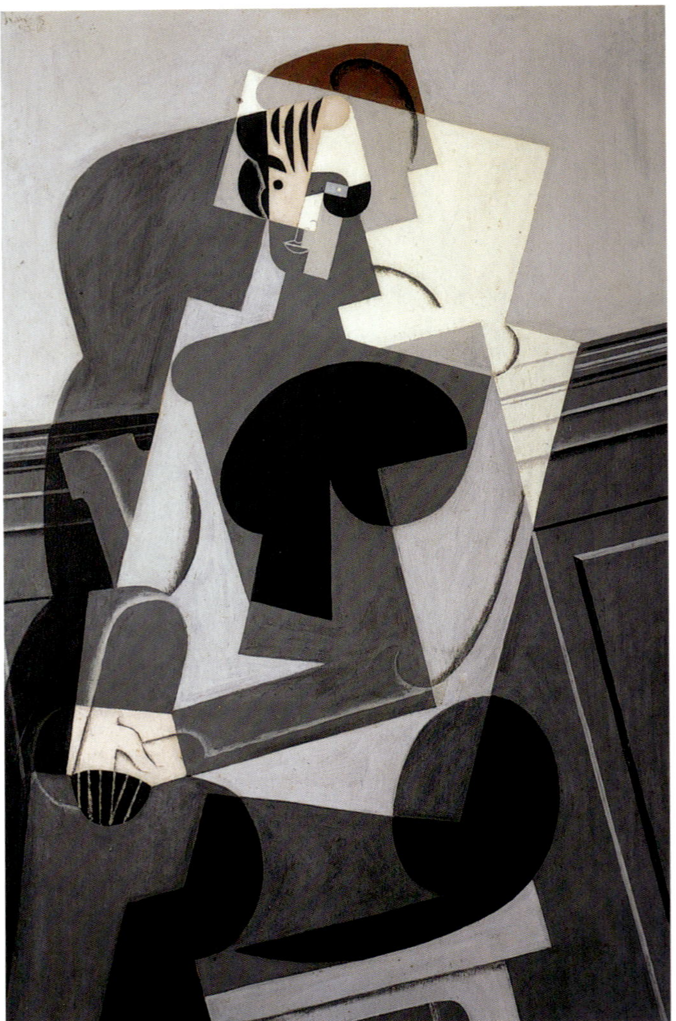

239. Juan Gris, *Portrait of Mme. Josette Gris*, 1916. Oil on canvas, 116.5 × 54 cm. Telefónica de España, S.A.

tion for the fiteenth-century Touraine painter, Jean Fouquet. One of these was *The Man from the Touraine* [240]. Lipchitz, by then a close friend, was with Gris in the Touraine; his *Seated Man with a Guitar* is in some ways the sculpted pair to Gris's picture. All of Gris's allusions to the past connect with a specifically French notion of tradition, a notion which brings together the 'French Primitives' (including Fouquet, an artist from a region crucial to the joining of South to North) and Latin classicism.

The period 1916–21 saw Gris also pay respectful attention to the economy of Ingres's graphic line in a series of crisp pencil portraits.[41] For him, as for so many, Ingres belonged together with Fouquet, Corot and Cézanne. Gris's interest in Ingres as a draftsman had been stimulated by Picasso, who followed the declaration of war in August 1914 with a two-track pursuit, on the one hand of the structural possibilities opened up by Cubist collage and papier-collé, and on the other of the lessons to be learned in 'traditional' figure drawing, with an eye sometimes on Cézanne and sometimes on Ingres. In one of the earliest of the Ingres-like portraits, Picasso took the ever-patient Vollard as sitter [241], updating in unabashed traditionalist terms his Cubist

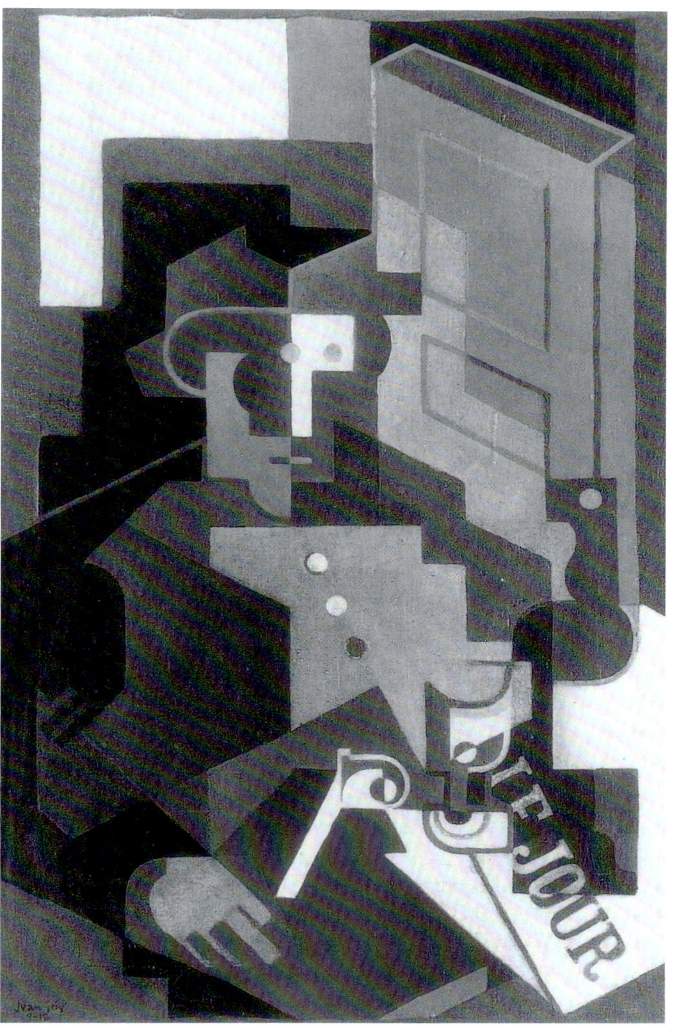

240. Juan Gris, *The Man from the Touraine*, 1918. Oil on canvas, 100 × 65 cm. Musée National d'Art Moderne, Paris

image of the dealer painted five years before [97]. In 1915 he too, anticipating Lipchitz as he did Gris, abandoned polychrome construction and at the same time collage for the more durable homogeneity of oil paint, and by 1918 he had cleaned up and straightened up his Cubist act to produce compositions just as 'architectural' as Lipchitz's and Gris's.

After the war, Jean Cocteau would coin the phrase 'Call to Order' ('rappel à l'ordre') for a change within the milieux of the Cubists and others after 1914, one that embraced music and literature as well as visual art. Certainly, by 1918–19 all but Léger among Léonce Rosenberg's 'L'Effort moderne' Cubists were part of such a change: besides Lipchitz and Gris, artists as different as Braque, Severini (the one-time Futurist), Herbin, Laurens, Metzinger and Maria Blanchard. Metzinger (b.1883) and Blanchard (b.1881) were both with Gris and Lipchitz in the Touraine in 1918; it is not surprising, therefore, that Metzinger's 1918 *Still-life with Fruit-bowl* and Blanchard's *Still-life with Guitar*, possibly of that date, share the sturdy structured qualities of their most architectural work [242, 243].[42]

By 1917, this 'Call to Order' in Cubism had been directly aligned with the idea of classicism. In the opening issues of the little magazine *Nord-Sud*, founded and edited by Pierre Reverdy, the Belgian poet Paul Dermée announced, as if stating the obvious: 'A period of exuberance and force must be succeeded by a period of organisation, classification, of science, that is to say a classical age.'[43] Both Reverdy and Dermée were deeply involved in the new Cubist milieu around the galerie de l'Effort Moderne. Not long recovered from terrible injuries sustained on the front, Braque set out a series of 'Thoughts and Reflections' in *Nord-Sud* in 1917. They were numbered as Cézanne's 'Opinions' had been when Emile Bernard published them in 1904. Predictably perhaps, Braque made the link between this classical 'Call to Order' in Cubism, and Cézanne as the model of a modern classicism, at least by implication. He reworked in Cubist terms Cézanne's now widely familiar demand that 'sensation' should be 'organised', that 'eye' and 'brain' should work together. 'The senses deform,' Braque said, 'the mind forms'. And: 'I love the rule which corrects emotion.'[44]

Albert Gleizes, who as a pacifist was fortunate to be released from the forces in 1915, lived and worked in Spain and the USA from that date to 1919.[45] When he returned to France after the Armistice he found a newly classicised Cubism, and at the same time a dominant cultural nation-

241. Pablo Picasso, *Portrait of Ambroise Vollard*, 1915. Pencil, 46.7 × 32 cm. The Metropolitan Museum of Art, New York. Elisha Wittelsey Fund

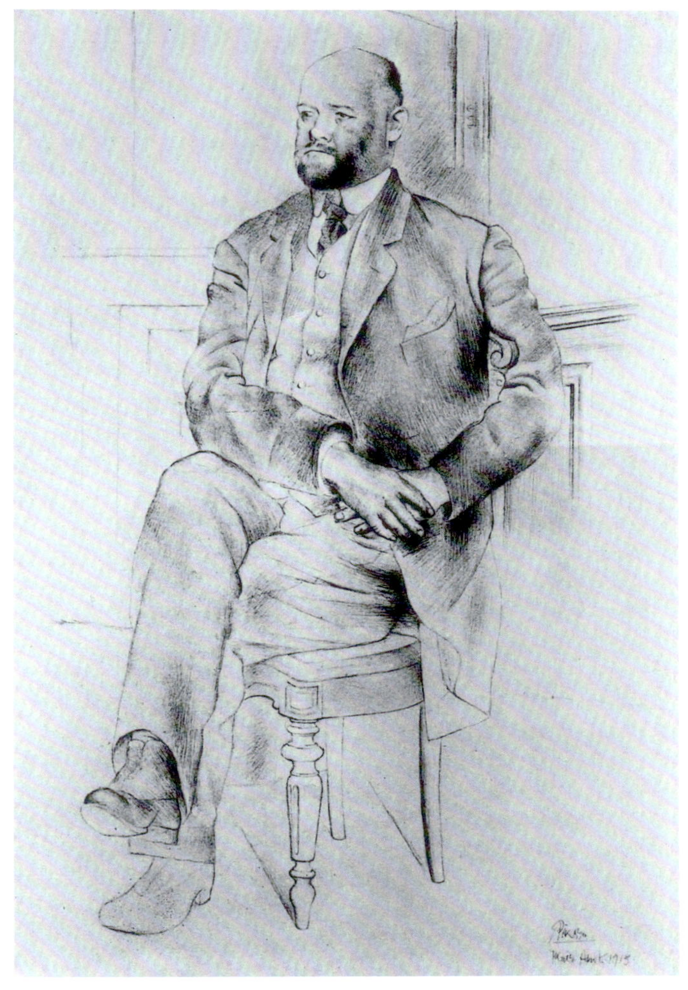

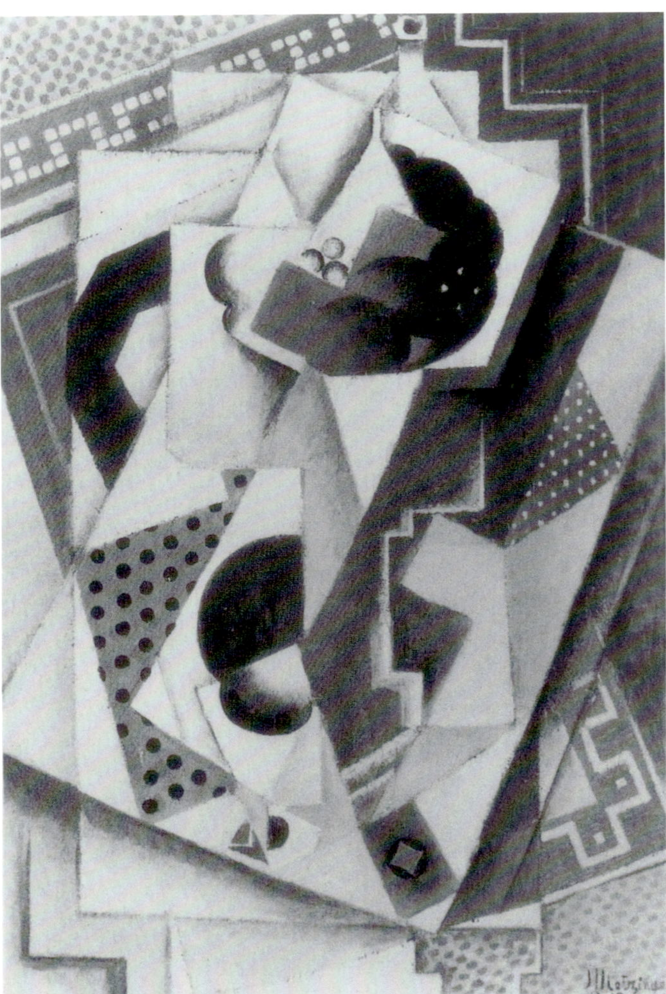

242. Jean Metzinger, *Still-life with Fruit-bowl*, 1918. Oil on canvas, 79.2 × 59.5 cm. Private Collection

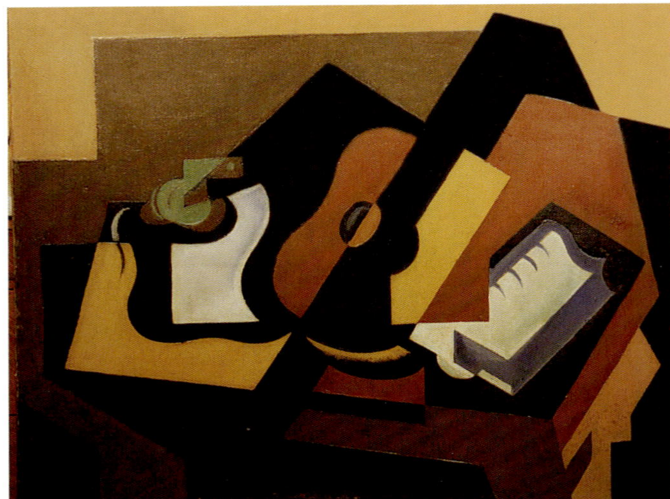

243. Maria Blanchard, *Still-life with Guitar*, 1918. Oil on canvas, 73 × 92 cm. Private Collection

alism inside and outside the avant-garde milieux which emphatically stressed not the Celtic but the Latin myth of national identity. Right across French culture, from propaganda texts and images aimed at the mass public, to the writings of academics like Henri Focillon and Émile Mâle (quite apart from those of literary modernists like Paul Dermée), France at war was more and more characterised as a Latin nation, illuminated by reason.

Léon Daudet's argument that this classical France faced an invasion not only by German armies but also by German culture increased in stridency. In 1915 there was a book-length polemic, *Hors du joug allemand* (Out from Under the German Yoke), to join his harangues in *L'Action française*. And that argument was quickly normalised. Germany came to stand for unimaginative regimentation on the one hand – a nation incapable of creative élan – and irrational barbarism, on the other – a brutalised nation inured to destruction (the bombardment of Rheims cathedral in 1914 was taken as an early proof). Maurras's, Daudet's, and Barrès's Latin France became the France celebrated by the historian Ernest Lavisse as well as Focillon, and by Apollinaire as well as Dermée.[46] Thus, in 1917 Apollinaire made no bones about claiming Cubism as a creation of 'a school which could . . . be described as Franco-Spanish or, more simply, Latin'.[47] Thus too, in 1919, Focillon could sum up all that separated France from Germany as the difference between 'the Greco-Roman mind, the French classical mind' and 'German reason, German nature', a nature inconceivably far from 'Greco-Latin method'.[48]

Midway through the war, Maurras published *Quand les français ne s'aimaient pas* (When the French did not Love Themselves), a book in which he traced the inexorable growth of nationalism and the takeover of the centre of republican politics by Action français's Latin myth of the French nation. He claimed that it was possible, even before 1914, to speak of this new kind of republican nationalism as Action française 'without the king'. In 1916, as circulation of the newspaper *L'Action française* boomed, Maurras boasted that the Right was changing mentalities, and he quoted a letter from a supporter on the front. 'Today . . . it's done: what seemed impossible is accomplished slowly before our eyes: the ideas of *L'Action française* are everywhere . . .'.[49] Are we then to see the Cubists' 'Call to Order', their growing wish to be placed in traditional contexts, and the erection of 'classical' notions of art around them stiffened by the rhetoric of Latinity, as the absorption of the Cubist avant-garde into what can only be called the political culture of the Right?

This is how some (including myself) have seen it.[50] It is as easy, however, to see the burgeoning fortunes of the Latin myth in France during the 1914–18 war not as one symptom of a broad-based shift to the Right but rather as the successful re-appropriation of a right-wing myth by the democratic republican centre of French society. The styles and images of so-called Latin classicism had, after all, never been entirely lost by that liberal centre to the extreme monarchist Right at any point. Foreign artists like Picasso, Gris, Lipchitz and Blanchard may well have realised that by identifying with classical notions of tradition, they were identifying with cultural and political nationalism. And to identify with nationalism was to set aside the internationalism of the Left, whether anarchist or socialist. But, if the republican centre rejected Action française's restrictive ethnocultural idea of the French nation for the expansive assimilationist idea inau-

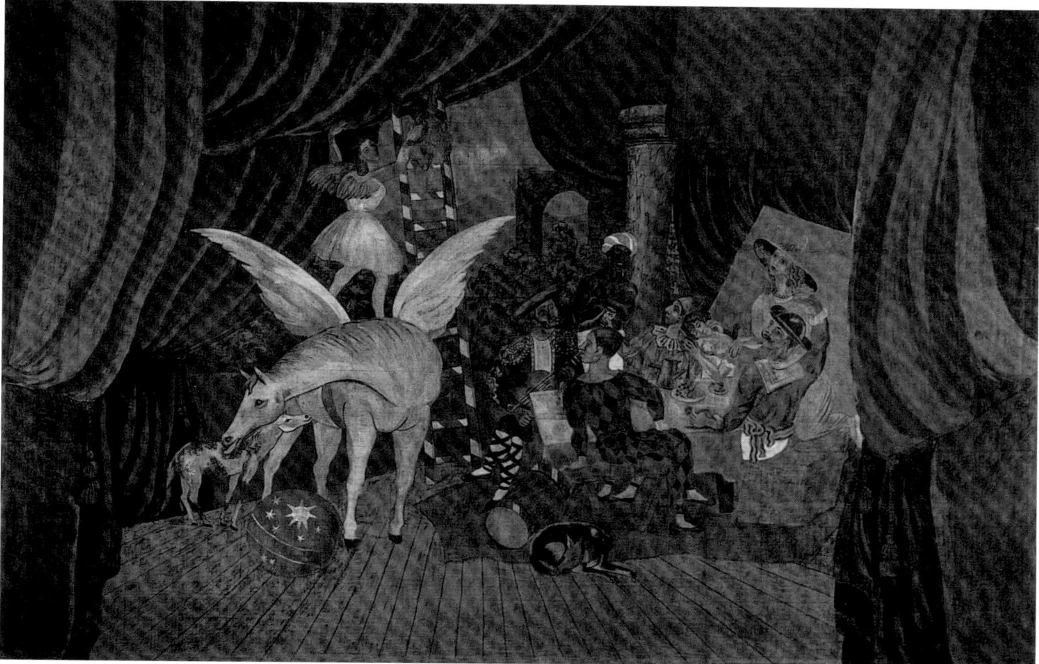

244. Pablo Picasso, Overture curtain for *Parade*, 1917. Musée National d'Art Moderne, Paris

gurated in 1789, its pride in French civilisation as a beacon of liberty had always given it a taste for national and cultural myths, which with only a small admixture of paranoia could become fervent nationalism. First the threat of war and then the actual invasion of many of the north-eastern 'départements' of the country in 1914 turned millions into nationalists apparently inspired by the myth of a Latin France, without turning them into believers in an organic, hierarchical nation, defined by ethnicity, the core convictions of the Right.[51] When Dermée advocated classicism to the readers of Reverdy's *Nord-Sud*, he made a point of dissociating himself from those who believed 'that classicism is an ideal that we cannot obtain without a king'.[52] By doing so, he shows his awareness of the danger that to preach classicism was to risk association with Action française; but he also expresses his confident conviction that being classical need not bind an artist or writer to the Right. By the last years of the Great War, the politics of culture had acquired a clearer thrust, impelled above all by nationalism and its myths; but there remained room for more than one kind of response to a work, even when the Latin connection was made.

In 1917 Picasso collaborated with the composer Erik Satie on the production of Cocteau's ballet *Parade* for Serge Diaghilev's Ballets Russes. It is accepted now to have been a witty attempt to charm the society of the 'beau monde' into acceptance of the delights of Cubism.[53] There was a wonky Cubist townscape set and two of the characters, the French and American managers, had to clatter about on stage encased in over-lifesize Cubist constructions. But there were bright, decorative costumes for the other characters (performers ostensibly managed by the managers) and the piece was introduced by the showing of a huge safety curtain [244] painted in a style loosely evocative of classicism whose 'dramatis personnae' included a winged horse (Pegasus), a blackamoor and characters from the *Commedia dell'arte* (the Italian theatre which had been taken into the French court in the eighteenth century). Antique architectural fragments and a Mediterranean landscape in the background were there to remove any lingering doubts about the curtain's Latin credentials. Everything was done to bring Cubism and the Latin myth of France together. Yet still, on 18 May 1917, the Parisian first-night audience in the Théâtre du Châtelet, among them troops from the front, received the ballet in uproar, at times the detractors drowning out the supporters with howls of 'Boches' ('Huns'), 'métèques' and 'treason'. For some, however Latin the allusions, all modernism, especially Picasso's Cubism, would never be anything else but a foreign invasion from the Left.

CHAPTER 10

From Peace to Crisis: Traditions in Conflict, 1918–40

FRANCE, FOREIGNERS AND 'THE ART OF THE OCCIDENT'

In February 1920, the German D-H. Kahnweiler returned to Paris. He had spent the war years in Bern, outside France. Between 1921 and 1923 his entire stock was sold by public auction as the goods of an enemy alien; it included literally hundreds of works by Vlaminck, Derain, Braque, Picasso, Léger and Gris.[1] A Jew as well as a German, Kahnweiler was one of those against whom Charles Maurras directed his most merciless bile, but Maurras referred to the territories of the destroyed Austro-Hungarian Empire and of Bolshevik Russia, when he wrote in March 1920: 'Like Macbeth's forest, one might say that the immense ghettos of central Europe are on the march in the direction of Paris. There will be new bohemians within our walls, and new pathogenic, political, moral, social microbes.'[2] By 1930, Camille Mauclair had convinced himself that the failure of his 1906 prescription for the future of French art was the result of a commercial 'consortium' involving critics and dealers, masterminded by cosmopolitan Jews intent on undermining the 'ethnic aspirations' of France by means of 'pictorial Communism'. Comfortable now with the rhetoric of neo-classicism, he acknowledged that a few 'foreigners' had come to France out of love for its 'ideal of latinity', but condemned what he called the 'Montparnassian cancer'. Paris had been, he explained to the 3,000,000 readers of the quasi-fascist newspaper *l'Ami du peuple*, invaded by 'Mittel-Europa'.[3] In 1936, the results of a national population census were published; 2,453,000 foreigners were shown to be living in France. The right-wing press claimed that a further 500,000 were there illegally. 'The number of foreigners,' wrote a commentator in *le Petit Journal*, 'constitutes a national menace, . . . in 50 years they have gone from one million to three . . . As an invasion in peacetime, this fact is without precedent.'[4]

In November 1918, French nationalism emerged from the terrible victory of the Great War with its potential for xenophobic paranoia hugely increased. Yet the war could not have exposed more brutally the danger of nationalism as a destructive force, something of which André Breton and his young Dada friends were bitterly aware. The raw casualty figures for those four years of French resistance to German invasion are without equal in the twentieth century: 1.4 million French dead, 10.5% of the active male population (higher than for any other combatant nation), with a further 1.1 million maimed or gassed.[5]

Very soon after the Armistice, politicians in the centre were planning to redress the effects of this human disaster on the French labour force by the encouragement of immigration, and employers were already bringing in workers, especially from Poland and Italy. Where, before 1914 the rate of growth of the foreign population in France had been two per cent annually, between 1921 and 1926, it was ten%. By 1930, France had passed the USA as the leading country of immigration in the world, and there were indeed around three million resident immigrants. When, in 1937, *Le Petit Parisien* focused attention on that figure, the total had, in fact, dropped, but the huge increases in unemployment from 1931 caused by the Depression turned foreign workers into a 'problem' as never before, on the unionised Left as well as the Right, as I shall show at the end of this chapter. Hitler's takeover in Germany in 1933, brought a new influx of Jewish refugees, so that between 1930 and 1939 the Jewish population in France grew from 200,000 to 300,000. Jewish immigration, however, added to a minority which still remained tiny. It was an active and successful minority in areas that included the arts, but only deep-rooted racism, fuelled by xenophobia, can explain the widespread tendency to bring the words 'Jew', 'métèque' and 'invasion' together, as Mauclair did half a decade before the beginning of the exodus from Germany.[6]

In Chapter 9 I showed how even before 1914, notions of tradition linked to the idea of the French nation were caught up in debates which attracted the super-heated rhetoric of racism and xenophobia. From 1918, it became increasingly difficult to claim successfully for tradition an idealised and universal status out of reach of the issues so sharply focused by that rhetoric. By 1930 the invocation of tradition almost inevitably carried with it racial as well as national connotations; they were often explicitly stated even by supporters of 'independent art' (Mauclair still claimed to be one). Yet, throughout the interwar period, the notion of a French tradition disseminated by the conservative republicans in control of the Louvre and academic art history in France remained firmly associated with the expansive, assimilationist idea of the French nation and profoundly hostile to the closed ethnic xenophobia that was so swiftly gaining ground. Cultural orthodoxy remained in tune with the government support of immigration that continued at least until 1931, and from many in the Radical centre all the way through the 1930s. The clearest indication of this is the prolific publishing career of Henri Focillon, who succeeded Emile Mâle in the chair of art history at the Sorbonne in the mid-1920s; it ran from his polemics of 1919, *Technique et sentiment* and *Les Pierres de France* (Stones of France), reprinted in 1928, to his magisterial study of the Romanesque and the Gothic, *Art d'Occident* (Art of the West), published in 1938 by Lavisse's and Vidal de la Blanche's publisher, Armand Colin. Focillon wrote commentaries on contemporary and recent art too, as supporter of the 'independents', and was a leading light, with Paul Valéry, in France's contribution to League of Nations sponsored 'intellectual cooperation' between countries in the 1930s. After the defeat of 1940, he accepted an invitation to teach in the USA, becoming an energetic supporter of general de Gaulle's Free French rebels against Vichy France.

Les Pierres de France was a patriot's celebration of France in wartime as a nation and a culture. *Art d'Occident* was a measured scholarly argument for France as the site of the beginning of 'Occidental art' and of its most quintessential early achievements in the Middle Ages; its context was the menace of the new ultra-nationalist dictatorships. Yet, the deep nationalist convictions so ardently expressed in 1919 still lie behind the picture painstakingly constructed in 1938: at the end of the 1930s, those convictions define themselves against fascism by their accent on liberal individualism and an outward-looking openness to the evidence of foreign influence. That openness, however, does not extend to Germany, though the germanophobia is everywhere muted in the later book. In 1917, galvanised by the destruction of the cathedral of Rheims, Mâle had published a book which step-by-step refuted the case for Germany as the starting point of any significant artistic development in the Middle Ages: the creation of 'barbaric' metalwork, illuminated manuscripts, Romanesque and above all Gothic architecture.[7] In *Les Pierres de France*, Focillon condenses Mâle's case for the Ile-de-France as in every respect the birthplace of Gothic. Moreover, his definition of French art echoes the one Mâle

245. Georges Braque, *Basket-carrier*, 1922. Oil on canvas, 180.5 × 73.5 cm. Musée National d'Art Moderne, Paris

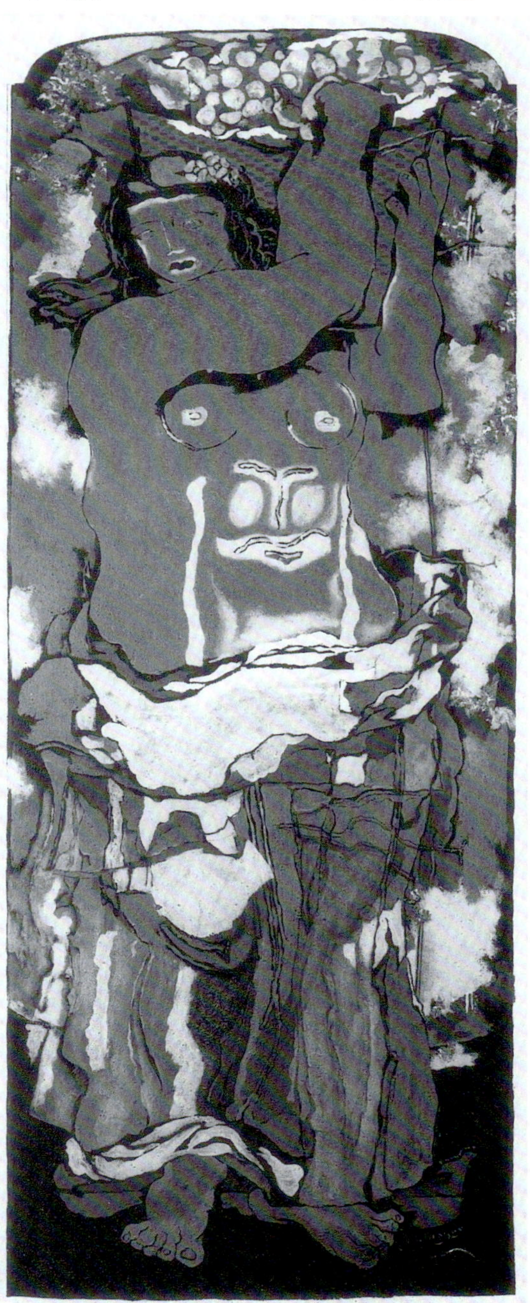

246. Jean Goujon, *Rivers of France*, *c.*1549. Plaster cast of original stone relief on the Fontaine des Innocents, Paris

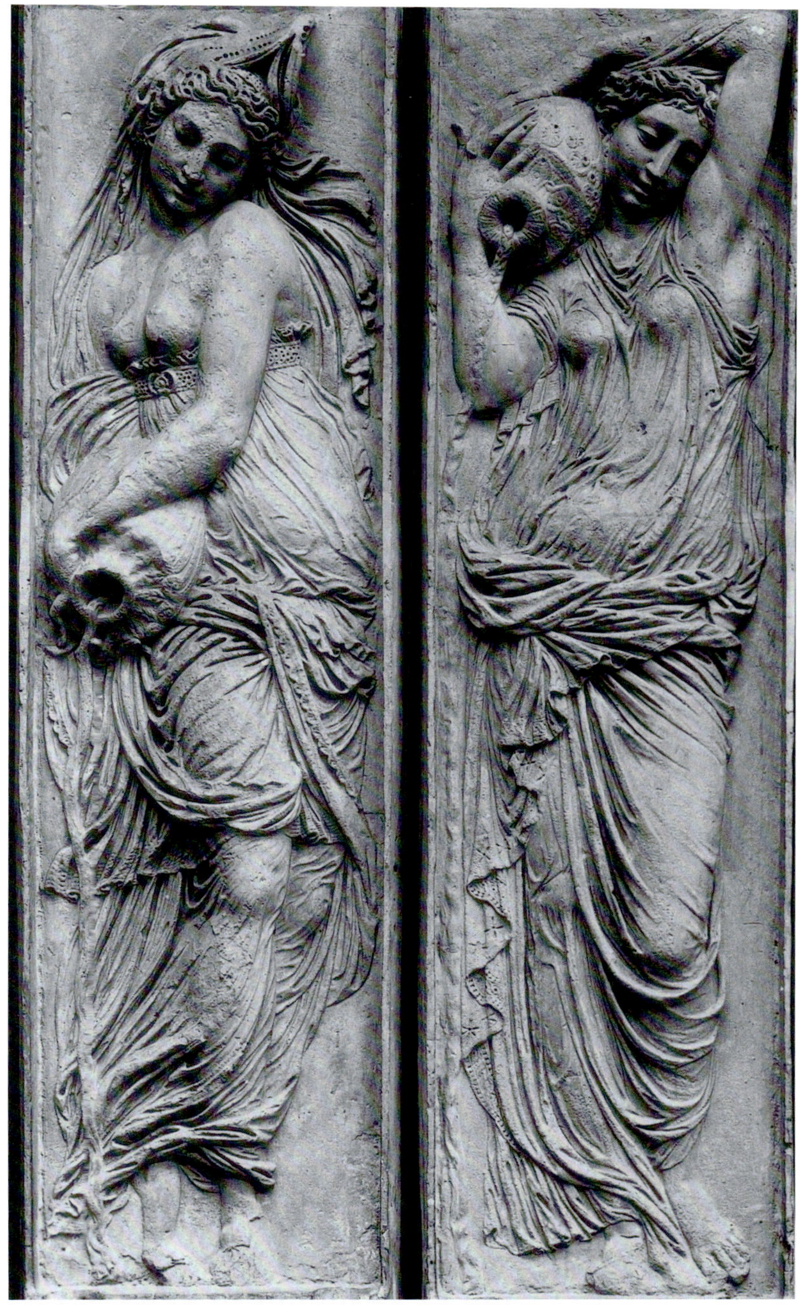

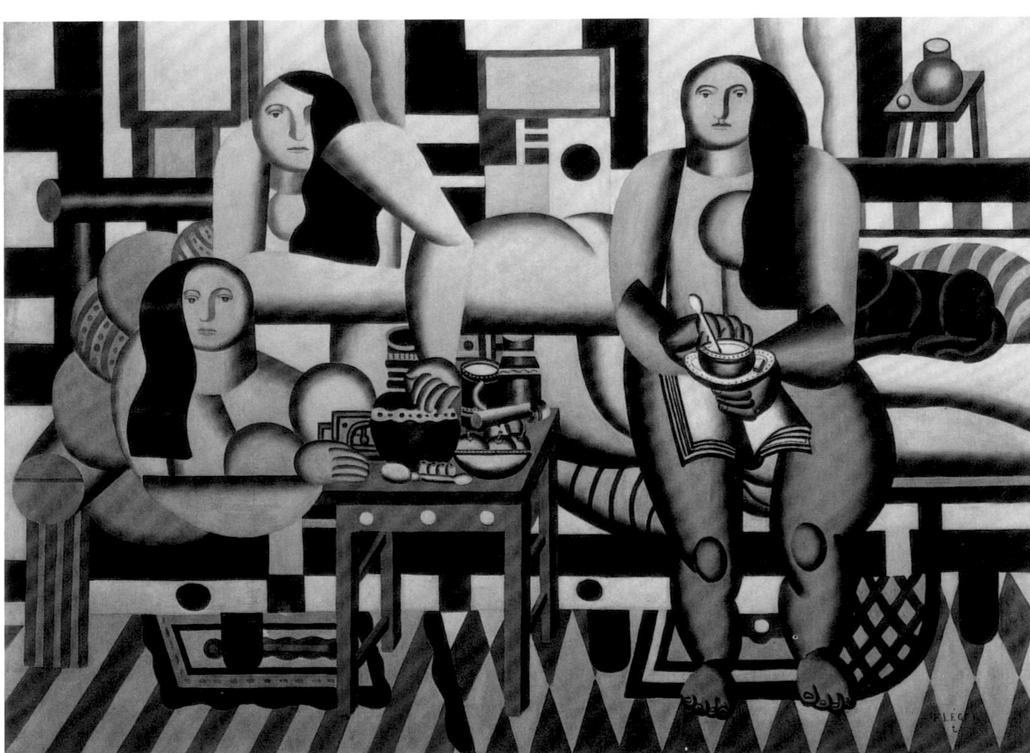

247. Fernand Léger, *Le Grand Déjeuner* (*Breakfast*, Large version), 1921. Oil on canvas, 183.5 × 251.5 cm. The Museum of Modern Art, New York. Mrs Simon Guggenheim Fund

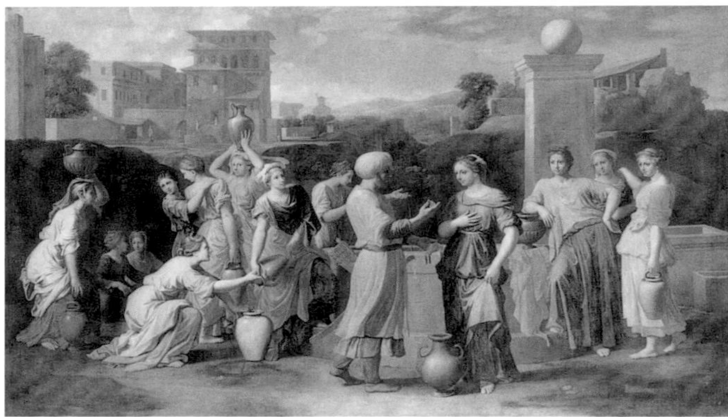

248. Nicolas Poussin, *Eliezer and Rebecca*, 1648. Oil on canvas, 118 × 197 cm. Musée du Louvre, Paris

had arrived at in explicit contradistinction to the hostile stereotype of German culture as imitative, regimented and drawn to the irrational. For Focillon too, the Romanesque and the Gothic are 'classical' in a special sense that allows for the 'vitality' of individual innovation and expression; and in this, they are consistent with the Latin idea of the classical as it had been promoted before 1914. France's Medieval architecture – the stones of France – becomes the symbol of the coming together of the Celtic and Mediterranean peoples in the territory first unified by the Romans. In 1938, Focillon would write of the cathedrals of France as the embodiment of a 'classical mentality' ('pensée'); in 1919, he argued that the 'French genius' had reconciled a 'Roman' respect for 'order' with the 'free humour' and the 'gift of renewal' which set the Celts apart. 'Conquered by the Romans but not destroyed,' he writes in 1919, 'the Celts of Gaul accepted Rome and with her worked to civilise the Occident'.[8] The Celtic Gleizes and the Roman Maurras were brought together in the nationalist centre.

'The Stones of France' is a metaphor which fuses the country's architecture with its physical geography. Focillon's 1919 *Pierres de France* is a small-scale architectural companion to Vidal de la Blanche's famous *Tableau de la géographie de la France*. It defines the 'classical' French tradition as a unity in diversity, and tours the territory of France to bring out the sheer richness of that diversity, never losing contact with the relation of buildings to local landscapes and local materials.[9] Even caught up in this supremely nationalist moment, his idea of France was territorial; and in *Technique et sentiment* (Technique and Feeling) he made an unequivocal disavowal of the ethnic idea of nation for which Germany stood. He ridiculed German claims of racial purity and the science on which they were based, and it was in this context that he set up the 'Greco-latin method' against all that was German, concluding that it was a way of thought 'invented, not for the tribe, but for all humanity'.[10] This classical France of orthodox art history was not only defined against German culture; it was also taken to stand for a territorial and political idea of the nation – a unity in diversity – against the ethnic idea of the German nation and, of course, against Maurrasian 'integral nationalism'. Focillon's pride in the diversity of French art as the representation of a nation and the model for all Western art, was undiminished when he published *Art d'Occident* in 1938.

By that date, however, anti-Semitism and xenophobic rhetoric against the 'foreign invasion' had reached far enough across the spectrum of French opinion to touch, as we shall see, even the French Communist Party on the far Left.

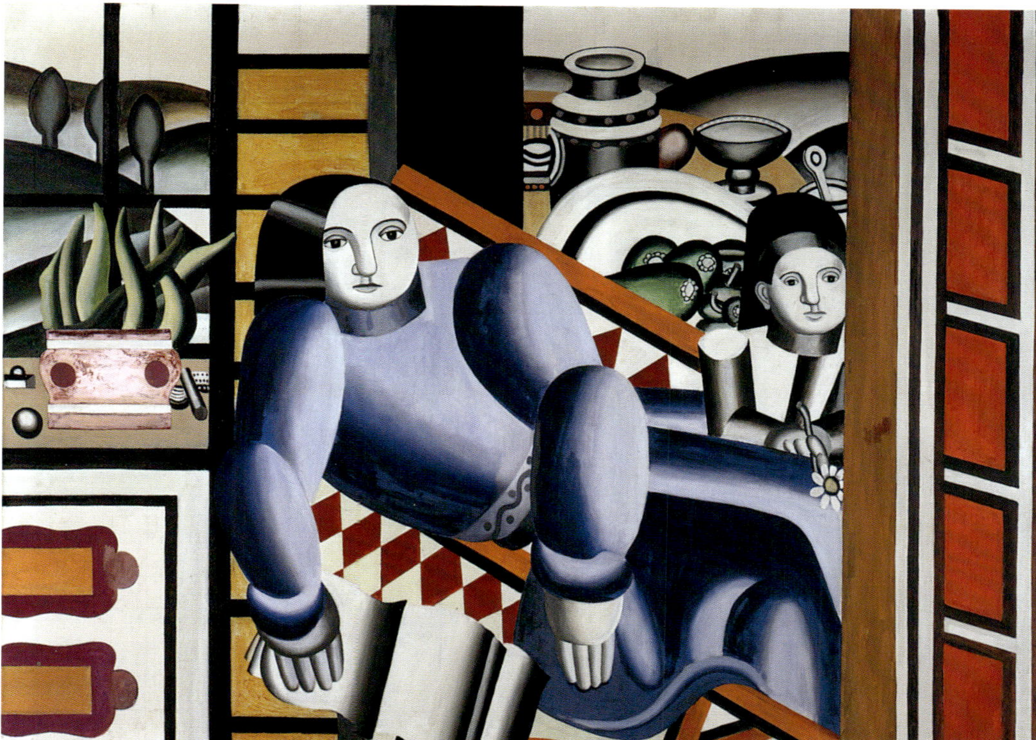

249. Fernand Léger, *Mother and Child*, 1922. Oil on canvas, 171 × 241.5 cm. Oeffentliche Kunstsammlung Basel, Kunstmuseum

THE UNITY IN DIVERSITY OF FRANCE: THE 'CALL TO ORDER' IN PARIS AND THE REGIONS, 1918–30

By the early 1920s, the Cubist 'revolutionaries' of the pre-war decade were established enough for one of them at least to become the subject of a Salon d'automne special exhibition. Georges Braque (b.1882) was given the honour in 1922. The most ambitious of the recent pictures he showed were two of that year, catalogued as 'Decorations'. They have become known as *The Basket-carriers* (Canéphores), and each one of them [245] features a generously proportioned woman rendered in earth browns spread out across the canvas in loosely worked organic forms as if flattened under pressure. Paul Fierens, writing in the Brussels magazine *Sélection*, accepted Braque's invitation to find classical precedents by comparing them to the nymphs which symbolised the rivers of France sculpted in the sixteenth century by Jean Goujon [246].[11] The Cubists' old supporter André Salmon found Braque's figures puzzlingly unresolved, but praised their 'extraordinary dignity', and used them as an excuse to launch a passage on Braque's Cubism which brings together the vocabulary of nationalism and traditionalism around the idea of Cubism in a distinctly revealing way. Echoing the Maurrasian phrase 'integral nationalism', he writes of 'integral Cubism', and then refers to what he calls 'essentially French qualities received from the wealth of classicism (fonds classique)'. Forgetting the figure, and remembering the still-lifes, he calls Braque 'the Chardin of Cubism'.[12] Among the pre-war Cubist leaders, Braque was not alone in inviting such a nationalist and traditionalist response.

Fernand Léger's sole exhibit at the Salon d'automne the year before (1921) had been an extra-large figure painting, *Le Grand Déjeuner* (*Breakfast*, Large version) [247]. It made a confident public spectacle of his decisive shift during 1920–1 away from the simultanist celebration of modernity in peacetime to his own mechanised version of neo-classicism. As a group of 'odalisques', this was a work that invoked Ingres; in its cooled-down skin tones and polished surfaces it invoked David; and in its taut yet swollen volumes it invoked Poussin, specifically the Poussin of the *Eliezer and Rebecca* of 1648 [248] a detail of which, featuring the three figures on the right, was illustrated in the Purist magazine *L'Esprit nouveau* earlier in 1921.[13] In 1922, the year of the Braque show at the Autumn Salon, Léger (b.1881) consolidated his move by exhibiting another extra-large figure painting there, *Mother and Child* [249]. It placed a comparable neo-classical woman, this time dressed off the peg, in a family context, on a suburban terrace. The most obvious allusion here, beyond Poussin, David and Ingres, was to the seventeenth-century painters of peasant scenes, the Le Nain brothers, also thought of then as classical, above all Louis Le Nain's *Peasant Family in an Interior* (*c.*1642), which had entered the Louvre in 1919. *Mother and Child* made a statement about the upward mobility of the French people (from peasants in their regions to the beneficiaries of mechanisation in their nation) as well as about the new modernity of classicism.

The year that Léger painted *Le Grand Déjeuner*, Paul Rosenberg put on a Picasso exhibition featuring his neo-classical alongside his Cubist work; his, of course, had been the stimulus behind both Léger's and Braque's decision to use figurative classicism in making their applications for membership of the French tradition. In the period from his involvement with Diaghilev in 1917, Picasso had moved from being a paper classicist, content with drawing, to being

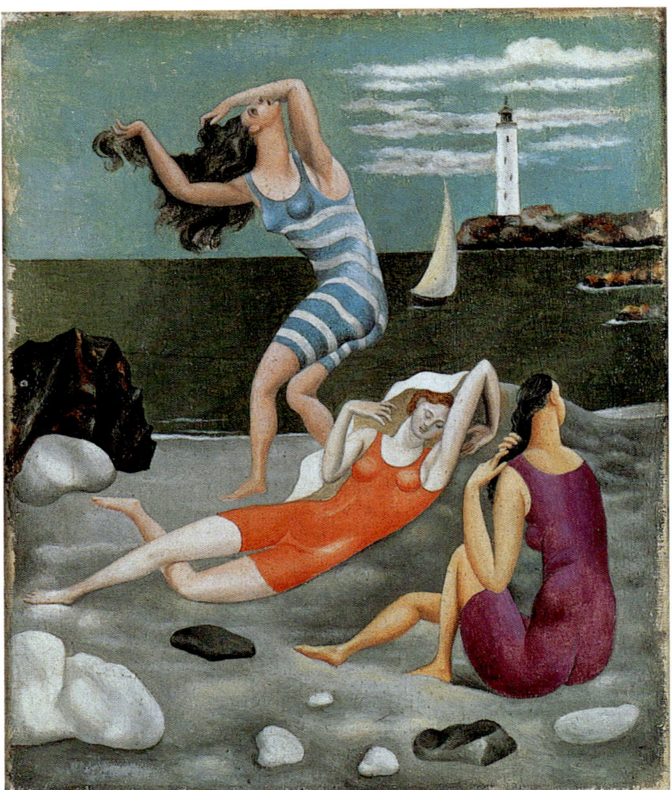

250. Pablo Picasso, *Bathers*, 1918. Oil on canvas, 26.3 × 21.7 cm. Musée Picasso, Paris

251. Pablo Picasso, *Olga in an Armchair*, 1917. Oil on canvas, 130 × 88 cm. Musée Picasso, Paris

a classical painter in the full-blown sense. Among the pictures he showed in May 1921, were a tiny, carefully finished beach scene *Bathers* painted at Biarritz in 1918, and a full-scale, carefully unfinished portrait from 1917 of his brand new Russian wife Olga in an armchair [250, 251]. The *Bathers* exaggerated to the point of Mannerist caricature the contorted poses for which Ingres was reputed, and underlined the connection by quoting figures from Ingres' *Turkish Bath* in the Louvre. Picasso painted *Olga in an Armchair*, as if this colonel's daughter from old Imperial Russia were one of Ingres' sitters in Rome in the early nineteenth century. The summer following the Paul Rosenberg exhibition, as Léger was no doubt at work on the *Grand Déjeuner*, Picasso painted his personal Salon-scale riposte to the Poussin of the 1640s, *Three Women at the Spring* [252]. It was laden with its own allusions to a Greco-Roman yet French Latinity, which included also both the Parthenon frieze and Jean Goujon's *Rivers of France* [246].[14]

Picasso's sometimes serious, more often ironic applications to belong as a French classicist were, of course, given a quite different inflection by the fact that he was a Spaniard and that he continued to paint Cubist alongside neo-classical canvases. His case raised a twofold question: how could a Spaniard paint, as it were, in French, and how 'classical' and therefore French was Cubism? One commentator in particular was provoked by the 1921 exhibition to reflect on Picasso's relationship with the French tradition as a foreigner, and on the character of Cubism in the context of nationality. This was the artist-critic Roger Bissière, articles by whom on Corot and Ingres were appearing in *L'Esprit nouveau* that year. In Picasso, he diagnosed an unstable personality, oscillating between an essentially 'realist', French neo-classicism, and an essentially 'mystical' (abstract) Cubism which was Spanish. Picasso aims, said Bissière 'to fuse two souls and two races . . .'.[15] He uses the term 'race' here, of course, in the manner sanctioned by Michelet, to refer to the French as one 'race' made up of many, whose cultural unity transcends its ethnic diversity. One can, therefore, discern underlying the article that assimilationist theme so characteristic of the conservative centre (Bissière had been the art critic of the right of centre *Le Temps*). But it is a theme broached with scepticism as to Picasso's ability actually to succeed in assimilating his 'abstract' Spanishness to the 'realism' Bissière believes so central a feature of the French 'race'.

As in all discussions of modern art as a classical art, Bissière made the relation between the 'abstract' and the 'real' the core issue. His 'Notes on Ingres' for *L'Esprit nouveau*, published just before the Picasso piece, revolves around a comparison of Ingres's 1814 *Portrait of Mme. Senones* and Raphael's sixteenth-century *La Fornarina* designed to bring out the distance between the French and the Italian forms of Latinity in these terms.[16] Both artists, he argues, are dominated by 'the need for order', but the one proceeds *from* an abstract structuring idea, while the

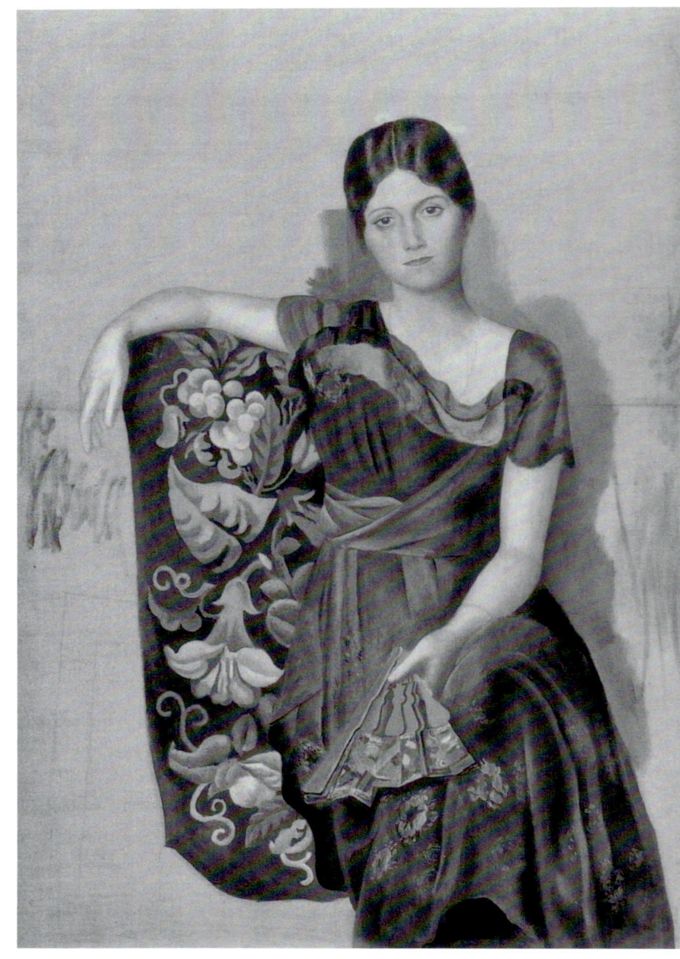

other (Ingres) only decides on his structuring idea 'after close contact with nature'.[17] We are back with Cézanne's 'Opinions' on the interaction of 'eye' and 'brain', 'sensation' and 'organisation'.[18]

Bissière's analysis of French as against foreign Latinity was reiterated in different ways right across the conservative centre of the 'independent' art world in the 1920s, and was a key tactic in ostracising Cubism (abstract and therefore foreign) from the protection of the French tradition as conventionally understood. It was a view of Cubism that could give a touch of gravitas to the cocktail of racist paranoia and anti-modernist fury mixed by Mauclair, so that it could sometimes be spilled over the 'cosmopolitan' Cubists; but it could be developed with real sophistication too. Most influential among those who produced sophisticated versions were, Louis Vauxcelles writing primarily in *Le Carnet de la semaine* and *L'Amour de l'art* from 1918, and the artist-critic, André Lhote, writing from 1919 in the *Nouvelle Revue française*. And then a cluster of critics writing for *les Nouvelles Littéraires* and later its offspring *L'Art vivant* from the early 1920s, led by Florent Fels and Jacques Guenne. Vauxcelles, adding provocative nuance to an anti-Cubist line begun before 1914, searched for signs that the Cubists were capitulating to the strength of the French tradition (in other words, finally assimilating). He found them in Braque's *Basket-carriers* at the Autumn Salon of 1922 and in the easy

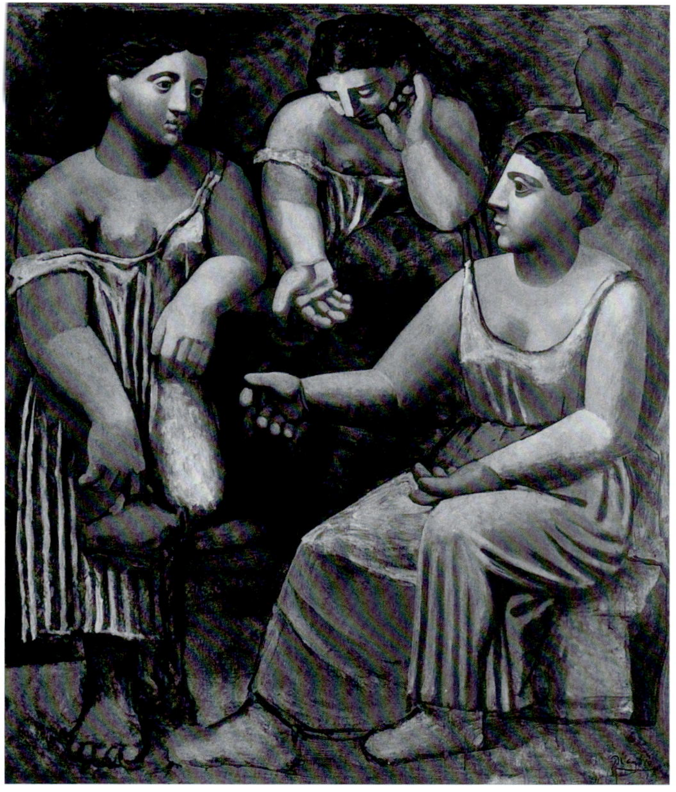

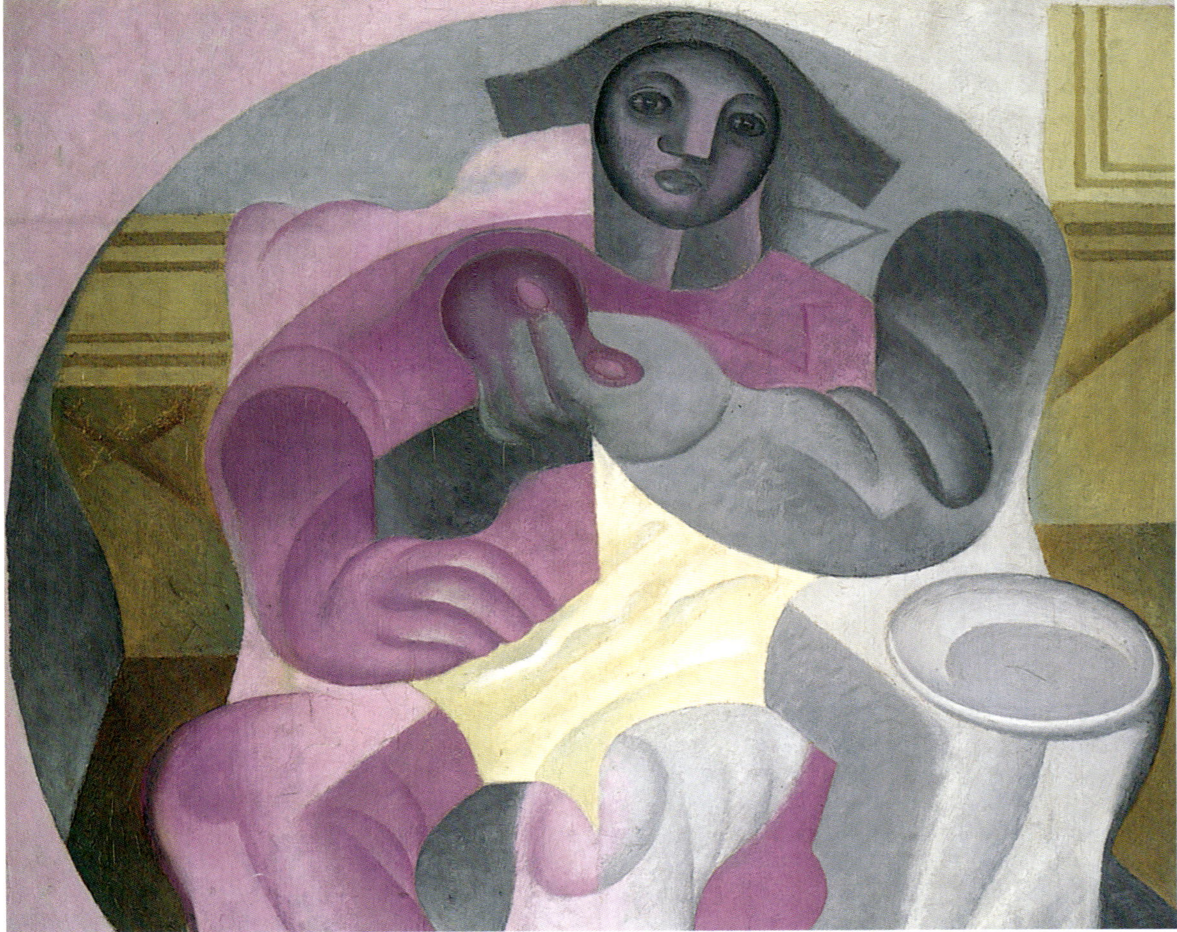

252. Pablo Picasso, *Three Women at the Spring*, 1921. Oil on canvas, 203.9 × 174 cm. Museum of Modern Art, New York Gift of Mr and Mrs Allan D. Emil

253. Juan Gris, *Seated Harlequin*, 1923. Oil on canvas, 73 × 92 cm. University of Michigan Museum of Art, Gift of the Carey Walker Foundation, 1994/1.71

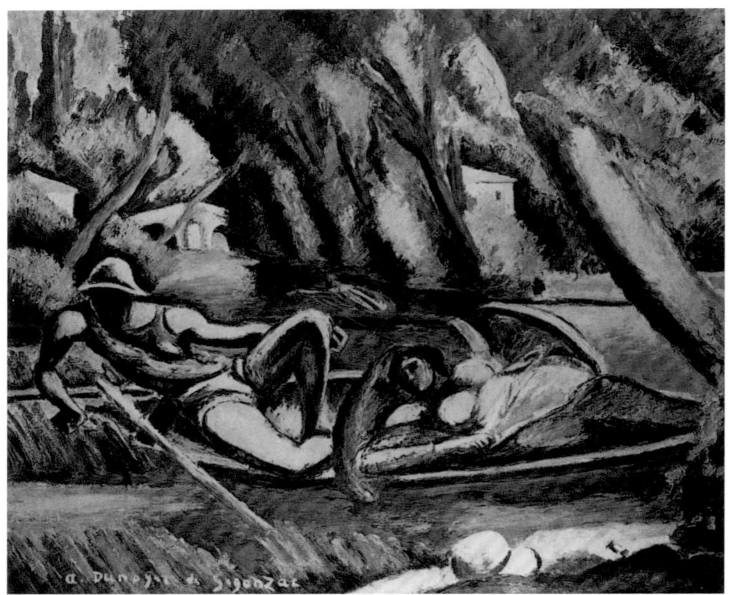

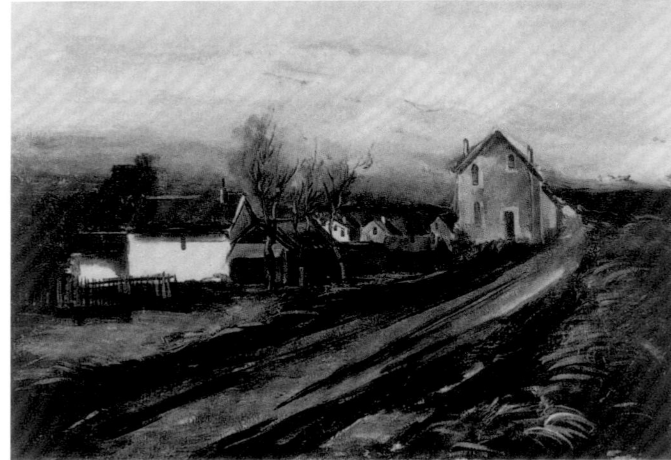

254. André Dunoyer de Segonzac, *Boating*, 1924. Oil on canvas, 200 × 210 cm. Private Collection

255. Maurice Vlaminck, *The Nantes Road*, c.1922–3. Oil on canvas. Measurements and whereabouts unknown

legibility and the evocative colour of Gris's new work when it was shown at Kahnweiler's galerie Simon in 1923 [253].[19] The implication was always clear: Cubism needed to accept the primacy of nature if it was to become French. And the example repeatedly brought to bear was Cézanne.[20]

For Guenne, Fels and those who wrote for them in *L'Art vivant*, the modern French antidote to Cubism was to be found in what was identified as the 'naturalism' of those artists who had resisted Cubism's abstraction. Foreigners like Modigliani and Kisling (now a naturalised Frenchman) were included among their elect, but above all they placed at the forefront artists who were unimpeachably French: Derain, Vlaminck, Gromaire, Utrillo (whose father was Spanish) and Dunoyer de Segonzac. In these cases too, with the exception of Derain, they stressed above all these artists' sense of regional identity and their painting of the local: sometimes local types (especially in the case of Gromaire), more often landscape, drenched in a sense of place.

In January 1925, in the second number of *L'Art vivant*, Edmond Jaloux named André Dunoyer de Segonzac (b.1884) together with Derain, Utrillo and Vlaminck as painters who had found another route, distinct from that of Picasso and the Cubists, away from Impressionism, towards the modernist grail of 'a new plastic truth'. It is a 'plastic truth' which de Segonzac, the subject of Jaloux's article, finds in 'muddy landscapes . . . , many of which seem to ooze water, river banks where the thick water flows like oil . . .'[21] Pictures like the ambitious *Boating* of 1924 fitted the bill, though the scene is invaded by people who seem not to be country people at all and have ample time for leisure [254]. Vlaminck (b.1876), who insisted on an unmediated, direct relationship with his motifs, was photographed in 1925 for *L'Art vivant* leading a horse and plough, with the caption: 'Vlaminck returns to the earth.' The same year, Roger Allard wrote of him: 'Vlaminck is our great bucolic painter. His Arcadia is on the banks of the Oise.'[22] Vlaminck's bluster allowed him to claim authenticity in the countryman's guise more plausibly than the aristocratically connected de Segonzac, despite his passion for cars, and the fact that his landscapes often acknowledged the presence of modernity in the country (roads, garages, telegraph poles), where de Segonzac's did not [255].

The phrase 'rusticising the modern' has been coined for this kind of painting: its concern with 'plastic truth' certainly identified it as modernist as well as 'rustic'.[23] Its immersion in a strong ideological current, flowing along with the broad current of nationalism, that of regionalism, has also been brought out. It is certainly true, that a strong element in this current had been set going by Maurice Barrès' seminal nationalist text of 1902, *Scènes et doctrines du nationalisme*, with its contrast between a centralised Germany and a France of 'petites patries' (little homelands), and that, on the extreme Right, Maurras too advocated the preservation of regional identities, including his own Provence. But one must remember also the core role played by the idea of a diverse France of local 'pays' across the entire centre of French opinion, so indelibly underlined, also early in the century, by Vidal de la Blanche, and so influentially sustained by expansive, liberal nationalists like Focillon. Shanny Peer has shown how regionalism in France between the 1900s and 1940 in the form of the Fédération régionaliste française (French Regional Federation) attracted members all the way from the Maurrasian Right to the Centre-Left Radicals, with even the occasional Socialist thrown in. It was this organisation that had most to do with the popularisation of the term 'regionalism', not the writings of Maurice Barrès.[24] The northern landscapes of Vlaminck or de Segonzac, and, say, Derain's Corotesque landscapes of the Roman Campagna of 1921 and Provence of around 1930 [256] were indeed deeply conservative in their nationalist connotations, but, however easily appropriated on the far Right, they could give sustenance to orthodox republican nationalism as much as to 'integral nationalism'.

So could 'realist' depictions of peasants, whether they were by out-and-out conservatives in matters of style like the sculptor Paul Niclausse (b.1879) or by accepted (if

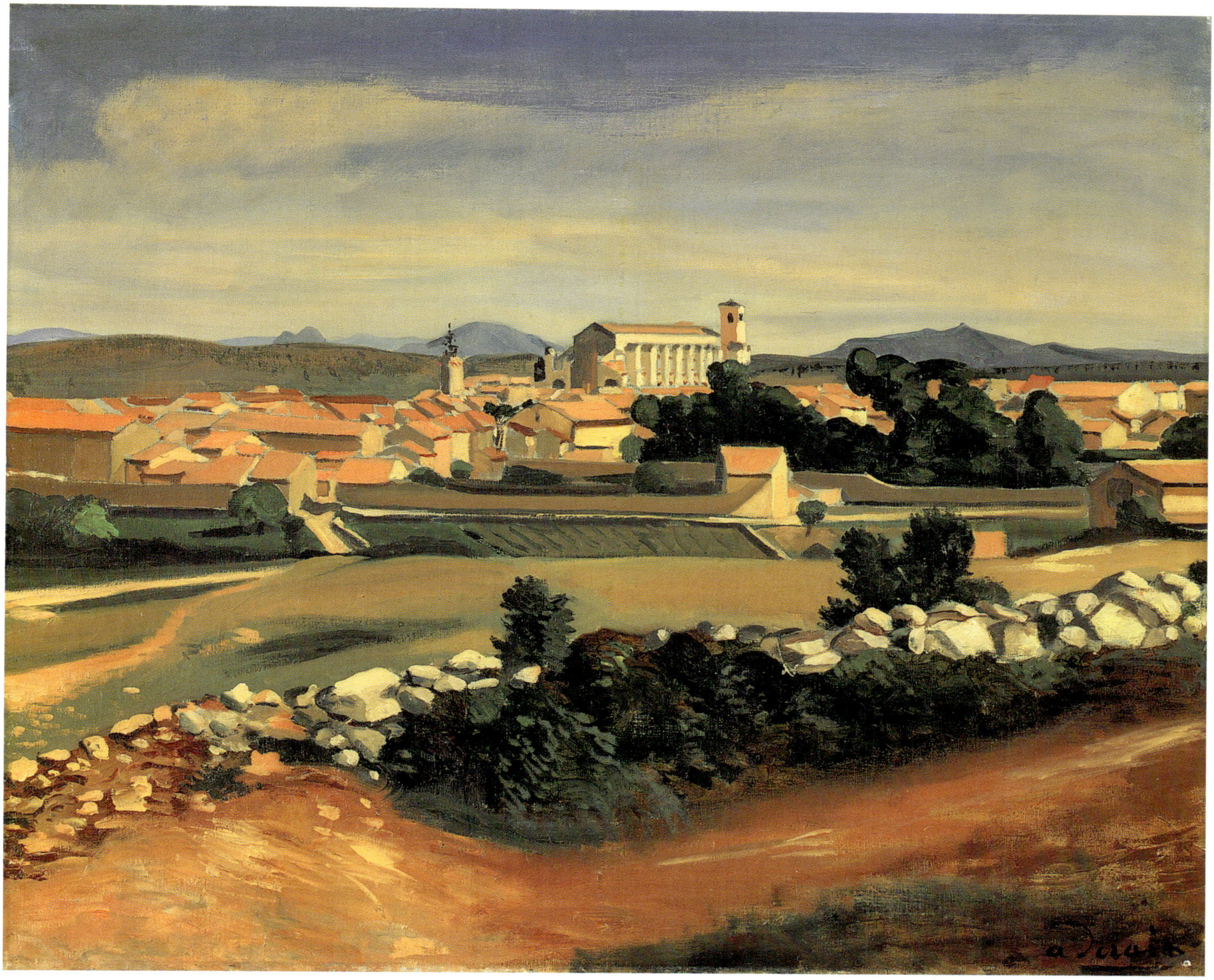

256. André Derain, *View of Saint Maximin*, 1930. Oil on canvas, 60 × 73 cm. Musée National d'Art Moderne, Paris

unchallenging) independents like Marcel Gromaire (b.1892). Indeed, in these two cases regionalist subjects could actually be seen in a Left Republican context. Niclausse took the peasants of the Brie region where he worked, as models from 1904 onwards; he showed his pungent depictions of them at the Artistes français throughout the 1920s. The bust *The Woodcutter* of 1924–5 [257] was shown at the Salon des Tuileries in 1926; the figure to which it related had already been bought by the Ville de Paris. Two years later Niclausse was included in A.H. Martinie's history of modern sculpture under the heading 'Social Tendencies and Realism', in the context of two major precedents from the Left, the Communard Dalou and the socialist sculptor of the miners of the North Constantin Meunier. He was equally prepared to enter and win the State competition in 1918–19 to produce a medal commemorating Marshall Foch and the wartime leader Georges Clemenceau

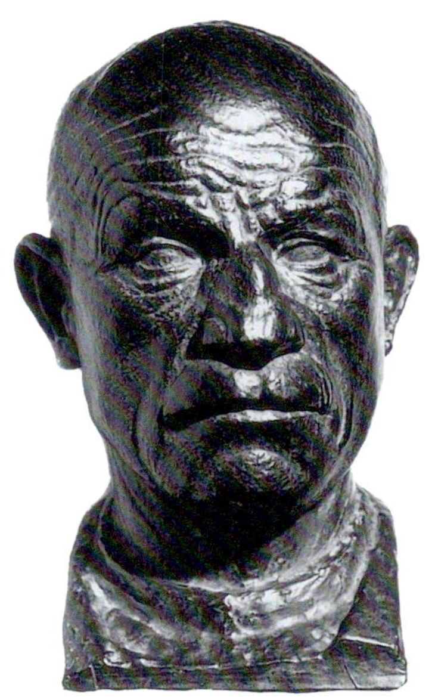

257. Paul Niclausse, *The Woodcutter*, 1924–5. Bronze. 52.4 × 18 × 18 cm. Musée Despiau-Wlérick, Mont-de-Marsan

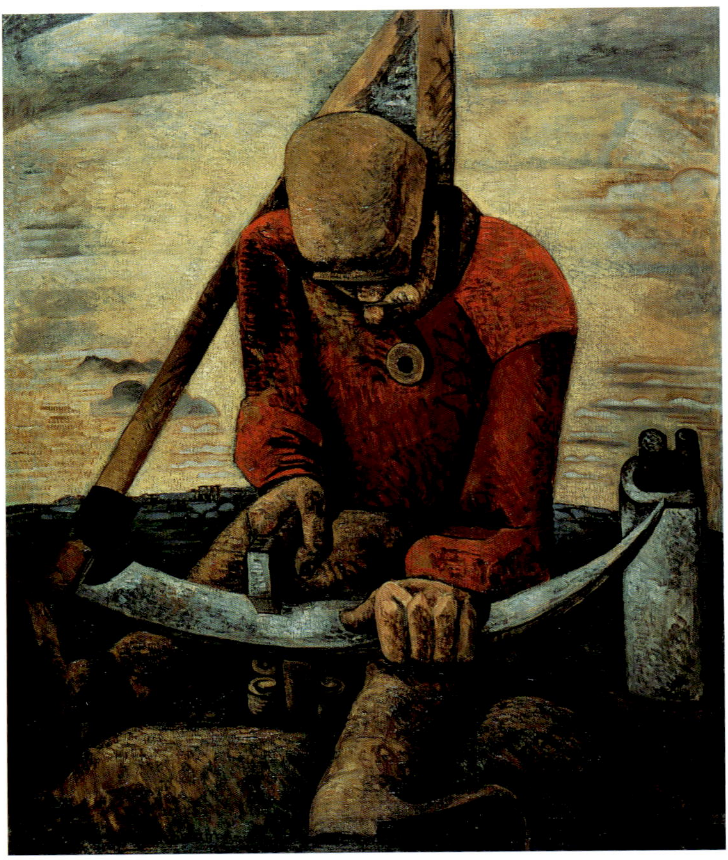

258. Marcel Gromaire, *Man with a Scythe*, 1924. Oil on canvas, 100 × 81 cm. Girardon Bequest, Musée d'art moderne de la Ville de Paris

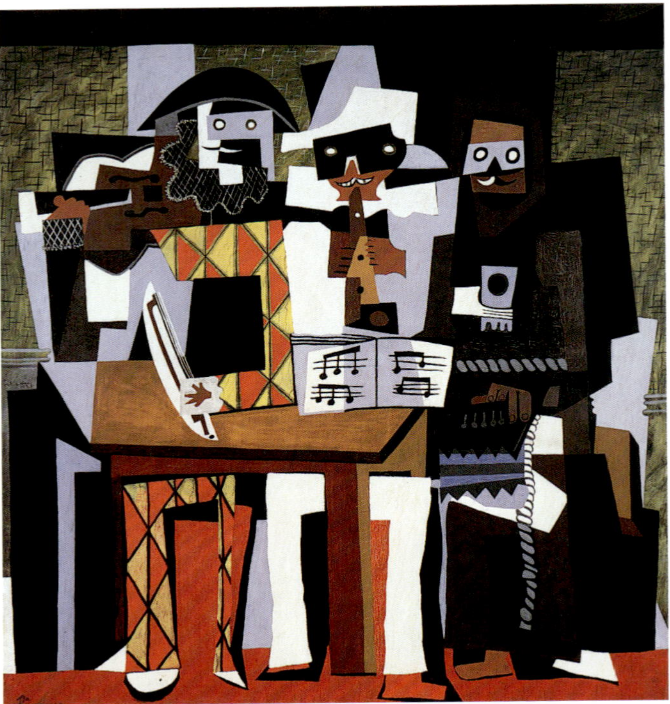

259. Pablo Picasso, *Three Musicians*, 1921. Oil on canvas, 203 × 188 cm. Philadelphia Museum of Art, A.E. Gallatin Collection

260. Right. Henri Laurens, *Bas-relief on pillar, Hall of the de Noailles Villa at Hyères*, 1925–6

(which had the alternative title 'The Liberation of the Territory'), *and* to enter and win a competition in 1919 for a commemorative bust of the pacifist socialist leader Jean Jaurès for the Paris Bourse du Travail. His 'rustic realism', compulsively recording the physiognomies of Briard peasants, was actually viewed in a socialist context. In 1923, he showed a selection of his regionalist sculptures at the Salon de l'art organised by the Socialist CGT, where 'integral nationalist' readings would simply have been impossible.[25] Later in the decade, the convergence of socialism and nationalism, especially where connected with syndicalism, would produce France's first imitations of Mussolini's Italian fascism, but this would never take the form of an authoritarianism to be confused with that of the traditionalist and the Royalist Right. Its rhetoric was more modernising and egalitarian than conservative and hierarchical.[26] Niclausse's rustic realism was certainly not modernising, but neither was it hierarchical: it made the peasant the centre of admiring attention.

Niclausse avoided Paris and urban subjects. Gromaire painted both the urban and the rustic. His *Man with a Scythe* of 1924 [258] was seen in 1926 at his galerie Barbazanges solo show alongside urban subjects which included factories and the Métro. Responding to an earlier exhibition in 1925, Florent Fels had acknowledged the urban in his work, and yet still called it 'the art of the earth', remarking: 'This is a character that the city has in no way distorted.'[27] He was, thus, another artist identified with regional origins, and this certainly was what was stressed when Jacques Guenne responded to his exhibition of 1926. Gromaire is, writes Guenne in *L'Art vivant*, a man of 'the North', from 'that country of eternally grey skies, where the spring seems to have difficulty in coming among those heavy clods of wet black earth . . .'.[28] And yet, like Niclausse, his connections with the Left were clear too; his regionalism, besides tying city to country, dug nationalism into a ready-made social realist lineage, going back to Millet, with strong egalitarian as well as republican associations.

The case of Gromaire is a reminder that for all the efforts of historians led by Henri Focillon to bring the Latin South and the Gallic North together under the notion of a single classical French tradition, there were still some who preserved a sense of difference, cultivating a northern rather than Latin notion of their cultural identity. Golan quotes Gromaire from his diary in 1926 calling 'the legend of France as a Latin country' 'a noxious political heresy spread by Southerners'. It is only because southerners were 'racially affected' by the Roman invaders, he tells himself, that they insist on their Latinity. He identifies, rather, with the 'prehistoric races which in certain regions have remained almost pure', those who preceded even the Celts.[29] In an interview included with Guenne's 1926 *L'Art vivant* article, Gromaire, however, makes a point of both aligning himself with 'the great Franco-Flemish tradition' embracing Breughel the Elder and Fouquet, and calling himself 'occidental'. Despite his refusal of Latinity, he is, he claims, 'within the French tradition, that order and that measure which rule the enthusiasm of our artists'.[30] Focillon would have recognised the 'classicism' in his claims to Frenchness easily enough.[31]

There might have been a concerted and powerful critical campaign to ostracise the Cubists from the French tradition, as it was conventionally conceived. The fact remains, however, that the Cubists and their defenders almost without exception claimed membership of 'Tradition', and were usually careful to make it clear that this tradition was French as well as 'universal'. Once back in France in 1919, Gleizes made a special effort, now as a converted Catholic, to develop his pre-war Celtic view of the French tradition into a sophisticated aesthetic which gave central authority to French Medieval wall-painting. He published extensively before and after abandoning Paris in the mid-1920s to found a small commune, Moholy-Sabata, on the model of the Medieval monastic community; it was near Sablons just south of Lyon in the Rhone valley. The greater impact was made, however, by those who invoked the classical, especially where they did not relinquish their Cubism. Here, it was usual to claim that Cubist and neo-classical work were equally solidly sanctioned by tradition.

Salmon's comment on Braque as the 'Chardin of Cubism' might possibly have caused an instant of envy in Juan Gris, who revealed how he identified his Cubism with Chardin when he wrote to Kahnweiler in 1919.[32] From 1917 especially, Gris's choice of subjects was designed to make links with the past: not only in those Cubist figure paintings evocative of Corot and Fouquet discussed in Chapter 9, but also in his ubiquitous fruit-bowls and napkins evocative of Cézanne, and his *Commedia dell'arte* characters evocative of Watteau's Pierrots and Cézanne's Harlequins [112, 239, 240, 253]. The fact that Picasso himself chose a *Commedia dell'arte* subject for his most ambitious Cubist endeavour of the early 1920s again made a point about Cubism and 'tradition'. His Cubist antithesis to *Three Women at the Spring* was a pair of large canvases which turned a threesome of *Commedia dell'arte* musicians into spatially dislocated but still clearly legible planar constructions [259]; it had been he, in 1915, who had painted the first Cubist Harlequin.

There is nothing surprising, thus, in the fact that the Cubists who replied to an art press Enquête on Cubism in 1924, repeatedly underlined their concern with 'tradition'. Auguste Herbin announced: 'True Cubism was invented from the first steps taken by humanity onwards.' Henri Laurens explained further: 'To retain and express the essential with simple and personal means; to rejoin tradition; there you are, that's what seems to me the aspiration of Cubism. Tradition is continuous beneath the different appearances of the epochs.'[33] That year Laurens had completed a fountain sculpture for Jacques Doucet's garden which was recognisably a cubist response to Jean Goujon's *Rivers of France* with Braque as intermediary; he was to produce comparable work for the Vicomte and Vicomtesse de Noailles [260] His move from polychromatic multi-media construction to working in stone and terracotta in 1919 prefaced a growing engagement in sculpture for architecture, which paralleled Lipchitz in the 1920s, and which in his case declared a profound identification with the idea,

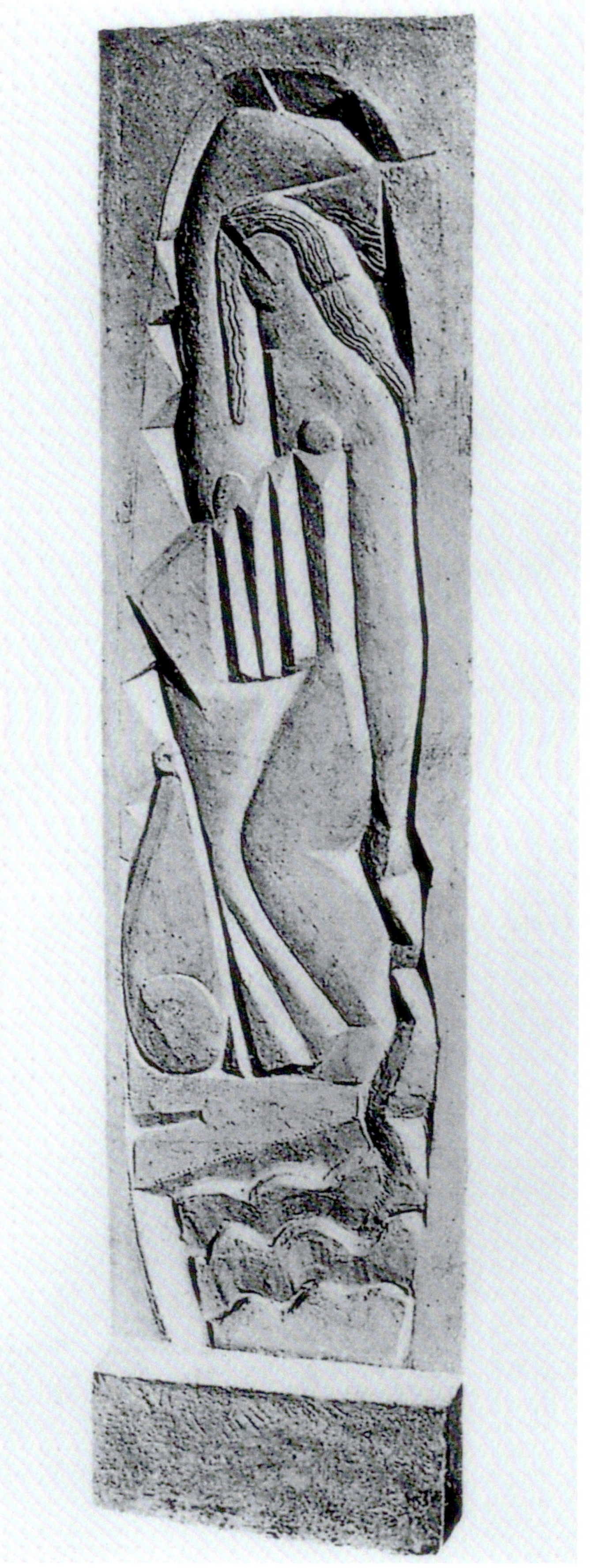

disseminated especially by Focillon, that French sculpture was from its Romanesque beginnings essentially 'architectural'.[34]

The Purists provided one important platform for the dissemination of a traditionalist understanding of Cubism and its significance; the dealer Léonce Rosenberg provided another. As we have seen, the Cubists and their supporters published in *L'Esprit nouveau* alongside articles on everything from Poussin and Ingres to Corot and Cézanne; and, it should be added, on everything from Greek vases to Roman mosaics. Between 1918 and 1925, Ozenfant and Le Corbusier balanced their fervent pursuit of modernity with an equally fervent pursuit of what they called the 'constants' underlying aesthetic experience. They brought together the promotion of the classical notion of the French tradition via the views of a Roger Bissière with the elaboration of what they believed were universal aesthetic principles. This pan-cultural stress on the universal is, of course, there in both Herbin's and Laurens's statements of 1924 quoted above. It allowed a Eurocentric faith in the art of the Occident, and especially in the French tradition, to cohabit with the modernist commitment to the non-European and to so-called 'primitive art'. And it opened the way to the kind of internationalism, transatlantic and European, that was Camille Mauclair's excuse for his furious attacks on 'cosmopolitan' consortia.

The first to make the case for the place of Cubism in tradition from the platform provided by Léonce Rosenberg's publishing ventures was Maurice Raynal. He did so in a pamphlet published in 1919 by the Editions de l'effort moderne with the modest title, *Quelques Intentions du cubisme* (Some Aims of Cubism). He summons up Egyptian art and Giotto as well as Chardin and Watteau, but is careful at this immediately post-war moment to accent the links with the 'French tradition', his language echoing that of Mâle and Focillon as he writes of the 'spirit of equilibrium' and 'the science of measure'. Crucially, his concept of this 'science of measure' does without measurement per se; it is, for Raynal, an internally and intuitively felt sense of structure, something like, of course, the 'spontaneous classicism' Denis had found in Cézanne.[35]

A year later, in 1920, Léonce Rosenberg made public his absolute conviction that by supporting Cubism commercially he was contributing to the ongoing development of 'tradition', and that his notion of tradition was both French and in the largest sense 'universal'. He argued his case in a pamphlet called *Cubisme et tradition*, the title an unequivocal statement in itself. The dealer was decidedly more prescriptive than Raynal, happy to use the word 'rules'; he was also more concerned with fitting Cubism into an historical picture. He sketches a master narrative of 'tradition', which begins in the Middle East (the Orient) comes to the West in the Middle Ages and is then nurtured and developed by 'a humanity jealously smitten with clarity, measure and intimacy', namely the French, until it re-emerges in the twentieth century with Cubism. Rosenberg, it should be added, had specialised in medieval and ancient art before beginning to buy Cubist art just prior to the Great War; the story he told was an idealised gloss on his own history as a dealer.

There are three questions raised by the Cubists' pursuit of tradition that need to be addressed finally here. First, was the pursuit of tradition by these radical modernists always entirely in earnest? Second, were the issues of cultural identity bound up in the wider discourse of tradition and nationalism of real importance to the Cubists within their milieux? And third, how far does their pursuit of tradition constitute an ideologically as well as an aesthetically conservative reaction? I shall use two instances to approach these questions: first, the case of Picasso, and then an exchange of letters between Léger and Rosenberg.

I have mentioned already the exaggerated posturing in Picasso's jewel-like *Bathers* of 1918 [250]. When one adds to this the sluggish movements, the thickening of the limbs and the massive proportions of the hands in *Three Women at the Spring* [252], doubts as to Picasso's absolute seriousness in invoking a classical past, whether working on an intimate or a monumental scale, must be raised. On the one hand, we have unimpeachable clarity of reference where the relevant models from the past are concerned – very precise comparisons can be made – and on the other hand, we have what seems to be the deliberate transformation of these figurative models into two kinds of monster, one caught up in a frenzy of dancing which yet remains elegant, the other weighed down by superfluous fleshly swellings, stolidly inelegant. Alexandra Parigoris, in a brilliant essay on the conundrum left by Picasso, writes of the 'language of pastiche', and certainly these paintings exploit such a 'language', especially if pastiche is understood in its negative sense as a kind of satire of the generally admired.[36] Where, before 1914 he had often challenged the past by vandalising its memory, in the neo-classical works of 1917–24, Picasso seems often to have challenged the past by approaching it so closely that the slightest deviation can be felt as ironic and deflationary. This is indeed how satirical pastiche works. And there can be no doubt that his decision to show his Cubist and his neo-classical work together, first of all at Paul Rosenberg's exhibition in 1921, provoked many not to take his neo-classicism as seriously as Roger Bissière did. Of course, there are works where he almost approaches earnestness in his respect for a source: his *Portrait of Olga in an Armchair* of 1917 is such a painting [251]. But even in these cases, their coexistence with the Cubist work cannot be forgotten, and was not.

Picasso, then, gave both his neo-classical and his Cubist work an ironic edge that invariably threatened to undermine the very idea of tradition. As he emulated, he relativised, equivocating about the status and distinctness of every lineage he invoked. And yet, even his most obvious pastiches, by their allusions to current notions of tradition, just as invariably raised issues of cultural identity which could not be ignored and whose implications were profound.

Nothing could better demonstrate this than a vigorous debate carried on between Léger and Léonce Rosenberg which acted as a preface to and then a commentary on Léger's own neo-classical figure paintings. This was a debate carried on by letter, but it began in the summer of 1919 as a semi-public affair, set in motion by Léger's pugnacious assertion of his 'northern' identity as a Norman against what he saw as the cold 'southern' culture of the Mediterranean defended by Rosenberg. Léger accused his dealer of liking the straight and narrow, and advised him to 'face

Northwards' more often. Rosenberg replied with an open letter sent to all the galerie de l'Effort Moderne artists. Here he identifies himself with 'Tradition' as a Jew (a southerner originally from the 'Orient'), and gives a specifically Semitic gloss to the argument he would develop the following year in *Cubisme et tradition*. He writes of a 'Mediterranean culture' founded on 'eternal principles' first brought to the 'Occident' by the 'Semitic Moslems and the Jews' of the 'Orient'. It is a culture which opposes the 'passion' and 'brutality' of the North with order. This provokes Léger to claim that the vitality and materialism of 'the North' had actually won the war and produced the Soviet Revolution, to dismiss the 'inferior Southern races' as exhausted, and to call their brand of order 'the bourgeois condition'. Rosenberg was unfazed; he predicted that Léger would 'end up like your predecessors: Poussin, Watteau, Fragonard, who began Nordic and ended their careers as Mediterraneans'. Léger's odalisques of 1920–1, culminating in *Le Grand Déjeuner*, might seem to have given Rosenberg satisfaction almost instantly, but Léger insisted on setting them up in rivalry to the Mediterranean Picasso, and when the question of North and South was raised again between artist and dealer in 1923, he refused the whole idea of fixing 'values' and 'temperaments'. He remains 'connected with the North, which is for ever making things happen (bougeant),' he tells Rosenberg, 'and yet I love order, dryness, plastically speaking'.[37] He is both northern *and* southern. In 1924 Rosenberg published another letter which had been sent him by the painter in 1921 where Léger echoed every modernist notion of tradition by singling out just one factor as crucial: 'invention'. Among the inventors from the past, he listed Ingres and Poussin alongside Clouet and Fouquet: he placed 'southerners' and 'northerners' together.[38]

What this remarkable exchange shows is the depth of feeling released by what seems now the arcane question of North and South, the 'Occidental' and the 'Oriental', the degree to which these categories were interactive, and the inevitability with which such discussions took in issues of class and race as well as nationality. Rosenberg, as a Jew, interprets the history of Medieval art in relation to the Middle East as a parable of assimilation, bringing 'Orient' and 'Occident' together, in which the Jews are originators, before being absorbed into the French nation, that people 'smitten with clarity' and 'measure', as he would put it in *Cubisme et tradition*. Cubism is 'Occidental', but in origin it is 'Oriental'; and it is French, as he is. In another letter to Léger, he points out that, compared with the Jews, the Normans were latecomers to France. As to Léger, he thinks of the North as 'the people' and the South as 'bourgeois', but he cannot in the end separate North from South. He brings them together as the 'warm' and the 'vital' in interaction with the 'dry' and the ordered. And this is an interaction that is there to be seen in his paintings.

The references to Poussin, David and Ingres incorporated into the figure style of the *Grand Déjeuner* and *Mother and Child* are juxtaposed with the tipped-up tables and simply modelled domestic objects typical of northern-European painting in the fourteenth and fifteenth centuries, of Campin's Merode altarpiece or Jean Fouquet's miniatures in the Bibliothèque Nationale. In *Mother and Child*, the invocation of the brothers Le Nain is northern too: they painted peasant scenes from the region of Gothic Laon. Then too, the dry orderliness of these compositions is set in motion by the sheer stridency of the collisions between colours and forms, by contrasts which 'make things happen'. Braque, Gris, Laurens, all the Cubists, including Picasso, who called up notions of tradition, inevitably opened their work to responses shaped by notions of tradition which placed North and South, 'Occident' and 'Orient', in relation to one another, and which inevitably went with some idea of France, an idea which carried its own baggage of assumptions and prejudices. Finally, Léger's robustly pro-Soviet, anti-bourgeois stance makes it clear that these assumptions and prejudices did not necessarily go together in an ideologically conservative package.

A last observation needs to be made before concluding this section. Within the milieu of the Cubists and their sympathisers, the dominant ethos was assimilationist, as it was in the centre of French opinion. When, in 1924 the Société des Indépendants made the decision to hang its Salons by nationality, thus for the first time making national difference an organising principle, Léger was one of the leaders of the dissenters who resigned. Asked for his opinion on the decision, Lipchitz published a memorable response. 'I know that if there were sitting on the Committee of the Indépendants Fouquet, Poussin, the Le Nain brothers, Philippe de Champaigne (sic), Chardin, Boucher, Watteau, Ingres, Delacroix, Corot, Manet, Cézanne, their decision would have been completely different.'[39] As a foreigner and a Jew, his assumption was that the French tradition, reduced here to a list of names (all of Frenchmen), had always assimilated the foreigner. Recalling the controversy a year later, André Salmon pointed to the fact that the huge exhibition 'Fifty Years of French Art' organised to coincide with the Exposition Internationale des Arts Décoratifs had given key roles to Picasso, a Spaniard, Modigliani, an Italian, and Van Dongen, a Dutchman.[40] His inference was simple: the very idea of a pure 'national school' was ridiculous; foreigners were part of it.[41]

'GREATER FRANCE' AT THE 1931 COLONIAL EXHIBITION; MATISSE AND ORIENTALISM

Between 1919 and 1923, the Treaty of Versailles and the agreements that followed it facilitated a huge expansion of France's colonial empire. Control of Syria and Lebanon in the Middle East and of Germany's African colonies of Togo and Cameroon (all of them mandated by the League of Nations) was added to France's pre-war colonial control of territories which included Algeria, Morocco and, in Southern Asia, modern Vietnam (then called Annam), Cambodia and Laos.[42]

Since the first flush of colonial enthusiasm under the 'civilising' ethos of Jules Ferry in the 1880s, French voters had proved resistant to the expansionist ambitions that went with it; another measure of French absorption in France as a geographical territory, sufficient to itself. Between the wars, partisans of colonialism committed funds which rivalled those that financed the great Universal Exhibitions to organise two huge colonial exhibitions: a national affair held in 1922 in Marseilles (the key maritime point of contact with colonies), and the far more extensive 'International Colonial Exhibition' of 1931 in Paris, for which the park of the Bois de Vincennes was transformed and a new Métro station built. They were an attempt to win over public opinion by spectacle (to induce wonder at the cultural riches controlled by France) and by facts (to aid appreciation of the economic benefits of empire and to enhance the idea of a civilising mission disseminating France's republican values across the world). The enterprise of 1931 was overseen by the Radical administrations of the centre, with the liberal politician Albert Sarraut (an important collector of 'independent' art) a leading figure. But in the final year of the Great War, Maurice Barrès, from the nationalist Right, captured both the expansionist ambitions and the sense of republican rectitude behind the Imperial propaganda of 1931: 'We shall open a world haunted by the obsession with German *kultur*,' he wrote, 'to the peaceful penetration of the French spirit . . . The principles which we shall spread are the same as those for which the Entente took up arms: Right, Justice and Freedom.'[43]

The most spectacular exhibit in 1931 was a gigantic plaster model of the Khmer temple Angkor Wat [261]. It covered fifteen acres and its five towers reached a height of nearly 150 feet, while the central tower soared thirty feet higher still. Outside, the accent was on authenticity and romance; visitors were counselled to stay on for an unforgettable experience as the sun set behind the towers. Inside, the accent was on information: graphs, photographs, statistics, displays of products designed to demonstrate Indo-Chinese growth under the French. The five towers of Angkor Wat, reconstructed in less than a year in the Bois de Vincennes, were presented by the official Guide to the Exhibition as symbol of France's colonial role in bringing together 'the five "pays" of the Indo-Chinese Union'.[44] As such, it became the expression of a concept of empire which was a vastly expanded reflection of the concept of France as a unity in diversity.

The entire exhibition was shaped to create a 'tableau' of the empire as a far-flung extension of France: like the mother country, made up of extraordinarily varied 'petits pays', and brought together by the French nation to form a newly unified La Plus Grande France ('Greater France').[45] As the Minister of the Colonies, Paul Reynaud, put it at the State opening in 1931, the event was to help everyone 'understand himself to be a citizen of Greater France'. And as the Guide put it when alluding to plans to introduce new transport links between West African towns and France: 'These names will be more familiar to your ears than Provençal or Gascon names became to Parisians in the seventeenth century.' The Guide adds that: 'Our Africa tightly bound to us now for both its defence and its prosperity, will become a magnificent and direct extension of our French humanity.'[46]

From the 1900s, French colonial policy had been dominated by two major alternatives: assimilationism and associationism. The first was, like the idea of 'Greater France', an extension of the expansive concept of French national identity into the colonial field. It was based on that blithe confidence in French civilisation which assumed both the desire of outsiders to become French and the capacity of France to assimilate anyone. It envisaged a time when education and modernisation would have turned all the colonised peoples into citizens of 'Greater France'. Associationism amounted to a policy, first seriously taken up in 1906, aimed at reconciling the civilising mission with the need for domination. The stress was on preserving the 'authentic' local traditions

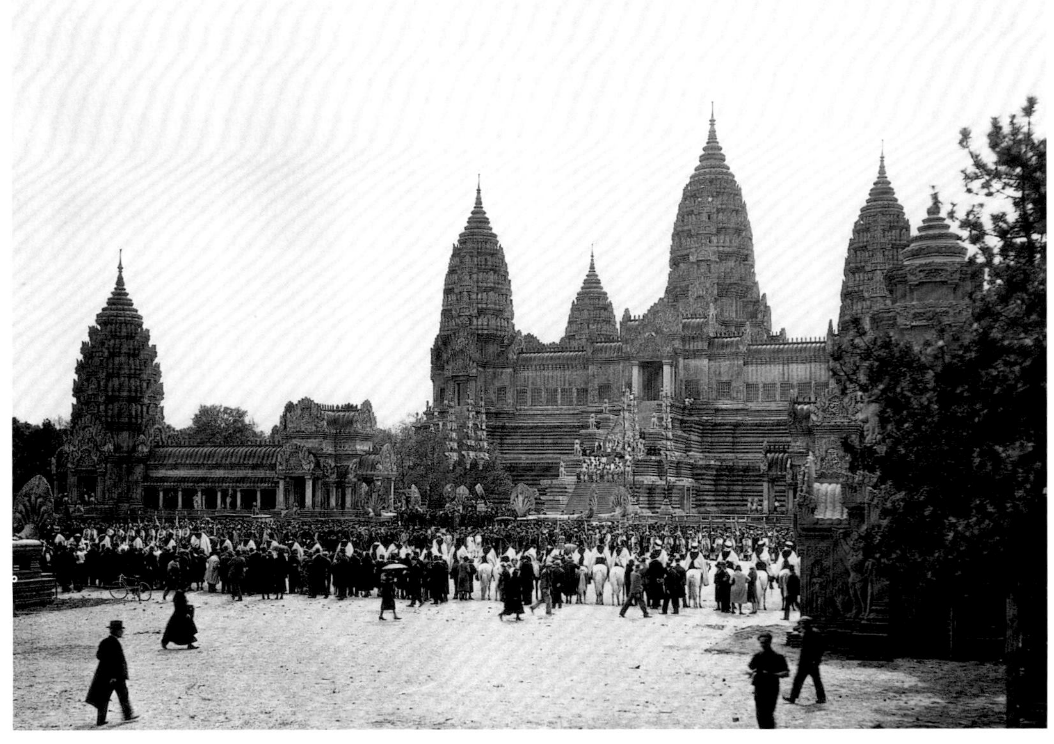

261. Reconstruction of the temple of Angkor Watt, Cambodia. Exposition Coloniale, Parc de Vincennes, Paris, 1931

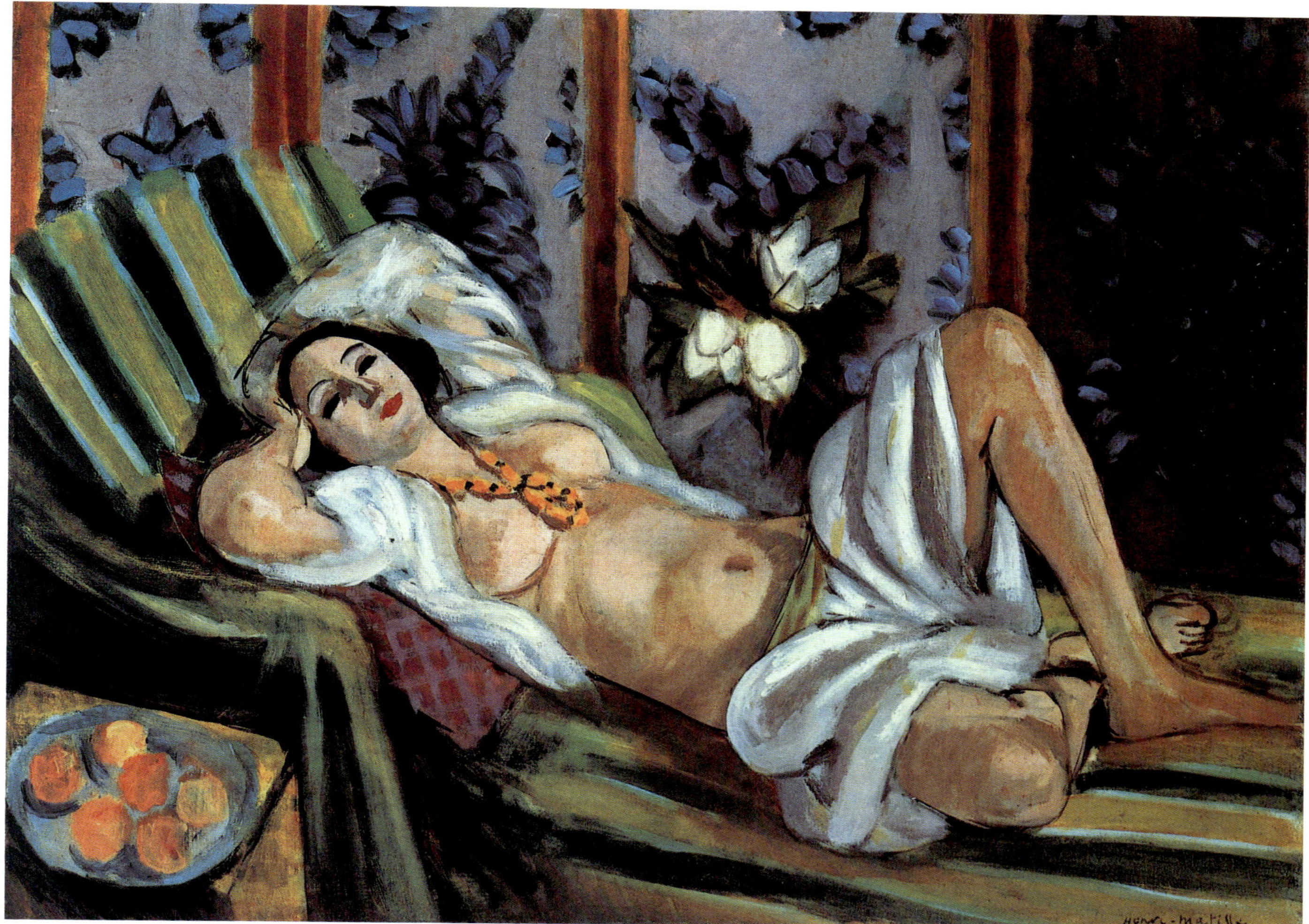

262. Henri Matisse, *Odalisque with Magnolias*, 1923 or 1924. Oil on canvas, 65 × 81 cm. Private Collection

and skills of the 'natives' rather than educating them as 'Frenchmen'. Education ideally was restricted to encouraging and reviving local traditions, and training just enough 'natives' in practical subjects for them to help run the colonies in association with their French rulers. Between the mid-1890s and the election of the Popular Front in 1936, assimilationism was ousted by associationism as the guiding principle of French policy. A leading exponent of it was Sarraut as Minister of the Colonies between 1920 and 1924, and then again in 1933. The creation in the 1920s of an Indo-Chinese Communist Party intent on fomenting insurrection, and serious unrest in Annam led by French-educated revolutionaries, encouraged such a policy in southern Asia especially: educating the colonised to be fully French was seen to encourage revolt, not conformity. Newly encouraged traditional crafts alongside imported French modernisation dominated the 1931 Indo-Chinese showing: the 'authentically' Oriental alongside the results of French modernity and control.[47]

One section of the Exhibition, however, betrayed something like an assimilationist character, the section devoted to France's oldest and closest colonial possession, Algeria. The Algerian pavilion was not an 'authentic' reconstruction or approximation, it was what Lebovics describes as a 'stylised synthesis of Algerian architecture'.[48] The French capacity for style and synthesis made something new of traditional Algerian forms. To some extent, Algeria was allowed to be French. And indeed, in 1931 Maurice Violette, Governor-General of the colony, made plain his strong assimilationist faith, his conviction, moreover, that it was France's duty to absorb indigenous cultures into its own, allowing the modern to supplant the old, French culture to destroy indigenous cultures.[49]

In Part Six, I consider the question of the 'authentically' native in the context of so-called 'Primitivism', and so return to the question of associationism and non-European culture. Here it is worth noting that the accent on the authentic stature of southern-Asian culture at the exhibition of 1931 and on its distinctive contribution as the achievement of a separate civilisation to be compared with, say, medieval France, left it in a kind of priviliged, sacrosanct isolation.[50] No significant modernist artist or architect in France made Angkor Wat or South Asian art an obvious source of inspiration comparable to African and Oceanic art; in a sense, this was a compliment.[51] There was, however, one major modernist who took what can be called an assimilationist approach to certain of France's colonies as cultural centres and as places, Henri Matisse (b.1869); and his inspiration

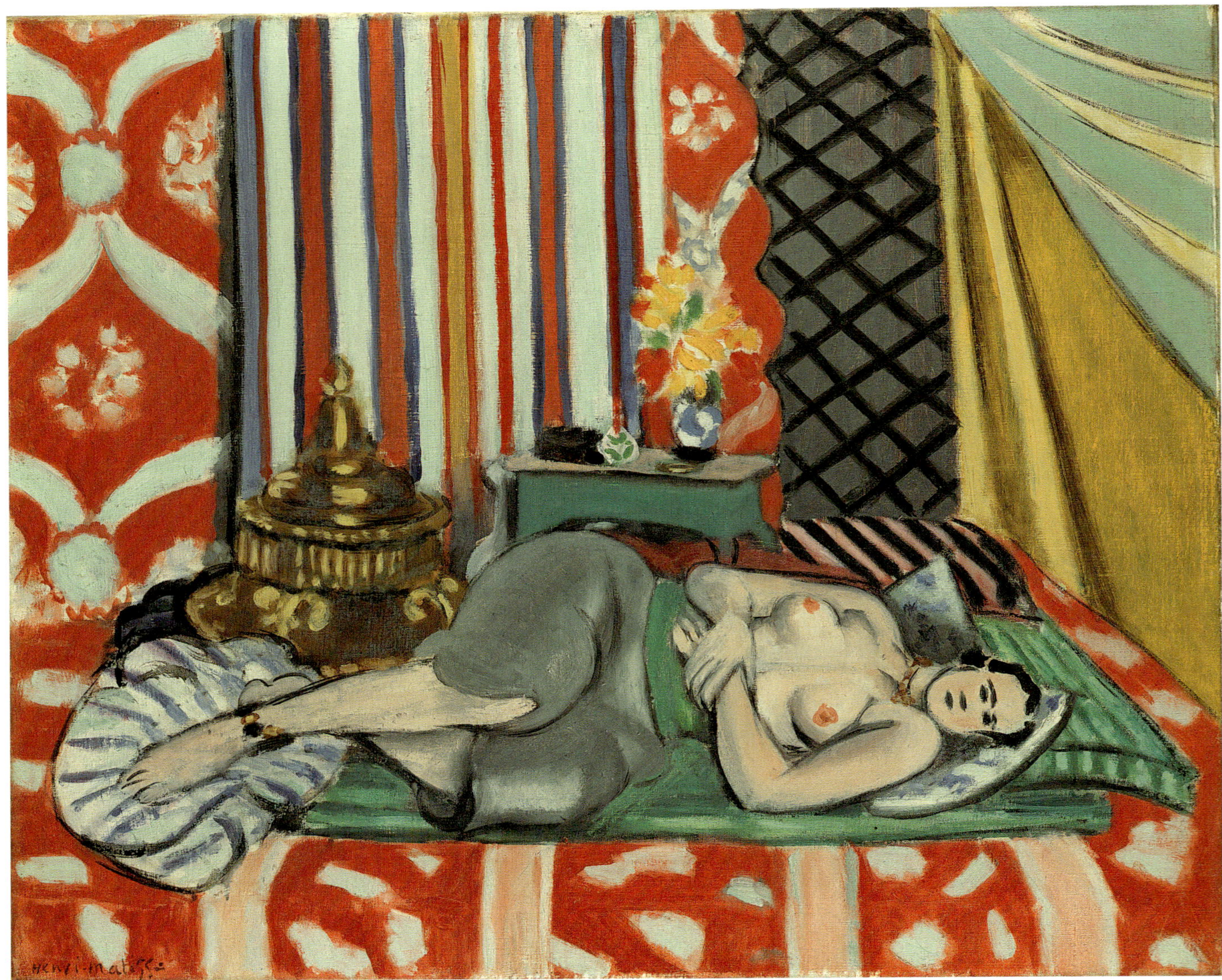

263. Henri Matisse, *Odalisque in Grey Culottes*, 1926–7. Oil on canvas, 54 × 65 cm. Musée de l'Orangerie, Paris

came initially from North Africa, first of all Algeria. What was quickly called Matisse's Orientalism went public to great acclaim with an exhibition at the galerie Bernheim-Jeune in 1913, though it had been a feature of his art since at least 1906, the date of his visit to Algeria. It became a dominant feature of his work especially in the 1920s, reaching its climax between 1926 and 1928, just before the 1931 Exhibition.

The first purchase of a Matisse for the Luxembourg by the State was of an Orientalist odalisque and it occurred in 1922, the year of the Marseilles Colonial Exhibition.[52] It seems indeed that by the early 1920s the significance of Matisse's revival of Ingres's and especially Delacroix's Orientalism could only be viewed in the context of France as a confident colonial power. His return to Orientalism at the end of the war had been encouraged by the ease with which his new French model Lorette could be orientalised, and then by a concatenation of pictorial and erotic desires. But works like *Odalisque with Magnolias* of 1923 or 1924 and *Odalisque in Grey Culottes* of 1926–7 [262, 263], painted in his successive studios at place Charles-Félix in Nice were inextricably caught up at once in a French Orientalist past and in a French colonialist present. When, in 1928, Matisse was given a room at the Venice Biennale, his Orientalism was a major feature of his showing; Italy too had ambitions in North Africa, and would be one of the foreign Imperial powers invited to the 1931 Exhibition.

Matisse's room at the Biennale was picked out by Camille Mauclair as one of his targets in his attack on the 'pictorial Communism' and the 'cosmopolitan' consortia of modern art between 1928 and 1930. It was the odalisques that provoked the insults, and what most infuriated him was their inauthenticity: 'They haven't even the semblance of oriental truth that those of Ingres have: they've never left Montmartre.'[53] This horror at the want of authenticity is telling; it indicates the effectiveness of Matisse's refusal of the 'authentic' in favour of obvious set-ups where European models either accept a touch of the 'Oriental' as they might a cosmetic, for instance in *Odalisque with Magnolias*, or play the 'Oriental' part to the hilt, as in *Odalisque in Grey Culottes*. It is the response of one who cannot accept the

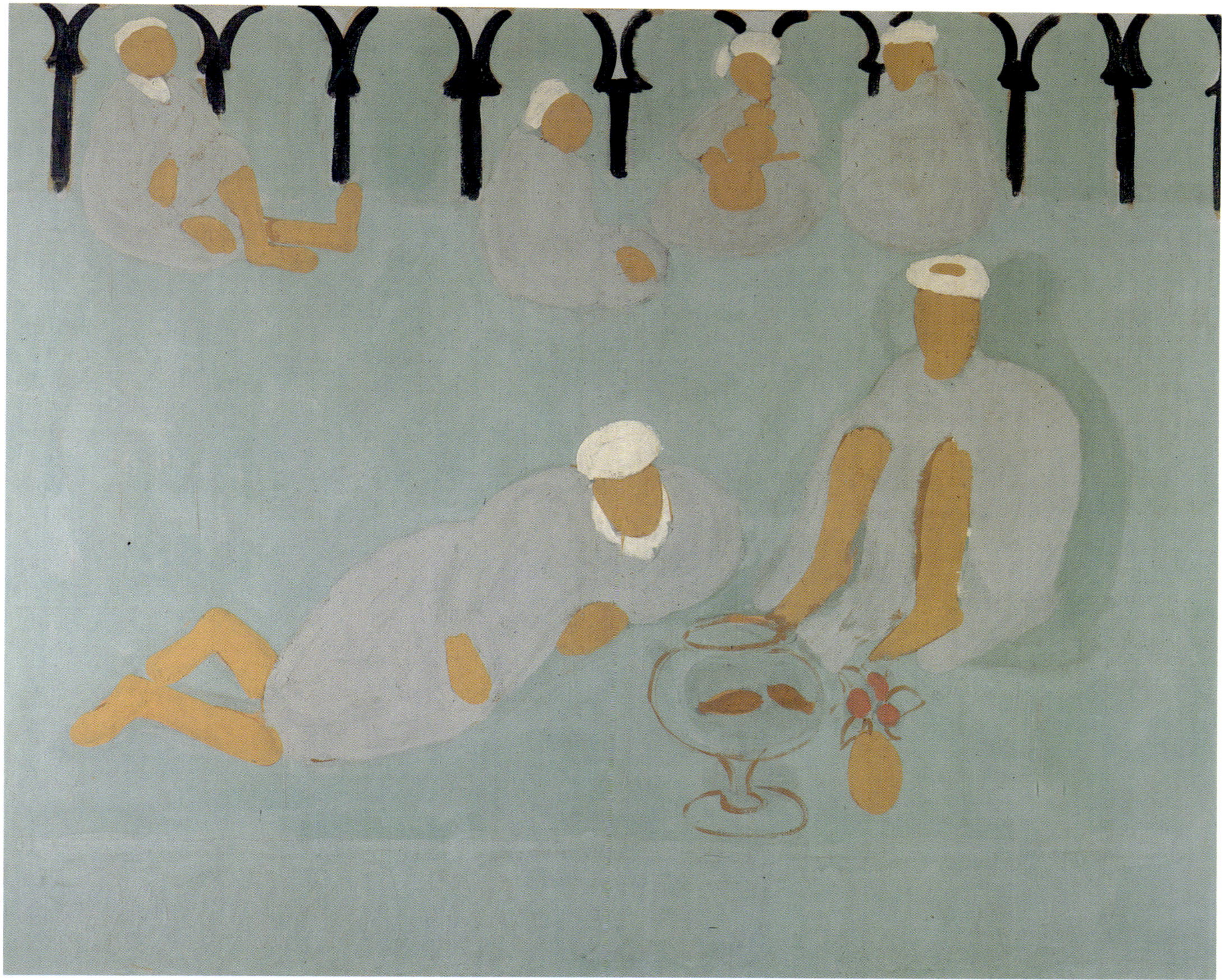

264. Henri Matisse, *Moroccan Café*, 1912–13. Distemper on canvas, 176 × 210 cm. The State Hermitage Museum, St Petersburg

hybridity of a mingling of cultures: the implications of images where what could be North African is absorbed into a French vision that asserts its French identity, even if, by doing so, it takes control. For Mauclair such images demean, indeed threaten his idea of French culture.

Just how far Matisse's Orientalism was caught up from the outset in assimilationist attitudes to North Africa is underlined both by the paintings he executed in Morocco and showed at the 1913 exhibition and by one of the published responses to them. The Orientalist paintings he made in 1912–13 were not based on artificial set-ups where the Moroccan was absorbed into some French fantasy. Instead they took 'authentic' Moroccan subjects, as seen by a tourist-painter, and metamorphosed them according to the imperatives of a highly sophisticated style informed by everything from Persian miniatures and North African pottery to Signac and Cézanne (besides North Africa, in 1910 he visited Munich for the huge 'Islamic Art' exhibition). Modernism as a practice was itself here assimilationist, capable of absorbing into its constantly renewed synthetic hybridity almost any other style, French or otherwise; and yet such a modernist practice was, almost by definition, above all French.

So in a sense what viewers saw in, for instance, *Moroccan Café*, completed in France in 1913 [264], was a genuine North African scene absorbed into the kind of flat chromatic field which was Matisse's own invention – a French invention. Into this field too were absorbed fragmentary patterns strongly evocative of Islamic ornamental styles. It was this picture that was the subject of key passages in an article written at the time of the Moroccan show by Marcel Sembat, Socialist deputy, and major collector of modernism, especially Matisse. Sembat describes how Matisse the painter takes control: how the details of the café scene in Tangiers – a pipe, a line of slippers – vanish as he simplifies in order 'to perfect'. Matisse becomes a force which takes things in and absorbs them, especially influences. 'I don't know anyone,' writes Sembat, 'who insists more on the necessity of influences and on the foolishness of trying to escape . . . them. Rather, he feels himself strong enough to assimilate, digest, and incorporate all that comes from outside.'[54] Matisse as an artist becomes a coloniser, one who makes everything his by simply 'incorporating' it.

When Matisse painted colonial subjects having absorbed colonial cultures, the way he assimilated everything to himself made a statement about the French and 'Greater France'. Fifteen years later, it was to this that Mauclair responded so furiously. By the 1920s, Matisse's Orientalism stood for an openness to the foreign and a capacity to absorb its influences that inevitably was a provocation to xenophobes. It is worth adding that Nice, where Matisse painted his odalisques in the 1920s, was itself a special case in the rapidly worsening climate of xenophobia at the end of that decade. By 1931, the city had one of the highest immigrant populations in France: 25% of its inhabitants were foreign, many of them North Africans.[55]

THE CULT OF THE PAST, THE 'ÉCOLE FRANÇAISE' AND THE 'MÉTÈQUES': HUMANISM AND XENOPHOBIA, 1926–40

The overwhelming competence of the educational displays at the Colonial Exhibition of 1931 was a product of the invention and development of professional museology between the wars. The leading part France played in this was, in its turn, a product of the profound seriousness with which the art of the past was taken by the French cultural establishment: the art of the European past, above all the French past, far more than 'native traditions' in the colonies.

By 1931 plans were being implemented for the reorganisation and reinstallation of almost all the major French museums. Between 1930 and 1937, a new installation of the Louvre was masterminded by its director, Henri Verne; the emphasis was on clarity in laying out a master narrative room by room. Besides the opening of the new museums of modern art at the Palais de Tokyo, the International Exhibition of 1937 saw the opening of new museums in the brave new Palais de Chaillot [13]. Besides the Musée de l'Homme, which was an expanded and re-shaped version of the Ethnographic Museum of the Trocadéro, there was an altogether more spectacular version of the Musée de Sculpture Comparée, first opened in 1882 and originally conceived by the architect and architectural historian Viollet-le-Duc as a museum of plaster casts of sculpture from the past. The new museum was cleared of non-French examples and renamed the Musée des Monuments Français to underline the exclusiveness of its focus.[56] The plan was to use full-scale reproductions to make possible a tour within a single suite of rooms (as if within book covers) of the greatest 'stones of France' and the greatest medieval French wall paintings, taking in every region, every 'pays' with a major monument. When the museum opened in 1937, a splendidly authentic plaster cast of the twelfth-century tympanum of Vézelay in the Morvan, a 'petit pays' in Burgundy, was already installed, and copies of portions of the twelfth-century mural cycle from the vault of the nave of Saint-Savin in the South West had been commissioned from the fresco specialist Julien Socard. This was the museological counterpart of Henri Bouchard's neo-Romanesque tympanum just completed for the church of Saint-Pierre de Chaillot [220]; it made a statement too that a modernist sculpor like Henri Laurens could appreciate.

Education coupled with populism gave the new museology its ethos from the 1920s. Under the Popular Front and faced with the threat of the new Totalitarian States, that ethos was given a keen edge whenever it was invoked. Thus, in March 1937, an editorial in *L'Amour de l'art* declared that: 'the Museum is called to play a new and ceaselessly expanding role in the new society. The revolutionary states however opposed they may be, dictatorial or communist, have understood that the museum is made for a more universal public, that it is not only a place of pleasure but a precious instrument for the education of the people'.[57] What the museum taught, of course, was so crucial because it bedded down the values promoted by governments and could give strong cultural form to ideas of nation. On the Left, curatorial innovators like Georges-Henri Rivière, Jean Cassou and René Huyghe came together to found the Association Populaire des Amis des Musées (APAM), affiliated to the Maisons de la culture, whose aim was to open the museums to 'the masses'. Henri Verne's decision to open the Louvre regularly on certain weekday evenings was one manifestation of this Popular Front commitment to the opening up of 'high culture' to the French 'people'.

Despite such a populist context, notions of tradition in the French cultural politics of the 1930s remained uncompromisingly elitist, to some extent even on the Communist Left, quite apart from the Socialist Left, the Radical Centre and on the Right. However, the new Right, where fascism actually impinged on 'independent art', is the most revealing direction from which to explore the politicised role given to the past in the French modern art world from the late 1920s. For what happened was the final absorption by majority French opinion of what had been the Right's myth of the French tradition, and there was one critic on the new Right, respected across a wide spectrum of moderate opinion, who put together a particularly coherent polemic in favour of the active presence of the past in the present. This was Waldemar George. As editor of *L'Amour de l'art* in the mid-1920s he had added real modernist spice to Louis Vauxcelles' francocentric traditionalism. By the early 1930s, now an enthusiastic supporter of Mussolini and the Italian Fascist Party, he identified modernism as a symptom of the 'crisis' brought on by liberal democracy and capitalism, and advocated instead a fresh appreciation of the past as the foundation of a European cultural renewal. Between 1930 and 1933 he founded and edited a new art magazine, *Formes*; it became the vehicle of a campaign that politicised art from the start. Appropriating a term with wide intellectual appeal in the thirties, George named his creed for the fascist future Neo-Humanism.[58]

The demon of modernism in *Formes* – admired as well as feared – was Picasso; and modernism in its typical and most dangerous forms was to be found in Cubism and 'Primitivism'. In January 1931, George set out his programme for the new year in *Formes*. His object, he announced, was to find a way out of a dehumanised culture, on the one hand mechanistic and abstract (Cubism), on the other hand (by way of compensation) lost among 'the idols of the barbarians . . . in the domain of the dream, of halluci-

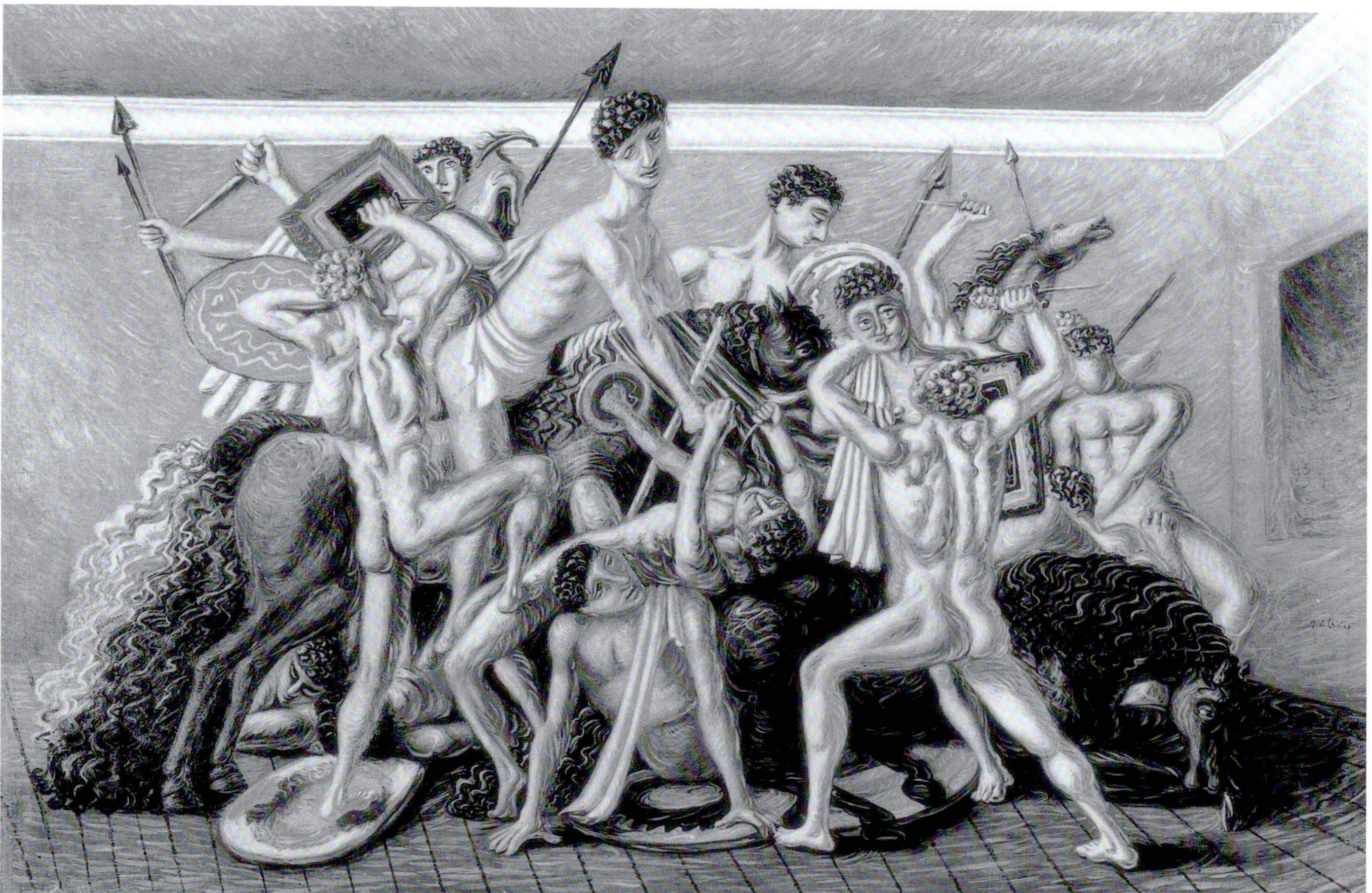

265. Giorgio de Chirico, *Combat*, 1928. Oil on canvas, 164 × 240 cm. Civica Galleria d'Arte Moderna, Collezione Boschi, Milan

nation' (Primitivism).[59] The following month, he underlined the ideological dimension of his polemic. Modernism had become a purposeless pursuit of individual experiment whose success depended on its commitment to 'the myth of progress and of freedom, those orthodoxies of democracy', which flattered 'bourgeois' aspirations. 'The young people of today,' George insisted, 'are left absolutely cold' by 'the myth of the new spirit. They are in search of constants, not shock values.'[60]

Such scorn for progress and modernity did not diminish George's typically fascist desire to identify both with the young and with an idea of the nation believed to be inherited from its cultural past. In the opening issue of *Formes* he followed the familiar claim that the French tradition brought together the Gothic and the classical by aligning it with 'our young school', which was, he declared, oriented towards 'a humanist art'. He named as members of this 'young school' the not-so-young Italians Giorgio de Chirico and his brother Alberto Savinio alongside the genuinely emergent Christian Bérard, Eugène Bermann and Paul (Pavel) Tchelitchew.[61] Later in 1930, George devoted monographic pieces to Bermann and Tchelitchew, using their work to help clarify what he meant by Neo-Humanism, but between 1930 and 1933 the prophets and leaders of Neo-Humanism in the pages of *Formes* were above all Derain and Maillol alongside de Chirico.

For George, where modernism had replaced God with formal experiments (abstraction) and 'cabalistic' superstition (Primitivism), Humanism would restore that sense of each individual's human relationship with the world which had been threatened by the machine. He idealised this relationship as a perfect equilibrium between the 'inner' and the 'outer', an ideal which was endemic across the cultural theories of the fascisizing Right in France during the Thirties. Humanist art, he proclaimed in his January 1931 programme for *Formes*, would use composition to affirm the 'cosmic' sense of 'general harmony', would restore the figure and the portrait in art, the one as 'microcosm of the universe', the other as the sign of 'individual life', and would restore landscape, in the lineage of Poussin and Corot, as sign of 'the accord between man and the world'.[62]

De Chirico's role in ushering in this new Humanist art for the future fascist society was, for George, that of herald. In 1930, he compared the Italian's recent paintings of gladiators, commissioned for Léonce Rosenberg's private apartment [265], with the Roman sculpture of the 'Lower Empire', a period of preparation, as he saw it, for the spirituality of Christian art after the materialism of Rome. According to George, de Chirico's insubstantial, oddly ineffectual fighters conveyed the exhaustion of a world in crisis, and the onset of a deepening realisation that the physical alone could not be enough.[63] His writing on Derain and Maillol makes of them the two modern artists who have already achieved a fully Humanist art. Thus, in a piece with

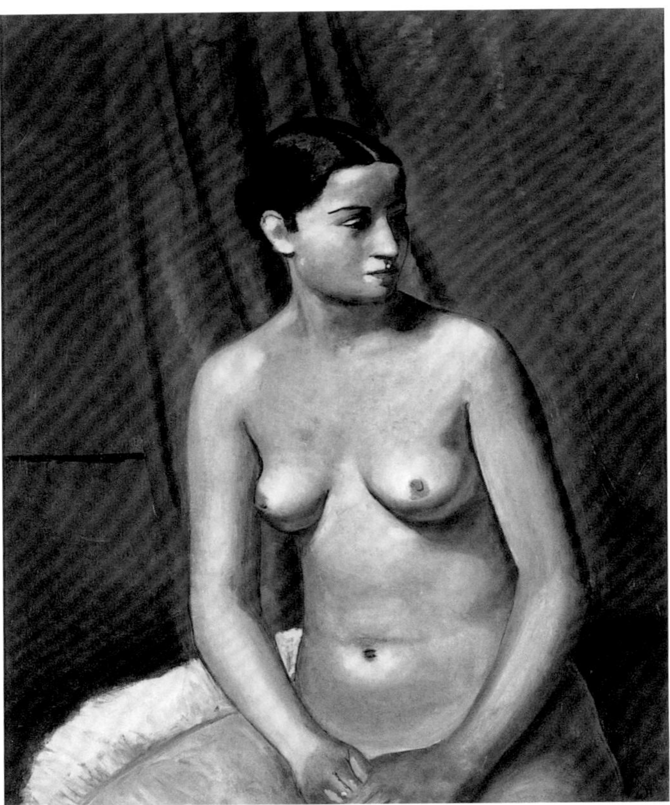

266. André Derain, *Woman in front of a Green Curtain*, 1923. Oil on canvas, 92 × 73 cm. Musée National d'Art Moderne, Paris

the title 'The Message of Derain' (pressing near-divine status upon the artist), the two of them are set up as the antitheses of Picasso. Derain is 'timeless', 'an *un*contemporary (inactuel) painter' (my italics); Picasso is so contemporary that he represents 'a collective psychosis'. Derain stands for the persistance of the past even in the mechanised present: 'His landscapes, figures, portraits . . . prove the persistance and vitality of a culture which has rounded the cape of americanism [machinism] and africanism [Primitivism] . . .' Maillol has achieved this with nothing more than a 'naïve faith' in the ordered, he is an unwitting, saintlike classicist; Derain by contrast has achieved it despite his acute awareness of the 'crisis'.[64]

It was not difficult to press the work produced by Derain and Maillol during the 1920s and early 1930s into this carefully shaped conceptual mould. To take just the case of Derain, his painting of that period was so clearly proof against the abstractions of Cubism and so openly aligned with easily recognised French classical sources that in 1927 Maurice Raynal had already placed him at the head of a tendency in French art that he called 'Eclecticism': a tendency which linked 'Naturalism with the Idealist tradition of the museums . . . to construct a sort of Classicism'.[65] The Corotesque landscapes of Provence [256] and figure paintings like the 1923 *Woman in front of a Green Curtain* [266] could be claimed easily enough both for such a category, which had distinctly negative connotations, and for George's Neo-Humanism, whose connotations were distinctly positive. Derain himself made very few public statements to clarify his position, but in the 1920s he did not conceal a continuing modernist commitment to formal questions, while after 1933 he was happy to be involved with the Surrealist-oriented periodical *Minotaure*, one of the main forums for the promotion of so-called 'primitive art' in France. It is difficult to connect what we know of his own convictions with the stance taken by *Formes* against modernism and 'Primitivism'. George's appropriation of not only Derain and Maillol but also of de Chirico and the 'young school' was one of many attempts in the 1930s to appropriate artists and their art for overweening political agendas. This is an important point to grasp before considering the national and racial implications of these agendas, especially given the anti-Semitism and xenophobia rampant in France at that moment. We are concerned not with what artists necessarily *wanted* their work to say, but with what a strong critical voice wanted it to say and with a body of viewers who were ready to listen to *his* message.

Waldemar George was himself an immigrant. A Polish Jew, he had arrived in France in 1911 as a political refugee from the Russian empire. Studies in French literature at the Sorbonne had allowed the fullest of assimilations, underlined by his decision to replace his surname Jarocinski with his first name George. He had fought in the Great War as a naturalised French citizen.

In the summer of 1931, he published in *Formes* his two-part response to Camille Mauclair's anti-Semitic defence of the 'Ecole Française' against the 'invasion' of the 'métèques' of the 'Ecole de Paris'. George has been accused of a brand of xenophobia here which, while not singling out Jews, was transparently anti-Semitic.[66] In fact, his stance was that of many French Jews whose families had been in France for generations and who feared the 'foreignness' of immigrant Jews would encourage anti-Semitism. Nationalism in France, even on the extreme Right, had its Jewish supporters; the 'Union Patriotique des Français Israélites' organised meetings with the Right-wing 'Solidarité Française' to protest against 'undesirable' foreigners.[67] George's arguments were, in fact, the typically assimilationist arguments of a naturalised immigrant who wanted to embed himself deeper in French society, protected by the idea of an expansionist nation. His hostility was against those of the 'Ecole de Paris' who had refused what he understood to be the 'living' Humanism of the 'Ecole Française', who had refused therefore to assimilate on the terms he set for himself. These unassimilable foreign artists, of course, included many of those Mauclair despised as 'métèques', for they were by definition the 'rootless' modernists. George begins by making a point of the importance of assimilated foreigners to the 'Ecole Française'; he dismisses Louis Dimier's Action française view that the Italians who worked at Fontainebleau in the sixteenth century weakened French art and claims instead that their proper respect for 'French sentiment' actually strengthened it. For him, Rosso Fiorentino and Primaticcio prove 'that the origin, the nationality of a painter or sculptor in no way determines the nature of their art . . . France,' he continues, 'is not just a nation . . . France stands for a spiritual and intellectual order. French art welcomes and assimilates all those who adapt to its mode of feeling'. This 'mode of feeling' is ordered, but it is an order that resists definitions, where Italy's is 'absolute'. Now, in the twentieth century, it is again to be Italy and France together who will lead the way to a Humanist art; they are to do so against the threat of a twentieth-century 'barbarian invasion' (by unassimilable modernists).[68]

Ultimately, for George, France's cultural role is to be the champion of *European* civilisation, a role he declares only France can fulfil precisely because French art has absorbed into itself all the qualities essential to European culture as a whole. In an earlier article he called French art the last hope 'for an Occidental art which has been set adrift'. The absolutism of Italian art becomes a flaw, Spanish art is too idiosyncratic, German art too much 'the expression of a race'. Only French art 'satisfies all the conditions of European art . . .'.[69]

This was neither xenophobia in the sense applicable to Mauclair nor anti-Semitism in any sense, yet it absorbed into an elaborately historicised notion of the European and French tradition attitudes and arguments that with the smallest adjustment could become both. George, the assimilated immigrant Jew, shows just how vulnerable to the racist Right the orthodox expansive view of French nationality and culture was. And, in a broader sense, he stands for a racist understanding of European culture which was often clearly aligned with anti-Semitism and which was widespread. In the final analysis, 'Primitivism' was to be rejected, George told his readers, because it was alien to the 'white races', that Europe-wide ethnic melting pot which included the Jews, but excluded the 'black races'. The penultimate issue of *Formes* carried the following warning: 'When the white race forgets itself so far as to sacrifice the Greeks and the Goths to the idols of the black continent, it signs its own death warrant.' George went on here to approve the Nazis' closure of the Bauhaus at Weimar. For him, this was a laudable act of aggression by 'white' civilisation against 'the cult of abstract language, magic, [and] spiritual, moral and aesthetic disintegration'.[70]

Within the 'independent' art world, Mauclair's anti-Semitism was an extreme minority position, and few shared his view of what the legitimate 'Ecole Française' of the twentieth century was (for Mauclair, it comprised belated Impressionists like Besnard and the Nabi generation). George's assimilationist defence of an 'Ecole Française' led by Derain and Maillol was, on the other hand, easily accepted in the middle ground. His open fascist sympathies as a supporter of Mussolini, did not prevent the Beaux-Arts administration giving him an official role in the commissioning of work for the 1937 International Exhibition; he kept that role under the Popular Front. His case aids understanding of the almost universal assimilationist approach adopted by Jewish immigrant artists in France between the wars, especially as the xenophobic and anti-Semitic attacks mounted in French society generally from the end of the 1920s on. Persuasive arguments have been deployed to demonstrate that there was a 'double-bind' involved in assimilation for Jews: the fact that to assimilate is to acknowledge the power of those who will always see only inferiority and difference – the colonised were, of course, in the same position.[71] France's expansive idea of nationality does, however, distinguish the French from the German situation in particular: assimilation was thought of by Jews like George as a positive act of affirmation, not the acquisition of a disguise. What then of those Montparnassian Jewish immigrants whose foreignness remained more or less at issue and yet whose art can seem now to disclose the dominant assimilationist impulse? I have touched already on the case of the Cubist Lipchitz, here I shall pick out three other examples, each of whom had achieved considerable success by the mid-1920s: Moise Kisling, Chaim Soutine and Marc Chagall.

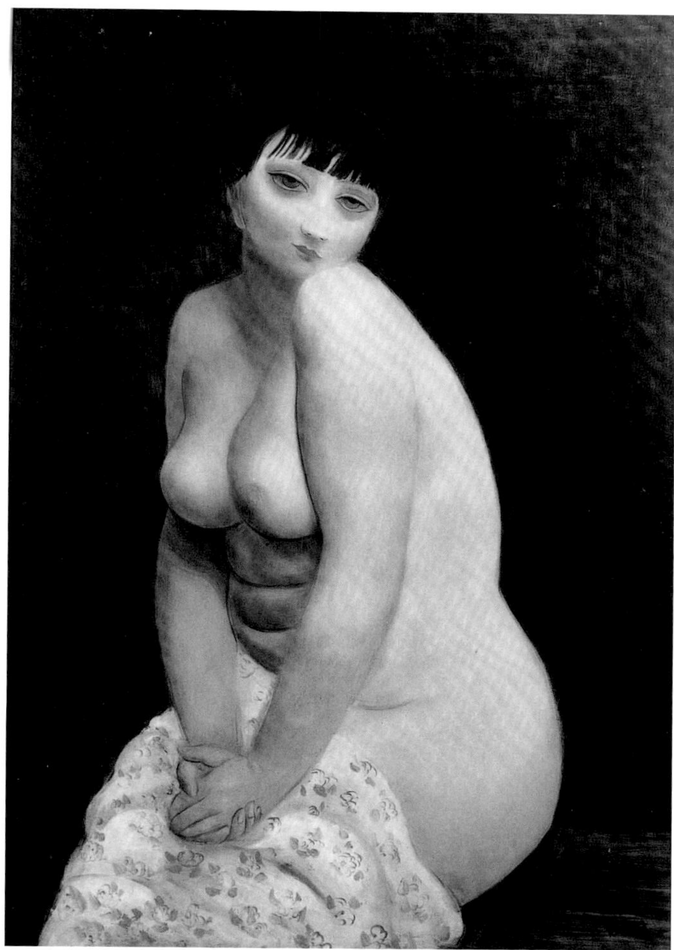

267. Moise Kisling, *Nude*, 1924. Oil on canvas, 113.2 × 78.2 cm. Private Collection

Adolphe Basler was another immigrant Jew who wrote for the 'Ecole Française' and against the 'Ecole de Paris'. As early as 1925, Basler used a reply to an Enquête on the 'Jewish question' in *Mercure de France* to argue that the Jews had a special gift of reflecting 'the artistic culture of the country in which they lived', and among the artists he named in evidence was Kisling (b.1891), who the year before had showed with considerable success at Paul Guillaume's gallery on the Right Bank.[72] A Polish Jew like George, Kisling was just as wholesome a model of assimilation, if his taste for bohemian exhibitionism was forgiven. Service on the front in 1914–15 gave him French citizenship, and in 1916 he married the daughter of a high-ranking French officer. Close to Modigliani in the war years, he developed a comparably Francophile style, synthesizing from Cézanne, Renoir and Gauguin and ignoring the Cubists, while adding landscapes with French provincial motifs to a repertoire of

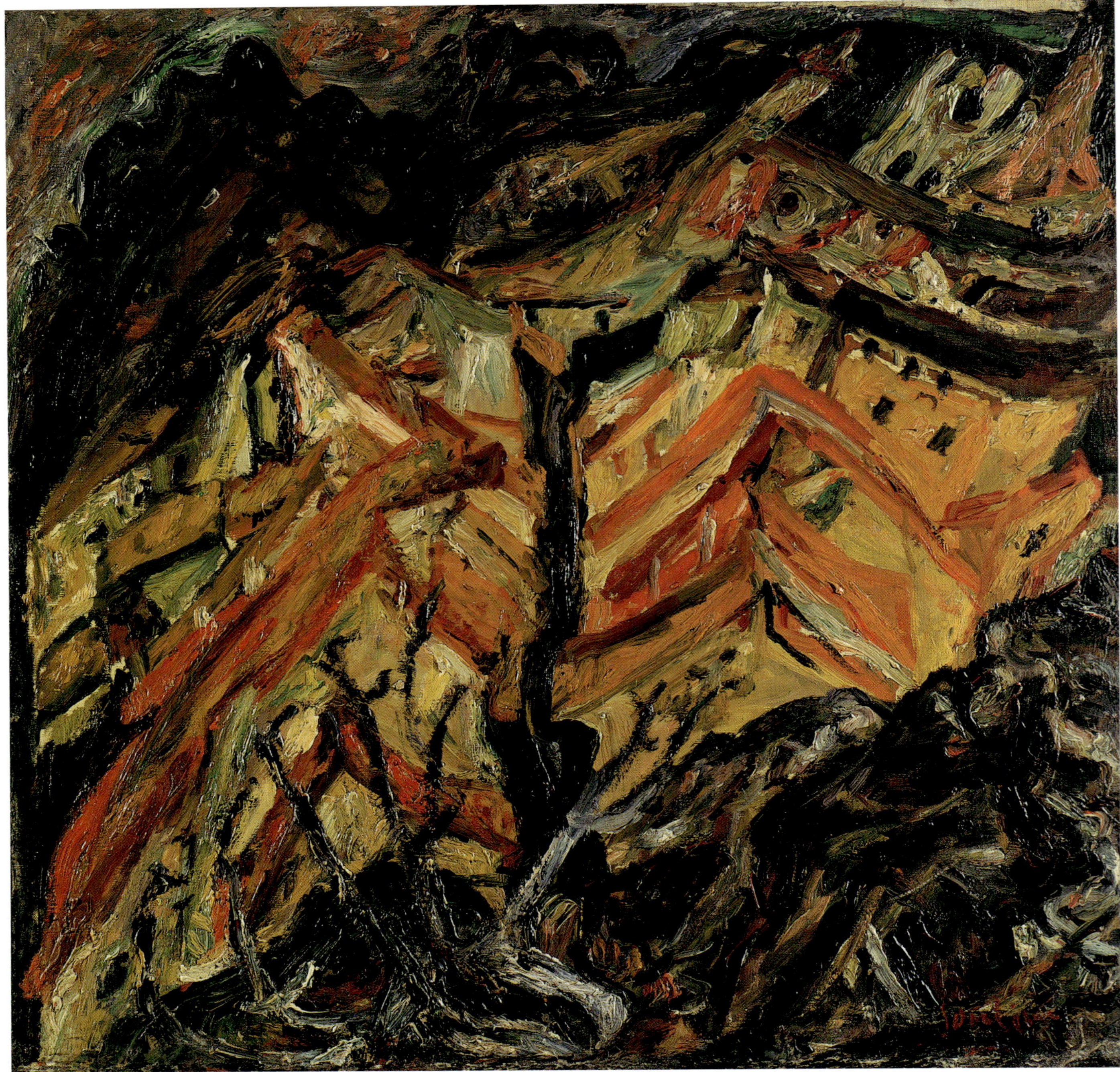

268. Chaim Soutine, *View of Céret*, *c*. 1922. Oil on canvas, 73.7 × 74.9 cm. The Baltimore Museum of Art, Gift of Mabel Garrison Siemonn.

nudes and portraits [267]. The word 'French' rings out when his friend André Salmon responds to the 1924 exhibition thus: 'Kisling is . . . one of the most complete representatives of the young French school'.[73]

Soutine (b.1893), a Lithuanian Jew also close to Modigliani in the war years, could not assimilate with anything like comparable success after his arrival in Paris in 1913, and his work along with the responses it excited reveals the tensions that could accompany less comfortable experiences of France and French culture. No foreign artist in France in the period related more intensely yet awkwardly to the French world he lived in; and no French artist of the period more conscientiously founded his art upon models from the European past easily adapted to current notions of tradition. When success came in the person of Dr Albert C. Barnes in 1923, Soutine intermittently made efforts to enjoy its bourgeois fruits in appropriate style, but with none of Kisling's convivial ease. His painting is always the product of acutely felt experiences of things seen – people, places and things in France – and often things seen *as* art, selected, positioned and treated with specific paintings from the past in mind. Van Gogh at Arles and Auvers along with late Cézanne shape the way he paints Céret, where he lived between 1919 and 1922 [268]. Rembrandt's *Carcass of Beef* in the Louvre finds its response

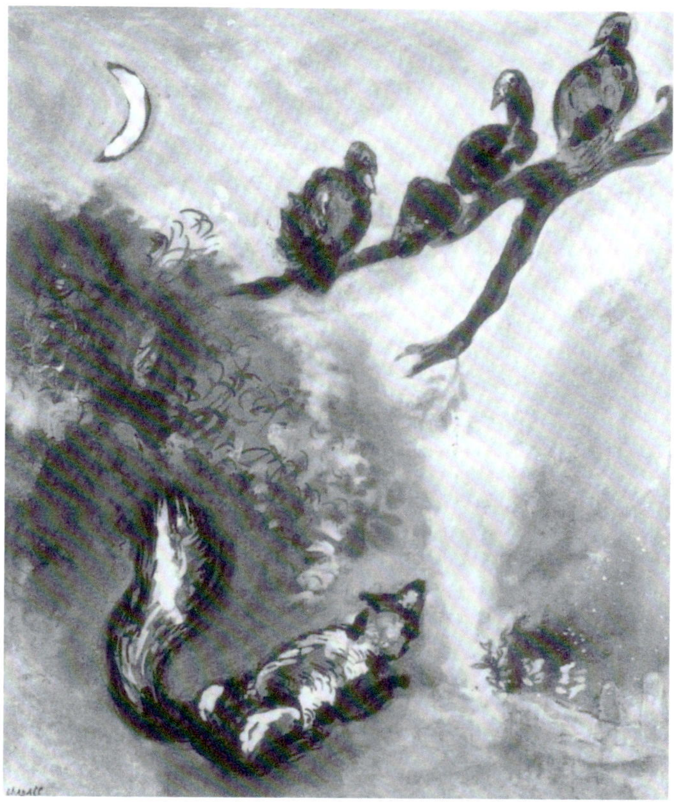

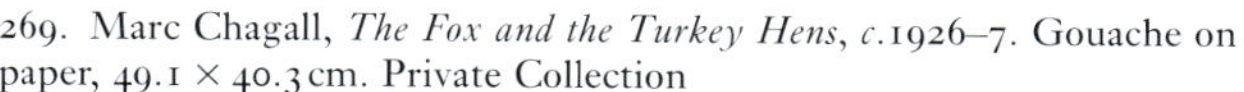

269. Marc Chagall, *The Fox and the Turkey Hens*, *c.*1926–7. Gouache on paper, 49.1 × 40.3 cm. Private Collection

270. Top Right. Marc Chagall, *The Cock*, 1928. Oil on canvas, 81 × 65.5 cm. Museo Thyssen-Bornemisza, Madrid

271. Right. Chaim Soutine, *Still-life with Skate*, 1925. Oil on canvas, 79.1 × 99.7 cm. Perls Galleries, New York

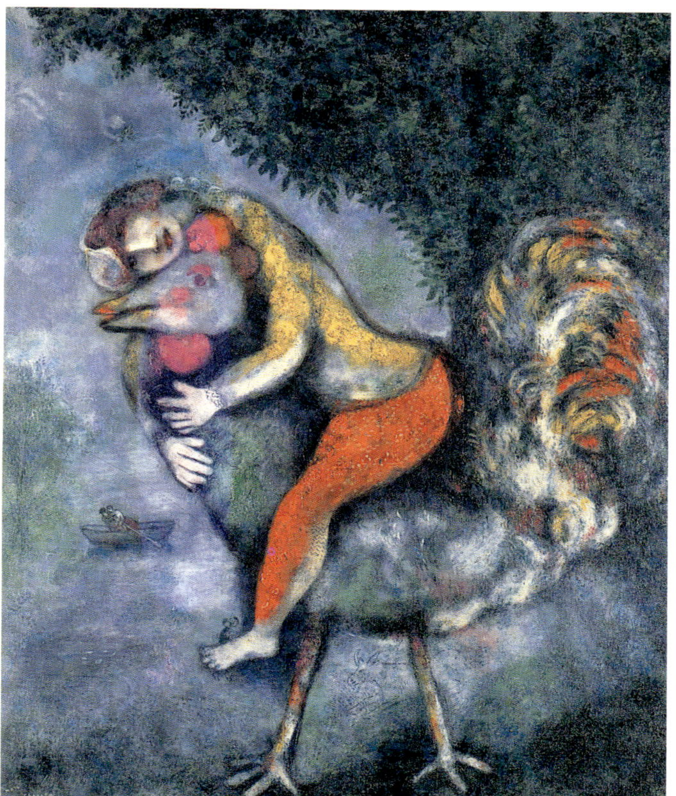

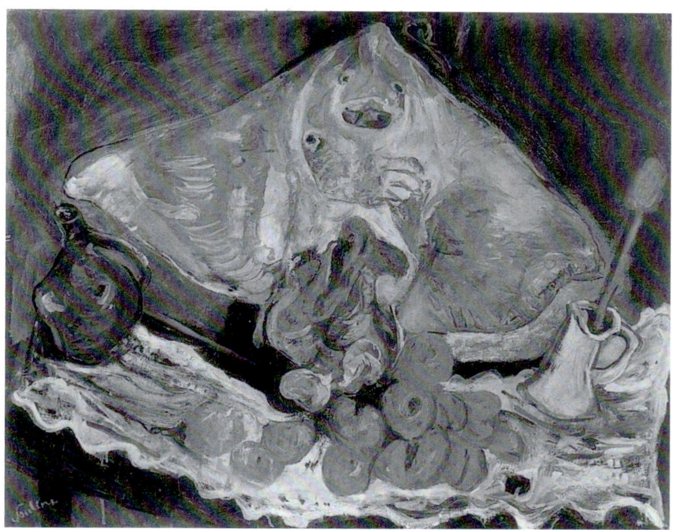

in his series of *Carcasses* in 1925; Chardin's *Still-life with Skate* in the Louvre, assiduously copied over several years by Matisse in the 1900s, finds another response in his *Skate* series of 1925–6 [271].[74] Such images are embedded in a past Focillon or George would have called thoroughly Occidental, and engaged with an often very particularised French present. And yet, when George wrote a short monograph on Soutine in 1929, a contribution to a series called 'Les Artistes Juifs', he finds in his work only the restless anxiety of the eternal alien. Golan quotes him tellingly:

> I challenge anyone to trace the filiation of Soutine's art . . . The curse that weighs on his oeuvre extends to his whole race . . . A muted wind of revolt blows through this dramatic oeuvre. (Isn't the wandering Jew the archetype of the eternal rebel?) . . . What can we say of this *déraciné*? . . . Soutine owes nothing to France, except his thirst for internal balance, which, thank god, he will never reach.[75]

Here was one artist who George was happy to see remain unassimilated, because his energy, he believed, originated in his very rootlessness. Soutine becomes an opposite against which the 'measure' of the French tradition can be defined.

As for Chagall (b.1887), a Russian Jew from Vitebsk, he was perhaps unique among prominent immigrant artists in France for holding in balance allusions at once to his foreignness, as a Jew, and to his identification with the French, both presented to the viewer as loaded with positive significance. And the dealer Ambroise Vollard, engineer of Cézanne's reputation as a classic French artist, himself sponsored the project which most effectively brought out such a conjunction as a positive and fruitful fusion. It was Vollard's plans for Chagall as an illustrator that persuaded him to return to Paris late in 1923, and the most important of the series that he produced with Vollard's backing was the 100 plate cycle illustrating La Fontaine's *Fables*. A Russian and a Jew took on, in George's words, 'our old fables which the little village schoolchildren recite like dull paternosters': one of the most sacrosanct literary monuments of French culture.[76]

Chagall produced the black-and-white La Fontaine etchings between 1929 and 1931; they were based on gouaches executed in 1926–7 [269]. The project dominated his work from the mid-1920s to the early 1930s, and provided the excuse for important exhibitions in Paris, Brussels and Berlin in 1930, generating real debate. He continued to paint subjects evocative of his Russian past as a Hasidim in Vitebsk, but now French subjects, often associated with the creatures and landscapes of the La Fontaine illustrations, entered his painting as they never had in his first French period between 1910 and 1914. An example is *The Cock* of 1928 [270]. Its moist landscape is temperate and verdant, suggestive both of Lake Chambon in the Auvergne where he worked on the gouaches and of the Bois de Boulogne close to where he lived in the twenties: French places and a French climate. The skittish cow and the lovers on the lake might be Russian, might be French, and the strutting cock with his amorous rider evokes both the Gallic cock of the French nation and the cocks and riders of popular Russian prints (the *lubok*). This fusion of French places and imagery with Russian fantasy was precisely what the La Fontaine illustrations were seen to offer, and predictably the discussion they generated centred on the Russianness, Frenchness and Jewishness of Chagall's art.

Waldemar George was the one important commentator to suggest that Chagall had met the Frenchness of La Fontaine with an antipathetic, a foreign vision, 'the taste for the dream . . . proper to the Jewish East'.[77] Otherwise criticism around 1930 found fusion. Salmon, bringing in the whole range of Chagall's work, wrote of his lovers flying above both 'Russian roof-tops and the little churches of France'. Jacques Maritain found in the La Fontaine illustrations at once 'the bonhomie of the Ile-de-France' and 'the rêverie of the Russian forests'; La Fontaine brought together with the Russian fabulist Krylov.[78] This was precisely how Vollard wanted Chagall's La Fontaine to be seen. His introduction

272. Pierre Dureuil, Dufour, Féray, Jean Hébert, André Robinne, Normandy Pavilion, 1937. Exposition internationale des arts et des techniques dans la vie moderne, Paris

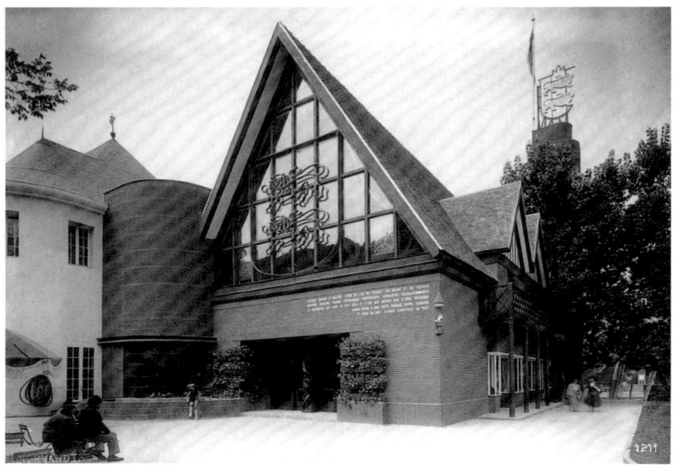

to the cycle confronted the question of foreignness almost brutally: why pick 'a foreigner' to illustrate 'so specifically French a genius?' For him, the universality of the *Fables* opened them up to every kind of response, including Chagall's. What is more, their origins lay in the East, in Aesop and in Hindu, Persian and Arab fables. According to Vollard, Chagall has restored the link between La Fontaine and the 'Orient', another instance of East and West meeting in French culture.[79]

Kisling, Soutine and Chagall, like most of the immigrant population of the art world, remained in France throughout the 1930s, as ideas of national identity reacted more and more explosively with antagonism towards foreigners, especially Jews. The Popular Front brought to a climax the museological movement begun in the 1920s, and the great exhibition 'Chefs-d'oeuvre de l'art français', so much Léon Blum's special cultural project for 1937, placed France's cultural role within world civilisation at the core of the Left's as much as the Right's image of the nation. Blum's Socialist Party remained internationalist, resisting xenophobia and working for a 'humane' immigration policy (while accepting restriction). The decision to commission Focillon to write the catalogue introduction for the 'Masterpieces' show was significant, because his liberal brand of Humanism was pan-cultural enough to stress France's national importance on an international stage characterised by 'intellectual cooperation'. But in the mid-1930s and even after the election of the Popular Front in 1936, there were continuous detonations of xenophobic violence against foreign workers from within the socialist and communist labour movements, and, most remarkable of all, the French Communist Party, dogged partisan of internationalism since its formation in 1920, veered towards a decisively nationalist identification with the 'French tradition' in 1936–7.[80]

This can be considered as simply opportunism, but nothing could better demonstrate the pulling power of the idea of tradition in France across all sectors of opinion by that date. Maurice Thorez, leader of the party, not only extended his 'hand' to his old enemies on the Left and in the Radical centre, but publicly embraced the Republic and the Tricolore. In 1936 Aragon spoke of taking back the idea of the nation that Maurice Barrès had 'audaciously arrogated' for the Right. And Paul Vaillant-Couturier, editor of *L'Humanité*, addressed the party's Central Committee on its duty to ensure the continuity of 'generous, welcoming, all-embracing, shining France, all measure and taste', whose 'traditional humanism draws its energies from its roots plunged deep into the earth . . .'. At the Second International Congress of Writers in 1937, he reached a climax unimaginable for a Communist less than half a decade before: 'My blue-eyed France, my France of Joan of Arc and Maurice Chevalier'.[81] This was a rhetoric now of the extreme Left as well as the extreme Right, as mass politics focused from both directions at once on the nationalist centre.

By 1937 this was true too of the rhetoric of regionalism, for at the International Exhibition regionalism, still steeped in conservative social and cultural values, confirmed its weight as an ideology not exclusively of the Right but of the radical centre and the Left too. As France slowly made the transition from a predominantly rural to a predominantly urban society in the 1930s, strong political and cultural forces combined to conserve its image as a nation defined by its pre-industrial territories and its rural peoples, thus consolidating the growing hostility to foreigners. Albert Sarraut's colonialist ambition to preserve 'native' traditions while modernising from the centre, was duplicated by Radical policy at home. He himself is typical as a moderniser from the Radical Party whose deepest idea of France remained untouched by modernity. Speaking at the funeral of the Radical senator Jean Durand in 1936, he quoted approvingly from Durand: 'When I want to picture the Republic for myself in my dreams, I see her as a beautiful peasant woman from home, her forehead high, her cheeks fresh, her breasts firm, who walks strongly across the furrows where her hand scatters fistfuls of grain from which will rise splendid shoots.' This is the late nineteenth-century image of the Republic as Marianne the sower: a France organically growing out of her 'pays' and her past.[82]

Despite the glamorous spectacle of science and technology offered by, for instance, the Palais de la Découverte and the Aeronautical Pavilion at the 1937 Exhibition [12], a special effort was made to show the world the diversity and rootedness of regional France in order to substantiate the Radicals' case for preserving local craft traditions at the same time as opening the countryside to modernisation. Behind this strategy was the civil servant given overall charge of the Exhibition in 1934, Edmond Labbé, very much a Radical in his sympathies. Labbé had run the national programme of specialist craft training in the regions from 1919; he was an active regionalist, ardently committed to preserving the artisanal crafts in the country against factory methods.[83] His major initiatives in 1937, the Centre Régional, the Centre Artisanal and the Centre Rural, constituted a grand demonstration of the hope for a future of 'petits pays' preserving a Vidalian France shaped by the interaction of peoples and geographies. The vision was of local vernacular styles using local crafts and materials in tastefully modernised forms, as in the Normandy Pavilion in the Centre Régional [272], or as in the juxtaposition of regional vernacular village buildings and modern grain silos in the Centre Rural.[84]

Regionalism could sustain a variant of fascism to the far Right of Sarraut and Labbé, with Henri Dorgères' Green Shirts of the 1930s. By 1937, it had also been taken up on the far Left, becoming just as politically polysemic as the idea of the French tradition in art. The Congress of the French Communist Party that year was held at Arles in Provence, and made a great show of celebrating Frédéric Mistral and the Provençal poets of the literary society the Félibrige, heroes of Action française from the 1900s. 'These sunlit treasures,' announced *l'Humanité*, 'are not the private property of MM.Daudet and Maurras'.[85] Already by 1937, Jean Giono, the hugely popular regionalist novelist, had been elected honorary president of the Marseilles Maison de la culture. Indeed, the major museological initiative from the Left during the Popular Front's brief period in power was a regionalist and folkloric enterprise, Georges-Henri Rivière's brainchild, the Musée des Arts et Traditions Populaires, which opened in embryo form alongside the Musée des Monuments Français in the Palais de Chaillot. Rivière's

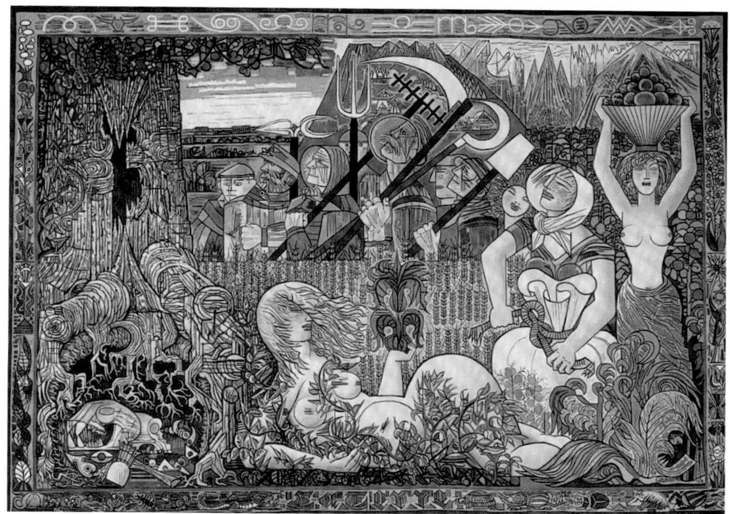

273. Marcel Gromaire, *The Earth*, 1939–43. Tapestry, Mobilier national, Paris

mission, as he repeatedly underlined, was not merely to collect and display the artefacts of rural 'traditions', but to record ways of life in town as well as country, and the penetration of the urban into the rural. He brought an up-to-date ethnographic modernism to bear on Sarraut's rural France, one grounded in socialist values.[86]

When in 1938, Jean Cassou backed Jean Lurçat's idea of reviving tapestry as a popular public art by reorganising the State-run 'Manufactures Nationales', the first cartoons designed for this Popular Front initiative took subjects with strong regionalist associations. Marcel Gromaire, who was, as we have seen, a painter who moved between town and country, was among those commissioned. He and Lurçat had been involved in organising new tapestry-weaving studios for the 'Manufactures' at Aubusson, a town in the rural West with a Popular Front council and a long-established but run-down tradition in the craft.[87] One of Gromaire's first tapestries (actually woven in Paris at the Gobelins rather than Aubusson) was *The Earth* [273]; it was one of a planned cycle on *The Four Elements* which was halted by the war. The hammer and sickle centrepiece and the massing together of peasants young and old, emblematically appropriates for the Left an otherwise deeply conservative image of the country as female cornucopia. The fact that it could sustain deep traditionalist sentiments on the Right, despite this blatant embrace of socialist aspirations, is demonstrated by its inclusion in an exhibition of tapestry cartoons at the Orangerie in 1943, an exhibition organised to bolster what by then had become the Vichy policy of reviving traditional crafts.[88]

Through the whole of the 1900–40 period, it is the sheer power and ubiquity of the myths of national identity invoked by artists in France that is so striking. By the 1930s, a layering of rhetorics had been produced which spoke for every political position, from George and Mauclair to Labbé and Sarraut to Blum and Vaillant-Couturier. Some have suggested that this history reveals above all the readiness of French society in 1940 for the 'New Order' of Vichy. The evidence is, in fact, that the Vichy regime could never count on anything like majority support for its vision of an 'organic' France worthy of Barrès and Maurras.[89] But still this his-

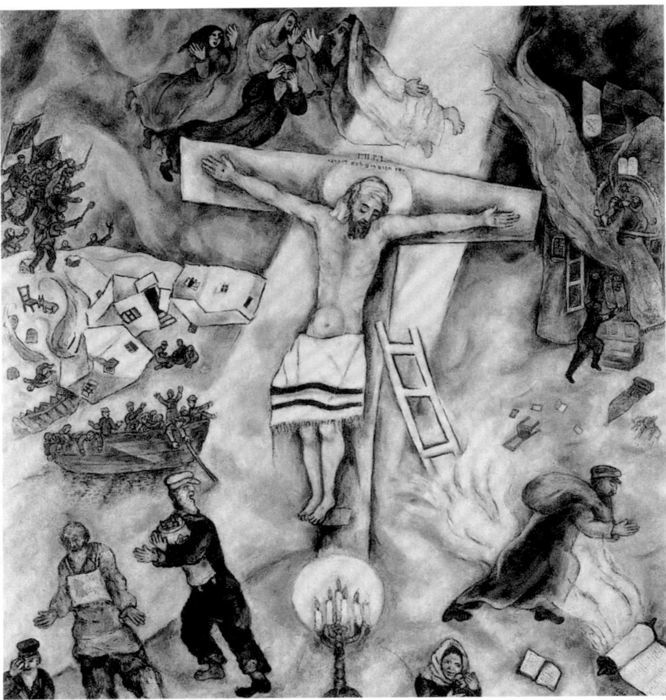

274. Marc Chagall, *White Crucifixion*, 1938. Oil on canvas, 155 × 139.5 cm. The Art Institute of Chicago, Gift of Alfred S. Alschuler

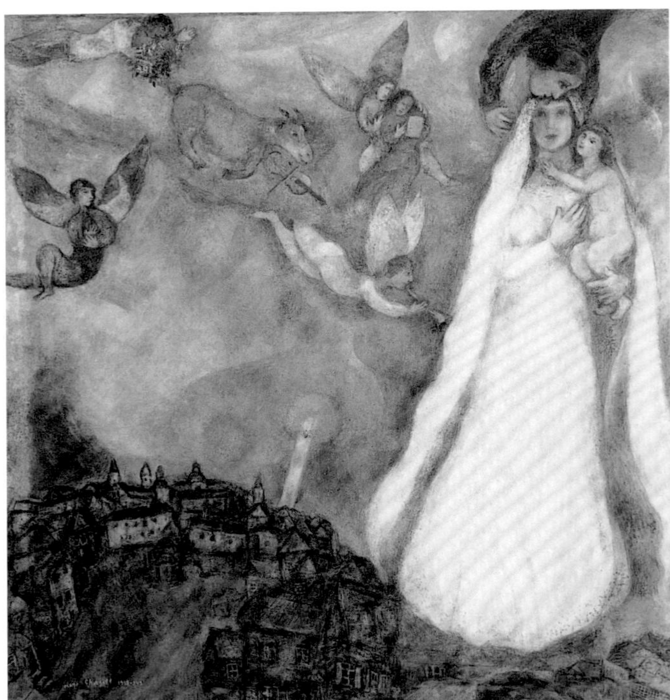

275. Marc Chagall, *Madonna of the Village*, 1938–42. Oil on canvas, 102.5 × 98 cm. Museo Thyssen-Bornemisza, Madrid

tory reveals clearly enough the fragility of the libertarian expansionist vision of France which until 1940 remained dominant: the ethos of assimilation.

These were rhetorics which could indeed be used to smother that dominant ethos and to make xenophobic and racist bigotry seem acceptable, and this was just one factor in easing the way to passive acquiescence when deportation and murder became the fate of thousands of Jews and other 'undesirables' after 1940.

FROM MODERN MASTER TO REFUGEE: CHAGALL, 1938–41

In the late 1930s, as news of the beginnings of the holocaust accompanied the tide of Jewish refugees from the Third Reich, Marc Chagall added a new dimension and force to his fusion of Russian, Jewish and French imagery. In 1938, he painted the Christian crucifix, with a Christ dying upon it who wears a Jewish prayer shawl, amidst scenes of flight, savagery and the burning of synagogues [274]. In May 1940, the month the Germans invaded Holland and Belgium before advancing across France, he settled at Gordes in the Provence of Mistral and the Félibrige. Briefly, he was safe. There he continued to work on a large canvas he had begun in 1938, *Madonna of the Village* [275]. X-rays show that originally the village in the picture was Vitebsk. By the time he left Gordes, he had repainted it, bringing together the stone houses with shuttered windows of Northern France and the domed churches of Orthodox Russia. In the celestial sphere above, both fabulous and sacred, he suspended angels from the Old Testament, a violin-playing cow and a Madonna dressed as a bride. This is the Madonna of Christian votive paintings, whose function is to protect against catastrophe.[90] In April 1941, less than a year after his move to Gordes, Chagall fled the catastrophe which had now enveloped France; the picture was completed in New York.

The Third Republic had welcomed Chagall and had given his Jewish-Russian-French painting success; Pétain's France turned him and many others who had achieved modernist success into refugees. Among them were, for instance, the German Max Ernst, and the Frenchman Fernand Léger too.

PART SIX

Resisting Modernity; Resisting Civilisation

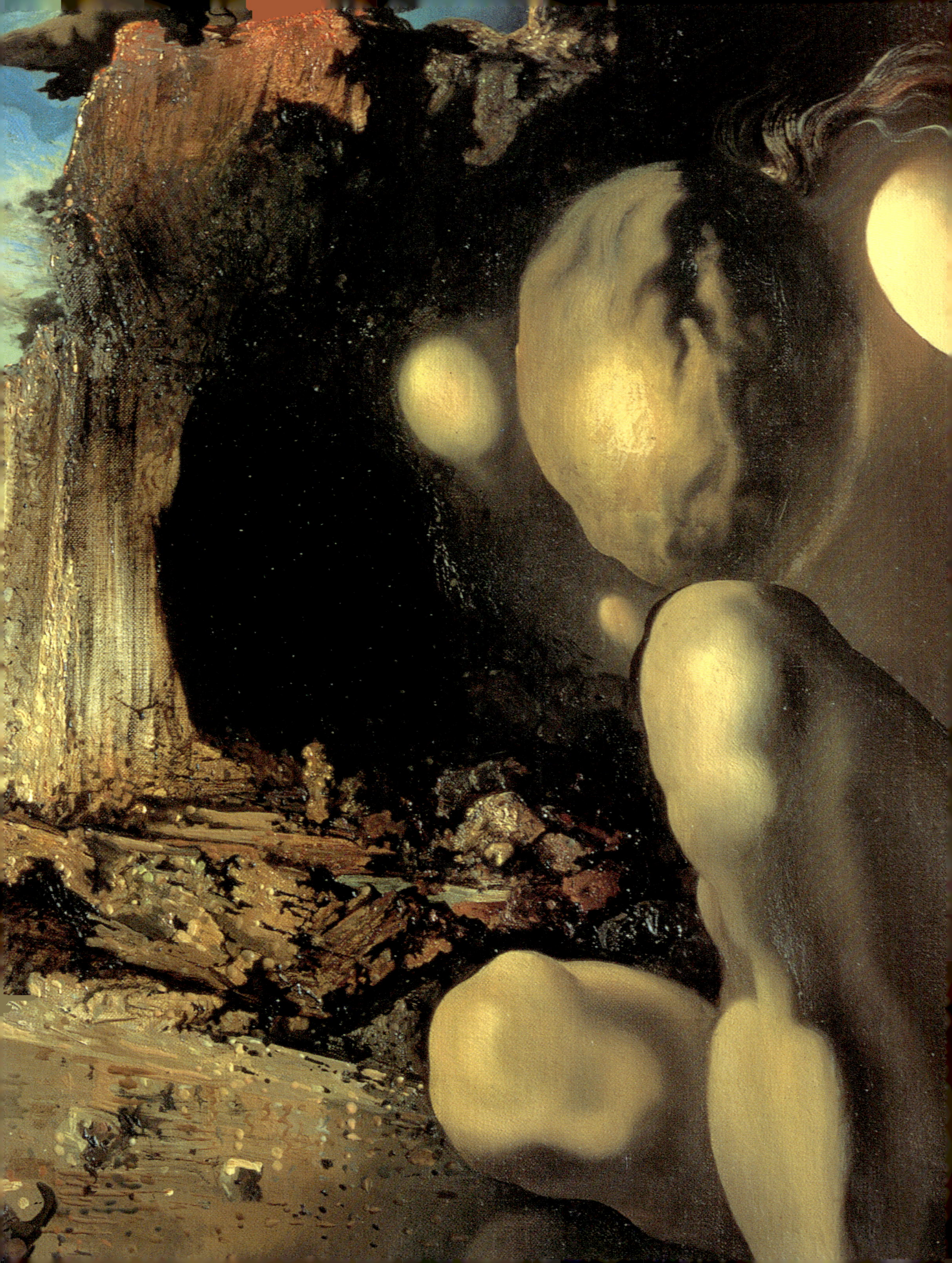

PART SIX

Resisting Modernity; Resisting Civilisation

INTRODUCTION

> Civilisation is a process in the service of Eros [love], whose purpose is to combine single human individuals, and after that families, then races, peoples, nations, into one great unity . . . But man's natural aggressive instinct, the hostility of each to all and of all against each, opposes this programme of civilisation. This aggressive instinct is the derivative and the main representative of the death instinct . . . which shares world-domination with [Eros].
>
> Sigmund Freud, *Civilisation and its Discontents* (1930)[1]

The 'dissident Surrealist' Georges Bataille reacted almost instantly to Freud's *Civilisation and its Discontents*, which appeared in French in the year of its first German edition. In 1930, the penultimate issue of the periodical Bataille edited, *Documents*, carried a short but startling article by him on Joan Miró's 'Recent Paintings', seven of which were illustrated; they included *Head* [276]. Like all the others, it was simply captioned 'Painting'. Miró's driving desire, declared Bataille, was to 'kill painting', and perhaps most aggressively of all the pictures illustrated, *Head* showed what this could mean. In the middle of a huge canvas, Miró has drawn a graffiti head, lividly coloured-in, which he has then erased with disfiguring smudges and scribbles, and brutal slashing strokes of pencil and brush. He has begun by making an image which refuses all technical sophistication, and then destroyed it. His 'Painting' is the remains of a painting. For Bataille, these pictures were compelling evidence of the force of Freud's 'aggressive instinct' and the depth of the hostility to civilised values – including aesthetic values – within civilised society.[2]

Facing page. Detail of Salvador Dalí, *Metamorphosis of Narcissus*, 1937 [325]

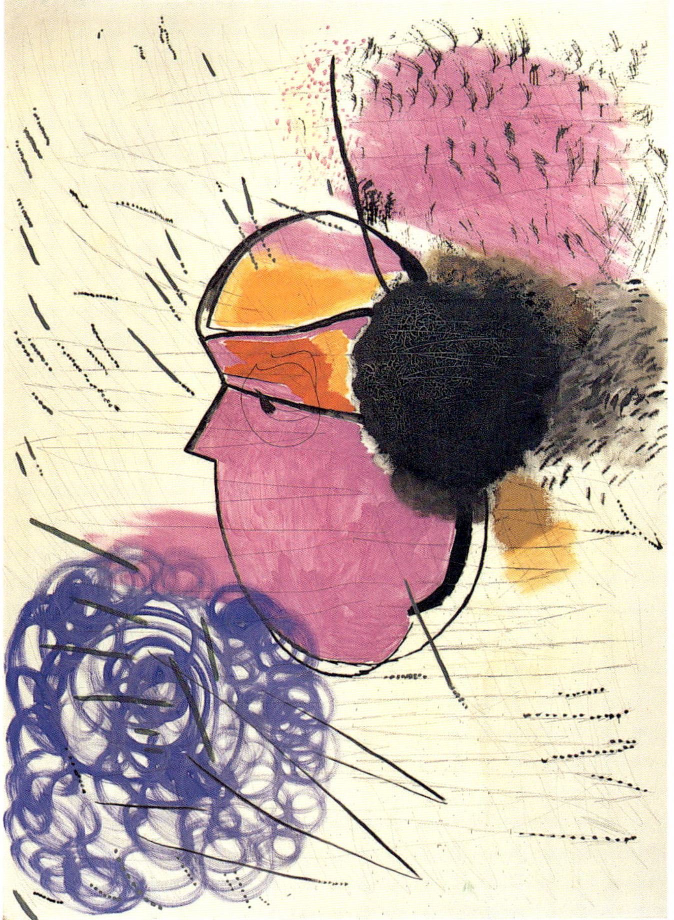

276. Joan Miró, *Head*, 1930. Oil on canvas, 230 × 165 cm. Musée de Grenoble

Before considering the reasons for the hostility of so many to civilisation, Freud sketches a definition in *Civilisation and its Discontents*. Technological development, the product of man's need to control nature, is a key factor in his definition of civilisation, and technology entails the continual extension and improvement of 'man' himself (his motor and sensory organs) in the form of tools. Civilisation, furthermore, reveres 'beauty', demands order, and is obsessed with cleanliness. Finally, civilisation requires the regulation of individuals within communities by law: submission to authority.[3]

In France during the 1920s, there was a particular modernist phenomenon that stood for just such an idea of civilisation: the Purism of Ozenfant and Le Corbusier. In Part Four, I show how the Purist periodical, *L'Esprit nouveau*,

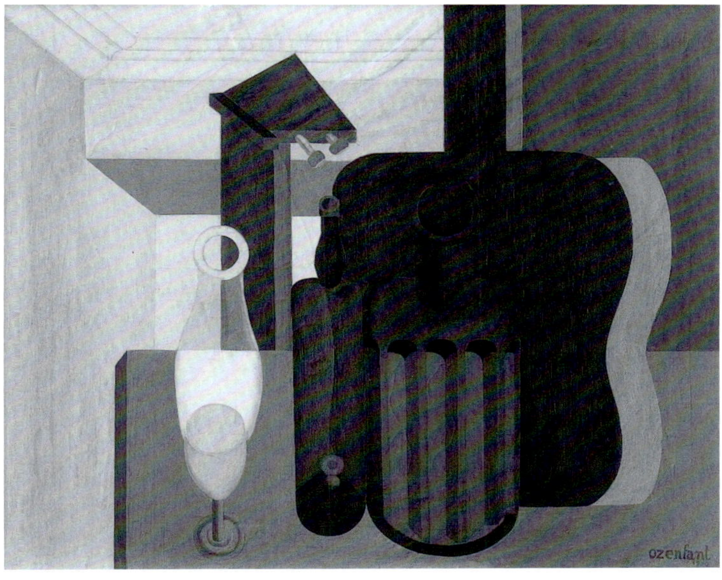

277. Amédée Ozenfant, *Guitar, Glass and Bottle on a Grey Table*, 1920. Oil on canvas, 81 × 101 cm. Oeffentliche Kunstsammlung Basel, Kunstmuseum

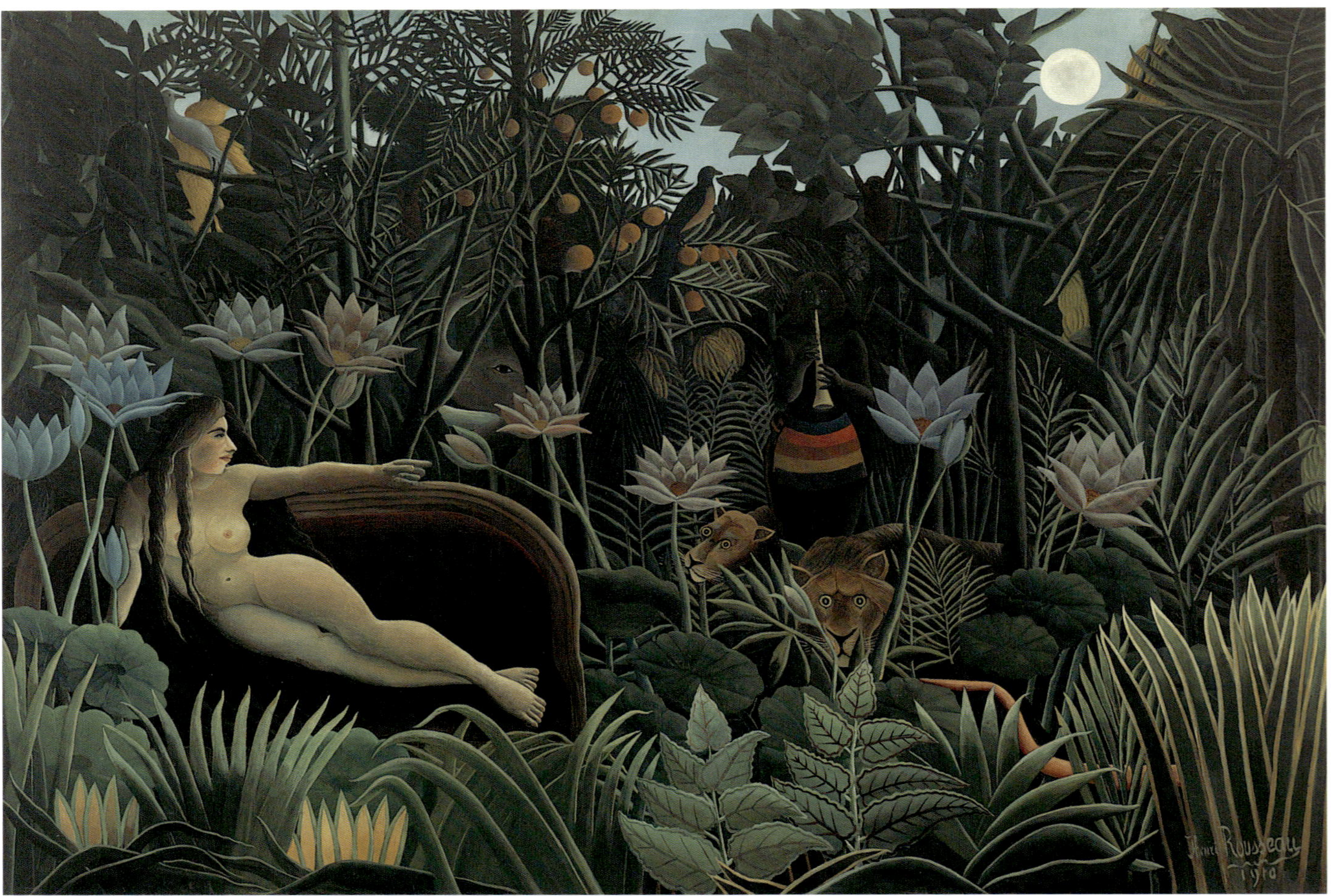

278. Henri Rousseau, *The Dream*, 1910. Oil on canvas, 204 × 298 cm. The Museum of Modern Art, New York. Gift of Nelson A. Rockefeller

represented modernity as an ideal order, an on-going manifestation of evolution towards ever-greater control of nature, to be achieved by tools which enhance exponentially the powers of human limbs and sensory organs, and so the dominance of the human body in the world. In Part Five, I show how the Purists promoted a universal notion of tradition, which held up constant aesthetic principles as the elements of a transcendent beauty. Ozenfant's Purist still-lifes [277], like Le Corbusier's, are ordered and 'beautiful'; their carefully finished surfaces and the unblemished objects they represent are also perfectly clean. Finally, Le Corbusier's urbanism reveals an overriding respect for regulation and authority, again as shown in Part Four.

The Purists' commitment to order, beauty, cleanliness and authority depended in no way upon Freud; they anticipated *Civilisation and its Discontents*. But Freud's analysis helps bring out the terms of, on the one hand, a confident affirmation of 'civilisation' in the period, and on the other, its violent rejection. It also helps underline the point that 'civilisation', like 'tradition', is a notion, which between 1900 and 1940 was shaped by figures like Ozenfant, Le Corbusier and Freud, who believed in its benefits, as well as by some like Bataille, who rejected them.

As Freud sees it, civilisation develops in a way comparable with the individual: it is a social condition in which sexual instinct and the anti-social aggressive instinct have come under the control of various mechanisms of displacement and repression. And among civilised values, only the desire for 'freedom' retains traces of humanity's 'original personality, which . . . [was] still untamed by civilisation'. It is, he argues, this 'original personality', driven by the sexual and the aggressive instinct, that resurfaces in the 'discontents' of civilisation: the repressions of civilisation are resisted.[4] When, in 1929, Miró's friend Michel Leiris supplied his own definition of civilisation in *Documents*, it was this aspect of Freud's argument that he anticipated.

> 'Civilisation,' he wrote, 'can be compared without too much imprecision to the thin greenish layer . . . which forms on the surface of calm waters and sometimes solidifies into a crust . . . All our moral habits and our polite usages, all that covering of fresh colour which veils the crudity of our dangerous instincts, all the beautiful forms of culture of which we are so proud . . . are ready to vanish at the least disturbance . . . , allowing to appear a terrifying savagery, revealed in the cracks, as the inferno is by earthquakes . . .'.[5]

There was a continuing presence in France of a powerful antagonism towards all that was modern, orderly and controlled about French society. This was not a unitary phenomenon, and its manifestations were by no means always as aggressive as Miró's 'murder of painting' or as threatening as Leiris's evocation of the uncivilised, but in its various forms it almost always mounted a challenge against the values associated with modernity and tradition: against modernity as the representative of control, and tradition as the lineage of beauty, both of them protected by authority (political and cultural). This can be considered just another minority counter-view like the anti-democratic nationalism of the Right, a counter-view also directed against dominant progressive, rationalist values, but it is, of course, in every other way to be defined against that extreme authoritarian position. And, most important for this book, it generated extraordinary creative energy, becoming the stimulus for much of the avant-garde work that continues to impress, excite and disturb at the turn of the millennium. The challenge of that work was originally given its edge against the grain of the Third Republic between 1900 and 1940: against the grain of a still traditionalist society increasingly in danger of stagnation, whose institutions and representatives consistently held France up as *the* model of civilisation.

Chapter 11 will explore this counter-cultural thrust in the period before 1918; a major theme will be so-called 'Primitivism'. Chapter 12 will do so for the period between 1918 and 1940, taking in many of the artists associated with Dada and Surrealism, as well as such 'dissidents' as Georges Bataille and Michel Leiris.

CHAPTER 11

Primitivising the Modern, 1900–18

THE 'NAÏVE', THE 'SINCERE' AND THE 'SAVAGE': FROM ROUSSEAU IN THE 'CAGE DES FAUVES' TO THE 'DEMOISELLES D'AVIGNON'

In 1930, Michel Leiris made the transition between poet and poet-anthropologist. A contributor to *La Révolution surréaliste* and then to Georges Bataille's 'dissident Surrealist' *Documents*, he became a member of a major ethnographic expedition across Africa, later known as the Dakar-Djibouti expedition.[1]

What is relevant here is Leiris's account, published in *Documents* that year, of the beginning of his obsession with Africa. He tells the story of a seduction which began in 1912 at the Parisian Théâtre Antoine, where, as a child, he saw *Impressions d'Afrique*, a play privately put on by its author, his uncle, Raymond Roussel. Also among those who saw it were Apollinaire, Picabia and Duchamp. For Duchamp (b.1887), the bizarre improvised mechanisms devised by shipwrecked Europeans for the triumphant African Emperor Ponukéle's entertainment would be one of the germs of his extravagantly imagined bridal machine, *The Large Glass* [302]. For Leiris, it was the fear and fascination engendered by the play's fantastic exoticism that attracted: the vision of a far-off tropical place, populated by savages who engage in macabre dreamlike rituals featuring severed heads. From this, he confesses, emerged his interest in African art. He uses the term 'Art Nègre' (Negro Art), the now unacceptably offensive term habitually used in France in the period up to 1940.[2] And from that fascination with African art had come his metamorphosis into professional anthropologist.

Looking back, he was struck by two aspects of his own story: the role of fantasy in it, and the role in that fantasy of racist stereotype. As a social anthropologist, he was determined to study Africa with the scientific even-handedness of those trained according to Durkheim's sociological principles. Now, in 1930, what struck him about Roussel's *Impressions d'Afrique* was not only his experience, in a 'white childhood', of Africa as a dream, but also the way the play, with its European entertainments for Emperor Ponukéle, exposed the fantastic character of European 'inventions' for 'those we disdainfully call "primitives"' – for them, *Europe* was the dream. Ethnography offered the hope, he suggested, of 'placing all civilisations on the same footing', without any assumption of European superiority; 'civilisation' was a word that he could apply to the peoples of Africa. He could not deny, however, that in 1912, he had been pulled towards Africa by a European fantasy of the 'primitive'.[3]

The Africa that France was competing for as a colonial power in the 1900s was, for most Frenchmen, divided into two oneiric regions, one altogether more fantastic and dangerous than the other. North Africa (Morocco and especially Algeria) was easily assimilable to the richly decorative 'Orientalist' imagination of Henri Matisse, and to the idea of a 'Greater France'.[4] 'Afrique noir' (Black Africa) – especially the new Central and West African colonies, the Congo and Dahomey – was an unassimilable Other, a place of legend, where the dark lushness of tropical forests went with savagery. Dahomey in particular became the crucible of a mythology of magic and cannibalism created at the turn of the century by the popular press to feed the appetite for horror and, as an incidental bonus, to confirm the superiority of the 'white races' and the rectitude of the French civilising mission.[5] So alien to civilised Europe was this 'Black Africa' that even after the Treaty of Versailles, when in 1922 France gained the ex-German colonies Cameroon and Togo as mandates from the League of Nations, they were designated 'B' mandates, i.e. incapable of self-government. Lebanon and Syria in the Middle East were, by contrast, designated 'A' Mandates, i.e. capable of self-government.[6] Fantasy exploits the mysteriously indistinct, and this Africa was geographically as well as culturally ill-defined: France's more remote Pacific possessions, which went under the suggestive name Oceania (Océanie), were often popularly treated as inseparable from 'Africa'.

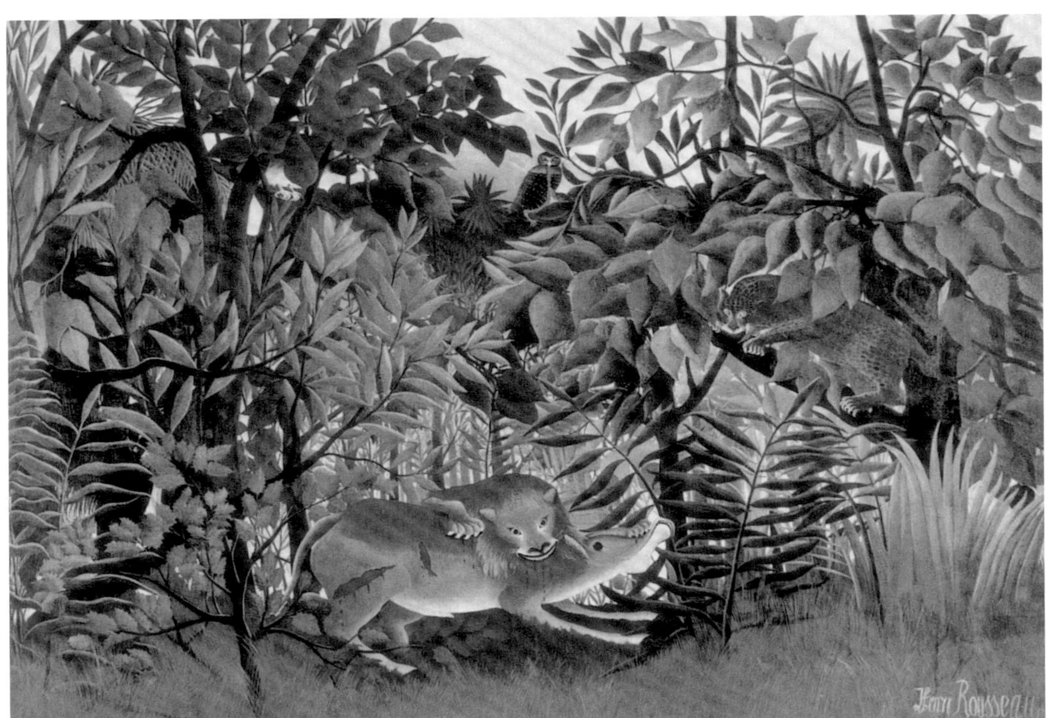

279. Henri Rousseau, *The Hungry Lion*, 1905. Oil on canvas, 201.5 × 301.5 cm. Private Collection

One painter who fed the French appetite for a tropical dream of savagery was the autodidact Henri Rousseau (b.1844), whose contributions to the Indépendants and the Salons d'automnes regularly included jungle fantasies. These began in 1891 and continued up to the Indépendants of 1910, a few months before his death, where he showed *The Dream* [278], an image whose inclusion of an 1830's sofa, complete with dreaming nude, in a jungle populated by wild cats and a piping 'native' Orpheus, would later attract the praise of the Surrealist leader, André Breton. From 1907, Rousseau was taken up by those avant-garde milieux which bridged Montmartre and Montparnasse; Apollinaire, Salmon, Picasso, Delaunay and many others became his admirers. It was Apollinaire especially who propagated the legend that his jungles were inspired by two years spent in Mexico with Napoleon III's military expedition to aid Emperor Maximilien in the 1860s. Rousseau was the source of this 'fact', though his four years as an infantryman had been spent safely in France and he had never visited anywhere tropical.[7] His jungles were actually inspired by visits to the zoo and the glasshouse displays of tropical vegetation in Paris's Jardin des Plantes. Evidently, his fantasies of a Mexico which might be 'Afrique noir' were so real to him that he needed his public to believe they were real too.

In *The Dream*, Yadwiga, Rousseau's strangely named nude, drawn by the piper into an exotic dream, is the centre of an image of calm pervaded by menace. The sofa establishes her European credentials; the picture is, in fact, the last of a series begun around 1905 which features smartly clothed rather than naked European ladies placed in silent jungles, whose peaceful luxuriance is equally full of menace. They too are dreamers. The menace sensed in all of these works is an echo of Rousseau's dominant jungle fantasy, of a place where the wild means the savage, a place of bestial violence, where big cats rip apart their prey. In 1905, the most ambitious of the three pictures he showed at the Salon d'automne, *The Hungry Lion* [279], featured such a scene. The long caption and catalogue entry supplied by Rousseau captures the relish with which he imagined every horrific detail: 'The lion, being hungry, hurls itself on the antelope, [and] devours it, the panther anxiously awaits the moment when she too will have her turn. Carnivorous birds have each torn off a piece of flesh from the underside of the poor animal as it lets fall a tear! Sunset.'[8] It is this that the moonlit peace of *The Dream* conceals, a savage bestiality that rivals the sculptural dramas starring wild animals commissioned for the zoo of the Jardin des Plantes from the academic sculptor Emmanuel Frémiet [46].

The Hungry Lion was given a privileged place at the 1905 Salon d'automne, in the large room where Matisse (b.1869) engineered the group showing of his own and Derain's Collioure landscapes with work by their friends Camoin, Puy, Rouault and Vlaminck [16, 87]. It has often been suggested that its presence there put the idea of a 'cage des fauves' (a cage of wild beasts) into the critic Vauxcelles' head, and so triggered the label 'Fauves'. But it was not so much Rousseau's dreams of exotic savagery that connected with the new values represented by the Fauves, it was the other primitivising myth habitually associated with him from the 1890s: the myth of the untaught naïf. Critical responses show how important spontaneity and immediacy were to perceptions of Fauve painting; that they were important to Matisse's own perception of his work is demonstrated by the vigour with which, between 1906 and 1908, he fought off accusations from Maurice Denis and others that he had allowed intellect to smother instinct. Those grouped around him were almost all skilled products of academic teaching, who had chosen to refuse its principles, but they included one autodidact, Vlaminck (b.1876), who would always exaggerate his cultural ignorance as

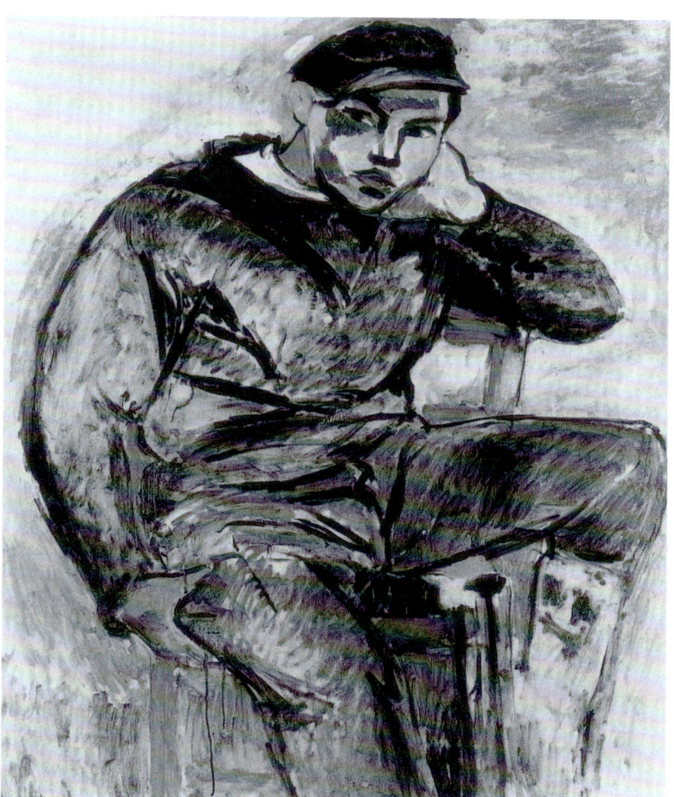

280. Henri Matisse, *Young Sailor I*, 1906. Oil on canvas, 100 × 82 cm. Private Collection

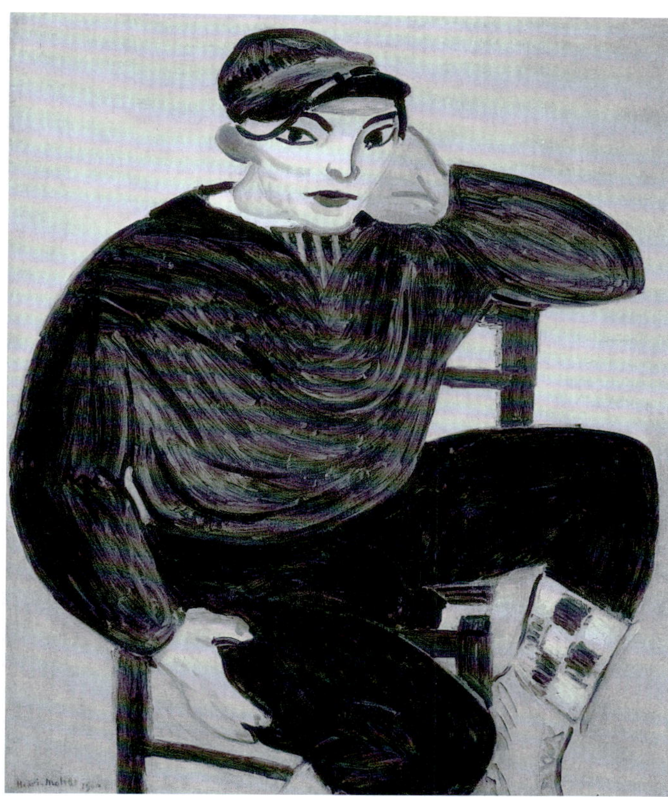

281. Henri Matisse, *Young Sailor II*, 1906. Oil on canvas, 101.5 × 83 cm. The Metropolitan Museum of Art, New York, Jacques and Natasha Gelman Collection, 1999

something to boast about rather than regret.

Naïvety was the characteristic attached to Rousseau's painting by all who were positive about it from the very first such press response, the Swiss painter Félix Vallotton's in 1891, who wrote of 'so much infantile naïvety'.[9] For such enthusiasts, his humble petty bourgeois origins and lack of instruction were an advantage. He was the son of an ironmonger in provincial Laval, and, before his retirement in 1893 to paint full-time, had worked in the uniformed 'octroi' service of Paris, an antiquated system which imposed tarrifs on goods brought into the city for trade (his nickname, 'le Douanier' [the customs officer], was not quite accurate). In this affirmative discourse too, 'naïve' was an epithet habitually coupled with 'sincere', as it had been in critical writing about art since at least the 1880s.[10] One newspaper response to Rousseau's *The Hungry Lion* in 1905 called the landscape 'quasi-prehistoric' and categorised him not as an 'independent' but as one of the 'sincere'.[11]

Such a positive pairing of the terms 'naïve' and 'sincere' is characteristic of the critical writing that affirmed another major reputation in the period between 1904 and 1910, Cézanne's. 'True sincerity' is a quality given him by Gustave Geffroy in 1894, and this was made the necessary complement to naïvety when a decade later Emile Bernard published his major appreciation in *L'Occident*. Bernard endows him with Christ-like humility, portraying, as others would, his isolation in Aix-en-Provence as a defence against the erosion of his truthfulness by Parisian sophistication: 'His frank, naïve, honest, precise painting speaks his genius as an artist.'[12] This, of course, was the 'spontaneous' aspect of the 'spontaneous classicism' Maurice Denis would find in his work.[13] The awkwardness of his drawing was already taken as the mark of his naïvety, and the overt hesitancy of his handling as the mark of his sincerity; the artist whose work most clearly betrays this is Matisse. The unabashed gaucheness of the drawing in *Music* [82] and the hesitancy so evident in *Bathers by a Stream* [84] show how he learned from his own little Cézanne [90] to value both as qualities. In his case, such refusals of overt refinement and sophistication went with the priority he gave to 'expression' in his 'Notes of a Painter' of 1908: honesty and directness of expression were, of course, closely related for him.

Matisse was the one modernist whose work Rousseau is said to have positively disliked, and there is no evidence that he learned from the 'Douanier' as he learned from Cézanne. But there is strong evidence that Matisse himself valued the look of naïvety in his own work in the sense much more associated with the uneducated Rousseau than with Cézanne, the Lycée educated son of a banker. In 1906 Matisse painted a portrait of a young fisherman at Collioure, a work whose heavily built-up complexities carry echoes of Cézanne's paintings of peasant sitters [280]. It was followed by *Young Sailor II* [281], a second version which used the first version rather than the youth as the model, and achieved both a greater simplicity and a higher degree of distortion. Leo Stein reports that when the artist brought it back to Paris, at first he pretended that it had been painted by the Collioure postman, before admitting it was an 'experiment of his own'. The joke was in earnest: Matisse was happy to make a painting that could be passed off as the

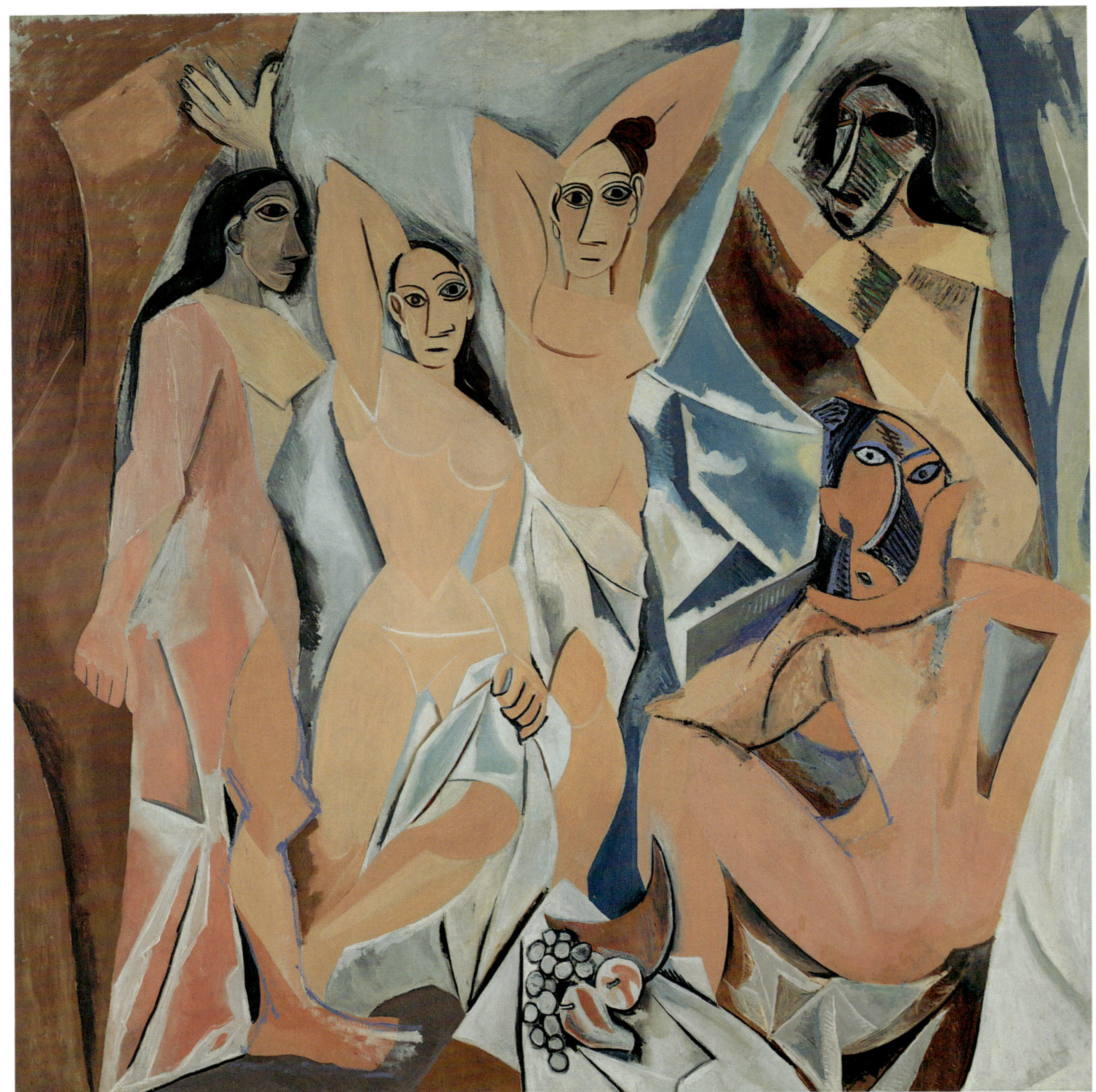

282. Pablo Picasso, *Les Demoiselles d'Avignon* (*The Young Ladies of Avignon*), 1907. 243.9 × 233.7 cm. The Museum of Modern Art, New York. Acquired through the Lillie P. Bliss Bequest

work of an authentic naïf.[14]

Cézanne and the 'Douanier' were seldom spoken of as a pair. They taught their lesson of naïvety and sincerity in very different ways, a point summed up by the American artist Max Weber's story of accompanying Rousseau to the 1907 Cézanne retrospective at the Salon d'automne and hearing his earnest claim that he could finish one of the large *Bathers*.[15] If Cézanne's naïvety was seen in his drawing and his handling, Rousseau's was seen in his 'mentality' and pictorial conception. His finish was impeccably smooth and unhesitating, to a degree that inevitably raises the question: just how naïve was his naïvety?

Both painters, however, became associated with the Fauves and Picasso just at the moment when those artists began to acknowledge the 'primitive' in a sense that included 'Africa'. And it is clear that the qualities of naïvety and sincerity which both were believed to exemplify were from the outset features of the European notion of the 'primitive'

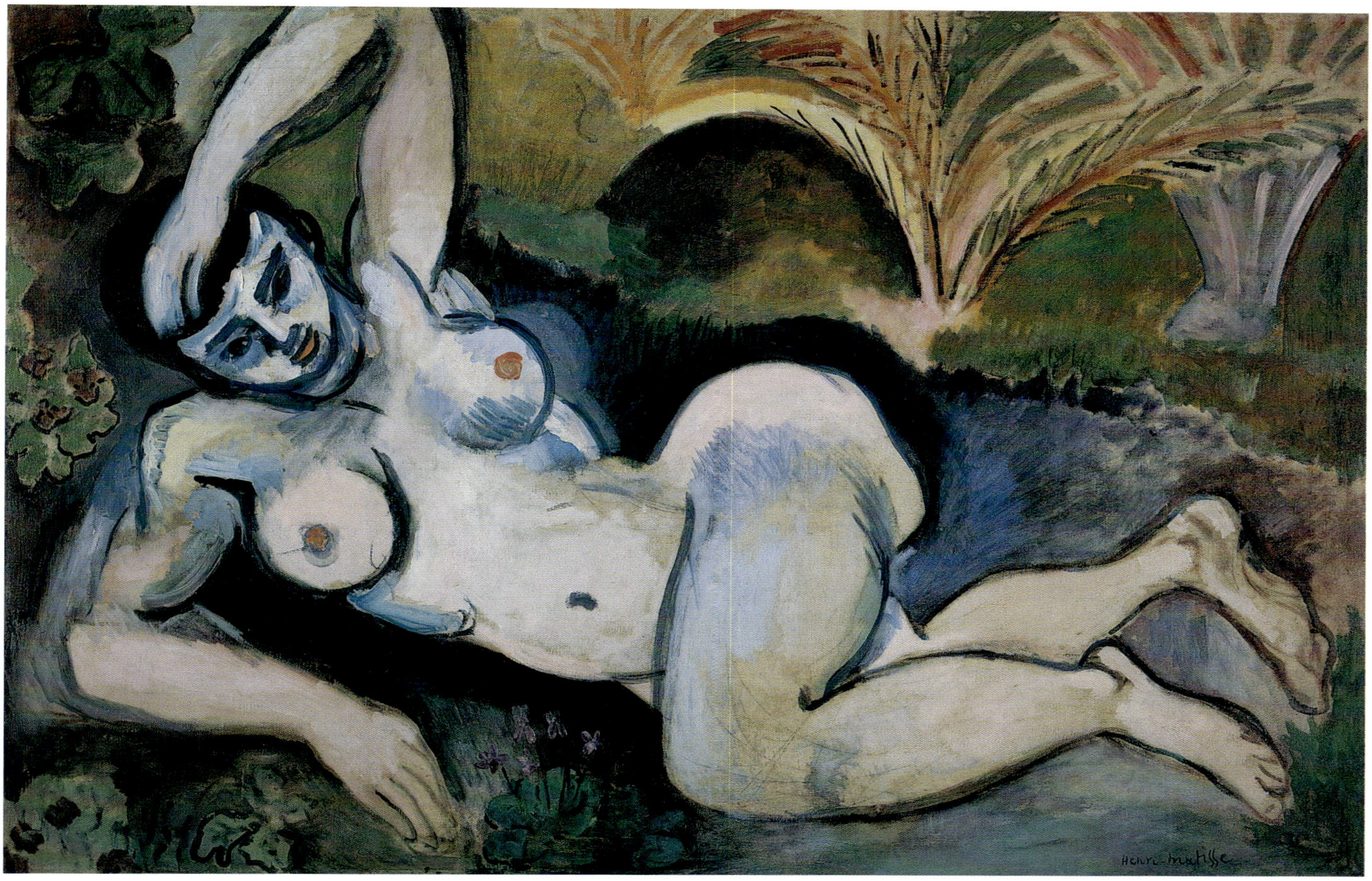

283. Henri Matisse, *Blue Nude: Memory of Biskra*, 1907. Oil on canvas, 92.1 × 140.4 cm. The Baltimore Museum of Art. The Cone Collection

that guided these emergent modernists in their initial approaches to African sculpture. The 'Africa' they dreamed of when they first responded to African carvings was in part a fantasy comparable with Rousseau's jungles, a savage place where the repressions of civilisation had not taken hold. But it was also in part a place where sculptors imagined as artists in the European sense produced direct, expressive images, whose 'naïvety' guaranteed sincerity, a place whose culture was compatible with civilisation. As Leiris realised when he looked back from 1930, at first the modernist enthusiasm for the non-European tended to primitivise everything in its path according to a European aesthetic ideal of the 'primitive', while by contrast, at a deep level the impulse behind primitivisation was often disruptive and even dangerous, blatantly opposed to the aesthetic. On the one hand, the 'primitive' was exploited to enrich European modernism, assimilating it to the idea of art's role in civilised society. On the other, modernists were drawn to all that threatened the notion of civilisation in the dream of a 'primitive' savagery. 'Primitivism' would always bring into play irreconcilable contradictions.

It was Matisse and especially Derain (b.1880) who stimulated Picasso's interest in African and Oceanic ritual masks and figures; and the first major product of that interest on Picasso's part was his attempt single-handedly to refashion European figure painting, *Les Demoiselles d'Avignon* [282]. Picasso (b.1881) probably stopped work on the enormous canvas in late July 1907, leaving it in a state which may or

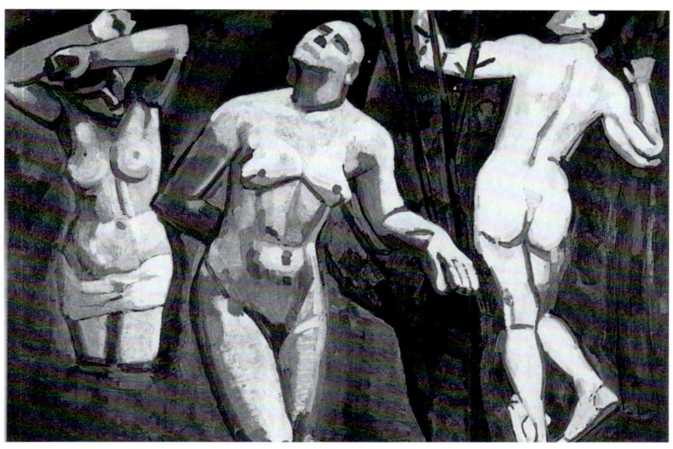

284. André Derain, *Bathers*, 1907. Oil on canvas, 132.1 × 195 cm. The Museum of Modern Art, New York. William S. Paley and Abby Aldrich Rockefeller Funds

may not be finished. This was some months after both Matisse and Derain had shown important paintings at the Indépendants which more or less obviously exploited African references, Matisse's *Blue Nude* and Derain's *Bathers* [283, 284]. Derain seems to have triggered Matisse's interest in things African by showing him a large white-faced Fang mask which he had bought from Vlaminck. Vlaminck seems to have been the first to collect such objects, possibly as early as 1905. Certainly by the end of 1906, all three possessed their own examples of African carving, and Picasso could well have seen pieces either in Derain's or Matisse's studio before he visited the ethnographic museum at the Trocadéro, the experience which later he would say was truly revelatory for him. It is now agreed that this visit, possibly made at Derain's instigation, occurred just before his last campaign of work on the *Demoiselles*, which involved the repainting of the two nudes on the right with new Africanised heads.[16]

African and Oceanic 'art' was never an exclusive interest of any of these artists, and the way it functioned in relation to their other interests, European and non-European, is especially revealing of the way their 'primitivism' could be responded to in relation to the 'civilised'.

By his own account, Vlaminck came to it via an enthusiasm for the 'instinctive' and the 'expressive' found in untutored art in France; he had already started collecting child drawings and the popular, coloured woodcuts produced at Epinal (the latter, incidentally, promoted in the mid-1890s by the anarchist writer Alfred Jarry, alongside Rousseau).[17] Such a view, pairing the childlike and the African under the label 'primitive', is at once affirmative and, typically for the time, derogatory towards many non-European peoples. It accepts the evolutionary picture of cultural development from simple and ignorant beginnings in 'savage' societies to complexity and knowledge in 'advanced' societies, even if it takes a hostile stance against knowledge. African sculpture acted not so much as a source for Vlaminck, but as a further confirmation of his advantages as an autodidact in a society which overvalued knowledge. His brutally coloured painting of 1905–7 almost never alludes directly to 'Africa' [15, 20]; its expressive directness said enough about his naïvety.

Both Derain and Matisse came to African 'art' as painters deeply aware of the European and French tradition; they would develop self-consciously traditional approaches, as I show in Part Five. But they also came to it encouraged by the enthralling example of Gauguin, who held up the possibility not only of a new expressive art characterised by 'deformation' and technical directness, but of a new 'decorative' art founded on 'universal' formal principles which applied across all cultures, ancient Egyptian, Hindu, Javanese, Polynesian and European. Derain's primitivising *Bathers* at the 1907 Indépendants, was preceded by ceramics, painted wooden panels with dancer subjects and a large frieze-like painting, *Dance*, all of them the work of 1906, which could as well be called Gauguinist as Fauve. He and Matisse had seen a rich body of Gauguin's work, including ceramics and some of his crudely carved wood sculptures, during their summer at Collioure, in the nearby home of Gauguin's old friend

285. André Derain, *Crouching Man*, 1907. Sandstone, 33 × 28 × 28 cm. Museum Moderner Kunst Stiftung Ludwig, Vienna

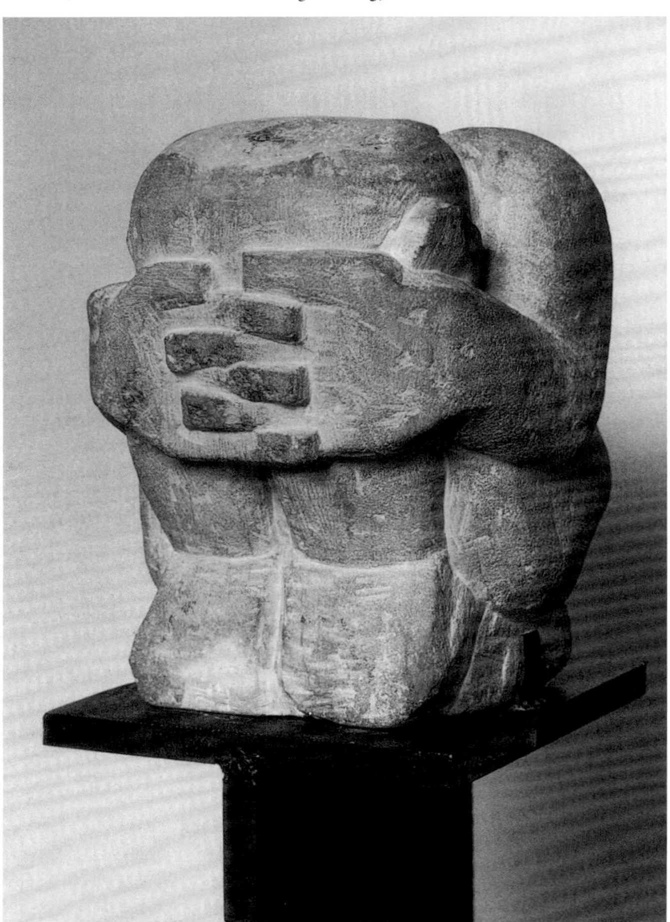

286. Kota Reliquary Figure, Gabon or People's Republic of the Congo. Musée de l'Homme, Paris

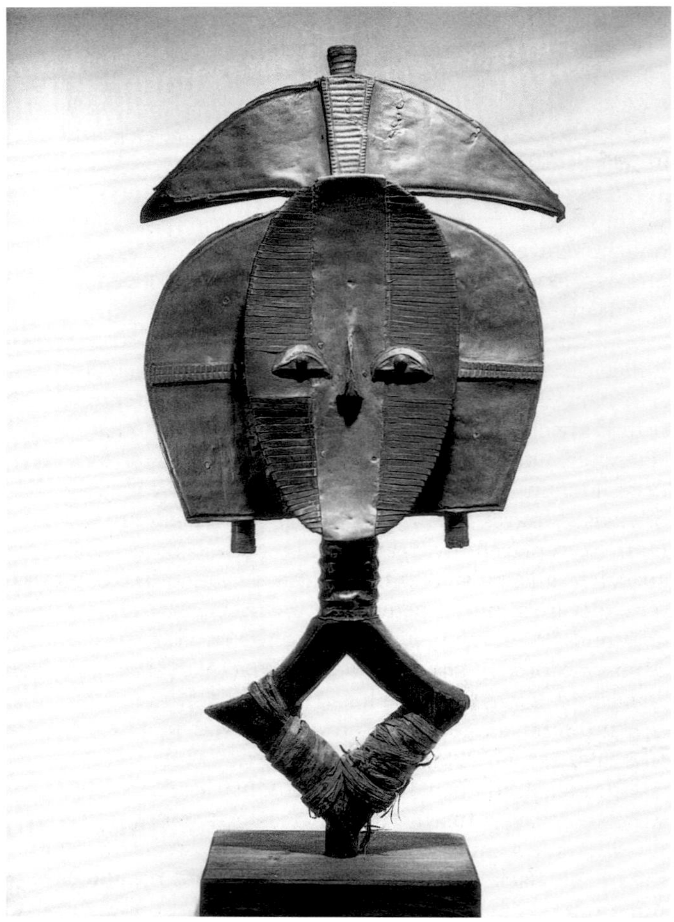

Daniel de Monfried. To that experience was added the Gauguin retrospective at the 1906 Salon d'automne.

Responses to that retrospective demonstrate how both Gauguin's departure for Polynesia and his later work were taken as the clearest of rejections of Europe and civilisation, despite the evident European exoticism of Polynesia as he painted it. He had 'purged himself of [vomissait] the whole of civilisation', in Vauxcelles' words.[18] Neither Derain nor Matisse wished the 'primitive' in their work, even the African, to encourage such a response. They absorbed Gauguin's pan-cultural openness to ancient and non-European stimuli, but retained their loyalty to the European, bringing both together in one brilliant synthesis after another.

In the spring of 1908 an American journalist Gelett Burgess visited Derain, along with other artists (including Picasso and Braque); he published an account two years later. 'Notice,' he wrote, 'his African carvings, horrid little black gods and goddesses with conical breasts, deformed, hideous. Then, look at Dérain's (sic) imitations of them . . . Here's the cubical man himself, compressed into geometrical proportions, his head between his legs.'[19] He placed one of Derain's first sculptures, his *Crouching Man* of 1907 [285], in close proximity to his African carvings, calling it an imitation, and implied that one was as uncivilised as the other. And yet even this piece is a synthesis that includes the African but not to the exclusion of other cultural allusions. Its block-like symmetry could be called Africanising, but it is carved in stone, not wood (the material most associated with African art), and it is worked with a simplifying vigour that invites comparison with early Romanesque capitals. Moreover, its crouched figure, still contained in the block, alludes more obviously to Egyptian cube figures, which were well represented in the Louvre, than to anything produced in 'Black Africa'. The raised face of the central nude in the 1907 *Bathers* has the angularity and pallid flatness of the white-faced Fang mask Derain had bought from Vlaminck, but the figures take up Cézannian bather poses and, however distorted, are given bodies plainly sanctioned by studio life-drawing sessions.

Matisse's *Blue Nude* invokes Africa most obviously by the dulled flesh-colours of the nude and the sub-tropical vegetation behind her, and less obviously by the simplified facial features which suggest masking, without any precise tribal reference. Otherwise, this is a nude which takes on as directly as Derain European post-Renaissance precedents, most obviously Ingres' odalisques. Conventional Orientalist langour is replaced by animal vigour, and body parts are stretched and twisted within brittle Cézanne-like contours. The picture's Ingrist pedigree is underlined by the fact that this nude is developed from a sculpture, itself developed from one of the two central reclining nudes in Matisse's *Bonheur de vivre* [227]; and the picture's Cézannism is to be seen in every altered line and overpainted surface. No less than in Derain's *Bathers*, here it seems more that the African is Europeanised than the European Africanised. And just which 'Africa' is fused with the European is left uncertain, for the nude's animal energy might exploit racist stereotyping of the black, and the masking might add pseudo-savage undertones, but the subject is North African and the title

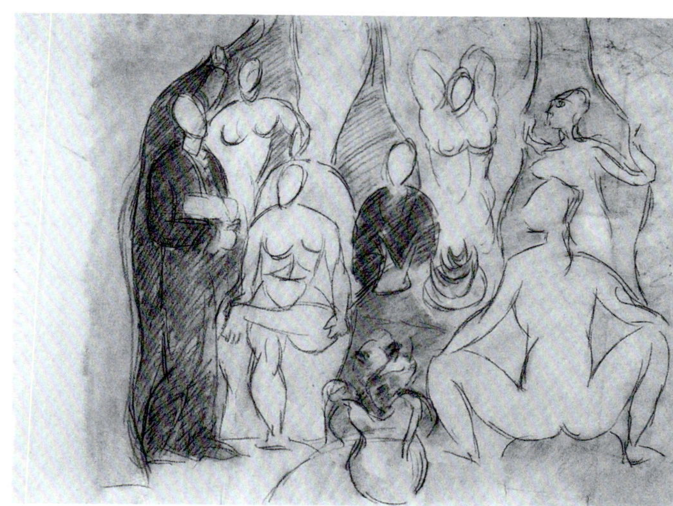

287. Pablo Picasso, *Study for 'Les Demoiselles d'Avignon'*, 1907. Pencil and pastel on paper, 47.7 × 63.5 cm. Oeffentliche Kunstsammlung Basel, Kupferstichkabinett

makes a point of the fact. Matisse's full title was: *Blue Nude, Souvenir of Biskra*, a reference to an oasis town in Algeria developing as a tourist attraction and noted in contemporary travel literature for its 'Uled-Naryls', North African prostitutes who, one writer enthused, would give themselves to Arabs and Europeans 'without self-degradation'.[20] 'Black Africa' and North Africa are fused as both are given lead roles in re-invigorating a still-European pictorial genre.

The sheer violence of the bodily and facial distortions in the croucher on the right of Picasso's *Demoiselles d'Avignon*, can seem like a response to the challenge of *The Blue Nude*, and the savagery of the work as a whole has often been analysed as a brutal response to Matisse's arcadian idyll at the Indépendants of 1906, the *Bonheur de vivre*. If it is confrontational in the way it invokes Titian and the Ingres of *The Turkish Bath*, using modernist distortion destructively against 'tradition', it is also confrontational in the way it uses Africanisation with and against the European. The contrast here with the cultural fusions of Derain and Matisse is extreme; it reveals in Picasso's case a strikingly distinct and in 1907 a unique grasp of the relationship between the 'primitive' and the 'civilised'.

Where differences are absorbed into figurative and stylistic syntheses by Derain and Matisse, the Picasso of the *Demoiselles* dramatises them by confrontational juxtaposition. The range of cultural allusion is bewilderingly wide: not only to Cézanne's *Bathers*, to El Greco or Ingres or Titian, but also to ancient Egyptian art, to two distinct epochs of ancient Iberian sculpture, and to both African and Oceanic sculpture. All these extraordinarily disparate cultural products have been convincingly related to aspects of the picture, and where the relationships are most obvious, the stylistic differences are so emphatic that they threaten to pull the composition apart.[21]

Most obvious of all are the allusions to Mediterranean antiquity and to African forms. The bodies of the two central nudes are styled to recall both Egyptian reliefs and archaic Greek *kouroi*; on them are mounted heads given features adapted from ancient Iberian sculpture: almond eyes,

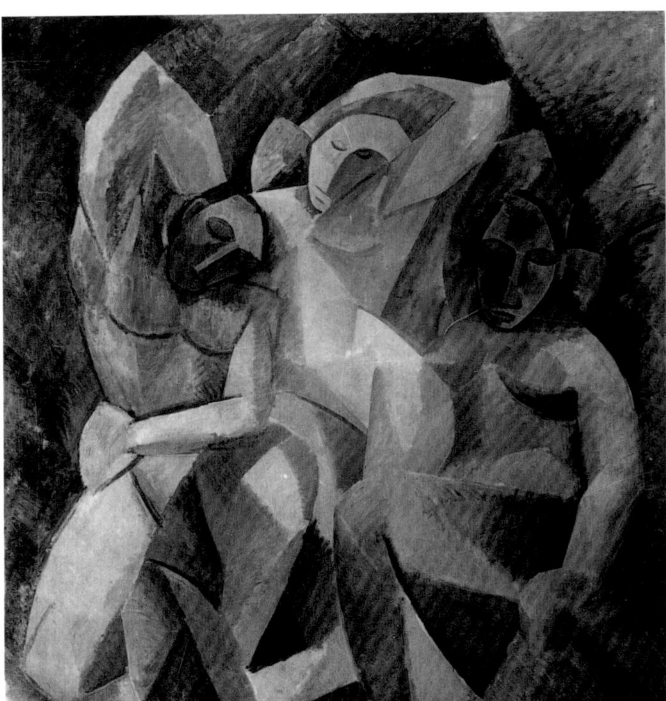

288. Pablo Picasso, *Three Women*, 1908. Oil on canvas, 200 × 178 cm. The State Hermitage Museum, St Petersburg

noses joined to brows, and grossly elongated ears. After the first campaign of work on the canvas, all the figures were styled thus, but with its repainting in July 1907, the two figures on the right were given wedge-shaped noses, snoutlike and bestial, thrown into relief by strident hatchings. The brutal colouring echoes that of masks from Vanuatu in Oceania, the striations, like ritual scarring, echo the copper strips characteristic of Kota reliquary figures [286]: examples of both were on display in the Ethnographic Museum of the Trocadéro. The ancient and 'primitive' European is juxtaposed forcefully with the African and Oceanic. Difference becomes a source of energy on many different levels, stylistic, cultural, expressive. And the racial dimension of difference is not concealed by cross-cultural fusion: these bodies, including those that carry Africanised heads, are startling pink (white bodies with black masks).

Matisse's model in *Blue Nude* was a prostitute; the animal vigour of his 'African' was blatantly sexual. Derain's alignment of Dionysiac dance themes with 'primitivised' styles similarly brought together the 'primitive' with a fantasy of sexual release: Eros in some ideal nowhere free of repression. Picasso's subject is five prostitutes on display in a brothel. In the earlier of the hundreds of studies that led up to the picture, the prostitutes entertained a sailor client and another visitor, entering from the right [287]. Some sketches show the visitor holding a book or a skull under his arm, introducing the allegorical theme of the wages of sin; Picasso later told Alfred H. Barr Jr. that this figure was a medical student. With the removal of the two males all suggestion of allegory vanishes, and, as Leo Steinberg famously demonstrated, we, the viewer, become the client; the gazes of the prostitutes are levelled outwards, each individually, to engage directly with ours.[22] Their exaggerated posturing attracts, the hostility of their collective gaze terrorises, the savage bestiality of the croucher adding a special menace. The picture, thus, exploits the potential for nightmare in the early twentieth-century European idea of 'Africa' to create a new kind of pictorial engagement with sexuality, one that implicates the viewer more immediately and disturbingly than anything in the erotic 'primitivism' of Gauguin, Matisse and Derain.

A concatenation of events in Picasso's life has been hypothesised as the trigger for the sudden convergence of 'Africa' and European sexuality in this image of prostitutes for sale. The case for this is based on the temporary breakdown of the artist's relationship with Fernande Olivier, and the deep fear of venereal disease he must have suffered in the face of frightening public-awareness campaigns of the 1900s aimed at frequenters of brothels like him. On this basis, the suggestion is made that the 'epiphany' of Picasso's experience in front of the ritual objects amassed in the Trocadéro came of a need for the magic protection against danger they offered.[23] The evidence is a statement purportedly made in 1938 to André Malraux, but not recollected for publication until 1974. Here he spoke of the *Demoiselles* as 'my first exorcism picture', and of his realisation that the African and Oceanic masks he saw in 1907 were 'magic things', made as 'weapons' against 'unknown, threatening spirits'. 'If you give spirits a shape,' he said, 'you break free of them. Spirits, the unconscious, . . . emotion, they're all the same thing'.[24]

Seen thus, the work marks not only the beginning of a new, 'uncivilised' representation of sexuality, which demands viewer-participation at every level, but the sudden appearance of a 'primitivism' that borrows the magical force of non-European ritual objects, applying it to exorcise the accumulated neuroses produced by the 'civilised' condition. Picasso's invocation of the 'unconscious', however, reveals an awareness of Freudian psychoanalysis, as does his observation that exorcism is to be achieved by giving shape to 'spirits', to one's unconscious fears and desires (he applies the Freudian notion of the displacement of repressed wishes onto fetish objects). In 1938, he had such an awareness; in 1907, he certainly did not. He may indeed have responded to African art with real personal involvement – the 'Africa' of early twentieth-century French myth was, after all, a magic place – but it is difficult to believe that the menace of his primitivised 'demoiselles' could have given its first viewers any sense of protection against danger: here female sexuality *is* danger. 'Africa' is, in Joseph Conrad's phrase, the 'heart of darkness'.

It has also been suggested that the confrontation of the seductively posturing 'European' nudes in the centre and the hideously deformed Africanised nudes on the right can be read as the confrontation of Eros (Love) and Thanatos (Death).[25] The grounds for such a suggestion are found in the theory of the sexual and aggressive instincts developed by Freud after 1918, to which the quotation at the start of Part Six alludes. Picasso could not have thought of it in these terms, but his picture patently brings together forces of attraction and repulsion, desire and violence, in a way open to such an analysis, and implicates in this confrontation the European and the non-European experienced as a potentially catastrophic meeting of opposites.

What then did Picasso's simultaneous affirmation of cultural and sexual difference in the *Demoiselles d'Avignon* say about cultural and racial difference in the context of French colonialism before 1914? The first and most obvious point to make is that 'primitivism' here has nothing to do with the expansive impulse to assimilate other cultures that is so much a factor in Derain's and Matisse's work. Neither has it anything to do with the pan-cultural Humanism, in search of some fundamental aesthetic unity, represented by both their work and the example of Gauguin. Instead, in the *Demoiselles* Picasso confronted his viewers with difference as a potent sexual, racial and cultural reality; he accepted something that directly threatened the values underpinning the colonialist civilising mission.

The picture was not to be publicly exhibited until 1916, and not to make its global reputation as the birthplace of twentieth-century modernism until the late 1930s, when it was bought by the Museum of Modern Art in New York. But the few who saw it in the studio in 1907–8 almost unanimously greeted it with fascinated horror, a horror expressed in a sensationalist vocabulary that disqualified any cool assessment. In 1912, André Salmon wrote tellingly of 'images from . . . Dahomey', and of 'masks almost entirely freed from humanity'.[26] Gelett Burgess, who visited Picasso as well as Derain in 1908, wrote of seeing 'sub-African caricatures'.[27] Only one or two exceptions, notably Gertrude Stein and D-H. Kahnweiler, did not experience the picture as a negative force.

A case has been put for seeing Picasso's decision to Africanise prostitutes as an attempt to identify both as victims of modern society, and to declare solidarity with the anti-colonial campaigns of the revolutionary Left, which had been stepped up in 1905 because of the exposure of the brutal exploitation of local populations in the Congo.[28] An equally convincing counter-case has been put for seeing it as an image of difference that reinforced existing fears and prejudices of a fundamentally racist kind: the fear above all, propagated by the writings of Max Nordau and Cesare Lombroso at the end of the nineteenth-century, that evolution could go into reverse, bringing the degeneration of the European races, and that prostitution and sexually transmitted diseases threatened to trigger the process.[29] It is possible that the work was open to both kinds of response. Certainly, for those at the heart of the modernist enterprise, it played a major part in the positive revaluation of African and Oceanic 'art' in relation to European art – a development that would later work against racism – and certainly it possessed the power to disturb, a power that did not only follow from the violence of its rejection of naturalism. Most importantly, however, it opened the way to a modern 'primitivism' that would operate forcefully against assimilation on the side of difference.

There is no simple explanation for the fact that the *Demoiselles d'Avignon* did not lead immediately to further developments focused on the challenge of sexual and cultural difference. Its implications, at least in this register, would not be followed up by any artist, including Picasso, until the mid and late 1920s. The most ambitious sequel to the work

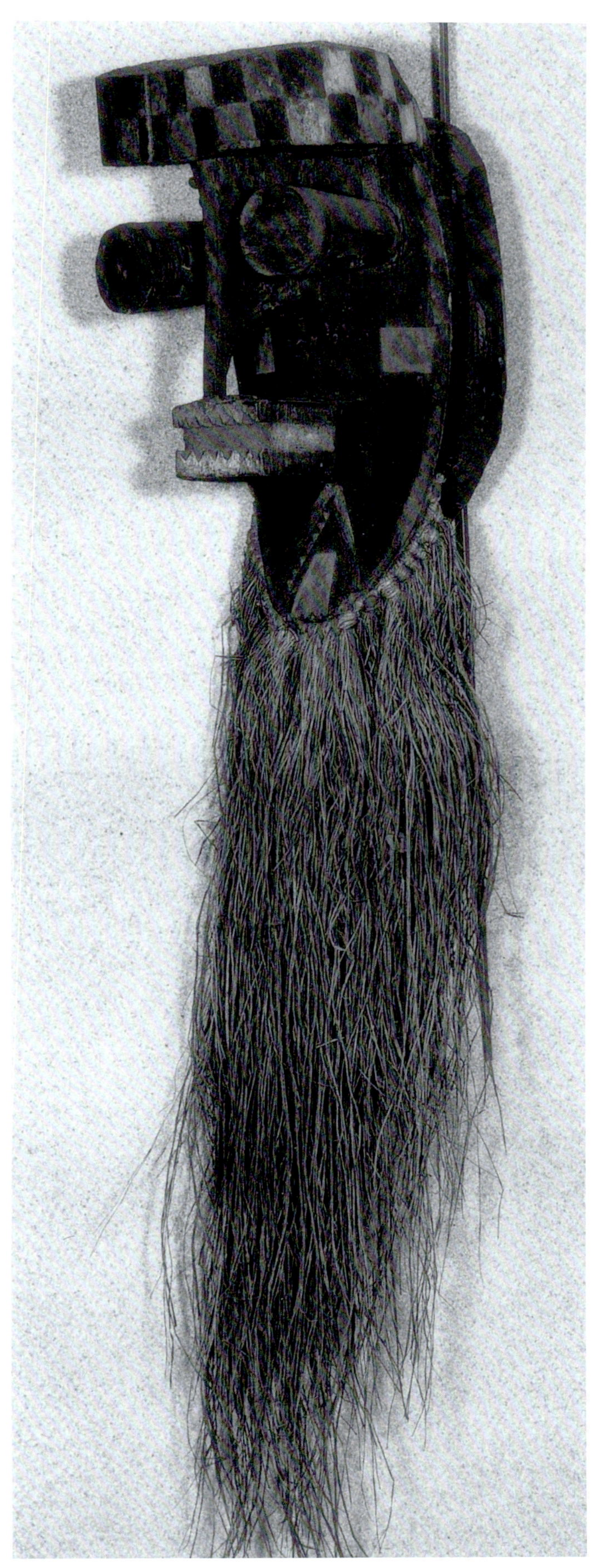

289. Mask. Grebo. Ivory Coast or Liberia. h. 37 cm. Claude Picasso Collection

was another large canvas developed from many studies which was completed a year later. Although it includes at least one male figure, it is known as *Three Women* [288]. It features obviously Africanised nudes, the faces of the central one reminiscent of a particular type of Fang mask with concave cheeks, an example of which Derain owned. But here confrontational stylistic difference is not a factor, the figures are together crystallised to construct a cohesive geometric structure of planes, flattened up against the picture plane. What is more, they are no longer prostitutes but nudes who might be bathers, in nature, and their ochre and terracotta colouring as well as their hard angularity allow them to merge with the rocks around them. Sexuality and the 'primitive' are brought together again, but now in what reads as an image of origins and of the instinctual as a natural force. Picasso here anticipated the overt modernisation of 'primitivism' in terms of a Cézannist geometry found in Fernand Léger's image of a modern moment of origin, his *Nudes in the Forest* shown at the Indépendants of 1911 [28].

It was this development out of the *Demoiselles* towards a geometric, conceptual art, increasingly focused on the pictorial possibilities opened up by Cézanne, that allowed Kahnweiler in 1920 to stress the link between the painting and Cubism.[30] It was this too that allowed Salmon in his 1912 account of the *Demoiselles* to refer not only to 'images from . . . Dahomey' but also to the prostitutes as 'naked problems, white numbers on the blackboard'.[31] With Picasso's replacement of the problems of difference by the myth of origins, his own work arrived at a new starting point.

It is significant that this was the moment, in the summer and autumn of 1908, that Picasso responded in his work to Rousseau, above all in the little still-lifes and the *sous bois* landcapes he painted at La Rue des Bois to the north of Paris; for him Rousseau and Cézanne made their impact as a pair. 'Primitivism' in his work now meant more the simple and the naïve than the disruptive and the different: a return to beginnings. It went with the enterprise of developing new first principles for art, the remaking of art as a language conveying ideas, not as an imagery that touched the rawest of nerves. Surprisingly perhaps, however, African carving did have a role in this enterprise, one that has been considered by some commentators more profoundly important than the role of 'Africa' in the *Demoiselles*. There is something appropriate in the fact that this role was not publicly recognised until more than thirty years afterwards, for the African in this case operated at the most abstract of conceptual levels. 'Africa' as a visible manifestation of sexual, cultural and racial difference no longer had a place in his work.

In 1948, Kahnweiler published an essay which explicitly brought African carving and Cubism together as art. The revelation of this article was that the sudden breakthrough produced in the autumn of 1912 when Picasso cut, tore and bent into shape the cardboard model for his metal *Guitar* [129] was made possible by his thoughtful study of a 'Wobé' mask from the Ivory Coast. In fact, the mask in question is now known to be from the Grebo tribe [289], and Picasso actually owned two of them, one bought on a trip with Braque to Marseilles on 9 August 1912. The guitar subject, the rusted metal of the final version, the look the work has of discarded urban equipment, nothing about it says that it relates to African carvings, and when Salmon used it to introduce his book *La Jeune Sculpture française* he put it in the context of construction sites, not Africa. But since Kahnweiler made the connection the importance of the Grebo mask's role has been obvious. The lessons Picasso learned from it have nothing to do with magic, ritual or 'Africa', they follow from his capacity to conceptualise, to draw profound European conclusions from it. As Kahnweiler pointed out, the mask produced the idea of a face without a single element that imitated the appearance of facial features, and, most remarkable of all, it allowed the viewer to 'read' the presence of the head's volume by an absence: the mind filled in what was not there between the cylinders of the eyes, the triangle of the nose and the jutting wooden slab of the mouth.[32]

It is only a small exaggeration to say, with Kahnweiler, that the entire history of modernism as the self-conscious exploration of the metamorphic potential of signs explored in Part Three began here, with Picasso's conclusions about the way Grebo masks worked as images. And it is certainly true to say that between the moment he stopped working on the *Demoiselles* and the emergence of Surrealism in 1924, it was the conceptual implications of all so-called 'primitive' art that took priority in its exploitation by modernists in France. When André Salmon looked back to the *Demoiselles* in 1912, he referred, as we have seen, to its 'Dahomeyan' aspect, but, from a vantage point exactly contemporary with the *Guitar*, he played down its capacity to mystify or to terrify. 'Those who see in Picasso's work the masks of the occult, of symbolism or mysticism,' he instructed his readers, 'are in great danger of never understanding it'.[33] He had moved on with Picasso, and even when he considered the relevance of African sculpture to the *Demoiselles* he was willing now to allow the conceptual to supersede the 'sorcery' that he still associated with 'Africa'. Oceanic and African ritual carvings had become the most *abstract* of Cubism's precedents: the process of their Europeanisation as art could not have been taken further.

What happened with *Guitar* was more than the assimilation of the Grebo mask. The work of artists like Matisse and Derain in which the assimilation of other cultures is a feature always leaves clearly legible traces of those cultures, either stylistic or in fragments of them incorporated as subject matter (in Matisse's case, North African carpets, tiles or pottery). Assimilation meant the enrichment of the home culture by other cultures; this had to be seen to be appreciated. When he made *The Guitar* Picasso left no trace of the Grebo mask. He absorbed it so completely that it was obliterated.

BEING 'PRIMITIVE' IN EARLY TWENTIETH-CENTURY PARIS: HENRI ROUSSEAU, 'LE DOUANIER'; CONSTANTIN BRANCUSI, 'THIS PEASANT FROM THE DANUBE'

Given the special charge carried by the word 'primitivism' in the context of colonialism, I have used it and related terms with care here. As should be clear by now, this chapter is concerned more with an active process by which European artists 'primitivised' the cultures of less technologically developed societies, than with any actual condition that can be called authentically 'primitive' in the way they understood that word. This was a process, however, which was dependent on the belief that such a condition did actually exist. In France itself there were two major artists who were taken to be authentic 'primitives' despite their modern urban surroundings: Rousseau and Constantin Brancusi. Both conformed so successfully to an idea of primitiveness that they actually primitivised themselves, and, although they internalised the process to a large extent, they seem in their different ways to have been conscious of what they were doing.

Rousseau's particular form of primitiveness went under the heading naïve. His letters demonstrate that he was more than adequately literate, but he lacked the Lycée culture of the educated bourgeois, quite apart from the training of an artist. Brancusi was in no sense a naïf. Ample evidence exists to show just how sophisticated and demanding his formation was, first at the craft school in Craiova, then at the Bucharest Academy of Fine Art and finally in the studio of Antonin Mercié at the Paris Ecole National des Beaux-Arts. The Bucharest Academy was modelled on ENBA, and there he learned all the technical skills of a monumental sculptor, becoming adept at working both from antique and from live models, and at preparing plasters for the semi-industrial processes of the bronze foundry. The Academy had never awarded a gold medal before Brancusi left it in 1902. He was winner of several bronze medals and a silver: he was the outstanding academic sculptor of his year.[34] Moreover, soon after his arrival in Paris in 1904, he was accepted as an exhibitor at the most selective of the 'official' Salons, the Société Nationale, and there attracted the attention of Rodin with busts whose expressive Romanticism revealed a talent verging on the virtuoso. Brancusi qualified as an authentic 'primitive' not because he was ignorant, but because from around 1907–8 he steadily built a reputation based on the apparent renunciation of his laboriously acquired knowledge and on a deeply committed attempt to retrieve the simplicity that he associated with his peasant origins. If Rousseau was a petty-bourgeois naïf, Brancusi refashioned himself as a Romanian peasant in Paris.

Brancusi was the fifth of seven children born to a relatively well-off peasant family from the hamlet of Hobitza in the remote Gorj region of Romania. His early life there cannot have been especially happy, since he ran away from it well before adolescence. Yet it has been recorded that he liked to tell visitors to his studio that 'in my native village in the Carpathians life was happy, without quarrels or illness', adding that 'civilisation . . . [which] spoils everything had not yet arrived'.[35] After he moved into the Impasse Ronsin in 1916, he carefully crafted the furniture and fittings of his studio dwelling to create an evocation of the wooden peasant house in which he had been brought up; not a single piece of French bourgeois furniture was allowed in. In 1929, the critic Benjamin Fondane was subscribing to a well-established orthodoxy in the still limited range of critical writing on Brancusi when he wrote lyrically of 'this peasant from the Danube'. He was less orthodox, but extremely revealing, when he went on to pair Brancusi with Rousseau, 'le Douanier', and to tackle head-on the contradiction of peasant simplicity and highly refined knowledge. Rousseau, he declares, 'was an unschooled painter' and 'it stood him in marvellous stead. I could not say the same for Brancusi: no-one could match him for knowledge of 'high fashion'. Yet, for all that skill – skill that has been instilled in him from without – when he stands before his plaster he is as pure as Henri Rousseau . . . It will be said that he lived a simple life, like those worthy souls who . . . are canonised three centuries later'.[36]

The contradictions acknowledged here in Brancusi's case were complex, and I shall return to them. Fondane saw no contradictions to complicate the simplicity he associated with Rousseau's naïvety; he believed, like most, in its total authenticity. And yet, there are many indications that Rousseau realised from an early date that naïvety was a quality considered especially precious by artists: that, in a sense, he *refused* to develop, deliberately neglecting to acquire the kind of knowledgeable skill he deeply admired in the work of 'official' painters like Bonnat, Bouguereau and his early mentor, the Prix de Rome laureat Félix Clément. Certainly, when Jarry began to promote him in the mid-1890s Rousseau knew that the writer and his friends valued especially his lack of instruction. But most telling of all is a letter he wrote to a friend of Apollinaire surprised by the presence of the 1830 sofa in *The Dream*. 'Thank you for your good appreciation,' he writes politely, 'and if I have conserved my naïvety, it is because M. Gérome, who was professor at the Ecole des Beaux-Arts, like M. Clément, director of Fine Arts at the School of Lyon, always told me to keep it . . . I would not be able to change my manner, which I have acquired by committed application (un travail opiniâtre) . . .'.[37]

The contradictions in Rousseau's case turn out to be almost as complex as in Brancusi's: we have a refusal of education rather than a renunciation. In the work itself, perhaps the most visible evidence of the deliberation involved in the 'manner' he 'acquired' is the relationship between his landscape sketches and the finished pictures they led to.[38] *View of Malakoff* [290], a suburban landscape shown at the Indépendants of 1908, has the familiar disjunctions of scale and oddities of perspective associated with Rousseau's Salon 'manner'. Huge telegraph poles loom over tiny figures lost in an apparently vast area of road, while figures which are giants by comparison proceed along the pavement. The road and the buildings are stacked up across the canvas without perspective. Yet, the perspective and the scale of the figures is almost convincing in the tiny oil sketch [291], which reveals a real ability to capture light and atmosphere in late nineteenth-century naturalist terms. Knowledge and skill of a naturalist kind is useful at the stage of recording *sur le motif*; its role is resolutely denied in the finished picture painted for the public eye.

Ironically, by the deliberate conservation of his naïvety so that it became a 'manner', Rousseau promoted a kind of response on the part of his modernist admirers which in a fundamental way actually contradicted the values for which his painting very explicitly stands. They responded to the 'primitive' in him, as he celebrated the virtues of the civilised Third Republic.

His urban landscapes are the complement to his jungle pictures; he regularly showed them together. Against the

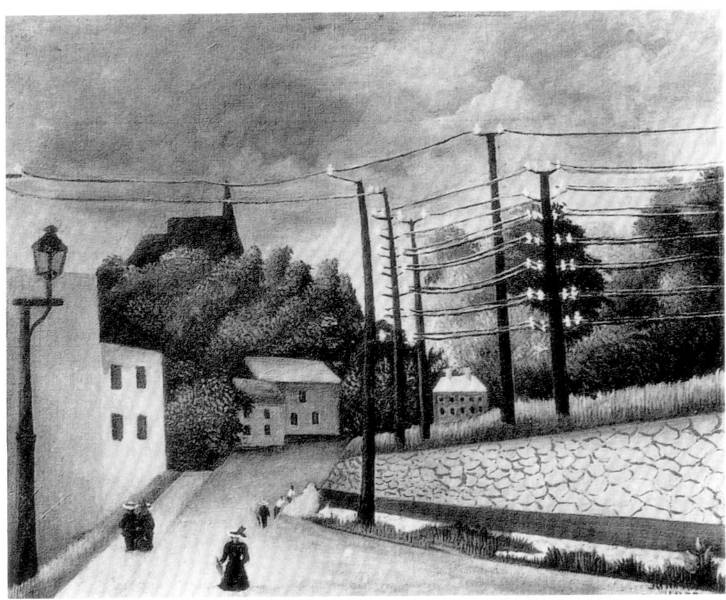

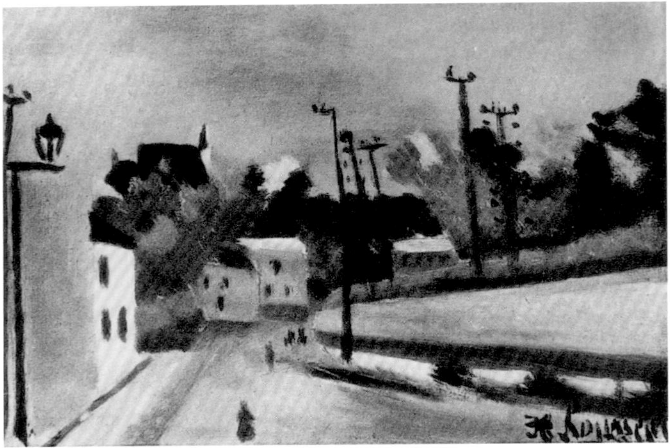

290. Henri Rousseau, *View of Malakoff*, 1908. Oil on canvas, 46 × 55 cm. Private Collection, Switzerland

291. Henri Rousseau, *View of Malakoff (Sketch)*, 1908. Oil on canvas, 19 × 26 cm. Private Collection

fantastic cruelties of the savage state as he dreams it, he opposes a modern French reality painted at first hand which is invariably at peace, populated by law-abiding, properly attired types of all classes, and free of any sign of conflict. Often there are the trappings too of modernity in the form not merely of telegraph poles (a real novelty in 1908) but of the strange new flying objects sometimes to be seen in the suburban sky, airships and aeroplanes. Rousseau proudly stands for France as the centre of modern civilisation, and on a few occasions he painted elaborate allegories as loyal expressions of a strong Republican faith to make his allegiance absolutely clear.

The most elaborate of these was *The Representatives of the Foreign Powers Coming to Salute the Republic as a Sign of Peace* [292]; it was shown at the Indépendants of 1907 (the same Salon as Matisse's *Blue Nude* and Derain's *Bathers*). In her Phrygian bonnet, cloaked in the red of the Revolution, the Republic offers the olive branch of peace above a roll-call of the presidents, including the current incumbent, Armand Fallières (elected 1906), who have been 'visited' by such foreign leaders as the Russian tzar, the German, Austrian and Ethiopian emperors, and the kings of Greece, Belgium and Serbia. The 'concert of nations', led by the peacemaking Republic, is joined by black and Asian children who dance around the monument to Etienne Dolet, a sixteenth-century martyr burned at the stake for 'free thought'. They are welcoming, of course, the civilising mission of the Republic. This encomium to all that was right and proper for a zealous Republican in the 1900s found a buyer not long afterwards, Picasso.

It was not, of course, the right and proper aspect of Rousseau's *Representatives of the Foreign Powers* that attracted Picasso, or any of the modernists drawn to Rousseau's painting before his death in 1910. It was his refusal, as a painter, of one of the central ideals of the Republic, namely education, and everything that followed from it in his work. The disjunctions of scale, the sudden spatial compressions, expansions and flattenings that accompanied his perspectival distortions, the pictorial cohesion that so strangely coexisted with these passages of incoherence, and the appetite for dreams. This allegory was a dream quite as fantastic as his jungle scenes. Rousseau accumulates the bizarre juxtapositions sanctioned by allegory more indefatigably than any 'official' painter and deploys none of their normalising skills to make them acceptable. In the end, his refusal of knowledge struck not only at the ideal of education, but at the very qualities of consistency and coherence. Nowhere is this more striking than in *The Dream*, whose displaced sofa anticipates Giorgio de Chirico's enigmas and Max Ernst's Dada collage paintings [139, 146]. Consistency and logical coherence was central to the teaching of every discipline in the Republic's educational institutions from the new primary schools to the reformed and expanded Universities. Salmon was in earnest when he remarked in 1912 that the enthusiasm for Rousseau had amounted to 'a beautiful revolutionary act'.[39] And the force with which his naïvety could seem to threaten the most central educational values is to be discerned in the virulence with which the critics who rejected him did so. Responding to the Indépendants of 1907, the Right wing *Le Soleil* was appalled at the encouragement that his example gave for 'regrettable experiments', and interpreted his naïvety as culpable ignorance: 'Rousseau paints puppets like a primary school pupil with no gift for painting.'[40]

Whether his viewers at the Indépendants and the Salon d'automne were for him or against him, they were in no doubt about Rousseau's identity as a naïf. By asserting his naïvety as a quality, Rousseau asserted his 'primitiveness' as difference, a desirable form of difference for some. At first, Brancusi primitivised his work away from the public eye. His earliest showing in public of such work came in 1910, two or three years after his earliest primitivised pieces, with the exhibiting of a small stone carving, *The Kiss* [293] in Bucharest at the Romanian equivalent of the French 'independent' exhibiting societies, Tinerimea Artisticã. This was followed in 1911 by the showing at the Indépendants in Paris of a work with an overtly folkloric subject evoking his peasant beginnings, the *Maiastra* [297], and then at the 1913

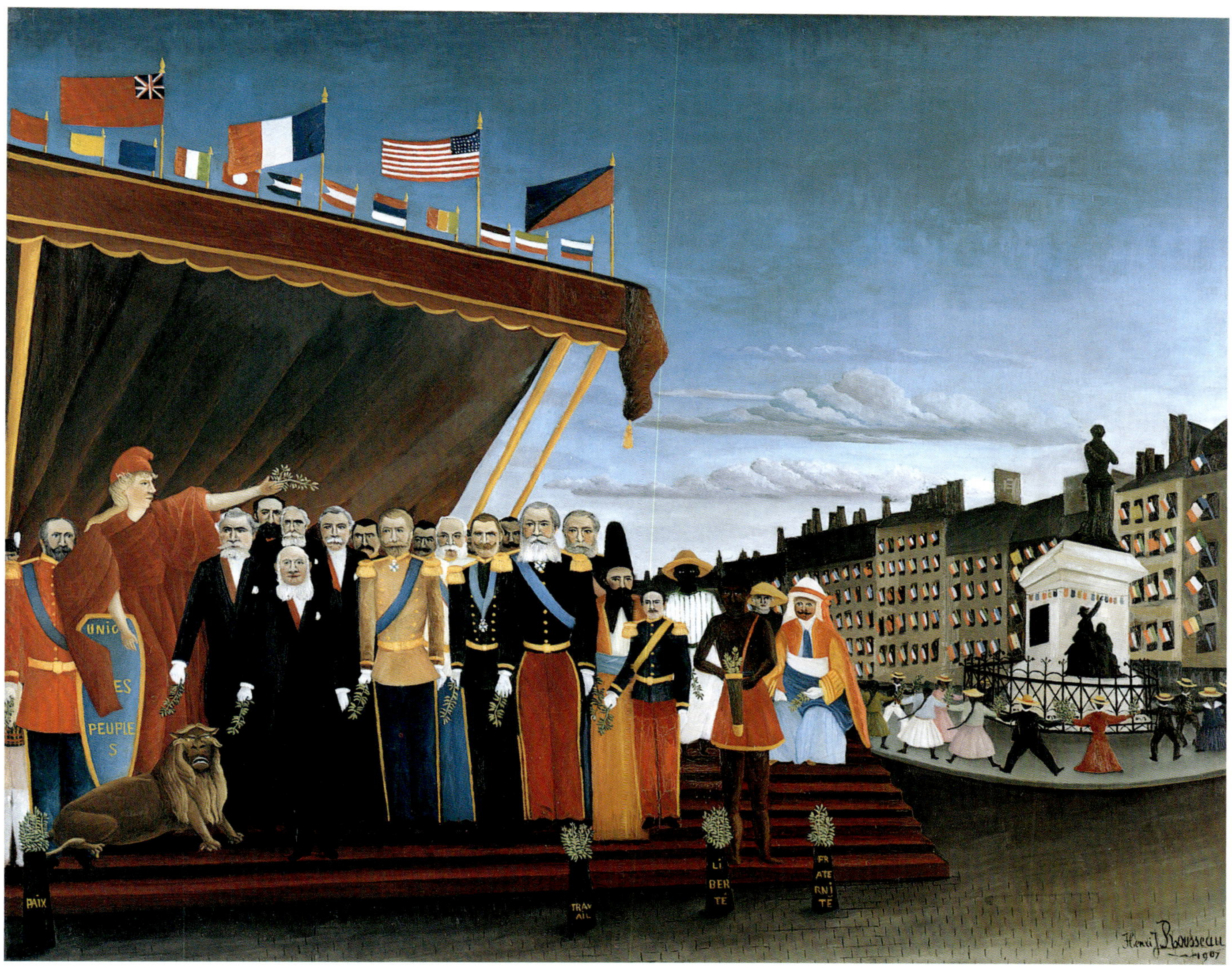

292. Henri Rousseau, *The Representatives of the Foreign Powers Coming to Salute the Republic as a Sign of Peace*, 1907. Oil on canvas, 130 × 161 cm. Musée du Louvre, Paris

Indépendants by the showing of a larger version of *The Kiss*. But at every stage, these primitivised pieces were placed in the context of a sculptural production dominated by Brancusi's highly refined abstracted form of classicism, a classicism aligned with the explicitly Hellenistic busts of the then fashionable Polish modernist Elie Nadelman.[41] In 1913, *The Kiss* was shown in Paris with two such works, *Prometheus* and *Sleeping Muse*. It would not be until after 1914 that Brancusi's 'primitivism' began to assert without qualification his renunciation of the knowledge instilled by the academies and his commitment to the retrieval of a lost 'primitive' identity. And even then, the re-primitivisation of his own identity would not entail the rejection of his commitment to 'ideal beauty', as I shall show at the end of this discussion.

Because of the lack of exhibition evidence, we have only an approximation for the date of Brancusi's first primitivising sculptures. The date ascribed is usually 1907, because that date was given in a statement of 1925 where Brancusi named *The Kiss* with another piece, *The Wisdom of the Earth*, as the first examples in his work of 'direct carving'. The version associated with this statement has usually been the small half-length version shown in 1910 [293], but a strong argument has been made for the full-length version used for a memorial in the Montparnasse Cemetery in 1911 as being actually the first one.[42] It is possible to say only that Brancusi carved his first primitivising sculptures in 1907 or 1908, and that the small *Kiss* was among them. Of course, 1907 was the date of Matisse's *Blue Nude*, Derain's *Bathers* and Picasso's *Demoiselles d'Avignon*, and it is easy to see the connection between Derain's carving *The Crouching Man* and the small *Kiss*. Brancusi certainly contributed to the climax in 1907–8 of the first phase of twentieth-century 'primitivism' in France, and did so alongside Matisse, Derain and Picasso. And certainly by 1908, he was directly in touch with Picasso, Derain and the milieux around Apollinaire; in November that year he was one of those who honoured Rousseau at a rumbustous banquet in Picasso's Bâteau-lavoir studio. He was himself already an admirer of the 'Douanier'.

Brancusi's early, private 'primitivism' was not at all culturally specific in its allusions. Its subjects connected with the kind of 'universal' subjects favoured by Matisse and Derain in their 'primitive' and Golden Age idylls, in Brancusi's case, wisdom, love and procreation. At the same time, Brancusi too took up a pan-cultural stance in the line of Gauguin, fusing multiple cultural allusions, refusing the clear statement of difference. *The Kiss* has been shown to be a response in stone to a cylindrical wooden carving by Gauguin included in the retrospective at the 1906 Salon d'automne, *Hina and Te Fatou*.[43] But it is a response to many other 'primitivised' stimuli too: Derain's *Crouching Man*, and, as with that piece, Egyptian cube figures, the Romanesque and perhaps African carving (the block-like four-façade symmetry suggests the connection). The allusion to the Romanesque was underlined when the small version was shown in Bucharest in 1910 by the title given it there: 'Fragment of a Capital'. At this stage, however roughly and directly worked his stone carvings were, Brancusi took the dominant all-knowing vantage point of his sophisticated modernist friends and their 'primitivist' paradigm, Gauguin.

As in Picasso's case, there was a second beginning for Brancusi's 'primitivism', but where Picasso's of 1912 involved the rejection of the overt 'primitivism' of 1907–8 for a concealed engagement with the lessons of African sculpture, Brancusi's involved a far more explicit identification with the 'primitive' as such. In his case, this second 'primitivist' beginning happened in 1913, and it accompanied his decision to carve in wood. The earliest known of his 'woods' was a figure, *The First Step*, only the head of which survives. Among those that followed in the 1914–18 war, was *Little French Girl* [294]. The subjects that dominate in the early wood carvings are infancy and childhood – beginnings – and the cultural allusions made by all the wood carvings in the period when they

293. Constantin Brancusi, *The Kiss*, 1907–8. Stone, 28 × 26 × 21.5 cm. Muzeul de Artă, Craiova

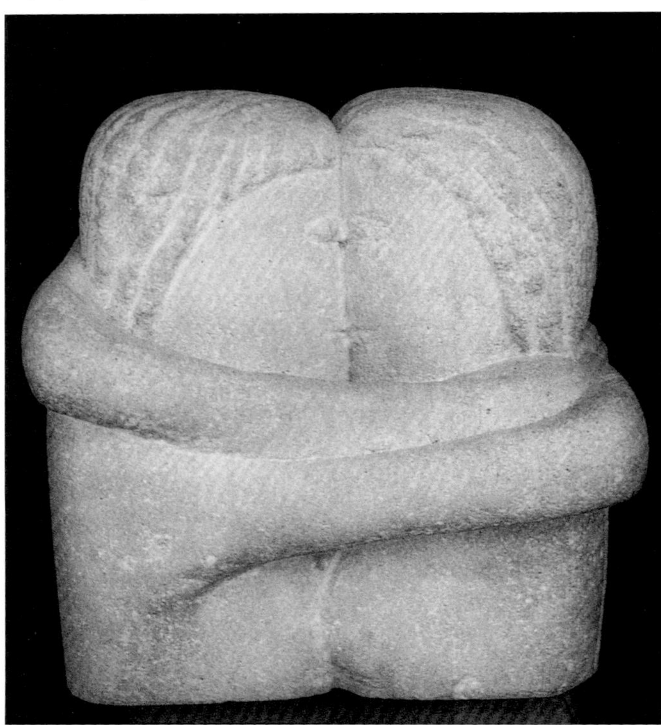

were most important in Brancusi's production, between 1914 and the early 1920s, were exclusively to black African and European peasant cultures.

At first, in 1913–14, the African allusions were especially clear. *Little French Girl* is not specific in its African references, although striking similarities have been found between it and a Senufo helmet mask; but however generalised the references, the 'Africanness' of the work is overwhelming.[44] The later figures that Brancusi developed on the basis of this piece, *Plato* and *Socrates* [298, 295], are in this sense African too, but during the 1914–18 war he became less at ease with such invocations of 'Africa', and this seems to have been the reason for the destruction of the torso and limbs of *First Step*. It was now that Romania and Brancusi's peasant identity came into its own. His engagement with woodcarving in emulation of the 'primitive' in the carving traditions of black Africa opened the way to a complete reassessment of his own identity as a highly trained, widely knowledgeable sculptor in Paris. He was able to appreciate fully the profound importance to him as a modernist of the values he associated with the peasant culture he had once rejected.

When he began to make aphoristic statements for the record, during the 1920s, carving as the key to truth, simplicity as essence, and the natural as against the artificial became ever-present themes in them, always expressed in the elementary language of proverbs. Direct carving is 'the true road to sculpture, but the worst for those who have not learned how to walk,' says one of his four aphorisms in the catalogue of his 1926 New York exhibition. 'In art, one does not aim for simplicity', says another, 'one achieves it unintentionally as one gets closer to the real meaning of things'.[45] His skill and 'honesty' as a carver was by then widely associated with his Romanian peasant identity, which he was happy to relate to his primitivised idea of Africa. In 1927, he told an American journalist that the affinity he felt with African carving came of the fact that, like his work, it had 'the look of being made . . . by one inside of things, who stands on the ground an equal among rocks, trees, people, beasts, and plants, never above or apart from them'.[46]

The primitivisation of Brancusi's own surroundings was triggered thus by the convergence of an idea of Africa with memories of a peasant childhood in Romania, the two concretised in the form of woodcarving, its practice as well as its forms. That process of renunciation and retrieval began in 1915 with the carving of a bench and a gateway using oak beams salvaged from demolition sites. Neither merely imitated the peasant forms of the Gorj region of Romania, but both are plainly artisanal artefacts in tune with peasant ways. There followed in January 1916 Brancusi's move from 54, rue du Montparnasse to 8, Impasse Ronsin, and the comprehensive primitivisation of his studio as a Romanian peasant world for him to live in. 'Africa', as something new in Paris which belonged to no modernist exclusively, showed

294. Constantin Brancusi, *Little French Girl*, *c.*1914–18. Oak, 124.5 × 22.2 × 21.6 cm. Solomon R. Guggenheim Museum, New York. Gift, Estate of Katherine S. Dreier, 1953

295. Constantin Brancusi, *Socrates*, 1922. Oak, h. 130.2 cm. The Museum of Modern Art, New York. Mrs Simon Guggenheim Fund

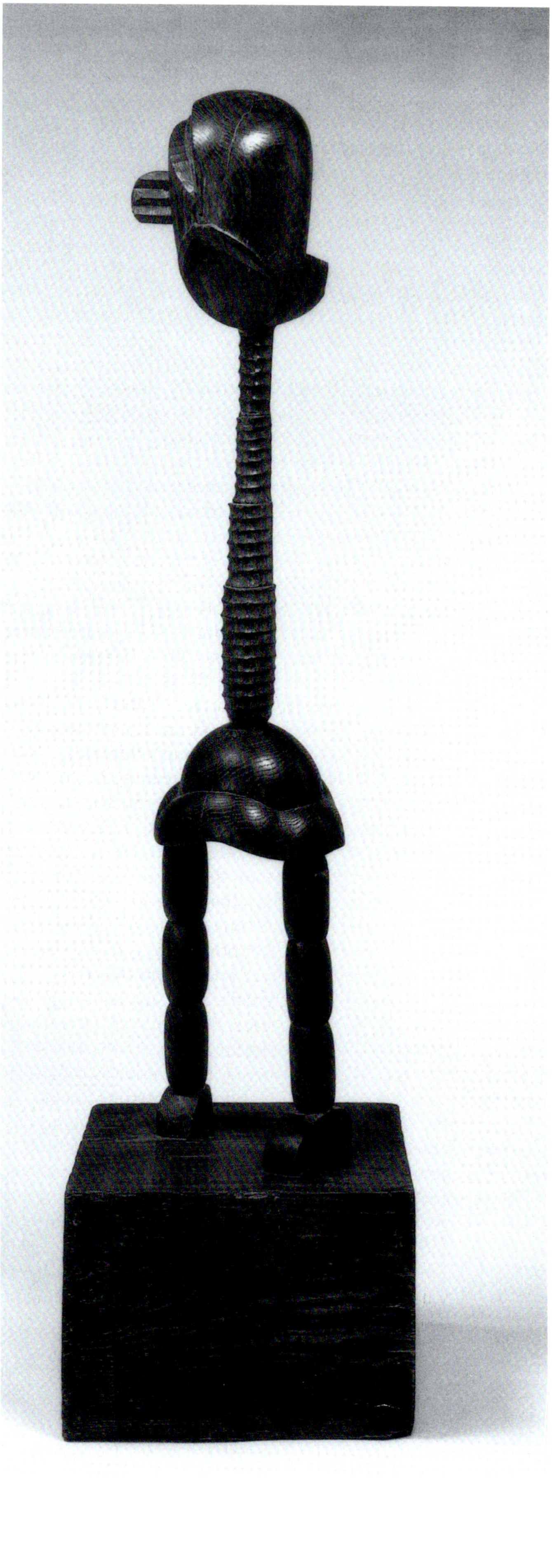

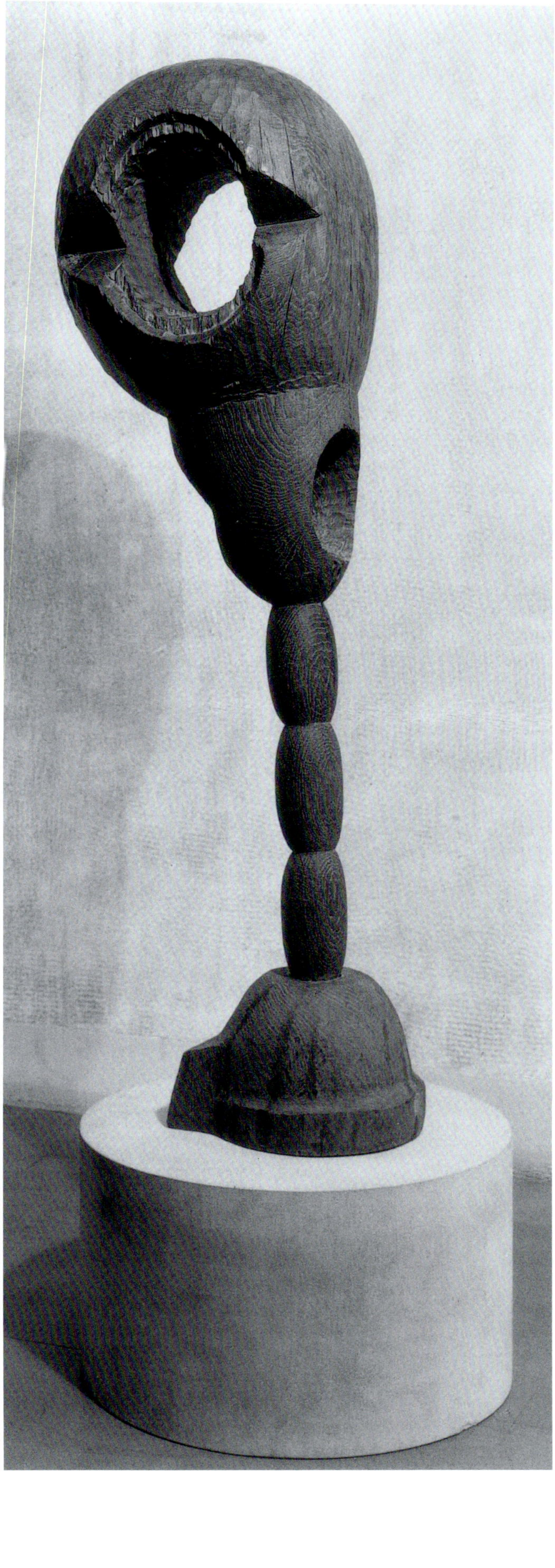

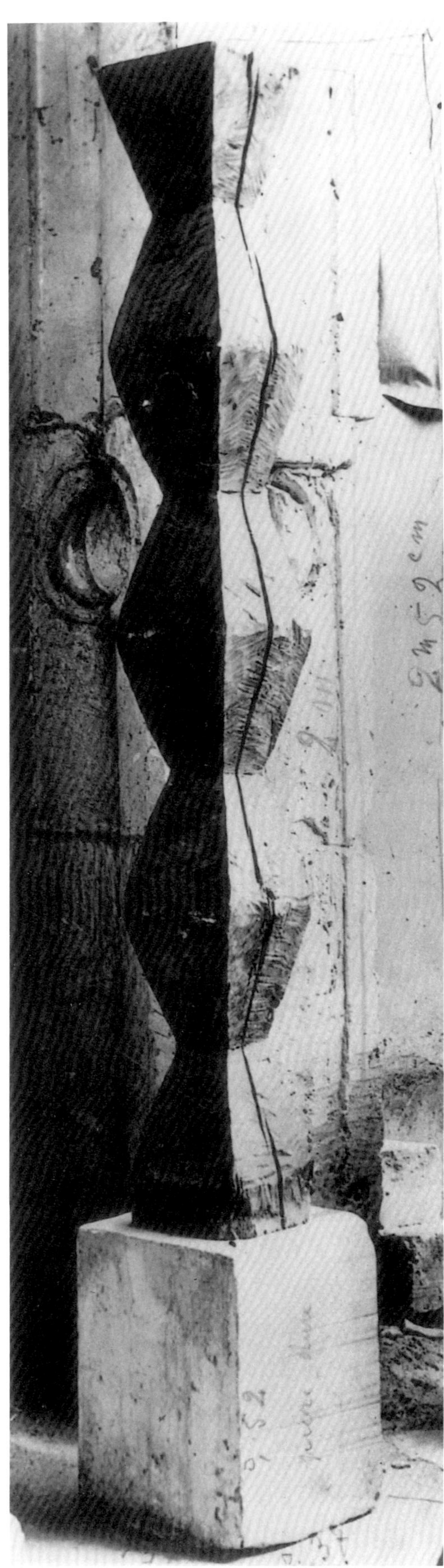

296. Constantin Brancusi, *Endless Column*, 1918. Oak, 202 × 25.4 × 25.4 cm. Collection Mary Sisler, Palm Beach, Florida

the way for him to find in peasant Romania something old which was both authentically and, among Parisian artists, exclusively his.

Even in the early wooden figures like *Little French Girl* there are echoes of Romanian peasant carving. In this case, the thin screw-like torso, its turning grooves gouged out with precise vigour, echoes across the distance of separation, memories of the carved supporting posts ('spindles') found on the open terraces of timber houses like his parents' in Hobitza.[47] Such echoes are stronger and more explicit in the wooden bases that became a feature of his work during the 1914–18 war. From one of the simpler types of base there emerged in 1916 or 1917 the idea of the wooden column as a separate, self-sufficient sculpture [296], the germ of *The Endless Column* erected in the photographer Edward Steichen's garden in 1920. The modular repetitions of the carved posts in the cemeteries or for the gateways and terraces of dwellings in the Gorj region were here Brancusi's model almost to the exclusion of African sculpture, though African echoes have been found even in this instance.[48]

Brancusi's primitivisation of himself and his work in pursuit of a lost peasant identity inevitably led to an assertion of that identity in terms of difference. Just as Rousseau was 'authentically' different from trained artists in his petty-bourgeois naïvety, Brancusi was 'authentically' different from all other Parisian modernists in his peasant simplicity. Again like Rousseau, Brancusi's work made powerful challenges to the accepted values of civilised orthodoxy, especially after he turned to woodcarving in 1913.[49] But here, where questions of authenticity and cultural identity are at issue, it is important to realise that the 'primitivism' of both artists, Brancusi as well as Rousseau, did not involve the rejection of modern French society – of civilisation – and that their work could actually be accommodated within notions of tradition. Indeed, it could be accommodated within notions of progress – even if modernity as such was rejected – since to primitivise oneself was, in a sense, to be modern.[50]

In Rousseau's case, as we have seen, his acceptance of modern French society could not be more fulsome, and it was hardly more than a decade after his death that his work was rendered eminently assimilable to the most conservative notions not merely of tradition but of the French tradition. He was, after all, a *French* 'primitive'. His sure mastery of what became the key 'classical' values of pictorial modernism easily overrode the challenge presented by his refusal of education. Already in 1918, Ozenfant and Jeanneret (Le Corbusier) could call his art 'purely traditional'.[51] In 1925, the State accepted the gift of his *Snake Charmer* for the Louvre, to the triumphalist delight of the independent art press. Rousseau's lesson had been made safe: Salmon's 'beautiful revolutionary act' was seen to have delivered a new set of standards endorsing conservative notions of tradition. As Salmon put it in an article celebrating the Douanier's imminent entrance into the Louvre: 'All he did was to try to paint as well as he could. For that and because the Museums babbled in his soul, he had a classical bearing and gave directions to the revolutionary young against the professors of formulae.'[52]

Rousseau simply maintained an identity as 'le Douanier'; Brancusi had to retrieve one as 'this peasant from the

Carpathians'. He could never, of course, fully retrieve what had been erased by his education, and never lost his identity as a modern (or wished to). In his primitivised way, he lived productively in Paris as a fully aware modern keeping in touch with an idealised peasant past. He retained his links with Romania, travelling there several times before and after the 1914–18 war, keeping in touch with his siblings, and singing in the Romanian Orthodox church in Paris on Sundays. But when he travelled after 1918 he stayed in exceedingly comfortable hotels, and in 1926 he was as ready to go to New York for his exhibitions there as he had been to return to the Gorj. He was even willing to endorse the security that civilisation brought. In New York, he jotted down the following note (it has slightly chilling undertones in view of what would happen in the 1930s): 'What we call civilisation is nothing but maintaining an order that the masses need or make necessary.'[53] Among his closest friends from the pre-1914 years were Duchamp, the most sophisticated of modern sceptics, and Léger, the most optimistic of modernity's champions.

He himself was never in any doubt that his 'primitivism' was assimilable to a European classical ideal, one whose intellectual foundations lay in Socratic and Platonic philosophy. His engagement with the 'primitive' from the beginning in 1907/8 was closely in tune with his idealist pursuit of perfection through refinement, because his 'primitivism' went with direct carving and direct carving went with another kind of idealist pursuit, the extraction from any and every material of its 'essence'. Already in the period 1916–19, his correspondence with Walter Pach and then John Quinn makes it clear that, for him, 'truth to material' applied not just to the direct carving of stone and wood – his 'primitivist' work – but to the perfected forms of marble and bronze too. 'I cannot say with a block of marble what I can with a piece of wood,' he wrote in a 1918 draft of a letter to Quinn . . . 'all I am trying to do is attune what is in my mind [ideal forms] to the materials that come my way. Each material has a particular language that I do not set out to eliminate and replace with my own, but simply to make express what I am thinking, what I am seeing, in its own language, that is its alone (which is part of the beautiful).'[54] His 'primitivist' recuperation of direct carving meshed seamlessly, thus, with his pursuit of 'the beautiful': essences and origins were pursued together, in the material.

Brancusi was ultimately an idealist whose commitment to a pan-cultural Humanist view of art was maintained. In this context, his Romanianness was no more than a token of his good faith as a seeker after beauty. Yet, the appearance of abstraction in much of his exhibited work, however 'classical' its simplicity, encouraged the view among independent critics in France that he had turned his back on the real, and so could not be assimilated into their understanding of the 'spontaneous classicism' of the French tradition.[55] He was not accepted as a major sculptor by French institutions until after 1945. Brancusi's livelihood and the future of his modernist reputation depended on his American supporters, above all John Quinn. His correspondence shows how skilfully he cultivated them. An artist keeping up with the rising cost of living in modern Paris, he was as far from being a naïf in financial matters as he was in his art.

AGAINST MODERNITY, AGAINST LOGIC: 'PRIMITIVE MENTALITY' AND BERGSONIAN INTUITION

When in 1912 Picasso made his *Guitar* out of cardboard and sculptural 'signs', and André Salmon called his 'demoiselles' 'white numbers on a blackboard', Cubism, as Part Three shows, had come to stand for an uncompromisingly conceptual approach to representing things. By that date, the 'primitive' too was predominantly thought of within the milieux around Picasso, Salmon and Apollinaire (inclusive of Brancusi) as conceptual. For Apollinaire in autumn 1912, a 'god of war' from Dahomey in the Ethnographic Museum at the Trocadéro was to be celebrated as a specimen of proto-Cubist conceptual art. 'The human figure,' he writes, 'certainly provided the inspiration for this singular work. And yet, by a stroke of invention as funny and profound as a page of Rabelais, not one of the elements that compose it resembles any part of the human body. The African artist was obviously a "creator".'[56] By that date, an entirely European and highly abstract view of the 'primitive' had brought together everything from Giotto to Rousseau and African carving as demonstrations of the impoverishment of 'naturalism' and the potential of pictorial and sculptural conceptualism. The sexual or political charge that could accompany the invocation of other cultures was rarely mentioned.

With this development came claims that the Cubists, as the most advanced and abstract of the modernists, were to be aligned with science and their practices with logic. In 1911 Michel Puy, wrote: 'Cubism seems to be a system with a scientific foundation, which enables the artist to support his effort by reliable data.'[57] Such a context can seem to re-situate the 'primitive' in the most inappropriate possible of modern surroundings, so that it becomes an encouragement to everything rational as well as conceptual in modernism. After all, in 1912 Salmon quotes Picasso himself calling African art, 'raisonnable' (reasonable).[58] In fact, however, the kind of conceptualism for which both the Cubists around Picasso and those who showed at the Salons stood, was far from reasonable, and was profoundly antagonistic to logic. For modernists generally, the 'primitive' was always to be used to endorse critiques – serious, savage or funny critiques – of the common-sense logics and mechanistic mentalities dominant in Third Republic France.

Certain developments in both mathematics and theoretical science had, in fact, become open to anti-common sense, anti-positivist interpretation, and many in the Symbolist and Cubist groupings were aware of this. One major liberating contribution here was Henri Poincaré's writings on science, published between 1902 and 1908, which emphasised the inventive and hypothetical character of science, its uncertainties.[59] Picasso and his friends were introduced to Poincaré's ideas before 1912.[60] Another lighter yet sharper liberating contribution was Alfred Jarry's knowing satirisation of scientific thinking *Gestes et opinions du docteur Faustroll*, in which the fantastic yet 'logical' science of 'pataphysics' is introduced, and which, Linda Henderson notes, ends with Dr Faustroll assuming 'the realm of the unknown dimension', so 'abstract and nude' is his soul.[61] Jarry, Rousseau's first promoter in Paris, was also the inventor of 'Ubu', the French bourgeois soul caricatured as an tor of 'Ubu', the French bourgeois soul caricatured as an offensive grotesque. In 1911, the year that the complete *Gestes et Opinions du docteur Faustroll* appeared in book form, Louis Vauxcelles made a point of calling Juan Gris's *Homage to Pablo Picasso* [31] a portrait of 'Père Ubukub'.[62]

Alongside the freeing of mathematics and science from empirically based positivism, important groupings in the post-Symbolist and Cubist avant-gardes were drawn to pre-modern models of science, informed by magic and religion, which endowed number with mysterious properties and turned chemistry into a kind of metaphorical poetry. The dice and playing cards of Picasso's, Braque's and Gris's still-lifes are echoes of the experiments in divination that Max Jacob adored. Alchemical imagery enters the poetry of Apollinaire in the 1900s, as does the figure of the magician in his *L'Enchanteur pourrissant*, illustrated in 1909 by Derain using the 'primitivist' technique of woodcut. Though Mondrian's and Kupka's engagement with Theosophy was exceptional for artists within the Cubist milieux, it is also significant that among the writers involved with the Puteaux and Passy groups, Alexandre Mercereau was actively involved in that attempt to bring together Eastern and Western religious traditions.

If by 1912 'primitivism' was an underpinning for the conceptual ambitions of modernists, it functioned thus very much in the context of these anti-positivist, quasi-mystical and often anti-rational concerns of the Cubist avant-garde, concerns which were given real impetus above all by Bergsonism, as will become clear. And its anti-rational import was paralleled by, though almost certainly not influenced by, important developments at the time in the anthropological and the psychological study of the 'primitive'. Despite the lack of causal connection, these parallels are important to this discussion for two reasons. First, they show how the primitivisation of the modern in art was part of a deep change in attitudes to the undeveloped and the 'uncivilised' that involved the disciplines most concerned with the systematic investigation of pre-modern societies outside Europe and of psychological development. Second, although the changes in the understanding of the 'primitive' produced within anthropology and psychology were almost certainly unknown to the modernists of the pre-1914 period, those engaged with the 'primitive' from the mid-1920s on would be very much aware of them. Certainly by the end of that decade they would be a crucial factor in both the production and the reception of primitivised art.[63]

The challenge offered by Rousseau's naïvety resulted from, as we have seen, the refusal of consistency and coherence in his painting. This openness to the contradictory was also, in fact, a feature of Brancusi's sculpture.[64] It was fundamental, indeed, to the practices of the Cubists, and became even more emphatic with the 'synthetic' developments that followed the making of Picasso's *Guitar*. Everything about Cubist construction, collage and papier–collé represented a renunciation of consistency, and an acceptance of the contradictory.

This acceptance of contradiction as a feature of a conceptual rather than a naturalistic art paralleled remarkably closely the findings concerning child art of G.H. Luquet in a book devoted to developmental psychology, which was published in 1913, *Dessins d'un enfant* (A Child's Drawings). Luquet used the systematic recording of his daughter Simone's drawings to establish a clear distinction between adult and child 'realisms'. In children up to the age of six, he found, not a 'photographic realism', but a conceptual 'realism' which aimed to 'contain all the details of an object' from every viewpoint, and 'to give each of these details in its characteristic form'.[65] This conceptual realism throve on contradiction: multiple viewpoints, 'impossible' juxtapositions, things seen through other things, etc. There is an unwritten inference in the book that adult 'photographic realism' represents a desirable advance, but nonetheless Luquet demonstrates that child art is not a feebler, undeveloped version of adult art. Instead it is the product of a structurally distinct way of seeing, and that, by instruction, the child learns to replace the contradictions inherent in infantile subjectivity by the consistency of adult objectivity. It was this 'objective' consistency that Rousseau refused as an untaught adult, preferring to conserve that state of 'childlike' ignorance which Luquet showed was to be found everywhere, even among adults in modern France, in the phenomenon of graffiti.

Luquet's conclusions echoed those of a major anthropological study published three years earlier in 1910, Lucien Lévy-Bruhl's *Fonctions mentales dans les sociétés inférieures* (Mental Functions in Inferior Societies), though he does not mention it. Despite the neo-colonialist use of the term 'inferior societies', Lévy-Bruhl directly challenged the evolutionism then dominant in social anthropology. He dismissed the hypothesis of J.G. Fraser's *Golden Bough* that 'primitive' thought employed simpler forms of logic premised on false perceptions (the perception, for instance, that the spirit does not die because it lives in dreams). For him, such a hypothesis merely projected European logical notions onto non-European mechanisms of thought. His contention was that 'primitive' thinking is just as complex but entirely without the essentials of logic. And the major differences between 'primitive' and 'civilised' thought are to be located, he argued, in mysticism – the belief that everything possesses spirit or life – and magic.

In the case of magic, Lévy-Bruhl focused on a particular aspect: the 'illogical' notion of causation required by the belief that two demonstrably unconnected things are causally connected, that, say, in an instance recorded from Northern Australia, a portrait of Queen Victoria hung in one place *caused* misfortune in another a long way away. In such instances, he stressed, things can be associated causally when they are in different places and contiguous in time. This capacity of magical thinking was to be understood, according to Lévy-Bruhl, in terms of what he called 'the law of participation', and that law simply ignored the logician's fundamental rule whereby two objects cannot occupy the same space at the same time, the rule of 'non-contradiction'. As he put it, in the representations of 'primitive mentality' (a term he invented), 'phenomena can be . . . at once themselves and other than themselves . . . they emit and receive forces . . . , which are felt to be outside them, without ceasing to be what they are'.[66] Though he accepted that so-called 'primitives' used logic to solve practical problems daily, he coined the term 'pre-logical' for such magical thinking. Lévy-Bruhl was well aware of the derogatory racist implications that followed from the tendency to conflate the 'primitive' and the infantile, and he dismissed such conflations vehemently. But, in the 1920s, the alignment between his and Luquet's conclusions on child 'realism' would be remarked on by the great child psychologist Jean Piaget.

In the 1900s and the 1910s, the avant-gardists engaged with the 'primitive' still betray an essentially nineteenth-century Romantic attraction to the child and the 'primitive' as 'innocent' and therefore free, an attitude rooted in the eighteenth-century convictions of Jean-Jacques Rousseau rather than in the writings of Lévy-Bruhl and Luquet. The new anthropological and psychological theory of different mentalities that inevitably separates the educated European adult from the child and the 'primitive' was not shared. There was a faith instead in the possibility of retrieving earlier states of 'innocence' and therefore 'freedom', and an appreciative openness to the 'genius' of child art. One especially telling manifestation of this was the couturier Paul Poiret's instantly successful 1911 enterprise, the Atelier Martine, where young teenage girls produced decorative designs for wallpapers, textiles and carpets based on their drawings after nature and where the policy was *not* to give them instruction in art. And yet, the modernists' identification of the 'primitive' with a kind of conceptual representation that struck at the foundations of educated good sense in the Third Republic, above all the 'rule of non-contradiction' basic to logic, carried strong echoes of the findings of both Luquet and Lévy-Bruhl. It may not have been how he viewed it, but what Picasso extracted from his Grebo masks was the freedom of magical thinking as Lévy-Bruhl had already analysed it. Emptyness could be fullness, projection recession, wallpaper could be shaped to make a guitar or the wine in a glass while remaining wallpaper, one thing could change into another. The law of participation operates in Cubist collage and papier-collé, even if it is not invoked. Anything can be anything else, anywhere.

There is, finally, one further parallel which illuminates the anti-logical in the modernist notion of 'the primitive' between 1907 and 1914: the obvious parallel between Lévy-Bruhl's 'primitive mentality' and Henri Bergson's 'intuition'. In this case the direct relevance of Bergson's thinking to the milieux of the Salon Cubists above all is clear enough, as I show in Chapter 7. At the same time, the direct relevance of Bergson to Lévy-Bruhl is clear too, for the latter explicitly based his distinction between 'primitive' and European mentalities on Bergson's distinction between art as 'intuition' and the logical positivist forms of science. For Bergson, logical thought had a strictly pragmatic role, it could not penetrate to essences. Such penetration was only possible if the systematic measuring of time could be ignored and 'our inner experience of time' regained as the ground of contemplation. 'If', he wrote in 1889, 'we penetrate into the depth of organised and living intelligence, we shall witness the joining together or rather the blending of many ideas which, when once dissociated, seem to exclude one another as logically contradictory terms'. His belief was that the artist's capacity for intuition took him or her beyond logic, offering access to 'living intelligence', to a grasp, however momentary, of one's 'unmeasurable duration in which nothing is repeated'.[67] The parallel between his notion of artistic 'intuition' and Lévy-Bruhl's notion of a pre-logical primitive mentality was close.

Directness, spontaneity and access to essences were qualities as often ascribed to the 'primitive' as they were to Bergsonian 'intuition', and in the way that the notions of the 'primitive' and of 'intuition' were applied to modernism, process was central. In a very broad sense, the open-ended processes of Matissian expressive painting and of Picasso and Braque's painting-as-drawing or collage assemblage, were 'primitive' in their 'intuitiveness'. The primitivisation of the modern became, thus, implicated in a much more all-embracing modernist challenge to the Enlightenment foundations of French rationalism. It was a challenge that worked both in the temporal and the spatial dimension, by refusing calculation and by accepting contradiction.

CHAPTER 12

Counter-Cultural Art, 1918–40

CHANGE AND CONTRADICTION: THE PROVOCATIONS OF BRANCUSI, DUCHAMP AND PICABIA

There was at least one vantage point from which Brancusi's sculpture represented a challenge to the essentialism for which it ostensibly stood, that of Marcel Duchamp (b.1887). The close friendship between the two had begun by 1912; from Duchamp's first trip back to Paris from New York in 1919 it was fastened tighter. Much about Brancusi's work could be seen as the very opposite of finite and consistent – a confirmation, indeed, of that love of contradiction which was so central to Duchamp's quiet counter-cultural critique of liberal bourgeois assumptions and values. Fundamental to this was Brancusi's use of bases in his sculptures.

Between 1917 and 1919, Brancusi (b.1876) was in correspondence with John Quinn in New York about the possible sale to him of a number of sculptures, including his 1910 marble *Maiastra*, which he offered with a wooden base. When Quinn eventually bought the piece, it came with three stone bases, one of which was a stone carving from around 1908 left by Brancusi in a very rudimentary state, *The Caryatids*. This was the base the collector used [297].[1] The earliest evidence of the sculptor treating his bases as independent pieces that worked *with* his pieces, is from 1914, when he was negotiating his solo show at Alfred Stieglitz's Photo-Secession Gallery in New York. *The Maiastra* Quinn bought later was exhibited on that occasion, and the base it was given there was sent as a separately itemised piece, invoiced as an original sculpture'. Already in 1914, Brancusi saw the sculpture-and-base combination as flexible, because, when there was the suggestion of a buyer for the *Maiastra* from the show, he wrote offering alternative bases, including a 'big stone', which might have been *The Caryatids*.[2]

For an artist so apparently committed to the refinement of ideas within a neo-Platonic aesthetic, this openness to change in the way his work was displayed was profoundly contradictory. His juxtapositional use of base-and-sculpture combinations clearly exploited the freedoms of collage and assemblage opened up by Picasso, Braque and Gris. And Duchamp was also probably himself a factor, for his very first readymade, the *Bicycle Wheel* of 1914, involved just such a juxtaposition: it spun, mounted on a stool.[3] Strikingly, at a moment when Picasso and Gris dropped collage, Brancusi developed an entirely fresh application of collage practice to sculpture.

Besides *The Maiastra*, among the pieces that Brancusi offered Quinn in 1917 was a group of three sculptures, one of which was a base that threatened to exceed its supporting function altogether. These sculptures were offered as a juxtapositional composition: a single work. The composition came to Quinn in the form of a photograph specially taken by Brancusi titled: *Child of the World, Mobile Group* [298]. The three constituent sculptures were all woods: a figure developed from *Little French Girl* [294], an intermediary stage of the first *Column* (the modules not yet hacked-out fully in the round), and perched on top of the *Column*, a sculpted *Cup*.[4] The implication of the phrase 'Groupe mobile' (Mobile Group) was that Quinn could make his own juxtapositional compositions so long as he kept these three sculptures together and also kept Brancusi's title.[5]

New juxtapositions of the kind invited in the cases of *Child of the World* and *The Maiastra* did not merely produce new formal and material combinations, they opened up new possible meanings. *The Maiastra* emerged from Brancusi's pancultural 'primitivist' first phase; it invoked not only the Romanian folk tale of an all-seeing magic bird which gives protection, the 'Maiastra', but also Egyptian sculptures representing the fierce falcon-god Horus. Quinn's decision to raise it above the bent and broken figures of the *Caryatids* invited imaginary narratives of protection attuned especially to the 'Maiastra' story. Titles were crucial here, and if meanings could be inflected differently by new juxtapositions, they could be completely changed by new titles. The title *Child of the World* identifies the figure sculpture in the group as a child. Soon, however, the same figure would acquire the title *Plato*, and already in 1917 it seems likely that Brancusi thought of the cup as Socrates' cup, out of which the philosopher drank the hemlock to kill himself. In around 1922, he carved one more version of the *Little French Girl*, which he called *Socrates* [295]. Briefly, *Cup* and *Socrates* were brought together to form another 'mobile group' for Brancusi's camera; here the cup was balanced precariously on the philosopher's head, the very oddity of the juxaposition stimulating unanticipated new responses.[6] Other photographs of 'mobile groups' place the erect, assertive *Socrates*, as it were in conversation with the toddler *Plato* accompanied by a changing cast of sculptures, suggesting one new scenario after another.

Brancusi's use of photography to record 'mobile groups' was a relatively private activity; it was for his clients and himself. One must remember, however, that from 1914 he kept almost total control over the photographing of his work, and, through his photography, consciously sought to guide his clients as his primary spectators. At the same time, even when his sculptures are approached singly, neither with their bases nor in groups, they often resist unitary, consistent interpretation, something again underlined by his photography. His use of light, reflection and multiple exposures tends to enhance the mysterious and the suggestive. Yet, the most notorious instance of a work that triggered conflicting responses did not require photography to emphasise its polysemic openness, the work itself was enough. This was *Princess X*, one of Brancusi's slowly perfected sculptures, the first version of which was produced in polished marble between 1910 and 1916. Its capacity to provoke conflicting responses led famously to actual public conflict when the polished bronze version [299] was shown at the Paris Indépendants of 1920.

Princess X was removed from the Salon on the orders of the Indépendants' President, Paul Signac (b.1863), as an indecent object liable to provoke disorder. Anticipating perhaps the charge that his *Princess* was a phallus, Brancusi had already made earnest idealist claims for her. 'You see . . . ,' he told an interviewer in January 1920, 'my statue is of Woman, all women rolled into one, Goethe's Eternal Feminine reduced to its essence'.[7] When first shown at the New York Independents of 1917 no scandal occurred, but even then *Vanity Fair* treated the work as 'erotica', and one critic called it a 'phallic symbol' remarking that 'America . . . demands clean art'.[8] Today, Brancusi's behaviour in utterly rejecting the possibility that it could be seen as a phallus seems positively obtuse; then, the furious indignation with which he condemned the police and artistic authorities was supported by almost the entire modernist community. A letter of protest, published in *Paris-Journal*, recorded among its dozens of signatories Picabia and Picasso, Léger and Derain, Lhote and Salmon (Duchamp was in New York).

Picabia (b.1879) was not the only close associate of Duchamp to sign; so did Quinn's agent in Paris, Henri-Pierre Roché. Perhaps the reason why *Princess X* had not caused a scandal in 1917 was that another scandal had dom-

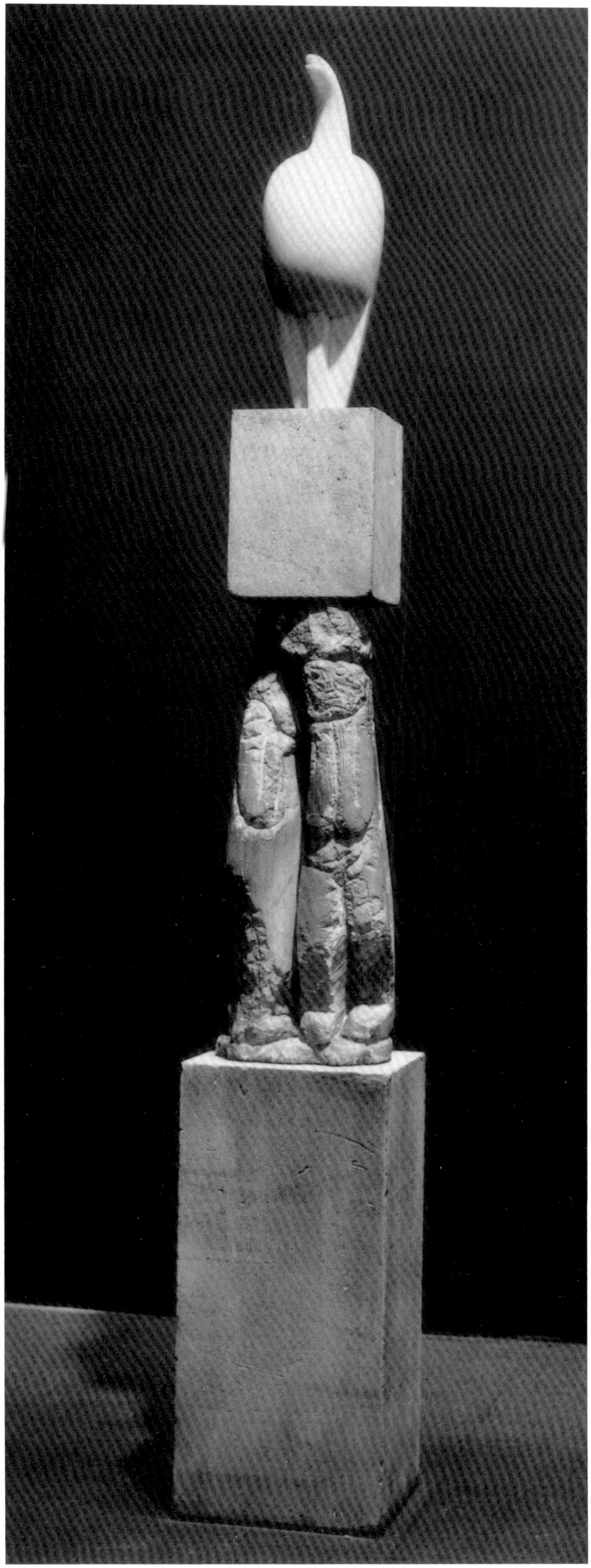

297. Constantin Brancusi, *Maiastra (Magic Bird)*, 1910–12. White marble, h. 55.9, max. circum. 60.3 cm; on three-part limestone pedestal, h. 177.8 cm, of which the middle section is the *Double Caryatid*, *c.*1908, stone, h. 75.2 × 26.6 × 16.5 cm. The Museum of Modern Art, New York. Katherine S. Dreier Bequest

298. Constantin Brancusi, *Child in the World* (incorporating *Plato* and *Cup*), 1917. Photograph by Brancusi. Musée National d'Art Moderne, Paris

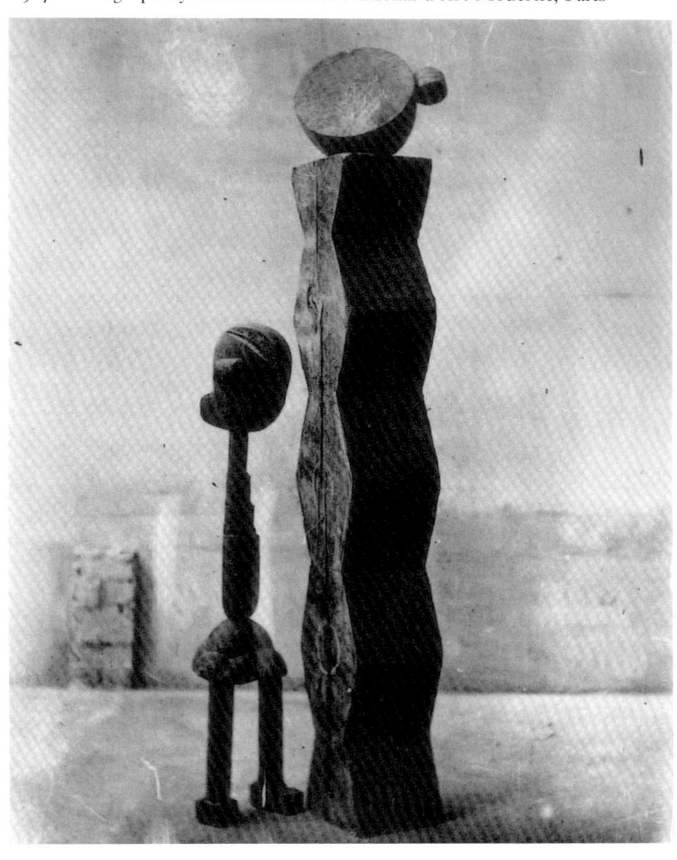

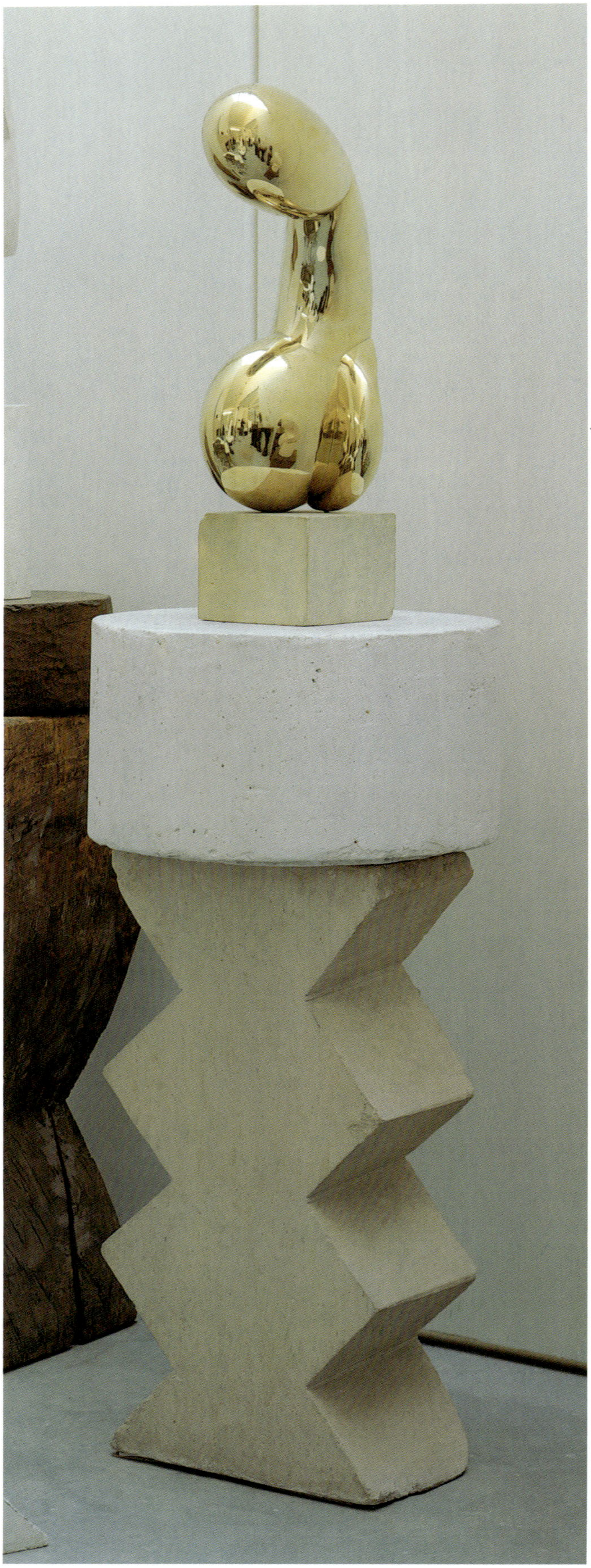

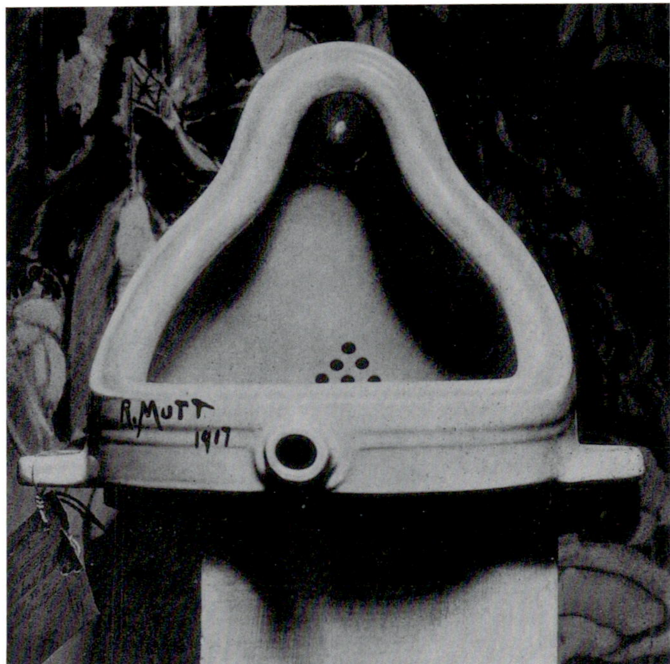

299. Constantin Brancusi, *Princess X*, 1916. Polished bronze, 56.5 × 42 × 24 cm. Musée National d'Art Moderne, Paris

300. Marcel Duchamp, *Fountain*, 1917. Photograph by Alfred Stieglitz, as published in *The Blind Man*, no. 2 (New York, May 1917)

inated responses to the New York Independents, one engineered and exploited by Duchamp and Roché together. This scandal was triggered by something else which attracted the charge of indecency, the urinal signed 'R. Mutt', sent in by Duchamp with the title *Fountain* [300]. I shall return to this scandal later, here what are significant are the multiple responses generated among Duchamp's supporters by *Fountain*, and the uncanny way they anticipate responses to *Princess X*. Published as evocatively photographed by Stieglitz [300], *Fountain* was instantly praised by its champions both in idealised formal terms and as a gendered image: 'chaste' in 'the simplicity of its line and colour', yet suggestive of 'the legs of the ladies by Cézanne', quite apart from Madonnas and Buddhas.[9] A piece of plumbing for men becomes both formally perfect and a 'sculpture' that fuses male and female properties; this is precisely what *Princess X* became.[10]

It remains just possible to take Brancusi's injured innocence on trust, but the attitude of Roché in 1920 is much more questionable. It is difficult to believe that Roché, prepared by Duchamp's indiscrete and ambivalent *Fountain* in 1917, did not see the contradictions in *Princess X*: the fact that it combined utterly opposed possible meanings, the ideal and the erotic, 'Woman' reduced to 'her essence' and a phallus in a state of semi-arousal. There was surely relish in the way he and, for instance, Picabia fuelled the controversy by adding their support to the sculptor's uncompromising idealism. At the same time, given his Dada associates, it is certainly possible that Brancusi himself knowingly showed the work as a Dada gesture. He must surely have been aware of its capacity to shock by double-entendre, since the piece

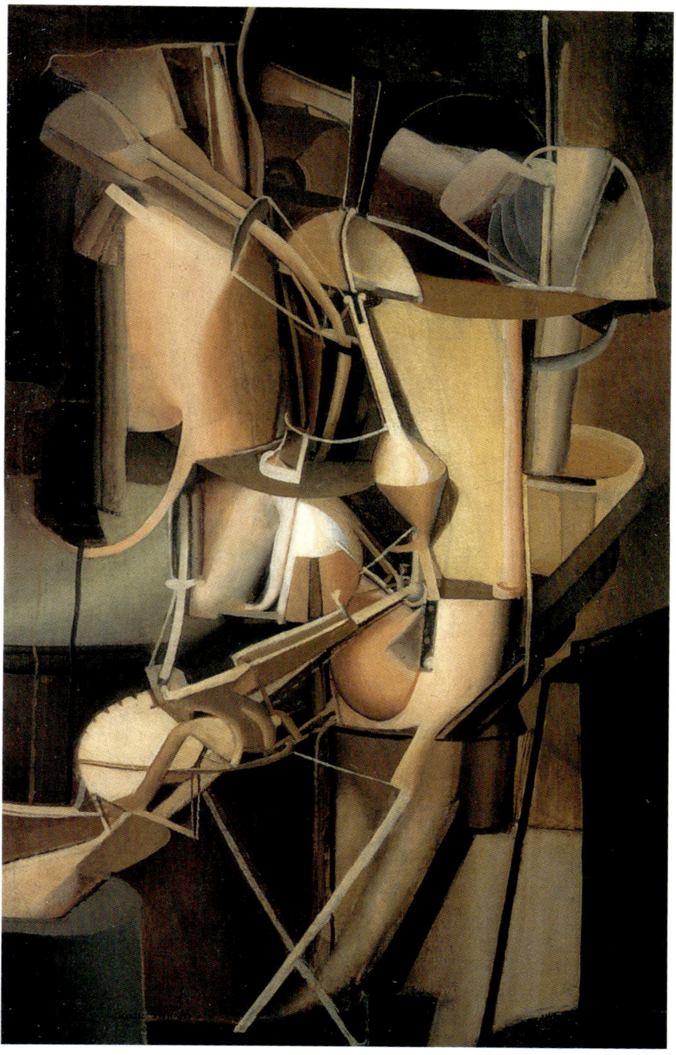

301. Marcel Duchamp, *The Bride*, 1912. Oil on canvas, 90 × 55 cm. The Philadelphia Museum of Art, The Louise and Walter Arensberg Collection

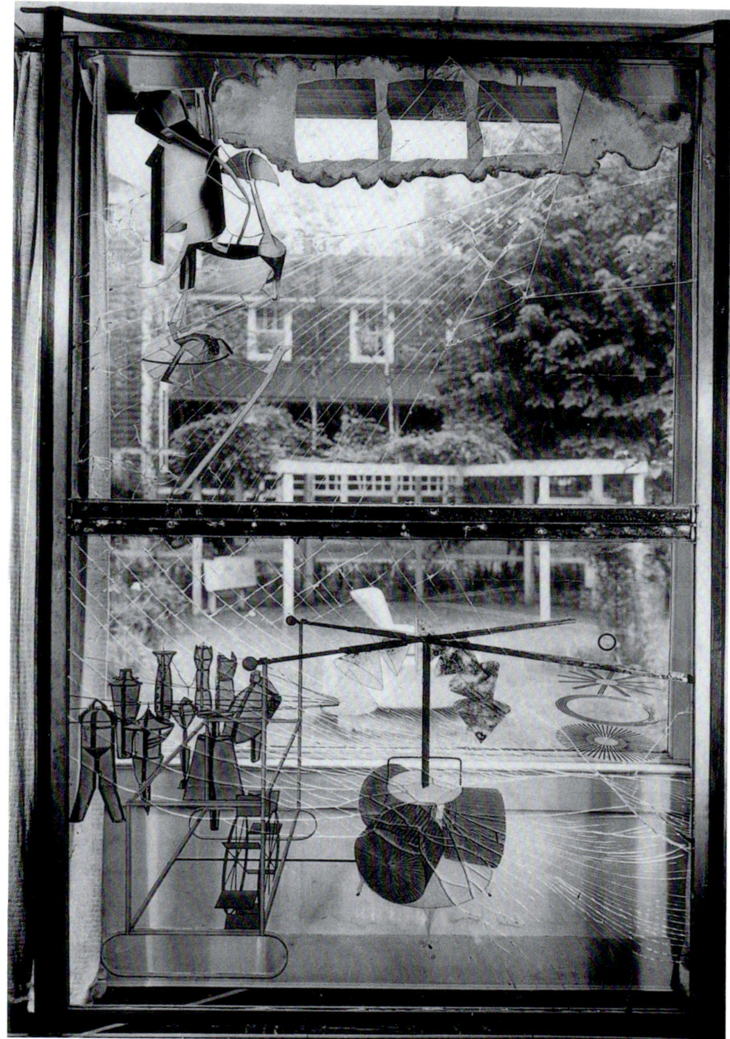

302. Marcel Duchamp, *The Bride Stripped Bare by her Bachelors, Even*, 1915–1923. Oil, lead wire and foil, dust and varnish on glass, in two parts, 272 × 170 cm. Philadelphia Museum of Art, The Louise and Walter Arensberg Collection

had already been removed once by the police from public exhibition in Paris: in 1916, from a wartime exhibition organised by André Salmon, his Salon d'Antin.[11]

Moreover, the carved effigies which were titled *Plato* and *Socrates* and then were given changing roles in Brancusi's 'mobile groups' suggest that he was fully aware of the provocation his practice presented generally to those who wished to see only fixed meanings, petrified essences in art. *Plato*, the philosopher of essences, is an Africanised infant; *Socrates*, his teacher, is even more strongly Africanised, his face emptied out as either a bizarre or a comic image of the unstoppable flow of wisdom, a mouth speaking.[12] Perhaps for Brancusi there was some fundamental truth in the bringing together of Greek idealism and the 'primitive' – a truth consonant with the pan-cultural 'truth' he ascribed to 'direct carving'. His friend Eric Satie's cantata *Socrate*, three of Plato's dialogues put to music, was indeed a homage dedicated without irony to the 'white' and the 'pure' in the Antique, and provides a positive context for Brancusi's carvings; its first performance was in 1919.[13] Brancusi, after all, owned Plato's dialogues in a 1916 French translation, and the composer used to call the Romanain the brother of Socrates. Yet, Satie's own highly developed taste for provocation always invited counter-provocation – he too was close to Duchamp – and it seems unlikely that Brancusi did not realise just how subversive his 'black African' images of his own and Satie's heroes from Greek philosophy were.

The precise degree to which Brancusi was Dada, whether he *wanted* his work to be subversive, are questions which will never be definitively answered. In Duchamp's case, nothing could be clearer: from 1912, the subversion of consistency in all its logical positivist forms (including modernist aesthetics) was the object of everything he produced in the context of art: he refused all definitive answers.

If Brancusi infuriated many by denying his eroticism, Duchamp provoked by making his eroticism explicit, and using it as a weapon. For him, it was a weapon not so much against decency as against idealism, the idealism that goes with the promise of love. Already, in his *Bride* of 1912 [301], 'Woman' has become an incomprehensible mélange of

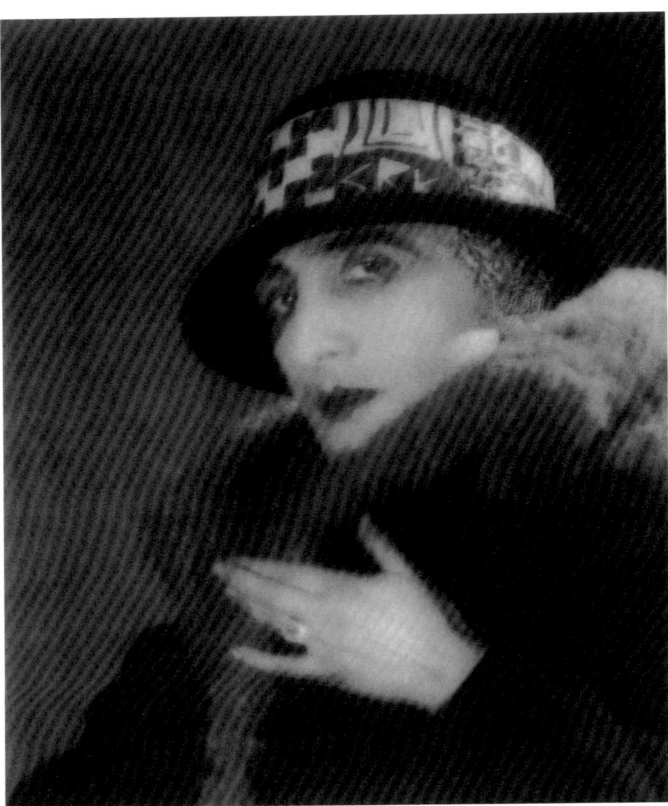

303. Marcel Duchamp and Man Ray, *Marcel Duchamp as Rose Sélavy*, *c.*1921. Gelatin silver print. The J. Paul Getty Museum, Los Angeles

internal body parts and mechanisms. The *Large Glass*, *The Bride Stripped Bare by her Bachelors, Even* [302], whose conception began that year, was to stretch to the utmost every analytical and inventive skill he possessed to make of love a pointless mechanical operation. But love was not Duchamp's main target: the erotic was his route to the subversion of the very foundations of all essentialism. As Rudolf Kuenzli has put it, his works function 'as machines that de-essentialise essentialist concepts'.[14] And, just as the ambivalence of Brancusi's sculpture resists fixed interpretations, Duchamp works against essentialism by multiplying identities and thus putting in question *all* identity as such.

The *Fountain* controversy put in question 'art' and the 'artist', and did so by multiplying the possible identities of something hitherto considered nothing to do with art. As reported by the *New York Herald*, the Independent Society of Artists voted against its inclusion in their exhibition, because the urinal, while 'a very useful object', 'is, by no definition, a work of art'.[15] Katherine Dreier, who voted against it, wrote to Duchamp, that she did so because 'I did not see anything pertaining to originality in it'.[16] The Duchamp-and-Roché-backed *Blind Man* magazine replied by adding to the principle of individual artistic creation, that of personal choice: 'Whether Mr. Mutt with his own hands made the fountain or not has no importance. He CHOSE it. He took an ordinary article of life, placed it so that its useful significance disappeared under the new title and point of view – created a new thought for that object.'[17] The urinal remained a urinal and so *not* a work of art, but *was* also a work of art, because it was chosen for an exhibition. Its new identity, which was itself multiple (ideal, male, female), put *both* its identities in question.

Duchamp multiplied his own identity too: he 'himself' was to induce uncertainty. After signing *Fountain* 'R. Mutt', he played along with the deception not only for the New York press, but even in correspondence with his sister Suzanne. He went a step further for Suzanne, informing her solemnly that 'Richard Mutt' was the 'masculine pseudonym' of 'one of my female friends'.[18] A few years later, he added to the sexually ambiguous 'Mutt', a third identity, this time decisively changing sex: he dressed up as a stylish modern woman, had Man Ray photograph him, and signed the photographs 'Rose Sélavy' [303]. Richard Mutt never worked again, but Rose was prolific between the wars, and when in 1921 'she' added a faint inscription to Picabia's graffiti picture, *The Cacodylic Eye* (*L'Oeil Cacodylate*), she became 'Rrose Sélavy', punning (when spoken in French) both 'arrose' (the verb 'waters') and Eros: 'Eros C'est la vie' – (Eros, that's life). From 1922 to 1924, and then more intermittently into the 1930s, Rrose was the author of a particular genre of word game, which had a bizarre spin-off in the word games of one of Breton's circle, Robert Desnos, who, in 1922, claimed to be in touch with 'her' when in trance states (either hypnotic or self-induced).

Duchamp's starting point could be said to be Henri Poincaré's insight that the truths derived from observation and logical reasoning (however scientifically controlled) are no more than hypotheses, always uncertain. Everything he was and everything he produced was designed to induce uncertainty; and, in order to avoid the essentialist danger of taking clear positions for or against other positions, nothing he was and nothing he produced was in earnest. Brancusi's high seriousness has its foil here in lightness of touch and irony. The intricately conceived and laboriously executed *Large Glass* was projected in one of Duchamp's early notes as a 'hilarious picture'.[19] The question posed by his friend and ally Louise Norton, regarding *Fountain*, was: 'Is he serious or is he joking?' Her answer was: 'Perhaps he is both!'[20]

Duchamp worked on the *Large Glass* for eleven years, between 1912 and 1923, leaving it 'definitively unfinished' in New York when he decided to settle again in Paris. It did not become a public work of art in France until 1934–5, with the publication of many of the notes for it in the *Green Box* facsimile edition, and then with Breton's presentation of the work in *Minotaure*, 'The Lighthouse of the Bride'. Even attributing a date to the *Glass* is thus uncertain.

From the start, its meanings depended on the notes, and the notes acted as a defence against any kind of definition or explanation. They survive in three sets, all produced between 1912 and some time towards the middle of the 1914–18 war: 'The Box of 1914', the *Green Box*, and 'Towards the Infinitive. White Box'. The very manner of their appearance and publication induces uncertainty. Duchamp's painstakingly exact facsimile scraps of paper covered in his jottings were deposited in the *Green Box* in random disorder, discouraging the pursuit of coherence. But Michel Sanouillet's edition of his writings claims to reconstitute 'the order, if not the chronology, of their drafting', and to have done so actually with Duchamp's help.

Sanouillet remarks, further, that the order arrived at is not 'without relation' to the order proposed by Breton; so it seems likely that Breton too, in 1934–5, had Duchamp as a guide.[21] Are we to accept, then, randomness or direction as the desired mode for approaching the notes and the meanings they might give the work? Once again the best answer is both – sometimes one and sometimes the other – and even if, as outlined in Chapter 6, Breton did arrive at an itemisation of the parts and an analysis of the functioning of the *Glass*, the result is nothing if not uncertain.

Within the notes, two major concerns are repeatedly addressed. One is measurement and the perception of space. The other is words and language. The standardised sign-systems of measurement and language are the very foundations of civilised thinking and communication in modern logocentric societies, now as in the early twentieth century when France and the United States were the model democratic republics, setting examples for the World. Duchamp's notes for the *Glass* suggest strategies (sometimes followed in its fabrication, sometimes not) aimed at undermining the grounds for certainty offered by both kinds of sign-system.

Notes in the *Green Box* and 'The Box of 1914', outline the procedure to be followed in arriving at what Duchamp calls the *Three Standard Stoppages*, a procedure designed to expose the arbitrariness of the metre as the standard unit of measure. It is typically rigorous, and eminently practicable. This is his most fundamental challenge to systems of measurement. A one-metre-long piece of string, held horizontally, is to be dropped from a height of one-metre, and its form on landing recorded. This is to be done to produce not one, but three 'standard' units of measurement, so that there is neither one measure, nor two alternative measures, but the possibility of any number. Duchamp produced wooden templates from his experiment, exactly reproducing the wavering contour taken by the string, and used them as the modules for the capillary tubes attached to the top of the nine malic moulds of the bachelor machine.

More than once, the notes take up the question of words and definitions by envisaging entire new vocabularies and languages, which by their obvious arbitrariness would expose the relativity of all sign-systems. Thus, the *Green Box* contains an elaborate suggestion for producing a vocabulary of 'standard signs', each one arbitrarily selected to stand for an abstract word from the Larousse dictionary. Colour is then to be used to designate these signs in linguistic terms as substantives, verbs, adverbs, etc., and they are to be grouped in new relationships, as if syntactically and grammatically, in ways 'inexpressible in . . . present and future living languages'.[22]

The measurable and the definable are constantly at issue. Consequently, at one point in the *Green Box*, Duchamp floated the idea that the bride's 'milky-way' – the vague, vapourous cloud of her 'blossoming' which crowns the composition – should be realised using his 'standard signs' for the abstract words in the Larousse dictionary captured photographically moving through space, a process designed expressly to enhance its ineffability. And thus at another point, he contrasts the 'unmeasurable' imprecisions of the bridal machine above with the exact precision of the bachelor machine below, commenting that, because 'measured', the rectangles, circles, parallelopipeds, etc. of the latter are necessarily 'imperfect'. The 'White Box' is packed with speculations concerning the translation of three into four dimensions. They are based on the fashionable theories of 'hyperspace' that attracted others in the Cubist milieu, but are geared not towards revealing some 'absolute' Platonic dimension, but rather towards discrediting everyday perception – the measurable 'imperfection' of three-dimensions.

Duchamp's elaborate procedures are almost always defence strategies aimed against the ideal, the consistent and the definite. One note in the *Green Box* records his preference for the word 'indefinite' over the word 'infinite'.[23]

Even when Breton's guided tour of the operations of the Bachelor and Bride machines is followed, no consistent application of mechanical, physical or chemical laws can be found, only bizarre and improbable combinations of all three. Here Alfred Jarry's Dr Faustroll and his 'pataphysics' is the springboard for a playful science, a 'science' which skates across invented physical, chemical, biological and mathematical principles. At every stage and in every detail it is developed with remarkable rigour, guying scientific 'method'. A single instance is demonstration enough.

There is, for example, the blossoming of the bride, essential to her stripping, as expounded early in Sanouillet's publication of the *Green Box* and so presumably at an early stage in the *Glass*'s conception. This is presented as threefold. The first blossoming is activated by the 'electrical stripping' initiated by the bachelors. The bride is rooted into the cogs-of-desire of the bachelors by a 'standard tree' up whose trunk their desire rises. The second blossoming is 'imaginative-wilful'; it involves the transmission of the bride's own 'feeble power . . . a sort of . . . petrol of love', to her 'very feeble cylinders'. The third is the coming together of the two. Altogether, the blossoming is 'cinematic': something filmed, not seen.[24]

Duchamp comments on the triple blossoming of the bride: 'Mixture, physically composed of two causes (bachelor and imaginative desire) unanalysable by logic.'[25] Everything about the notes and the *Glass* was rigorously developed, though often differently at various stages, but, in the end, everything was 'unanalysable by logic'. The logician's law of non-contradiction was flouted as a matter of principle. And even the modernity of the *Glass* – its mechanisms – were subversive. For many were downright old-fashioned, from the water-mill to the chocolate-grinder – and where they were not, they were absurd, like the Bride's 'feeble cylinders'. While altogether, they can never achieve their goal: the satisfaction of desire.

As a 'machine for de-essentialising essentialist concepts', the *Large Glass* reached beyond logical positivism, even. It took as one of its targets for ironical demolition the philosophical mainstay of optimistic modernism, Henri Bergson. For Bergsonist champions of modernity, after all, Bergsonian 'intuition' was simply a faster, surer route to the 'essence' of reality, beyond logic. One of the earliest notes in Sanouillet's *Green Box* sequence suggests a subtitle for his 'hilarious picture', 'Delay in Glass'.[26] The word 'delay' is used as substitute for the word 'picture' (tableau). It was as if Duchamp was claiming for the *Glass* the capacity to stop change, to free its ideas and its images from time by fixing

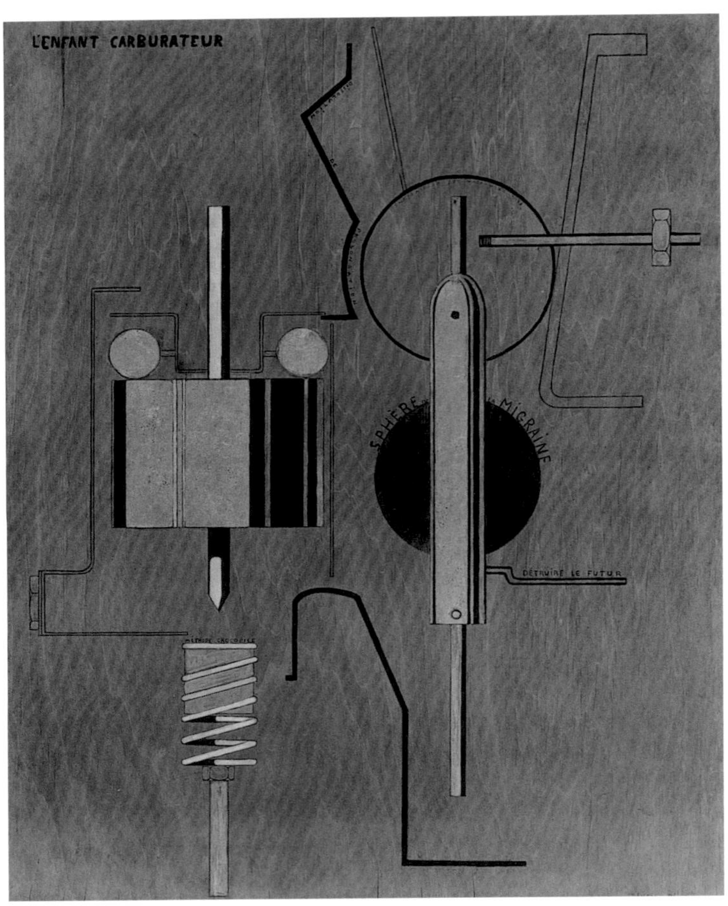

304. Francis Picabia, *Child Carburettor*, 1919. Oil and gold leaf on wood, 126.3 × 101.3 cm. Solomon R. Guggenheim Museum, New York

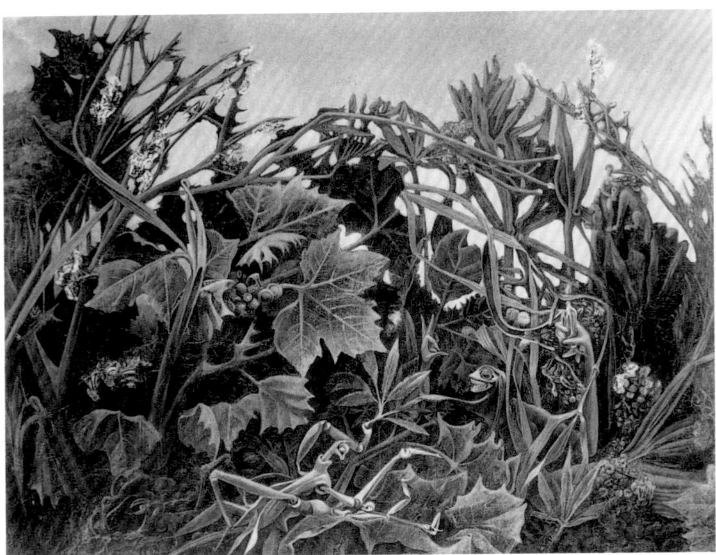

305. Max Ernst, *The Joy of Life*, 1936. Oil on canvas, 73.5 × 93 cm. Private Collection

them in the glass and in the boxes of notes. As a 'delay', the *Glass* escaped even Bergson's pursuit of essences in 'creative evolution'.

At the beginning of this chapter, I described Duchamp's critique of progressive liberal assumptions as quiet. After the excitement generated by *Fountain*, it was pursued largely in private spaces away from the public eye, and in that sense it was indeed quiet. But its echoes were received by the Paris audience of independent art, amplified sometimes to create a cacophony of noise, through the work of Duchamp's friend and ally Francis Picabia. It might in its most far-reaching effects have amounted to another kind of 'delay', but it had begun to make an impression, at one remove, by the early 1920s. The relationship between the two was so close and interactive that one cannot describe Picabia as in any way Duchamp's follower, but many of Picabia's concerns were Duchamp's, and he gave them textual and pictorial forms that were much more instantly consumable in the public sphere. Moreover, alongside Breton, from 1919 into the mid-1920s, it was he who provided Duchamp with a public platform when he needed it. Besides publishing *L.H.O.O.Q.*, Duchamp's hirsute version of the *Mona Lisa*, in his short-lived Dada periodical *Cannibale*, Picabia included his word games in his more long-lived *391*. Among them was the 1924 publication of Rrose Sélavy's terse two liner: 'Oh! Do shit again! . . . /Oh! Douche it again! . . .'.[27]

Between 1919 and 1922, Picabia's aggressive yet always humorous provocation of scandals at the Indépendants and the Autumn Salons often involved images which sharpened Duchampian barbs with Picabian wit. The very first, provoked by the unadvantageous showing of Picabia's painting *Child Carburettor* [304] at the Salon d'automne of 1919, revolved around a work which now can be read as a commentary on aspects of the *Large Glass*, including the notes. His painting is an edited enlargement of a diagram of a carburettor. It is partly executed in metallic paint. As such it echoes the readymade aspects of the *Glass*, the chocolate grinder especially, with all the subversive implications they carry for the category 'art'. The mechanism depicted has obvious erotic overtones, and lacks the connections to make it function. There are fragments of text, apparently added to clarify matters, which actually defy sense by failing to combine. The scientific penchant for naming is gently mocked with the identification of the central disc as a 'sphère de migraine' (migraine sphere). And overall, the concept of the 'enfant carburetteur' (child carburettor) carries a private echo of an especially striking passage in the *Green Box*. Here Duchamp records the ideas sparked off by a night drive with Picabia in 1912 (the year after their meeting) from the Jura to Paris, and imagines them translated into a mechanism of nickel and platinum. He dubs the central personage of this imagined work, the 'head-light child' (enfant phare).[28] Duchamp was there to approve of the noise Picabia orchestrated around *Child Carburettor* – a child of his 'child' – in the press. He spent the months of his 1919 stay in Paris in Picabia's apartment.

RELEASING IMAGES: SURREALIST STRATEGIES OF LIBERATION

In October 1925, *La Révolution surréaliste* published a manifesto which was signed by political activists on the revolutionary Left as well as André Breton's Surrealist cohort: 'Revolution Now and Always' (La Révolution d'abord et toujours). They signed up to 'deliverance'

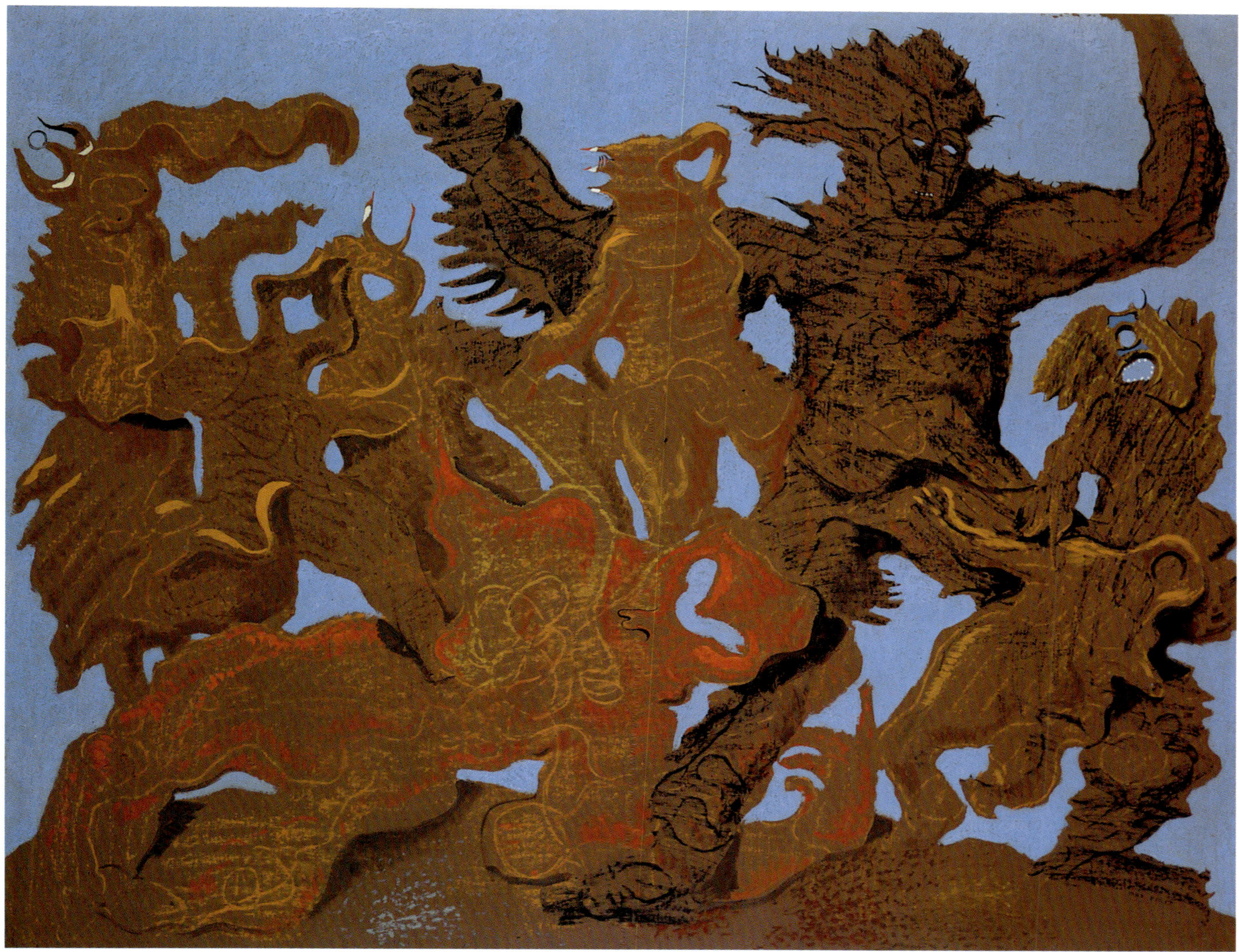

306. Max Ernst, *The Horde*, 1927. Oil on canvas, 115 × 146 cm. Stedelijk Museum, Amsterdam

through revolutionary social change, and proclaimed their rejection of 'the ideas which are fundamental to European civilisation'. They were, they declared, 'Barbarians'.[29]

Endemic within Surrealist writing and visual art was an imagery of ruins, barbaric violence and of worlds returned to the wild. In 1927, Max Ernst (b.1891) used his paint-scraping technique, *grattage*, to generate images of collective male savagery, as in *The Horde* [306]. Communist revolution was pictured as the barbaric destruction of Latin civilisation. The mid-1930s saw him return to the realism of his collage paintings with heightened precision to produce Surrealist versions of Rousseau's jungles. They followed a series obsessively focused on the image of a honeycomb city being swallowed by rampant nature. The title of one jungle picture, *Joy of Life* [305], ironically invokes Matisse's Arcadian idyll of 1906 [227]; a praying mantis and carniverous plants replace the Douanier's wild cats. In 1934, *Minotaure* carried a short text by Ernst on forests. 'What will be the death of forests?' he asks himself, and answers: 'The day will come when a forest, until then the friend of dissipation, will decide to frequent only well-behaved places, tarmacked roads, and Sunday strollers . . . She will become geometric, conscientious, dutiful, grammatical, judicial, pastoral, ecclesiastical, constructivist and republican.'[30] For him, the civilisation Rousseau had portrayed with such faith [290] was the threat, the barbarians and the forest the promise.

The Surrealists did not only use images of savagery and ruin against the civilisation of republican France. Like Duchamp, they used its own most-respected systems and institutions, turned against themselves by parody. As with Duchamp too, the leading candidates for parodic appropriation were language, science and technology. In 1929, Magritte (b.1898) presented the most deadpan image possible of a bakelite pipe above the elementary school caption 'This is not a pipe', and called it *The Treason of Images* [307]: their treason was against the tyranny of words. Early issues of *La Révolution surréaliste* carried spoofs of glossaries by Leiris and Jacques-André Boiffard featuring words and names. Leiris's 'Glossaire: j'y serre mes gloses', serialised from April 1925, defined 'vocable' (word) as 'le cable ou le volcan' (cable or volcano). The accepted formats used for elucidating words and concepts were borrowed and fantasti-

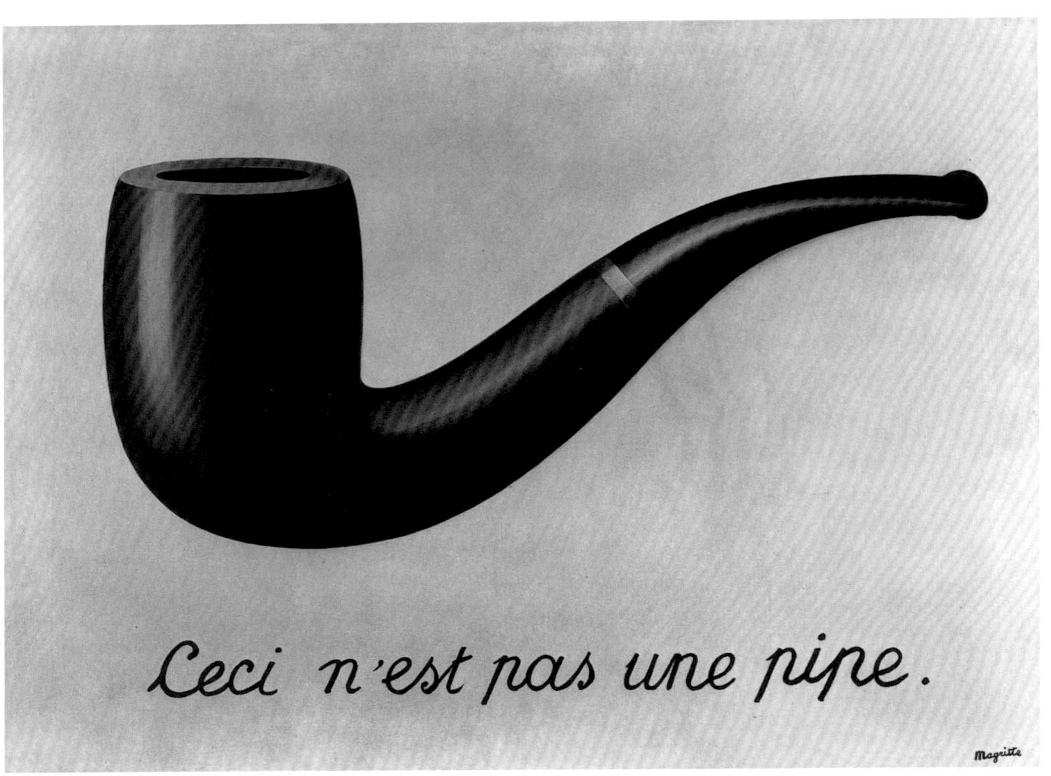

307. René Magritte, *The Treason of Images (Ceci n'est pas une pipe)*, 1928–9. Oil on canvas, 64.5 × 94 cm. Los Angeles County Museum of Art. Purchased with funds provided by the Mr and Mrs William Preston Harrison Collection

cally deformed by parodic substitutions. The word games of Rrose Sélavy were the stimulus for new games whose targets were altogether more programmatically identified.

And Duchamp's playful physics and mechanics, made public property by Picabia's tactical provocations after 1918, produced subversive Surrealist glosses too, from Ernst's often disquieting mechanisms in the collages and collage paintings of the early 1920s [138, 139] to Roberto Matta's diffuse evocations of a fourth dimension in 1938–9 [308]. Referring to the brand-new Surrealist work of Matta (b.1911) in 1939, Breton acknowledged that the Cubists had also dabbled in the fourth dimension (he did not mention Duchamp by name), but added that the problems it posed to normal perception in its later Einsteinian form, where space and time fuse as 'space-time', were 'much more acute'.[31] Science was pressed into service by means of painterly parody on the side of the fantastic against the reasonable.

The Surrealists, however, targeted one institution left largely alone by Duchamp (though not Picabia): the church. Late in 1926, *La Révolution surréaliste* no. 8 was dedicated both to Breton's case for Surrealism against the repressive discipline of the French Communist Party and to sacrilegious resistance against the repressive discipline of the church. Max Ernst's sado-masochistic substitution of the Madonna by a punishing mother [40] was published; Marcel Noll railed against pious women; and three letters appeared from a priest who had been expelled from a Jesuit seminary for sexual misdemeanours, the Abbé Gengenbach. The 1920s had seen the conversion of several leading avant-gardists to Roman Catholicism, helped by the Thomist writer Jacques Maritain; Jean Cocteau, Pierre Reverdy and Max Jacob were among them. Gengenbach was held up as a counter-convert to Surrealism. In 1927, as Jean Genbach, he published a surrealised account of his conversion, *Satan à Paris*, which features a young abbé buried alive, who is resuscitated with the aid of pyjamas formerly worn by a rake, and led into his new life by Satan in the form of a black banjo player from Josephine Baker's *Revue nègre*.[32]

Just as Duchamp evaded the reinforcement of the positions he opposed by using the humour of parodic substitutions, Surrealist inversions of Catholic language and imagery are infused by humorous irony to the same effect. Breton wrote a preface for *Satan à Paris* where he recorded Gegenbach's belief that he, Breton, was a reincarnation of Benoît XIII, one of the Avignon popes. Metaphorically apt this might have been, but to believe Breton an *actual* pope was so ridiculously presumptuous that it exposed the presumption of actual popes too, including the then current incumbent, Pius XI. Besides ironic parody, the other weapon used to protect against any possibility that opposition might reinforce the legitimacy of Catholic authority was blasphemy. Ernst's *Infant Jesus Chastised by the Virgin Mary* is not merely a parodic inversion of the Pietà, it is a gratuitous blasphemy designed to shock as only one brought up in a pious Catholic family could. Parody and blasphemy stew together in his 1930 surrealisation of the early life of the Carmelite nun Sainte Thérèse de Lisieux, his collage novel *Rêve d'une Petite Fille qui voulut entrer au Carmel* (Dream of a Little Girl who wanted to Enter Carmel). Sainte Thérèse's much read *Histoire d'une âme* of 1898, told her story as one of a girl's chaste love of God; Ernst makes of it an erotic adventure with the father as the object of unbridled desire.

In France, anti-clericalism and the republicanism of the Radical centre went together. The Surrealists' taste for sacrilege was, in fact, an excessive version of the antipathy to the Catholic Church dominant in the secular Third

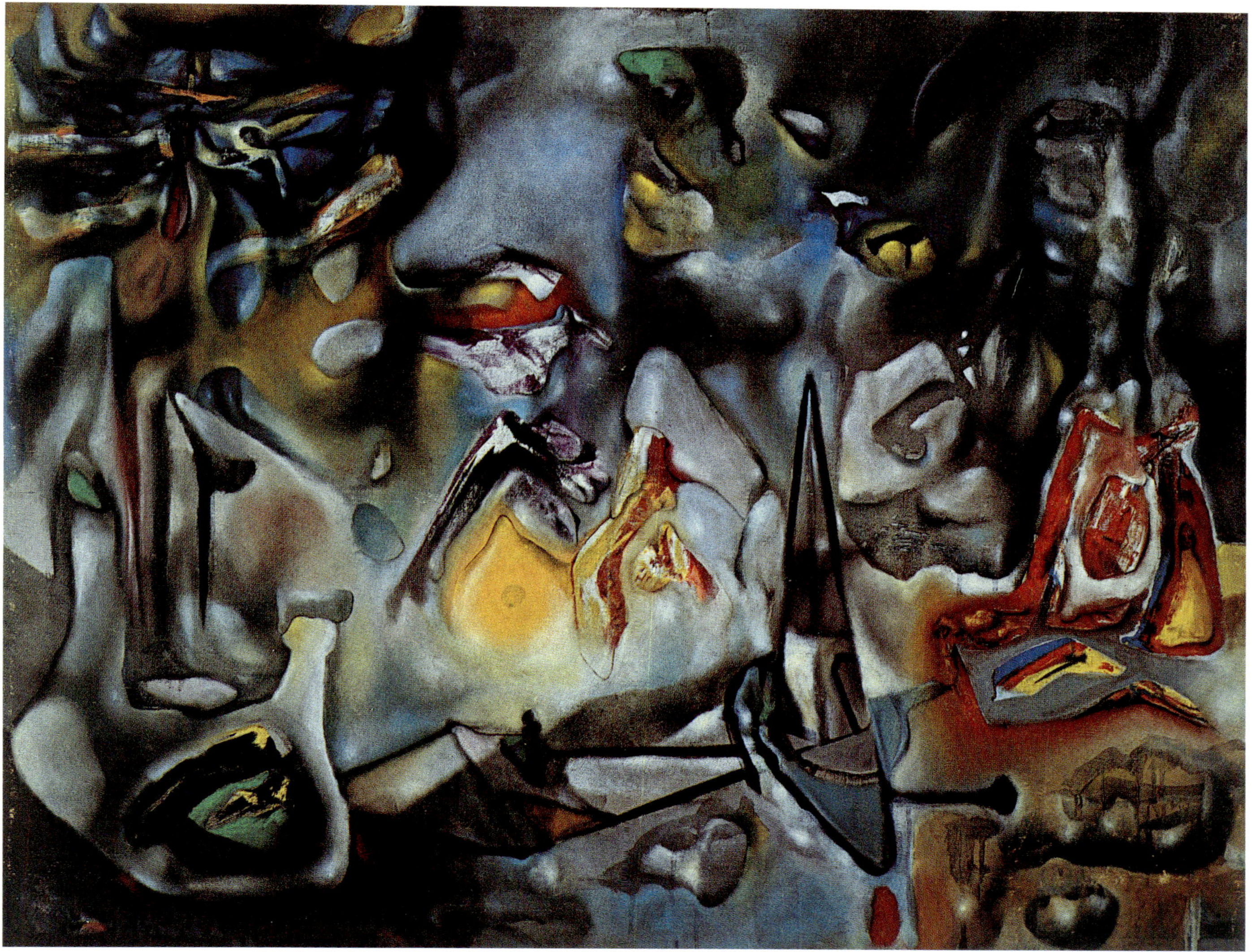

308. Roberto Matta, *Psychological Morphology, no. 104*, 1938. Oil on canvas, 73 × 92.7 cm. Private Collection

Republic, which was given new government backing when the Cartel des gauches came to power in 1924 under the fervently anti-clerical Edouard Hériot. There may have been an alliance between the extreme nationalist Right and some leading Catholic zealots, but in 1926 Pius XI refused the sacrament to the adherents of Action française. And during the 1930s, with the pope's encouragement, Catholic youth movements grew up which were oriented to the Christian democratic Left, leaving French Catholicism in an increasingly ambiguous political position.[33] Surrealist anti-clericalism was, therefore, itself ambiguously placed in relation to what was 'constructivist and republican'. It went more with the development of individual oeuvres which resisted the remembered moral authority of Catholicism in childhood, like Ernst's, than with any consistently sustained countercultural strategy.

The Surrealist subversion of the idea of modernity was both more extensive and more far-reaching in its implications. It involved the very notions of modernity that constituted the orderly 'New Spirit', which Part Four showed were so important to many modernists. Even these could be surrealised. The very centre of Fernand Léger's modernity, the city of Paris, became filled for the Surrealists with places that invited the imagination to work against the forward thrust of progress. Nowhere is this more compellingly so than in two texts of the 1920s: Louis Aragon's *Paysan de Paris* and Breton's *Nadja*, the first published in 1926, the second in 1929.

Aragon wrote of a 'poetic divinity' that dwelt unsuspected in places through which thousands passed without seeing anything, a 'divinity' that 'all of a sudden becomes responsive, and dreadfully haunting, for those who just once inadvertently see it'. His book is dedicated to two such places: a glass sky-lit shopping arcade under threat of demolition, the Passage de l'Opéra, and a romantically landscaped park in a working-class Paris neighbourhood, the Buttes-Chaumont. Within modernity, Aragon refused his own modernity, becoming a 'peasant' in Paris. He scorned the 'new aesthetic' based on the 'principle of utility', and wrote of the apparatus in hairdressers' as 'great modern wild animals', and of petrol pumps as 'metallic phantoms', 'barbarous' in their 'appearance of destiny and force'. Instead of finding in the city the practical and the commodified, he found the stimulus for dreams everywhere. In the Passage de l'Opéra, the way acquisitive desire over-values things for sale, what Karl Marx called 'commodity fetishism', is re-directed: everything is excessively overvalued by Aragon's imagination in response to fears and desires of a different kind. The arcade is, he writes, 'a great coffin of glass' in which 'Libido' [the sex drive] strolls . . . followed by the little dog Sigmund Freud'.[34]

Breton's *Nadja* is the record of his pursuit of and his encounters with a woman who, in the end, loses her sanity. The places in the city through which his pursuit passes, like the hairdressers, the café, the umbrella shop and the vaudeville in Aragon's shopping arcade, are haunted by 'Libido': Breton's desire. In this case, the surrealisation of the city generated visual as well as verbal images. Embedded in Breton's text were photographs by Jacques-André Boiffard [b.1902] which in the most literal fashion recorded the places transformed by Breton's and Nadja's passage [309]; their very banality becomes an invitation for the imagination as the eye moves from text to image, like a blank page that suddenly fills.

In visual art, Surrealism's subversion of modernity was always at its most effective when dealing most literally *with* the modern, above all, in photography. In 1926, the cover image of *La Révolution surréaliste* no.7 was a photograph by

309. Jacques-André Boiffard, *Outside the Sphinx Hotel*, photograph published in André Breton's *Nadja* (Paris, 1928)

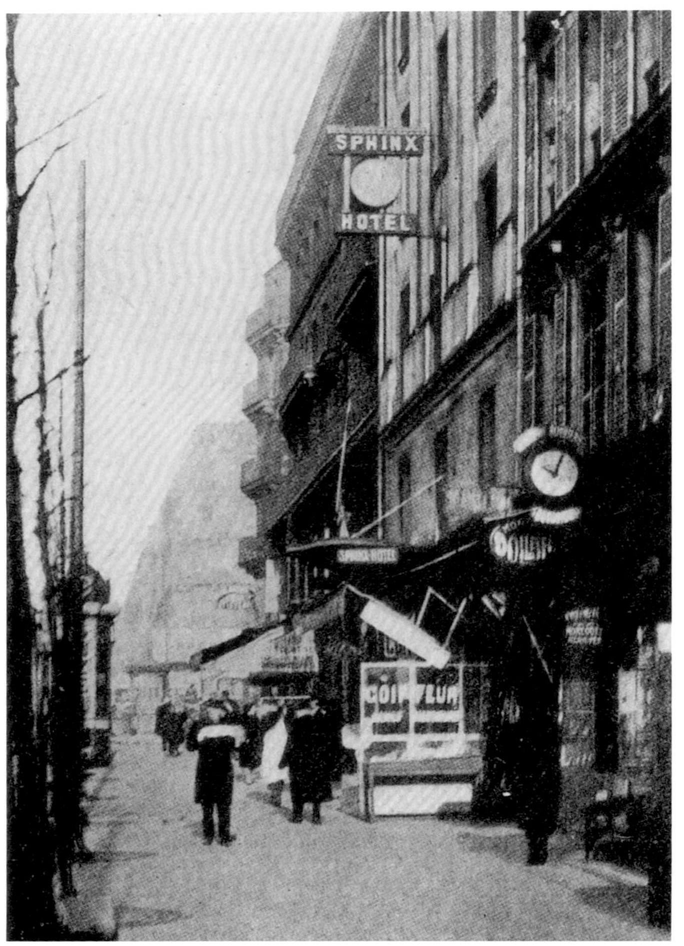

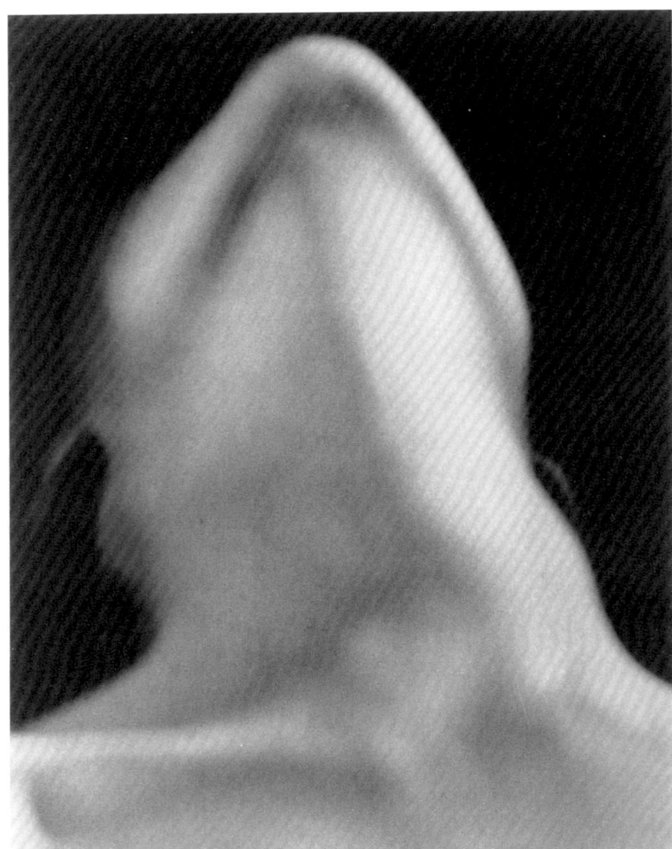

310. Man Ray, *Anatomies*, 1929. Photograph, Gelatin silver print, 22.6 × 27.2 cm. The Museum of Modern Art, New York. Gift of James Thrall Soby

Eugène Atget (though Atget (b.1857) asked not to be credited). The photograph showed ordinary pre-war Parisians gathered around a lamp-post; they all have their hands held up in front of their eyes which are raised fixedly to the sky. No explanation was given for this extraordinary behaviour. With a wry eye on Jacques Maritain's activities, the caption read: 'The Latest Conversions'. Atget, whose albums were intended as the most literal of records of Paris, called his print *The Eclipse – April 1912*; detached from its title, a simple-minded response to scientific curiosity becomes an event charged with mystery. Inside the magazine was one of Atget's shopfront photographs, comparable with *Au Tambour* [169], it appeared captionless in a body of text headed 'Dreams'.

In the mid-1980s, one powerful arbiter of global judgements concerning modernism, a group of academic critics and art historians centred on New York, gave photography the lead role not only in the visual surrealisation of modernity, but in Surrealist visual art across every sector of its revolt against European civilisation. Before I move on to look more fully at that revolt in its visual register, this historical claim needs to be addressed; its corollary is, of course, the removal of painting from centre stage.

The argument was launched with compelling force by Rosalind Krauss and was sustained within the milieu of *October* magazine; its vehicle was the exhibition *L'Amour fou: Photogaphy and Surrealism* (1985–6). In the catalogue Krauss

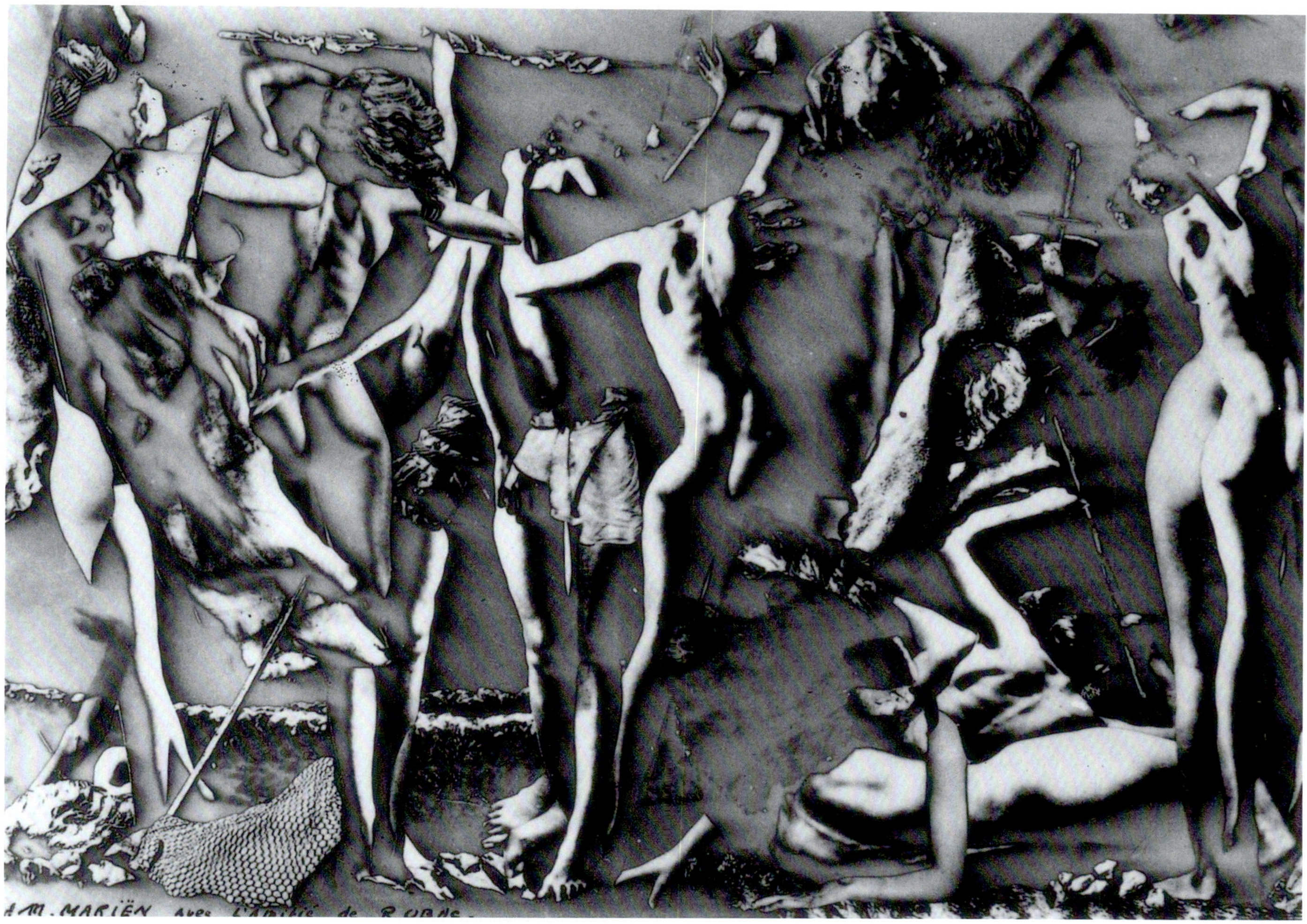

311. Raoul Ubac, *The Battle of the Amazons*, 1939. Photograph. Galerie Adrien Maeght, Paris

asserted that Surrealist photography was 'the *great* production of the movement', displacing the increasingly 'labored paintings and drawings' produced within Breton's sphere. Her argument centres on the exploitation by Surrealist photographers of a duality within photography: its literalness as 'a photochemically processed trace' of reality, and its openness to techniques which expose the intervention of the photographer. In the language of semiology, Surrealist photography can simultaneously be a 'message without a code' – a physical trace of reality – *and* produce 'the mark of the sign' – reveal the transformation of that reality into representation by the imagination.[35] Surrealist photographers are shown to have exploited a stunning repertoire of techniques to register the repossession of the real for the imagination: unexpected angles, which defamiliarise the familiar, double images (using mirrors, double exposures, etc.), which put any 'original' reality into question, rayography (the placing of objects on sensitised paper before exposing it to light), solarisation (brief exposures of developing prints to light), *brûlage* (the partial burning of negatives), and negative printing. As we have seen, the interaction of text and image could transform even the blandest photographic records of reality, Boiffard's in *Nadja* for example.

Two of the instances Krauss singles out are a straight print of around 1930 by Man Ray (b.1890), *Anatomies* [310], and a print by Raoul Ubac (b.1909) of 1939 which is the result of repeated solarisations using fragments of shots of a single nude body, *Battle of the Amazons* [311]. In the first, a head of uncertain gender is photographed from below. Thrown back, 'its' chin becomes the apex of a column of flesh without any clear corporeal identity, perhaps phallic, perhaps not: it is many possible anatomies. In the second, the fragments of bodies are eaten into by the space around them, each fragment still but, when seen together, frenetically, violently mobile: in savage conflict as they dissolve into one another.

The ambivalence of defamiliarised images frees them from fixed definition of any kind. In this way they become what Krauss calls 'informe'. Here, she uses a concept first broached by Georges Bataille in 1929, where the 'informe' is given a distinctly Duchampian job: to resist that mainstay of civilised reason, classification. In Bataille's words: 'For academics to be happy, the universe has to have form . . . By contrast, to affirm that the universe is nothing but '*informe*' amounts to saying that the universe is something like a spider or a gob of spit.'[36] The *informe* and the unclean go together: the *informe de*civilises. For Krauss, nothing does the *informe*'s job more forcefully than photography, because

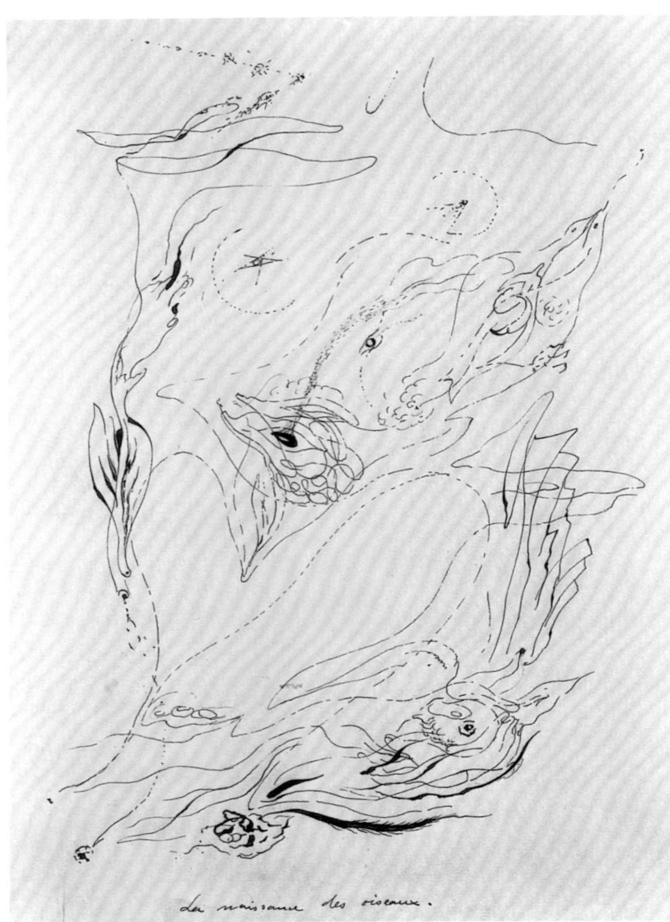

312. André Masson, *Birth of Birds*, *c.* 1925. Ink on paper, 41.9 × 31.4 cm. The Museum of Modern Art, New York. Purchase

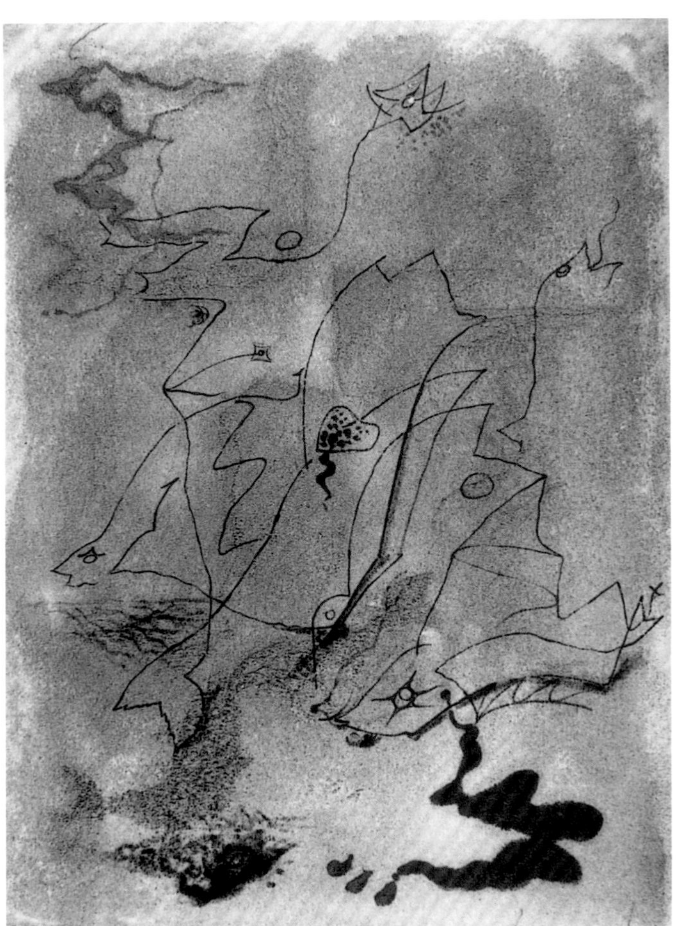

313. André Masson, *Fish Drawn on the Sand*, 1926–7. Oil and sand on canvas, 100 × 73 cm. Kunstmuseum, Bern, Hermann und Margit Rupf-Stiftung

it can simultaneously present the traces of classifiable reality – including the reality called modernity in the early twentieth century – and dissolve it into the unclassifiable, as *re*presentation.[37] Within reach of classification, places, people and things become unclassifiable before our eyes.

More than merely a claim, Krauss's argument has reclaimed the force of Surrealist photography and brought it in from the margins, but her denial of the significance of painting in Surrealist activity between the wars is plainly an historical distortion. This distortion (shaped by critical rather than historical priorities) follows from her focus on the image produced rather than on the processes behind and inscribed in the image. Those processes and the possibility of their inscription in the image were, in fact, key elements of the Surrealists' campaign against their logocentric society. If photography's advantage came of, in Krauss's words, its 'privileged connection to the real', painting's advantage came of its privileged connection to the processes of its making.

Krauss's focus on the image and its effect is supported historically by one of Breton's attempts at counter-definition. In 1934, he published an article in *Minotaure* entitled 'Beauty will be Convulsive', where he supplanted the aesthetic notion of 'beauty' with one entirely centred on the capacity of images to excite: to produce a 'frisson' comparable to 'that of erotic pleasure'. Convulsive beauty, he contended, was to be found in both 'the spectacles of nature and works of art'; the article was illustrated entirely with photographs recording 'spectacles of nature'. There were examples of all three of his categories of convulsive beauty: the 'veiled erotic', where one natural phenomenon looks like another (states of ambivalence and transition, where, for instance, the inanimate borders on the animate); the 'exploding-yet-fixed' (explosante-fixe), the freezing of motion (a spinning dancer photographed, for instance); and the 'magical-circumstantial', where objects seem to carry 'a message informing the recipient of his own desire' (a glove found in *Nadja*, for instance).[38] In every case, as Krauss points out, the real is experienced in 'the process of contorting or convulsing itself into its apparent opposite, namely a sign' – a representation rather than a reality. For Krauss, the concept of convulsive beauty is 'at the core' of Surrealism's 'aesthetic'; it follows that photography, given its 'privileged connection with reality', is at the core of Surrealism.[39]

The concept of convulsive beauty was certainly crucial to Breton in the mid-1930s; he used his *Minotaure* article to open his major publication of 1936, *L'Amour fou*, another text illustrated by photographs (Man Ray's and Brassaï's). However, Breton originally defined Surrealism in the *Manifesto* of 1924 as 'psychic automatism'; he placed his emphasis not on the image as such, but rather on the processes by which 'all control by reason' could be relinquished allowing the release of images. Surrealism existed not merely in images but in activities; modes of behaviour by which writers and artists could override the civilised impulses towards rational, 'aesthetic' and 'moral' order. Its counter-culture entailed not merely an alternative 'beauty', which challenged the real, but automated modes of thinking and doing, which subverted creativity and which challenged, therefore, the very idea of the creative artist as a 'genius' willing new forms.

The theory of automatism certainly dominated Surrealist theory and practice between 1922 (before the manifesto) and the late 1920s. From the second *Manifesto* of 1929 until the later 1930s, it was given a much less central role, especially with Dalí's assertive advocacy of a more active, 'paranoid' imposition of the artist's hallucinatory 'reality' upon appearances, and with the craze for making, finding and assembling 'objects'. Dalí (b.1904) himself, however, saw his practice as running alongside, not displacing, the more passive practices of automatism; and there is, as we shall see, an automatist aspect to the Surrealist object. Moreover, in 1933, in the number of *Minotaure* preceding 'Beauty will be Convulsive', Breton published 'The Automatic Message', an essay which ensured that the question of automatism would remain a legitimate Surrealist concern. Here the automatists who he lifted into the Surrealist limelight were not 'artists' but mediums; in themselves they challenged the elevation of the artist-as-'genius'. It was with relish that Breton reported 'a marked return to *automatism*' in 1939, looking back in the joint final number 12–13 of *Minotaure* to his call for 'psychic automatism' fifteen years before, as he welcomed a new generation of automatist painters, among them Matta.[40]

Early Surrealist writing on automatism makes it clear that it entailed for the group not only the development of specialist procedures for cutting out 'all control by reason', but the cultivation of alternative values and behaviours in the modern world. Counter-cultural priorities – indeed, a counter-cultural morality – produced automatist activity. Surrealism would always be geared not simply to the release of images in texts and in visual art, but to a way of life whose first priority was their *pursuit*, not their collection. Breton's *Nadja* is not about finding what this always-unexpected woman means to him in any definitive sense; it is about the pursuit of what she *can* mean. Activities with a goal were replaced by energetic aimlessness; the structures of reason by the *informe* of the imagination. In *Le Paysan de Paris*, Aragon included a mock drama featuring 'Sensibility', 'Will', 'Intelligence' and 'Imagination'. 'Imagination' offers Surrealism like a commodity, a new drug with the power to free everyone's 'faculties in the void'.

Reason demolished by imagination, form by the *informe*, brought with them contradictions which were left unresolved in the theory and practice of automatism. The aim of this *activity* was a perfect *passivity* (always beyond reach), and it required an uncompromising individualism to achieve the unwilled, and so to *diminish* the role of individual creativity and undercut the ideal of genius. In the first *Manifesto* Breton proudly claimed: 'We have no talent . . . , we who have made ourselves, in our works, the deaf receptacles of so many echoes, the modest *recording devices* that are not hypnotised by the designs they trace . . .'.[41] The editorial of the first number of *La Révolution surréaliste* announced that the loss of control meant the disappearance of the author from the text.

And yet, the pursuit of this ideal state of absence necessarily involved placing one's own imaginative activity above everything else, especially the demands of society (hence Surrealism's moral dimension). The Marquis de Sade's willingness to endure imprisonment rather than betray the anti-social violence of his imagination is what made him a Surrealist hero from the mid-1920s. As Aragon brought *Le Paysan de Paris* to an end, he wrote: 'The first person singular expresses for me all that is concrete about man. All metaphysics is in the first person singular. All poetry too.'[42]

If Surrealist photography was able to bring together reality and representation with special force, Surrealist painting was able to bring together the creative individual and his or her dissolution with special force. It did so because of modernist painting's capacity to be both the record of a process and its representation.

When in 1939 Breton wrote of a return to automatism, he asserted that '*absolute* automatism' was only then being achieved on the 'plastic plane'; he mentioned recent technical procedures, 'décalcomania' and '*fumage*', as well as those painters like Matta who he grouped around the older Yves Tanguy (b.1900). Among the examples he illustrated was Matta's *Psychological Morphology* [308]. Of earlier techniques like collage, Ernst's pencil-rubbing technique 'frottage' and Dalí's paranoid-critical method, he wrote: '[they] have not ceased to maintain a certain equivocation between the willed and the unwilled . . .'.[43] Perhaps surprisingly, he did not mention either André Masson (b.1896) or Joan Miró (b.1893) whose work had made the most convincing claim to '*absolute*' pictorial automatism in the 1920s heyday of the theory.

The kind of pictorial automatism to which Breton referred in 1939 concerned not the painting of dreams but the 'automatic' marking of paper or canvas with whatever implement there was available. This kind of pictorial automatism brought together activity and passivity, the individual and his or her dissolution with particular immediacy. In the mid-1920s, this mark-making automatism came closest to Breton's 'absolute' in such drawings by Masson as *Birth of Birds* of 1925 [312] and in his sand-paintings of 1927, the largest of which was *Fish Drawn on the Sand* [313], as well as in Miró's so-called 'dream paintings' of 1924–7, works like *Circus Horse* of 1927 and the most ambitious of all, the 1925 *Birth of the World* [314, 316]. In the making of none of these works was the 'aesthetic' and the 'willed' completely cut out, however.

The elegant economy with which images emerge from the play of line in Masson's *Birth of Birds* betrays control allied to skill, however open the process might have been. The procedure that produced *Fish in the Sand* allowed no room for manual skill except at the very last moment. Glue was randomly applied, sand was then sprinkled over the canvas, remaining where fixed by the glue; this was repeated more than once. Only then did Masson draw and add colour, responding to the suggestions in the sand. But still he found his images of submarine violence with pointed cogency.

Miró's automatism was always at one remove in the 'dream paintings'. He worked on canvas from tiny sketches

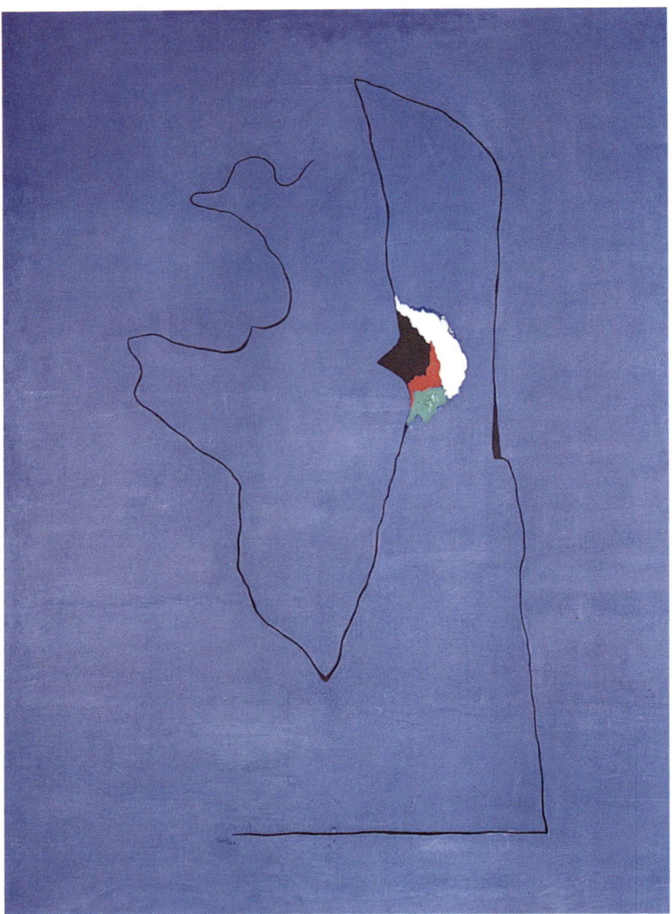

314. Joan Miró, *Circus Horse*, 1927. Oil on canvas, 130 × 95.8 cm. Whereabouts unknown

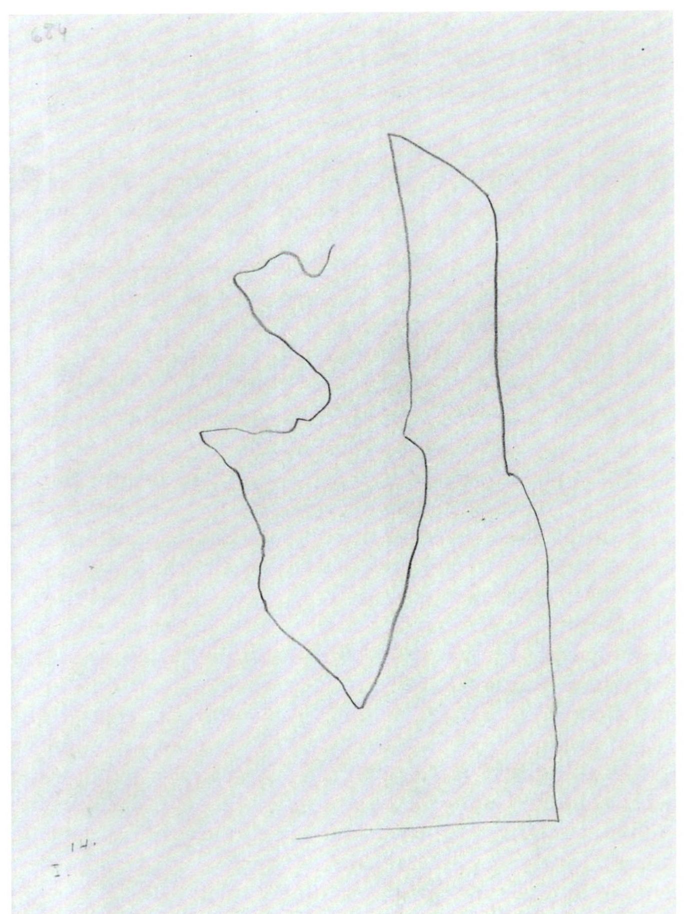

315 Joan Miró, *Sketch for 'Circus Horse'*, 1926–7. Pencil on paper, 27 × 26.1 cm. Fundació Joan Miró, Barcelona, FJM684

in notebooks, transferring his pencil jottings onto suggestively worked grounds, usually painted in one colour, yellow, blue or brown. Such sketches lie behind both *Birth of the World* and *Circus Horse* [314–316]. At the stage of drawing, Miró worked hard to exclude control. Allowing his hand to move, possibly with eyes shut, seems to have produced the wavering, unravelling line in the larger-than-usual sketch transcribed for *Circus Horse*. His translations from notebook to painting are often remarkably exact, but the clarity of the drawing with the brush, the precise placing of elements within the format, quite apart from the colours used, are painterly procedures open to 'conscious' editorial control; and sometimes, as in *Circus Horse*, he made significant additions when he painted.

Neither artist, therefore, can be said to have produced works in which the marks are in any absolute sense automatic: 'unwilled'. The authentic, however, was not at issue among the Surrealists. As Aragon put it in *Une Vague de rêves*: 'To simulate something, is it anything else than to think it so? And what is thought, is.'[44] All that mattered was the convincing representation of automatism. In this these drawings and paintings often succeed, given an open and responsive viewer. They erase, obscure or minimise all the most telling markers of control. And yet, simultaneously the capacity of the drawn or painted mark to signify the artist's hand remains. Grounded as Masson and Miró were in Cubist painting-as-drawing and the notion of the *tableau objet*, from the start they inscribed the process of making within each work. The viewer is invited to read that process and to feel it empathetically as an activity, one in which images are pursued, reason is derailed and creativity gives way to passive receptivity. Even as the artist leaves his own, distinctly personal traces – those marks on the surface – he produces a representation of his dissolution: he represents himself as nothing more than Breton's 'modest recording device'. Viewers can emulate the process imaginatively, 'losing' themselves in the work, like the artist.

Manually fabricated art objects could do this with such immediacy, because of the directness with which they incorporated traces of identity. Yet, even Surrealist techniques which minimised or actually excluded altogether direct traces of the artist's hand did not take away from pictorial or sculptural work its capacity to inscribe process *and personality*, with all that could imply. Ernst's *frottage* and *grattage* techniques were designed more or less to exclude the personalised mark of the pencil or the brush, producing drawings and paintings without a 'hand'. Their densely worked surfaces seem, however, to disclose the process of their making *as* personal, while the actual complexities of the quasi-automated processes involved are concealed. This is especially so of the *grattages* like *The Horde* which include lines achieved by dropping paint-soaked string on the canvas,

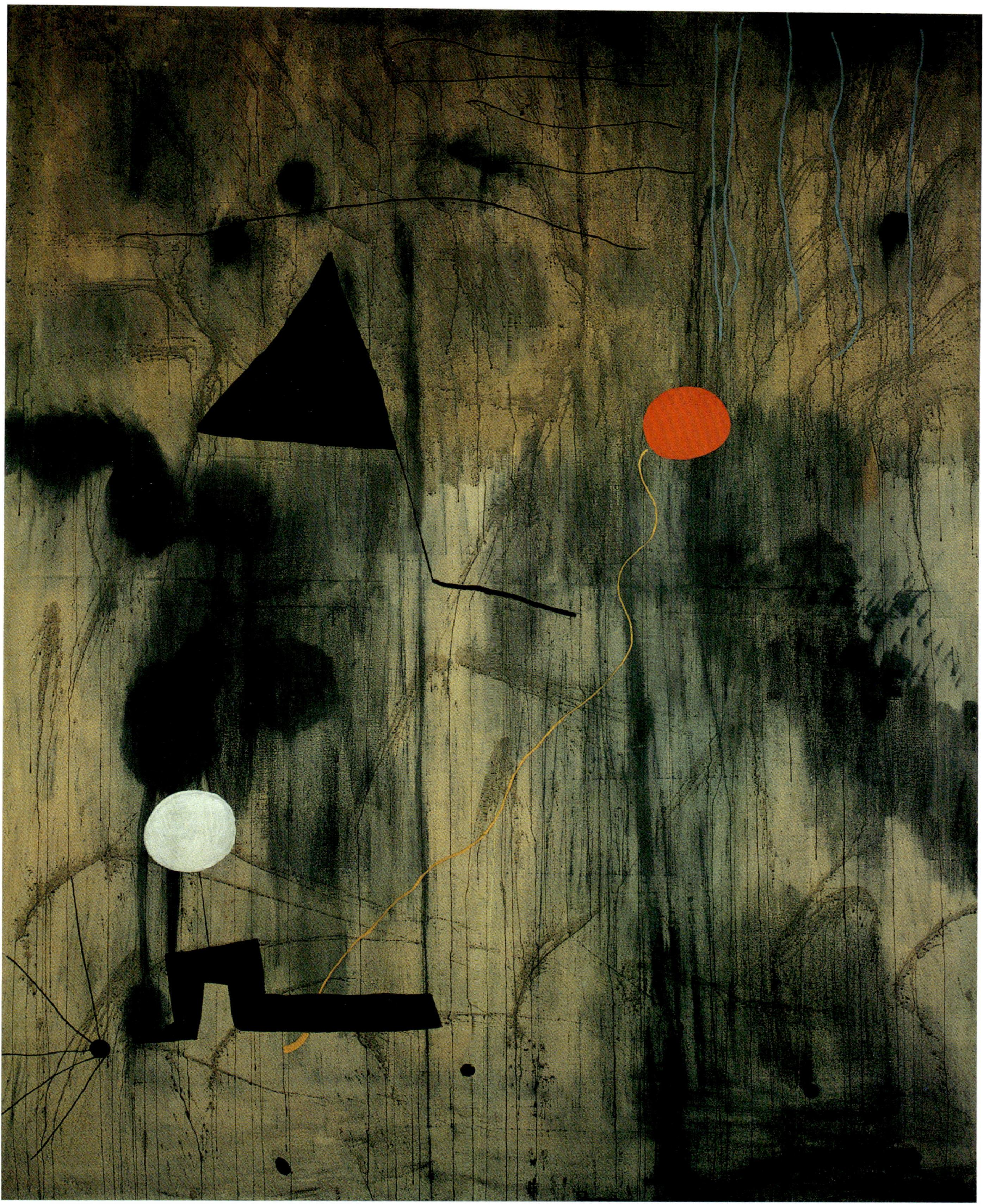

316. Joan Miró, *Birth of the World*, 1925. Oil on canvas, 250.8 × 200 cm. The Museum of Modern Art, New York. Acquired through an anonymous fund, the Mr and Mrs Joseph Slifka and Armand C. Erpf Funds, and by gift of the artist

where the look of a personal calligraphy is almost too plausible to doubt. Even here, the idea of the artist and his dissolution come together in confrontation; they do so as a result of the deliberately mendacious exploitation of the expected association between pencil or paint marks and personality in modernism.

In 1930, Aragon's important text on collage, *La Peinture au défi* (In Defiance of Painting), emphasised above all the exclusion of 'personality-through-technique' from collage, and offered in its place 'the personality of choice'.[45] Before the first 'Surrealist Objects' in 1930–1, work like Ernst's Dada collages of the early 1920s [37], his later collage novels and Picasso's rubbish collages of 1926 [317] constituted the most uncompromising demonstrations of such a denial of the 'hand' as the mark of the artist. Yet, the force of that denial could only be increased by the fact that it took place within the conventional formats of pictorial art, print making and book illustration, because those formats inevitably invoked the idea of autograph techniques and styles. The expectation of 'personality-through-technique' was aroused only to be denied. Precisely the same confrontation between conventional expectations and their denial was exploited in those Surrealist objects that were not found or assembled, but produced out of the imagination and then fabricated. Giacometti made a point of not crafting his object works of 1930–2 himself. Significantly, however, when his *Suspended Ball* [155] was included in the 1931 number of *Le Surréalisme au service de la révolution* dedicated to the Surrealist object, it was one of only two works illustrated to be captioned 'Sculpture'. The other was a work by Miró which incorporated found items (artificial flowers and an umbrella), but whose major elements were also fabricated by a carpenter to his designs. By placing these impersonal productions in the category 'sculpture', once again the idea of the artist as creator was invoked only to be denied. Objects displayed outside the context of sculpture, as they were in the 1936 exhibition at the galerie Charles Ratton [157], derived the force of denial, like photography, from their privileged connection to the real. By contrast, *all* Surrealist images displayed as painting or sculpture, the 'hand-painted photography' of Dalí included, derived part of their force from their privileged connection to 'art' and 'artists'.

317. Pablo Picasso, *Guitar*, 1926. Cloth, paper, string, nails and oil on canvas, 130 × 97.5 cm. Musée Picasso, Paris

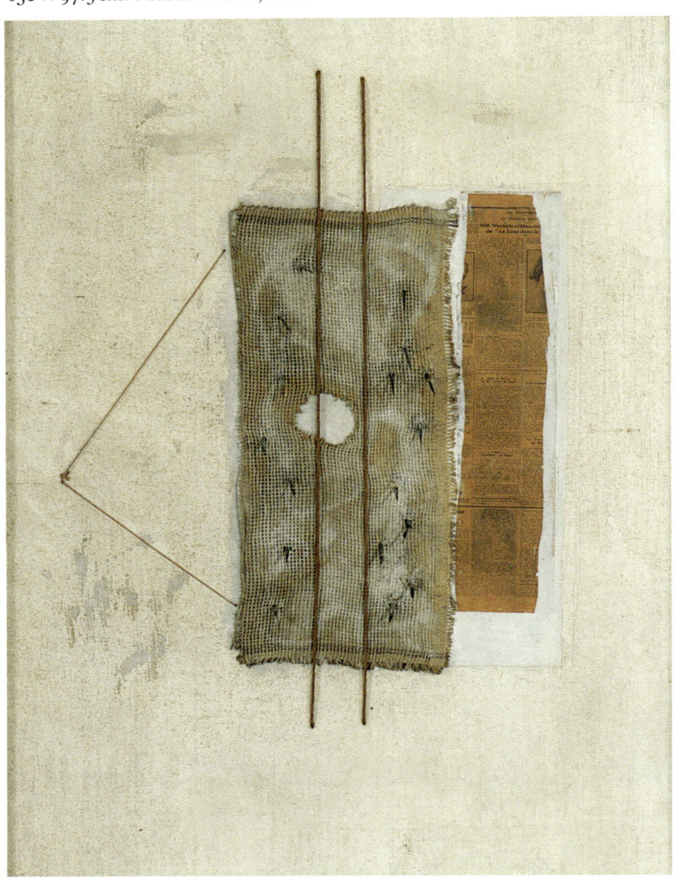

The Surrealists worked to subvert their progressive and rationalist society by generating textual or visual productions that parodied its forms, from language to art, that gave imagination hegemony over all the categories of the real to the extent of threatening their dissolution, and that replaced willed creation with the aimless yet determined pursuit of the unexpected and the thrilling. Their textual and visual productions have increasingly been treated as ends (perhaps an inevitable development): works of art, to be analysed in terms of their capacity to make meanings, to represent. They are, in fact, what has been left behind by writers and artists (including photographers) whose first priority was to make their work an activity, one of many ways of living against the grain in what they thought of contemptuously as civilised society.[46]

THE WORLD AS MYTH: PSYCHOANALYSIS AND OTHER SURREALIST PREOCCUPATIONS

In 1932, Christian Zervos, editor of *Cahiers d'art*, published the following 'confidence' taken from conversations with Picasso (b.1881): 'Each time that I take up a picture I have the sensation of throwing myself into the void.' Zervos comments: 'when Picasso works, it is the action of creating that counts for him far more than the result obtained'.[47]

When Breton attempted his appropriation of Picasso for Surrealism in 1925, among the works that he illustrated to mark the event in *La Révolution surréaliste* was Picasso's latest major painting, *The Three Dancers* [318]. He had already illustrated a page of drawings from one of Picasso's 1924 sketchbooks as if they were fully 'automatist'. Picasso's refusal actually to enter the group, however, went with a clear determination, as an artist, never to allow his engagement with process to mask his supreme confidence in his creative uniqueness. Yet, there is no mistaking the presence of Surrealist priorities in his work and behind his statements from the mid-1920s. He was, after all, close to such important figures from both the Surrealist and the so-called dissident Surrealist groupings, as Miró, Leiris and, especially from the mid-1930s, Paul Eluard.

The disposition of the figures of *The Three Dancers* in front of the frames of an open window unmistakably evoke the crucifixion format, complete with paired mourners. The frenzied dance of the figure on the left has, as a result,

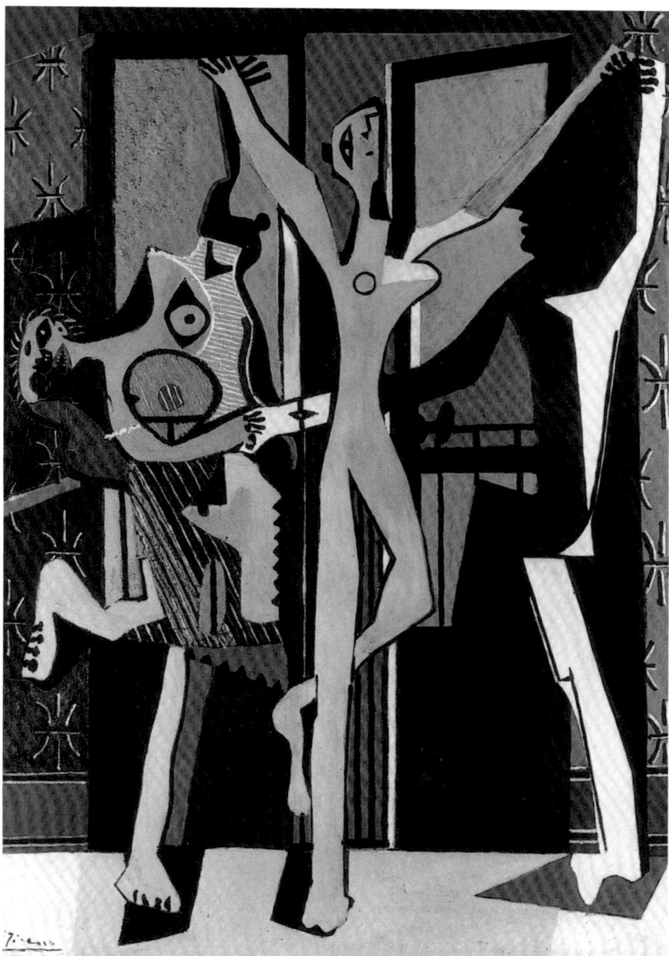

318. Pablo Picasso, *The Three Dancers*, 1925. Oil on canvas, 215 × 142 cm. The Tate Gallery, London

been identified with Renaissance adaptations of Hellenic Bacchantes for the role of Mary possessed by grief: what is termed the 'Maenad under the Cross'. Picasso fuses an allusion to religious sacrifice and grief with the release of sexual ecstacy in dance.[48] From his beginnings in Barcelona, Picasso had been aware of the writings of Friedrich Nietzsche. The Maenad of *The Three Dancers* echoes unmistakably the Nietzschean notion of creativity as release through complete loss of control, a notion the philosopher identified with the dance of the Maenads, females possessed by the god Dionysos.

Mythic figures representing loss of control – frenzied, monstrous or both – abound in Picasso's work alongside that of many Surrealists from the mid-1920s. The periodical *Minotaure*, dominated by the Surrealists throughout its existence (1933–9), brought the figure of the bull-headed monster to the fore: the seat of reason transformed into an image of dark instinct and bestiality. Picasso provided the Minotaure image for the first number in 1933, by which time this figure from the story of Theseus and Ariadne and the Cretan labyrinth was becoming a leading character in the series of etchings he began that year, the 'Vollard Suite'. One of the monster's many appearances would be as the anti-hero of the *Minotauromachy* in 1935 [147]. Masson was the Surrealist artist most engaged with the figure of the Minotaure besides Picasso, and his treatment of it was very much his own. In 1938, no longer predominantly a mark-making automatist, he painted *The Labyrinth* [319], the Minotaure as a half-built, half-ruined monument in nature, with the labyrinth contained inside him. Minotaure and labyrinth come together as an image of the unfathomable *informe* within us.

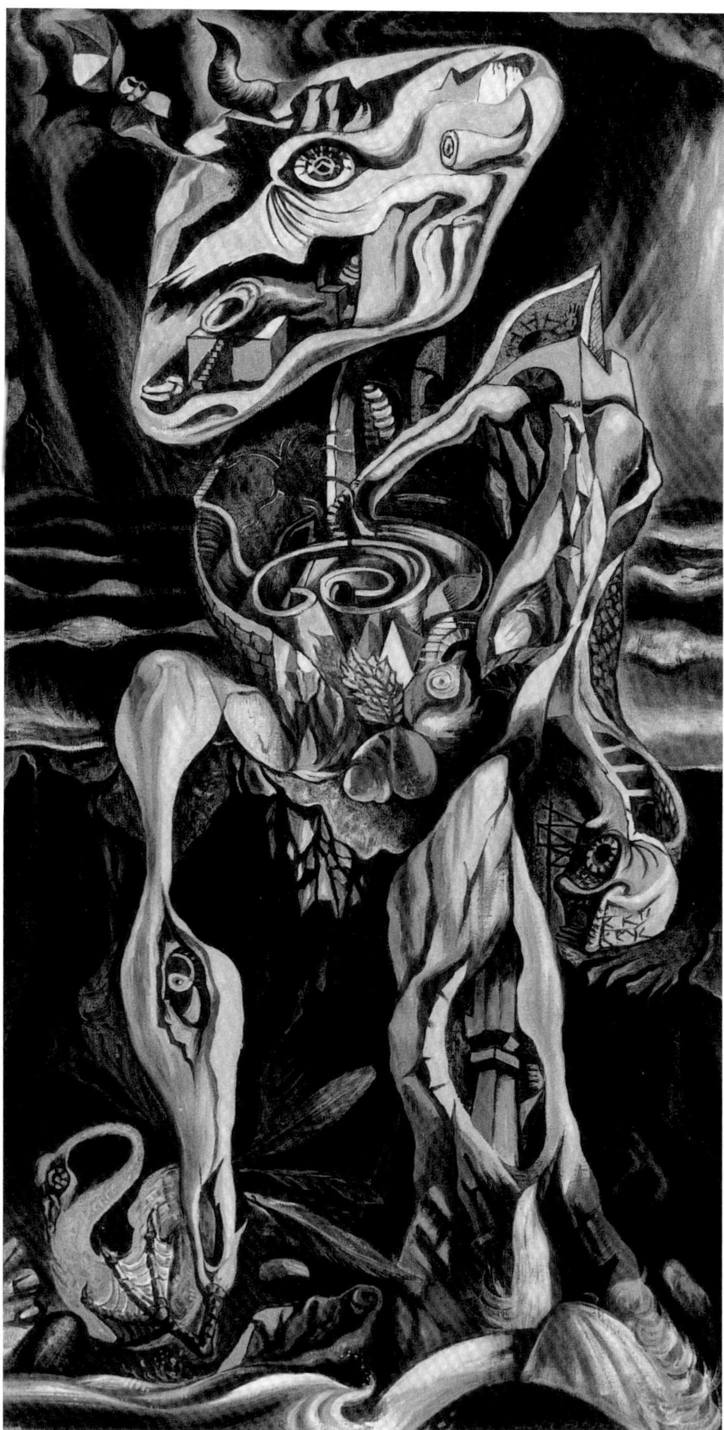

319. André Masson, *The Labyrinth*, 1938. Oil on canvas, 120 × 61 cm. Musée National d'Art Moderne, Paris

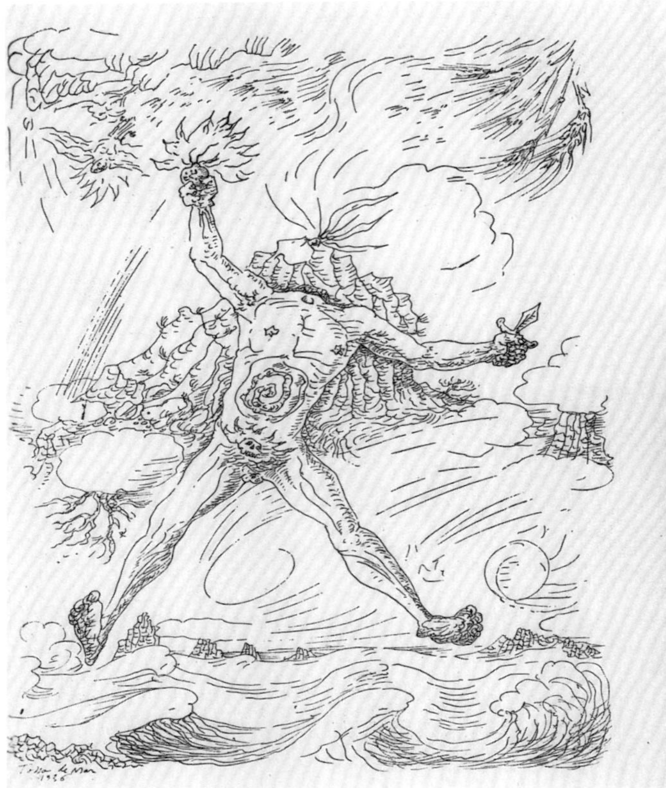

320. André Masson, *'Acéphale'. Reappearance to Nietzsche*, 1937. Illustration from *Acéphale*, double number, 21 January 1937, p. 19. Bibliothèque nationale, Paris

By 1938, Masson was involved with Georges Bataille and a philosopher friend, Pierre Klossowski, in a smaller, more occasional magazine than *Minotaure*, *Acéphale*, whose title referred to a headless god, a figure who had attracted Bataille since the days of *Documents* (1929–30). From Spain, where Masson was based between 1934 and 1936, the painter had sent the drawing used for the cover of its opening issue (July 1936); he was Bataille's closest painter-friend. The cover image is the springboard for an illustration he provided in number 2 (January 1937), *'Acéphale'. Reappearance to Nietzsche* [320]. In Masson's own account of the cover image, the god's severed head – a skull – takes the place of his genitalia: as death, the head becomes the place of erotic passion. Masson opens the belly to show the god's guts as a labyrinth, and places in his hands a sword and a flaming heart. The latter is not, he stresses, 'that of the crucified [god], but that of our master Dionysos'.[49] Acéphale, the Minotaure and Dionysos become a single image of headless frenzy, in an issue of the magazine dedicated to Nietzsche. *Acéphale*'s next issue (July 1937) was dedicated to Dionysos.

The acephalic image of release was aggressively masculine; its dionysian equivalent, in the frenzied figure of the Maenad, was usually feminine. If the outcome of release could be male savagery, the condition of release as such was more often pictured as female. The most striking early display of Surrealist liberation from control as a feminine condition came with a joint article by Aragon and Breton published in *La Révolution surréaliste* in 1928, 'The Fiftieth Anniversary of Hysteria (1878–1928)'. Their text begins:

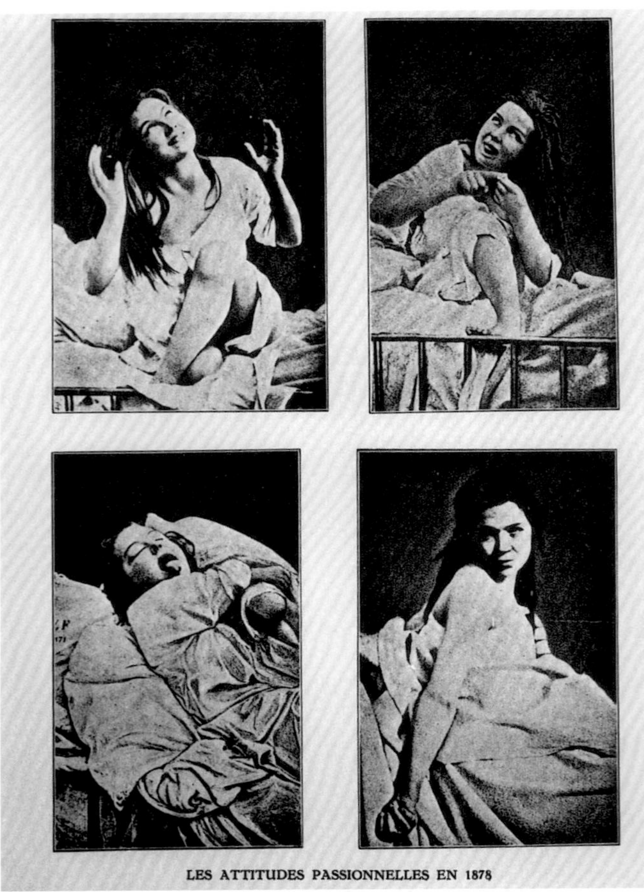

321. *Passionate Poses in 1878 (Les Attitudes Passionnelles en 1878).* Photographs illustrated in André Breton & Louis Aragon, 'Le cinquantenaire d'hystérie, 1878–1928', *La Révolution Surréaliste*, no. 11 (Paris, 1928)

'We, Surrealists, undertake to celebrate here the fiftieth anniversary of hysteria, the greatest discovery of the end of the 19th century'. Illustrated were photographs of 'Augustine', a young patient of the French psychiatrist Jean-Marie Charcot (an early influence on Freud), subject of a study of hysteria at the Salpêtrière assylum in 1878 [321]; they were captioned 'attitudes passionnelles' (passionate poses). For Aragon and Breton, hysteria was not so much a 'discovery' as a psychiatric invention. They went on to reject the idea that hysteria is a pathological condition open to clinical definition (the view of Joseph Babinski, a pupil of Charcot who Breton had assisted in 1917). They saw it rather as a 'mental state' of rebellion against 'the world of morality', which made it, of course, a Surrealist invention. As Briony Fer has contended, to hold up 'the delicious X.L (Augustine)' as 'the perfect type' of the 'hysteric', freed from reason, was to reinforce a distinctly negative stereotype of the feminine, but to hold up such a condition as a model of revolt against morality was to give that stereotype a new and not necessarily negative inflection.[50]

Hysterics were not the Surrealists' only models of release from control. There were many more, often (but not always) female. They included the mental patients whose drawings the German psychiatrist Hans Prinzhorn published in 1922 (introduced in Paris by Ernst); the celebrated medium from the turn of the century, Hélène Smith, who was among

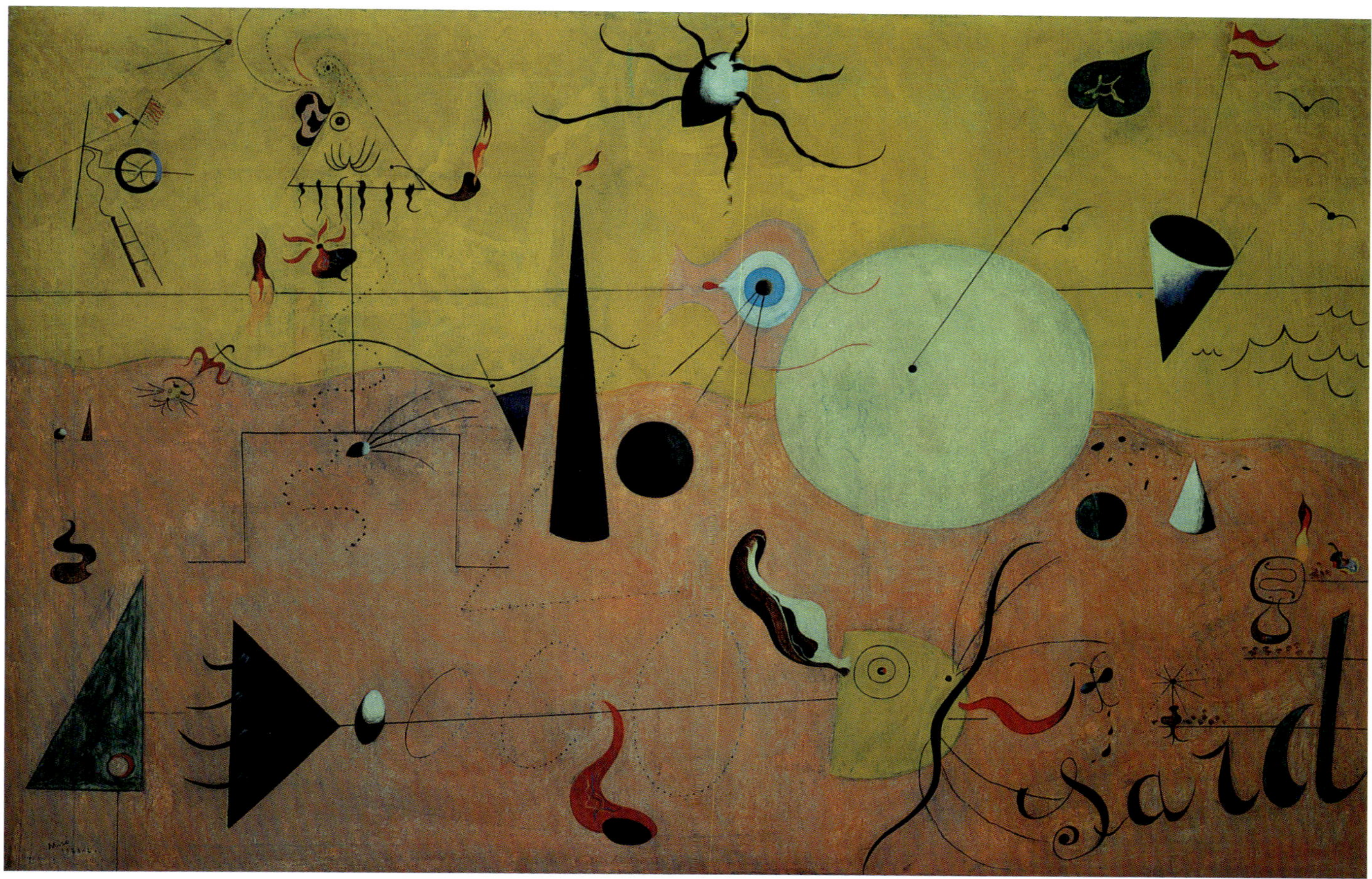

322. Joan Miró, *Catalan Landscape (The Hunter)*, 1923–4. Oil on canvas, 64.8 × 100.3 cm. The Museum of Modern Art, New York

those singled out by Breton in his 1933 article 'The Automatic Message'; and even the murderers, the Papin sisters, domestic servants whose revenge against their employers ended with the ripping out of their eyes.[51] All stood outside the established categories of the normal and the acceptable, some far enough outside to shock.

At the same time, Breton and his group periodically alluded to figures from the past as liberated in exemplary ways from the 'control of reason', occasionally even erecting part-serious, part-parodic cultural lines of descent – traditions. One of the first and most complete of these was a chart of names printed in different sizes to indicate importance, which appeared in 1923 under the heading 'Erutaréttil' ('littérature' backwards) in the periodical *Littérature*. These counter-lineages were conceived against the grain of the dominant Humanist notions of tradition; and figures rarely stayed in favour permanently. They gave prominence to the irrationally inspired, acknowledging not only the German Romantics and such French Romantic and Symbolist figures as Baudelaire and Rimbaud, but marginal undesirables like Breton's own discovery, Isidore Ducasse, known as the Comte de Lautréamont, author of the *Chants de Maldoror*, a prose work which combines the Sadean and the dionysiac with unparalleled imaginative élan.

When, in the *Second Manifesto of Surrealism*, Breton cited Arthur Rimbaud's famous statement of 1871 – 'The poet becomes a seer by a long, enormous and reasoned derangement of the senses' – he did so to underscore the convergence of the mediumistic and the poetic, a convergence that would remain consistently crucial to the Surrealist counter-aesthetic.[52] Breton's reference to Rimbaud's so-called 'Lettre du voyant' (Letter of the Seer) is made, significantly, in a passage of the manifesto dedicated to drawing out an arcane analogy between Surrealism's transformation of the raw material of reality and the Medieval alchemists' pursuit of the 'philosophical stone' by the transformation of the *prima materia*. Here Rimbaud, alongside Lautréamont, is placed in the context not only of alchemists but of the sixteenth-century occultist Cornelius Agrippa. At the end of the passage, Breton demands 'the deep, and true occultation of Surrealism'.[53] In the 'Erutaréttil' chart of 1923, five alchemists and occultists are named in company with such literary figures as Baudelaire, Lautréamont and Rimbaud. They include Cornelius Agrippa, and also Hermes Trismegistus, an alchemist cited by Apollinaire well before 1914, besides the Catalan mystic Raymond Lull.

There is strong evidence that this enduring Surrealist interest in the occult and alchemy, tied in as it is with the Surrealists' commitment to the visionary in all media, finds echoes in the work of major artists associated with the group. Allusions to Lull have been found in Miró's work, for instance in his use of the ladder image. The ladder that hangs crazily from the aeroplane in the sky of *Catalan Landscape (The Hunter)* may be more than comic [322]. Indeed, the hunter himself here has been associated with the *Zohar*, one of the most important books of the Kabbalah: the separate hairs of his beard and the opening out of his head into the sky conform strikingly to the Kabbalic image of God in Heaven, the 'Ancient One'.[54] Most telling, however, is the case for seeing allusions to hermetic and alchemical symbolism in the work of both Duchamp and Ernst. An unproven but compelling circumstantial case has been made for linking the bizarre blend of sexual and scientific imagery in the *Large Glass* to the alchemical symbolism of the stripping of the virgin (a rite of purification), and specifically to an illustration of the event in the treatise of the philosopher Solidonius.[55] The furnaces and chemical apparatus of the alchemists, coupled with the alchemical image of the *conjunctio* – the fusion of man and woman – certainly acted as a stimulus for Ernst, while works like *Paris-Dream* and its direct *frottage* relative, *Earthquake*, [140, 141] deploy an alchemical symbolism of the heavenly spheres, summed up in the adage of Hermes Trismegistus: 'What is below is like what is above.'[56] It is possible that both Duchamp and Ernst were aware of the research into alchemical symbolism undertaken before the 1914–18 war by Herbert Silberer. This was to be one of the germs of C.G. Jung's analytical psychological interpretation of alchemy from the end of the 1920s as a compendium of archetypal symbols of the formation of the self.[57]

For Jung, alchemy was not interesting as science but only as symbol. For the Surrealists too, it was an edifice of metaphor engaging the erotic and processes of metamorphosis, not a system with the explanatory power of science. Both Jung's analytical psychology and Freud's psychoanalysis were, of course, systematic attempts to explain our most profound unconscious instincts by the study of symbols produced in myths, dreams and in other states of diminished rational control. The Surrealists and the dissident Surrealists *were* interested in such notions as the unconscious, libidinal energy, the complexes, and the drives or instincts, but they were not so much interested in the explanatory potential of the new traditions of psychological analysis as in the emphasis they placed on the symbolic rather than the functional, the concealed rather than the apparent, the imagination rather than reason. Jung's notions of the archetype and especially of the collective unconscious seem gradually to have penetrated Surrealist circles during the inter-war period. Ernst certainly arrived in Paris with an awareness of them, perhaps linked to his interest in alchemy, and by 1933 Jung and the collective unconscious were being cited in *Minotaure*. But, though major texts by Jung began to appear in French around 1930, by then Breton, Bataille and their friends were first and foremost committed to Freudian psychoanalysis as the psychological grounding on which to erect a world of images: the world as myth.[58] If Surrealism produced anything as systematic as a mythology (and this is questionable), it was a mythology whose structures were based on Freudian psychoanalysis.

Ernst may have been aware of Jung when he left Cologne in 1922, but his knowledge of Freud has been shown to have been far more exacting.[59] At that point his new French friends could only skim the surface of Freudian theory, because, though Freud's major texts were translated from German significantly earlier than Jung's, they still did not begin to appear until the 1920s.[60] There can be no doubt, however, that Breton's earliest experiments with 'psychic-automatism', the writing of *Les Champs magnétiques* with Philippe Soupault in 1919, were triggered by accounts of Freud's free-association technique in pioneering French introductions to psychoanalysis read some three years earlier, and that it was then that the ideal of perfect passivity emerged. In letters of 1916 to an old lycée friend, he copied out page after page on Freud from Dr Régis' *Précis de psychiatrie* (1914), including a passage unmistakably echoed in the first *Manifesto* where the 'subject', noting down the thoughts that come to him spontaneously in response to words and questions, is likened to 'a simple recording device'. Breton's phrase 'psychic automatism' came, in fact, from a French psychologist, Pierre Janet, but it was in Freud that he found a theory that gave real positive significance to the undirected release of images achieved by automatist activity.[61] From the very beginning, however chary Breton might have been of the curative and explanatory agenda of Freudian psychoanalysis, it was a formative feature embedded in both Surrealist theory and practice, as it would be for the 'dissidents' too.

Again and again for the Surrealists, Freud's writings confirmed the central significance of the 'sex instinct' and so of the sex organs and the sex act (actual or metaphorical) in Surrealist art. Man Ray's head-as-phallus, his *Anatomies* [310], Giacometti's allusive simulacrum of failed coitus, *Suspended Ball* [155], and the constellation of images evoking genitalia, male and female, in *Catalan Landscape (The Hunter)* are three from countless instances that could be given in support of that centrality. None of these are directly explicit, they exploit the ambivalence of analogy. Even when thus focusing on the organs and the act, Surrealist artists tended to reject the explicit and the manifest, preferring the openness that came of leaving sexual meanings latent. The Surrealist object is perhaps the most obvious demonstration of this preference for the latent over the manifest; it is a point Breton stressed in his contribution to the 1931 number of *SASDLR* that launched the object, including *Suspended Ball*.

Freud's thinking on the fetish and especially on the 'uncanny' has recently been applied to the Surrealists' compulsive investment of such significance in fabricated or found objects, though it is acknowledged that they may not have known the essay concerned (the 'Essay on the Uncanny' [1919] did not appear in French until 1933).[62] Establishing a cause-and-effect link here is not as important as the insight offered by Freudian theory, so deeply penetrated were Surrealist ways of thinking about the latent by the general notions basic to that theory.

'Uncanny' is the English translation of the German 'unheimlich', literally 'unhomely'. Freud applies it to everything that induces an unexplained discomfiture, from coincidences to automata. Things are uncanny, for Freud, because their manifest identity conceals a latent content. This concealed content is a repressed fear which threatens to surface from that early stage in infancy when desires and fears can seem to possess anything, what he calls the period of 'omnipotence of thoughts', or animism. Freud uses an existing definition as his own: the uncanny is 'the name for everything that ought to have remained . . . secret and hidden but has come to light'. The fetish, as defined since the nineteenth century, was an extreme instance of the uncanny, an object excessively over-valued for reasons associated with early sexual experiences. In the Freudian scheme, the mechanism involved is substitution and is activated by the infantile trauma of seeing for the first time the mother's lack of a phallus, and with it the onset of the fear of castration. The fetish substitutes the desired and lost object, the missing phallus.

For the Surrealist (artist or viewer) any object could become fetishised, harbouring within it the desired and lost object and so disturbingly 'alive'. In the same way, all Surrealist objects, along with the images and encounters between images found in Surrealist photography and in those Surrealist paintings that evoke dreams, can be described in the Freudian sense as uncanny. For all such works are, in one way or another, examples of the psychological operations described by Freud as 'displacement' and 'condensation' in action. As in dreams, attention is shifted from the important to the seemingly unimportant (displacement), and many meanings can be crowded into a single object, image or event (condensation); in dreams, Freud called these operations of repression combined with overvaluation, the dream work.[63]

In the context of Surrealism, the release of images by 'psychic automatism', dreaming, choosing objects, paranoiac-critical method, or whatever means, inevitably exposed the fears and desires repressed within the unconscious. Since in a Freudian as well as a Jungian framework, these were believed to be common across the human psyche, this was approached as something far more than merely personal, it was collective too. As Breton put it in 1935: 'Art is no longer a question of the creation of a personal myth, but rather, with Surrealism, of the creation of a collective myth.'[64] Freud had already adapted long-familiar 'collective myths' from antiquity to his analysis of the complexes and the drives – most crucially the story of Oedipus – underlining thus his confidence in the collective force of his findings. As the artists associated with Surrealism generated their imagery, they increasingly followed suit, openly invoking classical myth; we have already encountered Dionysos, the Minotaure and Acéphale as examples. Just as the most familiar of objects were found to harbour uncanny secrets, so the myths of Latin culture with which European society had grown comfortable were re-worked as the repositories of a powerfully disruptive latent content open to all.

Max Ernst and Salvador Dalí were the most adept of the Surrealist artists at both the knowing manipulation of psychoanalytic imagery and the reworking of myths.

Automated techniques certainly played a part in Ernst's activity, as in his *frottages* and *grattages*, but the degree to which he *consciously* applied his reading of Freud has been revealed, and nowhere more subtly yet disturbingly than in his collage painting of 1922 *Oedipus Rex* [139]. The work does not portray Oedipus or tell any part of the story of Sophocles' play in which the Theban king unknowingly marries his own mother and kills his own father, before having his eyes put out. It is a collection of images presented as if recorded from a dream. The title acts as an invitation to recognise in them the potential presence of a latent content that connects with the Freudian Oedipal predicament: the desire for the mother and the fear coupled with murderous hatred of the father that Freud believed common to all male infants. The bird-heads, one horned, can be read as 'vigilant' parental presences, their stare inducing guilt. The walnut can be read as a possible reference to the womb, and through that to the infant's eternal question: where do babies come from? – a question directly associated by Freud in his 'Little Hans' case history with the riddle that the sphinx posed Sophocles' Oedipus. In Freud's view, that question inevitably relates to the infant's desire for the mother, since it is ultimately the desire to return to the satiation of the womb.[65] Furthermore, the giant hand can be seen as related both to the blinding of Oedipus and to the Freudian fear of castration, the punishment of those who desire the mother and wish to kill the father (blindness – the cutting off of the gaze – and castration are linked in Freud).[66] These themes, the Oedipal predicament and the fear of castration, are often close beneath the surface of Ernst's imagery even where he offers no explicit Freudian invitation. This is obviously the case in *The Infant Jesus Chastised*, for instance [40].

It did not require titles or elaborately developed imagery to situate a Surrealists' work in relation to the Oedipus myth as remade by Freud. Among Giacometti's sculptural production in the early years of his involvement with the Surrealists (1931–2), were bulky upright forms, like glacial moraine, and flat, horizontal sculptures, one of which combined hollows and pyramidal excrescences [323]. In 1933, Giacometti (b.1901) published a text entitled 'Hier, sables mouvants' (Yesterday, Shifting Sands). Here he recounts childhood memories featuring the mountain country around his parents' summer villa at Maloja in the Alps. He remembers a great stone which his father took him to, with beneath it a cave, and within that a second, inner chamber. He writes of the joy he felt to be crouched in the inner chamber. Then

323. Alberto Giacometti, *La Vie Continue*, 1932. Original plaster, 25.5 × 37.5 cm. Musée Nationale d'Art Moderne, Paris

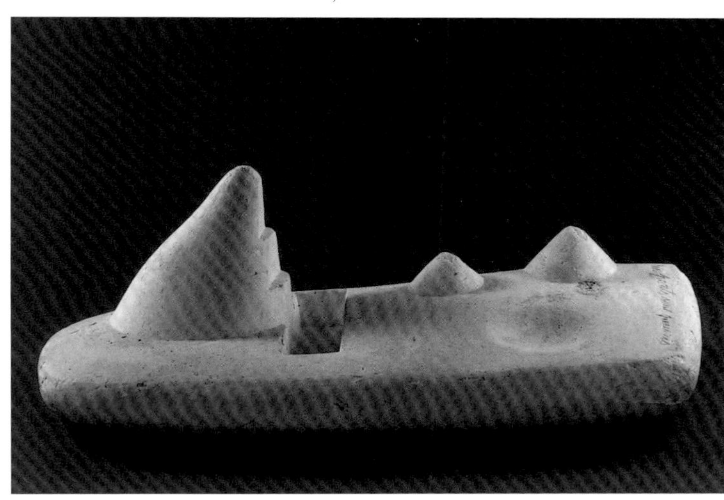

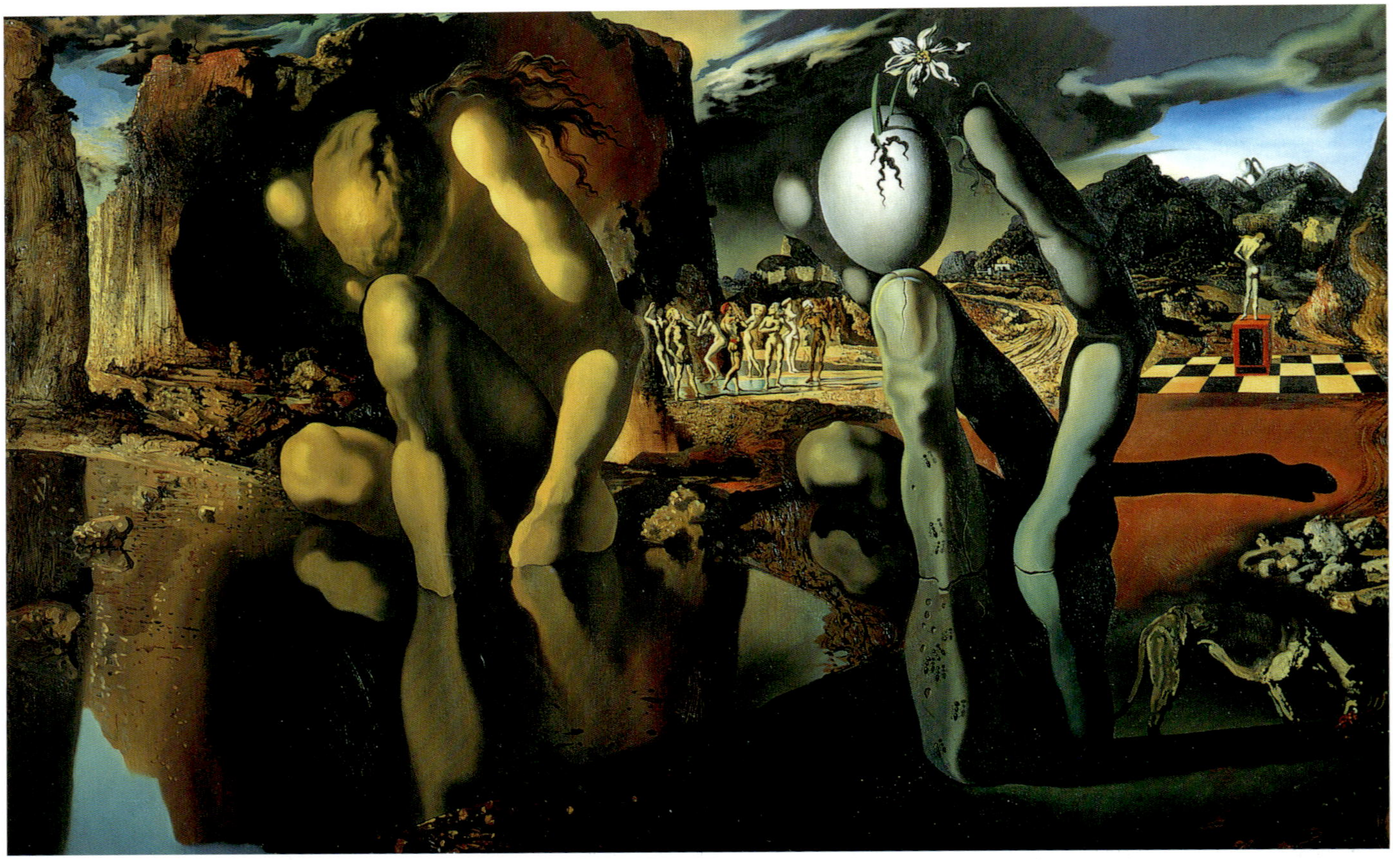

324. Salvador Dalí, *Metamorphosis of Narcissus*, 1937. Oil on canvas, 50.8 × 78.2 cm. The Tate Gallery, London

325. Alberto Giacometti, *Palace at 4.a.m.*, 1932. Construction in wood, glass, wire and string, 63.5 × 71.8 × 40 cm. The Museum of Modern Art, New York. Purchase

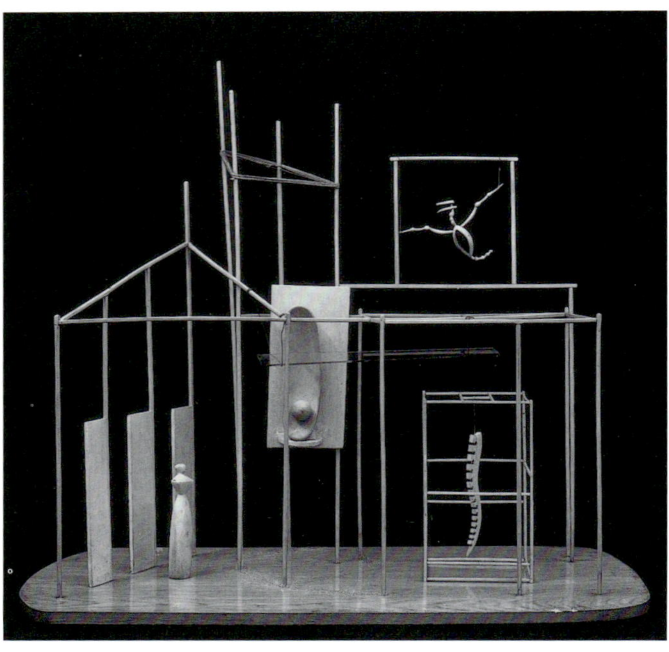

he remembers exploring for himself and finding another stone further off, black and 'in the form of a pyramid narrow and pointed', which impressed itself upon him 'like a living being, hostile and menacing,' a threat even to his 'little cave'. He writes of how he felt compelled to approach and touch it, and how afterwards he fled in horror, unable to speak of it to anyone. Anxiety and guilt succeed contentment in a scenario which gives Freudian maternal and paternal roles to caverns and rocks in memories of childhood.[67] No explicit connection is made with a work like *La Vie Continue (Life Continues)* [323]; but there is no missing the invitation.

Much more obviously placed in a context of dream imagery and infantile memories was Giacometti's quickly celebrated piece, *Palace at 4.a.m.* [325]. The title he gave the text with which his *Palace* was illustrated in *Minotaure* in 1933 was 'I can only speak indirectly about my sculptures'. It is thus that he writes about the work, having stressed that all his sculptures appear to him 'completely finished in my mind (esprit)', and then are made without a single change and 'without asking myself what they could mean . . .'. Item by item, he describes what is in his *Palace* with minimal comment, from the spinal column in a cage to the bird-skeletons and the basin of water he imagines filled with skeletal fish, until he comes to the 'statue of a woman'. Suddenly more than description is required, for in her he finds 'my mother, as she left her mark on my first memories'. And his feelings have to be acknowledged: 'I was troubled by the long black dress that touched the ground because of its

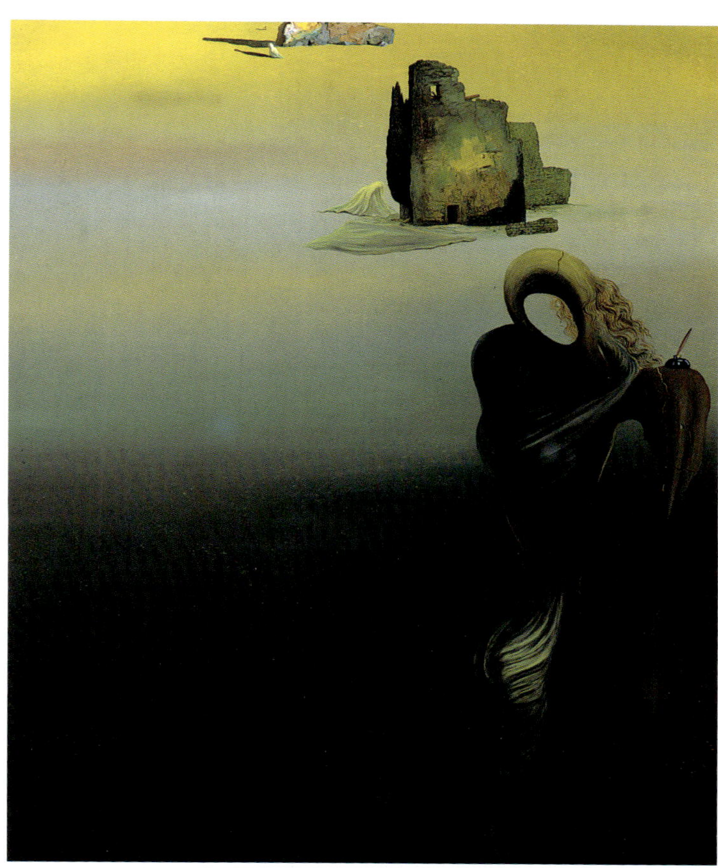

326. Salvador Dalí, *Gradiva Rediscovers the Anthropomorphic Ruins (Retrospective Fantasy)*, *c.*1931–2. Oil on canvas, 65 × 54 cm. Museo Thyssen-Bornemisza, Madrid

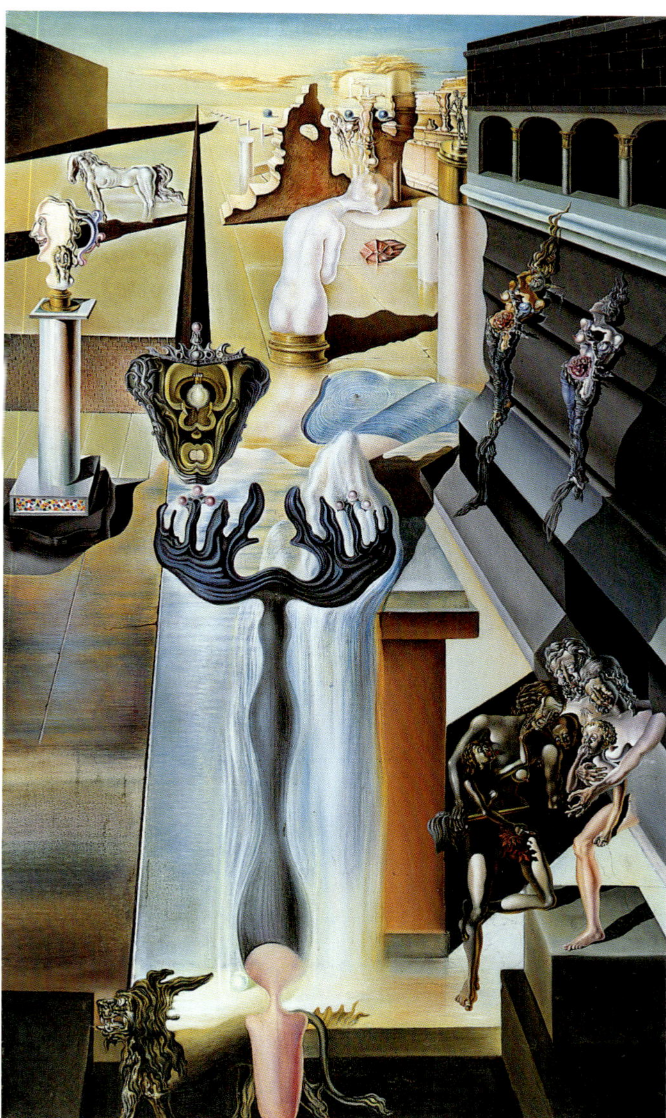

327. Salvador Dalí, *The Invisible Man*, 1929–31. Oil on canvas, 143 × 81 cm. Museo Nacional Centro de Arte Reina Sofia, Madrid

mystery; it seemed part of the body and that caused me a sensation of fear and disturbance; everything else . . . escaped my attention'.[68] They are the feelings aroused, of course, by the uncanny, which for Freud always involved the recollection of repressed experiences from infancy. These feelings and the figure of his mother have to be recognised.

From the moment of his arrival in Paris in 1929, Dalí's appropriation of Freud and his elaboration of mythologies reaching back to infancy proceeded with an explicitness and concern for detail that rivalled Ernst at his most ambitious. A culminating point was reached in 1937 with his appropriation of the Ovidian myth of Narcissus in *The Metamorphosis of Narcissus* [324]. This was Dalí's classical addenda to a series of earlier works which brought together a mythic version of his own biography, beginning in childhood, and a romantic novel analysed by Freud, the story of Gradiva. A work of 1931–2 dedicated to this conjunction was *Gradiva Rediscovers the Anthropomorphic Ruins (Retrospective Fantasy)* [326]. The personal myth involved would not be recounted in detail until the publication of Dalí's autobiography in 1942, but from 1931 Freud's 1907 study 'Delusions and Dreams of Jensen's "Gradiva"' was available in French, and the themes the painter drew from it – above all, the loved one as the repressed object of desire made visible – were planted in his texts from 1930.

Dalí's *Gradiva Rediscovers* leads the viewer stage by stage into a plunging perspectival space, passing ruins and phantoms, until in the very distance the tiny figures of a father and son are encountered. The picture's space is the analogue of Freud's idea of regression into infancy, linking the kiss that revives the hollow wax mannequin in the foreground, Dalí's present, to his distant past. The novel Freud analysed in 1907 tells the story of an archaeologist, Hanold, who develops an obsession with the figure of a young woman in a Roman relief, fixing his attention especially on her heel, raised free of her drapery as she strides along. Hanold calls her Gradiva, 'the girl splendid in walking'. Not knowing why, he is drawn to Pompeii, and there he meets her, believing her to be a ghost who only appears in the midday hour. She finally becomes real when she reveals herself to be his childhood friend, Zoë Bertgang; this happens with a passionate embrace. For Freud, Jensen's story is a fable of delusion and its cure, and the ruins of Pompeii are the ruins of Hanold's past out of which he digs the *real* Zoë.

Just as Dalí 'paranoiacally' imposed his myths upon the world of space around him, so here he imposed the shape of the Gradiva myth, complete with its Freudian interpretation, upon the development of his personality in time: upon his life. His Gradiva is Gala Eluard, who, with a passionate embrace, cured him of the neurosis that accompanied his father's final rejection of him in 1929. By doing so, she made real his own unrealised desires for narrow-waisted girls from early childhood through adolescence, thus becoming his 'Visible Woman' and restoring him to life. One of the themes in *The Invisible Man* [327], among the most important of his early Surrealist paintings, is the delusion of his own 'invisibility'. Sanctioned by Freud, a personal myth is offered as a new collective myth, resonating, at least potentially, with other (male) autobiographies.

The Metamorphosis of Narcissus lifts Dalí's personal myth onto a more 'universal' plane still, by linking his own paranoid compulsions to the classical figure of Narcissus but also by linking them to the Freudian notion of the Narcissitic stage in ego-formation. The work offers a paranoiac image symbolic of a need to regress to that stage when, in Freud's theory, the child becomes aware of itself as a source of pleasure and pain distinct from the world, and makes itself the object of its own love in auto-eroticism. For Freud, incidentally, this is the stage, just prior to the decisive separation of the self from others, when the child believes its thoughts 'omnipotent' and everything in the world, therefore, subject to them: the stage of animism.

There is a final point to be made about the Surrealists' reconstruction of the world and themselves as myth in the context of psychoanalysis, it brings us back to the loss of self considered a corollary of the release from 'all control by reason'. It is that Surrealist myths of the self characteristically involve its dissolution or its fragmentation.

1923 saw the publication of Freud's *The Ego and the Id*, which consolidated in the clearest terms his view of the personality as irredeemably split; it appeared in French in 1927. When Ernst inserted himself into his work in 1929–30, he did so in the person of an alter-ego, 'Loplop, the *Bird Superior*', a self which had developed from early infancy separate from 'himself', though it often 'visited' him. Superficially, Dalí's *Metamorphosis of Narcissus* might seem to represent the reinforcement of a unified ego through self-love. In the context of psychoanalysis it cannot, however, for the doubling of the self in mirror reflection inevitably serves, like the mannequin or the automaton, as, in Freud's words, 'a ghastly harbinger of death'.[69] The self is doubled by its own lifeless image. Dalí's painting proliferates doubles, and in them represents Narcissus's death at the moment of his birth (the moment of the ego's birth in infancy). His head is doubled by an egg; it is this that sprouts the narcissus flower which is all that is left of him when, trapped by his beloved reflection, he dies. Contemporary with *Metamorphosis of Narcissus*, Dalí's friend, the psychoanalyst Jacques Lacan, developed his theory of ego-formation known as the 'mirror stage'. In Lacan's extension of the Freudian scheme, the ego is first separated from the world actually during the Narcissistic stage. The trigger is the infant's recognition of itself as a distinct being when it sees its own image reflected. As Lacan presented the process, this can only mean that the ego never achieves real self-sufficiency: it is always an image, a representation.[70]

DE-CIVILISING CULTURE: FROM MAGIC TO *BASSESSE*

'Latin civilisation,' André Breton writes in 1924, '. . . seems just now to be the last rampart of bad faith, senility and cowardice'.[71] With 'Latin civilisation', for Breton, went the refusal of risk and an acceptance of Europe as an ageing culture. By taking the risk of setting aside the controls of civilisation and with them repression, one could, in the Freudian scenario, regress to the 'primitive' state of infancy and reactivate its animistic powers.

For Freud, infant narcissism was characterised by 'the omnipotence of thoughts', i.e. the child's 'unshakeable confidence in the possibility of controlling the world': magic. In *Totem and Taboo*, Freud identifies adult regression to animism with such neurotic behaviours as fetishism or 'obsessional prohibitions' (taboos); but he makes one exception. 'In only a single field of our civilisation has the omnipotence of thoughts been retained, and that is in the field of art. Only in art does it still happen that a man who is consumed by desires performs something resembling the accomplishment of those desires and that what he does in play produces emotional effects – thanks to artistic illusion – just as though it were something real. People speak with justice of the 'magic of art' and compare artists to magicians.'[72] In the Freudian scheme, all artists were Narcissistic – another Freudian feature of Dalí's regressive self-portrait as Narcissus – and all artists were magicians, because in art they could regress to an infant stage where everything was subject to the transforming power of their desires.

From the mid-1920s, the image of the artist as magician was a constant feature in the milieux of Breton and the dissident Surrealists. It was an image which went with that of the artist as alchemist, and it had a long poetic pedigree in France, reaching back through Apollinaire and Mallarmé to the Masonic mystics of the eighteenth century. When Breton called for the 'occultation of Surrealism' in the second *Manifesto*, he deepened the sense of identity that existed within a psychoanalytic context between artists and magicians. By that date, there was one artist who above all was held up as the exemplary modern artist-magician, Picasso.

In 1912, André Salmon had written of the *Demoiselles d'Avignon* in the context of African 'sorcery', but ultimately had preferred to present him as the inventor of new pictorial geometries. When the image of the magician was invoked for Picasso after the mid-1920s, it was not thus qualified. The exhibition of Cubist and Surrealist collage put on at the galerie Goemans in 1930 included two large Picasso *Guitars* of 1926; one, according to Aragon's text for the catalogue, incorporated a piece of the artist's own shirt, the other incorporated a piece of dishcloth with long nails hammered through the support *at* the viewer [317]. The use of things stained with his own dirt clearly invoked sympathetic magic. From a position of authoritarian traditionalism, Waldemar George was in no doubt that Picasso's new primitivising work was profoundly different from the 'conceptual' Cubism which had emerged in the sequel to the *Demoiselles*, and far more dangerous. 'Years ago,' he wrote in 1930, 'Picasso asked of the blacks a lesson in advanced geometry. Today, he asks of their masks and ritual dances a lesson in magic.' Even from

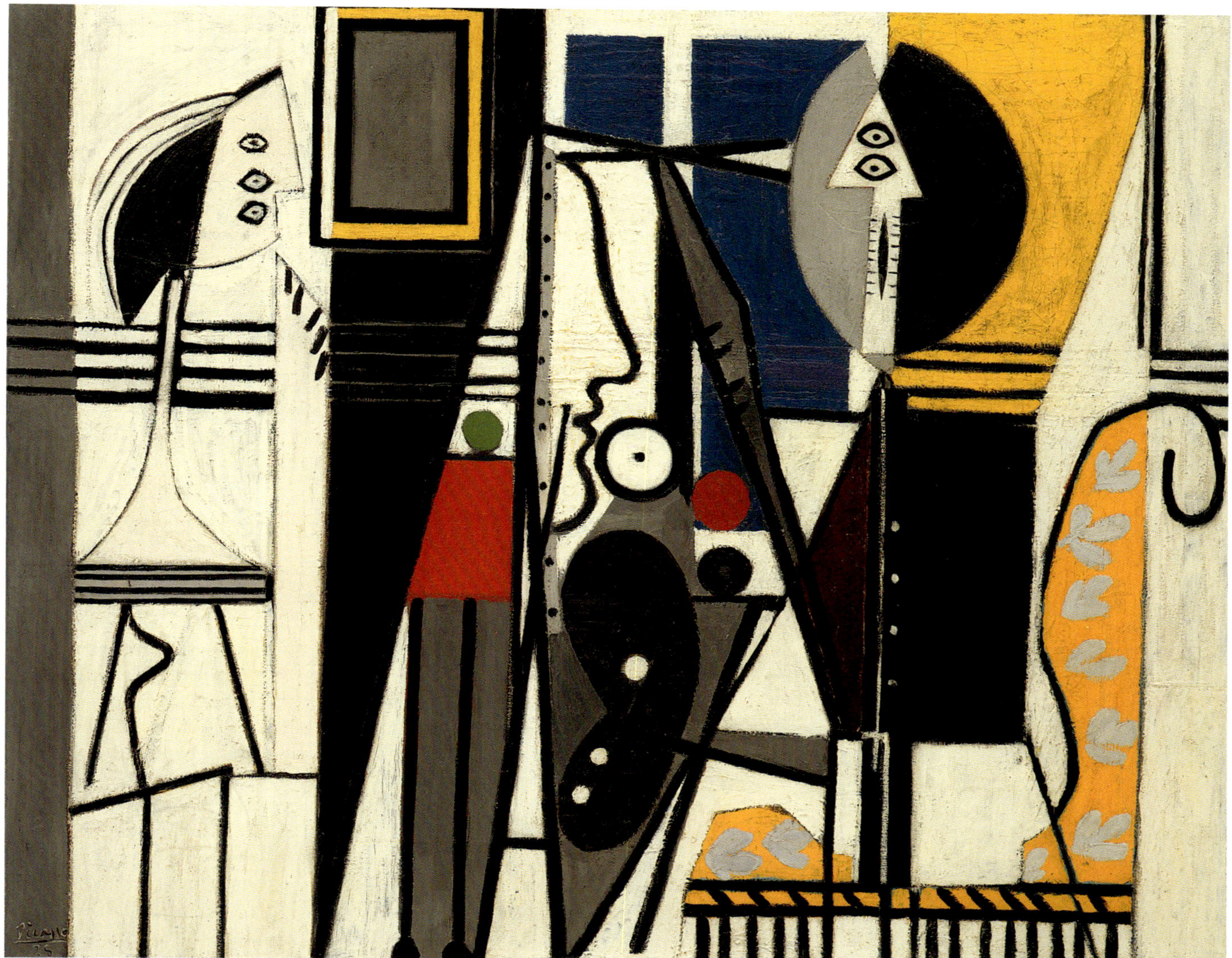

328. Pablo Picasso, *Painter and Model*, 1928. Oil on canvas, 129.8 × 163 cm. The Museum of Modern Art, New York. The Sidney and Harriet Janis Collection

the official Communist standpoint of *L'Humanité* in 1930, Picasso was not merely among the 'greatest artists of all time', he was also 'this demon of a magician'.[73]

More than African carvings, Breton and the Surrealists favoured Oceanic and Eskimo masks, along with Pre-Columbian sculpture, especially that of the Aztecs. These were non-European artefacts less compromised by the imposition on them of the formalist 'conceptual' aesthetics of pre-1914 'primitivism'. When Picasso started once again to primitivise his figure painting in 1925, he continued to respond to the kind of Oceanic and African images that had thrilled him at the ethnographic museum of the Trocadéro in 1907. An Oceanic mask from Vanuatu with sharpened teeth in his own collection inspired the skull-like howling head of the Maenad on the left of *The Three Dancers* [318]. Kota reliquary figures from West Africa [286], which had been invoked in the striated patterns of the masks worn by the nudes on the right of the *Demoiselles*, are invoked again by the flat, spread-out disk of the painter's head in his 1928 *Painter and Model* [328].

These are both major works, and they make their non-European 'primitivising' aspect brutally clear. If the former connects the 'primitive' to the Nietzschean notion of ecstatic release, as a work like Derain's *Bathers* of 1907 had [284], the latter makes the 'primitive' integral to a representation of the artist as magician. The fivefold female stare of the naked 'demoiselles' is replaced by the male stare of a single, controlling painter-sorcerer. That stare's unwavering challenge to the viewer evokes the magician's 'evil eye', while behind the model (on the left) a blank mirror – highly significant in the context of magic – hangs on the wall of the studio. This male artist and his art, moreover, are above all sexually driven. He has a vertical vaginal mouth, and his brush is held like a wand, extending an arm which rises straight from his midriff like a huge phallus. This is an image of the artist-magician that invites (probably consciously in 1928) Freudian corroboration. For Freud, since desire was the energy behind 'the omnipotence of thought', magic – and therefore art – was fundamentally 'sexualised thinking'.

If there was, besides the so-called 'primitive', another model of the artist as magician, it could be no other than the child. By 1930, the infantile counterpart of Picasso's savage

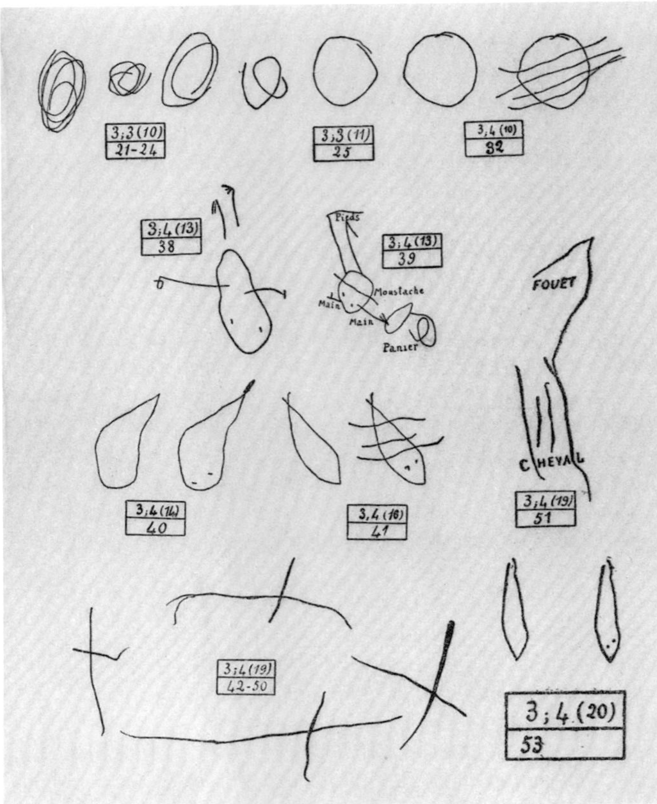

329. Child's drawings (Simone Luquet), Plate I from G.-H. Luquet, *Les Dessins d'un enfant, étude psychologique*, (Paris, 1913)

artist-magician was Miró. His success in infantilising his art and persona was consummate. That year in *Documents*, the critic Carl Einstein, author of an early study on African art, writes of 'dream paintings' like *The Birth of the World* [316] as 'the starry songs of children,' and goes on to call his more recent renunciation of charming colour in works like *Head* [276] a return to 'prehistoric simplicity', a return not merely to infancy but to all our beginnings: 'The end rejoins the beginning'.[74] In 1929, Michel Leiris had described the emptying out of Miró's work as a route back to magic. Miró achieves, he writes, 'a void in himself . . . in order to rediscover an infancy . . . founded on the metonymy of stones, plants, animals, a little like the stories of savage peoples, where all the elements of the globe encounter unlikely transformations'.[75]

As in the relationship between pre-1914 'primitivism' and developments in psychology and anthropology, Miró's infantilism ran parallel with, but was probably little influenced by, important post-1918 developments in both fields. Again in this case, those developments demonstrate the degree to which his work was part of deep changes in attitudes to the 'pre-logical' and the 'uncivilised' within the French intelligentsia. Moreover, because awareness of developments in these fields was beginning to penetrate avant-garde milieux in Paris, they were increasingly a real factor in what might be called the conditions of reception for both primitivising work in general and his infantilism in particular. They changed the way the 'naïve' and the 'primitive' could be understood and therefore responded to.

As a contribution to psychology, most important by far was Jean Piaget's rigorous research into child development in the 1920s, which found a new application for Lucien Lévy-Bruhl's notion of 'primitive mentality'. This research was carried out in Switzerland, but it was first published in France and was highly influential in French psychology. There is no evidence of serious interest within the counter-cultural avant-garde in Piaget's work, but G.H. Luquet's development of the ideas broached in his 1913 *Dessins d'un enfant* during the 1920s produced at least one significant response. In 1930, he published *Art primitif*, a wide-ranging popularising book in which he applied his observations concerning child art to the whole gamut of 'primitive art', going back to prehistory. It led instantly to a review by Georges Bataille in *Documents*. Bataille's review appeared immediately before the only article he published on Miró.

Bataille's review of Luquet's new book took as its springboard, not his analysis of 'primitive art' in terms of 'conceptual realism' with its stress on multiple viewpoints and so on, but rather his analysis of the origins of art in cave painting. Luquet argued that the manner of the discovery of figurative art in the beginnings of human culture and in the early development of children was identical, a simple parallel between prehistory and childhood that Bataille rejected, as we shall see later. According to his theory, the figure of the 'first artist' returns in the infancy of every individual. He pointed to cases of apparently purposeless mark-making on the walls of caves (palm-prints and finger-marks), in order to hypothesise a process of development precisely analogous to the one he had followed before 1914 in his daughter Simone's development, from scribbles made *without* any depictive intent, to signs for things made *with* depictive intent. For him, infants (in Simone's case at the age of three) and prehistoric cave-dwellers alike can be shown to discover figurative art by seeing resemblances in undirected scribbles and then, with directed industry, by producing signs with referential meanings.

This was, of course, precisely how Miró often worked in the notebooks from which he produced his 'dream paintings' in the mid-1920s, though he tended to keep directed industry for the translation of drawings into paintings, not use it to develop definitive signs. And the least definitive of the dream paintings, for instance *Birth of the World* and *Circus Horse* [314, 316], actually recreate for every viewer the moment of the 'first artist': it is for the viewer to see resemblances and signs. So close, indeed, is the sketch behind the *Circus Horse* [315] to a scribble Luquet's daughter Simone made when she was 3 years and 4 months old, and published in *Dessins d'un enfant* that the possibility of something more than coincidence emerges, especially since Simone saw in her own random marks a whip (fouet) and a horse (cheval) [329].[76]

Miró's infantilism was not confined to the 'dream paintings'. With the look of adult graffiti, it is found in 1930 in, for instance, *Head* [276]; and with the look of the detailed drawings of older children, it is found in paintings like *Catalan Landscape (The Hunter)* [322]. Piaget's new thinking on child psychology may not have been a demonstrable influence, but it is relevant to the whole range of Miró's infantilism. What the Swiss psychologist found in children was Lévy-Bruhl's 'law of participation' everywhere in action: an unwavering belief in magic. He was well aware of psychoanalytic theory, and there is a clear parallel between his picture of child mentality (from three to seven) as 'pre-logical' and Freud's picture of the animistic stage preceding the separate formation of the ego: the 'primitive' stage of 'omnipotence of thought'.[77] It was, for Piaget, the 'egocentricity' of child thought that produced its magical qualities: the child's inability to separate itself from others and the world, and its capacity therefore to see everything as subject to its ego. From this followed the child's 'mystical' belief that even inanimate things are invested with spirit (animism), and a magical mode of thinking which relates things not in the logical terms of cause-and-effect, but in chains of analogies. This latter was termed 'syncretic thinking', and had already been analysed as such by earlier writers on magic. For Lévy-Bruhl, it was the mechanism by which the 'law of participation' is actually put into action. One thing is experienced as so like another that the two can partake of each other's force, or can even be thought one and the same: an animal can *become* a root found in the earth or a star-system.[78]

Piaget's theory of child development, like Luquet's notion of conceptual realism in primitive art, erected a structural barrier between the condition of children and that of adults: the mentality of children was, he argued, structurally different. Luquet and Piaget together underlined the fact that even a Miró could not think *as* a child, but only *as if* a child: the promise of an authentic return to the 'innocence' of childhood as Jean-Jacques Rousseau conceived it was denied. Freud's theory of regression, however, held up the possibility of a return to the magic of infancy in another sense. For him, early experiences remain to be excavated from the unconscious in all their intensity; they are there, whole, beneath the ruins of the past. What Miró produced was a kind of syncretic thinking in pictorial images that could *seem*, in Leiris's words, to 'rediscover infancy' and with it a magical world of 'unlikely transformations': the animism of infancy.

Catalan Landscape (The Hunter) can appear put together by magical thinking above all. On an imaginative level, syncretic chains of analogy suggest the possibility of metamorphoses everywhere. The triangles of the boat, the sardine's tail, the hunter's gun and head, echo one other, as do the flame of the gun, the burning heart and pipe. Miró paints *as if* the world is subject in every detail to his 'omnipotent thoughts'. And with this willed and therefore simulated return to infancy, he leaves the unmistakable inference that he is willing a return to that state of undifferentiated oneness between self and world central to the Piagetian and the Freudian notion of the infantile. Miró is, as it were, *in* everything. When at the end of the 1930s, he painted a pair of self-portraits, he painted 'himself' and the landscape of his imagination as one and the same.

Syncretic thinking, where analogies make possible metamorphoses, is a constant feature of much of Picasso's Cubist and post-Cubist work too. In Picasso's case, where the frame of reference was the magic of so-called 'primitive' peoples, not children, the relevant developments were in anthropology alongside psychoanalysis, and their direct impact on him as well as his immediate circle cannot be doubted. From around the date of *Painter and Model*, in the later 1920s, Picasso became part of a milieu that was actively involved in bringing together psychoanalysis and social anthropology (the latter known as ethnology in France). It was a milieu that crossed the divisions between the Surrealists and the dissident Surrealists, though the latter were initially more central. Within this milieu, Picasso's closest relations were with Leiris. In 1929–30 it was centred on Georges Bataille and the periodical *Documents*; in the mid-1930s, it came to be associated with *Minotaure* and *Acéphale*, bringing in Breton as well as Bataille (though not bringing them together). It was a milieu that included other artists as well as Miró and Picasso, most importantly Masson and Giacometti. The late 1920s work of the latter often invoked African sculpture as overtly as Picasso's.

The degree of overlap between this milieu and the emerging professional science of social anthropology is, from the late 1920s, remarkable. Leading archaeologists and social anthropologists were among *Documents*' contributors throughout its two-year life. Leiris's decision to become an anthropologist as well as a poet was made in the most conducive of situations. The leader of the expedition across Africa from Dakar and to Djibouti, which, between 1931 and 1933, gave him his first experience as a professional anthropologist, was Marcel Griaule, an anthropologist who had regularly contributed to *Documents*. Other contributors included the Director and Deputy Director of the Ethnographic Museum at the Trocadéro, Paul Rivet and Georges-Henri Rivière, with whom Leiris would be involved in the foundation of the Musée de l'Homme in 1937. The second number of *Minotaure* in 1933 was dedicated to the Dakar-Djibouti expedition. Leiris was guest editor for it, while he, Griaule and other members of the team supplied highly professional articles lavishly illustrated with photographs of some of the thousands of objects collected on the expedition for the future Musée de l'Homme. This engagement with professional anthropology went with an equally serious engagement with psychoanalysis. In 1927, Bataille embarked on analysis with the French Freudian Adrien Borel, and in 1929, on Bataille's advice, so did Leiris. One of Borel's interests, tellingly, was magical thinking in art; in 1934, he published on the subject.[79]

Miró, it could be said, pursued an assimilationist strategy in relation to child art. He so completely absorbed it into his adult Surrealist practice that the question of difference was simply erased: Surrealist painting was infantilised and child art was surrealised. Like the *Demoiselles d'Avignon*, Picasso's major primitivising images of the late 1920s and early 1930s confronted the question of difference head-on, and with it all the racial, cultural and political implications this entailed when the reference was to the colonised.

Three Dancers [318] was illustrated as a 'finished' work by Breton in 1925, and so the stylistic disjunction which amplifies the confrontational relationship between the ecstatic Maenad on the left and her solemn companions was certainly something Picasso made happen. There is no possibility, as there is in the *Demoiselles*, that this stylistic heterogeneity is merely the incidental result of incompletion, accepted but not willed. Savagery and release in a figure whose head brandishes non-European references, confronts post-Cubist structure: 'primitive' magic against European

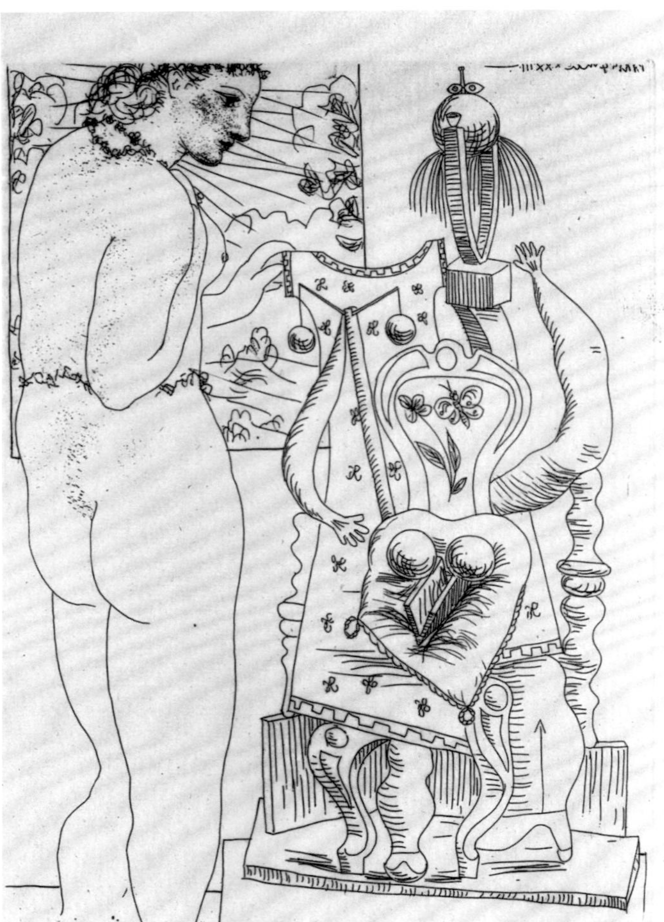

330. Pablo Picasso, *Nymph and Surrealist Sculpture*, May 4, 1933, printed 1939. Etching, 26.8 × 19.3 cm. The Museum of Modern Art, New York. Abby Aldrich Rockefeller Fund

'geometry'; sacrifice (the crucifixion) and dionysiac frenzy against 'classical' dance. In *Painter and Model*, the phallic artist with Africanised head paints an absurd three-eyed female model, but the image he produces on the canvas in front of him is an eyeless 'classical' profile, male, traditional and European. Half a decade later, in 1933, one of the etchings Picasso produced as part of the Vollard Suite [330] shows a 'classical' nymph contemplating a strange assemblage, partly thrown together from fragments of European furniture, whose head is crowned by disembodied staring eyes. The head is adapted from a particular Dogon dance mask from Mali brought back from the Dakar-Djibouti expedition, and illustrated in the special number of *Minotaure* edited by Leiris.[80] In all these cases, the non-European confronts and dominates the European, both on a stylistic and an iconographic level: the Maenad, the artist-sorcerer and the magic sculpture all take control.

As is shown in Leiris's discussion of his own seduction by African art, *Documents* too confronted the question of racial and cultural difference directly. The period 1925–31 brought the craze for the black to a climax in France, bracketed as it was by the smash hit *Revue nègre* in 1925, starring Josephine Baker, and the 1931 Colonial Exhibition. Leiris's guilt on account of both his own earlier exoticism and the colonial abuse of power had grounds. 'Joséphine', jazz, black boxing champions and fashionable cosmopolitan Paris led by Nancy Cunard had given black exoticism an unprecedented glamour, while the pro-colonial lobby, led by figures like Albert Sarraut, in alliance with the colonial ministry was the major source of funding for the Dakar-Djibouti expedition, as it would be for the Musée de l'Homme. The exotic and the colonial went together, and the new alliance between the counter-cultural avant-garde and social anthropology was one beneficiary. The position of the *Documents* circle was ambiguous to say the least.

Be that as it may, throughout its short life the magazine consistently and aggressively took the side of black against white culture. In this it was aligned with the equally vigorous anti-colonialism of the Bretonian Surrealists, which in 1931 took the form of a counter-exhibition, 'The Truth about the Colonies', organised as a protest against the Colonial Exhibition. In *Documents*, the idea of 'the primitive' became, indeed, a de-civilising weapon on the side of the *informe* against European civilisation. There is, for instance, Marcel Griaule's 1930 article on a drum of the Baule tribe from West Africa which includes a figure carrying a European gun. Griaule is angered by the tendency for European good taste to dismiss such a piece as inauthentic because of its inclusion of something European. He contrasts, to its obvious disadvantage, the white commercialised appropriation of black artefacts as art with the black appropriation of everything from oil drums to Chianti bottles, not for commerce but to fulfil their 'sense of the sacred'. He especially despises the differentiation of European 'popular' artefacts from black artefacts under the heading 'folklore', and ends contemptuously thus: 'I call folklore the ethnography of pretentious peoples, those peoples without colour, whose habitat is to the north of a sea with restricted tides and moderate storms, the Mediterranean, peoples who fear things and words, who do not wish to call themselves natives, and who, in their dictionaries, explain anything shocking in Latin so as to reserve the little pleasures of shame for their elites.'[81] For Griaule, as for Leiris, Europe – so-called 'civilisation' – was hopelessly sick, but the answer lay not in the resurrection of 'classical' forms, as it did for a Humanist authoritarian like Waldemar George, but in the lessons to be learned from so-called 'primitives'.

Within social anthropology such attitudes to racial and cultural difference were grounded not so much in Lévy-Bruhl's alternative to Darwinian evolutionism but rather in the work of Griaule's teacher and mentor, Marcel Mauss, professor at the Ecole Pratique des Hauts-Etudes, and co-author with Henri Hubert in 1902–3 of a major study of magic. Bataille too attended Mauss's famous lectures in the 1920s. Mauss's writing explores not the structural differences separating cultures, as in the notion of 'primitive mentality', but deeper structures, which reveal profound principles underlying *all* human social and cultural activity.

Thus, when Mauss and Hubert discussed syncretic thinking in their study of magic, they did not stress its 'illogicality' but rather its structural similarities with even the most 'advanced European thinking'. They pick out, for instance, the way connections by analogy in magical systems always involve the transference of properties – to the child who cannot speak, say, is transferred 'the loquacity of the parrot'. They note how the grouping of phenomena according to 'properties' is basic to such rites as rain-making – fire is used to make rain because it is the contrary of water – and observe that the grouping of properties is fundamental both to the ancient European science of alchemy and to modern science.[82] To bring together magical thinking and science was to counter social Darwinism far more radically than Lévy-Bruhl, and one aspect of Freud's adaptation of anthropological material to psychoanalysis, unacceptable both to Mauss and to the *Documents* circle, was its evolutionism. The derogatory racist parallel Freud drew in *Totem and Taboo* between the 'evolution' of humanity and that of individuals, between ontogenetic and philogenetic evolution, was set aside. So-called 'primitive' peoples were not to be thought of as 'equivalent' either to European neurotics or to European infants at the narcissistic stage of development, even if regression to that stage was a goal.

Within the *Documents* circle there was certainly a level at which cultural difference was confronted in order, along with Mauss, to reveal the fundamental similitudes underlying difference. Mauss's committed socialism gave his work a strong Humanist agenda dedicated to a pan-cultural ideal of equality, very different from the eurocentric Humanism of a Waldemar George; it was given institutional form in the Musée de l'Homme, enshrined in that very name. But, nonetheless, as editor Bataille took every opportunity in *Documents* to use confrontational juxtaposition, especially in the layout of illustrations, to bring out difference disruptively, for instance in the absurd yet deeply disturbing juxtaposition of white chorus-line performers and regimented black 'children' under French military orders in the fourth issue of 1929 [331].

Picasso's confrontational images juxtaposing the European and the non-European could have been responded to on both levels: as images of encounter, where the similitude underlying difference emerges (the nymph makes contact with the half-European, half-African 'Surrealist sculpture', by touching it however gingerly), or as images where the encounter merely deepens the sense of difference and the awareness of the grotesque assymmetries of power. In either case, they are images that threaten the formal stability and cultural longevity of European aesthetic modes with the power of magic; one can understand why Waldemar George found Picasso's replacement of geometry by magic so dangerous. Lydia Gasman has argued that Picasso did not merely allude to magic, but consciously used it as a means of self-protection against fate and death.[83] More important than such a possibility, which can never be proven, is the way magic and the erotic are always brought together, sometimes in the presence of death (in the form of the crucified Christ or that doll-like, animate/inanimate assemblage in the 1933 etching). Magic, thus, is always given its head by Picasso in a distinctively Freudian scenario. As in Miró's infantilism, it is offered as the route back to the 'sexualised thinking' of childhood, a manifestation of what was believed to be the regressive narcissism of all art and artists. As such, in the context of psychoanalysis and Surrealism, it brings Picasso's personal obsessions onto the collective level of myth.

The bringing together of sexuality and mortality has been shown to be a feature of the *Demoiselles d'Avignon* [282].[84] It did not require a conscious Freudian agenda for such a confrontation to occur. *Beyond the Pleasure Principle* of 1920, saw Freud's arrival at his final notion of the instinctual drives. Here he asserted that the positive, self-preservative sex instinct existed in opposition to a self-destructive, aggressive drive, a compulsion to 'restore an earlier state of things', to return ultimately to the condition preceding life: death. As ever, he invoked the classical gods: against Eros was pitched the god Thanatos.[85]

The quotation and the discussion that opens my Introduction to Part Six demonstrates how this idea of competing creative and destructive instincts was applied to the relation between 'civilisation' and its 'discontents' in Freud's 1930 analysis of the topic, and how, almost instantly, it was then applied to Miró's latest work by Bataille in the article which accompanied his review of Luquet's *Art primitif*. In both articles by Bataille, it is Freud's notion of the aggressive instinct that takes charge over the creative instinct, Thanatos

331. Above: 'Bessie Love in the talkie "Broadway Melody", currently on constant show at the Madeleine-Cinéma'; below: 'Children from the school at Bacouya, Bourail (Photograph Albums of E. Robin, 1869–71 – Musée d'ethnographie du Trocadéro)'. Page from *Documents*, no. 4 (Paris, 1929)

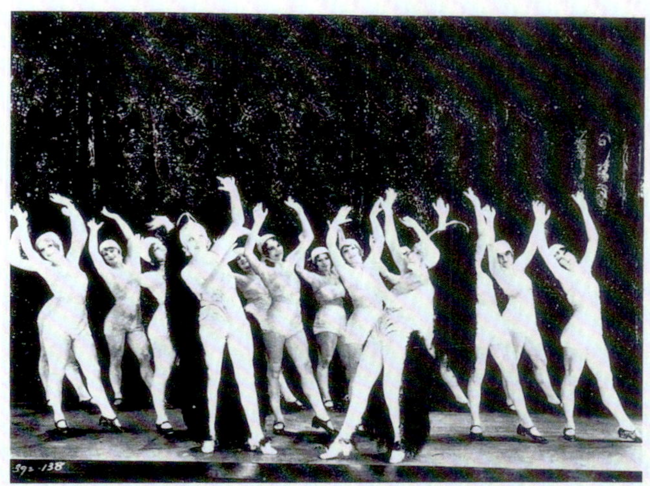

Bessie Love dans le film parlant " Broadway Melody " qui passera incessamment au Madeleine-Cinéma.

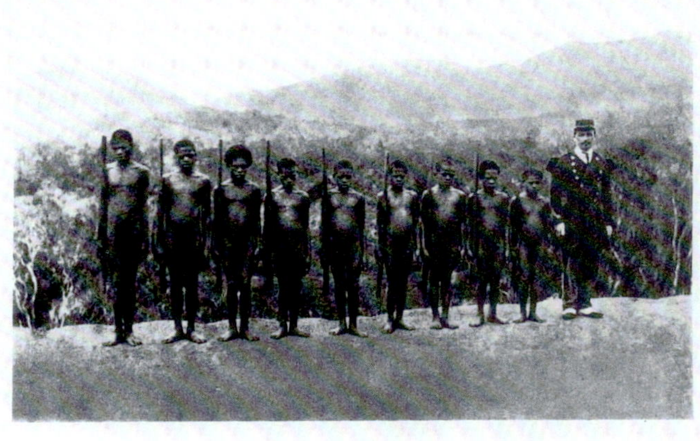

Enfants de l'École de Bacouya, Bourail.
(Albums de photographies de E. Robin, 1869-1871. — Musée d'ethnographie du Trocadéro.)

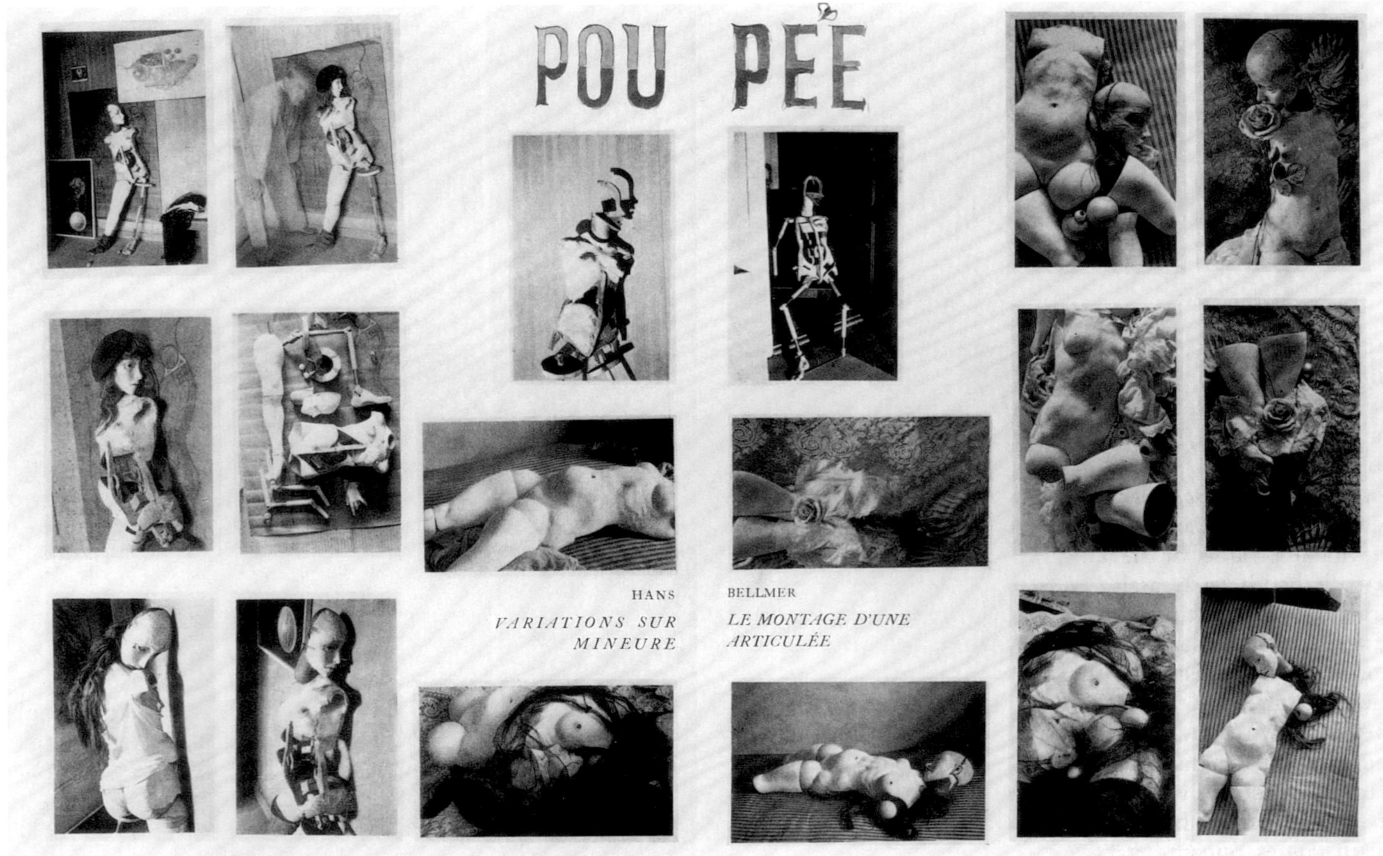

332. Hans Bellmer, *Doll: Variations in the montage of an articulated minor*, double-page spread from *Minotaure*, no. 6 (Paris, winter 1935)

over Eros. For Bataille, the initial impulse behind the infant's desire to draw is not creative at all, but an aggressive impulse to 'alter' things by vandalistically marking surfaces. At the same time, the parallel between the infantile and the prehistoric artist falls down, because in the latter case prehistoric adults *choose* an aggressive 'conceptual realism', usually in their treatment of the human figure, rather than 'naturalism'. Bataille points to the co-existence of the two modes from the same epochs in the same caves as evidence.

For him, Miró's decision in the late 1920s to 'kill painting' wilfully took his art back to a stage when the desire 'sadistically' to destroy *overrode* the desire to create. Bataille saw in pictures like Miró's *Head* [276] a brutal process of 'decomposition pushed to such a point that nothing is left but the formless [informe] stains on the lid (or on the tombstone, if you will) of the box of spells'.[86] With the release of the aggressive instinct came, inevitably, the *informe*, as it had in Picasso's *Guitars* of 1926, especially the dishcloth guitar stabbed by nails [317].

During the 1930s, Thanatos, set in opposition to Eros, became a theme in Bretonian Surrealism too, and in *SASDLR* and *Minotaure* the Marquis de Sade's star, as champion of the aggressive death-drive, rose still higher than it had in *La Révolution surréaliste*, where he throve more as a counter-moralist. One savage manifestation of this was the publication of Hans Bellmer's photographs of horribly contorted and dismembered dolls in *Minotaure* in 1935 [332]. But Breton never advocated a confrontation between the destructive and the creative in which the death drive would, even at the level merely of inference, 'kill' Eros. Just as his dialectical thinking held up the promise of a point at which the contradiction between dream and reality would be resolved, so he wished for the resolution of the sex and death instincts. Bataille took the risk of confronting and even desiring the possible victory of Thanatos.

This was an increasingly dominant aspect of what he called in *Documents* 'base materialism', the preference for all that is 'base' in 'Man', all that is bestial and earthbound, not directed upwards to the heavens. It was Bataille the 'materialist' with his liking for 'flies' – decomposition – who Breton attacked most uncompromisingly in the purge of the Surrealist group that culminated in the second *Manifesto*. *Documents* was full of violence, putrescence and death. Boiffard supplied photographs for articles by Bataille on slaughterhouses and on the taboo represented by that lowest of human features, the big toe. Bataille opposed the ideal of beauty – later to be surrealised as 'convulsive' by Breton – with what he called *bassesse* (baseness). In 1930, he published a scholarly contribution in *Documents* on Aztec blood-sacrifice which followed up his own earlier writing on the topic and anticipated Leiris's most extensive contribution to the Dakar-Djibouti special number of *Minotaure* in 1933, an account of a bull sacrifice in East Africa.[87] Picasso's invocation of sacrifice in *The Three Dancers* [318] was prophetic: blood sacrifice, especially in the bull fight, descendent of the kind of bull sacrifice recorded by Leiris, became one of his central obsessions in the 1930s.

The bull, living not dead, but potentially both killer and sacrificial victim, is given its most resonant role in Picasso's painting of the 1930s with *Guernica* [333]. Here, Freud's aggressive instinct impelled by the death drive is harnessed in a major statement on the inhumanity of war. It was a statement made at just the moment when Bataille and André Masson were most involved in the enterprise they initiated in 1936, *Acéphale*. With the five numbers of that little magazine, Bataille allowed Thanatos total dominance over Eros in the murderous image of his headless god of *bassesse* [320]. At the same time, he brought together his friends, a few (including Leiris) from the period of *Documents*, for a series of meetings and lectures dedicated to the serious study of such topics as the sacred and sacrifice in modern life. In tune with the social anthropological and counter-cultural alliance represented by *Documents*, it was dubbed the 'Collège de sociologie'. In these forums, war was not inhuman, it was an inevitable product of the acephalic (base) human condition. Bataille had been a passionate anti-fascist from early in the decade (briefly in 1935 alongside Breton) and yet in an essay of 1933 he betrays a fascination with fascism as a phenomenon, even if he dismisses it as an extreme manifestation of the authoritarian demand for order.[88] Indeed, his continuing obsession with violence and death in the later 1930s can seem in tune to a disquieting extent with all that was aggressive and destructive in fascism. In the end, Bataille and *Acéphale*'s harnessing of the self-destructive drive towards death comes uncomfortably close to an acceptance of the rush towards war.

THE VISUAL ART OF OPPOSITION: PICASSO AND 'GUERNICA', SURREALISM AND POLITICS, COLLAGE AND WAR

Guernica was Picasso's first propaganda painting. In it, he later said, 'there is a deliberate appeal to people, a deliberate sense of propaganda'.[89] It was his attempt to stop the rush to war. His weapon was the terror of a confrontation with Thanatos in the context of real events.

In July 1936, General Francisco Franco led a military uprising against the five-year-old Spanish Republic from Spanish Morocco; it was supported by garrisons across Spain. The opposition of the Right to the Republic's anticlerical, democratic-socialist policies escalated into civil war. By November, troops and aircraft from the Nazi and Italian fascist regimes were involved with Franco's Nationalist forces in a powerful assault on Madrid; Soviet aircraft and leftists from across the world (the 'International Brigade') helped the Republicans in the city's successful defence. The victory (which would be reversed in 1939) was immediately followed by the Republic's appointment of Picasso as director of the Prado, an entirely symbolic act, since the Museum's great collections had been removed to Valencia for safe keeping. This active policy of involving Picasso in the propaganda effort of the Spanish Republic was taken further in January 1937, when Josep Lluis Sert, architect of the Republic's pavilion for the International Exhibition in Paris, commissioned Picasso to paint a mural for the building, to occupy a key site dominating the entrance hall. *Guernica* was the result [333], but it needed an unprecedented event to arouse Picasso to the furious engagement with the Republican cause that gave the picture its force.

On 29 April 1937, Picasso read the graphically illustrated front-page reports in *L'Humanité* of the bombing three days before by Nazi Condor squadrons of the little town of Guernica, ancient Basque capital and site of the first democratic Parliament in Spain. Most vivid and accurate was a French translation of the eyewitness account by George Steer, war correspondent of *The Times*. Steer wrote of women and children burned to death in shelters under bombed buildings and of those in flight machine-gunned in the surrounding fields. This was, he stressed with devastating coolness, an event 'unparalleled in military history': the systematic destruction of an undefended town behind the lines, ignoring possible military targets, whose object was 'the demoralisation of the civilian population'.[90] The real shock the destruction of Guernica caused internationally was quickly recognised by Franco as a propaganda disaster. The Nationalist Junta issued denials of all involvement, accusing the Republican militia of torching the town itself.

1 May 1937, saw Picasso make the first sketches for his mural. He completed a canvas more than twenty-five feet long and eleven feet high – the size of a cinema screen – in just five weeks. When Christian Zervos's key modernist periodical *Cahiers d'art* dedicated a whole issue to *Guernica* immediately after its completion in June 1937, the French and Spanish supporters of the Republic who contributed made Picasso's anger one of their themes: it was a measure of his real political engagement. For Zervos, it was fear as well as anger that drove Picasso to make so public a political statement, a statement that externalised his most 'inner' obsessions in the service of the 'outer' world of events.[91] For the supporters of modernism, the work's force (and success) would always derive from this convergence of private obsession – the generator of the imagery of the bull, the horse, the broken statue of the warrior, grief as feminine frenzy – and public political commitment. It had begun in the most private of sketches, where almost immediately Picasso fashioned from the cast of the 1935 *Minotauromachy* etching [147] an imagery of disaster.[92] It was painted almost in public, in the barn-like new studio he had taken specially for the commission at 7 rue des Grands Augustins. Friends and allies came in numbers to see progress, on one occasion an audience of 'some fifteen well-known persons' bursting into applause as if at the theatre when he tore off pieces of coloured paper which he had stuck on experimentally.[93] The picture's making was recorded as if a news event: in the *Cahiers d'art* special number, the Surrealist photographer Dora Maar, Picasso's new lover, published a photographic record in seven moments of its progress. The magician in his cell had become a performer in public.

Outside the circles who read *Cahiers d'art* and supported Picasso, however, the success of the picture was quickly questioned. The Communist press in France resisted any temptation to criticise, so as not to weaken its propaganda value, but Spanish Republican officials expressed serious doubts about its capacity to reach a proletarian public, and even Sert recalled later that the majority of visitors to the pavilion 'didn't understand it'.[94] When it was shown in London in

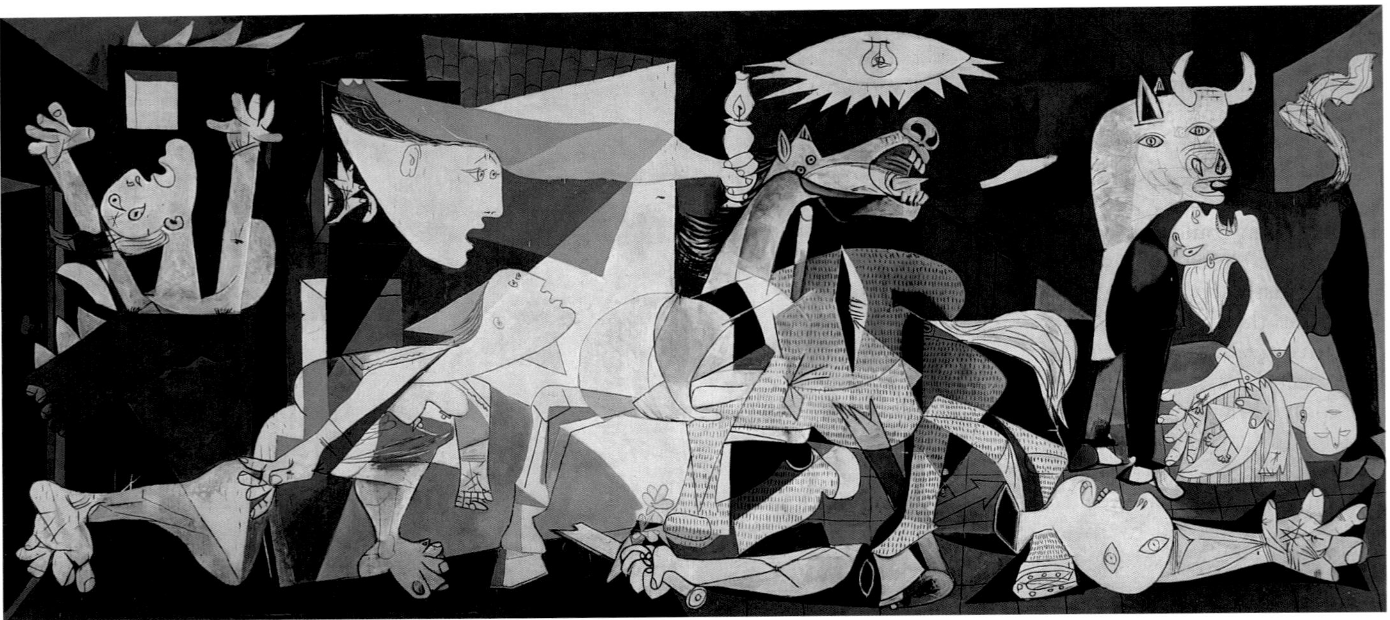

333. Pablo Picasso, *Guernica*, 1937. Oil on canvas, 349.3 × 776.6 cm. Museo Nacional Centro de Arte Reina Sofia, Madrid

October 1937, Anthony Blunt raised the issue without compromise. For him, then a Stalinist supporter of socialist realism, Picasso's private imagery, however strong the horror that infused its pictorial treatment, could only reach a 'limited coterie of aesthetes'.[95] Picasso's anger and his unquestioned political commitment was not enough, Blunt believed, to transform a private into a public political art with real propaganda potential.

Guernica was the most ambitious modernist painting of the 1930s to marshal the weapons of attack honed in the interwar avant-gardes for an explicit political purpose, aimed against a specific target, the fascist Right. It posed – and continues to pose – a major question: how effectively could modernist art be an art of opposition in the political arena? And the way it poses that question, focusing attention on the public efficacy of a private imagery, above all raises the issue of the role of the individual in collective political action.

When Sert visited Picasso to offer the commission in January 1937, he was accompanied by Louis Aragon. With one of the groups that saw the painting in progress was André Breton. It was in the relationship between Surrealism and the Communist organisations of the 1930s that the issue of the individual artist's role in collective political action was exposed most starkly as a problem where modernism was concerned. Aragon and Breton, relations between them irrevocably broken by 1937, represented two opposing positions whose fundamental principles were not negotiable. Aragon had become a Communist activist at the expense of Surrealism; he was one of those who directed the cultural policy of the PCF (French Communist Party) within the Popular Front. In 1935, after a decade of uncomfortable fellow-travelling with the PCF, Breton had severed all links with Communist organisations to keep faith with Surrealism. Early in 1938, he would visit Leon Trotsky in Mexico, underlining thus his total rejection of the cultural politics of Stalin and the Moscow-led Fourth International. Picasso was so prestigious a figure that he could operate above such conflicts, accepted by both sides, but even Picasso and *Guernica* could not override the conflict between private individual impulse and collective public action exposed by the Surrealists' quarrel with the Communists.

The Surrealists' relations with Communist organisations had begun in 1925, as a result of their aggressive anti-colonialist reaction to the Franco-Spanish war against the uprising of Abd-el-Krim and the Riff tribesmen in Morocco (in which, incidentally, General Franco played a determining role). It had started with whole-hearted collaboration between *La Révolution surréaliste* and the Marxist periodical *Clarté* in 1925–6, a period when Breton and his friends, including Aragon, learned the terminology and arguments of dialectical materialism. But even then, the elements of the Surrealists' problem in relation to the collective discipline of French Communists were brought into the open. It took an early defector from the Surrealists, Pierre Naville, to expose the differences between the two movements as an irreconcilable dichotomy.

Naville published a pamphlet, *La Révolution et les intellectuels: Que peuvent faire les surréalistes?* (The Revolution and the Intellectuals: what can the Surrealists do?). Here he charged Breton and his group with placing 'the sacred character of the individual' above the 'disciplined action of *class* struggle'. For him, there could be no revolution of 'the spirit' of the kind pursued by the Surrealists until *after* 'the abolition of bourgeois conditions of material life'. 'Yes or no,' he asked rhetorically, 'this desired revolution, is it of the mind *a priori*, or of the world of facts? Is it linked to Marxism, or to contemplative theories about the purification of the inner life?'[96] Breton answered in December 1926 with an essay which appeared both as a pamphlet and in *La Révolution surréaliste*, 'Legitimate Defence'. The position he established here would be the position he kept to until forced to relinquish his Communist links in 1935. He dismissed Naville's dichotomy as 'a completely artificial opposition'. 'In the realm of facts,' he argued, '. . . no ambiguity is possible; all of us seek to shift power from the hands of the bourgeoisie to those of the proletariat. Meanwhile, it is . . . necessary that experiments of the inner life continue, and do so, of course, without external or even Marxist control'.[97] For Breton, the Communist and Surrealist projects were revolutionary forms of action that could run parallel with one another. He ended 'Legitimate Defence' by stating that he remained outside the Communist Party in order to preserve his independence, an admission that in 'the realm of facts' Communist-Surrealist relations *were* inherently problematic.

Within a few months, Breton and four other Surrealists, including Aragon, had joined the PCF, and 'Legitimate Defence' in its pamphlet form had been withdrawn from circulation. The problem of the conflict between the freedom of the individual imagination and the commitment to social revolution led by the Communist International did not, however, go away. The moment when, Aragon later recalled, he realised that his loyalties had switched from the Surrealist group to the International came late in 1930, on his return from the Second International Congress of Revolutionary Writers at Kharkov in the Soviet Union. But he vacillated between his old and new loyalties until the end of 1932, when Breton's refusal to follow PCF instructions in a controversy involving both of them triggered their final separation. It was in the context of his Stalinist promotion of socialist realism in 1935 that Aragon summed up what in his experience had forced the break. For Aragon, the Surrealists' attempt to 'bend Marxism to fit the theories of Freud' merely spoke of a refusal to bow to the social revolutionary imperative. Their 'inner' lives had remained their primary concern: poetry and 'Freudism', not the 'new world' in whose service he now placed his art.[98] Breton continued with stubborn brilliance to deny the existence of Naville's and Aragon's either/or dichotomy. He ended his speech to a hostile audience of French and Soviet writers convened to 'defend culture' in 1935: '"Transform the world", said Marx: "Change Life", said Rimbaud; for us, these two commands are the same.' In 1938, the manifesto he wrote with Trotsky included a vision of a 'new world' where a '*socialist* regime' would be built on 'centralised control', but where 'intellectual creation' would be based on 'an *anarchist* regime of individual liberty': where the two revolutions would finally be resolved, without the one losing its collectivist or the other its individualist essence.[99]

That term 'anarchist' is telling, for, in the last analysis, the role given to culture in Breton's idea of a politics of culture was that given to it at the turn of the century by writers and artists building on the texts of the major anarchist theorists of the nineteenth century, Joseph Proudhon and Peter Kropotkin especially. Anarchist aesthetics in the late 1890s and early 1900s valued individual liberty too highly for its sacrifice to be contemplated, and endowed culture with the capacity to subvert capitalist society both by exposing its miseries and injustices, and by clearing a space in society, however small, for the free-living, free-thinking individual artist. In this politics of culture, the very individualism of a text or painting could of itself act subversively. As Pierre Quillard, a friend of Alfred Jarry, put it in 1892: 'good literature is an outstanding form of propaganda by the deed . . . Whoever communicates to his brothers in suffering the secret splendour of his dreams acts upon the surrounding society in the manner of a solvent and makes all those who understand him, often without realisation, outlaws and rebels.'[100]

What separated early twentieth-century anarchist aesthetics – that of Paul Signac or Pierre Bonnard – from the Surrealists' strategies of subversion was its commitment to harmony in art as the analogue of a utopian vision of a harmonious society, where the savagery of capitalist competition would be replaced by the peaceful cooperation of mutuality. As Signac noted in 1902: 'Justice in sociology, harmony in art: same thing.'[101] Surrealist cultural politics was driven more by a post-1914–18 anger than by utopian hope: it placed its faith in the capacity of a totally liberated culture to subvert values by displaying their brutal demolition; it rejected altogether the Golden Age dream of Signac's *In Time of Harmony* or Bonnard's summer idylls [94, 230]. This is even more the case of Bataille's cultural politics: destructive anarchism was pitched directly against fascism in his brief collaborative enterprise of 1935–6 with Breton, the periodical *Contre-attaque*. What linked the Surrealists and the early twentieth-century anarchists was their belief that culture could act politically without becoming explicitly propagandistic: that subversion, driven by 'the secret splendour' of individual 'dreams', was a more powerful weapon than propaganda. For the Surrealists, by placing imagination above logic, art was made to function subversively, and sometimes, in the specific way it did so, art could also undermine the values of progressive democracy, of Catholicism, nationalism and colonialism.

In 1930 one unforgettably violent event underlined how potent Surrealist subversion could be. On 3 December, Buñuel and Dalí's ironically titled film *L'Age d'or* (The Golden Age) was given its first public showing at Studio 28 in Paris. An exhibition, including work by Dalí, was organised to accompany it. The film's sustained demolition of the dignity of the Church and the values of the family attracted the furious attention of the extreme right-wing 'Ligue des patriotes'. The theatre was invaded, members of the audience were assaulted (most of the Surrealist and dissident Surrealist groups were present), ink was thrown at the screen, the projection equipment was destroyed, and several paintings, especially Dalí's and Ernst's, were ripped to pieces. This was followed by a vandalistic attack on the editorial offices of *SASDLR* and calls for the suppression of Surrealism from the newspaper *Le Figaro*, while the quasi-fascist *L'Ami du peuple* indignantly dismissed Dalí and Buñuel as 'the refuse of their countries of origin'.[102] Finally, the official censor banned the film. Surrealist work could and did provoke the political enemies both of the Surrealists and of the communist Left. Indeed, the *L'Age d'or* affair was one event that persuaded the communist press openly to support the group. '*L'Age d'or* is not a film for the proletariat,' announced *L'Humanité*, 'but one may affirm that . . . it serves the revolutionary purposes of the working class'.[103]

When in 1944, with the liberation of France from Nazi occupation, Picasso joined the Communist Party, the political role he claimed for art despite the propaganda paintings he was to produce occasionally in the context of the

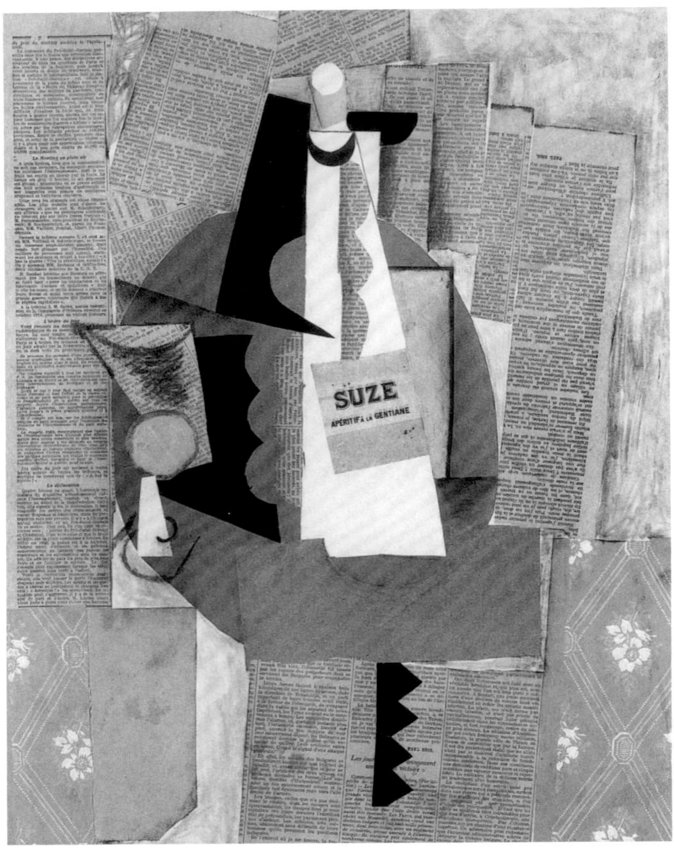

334. Pablo Picasso, *Bottle of Suze*, 1912. Charcoal, gouache and pasted paper, 64 × 50 cm. Washington University Gallery of Art, St Louis, University Purchase, Kende Sole Fund, 1946

peace movement, amounted once again to anarchist subversion, and in his case the echoes of early twentieth-century anarchism were stronger than they had been within Surrealism. Interviewed for *L'Humanité*, he claimed that membership of the PCF was 'the logical outcome of my whole life,' and went on to say that he had always used 'drawing' and 'colour' as 'my weapons' by which to 'liberate us all more each day . . .'.[104] In the period 1900–40, the explicit propagandistic character of *Guernica* was a rare exception; it was by saying things 'in my own way', by the individual freedom of work which almost never directly invoked politics, that he believed he had used art as a weapon against the dominant values of society.

Before the Spanish Civil War set his anger alight and drove him to paint *Guernica*, there was just one phase in his Cubist and post-Cubist work when he directly invoked politics. Surprisingly, it was at the moment of his most recondite and private Cubist experiments, the moment of his first papiers-collés, at the end of 1912. The relation between the individualistic, inventive aspect of the works in question and the political material they contain can take me back to a final look at the effectiveness of *Guernica* as a political statement, in particular because they have been considered explicitly anarchist works aimed, like *Guernica*, against militarism and war.

It has been demonstrated that a high proportion of the news cuttings glued to Picasso's first papiers-collés in the autumn and winter of 1912 are reports on the Balkan wars and that the news items incorporated are invariably left legible, however fragmentary.[105] The Balkan wars began in October 1912 with Serbian and Bulgarian campaigns against the Ottoman and Austro-Hungarian Empires. Like the Spanish Civil War, they threatened to trigger a full-scale European war, in this case with the French drawn in as the allies of Tzar Nicholas II against the Germans and the Austro-Hungarians. These abruptly ended hostilities were a false start before the actual beginning of the Great War in August 1914, and filled the French press with black portents for months, fuelling the growing mood of bellicose nationalism (a very different mood from the confused anger, anxiety and pacifist dread of 1936–7).

Picasso's incorporation in his papiers-collés of Balkan war reports can be placed in the context of his connections with anarchist activists in both Barcelona and Paris between 1898 and 1914, anarchists whose social utopianism went with uncompromising anti-militarism. Especially rich in its references to the Balkan wars is a work of late 1912, *The Bottle of Suze* [334], which incorporates cuttings that give accounts of a thwarted Bulgarian advance against the Turks, the horror of a cholera epidemic among the Turkish forces (upside down), and the well-organised clamour of a peace demonstration in Paris addressed by prominent pacifists, anarchists and socialists (including the Cubists' champion in the Chamber of Deputies, Marcel Sembat). The references to contemporary political events are far more explicit than anything in *Guernica* and yet, despite strong circumstantial evidence of Picasso's anarchist sympathies, the political message of the work remains ambivalent in a way that *Guernica* was not.[106]

Nothing in the work itself demands that these references be read necessarily as a statement of solidarity with Marcel Sembat and the Parisian peace demonstrators. Picasso made no decisive political gesture or statement at the time to establish his engagement with the issues, and, though his dealer Kahnweiler recalls attending peace demonstrations as a committed supporter of the Left, it is he also who recalls the Picasso of those years as emphatically apolitical. Moreover, the cuttings come from *Le Journal*, a mass-circulation newspaper of the nationalist centre Right, no supporter of pacifism. Certainly the choice of cuttings demonstrates interest, but it neither demonstrates an overriding interest in these events as against pictorial events nor conveys the passion of commitment. The cuttings are left open to the viewer, to be read with whatever bias he or she might add, if they are read at all.[107] And indeed, their very relationship with the café setting in which they are placed threatens to reduce their contents to mere background noise, peripheral to the crisply shaped objects that occupy centre-stage on the table top, the glass and the bottle of Suze, and to the arresting pictorial experience offered.

If *Bottle of Suze* is an anarchist work aimed against militarism and war, its aim is far from unerring. Like all Picasso's papiers-collés of late 1912, it squares much more obviously with the anarchist notion of art as the analogue of libertarian revolution, the notion the artist referred to in 1944 when he spoke of his 'drawing' and his 'colour' as his 'weapons' by which to 'liberate us all more each day'. So ambivalent a use of political reference could never function effectively as propaganda for a cause; and so playful yet intellectually demanding a practice could never express fear or fury.[108]

One of those to visit Picasso's studio in 1937 to view *Guernica* in progress was the Spaniard José Bergamin. He was with the group that saw the artist tear the pieces of coloured papier-collé off the canvas. For Bergamin, papier-collé was nothing more than an aesthetic distraction in the black, grey and white starkness of *Guernica*, an attempt 'to hide . . . the terrible truth . . . [Picasso's] hands revealed'.[109] And yet, arguments for the success of Picasso's 'inner' imagery as an effective imagery of political propaganda in the painting have centred on its ambivalence, an openness that recalls the ambivalence of papier-collé in *Bottle of Suze*. Where the political significance of explicit political material was left open in 1912, here the meanings of images that carry almost no explicit political markers are left open.

The most devastating early Marxist critique of the picture is Max Raphael's, written from a decade's distance, when its fame as a cultural icon was assured. It is this ambivalence that Raphael sees as the key, not to *Guernica*'s success, but to its failure. He notes how the bull can be seen both as male life force, symbol of rebirth, and as symbol of 'Franco's (and all other 'Führer's') impassive sadism,' in the same way that the horse can be defeated fascism as well as the people in sacrificial defeat. 'The viewer,' he asserts, 'is made the victim of an allegory which is not self-evident: his emotions and his judgement are being torn apart . . . , so that he is stultified rather than stimulated to creative action'. The blame for this lies squarely, for Raphael, in Picasso's commitment to his 'inner' obsessions in all their 'mysteriousness' rather than to those outside his circle 'who respect real action in the real world'.[110]

Psychoanalysis figures nowhere in Raphael's argument. It was psychoanalysis' claim to reveal the universality of myths as the metaphors of collective human truths that provided the grounding for one set of arguments produced in support of *Guernica*, for instance those of Herbert Read and Roland Penrose in England. By their very *lack* of specificity, Picasso's symbols, instantly recognisable because of their generalised banality (a bull, a horse, a fallen warrior) can transcend their historical moment and attain universality; this is the argument. As William Rubin was the first to show, Picasso's cast of performers connect the work with three entire systems of mythology: the grieving women with the Christian crucifixion (an allusion confirmed by the tripartite composition), the bull with the classical myth of the Minotaur, and the bull and the horse with the Spanish myth of bull sacrifice in the bull fight.[111] The cultural span of its allusions is indeed vast. And yet, what is striking about the positive responses to the picture published early on is not vague invocations of universal myths, but the specificity and the decisiveness of the opinions expressed. This is already clear in the *Cahiers d'art* special number. From the start, responsive viewers found clear political meaning in the allegory, they did not succumb to its ambivalence as its 'victims': they decided what the bull and the horse and the imagery of disaster said for them. In the case of Bergamin, the 'truth' revealed when Picasso tore off the masking papier-collé was 'revealed . . . like raised fists'. 'Doubt,' he wrote, 'is no longer possible'.[112]

The reason for this decisiveness is clear. Unlike the papiers collés of 1912, which remained in the closed private space of the studio and Kahnweiler's gallery, *Guernica* was seen in a public space which insisted on a political response at a moment when pressure was mounting for France's Popular Front government to enter the war on the side of the Spanish Republic. The picture's fury and its allegorical drama came as one item, however dominant, in a display

235. Julio González, *The Montserrat*, 1936–7. Forged iron, 165 × 47 × 47 cm. Stedelijk Museum, Amsterdam

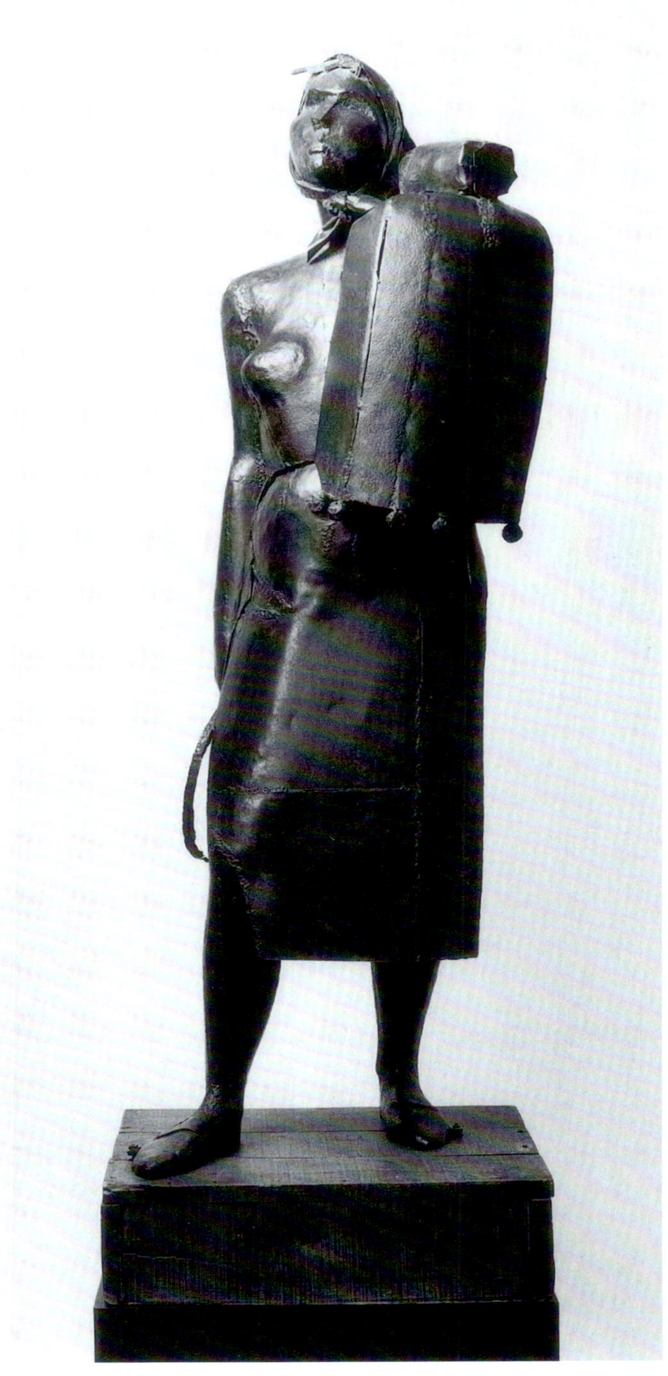

which included not only the Surrealism of Joan Miró and the playful formalism of Alexander Calder, but the socialist realism of Julio González. Before seeing *Guernica*, every visitor was confonted by González's socialist realist *Montserrat* at the entrance, the iron figure of a peasant woman, standing firm against all comers with her scythe and shield [335]. On a floor above were photographs of Guernica in flames alongside a wall-panel bearing Paul Eluard's poem 'La Victoire de Guernica'. Photography and socialist realist art worked with, not against the huge modernist mural; together they demanded a political response. The Spanish Pavilion in 1937 was a place where Aragon's socialist realism and the Surrealists' individualist anarchism functioned in tandem.

In this context, the openness of Picasso's imagery could actually add to its propandistic force. It demanded not passive acquiescence, but active engagement from its viewers: decisions. Only in the seventh and last stage of the picture's development as recorded by Dora Maar's photographs was the head of the fallen warrior finalised. He is given lidless eyes that stare out lifeless at the viewer. They echo the lidless eyes of the bull that stare out full of life, and both echo the staring elipse of the sun above with its electric-light-bulb pupil, the light that reveals all even for the torch-bearing figure of Truth on the right. These gazes directed outwards draw in the viewer, as did the magician's gaze in *Painter and Model* and the prostitutes' gazes in the *Demoiselles d'Avignon*, and by crossing the threshold of the picture plane into the viewer's space they separate *Guernica* as an open modernist work from the pre-twentieth-century sources that have often been associated with it: such depictions of disaster as, for instance, Guido Reni's and Nicolas Poussin's *Massacres of the Innocents* and even Francisco Goya's *Disasters of War*. The politics of the painting is the viewer's decision.

Many early responses to the work balanced hope against the horror of catastrophe. When read as the noble symbol of the people, the bull invariably became a symbol of hope, and so did the bird flying upwards beside him. But *Guernica*, unlike the *Minotauromachy*, excludes Eros altogether to allow Thanatos a fearful victory. It has been pointed out that between 22 April and 6 May, at the moment when Picasso began work on the mural, Jean-Louis Barrault put on in Paris Miguel Cervantes' sixteenth-century tragedy, *El Cerco de Numancia* (The Siege of Numancia), with sets by André Masson, and that links can be drawn between the play and the painting. The story of the Roman destruction of Numancia, sacred town of the Iberian Celts, became in Barrault's production a statement of Republican resistance even in defeat.[113] Yet, *Guernica* as an image of destruction and defeat could provoke at least one contributor to the *Cahiers d'art* special number to a response which is devastating in its refusal of hope. Michel Leiris called his contribution 'Death Notice' (Faire-part). *Guernica*'s openness to the most negative responses made it one of many works that can seem to anticipate the German defeat of France in 1940: others included Ubac's *Battle of the Amazons* and Masson's *Acéphale* [311, 320].

Finally, *Guernica* brings out another kind of defeat which the entire avant-garde oppositional enterprise inevitably faced within not only French society but liberal democratic societies in general: the adaptation of its weapons to serve the very values it opposed. For Picasso's pictorial weaponry had been developed alongside the verbal and visual armouries of those intent on the demolition of civilised French values, the circles of *Documents* and *Acéphale* included, and in *Guernica* that weaponry was used *in defence* of civilisation. Zervos, speaking for Picasso, was unequivocal: the artist's anger was directed against forces that threatened to extinguish 'the last hopes of civilisation'.[114]

Notes

PART ONE INTRODUCTION

1. Founded in 1871, the Third Republic was the successor to the Republics of 1793 and 1848.

2. Jules Roches, cited from *Exposition Universelle Internationale de 1900 à Paris. Actes Organiques* (Paris, June 1896), 7; in Yvonne Brunhammer, *1925*. Exh. cat. (Musée des arts décoratifs, Paris, 1976), 22.

3. The suggestion is Ory's, see Pascal Ory, *Les Exposition Universelles de Paris. Panorama raisonné avec des aperçus nouveaux et des illustrations par les meilleurs auteurs* (Paris, 1982), 144.

4. Cited in Philippe Rémond, 'Le pacifisme et la Tour de la Paix', in Musée d'art moderne de la Ville de Paris, Exh. cat., *Cinquantenaire de l'Exposition Internationale des arts et des techniques dans la vie moderne* (Paris, 1987), 308–17.

CHAPTER 1

1. Central Paris, in the late nineteenth century famously republican, moved to the nationalist Right in 1900, against the trend. See Jean-Marie Mayeur and Madeleine Reberioux, *The Third Republic from its Origins to the Great War* (Cambridge, 1984), 206.

2. Cited from Paul Morand, *1900* (Paris, 1931), in Pascal Ory, *Les Expositions Universelles de Paris. Panorama raisonné avec des aperçus nouveaux et des illustrations par les meilleurs auteurs* (Paris, 1982), 118.

3. *Ibid.*, 56. An approximate figure of 83,000 is given by Ory for the number of visitors; there were 4.8 million recorded 'entrées', 25.

4. Useful accounts of France's industrial development in this period are to be found in Mayeur and Reberioux (1984) *op.cit.*, and James F. McMillan, *Dreyfus to De Gaulle: Society in France 1898–1969* (London, 1985). For the 'Belle Époque' and social and political change, see David Cottington, *Cubism in the Shadow of War. The Avant-Garde and Politics in Paris, 1905–1914* (New Haven and London, 1998), 13–32.

5. Emile Molinier, Preface to Roger Marx, *Exposition Centennale de l'art français 1800–1900* (Paris, 1900), np.

6. Proust became the first and only minister of the arts in the Third Republic in 1881. His ideas on art and industry were published in his *L'Art sous la République* (Paris, 1892).

7. The quotation used here comes from Anatole France's Preface to 'L'Art social'; it is cited in Fay Brauer, *L'Art révolutionnaire: The Artist as Alien, The Discourses of Cubism, Modern Painting and Academicism in the Radical Republic*, Ph.D. thesis. Courtauld Institute of Art London, 1997, 157.

8. The positions of Roger Marx and Paul-Boncour are discussed in *ibid.*, 156ff., and in Cottington (1998) *op.cit.*, 29–30.

9. Both Marx and Guilleré are cited in Yvonne Brunhammer, *1925*, exh. cat. (Musée des arts décoratifs, Paris, 1976), 14–18.

10. Waldemar George, 'L'Exposition des arts décoratifs et industriels de 1925 – les tendances générales', *L'Art vivant* (1925) 285–8.

11. See Le Corbusier, *Almanach d'architecture moderne* (Paris, 1926).

12. George (1925), *op.cit.*

13. Serge Berstein, *La France des années 30* (Paris, 1988), 10, 16.

14. Mayeur and Reberioux (1984), *op.cit.*, 341.

15. Secondary sources disagree on the figures. My figures here are taken from Pascal Ory, *La Belle Illusion. Culture et Politique sous la signe du Front Populaire 1935–1938* (Paris, 1994), 282.

16. Georges Huisman, Lecture delivered at the Salle Pleyel, 29 April 1937, in *Europe* (Paris, June 1937); as cited in Ory (1994), *op.cit.*, 156. For the commissioning and monitoring committees and the conflicts within them, see: Bruno Foucart, 'Les artistes et la commande publique: Le cas du palais de Chaillot', in Jean-Louis Cohen (ed.), *Les Années Trente: L'architecture et les arts de l'espace entre industrie et nostalgie*, exh. cat. (Musée des monuments français, Paris, 1997), 71–83.

17. Drieu la Rochelle in *La Lutte des jeunes*, 4 March 1934; cited in Zeev Sternhell, *Ni Droite ni gauche: L'idéologie fasciste en France* (Paris, 1987), enlarged edition, 285–6.

18. For Labbé's views on regionalism and the crafts, and early career, see: Madeleine Rebérioux, 'L'Exposition de 1937 et le contexte politique des années trente', in Musée d'art moderne de la Ville de Paris, *Cinquantenaire de l'Exposition Internationale des arts et des techniques dans la vie moderne*. Exh. cat. (Paris, 1987), 28.

19. For the rural and provincial aspects of the 1937 Exhibition, see: Shanny Peer, *France on Display. Peasants, Provincials and Folklore in the 1937 World's Fair* (New York, 1998). She discusses regionalism and the 'Centre régional' in Chapter 2.

20. For Blum's interventions, see: Ory (1994), *op.cit.*, 284–6, 477ff. Perrin had a 'sous-secrétaire' post in the Blum administration, and so himself pushed through the Palais de la Découverte initiative, though, of course, with Blum's backing.

21. This is succinctly demonstrated in Berstein (1988), *op.cit.*, 29–37.

22. A very full account of the beginnings of the Musée des arts et traditions populaire is given in Ory (1994), 499–509.

23. Figures from Berstein (1988), *op.cit.*, 5–7.

24. Raymond Escholier, 'Préambule', *Les Maîtres de l'art indépendant, 1895–1937*, exh. cat. (Petit Palais, Paris, 1937), np.

25. Also given a key formative role in the catalogue and the installation was so-called 'primitive art'. African and Oceanic objects were lent generously by, among others, Matisse and Eluard.

26. André Salmon, *La Jeune Peinture française* (Paris, 1912), 1–2.

27. André Fontainas and Louis Vauxcelles (with contributions by Waldemar George), *Histoire générale de l'art français de la Révolution à nos jours. I. La Peinture, la gravure – le dessin* (Paris, 1922). The loose chapter structure reveals this clearly enough. Vauxcelles' coverage of the moderns was an addition to a survey history first published in 1906, leading to this 1922 edition.

28. Henri Focillon, *La Peinture au XIXe et XXe siècles. Du Réalisme à nos jours* (Paris, 1928), and René Huyghe, *Histoire de l'art contemporain* (Paris, 1935).

29. *Ibid.*, Chapter 1, 'Les Origines de la peinture contemporaine'.

30. Germain Bazin and René Huyghe, *Les Contemporains* (Paris, 1939).

CHAPTER 2

1. The passage in *La Nouvelle Revue* is cited in Sarah Whitfield, *Fauvism* (London, 1991), 56. See also, Louis Vauxcelles, *Gil Blas* (Paris, 23 March 1905), also cited by Whitfield and by John Elderfield, *The 'Wild Beasts'. Fauvism and its Affinities*, exh. cat. (Museum of Modern Art, New York, 1976), 32.

2. For the formation and operation of the Salon d'automne and both its and the Indépendants' relationship to the other Salons, see Part II, Chapter 3.

3. The passage is cited as excerpted and translated in Whitfield (1991) *op.cit.*, 82.

4. Denis' views on Matisse at the Salon d'automne were published in *L'Hermitage* (Paris, 15 November 1905). Vauxcelles was to warn of the danger of Matisse becoming too abstract and theoretical in *Gil Blas* (Paris, 20 March 1906). This is discussed in the context of a wide range of critical responses to the Fauves in Roger Benjamin, 'Fauves in the Landscape of Criticism, Metaphor and Scandal at the Salon', in Judi Freeman (ed.), *The Fauve Landscape*. Exh. cat. (Los Angeles, Los Angeles County Museum of Art, 1990).

5. Henri Matisse, 'Notes d'un peintre', *La Phalange* (Paris, December 1907), 481–5; published in English translation in Jack D. Flam, *Matisse on Art* (London, 1973). Also see Roger Benjamin, *Matisse's 'Notes of a Painter': Criticism, Theory and Context, 1891–1908* (Ann Arbor, 1987).

6. James Herbert dedicates a study of Fauvism to Matisse, Derain and Vlaminck alone. See James D. Herbert, *Fauve Painting. The Making of Cultural Politics* (New Haven and London, 1992).

7. Georges Duthuit, *Les Fauves* (Geneva, 1949), 35.

8. André Fontainas and Louis Vauxcelles (with contributions from Waldemar George), *Histoire général de l'art français de la Révolution à nos jours* (Paris, 1922), Chapter XV, 'Les Salons de la jeune peinture', 264–6.

9. Elderfield (1976) *op.cit.*, 83.

10. See André Salmon, *La Jeune Peinture français* (Paris, 1912), 9–40; Anon., 'Introduction', *Origines et développement de l'art international indépendant*, exh. cat. (Jeu de Paume, Paris, 1937); and Elderfield (1976) *op.cit.*

11. *Ibid.*, 14, 56.

12. *Ibid.*, 52.

13. This is discussed more fully in Judi Freeman, 'Surveying the Terrain. The Fauves and Landscape'; in Freeman (1990) *op.cit.*

14. *Ibid.*, 24–9.

15. Jeffrey Weiss, *The Popular Culture of Modern Art. Picasso, Duchamp and Avant-Gardism* (New Haven and London, 1994), Chapter II.

16. As cited, ibid., 83.

17. The exhibition, held 9–28 November, showed twenty-seven works including many of the landscapes. Vauxcelles' remarks were in *Gil Blas* (Paris, 14 November 1908).

18. Charles Morice, in *Mercure de France* (Paris, 16 April 1909), 709. The word 'cubism' is used a month earlier in Anon., 'Echos', *Le Figaro* (Paris, 24 March 1909).

19. Anon., in *La Phalange*, 4, no. 48 (Paris, 20 June, 1910), 728–30; cited as

translated in Judith Cousins, 'Chronology', in William Rubin (ed.), *Picasso and Braque: Pioneering Cubism*, exh. cat. (Museum of Modern Art, New York, 1989), 365. The review refers to Picassos shown at the dealer Wilhelm Uhde's galerie Notre-Dame-des-Champs in May 1910.

20. André Salmon, 'Le Salon d'automne', *Paris-Journal* (Paris, 30 September 1910), 5.

21. Jean Metzinger, 'Note sur la peinture', *Pan* (October–November 1910), 649–52. Cited as in Cousins (1989).

22. Roland Dorgelès, 'Ce que disent les cubes . . .', *Fantasio* (Paris, 1 November 1911).

23. It appeared with his *Paysage* in *Le Matin* (Paris, 6 October 1911).

24. Fay Brauer is the first to have noticed the mention of Lampué's career as an Indépendants artist. See Brauer (1997) *op.cit.* She discusses the debates provoked by the 1912 Salon d'automne in detail in Chapter 4. His open letter, dated 5 October 1912, was circulated to all the major national dailies, and was addressed to the Sous-Secrétaire d'Etat aux beaux-arts, Bérard, in the hope of an official government response. The nationalist press of the Right, for instance *Le Matin*, gave him unequivocal support; *Le Matin* published the letter in full on 5 October. The Chamber debate took place on 28 November and 3 December.

25. *Le Petit Parisien* (Paris, 23 April 1911). Cited in Cousins (1989) *op.cit.*

26. See also Chapter 4.

27. Guillaume Janneau, *L'Art cubiste. Théories et réalisations. Etude critique* (Paris, 1929), 3, 19.

28. André Salmon (1912) *op.cit.*, 44.

29. Maurice Raynal, 'Conception et vision', *Gil Blas* (Paris, 29 August 1912).

30. See especially the analysis in Golding's fundamental history: John Golding, *Cubism: a History and an Analysis, 1907–1914* (London, 1959, 1968 and 1988).

31. Janneau (1929) *op.cit.*, 3, 10–11.

32. The key texts are: Rosalind E. Krauss, 'In the Name of Picasso', in Krauss, *The Originality of the Avant-garde and Other Modernist Myths* (Cambridge, Mass., and London, 1987); and Yve-Alain Bois, 'Kahnweiler's Lesson', in Bois, *Painting as Model* (Cambridge, Mass., and London, 1993).

33. Guillaume Apollinaire, 'Les trois vertus plastiques', in the catalogue of the IIIe Exposition du Cercle de l'art moderne, Mairie, Le Havre, June 1908; cited as translated in Leroy C. Breunig (ed.), *Apollinaire on Art: Essays and Reviews 1902–1918*, translated from the French by Susan Suleiman (London, 1972), 47.

34. Daniel Robbins, 'Jean Metzinger: At the Centre of Cubism', in Ann Moser (ed.), *Jean Metzinger in Retrospect*, exh. cat. (The University of Iowa Museum of Art, Iowa City, 1985).

35. I have demonstrated as much at length in: Christopher Green, *Cubism and its Enemies. Modern Movements and Reaction in French Art, 1916–1928* (New Haven and London, 1987), Part I.

36. See *ibid.*, Part III, Chapters 9 and 10.

37. André Lhote, 'Le Cubisme au Grand Palais', *La Nouvelle Revue française*, 7th Year, 78 (Paris, 1 March 1920), 467–71; and quoted in Jacques Guenne, 'André Lhote', *L'Art vivant* (Paris, 1 March 1926).

38. André Breton to Louis Aragon, 13 April 1919. As cited in Marguerite Bonnet, *André Breton. Naissance de l'aventure surréaliste* (Paris, 1975), 153. Author's translation.

39. Tristan Tzara to André Breton, 21 September 1919. Cited in Michel Sanouillet, *Dada á Paris* (Paris, 1965), 449.

40. Francis Picabia, 'Manifeste Dada', *391*, 12 (Paris, March 1921), 1.

41. Sanouillet (1965), *op.cit.*

42. André Breton, 'Caractères de l'évolution moderne et ce qui en participe'. Lecture given at the 'Ateneo' in Barcelona, 17 November 1922, in Breton, *Les Pas perdus* (Paris, 1924), 157–8.

43. 'Après Dada' is the title of a piece published by Breton in *Comoedia* (Paris, 2 March 1922).

44. André Breton, 'Entrée des médiums', in Breton (1924) *op.cit.*, 123–4.

45. André Breton, 'Manifeste du Surréalisme' (1924), in Breton, *Manifestes du surréalisme* (Paris, 1972), 37.

46. David Sylvester, 'Regarding the Exhibition', in Dawn Ades, *Dada and Surrealism Reviewed*, exh. cat. (Arts Council of Great Britain, Hayward Gallery, London, 1978), 1.

47. Jacqueline Chénieux-Gendron, *Surrealism*, translated by Vivian Folkenflik (New York, 1990; French ed. 1984), 10–11. Alluded to here is Breton's own use of these quotations from Marx and Rimbaud in 'Discours au congrès des écrivains', in André Breton, *Position politique du surréalisme* (Paris, 1935), 98.

48. André Breton, 'Second Manifeste du surréalisme' (1929), in Breton, *op.cit.*, (1972), 78.

49. Figures from Ades (1978) *op.cit.*, 251.

50. Breton (1972) *op.cit.*, 149–50.

51. As cited in Maurice Nadeau, *The History of Surrealism*, translated by Richard Howard (London, 1968; French editions 1944 and 1968), 154–8.

52. Breton (1972) *op.cit.*

53. *Ibid.*, 146.

54. See Bibliography.

55. Maurice Raynal, *Anthologie de la peinture en France de 1906 à nos jours* (Paris, 1927), 34–7. Author's translation.

56. Guillaume Apollinaire, *Méditations esthétiques. Les Peintres cubistes* (Paris, 1913), L-C. Breunig and J-Cl. Chevalier (eds.) (Paris, 1965), 57. Author's translation.

57. I am grateful to Gladys Fabre for information given me on Kupka, Del Marle and Gallien. See also: Gladys Fabre, 'La Création artistique comme métaphore du vivant: de l'oeuvre de Kupka comme organisme au sein du milieu artistique parisien', in *František Kupka 1871–1957, ou l'invention d'une abstraction*, exh. cat. (Paris, Musée d'art moderne de la Ville de Paris, 1989–90), 34–5.

58. See Part II, Chapter 4.

59. Peter Bürger, *The Theory of the Avant-Garde* (Minneapolis, 1983; 1st English ed.).

60. Jean-Marie Mayeur and Madeleine Reberioux, *The Third Republic from its Origins to the Great War, 1871–1914*. Translated by J.R. Foster (Cambridge, 1984; 1st French ed. 1973), 195.

PART TWO INTRODUCTION

1. Roger Marx, 'Preface', exh. cat. (Galerie Vollard, Paris, 1904). As cited in translation in Jack Flam, *Henri Matisse. The Man and his Art, 1869–1918* (London, 1986), 109.

CHAPTER 3

1. Emile Zola, 'Le Naturalisme au Salon', *Le Voltaire* (Paris, 18 June 1880). As cited in Patricia Mainardi, *The End of the Salon. Art and the State in the Early Third Republic* (Cambridge, 1993), 82.

2. *Ibid.*

3. Those elected onto juries were almost exclusively previous medal-winners, who did not have to submit for selection (who were 'hors concours'). Medals, however, were given generously: forty could be won in the painting section alone. I am indebted here to Fay Brauer. See Fay Brauer, 'L'Art révolutionnaire. The Artist as Alien: The Discourses of Cubism, Modern Painting and Academicism in the Radical Republic'. Ph.D., thesis, Courtauld Institute, University of London, 1997. Chapter 2 and appendices. Material in this section is drawn most of all from Brauer, Marie-Claude Genet-Delacroix, *Art et Etat sous la IIIe République. Le système des Beaux-Arts 1870–1940* (Paris, 1992), Mainardi (1993) *op.cit.*, and Pierre Vaisse *La Troisième République et les peintres* (Paris, 1995).

4. For a fuller account of the Salons and 'Salonnets', see David Cottington, *Cubism in the Shadow of War. The Avant-Garde and Politics in Paris, 1905–1914* (New Haven and London, 1998), 40–3. For the 'Femmes peintres', see Tamar Garb, *Sisters of the Brush: Women's Artistic Culture in Late Nineteenth-Century Paris* (New Haven and London, 1994).

5. Cited in Vaisse (1995) *op.cit.*, 61.

6. See Genet-Delacroix (1992) *op.cit.*

7. *Ibid.*, 15–16.

8. These changes are recounted in: Pascal Ory, *La Belle Illusion. Culture et Peinture sous le signe du Front Populaire* (Paris, 1994), 274ff.

9. He records these views in his Report of 1938. See Genet-Delacroix (1992) *op.cit.*, 105.

10. This is apparent in the campaign of 1925 to resist a civil-servant successor to Léonce Bénédite at the Luxembourg, and the support given by writers and artists to Louis Vauxcelles' canditature.

11. They included, for instance, Matisse's *Luxe I*, Braque's *Still-life on a Mantlepiece* and Picasso's *Aubade*.

12. Cassou's purchases are surveyed in Jeanne Laurent, *Arts et pouvoirs en France de 1793 à 1981* (Saint-Etienne, 1982), 151ff.

13. Léonce Rosenberg to Fernand Léger, 27 October 1926; in Christian Derouet (ed.), *Une Correspondance d'affaires. Correspondances Fernand Léger – Léonce Rosenberg 1917–1937* (Les Cahiers du Musée national d'art moderne, Paris, 1996), Letter 354, 222. This correspondence, as published by Derouet, is extremely revealing for the painters' and dealers' attitudes to the Salon paintings and their smaller variants.

14. Mainardi (1993) *op.cit.*, Chapter 6.

15. See Chapter 1.

16. 12 April 1881. Cited in Mainardi (1993) *op.cit.*, 82.

17. 7.7% of the Education budget in 1912; 4.35% in 1927; 3.65% in 1937;

6.53% in 1939. Figures from Genet-Delacroix (1992) *op.cit.*, Chapter 6, who also gives the figures for the relationship with the national budget overall.

18. See Derouet (1996) *op.cit.* Prices for the works in the 1919 exhibition are given, 285–7.

19. Figures from Laurent (1982) *op.cit.*, 108, and in the case of Laurens and Toulouse from Musée d'Orsay, exh. cat., *Jean-Paul Laurens, 1838–1921. Peintre d'histoire* (Paris, 1997–8), 154.

20. Brauer (1996) *op.cit.*, 113.

21. Vaisse (1995) *op.cit.*

22. There are one or two cases of genuine fresco, Paul Baudouin's vaults for the loggia around the Petit Palais garden most notably. Otherwise, the technique used was almost exclusively oil on canvas fixed to the wall surface (*toile marouflée*).

23. Material on the commissioning of monumental sculpture in this section comes largely from the following secondary sources: June Hargrove, *Les Statues de Paris. La représentation des grands hommes dans les rues et sur les places de Paris* (Antwerp and Paris, 1989); Penelope Curtis, 'E.A. Bourdelle and Monumental Sculpture'. Ph.D., thesis, Courtauld Institute, London, 1990; and Patrick Elliott, 'Sculpture in France, 1918–1939'. Ph.D., thesis, Courtauld Institute, London, 1991.

24. See Elliott (1991), Chapter 2.

25. Instance given by Curtis (1990) *op.cit.*, Chapter 1.

26. Figures from Elliott (1991) *op.cit.*, Chapter 1.

27. See Vaisse (1995) *op.cit.*, Introduction.

28. André Salmon, 'Dessins de Picasso (galerie Paul Rosenberg)', 'Peintures de Kisling (galerie Druet)', *L'Europe nouvelle* (Paris, 25 October 1919), 2065. The passage is lifted by Salmon from his preface to Picasso's galerie Paul Rosenberg catalogue.

29. Maurice Raynal, 'Juan Gris', *L'Esprit nouveau* no. 5, February 1921.

30. Monet's doubts are expressed in a letter to Durand-Ruel of 17 February 1900, cited in Vaisse (1995) *op.cit.*, 126.

31. Louis Vauxcelles, *Gil Blas* (Paris, 30 April 1910); as cited in Brauer (1997) *op.cit.*, 88. Author's translation.

32. Vaisse (1995) *op.cit.*, 139; Curtis (1990) *op.cit.*, Chapter 2.

33. Guillaume Apollinaire, *L'Intransigeant* (Paris, 13 May 1913).

34. André Salmon, 'Cinquante ans de peinture française, 1875–1925', *L'Art vivant* (Paris, 15 June 1925), 1.

35. Vauxcelles, already a chevalier, became an officier in 1925. Matisse, who had refused previous invitations, became a chevalier.

36. Information from Vaisse (1995) *op.cit.*, 166.

37. Information from Genet-Delacroix (1992) *op.cit.*, 99.

38. André Salmon, *La Jeune Sculpture française* (Paris, 1919), 2.

39. A.-H. Martinie, *La Sculpture* (Paris, 1928).

40. Louis Vauxcelles, in *Les Nouvelles Littéraires* (Paris, 15 April 1911). Schnegg died in 1909. For a full discussion, see Elliott (1991) *op.cit.* He gives a briefer account in Patrick Elliott, 'Sculpture in France and Classicism, 1910–39'; in Elizabeth Cowling and Jennifer Mundy (eds.), *On Classic Ground. Picasso, Léger, de Chirico and the New Classicism 1910–1930*. Exh. cat. (London, Tate Gallery, hardback ed. 1990).

41. A.H. Amann, *Charles Despiau 1874–1946* (Collections du Musée municipal de Mont-de-Marsan, 1982), 16.

42. Elliott (1991) *op.cit.* He also cites Henri Focillon from the *Gazette des Beaux-Arts*, 1 (Paris, 1926), and Raymond Bouyer from *Revue de l'art*, II (Paris, 1925).

43. Salmon (1919) *op.cit.*, 54.

44. 'Metteurs au point' specialised in the use of pointing mechanisms for the scaling-up of modelled maquettes to produce finished statues in stone or marble.

45. Adolphe Basler, *La Sculpture moderne en France* (Paris, 1928), 53, 57.

46. Roger Vitrac, 'Constantin Brancusi', *Cahiers d'art*, 8–9 (Paris, 1929), 383–5.

47. André Breton (with photographs by Brassaï), 'Picasso dans son élément', *Minotaure*, 1 (Paris, 1933), 8–29; Maurice Raynal (with unattributed photographs and a statement by Alberto Giacometti), 'Dieu-Table-Cuvette', *Minotaure*, 3 (Paris, 1933), 39–53.

48. The first was Louis Chéronet, 'Affiches du mois', *L'Art vivant*, 2nd Year, 31 (Paris, 1 April 1926); Delaunay's and Léger's opinions appear on 1 December 1926.

49. Brauer makes this point. See Brauer (1997) *op.cit.*, Chapter 1. Also helpful on the art press are Malcolm Gee, *Dealers, Critics and Collectors of Modern Painting; Aspects of the Parisian Art Market, between 1910 and 1930* (London and New York, 1981), and in relation to the political left, Cottington (1998) *op.cit.*, 77ff.

50. André Salmon, *L'Art vivant* (Paris, 1920), 9.

51. It is Georges Charensol, a contributor to both *L'Amour de l'art* and *L'Art vivant*, who describes Fels and Guenne in this way. See Georges Charensol, *D'Une rive à l'autre* (Paris, 1973), 165.

52. André Breton, *Second Manifeste du surréalisme* (Paris, 1929); in Breton, *Manifestes du surréalisme* (Paris, 1972), 125.

53. Paul Guillaume in Georges Charensol, 'Pour un musée français d'art moderne', *L'Art vivant*, 1st Year, 18 (Paris, 15 September 1925), 38.

54. For information on this, see Marie-Blanche Pouradier Duteil, 'Le Livre d'or', in Musée de la Ville de Strasbourg, *Jeanne Bucher. Une galerie d'avant-garde, 1925–1946. De Max Ernst à de Staël*. Exh. cat. (Strasbourg, 1994), 134.

55. Louis Vauxcelles in *Cahiers de la semaine* (Paris, 10 January 1926); cited in Gee (1981) *op.cit.*, 15.

56. A detailed account of the Peau de l'ours operation is given in Michael C. Fitzgerald, *Making Modernism. Picasso and the Creation of the Market for Twentieth-Century Art* (Los Angeles and London, 1995), Chapter 1. See also Cottington (1998) *op.cit.*, 45–6.

57. For Kahnweiler, see especially Pierre Assouline, *L'homme de l'art. D.H. Kahnweiler, 1884–1979* (Paris, 1988); translated as *An Artful Life. A Biography of D.H. Kahnweiler* (New York, 1990).

58. For the art market generally, after 1910, see Gee (1981) *op.cit.* For Paul Rosenberg, *see* Fitzgerald (1995) *op.cit.*; for Léonce Rosenberg, see Christian Derouet, 'Juan Gris: A Correspondence Restored', in Christopher Green, *Juan Gris*, exh. cat. (Whitechapel Art Gallery, London, 1992), Christian Derouet, 'Exposition Henri Laurens, Décembre 1918', in *Henri Laurens*, exh. cat. (Musée d'art moderne, Villeneuf d'Ascq, 1992–3), and Christian Derouet, *Fernand Léger. Une Correspondance d'affairs* (Les Cahiers du Musée national d'art moderne, Paris, 1996).

59. For Guillaume, see Colette Giraudin, *Paul Guillaume et les peintres du Xxe siècle. De l'art nègre à l'avant-garde* (Paris, 1993).

60. Information from Fitzgerald (1995) *op.cit.*, 188.

61. For Doucet as modern collector and for his homes of the 1920s, see François Chapon, *Mystères et splendeurs de Jacques Doucet 1853–1929* (Paris, 1984), Chapters 8, 9 and 10.

62. Information on the de Noailles from: Shane Dunworth, 'The De Noailles as Collectors and Patrons', M.Phil. thesis, courtauld Institute, London, 1984.

63. Louis Aragon, 'Le Passage de l'Opéra', in Aragon, *Le Paysan de Paris* (Paris, 1926), 81.

CHAPTER 4

1. Jean Cassou, for instance, reveals not a particle of doubt when he declares that for the 'true artist', 'art will . . . retain its irreducible autonomy despite the modes and subjects he has believed he should adopt to fulfil the conditions of his contract.' *L'Art vivant* (Paris, 15 September and 1 November 1927).

2. Jean Grave, *La Société future* (Paris, 1895; 8th edition, Paris, 1908), 294, 367–8. As cited in James D. Herbert, *Fauve Painting: The Making of Cultural Politics* (New Haven and London, 1992), 50, 139.

3. Léon Werth, 'Chronique artistique. La peinture et l'époque', *L'Art vivant* (Paris, 1 June 1925), 19.

4. Léon Werth, 'Chronique artistique. La peinture en province', *L'Art vivant* (Paris, 1 August 1925), 23.

5. *L'Art vivant* (Paris, 15 September 1927), 740.

6. Maurice Vlaminck, *Tournant dangereux* (Paris, 1929), 223–4; as cited in Herbert (1992), 94.

7. Fernand Léger, 'L'esthétique de la machine. L'objet fabriqué, l'artisan et l'artiste', lecture given in June 1923, published with this title in *Bulletin de l'Effort Moderne*, 1 and 2 (Paris, January and February 1924).

8. Georges Charensol, 'Pour un Musée français de l'art moderne. Conclusion', *L'Art vivant*, (Paris, 1 October 1925).

9. Billy Klüver and Julie Martin, 'Carrefour Vavin', in Kenneth E. Silver and Romy Golan, *The Circle of Monparnasse. Jewish Artists in Paris 1905–1945*. Exh. cat. (New York, The Jewish Museum, 1985), 69.

10. André Salmon, 'Cinquante ans de peinture française, 1875–1925', *L'Art vivant*, (Paris, 15 June 1912), 1.

11. Ossip Zadkine, *Le Maillet et le ciseau. Souvenirs de ma vie* (Paris, 1968), 75.

12. Figures from Jean-Marie Mayeur and Madeleine Reberioux, *The Third Republic from its Origins to the Great War, 1871–1914*, translated by J.R. Foster (Cambridge, 1984; 1st ed. Paris, 1973), 338.

13. Figures from Eugen Weber, *The Hollow Years: France in the 1930s* (London, 1995), 85.

14. Cited in Sylvain Lecombre, in collaboration with Helena Staub, *Ossip Zadkine. L'œuvre sculpté* (Paris, 1994), 36.

15. Ernest Renan, *Qu'est-ce qu'une nation* (Paris, 1882), 26; translated by Ida Mae Snyder in John Hutchinson and Anthony D. Smith (eds.), *Nationalism* (Oxford, 1994), 17.

16. Figures from Mayeur and Reberioux (1984) *op.cit.*, 338.

17. Laurencin as cited in José Pierre, *Marie Laurencin* (Paris, 1987), 23.

18. Letter from Joan Miró to J.F. Ràfols, 10 August 1919; in Margit Rowell, *Joan Miró. Selected Writings and Interviews*, translated from the Catalan by Patricia Matthews (London, 1986), 62.

19. Kenneth E. Silver, 'Jewish Artists in Paris, 1905–1945', in Silver and Golan (1985) *op.cit.*, 13–15.

20. A full account of these changes is in Marie-Claude Genet-Delacroix, *Art et Etat sous la IIIe République. Le système des Beaux-Arts 1870–1940* (Paris, 1992), 117. See also Tamar Garb, *Sisters of the Brush: Women's Artistic Culture in Late Nineteenth-Century Paris* (London and New Haven, 1994).

21. See Mayeur and Reberioux (1984) *op.cit.*, 340.

22. As cited in translation in Gill Perry, *Woman Artists and the Parisian Avant-garde. Modernism and 'feminine' art 1900 to the late 1920s* (Manchester and New York, 1995), 6–7.

23. René Gimpel, *Diary of an Art Dealer* (London, 1986), 261.

24. The costumes and sets for the ballet *Les Biches*, with music by Francis Poulenc and choreography by Bronislava Nijinska in 1923.

25. Perry, (1995) *op.cit.*, and Whitney Chadwick, *Woman Artists and the Surrealist Movement* (London, 1985).

26. André Breton, 'Second Manifeste du surréalisme' (1929); in Breton, *Manifestes du surréalisme* (Paris, 1972); cited as translated in *ibid.*, 37.

27. Maurice Agulhon, *Marianne au pouvoir. L'imagerie et la symbolique républicains de 1880 à 1914* (Paris, 1989), 299.

28. Mayeur and Reberioux (1984) *op.cit.*, 306.

29. Louis Vauxcelles in André Fontainas and Louis Vauxcelles, *Histoire générale de l'art français de la Révolution à nos jours. I. La Peinture, la gravure – le dessin* (Paris, 1922), 315.

30. Perry (1995) *op.cit.*, 21ff., 73.

31. Vauxcelles (1922) *op.cit.*, 321.

32. Marcel Jouhandeau, *Marie Laurencin* (Paris, 1928), np.

33. See Michael C. Fitzgerald, *Making Modernism. Picasso and the Creation of the Market for Twentieth-Century Art* (Berkeley, Los Angeles and London, 1995), 190–204.

34. Guy Hickok, 'He Keeps the Art Boys Guessing', *The Eagle Magazine* (New York, 17 July 1932), 7. Cited in *ibid.*, 190.

35. Christian Zervos, *Pablo Picasso*, 33 vols (Paris, 1932–78).

36. Brassaï, *Conversations avec Picasso* (Paris, 1964), 12–13. Author's translation.

37. Georges Charensol, *D'Une Rive à l'autre* (Paris, 1973), 89–94.

38. Man Ray, *Self-Portrait* (New York, 1963), 174–6.

39. The first modern master car-owner was Matisse, who inaugurated the genre of car-window landscapes in the spring of 1917.

40. Man Ray (1963) *op.cit.*, 109.

41. Melissa McQuillan, 'Pablo Goes to the Ball: Performance, Play, and Diversion in the 1920s', paper delivered at the Conference of the Association of Art Historians, London, April 1997. I am grateful to Melissa McQuillan for allowing me to see a printout of her paper; I am dependent on her for much of the material here on the Bals.

42. Léon Werth, 'La peinture en province', *L'Art vivant*, (Paris, 1 August 1925), 23.

43. Fernande Olivier, *Picasso et ses amis* (Paris, 1933). Quoted as translated by Jane Miller in *Picasso and his Friends* (London, 1964), 22.

44. *Ibid.*, 89–90.

45. John Richardson, with the collaboration of Marilyn McCully, *A Life of Picasso. Vol. I: 1881–1906* (London, 1991), Chapter 13.

46. Later that year, Picasso produced another, darker self-portrait inscribed simply: 'Yo'. See ibid., p. 228.

47. Amélie Matisse had married Henri in 1898. Both her parents, the Parayres, were faithful retainers of Frédéric and Thérèse Humbert, liberal Republicans whose banking interests were supported by fraud, and who implicated the Parayres in their dealings. The story is told for the first time and its effect on Matisse is assessed in Hilary Spurling, *The Unknown Matisse. A Life of Henri Matisse*, Vol. 1, *1869–1908* (London, 1998), especially 234–40.

48. Schukine to Matisse, letter of 10–11 November 1910; cited in Isabelle Monod-Fontaine and Claude Laugier, 'Eléments de chronologie, 1904–1918', in *Henri Matisse 1904–1918*, exh. cat. (Centre Georges Pompidou, 1993), 96.

49. Cited *ibid.*

50. Gertrude Stein, *Picasso* (London, New York, Toronto, Sidney, 1938), 9.

51. Fernande Olivier (1933) *op.cit.*, 48.

52. Fitzgerald publishes a detailed analysis of Picasso's scribbled notebook accounts, now in the Picasso Archive at the Musée Picasso in Paris. See Fitzgerald (1995) *op.cit.*, 44.

53. French canvases were numbered according to size, and each size is divided into three categories: *Figure* (F), *Landscape* (paysage – P) and *Seascape* (marine – M). Size 40 is 100 × 81 cm. (F); 100 × 73 cm. (P); 100 × 65 cm. (M).

54. Anne Baldassari, *Picasso Photographe 1901–1916*, exh. cat. (Musée Picasso, Paris, 1994), 229–43.

55. Isamu Noguchi, *A Sculptor's World* (London, 1967).

56. *Cercle et carré*, I, no. 3 (Paris, 1930), np.

57. Completed late 1926. First published in Dutch in *i10* (Amsterdam, January 1927). Published in French in *Vouloir*, 25 (Lille, 1925). In English in Harry Holtzman and Martin S. James (eds.), *The New Art – The New Life. The Collected Writings of Piet Mondrian* (London, 1987), 207–12.

58. Maurice Raynal, 'Dieu – Table – Cuvette', *Minotaure*, 3–4, (Paris, December 1933), 39–53.

59. For discussion of Breton, commerce and dealing, see Chapter 3.

60. A striking instance is Guillaume Janneau's opinion in his critical study of Cubism: 'Marcel Duchamp, an original talent, full of promise, has not been able either to realise or perhaps even to be in touch with his ability.' Guillaume Janneau, *L'Art cubiste. Théories et réalisations. Etude critique* (Paris, 1929), 24. The French includes a word-play involving 'se réaliser' and 'se connaître' which cannot be adequately translated into English.

61. Pierre Cabanne, *Dialogues with Marcel Duchamp* (London, 1971), 44; and Calvin Tomkins, *Duchamp. A Biography* (London, 1997), 81–3.

62. See *ibid.* (Tomkins), 154 and 199.

63. Breton had met him through Picabia in 1921, and had published the first major monographic article on him in *Littérature* (October 1922), which was reprinted in his influential anthology, *Les Pas perdus* (Paris, 1924).

64. Duchamp's use of 'delay' in preparing his future emergence as an historical figure is explored by Martha Buskirk in 'Thoroughly Modern Marcel', in Martha Buskirk and Mignon Nixon (eds.), *The Duchamp Effect. Essays, Interviews, Round Table* (Cambridge, Mass., and London, 1996), 191–203.

PART THREE CHAPTER 5

1. 11 March 1909, Matisse wrote to Shchukin suggesting three subjects for the murals, including the *Bathers*; 12 March, he sent sketches of the *Dance* and *Bathers by a Stream*. *Music* was conceived later. A statement referring to the scheme published in April 1909 indicates that Matisse mistakenly thought the staircase in the Trubetksoy Palace had three levels. In fact, it had only two. Only two could be hung: *The Dance* and *Music*. See: Charles Estienne, 'Des tendances de la peinture moderne: Entretien avec M. Henri-Matisse', *Les Nouvelles* (Paris, 12 April 1909), 4, in translation in Jack D. Flam, *Matisse on Art* (New York and London, 1972), 47–9. Also see Jack Flam, *Matisse. The Man and his Art, 1869–1918* (London, 1986), 254ff.

2. The programme for the 'Salle des fêtes' was fixed in 1888; Benjamin-Constant was commissioned for the central ceiling panel, Morot and Gervex for the flanking panels. See *Le Triomphe des mairies. Grands décors républicains à Paris, 1870–1914*. Exh. cat. (Musée du Petit Palais, Paris, 1987), 397–400, 406.

3. Henri Matisse, 'Notes d'un peintre', *La Grande Revue*, LII, 24 (Paris, 25 December 1908), 731–45. Cited as translated in Jack D. Flam, *Matisse on Art* (New York, 1972), 36.

4. Cited as translated in Nancy J. Troy, *Modernism and the Decorative Arts in France. Art Nouveau to Le Corbusier* (New Haven and London, 1991), 17.

5. *Ibid.*, 231, Note 38.

6. That he did so is shown by a small canvas depicting the murals in the dome, painted, it seems, to show how they would fit the space. See *Maurice Denis. 1870–1943*. Exh. cat. (Musée des Beaux-Arts, Lyon, 1994), 280, No.124.

7. Paul Signac, *D' Eugène Delacroix au néo-impressionnisme* (Paris, 1898) Part V, 7. Cited as translated in Catherine C. Bock, *Henri Matisse and Neo-Impressionism. 1898–1908* (Michigan, 1981), 19.

8. Matisse cared so much about process that he had photographs taken to record stages in the development of both *Music* and *Bathers by the Stream*. At first the latter was closely attuned to the flat simplified look of the Shchukin panels.

9. Most conspicuously in *Buffet and Table*, 1899. Oil on canvas, 67.5 × 82.5 cm. (Private Collection).

10. Cf. Signac (1898) *op.cit.*, Part IV, 4. As cited in Bock (1981), 24.

11. Signac writes that the dot had functioned in *pointillisme* 'to imitate, by optical mixture . . . the various tints of nature, without any desire for balance, without any concern for contrast.' Signac (1898) *op.cit.*, Part V, 4. As cited *ibid.*, 20.

12. Maurice Denis, 'De Gauguin, de Whistler et de l'excès de théories', *L'Ermitage* (Paris, 15 November 1905); in Denis, *Théories 1890–1910. Du Symbolisme et de Gauguin vers un nouvel ordre classique* (Paris, 1920, 1st edition 1912), 208. Cited as translated in Roger Benjamin, *Matisse's 'Notes of a Painter'. Criticism, Theory, and Context, 1891–1908* (Ann Arbor, Michigan, 1987), 94–5.

13. Signac's hostile reception to the painting is recorded in a letter to Charles Angrand dated 14 January 1906; it is cited in Alfred H. Barr Jr., *Matisse, His Art and His Public* (New York, 1951), 82.

14. 'All the qualities of the picture other than the contrast of lines and colours, everything not determined by the painter's'reason, everything that comes from our instinct and from nature, finally all the qualities of representa-

tion and sensibility are excluded from the work of art.' Denis (1905) *loc.cit.*, 208.

15. Stein's recollection is quoted in John Elderfield, *The 'Wild Beasts': Fauvism and Its Affinities.* Exh. cat. (The Museum of Modern Art, New York, 1976), 69.

16. Maurice Denis, 'De Gauguin et Van Gogh au classicisme', *L'Occident* (May 1909); in Denis (1920) *op.cit.*, 266–7; as translated and cited in Benjamin (1987), 97.

17. Maurice Denis, 'Cézanne', *L'Occident*, (Paris, September 1907).

18. Emile Bernard, 'Paul Cézanne', *L'Occident*, (Paris, July 1904).

19. Paul Cézanne cited in ibid., as cited in translation in Benjamin (1987) *op.cit.*, 180.

20. Matisse (1908) in Flam (1972) *op.cit.*, 36.

21. Sarah Stein, 'Notes', 1908. As cited in Flam, ibid., 45.

22. Matisse (1908) in Flam, ibid., 39.

23. Elderfield (1976) *op.cit.*

24. John Elderfield, 'Seeing Bonnard', in Sarah Whitfield and John Elderfield, *Bonnard.* Exh. cat. (The Tate Gallery, London, 1998), 33–52.

25. Louis Vauxcelles, 'Le Salon des Indépendants', *Gil Blas* (Paris, 20 March 1907), 1. Cited as translated in Flam (1987), 196.

26. André Salmon, *La Jeune Peinture français* (Paris, 1912), 43.

27. According to Marguerite Duthuit (Matisse's daughter) interviewed by Flam (26 November 1976). Flam (1987) *op.cit.*, 371.

28. André Salmon, 'Le Salon', *Montjoie!* (Paris, November–December 1913), 4.

29. G. Sailles, *L'Illustration* (Paris) 1888. Cited in *Equivoques.* Exh. cat. (Musée des arts décoratifs, Paris, 1973).

30. Matisse (1908) in Flam (1972) *op.cit.*, 37.

31. Flam quotes a letter of 12 July 1914 from Pritchard to Isabella Stewart Gardner describing this. See Flam (1987) *op.cit.*, 503, Note 22.

32. The conceptual view of Cubism is discussed also in Chapter 2.

33. Albert Gleizes, 'Art et ses représentants, Jean Metzinger', *La Revue Indépendante* (Paris, 1911), 161–72.

34. Maurice Raynal, 'Conception et vision', *Gil Blas* (Paris, 29 August 1912). Cited as translated in Edward F. Fry, *Cubism* (London, 1966), 95.

35. Maurice Raynal, 'L'Exposition de la Section d'Or', *Bulletin de la Section d'Or* (9 October 1912).

36. Studies are reproduced in Juan Antonio Gaya-Nuño, *Juan Gris*, translated by Kenneth Lyons (London, 1975), 27, no.43, and in Green (1992) *op.cit.* 178–9, Plates 18–20.

37. Gris and Raynal were close friends and would remain so until Gris's death in 1927.

38. 'Analysis' and 'synthesis' in Cubism is discussed also in Chapter 2.

39. The clearest indication that Picasso started with a simple schema of this kind is the etching *Mlle. Léonie.* Here, basically the same schema for the head is used, although the etching is known to have been produced as an illustration for Max Jacob's *Saint-Matorelle* in the summer of 1910, before the Kahnweiler portrait, which was painted in the autumn.

40. This drawing is reproduced in Juan Gaya Nuño, *Juan Gris*, translated from the Spanish by Kenneth Lyons (London, 1975), 27, no.43.

41. A letter from Braque to Kahnweiler, sent between late September and early October 1911, records that the subject initially was 'an Italian [not Portuguese] emigrant standing on the bridge of a boat with a bridge in the background'; the switch to the café occurred during the work's development. Cited in Judith Cousins, in collaboration with Pierre Daix, 'Documentary Chronology', in William Rubin (ed.), *Picasso and Braque. Pioneering Cubism.* Exh. cat. (Museum of Modern Art, New York, 1989), 380.

42. The painting-out of a more elaborate scaffold of planes has been revealed by infra-red examination. For a fuller discussion, see Christopher Green, *The Thyssen-Bornemisza Collection. The European Avant-gardes. Art in France and Western Europe 1904–c.1945* (London, 1995), 390–3.

43. Juan Gris, Statement, in 'Vauvrecy' (pseudonym for Amédée Ozenfant), untitled, *L'Esprit Nouveau*, 5 (Paris, February 1921), 533–4. Translated in Daniel-Henry Kahnweiler, *Juan Gris: His Life and Work* (new enlarged edition, London, 1968).

44. Paul Dermée, 'Jean Metzinger', *S.I.C.*, 42, 43 (30 March 7 15 April 1919), and 'Lipchitz', *L'Esprit Nouveau*, 2 (Paris, November 1920).

45. Pierre Reverdy, 'Sur le cubisme', *Nord-Sud*, 1 (Paris, 15 March 1917), in Etienne-Alain Hubert (ed.), *Pierre Reverdy, Oeuvres complètes, Nord-Sud, Self-Defence et autres ecrits sur l'art et Nord-Sud, 1917–26* (Paris, 1975).

46. André Lhote quoted in Jacques Guenne, 'André Lhote', *L'Art vivant* (Paris, 1 March 1926).

47. Picasso quoted by Rubin, in William Rubin, *Picasso in the Collection of The Museum of Modern Art* (Museum of Modern Art, New York, 1972).

48. Mallarmé quoted by Jules Huret, 'Enquête sur l'èvolution littéraire', *L'Echo de Paris* (14 March 1891), 2. In Dieter Schwarz (ed.), *Les Interviews de Mallarmé* (Neuchâtel, 1995), 30–1.

49. For his early notion of purity in painting, see Guillaume Apollinaire, 'Les trois vertus plastiques', in the *Catalogue de la IIIe Exposition du Cercle de l'art moderne* (Hôtel de Ville, Le Havre, June 1908). Translated by Susan Suleiman in Apollinaire (Leroy C. Breunig, ed.), *Apollinaire on Art: Essays and Reviews 1902–1918* (London, 1972), 47–9.

50. Guillaume Apollinaire, 'Sur le sujet dans la peinture moderne', *Soirées de Paris* (Paris, 1 February 1912). In ibid., 197–8.

51. Guillaume Apollinaire, *Méditations esthétiques. Les Peintres cubistes* (Paris, 1913). Edition edited and annotated by L.C. Breunig and J.Cl. Chevalier (Paris, 1965), 57.

52. Buckberrough has noted that the initial French version of the text was more uncompromisingly 'pure'. She translates his words thus: 'If it departs from an object, art is descriptive.' See Sherry A. Buckberrough, *Robert Delaunay: The Discovery of Simultaneity* (Ann Arbor, Michigan, 1982), 118.

53. Buckberrough establishes his dependence on Rood convincingly, and discusses his use of these techniques with admirable clarity. *Ibid.*, 126.

54. This information is given, it would seem, with the support of Sonia Delaunay, in Gustav Vriesen and Max Imdahl, *Robert Delaunay, Colour and Light* (Cologne and New York, 1967), 6.

55. Fernand Léger, 'Les Origines de la peinture et sa valeur représentative', *Montjoie!* (Paris, 29 May and 14–29 June 1913). Translated by A. Anderson in Edward Fry (ed.), Fernand Léger, *Functions of Painting* (New York and London, 1965).

56. I have written on the processes involved, in Christopher Green, *Léger and the Avant-garde* (New Haven and London, 1976) Chapter 2.

57. See Flam (1987) *op.cit.*, 402.

58. Juan Gris, 'Sur les possibilités de la peinture', lecture delivered at the Société des études philosophiques et scientifiques in the Sorbonne, 15 April 1924. First published in *Transatlantic Review* vol.1, 6 (Paris, June 1924). Translated in Kahnweiler (1969) *op.cit.*

59. There is a later eye-witness account of Apollinaire lecturing in front of Kupka's paintings at the Section d'Or, and certainly the poet gave a lecture there in October 1912 and that month inserted his definition in the proofs of *Les Peintres cubistes.* On the other hand, no items by Kupka are recorded in the catalogue. If he showed, it can only have been a last-minute decision, and we do not know what he sent. The evidence is discussed fully in Meda Mladek and Margit Rowell, 'Chronology', *František Kupka 1871–1957. A Retrospective.* Exh. cat. (Solomon R.Guggenheim Museum, New York, 1975), 310–11, note 6. The second work shown at the Automne was *Amorpha, Warm Chromatics.*

60. What is referred to here is a set of notes in manuscript form are described as a 'notebook' and dated 1910–11(?) by Margit Rowell (C. Rowell, in *ibid.*, 60–1, note 19), and a book written in French by Kupka between 1910 and 1913, published as *Tvoreni v umení Vytvarném* (Prague, 1924). The book has been re-issued in French: František Kupka, *La Création dans les arts plastiques*, translated and edited by Erika Arams (Paris, 1989).

61. I discuss the dating and the origins of this work fully in Green (1995) *op.cit.*, 244–9.

62. Both in the manuscript and in the book. See note 60, above.

63. Kupka (1924/1989) *op.cit.*, 251.

64. Kupka's personal notes suggest that it was only when he was working on the *Positioning of Mobile Graphic Elements* in July 1913, that his friend the musician Morse-Rummel introduced him to Kandinsky's book. 'Inner impulse' is an approximation in English of the untranslateable 'mobile interne' in Kupka's inventive French. See Notebook (1910–11 [?]), 30–5.

65. Kupka (1924/1989), 168, 164.

66. *Ibid.*, 19.

67. Welsh (1969) suggested 1913–14 as the date of the annotations in both sketchbooks; Joosten (1981) has suggested summer 1914 for the annotations in the so-called Sketchbook I. Joop Joosten (ed.), with an introduction and translations by Robert Welsh, *Two Mondrian Sketchbooks 1912–14* (Amsterdam, 1969); and Joop Joosten, 'Mondrian's lost sketch-books from the years 1911–1914', in *Mondrian: Drawings, Watercolours.* Exh. cat. (Stuttgart Staatsgalerie, the Gemeentemuseum, The Hague and the Baltimore Museum of Art, 1981), 69.

68. Mondrian to Bremmer, 14 January 1914. Cited in Joop Joosten (ed.), 'Documentatie over Mondrian (I)', *Museumjournaal*, 12, 4 (1969), 211–12. Translated from the Dutch by Michael White.

69. This is argued persuasively by Joosten, in Joosten (1981) *op.cit.*

70. Sketchbook II. Cited in Joosten and Welsh (1969) *op.cit.*, 35–6.

71. Yve-Alain Bois, 'The Iconoclast', in *Piet Mondrian 1872–1944.* Exh. cat. (The Gemeentemuseum, The Hague; National Gallery of Art, Washington, D.C.; and The Museum of Modern Art, New York, 1995–6), 338.

72. Bois quotes an especially telling passage from Mondrian's trialogue, 'Natuurlijke en abstracte realiteit', *De Stijl* II, 12 (Amsterdam, October 1919) to substantiate this point. *Ibid.*, 321.

73. Infra-red examination has confirmed this in at least one case. See Green (1995) *op.cit.*, 343.

74. Piet Mondrian, 'L'Art réaliste et l'art superréaliste', *Cercle et carré*, 2 (Paris, April 1930), in Harry Holtzman and Martin S. James, *The New Art – The New Life. The Collected Writings of Piet Mondrian* (New York, 1986/7), 239.

75. He writes of light thus in *ibid.*, 228–9.

CHAPTER 6

1. The cardboard version of *The Guitar* was made in the late autumn of 1912. It served as the model for the metal version, which was made later.

2. That the cardboard version of *The Guitar* represents a first step in this respect, is most strongly argued in Yve-Alain Bois, 'Kahnweiler's Lesson', *Representations*, 18 (California, spring 1987), reprinted in revised form in Bois, *Painting as Model* (Cambridge, Mass., 1993). The dating of both the cardboard and metal versions is exhaustively discussed in Edward Fry, 'Picasso, Cubism and Reflexivity', *Art Journal*, vol.47, 4 (Winter 1988), 305–6, note 24. Braque is known to have made paper constructions in the period leading up to the making of the first papier-collé.

3. A review makes it clear that photographs of 'cigar boxes and other object medleys' were shown in the exhibition of the Grafton Group at the Alpine Gallery in London very early in 1913. See G.R.H., 'Gallery and Studio/The Grafton Group at the Alpine Gallery', *Pall Mall Gazette* (London, 8 January 1913).

4. André Salmon, *La Jeune Sculpture française* (Paris, 1919), 103. Author's translation. Salmon asserts that the book had been almost entirely written before the 1914–18 war.

5. Picasso's earlier Cubist sculptures, most notably *Head* of 1909, which was cast in bronze, explore the possibilities and limitations of painting by translating pictorial into sculptural ideas. The painting most closely related is *Woman with Pears*, 1909 in Pierre Daix and Joan Rosselet, *Picasso. The Cubist Years 1907–1916*. A catalogue raisonné of the paintings and related works (London, 1979) cat. no. 290. In this respect, these sculptures are comparable with Matisse's.

6. The term 'Language' is used here as Ferdinand Saussure uses the term 'Langue' in his *Cours de linguistique générale* in contradistinction to the term 'parole'. It denotes language considered in terms of its most general principles, rather than in terms of everyday utterance.

7. Bois (1987) *op.cit.*

8. As Bois puts it: 'Picasso realised . . . that a sign, because it has a value, can be entirely virtual, or nonsubstantial.' Bois (1987) *op.cit.*, 14.

9. For a fuller discussion of this, see the penultimate section of Chapter 5.

10. Gris's papier-collés, by contrast, are finished with perfectionist care, and conceal all traces of the process of fabrication; they are wholly conceptual in this sense.

11. Maurice Raynal, 'Juan Gris', in Raynal, *Anthologie de la peinture en France de 1906 à nos jours* (Paris, 1927), 176. Author's translation. The article was first published in *Feuilles libres*, 31 (Paris, April 1923).

12. Paul Dermée, 'Jean Metzinger', *S.I.C.*, 42 and 43 (Paris, 20 March–15 April 1919), 13.

13. Pierre Reverdy, 'L'Image', *Nord-Sud*, 13 (Paris, March 1918). In Reverdy, *Oeuvres complètes, Nord-Sud, Self Defence et autres écrits sur l'art et la poésie*, edited with notes by Etienne-Alain Hubert (Paris, 1975), 73.

14. This image comes from Reverdy's poem 'Façade' in the collection *Les Ardoises du toit* (Paris, 1918), for which illustrations by Gris were made in 1916 for an illustrated edition planned by Léonce Rosenberg. An edition based on this project was not actually to be published until the 1950s.

15. Marguerite Bonnet, *André Breton. Naissance de l'aventure surréaliste* (Paris, 1975), 362.

16. André Breton, *Manifeste du surréalisme* (Paris, 1924), in Breton, *Manifestes du surréalisme* (Paris, 1972), 52. Author's translation.

17. Raynal (1923/1927) *op.cit.*, 174.

18. Breton (1924/1972) *op.cit.*, 51–4. Breton uses the French 'se disconcerter'.

19. André Breton, 'Le Surréalisme et la peinture', *La Révolution surréaliste*, 4 (Paris, 15 July 1925), 28.

20. *Ibid.*, 29–30.

21. It is worth noting that from 1914 Picasso and Gris would drop collage and papier-collé, though Picasso would return to it and to construction from time to time after 1918. Braque dropped it too, when he started to paint again after his return from the front in 1917. All of them, however, continued to use the lessons in sign-making and the planar creation of pictorial space drawn from those practices.

22. Max Morise, 'Les Yeux enchantées', *La Révolution surréaliste*, 1 (Paris, 1 December 1924), 27.

23. Miró to Leiris, 10 August 1924. Translated into English in Margit Rowell (ed.), *Joan Miró. Selected Writings and Interviews* (London, 1987), 86–7.

24. The question of whether or not the sketch related directly to *The Birth of the World* itself came after a more legible sketch depicting a male figure reclining beneath a tree bearing a single fruit has caused some controversy. Technical examination of the sheets of the drawings in the relevant sketchbook have established beyond doubt that Miró worked from the more legible sketch, to the sketch directly related to the painting. See Christopher Green, *Cubism and its Enemies. Modern Movements and Reaction in French Art, 1916–1928* (New Haven and London, 1987), 269; Carolyn Lanchner, '*Peinture-Poésie*, Its Logic and Logistics', in Lanchner, *Joan Miró*. Exh. cat. (The Museum of Modern Art, New York) 1993, 78, note 135; and Christopher Green, 'Un Campesino catalán entre los campesinos catalanes: El "Campesino catalán con guitarra" de Miró y La serie del Campesino catalán de los años 1924–1925', in *Joan Miró: Campesino catalán con guitarra, 1924*. Exh. cat. (Museo Thyssen-Bornemisza, Madrid, 1997–8), 28–9, note 37.

25. André Breton, 'Max Ernst', preface to the catalogue of the exhibition *Max Ernst* (galerie Au Sans Pareil, Paris, 1921); in Breton, *Les Pas perdus* (Paris, 1924), 86–8.

26. The collaboration is discussed in Patrick Waldberg, *Max Ernst: Peintures pour Paul Eluard* (Paris, 1969) and Werner Spies, *Max Ernst, Collagen: Inventar und Widerspruch* (Cologne, 1975). English edition: *Max Ernst: Collages–The Invention of the Surrealist Universe* (New York and London, 1991)

27. For the walnut source, see *ibid.* (Spies, 1975–91) plate 575.

28. Aragon wrote a piece on the collages with this title, though it would only be published later. Louis Aragon, 'Max Ernst, Peintre des illusions', August 1923, in Aragon, *Ecrits sur l'art moderne, les écrits d'Aragon sur l'art publiés sous la direction de Jean Risart* (Paris, 1981), 12–16.

29. Ernst's account of the 'discovery' of frottage is given in 'Au-delà de la peinture' (1936). See Max Ernst, *Ecritures* (Paris, 1970), 242–3.

30. The identification of the combing technique was made by Matthew Gale. I discuss it and its implications in Christopher Green, *The Thyssen-Bornemisza Collection. The European Avant-gardes. Art in France and Western Europe 1904–c. 1945* (London, 1995), 182–3.

31. Breton also gives a technical description of the practice. André Breton, 'D'une décalcomanie sans objet préconçu (décalcomanie de désir)', *Minotaure*, 8 (Paris, June 1936), 18.

32. The letter (written to the Belgian writer Paul Nougé) is cited and the probability that this was Magritte's first Paris painting is discussed in David Sylvester and Sarah Whitfield, *René Magritte. Catalogue Raisonné. I: Oil Paintings. 1916–1930* (London, 1992), 235 (no. 166).

33. The postcard source is illustrated in *ibid.*, 249.

34. Florent Berger (René Magritte), 'Georges Braque', *La Voix du peuple* (Brussels, 1 December 1936); in Magritte, *Ecrits complètes*, edited and annotated by André Blavier (Paris, 1979), 93.

35. André Breton and Paul Eluard, 'Prière d'insérer', in Salvador Dalí, *La Femme visible* (Paris, 1930); as cited in Musée national d'art moderne, *La Vie publique de Salvador Dalí*. Exh. cat. (Centre Georges Pompidou, Paris, 1980), 25.

36. This is suggested in Dawn Ades, *Dalí* (London, 1982), 70.

37. Salvador Dalí, 'L'âne pourri', *Le Surréalisme au service de la révolution*, 1 (Paris, July 1930), 9–12.

38. Lacan's thesis, *De la psychose paranoïaque dans ses rapports avec la personnalité*, is dated September 1932. Dalí read it before the end of the year. Their first meeting, with Breton as intermediary, is discussed in Patrice Schmitt, 'De la psychose paranoïaque dans les rapports avec Salvador Dalí', in Musée national d'art moderne (1980) *op.cit.*, 262–6.

39. The term appears in Dalí's article 'Interprétation paranoïaque-critique de l'image obsédante 'L'Angélus' de Millet', *Minotaure*, 1 (Paris, May 1933), 65–7.

40. Salvador Dalí, *La Conquête de l'irrationnel* (Paris, 1935).

41. Michel Leiris, 'Métaphore', *Documents*, 1st Year, 3 (Paris, 1929), 170.

42. Ernst's conscious manipulation of psychoanalytic images is demonstrated in Elizabeth Legge, *Max Ernst. The Psychoanalytic Sources* (Ann Arbor and London, 1989).

43. He claimed to be a madman without being mad in the lecture he gave at the opening of his exhibition of 1934 at the Wadsworth Atheneum in Hartford, Connecticut.

44. The dating of Ernst's first encounter to 1919 in Munich has long been agreed. The monograph in question was published by the Roman periodical *Valori Plastici* that year. The work Magritte saw in reproduction was *Song of Love* (1914); the circumstances and dating of this experience are fully discussed in Sylvester and Whitfield (1992), *op.cit.*, 38–9.

45. Salvador Dalí, Preface of the catalogue of the Dalí exhibition, galerie Pierre Colle, Paris, 1933. Author's translation.

46. My reading here is indebted to Matthew Gale, 'De Chirico, the Enigma of Fatality: A Contexualised Interpretation, 1906–1926'. Ph.D. Thesis Courtauld Institute, London, 1992, section 3, Chapter II. For a related analysis, see Maurizio Fagiolo dell'Arco, 'De Chirico à Paris', in Musée national d'art moderne, *Giorgio de Chirico*. Exh. cat. (Centre Georges Pompidou, Paris, 1983).

47. His brother Andrea (known as Savinio) was a musician and composer,

who produced a body of painted work too.

48. Jean Cocteau, *Giorgio de Chirico: Le Mystère laïque* (Paris, 1928). The same view is taken in Roger Vitrac, *Giorgio de Chirico* (Paris, 1927).

49. Masson is the other leading artist in and around Surrealism who becomes engaged in Classical myth.

50. As cited in Alfred H. Barr, Jr., *Symposium on 'Guernica'* (The Museum of Modern Art, New York, 1947).

51. Guillaume Apollinaire, 'Pablo Picasso', *Montjoie!* (Paris, 14 March 1913). Cited as translated by Susan Suleiman in Leroy C. Breunig (ed.), *Apollinaire on Art: Essays and Reviews 1902–1918* (London, 1972), 279.

52. Guillaume Apollinaire, *Méditations esthétiques. Les Peintres cubistes* (Paris, 1913). Edition edited and annotated by L.C. Breunig and J.Cl. Chevalier (Paris, 1965), 89. The first edition appeared on 17 March 1913.

53. Louis Aragon, 'La Peinture au défi', preface to the catalogue of the *Exposition de collages* (Galerie Goemans, Paris, 1930), in *Aragon, Ecrits* (1981) *op.cit.*, 35.

54. A.B. (André Breton) and Marcel Duchamp, 'La Mariée mise à nu par ses célibataires mêmes', *Le Surréalisme au service de la révolution*, 5 (Paris, 15 April 1933), 1–2.

55. André Breton, 'Phare de la Mariée', *Minotaure*, 6 (Paris, winter 1935), 48.

56. *Ibid.*, 46.

57. Paul Nougé, 'René Magrite ou la révélation objective', *Les Beaux-Arts*, 1, V (Brussels, 1936). Cited as translated in Emmanuel Guigon, 'El Objeto Surrealista', in *El Objeto Surrealista*. Exh. cat. (IVAM Centre Julio González, Valencia, 1997–8), 279.

58. Marcel Duchamp, *Ingénieur du temps perdu* (Paris, 1967), 84–5.

59. This is linked to *The Treason of Images* in Guigon (1997–8) *op.cit.*, 279.

60. This recent reading is in Simon Dell, 'The Personality of Choice: Subjectivity and Commodity Culture, France c.1918–1935'. Ph.D. Thesis Courtauld Institute, London, 1995. The painting of 1928 is Sylvester and Whitfield (1992) *op.cit.*, no. 204.

61. Cited as in Guigon (1997–8) *op.cit.*, 279.

62. He ended his 1919 collection of poems, *Mont de piété* (Pawn Shop), with 'Le Corset mystère', a poem first published in *Littérature*, composed entirely of fragments reproduced in facsimile from newspaper advertisements.

63. André Breton, 'L'Introduction au discours sur le peu de réalité', *Commerce* (Paris, 1924); republished independently in 1927; cited from Breton, *Point du jour* (Paris, 1934/70), 24.

64. The section of *Le Paysan de Paris* entitled 'Le Passage de l'Opéra' is dated 1924.

65. Yves Tanguy, 'Poids et couleurs', *Le Surréalisme au service de la révolution*, 3 (Paris, December 1931), 27.

66. Salvador Dalí, 'Objets Surréalistes', *Le Surréalisme au service de la révolution*, 3 (Paris, December 1931), 16–17.

67. André Breton, *Qu'est-ce que le surréalisme* (Paris, 1934). Cited as translated in Guigon (1997–8) *op.cit.*, 270.

68. Paul Nougé, *La lumière, l'ombre et la proie* (Brussels, 1930). Cited as translated in *ibid.*, 280.

69. The remakes are recorded and their significance is explored in William A. Camfield, *Marcel Duchamp. Fountain* (Houston, 1989).

70. See Rosalind Krauss, 'Photography in the Service of Surrealism', in *L'Amour fou: Photography and Surrealism*. Exh. cat. (Hayward Gallery, London, 1986).

71. André Breton, 'Il y aura une fois', *Le Surréalisme au service de la révolution*, 1 (Paris, July 1930), 3.

72. André Breton, 'L'Objet fantôme', *Le Surréalisme au service de la révolution*, 3 (Paris, December 1931), 22.

73. André Breton, 'Crise de l'objet', *Cahiers d'art*, special number 'Pour l'objet' (Paris, 1936).

74. Anne Baldessari, *Picasso Photographe 1901–1916*. Exh. cat. (Musée National Picasso, Paris, 1994), 229–43.

75. Louis Aragon (1930/1981), 30–1.

76. This is Dell's persuasive argument. He discusses at length advertising theory and practice in France between the 1900s and the end of the 1920s. See Simon Dell (1995) *op.cit.*

PART FOUR INTRODUCTION

1. Blaise Cendrars, 'Prose du Transsibérien et de la petite Jehanne de France' (1913), in Cendrars, *Du Monde entier* (Paris, 1947), 38.

2. Amédée Ozenfant and Charles-Edouard Jeanneret, *Après le cubisme* (Paris, 1918) np.

CHAPTER 7

1. Dr R. Allendy, 'L'orientation des idées nouvelles', *La Vie des lettres* (Paris, February 1923), 10–15.

2. Piet Mondrian, *Le Néo-Plasticisme: principe général de l'équivalence plastique* (Paris, 1920); in Harry Holtzman and Martin S. James (eds.), *The New Art – The New Life. The Collected Writings of Piet Mondrian* (New York and London, 1986–7), 134–47.

3. Piet Mondrian, 'Le Cubisme et le néo-plastique', *Cahiers d'art* (Paris, January 1931); in *ibid.*, 239–40. Holtzman and James establish that the typescript of this text is dated 25 March 1930 (*ibid.*, 236).

4. Camille Mauclair, *Albert Besnard: L'homme et l'œuvre* (Paris, 1914), 28.

5. *Ibid.*, 58.

6. *Ibid.*, 42.

7. Paul Adam, 'Le symbolisme dans l'œuvre d'Albert Besnard', *Gazette des Beaux-Arts* (Paris, 1911–12), 437–53. Though confusion is created by his use of inverted commas, Adam cites Bergson's 1904 study of Félix Ravaisson, reprinted in the anthology *The Creative Mind*. Translated by Mabelle L. Andison (New York, 1946), 261–300, and Tancrède de Visan's 'La philosophie de M. Bergson et le lyrisme contemporaine', *Vers et prose* (April–June 1910), 125–40.

8. See Chapter 2.

9. Antliff's important reassessment of Bergsonism's role in Salon Cubism appeared in partial form in Antliff, 'Bergson and Cubism: A Reassessment', *Art Journal*, vol. 47, 4 (Winter 1988), 341–9. The most complete statement of his case is Mark Antliff, *Inventing Bergson. Cultural Politics and the Parisian Avant-garde* (Princeton, NJ, 1993).

10. The first to do so was Petrie. See Brian Petrie, 'Boccioni and Bergson', *The Burlington Magazine*, 116 (March 1974), 140–7.

11. Robert Delaunay, 'La Lumière' (1913); Cited as translated in Gustav Vriesen and Max Imdahl, *Robert Delaunay: Light and Color* (New York, 1967), 9.

12. Adam (1911–12) *loc.cit.*, 449.

13. Alexandre Mercereau, 'Paroles devant la vie', *Vers et prose* (Paris, July–August–September 1911), 128–9.

14. Albert Gleizes and Jean Metzinger, *Du Cubisme* (Paris, 1912); as republished with a preface by Daniel Robbins (Paris, 1980), 44. Author's translation.

15. *Ibid.*, 68.

16. Linda Dalymple Henderson, *The Fourth Dimension and Non-Euclidean Geometry in Modern Art* (Princeton, NJ, 1983). My account is especially indebted to Henderson's book.

17. Gleizes and Metzinger (1912/1980) *op.cit.*, 50.

18. Flam has established the role of an Englishman, Matthew Stewart Prichard, who studied at Matisse's school and who admired Bergson, attending his lectures at the Collège de France. See Jack Flam, *Matisse. The Man and his Art 1869–1918* (London, 1986), 242.

19. This letter of early 1916 is cited in Raymond Escholier, *Henri Matisse, ce vivant* (Paris, 1956), 112–13.

20. An account of this process of dissemination and popularisation can be found in Henderson (1983) *op.cit.*

21. Gaston de Pawlowski, 'Le Léviathon', *Comoedia* (Paris, 24 December 1909). As cited in *ibid.*, 51.

22. Gaston de Pawlowki, 'L'Ame de silence', *Comoedia* (Paris, 24 February 1912), 1. As cited in *ibid.*, 52.

23. E. Jouffret, *Traité élémentaire de géométrie à quatre dimensions* (1903), and *Mélange de géométrie à quatre dimensions* (1906).

24. Henderson (1983) *op.cit.*, 57, 69–70, 87–91.

25. The manifesto was published in French in Gaston de Pawlowski's *Comoedia* (Paris, 18 May 1910).

26. For a full account of Marey's development of chronophotography, see Marta Braun, *Picturing Time. The Work of Etienne-Jules Marey (1830–1904)* (Chicago and London, 1992), especially Chapter 3.

27. The first to make this connection was Golding, from whom the phrase 'pervasive melancholy' comes. See John Golding, *Marcel Duchamp: The Bride Stripped Bare by her Bachelors, Even* (London, 1973), 25.

28. The phrase was made by the astronomer Jules Jansson and was cited in Albert Londe's *La Photographie moderne* (Paris, 1896), 546. It is cited here as in Georges Didi-Huberman, 'Photography – scientific and pseudo-scientific', in Jean-Claude Lemagny and André Rouillé (eds.), *A History of Photography. Social and Cultural Perspectives* (Cambridge and New York, 1987), 71, to which this discussion is indebted.

29. See Jean-François Chevrier, 'Bonnard photographe', in *Bonnard*. Exh. cat. (Paris, Centre Georges Pompidou, Musée national d'art moderne, 1984), 218–39); and Anne Baldassari, *Picasso photographe 1901–1916*. Exh. cat. (Paris, Musée National Picasso, 1994).

30. See Claude Nori, *La Photographie française dès origines à nos jours* (Paris, 1978), 14, and especially Marc Mellon, 'Beyond reality: art photography', in Lemagny and Rouillé (1987) *op.cit.*, 82–101.

31. Fernand Léger, 'Les origines de la peinture et sa valeur représentative', *Montjoie!* (Paris, 29 May and 14–29 June 1913), and 'Les réalisations picturales actuelles', *Soirées de Paris*, 25, 15 June 1914; in Léger, *Fonctions de la peinture* (Paris, 1965), 18–29.

32. The collection published in Paris in 1908 was *La Ville charnelle*. Marinetti dedicated *La roi Bombance* (Paris, 1905) to 'mon cher maître Paul Adam'.

33. Blaise Cendrars 'Tour', August 1913, in Cendrars (1947) *op.cit.*, 73.

34. Umberto Boccioni, 'Preface', catalogue of the exhibition of Futurist painting at the galerie Bernheim-Jeune, Paris, 1912; in *Archivi del Futurismo*, 1 (Rome, 1958), 106.

35. One of Besnard's four panels for the dome of the Petit Palais was *Plastique* (freely translated as 'Beauty'). Its iconography was partially adapted from the Judgement of Paris, with 'Poetry' replacing the shepherd Paris and only the chosen one of the Three Graces represented. Paris and the beautiful are equated using the conventional allegory of the Judgement of Paris.

36. Cendrars' *Paques à New York* was published in October 1912.

37. The press photograph is reproduced in Vriesen and Imdahl (1967) *op.cit.*, opposite, 109.

38. Alexandre Mercereau, *La Littérature et les idées nouvelles* (Paris, 1912), 101–45. Especially important was Michel Bréal's *Essai de sémantique* (Paris, 1904). Meillet published with Emile Durkheim's 'Année sociologique'.

39. Eugen Weber, *The Hollow Years: France in the 1930s* (USA, 1994, London, 1995), 209.

40. Fernand Léger (1914/1965) *op.cit*, 20–9. The early campaigns against hoardings in the countryside are fascinatingly discussed in Jeffrey Weiss, *The Popular Culture of Modern Art. Picasso, Duchamp, and Avant-gardism* (New Haven and London, 1994), 62–70.

41. Lista has shown the clear debt to Boccioni's book *Dinamisme plastique et sculpture française*, published a couple of months before the lecture was given. See Giovanni Lista, in Hélène Lassalle (ed.), *Fernand Léger*. Exh. cat., Musée d'art moderne (Villeneuve d'Asq, 1990).

42. Figures taken from Jean-Marie Mayeur and Madeleine Rebérioux, *The Third Republic from its Origins to the Great War, 1871–1914*, translated by J.R. Foster (Cambridge, 1984), 334–5. See also Emmanuel Chadeau, *L'industrie aéronautique en France* (Paris, 1987).

43. I set out the evidence for his visit to the Salon de l'aviation of 1912 in Christopher Green, *Léger and the Avant-garde* (New Haven and London, 1976), 324, note 52.

44. For the war correspondence, see Christian Derouet (ed.), *Fernand Léger: une correspondance de guerre à Louis Poughon, 1914–1918* (Paris, 1990).

45. See Roger Magraw, *France 1815–1914, The Bourgeois Century* (London, 1983), 359.

46. The reasons given in his letters to Poughon for his hospitalisation are rheumatism and gastric problems. See Derouet (1990) *op.cit.*

47. Letter 13, 30 March 1915, in *ibid.*, 35–6.

48. Fernand Léger, 'Pensées', *Valori Plastici* (Rome, February–March 1919), 3.

49. Letter 12, 12 April 1915, in Derouet (1990) *op.cit.*, 35.

50. Paul Dermée, 'Quand le symbolisme fut mort', *Nord-Sud*, 1 (Paris, 15 March 1917), 3.

51. Some of these stills were edited out of the four reels of the film that survive.

52. Ozenfant and Jeanneret (1918) *op.cit.*

53. Amédée Ozenfant and Le Corbusier, 'Formation de l'optique moderne', *L'Esprit nouveau*, 21 (Paris, March 1924).

54. Le Corbusier, 'Statistique', *L'Esprit nouveau*, 24 (Paris, June 1924).

55. Le Corbusier, 'Pérenité', *L'Esprit nouveau*, 20 (Paris, February 1924). Le Corbusier's 'Trois rappels à MM. les architectes' in nos. 1, 2, 3 eulogise the engineer as the model for the modern architect. These articles were adapted for his book *Vers une architecture*, published in 1923.

56. Le Corbusier elaborates the idea in: '1925. Exposition des Arts Décoratifs. Besoins, types, meubles, types', *L'Esprit noveau*, 23 (Paris, May 1924).

57. See Mary McLeod, '"Architecture or Revolution': Taylorism, Technocracy, and Social Change', *Art Journal*, vol. 43, 2 (New York, summer 1983), 132–47.

58. Ozenfant and Le Corbusier (1918) *op.cit.*

59. As McLeod notes, Herriot's progressive technocratic vision of France was set out in his book *Créer* in 1919. As mayor of Lyon, he sponsored the career of the Lyonnais modernist architect Tony Garnier.

60. McLeod presents the evidence scrupulously and persuasively. See McLeod (1987) *loc.cit.* Support for the 'cartel des gauches' was given by Jean Lurçat and Henri Hertz in *L'Esprit nouveau*, 24 (Paris, May 1924).

61. This admiration is clear in a letter of 4 June 1924, in reply to one from Rosenberg of 2 June where the dealer suggests that only Cubist art can touch 'the kings of the railway, of oil, of coffee, cotton, etc.' who spend their days 'glued to the telephone, surrounded by 50 secretaries . . .'. See Christian Derouet (ed.), *Une correspondance d'affairs. Correspondances Fernand Léger – Léonce Rosenberg 1917–1937* (Paris, 1996) Letters 205, 207, 137–40.

62. Amédée Ozenfant, 'Certitude', *L'Esprit nouveau*, 22 (Paris, April 1924).

63. Fernand Léger, 'L'esthétique de la machine. L'object fabriqué, l'artisan et l'artiste'. Lecture given in June 1923, first published in *Der Querschnitt*, vol. III (Berlin, 1923) and *Bulletin de l'Effort moderne*, 1 and 2, January and February 1924. In Léger (1965) *op.cit.*, 53–62.

64. *Ibid.*, 53.

65. See McLeod (1987) *loc.cit.*

66. An account of Le Corbusier's relations with Valois' movement and of the praise for his urbanism in *Nouveau Siècle* is given in Mark Antliff, '*La Cité française*: Georges Valois, Le Corbusier, and Fascist Theories of Urbanism', in Matthew Affron and Mark Antliff (eds.), *Fascist Visions. Art and Ideology in France and Italy* (Princeton, NJ, 1997), 134–70.

67. Figures from Pacal Ory, *La belle illusion. Culture et politique sous la signe de la Front Populaire 1935–1938* (Paris, 1994), 482. My account here is indebted to Ory.

68. Jean Perrin, 'Préambule', Groupe 1, Classe 1: Palais de la Découverte', archives of the commissariat of the Exhibition, Archives Nationales. As cited in Gilles Plum, 'Le Palais de la Découverte', in Bertrand Lemoine (ed.), *Cinquantenaire de l'Exposition Internationale des arts et des techniques dans la vie moderne*. Exh. cat. (Musée d'art moderne de la ville de Paris, 1987), 294.

69. Cited in Ory (1994) *op.cit.*, 477.

70. *Le Matin* (Paris, 2 May 1938). Cited in *ibid.*, 282.

71. My account follows Plum (1987) *op.cit.*

72. Figures on car production from Serge Berstein, *La France des années 30* (Paris, 1988), 32; otherwise, see Eugen Weber, *The Hollow Years: France in the 1930s* (New York and London, 1994 and 1995), 252.

CHAPTER 8

1. For the impact of the department store, see Michael B. Miller, *The Bon Marché. Bourgeois Culture and the Department Store 1869–1920* (Princeton, NJ, 1981) and Philip Nord, *Paris Shopkeepers and the Politics of Resentment* (Princeton, NJ, 1986). The latter keeps to the period before 1900.

2. *Ibid.*

3. The approach, work and reputation of the 'coloristes' is analysed in Nancy J. Troy, *Modernism and the Decorative Arts in France. Art Nouveau to Le Corbusier* (New Haven and London, 1991).

4. The most discerning and informative account of the 'Maison Cubiste' is given by Troy. *Ibid.*

5. Fernand Léger to André Mare, 7 August 1912. Given as cited in translation by Troy. *Ibid.*, 94.

6. Among these are Kirk Varnedoe and Adam Gopnik (eds.), *High and Low. Modern Art and Popular Culture*. Exh. cat. (Museum of Modern Art, New York), which devotes a chapter to advertising. Jeffrey Weiss, *The Popular Culture of Modern Art. Picasso, Duchamp and Avant-Gardism* (New Haven and London, 1994). And Simon Dell, 'The Personality of Choice: Subjectivity and Commodity Culture in France, c.1918–1930'. Ph.D. thesis, Courtauld Institute, London, 1995.

7. *Ibid.* My account here is indebted to Dell.

8. See Charles Gide, *La consomption* (Paris, 1921).

9. Cited in Dell (1995) *op.cit.*, from Francis Elvinger, *La Marque* (Paris, 1922).

10. These articles were incorporated into the book *L'Art décoratif d'aujourd'hui* in 1925 (English ed. *Decorative Art of Today*, translated by J. Dunnett (London, 1987)).

11. His agenda for the pavilion was set out in *L'Almanach de l'architecture moderne* (Paris, 1925).

12. A point Le Corbusier makes himself in *ibid.*, 194.

13. This is made clear in Le Corbusier, *Urbanisme* (Paris, 1925) (English ed. *The City of Tomorrow*, translated by Frederick Etchells (London, 1929)).

14. The sexual dimension is discussed in Tag Gronberg, 'Speaking Volumes: The Pavillon de l'Esprit Nouveau', *Oxford Art Journal*, vol.15, 2 (Oxford, 1992).

15. De Fayet (Amédée Ozenfant), 'La Sixtine de Michel-Ange', *L'Esprit Nouveau*, 14 (Paris, 1922); and Le Corbusier, *Vers une architecture* (Paris, 1923) (English ed. *Towards a New Architecture*, translated by Frederick Etchells [London, 1927]).

16. Guillaume Apollinaire, 'Pablo Picasso', *Montjoie!* (Paris, 14 March 1913). In Leroy C.Breunig (ed.), *Apollinaire on Art: Essays and Reviews 1902–1918*, translated by Susan Suleiman (London, 1972), 279.

17. The posters and the question of suggestion are discussed in Pascal Rousseau, 'Les couleurs "suggestives" de l'affiche. *L'Equipe de Cardiff* de Robert Delaunay et la querelle des "panneaux-réclame",' *Histoire de l'art*, 39 (Paris, October 1997), 77–89.

18. The first to suggest this reading was Rosenblum. See Robert Rosenblum, 'Picasso and the Typography of Cubism', in Roland Penrose and John Golding (eds.), *Picasso in Retrospect* (New York and Washington, 1973), 53.

19. Fernand Léger, Blaise Cendrars and Louis Carré, *Le Paysage dans l'oeuvre de Léger* (Paris, 1956) np.

20. This connection was first identified in Christopher Green, *Léger and the Avant-Garde* (New Haven and London, 1976), 273.

21. Maurice Hiver excerpted from *Montparnasse* in André Salmon, 'La Peinture et la sculpture', *La Revue de France* (Paris, 1 September 1923), 190–1.

22. Quoted in Florent Fels, 'Propos d'artistes, Fernand Léger', *Les Nouvelles Littéraires* (Paris, Saturday, 30 June 1923), 4.

23. Louis Aragon, 'La Peinture au défi', preface to the catalogue of the *Exposition de Collages* (Galerie Goemans, Paris, 1930); in Jean Risart (ed.), *Aragon. Ecrits sur l'art moderne* (Paris, 1981), 34. This is a point suggested in Dell (1995) *op.cit.*

24. The attention given to this phenomenon in, for instance, Paul Dubuisson's *Les Voleuses de grands magasins* (1902) and the academic psychology of Roger Dupouy is fully discussed in Miller (1981) *op.cit.*, 197ff.

25. Zola's notes are cited by Miller. *Ibid.*, 177.

26. Fernand Léger to Léonce Rosenberg, 4 September 1921, published in *Bulletin de l'Effort moderne*, 4 (Paris, April 1924). Cited as translated by Charlotte Green in *Léger and Purist Paris*. Exh. cat. (The Tate Gallery, London, 1970–1), 86.

27. See Françoise Thébaud, *La Femme au temps de la guerre de 14* (Paris, 1986), 34.

28. Figures from James F.McMillan, *Dreyfus to De Gaulle. Politics and Society in France 1898–1969* (London, 1985), 56.

29. For department store 'demoiselles', see Miller (1981) *op.cit.*, 193–7.

30. See Léon Abensour, *Les Vaillants* (Paris, 1917) and Marie de la Hire, *La Femme français, son activité pendant la guerre* (Paris, 1917).

31. Léon Abensour, *Histoire générale du Féminine. Des origines à nos jours* (Paris, 1921), 310.

32. Figures from Thébaud (1986) *op.cit.*, 195.

33. This is Georges Blanchet (an academic 'philosopher'). Victor Margueritte, *La garçonne* (Paris, 1922), 63.

34. Where 72% of abortion cases ended in acquittal between 1880 and 1910, Eugen Weber points out that only 20% did between 1925 and 1934. See Eugen Weber, *The Hollow Years: France in the 1930s* (London, 1994/5), 77–8.

35. Figures from Weber. Ibid., 80.

36. Perry demonstrates as much by quoting from Marevna's *Life in Two Worlds* (London, 1962). See Gill Perry, *Women Artists and the Parisian Avant-garde. Modernism and 'feminine' art, 1900 to the late 1920s* (Manchester and New York, 1995), 73–4.

37. For Marval see Perry. *Ibid.*, 19–20.

38. For Marthe Bonnard see Sarah Whitfield, 'Fragments of an Identical World', in *Bonnard*. Exh. cat. (The Tate Gallery, London, 1998), 15. For Josette Gris see Christopher Green, *Juan Gris*. Exh. cat. (Whitechapel Art Gallery, London, 1992), 123–4.

39. John Richardson, *A Life of Picasso*, vol. I: 1881–1906 (London, 1991), 201.

40. Perry is responsible for the re-discovery of Charmy, who she shows had a considerable reputation by the early 1920s. She also brings out the importance of Marval, noting especially her contribution to the harem theme developed by Ingres in the nineteenth century, her huge *Odalisques* shown at the Indéndants of 1903. See Perry (1995) *op.cit.*, Chapter 4.

41. Chapon discusses the expenses involved. See François Chapon, *Mystères et splendeurs de Jacques Doucet* (Paris, 1984), 58.

42. Blanchard returned to the maternity subject repeatedly through the 1920s. See Liliane Caffin Madaule, *Catalogue raisonné des oeuvres de Maria Blanchard*. Vol. II (London, 1994), 225–39.

43. Le Corbusier, as cited from Le Corbusier (1923/27) *op.cit.* in McLeod (1983) *loc.cit.*, 138.

44. Le Corbusier (1925/29) *op.cit.*, especially 'The Great City' and 'A Contemporary City'.

45. Le Corbusier-Saugnier (Le Corbusier and Ozenfant), 'Des Yeux qui ne voient pas', *L'Esprit nouveau*, 8 (Paris, May 1921) np.

46. Le Corbusier, in *Le Corbusier, oeuvre plastique. Peintures et dessins*. Exh. cat. (Galerie Balaÿ et Carré, Paris, 1938), 17.

47. Le Corbusier as cited from Le Corbusier, *La Ville radieuse* (Paris, 1935/64), in Robert Fishman, 'From the Radiant City to Vichy: Le Corbusier's Plans and Politics, 1928', in R. Walden (ed.), *The Open Hand: Essays on Le Corbusier* (Cambridge, Mass., 1977), 259. Fishman is an essential secondary source on Le Corbusier and politics in the 1930s. The other is Mary McLeod, 'Urbanism and Utopia: Le Corbusier from Regional Syndicalism to Vichy'. Ph.D. thesis, Princeton University, 1985.

48. In a eulogy to the modernist and Taylorist Van Nelle factory in Rotterdam, he wrote: 'But here there is no proletariat. There is the hierarchical scale . . . , established and respected'. Le Corbusier (1935/64) *op.cit.*, 179.

49. I have used two major secondary sources on the Left and cultural debates in the period of the Popular Front: Sarah Wilson, 'Art and the Politics of the Left in France, c.1935–c.1955'. Ph.D., thesis (Courtauld Institute, University of London, 1992). And Pascal Ory, *La Belle Illusion. Culture et politique sous le signe du Front Populaire 1935–1938* (Paris, 1994).

50. Paul Vaillant Couturier, speech delivered on 23 October 1934, published in *Commune* (Paris, November 1935). Quoted as cited in Ory (1994), 118.

51. Both signed this 'déclaration' published by Emmanuel Mounier in *L'Esprit* (Paris, October 1934). Quoted as cited in *ibid.*, 99.

52. Quoted as cited in Wilson (1992) *op.cit.*, from Louis Aragon, 'De Vigny à Aducenko', in Aragon, *Pour un réalisme socialiste* (Paris, 1935).

53. Moussinac's statement was made in answer to an enquiry held in *Commune* (May–June 1935), 'Où va la peinture'.

54. Louis Aragon (ed.), *La Querelle du réalisme* (Paris, 1936), 66–7.

55. As Wilson notes, Aragon edited out this passage from *La Querelle du réalisme* as published. It is quoted as she cites it from Roger Garaudy, *Pour un réalisme du XXe siècle*, in Wilson (1992) *op.cit.*

56. Louis Aragon, 'Le réalisme à l'ordre du jour', *Commune*, 37 (Paris, September 1936). Cited in *ibid.*

57. Jean-Marc Campagne, interview with Fernand Léger, in *Marianne* (Paris, 13 October 1937). Cited in Giovanni Lista, 'Léger scénographe et cinéaste', in *Fernand Léger et le spectacle*. Exh. cat. (Musée national Fernand Léger, Biot, 1995), 72.

58. The latter was for the hall of a proposed French Embassy for a foreign capital. Delaunay also contributed a painting for the installation. Attention was drawn to Léger's and Delaunay's contributions when Paul Léon, director of the Beaux-Arts administration criticised them and they were temporarily withdrawn

59. See especially Fernand Léger, 'L'architecture polychromie', *L'Architecture vivante* (Paris, autumn–winter 1923). Translated into English by Charlotte Green in Tate Gallery (1970–1) *op.cit.*

60. Saint-Maur's name was actually Samuel Guyot. For 'L'art mural', see Ory (1994) *op.cit.*, 235.

61. Technical experimentation was a feature of the muralist effort. Both Delaunay and Ozenfant were involved in this, but it was not necessarily modernist, as the use of frescoed cement for Billotey's *Tragedy* mural in the Palais de Chaillot shows [6].

62. This attendance figure is given by Ory. *Ibid.*, 238.

63. Léger (13 October 1937) *loc.cit.*; as cited in Lista (1994) *op.cit.*, 72.

64. Jean-Richard Bloch, mss. (Fonds Jean-Richard Bloch, Bibliothèque Nationale, Paris). Cited as transcribed in *Léger et le spectacle* (1994) *op.cit.*, 148. Author's translation.

65. A very full account is given in Peter de Francia, *Fernand Léger* (New Haven and London, 1983) Chapter 8.

66. As cited in Ory (1994) *op.cit.*, 187.

67. Léger (13 October 1937) *loc.cit.*; as cited by Lista (1994) *op.cit.*, 72.

68. Wilson (1992) *op.cit.*

69. For 'Les Indélicats', see ibid.

70. Information from ibid.

71. See ibid.

72 Statement made at the 2nd Congress of the Fédération musicale populaire, May 1937. Cited in Ory (1994) *op.cit.*, 65.

73. Gleizes turned to rugby players as a subject in 1912, and Metzinger to cycling in 1911.

74. Bloch mss. Cited as transcribed in *Léger et le nouvel spectacle* (1994) *op.cit.* 146.

75. Ory draws attention to both these events. See Ory (1994) *op.cit.*, 52–3.

76. Fernand Léger, 'L'avis d'un peintre. Si tu n'aimes pas les vacances', *L'Intransigeant* (Paris, Monday 21 October 1929).

77. Le Corbusier (1935/64) *op.cit.*, 68–9.

78. Quoted as cited in Ory (1994) *op.cit.*, 65.

79. Information from Wilson (1992) *op.cit.*

PART FIVE INTRODUCTION

1. Henri Focillon, *La Peinture au XIXe et XXe siècles. Du Réalisme à nos jours* (Paris, 1928), 302.

2. Elie Faure, 'Preface', catalogue of the Salon d'automne, 1905. As cited in translation in James D. Herbert, *Fauve Painting: The Making of Cultural Politics* (New Haven and London, 1992), 8.

3. Elie Faure, *History of Art*. II *Medieval Art*, translated by Walter Pach (London, 1922), 302–3.

4. Henri Focillon, Preface, *Chefs-d'oeuvre de l'art français*. Exh. cat. (Palais National des arts, Paris, 1937), xiii–xiv.

5. This account of Lavisse's and Vidal's studies is based on Pierre Nora,

'Lavisse, the Nation's Teacher', and Jean-Yves Guiomar, 'Vidal de la Blanche', both in Pierre Nora (ed.), *Realms of Memory. The Construction of the French Past*, II Traditions, translated by Lawrence D. Kritzman (New York, 1997).

6. As cited from the 1912 edition by Nora. *Ibid.*, 174.

7. As cited from the 1979 edition by Guiomar. *Ibid.*, 187.

8. See Rogers Brubaker, *Citizenship and Nationhood in France and Germany* (Cambridge, Mass., and London, 1992).

9. As cited in *ibid.*, 101.

10. This is a point underlined by Lebovics. See Herman Lebovics, *True France. The Wars over Cultural Identity, 1900–1945* (Ithaca and London, 1992), xii–xiii.

CHAPTER 9

1. Camille Mauclair, *Trois crises de l'art actuel* (Paris, 1906), 280. See also 270.

2. *Ibid.*, 280–3.

3. *Ibid.*, 308.

4. Emile Bernard, 'Paul Cézanne', *L'Occident* 31 (Paris, July 1904).

5. Maurice Denis, 'Cézanne', *L'Occident*, 12 (Paris, September 1907). Cited as translated in Richard Schiff, *Cézanne and the End of Impressionism. A Study of the Theory, and Critical Evaluation of Modern Art* (Chicago, 1984), 136.

6. The link to *The Dying Niobid* is made by Sasha Newman in *Bonnard*. Exh. cat. (The Phillips Collection, Washington DC and Museum of Art, Dallas, 1984).

7. This circle and the positions of both Gide and Mithouard are discussed in David Cottington, *Cubism in the Shadow of War. The Avant-Garde and Politics in Paris, 1905–1914* (New Haven and London, 1998), 63–4.

8. Maurice Denis, 'Aristide Maillol', *L'Occident* (November 1905), 241–9. In 1908 Kessler took Maillol on a trip to Greece, where he was especially attracted to pre-Hellenic sculpture, and was said to have recognised his native Catalonia in the landscape. For Maillol and Denis, see Jean-Paul Bouillon, 'Maillol et Denis', in Ursel Berger and Jörg Zutter, *Aristide Maillol*. Exh. cat. (Georg-Kolbe Museum, Berlin, and Musée cantonal des Beaux-Arts, Lausanne, 1996).

9. Clara T. MacChesny, 'A Talk with Matisse, Leader of the Post-Impressionists', *New York Times Magazine* (New York, 9 March 1913); in translation in Jack D. Flam, *Matisse on Art* (New York and London, 1973), 52. And Jacques Guenne, 'Entretien avec Henri Matisse', *L'Art vivant*, (15 September 1925); cited in translation from Flam (1973), 52.

10. *Ibid.*, (1925/1973), 55.

11. James D. Herbert, *Fauve Painting: The Making of Cultural Politics* (New Haven and London, 1992), 82–3.

12. *Ibid.*

13. Vidal de la Blanche's *Tableau de la géographie de la France*, published in 1903, is discussed in the Introduction to Part IV. For the landscapes painted by the Fauves, see the essays by Judi Freeman and James Herbert in Judi Freeman (ed.), *The Fauve Landscape*. Exh. cat. (Los Angeles, Los Angeles County Museum of Art, 1990).

14. It is worth noting that Matisse's appropriation of Ingres was treated as a direct provocation by Mauclair, whose *Trois Crises de l'art actuel* ends with a chapter on 'The Crisis of Ugliness in Painting'. Matisse is not named, but it is here that the idea of Ingres and Cézanne belonging to the same French lineage is held up to ridicule. See notes 1 and 3, above.

15. For Count Kessler Maillol titled it *Statue for a Shaded Garden*. *La Pensée latine* came after this, Cladel says, and so after 1904–5, but she also places it in the period of the 'Affaire' (Dreyfus), which was largely over by then; it is likely, therefore, that she means the mid-1900s at the latest. The story clearly comes from Maillol himself. See Judith Cladel, *Aristide Maillol; Sa vie – son œuvre – ses idées* (Paris, 1937), 74.

16. Charles Maurras, 'Les Chansons Provençals' (1903); in *L'Etang du Berne* (Paris, 1915), 155. Cited as translated in Herbert (1992) *op.cit.*, 125–6.

17. Camille Mauclair, 'La réaction nationaliste en art et l'ignorance de l'homme de lettres', *La Revue*, 54 (15 January 1905). Cited as translated in *ibid.*, 124.

18. Jack Flam, *Matisse. The Man and his Art, 1869–1918* (London, 1986), 156–7. The opening from Mallarmé is quoted as cited in translation by Flam.

19. These events and their impact on the cultural politics of the period are examined in Cottington (1998) *op.cit.*, 20–32.

20. Guillaume Apollinaire, 'Henri Matisse', *La Phalange* II, 18 (December 1907), 481–5. Cited from the translation in Flam (1973) *op.cit.*, 32.

21. André Salmon, *La Jeune Peinture française* (Paris, 1912), 47.

22. The El Greco in question is *Apocalyptic Vision*, 1608–14, now in The Metropolitan Museum of Art, New York. In 1907, it was in the Paris home of Ignacio Zuloaga, a painter friend of Picasso. For a discussion of this, see Robert S. Lubar, 'Narrating the Nation: Picasso and the Myth of El Greco', in Jonathan Brown (ed.), *Picasso and the Spanish Tradition* (New Haven and London, 1996).

23. See especially the articles signed Ozenfant and Jeanneret (Le Corbusier) on 'Le Cubisme' in *L'Esprit nouveau*, 23 and 24, 1924, where 1912 is identified as the high point of Cubism.

24. Leighten has also argued that Picasso's invocations of past models in the pre-1914 period have a vandalistic aspect. See Patricia Leighten, *Reordering the Universe. Picasso and Anarchism, 1897–1914* (Princeton, NJ, 1989), 91–5.

25. See Cottington (1998) *op.cit.*, 61–4. Cottington brings out the links between Barrès' and Denis' notions of classicism, and their adaptability to modernist notions of order balanced by sensibility in art.

26. Léon Daudet, in *L'Action française* (Paris, 13 September 1911). As cited in Fay Brauer, 'L'Art révolutionnaire. The Artist as Alien: The Discourses of Cubism, Modern Painting and Academicism in the Radical Republic' Ph.D., thesis, Courtauld Institute, 1997, 201. My account here is indebted to Brauer.

27. *Ibid.*

28. For Gleizes and Metzinger's Bergsonism, see Chapter 7.

29. Albert Gleizes, 'Le Cubisme et la Tradition', *Montjoie!* 1 (10 February 1913), 4.

30. Albert Gleizes, 'L'art et ses représentants: Jean Metzinger', *Revue indépenante* 4 (September 1911), 161–72. I excerpt here from the article as cited in Mark Antliff, *Inventing Bergson. Cultural Politics and the Parisian Avant-garde* (Princeton, NJ, 1993), 125. My account here of Gleizes and Celtic nationalism is indebted to Antliff.

31. Most notably, Alexandre Mercereau, Henri-Martin Barzun, founder-editor of the periodical *Poème et drame*, and Eugène Figuière, publisher of *Du Cubisme*. See ibid., Chapter 4.

32. As Antliff shows, this was a social and political vision developed above all by Robert Pelletier and others in the periodicals of the Ligue Celtique, *L'Entendard celtique* and the *Revue des nations*. See *ibid.*

33. This is argued strongly by Barzun in *Poème et Drame* 1 (November 1912). This first issue of the periodical also carried a section from Gleizes and Metzinger's *Du Cubisme*.

34. Gleizes (1913) *loc.cit.*

35. Aristide Maillol to Maurice Denis, postcard dated 29 January 1910. Cited in Bouillon (1996) *op.cit.*, 130.

36. Waldemar George, 'André Derain', in René Huyghe (ed.), *Histoire de l'art contemporaine* (Paris, 1935), 158–9.

37. Jane Lee is the one to have brought out most usefully the range of Derain's sources and the richness of their implications. See Jane Lee, *Derain* (Oxford and New York, 1990), 27–45. It is Lee who has established the importance of Roman Catholic iconographies in his painting before the 1914–18 war. Her work offers a new starting point for Derain studies.

38. For a much fuller discussion of these pictures in these terms, see ibid., 40–5.

39. Georges Lefenestre, 'Introduction', in Henri Bouchot (ed.), *Exposition des Primitifs français au Palais du Louvre (Pavillon de Marsan) et à la Bibliothèque Nationale*. Exh. cat. (Paris, April 1904), xii, xii–xiii.

40. Jacques Lipchitz to Léonce Rosenberg, 'Tuesday' (dateable to December 1916). Cited in Christopher Green, 'Lipchitz and Gris: The Cubisms of a Sculptor and a Painter'; in *Lipchitz. Un mundo sorprendido en el espacio*. Exh. cat. (Museo Nacional Centro de Arte Reina Sofía, Madrid, 1997. Cited in French in the English translation of the text, 207, 210, note 36.

41. A letter indicates that these actually began in 1915, though none survive from that year. Juan Gris to D.-H. Kahnweiler, 7 September 1915. In Douglas Cooper (ed. and trans.), *Letters of Juan Gris (1913–1927)* (London, 1956), 31.

42. Caffin Madaule dates this picture 1919. Its dark palette, formal rhymes and simple vocabulary are, however, compatible with Gris's work of both 1918 and 1919, indicating that it could be the earlier date. See Liliane Caffin-Madaule, *Catalogue raisonné des oeuvres de Maria Blanchard*, vol.1 (Paris, 1992), 184.

43. Paul Dermée, 'Quand le symbolisme fut mort', *Nord-Sud*, 1 (March 1917), 3.

44. Georges Braque, 'Pensées et réflexions sur la peinture', *Nord-Sud*, 10 (December 1917), 3, 5.

45. He married in September 1915, and his new father-in-law, the powerful radical politician, Jules Roches, helped obtain an honourable discharge for him.

46. The story of the increased influence of the Latin myth is well told in Kenneth Silver, *Esprit de Corps. The Art of the Parisian Avant-Garde and the First World War, 1914–1925* (Princeton, NJ, and London, 1989).

47. Guillaume Apollinaire, open letter dated 22 September 1917, *Mercure de France* (Paris, 16 October 1917).

48. Henri Focillon, *Technique et sentiment. Etudes sur l'art moderne* (Paris, 1919), 167, 175. Quoted from the excerpted citations in Silver (1989) *op.cit.*, 101.

49. Charles Maurras, *Quand les français ne s'aimaient pas* (Paris, 1916), 392. Cited in Herbert (1992), 144.

50. See Silver (1989), *op. cit.*, and Christopher Green, *Cubism and its Enemies: Modern Movements and Reaction in French Art, 1916–1928* (New Haven and London, 1987). Chapter 12 especially.

51. Just how deeply the images and ideals disseminated by propaganda influenced individuals is open to question, as Becker's work has demonstrated, so the adverb 'apparently' here is to be taken seriously. See Jean-Jacques Becker, *The Great War and the French People*, translated by Arnold Pomerans (Leamington Spa, Heidelberg and Dover, NH, 1985 (French 1st ed., 1983)).

52. Dermée (March 1917) *loc.cit.*, 3.

53. The argument is persuasively put in Silver (1989) *op.cit.*, 115–23.

CHAPTER 10

1. The sequestration of Kahnweiler's stock and the sales are examined in great detail in Malcolm Gee, *Dealers, Critics and Collectors of Modern Painting: Aspects of the Parisian Art Market between 1910 and 1930* (London and New York, 1981).

2. Charles Maurras, *L'Action française* (Paris, 9 March 1920). Cited in Ralph Schor, *L'Opinion française et les étrangers en France 1919–1939* (Paris, 1985), 78.

3. In 1928–9, Mauclair mounted a campaign in support of these views in *Le Figaro* and especially the extreme right wing *l'Ami du peuple*, for the latter of which he had editorial responsibilities. These were brought together in two volumes published in 1929 and 1930. The phrases cited here are from the first of these: Camille Mauclair, *La farce de l'art vivant*. Une campagne picturale, 1928–9 (Paris, 1929), 33, 38, 153. For further discussion of this anti-semitic campaign, see below.

4. Pierre Apesteguy, *Le Petit Journal* (Paris, 19 September 1937). Cited in Schor (1985), 663.

5. Figures from Schor. *Ibid.*, 28. This paragraph is reliant for its material on this fundamental secondary study of the 'foreigner problem' in France between the wars.

6. The second of Mauclair's two volumes collecting the articles of his 'campaign' was: *Les Métèques contre l'art français* (Paris, 1930). For anti-semitism in France, see also Ralph Schor, *L'Antisémitisme en France pendant les années trente* (Paris, 1992).

7. Émile Mâle, *L'Art allemand et l'art française du Moyen Age* (Paris, 1917).

8. Henri Focillon, *Les Pierres de France* (Paris, 1919), 59, 117, 13.

9. Of the Romanesque, he writes: 'Provence, Auvergne, Périgord, Poitou, Saintogne, Normandy, Burgundy, what beautiful paths open up for the traveller of the Roman land! And what a complete lesson for whoever wishes to grasp our diverse fashions of understanding and creating.' *Ibid.*, 58.

10. Henri Focillon, *Technique et sentiment* (Paris, 1919), 175.

11. Paul Fierens, 'Lettre de Paris – Salon d'automne (le 1er novembre)', *Sélection*, 9–10 (Brussels, 15 December 1922).

12. André Salmon, 'Le Salon d'automne', *La Revue de France* (Paris, December 1922), 618.

13. It accompanied an article by Amédée Ozenfant signed 'de Fayet' in *L'Esprit Nouveau*, 7 (Paris, April 1921).

14. The first among recent commentators to make the Goujon link was Parigoris. See Alexandra Parigoris, 'Pastiche and the Use of Tradition', in Elizabeth Cowling and Jennifer Mundy (eds.), *On Classic Ground: Picasso, Léger, de Chirico and the New Classicism 1910–1930*. Exh. cat. (Tate Gallery, London, 1990, hardback edition only), 303. She draws attention also to Jean Cocteau's recollection that when he met Picasso in 1916, the artist had suspended in the stairwell outside his studio a photograph of the Parthenon frieze.

15. Roger Bissière, 'L'Exposition Picasso', *L'Amour de l'art* (Paris, July 1921), 210.

16. In *l'Esprit nouveau*, 4 (January 1921).

17. Roger Bissière, 'Notes sur Ingres', *l'Esprit nouveau*, 4 (Paris, January 1921).

18. *L'Esprit nouveau* re-published Cèzanne's 'Opinions' in 1921.

19. 'Pinturichio' (Louis Vauxcelles), 'Carnet des ateliers. Braque', *Le Carnet de la semaine* (Paris, 5 November 1922), 10ff.; 'Pinturicchio (Louis Vauxcelles), 'Mort de quelqu'un', *Le Carnet de la semaine* (1 April 1923), 8ff.

20. Especially important was an attempt to defend Cézanne from the Cubists' claims to be his legitimate successors, where he accuses them of being 'possessed by the demon of abstraction'. See: Louis Vauxcelles, 'De Cézanne au cubisme, à propos de la "section d'or"', *Eclair* (Paris, 18 March 1920). The piece was provoked by a revival of the pre-war Cubist Salon de la Section d'Or.

21. Edmond Jaloux, 'Dunoyer de Segonzac', *L'Art vivant* (Paris, 15 January 1925), 1–3.

22. *L'Art vivant* (Paris, 1 June 1925), 37; and Roger Allard, 'Maurice de Vlaminck', *L'Art vivant* (Paris, 1 April 1925), 2.

23. Romy Golan, *Modernity and Nostalgia: Art and Politics between the Wars* (New Haven and London, 1995) Chapter 2. I have taken account of Golan's important analysis in this section although, in my view, the evidence does not support the conclusion that all regionalist work was necessarily on the Right ideologically.

24. Shanny Peer, *France on Display. Peasants, Provincials and Folklore in the 1937 World's Fair* (New York, 1998), 61–2.

25. I am reliant for material concerning Niclausse on *François Paul Niclausse, 1879–1958* (Collections du Musée Municipal de Mont-de-Marsan, Musée Despiau Wlérick, Mont-de-Marsan, 1987).

26. This is discussed in Chapter 8.

27. Florent Fels, 'Les expositions', *L'Art vivant* (Paris, 1 June 1925), 22.

28. Jacques Guenne, 'Marcel Gromaire', *L'Art vivant* (Paris, 15 May 1926), 380.

29. Cited in Golan (1995) *op.cit.*, 34.

30. Gromaire quoted in Guenne (1926) *loc.cit.*, 382.

31. Others who identified with regionalism and with a northern rather than a Latin cultural identity included sculptors dedicated to direct carving who were associated with *La Douce France*, a periodical founded in 1913, which organised exhibitions of direct carving in 1922 and 1923, and brought together a team of sixteen sculptors, including Zadkine, to produce a collaborative work called the *Pergola de la douce France* for the 1925 Exposition Internationale des Arts Décoratifs. It is discussed in Golan (1995) *op.cit.*, 33–6.

32. Juan Gris to D.H. Kahnweiler, 25 August 1919; in Douglas Cooper (editor and translator), *Letters of Juan Gris [1913–1927]* (London, 1956), 65.

33. Auguste Herbin, in 'Chez les cubistes – Notre enquête I', and Henri Laurens, in 'Chez les cubistes – Notre enquête III', *Bulletin de la Vie artistique* (Paris, 1 November and 1 December 1924), 485 and 509. Also cited in Christopher Green, *Cubism and its Enemies: Modern Movements and Reaction in French Art, 1916–1928* (New Haven and London, 1987), 193. My discussion of Cubism and the notion of tradition is developed here from my treatment of the topic in Chapter 12 of that book.

34. The key study here was Henri Focillon, *L'Art des sculpteurs romanes* (Paris, 1931), which was based on lectures given at the Sorbonne between 1926 and 1929. Focillon's views and their relevance to Laurens and Lipchitz are very fully discussed in Cathy Pütz, 'Cubist Sculpture and the Circularity of Time. The Work of Jacques Lipchitz and Henri Laurens in interwar Paris'. Ph.D., Thesis Courtauld Institute, London, 1998, especially Chapters 3 and 10.

35. Maurice Raynal, *Quelques intentions du cubisme* (Paris, 1919). Cited as reprinted in *Bulletin de l'Effort moderne*, 3 (March 1924).

36. Parigoris (1990) *op.cit.* In her lengthy essay 'Picasso/Pastiche', Rosalind Krauss neither acknowledges nor responds to Parigoris' piece, a mystifying exclusion. See Rosalind Krauss, *The Picasso Papers* (London, 1998).

37. Letters 54, 55, 56, 173 (16 and 24 August, and 6 September 1919; 21 August 1923) in Fernand Léger, *Une Correspendance d'affaires. Correspendances Fernand Léger–Léonce Rosenberg 1917–1937.* Christian Derouet (ed.) (Paris, Cahiers du Musée nationale d'art moderne, 1996), 52–60, 118–19.

38. This letter is dated 4 September 1921. It is Letter 109 in *ibid.*, 90–1. It was published with the mistaken date 'March 1922' in *Bulletin de l'Effort moderne*, 4 (Paris, April 1924).

39. Jacques Lipchitz, Reply to an 'Enquête', *Bulletin de la Vie artistique* (Paris, 15 January 1924) 31–2.

40. André Salmon, 'Vingt ans après', *L'Art vivant* (Paris, 15 October 1925), 10.

41. This is a point Salmon had made as early as 1912, see: André Salmon, 'Les artistes étrangers de Paris', *Gil Blas* (Paris, 1 June 1912), 4. I am grateful to Fay Brauer for bringing this to my attention.

42. For the colonial expansion allowed by the Treaty and these agreements, see Christopher M. Andrew and A.S. Kanya-Forster, *France Overseas: The Great War and the Climax of French Imperial Expansion* (London, 1981), Chapters 8 and 9.

43. Maurice Barrès, 'Preface' to Camille Fidel, *La Paix coloniale française* (Paris, 1918). Cited in ibid., 164.

44. Cited in Herman Lebovics, *True France. The Wars over Cultural Indentity, 1900–1945* (Ithaca and London, 1992), 74. I am indebted in this discussion of the reconstruction of Angkor Wat and in this entire discussion of the Exhibition to Lebovics.

45. The point is comprehensively made in ibid.

46. Both quotations cited in *ibid.*, 64, 79.

47. Lebovics goes into the impact on policy in Indochina of the agitation for independence and the changes in education policy introduced in the 1920s. See *ibid.*, 98ff. For assimilationism and associationism, see especially Charles-Robert Ageron, *France coloniale ou parti coloniale* (Paris, 1978).

48. *Ibid.*, 81.

49. Violette is quoted to this effect from *Les Cahiers des Droits de l'Homme* in Ageron (1978) *op.cit.*, 200.

50. Lebovics shows how such a comparison with medieval France was invited by the Angkor Wat reconstruction. See Lebovics (1992) *op.cit.*, 59.

51. The one possible exception is Max Ernst, but his response has yet to be investigated.

52. Kenneth E. Silver, *Esprit de Corps. The Art of the Parisian Avant-Garde and the First World War, 1914–1925* (Princeton NJ and London, 1989), 264.

53. Camille Mauclair, *La Farce de l'art vivant*, Une campagne picturale,

1928–1929 (Paris, 1929), 154.

54. Marcel Sembat, in *Cahiers d'aujourd'hui* (Paris, April 1913). As cited in Jack Flam, *Matisse. The Man and his Art, 1869–1918* (London, 1986), 360.

55. Figures from Schor (1985) *op.cit.*, 34.

56. Sophie Bowness, 'The Presence of the Past: Art in France in the 1930s, with Special Reference to Le Corbusier, Léger and Braque'. Ph.D. Thesis, Courtauld Institute, London, 1996. My discussion of museology here relies on Bowness's section on the topic, which is the best account and analysis now available.

57. Editorial, *L'Amour de l'art* (Paris, March 1937). Cited as in Bowness. *Ibid.*

58. George's passionate advocacy of Italian fascist principles is revealed in a major contribution by Affron. See Matthew Affron, 'Waldemar George: A Parisian Art Critic on Modernism and Fascism', in Matthew Affron and Mark Antliff (eds.), *Fascist Visions. Art and Ideology in France and Italy* (Princeton, NJ, 1997), 171–204.

59. Waldemar George, 'Homo sum humani nihil a me alienum puto', *Formes*, XI (Paris, January 1931), 2. My treatment of George's stance relates to my 1990 analysis, though I take the analysis further here. See Christopher Green, 'Classicisms of Transcendence and of Transience: Maillol, Picasso and de Chirico', in Cowling and Mundy (1990) *op.cit.*, 267–82.

60. Waldemar George, 'La crise de l'optimisme moderne et l'agonie d'un mythe', *Formes*, XII (Paris, February 1931), 19.

61. Waldemar George, 'Appels du Bas-Empire, Georges de Chirico', *Formes*, I (Paris, January 1930), 12.

62. George (January 1931) *loc.cit.*, 2.

63. George (January 1930), *loc. cit.*, 12–14.

64. Waldemar George, 'Le message de Derain', *Formes*, XIX (Paris, November 1931), 145–6.

65. Maurice Raynal, *Anthologie de la peinture en France de 1906 à nos jours* (Paris, 1927), 21.

66. This is Golan's argument initially in: Romy Golan, 'The "Ecole Français' vs. the "Ecole de Paris": the Debate about the Status of Jewish Artists in Paris between the Wars', in Kenneth E. Silver and Romy Golan, *The Circle of Montparnasse. Jewish Artists in Paris, 1905–1945*. Exh. cat. (The Jewish Museum, New York, 1985), 86. The analysis is reprised and extended in Romy Golan, 'From Fin de Siècle to Vichy: The Cultural Hygienics of Camille (Faust) Mauclair', in Linda Nochlin and Tamar Garb (eds.), *The Jew in the Text: Modernity and the Construction of Identity* (London, 1995), 167–9.

67. Schor (1985) *op.cit.*, 195.

68. Waldemar George, 'Ecole Française ou Ecole de Paris, I', and 'Ecole Française ou Ecole de Paris, II', *Formes*, nos. XVI and XVII (Paris, June and September 1931), 92–3, 110–11.

69. Waldemar George, 'Le Gouvernement de la France contre l'art français', *Formes*, XV (Paris, May 1931), 74.

70. Waldemar George, 'Un bilan et un programme: peinture, architecture, art décoratif', *Formes*, XXXI (Paris, 1933), 340.

71. See especially Sander L. Gilman, *Jewish Self-Hatred: Anti-Semitism and the Hidden Language of the Jews* (Baltimore, 1986). Cited in Golan (1995), *op.cit.*, 165.

72. Cited by Golan. *Ibid.*, 169.

73. André Salmon, in *La Revue de France* (Paris, 15 July 1924), 377.

74. For Soutine's sources, see: Ernst-Gerhard Güse (ed.), *C. Soutine, 1893–1943*. Exh. cat. (Arts Council of Great Britain, Hayward Gallery, 1981), 130–3.

75. Waldemar George, *Soutine* (Paris, 1929), 14–18. As cited in Golan (1995) *op.cit.*, 167.

76. Waldemar George, 'Lettre ouverte à André de Ridder sur Marc Chagall et la génie du Nord', *Sélection*, Cahier 6 (Antwerp, 1929), 22.

77. *Ibid.*

78. André Salmon, *Chagall* (Paris, 1928), 18; Jacques Maritain, 'Chagall', in *Sélection* (1929) *op.cit.*, 28.

79. Ambroise Vollard, 'Chagall, illustrateur des Fables de La Fontaine', as published in *ibid.*, 35–6.

80. See Schor (1985), 549ff.

81. Thorez, Aragon and Vaillant-Couturier cited in Pascal Ory, *La Belle Illusion. Culture et politique sous le signe du Front populaire* (Paris, 1994), 71.

82. Sarraut cited in Maurice Agulhon, *Marianne au pouvoir. L'imagerie et la symbolique républicains de 1880 à 1914* (Paris, 1989), 30–1. Agulhon also discusses the image of Marianne the sower.

83. Labbé's career, regionalist beliefs and policies are discussed in Madeleine Rebérioux, 'L'Exposition de 1937 et le contexte politique des années trente', in Bertrand Lemoine (ed.), *Cinquantenaire de l'Exposition Internationale des arts et des techniques dans la vie moderne*. Exh. cat. (Musée d'art moderne de la Ville de Paris, 1987), 26–9.

84. This aspect of the 1937 Exhibition is very fully explored in Peer (1998) *op.cit.*, Chapters 2 and 3.

85. Cited in Ory (1994) *op.cit.*, 80–1.

86. Rivière's socialist orientation as the protegé of the ethonographer and Socialist Party activist Paul Rivet, as well as his maintenance of such a position even under the Occupation, is discussed with a full awareness of the issues, including the charge of collaboration sometimes levelled against him, in Lebovics (1992) *op.cit.*, 136–77.

87. For the 'Manufactures Nationales' and the Popular Front, see Ory (1994) *op.cit.*, 278–9.

88. This is a point made by Golan in Golan (1995) *op.cit.*, 160–2.

89. Especially convincing in this respect is Sweets's study of Clermont-Ferrand and the Auvergne. See John F. Sweets, *Choices in Vichy France: The French under Nazi Occupation* (New York, 1986; New York and Oxford, 1994).

90. I have analysed the x-ray evidence and supported the argument that this is a work modelled on votive paintings in Christopher Green, *The European Avant-gardes. Art in France and Western Europe 1904–c. 1945* (London, 1995), 84–91.

PART SIX INTRODUCTION

1. Sigmund Freud, *Civilisation and its Discontents* [1930]; in James Strachey (ed.) *The Pelican Freud Library*, 12 (Albert Dickson (ed.)) (Harmondsworth, 1985), 313–14.

2. G[eorges] B[ataille], 'Joan Miró: Peintures récentes', *Documents* 2nd Year, 7 (Paris, 1930), 399. Bataille most tellingly demonstrates his awareness of Freud's argument concerning the 'aggressive instinct' in an article juxtaposed with the Miró piece: 'L'Art primitif', 389–97.

3. Freud (1930/1985) *op.cit.*, 279–88.

4. *Ibid.*, 285.

5. Michel Leiris, 'Civilisation', *Documents*, 1st Year, 4 (Paris, 1929), 221.

CHAPTER 11

1. For a fuller discussion of the Dakar-Djibouti expedition, see Chapter 12.

2. There may be a temptation to translate 'art nègre' as black art, but in English too, the term 'negro art' was habitually used, as, for instance, in the title of one of the most influential English language writings on the subject of African sculpture, Roger Fry's essay 'Negro Art', first published in *The Athenaeum* (16 November 1920), and reprinted in his widely read anthology *Vision and Design* (London, 1920). Fry was an anti-Imperialist with relatively advanced liberal attitudes to race, but I find the term too offensive to use in my own account here, and so, at the risk of masking real cultural and social differences between Europe at the turn of a new Millennium and at the beginning of the twentieth century, I will substitute the terms African art, African carving or African sculpture where possible.

3. Michel Leiris, 'L'oeil de l'ethnographe', *Documents*, 2nd Year, 7 (Paris, 1930), 405–14.

4. For Matisse, assimilation and Orientalism, see Chapter 11.

5. This is comprehensively demonstrated by Patricia Leighten in Patricia Leighten, 'The White Peril and *L'Art nègre*: Picasso, Primitivism, and Anticolonialism', *Art Bulletin*, LXXXII, 4 (December 1990), 609–30.

6. Christopher M. Andrew and A.S. Kanya-Forstner, *France Overseas: The Great War and the Climax of French Imperial Expansion* (London, 1981), 226.

7. Apollinaire's myth-making was especially influential in the special number devoted to Rousseau of *les Soirées de Paris* (Paris, January 1914). For Rousseau's actual career as a 'soldier 2nd class', see Henry Certigny, *La Vérité sur le Douanier Rousseau* (Paris, 1961), Chapter XI.

8. Cited in *ibid.*, 248.

9. In *le Journal Suisse* (Lausanne, 25 March 1891).

10. Lanchner and Rubin point out that in 1886 Emile Verhaeren praised Seurat's *Sunday Afternoon on the Grande Jatte*, shown in the same Salon des Indépendants as Rousseau's first exhibits there, as 'painted with the naïvety and honesty of the primitives . . .'. See Carolyn Lanchner and William Rubin, 'Henri Rousseau et le modernisme', in *Le Douanier Rousseau*. Exh. cat. (Galeries nationales du Grand Palais, Paris, and The Museum of Modern Art, New York, 1985), 45.

11. *L'Evènement* (Paris, 18 October 1905). Cited in Certigny (1961) *op.cit.*, 250–1.

12. Gustave Geffroy, 'Paul Cézanne', le *Journal* (Paris, 25 March 1894); Emile Bernard, 'Paul Cézanne', *L'Occident* (July 1904).

13. See Chapter 9.

14. Leo Stein, *Appreciations: Painting, Poetry, and Prose* (New York, 1947), 192. Cited in Jack Flam, *Matisse. The Man and his Art, 1869–1918* (London, 1986), 175.

15. Cited in Lanchner and Rubin (1985) *op.cit.*, 53.

16. The fullest discussion of the African and Oceanic sources for Picasso's painting from 1906–7, including the problem of the *Demoiselles d'Avignon*, is William Rubin, 'Picasso', in William Rubin (ed.), *'Primitivism' in 20th Century*

Art. Vol. I. (The Museum of Modern Art, New York, 1984).

17. See Maurice de Vlaminck, *Tournant dangereux* (Paris, 1929), 71. For Rousseau and Jarry, see Henri Béhar, 'Jarry, Rousseau et le populaire', in *Rousseau* (1985), 25ff.

18. Louis Vauxcelles, 'Le Salon d'automne', *Gil Blas* (Paris, 5 October 1906). Cited in James D.Herbert, *Fauve Painting: The Making of Cultural Politics* (New Haven and London, 1992), 28.

19. Gelett Burgess, 'The Wild Men of Paris', *The Architectural Record* (New York, May 1910), 410.

20. René Fage, *Vers les steppes et les oasis: Algérie-Tunisie* (Paris, 1906), 183. Cited in Herbert (1992) *op.cit.*, 160–1. I am indebted to Herbert in this discussion.

21. An illustrated summary of the accepted possible sources, European as well as non-European, for the *Demoiselles d'Avignon* is to be found under the heading 'Choses vues' in *Les Demoiselles d'Avignon*. Exh. cat. (Musée Picasso, Paris, 1988), 4–13. A summary is also supplied in William Rubin, *Les Demoiselles d'Avignon* (Studies in Modern Art 3, The Museum of Modern Art, New York, 1994), Chapter 1, 'The Critical Heritage'.

22. Leo Steinberg, 'The Philosophical Brothel', *October*, 44 (New York and Cambridge, Mass., Spring 1988), 7–74. Revised version of an essay first published in *Art News* vol. 71, 5, 6 (New York, September and October 1972). No analysis of the *Demoiselles* can ignore this contribution.

23. The hypothesis is most fully explored by William Rubin, who is the art-historian to have made the most important contribution to knowledge about the picture. See Rubin (1994) *op.cit.*

24. André Malraux, *La Tête d'obsidienne* (Paris, 1974), 18.

25. Rubin (1994) *op.cit.*

26. André Salmon, *La Jeune Peinture française* (Paris, 1912), 43.

27. Burgess (1910) *loc.cit.*, 408.

28. The case is persuasively put in Leighten (1990). I am indebted to Leighten for my discussion on questions of race and the functioning of the myth of 'Africa' in the *Demoiselles*.

29. The counter-case is equally persuasively put in David Lomas, 'A Canon of Deformity: *Les Demoiselles d'Avignon* and Physical Anthropology', *Art History*, vol. 16, 3 (September 1993), 424–46. It should be added that Leighten herself does discuss at length the negative and racist side of modernism altogether.

30. D-H. Kahnweiler, *Der Weg zum Kubismus* (Munich, 1920).

31. Salmon (1912) *op.cit.*, 43.

32. Daniel-Henry Kahnweiler, 'L'art nègre et le cubisme', *Présence Africaine*, 3 (Paris-Dakar, 1948); in Kahnweiler, *Confessions esthétique* (Paris, 1963), 222–36.

33. Salmon (1912) *op.cit.*, 43–7.

34. Miller is the scholar who has presented the evidence most comprehensively. See Sanda Miller, *Constantin Brancusi. A Survey of his Work* (Oxford, 1995), 24–34.

35. Edith Balas, *Brancusi and Romanian Folk Traditions* (Boulder, Col., 1987), 1.

36. Benjamin Fondane, in *Cahiers de l'Etoile* (Paris, September/October 1929). Cited in Pontus Hulten, Natalia Dumitresco, Alexandre Istrati, *Brancusi* (London, 1986), 192.

37. Henri Rousseau to André Dupont, in *les Soirées de Paris*, 20 (Paris, January 1914), 57.

38. This point was first made in Lanchner and Rubin (1985) *op.cit.*

39. Salmon (1912) *op.cit.*

40. Funetières, *Le Soleil* (Paris, 2 April 1907). Cited in Certigny (1961) *op.cit.*, 271.

41. Miller argues persuasively for the importance to Brancusi of Nadelman, who scored a major success among modernists with a solo show at the galerie Druet in 1909. Miller (1995) *op.cit.*, 123–7.

42. Brancusi's statement appears in *This Quarter*, Art Supplement, vol. 1, 1 (1925). The argument against the small version as the first is put in *ibid.*, 69ff.

43. See Sidney Geist, *Brancusi/The Kiss* (New York, Hagerstown, San Francisco and London, 1978), 37.

44. The Senufo comparison is seriously undermined by the fact that such pieces seem not to have arrived in Paris until later. The comparison is made in Sidney Geist, 'Brancusi', in William Rubin (ed.), *'Primitivism' in 20th Century Art: Affinity of the Tribal and the Modern*, II. Exh. cat. (The Museum of Modern Art, New York) 1984, 348–51.

45. Constantin Brancusi, 'Aphorisms', in *Brancusi*. Exh. cat. (Brummer Gallery, New York, 1926).

46. Brancusi quoted in Dorothy Dudley, 'Brancusi', *Dial* (February 1927). Cited in Anna C. Chave, *Constantin Brancusi. Shifting the Bases of Art* (New Haven and London, 1993), 166.

47. The structural and decorative forms of peasant architecture in the Gorj region of Romania are fully introduced in Miller (1995) *op.cit.*, Chapter 1. The most comprehensive discussion of Brancusi's sculpture in relation to Romanian folk art and folklore is Edith Balas, 'The Sculpture of Brancusi in the Light of his Romanian Heritage'. Ph.D. Thesis, University of Pittsburgh, 1973, whose findings are more accessibly available in Edith Balas, 'The Sculpture of Brancusi in the Light of his Romanian Heritage', *Art Journal*, vol. 35, 2 (1975–6), 94–104.

48. Geist finds an echo of a pattern in the background of a 1911–12 Modigliani portrait, which is possibly from an African textile owned by the sitter, Dr Paul Alexandre, who knew Brancusi. Modigliani and Brancusi met in 1909. See Geist (1984) *op.cit.*, 356–7. Geist argues that the stimulus of African sculpture was important to the exclusion of Romanian memories. I disagree.

49. For discussion of this challenge, see Chapter 12.

50. My thanks to Patricia Leighten for suggesting this possibility.

51. Charles-Edouard Jeanneret (Le Corbusier) and Amédée Ozenfant, *Après le cubisme* (Paris, 1918), 16.

52. André Salmon, 'l'entrée au Louvre du Douanier Rousseau', *L'Art vivant* (Paris, 1 November 1925), 30. The picture was bequeathed by Jacques Doucet. It did not enter the Louvre until 1936.

53. Undated jotting from notebook, cited in Dumitrescu et al. (1986) *op.cit.*, 177.

54. Draft of a letter from Constantin Brancusi to John Quinn, December 1918. Cited in *ibid.*, 121.

55. These negative responses are discussed in Christopher Green, *Cubism and its Enemies: Modern Movements and Reaction in French Art, 1916–1928* (New Haven and London, 1987), 81.

56. Guillaume Apollinaire, 'Exoticisme et ethnographie', *Paris-Journal* (Paris, 12 September 1912); in *Guillaume Apollinaire on Art: Essays and Reviews, 1902–1918*, Leroy C. Breunig (ed.), translated by Susan Suleiman (New York and London, 1972), 144.

57. Michel Puy, 'Les Indépendants', *Les Marges* (Paris, 1911). Cited as translated in Edward F. Fry, *Cubism* (London, 1966), 65.

58. Salmon (1912) *op.cit.*

59. Poincaré's books were: *La Science et l'hypothèse* (1902), *La Valeur de la science* (1904), and *Science et méthode* (1908). The relevance of his ideas to the Cubist milieux are very fully discussed in Linda Dalrymple Henderson, *The Fourth Dimension and Non-Euclidean Geometry in Modern Art* (Princeton, NJ, 1983). I am indebted to Henderson in my discussion here.

60. For a fuller discussion of this, see Chapter 7.

61. Jarry as cited by Henderson. Ibid., 47.

62. Vauxcelles as cited from D-H. Kahnweiler's press albums at the galerie Louise Leiris in Judith Cousins, with the collaboration of Pierre Daix, 'Documentary Chronology'; in William Rubin, *Picasso and Braque: Pioneering Cubism*. Exh. cat. (The Museum of Modern Art, New York, 1989), 389.

63. This is demonstrated in Chapter 12.

64. For a discussion of this, see Chapter 12.

65. G.H. Luquet, *Dessins d'un enfant* (Paris, 1913), 186.

66. Lucien Lévy-Bruhl, *Les Fonctions mentales dans les sociétés inférieures* (Paris, 1910), 77.

67. Henri Bergson, *Time and Free Will: An Essay on the Immediate Data of Consciousness*, authorised translation by F.L. Pogson (London and New York, 1959; 1st French ed. 1889). As cited in Mark Antliff, 'Bergson and Cubism: A Reassessment', *Art Journal* (Winter 1988), 343.

CHAPTER 12

1. The correspondence in question is excerpted in Pontus Hulten, Natalia Dumitresco, Alexandre Istrati, *Brancusi* (London, 1986), 110–22. It is Miller who records that Quinn was sent three bases for *The Maiastra*. See Sanda Miller, *Constantin Brancusi. A Survey of his Work* (Oxford, 1995), 177.

2. The correspondence between Brancusi and Alfred Stieglitz is excerpted in Hulten et al. *Ibid.*, 94–8.

3. The connection is made in Miller (1995) *op.cit.*, 178.

4. The letter in which Brancusi itemises and prices *Child in the World*, enclosing the photograph, is dated 27 December 1917. See Hulten et al. (1986) *op.cit.*, 110.

5. Quinn did not buy *Child of the World*. Brancusi was never to sell a 'mobile group' as such.

6. Brancusi's photograph of this 'mobile group' is reproduced in Anna C. Chave, *Constantin Brancusi. Shifting the Bases of Art* (New Haven and London, 1993), 152.

7. Brancusi interviewed by Roger Devigne in *L'Ere nouvelle* (Paris, 28 January 1920). Cited in Hulten et al. (1986) *op.cit.*, 130.

8. W.H. de B. Nelson, 'Aesthetic Hysteria', *International Studio*, vol. 61, 244 (New York, June 1917), ccxxi–ccxxv. Cited in William A. Camfield, *Marcel Duchamp. Fountain* (The Menil Collection, Houston, 1989), 56. The *Vanity Fair* reference is made in Alexandra Parigoris, 'Brancusi, A Peasant in Paris: A Study of the Persona and Work of Constantin Brancusi from a Post-Symbolist

Perspective' Ph.D. Thesis, Courtauld Institute, London, 1998, Chapter 4.

9. I cite here from Louise Norton, 'Buddha of the Bathroom', *The Blind Man*, 2 (New York, May 1917), 6. The reference to a Madonna comes from an undated letter, attributed to April 5 1917, from Carl Van Vechten to Gertrude Stein. See Carl Van Vechten, *The Letters of Gertrude Stein and Carl Van Vechten*, Edward Burns (ed.) (New York, 1986), 58–9. Both sources are cited by Parigoris in ibid., 35 and 40.

10. The first to bring out the connections between *Fountain* and *Princess X* was Camfield in his exhaustive study of the former. Ibid., 54–6.

11. Parigoris notes the fact that it was removed from the Salon d'Antin. She argues, further, that the work was conceived and refined in the context of the suggestive eroticism practiced by Apollinaire, Picabia and Duchamp before 1912, and that it was, therefore, from the beginning knowingly erotic. I find her case for seeing *Princess X* as a Dada gesture persuasive. See Parigoris (1998) *op.cit.*, Chapter 4.

12. The face-as-hole was apparently said by Brancusi himself to be a passageway through which 'the whole universe flows'. See Hulten et al. (1986) *op.cit.*, 148. Chave brings out the challenge in *Socrates*. See Chave (1993) *op.cit.*, 175.

13. This point is made by Chave, see *ibid.*, 181.

14. Rudolf Kuenzli, 'Introduction', in Rudolf Kuenzli and Francis M. Naumann (eds.), *Marcel Duchamp. Artist of the Century* (Cambridge, Mass., and London, 1990), 5.

15. Anon., 'His Art Too Crude for Independents', *The New York Herald* (New York, 14 April 1917), 6; cited in Camfield (1989) *op.cit.*, 27.

16. Letter from Katherine S. Dreier to Marcel Duchamp, 13 April 1917. Archives of the Société Anonyme. Cited in *ibid.*, 31.

17. Unsigned editorial (probably by Beatrice Wood), *The Blind Man*, 2 (New York, May 1917).

18. Marcel Duchamp to Suzanne Duchamp, 11 April 1917; in Francis M. Naumann, 'Affectueusement, Marcel', *Archives of American Art Journal*, vol. 22, 4 (Washington, DC, 1982), 8.

19. Note from the *La Boîte de 1914*. In Michel Sanouillet (ed.), Marcel Duchamp, *Duchamp du signe. Ecrits* (Paris, 1975), 45.

20. Norton (1917) *loc.cit.*, 6. Cited in Camfield (1989) *op.cit.*, 39.

21. Sanouillet in Sanouillet/Duchamp (1975) *op.cit.*, 39.

22. Duchamp in *Ibid.*, 46.

23. *Ibid.*, 42.

24. *Ibid.*, 62–3.

25. *Ibid.*, 63.

26. *Ibid.*, 41. The key to Bergson's notion of 'duration' as grasped by 'intuition', is the experience of time as unmeasurable flux. Duchamp's notes repeatedly suggest procedures using the timed recording of results. Time throughout is measurable; it is space that is sometimes not. In this way, he reverses Bergson's idea of the nature of time and space. The first to discuss Duchamp as an anti-Bergsonian was Ivor Daries, in 'New Reflections on the "Large Glass",' *Art History* (Oxford, March 1979) pp. 85–94. For a very full discussion of Bergson and Duchamp, see Linda Dalrimple Henderson, *Duchamp in Context. Science and Technology in the 'Large Glass' and Related Works* (Princeton, NJ, 1998).

27. *391*, 18 (Paris, 1 July 1924).

28. This text, headed 1912, is usually referred to as 'The Jura-Paris Road'. Sanouillet/Duchamp (1975) *op.cit.*, 41–2.

29. André Breton et al., 'La Révolution d'abord et toujours', *La Révolution surréaliste*, 5 (Paris, 15 October 1925), 31.

30. Max Ernst, 'Les mystères de la forêt', *Minotaure*, no. 5 (15 February 1934), 6.

31. André Breton, 'Des tendances les plus récentes de la peinture surréaliste', *Minotaure*, 3rd series, 12–13 (Paris, May 1939), 17.

32. Fiona Bradley, 'An Oxymoronic Encounter: Surrealism and Catholicism in France between the Wars' Ph.D. Thesis, Courtauld Institute of Art, London, 1995. I am indebted to Bradley here for her brilliant analysis of the way parody, blasphemy and sacrilege are used in the Surrealist encounter with Roman Catholicism.

33. This is a point made by Bradley. *Ibid.* Also important for this topic is René Rémond, *L'Anticléricalisme en France de 1815 à nos jours* (Paris, 1976).

34. Louis Aragon, *Le Paysan de Paris* (Paris, 1926), 90, 144–6, 49–53, 30–33 (in order of citation).

35. This aspect of the argument is largely put in Rosalind Krauss, 'Photography in the Service of Surrealism', in Rosalind Krauss and Jane Livingstone (eds.), *L'Amour fou: Photography and Surrealism*. Exh. cat. (Hayward Gallery, London, 1986), 15–42.

36. Georges Bataille, 'Informe', *Documents*, 1st Year, 7 (Paris, 1929), 382.

37. The *informe* is dealt with in Rosalind Krauss, 'Corpus Delicti', in *ibid.*, 57–100. Krauss had previously invoked the concept in 'Giacometti', in William Rubin (ed.), *'Primivism' in 20th Century Art: Affinity of the Tribal and the Modern*, II. Exh. cat. (Museum of Modern Art, New York, 1984), 514–15; revised as 'No More Play', in Rosalind Krauss, *The Originality of the Avant-Garde and Other Modernist Myths* (Cambridge, Mass., and London, 1985).

38. André Breton, 'La beauté sera convulsive', *Minotaure*, 5 (Paris, 1934), 9–16.

39. Krauss (1986) *op.cit.*, 31–5. The centrality of the notion of convulsive beauty is affirmed at length in Hal Foster, *Compulsive Beauty* (Cambridge, Mass., and London, 1993).

40. Breton (1939) *loc.cit.*, 16.

41. André Breton, *Manifeste du surréalisme* (Paris, 1924), in Breton, *Manifestes du surréalisme* (Paris, 1972), 40.

42. Aragon (1926) *op.cit.*, 78.

43. Breton (1939) *loc.cit.*, 16.

44. Louis Aragon, *Une Vague de rêves* (Paris, 1924), 23.

45. Louis Aragon, 'La Peinture au défi', preface to the catalogue of the *Exposition des collages* (Galerie Goemans, Paris, 1930), in Aragon, *Écrits sur l'art*, Jean Risart (ed.), (Paris, 1981).

46. It is worth observing, as Krauss does, that, though the mechanistic character of photography always prevented the photographer from leaving his or her mark, Surrealist photography often did inscribe the process within its images: by, for instance, the angling of the camera, the manipulation of light and the intervention of the photographer in the processes of development. Much photography which is not Surrealist uses such techniques to inscribe the active presence of the photographer in what is too easily taken to be a mechanical image.

47. Christian Zervos, 'Picasso', *Cahiers d'art*, 3–5 (Paris, 1932), 87.

48. I am indebted here to Gasman's analysis of *The Three Dancers*. See Lydia Gasman, 'Mystery, Magic and Love in Picasso, 1925–1938. Picasso and the Surrealist Poets.' Ph.D. Thesis, Columbia University, 1981, Chapter IX.

49. André Masson in Françoise Will-Levaillant (ed.), *Le Rebelle du surréalisme. Ecrits* (Paris, 1976), 12.

50. Louis Aragon and André Breton, 'Centennaire de l'hystérie (1878–1928), *La Révolution surréaliste*, 4th Year, 11 (15 March 1928), 20–1. See also Briony Fer, 'Surrealism, Myth and Psychoanalysis', in Briony Fer, David Batchelor and Paul Wood, *Realism, Rationalism, Surrealism. Art between the Wars* (New Haven, Conn., and London, 1993), 212.

51. Hans Prinzhorn, *Bildenrei der Geisteskranken* (Berlin, 1922), translated as *Artistry of the Mentally Ill: A Contribution to the Psychology and Pathology of Configuration* (Berlin, Heidelberg and New York, 1972). The Surrealists responded to the Papin sisters in *Le Surréalisme au service de la révolution*, 5 (Paris, May 1933).

52. André Breton, *Second manifeste du surréalisme* (Paris, 1929); in Breton (1972) *op.cit.*, 135.

53. *Ibid.*, 139.

54. These connections are made in R.T. Doepel, 'Zoharic Imagery in the Work of Miró (1924–1933), *South African Journal of Cultural and Art History*, vol. 1, 1 (1987).

55. The case for alchemy in the *Large Glass* is succinctly put in John Golding, *The Bride Stripped Bare by her Bachelors, Even* (London, 1973), 85ff. Duchamp and alchemy is a theme explored further in David Hopkins, *Marcel Duchamp and Max Ernst: the Bride Shared* (Oxford, 1998).

56. Hermes Trismegistus', text the *Emerald Table* appeared in French in 1921. For Ernst and alchemy, see: Geoffrey Hinton, 'Max Ernst: "Les Hommes n'en Sauront Rien"', *The Burlington Magazine*, CXVII (London, May 1975), 292; Elizabeth M. Legge, *Max Ernst: The Psychoanalytic Sources* (Ann Arbor, 1989), 84–98; and William A. Camfield, *Max Ernst: Dada and the Dawn of Surrealism* (Munich/Houston, 1993), 136.

57. See Herbert Silberer, *Probleme der Mystik und Ihrer Symbolik* (Vienna, 1914); C.G. Jung, *Das Geheimnis der goldenen Blüte* (Zurich, 1929) and *Psychologie und Alchemie* (Zurich, 1944), translated by R.F.C. Hull as *Psychology and Alchemy* (Princeton, NJ, 1968). The Silberer connection was first made by David Hopkins. See Hopkins (1998) *op.cit.*

58. The case for the importance of Jung to the Surrealists is persuasively made in Clio Mitchell, 'Secrets de l'art magique surréaliste: Magic and the Myth of the Artist-Magician in Surrealist Aesthetic Theory and Practice', unpublished dissertation submitted for the degree of Ph.D., (Courtauld Institute of Art, University of London, 1993) especially 140–51, 178–83. Roudinesco argues that Jung's interest in the beyond was not compatible with Surrealist priorities. See Elisabeth Roudinesco, *La bataille de cent ans. Histoire de la psychanalyse en France*, vol. II, *1925–1985* (Paris, 1986), 27–8.

59. See Legge (1989) *op.cit.*

60. Important instances are: *Psychopathology of Everyday Life* (1901); French translation, 1922; *Totem and Taboo* (1913), 1924; *The Interpretation of Dreams* (1901), 1925; *Three Essays on Sexuality* (1905), 1927. A list of the dates of French translations of Freud's works between 1920 and 1940 is given in Roudinesco (1986) *op.cit.*, 477–9.

61. The letters of 1916 are to Théodore Fraenkel. They are cited by Bonnet, who discusses the evidence fully and argues against Janet as a positive influence. The Janet source referred to is his *L'Automatisme psychique*. See

Marguerite Bonnet, *André Breton. Naissance de l'aventure surréaliste* (Paris, 1975), 98–111.

62. It appeared in *Essais de psychanalyse appliqué* (Paris, 1933).

63. The first to bring into the reckoning Freud's 'Essay on the Uncanny' was Krauss in 'Giacometti' (1984/5) *op.cit.* She elaborated on this in Krauss (1986) *op.cit.* More recently, important discussions of the concept applied to Surrealism have appeared in Fer, in Fer et al. (1993) *op.cit.*, and in Foster (1993) *op.cit.* The notion of fetishism is discussed both revealingly and in a fuller historical context in Dawn Ades, 'Surrealism: Fetishism's Job', in Anthony Shelton (ed.), *Fetishism. Visualising Power and Desire*. Exh. cat. (Brighton Museum and Art Gallery, 1995).

64. André Breton, 'Position politique de l'art d'aujourd'hui' (Prague, 1935). As cited in Whitney Chadwick, *Myth in Surrealist Painting, 1929–1939* (Ann Arbor and London, 1980), 9.

65. Elizabeth Legge is the scholar who has suggested these readings, see Legge (1989) *op.cit.*, 36–48.

66. See Werner Spies, 'Une Poétique du collage', in *Paul Eluard et ses amis peintres* Exh. cat. (Musée national d'art moderne, Centre Georges Pompidou, Paris, 1982), 64; and Jeanne Siegel, 'The Image of the Eye in Surrealist Art and its Psychoanalytic Sources. Part One. The Mythic Eye', *Arts Magazine*, 56 (February 1982), 102–6.

67. Alberto Giacometti, 'Hier, sables mouvants', *Le Surréalisme au service de la révolution*, 5 (Paris, 15 May 1933), 15.

68. Alberto Giacometti, 'Je ne puis parler qu'indirectement de mes sculptures', *Minotaure*, 3–4 (Paris, 12 December 1933), 46.

69. Cited from Freud's 'Essay on the Uncanny', in Krauss (1986), 82.

70. Lacan's theory of the 'mirror stage' was first presented publicly in 1936, though not published until 1949. For an introduction to this, see: Bice Benevuto and Roger Kennedy, *The Works of Jacques Lacan: An Introduction* (London, 1986), Chapter 2.

71. André Breton, *Introduction au discours sur le peu de réalité* (Paris, 1924).

72. Sigmund Freud, *Totem and Taboo* (1913); in Freud, *The Origins of Religion*, James Strachey (ed.), The Pelican Freud Library, 13 (London, 1985), 148–9.

73. Louis Aragon, 'La Peinture au défi' (Paris, 1930); in Aragon, *Ecrits sur l'art moderne*, Jean Risart (ed.) (Paris, 1981), 44; Waldemar George, 'Franc jeu. La Passion de Picasso', *Formes*, 4 (Paris, April 1930), 9; Anon., *L'Humanité* (Paris, 22 May 1930).

74. Carl Einstein, 'Joan Miró (papiers collés à la galerie Pierre)', *Documents*, 2nd Year, 4 (Paris, 1930), 243.

75. Michel Leiris, 'Miró', *Documents*, 1st Year, 4 (Paris, 1929), 263–4.

76. These connections and the topic of Miró and infantilism as a whole are fully discussed in Christopher Green, 'The Infant in the Adult: Joan Miró and the Infantile Image'; in Jonathan Fineberg (ed.), *Discovering the Child. Essays on Childhood, Primitivism and Modernism* (Princeton, NJ, 1998), 210–34.

77. It should be noted, however, that Freud implied that this was at a much earlier age.

78. The key books in the presentation of Piaget's theory are: *Le Langage et la pensée chez l'enfant* (Paris, 1923) and *La Représentation du monde chez l'enfant* (Paris, 1926).

79. This is discussed in Mitchell (1993) *op.cit.* 126–30.

80. The 'white monkey mask of the Ireli', which Leiris's diary shows especially impressed him. *See* Michel Leiris, *L'Afrique fantôme* (Paris, 1981; 1st ed. 1934), 151.

81. Marcel Griaule, 'Un coup de fusil', *Documents*, 2nd Year, 1 (Paris, 1930), 46.

82. Marcel Mauss & Henri Hubert, *Esquisse d'une théorie de la magie* (Paris, 1902–3); in Marcel Mauss, *Sociologie et anthropologie* (Paris, 1966), 60–71.

83. See Gasman (1981) *op.cit.*

84. See Chapter 11.

85. This development, its relation to Freud's ideas on the 'uncanny', and to Surrealist theory and practice is discussed in Foster (1993) *op.cit.*, Chapter 1.

86. Georges Bataille, 'Joan Miró: Peintures récentes', *Documents*, 2nd Year, 7 (Paris, 1930), 309.

87. Bataille's key article on materialism is: 'Le bas-matérialisme et la gnose', *Documents*, 2nd year, 1 (Paris, 1930), 1–8. See also: Roger Hervé, 'Sacrifices humains du centre-Amérique', *Documents*, 2nd Year, 4 (Paris, 1930), 205–13; and Michel Leiris, 'Le taureau de Seyfou Tchenger', *Minotaure*, 2 (Paris, May 1933), 75–82.

88. Georges Bataille, 'La structure psychologique du fascisme', *La Critique sociale*, 10 (Paris, November 1933), 159–65, and 11 (Paris, March 1933), 205–11.

89. Cited in Jerome Seckler, 'Picasso Explains', *New Masses* (New York, 13 March 1945), 7. In Ellen C. Oppler (ed.), *Picasso's 'Guernica'* (New York and London, 1988), 151.

90. George L. Steer, 'The Tragedy of Guernica', *The Times* (London, 28 April 1937); in *ibid.*, 160–3.

91. Christian Zervos, 'Histoire d'un tableau de Picasso', *Cahiers d'art*, vol. 12, 4–5 (Paris, 1937), 105–11.

92. In broad terms, the composition of *Guernica* repeats that of the etching, in reverse, i.e., as it was drawn by Picasso onto the plate.

93. Information from a letter to Ellen C. Oppler from Juan Larrea, 10 December 1970, in Oppler (1988) *op.cit.*, 201.

94. Josep Lluis Sert, typescript of a statement made at a symposium held in the Museum of Modern Art, New York, 25 November 1947. In *ibid.*, 199–200.

95. Anthony Blunt, 'Picasso Unfrocked', *The Spectator* (London, 8 October 1937).

96. Pierre Naville, *La Révolution et les intellectuels: que peuvent faire les surréalistes?* (Paris, 1926), 30.

97. André Breton, 'Légitime défence', *La Révolution surréaliste*, 8 December 1926).

98. Louis Aragon, *Pour un réalisme socialiste* (Paris, 1935), 53 and 74. As cited in translation in Helena Lewis, *The Politics of Surrealism* (New York, 1988), 115.

99. André Breton, 'Discours au congrès des écrivains', in Breton, *Position politique du surréalisme* (Paris, 1935), 96–8; and André Breton and Leon Trotsky, *Pour un art révolutionnaire indépendant* (1938), in Trotsky, *Culture and Socialism and a Manifesto: Art and Revolution* (London, 1963), 37–8. Both texts cited from *ibid.*, 131 and 146.

100. Pierre Quillard, 'L'anarchie par la littérature', *Entretiens politiques et Littéraires* (April 1892), 150–1. Cited from Patricia Leighten, *Reordering the Universe. Picasso and Anarchism, 1897–1914* (Princeton, NJ, 1989), 40.

101. Paul Signac, unpublished mss., *c.*1902. Cited *ibid.*

102. *L'Ami du peuple* (Paris, 7 December 1930). Cited from Lewis (1988) *op.cit.*, 93.

103. *L'Humanité* (Paris, 7 December 1930). Cited from *ibid.*, 94.

104. Interview with Pol Gaillard, *L'Humanité* (Paris, 29–30 October 1944). Cited as translated in Leighten (1989) *op.cit.*, 97.

105. The point is made by Leighten, to whose work I am indebted here. See ibid., Chapter 5.

106. For Leighten's argument see *ibid.* Richardson disagrees with Leighten on several points and downplays Picasso's anarchist links, but agrees that he was a pacifist from early on. See John Richardson, with the collaboration of Marilyn McCully, *A Life of Picasso. Volume II: 1907–1917* (New York and London, 1996), 343ff.

107. Another reading of *Bottle of Suze* and of the collages which include cuttings referring to the Balkan wars which also brings out their openness is David Cottington, *Cubism in the Shadow of War. The Avant-Garde and Politics in Paris, 1905–1914* (New Haven and London, 1998), 128–30.

108. Leighten herself notes that Picasso did not use cuttings from anarchist or radical newspapers; she argues that descriptive accounts aimed at a mass readership could act more effectively than political rhetoric in his collages. Though she insists that the newspaper cuttings in a work like *Bottle of Suze* gave voice to an explicitly anarchist position on the Balkan wars, she accepts that much of his work in 1912–14 followed the anarchist strategy of subversion through the free practice of art rather than the practice of propaganda.

109. José Bergamin, 'Introduction', Klaus Gallwitz, *Picasso at 90: The Late Work* (New York, 1971), 9. Cited from Oppler (1988) *op.cit.*, 201–2.

110. Max Raphael, *The Demands of Art* (Princeton, NJ, 1968) Chapter V. Excerpted in *ibid.*, 261–7.

111. Herbert Read in *London Bulletin*, vol. VI (October 1938), 6 (in *ibid.*, 217–18); Roland Penrose, *Picasso: His Life and Work* (London, 1958); William Rubin, *Dada and Surrealist Art* (New York, 1968), 290–309.

112. 'Le mystère tremble: Picasso furioso', *Cahiers d'art*, vol. 12, 4–5 (Paris, 1937), 135–9. Cited as translated in Oppler (1988) *op.cit.*, 212.

113. Public attention was first drawn to the significance of the performance of *El Cerco de Numancia* by Sarah Wilson, who was alerted by a Sorbonne doctorate by François Moulignat. See Sarah Wilson, 'Problèmes de la peinture en marge de l'Exposition Internationale', in Musée nationale d'art moderne, *Paris-Paris*, exh. cat. (Paris, Centre Georges Pompidou, 1981) 44–5. For a recent discussion which especially suggestively makes the case for *Guernica* as, at one level, simultaneously a response to Barrault's production of the play and to the destruction of the town, see: Kathleen Brunner, 'Picasso Rewriting Picasso: Poetry and Plays 1935–1959'. Unpublished dissertation submitted for the degree of Ph.D. (Courtauld Institute, University of London, 1997) 131–6.

114. Zervos (1937) *loc cit.*

Select Bibliography

BIBLIOGRAPHICAL NOTE

This bibliography is divided into three sections: I. General Historical Matierial, II. Source Material, and III. Secondary Material: Books, Exhibition Catalogues and Articles. The items are individually numbered I.1 etc., II.1 etc., and III.1 etc. Despite the importance of contextual material involving such fields as literature, philosophy and psychoanalysis to the study of art in France in this period, this bibliography only includes such material where it directly bears on the history of visual art, for instance in the case of major writings by André Breton. Otherwise, with the exception of the general historical section, it focuses exclusively on material on art and material produced by or dealing with artists. Much important work in the field has been produced in the form of doctoral theses. I have not included theses in this bibliography, because, given my own teaching position, my listing would inevitably be biased towards theses produced in English universities, and so would not be a balanced sample. Those theses I have found especially important in the writing of this book are, of course, acknowledged and referenced in the footnotes in the body of the text.

Since the items in each of the three sections are arranged alphabetically by author or publishing institution, an index is given at the end of the Bibliography as a guide to material on individual artists and the major modern movements. In this index references to the Bibliography are given by number.

I. GENERAL HISTORICAL MATERIAL

I.1. AGERON, CHARLES-ROBERT. *France coloniale ou parti coloniale*, Paris, 1978.

I.2. ALDRICH, ROBERT. *Greater France. A History of French Overseas Expansion*, London, 1996.

I.3. BECKER, JEAN-JACQUES. *Les Français dans la grande-guerre*, Paris, 1983; translated by Arnold Pomerans as *The Great War and the French People*, Leamington Spa, Heidelberg and Dover, NH, 1985.

I.4. BERSTEIN, SERGE. *La France des années 30*, Paris, 1988.

I.5. BRUBAKER, ROGERS. *Citizenship and Nationhood in France and Germany*, Cambridge, Mass and London, 1992.

I.6. JACKSON, JULIAN. *The Popular Front in France. Defending Democracy, 1934–38*, Cambridge, 1988.

I.7. KRIEGEL, ANNIE. *Les Communistes français*. Paris, 1968; translated by Elaine P. Halperin as *French Communists: Profile of a People*, Chicago and London, 1972.

I.8. LEBOVICS, HERMAN. *True France. The Wars over Cultural Identity, 1900–1945*. Ithaca and London, 1992.

I.9. MCMILLAN, JAMES F. *Housewife to Harlot: The Place of Women in French Society 1870–1940*, Brighton, 1981.

I.10. MCMILLAN, JAMES F. *Dreyfus to De Gaulle: Society in France 1898–1969*. London, 1985.

I.11. MAJEUR, JEAN-MARIE and REBERIOUX, MADELEINE. *Les Débuts de la Troisième République* and *La République radicale?*, Paris, 1973 and 1975; translated by J.R.Foster as *The Third Republic from its Origins to the Great War 1871–1914*. Cambridge, 1984.

I.12. MILLER, MICHAEL B. *The Bon Marché. Bourgeois Culture and the Department Store 1869–1920*, Princeton, 1981.

I.13. MORTIMER, E. *The Rise of the French Communist Party 1920–1970*, London, 1984.

I.14. NORA, PIERRE (ed.). *Les Lieux de mémoire* (7 vols) Paris, 1984–92; translated in 3 vols by Arthur Goldhammer as *Realms of Memory*, New York, 1996–7.

I.15. ORY, PASCAL and SIMINELLI, JEAN-FRANÇOIS. *Les Intellectuels en France, de l'Affaire Dreyfus à nos jours*, Paris, 1986.

—— REBERIOUX, MADELEINE, see Majeur, Jean-Marie.

I.16. ROUDINESCO, ELISABETH. *La Bataille de cent ans. Histoire de la psychanalyse en France* (2 vols), Paris, 1986, vol.2 translated as *Jacques Lacan and Co.: a History of Psychoanalysis in France*. London, 1990.

I.17. SAID, EDOUARD. *Orientalism*, New York, 1978.

I.18. SCHOR, RALPH. *L'Opinion française et les étrangers en France 1919–1939*, Paris, 1985.

I.19. SCHOR, RALPH. *L'Antisémitisme en France pendant les années trente*, Paris, 1992.

—— SIMINELLI, JEAN-FRANÇOIS, see Ory, Pascal.

I.20. STERNHELL, ZEEV. *Maurice Barrès et le nationalisme français*, Paris, 1972.

I.21. STERNHELL, ZEEV. *Ni droite, ni gauche. L'idéologie faciste en France.* Paris, 1983 and 1987.

I.22. THÉBAUD, FRANÇOISE. *La Femme au temps de la guerre de 14*, Paris, 1986.

I.23. TOMBS, ROBERT (ed.). *Nationhood and Nationalism in France, from Boulangism to the Great War, 1889–1918*, London, 1991.

I.24. WEBER, EUGEN. *Action française: Royalism and Reaction in Twentieth-Century France*, Berkeley and Los Angeles, 1962; French edition *L'Action française*, Paris, 1962.

I.25. WEBER, EUGEN. *Peasants into Frenchmen. The Modernisation of Rural France, 1870–1914*, London, 1977.

I.26. WEBER, EUGEN. *The Hollow Years: France in the 1930s*, London, 1995.

I.27. ZELDIN, THEODORE. *France 1848–1945* (2 vols) London, 1973 and 1977.

II. SOURCE MATERIAL

(A) *Periodicals*

Note: for periodicals which continued beyond 1940, no end-date is given

II.1. *L'Amour de l'art* (1920–).

II.2. *L'Art vivant* (1925–1939).

II.3. *Art concret* (1930).

II.4. *Bulletin de l'Effort moderne* (Paris, 1924–8).

II.5. *Cahiers d'Abstraction-Création* (Paris, 1932–6).

II.6. *Cahiers d'art* (Paris, 1926–).

II.7. *Cercle et carré* (Paris, 1930). Reprinted, Michel Seuphor (ed.) (Paris, 1971).

II.8. *De Stijl* (Amsterdam and Paris, 1917–28). Reprinted, Ad Peterson (ed.) (Amsterdam and The Hague, 1968).

II.9. *Documents* (Paris, 1929–30). Reprinted, Denise Paulme-Schaeffner, Arlette Albert-Birot and Bernard Noël (eds.) (Paris, 1987).

II.10. *L'Esprit nouveau* (Paris, 1920–5). Reprinted (New York, 1968).

II.11. *Formes* (Paris, 1930–3).

II.12. *Minotaure* (Paris, 1933–9). Reprinted in 3 vols, (Geneva, nd.).

II.13. *Montjoie!* (Paris, 1913–14).

II.14. *La Révolution surréaliste* (Paris, 1924–9). Reprinted (New York, 1968).

II.15. *Soirées de Paris* (Paris, 1913–14).

II.16. *Le Surréalisme au service de la révolution* (Paris, 1931–3). Reprinted (Paris, 1976).

II.17. 391 (Barcelona, New York, Zurich and Paris, 1917–24). Reprinted in 2 vols, Michel Sanouillet (ed.), with, as vol.II, accompanying notes: Sanouillet (Michel), *Francis Picabia et 391* (Paris, 1960).

(B) *Artists' Statements, Writings and Correspondence; Contemporary Texts by Critics, Commentators and Historians; Memoirs*

II.18. APOLLINAIRE, GUILLAUME. *Méditations esthétiques. Les Peintres cubistes* (Paris, 1913); L.C. Breunig and J-Cl. Chevalier (eds), Paris, 1965; translated by Lionel Abel as *The Cubist Painters. Aesthetic Meditations*, New York, 1944, 1949.

II.19. APOLLINAIRE, GUILLAUME. *Chroniques d'art, 1902–1913*, L.C.Breunig (ed.). Paris, 1960; translated by Susan Suleiman as *Apollinaire on Art: Essays and Reviews 1902–1918*, L.C.Breunig (ed.), London, 1972.

II.20. ARAGON, LOUIS. *Une Vague des rêves*, Paris, 1924.

II.21. ARAGON, LOUIS. *Le Paysan de Paris*, Paris, 1926; translated by Simon Watson Taylor as *Paris Peasant*, London, 1971.

II.22. ARAGON, LOUIS. *La Querelle du réalisme*, Paris, 1936.

II.23. ARAGON, LOUIS. *Écrits sur l'art*, Jean Risart (ed.), Paris, 1981.

II.24. ARP, JEAN/HANS. *Collected French Writings: Poems, Essays, Memories*, translated by Joachim Neugrosolel, Marcel Jean (ed.), London, 1974.

II.25. BASLER, ADOLPHE. *La Sculpture moderne en France*, Paris, 1928.

II.26. BATAILLE, GEORGES. *Oeuvres complètes*, vol.1 *Premiers écrits* 1922–1940. *Histoire de l'oeil – L'anus solaire – sacrifices – articles*, Michel Foucault (ed.), Paris, 1970.

II.27. BATAILLE, GEORGES. *Visions of Excess (Selected Writings, 1927–39)*, translated and edited by Allan Stoekl, Minneapolis, 1985.

II.28. BAZIN, GERMAIN and HUYGHE, RENÉ. *Les Contemporains*, Paris, 1939.

II.29. BRAQUE, GEORGES. 'La Peinture et nous, propos de l'artiste . . .', *Cahiers d'art*, 1 Paris, 1954.

II.30. BRASSAÏ, *Conversations avec Picasso*, Paris, 1964, translated by Francis Price as *Picasso and Co*. London, 1967.

II.31. BRETON, ANDRÉ. *Les Pas perdus*, Paris, 1924.

II.32. BRETON, ANDRÉ. *Le Surréalisme et la peinture*, Paris, 1928; translated by Simon Watson Taylor as *Surrealism and Painting*, New York, 1972.

II.33. BRETON, ANDRÉ. *Nadja*, Paris, 1929; translated by Richard Howard, New York, 1960.

II.34. BRETON, ANDRÉ. *L'Amour fou*, Paris, 1937; translated by Mary Ann Caws as *Mad Love*, Lincoln, 1987.

II.35. BRETON, ANDRÉ. *Entretiens*, Paris, 1952.
II.36. BRETON, ANDRÉ. *Manifestes du surréalisme*, Paris, 1972; translated by Richard Seaver and Helen R.Lane as *Manifestoes of Surrealism*, Ann Arbor, Michigan, 1972.
II.37. BRETON, ANDRÉ. *What is Surrealism? Selected Writings*, Franklin Rosemont (ed.), New York, 1978.
II.38. CABANNE, PIERRE. *Entretiens avec Marcel Duchamp*, Paris, 1967; translated by Ron Padgett as *Dialogues with Marcel Duchamp*, London, 1971.
II.39. CENDRARS, BLAISE. *Profond aujourd'hui*, Paris, 1931.
II.40. CLADEL, JUDITH. *Aristide Maillol: Sa vie – son oeuvre – ses idées*, Paris, 1937.
II.41. DALÍ, SALVADOR. *La Femme visible*, Paris, 1930.
II.42. DALÍ, SALVADOR. *The Secret Life of Salvador Dalí*, translated by Haakon M.Chevalier, New York, 1942.
II.43. DELAUNAY, ROBERT. *Du Cubisme à l'art abstrait*, Pierre Francastel (ed.), with a catalogue raisonné by Guy Habasque, Paris, 1957.
II.44. DENIS, MAURICE. *Théories 1890–1910. Du symbolisme et de Gauguin vers un nouvel ordre classique*, Paris, 1912 and 1920.
II.45. DERAIN, ANDRÉ. *Lettres à Vlaminck, suivies de la correspondance de guerre*, Philippe Dagen (ed.), Paris, 1994.
—— DUCHAMP, MARCEL, see Cabanne, Pierre.
II.46. DUCHAMP, MARCEL. *Duchamp du signe. Ecrits*, Michel Sanuouillet (ed.), Paris, 1975.
II.47. DUCHAMP, MARCEL. *Salt Seller. The Essential Writings of Marcel Duchamp*, Michel Sanouillet and Elmer Peterson (eds). London, 1975.
II.48. EINSTEIN, CARL. *Georges Braque*, Paris, 1938.
II.49. ERNST, MAX. *Beyond Painting*, New York, 1948.
II.50. ERNST, MAX. *Écritures*, Paris, 1970.
II.51. FOCILLON, HENRI. *Les Pierres de France*, Paris, 1919.
II.52. FOCILLON, HENRI. *L'Art des sculpteurs romanes*, Paris, 1931.
II.53. FOCILLON, HENRI. *L'Art d'Occident*, Paris, 1938.
II.54. FONTAINAS, ANDRÉ and VAUXCELLES, LOUIS. (with contributions by Waldemar George), *Histoire général de l'art français de la Révolution à nos jours*, Paris, 1922.
II.55. FRY, EDWARD F. *Cubism* [an anthology of primary texts in translation], London, 1966.
II.56. GIACOMETTI, ALBERTO. *Alberto Giacometti. Écrits*, Michel Leiris and Jacques Dupin (eds). Paris, 1990.
II.57. GLEIZES, ALBERT and METZINGER, JEAN. *Du Cubisme*, Paris, 1912; re-printed with a preface by Daniel Robbins, Paris, 1980.
II.58. GLEIZES, ALBERT. *Souvenirs: le cubisme 1908–1914*, Paris, 1957.
II.59. GRIS, JUAN. *Letters of Juan Gris (1913–1927)*, translated and edited by Douglas Cooper, London, 1956.
II.60. GRIS, JUAN. *Juan Gris. Correspondances avec Léonce Rosenberg*, Christian Derouet (ed.), Paris, *Les Cahiers du Musée national d'art moderne*, 1999.
II.61. HUYGHE, RENÉ. *Histoire de l'art contemporain*, Paris, 1935.
II.62. JANNEAU, GUILLAUME. *L'Art cubiste. Théories et réalisations. Étude critique*, Paris, 1929.
II.63. KAHNWEILER, DANIEL-HENRY. as Daniel Henry, *Der Weg zum Kubismus*, Munich, 1920; translated as *The Rise of Cubism*, New York, 1949, and as *Les années héroïques du cubisme*, Paris, 1950.
II.64. KAHNWEILER, DANIEL-HENRY. *Confessions esthétiques*, Paris, 1963.
II.65. KUPKA, FRANTIŠEK. *La Création dans les arts plastiques*, Paris, 1989, translated and edited by Erika Adams from *Tvoreni v umení Vytvarném*, Prague, 1924.
—— LE CORBUSIER, JEANNERET, CHARLES-EDOUARD, see Ozenfant, Amédée.
II.66. LE CORBUSIER. *Vers une architecture*, Paris, 1923; translated by Frederick Etchells as *Towards a New Architecture*, London, 1927.
II.67. LE CORBUSIER. *L'Art décoratif d'aujourd'hui*, Paris, 1925; translated by J.Dunnett as *Decorative Art of Today*, London, 1987.
II.68. LE DORBUSIER. *Urbanisme*, Paris, 1925; translated by Frederick Etchells as *The City of Tomorrow*, London, 1929.
II.69. LE CORBUSIER. *La Ville radieuse*, Paris, 1935 and 1964; translated by Pamela Knight, Eleanor Levieux and Derek Coltman as *The Radiant City. Elements of a doctrine of urbanism to be used as a basis for our machine civilization*, London, 1967.
II.70. LÉGER, FERNAND. *Fonctions de la peinture*, Paris, 1965; translated by Alexandra Anderson as *Functions of painting*, Edward F.Fry (ed.), New York and London, 1973.
II.71. LÉGER, FERNAND. *Lettres à Simone*, Christian Derouet (ed.), Geneva and Paris, 1987.
II.72. LÉGER, FERNAND. *Fernand Léger. Une Correspondance de guerre à Louis Poughon, 1914–1918*, Paris, *Cahiers du Musée national d'art moderne*, 1990.
II.73. LÉGER, FERNAND. *Une Correspondance d'affaires. Correspondances Fernand Léger – Léonce Rosenberg 1917–1937*, Christian Derouet (ed.), Paris, *Cahiers du Musée national d'art moderne*, 1996.
II.74. LIPCHITZ, JACQUES. with H.H.Arnason, *My Life in Sculpture*, London, 1972.
—— LIPCHITZ, JACQUES, see Yvars, J.F.
II.75. MAGRITTE, RENÉ. *Écrits complètes*, André Blavier (ed.), Paris, 1979.
II.76. MÂLE, EMILE. *L'Art allemand et l'art français*, Paris, 1917.
II.77. MASSON, ANDRÉ. *Le Rebelle du surréalisme. Écrits*, Françoise Will-Levaillant (ed.), Paris, 1976.
II.78. MASSON, ANDRÉ. *Les Années surréalistes. Correspondance 1916–1942*, Françoise Levaillant (ed.), Paris, 1990.
II.79. MATISSE, HENRI. *Henri Matisse: écrits et propos sur l'art*, Dominique Fourcade (ed.), Paris, 1972.
II.80. MATISSE, HENRI. *Matisse on Art*, Jack Flam (ed.), London, 1973, New York, 1978.
II.81. MAUCLAIR, CAMILLE. *Trois Crises de l'art actuel*, Paris, 1906.
II.82. MAUCLAIR, CAMILLE. *Albert Besnard: L'homme et l'oeuvre*, Paris, 1914.
II.83. MAUCLAIR, CAMILLE. *La Farce de l'art vivant* and *Les Métèques contre l'art français*, Paris, 1929 and 1930.
II.84. MARTINIE, (A-H.), *La Sculpture*, Paris, 1928?.
II.85. MARX, ROGER. *L'Art social*, Paris, 1912.
II.86. MCCULLY, MARILYN (ed.), *A Picasso Anthology*, London, 1981.
—— METZINGER, JEAN, see Gleizes, Albert.
II.87. MIRÓ, JOAN. *Joan Miró. Selected Writings and Interviews*, translated from the Catalan by Patricia Matthews, Margit Rowell (ed.), London, 1986.
II.88. MONDRIAN, PIET. *The New Art – The New Life. The Collected Writings of Piet Mondrian*, Harry Holtzman and Martin S.James (eds). London, 1987.
II.89. OLIVIER, FERNANDE. *Picasso et ses amis*, Paris, 1933; translated by Jane Miller as *Picasso and his Friends*, London, 1964.
II.90. OLIVIER, FERNANDE. *Souvenirs intimes*, Paris, 1988.
II.91. OZENFANT, AMÉDÉE and JEANNERET, CHARLES-EDOUARD. *Après le cubisme*, Paris, 1918.
II.92. OZENFANT, AMÉDÉE. *Mémoires 1886–1962*, Paris, 1968.
II.93. PAUL-BONCOUR, JOSEPH. *Art et démocratie*, Paris, 1911.
II.94. PICASSO, PABLO. *Picasso on Art: A Selection of Views*, Dore Ashton (ed.), London and New York, 1972.
—— PICASSO, PABLO, see McCully, Marilyn.
II.95. PICASSO, PABLO. *Picasso/Apollinaire. Correspondance*, Pierre Caizergues and Hélène Seckel (eds). Paris, 1992.
II.96. RAY, MAN. *Self-Portrait*, New York, 1963.
II.97. RAYNAL, MAURICE. *Quelques Intentions du cubisme*, Paris, 1919; reprinted in *Bulletin de l'Effort moderne*, no.3 Paris, 1924.
II.98. RAYNAL, MAURICE. *Anthologie de la peinture en France de 1906 à nos jours*, Paris, 1927.
II.99. REVERDY, PIERRE. *Pierre Reverdy, Oeuvres complètes. Nord-Sud, Self-Defence et autres écrits sur l'art et Nord-Sud, 1917–26*, Paris, 1975.
II.100. ROUAULT, GEORGES. *Sur l'art et sur la vie*, Paris, 1971.
II.101. SALMON, ANDRÉ. *La Jeune Peinture française*, Paris, 1912.
II.102. SALMON, ANDRÉ. *La Jeune Sculpture française*, Paris, 1919.
II.103. SALMON, ANDRÉ. *L'Art vivant*, Paris, 1920.
II.104. SEVERINI, GINO. *Tutta la vita di un pittore*, Rome and Paris, 1947; *Tempo de l'Effort Moderne* (Paris,1968), both vols. translated by Jennifer Franchina as *The Life of a Painter. The Autobiography of Gino Severini*, Princeton, NJ, 1995.
II.105. SEVERINI, GINO. *Severini. Écrits sur l'art*, Serge Faucherau (ed.), Paris, 1987.
II.106. SIGNAC, PAUL. *D'Eugène Delacroix au néo-impressionnisme*, Paris, 1898; re-printed, Françoise Cachin (ed.), Paris, 1964 and 1978.
II.107. STEIN, GERTRUDE. *The Autobiography of Alice B.Toklas*, London, 1933 and 1960.
II.108. STEIN, GERTRUDE. *Picasso*, London, New York and Sidney, 1938.
II.109. VLAMINCK, MAURICE. *Tournant dangereux*, Paris, 1929.
II.110. YVARS, J.F and YBARRA, LUCÍA. *Letters to Lipchitz, and some personal notes by the artist*, texts in English (translated by Lucía Jones) and French, Valencia, 1997.
II.111. ZADKINE, OSSIP. *Le Maillet et le ciseau. Souvenirs de ma vie*, Paris, 1968.

III. SECONDARY MATERIAL: BOOKS, EXHIBITION CATALOGUES AND ARTICLES

III.1. ADES, DAWN. *Dada and Surrealism Reviewed*. Exh. cat. London, Arts Council of Great Britain, Hayward Gallery, 1978.
III.2. ADES, DAWN. *Dalí*, London, 1982.
—— ADES, DAWN, see Krauss, Rosalind.
III.3. ADES, DAWN. *André Masson*, Barcelona, 1994.
III.4. ADES, DAWN and BRADLEY, FIONA. (eds), *Salvador Dalí. A Mythology*. Exh. cat. Liverpool, Tate Gallery, 1998.
III.5. ADES, DAWN, COX, NEIL and HOPKINS, DAVID. *Marcel Duchamp*, London, 1999.
III.6. AFFRON, MATTHEW and ANTLIFF, MARK. *Fascist Visions. Art and Ideology in*

France and Italy, Princeton, NJ, 1997.
III.7. AFFRON, MATTHEW. 'Léger's Modernism: Subjects and Objects', in Lanchner, Carolyn. *Fernand Léger*. Exh. cat. Museum of Modern Art, New York, 1998.
III.8. AGEE, WILLIAM C. and HAMILTON, GEORGE, H. *Raymond Duchamp-Villon 1876–1918*. Exh. cat. New York, Knoedler Gallery, 1967.
III.9. AGULHON, MAURICE. *Marianne au pouvoir. L'imagerie et la symbolique républicains de 1880 à 1914*, Paris, 1989.
III.10. ANTLIFF, MARK. *Inventing Bergson. Cultural Politics and the Parisian Avant-Garde*, Princeton, NJ, 1993.
—— ANTLIFF, MARK, see Affron, Matthew.
III.11. ARAGON, LOUIS. *Henri Matisse. Roman*, Paris, 1971; translated by Jean Stewart as *Henri Matise: A Novel*, London and New York, 1972.
III.12. ASSOULINE, PIERRE. *L'Homme de l'art. D-H.Kahnweiler, 1884–1979*, Paris, 1988; translated as *An Artful Life. A Biography of D-H.Kahnweiler*, New York, 1990.
III.13. BACHELOR, DAVID, FER, BRIONY and WOOD, PAUL. *Realism, Rationalism, Surrealism. Art between the Wars*, New Haven and London, 1993.
III.14. BALAS, EDITH. *Brancusi and Romanian Folk Traditions*, Boulder, Col., 1987.
III.15. BALDASSARI, ANNE. *Picasso photographe 1901–1916*. Exh. cat. Paris, Musée Picasso, 1994.
III.16. BALDASSARI, ANNE. *Picasso and Photography. The Dark Mirror.* translated from the French by Dete Dusinberre, Paris and Houston, 1997.
III.17. BAUQUIER, GEORGES. *Fernand Léger. Catalogue raisonné de l'oeuvre peint*, vol.I, *1903–19*, vol.II, *1920–24*, vol.III, *1925–28*, vol. IV, *1929–31*, Paris, 1990, 1992, 1993 and 1995.
III.18. BARR, JR. ALFRED H. *Cubism and Abstract Art*, Museum of Modern Art, New York, 1936; Cambridge, Mass., and London, 1986.
III.19. BARR, JR. ALFRED H. *Matisse. His Art and His Public*, New York, 1951.
III.20. BENJAMIN, ROGER. *Matisse's 'Notes of a Painter': Criticism, Theory and Context, 1891–1908*, Ann Arbor, Michigan, 1987.
III.21. BENJAMIN, ROGER. 'The Decorative Landscape, Fauvism, and the Arabesque of Observation', *Art Bulletin*, LXXV, 2 New York, June 1993.
III.22. BERGER, URSEL and ZUTTER, JÖRG. (eds), *Aristide Maillol*. Exh. cat. Berlin, Georg-Kolbe Museum and Lausanne, Musée cantonal des beaux-arts, 1996.
III.23. BERNIER, GEORGES and SCHNEIDER-MAUNOURY, MONIQUE. *Robert et Sonia Delaunay. Naissance de l'art abstrait*, Mesnil-sur-l'Estrée, 1995.
III.24. BLOTKAMP, CAREL. *Mondrian. The Art of Destruction*, London, 1994.
III.25. BOCK, CATHERINE C. *Henri Matisse and Neo-Impressionism. 1898–1908*, Ann Arbor, Michigan, 1981.
III.26. BOIS, YVE-ALAIN. 'Kahnweiler's Lesson', *Representations*, 18, California, spring 1987; reprinted in revised form in Bois, *Painting as Model*, Cambridge, Mass., and London, 1993.
III.27. BOIS, YVE-ALAIN. et al., *Piet Mondrian 1872–1944*. Exh. cat. The Gemeentemuseum, The Hague; National Gallery of Art, Washington, DC; Museum of Modern Art, New York, 1995–6.
III.28. BOIS, YVE-ALAIN and KRAUSS, ROSALIND. *L'informe. Mode d'emploi*. Exh. cat. Paris, Musée national d'art moderne, Centre Georges Pompidou, 1996.
III.29. BOIS, YVE-ALAIN. *Matisse and Picasso*. Exh. cat. Fort Worth, Tex., Kimbell Art Museum, 1999.
III.30. BONNET, MARGUERITE. *André Breton. Naissance de l'aventure surréaliste*, Paris, 1975.
III.31. BORRÀS, MARIA LLÜISA. *Picabia*, Barcelona and London, 1985.
—— BRADLEY, FIONA, see Ades, Dawn.
III.32. BRAUN, MARTA. *Picturing Time. The Work of Etienne-Jules Marey (1830–1904)*. Chicago and London, 1992.
III.33. BROWN, JONATHAN (ed.), *Picasso and the Spanish Tradition*, New Haven and London, 1996.
III.34. BRUNHAMMER, YVONNE. 1925. Exh. cat. Paris, Musée des arts décoratifs, 1976.
III.35. BUCHLOH, BENJAMIN. 'Figures of Authority, Ciphers of Regression', *October*, 16 New York and Cambridge, Mass., spring 1981.
III.36. BUCKBERROUGH, SHERRY A. *Robert Delaunay: The Discovery of Simultaneity*, Ann Arbor, Michigan, 1982.
III.37. CAFFIN MADAULE, LILIANE. *Catalogue raisonné des oeuvres de Maria Blanchard*, 2 vols. London, 1992 and 1994.
III.38. CAMFIELD, WILLIAM A. *Francis Picabia. His Art, Life and Times*, Princeton, NJ, 1979.
III.39. CAMFIELD, WILLIAM A. *Marcel Duchamp. Fountain*, Houston, 1989.
III.40. CAMFIELD, WILLIAM A. *Max Ernst: Dada and the Dawn of Surrealism*, Munich and Houston, Texas, 1993.
III.41. CARMEAN, JR. E.A. and MONOD-FONTAINE, ISABELLE. (eds), *Braque: The papiers collés*. Exh. cat. Washington, DC, National Gallery of Art, 1982; French edition, Paris, Musée national d'art moderne, Centre Georges Pompidou, 1982.
III.42. CERTIGNY, HENRI. *La Vérité sur le Douanier Rousseau*, Paris, 1961.
III.43. CHADWICK, WHITNEY. *Myth in Surrealist Painting, 1929–39*, Ann Arbor, Michigan and London, 1980.
III.44. CHADWICK, WHITNEY. *Woman Artists and the Surrealist Movement*, London, 1985.
III.45. CHAPON, FRANÇOIS. *Mystères et splendeurs de Jacques Doucet, (1853–1929)*, Paris, 1984.
III.46. CHAVE, ANNA C. *Constantin Brancusi. Shifting the Bases of Art*, New Haven and London, 1993.
III.47. CHAVE, ANNA C. 'New Encounters with *Les Demoiselles d'Avignon*: Gender, Race, and the Origins of Cubism', *Art Bulletin*, vol.76, 4, New York, 1994.
III.48. CHÉNIEUX-GENDRON, JACQUELINE. *Le Surréalisme*, Paris, 1984; translated by Vivian Folkenflik as *Surrealism*, New York and Chichester, 1990.
III.49. CLIFFORD, JAMES. *The Predicament of Culture. Twentieth-Century Ethnography, Literature and Art*, Cambridge, Mass., and London, 1988.
III.50. COHEN, JEAN-LOUIS (ed.), *Les Années Trente: L'architecture et les arts de l'espace entre industrie et nostalgie*. Exh. cat. Paris, Musée de monuments français, 1997.
III.51. COMPTON, SUSAN. *Chagall*. Exh. cat. London, Royal Academy of Arts, 1985.
III.52. COOPER, DOUGLAS. with the collaboration of Margaret Potter, *Juan Gris. Catalogue Raisonné of the Painted Work*, (2 vols), Paris, 1977.
III.53. COTTINGTON, DAVID. *Cubism in the Shadow of War. The Avant-Garde and Politics in Paris 1905–1914*, New Haven and London, 1998.
III.54. COWART, JACK (ed.), *Henri Matisse: The Early Years in Nice, 1916–1930*. Exh. cat. Washington, DC, National Gallery of Art, 1986.
III.55. COWLING, ELIZABETH and MUNDY, JENNIFER. (eds), *On Classic Ground. Picasso, Léger, de Chirico and the New Classicism 1910–1930*. Exh. cat. London, Tate Gallery, 1990.
III.56. COWLING, ELIZABETH and GOLDING, JOHN. *Picasso: Sculptor/Painter*. Exh. cat. London, Tate Gallery, 1994.
—— COX, NEIL, see Ades, Dawn.
III.57. DAIX, PIERRE and BOUDAILLE, GEORGES. with the collaboration of Joan Rosselet, *Picasso 1900–1906, catalogue raisonné de l'oeuvre peint*, Neuchâtel, 1966.
III.58. DAIX, PIERRE and ROSSELET, JOAN. *Le Cubisme de Picasso. Catalogue raisonné de l'oeuvre 1907–1916*, Neuchâtel, 1979; translated by Dorothy S.Blair as *Picasso. The Cubist Years 1907–1916*. A catalogue raisonné of the paintings and related works, London, 1979.
III.59. DIDI-HUBERMAN, GEORGES. *L'Invention de l'hystérie*, Paris, 1982.
—— DUFET, MICHEL, see Ianou, Ionel.
III.60. DUMITRESCO, NATALIA, ISTRATI, ALEXANDRE and HULTEN, PONTUS. *Brancusi*, London, 1986.
III.61. DUTHUIT, GEORGES. *Les Fauves*, Geneva, 1949.
III.62. DUPIN, JACQUES. *Miró*, Paris, 1993.
III.63. ELDERFIELD, JOHN. *The 'Wild Beasts'. Fauvism and its Affinities*. Exh. cat. New York, Museum of Modern Art, 1976.
III.64. ELDERFIELD, JOHN. *Matisse in the Collection of the Museum of Modern Art*, New York, Museum of Modern Art, 1978.
III.65. ELDERFIELD, JOHN. *Henri Matisse. A Retrospective*. Exh. cat. New York, Museum of Modern Art, 1992.
III.66. ELDERFIELD, JOHN. *Pleasure Painting. Matisse's Feminine Representations.* The 27th Walter Neurath Memorial Lecture, London, 1995.
—— ELDERFIELD, JOHN, see Whitfield, Sarah.
III.67. ELLIOTT, PATRICK. 'Sculpture in France and Clssicism, 1910–1939'; in Elizabeth Cowling and Jennifer Mundy (eds), *On Classic Ground. Picasso, Léger, de Chirico and the New Classicism 1910–1930*. Exh. cat. London, Tate Gallery, hardback edition, 1990.
III.68. ELLIOTT, PATRICK and STOOS, TONI. *Alberto Giacometti, 1901–1966*. Exh. cat. Edinburgh, National Galleries of Scotland and London, Royal Academy of Arts, 1996.
III.69. FAVELA, RAMÓN. *Diego Rivera. The Cubist Years*. Exh. cat. Phoenix Art Museum, 1984.
—— FER, BRIONY, see Bachelor, David.
III.70. FISHMAN. ROBERT. 'From the Radiant City to Vichy: Le Corbusier's Plans and Politics'; in R.Walden (ed.), *The Open Hand: Essays on Le Corbusier*, Cambridge, Mass., 1977.
III.71. FITZGERALD, MICHAEL C. *Making Modernism. Picasso and the Creation of the Market for Twentieth-Century Art*, Berkely, Los Angeles and London, 1995.
III.72. FLAM, JACK. *Henri Matisse. The Man and his Art, 1869–1918*, London, 1986.
III.73. FONTI, DANIELA. *Gino Severini. Catalogo ragionato*, Milan, 1988.
III.74. FORSTER, HAL. *Compulsive Beauty*, Cambridge, Mass., and London, 1993.
III.75. FREEMAN, JUDI. *The Fauve Landscape*. Exh. cat. Los Angeles, Los Angeles County Museum, 1990.

—— FRASCINA, FRANCIS, see Harrison, Charles.

III.76. FRY, EDWARD F. 'Picasso, Cubism and Reflexivity', *Art Journal*, vol.47, 4 Winter 1988.

III.77. FUNDACIÓ JOAN MIRÓ, *Joan Miró 1893–1993*. Exh. cat. Barcelona, 1993.

III.78. GEE, MALCOLM. *Dealers, Critics and Collectors of Modern Painting: Aspects of the Parisian Art Market between 1910 and 1930*, London and New York, 1981.

III.79. GEE, MALCOLM (ed.), *Art Criticism since 1900*, Manchester and New York, 1993.

III.80. GEIST, SIDNEY. *Brancusi. A Study of the Sculpture*, New York, 1983.

III.81. GEIST, SIDNEY. *Brancusi/The Kiss*, New York, Hagerstown, San Francisco and London, 1978.

III.82. GENET-DELACROIX, MARIE-CLAUDE. *Art et Etat sous la IIIe République. Le Système des Beaux-Arts, 1870–1940*, Paris, 1992.

III.83. GIBSON, IAN. *The Shameful Life of Salvador Dalí*, London, 1997.

III.84. GIRY, MARCEL. *Le Fauvisme: ses origines, son évolution*, Neuchâtel, 1981.

—— GOLAN, ROMY, see Silver, Kenneth E.

III.85. GOLAN, ROMY. *Modernity and Nostalgia: Art and Politics between the Wars*, New Haven and London, 1995.

III.86. GOLDING, JOHN. *Cubism: a History and an Analysis, 1907–1914*, London, 1959, 1968, 1988.

III.87. GOLDING, JOHN. *Marcel Duchamp: The Bride Stripped Bare by her Bachelors, Even*, London, 1973.

—— GOLDING, JOHN, see Cowling, Elizabeth.

—— GOPNIK, ADAM, see Varnedoe, Kirk.

III.88. GREEN, CHRISTOPHER. *Léger and the Avant-garde*, New Haven and London, 1976.

III.89. GREEN, CHRISTOPHER. *Cubism and its Enemies. Modern Movements and Reaction in French Art, 1916–1928*, New Haven and London, 1987.

III.90. GREEN, CHRISTOPHER. 'Classicisms of Transcendence and of Transience: Maillol, Picasso and de Chirico'; in Elizabeth Cowling and Jennifer Mundy (eds), *On Classic Ground. Picasso, Léger, de Chirico and the New Classicism 1910–1930*, London, Tate Gallery, hardback edition, 1990.

III.91. GREEN, CHRISTOPHER. *Juan Gris*. Exh. cat. London, Whitechapel Art Gallery, 1992.

III.92. GREEN, CHRISTOPHER. 'The Infant in the Adult: Joan Miró and the Infantile Image'; in Fineberg (Jonathan) (ed.), *Discovering the Child Essays on Childhood, Primitivism and Modernism*, Princeton, 1998, 210–34.

III.93. GRONBERG, TAG. 'Speaking Volumes: The Pavillon de l'Esprit Nouveau', *Oxford Art Journal*, vol.15, 2 Oxford, 1992.

III.94. GUIGON, EMMANUEL. *El Objeto Surrealista*, with English translation. Exh. cat. Valencia, IVAM Centre Julio González, 1997–8.

III.95. HARGROVE, JUNE. *Les statues de Paris. La représentation des grands hommes dans les rues et sur les places de Paris*, Antwerp and Paris, 1989.

III.96. HARRISON, CHARLES, FRASCINA, FRANCIS and PERRY, GILL. *Primitivism, Cubism, Abstraction. The Early Twentieth Century*, New Haven and London, 1993.

III.97. HENDERSON, LINDA, DALRYMPLE. *The Fourth Dimension and Non-Euclidean Geometry in Modern Art*, Princeton, 1983.

III.98. HENDERSON, LINDA, DALRIMPLE. *Duchamp in Context. Science and Technology in the 'Large Glass' and Related Works*, Princeton, 1998.

III.99. HERBERT, JAMES. *Fauve Painting. The Making of Cultural Politics*, New Haven and London, 1992.

III.100. HERGOTT, FABRICE and WHITFIELD, SARAH. *Georges Rouault. The Early Years* 1903–1920. Exh. cat. London, Royal Academy of Arts, 1993.

III.101. HODEIR, CATHERINE and MICHEL, PIERRE. *L'Exposition coloniale*, Paris, 1991.

III.102. HOHL, REINHOLD. *Alberto Giacometti*, London, 1972.

III.103. HOLLIER, DENIS (ed.), translated by Betsy Wing, *The College of Sociology*, Minneapolis, 1988.

III.104. HOLLIER, DENIS. *La Prise de la concorde. Essais sur Georges Bataille*, Paris, 1974; translated by Betsy Wing as *Against Architecture: The Writings of Georges Bataille*, Cambridge, 1989.

III.105. HOPKINS, DAVID. *Marcel Duchamp and Max Ernst: the bride shared*, Oxford, 1998.

—— HOPKINS, DAVID, see Ades, Dawn.

—— HULTEN, PONTUS, see Dumitresco, Natalia.

III.106. IMDAHL, MAX, see Vriesen, Max.

—— ISTRATI, ALEXANDRE, see Dumitresco, Natalia.

III.107. JIANOU, IONEL and DUFET, MICHEL. *Bourdelle*, 3rd edition, Paris, 1984.

III.108. KAHNWEILER, DANIEL-HENRY. *Juan Gris. Sa vie et son oeuvre*, Paris, 1946; translated by Douglas Cooper as *Juan Gris: His Life and Work*, New York, 1947; new enlarged edition, in German, French and English, Stuttgart, Paris, London and New York, 1969.

III.109. KELLERMANN, MICHEL. *André Derain. Catalogue raisonné de l'oeuvre peint*, Paris, 1992.

III.110. KRAUSS, ROSALIND. *Passages in Modern Sculpture*, Cambridge, Mass., 1977.

III.111. KRAUSS, ROSALIND, ADES, DAWN and LIVINGSTONE, JANE. *L'Amour fou: Photography and Surrealism*. Exh. cat. London, Arts Council of Great Britain, Hayward Gallery, 1986.

III.112. KRAUSS, ROSALIND. 'In the Name of Picasso' and 'No More Play'; in Krauss, *The Originality of the Avant-Garde and Other Modernist Myths*, Cambridge, Mass., and London, 1993.

—— KRAUSS, ROSALIND, see Bois, Yve-Alain.

III.113. KRAUSS, ROSALIND. *The Picasso Papers*, London, 1998.

III.114. KUENZLI, RUDOLF and NAUMANN, FRANCIS M. *Marcel Duchamp. Artist of the Century*, Cambridge, Mass., and London, 1990.

—— LANCHNER, CAROLYN, see Rubin, William.

III.115. LANCHNER, CAROLYN. *Joan Miró*. Exh. cat. New York, Museum of Modern Art, 1993.

III.116. LANCHNER, CAROLYN. *Fernand Léger*. Exh. cat. New York, Museum of Modern Art, 1998.

III.117. LANTHEMAN J. *Modigliani. Catalogue Raisonné*, Barcelona, 1970.

III.118. LASSALLE, HÉLÈNE (ed.), *Fernand Léger*. Exh. cat. Villeneuve d'Asq, Musée d'art moderne, 1990.

III.119. LAUDE, JEAN. *Les arts de l'Afrique noire*, Paris, 1979.

III.120. LAUDE, JEAN and WORMS DE ROMILLY, NICOLE. *Braque: Cubism, 1907–1914*, Paris, 1982.

III.121. LAUGIER, CLAUDE and RICHET, MICHELLE. *Oeuvres de Fernand Léger. Collections du Musée national d'art moderne*, Centre Georges Pompidou, Paris, 1981.

III.122. LAURENT, JEANNE. *Arts et pouvoirs en France entre 1793 et 1981*, Saint-Etienne, 1982.

III.123. LECOMBRE, SYLVAIN. in collaboration with Helena Staub, *Ossip Zadkine. L'oeuvre sculpté*, Paris, 1994.

III.124. LEE, JANE. *Derain*, Oxford and New York, 1990.

III.125. LEGGE, ELIZABETH M. *Max Ernst. The Psychoanalytic Sources*, Ann Arbor, Michigan and London, 1989.

III.126. LEIGHTEN, PATRICIA. *Reordering the Universe. Picasso and Anarchism, 1897–1914*, Princeton, 1989.

III.127. LEIGHTEN, PATRICIA. 'The White Peril and *L'Art nègre*: Picasso, Primitivism and Anticolonialism', *Art Bulletin*, vol.LXXXII, 4 (December 1990), 609–30.

III.128. LEIGHTEN, PATRICIA. 'Cubist Anachronisms: Ahistory, Cryptoformalism, and Business-as-Usual in New York', *Oxford Art Journal*, vol.17, 2 1994.

III.129. LEMAGNY, JEAN-CLAUDE and ROUILLÉ, ANDRÉ. (eds), *A History of Photography. Social and Cultural Perspectives*, Cambridge and New York, 1987.

—— LEMNY, DOÏNA, see Tabar, Marielle.

III.130. LEMOINE, SERGE (ed.), *Theo van Doesburg. Peinture, architecture, théorie*, Paris, 1990.

—— LIVINGSTONE, JANE, see Krauss, Rosalind.

III.131. LOMAS, DAVID. 'A Canon of Deformity: *Les Demoiselles d'Avignon* and Physical Antropology', *Art History*, vol.16, 3 Oxford and Cambridge, Mass., September 1993.

III.132. LORD, JAMES. *Giacometti. A Biography*, London, 1983, 1985 and 1986.

III.133. LUBAR, ROBERT S. 'Miró's Mediterranean: Conceptions of Cultural Identity', in *Joan Miró 1893–1993*. Exh. cat. Barcelona, Fundació Joan Miró, 1993.

III.134. LUBAR, ROBERT S. 'Picasso, El Greco, and the Body of the Nation'; in Jonathan Brown (ed.), *Picasso and the Spanish Tradition*, New Haven and London, 1996.

III.135. MAINARDI, PATRICIA. *The End of the Salon. Art and the State in the Early Third Republic*, Cambridge, 1993.

III.136. MANDELL, RICHARD. *Paris 1900. The Great World's Fair*, Toronto, 1967.

III.137. MCLEOD, MARY. ' "Architecture or ": Taylorism, Technocracy, and Social Change', *Art Journal*, vol.43, 2 New York, summer 1983.

III.138. MCLEOD, MARY. 'Le rêve transi de Le Corbusier: L'Amérique "Catastrophe féerique" '; in Jean-Louis Cohen and H. Damisch (eds), *Amérique et modernité. L'idéal américain dans l'architecture*, Paris, 1993.

—— METKEN, SIGRID and GÜNTER, see Spies, Werner.

III.139. MEYER, FRANZ. *Marc Chagall. Life and Work*, London, 1964.

—— MICHEL, PIERRE, see Hodeir, Catherine.

III.140. MILLER, SANDA. *Constantin Brancusi. A Survey of his Work*, Oxford, 1995.

III.141. MONOD-FONTAINE, ISABELLE and POUILLON, NADINE. *Braque*, Collections du Musée national d'art moderne, Paris, 1982.

III.142. MONOD-FONTAINE, ISABELLE, see Carmean, Jr. E.A.

III.143. MOSER, ANN (ed.), *Jean Metzinger in Retrospect*. Exh. cat. Iowa City, The University of Iowa Museum of Art, 1985.

—— MUNDY, JENNIFER, see Cowling, Elizabeth.

III.144. Musée carnavalet. *Henri Gervex*. Exh. cat. Paris, 1993.

III.145. Musée de l'annonciade, *Signac et St Tropez, 1892–1913*. Exh. cat. St Tropez, 1992.

III.146. Musée d'art moderne de la Ville de Paris, *Abstraction Création 1931–1936*. Exh. cat. Paris, 1978.

III.147. Musée d'art moderne de la Ville de Paris, *Léger et l'esprit moderne*. Exh. cat. Paris, 1982; translated as *Léger and the Modern Spirit* for Museum of Fine Arts, Houston, Houston, Texas, 1982.

III.148. Musée d'art moderne de la Ville de Paris, *Cinquantenaire de l'Exposition Internationale des arts et des techniques dans la vie moderne*. Exh. cat. Paris, 1987.

III.149. Musée d'art moderne de la Ville de Paris, *František Kupka 1871–1957, ou l'invention de l'une abstraction*. Exh. cat. Paris, 1989–90.

III.150. Musée d'art moderne de la Ville de Paris, *André Derain. Le peintre du 'trouble moderne'*. Exh. cat. Paris, 1994–5.

III.151. Musée d'art moderne de la Ville de Paris, *Années 30 en Europe. Le temps menaçant* 1929–1939. Exh. cat. Paris, 1997.

III.152. Musée d'art moderne, Villeneuf d'Asq, *Henri Laurens*. Exh. cat. Villeneuf d'Asq, 1992–3.

III.153. Musée des Beaux-Arts, Lyon. *Maurice Denis. 1870–1943*. Exh. cat. Lyon, 1994.

III.154. Musée municipal de Mont-de-Marsan, *Charles Albert Despiau (1874–1946)*. Mont-de-Marsan, 1982.

III.155. Musée national d'art moderne, *Georges Rouault. Exposition du Centenaire*. Exh. cat. Paris, 1971.

III.156. Musée national d'art moderne, *Salvador Dalí, rétrospective*. Exh. cat. Paris, Centre Georges Pompidou, 1979–80.

III.157. Musée national d'art moderne, *Paul Eluard et ses amis peintres*. Exh. cat. Paris, Centre Georges Pompidou, 1982.

III.158. Musée national d'art moderne, *Yves Tanguy: Rétrospective 1925–1955*, Paris, Centre Georges Pompidou, 1982.

III.159. Musée national d'art moderne, *Giorgio de Chirico*. Exh. cat. Paris, Centre Georges Pompidou, 1983; see also Museum of Modern Art for the English version.

III.160. Musée national d'art moderne, *Bonnard*. Exh. cat. Paris, Centre Georges Pompidou, 1984.

III.161. Musée national d'art moderne, *Matta*. Exh. cat. Paris, Centre Georges Pompidou, 1985.

III.162. Musée national d'art moderne, *André Breton. La beauté convulsive*. Exh. cat. Paris, Centre Georges Pompidou, 1991.

III.163. Musée national d'art moderne, *Henri Matisse* 1904–1918. Exh. cat. Paris, Centre Georges Pompidou, 1993.

III.164. Musée national d'art moderne, *Face à l'histoire, 1933–1996*. Exh. cat. Paris, 1996–7.

III.165. Musée national d'art moderne, *Fernand Léger*. Exh. cat. Paris, Centre Georges Pompidou, 1997.

III.166. Musée national Fernand Léger, *Fernand Léger et le spectacle*. Exh. cat. Biot, 1995.

III.167. Musée d'Orsay, *Maillol: La Méditerranée*. Exh. cat. Paris, 1986.

III.168. Musée d'Orsay, *Jean-Paul Laurens*, 1838–1921. *Peintre d'histoire*. Exh. cat. Paris, 1997–8.

III.169. Musée du Petit Palais, *Le triomphe des mairies. Les Grands Décors républicains à Paris, 1870–1914*. Exh. cat. Paris, 1987.

III.170. Musée de la Ville de Strasbourg, *Jeanne Bucher. Une galerie d'avant-garde, 1925–1946. De Max Ernst à de Staël*. Exh. cat. Strasbourg, 1994.

III.171. Museum of Modern Art, *De Chirico*. Exh. cat. New York, 1982; see also Musée national d'art moderne for the French version.

III.172. Museum of Modern Art and Galeries nationales du Grand Palais, *The Douanier Rousseau*. Exh. cat. New York and Paris, 1985, English and French editions.

III.173. Musée Picasso, *Les Demoiselles d'Avignon*. Exh. cat. 2 vols. (Paris, 1988).

III.174. NADEAU, MAURICE. *L'Histoire du surréalisme*, Paris, 1944 and 1968; translated by Richard Howard as *The History of Surrealism*, London, 1968.

III.175. National Gallery of Art, *Matisse in Morocco. The Paintings and Drawings, 1912–1913*, Washington, DC, 1990.

—— NAUMANN, FRANCES, M, see Kuenzli, Rudolf

III.176. NESBIT, MOLLY. 'The Language of Industry'; in Thierry de Duve (ed.), *The Definitively Unfinished Marcel Duchamp*, Cambridge, Mass., and London, 1991.

III.177. NESBIT, MOLLY. *Atget's Seven Albums*, New Haven and London, 1992.

III.178. NORI, CLAUDE. *La Photographie française dès origines à nos jours*, Paris, 1978.

III.179. OPPLER, ELLEN C. *Fauvism Reexamined*, New York and London, 1976.

III.180. OPPLER, ELLEN C. (ed.), *Picasso's 'Guernica'*, New York and London, 1988.

III.181. ORY, PASCAL. *Les Expositions Universelles de Paris. Panorama raisonné avec des aperçus nouveaux et des illustrations par les meilleurs auteurs*, Paris, 1982.

III.182. ORY, PASCAL. *La Belle Illusion. Culture et politique sous la signe du Front Populaire 1935–1938*, Paris, 1994.

III.183. PARIGORIS, ALEXANDRA. 'Pastiche and the Use of Tradition, 1917–1922'; in Elizabeth Cowling and Jennifer Mundy (eds), *On Classic Ground. Picasso, Léger, de Chirico and the new Classicism 1910–1930*. Exh. cat. London, Tate Gallery, hardback edition, 1990.

III.184. PEER, SHANNY. *France on Display. Peasants, Provincials and Folklore in the* 1937 *Paris World's Fair*. New York, 1998.

—— PERRY, GILL. see Harrison, Charles.

III.185. PERRY, GILL. *Women Artists and the Parisian Avant-garde. Modernism and 'feminine' art 1900 to the late 1920s*, Manchester and New York, 1995.

III.186. POGGI, CHRISTINE. *In Defiance of Painting: Cubism, Futurism and the Invention of Collage*, New Haven and London, 1992.

—— POUILLON, NADINE, see Monod-Fontaine, Isabelle.

III.187. POTTER, MARGARET. *Four Americans in Paris: The Collection of Gertrude Stein and her Family*. Exh. cat. New York, 1970.

III.188. READ, PETER. *Picasso et Apollinaire. Les métamorphoses de la mémoire 1905–1973*, Paris, 1995.

III.189. RICHARDSON, JOHN. with the collaboration of Marilyn McCully, *A Life of Picasso*, vol.1: *1881–1906*, London, 1991; vol.2: *1907–1917: The Painter of Modern Life*, London, 1996.

—— RICHET, MICHELLE, see Laugier, Claude.

III.190. ROBBINS, DANIEL. *Albert Gleizes, 1881–1953. A Retrospective Exhibition*. Exh. cat. New York, Solomon R.Guggenheim Museum, 1964.

III.191. ROBBINS, DANIEL. 'Jean Metzinger: At the Centre of Cubism'; in Ann Moser (ed.), *Jean Metzinger in Retrospect*. Exh. cat. Iowa City, The University of Iowa Museum of Art, 1985.

III.192. ROSENBLUM, ROBERT. 'Picasso and the Typography of Cubism'; in Roland Penrose and John Golding (eds), *Picasso in Retrospect*, New York and Washington, DC, 1963.

—— ROSSELET, JOAN, see Daix, Pierre.

III.193. ROUSSEAU, PASCAL. 'Les couleurs "suggestives" de l'affiche. *L'Equipe de Cardiff* de Robert Delaunay et la querelle des "panneaux-réclame" ', *Histoire de l'art*, 39, Paris, 1997.

III.194. ROWELL, MARGIT (ed.), *František Kupka 1871–1957*. Exh. cat. New York, Solomon R.Guggenheim Museum, 1975.

III.195. RUBIN, WILLIAM. *Dada and Surrealist Art*, New York, 1968.

III.196. RUBIN, WILLIAM. *Picasso in the Collection of the Museum of Modern Art*, New York, Museum of Modern Art, 1972.

III.197. RUBIN, WILLIAM. *Miró in the Collection of the Museum of Modern Art*, New York, Museum of Modern Art, 1973.

III.198. RUBIN, WILLIAM and LANCHNER, CAROLYN. Exh. cat. *André Masson*, New York, Museum of Modern Art, 1976.

III.199. RUBIN, WILLIAM (ed.), *Cézanne. The Late Work*. Exh. cat. New York, Museum of Modern Art, 1977.

III.200. RUBIN, WILLIAM (ed.), *'Primitivism' in 20th Century Art: Affinity of the Tribal and the Modern*, 2 vols. Exh. cat. New York, Museum of Modern Art, New York, 1984.

III.201. RUBIN, WILLIAM (ed.), *Picasso and Braque: Pioneering Cubism*. Exh. cat. New York, Museum of Modern Art, 1989.

III.202. RUBIN, WILLIAM and ZELEVANSKI, LYNN (eds), *Picasso and Braque: A Symposium*, New York, 1992.

III.203. RUBIN, WILLIAM (ed.), *Les Demoiselles d'Avignon*, Studies in Modern Art 3, Museum of Modern Art, New York, 1994.

III.204. RUBIN, WILLIAM (ed.), *Picasso and Portraiture. Representation and Transformation*. Exh. cat. New York, Museum of Modern Art, 1996; French edition, Paris, Grand Palais, 1996–7.

III.205. RYDELL, ROBERT. *World of Fairs. The Century of Progress Expositions*, Chicago, 1993.

III.206. SANOUILLET, MICHEL. *Dada à Paris*, Paris, 1965.

III.207. SCHIFF, RICHARD. *Cézanne and the End of Impressionism. A Study of the Theory, and Critical Evaluation of Modern Art*, Chicago, Ill., 1984.

III.208. SCHNEIDER, PIERRE. *Matisse*, Paris, 1984, translated by Michael Taylor and Bridget Strevens Romer, London, 1984.

—— SCHNEIDER-MAUNOURY, MONIQUE, see Bernier, Georges.

III.209. SCHWARZ, ARTURO. *The Complete Works of Marcel Duchamp*, revised and expanded edition, 2 vols, New York and London, 1997.

III.210. SEUPHOR, MICHEL. *Piet Mondrian. Life and Work*, London, 1957.

III.211. SILVER, KENNETH E. and GOLAN, ROMY (eds), *The Circle of Montparnasse. Jewish Artists in Paris 1905–1945*. Exh. cat. The Jewish Museum, New York, 1985.

III.212. SILVER, KENNETH E. *Esprit de Corps. The Art of the Parisian Avant-Garde and the First World War, 1914–1925*, Princeton, 1989.

III.213. SILVERMAN, DEBORA L. *Art Nouveau in Fin-de-Siècle France*, Berkeley, 1990.

III.214. SOLOMON, R.GUGGENHEIM. *Aristide Maillol. 1861–1944*. Exh. cat. New York, 1975.

III.215. SPATE, VIRGINIA. *Orphism. The Evolution of Non-Figurative Painting in*

Paris 1910–14, Oxford, 1979.
III.216. SPIES, WERNER. *Les sculptures de Picasso*, Lausanne, 1971.
III.217. SPIES, WERNER. METKEN, SIGRID and GÜNTER. *Max Ernst, Oeuvre Katalog: Werke* 1906–1925; *Werke* 1925–29; *Werke 1929–1938*, Cologne and Houston, Texas, 1975, 1976 and 1979.
III.218. SPIES, WERNER. *Max Ernst, Collagen: Inventar und Widerspruch*, Cologne, 1975; French edition, *Max Ernst. Les collages, inventeur et contradictions*, Paris, 1984; translated from the German by John William Gabriel as *Max Ernst: Collages – The Invention of the Surrealist Universe*, New York and London, 1991.
III.219. SPIES, WERNER. *Max Ernst. Loplop: The Artist's Other Self*, London, 1983.
III.220. SPURLING, HILARY. *The Unknown Matisse. A Life of Henri Matisse*, vol.1, *1869–1908*, London, 1998.
III.221. STAATSGALERIE, STUTTGART. *Mondrian: Drawings, Watercolours*. Exh. cat. Stuttgart, 1981.
III.222. STEINBERG, LEO. 'The Philosophical Brothel', *Art News*, vol.71, 5 and 6 New York, September and October 1972; reprinted in revised form in *October*, 44 New York and Cambridge, Mass., spring 1988.
III.223. STICH, SIDRA. *Joan Miró; The Development of a Sign Language*. Exh. cat. St Louis, Missouri, Washington University Gallery of Art, 1980.
III.224. STICH, SIDRA. *Anxious Visions. Surrealist Art*. Exh. cat. Berkeley, University Art Museum, 1990.
—— STOOS, TONI, see Elliott, Patrick.
III.225. SYLVESTER, DAVID and WHITFIELD, SARAH. *René Magritte. Catalogue Raisonné. I: Oil Paintings. 1916–1930*, London, 1992.
III.226. SYLVESTER, DAVID. *Magritte*, London, 1992.
III.227. SYLVESTER, DAVID. *Looking at Giacometti*, London, 1994.
III.228. TABAR, MARIELLE and LEMNY, DOÏNA. *L'Atelier Brancusi*, Musée national d'art moderne, Centre Georges Pompidou, Paris, 1997.
III.229. TOMKINS, CALVIN. *Duchamp. A Biography*, London, 1997.
III.230. TROY, NANCY J. *Modernism and the Decorative Arts in France. Art Nouveau to Le Corbusier*, New Haven and London, 1991.
III.231. VACHTOVÁ, LUDMILLA. *Frank Kupka*, London, 1968.
III.232. VAISSE, PIERRE. *La Troisième République et les peintres*, Paris, 1995.
III.233. VALLIER, THÉRÈSE. *Henri Bouchard*, Paris, 1943.
III.234. VARNEDOE, KIRK and GOPNIK, ADAM. *High and Low. Modern Art and Popular Culture*. Exh. cat. New York, Museum of Modern Art, 1990.
III.235. VRIESEN, GUSTAV and IMAHL, MAX. *Robert Delaunay. Colour and Light*, Cologne and New York, 1967.
III.236. WALDBERG, PATRICK. *Yves Tanguy*, Brussels, 1977.
III.237. WEISS, JEFFREY. *The Popular Culture of Modern Art. Picasso, Duchamp and Avant-Gardism*, New Haven and London 1994.
III.238. WELSH, ROBERT. *Two Mondrian Sketchbooks 1912–14*, Amsterdam, 1969.
III.239. WHITFIELD, SARAH. *Fauvism*, London, 1991.
—— WHITFIELD, SARAH, see Sylvester, David.
—— WHITFIELD, SARAH, see Hergott, Fabrice.
III.240. WHITFIELD, SARAH and ELDERFIELD, JOHN. *Bonnard*. Exh. cat. London, Tate Gallery, 1998.
III.241. WILKINSON, ALAN G. *The Sculpture of Jacques Lipchitz. A Catalogue Raisonné*, vol.1, *The Paris Years 1910–1940*, London, 1996.
III.242. WOOD, PAUL, see Bachelor, David.
—— WORMS DE ROMILLY, NICOLE, see Laude, Jean.
III.243. ZERVOS, CHRISTIAN. *Pablo Picasso*, 33 vols. Paris, 1932–78.
III.244. ZURCHER, B. *Braque: Life and Work*, New York, 1988.

Index

Photographic Acknowledgements

Artothek 233; Oeffentliche Kunstsammlung Basel, Martin Bühler 28, 30, 77, 105, 130, 236, 249, 277; The Bridgeman Art Library, London and New York 146; Groupement Documentation, Bibliothèque Royale Albert 1er, Brussels 85; Photographie Bulloz 74; Atget/ © Arch. Phot. Paris/ CNMHS 169; Baranger/Archives Photographique/ CNMHS 12, 272; Caroline Rose/CNMHS 5; © Cartier-Bresson H./Magnum Photos 218; Jean Dieuzade 47; Archives Durand-Ruel, Paris 73; Jacques Faujour 166; © Foundation Le Corbusier 7, 8, 188, 194, 195, 208; Giraudon 2, 214; Photographic Services, Harvard University Art Museums, © President and Fellows of Harvard College, Harvard University 229; Helga Kirchberger 225; The British Library, London 329; Photograph by Robert E. Mates © The Solomon R. Guggenheim Foundation, New York 305; Photograph by David Heald © The Solomon R. Guggenheim Foundation, New York 294; Photograph © 2000 The Museum of Modern Art, New York 91, 92, 99, 115, 117, 127, 129, 144, 156, 158, 178, 252, 278, 282, 284, 295, 297, 310 (copy print), 312, 316, 322, 325, 328, 330; Musée des arts décoratifs, Paris, Fonds Albert Lévy 10, 35, 57; Bibliothèque Nationale de France, Paris 132, 320; Musée Bouchard, Paris 48, 220, 221; Photothèque Mnam/Ccci, Paris 298; © Cliché Bibliothèque d'art et d'archéologie Jacques Doucet, Paris 56; © Photothèque des Musées de la Ville de Paris 42, 81, 84, 90, 165, 170, 205, 215, 217, 231, 258; © Ville de Paris - C.O.A.R.C. 14, 184; © Photo RMN 15, 46, 71, 86, 98, 128, 161, 164, 185, 189, 248, 250, 251, 263, 292, 317; Foto Saporetti 265; Telimage 41, 63, 66, 80, 163; © Collection Viollet 4, 261; © Branger-Viollet 148; © Lipnitzki-Viollet 209; © ND-Viollet 1, 62; © Roger-Viollet 11, 149.